Problems and Materials on
DECEDENTS' ESTATES AND TRUSTS

Problems and Materials on
DECEDENTS' ESTATES AND TRUSTS

Sixth Edition

Eugene F. Scoles
Max L. Rowe Professor of Law, Emeritus
College of Law, University of Illinois
Distinguished Professor of Law, Emeritus
School of Law, University of Oregon

Edward C. Halbach, Jr.
Walter Perry Johnson Professor
School of Law, University of California, Berkeley

Ronald C. Link
Dan K. Moore Professor of Law
University of North Carolina

Patricia Gilchrist Roberts
Professor of Law
Wake Forest University

ASPEN LAW & BUSINESS
A Division of Aspen Publishers, Inc.
Gaithersburg   New York

Permissions
Aspen Law & Business
1185 Avenue of the Americas
New York, NY 10036

Printed in the United States of America.

ISBN 0-7355-1235-3

1 2 3 4 5 6 7 8 9 0

Library of Congress Cataloging-in-Publication Data

Problems and materials on decedents' estates and trusts / Eugene F. Scoles . . . [et al.]. — 6th ed.
    p. cm.
    Rev. ed. of: Problems and materials on decedents' estates and trusts / Eugene F. Scoles, Edward C. Halbach, Jr. 5th ed. c1993.
    Includes bibliographical references and index.
    ISBN 0-7355-1235-3
    1. Decedents' estates—United States—Cases. 2. Trusts and trustees—United States—Cases. I. Title: Decedents' estates and trusts. II. Scoles, Eugene F. III. Scoles, Eugene F. Problems and materials on decedents' estates and trusts.

KF777.S34 2000
346.7305′6—dc21

00-032291

About Aspen Law & Business
Legal Education Division

With a dedication to preserving and strengthening the long-standing tradition of publishing excellence in legal education, Aspen Law & Business continues to provide the highest quality teaching and learning resources for today's law school community. Careful development, meticulous editing, and an unmatched responsiveness to the evolving needs of today's discerning educators combine in the creation of our outstanding casebooks, coursebooks, textbooks, and study aids.

ASPEN LAW & BUSINESS
A Division of Aspen Publishers, Inc.
A Wolters Kluwer Company
www.aspenpublishers.com

Summary of Contents

Contents

1
Introduction   1

2
Intestate Succession   32

3

Family Protection and Limits on Testation   76

6

Revocation and Revival   224

10

Introduction to Future Interests and Powers of Appointment   383

11

Constructional Problems in Estate and Trust Distribution   435

12
Creation of Trusts   525

13
The Nature of the Beneficiaries' Interests   605

14
Modification and Termination of Trusts   **664**

15
Charitable Trusts   709

17

The Fiduciary Office   815

19
Matters of Accounting and Successive Enjoyment   977

20
Rules Regulating Perpetuities 1072

Preface to the Sixth Edition

This sixth edition continues the time-tested approach of the earlier editions (see Preface to the First Edition, hereafter). Typically, text is used to set up a challenging problem, which is followed by selected statutory, case, or text material to be studied for insights into the issues presented. The problems are designed to develop and test the student's skills of advocacy and of doctrinal and statutory analysis; they also invite consideration of whether the planner or drafter could have prevented the controversy involved and whether the law could offer a better background for its avoidance or resolution.

In the most fundamental of its revisions, this edition incorporates the subject matter of the previously separate Halbach & Scoles, Problems and Materials on Future Interests (1977). This edition alone is therefore suitable for the now typical, all-inclusive course encompassing future interests as well as succession, trusts, and fiduciary administration. The goals of efficiently condensing and integrating, rather than just combining, the various bodies of material led us to reexamine the book's organization along pedagogical rather than topical lines. The results include chapters entitled "Introduction to Future Interests and Powers of Appointment" (Chapter 10), "Constructional Problems in Estate and Trust Distribution" (Chapter 11), and "Rules Relating to Perpetuities" (Chapter 20). Following Chapter 9's introduction to the trust device, Chapter 10 acquaints students with some of the most important distributive provisions of trusts. Chapter 11 then examines constructional issues arising from changes in a testator's property between execution of the will and distribution of the estate — matters formerly covered later in the book — and then proceeds to constructional issues resulting from changes among the potential beneficiaries prior to the distribution of an estate or trust. This permits an economical treatment and useful comparison of such matters as class gifts, lapse and other survivorship questions, and constructional issues involving powers of appointment. Having laid the groundwork for the time-divided ownership that is characteristic of trusts, the book proceeds to other aspects of trust law and fiduciary administration, with little *structural* change in these areas. In closing with a detailed study of rules regulating perpetuities (the outlines of which are introduced earlier), the book facilitates a review and pulling together of some of the previous material in the course and raises anew a major aspect of the dead hand control questions that pervade trust law.

Possibly the next most important change in this edition is the inclusion throughout of extensive materials reflecting the growing importance of professional responsibility issues in what has traditionally been thought of as a relatively nonadversarial field. In other structural and coverage changes, the materials on grounds for contesting a will have been moved up to Chapter 3 on Family Protection and Limits on Testation, and the treatment in that chapter of living wills has been significantly expanded to include other elder law issues. Of course, throughout the book there has been updating and adaptation to reflect recent developments, evolving themes, and shifts in emphasis within the field of donative transfers and estate planning.

Prior editions have reflected the upsurge of legislative reform in probate and trust law, especially through the Uniform Probate Code — still a focus of ongoing study and adaptation. The trend of change has accelerated and expanded since the publication of the fifth edition, with trust law receiving particular attention. The Uniform Prudent Investor Act of 1994 was followed by a significantly related 1997 Revised Uniform Principal and Income Act, and a comprehensive Uniform Trust Code is expected to be promulgated later this year. The 1999 Uniform Disclaimer of Property Interests Act and the earlier Uniform Statutory Rule Against Perpetuities also bear importantly on trust law, while the Uniform Health-Care Decisions Act evidences growing interest in legal issues associated with aging. The pace of reform in the field of estates and trusts has gained much of its momentum from ongoing projects of the American Law Institute: the Restatement (Third) of Trusts and the Restatement (Third) of Property — Wills and Other Donative Transfers, plus a Restatement (Third) of the Law Governing Lawyers.

To strike a balance between detail and brevity, and to avoid the need for a statutory supplement, uniform acts and other statutes are set out in full where the language is critical, but otherwise, relevant legislation is summarized. (Some instructors, of course, will wish to supplement the materials with local statutes.) While many new cases have been added, we did not engage in age discrimination: if the classic case is still the best, we kept it.

We hope the mix of the practical and the theoretical will continue to receive the acceptance reported by teachers and students who used the first five editions. The experience and observations of prior users are, we believe, reflected in pedagogical details as well as in content, with a goal of aiding students' independent mastery of much of the course material, both to protect classroom time and to advance the level of class discussion. We look forward to the comments of teachers who use this new edition, in which the original authors have been joined by Professors Link and Roberts.

We acknowledge with appreciation the authors and publishers who have granted us permission to reprint portions of their work and also the many helpful suggestions from teachers who have used prior editions. On the latter score we are particularly indebted to Professors Martin Begleiter and Richard Gould. We also wish to thank our student research assistants and the support staff at our respective institutions.

Eugene F. Scoles
Edward C. Halbach, Jr.
Ronald C. Link
Patricia Gilchrist Roberts

August 2000

Preface to the First Edition

This book is designed primarily for a combined course in Decedents' Estates and Trusts, including fiduciary administration, or for use, in conjunction with separate materials on future interests, in a more inclusive course encompassing the traditional subjects of Wills Trusts, and Future Interests.

The organization of the book is not necessarily a "logical" one. The materials are presented in a sequence calculated to make the study of them more meaningful, and also more efficient when possible. For example, matters relating to the termination of trusts are not presented at the end but are taken up earlier, because certain characteristics of trusts and certain rights of beneficiaries relating to termination are relevant to a thorough consideration of many aspects of trust administration. It will also be noted that much of the book is built around problems. The order in which some topics are taken up is dictated by the objective of adequately preparing students to approach the problems with an understanding of the legal and practical considerations that are relevant to public policy or to private solution through planning. In most instances the cases and other materials have been prepared not simply to be studied as such, but to be considered for the purpose of attacking a particular problem. We have tended to reverse the typical casebook format of cases followed by notes; usually we have placed text before the related cases, especially where basic doctrine can satisfactorily and more easily be imparted in this fashion. This organization, together with the more extensive use of textual material, is intended to make the experience of working with cases and problems more valuable and more interesting than if they were approached without some background in the basic rules involved. In other words, text is used to "set up" the cases and problems. Because a student does not come to them blindly, cases and problems which are more challenging can be used, or at least a more sophisticated discussion of a given case or problem can be expected. We believe that more is gained by this technique than is lost by what some teachers will consider a giving away of too much too readily. We hope, frankly, that a higher level of performance and interest can be stimulated concerning selected issues by having their practical and legal context, as well as by having a certain amount of general subject matter coverage, provided by text.

It is our objective that both the content and emphases of this book reflect the realities of present-day practice in the field of estates and trusts, while also revealing that the field is very much alive with new (as well as old) problems in need of solution. For example, although we do not seek in this book to teach tax planning, we do feel that course emphasis should reflect the types of current questions being opened up by various dispositions and fiduciary practices that are prompted by considerations of legitimate tax minimization. You may also note an effort in appropriate parts of the book to shift attention from the abundant case experience which grew out of the depression of the thirties to the largely unexplored issues arising from long-term inflation.

In the overall picture, however, a very important factor in determining the content, emphasis, and method of this book is a realization that growing demands upon lawyers, and hence upon law school curricula, require that significant features of this course area be covered in fewer classroom hours than in the past, without unduly sacrificing either depth of understanding in the field itself or fundamental insights which this course should offer concerning the law in general.

Finally, we wish to express our appreciation to the authors and publishers who have granted us permission to reprint portions of copyrighted texts and articles in this book.

Eugene F. Scoles
Edward C. Halbach, Jr.

1965

Acknowledgments

We are grateful to copyright holders for permission to reprint excerpts from the following items:

American Bar Association, Model Rules of Professional Conduct (1999), Rules 1.1, 1.3-1.4, 1.7-1.8, 1.14; Model Code of Professional Responsibility (1981); Statement of Principles Regarding Probate Practices and Expenses (1975); Report of the Fiduciary Accounting Standards Committee (1980). Reprinted by permission of the American Bar Association. Copies of the ABA Model Rules of Professional Conduct (1999) and the ABA Model Rules of Professional Responsibility (1981) are available from Service Center, American Bar Association, 750 North Lake Shore Drive, Chicago, IL 60611, 312-988-5522.

American Law Institute, Restatement of Trusts §§206, 184. Restatement (Second) of Trusts §§156, 171, 186, 330, 339, 342, 368, 375, 399, 400. Copyright © 1959. Restatement (Third) of Trusts §§2, 5, 11, 13, 16, 18-19, 21-26, 28-31, 35-37, 42-43, 45-47, 50, 56-60, 62, 171, 183, 227. Copyright ©1992. Restatement of Property, Introductory Note to Div. IV, 2129-2133; §242. Copyright © 1940. Restatement (Second) of Property §§2.1, 2.2, 11.1, 24.2, 25.3, 29.4; Part I Rationale at 8-18. Restatement (Third) of Property §§2.5, 3.3, 4.3, 5.2, 10.1, 11.1, 11.2, 12.1. Restatement of Restitution §182. Copyright © 1936. Reprinted with permission of the American Law Institute.

Atkinson, Thomas E., Handbook of the Law of Wills and Other Principles of Succession Including Intestacy and Administration of Decedents' Estates, Second Edition, 136. Copyright © 1953 West Publishing Company.

Bergin & Haskell, Preface to Estates in Land and Future Interests, Second Edition. Copyright © 1984 Foundation Press, University Textbook Series. Reprinted with permission.

Bogert, George G., Law of Trusts, Sixth Edition. Copyright © 1987 West Publishing Company.

Casner, A. James, ed., et al., American Law of Property: A Treatise on the Law of Property in the United States. Copyright © 1952 Little Brown. Reprinted with permission of Aspen Law and Business.

Comment, Wills, Undue Influence, 50 Michigan Law Review, 748, 758-60 (1952). Copyright © 1952. Reprinted by permission of the Michigan Law Review Association.

Mechem, Phillip, The Requirement of Delivery in Gifts of Chattels and of Choses in Action Evidenced by Commercial Instruments, 21 Illinois Law Review, 341-42, 348-50 (1926). Copyright © 1926 by Northwestern University School of Law, Vol. 21, No. 4. Reprinted by special permission of Illinois Law Review.

Nathanson, The Ethics of Inheritance, Social Meaning of Legal Concepts (No. 1): Inheritance and the Power of Testamentary Disposition, 74, 76, 85-89 (Cahn ed. 1948). Copyright © 1948. Reprinted by permission of New York University School of Law.

National Commission on the Observance of International Women's Year, To Form a More Perfect Union — Justice for American Women, U.S. Government Printing Office, 1976. Copyright © 1976.

Nussbaum, Liberty of Testation, 23 American Bar Association Journal, 183-86 (1937). Copyright © 1937. Excerpted by permission of the American Bar Association.

Posner, R., Economic Analysis of Law, Fourth Edition, 508-13. Copyright © 1992 by Aspen Law and Business.

Powell, Richard, et al., Powell on Real Property. Copyright © 1950 by Matthew Bender, Inc. Reprinted with permission.

————, Powell on Real Property, §27.01 n.8. Copyright © 1998 by Matthew Bender, Inc. Reprinted with permission from Powell on Real Property. All rights reserved.

Power, Wills: A Primer of Interpretation and Construction, 51 Iowa Law Review, 75, 76-87, 103-106 (1965). Copyright © 1965. Reprinted by permission.

Provisions for Dependents: The English Inheritance Act of 1938, Notes and Legislation, 53 Harvard Law Review, 465, 466-67 (1940). Copyright © 1940 by the Harvard Law Review Association. Reprinted by permission.

Shaffer, Nonestate Planning, 106 Trusts and Estates, 319-322 (1967). Copyright © 1967. Reprinted by permission.

Simes, Lewis M., Handbook of the Law of Future Interests, Second Edition, §§55, 69, 70, 91. Copyright © 1951, 1966. Reprinted with permission of the West Group.

Simes, Lewis M., and Smith, Allan F., The Law of Future Interests, Second Edition, Vol. 3, §1033 and Vol. 4, §1117. Copyright © 1956. Reprinted with permission of The West Group.

Sparks, Bertel M., Contracts to Make Wills: Legal Relations Arising Out of Contract to Devise or Bequeath, 27-28. Copyright © 1956 by New York University Press.

Stephenson and Gilbert, Drafting Wills and Trust Agreements: Dispositive Provisions, §17.12. Copyright © 1955, Little, Brown and Company. Reprinted with permission of Aspen Law and Business.

Sussman, et. al., The Family and Inheritance. Copyright © 1970 by the Russell Sage Foundation. Reprinted by permission.

Uniform Law Commissioners, Uniform Trust Act, Prefatory Note, §§102, 106, 107, 303-305, 408, 410-415, 501-506, 602, 604, 703, 803, 807, 810, 814-816, 1101, 1011. Uniform Probate Codes, §§1-108, 1-403, 2-101-103, 2-105-106, 2-109, 2-114, 2-202-209, 2-213, 2-404, 2-705, 2-803, 2-801, 3-203, 3-706, 3-709, 3-711, 3-714, 3-715, 3-719, 3-904, 3-916, 7-302, 7-303. Uniform Prudent Investor Act, Prefatory Note, §1-11. Uniform Principle & Income Act, TOC, Prefatory Note, §§102-103, 104, 201-202, 301-303, 401-403, 413-415, 501-503. Uniform Statutory Rule Against Perpetuities, Summary, Prefatory Note, §§1-5, 9. Uniform Marital Property Act, Prefatory Note, §§2-301-302, 2-502-507, 2-509-511, 2-512-514, 2-603-605, 2-608, 2-704, 2-707, 2-711, 3-902, 3-912, 3-1101, 3-1201-1204, 6-101, 6-211-216. Reprinted with permission of the Uniform Law Commissioners.

Westlaw internet site, excerpt. Reprinted by permission of the West Group from the Westlaw internet site.

Whitman and Hoopes, The Confidential Relationship in Will Contests, 122 Trusts & Estates, 53, 54 (1985). Copyright © 1985. Reprinted by permission.

Young, Russell, et al., Current Investment Questions, 13 Real Property, Probate & Trust Journal 650, Fall 1979, 664-668. Copyright © 1978 American Bar Association. Reprinted by permission.

Problems and Materials on
DECEDENTS' ESTATES AND TRUSTS

1

Introduction

A. Terminology

These first few paragraphs are not intended as a substitute for a dictionary. The definitions provided here are in part a cast of characters for the course. It is also hoped that these definitions, though not exhaustive, will help to prevent your carrying some misconceptions through the course. Even though it happens every year in possibly every law school, it never ceases to shock teachers to discover that some students in the middle of their second year in law school still believe that the heirs of a person who died testate are those who take under the will. This first section is calculated, among other things, to improve communication and to reduce the number of shocks experienced on both sides of the teaching rostrum.

A person who dies without a will is said to die *intestate*. A *testator* or *testatrix* is one who has died *testate* — i.e., leaving a will. Traditionally, a testator *devises* real property to a *devisee* and *bequeaths* personal property to a *legatee*. Strictly speaking, a *legacy* is a bequest of a sum of money, but you will regularly encounter the term used as broadly as *bequest*, the generic term for testamentary gifts of personalty. In fact, in statutes, opinions, and everyday usage, you will find the real and personal property lines disregarded; thus, many statutes today (including the Uniform Probate Code) use *devise* to refer to a bequest as well as a testamentary disposition of land. In this book, the term *devise* is used to refer to a gift by will of personal or real property, and the term *testator* is used to refer to a testator of either gender.

Persons who take or, but for a will, would have taken a decedent's personalty under the laws of intestacy are, traditionally, *next of kin;* intestate successors to realty are the decedent's *heirs*. Although the surviving spouse shares in the intestate property, the spouse may or may not be properly classified as an *heir*, depending on the local law. As real and personal property have come generally to be governed by a single statute of descent (referring to land) and distribution (personalty), it has become fully acceptable and usual to refer to the persons designated by statute to take intestate property, real and personal, as the decedent's *heirs*. A living person has no heirs.

The personal property of a decedent, whether testate or intestate, is generally supposed to pass through a court-supervised process of estate *administration*. Traditionally, real property has bypassed this process, descending directly to the devisees or heirs, but administration has been extended to realty by most statutes. Because the process of administration generally affects realty, even if not fully subject to administration, this distinction between real and personal property usually is disregarded for purposes of terminology. The term *probate* is often used interchangeably with *administration,* but the term strictly refers to the process of proving and deciding the validity of a will in the appropriate court. Probate, then, is a preliminary step in testate administration.

The person appointed to handle an estate — to collect assets, pay creditors, and distribute the remaining property — is the *personal representative.* The personal representative appointed by the court to administer an intestate estate is an *administrator* or *administratrix;* if for any reason a successor is required in this office, that person is called an *administrator d.b.n. (de bonis non,* i.e., of goods not administered). Wills usually nominate someone to serve as a personal representative; this nominee, if appointed, is called an *executor* or *executrix* of the will. Should the nominee predecease the testator or for other reason not be appointed, an *administrator c.t.a. (cum testamento annexo,* i.e., with will annexed) is appointed. If an executor or administrator c.t.a. ceases to serve after commencing administration, an *administrator c.t.a., d.b.n.* is appointed to finish the job. Again, casual usage is such that the term *executor* or *administrator* may be encountered in reference to any personal representative. In this book *executor* and *administrator* are used to refer to either gender.

A little genealogical terminology is also useful at the start. Relationship by blood is by *consanguinity;* relationship by marriage is by *affinity. Ascendants* or *lineal ascendants* are ancestors; *descendants* or *issue* are children, grandchildren, and others of all degrees in the descending line. *Collaterals* are relatives who are neither ascendants nor descendants but are related to the person in question through common ancestry; a sister (related through common parents), an uncle (via grandparents), a maternal cousin once removed, and the like are collateral relatives.

Throughout this course, reference will be made to *trusts.* The term is commonly and almost meaninglessly used, especially in judicial opinions, to connote a broad range of relationships, particularly of a fiduciary character but extending all the way from guardianship to agency to bailment. In this course, the term is used in the narrower sense. At this preliminary stage, an example, rather than a definition, is probably more useful to present the fundamental notion. *A* transfers certain securities to *T* "in trust to manage, invest, and reinvest and to pay *B* the net income for life, and, on *B*'s death, to distribute the principal to *C*." *A* has created an *express trust* by which *T*, called the *trustee,* is obligated to perform a function with regard to the trust property (of which *T* is generally legal owner) exclusively for the benefit of *B* and

C. The beneficiary is often called the *cestui que trust;* here the cestuis, *B* and *C,* would more specifically be called *income beneficiary* and *remainder beneficiary* (traditionally called *"remainderman"*) respectively. *A* is usually called the *settlor* (today, even when the trust is created by will) or, in some places, the *trustor.* The *subject matter of the trust* is the trust property and is usually referred to as the *res, corpus,* or *principal.*

Unless qualified by the words *constructive* or *resulting,* the term *trust* is used in this book to refer to express trusts, which may be charitable as well as private. The express private trust above is a *living trust* or *inter vivos trust* because it is created during the settlor's lifetime, while a *testamentary trust* is one that is created in the testator's (i.e., settlor's) will. Briefly, you may find it helpful for now simply to think of a resulting trust as a form of reversionary interest and to think of a constructive trust as a remedial device, typically for recovering or obtaining property to prevent unjust enrichment or to redress wrongful conduct.

Trustees and the various types of personal representatives are more broadly referred to as *fiduciaries,* a term properly applicable to persons in numerous other categories, including lawyers, agents, guardians, and directors of corporations. It is often asserted that the trustee's fiduciary duty to the beneficiary is of the highest order known in the law. You should consider why and to what extent this is so.

In considering the trust example above ("to *A* for life, then to *B*") you are revisiting the concept of ownership divided over time that you probably were introduced to in your first-year property course. *B* has a "future interest," but, remember, the only thing "future" about *B*'s interest is possession. In every other respect, it is a presently existing interest. *B* acquires her interest at the same time that *A* acquires the life estate. Although the law of future interests evolved at a time when most wealth was in the form of real property, the concept of time-divided ownership applies equally as well to personal property. Most sophisticated modern day wills and trusts create future interests, and this casebook covers an array of interesting future interests issues that the estate planner must understand.

Restatements of the Law and Uniform Acts

Throughout this book there will be references to Restatements of the Law and to various Uniform Laws, notably the Uniform Probate Code (UPC) and the Uniform Trust Code. The Restatements are produced under the auspices of the American Law Institute (ALI), and they purport to state a proper or recommended view of current American common law. They must receive formal approval of the Institute. The first series of Restatements began in 1923, and the Restatements (Second) began in 1952. The Third Restatement series is now in progress. Both a Restatement (Third) of the Law of Trusts and a Restatement (Third) of the Law of Property (Wills & Other Donative Transfers) are currently at various stages of drafting or approval by ALI.

Uniform acts are promulgated by the National Conference of Commissioners on Uniform State Laws (NCCUSL). Uniform acts are drafted by NCCUSL with the hope that they will be enacted by the legislatures of individual states. Because our society is so mobile, there is a great need for uniformity in this area of the law. The 1969 UPC (often referred to as the pre-1990 UPC) was enacted in many of the jurisdictions. Then, in 1990, there was an extensive revision and expansion of the UPC, motivated by the changes in the American family and by the "nonprobate revolution" that has taken place during the last three decades. Unless otherwise indicated, the references to the UPC in this book will be references to the 1990 UPC. A new Uniform Trust Code is near completion; it will be the first comprehensive uniform act dealing with the law of trusts.

B. Historical Background

We will now take a brief look at the English background against which so much of the American laws of succession and trusts developed. We are particularly concerned with the English history of wealth transmission up to the period in which the roots of our own systems developed. Even if it is acceptable to say that what happened in England after 1776 is not a part of our heritage, the influence of English case law and legislation certainly did not then and has not yet ceased.

As ancient societies came to recognize individual as distinct from family or clan ownership of property, the institution of succession came into being. Indications are that family ownership was never recognized among the Anglo-Saxons. Although wills were recognized in ancient Greece (and apparently the power of testation as well as intestate succession existed in earlier societies), the Roman law concepts of wills and the interests of the church influenced the gradual development of testamentary disposition of personalty in England. As we shall see, succession to land did not exist under feudalism in England until the system had matured somewhat. A review of developments beyond the Anglo-Saxon period requires a division of our study into personal property and real property categories at the outset. These two lines of development have largely been merged in modern times, but the influences of their "separate" though not unrelated histories remain with us today.

1. Personal Property

Centuries before the Norman Conquest, respect for the expressed wishes of a dying man produced a practice that might be termed testation. Also, the irrevocable post obit gift, made inter vivos but understood to take effect in possession at death, provided another starting point. The post obit gift was sometimes accompanied by instructions for disposition of the property. Supported by the authority of ecclesiastics, these two devices evolved into a system of executorship as a method of testamentary disposition, possibly by analogy to Roman law principles and to the Germanic salman (a transferee who undertook to carry out purposes specified by the transferor). Shortly after 1066 a separation of ecclesiastical courts from the king's courts left the former to develop rules for succession to personal property, while matters involving land fell within the functions of the king's court. The concept of an informal and revocable will applicable to chattels became well recognized in the ecclesiastical courts at an early time.

Intestacy was considered shameful, since the making of a will normally accompanied the confession of a dying person and it was customary for the will to show proper concern for the welfare of the soul. For centuries the ecclesiastical rules for intestate distribution of chattels remained uncertain, subject to local custom, and, in general, matters of loose practice. Thus, there was also a temporal incentive for having a will, because of the uncertainty of the family's rights as against those of the church and the feudal lord or king and also because of the peculiar patterns of distribution within the family. Rules similar to those of the Roman law, and still typical of civil law systems, were developed by the ecclesiastical courts to limit the extent to which wives and children could be deprived of inheritance. These limitations disappeared by the early fourteenth century in England, except as preserved by local custom. Over several centuries following the Norman Conquest, statutory reform was attempted in an effort to eliminate abuses by executors in the administration and distribution of personalty. This effort might be seen as a step in the development of a fiduciary concept in the process of wealth transmission. The decline of feudalism and the growing emphasis on commercial activities and on wealth in forms other than land created a need for effective procedures and rules affecting personal property. But reforms were slow in coming.

The Statute of Distribution, 22 & 23 Car. II, c. 10 (1670), and the Statute of Frauds, 29 Car. II, c. 3 (1677), established the pattern of succession to personalty for modern times. The Statute of Distribution clarified rules of intestate succession and removed objectionable features of the schemes of distribution developed in the ecclesiastical courts. The distributive pattern of the statute is examined in the next chapter, dealing with the modern rules of intestate succession. The Statute of Frauds introduced the requirement, with limited exceptions, of a writing for testamentary dispositions of personalty. After 1677, personal property owned at death could pass under a will executed prior to the acquisition of the particular personalty, and today this is true with regard to all property.

2. Real Property

At the outset, the character of feudal land holding in England delayed the development of succession to land. Because the relationship of lord and tenant was essentially a personal one, the "heir" of a deceased tenant did not succeed to the land but had to seek a re-grant. Even after the Conquest, there is evidence of lords refusing to re-grant to heirs of deceased tenants. Despite the absence of obligation, however, it became customary for the lord to accept the heir as tenant on the payment of a sum of money called a relief. Gradually, inheritance by the heir became a matter of right, and the relief paid the lord is recognizable as a predecessor of our succession taxes. "By 1100 it therefore appears that the hereditary principle was admitted by the king in favour of his tenants in chief, and by them in favour of their subtenants. Having gone that far, it must rapidly have spread all through the feudal network." T. Plucknett, A Concise History of the Common Law 524 (5th ed. 1956).

The feudal influence is reflected in the common law Canons of Descent as developed in the king's courts. Under these rules, male descendants excluded females of the same degree; among males of equal degree, only the eldest inherited (primogeniture); absent surviving sons or issue of deceased sons (for, under the principle of representation, issue, male or female, stood in the place of a deceased descendant), daughters took equally as coparceners. In the absence of issue, the land passed to collaterals, because, by the mid-twelfth century, ascendants were not allowed to inherit; among collateral relatives, the principle of representation was also adhered to, in what is called a *parentelic* system, but males were generally preferred over females. Whole-blood collaterals were preferred to half bloods, and the doctrine of ancestral property limited inheritance among collaterals to those of the blood of the "first purchaser" (usually the ancestor from whom the decedent had inherited the land). These canons were occasionally modified by local custom but essentially endured until beyond 1776. The Inheritance Act, 3 & 4 Wm. IV, c. 106 (1833), restored inheritance by ancestors and ended the preference for whole bloods over half bloods, but not until the Administration of Estates Act, 15 Geo. V, c. 23 (1925), was primogeniture abolished.[1] The same rules have governed intestate succession to real and personal property in England since 1925, and the preference for males over females has been eliminated.

---

1. Primogeniture's primitive origin was based on its effectiveness in avoiding inefficient dispersal of family wealth, power, and responsibility. In feudal England, it was valued for this same quality, and also for the spur it provided younger sons to make their own fortunes and thereby to enrich society. Its evident unfairness, plus possible skepticism about its supposed justifications, led to the system's eventual rejection.

In the United States, ancestors are allowed to inherit, and neither primogeniture nor preference for males is recognized; nevertheless, peculiarities of the English history of descent are reflected in varying degrees in our statutes.

The widow was not an heir at common law. She was provided for by dower, of which we know little of the history. Very early, husbands voluntarily gave portions of their property to their wives on marriage. Although church authorities may then have come to require such gifts, it was not until the thirteenth century that common law dower had fully developed. Dower, which endured in England until 1925, entitled the widow to a life estate in one-third of the lands of which her husband was seised at any time during the marriage and that were inheritable by his issue. Dower protected the wife against the husband's inter vivos conveyances, as well as against his testamentary dispositions after the power to devise land was created. See Haskins, The Development of Common Law Dower, 62 Harv. L. Rev. 42 (1948); Note, The Defeasibility of Dower, 98 U. Pa. L. Rev. 826 (1960). Until 1833, dower did not apply to equitable interests. The husband's curtesy, unlike dower, applied to equitable interests and to all, rather than one-third, of the wife's inheritable freeholds. As an extension of the marital right, by which he acquired an estate for the period of the marriage, the husband's curtesy gave him an estate for his life on birth of issue. The dower concept represents an early step in the development of modern restrictions on testation but, in this country, has been generally abolished in favor of a statutory forced share for surviving spouses.

Even when land became inheritable under the feudal system, testamentary disposition was allowed only by occasional local custom. In general, freehold interests in land could not be devised until 1540. But the centuries of intestate succession, unaccompanied by a right of testation, gave rise to some interesting and revealing developments that have left a significant mark on Anglo-American legal systems. The desire to devise property at death, together with efforts to avoid feudal incidents and certain inflexible legal rules, led to the practice of conveying land to several persons (jointly with right of survivorship) to hold title "to the use of" others. The use concept cannot be clearly traced, but its development in the ecclesiastical courts and later in chancery may be explained by reference to several possible sources, each of which may have had its influence. We have already noted the experience of ecclesiastics with executorship under wills of personal property; and the feoffee to uses also had its counterpart in the Germanic salman. In addition, institutions analogous to the use existed in the Roman and canon law, which were familiar to the prominent churchmen who long served the king in the office of Chancellor. Soon after the establishment of inheritance throughout the feudal system, it appears that a leading purpose of the use was to permit what amounted to testamentary disposition of land. Initially, feoffments to uses prescribed a particular beneficiary who was to receive the property after the feoffor's death. Later, conveyances to the use of such persons as the grantor might designate by will, followed by testamentary directions to the feoffee to uses, became a widespread method of "devising" land. This arrangement was a forerunner of our inter vivos trust with testamentary power of appointment.

Although the technique is easy to comprehend, the recognition and enforcement of uses were by no means a foregone conclusion in the courts that dealt with land in England. This was so despite the analogies available in the legal systems of other countries and in the ecclesiastical courts in England. The history of the use before the fifteenth century is particularly obscure. It is clear that uses were employed, relying on the feoffee's good faith, long before they became enforceable in the courts. In fact, statutes reflect a concern over the employment of unenforceable uses to defraud creditors and to circumvent such policies as that of the mortmain acts. Effective pressure, reinforcing a feoffee's good faith, resulted from the church's interest in the feoffee's honesty and in the use as a device for accomplishing social and religious objectives. Even after the king's courts excluded the ecclesiastical courts from the handling of matters involving land, the church could exert its influence through informal pressures. Later, the religious influence was felt through the Chancellor, to whom petitions addressed to the king came officially to be channeled. As chancery developed a body of equitable doctrine different from the inflexible substantive (as well as procedural) rules of the law courts, the use came and remained within the exclusive jurisdiction of equity. By the early fifteenth century, the Chancellor would enforce uses not inconsistent with public policy, and the body of rights of the cestui que use gradually took on the character of equitable ownership. A declining feudal system offered inadequate reason to withhold approval from the feoffment to uses to be declared by will. Consequently, of the many reasons why most of the land in England was held to uses by the early sixteenth century, this means of "testation" was at least one of the most important.

The Statute of Uses, 27 Hen. VIII, c. 10 (1535), which became effective in 1536, was the combined product of Henry's desire to replenish the treasury and the desire of lawyers in Parliament to recapture land litigation from chancery. The Statute of Uses transformed certain equitable estates into legal estates by executing uses where a person was "seised of land to the use of" another. In your first-year property course, you learned that this process created new methods of conveyancing and new legal future interests. We are particularly interested in two other effects ensuing from the enactment of the Statute of Uses. First, the statute upset the use device as a means of disposing of land at death. The immediate discontent among the landowning classes produced the Statute of Wills, 32 Hen. VIII, c. 1 (1540). The Statute of Wills created, subject to the usual feudal dues, the power to devise certain lands by a written will. Rather than following the administration process typical of succession to personalty in the ecclesiastical courts, lands passed directly. The validity of a devise was tested in a common law action of ejectment. A will operated only on land owned by the testator at the time the will was executed, and this disability survived the Statute of Frauds, 1677, which made wills ambulatory as to personal property.

A second result of the Statute of Uses was its spur to the development of the modern trust. The statute did not execute all uses, and the exceptions are extremely important. The three basic categories of unexecuted uses included the use on a use, the use in personal property, and the active use. The decision protecting a use on a use came a hundred years after the statute, when feudal dues had ceased to be significant as a source of the Crown's revenue. Because the statute operated only where the feoffee to uses was "seised," it had no application to a use raised on personal property, and personalty was constantly growing in importance as a form of wealth. Shortly after its enactment, the statute was held not to execute an active use; i.e., one in which the grantee was charged with affirmative duties such as managing the property and collecting and paying over the rents. Having done away with most of the uses at the time, particularly the more objectionable ones, the statute left chancery free to mold the unexecuted use or trust into an effective institution for the management and disposition of property. The Chancellor was in a position to develop a body of equitable doctrine applicable to this special type of fiduciary relationship. Thus, the Statute of Uses accelerated evolution of the modern trust.

The unexecuted use served numerous purposes in the centuries that followed the Statute of Wills. Although it no longer was necessary as a means of wealth transmission on death, it has continued to serve as a will substitute. In the more immediate aftermath of the Statute of Uses/Statute of Wills period but preceding the American Revolution, the use served as a device to avoid destructibility of contingent remainders and as an element of the ingenious strict settlement. Probably of greater significance, the trust served to counter the husband's right to exclusive possession and to the profits of the wife's property during their joint lives. A devise or inter vivos conveyance to a person to the sole and separate use of the married woman gave rise to a use that equity held unexecuted. The legal title was required to be held for the cestui's exclusive benefit and control, despite the fact that the husband's estate jure uxoris generally applied to the wife's equitable estates as well as to her legal estates. Under this institution of the married women's separate estate, which continued until removal of the wife's disability in 1882, chancery acquired long experience in supervising the relations between legal and equitable owners of property. Objectionable and rigid rules of the English common law thus led to the growth of the virtually unique Anglo-American concept of the trust. It has continued and in fact matured since the development of modern laws providing for testate and intestate succession.

C.   The Modern Role of Succession and Trusts

The most commonly expressed view regarding the source and constitutional standing of succession rights is typified by language found in Irving Trust v. Day, 314 U.S. 556, 562 (1942): "Rights of succession to the property of a deceased, whether by will or by intestacy, are of statutory creation, and the dead hand rules succession only by sufferance. Nothing in the Federal Constitution forbids the legislature of a state to limit, condition, or even abolish the power of testamentary disposition over property within its jurisdiction." See also Kornstein, Inheritance: A Constitutional Right?, 36 Rut. L. Rev. 741 (1984).

A different view is expressed in Nunnemacher v. State, 129 Wis. 190, 108 N.W. 627 (1906), which involved an action to recover inheritance taxes paid under protest. In challenging the constitutionality of the tax law, the taxpayer asserted, as the first of several propositions, that the right to take property by will or inheritance is constitutionally protected as a "natural right which cannot wholly be taken away or substantially impaired by the Legislature." In agreement, the court stated:

> We are fully aware that the contrary proposition has been stated by the great majority of courts of this country, including the Supreme Court of the United States. The unanimity with which it is stated is perhaps only equaled by the paucity of reasoning by which it is supported. In its simplest form it is thus stated: "The right to take property by devise or descent is the creature of the law and not a natural right." Magoun v. Bank, 170 U.S. 283. In Eyre v. Jacob, 14 Grat. (Va.) 422, 73 Am. Dec. 367, it is stated more sweepingly thus: "It [the Legislature] may tomorrow, if it pleases, absolutely repeal the statute of wills, and that of descents and distributions, and declare that, upon the death of a party, his property shall be applied to the payment of his debts and the residue appropriated to public uses." . . .
>
> That there are inherent rights existing in the people prior to the making of any of our Constitutions is a fact recognized and declared by the Declaration of Independence, and by substantially every state Constitution. Our own Constitution says in its very first article: "All men are born equally free and independent and have certain inherent rights; among these are life, liberty and the pursuit of happiness; to secure these rights governments are instituted among men deriving their just powers from

the consent of the governed." Notice the language, "to secure these (inherent) rights governments are instituted"; not to manufacture new rights or to confer them on its citizens, but to conserve and secure to its citizens the exercise of pre-existing rights. It is true that the inherent rights here referred to are not defined but are included under the very general terms of "life, liberty and the pursuit of happiness." It is relatively easy to define "life and liberty," but it is apparent that the term "pursuit of happiness" is a very comprehensive expression which covers a broad field. Unquestionably this expression covers the idea of the acquisition of private property; not that the possession of property is the supreme good, but that there is planted in the breast of every person the desire to possess something useful or something pleasing which will serve to render life enjoyable, which shall be his very own, and which he may dispose of as he chooses, or leave to his children or his dependents at his decease. To deny that there is such universal desire, or to deny that the fulfillment of this desire contributes in a large degree to the attainment of human happiness is to deny a fact as patent as the shining of the sun at noonday. . . . And so we also find that, from the very earliest times, men have been acquiring property, protecting it by their own strong arm if necessary, and leaving it for the enjoyment of their descendants; and we find also that the right of the descendants, or some of them, to succeed to the ownership has been recognized from the dawn of human history. The birthright of the firstborn existed long before Esau sold his right to the wily Jacob, and the Mosaic law fairly bristles with provisions recognizing the right of inheritance as then long existing, and regulating its details. The most ancient known codes recognize it as a right already existing and Justice Brown was clearly right when he said, in U.S. v. Perkins, 163 U.S. 626: "The general consent of the most enlightened nations has from the earliest historical period recognized a natural right in children to inherit the property of their parents." . . .

So clear does it seem to us from the historical point of view that the right to take property by inheritance or will has existed in some form among civilized nations from the time when the memory of man runneth not to the contrary, and so conclusive seems the argument that these rights are a part of the inherent rights which governments, under our conception, are established to conserve, that we feel entirely justified in rejecting the dictum so frequently asserted by such a vast array of courts that these rights are purely statutory and may be wholly taken away by the Legislature. . . .

But, while we utterly reject the doctrine of Eyre v. Jacob, and hold the right to demand that property pass by inheritance or will is an inherent right subject only to reasonable regulation by the Legislature, we are not thereby brought to the conclusion that inheritance or succession taxes can not be levied. They do not depend upon the right to confiscate. . . .

So we arrive at the conclusion that the general principle of inheritance taxation may be justified under the power of reasonable regulation and taxation of transfers of property.

HODEL v. IRVING
481 U.S. 704 (1987)

O'CONNOR, J. The question presented is whether the original version of the "escheat" provision of the Indian Land Consolidation Act of 1983, Pub. L. 94-459, Tit. II, 96 Stat. 2519, effected a "taking" of appellees' decedents' property without just compensation. . . .

. . . [The statutory provision] here amounts to virtually the abrogation of the right to pass on a certain type of property — the small undivided interest — to one's heirs. In one form or another, the right to pass on property — to one's family in particular — has been part of the Anglo-American legal system since feudal times. . . . The fact that it may be possible for the owners of these interests to effectively control disposition upon death through complex inter vivos transactions such as revocable trusts is simply not an adequate substitute for the rights taken, given the nature of the property. Even the United States concedes that total abrogation of the right to pass property is unprecedented and likely unconstitutional. . . . Moreover, this statute effectively abolishes both descent and devise of these property interests even when the passing of the property to the heir might [advance the statutory objectives]. . . . [Thus], a *total* abrogation of these rights cannot be upheld. . . .

In holding that complete abolition of both the descent and devise of a particular class of property may be a taking [in this situation], we reaffirm the continuing vitality of the long line of cases recognizing the States', and where appropriate, the United States', broad authority to adjust the rules governing the descent and devise of property without implicating the guarantees of the Just Compensation Clause. See, e.g., Irving Trust Co. v. Day, 314 U.S. 556, 562 (1942). . . . The difference in this case is the fact that both descent and devise are completely abolished . . . [even] when the governmental purpose sought to be advanced, consolidation of ownership of Indian lands, does not conflict with the further descent of the property.

There is little doubt that the extreme fractionation of Indian lands is a serious problem. It may well be appropriate for the United States to ameliorate fractionation by means of regulating the descent and devise of Indian lands. . . . What is certainly not appropriate is to take the extraordinary step of abolishing both descent and devise of these property interests even when the passing of the property to the heir might result in consolidation of property. Accordingly, we find that this regulation, in the words of Justice Holmes, "goes too far." . . .

Congress amended the Indian Land Consolidation Act in an attempt to make it pass constitutional muster, but in Babbit v. Youpee, 519

U.S. 234 (1997), the Supreme Court held that, under a fair reading of *Irving*, the amendment did not rehabilitate the Act.

Despite the prevailing view in the country that there is no natural or constitutional right of succession, it is recognized, with as near certainty as such matters permit, that succession in some form and in some types of property is virtually a universal institution of civilized societies, ancient and modern, including present and former communist nations.[2] On the other hand, there is no such universality of the right to dispose of property by will. We have just reviewed the struggle to establish testation in England. Modern civil and Anglo-American legal systems accept the right of testation in some form. Often-expressed notions that the power of testation is justified as an encouragement to industry and thrift have by no means gone unquestioned, but the will may be seen as a means of making succession more meaningful and responsive to the individual wishes of property owners. Through the will, succession can be adapted to the needs and circumstances of the particular decedent's family. The existence of succession having been more or less accepted, however, legislative attention has largely focused on the nature and extent of the power of testation and on the priority of potential claimants to intestate property.

The modern tendency in this country is slightly in the direction of narrowing the class of relatives entitled to succeed to the property of an intestate and of expanding the occasions of escheat. More significant inroads on succession may be found in the form of estate and inheritance taxation in the United States, but succession taxes today reflect little of earlier notions that such taxes should serve as major instruments of social and economic policy, particularly so far as concentration of inheritable wealth is concerned. (This function is more effectively being performed by the income tax.) Because of the intimate relationships between testation and inter vivos giving, especially through the trust device, any serious social policy or revenue-raising function of succession taxes must be implemented in such a way as to deal with the whole area of gratuitous transfers. Thus, modern death taxes deal with inter vivos dispositions, which are in effect will substitutes, and such taxes are often supplemented by a gift tax. Countries

---

2. The institution of succession appears to reflect a basic human urge, and its development accompanied that of private property as civilization evolved from the food-gathering to the hunting-fishing, pastoral, and then gardening stages. See E. Hoebel, The Anthropology of Inheritance, in Social Meaning of Legal Concepts (No. 1): Inheritance of Property and The Power of Testation 5-26 (1948), concluding: "Within the scope of our anthropological survey, we may conclude that inheritance is a mechanism of greater significance in early and simple primitive society than most writers on legal history have been prone to allow." Also see Tay, The Law of Inheritance in the New Russian Civil Code of 1964, 17 Intl. & Comp. L.Q. 472 (1968); L. Schwartz, The Inheritance Law of the People's Republic of China, 28 Harv. Intl. L.J. 433 (1987).

urgently concerned with land reform or with redistribution of economic power and opportunity may come to rely heavily on partial abolition of succession rights, directly or through taxes. This method of attacking concentrations of wealth — which might encounter less resistance than programs of more immediate change — would have to be accompanied by some provision for the property owner's family and by restriction on inter vivos transmission of wealth. Thus, any soul-searching about the proper role of succession in a modern society must concern itself with the whole of what we might call donative transactions in property.

The modest restrictions on testation and inter vivos giving in this country have largely dealt with such matters as protecting the family from disinheritance and restraining the dead hand. (Despite the historical background of the *use* as a means of "succession," you will see that nearly all but the most modern of statutes dealing with family protections have disregarded will substitutes.) Temptations to disinherit members of the immediate family or to tie up property in perpetuity are sufficiently rare that these restrictions represent no substantial impairment of the freedom of testation of most of our clients. For the most part the trust is a rather generous and flexible institution through which a property owner may extend his personality beyond his lifetime, either for the good or the detriment of his beneficiaries. Inter vivos and testamentary trusts today allow for the accomplishment of nearly any reasonable objective. It is fair to say that most of today's legislative efforts concerning testation and the use of trusts have been in the direction not of limitation but of making these institutions more effective as a means of accomplishing individually formulated objectives. You will see, however, that policy restrictions, along with certain formal safeguards, do sometimes upset improperly handled attempts to exercise the broad freedoms allowed.

On the private side, succession and trusts play a varied role in the affairs of individuals. Intestate succession provides a scheme of descent and distribution that is generally said to be calculated to approximate the probable wishes of most decedents. It is questionable how well this objective has been achieved. See Fellows, Simon, and Rau, Public Attitudes About Property Distribution at Death and Intestate Succession Laws in the United States, 1978 Am. B. Found. Res. J. 319; Plager, The Spouse's Nonbarrable Share, 33 U. Chi. L. Rev. 681, 710 (1966). A statutory scheme of intestate succession, or the so-called estate plan by operation of law, can hardly be expected to satisfy the needs of everyone. In fact, it is unlikely to satisfy completely the wishes of any individual. Nor can the simple outright gift satisfy the objectives of all persons desirous of making inter vivos gifts. Thus, lawyers are actively involved in making testamentary succession and inter vivos donation serve the diverse purposes of individual clients. The will, frequently including testamentary trust provisions, is called on to enable a client to tailor succession to his precise goals and to the best interests of his beneficiaries. The living trust is called on to fulfill the particular objectives of the donor or to fit a gift to the needs of the donee. It also can serve as a substitute for a will, avoiding some of the drawbacks of having property pass through estate administration proceedings. More specifically, inter vivos and testamentary trusts offer means of providing for successive enjoyment of property. The trust is also a vehicle for managing property while a donee or legatee is legally or practically unable to manage it. Individuals may also use trusts when they find it necessary or desirable to defer certain dispositive decisions concerning the property and to entrust these decisions to another as fiduciary or as holder of a power of appointment. Today, planned giving and tediously planned testamentary dispositions are widely used to reduce income and death taxation as far as the donor is concerned and, more frequently, as far as the beneficiaries are concerned.

The trust has been praised as a device for reform in the law, and it has been condemned as a device for evading legal policies. Historical and present-day usages reflect the role trusts can play in circumventing conscious policies of the law, such as early and modern fiscal policies and restrictions on testation. Some avoidance techniques have been eliminated by legislation, and some attempts have been thwarted by judicial decision. On the other hand, the trust has been notably successful and valuable as a device for escaping disabilities and limitations that are merely the product of rigidity of concept or outmoded "legal technicalities" that courts of equity are willing to undercut. See Scott, The Trust as an Instrument of Law Reform, 31 Yale L.J. 457 (1922). The flexibility of the trust is such that its modern purposes are nearly as unlimited as lawyers' imaginations.

Serious question can be and has been raised about the wisdom of preserving significant inequalities based on inherited wealth and of perpetuating economic power that significantly affects the lives of others even when it no longer reflects the qualifications and merit of the power holder. We are thus asked to consider the justification for a system that allows private wealth to pass from generation to generation, with some individuals, selected by accident of birth, enjoying comforts and power they have not personally earned. Reflecting on society's rationale for the institution of succession is also helpful in understanding and thinking about the taxation of gifts and inheritances, about "the dead hand" (including questions concerning the duration and the permissible purposes and characteristics of trusts), and about the appropriate extent, freedom, and nature of succession to private wealth.

An essay dealing with these and associated topics is excerpted at length below. Others, together with the related report of an American Assembly held in 1976, are collected in Death, Taxes and Family Property (E. Halbach ed. 1977). Of particular relevance are Friedman, The Law of Succession in Social Perspective, id. at 9; Shaffer, Death, Property and Ideals, id. at 26; Jantscher, The Aims of Death Taxation, id. at 40; and Boskin, An Economist's Perspective on Estate Taxation, id. at 56. The philosophical and economic crosscurrents are aptly highlighted by viewing the Boskin essay (supra) through an egalitarian's eyes. Professor Boskin argues that the goals of equality are retarded rather than advanced if we raise death taxes (the only meaningful vehicle through which our society restricts the amount of succession) to a level that induces the wealthy to increase consumption at the expense of the capital base, thereby diminishing productivity and employment opportunities for others. Despite disagreement as to the point at which this regression might occur — at best speculative given the present state of knowledge (e.g., about "elasticity of demand for bequests") — even egalitarian principles of income/wealth redistribution acknowledge this danger by accepting that degree of inequality that will, in the long run by reason of incentives to productivity, provide the most for the poorest in society. See, e.g., Rawls, A Theory of Justice 275 (1971). Also, see generally R. Chester, Inheritance, Wealth and Society (1982); A. Okun, Further Thoughts on Equality and Efficiency (Brookings General Series, Reprint 325, 1977); Mark L. Ascher, Curtailing Inherited Wealth in America, 89 Mich L. Rev. 69 (1990) (arguing that inheritance promotes inequality and that it should be abolished).

NATHANSON, THE ETHICS OF INHERITANCE
Social Meaning of Legal Concepts (No. 1): Inheritance and the Power of Testamentary Disposition, 74, 76, 85-89
(E. Cahn ed. 1948)

Does the system of inheritance have any ethical value? The simplest answer is, "Yes, it does." For on its best level, it is an expression of deep family ties which are indispensable to a good life and a good society.

The problem confronting us, however, is not so simple as this. We are rather called upon to decide whether the value it has outweighs or is outweighed by its disvalue. No simple answer to this problem could be satisfying, since it involves a complex of social relations about which it would be foolhardy to be dogmatic and set of ethical criteria which are at best indemonstrable. . . .

What, then, are the ethical criteria which we bring to bear on this question? First, that every human being counts or ought to count as a person. Second, that in human relations, concern with eliciting the best possibilities in another is essential to the best development of oneself. Third, that this is as applicable in the relations of groups to groups as it is in individual relations. . . .

[T]he drive for money . . . is only one among the many drives existing side by side in each of us, of which one or another may be dominant at different stages in our lives or, for that matter, in different moods. In a competitive economy such as ours, where a person's security and status depend so much upon the accumulation of money and the outward display of its possession, it is not surprising that the pecuniary incentive should play a major role. It is true that this incentive often breeds remarkable ingenuity, initiative, and creative powers. It is also true that insofar as it encourages self-reliance, it develops a strong moral fiber within us. But it is not true that all persons are stimulated to do their best by the goad of competition. Nor is it true that any of us, at all times, finds competition the best stimulus to our best efforts.

There is a cooperative, as well as a competitive, need in us. There is that which we do seemingly at our own expense, as well as to our own benefit. There is that which we do hoping for the approval of those whose judgment we respect, regardless of what the world at large may think. There is all that we do for those we love, when not even love reciprocated is in our minds. There are the sacrifices we make for an idea or cause, finding what satisfactions we can in contributing our mite to the larger end.

It would be impossible validly to generalize about the relation of the pecuniary incentive to these and other tendencies in human beings. Nor have we settled the problem on the economic level, let alone in ethical terms, when, as some do, we observe that the Soviet Union, for all its overall objectives, has had to resort to vast differences in financial reward to get the most out of its people. What any or all societies have done up to now can never be conclusive demonstration of what any or all societies must do in the future. . . .

The positive case for inheritance, viewed individually, rests on the desire of an individual to provide for his family after his death. In any form of society, this concern with one's family is a virtue, and in a competitive society the attempt to make provision for them comes from understandable and ethically laudable motives. Now in this capitalist economy of ours, the desire to provide for one's family is regarded as a major stimulus to the efforts of the individual. The average healthy person does wish his family to live as comfortably as possible, and he has a strong desire, as well, to accumulate sufficient savings to deal with unemployment, old-age retirement, and emergencies due to sickness, accident, or death.

The fact is, however, that despite the normal desire to achieve such protection, a tremendous percentage of workers . . . have been unable to do so. . . . At least for these people, therefore, bequests and the system of inheritance as a whole are, in personal terms, academic matters.

How is it for those whose economic status is higher? Everyone with a sufficient sensitivity to family obligations would like to make provision for dependent wives, children, and parents. To make as sure as possible that one's widow will be able to maintain the way of life to which she has been accustomed, that one's children will have the educational and vocational opportunities which will give them the best start in adult life, that one's parents in their declining years will not suffer from the threat or actuality of destitution — all this is a normal desire. The attempt to realize this ambition is unquestionably as much a stimulus to individual effort as is the concern with a family's immediate well-being. Socially, it is desirable as far as it helps to strengthen the family unit. Ethically, it is one phase of a person's attempt to express his best in family relations. In a competitive society, the power to insure the well-being of those closest to oneself is of great practical and ethical value.

On the negative side, however, there are considerations of major importance. In the first place, the power to provide for one's family is not an unequivocal good. If it often stimulates the valuable desire of helping to protect those who need protection, it also, not infrequently, plays into the hands of an unhealthy ego interest. It is commonplace, in speaking of inheritance, to talk of the way in which the dead hand of the past so often controls the present and future. What is not so often considered is the ethically destructive part such a desire to exercise control over the future can play in an individual. It ought to be axiomatic that nothing can be more unethical than the attempt to play god in the lives of other people. The relation of a husband to a wife, of a parent to children, of a child to parents, should never be one of control or domination. It should be one of stimulating their best qualities, developing in ways which are unique and surpass our perception. This is a hard truth, and it is one evidence of how difficult it is to achieve a genuinely democratic way of life.

The authoritarian habit of mind is more widespread than we like to believe. And it manifests itself in a desire to control the lives of others. The parent who wishes to "provide" for children sometimes does so on conditions that can be emotional strait-jackets for them, telling them what they must or must not do about education, vocation, or marriage. In these, and other relations, the testator makes a club of his bequest. He makes a legacy, not a means of showing his generous concern with those he cares about, but a tool of reward or punishment. . . .

For the legatees themselves, in addition, there are often consequences which go directly counter to the claims that our prevailing system best stimulates individual effort. Insofar as that effort derives from the pecuniary incentive, then it is evident that it must be largely vitiated for those who inherit fortunes, or whatever amount they do inherit which is in excess of their needs. . . .

Nor is this all. It can be argued that fortunes are accumulated through the superior ability or shrewdness or creativeness or good fortune of individuals, and that such power as goes with this accumulation is a justifiable reward. But the accident of birth is no argument in its behalf. For all the attempts to do so, it is not easy to justify the possession of power through inheritance. On feudal grounds, it can be done; it seems to me impossible on democratic grounds.

Our entire discussion has been in terms of the inheritance of property which plays an important part in our overall system of economic and social relations. The same considerations do not apply to the more personal possessions — the keepsakes, the books, and objets d'art, the trophies, yes, even jewels having a special significance — which are so much the expression of a person's individuality. In any society, one should have the right to dispose of all such things as he desires, as tokens of genuine regard and affection. The manner in which they are handled does not basically affect the ways we live together.

D.   *The Setting: An Illustrative Case History*

My name is Eugene Edwards. I practice with a small law firm in Willton, North Calinois. I'm going to discuss an estate I handled a few years ago, mainly to show you how the concepts from this course play out in real life. The state of North Calinois has a fairly representative probate code, and our trust law is probably not much different from that of your state, although variations certainly exist from state to state. The estate I am going to tell you about had the unusual quality of involving almost no real complications, which makes it an easy case to get you started in your course. Just don't get the idea that estates are normally this simple. I will also set out the terms of the will I drew for the client. Keep in mind that this will is not a model. As you go through the casebook, refer back to this problem periodically. I'm sure you will find several places where I could have drafted the document better.

1.   Planning the Estate

Harry Elder called me at the office about making a will before his departure on a vacation. He also wanted to know what information to bring with him to my office — deeds and so on — and whether his wife, Wilma, needed a will, since she had little property of her own. I explained that Wilma should have a will; for example, if she outlives Harry, she may not get around to seeing a lawyer before she dies.

I knew the Elders were well into their sixties and that Harry was retired, but when they came to my office many matters remained to be discussed. I learned that, in addition to social security, Harry was receiving $2,900 a month under his company's retirement plan and that Wilma would receive $1,850 a month for life if she survived him. Their two children, Sam and Doris (now Doris Young), were both married; there were four grandchildren. Neither client had living parents. Wilma's property consisted simply of her personal effects and her joint interests with Harry in a fluctuating checking account, in the family home, and in a small farm in an adjoining state. I verified that the checking account provided a right of survivorship and that the deeds to the home and farm created joint tenancies. In addition to personal effects and an automobile, Harry had some $3,400 in a savings account and about $510,000 worth of securities in his own name. His life was insured for $150,000. The home and farm were worth about $125,000 and $160,000 (net) respectively. Interviewing is partly a matter of "educating" your clients; you must lead them to formulate a sound and complete scheme of disposition, starting with their embryo of an idea about what they want done with their property. This part of your job cannot be overemphasized.

I asked Harry whom he wished to take his property on his death. He indicated that he would like to leave small gifts to his grandchildren but that he mainly wanted to benefit his wife and then the children. Next, I discussed the federal estate tax with the Elders and told them about the marital deduction, under which Harry could leave any property he wished to Wilma estate tax free (although a bit of North Calinois inheritance tax would be incurred). I also explained that, if he left enough to Wilma under that deduction, he could leave the rest of his estate free of federal tax essentially to anyone and in any way he might choose, because of a so-called unified credit that exempts $675,000[3] worth of transfers at death or major transfers during life that would otherwise be subject to gift taxation. We decided that if Harry died first we could obtain enough marital deduction to eliminate any federal tax on his estate simply by devising his car and other tangible personalty to Wilma, by letting the checking account and real estate pass to her by right of survivorship, and by having the insurance policies remain payable to her. The value of these assets would be comfortably below the amount her own unified credit would shelter from tax later at her death.

Except for the devises to Wilma and the grandchildren, Harry decided to leave the residue of his estate to the Willton Bank in trust for Wilma for her lifetime (planned in such a way as to keep that property from being includable in her taxable estate at death), with the trust remainder thereafter to go to Sam and Doris. If Wilma predeceased

---

3. This figure is scheduled to rise gradually until it reaches $1 million for persons dying in 2006 or thereafter.

Harry, he would leave everything directly to the children. Similarly, if Wilma survived, she wanted to leave everything to the children; but if she died first, she would leave what little she has outright to Harry. The way things stood, however, if Wilma died first, Harry's property holdings were sufficient to exceed his unified credit and to cause a substantial estate tax. (I talked further to Harry about this at a later time and pointed out that the tax under these circumstances could be avoided if he roughly divided his estate with Wilma during life, which he could do under the gift tax marital deduction; then whoever died first could use his or her unified credit to exempt the estate and establish a tax-planned trust for the survivor, whose estate could thereby be expected to remain small enough that no tax would have to be paid at the second death because of the survivor's own unified credit — but Harry was never quite prepared to do this.)

It surprised Harry to learn that part of the joint tenancy property and, in his situation, all of the life insurance proceeds would be includable in his estate for estate tax purposes (we call that the *gross estate*), even though they would pass to Wilma outside of his probate estate. Like other assets, though, these types of properties passing outright to a surviving spouse qualify for the marital deduction (which is also available to property passing into trusts, if the trusts are in qualifying form). Thus, for this purpose, and to avoid the delays and costs of probate in the process, we left the land in joint tenancy and left the insurance payable to Wilma. The reason for Wilma's having the home and checking account are probably obvious enough to you. By leaving the farm to her via joint tenancy the need for ancillary administration in the situs state was eliminated. Also, Wilma knew quite a bit about the farm, and this arrangement seemed better than converting it from joint tenancy in order to have Harry devise it to his residuary trustee. The insurance proceeds would provide Wilma some ready funds, but you must remember that estates also may have their liquidity problems. By having the proceeds paid to a named beneficiary, rather than to the estate, however, we also took advantage of an insurance exemption under the North Calinois inheritance tax.

Harry decided to name Wilma to serve as his executor, and vice versa. I don't always like to advise naming elderly widows or widowers to serve as executors, but the probate estate here was so simple — practically all securities. Anyway, I often find I have to handle most matters myself as attorney for an executor, so I might as well save the estate an executor's fee by recommending the surviving spouse for the job.

Incidentally, if either Sam or Doris should fail to outlive the clients, some provision was needed for their families. We decided to give Wilma a testamentary special power of appointment over the trust remainder under Harry's will to deal with the possibility of changed conditions, like this very question of a predeceased child. You will see what I ended up with when you read Harry's will.

2. Harry Elder's Will

As you read Harry's will, consider where I could have done better. Look for planning as well as drafting deficiencies. As you study particular problems during the course, look back to see what provision I made for them, if any, and try to understand why I used particular clauses. Again, I emphasize, this will is a sample, not a model. You can find many reasonably good "model" forms around. You may be able to obtain form books from local trust companies. I started out using a variety of recommended forms until I developed my own set which I know in detail now and which I *think* I fully understand. Yet you can never rely on forms to do your thinking for you. Individualized tailoring is always required.

LAST WILL AND TESTAMENT OF HARRY D. ELDER

I, Harry Dunwoodie Elder, of Willton, North Calinois, make this my last will, revoking all previous wills and codicils.

Article I

If my wife, Wilma, survives me, I devise to her all of my tangible personal property, but exclude intangible properties such as securities and bank accounts.

Article II

I devise the sum of one thousand dollars ($1,000) to each of my grandchildren who is living at the date of my death. At present my living grandchildren are Sam E. Elder, Jr., Amy X. Elder, Barbara Y. Young, and Charles Z. Young. All references in this will to children, grandchildren, or to other issue shall include persons who are adopted.

Article III

I devise the residue of my estate, but excluding any property over which I hold a power of appointment, to the Willton Bank, Willton, North Calinois, in trust, to be held, administered, and distributed as follows:

1. If my wife, Wilma, survives me, the trustee shall

a. distribute the net income of the trust estate to my wife for as long as she lives, payments to be made at times and intervals convenient to the trustee but not less frequently than quarterly, and

b. distribute to my wife principal in whatever amounts the trustee, in its discretion, deems appropriate for her health, maintenance, and support.

2. On the death of my wife, Wilma, if she survives me, the trustee shall distribute the trust estate to or for any one or more of my descendants and the spouses of my descendants, and in whatever interests, legal or equitable, my wife shall designate by her last will and testament.

3. If my wife, Wilma, does not survive me, or on the death of my wife, if she survives me but fails in whole or in part effectively to exercise the foregoing power of appointment, the trustee shall divide the trust estate into as many equal shares as there are children of mine then living and children of mine then deceased leaving issue then living. The trustee shall then allocate one equal share to each then living child; and one equal share shall be allocated among the then living issue, per stirpes, of each child then deceased leaving issue then living. Each share thus determined and allocated shall be retained in trust or distributed as follows:

a. Each share so allocated to a living child, grandchild, or other descendant of mine who is then over the age of twenty-one shall be distributed to that person free of trust.

b. Each share so allocated to a living child, grandchild, or other descendant of mine who is then under the age of twenty-one shall be retained by the trustee in a separate trust for that person. The trustee shall apply so much of the income or principal or both as he may deem advisable for the education, health, and support of the beneficiary until the beneficiary reaches the age of twenty-one, at which time the trust estate shall be distributed to the beneficiary; if the beneficiary should die before age twenty-one, the trust shall then terminate and the trust estate shall be distributed to his heirs at law.

4. If there are no issue of mine who are living at the time of my death or at the time of the death of my wife, Wilma, if she survives me, the trust estate shall then be distributed to those of my brothers and sisters who are then living and by right of representation to the issue then living of those of my brothers and sisters who are then deceased; and in the absence of these persons, the trust estate shall be distributed to the Regents of Blackstone University, White Rock, North Calinois, the whole or any part of the principal and income to be expended for purposes that the Regents may designate from time to time.

Article IV

To carry out the trusts, if any, created by Article III, above, the trustee shall possess the following powers affecting the trust estate, in addition to powers now or hereafter created by law or otherwise granted by this will: to manage, improve, sell, sell on deferred payments, exchange, grant options, and lease for periods within or extending beyond the duration of this trust; to retain property and to invest and reinvest in property and in the manner that the trustee in its discretion deems appropriate (including common and mutual funds and investment company shares); to borrow and to mortgage and encumber trust property; to hold bonds, stocks, and other securities in bearer form or in the name of a nominee; to receive additions to this trust; to employ counsel, custodians, brokers, and agents: to institute, defend, and compromise actions, proceedings, and controversies, including but not limited to those relating to taxes; and in making any division or partial or final distribution, I authorize the trustee to divide or distribute in cash or in kind, to decide what constitutes a proper division, and to fix values unless a particular method of valuation is otherwise specified.

Article V

I hereby nominate my wife, Wilma, as executor of this will, if she survives me. If she ceases, declines, or is unable to serve, I nominate my son, Sam, as my executor. I request that the above nominees, if appointed, be excused from bond; neither of these nominees shall be liable for his acts or omissions or for those of any agent, nor shall the trustee be under any obligation to contest the accounts of one of these nominees.

My personal representative shall have, with regard to my estate, the same powers as are conferred on the trustee under Article IV, above, in addition to those now or hereafter conferred by law. All powers conferred on my trustee under Articles III and IV, above, shall apply to substitute and successor trustees.

I, Harry D. Elder, on this fourteenth day of March, 1997, hereby subscribe my name, declaring this instrument to be my will.

Harry D. Elder /s/
Harry D. Elder

The foregoing instrument was, on this fourteenth day of March 1997, declared by the testator, Harry D. Elder, to be his last will in our presence; we, at his request and in his presence, have subscribed our names hereto as witnesses to the execution thereof.

Carleton B. Adams /s/ of Willton, North Calinois
Jasper I. Plankton /s/ of Willton, North Calinois

3. Administration of the Decedent's Estate

About a year later, Sam Elder phoned me to tell me that his father had died and that Wilma had asked him to get in touch with me. Sam would make the funeral arrangements, for which the estate would assume any reasonable costs and about which Harry's will made no special provision. North Calinois has a statute providing for summary (informal) administration of very small estates, but Harry's estate was well beyond the limits of the statute. Wilma agreed to serve as executor and asked me to act as her attorney.

I had retained Harry's will for safekeeping and proceeded, on behalf of Wilma, to petition for probate of the will and for issuance of letters testamentary. (In an intestate estate, the petition would be for letters of administration.) The petition, reciting the jurisdictional facts and the names and addresses of the heirs and testate beneficiaries, was filed in the Probate Court of Marshall County. Administration is in the court of probate, whatever it may be called, in the county and state where the decedent resided. Because, in general, under many existing statutes, a personal representative's authority as an arm of the appointing court may not extend to other states, ancillary administration may be required wherever the decedent owned assets that are subject to administration. You may recall that we eliminated this problem as to the Elders' only out-of-state asset by having the farm held in joint tenancy, but ancillary administration may have been required for any equipment or personal property on the farm or if Harry had owned other chattels or even intangibles in another state. Determining the situs of intangibles may pose problems. If ancillary administration is required, it usually helps to have the same person act as personal representative in all states. Statutes often pose restrictions on nonresidents in these positions; however, most statutes permit the domiciliary personal representative to serve as ancillary administrator or allow a person named in a will to serve as executor. After filing our petition, I saw to the giving of the prescribed notice to all interested parties of the time and place of the hearing on the petition, which was scheduled for some two weeks later. We have a typical provision for appointment of a special administrator for the period prior to the appointment of an executor or administrator, but this was unnecessary because Harry left no properties requiring prompt attention and there would be no will contest to unduly delay probate of the will.

In the meantime, I helped Wilma start the collection of insurance proceeds — the company's local agent took over and was most helpful. We also obtained the North Calinois inheritance tax release to have the joint checking account transferred to Wilma's name individually. Joint accounts, like other bank accounts and safe-deposit boxes, are frozen in many states following an owner's death, but usually clearances for transfer to the proper person are readily obtained through a local office of the state tax collection agency as long as payment of any taxes appears assured. I advised Wilma to go ahead and pay current bills and to keep receipts, but that any large or questionable debts of Harry's were to be filed and proved in the estate proceedings.

When the time arrived for proving the will in court, our witnesses were readily available. After some routine questions by the judge, the will was admitted to probate. As you will later learn, unless someone immediately wishes to contest, some states allow proceedings more informal than ours for prompt admission of a will to probate. Even under statutes like ours, providing for notice before the hearing, a period is allowed for subsequently setting aside the will. At the time of the hearing, Wilma also filed a petition requesting a family allowance so that estate funds could be distributed to her periodically during administration in amounts set by the judge on the basis of her needs and size of the estate. Once it is apparent that an estate is solvent, our courts will authorize limited preliminary distributions, but otherwise estate assets are in general tied up during administration. As you will learn in your tax course, the timing of distributions is complicated by income tax considerations. In addition, prior to the probate hearing, we had prepared a tentative inventory estimating the value of Harry's estate, and the judge set the amount of Wilma's bond as executor on this basis. You may recall that Harry's will purported to excuse bond; the effect of this in North Calinois is merely to dispense with the sureties on the bond, but this may represent a worthwhile saving. Wilma filed her bond — a promise to pay a stated sum to the court, subject to cancellation if she properly performs her duties — and qualified as executor. The court then issued letters testamentary, evidencing to others Wilma's authority to represent and act on behalf of the estate. For example, a copy of the letters accompanied Wilma's requests for reissuance of stock certificates standing in Harry's name at his death. The letters also enabled Wilma, on obtaining inheritance tax clearance, to have Harry's savings account placed in her name *as executor*.

Promptly after Wilma's appointment, notice to creditors was published, as prescribed by statute, to commence the running of the period within which creditors must file their claims or have them barred by the nonclaim statute, a special statute of limitations. In North Calinois, the period is four months. Proof of a claim is submitted when it is filed. The personal representative passes on these claims but usually does not pay them until later in the administration. A disallowed claim may have to be litigated. Disputed claims against a decedent's estate can be litigated in the probate courts in North Calinois, but in some states these claims are tried in courts of general jurisdiction. Incidentally, even in North Calinois, actions by the personal representative against a debtor of the estate and against others to recover or determine ownership of property must be brought in courts of general jurisdiction. Probate courts will authorize compromise of claims by or against the estate.

Wilma encountered no serious problems in collecting and preserving the assets of the estate. She opened a separate checking account in her name as executor. We had to prepare an inventory within sixty days showing the appraised values of probate assets, i.e., assets subject to estate administration. Inventory appraisals provide the basis of the personal representative's accounting and also are a factor in determining her compensation. Although these appraisals are not binding determinations of value, we had careful appraisals made (including nonprobate assets such as the farm and home) to serve our needs for estate tax reporting. I will not go into the details of federal estate tax returns or the audit by the Internal Revenue Service, but I will just observe that we were concerned with valuations at the date of death and that we had to file a detailed estate tax return within nine months of Harry's death. We also had to take care of state inheritance tax matters and to file fiduciary income tax returns and an income tax return for the year of Harry's death. I might add further that the valuations were necessary for purposes of estate accounting. We had to file interim accounts, and Wilma's entire stewardship was subject to review at the final accounting.

Somewhat more than a year after Harry's death, we were ready to close the estate. Pursuant to a court order authorizing sale, Wilma had liquidated some securities and had paid the few creditors of the estate. Sufficient cash was also raised to meet the estate's tax liabilities and to set aside a fund for the eventual payment of devises and expenses of administration. Where any doubt exists concerning the solvency of an estate, payments to unsecured creditors would be deferred until the time of termination of administration because the family allowance, funeral and administration expenses (including fiduciary commissions and attorney's fees), federal and state taxes, and sometimes claims for rent and wages are accorded priorities. The exact order of priorities varies from state to state.

In the final accounting at time of distribution, Wilma's administration was open to detailed examination through her accounts and reports. The Willton Bank, on behalf of the trust beneficiaries, was the party most interested in reviewing the accounts. In North Calinois, notice of the final accounting and petition for distribution of the estate is given to all interested parties. Hearing practices on these matters vary from county to county within the state, depending on the probate judge. The finality of final accountings and the res judicata effect of decrees discharging the personal representative or ordering distribution vary from state to state depending on statutory provisions. Our petition for distribution set forth Wilma's proposed distribution of the estate and requested the court to approve and decree distribution accordingly. You may recall that Harry's will included devises of $1,000 to each of his grandchildren. Under North Calinois statute, it was not necessary to have a legal guardian of the property appointed for the minor distributees since the devise was less than $2,500. The court authorized the sums, with interest at 6 percent from one year after Harry's death, to be paid over to the legatees' parents, the natural guardians of their persons. The court approved the distributions as proposed, and the Willton Bank receipted for the residue of the estate.

The court also approved my fee in the amount of $18,400 for services as attorney for the executor. Most of this fee was computed on the basis of the time I spent working on the estate coming into the control of the executor and accounted for by her. Had Wilma not waived her commission, she would have been entitled to slightly less than the amount of my fee, computed in the same manner but without the compensation I was awarded for extra services. My fee did not include the fee paid me by Wilma individually for my work in clearing the title to her home and in assisting an out-of-state firm in clearing title to the farm. When title to joint tenancy property passes by right of survivorship, administration is avoided, but it is necessary to clear land titles and to have stock certificates reissued in the name of the survivor. This usually involves obtaining certificates of death and tax releases and then placing these on record or submitting them to transfer agents when the outstanding stock certificates are surrendered.

4.   The Testamentary Trust

Traditionally, the administration of trusts, unlike that of decedents' estates, proceeds without any general involvement of the courts. If necessary for some reason, the procedure still used in some states is to invoke the jurisdiction of a court of equity by commencement of a suit in the usual manner. In North Calinois, as in some other states, our courts of probate retain continuing jurisdiction and supervision of testamentary trusts. Yet the law of trusts, not of decedents' estates, applies. Such trusts are commonly called *court trusts,* to be distinguished from noncourt trusts such as those created inter vivos. Controversy continues among North Calinois practitioners concerning the pros and cons of continuing jurisdiction — does this provision for court intervention and supervision result in harassment and greater expense in the long run, or are its disadvantages outweighed by the informality and simplicity of proceedings and the ready access to a court for instructions and periodic settlement of accounts? It must be obvious that the merits and impact of court involvement vary with the circumstances. But keep this question in mind during the course, because one can often control the character of a particular trust. In any event, Harry Elder's residuary trust was subject to the continuing jurisdiction of the Probate Court of Marshall County.

In North Calinois, a testamentary trustee must qualify and be confirmed before a probate court will authorize distribution to him by an executor. As you might have assumed, the Willton Bank had no problem in this regard. During estate administration, notices were sent to the trustee, and the bank kept informed by careful examination of Wilma's reports and accounts. (This watching by one fiduciary over the shoulder of another is eliminated in the common situation in which a trust company is named both as executor and as trustee.) When Harry's estate was being closed and the residue distributed, the trustee sought and obtained instructions to determine (1) whether certain earnings of the estate during administration were allocable to trust principal or constituted trust income distributable to Wilma as the life beneficiary and (2) whether the discretionary power of investment under Article IV of Harry's will enlarged the class of permissible investments beyond those normally authorized for trustees under North Calinois law. (I am sorry to confess that another provision of the will had to be construed later, but I leave it for you to guess which one.)

Following distribution of the residue of the estate to the Willton Bank, Wilma was invited to visit one of the trust officers of the bank, and later Sam and Doris also dropped in for a brief conference with him. At these conferences, the handling of trust affairs was explained to the beneficiaries, and the discussions also concerned the circumstances, wishes, and expectations of the beneficiaries. Most of the income that had accumulated during estate administration was promptly paid over to Wilma. Thereafter, the trustee so scheduled its income payments to provide her with monthly checks in nearly constant amounts. A balanced investment portfolio was maintained, consisting of stocks and bonds. From time to time some of the trust's investments were changed, reflecting the current views of the trustee's investment division concerning various securities. Unlike executors in North Calinois, trustees exercise their powers of sale and investment without court order. The trust produced an average yield over the period of Wilma's life of about 6 percent, showing some growth in the principal of the trust estate as well.

Our local probate judge directed submission of accounts annually by the trustee, accompanied by notice to the beneficiaries. The frequency of accountings by testamentary trustees and the hearing procedures rests largely in the discretion of the probate courts in North Calinois, unless a beneficiary exercises the right to compel accounting in court under various circumstances. At each of the accountings, the bank asked for and was granted reasonable compensation for its service as trustee. (These fees averaged about three-fourths of 1 percent of the principal each year.) In addition to submitting reports and accounts to the court, with copies to the beneficiaries, the trustee filed state and federal fiduciary income tax returns each year.

When Wilma died last year, without having exercised her power of appointment, the trustee filed its final account and requested the court's approval of its proposed distribution of the trust estate then in its hands, less commissions, attorney's fees, and expenses of termination. Because the persons beneficially interested in Wilma's individual estate (which, by the way, is still under administration) were the same as those entitled to the trust estate, the trust administration was smoothly concluded and the property was distributed promptly. Termination was also facilitated by the fact that the trustee had regularly accounted for its management of the trust estate in prior periods. Any questions concerning the binding effect of the court's decree, approving the final accounts, and discharging the trustee were for practical purposes rendered moot by the receipts and releases executed by the remainder beneficiaries, Sam Elder and Doris Young. The involvement of none but readily ascertained, adult beneficiaries certainly simplifies matters. Unfortunately, as you will see, all estate and trust administrations are not as trouble free, nor are all family situations as harmonious as in the case history I have just described for you.

E. *Professional Responsibility*

There are two sides to the professional responsibility coin: malpractice and ethics. Each is separate, but may relate to the other. For example, conduct that breaches the attorney's legal duty of care to the client may also implicate the attorney's ethical duty of competent representation.

Until 1961 malpractice was not a large concern for the estates and trusts lawyer. If the testator's or settlor's attorney failed to properly plan or draft, the lack of privity between the attorney and the intended beneficiaries was generally a successful defense against suit by them. Usually the donor was dead and had suffered no damages, so the risk of suit by the donor or the donor's estate was not significant. In 1961 California, as is often the case, signaled a change in American attitudes. Lucas v. Hamm, 56 Cal. 2d 583, 364 P.2d 685 (1961), said that a negligent drafter could be liable to the disappointed beneficiaries, despite the lack of privity. This case began a revolution in malpractice doctrine that, coupled with an increasingly litigious society, made malpractice exposure a reality to the estates and trusts bar.

As you study the materials in this book, keep in mind the issue of possible malpractice liability. What is the standard of care? To whom do the attorney's duties run? What constitutes a breach of duty? What is the measure of damages? More specifically, was the estate or trust competently planned? Were the instruments well drafted? Was the estate or trust properly administered? Was the case well argued? How, if at all, could the litigation have been avoided? Also consider the circumstances in which the lawyer is a fiduciary or becomes liable for assisting or participating in a breach of trust by a client.

Heightened sensitivity to the other side of the coin, ethics, probably dates from post-Watergate concerns about legal ethics, followed by the ABA's issuance of the Model Rules of Professional Conduct in 1983. Most states eventually adopted the Model Rules, often with revisions. In some instances, estates and trusts lawyers found incomplete or dubious guidance in the Model Rules. The dominant conception of the lawyer in the Model Rules was that of a litigator, a zealous advocate, while most probate practitioners conceived of themselves as planners and family counselors. Often the zealous advocate model does not work well for the estate planner, who often represents persons with potentially conflicting interests such as husband and wife or multiple generations of the same family, or for the estate or trust attorney, who may seem simultaneously to represent the donor, the fiduciary, and the beneficiaries. Potential conflicts in representation usually may be resolved by adequately informed client consent.

As you proceed through the book, watch for the ethical issues. Who was the client? What did the lawyer's duty of competence require? Did the lawyer act promptly? Did she keep the client reasonably informed? Did she maintain client confidences? Was there a conflict of interest among clients or between the client and the lawyer? Did the lawyer deal with it properly? How should the lawyer deal with a client who may be under a legal disability?

2

Intestate Succession

When a person dies without having made a valid will, or a will fails to make a complete disposition of the estate, the person is said to have died intestate or partially intestate. Statutes in each of the states provide a scheme of intestate succession under which intestate property will pass.

Intestacy laws of various states tend to follow a common pattern, having been derived mainly from the English Statute of Distribution, 1670, 22 & 23 Car. II, c. 10. Nevertheless, in each state it is necessary to examine the statutory language and its interpretation because there will be significant local variations. It is important to understand your state's statute of intestate succession because, in addition to the fact that many people die intestate, the statute is necessary background often invoked in a testate or inter vivos transfer setting.

The Statute of Distribution applied only to personal property in England. Subject to local custom, the descent of land, until the Administration of Estates Act, 1925, 15 Geo. V, c. 23, was principally characterized by its preference of males over females, the doctrine of primogeniture, and its exclusion of ancestors. See generally 2 W. Blackstone, Commentaries on the Laws of England 208-234 (1761). Although in many states the law of decedents' estates continues to distinguish between real and personal property for some purposes, the intestacy statutes in this country treat both types of property alike with rare exceptions.

A. General Patterns of Intestate Succession

There is a basic similarity in the patterns of intestate succession in all of the states, but there are also significant differences in these statutory schemes. Consequently, the rights of individuals may be different depending on which statutory scheme is applicable to a given estate. The traditional rules for deciding which state's intestacy law is to be applied may be summarized as follows: (the law of the decedent's domicile at death governs questions of succession to personal property or perhaps, more precisely, movables; the law of the situs of property governs such questions in relation to land or immovables. In recent years, however, there has developed an increasing acceptance of the view that the law of the decedent's domicile should determine succession to land as well as to personalty. Frequently expressed concerns with respect to land title records and land use appear, for the most part, to be unwarranted.

These choice of law rules must not be confused with the rule that a decedent's property is administered where it is located. Thus, if the decedent lives in State *A* but owns certain chattels situated in State *B,* this property will be administered in State *B,* but under its conflict of laws rule State *B* will determine who is entitled to succeed to the chattels by looking to the laws of State *A.*

In addition to the general textual survey and other contents of this chapter, meaningful study of intestate succession requires careful examination of statutory materials — and preferably an attempt to master some specific jurisdiction's legislation as a living unit. The materials that follow include illustrative and proposed statutes. Nevertheless, the legislation of your own or some other selected states should also be examined, using the materials in this chapter for guidance and comparison.

UNIFORM PROBATE CODE

§2-101. *Intestate Estate.*

(a) Any part of a decedent's estate not effectively disposed of by will passes by intestate succession to the decedent's heirs as prescribed in this Code, except as modified by the decedent's will.

(b) A decedent by will may expressly exclude or limit the right of an individual or class to succeed to property of the decedent passing by intestate succession. If that individual or a member of that class survives the decedent, the share of the decedent's intestate estate to which that individual or class would have succeeded passes as if that individual or each member of that class had disclaimed his [or her] intestate share.

§2-102. *Share of Spouse.*[1] The intestate share of a decedent's surviving spouse is:

(1) the entire intestate estate if:

(i) no descendant or parent of the decedent survives the decedent; or

---

1. For community property states this section is adapted so that these provisions for the spouse apply to separate property, while another subparagraph provides for inheritance of the decedent's share of community property, with the suggestion that this share pass to the surviving spouse. — EDS.

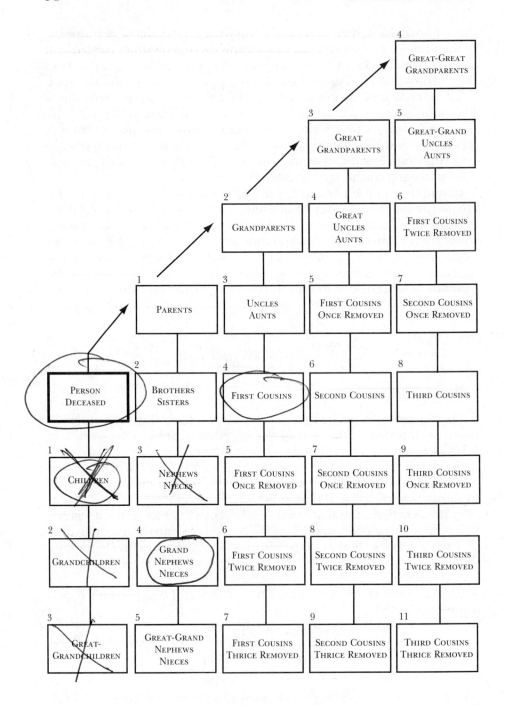

Table of Consanguinity
(Showing Degrees of Relationship)

(ii) all of the decedent's surviving descendants are also descendants of the surviving spouse and there is no other descendant of the surviving spouse who survives the decedent; *Ic step-children*

(2) the first [$200,000], plus three-fourths of any balance of the intestate estate, if no descendant of the decedent survives the decedent, but a parent of the decedent survives the decedent; *If parent survives $200K + 3/4 estate*

(3) the first [$150,000], plus one-half of any balance of the intestate estate, if all of the decedent's surviving descendants are also descendants of the surviving spouse and the surviving spouse has one or more surviving descendants who are not descendants of the decedent; *$150K + 1/2 estate*

(4) the first [$100,000], plus one-half of any balance of the intestate estate, if one or more of the decedent's surviving descendants are not descendants of the surviving spouse. *$100K + 1/2 estate*

§2-103. *Share of Heirs Other Than Surviving Spouse.*   Any part of the intestate estate not passing to the decedent's surviving spouse under Section 2-102, or the entire intestate estate if there is no surviving spouse, passes in the following order to the individuals designated below who survive the decedent:

(1) to the decedent's descendants by representation; *D - representation*

(2) if there is no surviving descendant, to the decedent's parents equally if both survive, or to the surviving parent; *no rep → D's parents*

(3) if there is no surviving descendant or parent, to the descendants of the decedent's parents or either of them by representation;

(4) if there is no surviving descendant, parent, or descendant of a parent, but the decedent is survived by one or more grandparents or descendants of grandparents, half of the estate passes to the decedent's paternal grandparents equally if both survive, or to the surviving paternal grandparent, or to the descendants of the decedent's paternal grandparents or either of them if both are deceased, the descendants taking by representation; and the other half passes to the decedent's maternal relatives in the same manner; but if there is no surviving grandparent or descendant of a grandparent on either the paternal or the maternal side, the entire estate passes to the decedent's relatives on the other side in the same manner as the half.

§2-105. *No Taker.*   If there is no taker under the provisions of this Article, the intestate estate passes to the [state].

Compare California Probate Code §6402(e), which, after setting out the substance of Uniform Probate Code §2-103, provides: "If there is no surviving issue, parent or issue of a parent, grandparent or issue of a grandparent, but the decedent is survived by the issue of a predeceased spouse, [then] to such issue. . . ." Absent these or other prior takers, §6402(f) provides that the decedent's "next of kin" take (under the modified civil law method, infra). And if this also fails, §6402(g) provides for the property to pass to certain of the decedent's in-laws, specifically to the parents or the issue of the parents of the decedent's predeceased spouse, before escheat to the state will occur. While ten other states include the issue of predeceased spouses in their schemes of intestate succession, none goes as far as California in extending inheritance rights to relatives by affinity.

Express Disinheritance. Assume that the testator's "will" consists of one sentence that says that his son John is to receive nothing from his estate. Assume also that the testator was survived by three sons, John, Ted, and Bill. The traditional view is one cannot "disinherit by fiat"; that is, the will must effectively devise the property, and if it does not or if there is a partial intestacy, the one expressly disinherited will take his intestate share. The typical judicial response has been that express disinheritance does not prevent intestacy. In this example, the testator's property would pass to his three sons equally.

The drafters of the UPC recognized that this tends to defeat the testator's intent. Section 2-101(b) departs from the traditional view by providing that the property passes as if the expressly disinherited person disclaimed his or her interest. In the example above, if John has no descendants, the testator's property passes to his two sons, Ted and Bill. If John has descendants, one-third of the property passes to them. See Uniform Probate Code §2-801.

What if the testator devises all to his brother and expressly disinherits all his other heirs, but his brother predeceases him with no issue surviving? Does the estate escheat or pass to his heirs in a UPC state? See Estate of Jetter, 1997 S.D. 125, 570 N.W.2d 26 (1997).

1. Share of Surviving Spouse

The provisions for the surviving spouse under the various state intestacy statutes differ considerably in detail.

One basic criticism leveled at most statutes is that the provision for a surviving spouse is grossly inadequate in the case of a small estate. The trend of reform is in the direction of increasing the surviving spouse's share. E.g., Uniform Probate Code §2-102, supra. The increased share reflects the fact that when married people do execute wills, most of them devise all to the surviving spouse, at least where all of the decedent's descendants are also descendants of the surviving spouse. The UPC's rationale for the increased share for the spouse is based on the "conduit" theory, which recognizes that the children probably will benefit from the inheritance upon the survivor's death. The UPC gives the spouse less if he or she has children from a prior marriage and even less if only the decedent had children from a prior marriage. The drafters felt that the potential for divided loyalties on the part of the surviving spouse is greater in the latter situation.

[handwritten margin note: if children from prior marriage]

Despite the trend to increase the share of the surviving spouse, it is still not unusual to find a statute that gives only one-third of the estate to the surviving spouse. Sometimes this share is enlarged (e.g., to half or to a dollar amount plus a fraction) when the decedent has left no descendants surviving.

In community property states, the intestate statutes generally provide a different treatment for separate and community property. Thus, it is common for the deceased spouse's separate estate to pass under provisions of the type described in the preceding paragraph, while the community property interest of the deceased spouse receives a different treatment. In some states, the survivor is entitled to both halves of the community property (e.g., Cal. Prob. Code §6401), while others provide that, if issue survive, the survivor does not participate in the intestate's half of the community property.

NATIONAL COMMISSION ON THE OBSERVANCE OF INTERNATIONAL WOMEN'S YEAR, TO FORM A MORE PERFECT UNION — JUSTICE FOR AMERICAN WOMEN
(1976)

When the decedent's only surviving children are those of the marriage to the surviving spouse, the committee believes the surviving spouse should receive the entire estate. If the children are minors or unable to earn a living, the surviving spouse will be responsible for their support. When they are able-bodied and grown, they are no longer dependent, and the surviving spouse is likely to be at least approaching old age.

The provision on disposition of an estate when there are surviving parents but no children is arbitrary and may result in great inequity. . . . Suppose the parent or parents of a decedent husband have been dependent completely on the couple for a number of years and the marriage is of long duration; shouldn't the wife receive everything? On the other hand, if the decedent husband is young and the marriage has been of short duration and the parents have been partially supporting the couple, shouldn't the parents receive all the estate?

The "forced share" provision [see Chapter 3, infra] of one-third may be equitable in some circumstances but not in many. Suppose a farm wife has worked along with her husband for 30 years to make the farm a success, and he becomes senile and tries to leave her out of his will. Shouldn't she be entitled to the whole estate? Any wife who has had a long marriage and has contributed to her husband's success is certainly entitled to at least the amount she would have received if he had died intestate. On the other hand, if a young woman has been married to a wealthy man for only a few years and has squandered his wealth during that period, contributing nothing to his welfare or to acquisition of the money, should she receive as much as one-third? Here again the committee believes that the law should be redrafted to recognize a variety of circumstances.

How much variation can a statute of general application accommodate? An early draft of the original Uniform Probate Code attempted to distinguish among spouses of differing "merit" and circumstances but met with widespread resistance. The justifications and content of that early effort are discussed in Fratcher, Toward Uniform Succession Legislation, 41 N.Y.U.L. Rev. 1037, 1047 (1966).

M. SUSSMAN, J. CATES, AND D. SMITH, THE FAMILY AND INHERITANCE
83, 89-90, 143-144 (1970)

In this chapter, the testate disposition of property is compared with the distribution that would have occurred if the testator were intestate. . . .

[In the most significant deviation from the intestate pattern, the survey revealed that, even where issue survived, the] large majority of testators altered the distribution by bequeathing all to the surviving spouse. . . . Male and female testators differed very little in this pattern of willing the entire estate to the spouse. . . .

Testators who deviated from the norm of bequeathing their entire estates to their spouses generally had higher incomes or larger estates than those who followed the norm. They could afford to remember other relatives or friends in their wills. . . . In large estates, tax considerations may be an important factor affecting the pattern of distribution. . . .

[In intestate situations] where the statute prescribed a division between spouse and lineal kin, there were a large number of deviations. . . . [A]dult children usually signed over their shares to the surviving parent. . . . Where the children could not [do so] because they were not of legal age, parents may actually have been hamstrung in caring for their children. Parents were universally chagrined at the position they were in. . . .

An exception to the spouse-all pattern occurred in the case of remarriage. In both testate and intestate cases, the estates were more likely to be divided between spouse and children than were those in which the spouse was the parent of the surviving children.

A *Share for the Decedent's Significant Other.* Unless the jurisdiction recognizes common law marriage, a domestic partner is usually unprotected if the decedent failed to execute a will. However, there has been some recent recognition of a need to protect nonmarital cohabitants. Similar to "palimony" cases, where the relationship ends during lifetime, nonmarital cohabitants have sometimes claimed a share of an intestate estate if the relationship continues throughout their joint lifetimes. Palimony cases so far have been based on contract, but some commentators argue that committed domestic partners should qualify as heirs. See Lawrence Waggoner, Marital Property Rights in Transition, 59 Mo. L. Rev. 21 (1994). See also the English statute in Chapter 3, section E.

Most commentators who argue for protection of committed partners include same-sex couples within the meaning of these partnerships. Even if a same-sex partner executes a will, there is risk that the survivor will face prejudice in court when disgruntled heirs challenge the will. See Chapter 3 infra. See also In re Kaufmann's Will, 20 A.D.2d 464, 247 N.Y.S.2d 664 (1964), aff'd, 15 N.Y.2d 941, 205 N.E.2d 864 (1965). An empirical study has found that same-sex partners usually have more generous intentions toward each other than opposite-sex partners (married or unmarried). See Mary Louise Fellows et al., Committed Partners and Inheritance: An Empirical Study, 16 Law & Inequality 1 (1998); an appendix sets out a draft statute by Professor Waggoner entitled "Intestate Share of Committed Partner." It provides an intestate share for a "committed partner" who had lived in a "marriage-like" relationship with the decedent.

In 1997 Hawaii enacted a statute that permits same-sex couples to register as "reciprocal beneficiaries." Haw. Rev. Stat. Ann. §572C. The statute provides the same intestate share for a surviving reciprocal beneficiary as for a surviving spouse. Id. at §560:2-201, 2-202. Opposite-sex couples may not register as "reciprocal beneficiaries." Do you see a reason for this distinction?

2. Share of Issue

Whatever property remains after the spouse's share, or the entire net estate if there is no surviving spouse, passes to the descendants of the intestate. Although the term *issue* includes descendants of all degrees, remote descendants do not compete with their own living ancestors who are also descendants of the intestate. Thus G, a *grandchild* of the decedent, will not share in the estate so long as G's parent, C, a *child* of the decedent, is still living. However, more remote descendants do share in the estate if they have no living ancestor who is also a descendant of the intestate. Thus, if C had predeceased the intestate, then G would participate in the intestate's property, even though he would thus share with the intestate's living children (C's brothers and sisters).

Statutory or judicially established methods for determining the intestate shares of descendants under various circumstances differ from state to state, and some statutes are unclear. The question is often stated in terms of whether issue take per capita (by head) or per stirpes (by stocks).[2] The question does not arise when all children of the intestate survive because they receive equal shares whether the local rule follows a per capita or per stirpes pattern.

Counting Roots. All systems in this country require counting roots (or stocks). The roots are counted by adding the number of living members in a generation plus deceased members of that generation who have descendants who survived the decedent.

Under a *strict per stirpes (or strict representation)* system, the roots are counted at the first generation after the intestate, even if they all predeceased the intestate. For example, assume that the intestate, I, had two children, C1 and C2. Assume also that they both predeceased I and that C1 had one child and C2 had four children, all of whom survived I. Under a strict per stirpes system, there are two roots. C1's child gets one-half and C2's children get one-eighth each. The argument against this result is that the five grandchildren are related equally to I and should therefore take equally.

Under a *modified per stirpes* (or *modified representation*) system, the roots are not counted until a generation is reached with at least one living member. In the example above, there are five roots, and each grandchild takes one-fifth.

If I had a third child, C3, who survived, there would be three roots. C3 takes one-third, C2's child takes one-third, and C2's children share a third, taking one-sixth each "by representation." Thus, even with modified per stirpes, there can be unequal shares among those related equally to the decedent.

The *per capita at each generation* (sometimes called *per capita with per capita representation*) system carries the idea of horizontal equality to what some consider to be its logical conclusion. Assume again that only C3 survives, with the roots again counted at the first generation having

---

2. It must not be assumed that these terms have the same meaning and application in all jurisdictions. See Kraemer v. Hook, 168 Ohio St. 221, 152 N.E.2d 430 (1958). See also Richland Trust Co. v. Becvar, 339 N.E.2d 830 (Ohio 1975).

a living member. Thus, there are three roots, and *C3* gets one-third. The remaining two-thirds drops to the next generation and the roots are counted again, excluding *C3*'s issue, of course. At this level, there are three grandchildren and each becomes a root, taking a third of the two-thirds, or one-ninth. Under this system, members of the same generation will never take different shares, and a more remote descendant will never take a larger share than a nearer descendant. A criticism of this system is that it aggravates the fortuitous consequences of order of deaths, which is inherent in any but the strict per stirpes method. Do you see why?

The 1990 UPC's intestacy provisions distribute property according to the "per capita at each generation" system, calling it "representation" (defined in §2-106, below). The 1969 UPC, which is still widely followed, adopted a form of modified per stirpes.

UNIFORM PROBATE CODE

§2-106. *Representation.*

(b) [Decedent's Descendants.] If, under Section 2-103(1), a decedent's intestate estate or a part thereof passes "by representation" to the decedent's descendants, the estate or part thereof is divided into as many equal shares as there are (i) surviving descendants in the generation nearest to the decedent which contains one or more surviving descendants and (ii) deceased descendants in the same generation who left surviving descendants, if any. Each surviving descendant in the nearest generation is allocated one share. The remaining shares, if any, are combined and then divided in the same manner among the surviving descendants of the deceased descendants as if the surviving descendants who were allocated a share and their surviving descendants had predeceased the decedent.

(c) [Descendants of Parents or Grandparents.] If, under Section 2-103(3) or (4), a decedent's intestate estate or a part thereof passes "by representation" to the descendants of the decedent's deceased parents or either of them or to the descendants of the decedent's deceased paternal or maternal grandparents or either of them, the estate or part thereof is divided into as many equal shares as there are (i) surviving descendants in the generation nearest the deceased parents or either of them, or the deceased grandparents or either of them, that contains one or more surviving descendants and (ii) deceased descendants in the same generation who left surviving descendants, if any. Each surviving descendant in the nearest generation is allocated one share. The remaining shares, if any, are combined and then divided in the same manner among the surviving descendants of the deceased descendants as if the surviving descendants who were allocated a share and their surviving descendants had predeceased the decedent.

PROBLEMS

2-A.   *I* was predeceased by her spouse and both of her children: *S*, who left a single child, and *D*, who left two children. Do the three grandchildren take equal one-third shares of the estate, or does *S*'s child take half, while *D*'s children take a quarter each under the statutes of your state? Under UPC §2-106(b)? — ⅓ each

2-B.   Determine the shares of each heir of *D* who died in a UPC jurisdiction survived by the following nine people: *C1*, child of *D*; *C2*, child of *D*; *G1*, child of *C1*; *G2*, child of *C3*, a deceased child of *D*; *GG1*, child of *G3*, a deceased sibling of *G2*; *GG2*, sibling of *GG1*; *G4*, child of *C4*, a deceased child of *D*; *G5*, sibling of *G4*; and *GG3*, child of *G6*, a deceased sibling of *G5*. See comment to UPC §2-106. The California Probate Code continues the earlier UPC concept of representation for intestacy in §240 but also seeks to facilitate testator selection of alternative patterns of distribution among issue in §§245-247, including the option of distributing per capita at each generation (§247).

3.   Shares of Ascendant and Collateral Relatives

American statutes typically provide that, in the absence of issue and subject to the share of a surviving spouse, intestate property passes to the parents or to the surviving parent of the decedent. In a few states, brothers and sisters (and the issue of any who are deceased) share with parents, while some others allow them to share with a parent if but one parent survives. If neither parent survives the intestate, the property is divided among living brothers and sisters and the issue of any who are deceased, the brothers and sisters taking equal shares and the issue taking by some form of representation.

The above-described shares of parents and the issue of parents are generally expressed in specific provisions of the statute. Most statutes, including the UPC, also provide expressly for grandparents and their descendants, but in others the "inner circle" of specifically mentioned relatives does not extend beyond parents and their descendants. These latter statutes typically provide that, beyond this inner circle, the property in question goes to the *next of kin* of the intestate. Frequently, some method of determining the next of kin is indicated. If not, the so-called civil law method of computation is used. The classic methods of determining degrees of kinship are given below, but it must be kept in mind that the degree of kinship does not become relevant until it is determined that the property is not disposed of under the specific terms of the statute. Thus, even though an uncle is only three degrees removed from the decedent under the civil law count, usually he would not share with the decedent's niece (also three degrees removed) because the latter is typically provided for either by the expressed terms of the statute, specifically referring to the intestate's nieces and nephews, or by specific reference to the children of brothers and sisters or to the issue of parents.

Under the *civil law* system of computation, used by the ecclesiastical courts in England and adopted by the Statute of Distribution in 1670, a claimant's degree of kinship is the total of (1) the number of the steps, counting one for each generation, from the decedent up to the nearest common ancestor of the decedent and the claimant, and (2) the number of steps from the common ancestor down to the claimant. The claimant having the lowest degree count (i.e., the nearest or next of kin) is entitled to the property. If there are two or more claimants who stand in equal degree of kinship to the decedent, they share per capita. However, under a widespread *modification* of this system, a statute may provide that, when there are several claimants of equal degree claiming through different ancestors, those claiming through the ancestor nearest the decedent take to the exclusion of those who claim through a more remote ancestor. The civil law system of computation and its modified form have been widely adopted by statute in the United States.

The *canon law* (sometimes called the *common law*) method of computation also involved counting the steps in the line from the claimant to the nearest common ancestor of the claimant and the decedent and then counting the steps in the line from that ancestor to the decedent. The number of steps in the *longer* of these two lines was the relevant degree of kinship. The claimant or claimants having the *lowest* degree of kinship thus determined took as next of kin. This system was used by the canon law to determine whether a marriage between relatives was prohibited and by the common law in limiting successive donees in frank-marriage.

Many states have enacted a form of parentelic system, resembling in part the rules for descent of land in England under the common law. Rather than mentioning certain near relatives and then providing that next of kin take in the absence of the specified relatives, these statutes require a determination of the nearest ancestors who either are alive or have issue living, and it is provided that the property goes to these nearest ancestors or their issue. These statutes do not involve the usual concept of next of kin. Universal representation eliminates the necessity of counting degrees of kinship. Statutes of this basic type vary in wording and detail. This, incidentally, is the approach of the UPC as far as it goes, i.e., to the issue of grandparents.

Beyond that inner circle of relatives who are specifically designated, the right to take by representation often is not recognized in states using the civil law methods. Under these statutes, when it becomes necessary to determine intestate succession by counting degrees of kinship, representation ceases.

rep is not usually det. by CL method

With but occasional and limited exceptions, intestate succession is confined to the surviving spouse and persons related to the decedent by blood (consanguinity) and adoption. If none of the relatives provided for in the statute are available to take the property, escheat will occur, and the property will go to the state or some subdivision or agency thereof. As a last resort prior to escheat, a few jurisdictions allow intestate property to pass to relatives by affinity. In a few other states certain property acquired by the decedent from a predeceased spouse passes to relatives of that spouse under various circumstances, and a few statutes provide for stepchildren in certain circumstances. However, the modern trend, exemplified by the UPC, is to confine intestate succession to near relatives of the decedent and to increase the occasions of escheat. What do you suppose is the reason for this?

PROBLEMS

2-C. *D* died intestate, survived only by the issue of a deceased sister and two deceased brothers. Altogether there were five nephews and nieces, one of whom predeceased *D* leaving issue. The living nephews and nieces claim equal shares of the estate and argue that one equal share should pass by representation and be divided among the issue of the deceased niece, i.e., that the number of primary shares is five. The deceased niece's issue contend that the nephews and nieces take by representation, in place of their respective parents, so that the number of primary shares should be three.

The pertinent statute provides: "(3) If there be no issue or parent, then in equal shares to his brothers and sisters, and to the descendants of any deceased brother or sister by right of representation." Paragraph (4) continues: "If there is no brother or sister or issue of such, then to the next of kin of equal degree and the lawful issue of such next of kin by right of representation."

(a) What argument should be advanced by each set of claimants? On what facts, language, and authorities?

(b) What result would be reached under the Uniform Probate Code? Your local statute?

(c) If the pertinent provisions are not adequate in the problem statute, what amendment would you suggest?

2-D. Consider the chart that follows and decide which of the three underlined (living) collateral claimants would receive the decedent's intestate property under (a) the civil law system, (b) the modified civil law system, (c) the canon law system, (d) the parentelic system, and (e) your local statute.

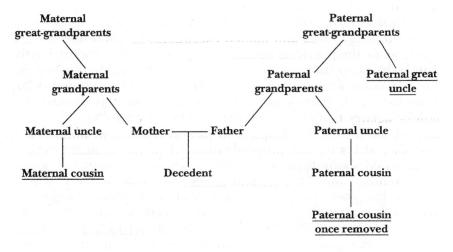

2-E.   (1) *D* died in a UPC jurisdiction survived by *D*'s grand niece, *A,* and two first cousins, *B* and *C.* Who are *D*'s heirs? (2) *D* died intestate in a UPC jurisdiction survived by two great uncles and one child of a deceased great aunt (first cousin once removed). Who are *D*'s heirs? (3) Inasmuch as the decedent did not bother to execute a will, who do you think should have the greater entitlement to the decedent's property — the state or distantly related blood relatives? In Estate of Brunel, 135 N.H. 83, 600 A.2d 123 (1991), the intestate decedent was survived by second cousins and the intestacy provisions were the same as UPC §2-103, but instead of an escheat provision as specific as UPC §2-105, the New Hampshire statute simply provided that when there is no heir or surviving spouse, the intestate property escheats to the state. The court held that the second cousins would take rather than the state because there was nothing in the statute that precluded them from qualifying as heirs.

2-F.   *D* died intestate in a UPC jurisdiction survived by three cousins, *A, B,* and *C. A* is a child of *D*'s predeceased Aunt Jane, who was *D*'s mother's sister. *B* is a child of *D*'s predeceased Aunt Karen, who was *D*'s father's sister. *C* is a child of *D*'s predeceased paternal Aunt Pam and *D*'s predeceased maternal Uncle Bill. Who takes and in what shares? See Estate of Adler, 175 Misc. 2d 357, 669 N.Y.S.2d 154 (1997). UPC §2-113 provides: "An individual who is related to the decedent through two lines of relationship is entitled to only a single share based on the relationship that would entitle the individual to a larger share."

B.   Questions of Definition and Status

1.   In General

Posthumous Heirs. The common law rule that a child in gestation at the death of the intestate is deemed to be in being, and thus entitled to inherit if subsequently born alive, has generally been codified in the United States. In cases involving collateral heirs conceived before the intestate's death, inheritance is also permitted, although statutory language may fail to provide for this situation. See also the discussion of children *conceived* after the decedent's death at page 63.

Simultaneous and Near-Simultaneous Death. Where two or more persons die in a common disaster, there may be little or no evidence of the order of deaths. Problems of this sort are not confined to intestate succession, of course, and must be resolved in some fashion. At common law the result usually turned simply on the inability of a claimant to carry his burden of proving that one through whom he claims survived the decedent. The Uniform Simultaneous Death Act (USDA), enacted in many states, originally provided that, absent contrary provision in the controlling instrument, where "title to property or the devolution thereof depends upon priority of death and there is no sufficient evidence that the persons have died otherwise than simultaneously, the property of each person shall be disposed of as if he had survived, except as otherwise provided by this Act." Specific provisions then deal with life insurance (providing for distribution as if the insured had survived the beneficiary), joint tenancy or tenancy by the entirety (treating each owner as the survivor with respect to half or other appropriate proportion of the property), and situations involving beneficiaries "designated to take successively by reason of survivorship under another person's disposition." Uniform Probate Code §2-104 requires that a relative survive the decedent by five days in order to inherit. Do you see the reasons for this innovation? The USDA has been amended to incorporate the five-day rule but many states have not amended their original versions of the Act. California has adopted the five-day rule, but only for intestacy. See Cal. Prob. Code §6403. Do you see why?

Aliens. Treaties or statutes frequently alter an alien's common law right to receive and dispose of personal property and his disability with regard to land. Despite serious doubt at the present time concerning their constitutionality, see Zschernig v. Miller, 389 U.S. 429 (1968), and Gorun v. Fall, 393 U.S. 398 (1969), some state statutes make this ability or disability depend on reciprocity or on the rights an alien will have with regard to the inheritance or both; these questions may pose legal questions that go to the very essence of property rights and concepts under the foreign law in question.

only in case of collateral relatives

Half-Blood Relatives. Generally in the United States, relatives of the ½ blood half blood inherit equally with those of the whole, and it appears that *inherits = whole blood* this is the rule in the absence of a statute covering the question. However, it is necessary to determine whether, when the applicable statute does discriminate against half bloods, the latter take a smaller share, are postponed to whole-blood relatives of the same degree, or are postponed in favor of whole-blood relatives only in the case of "ancestral property." Half-blood problems exist, of course, only in the case of collateral relatives.

Ancestral Property. In the descent of land under the common law in England, inheritance was limited to relatives of the blood of the ancestor who was the "first purchaser." The original doctrine is not applicable to personal property and is generally not recognized in the United States even as to land. Where the doctrine of ancestral property has been preserved by statute (in several states this has been done by a statute applicable only to the passage of ancestral property where the claimants include half-blood relatives who are not of the blood of the ancestor), it is necessary to examine the statute carefully, and also the decisions construing it. The tendency has been to construe such statutes narrowly.

2.   Adoption

Statutes typically create inheritance rights in adopted persons. The tendency is to treat the adopted child as if he or she had been born into the adopting family. See UPC §2-114 below. However, such statutes are often unclear in many respects. In examining a given statute, it is necessary to consider the question of inheritance *from* as well as *by* an adopted person and particularly to consider the adoptee's status with regard to the natural relatives as well as to the adoptive relatives.

The need to examine statutes carefully and the adoptee's long, uphill struggle against narrow construction of legislation in this area are aptly illustrated by In re Hewett's Estate, 153 Fla. 137, 13 So. 2d 904 (1943), involving the possible right of an adoptee to inherit *through* the adopting parents from other members of the adoptive family. In that case, the intestate's nearest relatives were two first cousins and the adopted daughter of a deceased first cousin. Applicable statutes provided (1) that intestate property should pass under these circumstances "to the uncles and aunts and the descendants of such of them as may be deceased" and (2) that an adopted child "shall be an heir at law and for the purpose of inheritance be regarded as a lineal descendant of its adopting parents." The court stated that "the statute says nothing about the adopting parents' ancestors" and that "we cannot add anything to the statute which is not expressly stated therein or which is not necessarily implied by the language used." It further stated:

> This statute is very liberal in its provisions in behalf of the adopted child. Such child inherits from its adopting parents as if it were their own natural child, and likewise inherits from its natural parents. Why should the legislature be *construed* to have gone further and intended by court-imposed implication, to give the adopted child the right to inherit from the adopting parents' ancestors or other blood kin? The legislature should not be construed to have intended this unless the language of the statute makes it plain that such was the legislative intent — which we do not think it does.

The opinion then refers to other cases indicating "that a statute which interrupts the natural course of the descent of property should be strictly construed" and that "to allow an adopted child to inherit from the ancestors of the adopter would often put property into the hands of unheard of adopted children, contrary to the wishes and expectations of such ancestors." 153 Fla. at 140-143, 13 So. 2d at 906-907.

Nearly all statutes today have expressly and clearly expanded the rights of adoptees to include inheritance "through" as well as "from" the adoptive parents. See Ralph C. Brashier, Children and Inheritance in the Nontraditional Family, 1996 Utah L. Rev. 93 (1996).

UNIFORM PROBATE CODE

§2-114.   *Parent and Child Relationship.*

(a) Except as provided in subsections (b) and (c), for purposes of intestate succession by, through, or from a person, an individual is the child of his or her natural parents, regardless of their marital status. The parent and child relationship may be established under [the Uniform Parentage Act] [applicable state law].

(b) An adopted individual is the child of his or her adopting parent or parents and not of his or her natural parents, but adoption of a child by the spouse of either natural parent has no effect on (i) the relationship between the child and that natural parent or (ii) the right of the child or a descendant of the child to inherit from or through the other natural parent.

(c) Inheritance from or through a child by either natural parent or his or her kindred is precluded unless that natural parent has openly treated the child as his or hers, and has not refused to support the child.

PROBLEM

2-G.   *H* and *W* were married and had a child, *C. H* and *W* were later divorced and *W* was awarded custody of *C*, with *H* being granted extensive visitation rights. Thereafter, *W* married *S*, who subsequently and with *H*'s consent adopted *C*, then age 11. *S*, *W*, and *C* have enjoyed a happy family relationship. Through the years, *C* also continued to spend considerable time with *H*, but *H* died intestate a week ago survived by his wife, *X*, and their daughter, *D*. (1) *C*, now age 24, asks you about his possible interest in *H*'s estate. How would you respond under the law of your state? Under the Uniform Probate Code? Or in a jurisdiction that has the statute set out below (Oregon R.S. §112.175)? Cf. Estate of Daigle, 642 P.2d 527 (Colo. App. 1982). (2) After *H*'s death, *G* (*H*'s widowed mother) died intestate; *H* was her only child. Does *C* have an interest in her estate under the law of your state? Under the UPC? Under the statute below?

(1) An adopted person, the issue and kindred of the adopted person shall take by intestate succession from the adoptive parents, their issue and kindred, and the adoptive parents, their issue and kindred shall take by intestate succession from the adopted person, the issue and kindred of the adopted person, as though the adopted person were the natural child of the adoptive parents.

[margin handwritten note: adopted kid takes from adopted parent]

(2) An adopted person shall cease to be treated as the child of the person's natural parents for all purposes of intestate succession by the adopted person, the issue and kindred of the adopted person and the natural parents, their issue and kindred, except:

[margin handwritten note: not from nat. parents]

(a) If a natural parent of a person marries or remarries and the person is adopted by the stepparent, the adopted person shall continue also to be treated, for all purposes of intestate succession, as the child of the natural parent who is the spouse of the adoptive parent.

(b) If a natural parent of a person dies, the other natural parent remarries and the person is adopted by his stepparent, the adopted person shall continue also to be treated, for all purposes of intestate succession by any person through the deceased natural parent, as the child of the deceased natural parent.

Even though legislation in most states has now clarified the more frequent of the intestacy problems involving adoptees, lawyers must still be conscious of analogous questions in drafting, for intestate succession statutes as such are not always controlling for purposes of ascertaining the meaning of class terminology such as *children* and *issue* in wills and trust agreements. For example, with respect to a testate counterpart of situation (2) in Problem 2-G, above, compare In re

Tracy, 464 Pa. 300, 346 A.2d 750 (1975) with First National Bank v. Schwerin, 54 Or. App. 460, 635 P.2d 388 (1981). See also Lockwood v. Adamson, 409 Mass. 325, 566 N.E.2d 96 (1991) (concluding that the testator's gift to the "issue" of another included that other person's blood descendant who had been "adopted out" of the family, despite an *intestate* succession statute providing in relevant part that a "person shall by adoption lose his right to inherit" from the biological family; the court also noted that "[e]ven if we assume that a devise or bequest to an adoptee somehow undermines the adoptive family relationship, . . . where the child's relationship to his natural parents is ordinarily known to all concerned," it is unlikely that the right to take as a class member in the biological family would have an "adverse effect on the family relationship" or otherwise "undermine the policy goals of integrating children as fully as possible into their adoptive families"). Consider Uniform Probate Code §2-705 below and the problems that follow.

adopted=no rt to biol family

UNIFORM PROBATE CODE

§2-705.   *Class Gifts Construed to Accord with Intestate Succession.*

(a) Adopted individuals and individuals born out of wedlock, and their respective descendants if appropriate to the class, are included in class gifts and other terms of relationship in accordance with the rules for intestate succession. Terms of relationship that do not differentiate relationships by blood from those by affinity, such as "uncles," "aunts," "nieces," or "nephews," are construed to exclude relatives by affinity. Terms of relationship that do not differentiate relationships by the half blood from those by the whole blood, such as "brothers," "sisters," "nieces," or "nephews," are construed to include both types of relationships.

(b) In addition to the requirements of subsection (a), in construing a dispositive provision of a transferor who is not the natural parent, an individual born to the natural parent is not considered the child of that parent unless the individual lived while a minor as a regular member of the household of that natural parent or of that parent's parent, brother, sister, spouse, or surviving spouse.

 (c) In addition to the requirements of subsection (a), in construing a dispositive provision of a transferor who is not the adopting parent, an adopted individual is not considered the child of the adopting parent unless the adopted individual lived while a minor, either before or after the adoption, as a regular member of the household of the adopting parent.

PROBLEMS

2-H.   Under *A*'s will, Blackacre was devised to *A*'s daughter, *D,* for life, remainder to such of *D*'s issue as survive her. At *D*'s death she is survived by two children, one of whom was adopted. In determining the adopted child's rights under *A*'s will, what is the relevance, if any, of a statute in the state in which Blackacre is situated providing that adopted children shall be treated the same as natural children for purposes of inheritance by, from, and through the adopting parent? For the traditional view, still adhered to in some states, see Restatement of Property §287 (1940); but see Restatement (Second) of Property §25.4 (1987); In re Trusts under Agreement with Harrington, 311 Minn. 403, 250 N.W.2d 163 (1977); and In re Coe's Estate, 42 N.J. 485, 201 A.2d 571 (1964).[3] *see UPC 2-114(b)*

3. In rejecting the traditional rule and in deciding that a person should take as a member of the class into which he has been adopted, the New Jersey court stated:

> [I]t is not important whether the adoption statute directly controls the interpretation of instruments. The important point is that the statute reflects the feeling and attitude of the average man and hence its policy should be followed unless the benefactor explicitly reveals a contrary purpose. . . . Hence even if the quoted provisions of the adoption statute . . . speak only of intestacy, they should nonetheless be accepted as a reflection of a common expectation and wish and hence as a guide to proper interpretation of a gift. . . .
>
> The trouble in our State began [with] an unwarranted assumption that when one who is not a party to the adoption makes a gift to a class consisting of children of the adopting parent, he probably intends to benefit only natural children. . . . We cannot believe it probable that strangers to the adoption would differentiate between the natural child and the adopted child of another. Rather we believe it more likely that they accept the relationships established by the parent whether the bond be natural or by adoption and seek to advance those relationships precisely as their parent would. . . .
>
> Finally, it is suggested that to depart from the stranger-to-the-adoption view would invite fraud by permitting a person to adopt someone solely to enable him to take under the will of another. . . . It seems to us that the prospect of fraud is quite remote and can be dealt with upon equitable principles if the circumstances are truly compelling.

42 N.J. 489-492, 201 A.2d 574-576. In Estate of Nicol, 74 N.J. 312, 372 A.2d 1201 (1977), the court did as suggested in *Coe* and found, on the basis of probable intent, that adult adopters were not included as recipients of a future-interest class gift.

As is readily apparent, adoptions have created an abundance of unique situations regarding the devolution of property. See Elliott v. Hiddleson, 303 N.W.2d 140, 144 (Iowa 1981) (rejecting the "stranger to the adoption" rule and holding that a testator had the right to distinguish between natural and adopted children but had to show such intent. Absent such a showing, the court assumes the testator wished to treat the adopted children in the same manner as natural children. The court would not permit the conscious use of adoption as a means of upsetting a transferor's normal expectations). This flexibility to deal with manipulative adoptions, however, may not be available under simple but explicit will provisions and statutes calling for the inclusion of adoptees in class gifts. See, e.g., Evans v. McCoy, 291 Md. 562, 436 A.2d 436 (1981)

See generally Halbach, Rights of Adopted Children Under Class Gifts, 50 Iowa L. Rev. 971 (1965).

2-I.   *A*'s will also left $500,000 in trust for his son, *S*, for life, remainder to such of *S*'s issue as survive him. *S* also had a small estate of his own. *S* died intestate survived by *X*, whom *S* had raised from infancy. It was generally believed, and believed by *S* and *X*, that *S* had adopted *X*, but the purported adoption was void. For the last ten years of *S*'s life he was a widower, and *Y* lived in *S*'s home, keeping house for him and generally caring for his needs. Out of gratitude, and with his father's trust in mind, *S* adopted *Y*. What are the rights of *X* and *Y* in *S*'s estate and in the trust?

MATTER OF HEIRS OF HODGE
470 So. 2d 740 (Fla. App. 1985)

DAUKSCH, J. . . .

This case involves the rarity, "virtual adoption." When someone gives his or her natural child to another with an agreement that the other will adopt the child then the child will be deemed to have an enforceable contractual right. . . .

[A]n oral or written promise to adopt may be enforced by the child in an intestacy proceeding to establish rights of inheritance. The elements to be proved include:

1. An agreement between the natural and adoptive parents;
2. Performance by the natural parents . . . in giving up custody;
3. Performance by the child by living [with] the adoptive parents;
4. Partial performance by the foster parents in taking the child into the home and treating the child as their child; and
5. Intestacy of the foster parents.

Appellee was three years old when her mother died and her father gave her to the Hodges. Although there was no one to testify directly

---

(elderly widow adopted adult neighbor, defeating her uncles' interests conditioned on her death without issue); Solomon v. Central Trust Co., 63 Ohio St. 3d 35, 584 N.E.2d 1185 (1992) (allowing a person adopted at age 44, long after settlor's death, to share with a biological child as "issue" of settlor's brother, the court expressly rejecting and seeking to remove the last vestiges of the "stranger-to-the-adoption" rule in Ohio); and the all-time shocker, Bedinger v. Graybill's Estate, 302 S.W.2d 594 (Ky. 1957) (life beneficiary adopted his wife, displacing other claimants under a remainder to his "heirs at law"), not followed in Minary's Estate, 419 S.W.2d 340 (Ky. App.1967).

Do recent construction statutes apply to class gifts under preexisting documents? See, e.g., New England Merchant's Natl. Bank v. Groswold, 444 N.E.2d 359 (Mass. 1983).

that they heard or read an agreement to adopt, there was sufficient evidence in the record for the trial judge to conclude that there was an agreement to adopt. When [Appellee] was nine the Hodges told her she was not their natural daughter but was adopted. She lived with the Hodges until she married at age seventeen and was always called Hodge, loved as a daughter and responded in kind. Mr. Hodge was the president of her P.T.A. when she was in school, he signed her report cards, she paid his funeral expenses and attended his funeral....

We agree with the trial judge that all elements were established....

Equitable Adoption. Comment k to §2.5 of the Restatement (Third) of Property: Wills, Trusts and Other Donative Transfers states:

> k. *Equitable adoption of foster children.* A foster child who has not been formally or legally adopted by his or her foster parents may nevertheless obtain inheritance rights under a doctrine called "equitable adoption." Courts also refer to this doctrine as "virtual adoption," "de facto adoption," or "adoption by estoppel." Courts in over half the states have recognized such a doctrine, but courts in at least eight states have rejected it....

In considering whether a child raised but not formally adopted by testator's niece could take under a trust provision for the niece's "child or children," the court in Wheeling Dollar Savings & Trust Co. v. Singer, 250 S.E.2d 369, 372-374 (W. Va. 1978) (recently affirmed in Welch v. Wilson, 516 S.E.2d 35 (W. Va. 1999)), stated:

> [W]e do not hesitate to hold that the concept of equitable adoption should be a viable theory for relief from injustice in West Virginia, as long as adequate care is taken to protect the tradition of our ancient law of future interests and inheritance. The status of adopted children long plagued this and other courts, but our holding in Wheeling Dollar Sav. & Trust Co. v. Hanes, 237 S.E.2d 499 (W. Va. 1977) ... settled the controversy in West Virginia. In *Hanes* we set the law by saying:
>
> > It appears to the Court that most testators and trustors establish trusts for the benefit of those persons they love and for the benefit of those persons yet unknown and yet unborn whom such testators and trustors infer that their loved ones will eventually love. While there may be testators and trustors who are so concerned with medieval concepts of "bloodline" and "heirs of the body" that they would truly be upset at the thought that their hard-won assets would one day pass into the hands of persons not of their blood, we cannot formulate general rules of law for the benefit of eccentrics.

Id. at 503. Since *Hanes* clearly establishes the right of adopted children
to be treated as natural children, the only remaining question presented
in the case before us is whether adherence to formal adoption procedures, W. Va. Code, 48-4-1 [1969] et seq. is the exclusive method by
which a person may be accorded the protections of adoptive status in
West Virginia. We find that it is not.

While formal adoption is the only safe route, in many instances a child
will be raised by persons not his parents from an age of tender years,
treated as a natural child, and represented to others as a natural or
adopted child. In many instances, the child will believe himself to be the
natural or formally "adopted" child of the "adoptive" parents only to be
treated as an outcast upon their death. We cannot ascertain any reasonable distinction between a child treated in all regards as an adopted child
but who has been led to rely to his detriment upon the existence of
formal legal paperwork imagined but never accomplished, and a formally adopted child. Our family centered society presumes that bonds
of love and loyalty will prevail in the distribution of family wealth along
family lines, and only by affirmative action, i.e., writing a will, may this
presumption be overcome. An equitably adopted child in practical terms
is as much a family member as a formally adopted child and should not
be the subject of discrimination. He will be as loyal to his adoptive parents, take as faithful care of them in their old age, and provide them
with as much financial and emotional support in their vicissitudes, as
any natural or formally adopted child.

However, the equitably adopted child and the formally adopted child
are not without differences. The formally adopted child need only produce his adoption papers to guarantee his treatment as an adopted child.
The equitably adopted child in any private property dispute such as the
case under consideration involving the laws of *inheritance* or *private trusts*
must prove by clear, cogent and convincing evidence that he has stood
from an age of tender years in a position *exactly* equivalent to a formally
 adopted child. Circumstances which tend to show the existence of an
equitable adoption include: the benefits of love and affection accruing
to the adopting party; the performances of services by the child; the
surrender of ties by the natural parent; the society, companionship and
filial obedience of the child; an invalid or ineffectual adoption proceeding; reliance by the adopted person upon the existence of his adoptive
status; the representation to all the world that the child is a natural or
adopted child; and the rearing of the child from an age of tender years
by the adopting parents. Of course, evidence can be presented which
tends to negate an equitable adoption. . . .

Most of the cited cases predicate the finding of an equitable adoption
on the proof of an expressed or implied contract of adoption. While the
existence of an express contract of adoption is very convincing evidence,
an implied contract of adoption is an unnecessary fiction created by
courts as a protection from fraudulent claims. We find that if a claimant
can, by clear, cogent and convincing evidence, prove sufficient facts to
convince the trier of fact that his status is identical to that of a formally

adopted child, except only for the absence of a formal order of adoption, a finding of an equitable adoption is proper without proof of an adoption contract.

In the case before us, appellant Singer alleges that she was taken from an orphanage when she was eight or nine by the Whartons; that she was given the surname of the Whartons; that she was raised as their child and that, until this action, she believed herself to be the adopted child of the Whartons. Furthermore it appears that Lyda Wharton [testator's niece] devised and bequeathed her residuary estate to "my daughter, Ada Bell Singer." If the appellant Singer can prove these allegations at the hearing below, she has a strong case for equitable adoption, and one of the most important elements in her proof is that she was held out to all the world as a natural or adopted child.

Many factors relevant to proof of equitable adoption are also relevant in proving acknowledgment in paternity actions. But, as you will see, the Constitution appears not to require a state to consider evidence that is less "trustworthy" than a paternity judgment in giving a nonmarital child an intestate share of the father's estate. The result in some states is that a court will not consider such factors unless the father is alive to defend (thus also apprising him of the possible desirability from his viewpoint of making a will).

Are there any circumstances in which it might be desirable for legislation to provide that stepchildren or foster children receive treatment similar to that accorded adoptees? Such statutes are almost nonexistent, but see California Probate Code §6454.

PROBLEMS

2-J. *M* and *F* were married and had a child, *C*. *M* and *F* were divorced and *F* was awarded custody of *C*. Then *F* married *W* and *W* adopted *C*.[4]

(a) *C* dies intestate without a surviving spouse or issue. *C* is survived by *M*, *F*, and *W*. Who are *C*'s heirs in a UPC jurisdiction? In your state?

(b) *M*'s mother died after *C*'s adoption leaving a will executed before the adoption devising all to her grandchildren. Does *C* share in this class gift in a UPC jurisdiction? In your state? See Miller v. Walker, 270 Ga. 811, 514 S.E.2d 22 (1999). If the devise to the grandchildren was of a future interest and *M*'s grandmother died before the adoption, what result? See Crumpton v. Mitchell, 303 N.C. 657, 281 S.E.2d 1 (1981). Do you think an adoption should have the effect of depriving

---

4. In most jurisdictions this would require *M*'s consent or her disqualification on grounds of nonsupport or noncommunication for a statutory period of time.

a child of an interest that she would have had prior to the adoption? What do you think *M*'s mother would have wished?

2-K.   *O* conveyed Blackacre "to *A* for life, then to *A*'s children." *A* married *B* and they had a child, *C*. *A* and *B* were divorced and *B* received custody of *C*. Then *B* married *X* who adopted *C*. *A* died. Does *C* share in the remainder in a UPC jurisdiction? In your state?

3.   Nonmarital Children

Statutes vary widely in clarity and coverage concerning the rights of persons born out of wedlock. Claims by unadopted, nonmarital children to share in intestate estates of or class gifts by members of the natural families, maternal and paternal, arise in contexts as varied as those involving adoptees — and each of these groups of issues are frequent sources of litigation in the probate and trust field today. The causes of controversy include not only bad lawyer work but also inadequately considered legislation and judicial opinions. In addition to this, the volume and seriousness of the litigation are reflections of the numbers of potential claimants of uncertain status. The demographic data are striking. Over 30 percent of American babies are born out of wedlock. Most out-of-wedlock births are to women age 20 or older, with the out-of-wedlock birth rate increasing most rapidly among women in their early twenties, reflecting both living-together arrangements and women wishing to raise children without a long-term relationship with a man, with the percentage given up for adoption declining.

The law's primary traditional line of distinction has been between relationships on the maternal side and those on the paternal side. The latter seem to raise the specter of the nonmarital offspring's surprise appearance at the natural father's funeral. Clearly, the circumstances of a person's birth will not affect inheritance from or by that person's own spouse and issue. In addition, an unadopted child born out of wedlock inherits from the mother, and statutes or decisions in most jurisdictions allow inheritance from maternal relatives; typical legislation also allows the mother, and now usually her relatives, to inherit from the child. The traditional rules, however, almost universally precluded inheritance from or by the father and his relatives, except that the subsequent marriage of the parents or the father's acknowledgment (often requiring a writing), and sometimes a judicial decree of paternity, have typically opened the lines of inheritance between child and father, and sometimes paternal relatives. Uniform Probate Code §2-114 represents recent trends to broaden the inheritance rights of these children. Meanwhile, concerns about the status of children of assisted conception as nonmarital children are beginning to be dealt with, if at all, by statutes. Cf. UPA (1987) and USCACA (1988) (section

4 below). At the present time, however, many of the traditional lines and distinctions in this entire area are giving way to reform and constitutional pressure, although the specifics of constitutional requirements remain unsettled.

Without holding that legislative classifications based on illegitimacy are strictly suspect, the United States Supreme Court decided in Trimble v. Gordon, 430 U.S. 762 (1977), that such classifications are invalid under the fourteenth amendment if they are not substantially related to permissible state interests. Accordingly, by a five-to-four vote the Court invalidated an Illinois inheritance statute requiring not only acknowledgment by the father but also the marriage of the parents in order for the child born out of wedlock to inherit from the father. Writing for the Court, Justice Powell rejected encouragement of legitimate family relationships as a purpose to be achieved by disadvantaging the child, but he recognized as permissible the aim of maintaining an accurate and efficient system for the transfer of intestate property. He conceded that the often difficult problem of proving paternity and the related danger of spurious claims "might justify a more demanding standard for illegitimate children claiming under their father's estates than that required either for illegitimate children claiming under their mother's estates or for legitimate children generally." In requiring the marriage of the parents, however, the statute excluded "at least some significant categories of illegitimate children of intestate men [whose] inheritance rights can be recognized without jeopardizing the orderly settlement of estates or the dependability of titles." The Court stated that the statute must be more "carefully tuned to alternative considerations" than were the broad rules of disqualification in the Illinois law. 430 U.S. at 770-772. An argument that the statute was justifiable as a reflection of the probable intention of decedents was not considered by the Court because it was procedurally improper, not having been raised and examined in the state proceedings.

Soon thereafter, in Lalli v. Lalli, 439 U.S. 259 (1978), the Supreme Court was confronted with New York's Estates, Powers, and Trusts Law §4-1.2, enacted in 1965. The statute allowed, as usual, "an illegitimate child and his issue [to] inherit from his mother and from his maternal kindred" but provided that "he and his issue inherit from his father [only] if a court of competent jurisdiction has, during the lifetime of the father, made an order of filiation, declaring paternity." (A further time limitation was not in issue in the case.) The statute also stated that "an agreement obligating the father to support the illegitimate child does not qualify such child or his issue to inherit from the father" in the absence of the prescribed order of filiation. Following the father's death, the nonmarital claimant offered evidence of his relationship to and with the decedent, including a notarized document in which the latter gave his consent to the marriage of "my son" and sev-

eral affidavits by persons who stated that the decedent had acknowledged his son openly and often. The New York Court of Appeals in In
re Lalli, 43 N.Y.2d 65, 371 N.E.2d 481 (1977), had found the statute
sufficiently related to the state's interest in "the orderly settlement of
estates and dependability of titles" to satisfy the dictates of equal protection.

By another five-to-four vote, the United States Supreme Court this
time upheld the statute. In a plurality opinion, Justice Powell found
the statute sufficiently related to its main purpose of providing "for the
just and orderly disposition of property at death." The statute, he wrote,
enhanced the accuracy of judicial fact-finding in paternity disputes, facilitated the administration of estates by making "the entitlement of
an illegitimate child to notice and participation a matter of judicial
record before the administration commences," and reduced the frequency of "fraudulent assertions of paternity." Incidentally, it also permitted a man "to defend his reputation against 'unjust accusations in
paternity claims.'" Justice Powell sought to distinguish his opinion in
Trimble by stressing that the legislative history disavowed any New York
intention to "discourage illegitimacy, to mold human conduct or to set
societal norms" and that, under the New York statute, "the marital status of the parents is irrelevant." He also emphasized that the statute
had been enacted mainly "to soften the rigors of previous law which
permitted illegitimate children to inherit only from their mothers," was
the product of a comprehensive and balanced study by individuals "experienced in the practical problems of estate administration," and had
been interpreted "liberally" by the New York courts. 439 U.S. at 269-
276. Petitioners argued that the New York law, like the Illinois law,
denied inheritance to children who could provide convincing proof of
paternity by other means than those prescribed in the statute, such as
by formal written acknowledgment of paternity. Justice Powell recognized that this was so but responded that the New York statute did not
disinherit as many deserving heirs as the Illinois statute.

Justice Blackmun, in a brief concurring opinion, found the distinctions between the two cases unconvincing, believed "the Court today gratifyingly reverts to [pre-*Trimble*] principles," and concluded: "I
therefore must regard *Trimble* as a derelict . . . offering little precedent
for constitutional analysis of State intestate succession laws. If *Trimble*
is not a derelict, the corresponding statutes of other States will be of
questionable validity until this court passes them, one by one, as being
on the *Trimble* side of the line or the . . . *Lalli* side." 439 U.S. at 277.

A four-Justice dissent notes a particular irony in the results of these
two cases, for the probabilities of intention (on which intestate law is
largely based) are most likely to favor the very nonmarital children the
New York law excludes. This opinion states: "[A]s a practical matter,
by requiring judicial filiation orders entered during the lifetime of the

father, the New York statute makes it virtually impossible for acknowledged and freely supported illegitimate children to inherit intestate."
439 U.S. at 278.

Reed v. Campbell, 476 U.S. 852 (1986), made clear that application
of an unjustifiably discriminatory Texas statute to bar a nonmarital
child's claim as a pretermitted heir (see Chapter 3, section D, infra)
was constitutionally impermissible, even though the father died before
the *Trimble* decision.

"A distinction between rights to inherit from a natural father and
. . . a natural mother may properly be based on the greater difficulty
of proving paternity than of proving maternity." But the alleged greater
difficulty of an administrator in "identifying and giving notice to the
illegitimate children of a man" was not a justification for the distinction, especially given that "notice by publication should be adequate"
for unknown claimants. The *state* constitution was thus held to be violated by a classification that denied an *openly admitted* illegitimate child
the right to inherit from the father because it went beyond what would
be necessary to "serve the State's interest in avoiding fraudulent claims"
in Lowell v. Kowalski, 380 Mass. 663, 405 N.E.2d 135 (1980).

On evidentiary and related aspects of these cases, see Proof of Heirship of Illegitimate Children of the Father—Estate of Daniel Finigan
(a Mock Trial), 13 Real Prop., Prob. & Tr. J. 733 (1978). See also Inheritance Rights for Extramarital Children, 65 U. Cin. L. Rev. 891 (1997).

Even less certainty, and much less experimentation and development, is reflected in decisions and legislation on the construction of
class gift terminology with respect to the rights of nonmarital descendants. (Incidentally, what is the effect of a formbook provision stating:
"For purposes of this will, the term 'issue' refers to lawful descendants
of all degree"? Contrast Harris Trust & Savings Bank v. Donavon, 145
Ill. 2d 166, 582 N.E.2d 120 (1991) with First Natl. Bank v. King, 165
Ill. 2d 533, 651 N.E.2d 127 (1995) (6-3 decision)). Strikingly lacking
in recent decisions is any discussion of a state's interests in effectuating
decedents' probable intentions as a permissible justification for state-
drawn distinctions in this area. Compare earlier recognition of that
interest in Estate of Pakarinen, 287 Minn. 330, 336-337, 178 N.W.2d
714, 717-718 (1970). Estate of Dulles, 494 Pa.180, 431 A.2d 208 (1981),
is a post-*Lalli* case involving a rule of construction. It held a statutory
presumption unconstitutional when the canon of construction flatly
allowed, absent contrary intention, a nonmarital child to hold class
membership through the mother but not through the father. The particular presumption then before the court would not have passed even
a more lenient test, but, in relying heavily on *Trimble,* the opinion addressed *Lalli* only in a superficial note, denying that it might be more
permissive. Of broader significance, however, is the opinion's generally
negative view of the permissibility of a purpose based on an attempt

to effectuate probable or typical, rather than universal, intentions of transferors.

ESTATE OF STERN v. STERN
311 S.E.2d 909 (N.C. App. 1984)

[Edward G. Stern died intestate, survived only by his maternal and paternal aunts and uncles. Stern's parents lived together in Canada when he was born but never married because of religious prohibitions in Canada at the time. Stern was nevertheless raised by both parents until his mother died when he was six. From the age of six on, Stern was raised by his father. Stern's father died in 1979, leaving his residuary estate worth over $500,000 to "my son" Edward Gordon Stern. Stern died intestate the following year. In a proceeding to determine who would inherit Stern's estate, the trial court ruled that Stern's maternal heirs were entitled to inherit to the exclusion of his paternal heirs. Stern's paternal heirs appealed.]

WEBB, Judge.

The question presented on this appeal is whether the heirs of the alleged natural father of Edward Gordon Stern have any rights to the decedent's estate. We believe they do not and affirm the order directing that the decedent's estate be distributed only to his maternal heirs.

G.S. 29-19(a) provides that for purposes of intestate succession, an illegitimate shall be treated as if he were the legitimate child of his mother so that he is entitled to inherit by, through and from his mother and his other maternal kindred, and they are entitled to take from him. There is no dispute that the decedent was illegitimate and that the respondent maternal heirs are entitled to some share of the decedent's estate.

The right of a putative father and the paternal heirs to inherit by, through and from an intestate illegitimate is governed by G.S. 29-19(b) and (c) which . . . (provide for such inheritance if the putative father has either been adjudged to be the father of the child or has acknowledged the child in a writing filed with the clerk of court.)

The record is devoid of any evidence indicating that Edward D. Stern was ever judicially adjudged to be the decedent's father . . . or that he ever acknowledged his paternity as provided in G.S. 29-19(b)(2).

G.S. 29-19(d) provides a further basis through which an illegitimate may inherit from his putative father. That section provides that:

(d) Any person who acknowledges himself to be the father of an illegitimate child in his duly probated last will shall be deemed to have intended that such child be treated as expressly provided for in said will or, in the absence of any express provision, the same as a legitimate child.

Edward D. Stern so acknowledged himself as the father of the decedent when he stated in his last will that he bequeathed his residuary estate to "my son, Edward Gordon Stern."

The appellant paternal heirs argue that since this acknowledgment of paternity by Edward D. Stern in his will is sufficient to permit the decedent to inherit from his putative father, it should also be sufficient to permit the putative father or his heirs to inherit from the decedent. . . .

We do not agree. G.S. 29-19(c) clearly and unambiguously provides that a putative father and his kindred are only entitled to inherit from an illegitimate child if paternity has been established by one of the methods prescribed in G.S. 29-19(b). Edward D. Stern's paternity was not established by either method; therefore, his heirs are not entitled to inherit from the decedent. . . . G.S. 29-19(d) . . . applies only when the child is taking under a will from the putative father and not when the putative father or his heirs are attempting to inherit from the child under the intestacy statutes.

[T]he father of an illegitimate has the ability to insure that he will be an intestate taker — he simply has to acknowledge his child in the prescribed manner. Unlike the illegitimate, the father can preserve his rights and he should not be rewarded for his failure to do so.

Affirmed.

paternity must be estb. by a prescribed method

failed to acknowledge

PROBLEM

2-L. *F* and *M* had a child, *C*, but were unmarried. *F* left town when *C* was six months old. He has had no contact with *C* and has provided no financial support. *M* raised *C*, who then died intestate survived by *F* and *M*. Who are *C*'s heirs in a UPC jurisdiction? In your state?

4. Assisted Reproduction

The ability that modern medical science has given people to conceive children without sexual intercourse has raised the question of whom the law should treat as parents.

Artificial Insemination by Donor (AID). The simplest form of assisted reproduction involves the introduction of sperm by means other than sexual intercourse. Where the sperm used is that of the woman's husband, the procedure is referred to as "artificial insemination by husband" (AIH) and does not complicate the inheritance picture since the two genetic parents are the only persons involved. However, where the sperm comes from someone other than the woman's husband, questions arise about the relationship between the child and the sperm donor and, if the mother is married, between the child and the moth-

[handwritten margin note: unmarried sperm donor ≠ father / married ⇒ thus is father IF consented.]

er's husband. The Uniform Parentage Act (1973) (UPA) and the Uniform Status of Children of Assisted Conception Act (1988) (USCACA) both provide that a sperm donor will not be regarded as a child's father and that, if the mother is married, her husband will be considered to be the child's father only if he consented to the procedure, (New uniform legislation is currently in process.)

There are two significant differences between the UPA and US-CACA. First, the UPA applies only to married women, thereby leaving in doubt the question of whether a sperm donor would be the father of an unmarried woman's child. Second, the UPA treats the mother's husband as the father only if he consented in writing while USCACA provides that the husband's consent is presumed unless he brings an action to deny it within two years of learning of the child's birth. See Helen S. Shapo, Matters of Life and Death: Inheritance Consequences of Reproductive Technologies, 25 Hofstra L. Rev. 1091 (1997); Ronald Chester, Freezing the Heir Apparent, 33 Hous. L. Rev. 967 (1996); and Ralph C. Brashier, Children and Inheritance in the Nontraditional Family, 1996 Utah L. Rev. 93. Because they refer to husbands, neither of the aforementioned statutes applies to lesbian partners. Thus, where one partner in a lesbian couple conceives a child via AID, the other partner will not be regarded as a parent of the child.

In Vitro Fertilization (IVF). Unlike the UPA, USCACA applies to IVF as well as AID. In one variant of IVF, an egg from a donor is fertilized and implanted in the womb of the woman who intends to raise the child. In this scenario, USCACA provides that an egg donor, like a sperm donor, is not a parent.

[handwritten margin note: egg donor ≠ parent]

Surrogacy. The problems for the law of estate distribution are most acute where assisted reproduction is used in combination with surrogacy. In traditional surrogacy, a couple unable to conceive a child contracts with a surrogate, who is impregnated with sperm from the husband. In the absence of a statute on point, the husband will be treated as the father and the surrogate is likely to be treated as the mother, unless and until adoption by the wife takes place. If the surrogate mother is married, the presumption of legitimacy is a problem because it creates a rebuttable presumption that the surrogate's husband is the child's father. Thus, legal action may be necessary to establish the child's paternity.

In gestational surrogacy, both sperm and egg are provided by the couple that wishes to raise the child, and the fertilized egg is implanted in the surrogate's womb. Thus, the child's genetic parents are the couple that contracted with the surrogate mother. Gestational surrogacy raises the question of who is a child's *natural* mother, the genetic mother or the gestational mother.

There are two alternative approaches to surrogacy under USCACA. One provides that the surrogate mother is the child's natural mother.

This equates the gestational surrogacy situation with traditional surrogacy and, as described above, makes adoption necessary for the woman who wants the child. Under the other alternative, if the surrogacy contract is approved by a court, the couple that contracted with the surrogate is treated as the child's natural parents. *K-approval*

Posthumous and Posthumously Conceived Heirs. The questions surrounding children who are conceived with frozen embryos or sperm are especially perplexing where conception occurs after the death of the donor of the embryo or sperm. This problem can be seen as a corollary to the posthumous heir situation where a person dies while a potential heir is in gestation. See page 46 above. In the latter situation, the child is generally allowed to share in the estate of the deceased parent if subsequently born alive. One of the arguments offered in favor of a different rule where a child is conceived after the death of one of the genetic parents is that allowing such a child to assert a claim against the estate of the deceased parent would create an administrative nightmare. Here, unlike the more conventional posthumous heir scenario, where the longest lapse between the decedent's death and the child's birth is about nine months, there is a high likelihood that the deceased parent's estate will be distributed prior to the birth, or even the conception, of the posthumously conceived child.

In Hecht v. Superior Court, 20 Cal. Rptr. 2d 275, 289 (Cal. App. 1993), a case dealing with the transferability of frozen sperm by will, the court mentioned in dicta its doubt that a posthumously conceived child would have a claim against the deceased parent's estate. Section 4(b) of USCACA provides that "[a]n individual who dies before implantation of an embryo, or before a child is conceived . . . , using the individual's egg or sperm, is not a parent of the resulting child." For a discussion of the *Hecht* case, see 47 Hastings L.J. 1081, 1128 (1996). See also Anne Reichman Schiff, Arising From the Dead: Challenges of Posthumous Procreation, 75 N.C. L. Rev. 901 (1997).

USCACA has been enacted in North Dakota and Virginia. See N.D. Cent. Code §14-18-01 to -07; Va. Code Ann. §20-156 to -165.

RESTATEMENT (SECOND) OF PROPERTY: DONATIVE TRANSFERS

§25.3 *Gifts to "Children" — Child Conceived by Means Other Than Sexual Intercourse.* When the donor of property describes the beneficiaries thereof as "children" of a designated person, the primary meaning of such class gift term includes a child conceived by means other than sexual intercourse who is recognized by the designated person as his or her child. It is assumed, in the absence of language or circumstances indicating a contrary intent, that the donor adopts such primary meaning.

5. Disqualification for Misconduct

misconduct & disqualification

As a general matter, the misconduct of an heir is not a basis for disqualification.[5] Under a few U.S. statutes, adultery or desertion by a spouse or abandonment by a parent may disqualify the offender from inheriting from the offended spouse or child. The English common law forfeiture of property rights by felons does not exist in the United States, and therefore inheritance rights are usually unaffected by the criminal activities of an heir. However, the right of one who commits homicide to take from the victim by will or inheritance, or under the terms of a life insurance policy or the survivorship provision of a deed, has been the subject of widespread legislation and litigation. See generally McGovern, Homicide and Succession to Property, 68 Mich. L. Rev. 65 (1969).

BRADLEY v. FOX
7 Ill. 2d 106, 129 N.E.2d 699 (1955)

DAVIS, J. . . .

ISSUE:

[The issue is whether a murderer becomes sole owner of property owned with the decedent as joint tenants with the right of survivorship.] . . .

The issue of whether a murderer may acquire or increase his property rights by the fruits of his crime is not a novel legal question. . . .

In the insurance cases the courts . . . construe the insurance policy in the light of the fundamental common-law maxim . . . that no man shall profit by his own wrong. . . . In conformity therewith, the Illinois courts . . . construed insurance contracts as though the public policy and this common-law maxim were part of the contract, and denied recovery on the policy to the murderer or his heirs.

There has not been the same unanimity in the case law, however, with reference to the right of a devisee or distributee who feloniously kills his ancestor to inherit from the decedent in the absence of a statute. 30 Harv. L. Rev. 622; 39 A.L.R.2d 498. The New York courts have

---

5. For example, a mother's abandonment of her child (who died at age 15) for a thirteen-year period following her divorce did not bar her right to share in the child's estate (absent formal termination of her parental rights) in Hotarek v. Benson, 211 Conn. 121, 557 A.2d 1259 (1989). For a criticism of this case, see Anne-Marie Rhodes, Abandoning Parents Under Intestacy, 27 Ind. L. Rev. 517 (1994).

consistently followed the case of Riggs v. Palmer, 115 N.Y. 506, 22 N.E. 188, 5 L.R.A. 340, and have construed the statutes of descent to preclude the murderer from inheriting from his victim . . . on the ground that all laws, as well as contracts, may be controlled in their operation and effect by the fundamental maxims of the common law that no one shall be permitted to acquire property by his own crime or iniquity. . . .

The Illinois court, however, in Wall v. Pfanschmidt [265 Ill. 180, 106 N.E. 785] . . . allowed a murderer to inherit from his victim on the theory that the statutes . . . did not preclude murderers from inheriting property, therefore the legal title which passed to the murderer must be deemed indefeasible.

The Illinois statute of descent, however, was modified in 1939, and provides in substance that a person who is convicted of the murder of another shall not inherit from the murdered person or acquire as surviving spouse any interest in the estate of the decedent by reason of the death. . . . Similar statutes have been enacted in most States, incorporating in effect the aforementioned common-law maxim as to the devolution of property. Wade, Acquisition of Property by Wilfully Killing Another — A Statutory Solution, 44 Harv. L. Rev. 715.

Defendants have questioned the constitutionality of the Illinois statute on the ground that it offends the constitutional prohibition against forfeiture of estate. Inasmuch as similar statutes in other States . . . have been uniformly sustained on the theory that they do not deprive the murderer of his property, but merely prevent him from acquiring additional property in an unauthorized and unlawful way . . . there is ample authority for sustaining the validity of the Illinois Law, and defendant's argument must be rejected.

However, the validity of that statutory provision is not determinative of the issue in the instant case, but at most indicates the broad policy of the State to prohibit a murderer from enjoying by descent the fruits of his crime, since at the time of the commission of the murder defendant held . . . a joint tenancy with the deceased, and his rights arise largely from the original instrument under which he had a right of survivorship, rather than by descent.

In this category of cases the courts have differed as to whether the murderer should be allowed his survivorship rights. Those courts which hold that he is entitled to the entire property as surviving joint tenant predicate their conclusion on the legal fiction [that] each tenant is deemed to hold the entire estate . . . and reason that the murderer acquired no additional interest by virtue of the felonious destruction of his joint tenant, of which he can be deprived. . . . Other courts, however, concerned with the equitable principles prohibiting a person from profiting from his own wrong . . . have abandoned the common-law fictions, and have either divested the killer of the entire estate; . . . or have deprived him of half the property; . . . or have imposed a constructive trust on the entire estate held by the murderer for the benefit of the heirs of the victim; . . . or a constructive trust modified by a life interest in half the property. . . .

The imposition of a constructive trust in the class of cases has been urged by legal scholars and is advocated by the Restatement of Restitution. Section 188b thereof provides in substance that when there are two joint tenants, and one of them murders the other, the murderer takes by survivorship the whole legal interest in the property, but he can be compelled to hold the entire interest upon a constructive trust for the estate of his cotenant, except that he is entitled to one half the income for life.

. . . Contracts and other instruments creating rights should properly be construed in the light of prevailing public policy evidenced in the statutes. . . . The Illinois statute prohibiting the devolution of property to a convicted murderer from his victim . . . [evinces] a legislative policy to deny the convicted murderer the fruits of his crime. That policy would be thwarted by a blind adherence to the legal fiction that a joint tenant holds the entire property at the date of the original conveyance, and acquires no additional interest by virtue of the felonious death of his cotenant, since that rationale sanctions in effect the enhancement of property rights through murder. For legal fictions cannot obscure the fact that before the murder defendant, as a joint tenant, had to share the profits of the property, and his right to complete ownership . . . was contingent upon surviving his wife; whereas, after . . . his felonious act that contingency was removed, and he became the sole owner of the property. . . .

In joint tenancy the contract that the survivors will take the whole necessarily presupposes that the death of either will be in the natural course of events and that it will not be generated by either tenant murdering the other. . . . Any act of a joint tenant which destroys any of [the four] unities operates as a severance of the joint tenancy and extinguishes the right of survivorship. . . . It is our conclusion that Fox by his felonious act destroyed all rights of survivorship and lawfully retained only the title to his undivided one-half interest in the property in dispute as a tenant in common with the heir-at-law of Matilda Fox, deceased. . . .

PROBLEMS

2-M. Consider the effect of the following statute: "No person convicted of the murder or voluntary manslaughter of the decedent may succeed to any portion of the estate; but the portion thereof to which he would otherwise be entitled to succeed goes to the other persons entitled thereto under the statutes of intestate succession."

[Margin notes: deprived of: 1) entire estate 2) 1/2 estate 3) restrictive trust on entire state; C/T hold; 1/2 income for life; share ⇒ after murder became sole owner of the property; act of J/T destroying (4) unities extinguishes right of survivorship; dependant on intestate succession laws]

murdered ✗ — G

D — Daughter

(a) *D* is murdered by his son, *S.* In addition to *S, D* is survived by a daughter and by a grandchild, *G,* who is the child of *S.* Under the statute, does *G* take anything, or does everything pass to the daughter, if *S* is convicted of murdering *D?* *G gets what entitled to through laws of intestate succession*

(b) Can *S*'s right to inherit be questioned if *S* commits suicide before he can be tried? If *S* had been convicted, could the question of his guilt be relitigated in an action by *S* to collect insurance proceeds on *D*'s life?

(c) What if *S* were a juvenile, found to be "delinquent" by the juvenile court, but not tried as an adult?

(d) What if *S* had been found "not guilty by reason of insanity"?

2-N.) In a state that has the Uniform Probate Code, *H* was killed by his wife, *W.* He left no will and was survived only by *W* and their two adult children. The district attorney has not and will not prosecute *W* because *H* had been terminally ill and begging for a "death with dignity."

(a) As administrator of *H*'s estate, should you bring this matter to the attention of the probate court? *yes* Do the wishes of the children matter? What if the children were minors?

(b) If you do not raise the issue, should the court raise it on its own motion? *yes*

(c) If *W*'s right to inherit is challenged, what result should the court *no inheritance* reach? For an argument that slayer statutes should not be applied to people who participate in mercy killings or assisted suicides, see Jeffrey Sherman, Mercy Killing and the Right to Inherit, 61 Cin. L. Rev. 803 (1993).

(d) If *W* had accepted a plea bargain, pleading guilty or nolo con- *no - still a felony* tendere to involuntary homicide, would that alter the result? Cf. Matter of Estate of Safran, 102 Wis. 2d 79, 306 N.W.2d 27 (1981). What if *W* had been charged with murder and acquitted?

UNIFORM PROBATE CODE

§2-803. *Effect of Homicide on Intestate Succession, Wills, Trusts, Joint Assets, Life Insurance, and Beneficiary Designations.*

(a) [Definitions.] . . .

(b) [Forfeiture of Statutory Benefits.] An individual who feloniously and intentionally kills the decedent forfeits all benefits under this Article with respect to the decedent's estate, including an intestate share, an elective share, an omitted spouse's or child's share, a homestead allowance, exempt property, and a family allowance. If the decedent died intestate, the decedent's intestate estate passes as if the killer disclaimed his [or her] intestate share.

(c) [Revocation of Benefits Under Governing Instruments.] The felonious and intentional killing of the decedent:

(1) revokes any revocable (i) disposition or appointment of property made by the decedent to the killer in a governing instrument, (ii) provision in a governing instrument conferring a general or nongeneral power of appointment on the killer, and (iii) nomination of the killer in a governing instrument, nominating or appointing the killer to serve in any fiduciary or representative capacity, including a personal representative, executor, trustee, or agent; and

(2) severs the interests of the decedent and killer in property held by them at the time of the killing as joint tenants with the right of survivorship [or as community property with the right of survivorship], transforming the interests of the decedent and killer into equal tenancies in common.

(d) [Effect of Severance.] A severance under subsection (c)(2) does not affect any third-party interest in property acquired for value and in good faith reliance on an apparent title by survivorship in the killer unless a writing declaring the severance has been noted, registered, filed, or recorded in records appropriate to the kind and location of the property which are relied upon, in the ordinary course of transactions involving such property, as evidence of ownership.

(e) [Effect of Revocation.] Provisions of a governing instrument are given effect as if the killer disclaimed all provisions revoked by this section or, in the case of a revoked nomination in a fiduciary or representative capacity, as if the killer predeceased the decedent.

(f) [Wrongful Acquisition of Property.] A wrongful acquisition of property or interest by a killer not covered by this section must be treated in accordance with the principle that a killer cannot profit from his [or her] wrong.

(g) [Felonious and Intentional Killing; How Determined.] After all right to appeal has been exhausted, a judgment of conviction establishing criminal accountability for the felonious and intentional killing of the decedent conclusively establishes the convicted individual as the decedent's killer for purposes of this section. In the absence of a conviction, the court, upon the petition of an interested person, must determine whether, under the preponderance of evidence standard, the individual would be found criminally accountable for the felonious and intentional killing of the decedent. If the court determines that, under that standard, the individual would be found criminally accountable for the felonious and intentional killing of the decedent, the determination conclusively establishes that individual as the decedent's killer for purposes of this section.

[Sections (h) (Protection of Payors and Other Third Parties) and (i) (Protection of Bona Fide Purchasers; Personal Liability of Recipient) are omitted.]

PROBLEMS

2-O. *K* killed himself and his mother (*M*) by intentionally driving off a cliff. The jurisdiction adopted the original version of the Uniform Simultaneous Death Act, providing that, if there is no sufficient evidence of the order of deaths, the decedent's property passes as if he survived the other. The jurisdiction's slayer statute provides that the victim's property passes as if he survived the killer, and also that the Simultaneous Death Act does not apply to cases governed by the slayer statute. *K* and *M* both died intestate. *K* had been *M*'s only lineal descendant. *M* had a sister, *S*, and *K*'s predeceased father had a brother, *B*. *B* and *S* survived *M* and *K*. How will *M* and *K*'s property be distributed?

2-P. *K* killed his father, *F*, whose will devised all of his property to his children. *F* was survived by five children including *K*. *K* had two children, *X* and *Y*, who also survived *F*. Who takes *F*'s property in a UPC jurisdiction? In your state? For a discussion of the applicability of an antilapse statute to a slayer's devise, see Estate of Van Der Veen, 262 Kan. 211, 935 P.2d 1042 (1997). Antilapse statutes are discussed in Chapter 11.

2-Q. *D* was murdered by his son, *S*. *D* is survived by a grandchild, *G1*, who is the child of *D*'s deceased daughter, and by *S* and *S*'s four children, *G2*, *G3*, *G4*, and *G5*. *D* died intestate in a jurisdiction that has general distribution taken from the Uniform Probate Code. The state's slayer statute provides that the victim's property passes as if the killer had predeceased. What result?

2-R. *W* was driving while intoxicated and ran off the road, killing her husband (*H*) who was a passenger. *H* died intestate. Can *W* take as his heir?

C. *Advancements, Releases, and Assignments* + Disclaimer + all affect succession

The preceding materials show how certain events prior to a decedent's death may affect succession and related matters. The material that follows deals with other types of activity that can affect succession: the concepts of advancement, release, assignment, and disclaimer. In Chapter 3, we shall examine some protections for family members and shall see that these protections may also be relinquished prior to a decedent's death. For example, a spouse may forgo the protection of a statutory "forced share" by a contract entered into while both spouses are alive or even before they were married.

Advancements. Nearly every state has a statutory provision relating to advancements. Despite differences in the terms of these statutes, the tendency of courts has been to construe them in a manner that eliminates potential differences in their application. The doctrine typically relates to instances of total intestacy. The related doctrine of satisfaction of testamentary dispositions is taken up later.

Nobles v. Davenport, 183 N.C. 207, 209-210, 111 S.E. 180, 181 (1922), states:

> In its legal sense an advancement is an irrevocable gift in praesenti of money or property, real or personal, to a child by a parent, to enable the donee to anticipate his inheritance to the extent of the gift; or, as somewhat differently defined, a perfect and irrevocable gift, not required by law, made by a parent during his lifetime to his child, with the intention on the part of the donor that such gift shall represent a part or the whole of the donor's estate that the donee would be entitled to on the death of the donor intestate. . . . The doctrine of advancements was the subject of statutory enactment in England as early as the reign of Charles II (22 and 23 Car. II, 1682-1683), and in this jurisdiction it is set forth as to both real and personal property in sections 138 and 1654(2) of Consolidated Statutes. This doctrine is based on the presumption that a parent who dies intestate intends equality among his children in the division of his property, but such presumption is subject to rebuttal by parol evidence. . . . In the determination of the question whether a transfer of property from parent to child is a gift, a sale, or an advancement, the intention of the grantor is the controlling element. . . . And only such intention as exists at the time of the transaction is to be considered. Therefore a parent's transfer of property to his child may constitute in part an advancement and in part a gift or a sale. . . . In endeavoring to discover the donor's intention, we must consider the circumstances surrounding the interested parties at the time the property is transferred; for the circumstances may be such as to create a presumption of advancement. Thus a substantial gift of property by a parent to his child, or a conveyance of land in consideration of love and affection, or a nominal sum, is ordinarily presumed to be an advancement. . . . But if the transfer is made for a valuable and adequate consideration there is no presumption of an advancement, but rather the contrary. . . . Nor is the doctrine of presumptions affected by the reservation of a life estate.

The doctrine of advancements is based on the "intention" of the intestate, but the major difficulty is in determining that intent. The presumption that a substantial gift to a child (and to other descendants under some applications of the common law rule) is intended as an advancement is a rebuttable one, but it is difficult to know what facts will serve to rebut the presumption.

The intestate's intent may be shown by his records, even informal ones, and by his declarations, even declarations subsequent to the alleged advancement if something of his state of mind at the time of the transfer may be inferred from them. Inferences as to intention may be drawn from the surrounding circumstances, the purpose, nature, and amount of the gift, and generally any factors that may be deemed persuasive as to the probable intent of the decedent at the time of making the gift.[6] The use of language of gift does not tend to rebut the presumption of advancement in an appropriate case, as an advancement is by its nature an irrevocable gift and merely attributes certain consequences to that gift.

The legislative trend is represented by a number of statutes that modify the general advancement rule by requiring a writing. See UPC §2-109(a) below. Is such a requirement desirable?

What if a person is incompetent to form an intent? In Guardianship of Hudelson, 18 Cal. 2d 401, 115 P.2d 805 (1941), a court had granted a daughter a living allowance out of her incompetent father's estate but provided that all amounts paid to her would be considered advancements when he died. The California Supreme Court affirmed, holding that a court acts for an incompetent as it supposes the incompetent would have acted had he been competent; if a court can find that the ward would have provided his child with an allowance, it can also find that he would have imposed conditions on the payments.

Unlike a loan, an advancement does not create an obligation on the part of the recipient, and it is not subject to statutes of limitations. It merely requires that, before participating in the estate, the recipient must bring the advancement into *hotchpot*. That is, the value of the advancement is added to the estate for purposes of computation, and the shares of the heirs in the mathematically "enlarged" estate are then determined. The recipient is then allowed to take from the estate the excess of that share over the advancement. If the advancement would exceed the share, the recipient would refuse to come into hotchpot, retaining the gift property without sharing in the estate.

The doctrine of advancements is generally said to apply to, and in favor of, children of the intestate. Statutes sometimes extend these rules to other heirs and to the surviving spouse. In the absence of such an extension of the doctrine, the share of the surviving spouse is not enlarged by the advancement (again, unlike a loan) to a child, nor is it diminished by inter vivos gifts to the spouse.

When an advancee predeceases the intestate, his or her issue are charged with the amount of the advancement in many states either by judicial decision or by statute (but cf. UPC §2-109(c) infra). Advancements are generally valued as described in the UPC, infra. Under some statutes, however, the valuation will be based on the value of like property as of the intestate's death. The value may be liquidated by agreement between the intestate and the donee.

---

6. Subsequent intent may be relevant, however. If the gift was not originally intended as an advancement, a change of intent will not alter the result, but what was originally intended as an advancement may by subsequent intent be converted into an outright gift.

UNIFORM PROBATE CODE

§2-109.　*Advancements.*

(a) If an individual dies intestate as to all or a portion of his [or her] estate, property the decedent gave during the decedent's lifetime to an individual who, at the decedent's death, is an heir is treated as an advancement against the heir's intestate share only if (i) the decedent declared in a contemporaneous writing or the heir acknowledged in writing that the gift is an advancement or (ii) the decedent's contemporaneous writing or the heir's written acknowledgment otherwise indicates that the gift is to be taken into account in computing the division and distribution of the decedent's intestate estate.

(b) For purposes of subsection (a), property advanced is valued as of the time the heir came into possession or enjoyment of the property or as of the time of the decedent's death, whichever first occurs.

(c) If the recipient of the property fails to survive the decedent, the property is not taken into account in computing the division and distribution of the decedent's intestate estate, unless the decedent's contemporaneous writing provides otherwise.

PROBLEMS

2-S.　*D* died intestate survived by his widow, *W*, and three children of a prior marriage, *A, B,* and *C.* His net estate is valued at $200,000. *W* had no children. Advancements were made to *A* in the amount of $50,000 and to *B* in the amount of $10,000. How should *D*'s net estate be distributed (a) under the Uniform Probate Code, and (b) under the law of your state (assuming community property is not involved)?

2-T.　*D*, an elderly bachelor, sent a check for $10,000 to *N*, his nephew. An accompanying letter stated in part: "That is a little down payment on your legacy. I know you need it now, and there will be more in my will for you." *D*, however, died intestate, survived only by nieces and nephews.

(a) Does the above check change the normal distribution of *D*'s estate under the Uniform Probate Code? Under the law of your state?

(b) How would you argue (i) for the nieces and nephews other than *N*, and then (ii) for *N*, under a statute that merely declares: "An advancement to any heir shall be charged against his share of the estate and to the extent of that share shall be included in the estate to be distributed"?

(c) Would it matter if *N*'s father *(D*'s brother) had been living at the date of the gift? Would the check affect the share of *N*'s child if *N* predeceased *D?* In the latter case would it matter if, in return for the check, *N* had executed a release of all his interest in *D*'s estate?

Releases and Assignments. Somewhat analogous to the problem of advancements is that of the *release* of an expectancy by a potential heir, devisee, or legatee. The general rule is that, when one who subsequently turns out to be an heir has released an expectant interest to the source (the intestate) before the latter's death, the release is binding on the heir if supported by a "fair and adequate consideration." It is also generally held that a purported *assignment* of an expectancy (to someone other than the source) for a fair and adequate consideration is binding on an heir or a beneficiary under a will.

An expectancy, being but a hope of succeeding to the property of another living person, is not treated as an existing property interest and therefore cannot be assigned gratuitously. Thus, in a true sense, no present transfer of an expectancy is possible. Statutes in some states expressly codify these common law principles. Consequently, releases and "assignments" of expectancies can be made binding only under some theory other than that of a present transfer. In appropriate transactions, the doctrine of estoppel by deed may apply; or a court of equity may label the purported assignment an *equitable assignment* or a specifically enforceable *contract to assign*. In the case of a release, it may be best to analyze the transactions as an advancement, the effect of which is fixed by agreement, and some courts have done so — possibly to avoid the necessity of a writing in certain factual situations.

Reference is made to *fair and adequate* consideration in the release and assignment cases. This requirement is not necessarily satisfied by consideration that would support a contract. Equity requires, before salvaging such a legally defective transfer, a greater showing of fairness and looks to the circumstances to discover any overreaching or bad faith. In the case of a release of an expectancy to the source, however, it is possible that a court would enforce the release without adequate consideration if it finds the basis of an estoppel in the release and in the reliance of the source in failing to make a will.

DONOUGH v. GARLAND
269 Ill. 565, 109 N.E. 1015 (1915)

[Thomas Garland died intestate, leaving a widow, Mary, and five children, Margaret Donough and Edward, Katherine, Mary Jane, and Lizzie Garland, as his heirs. Later, Mary Jane and Lizzie died, leaving their mother, brother, and sisters as heirs; thereafter Margaret quitclaimed to Edward and Katherine "all interest I now have or may hereafter acquire" in any lands owned by Thomas Garland at death or by Mary (his widow) at the date of the deed. After the deaths of Margaret and then Mary, Margaret's children sought to partition the lands Thomas and Mary had owned; the answer disputed their alleged title on the ground that Margaret had conveyed her interests in the lands to the defendants, who now appeal from a chancellor's decree in favor of Margaret's children. Clearly, Margaret conveyed all interests she had as a result of the deaths of her father and her sisters. The question was whether she also conveyed (and with what effect) her expectancy as heir of her mother, which on her mother's death, Margaret's children argue, passed to them.]

CARTWRIGHT, J. . . .

The expectancy of a prospective heir of a living person may be released to the ancestor or assigned to a stranger. In the case of a release to the ancestor a court of equity will enforce the contract for the benefit of the other heirs, and an assignment or transfer of an expectancy operates in equity as a contract by the assignor to convey the legal estate or interest when it vests in him, which will be enforced in equity when the expectancy has changed into a vested interest. 3 Pomeroy's Eq. Jur. §1287. . . .

. . . [Thus] a release by an heir presumptive of his expectancy operates as an extinguishment of the right of inheritance, cutting it off at its source. The line of inheritance is ended by the release made by the one having the expectancy at the time, and the release is binding not only upon him, but upon those who take as heirs in his place; otherwise a release would often be ineffective. That would always be the case where the one executing the release does not survive the one to whom the release is made, although he has himself received the consideration for the expectancy. If, however, the expectancy is assigned to another, the right of inheritance is not extinguished, but still exists, and the assignment is enforced as a contract to convey the legal estate or interest when it . . . becomes a vested estate. The assignee is regarded as bargaining for a legal interest depending on a future, uncertain, and contingent event. The assignee acquires a right to the legal estate if it ever vests in the assignor, but if it does not, he acquires nothing. In this case Edward Garland and Katherine Garland by the conveyance to them became entitled to enforce in equity a right to an interest in lands in case the interest should ever vest in Margaret Donough. The estate or interest did not vest in the grantor, and the chancellor did not err. . . .

———————————

As indicated by the result of the above case, one who takes by representation takes as a matter of personal right rather than through the person represented. As a result, a grandchild who takes in the place of a predeceased child of the intestate does not take subject to that child's assignments or the claims of the child's creditors. Can you explain why a release should be different in this regard from a purported assignment, as the above case indicates it would be?

Disclaimer. A beneficiary need not accept the benefits of an inheritance, and there can be both tax and non-tax reasons for disclaiming. Under the usual view at common law, however, the disclaimer by an heir was treated as a transfer while a disclaimer of a devise was not. This has been changed by statute in most jurisdictions and under UPC §2-801, generally to eliminate the "transfer" treatment. Also, the manner in which disclaimed property passes is generally prescribed by statute. A new Uniform Disclaimers Act was approved by NCCUSL in 1999. On disclaimers generally, see Chapter 13.

PROBLEM

2-U. *D* died intestate in a jurisdiction with a "per capita at each generation" distribution system. *D* is survived by one son, *S*, and a granddaughter, *X*, who is a child of a predeceased child of *D*. *S* has two children, *Y* and *Z*. *S* disclaims. The jurisdiction's disclaimer statute provides that the property passes as if the disclaimant predeceased. What result? UPC §2-801(d)(1) provides:

(d) [Effect of Disclaimer.] The effects of a disclaimer are:
     (1) If property or an interest therein devolves to a disclaimant under a testamentary instrument, under a power of appointment exercised by a testamentary instrument, or under the laws of intestacy, and the decedent has not provided for another disposition of that interest, should it be disclaimed, or of disclaimed or failed interests in general, the disclaimed interest devolves as if the disclaimant had predeceased the decedent, but if by law or under the testamentary instrument the descendants of the disclaimant would share in the disclaimed interest by representation or otherwise were the disclaimant to predecease the decedent, then the disclaimed interest passes by representation, or passes as directed by the governing instrument, to the descendants of the disclaimant who survive the decedent. A future interest that takes effect in possession or enjoyment after the termination of the estate or interest disclaimed takes effect as if the disclaimant had predeceased the decedent. A disclaimer relates back for all purposes to the date of death of the decedent.

3

Family Protection and Limits on Testation

Many of the policy conflicts in the area of decedents' estates and trusts concern the policies favoring freedom of property disposition as opposed to the policies favoring protection of the family and, incidentally, protection of the state from the burden of indigent families. Legislatures, reflecting general attitudes in society, often restrict the power of a person to dispose of property after death by requiring or encouraging some minimum provision for certain family members. The most common of these restrictions are considered in this chapter and raise the question whether a person should be able to dispose of property after death, by will or will substitute, without regard to the needs and expectations of spouse and children.

There are several basic types of protective provisions for family members. Some are *substantive* limitations on testamentary power. Others are *formal* requirements in that they are not really restrictions on the testator but merely provide that certain results must be accomplished in a way that tends to protect against oversight. In addition, there are temporary allowances during administration of a decedent's estate to assist the family through the administration period. We begin this chapter, however, with basic protections designed to assure that a property owner's actions are not the result of incapacity or of another's unlawful interference.

A. Testamentary Capacity and Autonomy: Grounds of Contest

Among the most fundamental of the safeguards provided for a property owner's immediate family members, or others the law designates as intestate successors, is the requirement that those who would make wills be competent and act free of deception or excessive imposition by others.

There are various grounds for contesting wills, and it is common that a contestant will assert several of these grounds in opposing probate or in seeking to set aside a will. The formal requirements of execution will be studied in the next chapter, although it is obvious that improper execution is a possible ground of contest. Usually the proponent of the will has the burden of proving its due execution. This burden, however, may readily be carried by aid of various presumptions, such as that arising from recitations in an attestation clause, or by inferences or even presumptions based on the appearance of the instrument once the required signatures have been identified. After a will has been admitted to probate, the contestant in a subsequent contest typically has at least the burden of going forward with the evidence in order to raise a question of fact on the matter of due execution.

Many statutes provide a right of jury trial as to at least some issues in will contests. As the materials involving grounds of contest are studied, consider the problems of proof, the way in which a party's burden is carried, and the quantum of evidence required to permit submission of a case on a question of fact. Consider whether there seems to be a different "feeling" for what constitutes a question of fact for a jury and for what is proper as a matter of appellate review in will contest cases as against the civil cases you have sampled in other courses, and whether there is a particular need for caution in submitting will contests to a jury. Under some statutes provision for jury trials in will contest cases is severely limited.

1. Testamentary Capacity

The age requirements for execution of wills rarely have been the cause of litigation, although under a few statutes the age requirement is unclear as a result of vague references to full or lawful age. Litigation concerning testamentary capacity generally centers on mental capacity. Basically, mental incapacity is of two types: (1) mental deficiency and (2) mental derangement.

Traditionally the burden of proof is on the proponent with regard to testamentary capacity. However, the burden of going forward with the evidence is often cast on the contestants as a result of a presumption of capacity arising from a mere showing of due execution. On the other hand, it is often held or at least stated that the burden of proof is on the contestant, particularly once the will has been admitted to probate. Judicial references to the "burden of proof" may only refer to the burden of going forward with the evidence, however, and the true burden of proof may remain with the proponent in many such cases. As you study the cases in this section consider the relationship between burdens of proof and procedure in will contest cases. An examination of many cases would suggest that the traditional relationships are sometimes overlooked or disregarded by probate courts and in appeals from probate decrees.

MATTER OF KUMSTAR
105 A.D.2d 747, 481 N.Y.S.2d 646 (1984)

Supreme Court, Appellate Division, Second Department. Nov. 13, 1984. . . . In a contested probate proceeding, the proponent of the purported will of the deceased Rose B. Kumstar, dated Sept. 1, 1982, appeals from a decree of the Surrogate's Court, Orange County (Green, J.), dated Jan. 5, 1984, which, after a jury trial, inter alia, denied probate to the purported will. Decree affirmed, with costs payable by appellant personally. The evidence on the record was sufficient to raise a jury question as to the issues of incompetence and undue influence, and there is no reason to disturb the jury's findings. We have considered appellant's other arguments and find them to be without merit. . . .

MATTER OF ESTATE OF KUMSTAR
66 N.Y.2d 691, 487 N.E.2d 271 (1985)

Memorandum.

The order of the Appellate Division [affirming denial of probate] should be reversed and the matter remitted to Surrogate's Court for entry of a decree granting the petition for probate.

It is the indisputable rule in a will contest that

> the proponent has the burden of proving that the testator possessed testamentary capacity and that the court must look to the following factors: (1) whether she understood the nature and consequences of executing a will; (2) whether she knew the nature and extent of the property she was disposing of; and (3) whether she knew those who would be considered the natural objects of her bounty and her relations with them. . . .

[handwritten marginalia: What Ct looks at to determine test. capacity]

When there is conflicting evidence or the possibility of drawing conflicting inferences from undisputed evidence, the issue of capacity is one for the jury. . . .

Here, there was insufficient evidence adduced at trial to warrant submitting that issue to the jury. The subscribing witnesses and those who were close to decedent when the will was drafted each testified that decedent was alert and capable of understanding the nature of her actions. Decedent's treating physician testified that it was his opinion, based on a reasonable degree of medical certainty, that decedent was competent when she signed the will. By contrast, a physician called by the objectant who reviewed decedent's medical records was unable to state with a degree of medical certainty that decedent was incompetent at the time in question. That the will contained a bequest to a "brother," long since deceased, "in Cuba, Cattaraugus County, New York" does not raise a question of decedent's competence in light of her attorney's testimony that, without knowing of the brother's death, he had assumed that the person referred to was decedent's brother. . . . Also without significance are the bequests establishing trust funds in relatively small amounts and the omission of a specific devise of certain land to a historical site contrary to a wish mentioned on several occasions by decedent. . . .

It was likewise error to submit the question of undue influence to the jury. That the will drafter stood to benefit by being named trustee of the estate and that he possessed an "opinionated and domineering personality," as indicated by his propensity to write "letters to the editor," is of no import. . . .

On review . . . order reversed, with costs payable out of the estate to all parties appearing separately and filing separate briefs. . . .

Mental Deficiency. In general, the test to be applied in the mental deficiency cases is well settled and agreed on by courts in this country. Of course, the real problems in these cases are those of fact and proof. The test of competence to make a will may be differently worded by different courts, but in substance the rule is generally accepted to be that a person is of sound mind for testamentary purposes if the person is able to understand "(1) The nature and extent of his property, (2) The persons who are the natural objects of his bounty, and (3) The disposition which he is making of his property," and if he is "capable of (4) Appreciating those elements in relation to each other, and (5) Forming an orderly desire as to the disposition of his property." T. Atkinson, Wills §51 (2d ed. 1953.)[1] "One may have testamentary capacity though he is under guardianship or lacks the ability to make

---

1. Compare Estate of Basich, 398 N.E.2d 1182, 1185 (Ill. App. 1979): "To have testamentary capacity, the testator must possess sufficient mental capacity to know the natural objects of his bounty, comprehend the kind and character of his property, understand the nature and effect of his act, and make disposition of his property according to some plan formed in his mind."

Occasionally statutes impinge on doctrine in this area, as in Georgia Code §13-106, providing that a will may disregard the testator's family and leave the entire estate to strangers but that in such a case "the will should be closely scrutinized and, upon the slightest evidence of aberration of intellect . . . probate should be refused." (This language may be of greater relevance in derangement cases, infra.) For purposes of this statute a common law spouse is not a stranger to the family. See Yuzamas v. Yuzamas, 241 Ga. 577, 247 S.E.2d 73 (1978).

a contract or transact business." Id.[2] For example, in Bye v. Mattingly, 975 S.W.2d 451 (Ky. 1998), the court found that the decedent did not lack capacity despite the fact that his business affairs had been placed under the control of a guardian. As emphasized in one opinion, a testator need only "have capacity to know and understand the nature and extent of his bounty" and other matters mentioned above, "as distinguished from [a] requirement that he have actual knowledge thereof." In re Estate of Jenks, 291 Minn. 138, 141, 189 N.W.2d 695, 697 (1971). Should these principles apply, or is adaptation required, in determining the validity of inter vivos gifts, the donative creation of joint tenancies, transfers in trust, and the like? Cf. Restatement (Third) Trusts §11 (Chapter 12 infra). See also Estate of Payton, 398 N.E.2d 977 (Ill. App. 1979); Re Beaney, [1978] 2 All Eng. Rep. 595.

Mental Derangement. The cases involving mental derangement or insane delusions cannot so easily be summarized. Note, however, that irrational beliefs *that do not affect the will* do not render the will invalid on the ground of insane delusion. Nevertheless, in such a situation the holding of beliefs that are clearly contrary to fact and reason may be some *evidence* of mental *deficiency*. The effect and definition of insane delusion, as widely recited in judicial opinions, are succinctly stated in In re Nigro's Estate, 243 Cal. App. 2d 152, 160, 52 Cal. Rptr. 128, 133 (1966), as follows:

> [T]he possession of an insane delusion which leads a testator to dispose of his property otherwise than he would have done had he not possessed such insane delusion is sufficient to invalidate a will. [A]n insane delusion is "the conception of a disordered mind which imagines facts to exist of which there is no evidence and the belief in which is adhered to against all evidence and argument to the contrary, and which cannot be accounted for on any reasonable hypothesis. One cannot be said to act under an insane delusion if his condition of mind results from a belief or inference, however irrational and unfounded, drawn from facts which are shown to exist."

2. See In re Estate of Teel, 14 Ariz. App. 371, 372, 483 P.2d 603, 604 (1971), where testator was found to be "mentally retarded," possessing a mental "age level of ten to twelve years," but where there was also a trial court finding that he "was aware of those who had some claim to benefit from his property"; "comprehended generally the kind and nature of his property"; "understood the nature and effect of his testamentary act"; and "could make [a] disposition of his property according to a plan formed in his mind." On that basis, the testator possessed testamentary capacity even though he was declared incompetent and had a guardian appointed not long after the will was executed, the court noting that even having a guardian when a will is executed does not necessarily preclude a testator from having the required capacity.

Is this distinction between "facts" and "beliefs" really a workable one? Try to apply it in the *Honigman* case, infra.

In Pendarvis v. Gibb, 328 Ill. 282, 159 N.E. 353 (1927), the testator bequeathed $1,000 to a cemetery association, $500 to each of two churches, $3,000 to the family physician, $500 to each of twelve persons "as slight recognition of kindness shown to me," $100 to his only surviving brother, William, and $250 to each of two nieces. The residue was left in equal shares to such of the children of the testator's deceased brothers and sisters as might be living at his death. The testator's brother William and several nieces contested the will; the jury found in their favor, and the will was set aside. On appeal, the Illinois Supreme Court reversed, holding the verdict based on unsoundness of mind to be "contrary to the manifest weight of evidence." As the facts appeared, the testator was a bachelor who lived alone on his farm and who had little contact with people, except for irregular visits by relatives and occasional visits by neighbors to help him or to play cards and drink whiskey. Some of these neighbors were remembered in the will by $500 devises. The testator's home and person were typified by filth and odor. Many witnesses testified he was sound of mind, while several testified he was not. The testator's own physician testified that testator was not of sound mind at a particular time that was more than eighteen months after execution of the will. Two doctors, who examined the testator just before a hearing on the appointment of a conservator shortly after the will was executed, testified that the testator was not of sound mind, but that he could name his brothers and sisters and some of his nieces and nephews and that he knew the size of his farm and had a general understanding of its condition. Substantial testimony evidenced that at the time the will was executed the testator believed that there were people in the trees around his house, that they were a threat to his property, that there were also cattle in the trees, and that the people were butchering them and hanging the beef in the trees. The testator recognized his need for a conservator and testified at the proceedings that his eyesight was bad, that there were things in the trees, and that he did not know whether they were people but that it looked like they were butchering out there.

The court stated at 291-295, 159 N.E.2d 357-358:

[A] testator does not have to be absolutely of sound mind and memory in every respect. . . . It is not every insane delusion that will avoid a will. In order to avoid a will the insane delusion must affect the testamentary disposition of the property. . . . Even if the testator has an insane delusion on certain subjects, still if he has mental capacity to know his property, the objects of his bounty and to make a disposition of his property according to a plan formed by him, the will cannot be set aside on the ground of mental incapacity. . . .

Apart from the evidence concerning this delusion [about the people in the trees] there is very little evidence on which a charge of unsoundness of mind could be sustained. Even if it be conceded that the testator had an insane delusion in the respect claimed, the evidence does not show that it in any way affected or entered into the execution of the will. The burden of proof was on appellees not only to overcome by the preponderance of the evidence the prima facie case made by appellants based upon the testimony of the subscribing witnesses to the will, but . . . to prove . . . that the testator was mentally incapable of making a will at the time it was executed. . . .

The preponderance of the evidence shows that the testator knew who were the objects of his bounty. He knew he had one brother living and two sisters who were dead, leaving children. He named . . . some of his nieces and nephews to Drs. Marshall and Babcock. He specifically named two of them in his will and none of them were omitted. The will stated that they were the children of his deceased brothers and sisters, who were named in the will. It is possible that he could not call each of these eleven nieces and nephews by name. One reason for this might have been that five of them were nonresidents, the children of his sister Eliza Fort.

The preponderance of the evidence also shows that the testator knew the kind and character of his bounty to be bestowed. He knew the amount of land he owned and that he had some personal property. . . . [T]he testator made disposition of his property according to a plan of his own. . . . The fact that he gave only $100 to the brother is in keeping with the facts. The brother was two years older than the testator. He had as much property as the testator. He had never been married and had no children. The heirs of each of the brothers were identical. The will, when considered as a whole, shows a rational and reasonable disposition of the estate under the facts in evidence.

Is there any doubt that a different result would be required by the *Pendarvis* case if the testator had also left $25,000 to Jones, a contractor, for the purpose of removing all the trees from the area of his home in order to protect his neighbors from the people residing in the trees (assuming, at least for purposes of discussion, that there were no people living and butchering in the trees)? In that event, to what extent would the court hold the will invalid? With this variation of the facts in *Pendarvis* compare the same court's earlier treatment of devises to promote spiritualism. In Owen v. Crumbaugh, 228 Ill. 380, 81 N.E. 1044 (1907), the testator, Crumbaugh, appeared to be a believer in spiritualism and purported to have frequent communications from residents of the spirit world, including mostly acquaintances long deceased and his spirit guide, Bright Eyes, his son who died in infancy but who had grown to manhood in the spirit world. In order to bring the benefits of spiritualism to his home town, the testator left most of his estate in trust to build a spiritualist church and public library. After hearing twenty-four lay witnesses and eight physicians for the contestants and fifty-five lay witnesses and twelve physicians for the proponents, the jury found against the will. At the conclusion of a thirty-page opinion reversing the lower court's decree setting aside probate, it was stated (228 Ill. at 413-414, 81 N.E. at 1055-1056):

> Proponents requested the court to direct a verdict in their favor, which was refused. If there was evidence requiring the court to submit the case to the jury the refusal of the request was not error. If, upon the whole case, there was evidence fairly tending to support contestants' bill the motion was properly denied. After giving this case the careful examination which its importance requires, we are firmly convinced that there is no evidence here even raising a suspicion in our minds that the testator was not entirely sane and as competent to make a will or transact any other kind of business as the average business man. We have examined the evidence with great care, and when it is all summarized and reduced to its final results it only proves that Crumbaugh was a believer in spiritualism; that he thought that he was doing a philanthropic work for his friends. . . and however much one may differ from him as to the advisability of such a devise, that has nothing to do with the legal status of the will. If the testator had the capacity to make the will he had the capacity to select the beneficiaries. . . .
>
> The court erred in refusing to direct a verdict for proponents, for which the decree must be reversed, which is accordingly done and the cause remanded to the circuit court, for further proceedings not inconsistent with the views herein expressed.

In considering the appropriate functions of the trial judge, the jury, and the appellate court in will contest cases, the rest of the litigation involving Mr. Crumbaugh's will, along with the above quoted opinion, affords considerable food for thought.

On remand, the circuit court dismissed the case, from which ruling the contestants successfully appealed. The supreme court again reversed the lower court and remanded for another jury trial.

On the second remand, the case was again submitted to the jury, which found for the contestants, and a decree was entered accordingly. Proponents appealed again, and again the court reversed but this time without remand, in Crumbaugh v. Owen, 238 Ill. 497, 87 N.E. 312 (1909). The court concluded its opinion by stating:

> This case has been submitted to two juries, and all the evidence which either of the parties to this litigation has been able to discover and bring forward, or can reasonably be expected to discover and bring forward upon another trial, is found in the record now before us. We are therefore satisfied that nothing will be gained by protracting this litigation and by submitting this case to another jury, as it is evident if a jury should

again return a verdict against the validity of the will that the court would be bound to set the verdict aside. We therefore think it to the interest of all the parties that this case should not be remanded for a new trial.

The decree of the circuit court will therefore be reversed but the cause will not be remanded, the result of which will be to leave the judgment of the county court of McLean county admitting the will of James T. Crumbaugh, deceased, to probate, in full force and effect.

238 Ill. At 509, 87 N.E. at 316. (About one-third of this estate was consumed by costs of litigation. Champaign-Urbana Courier, May 21, 1966, at 19.)

In re HONIGMAN'S WILL
8 N.Y.2d 244, 168 N.E.2d 676 (1960)

DYE, J.

Frank Honigman died May 4, 1956, survived by his wife, Florence. By a purported last will and testament, executed April 3, 1956, just one month before his death, he gave $5,000 to each of three named grandnieces, and cut off his wife, with a life use of her minimum statutory share, plus $2,500, with direction to pay the principal upon her death to his surviving brothers and sisters and to the descendants of any predeceased brother or sister, per stirpes. The remaining one half of his estate was bequeathed in equal shares to his surviving brothers and sisters and to the descendants of any predeceased brother or sister, per stirpes, some of whom resided in Germany.

When the will was offered for probate in Surrogate's Court, Queens County, the widow Florence filed objections. A trial was had on framed issues, only one of which survived for determination by the jury, namely: "At the time of the execution of the paper offered for probate was the said Frank Honigman of sound and disposing mind and memory?" The jury answered in the negative, and the Surrogate then made a decree denying probate to the will.

Upon an appeal to the Appellate Division, Second Department, the Surrogate's decree was reversed upon the law and the facts, and probate was directed. Inconsistent findings of fact were reversed and new findings substituted.

We read this record as containing more than enough competent proof to warrant submitting to the jury the issue of decedent's testamentary capacity. By the same token the proof amply supports the jury findings, implicit in the verdict, that the testator, at the time he made his will, was suffering from an unwarranted and insane delusion that his wife was unfaithful to him, which condition affected the disposition made in the will. The record is replete with testimony, supplied by a large number of disinterested persons, that for quite some time before his death the testator had publicly and repeatedly told friends and strangers alike that he believed his wife was unfaithful, often using obscene and abusive language. Such manifestations of suspicion were quite unaccountable, coming as they did after nearly 40 years of a childless yet, to all outward appearances, a congenial and harmonious marriage, which had begun in 1916. During the intervening time they had worked together in the successful management, operation and ownership of various restaurants, bars and grills and, by their joint efforts of thrift and industry, had accumulated the substantial fortune now at stake.

The decedent and his wife retired from business in 1945 because of decedent's failing health. In the few years that followed he underwent a number of operations, including a prostatectomy in 1951, and an operation for cancer of the large bowel in 1954, when decedent was approximately 70 years of age.

From about this time, he began volubly to express his belief that Mrs. Honigman was unfaithful to him. This suspicion became an obsession with him, although all of the witnesses agreed that the deceased was normal and rational in other respects. Seemingly aware of his mental state, he once mentioned that he was "sick in the head" ("Mich krank gelassen in den Kopf"), and that "I know there is something wrong with me" in response to a light reference to his mental condition. In December, 1955 he went to Europe, a trip Mrs. Honigman learned of in a letter sent from Idlewild Airport after he had departed, and while there he visited a doctor. Upon his return he went to a psychiatrist who Mr. Honigman said "could not help" him. Finally, he went to a chiropractor with whom he was extremely satisfied.

On March 21, 1956, shortly after his return from Europe, Mr. Honigman instructed his attorney to prepare the will in question. He never again joined Mrs. Honigman in the marital home.

To offset and contradict this showing of irrational obsession the proponents adduced proof which, it is said, furnished a reasonable basis for decedent's belief, and which, when taken with other factors, made his testamentary disposition understandable. Briefly, this proof related to four incidents. One concerned an anniversary card sent by Mr. Krauss, a mutual acquaintance and friend of many years, bearing a printed message of congratulation in sweetly sentimental phraseology. Because it was addressed to the wife alone and not received on the anniversary date, Mr. Honigman viewed it as confirmatory of his suspicion. Then there was the reference to a letter which it is claimed contained prejudicial matter — but just what it was is not before us, because the letter was not produced in evidence and its contents were not established. There was also proof to show that whenever the house telephone rang Mrs. Honigman would answer it. From this Mr. Honigman drew added support for his suspicion that she was having an affair with Mr. Krauss. Mr. Honigman became so upset about it that for the last two years of their marriage he positively forbade her to answer the telephone. Another allegedly significant happening was an occasion when Mrs. Honigman asked the decedent as he was leaving the house what time she might expect him to return. This aroused his suspicion. He secreted himself at a vantage point in a nearby park and watched his home. He saw Mr. Krauss enter and, later, when he confronted his wife with knowledge of this incident, she allegedly asked him for a divorce. This incident was taken entirely from a statement made by Mr. Honigman to one of the witnesses. Mrs. Honigman flatly denied all of it. Their verdict shows that the jury evidently believed the objectant. Under the circumstances, we cannot say that this was wrong. The jury had the right to disregard the proponents' proof, or to go so far as to hold that such trivia afforded even additional grounds for decedent's irrational and unwarranted belief. The issue we must bear in mind is not whether Mrs. Honigman was unfaithful, but whether Mr. Honigman had any reasonable basis for believing that she was.

In a very early case we defined the applicable test as follows:

> If a person persistently believes supposed facts, which have no real existence except in his perverted imagination, and against all evidence and probability, and conducts himself, however logically, upon the assumption of their existence, he is, so far as they are concerned, under a morbid delusion; and delusion in that sense is insanity. Such a person is essentially mad or insane on those subjects, though on other subjects he may reason, act and speak like a sensible man.

(American Seamen's Friend Soc. v. Hopper, 33 N.Y. 619, 624-625.)

It is true that the burden of proving testamentary incapacity is a difficult one to carry (Dobie v. Armstrong, 160 N.Y. 584, 55 N.E. 302), but when an objectant has gone forward, as Mrs. Honigman surely has, with evidence reflecting the operation of the testator's mind, it is the proponents' duty to provide a basis for the alleged delusion. We cannot conclude that as a matter of law they have performed this duty successfully. When, in the light of all the circumstances surrounding a long and happy marriage such as this, the husband publicly and repeatedly expresses suspicions of his wife's unfaithfulness; of misbehaving herself in a most unseemly fashion, by hiding male callers in the cellar of her own home, in various closets, and under the bed; of hauling men from the street up to her second-story bedroom by use of bed sheets; of making contacts over the household telephone; and of passing a clandestine note through the fence on her brother's property — and when he claims to have heard noises which he believed to be men running about his home, but which he had not investigated, and which he could not verify — the courts should have no hesitation in placing the issue of sanity in the jury's hands. To hold to the contrary would be to take from the jury its traditional function of passing on the facts. . . .

The proponents argue that, even if decedent was indeed laboring under a delusion, the existence of other reasons for the disposition he chose is enough to support the validity of the instrument as a will. The other reasons are, first, the size of Mrs. Honigman's independent fortune, and second, the financial need of his residuary legatees. These reasons, as well as his belief in his wife's infidelity, decedent expressed to his own attorney. We dispelled a similar contention in American Seamen's Friend Soc. v. Hopper, supra, 33 N.Y. at page 625, where we held that a will was bad when its "dispository provisions were or *might have been* caused or affected by the delusion" (emphasis supplied). . . .

The order appealed from should be reversed and a new trial granted, with costs to abide the event.

FULD, J. (dissenting).

I am willing to assume that the proof demonstrates that the testator's belief that his wife was unfaithful was completely groundless and unjust. However, that is not enough; it does not follow from this fact that the testator suffered from such a delusion as to stamp him mentally defective or as lacking in capacity to make a will. . . . "To sustain the allegation," this court wrote [in Clapp v. Fullerton,] 34 N.Y. 190, 197,

> it is not sufficient to show that his suspicion in this respect was not well founded. It is quite apparent, from the evidence, that his distrust of the fidelity of his wife was really groundless and unjust; but it does not follow that his doubts evince a condition of lunacy. The right of a testator to dispose of his estate, depends neither on the justice of his prejudices nor the soundness of his reasoning. . . .

In short, the evidence adduced utterly failed to prove that the testator was suffering from an insane delusion or lacked testamentary capacity. The Appellate Division was eminently correct in concluding that there was no issue of fact for the jury's consideration and in directing the entry of a decree admitting the will to probate. Its order should be affirmed.

DESMOND, C.J., and FROESSEL AND BURKE, J.J., concur with DYE, J.; FULD, J., dissents in an opinion in which VAN VOORHIS and FOSTER, J.J., concur.

———————

In Estate of Killen, 188 Ariz. 562, 937 P.2d 1368 (Ariz. App. 1996), the testator believed that her niece and nephews stayed in her attic, sprayed chemicals and parasites from the attic, were trying to poison her and take her property, and were in the mafia. They succeeded in contesting the will on grounds of insane delusion. The court noted that Arizona had no prior reported case where a will was invalidated on grounds of insane delusion.

Ante-Mortem Probate. Should there be some way by which these issues and those that follow could be determined while the testator is still alive? See Alexander and Pearson, Alternative Models of Ante-Mortem Probate and Procedural Due Process Limitations on Succession, 78 Mich. L. Rev. 89 (1979); Mary Louise Fellows, The Case Against Living Probate, 78 Mich. L. Rev. 1066 (1980); Beyer and Leopold, Ante-Mortem Probate, 43 Ark. L. Rev. 131 (1990). See also Ark. Stat. Ann. §§28-40-201 et seq. (1987); Ohio Rev. Code §§2107.081 et seq. (1981); N.D. Cent. Code §30.1-08.1-01 (Supp. 1977). Much support for legislation of this type comes from charities. Why? Is there a need for such legislation? Does determination of potential contest issues during life offer an option a testator would freely choose? Is such a procedure fair and humane to family members who have serious doubts about a living person's will, and is a genuine and hence just determination of the issues likely? In light of increasing interest in this subject, questions like these should be given thoughtful consideration not only with respect to the question of desirability but also with respect to matters of form and content.

2. Fraud

Although difficult factual problems arise in proving fraud, there has been little difficulty in defining it. "[F]alse representations . . . constitute fraud if it can be shown that they were designed to and did deceive the testator into making a will different in its terms from that which he would have made had he not been misled." Estate of Newhall, 190 Cal. 709, 718, 214 P. 231, 235 (1923). The fraud may be either in the execution of a will or in its inducement, and in either form it is similarly treated. (*Mistakes* in inducement, as well as in description, are examined as aspects of the extrinsic evidence problem in Chapter 5.)

The *remedy* for fraud poses a more difficult legal problem, especially in deciding whether and in what manner a disposition was, or — more realistically — should be deemed to have been, affected by deceit practiced upon a testator. Also, when is it sufficient merely to deny probate to the will or a portion of it? What other remedies are available? In what circumstances, and then how, must it be shown what the testator would have done but for the fraud?

In re CARSON'S ESTATE
184 Cal. 437, 194 P. 5 (1920)

[Alpha Carson's will left a number of bequests to relatives and her residuary estate to "my husband J. Gamble Carson." Within the statutory period following probate, her heirs petitioned to have probate revoked primarily on the ground of fraud, and contestants appeal the denial of their petition. The facts indicate that the testatrix and Carson had gone through a marriage ceremony a year before her death and that she made her will and died believing that he was her husband, which he was not because he was already married to and not divorced from another woman who was still living. It was alleged that Carson knew he was not free to marry but represented that he was.]

OLNEY, J. . . .

Was the evidence for the contestants, both what they introduced and what they sought to introduce, sufficient to justify revocation of the probate of the will?. . .

So far as the other beneficiaries are concerned . . . the will is perfectly valid. . . . [O]nly the portions of the will in favor of Carson should be revoked in case the contestants should succeed. . . . If it were not possible to separate the portions affected by the fraud from those unaffected, it may be that the whole will would have to fail, but that question is not present here. . . .

The gross fraud upon the testatrix is, of course, apparent. According to the evidence, she was seduced by a marital adventurer into a marriage with him which was no marriage in the eyes of the law. . . . There can be no question also that if the bequest to Carson were the direct fruit of such fraud, it is void.

The only question in the case, assuming the contestants' evidence to be true, as we must, is, was the bequest in fact the fruit of the fraud? This is a question of fact which it was for the jury to determine; and, unless it can be said that the jury could have reasonably reached but one conclusion concerning it, and that was that the bequest to Carson was not the direct fruit of his fraud, the evidence was sufficient to prevent a nonsuit.

Now a case can be imagined where, nothing more appearing, as in this case, than that the testatrix had been deceived into a void marriage and had never been undeceived, it might fairly be said that a conclusion that such deceit had affected a bequest to the supposed husband would not be warranted. If, for example, the parties had lived happily together for 20 years, it would be difficult to say that the wife's bequest to her supposed husband was founded on her supposed legal relation with him, and not primarily on their long and intimate association. It might well be that if undeceived at the end of that time her feeling would be, not one of resentment at the fraud upon her, but of thankfulness that she had been deceived into so many years of happiness. But, on the other hand, a case can easily be imagined where the reverse would be true. If in this case the will had been made immediately after marriage, and the testatrix had then died within a few days, the conclusion would be well nigh irresistible, in the absence of some peculiar circumstance, that the will was founded on the supposed legal relation into which the testatrix had been deceived into believing she was entering. Between these two extreme cases come those wherein it cannot be said that either one conclusion or the other is wholly unreasonable, and in those cases the determination of the fact is for the jury. Of that sort is the present.

We are not unmindful of the fact that the contestants offered no evidence other than that the testatrix had been tricked into the marriage; that in particular they did not offer any direct evidence that the inducing reason in her mind for her bequest to Carson was her belief that he was her legal husband, and that the bequest would not have been made except for that belief. But such direct evidence is not necessary, and not improbably could not possibly be had. It is not an unreasonable inference, from the fact that she has been so recently married when the will was made, that she left the bulk of her estate to Carson because she believed he was her lawful husband, and would not have so left it if she had believed otherwise. Such inference, of course, was subject to being strengthened or weakened by evidence of other circumstances throwing light upon the matter, such as the views of the testatrix upon the sanctity of marriage, her harmonious or other relations with Carson, and the strength of her affection for him. But in the absence of such circumstances the inference mentioned is yet not an unreasonable one from the facts that appear. Our conclusion therefore is that the order of nonsuit should not have been made. . . .

Judgment reversed.

Was the fraudulent marriage in the *Carson* case "designed to . . . deceive the testator into making a will"? (See quotation from Estate of Newhall at the start of this subsection.) Should a case such as this be an exception to that requirement? On the question of whether, if the truth were known to the testatrix before her death, she would have made a different disposition, should a jury be allowed to draw its own inferences from the circumstances?

ROOD v. NEWBERG
218 N.E.2d 886 (Mass. App. 1999)

SMITH, J. Dora Shaffer died on September 25, 1994, leaving a will in which she named her son ["Rood"] and her daughter ["Estelle"] as coexecutors. . . . Rood did not join in the petition [for probate, but objected] to the allowance of the will, claiming that [Newberg, who is]

Estelle's son and Shaffer's grandson, had used undue influence with respect to the will. . . . Rood also . . . sought an order requiring Newberg to turn over to the estate the proceeds of four [bank] accounts.

. . . In the equity action, the judge ruled that Newberg had committed fraud and exerted undue influence over Shaffer and, therefore, had obtained [survivorship rights in] the four bank accounts through improper means. . . . In the estate matter, the judge made the same finding of fraud and undue influence but allowed the will except for certain provisions benefitting Newberg. . . .

The judge found as a fact that Shaffer was opinionated, feisty, stubborn, and narrow-minded; if someone had "wronged" her, she would not likely forgive that person. He also found as a fact that Rood's testimony was more credible than Newberg's.

The judge ruled that Newberg was in a position of trust with Shaffer and had developed a confidential relationship with her and that Newberg violated that relationship by failing to correct Shaffer's mistaken belief that Rood had taken . . . items from [her] safe deposit box [when in fact Newberg had moved them into his own safe deposit box]. . . .

. . . [W]e do not set aside a judge's findings of fact unless they are "plainly wrong" (the standard applicable to probate proceedings to allow or set aside a will) or "clearly erroneous" (the standard applicable to equitable proceedings) [citation omitted, but a footnote states that there is "no essential difference between the two standards of review"]. . . .

We note that the judge considered fraud and undue influence together as the ground on which he could invalidate the will provision favoring Newberg and order the four joint bank accounts to be returned to the estate. However, "[i]t is well established that 'fraud' and undue influence are separate and distinct grounds for invalidating a testamentary provision, in the one case the testator proceeding of his own free will but affected by a false representation of fact which is the inducement for the disposition in question, and in the other the testator's own will and free agency being destroyed so that what he does he is constrained to do contrary to his own free will." [Citation omitted.] Therefore, either fraud or undue influence would invalidate the establishment of joint bank accounts or favorable provisions in a will.

The evidence in this matter does not refer to "influence exerted through coercion." Rather, it refers to "[f]raud, in the sense of deceit." [Citations omitted.]

In order to prove fraud by deceit, a plaintiff ordinarily must show that the defendant made a false statement of a material fact with the knowledge of its falsity in order to induce the plaintiff to act, together with a reliance by the plaintiff on the false statement to the plaintiff's detriment. Here, there is no evidence that Newberg made a false representation or statement of a material fact [citations omitted]. . . .

Usually, "nondisclosure does not amount to fraud. . ." [but may] if a party "is under a duty to the other [party] to exercise reasonable care to disclose the matter in question." . . . The duty may arise if there is a "fiduciary or other similar relation of trust and confidence between [the parties]." Restatement (Second) of Torts §551.

A confidential relationship does not arise merely by reason of family ties; however, such a relationship "may be found on evidence indicating that one person is in fact dependent on another's judgment in business affairs or property matters. Whether a relationship of trust and confidence exists is a question of fact. . . ." [Citations omitted.] In the present matter, . . . we agree with the judge that there was a confidential relationship between Newberg and Shaffer [discussion of relevant facts omitted].

Because of that relationship, Newberg had a duty to disclose to Shaffer that she was mistaken in her accusations against Rood. Newberg . . . remained silent when he repeatedly heard Shaffer voice her anger because she believed Rood had taken her property [and Newberg] was aware that . . . she was changing her will because of her erroneous beliefs. . . .

Newberg's nondisclosure also affected at least three bank accounts. . . .

3. Undue Influence

The effect of undue influence is to invalidate the portion of the will procured thereby. Unaffected portions of the will may be allowed to stand as written. "It has been stated in numerous cases that undue influence, such as will invalidate a will, must be something which destroys the free agency of the testator, at the time when the instrument is made, and which, in effect substitutes the will of another for that of the testator." Toombs v. Matthesen, 206 Okla. 139, 142, 241 P.2d 937, 940 (1952). Thus, it is generally said, an influence is not undue if it merely involves persuasion, pleas calculated to arouse the testator's sympathy, or the courting of favor, even with the intent to obtain benefits under a will. What actions then may constitute undue influence? Certainly the answer varies depending on the circumstances, particularly susceptibility of the testator as it appears from mental, emotional, and physical conditions at the time; but the answer is also likely to vary with the court's concept of undue influence.

It is self-evident that the actual facts of alleged acts of undue influence will rarely be known or provable by direct evidence. Undue influence must almost inevitably be shown by circumstantial evidence. The burden of proof, which generally rests on the contestant in the issue of undue influence, may be carried by a showing of facts from which an inference of undue influence may be drawn or that create a presumption of such influence, shifting to the proponent the burden of going forward with the evidence. Quite a few courts have taken the position that undue influence must be proven by clear and convincing evidence, but usually the preponderance-of-the-evidence requirement of ordinary civil litigation is held applicable.

Most cases of undue influence are proven, or sought to be proven, in one of two primary ways, as indicated by the fairly representative dicta set out below. But again the court's formulation and handling of doctrine can make a considerable difference in the outcome of a given contest.

(1) In Will of Leisch, 221 Wis. 641, 648, 650, 267 N.W. 268, 271-272 (1936), a showing of four elements is generally said to give rise to a permissible inference of undue influence:

raise a presumption

The proof of undue influence generally rests in circumstantial evidence. . . . The four elements necessary to be proved in order to establish undue influence are as follows: (1) a person unquestionably . . . . [susceptible] to undue influence; (2) opportunity to exercise such influence and [to] effect the wrongful purpose; (3) a disposition to influence unduly for the purpose of procuring an improper favor; and (4) a result clearly appearing to be the effect of the supposed influence. . . . [Y]et the clear establishment of three of these essential elements may with slight additional evidence as to the fourth compel the inference of its existence. This is especially true where the will is not what may be termed a natural one, such as relationship usually dictates.

(2) Compare In re Hopper, 9 N.J. 280, 282, 88 A.2d 193 (1952):

[I]f a will benefits one who stood in a confidential relationship to the testator and there are additional circumstances of a suspicious character, a presumption of undue influence is raised and the burden of proof is shifted to the proponent. A confidential relationship arises where trust is reposed by reason of the testator's weakness or dependence or where the parties occupied relations in which reliance is naturally inspired or in fact exists, as the relation between client and attorney.

See also Estate of Ausseresses, 178 Cal. App. 2d 487, 488, 3 Cal. Rptr. 124-125 (1960): " 'It is now settled that' . . . when the contestant has shown that the proponent of a will sustains a confidential relationship toward the testator, and actively participates in procuring the execution of the will, and unduly benefits thereby, the burden then shifts to the proponent to prove that the will was not induced by his undue influence." And see Estate of Osborn, 470 N.E.2d 1114, 1117-1118 (Ill. App. 1984):

The necessary fiduciary relationship exists where there is a special confidence reposed in one who, by reason of such confidence, must act in good faith and with due regard to the interests of the person reposing such confidence. This relationship "may exist as a matter of law between attorney-client, guardian-ward, trustee-beneficiary, and the like, or it may be the result of a more informal relationship — moral, social, domestic or even personal in its origin." . . . While the plaintiff . . . asserts that a confidential relationship arose from the Diocese's role as religious and spiritual adviser to the decedent, we are aware of no authority . . . that such a relationship is fiduciary as a matter of law. The further allegations . . . fail to indicate that the decedent reposed any "special confidence" in the Diocese or, indeed, that the relationship between the decedent and her religious advisors was any different than that between other elderly persons and their religious or spiritual advisers. . . .

Even if we were to assume the existence of a fiduciary relationship . . . [a] presumption of undue influence arises, not from the mere fact of a fiduciary relationship, but from the fiduciary's participation in procuring execution of the will . . . , as undue influence that will invalidate a will must be directly connected with its execution and operate at the time it was made.

For an argument that the doctrine of undue influence does not act to protect the intent of the testator, but rather to protect the testator's biological family from disinheritance, see Ray D. Madoff, Unmasking Undue Influence, 81 Minn. L. Rev. 571 (1997). Also see Melanie B. Leslie, The Myth of Testamentary Freedom, 38 Ariz. L. Rev. 235 (1996).

SANGSTER v. DILLARD
144 Or. App. 210, 925 P.2d 929 (1996)

DE MUNIZ, J.

Defendant, Dan Dillard, appeals from a judgment voiding the 1993 will of his mother, Evelyn Cochrane, on the grounds of undue influence. . . .

Defendant is Cochrane's only child. Plaintiff is defendant's daughter by his first marriage and Cochrane's granddaughter. Plaintiff contested Cochrane's 1993 will, which names defendant as sole beneficiary, and sought to probate a 1988 will naming her uncle, her siblings and herself as beneficiaries. . . .

[Cochrane left her first husband, Dillard's father, when Dillard was an infant. Dillard was raised by his father and rarely saw Cochrane until he went to live with her at the age of 15.]

In 1975, Cochrane, Gordon [her second husband], defendant and his second wife Sharon signed a real estate contract to purchase 160 acres of land on Mount Hood. This eventually became the Cooper Spur

Inn. . . . Defendant testified that he contributed half of the approximately $22,000 down payment, but the trial court found that Cochrane put up all the money.[3]

When Gordon retired around 1979, he and Cochrane moved to Cooper Spur and lived with defendant, Sharon and their two children. . . . There were frequent quarrels over management of the resort, particularly over the increasing investments by Cochrane and Gordon and defendant's indebtedness to them. Cochrane once estimated that she had loaned defendant approximately $400,000 for improvement and operation of the resort. . . .[4] There is no record of defendant paying back any of that money. . . .

In 1988, Cochrane executed a will explicitly disinheriting defendant, leaving her entire estate to Gordon and, if Gordon should die first, to her brother and [Dillard's children from his first marriage]. . . .

[After Gordon's death in 1989,] Cochrane remained at Cooper Spur with defendant, but continued to tell others that their relationship was strained and unpleasant. She reported that she rarely left the mountain because she did not trust defendant and needed to keep an eye on her investment. Cochrane lived in a 400-square-foot apartment above the resort's diner. The only telephone in her apartment was an extension that rang in the restaurant below and in defendant's home, located a few hundred feet away. Because she feared that defendant monitored her calls, Cochrane told relatives and friends not to call her there. Defendant also had access to her mail.

Although witnesses described Cochrane as tough, independent and shrewd, she became more reliant on defendant as her health failed. . . . Cochrane had no driver's license and relied almost exclusively on defendant for transportation to the pharmacy, doctor's office, bank, grocery store, hair dresser and all other contacts beyond Cooper Spur.

Sometime in February 1993, defendant told [his attorney] Bowe that Cochrane wanted to make a will leaving him all her property. Bowe told defendant that [Cochrane's attorney] should draft the will, but according to defendant's testimony, Cochrane insisted on Bowe. The trial court, however, did not believe defendant on this point. The court explicitly found that . . . it was defendant, not Cochrane, who selected Bowe. . . .

The next day, defendant drove his mother to Bowe's office. Bowe testified that she looked ill and weak. While defendant looked on in Bowe's lobby, Cochrane executed the will in the front seat of defen-

3. That same year, Cochrane and Gordon also formed a construction company with defendant in Hood River. Cochrane and Gordon again put up the money, and defendant supplied the equipment. After two or three years, the company failed. Cochrane covered a $60,000 default, and defendant liquidated the equipment.

4. There were also plans to build a house for Cochrane and Gordon at Cooper Spur. Only defendant's house was built. At trial, defendant estimated its value at $414,000.

dant's truck. There is no indication that either Bowe or defendant advised her to seek independent advice regarding the new will. No one knew about the new will except Cochrane, defendant, Bowe and Bowe's secretary.

Cochrane died about a month later, on March 6, 1993, at the age of 76. Within days, defendant filed a petition to admit the 1993 will to probate. Plaintiff then filed a petition contesting the will and seeking to have the 1988 will admitted. The trial court granted plaintiff's petition and voided the 1993 will. The sole issue on appeal is whether defendant used undue influence in persuading Cochrane to execute that will.

Underlying the doctrine of undue influence is the principle that "the law will not permit improper influences to control the disposition of a person's property." . . . Although undue influence is difficult to define, the question is generally whether the beneficiary, by his or her conduct, gained an unfair advantage by means that reasonable persons would regard as improper. . . . Undue influence is not the equivalent of coercion or duress; the focus is not so much on the testator's lack of consent as on the alleged influencer's lack of conscience in persuading the testator to act as he did. . . .

[A]n inference of undue influence arises where the evidence establishes the existence of a confidential relationship, the beneficiary's dominance over the testator and the presence of suspicious circumstances surrounding execution of the will. . . . The will's proponent then bears the burden of producing evidence negating that inference. . . .

Defendant concedes the existence of a confidential relationship, but argues that no evidence established his dominance over Cochrane. Dominance does not necessarily require proof of an authoritative, controlling person bullying or directing the actions of a subservient one. It may exist more subtly "such as by suggestion or persuasion or by fostering a sense of need and dependence." . . .

We have found dominance where the testatrix is isolated from the outside world and relies almost exclusively on the beneficiary to meet her daily needs. . . . [Cochrane was physically isolated, completely dependent on defendant for transportation, and lacked a private means of communication.]

Although aiding his elderly mother is commendable, defendant nonetheless fostered a sense of "need and dependence". . . . Such conduct by itself is not enough to question the 1993 will. Only when combined with defendant's less innocent behavior surrounding the will's execution do his actions become suspect.

Cochrane's extreme change in attitude toward defendant and . . . [her] grandchildren, as apparent from the disposition in the 1993 will, is also indicative of defendant's dominance over her. Although a "change in attitude" toward beneficiaries is one of the seven suspicious circumstances set out in Reddaway, 214 Or. at 423, 329 P.2d 886, it may also demonstrate dominance. . . .

Finally, dominance is found where the testator is guided by the beneficiary's judgment and advice in the period leading up to execution or destruction of a will. . . . The trial court found, and we agree, that it was defendant who selected his own attorney . . . to draft the new will. Cochrane's former lawyer . . . was not consulted. By accompanying defendant to [his attorney's] office, she apparently succumbed to her son's judgment and advice.

Based on the factors mentioned above, we conclude that plaintiff has established the existence of a confidential relationship such that defendant occupied a position of dominance over Cochrane.

Where such a confidential relationship exists, "slight evidence" of suspicious circumstances is sufficient to raise an inference of undue influence. . . . These circumstances include:

> (1) the participation of the beneficiary in the preparation or destruction of the will; (2) the lack of independent and disinterested advice regarding the will; (3) secrecy and haste in making the will; (4) an unexplained change in the donor's attitude toward those for whom he or she had previously expressed affection; (5) a change in the testamentary plan that ignores the natural objects of the testator's bounty or disregards the continuity of purpose running through former testamentary dispositions; (6) an unnatural or unjust gift, and (7) the donor's susceptibility to influence. . . .

We find several of these circumstances here. First, defendant participated in the preparation of the 1993 will. . . .

Second, as a beneficiary who was involved in a confidential relationship with Cochrane and who had participated in the procurement of her will, defendant had a duty to help her seek independent and disinterested advice. On this record, defendant breached that duty. . . .

Third, the 1993 will was executed in secrecy and haste. Cochrane had previously told several people about the 1988 will. . . . However, no one but defendant, Cochrane, Bowe and Bowe's secretary knew of the 1993 will until after defendant attempted to probate it. . . . Furthermore, within 24 hours of [the initial contact with Bowe], defendant had Cochrane sitting in the cab of his pickup truck in front of Bowe's office executing a new will. . . .

Fourth and fifth, the 1993 will drastically altered Cochrane's testamentary disposition, which indicated a change in attitude toward beneficiaries for whom Cochrane had previously expressed affection. The 1988 will left the bulk of Cochrane's estate to the . . . grandchildren, while explicitly disinheriting defendant. The 1993 will provided for the opposite disposition with no mention of the grandchildren. That in itself is a suspicious circumstance. . . .

We believe, as did the trial court, that it is more likely than not that Cochrane's change of heart, if any, resulted from defendant's influence.

Finally, as discussed under the "dominance" element above, Cochrane's failing health made her susceptible to influence by defendant, upon whom she relied heavily for her daily needs.

We find sufficient evidence of suspicious circumstances to raise an inference of undue influence. . . . On de novo review, we conclude that defendant produced insufficient evidence negating that inference. Accordingly, the trial court correctly invalidated the 1993 will on the grounds of undue influence.

Affirmed.

In re ESTATE OF KAMESAR
81 Wis. 2d 151, 259 N.W.2d 733 (1977)

[Samuel Kamesar died in 1974 at age 84, survived by his two daughters, Jeanette Feldman and Bernice Lee, his son Armon Kamesar, and his second wife, Doris, to whom he was married in March of 1971. The will in question was executed in June of 1971. It incorporated the terms of a prenuptial agreement with Doris, bequeathed $5,000 to a grandchild, and left the rest of his estate to Bernice, explaining that his omission of Armon and Jeanette was because he had made special provisions for them during life. The latest of his prior wills contained bequests to all of his grandchildren and would have left his residuary estate equally to his three children. The 1971 will was propounded by Bernice and contested by Armon and Jeanette, alleging it was the result of undue influence by Bernice. The trial court found in favor of Bernice and admitted the will to probate.

Samuel lived nearly all of his adult life in Milwaukee; Armon lived there until 1971 and managed his father's financial affairs until Armon moved to California that year. Jeanette also lives in California. Both did, in fact, receive substantial funds from their father during his lifetime. Bernice had lived abroad until 1968, when she returned to Milwaukee; after Armon's departure she managed her father's financial affairs and held a power of attorney executed by him in March 1971. There is no record of gifts to Bernice or her children, but after June 1971 she and her children received $3,000 apiece each year. Friends and relatives testified that Samuel had been forgetful and confused in 1971, but all except Armon testified that he was of sound mind when he married Doris. Armon doubted his father's mental capacity at the time but had never said so because he approved of the marriage and antenuptial agreement. A physician testified that Samuel had been in ill health for a number of years and that he lacked the ability to make a decision when he became hospitalized in 1973.]

DAY, J. . . .

While the record shows that there was much ill feeling between Bernice and her brother and sister, it seems clear that Samuel Kamesar had equal affection for all of them.

All of the wills were drawn by the deceased's lifetime friend and attorney, Mr. George Laikin. Mr. Laikin testified that on March 18, 1971, when Samuel Kamesar and Doris Kamesar executed the prenuptial agreement, Mr. Laikin recommended that Mr. Kamesar amend his will to incorporate the terms of the agreement. Mr. Kamsear told him that "other changes" should be made in the will also and that he would advise him of those changes later. Mr. Laikin testified that Mr. Kamesar did not personally contact him but communicated the changes to be made in the will by telephone through Bernice Lee. Mr. Laikin stated that Mr. Kamesar customarily communicated with him in that manner, first through Armon and later through Bernice.

When the June will was ready to sign, Bernice Lee made an appointment with Mr. Laikin and drove Samuel and Doris Kamesar to his office. Doris Kamesar and Bernice Lee were present when the will was executed. Mr. Laikin and Bernice Lee both testified that Mr. Laikin reviewed the specific terms of the will. Bernice Lee testified Mr. Laikin asked her to go through the terms again with her father and she read it to him. She testified Mr. Laikin told her father that the will would make some people unhappy but her father replied that one has to take a chance in life. Doris Kamesar testified that Mr. Laikin did not review the will but merely gave it to Samuel Kamesar to read and asked him if he understood it. She and Mr. Laikin testified Samuel Kamesar did ask to have the will changed to provide that his wife could remain in the apartment for one year after his death instead of six months.

Mr. Laikin testified that Samuel Kamesar said the will was what they had talked about and said, "let's proceed to sign the will." Mr. Laikin also testified he questioned Samuel Kamesar whether he knew this will left all to Bernice and he said he did. Mr. Laikin believed Samuel Kamesar was competent at the time and not under any undue influence.

Doris testified that some months after the will was signed, when she reminded Samuel Kamesar that he had cut his two children out of the will, he could not remember doing so. . . .

There are two avenues by which an objector to a will on the theory of undue influence may challenge its admission.

One is by proving the elements that this court has said show undue influence. Those are: (1) susceptibility to undue influence, (2) opportunity to influence, (3) disposition to influence, and (4) coveted result. The burden is on the objector to prove by clear, satisfactory and con-

vincing evidence that the will was the result of undue influence. However, when three of the four elements have been established by the
required quantum of proof, only slight evidence of the fourth is required.

The second method of challenge is to prove the existence of (1) a
confidential relationship between the testator and the favored beneficiary and (2) suspicious circumstances surrounding the making of the
will.

I.   Four Elements Test

A.   Susceptibility to Undue Influence

The objectors must establish by clear, satisfactory and convincing evidence that the testator in this case was susceptible to the influence of
Bernice Lee. Factors to be considered are age, personality, physical and
mental health and ability to handle business affairs. This court has
stated that the infirmities of old age, such as forgetfulness, do not inca-
pacitate one from making a valid will . . . [but] evidence of impaired
mental powers on the part of a testator is itself a circumstance which
gives rise to a reasonable inference that the testator is susceptible to
undue influence. . . .

The objectors argue that the fact that Samuel Kamesar entrusted
the management of his business affairs to Bernice, coupled with his
impaired mental powers, made him susceptible to her influence. But
the evidence is conflicting. The testator did suffer from arteriosclerosis,
and there was testimony that in June of 1971 he was forgetful and confused. But several witnesses testified he was of sound mind three
months before when he was married, and his wife testified he never
forgot what he owned or who his children were. Mr. Laikin, the attorney, who was present when all the wills were executed and had known
the testator for most of his own life, testified that the deceased was of
sound mind and not under any undue influence when the will in question was executed. At that conference the testator made one request
for a change with regard to his wife's occupancy of the apartment in
the event of his death. This request shows his awareness of the will's
provisions. The trial court's conclusion that the objectors did not establish susceptibility is not against the great weight and clear preponderance of the evidence.

B.   Opportunity to Influence

The trial court found and the proponents agree that Bernice Lee had
ample opportunity to exert undue influence on the decedent. This
conclusion is not against the great weight of the evidence.

C.   Disposition to Influence

Disposition to unduly influence means more than a desire to obtain a share of the estate. It implies a willingness to do something wrong or unfair.

The evidence in this case shows that Bernice Lee had taken over the decedent's business affairs completely, but as the trial court pointed out, she had merely taken up where her brother had left off when he moved from Milwaukee. Bernice Lee testified that in December 1973, she did consult another attorney other than Mr. Laikin and procured a declaration of intent signed by her father to give her and her children $9,000 in tax free gifts every year. This document was executed twenty-one days before Samuel Kamesar died, at a time when his attending physician testified that he was incapable of making any kind of decision. But this was remote in time from the date of execution of the will in question here. . . .

The evidence here is quite clear that Armon Kamesar and Jeanette Feldman received substantial gifts from their parents during the parents' lives and that Bernice Lee had not. Even if she had tried to influence her father to make his will more favorable to her than to her brother and sister who had already benefitted from Samuel Kamesar's generosity, such influence would not necessarily be undue. . . .

D.   Coveted Result

This element goes to the naturalness or expectedness of the bequest. The fact that the testator has excluded a natural object of his bounty is a "red flag of warning." But that fact alone does not render the disposition unnatural where a record shows reasons as to why a testator would leave out those who may be the natural beneficiaries of his bounty.

In the case at bar, the will expressly states that Armon Kamesar and Jeanette Feldman are excluded because the testator believed he had adequately provided for them during his lifetime. Mr. Laikin testified that it was he who suggested that this language be used in drafting the will. . . .

While conflicting inferences may be drawn from the evidence presented and even though the June 1971 will manifests a drastic change in attitude from that manifested just three months before when Armon Kamesar had been the close confidant of his father, the trial court's finding in favor of the proponent on this issue is not against the great weight and clear preponderance of the evidence.

We conclude, therefore, that on the basis of the four classic elements the trial court must be sustained.

II. . . . Presumption of Undue Influence . . .

Undue influence may also be proved by the existence of (1) a confidential relationship between the testator and the favored beneficiary, and (2) suspicious circumstances surrounding the making of the will. When the objector proves the existence of both elements by the required quantum of evidence, a presumption of undue influence is raised, which must be rebutted by the proponent. The trial court held that the record did not substantiate a finding of either element.

(1) Confidential Relationship

This court has described the confidential relationship that is sufficient to raise a presumption of undue influence as follows:

> The basis for the undue influence presumption lies in the ease in which a confidant can dictate the contents and control or influence the drafting of such a will either as the draftsman or in procuring the drafting. . . . If one is not the actual draftsman or the procurer of the drafting, the relationship must be such that the testator depends upon the advice of the confidant in relation to the subject matter of the will. . . .

Estate of Steffke, 48 Wis. 2d at 51, quoted in Estate of Velk, 53 Wis. 2d 500, 507, 192 N.W.2d 844 (1972).

The objectors argue that Bernice Lee's role in the execution of the June 1971 will made her the procurer of the drafting and execution of the will. To "procure" is "to initiate," "to instigate," or "to cause a thing to be done." Black's Law Dictionary 1373 (1968). However, the record shows that it was Mr. Laikin who recommended that Samuel Kamesar change his will to reflect the provisions of the pre-nuptial agreement. Samuel Kamesar himself stated that he intended to make "other changes" as well. Bernice Lee's role in communicating these changes to Mr. Laikin and in arranging for the execution of the will was a role customarily played by one of Samuel Kamesar's children.

The record is clear, however, that Bernice Lee did manage all of her father's business and personal affairs, and this court has held that where a child has also served as a testator's financial advisor that a confidential relationship can be found to exist. . . .

Bernice Lee testified that she took over the role that had previously been played by her brother and it appears to us that the reasonable inference to be drawn from the evidence is that Samuel Kamesar did rely on Bernice Lee in relation to the subject matter of the will. We conclude, therefore, the finding of the trial court, that there was no confidential relationship between Bernice Lee and her father is against the great weight and clear preponderance of the evidence.

(2)   Suspicious Circumstances

The suspect circumstances requirement is satisfied by proof of facts "such as the activity of the beneficiary in procuring the drafting and execution of the will, or a sudden and unexplained change in the attitude of the testator, or some other persuasive circumstance." "The basic question to be determined from the evidence is always whether 'the free agency of the testator has been destroyed.'". . .

[A]lthough Bernice Lee called the attorney, Mr. Laikin, made the appointment to see him to have the will signed, drove Samuel Kamesar to the lawyer's office and communicated to the attorney the terms of the will which made her the sole beneficiary, these were all routine practices for this particular testator. The evidence showed that at the time of execution, Samuel Kamesar was aware of the terms of his will. The will was also drafted by his long-time personal friend and attorney who testified there was nothing irregular in the drafting or in the execution. The will itself contained the explanation that Samuel Kamesar believed that he had adequately provided for his son and his other daughter during their lifetime, and the fact was that they had received substantial gifts and that Bernice Lee had not received such gifts. The will was not made in haste but over a period of three months. There was no reluctance shown in signing the will and while the testator was forgetful, he was functioning on his own, outside of a nursing home when the will was executed. It was also established that Armon Kamesar had been informed by Doris Kamesar of the new will before his father died and all parties were aware of the testator's failing health. The . . . court's conclusion that no suspicious circumstances were proven . . . is not against the great weight and clear preponderance of the evidence. . . .

By the Court, judgment affirmed.

In Will of Melson, 711 A.2d 783 (Del. 1998), the burden of proof on the issue of undue influence shifted to the proponent when the contestant established by clear and convincing evidence that the testator was in a weakened mental condition, the will was drafted by a person in a confidential relationship with the testator, and the drafter received a substantial benefit under the will. Estate of Gersbach, 960 P.2d 811 (N.M. 1998), reversed a trial court finding of undue influence for lack of clear and convincing evidence, despite the lower court's finding of suspicious circumstances and of secrecy surrounding a gift to a nonrelative. For a good discussion of both incapacity and undue influence, see the court's opinion in Kuster v. Schaumburg, 658 N.E.2d 462 (Ill. App. 1995).

COMMENT, WILLS, UNDUE INFLUENCE
50 Mich. L. Rev. 748, 759-760 (1952)

. . . Can it be said that an examination of the cases shows results consistent with the definition that undue influence is the destruction of the free agency of the testator so that he has lost his ability to weigh motivations and reach an independent decision? While the ultimate fact required by the courts may be in keeping with such a definition, it must be recognized that it is most difficult to prove that the free agency has been destroyed. As a result, the courts have been forced to accept a lower standard. It is clear that testators, especially when enfeebled, ought to be protected from certain "activity" on the part of others. Yet the courts are aware that many a disappointed heir attempts to break a will on any pretext handy even though no real grounds of undue influence exist; and the courts have observed that no jury should be permitted to rewrite a will merely because it disagrees with the propriety of the disposition made by the testator. These latter facts are borne out by the observations that in the great majority of cases appellate courts have either reversed jury findings of undue influence or have affirmed the trial judge in taking the case from the jury. . . . When a testator becomes old and mentally enfeebled, he is apt to be affected by the influences of others much more than in his younger days. While such a testator may not be a mere rubber stamp for the will of others, the courts have refused to permit such influences on the ground that society's interest is better served by allowing him to be free of importunities. . . .

WHITMAN AND HOOPES, THE CONFIDENTIAL RELATIONSHIP IN WILL CONTESTS
124 Tr. & Est. 53-54 (Feb. 1985)

The existence of a confidential relationship between a testator and beneficiary of a will can be an important factor in a will contest. Indeed, these rules often decide will contests. . . . While it has been suggested that we ultimately develop better legal rules by considering each state as a separate experimental laboratory, the confusion created by widely varying state rules also has been noted. The authors believe it is time to unify and standardize the rules of confidential relationship applied in will contests.

In many jurisdictions, courts now hold that if a substantial beneficiary is found to stand in a confidential relationship with a testator, and that beneficiary actively participated in the preparation or execution of the will, a rebuttable presumption of undue influence arises. But some jurisdictions additionally require that the benefits received be "undue" or "unnatural," or permit other "suspicious circumstances" to substitute for active participation. While the presumption of undue influence applies, in one form or another, in nearly every jurisdiction, the definition of what constitutes a confidential relationship clearly lacks uniformity.

Confusion also exists as to the effect of the finding of the existence of the presumption. Generally, if the proponent offers no evidence in rebuttal, the contestant is entitled to a directed verdict. If rebuttal evidence is presented, the presumption disappears from the case, leaving the burden of persuasion on the contestant. In a few jurisdictions, however, the presumption creates a prima facie case, permanently shifting the burden of persuasion to the proponents. . . .

While it is clear that a confidential relationship exists as a matter of law between a testator and his doctor, lawyer, clergyman or close business associate, when other categories of relationships are involved, each state's law must be consulted; for state law varies widely. . . .

When a rule of law does not govern the question of whether a particular relationship is confidential for purposes of will contests, then an issue of fact exists. A typical judicial statement of the standard to be used is that a confidential relationship exists "whenever trust and confidence is reposed by one person in the integrity and fidelity of another." In this area there is uniformity. The difficulty arises in determining whether one of the various rules of law applies to render a particular relationship either confidential, or not, as a matter of law.

Active Participation. There is also a lack of uniformity in the requirement of a showing of active participation in the preparation or execution of the will on the part of the person alleged to have unduly influenced the testator by means of a confidential relationship.

In some states, a showing of active participation is necessary in addition to the existence of a confidential relationship between a beneficiary and a testator. In other states, *additional* suspicious circumstances, such as a substantial gift or a weakness of mind of the testator, *must* be shown. And in still other jurisdictions, weakness of mind or other suspicious circumstances may serve as *substitutes* for active participation, in that *either* active participation *or* other suspicious circumstances may be shown.

Compounding the confusion, there are differing views as to what constitutes active participation. There appear to be two schools of thought. According to one, there is no active participation unless there is personal participation in the actual drafting or execution of the will. According to the other, active participation may be found to exist where there is only conduct by a beneficiary prior to the drafting or execution of the will.

It has been held, moreover, that a presumption of undue influence does not arise where a beneficiary participated in the preparation of the will at the request of the testator.

Unnatural Disposition. Another trap for unwary practitioners in the area of confidential relationship is the rule that, to raise a presumption of undue influence, it must be shown that the person alleged to have unduly influenced the testator received unnatural or undue benefits under the will. This is the law in some states, in others it is not, and, no doubt, in still others no one can be sure what the law is. . . .

The diversity of rules in the area of confidential relationship in will contests suggests a need for uniformity more than a need for any particular set of uniform rules.

The root issue is whether the presumption of undue influence is favored or disfavored. On the side of the presumption is a need to protect testators and the expectant objects of their bounty from the machinations of those who would thwart the free will of testators. Also on the side of the presumption is the fact that undue influence is difficult to prove affirmatively. The only evidence is usually circumstantial, and it is easy for wrongdoers to cover their tracks.

Other considerations, however, militate against too much enthusiasm for the presumption of undue influence. In particular, there is the policy, deeply rooted both in the common law and in Anglo-American notions of individual liberty, of freedom of testation. There is every reason to believe that when the issue of confidential relationship is one of fact, jurors will often allow their own feelings as to how the testator should have disposed of his property to influence their conclusion on the confidential relationship issue. Justice Tobringer of California has stated that "[i]t does appear, from the cases appealed, that the jury finds for the contestant in over 75 percent of the cases submitted to it. But the fact that juries exhibit consistent unconcern for the wishes of testators should come as no surprise. Indeed, the tendency of juries in this respect is so pronounced that it has been said to be a proper subject of judicial notice.". . .

B.   Allowances, Homesteads, and Exemptions

The statutory law of every state makes some provision to protect the family of a decedent against testamentary omission, the decedent's creditors, and the delays of administration. One or more and usually all of the following provisions exist in each state: (1) a support allowance for the families of the decedents, or sometimes just for widows and widowers, during a part or all of the period of estate administration; (2) a statutory or constitutional right of homestead in residential real estate; and (3) an exemption of certain personal property. See, e.g., Uniform Probate Code §§2-402 to 2-404. These provisions are typically, but not always, in addition to the intestate share or other statutory rights of the family. In most jurisdictions, it is presumed that any rights under the decedent's will are in addition to such provisions, although the terms of a will, particularly express disposition of the home or exempt property, may require a beneficiary to elect between an interest under the will and one or more of these statutory provisions.

C. Minimum Rights of the Surviving Spouse

1. Dower, Forced Shares, and Community Property

Protections afforded spouses vary from state to state. In some states, the surviving spouse's protective rights in land (immovables) are still determined by the law of the situs, whereas all spousal rights in other property (movables) are based on the law of the decedent's domicile at death. The application of situs law to land has been widely criticized, and the statutory trend is to provide, as does UPC §2-202(d), that in ancillary jurisdiction the situs state will determine the survivor's rights in immovables as well as movables according to domiciliary law.

At common law, the widow had a dower interest in all lands of which her husband was seised at any time during the marriage, entitling her, if she survived her husband, to a life estate in one-third of such property. Dower could not be defeated by the husband's will, the claims of his creditors, or his inter vivos conveyances in the absence of the wife's consent. Comparable to dower, but conditioned on birth of issue and relating to all of the wife's land, was the husband's common law *curtesy*. See generally R. Chused, Married Women's Property Law, 1800-1850, 71 Geo. L.J. 1359 (1983); H. Hartog, Marital Exits and Marital Expectations in Nineteenth Century America, 80 Geo. L.J. 95 (1991). A few jurisdictions still have statutes, relating to both husband and wife, that grant a spouse a right in all lands owned by the other spouse during the marriage. Nearly all of these interests ripen into fee interests in a third of such lands. See Committee Report, Spouse's Elective Share, 12 Real Prop., Prob. & Tr. J. 323 (1977); MacDonald, Fraud on the Widow's Share (1960).

In nearly all of the non-community property states, surviving spouses are protected by a form of statutory forced heirship entitling them to a share of the estate regardless of the deceased spouse's will. This nonbarrable right is generally a portion of the decedent's net estate, personal as well as real, subject to the debts and inter vivos transfers of the decedent. The forced share may be the same as the intestate share, but in many states it is less.

Where the community property system prevails, the main protection afforded spouses is their shared ownership of their community property. This system has long existed in eight states (Arizona, California, Idaho, Louisiana, Nevada, New Mexico, Texas, and Washington) and has now been adopted in a ninth state, Wisconsin, by legislation based on the Uniform Marital Property Act. It is important to note that there are substantive differences among the traditional community property states. All property owned before the marriage or acquired during marriage by gift or succession is separate property, as is income therefrom in most but not all of these states. All other property acquired during the marriage is community property. In most of these states, the spouses acting together are free to convert community property to separate and vice versa, sometimes with startling informality. With limited exceptions, the community property rights of husband and wife are present and equal, although until recent decades the husband generally had the management rights. As a result of this equal ownership, half of the community property belongs to the survivor and cannot be disposed of by the deceased spouse's will.

Migrating Couples. In community property states, dower and its counterparts are nonexistent, and generally there are no forced share provisions applicable to separate property. The community or separate character of a couple's property is determined by the law of the jurisdiction where they are domiciled when the property is acquired, and should not materially change if the couple moves to a jurisdiction with a different system. Under a blind application of the rule that the law of the decedent's domicile at death controls the succession, there may be times when the survivor would be left unprotected. For example, assume *H* and *W* lived in a common law state and *H* was the sole wage earner. After *H* retired, they moved to a community property state and shortly thereafter *H* died. If *H*'s will disinherits *W*, the community property state does not provide a forced share and there is no community property because the property was earned in the common law state.

California and Idaho have enacted "quasi-community property" statutes designed to give the surviving spouse rights equivalent to those the surviving spouse would have if the spouses had lived in a community property state at the time they acquired the property. See Cal. Prob. Code §§66, 101, 102; Idaho Code §§15-2201 to 15-2-209 (1978). A comparable "deferred marital property" regime exists in Wisconsin, which also deals with problems of transition from its pre-1986 common law system. See Wis. Stat. Ann. c. 766, §§851.055, 861.02. By other statutory provisions in these states, and by statutes and decisions in the other community and non-community property states, rules analogous to quasi-community property apply to the division of marital property on divorce.

The Uniform Disposition of Community Property at Death Act offers a solution to the inverse problems in common law states. In general, the Act provides that community property brought into a common law

[handwritten margin note: U DCPDA comm. prop unless agree to convert]

state remains community property (unless both spouses agree to convert it) and at the death of the first to die, half of the community property is subject to the will of the first to die, with the surviving spouse having no forced share in the decedent's half of the community property.

Waiver. The statutory rights of spouses may be modified or extinguished by antenuptial agreement and, in most states, by postnuptial agreement. These contracts generally must be either substantively fair and reasonable or based on full disclosure. In some states, all interspousal contracts are presumed to result from undue influence if one party obtains an "advantage" over the other. Uniform Probate Code §2-213, allowing waiver of elective rights either before or after marriage, focuses on fairness in the formation of the contract and the absence of unconscionability. Compare Uniform Marital Property Act §10 (1983) and Uniform Pre-Marital Agreements Act §6 (1983). See generally Haskell, The Premarital Estate Contract and Social Policy, 57 N.C.L. Rev. 415, 416-418, 437 (1979) (urging that premarital contracts not be enforced if "financial hardship" would result because the survivor's property and earning capacity are insufficient to maintain a "reasonable approximation" of the spouse's "accustomed standard" of living); J. Thomas Oldham, Premarital Contracts Are Now Enforceable Unless . . . , 21 Hous. L. Rev. 757 (1984).

[handwritten margin note: advantage = presump. of undue influence]

Federal law requires certain tax-favored retirement plans to provide for surviving spouses unless provision is specifically waived by the spouse. 29 U.S.C. §§1001 et seq. (ERISA), as amended by the Retirement Equity Act of 1984, 98 Stat. 1426 (1984).

2.   Election by the Surviving Spouse

As already indicated, rights in the nature of dower, forced heirship provisions, and community property interests cannot be defeated by will. However, a testator can require the spouse to choose between these rights and whatever provision is made for the spouse in the will — i.e., to elect whether to take under the will or to take (or retain) the statutory rights. Furthermore, in asserting statutory rights, the spouse may be required to choose between dower rights and some or all of the forced share.

The concept of election is one of long standing in equity and is relevant in many estate matters. For example, assume that *A* owns Blackacre, appraised at $100,000, and that *B* owns Whiteacre, worth $50,000. *A* dies and his will devises Blackacre to *B* and purports to devise Whiteacre to *C*. The doctrine of equitable election requires *B* to transfer Whiteacre to *C* if he chooses to accept the devise of Backacre from *A*. See Havens v. Sackett, 15 N.Y. 365, 369 (1857): "One who accepts the benefit under a deed or will must adopt the whole contents of the instrument." "The legacies and devises were acts of bounty merely. The testator was free to withhold them altogether, or to subject them to conditions, whether sensible or futile. The gift is to be taken as it is made or not at all." Oliver v. Wells, 254 N.Y. 451, 458, 173 N.E. 676, 679 (1930).

Today it is usually made clear by statute, or by judicial decision construing the statute, that the spouse cannot take dower or a forced share and also take under the will of the decedent, unless the contrary appears expressly or by clear implication from the will. At common law, it was presumed that any testamentary provision for the spouse was in addition to dower unless the will provisions were inconsistent with this result: generally, a like rule still prevails in regard to community property. Uniform Probate Code §2-209 resolves this issue by crediting any testate provision for the spouse against the forced share.

To illustrate, assume that *H*'s will provides, "All of my property shall go to my wife, *W*, for life and on her death to my issue per stirpes." *W* must elect to take the life estate in all of *H*'s property or to take only her dower or forced share. But where community property is involved, this language in *H*'s will would normally not be construed as requiring an election, and *W* would take a life estate in *H*'s separate property and in his half of the community property, while keeping her half of the community property as well.

Statutes often prescribe the time and method of making an election. The right of election is generally deemed personal to the surviving spouse. If the spouse dies without having made an election (expressly or impliedly by conduct) the right expires, and the spouse is deemed to have accepted the terms of the will. A few states, however, have adopted the view that a spouse takes the statutory share automatically unless "divested" by an election.

The Incapacitated Surviving Spouse. An issue that arises with increasing frequency is whether an election can (and if so, should) be made by another such as a guardian or a conservator on behalf of an incapacitated surviving spouse. Many statutes, as well as the UPC, allow an election on behalf of the incapacitated surviving spouse, based on the substituted judgment concept. But there are concerns about allowing, *or making,* such an election. Rarely does anyone know whether the spouse would have made the election if not under incapacity, and many spouses plan their estates together, with each acquiescing in the other's plan (e.g., for tax reasons) knowing that greater value would be available by election.

The Uniform Probate Code §2-212 provides that whatever is taken from the estate to satisfy the elective share of the incompetent spouse is held in a custodial trust. Only amounts needed for the spouse's support are expended; the remainder goes to the testator's residuary devisees. This prevents the election from benefitting the survivor's

successors in interest. Is this consistent with the "contribution" rationale of the elective share system? What result if the will of the first to
die devises the bulk of the estate to a sibling and the rest to charity?
See UPC §2-212 and §2-209.

The Traditional Elective Share Statute and the Need for Reform. There are
two primary, and sometimes competing, rationales for the elective
share system. The "support" rationale is that the surviving spouse may
need continuing support and should not become a burden on society
while the decedent's devisees enjoy the property. The other rationale,
the "partnership" or "sharing" rationale, is that regardless of the role
played by either spouse, each is viewed as making a significant contribution toward the acquisition of assets that are titled in the decedent's
name.

Although both of these rationales cannot be effectuated within the
context of every issue, traditional elective share statutes (usually giving
the spouse one-third of the estate), poorly reflect them in common
situations. For example, the surviving spouse might be many times
wealthier than the decedent, but can nonetheless take a forced share;
this is inconsistent with the support rationale. If the decedent dies a
week after the wedding, the surviving spouse can insist upon a forced
share; this is inconsistent with the partnership rationale.

Another problem with traditional elective share statutes is that they
do not, expressly at least, take nonprobate assets into account. If the
surviving spouse takes the nonprobate assets, the forced share has the
potential for overprotection. If a third party receives the nonprobate
assets, there is potential underprotection or even opportunity for evasion. Although some case law brings certain "illusory" or "fraudulent"
transfers within the spouse's reach, the statutes usually address only
probate assets. The original UPC gave the surviving spouse a one-third
elective share that reached most nonprobate assets other than life insurance.

The interest in reform has been heightened recently in most common law jurisdictions by the adoption of a system of "equitable distribution" that applies when the marriage ends in divorce. Equitable
distribution reflects a partnership theory of marriage. It is particularly
ironic for a spouse to be better off if the marriage ends in divorce than
if it ends in death.

With this obvious need for reform, the more recent statutory trend
is to effectuate a partnership theory both upon divorce and at death,
in a manner approximating a community property regime. The UPC's
revised elective share system has particularly influenced this trend. As
you study the UPC provisions, consider how they are both like and
unlike community property. What result if the sole wage earner is the
survivor? How would the UPC have to be amended to be consistent
with community property?

The UPC's elective share system deviates from the traditional approach in several respects. First, it takes the length of the marriage into account. Second, it takes account of the surviving spouse's own property. Third, it takes the decedent's nonprobate transfers into account in order to remedy the overprotection and underprotection problems. Finally, unless disclaimed, the property devised to the spouse is applied toward the satisfaction of the elective share. If the spouse is devised a life estate in trust, how should it be valued?

The effort to get the UPC's revised elective share provisions enacted in common law jurisdictions has met with considerable resistance, not only from the life insurance industry, but also from many members of the estate planning professions. Some balk at having to take the assets of the surviving spouse into account because of anticipated administrative problems such as valuation. However, their inclusion is essential if the objective of the statute is to be accomplished. (See Problem 3-A below.) Others simply disagree with the UPC's partnership theory of marriage, and even that the principle of free testation should be so inhibited. Cf. Jeffrey N. Pennell, Minimizing the Surviving Spouse's Elective Share, 32 Inst. on Est. Plan. Ch 9 (1998).

At the other end of this spectrum are opponents who believe that the only fair system is a community property system. As one critic of the common law has said, "spousal protection schemes are flawed by their premise: that the property being distributed is, insofar as the surviving spouse — generally assumed to be the wife — is concerned, a share *of someone else's property*." Barbara Ann Kulzer, Law and the Housewife: Property, Divorce, and Death, 28 U. Fla. L. Rev. 1, 37 (1975). See also Ronald R. Volkmer, Spousal Property Rights at Death: Re-Evaluation of the Common Law Premises in Light of the Proposed Uniform Marital Property Act, 17 Creighton L. Rev. 95 (1983); Note, The Revised UPC Elective Share: Missing Essential Partnership Principles, 13 Quinnipiac Prob. L.J. 225 (1998).

Even in jurisdictions that have enacted a form of the UPC elective share provisions, insurance industry lobbyists have had some success in getting life insurance proceeds excluded from the augmented estate, creating a loophole that can defeat the purpose of augmentation. See 1999 Fla. Sess. Law Serv. 343 (West). For a discussion of the UPC Joint Editorial Board's frustrations with the American Council of Life Insurance, see Waggoner, Alexander, and Fellows, Family Property Law 549 (2d ed. 1997).

PROBLEMS

3-A. Assume *H* and *W* have been married for fifty years and *H* dies with $500,000 representing savings from earnings during marriage. *W* also has $500,000 in a bank account representing her savings from

[handwritten: Dower]

earnings during marriage. *H*'s will devises all to his friend, *X*. What are *[handwritten: ½ in each]*
W's rights (1) in a common law jurisdiction that gives the spouse a
forced share of one-half (or more typically one-third), (2) in a community property jurisdiction, and (3) in a jurisdiction that has enacted
the UPC's elective share provisions? *[handwritten: takes considerations]*

3-B.[5]   *W* died survived by *H*, her spouse of thirty years, and two children of that marriage. Her estate consisted of $100,000 cash and mar-
ketable securities, Blackacre appraised at $200,000, and Whiteacre
appraised at $300,000. *W* had no debts. Her will devised $50,000 to *H*,
Blackacre to her oldest child, and the residue of her estate to her children in equal shares.

(a) What course of action would you recommend *H* take if his statu- *[handwritten: statutory right at com. law to ⅓ abate]*
tory rights permitted him to take against the will either an interest like
common law dower or a one-third forced share? What are *H*'s rights
under the law of your state?

(b) Would your advice differ if *W* left debts amounting to $500,000?

(c) What additional significance would you find in the fact that *W*
also had $500,000 worth of life insurance payable to *H*?

(d) What if *H* were independently wealthy? How would this question
be affected if the Uniform Probate Code sections set out below were
in effect in your state?

UNIFORM PROBATE CODE

Elective Share of Surviving Spouse

General Comment

The elective share of the surviving spouse is substantially revised. The
revised elective share has been endorsed by the Assembly of the National Association of Women Lawyers (NAWL), on the unanimous recommendation of NAWL's Executive Board.

The main purpose of the revisions is to bring elective-share law into
line with the contemporary view of marriage as an economic partnership. The economic partnership theory of marriage is already imple-

---

5. In addition to, or instead of, Problem 3-B, students from community property
states should consider whether, under the law of your state, the following facts require
the surviving spouse, *S*, to make an election and if so what the alternatives are: *D*'s will
leaves "all of my estate to *T* in trust for *S* for life, remainder to our issue by right of
representation." The properties involved are $200,000 of assets traceable to *D*'s recent
inheritance; $400,000 of securities traceable to *D*'s earnings during marriage, half being
traceable to a period when *D* and *S* lived in a non-community property jurisdiction;
pension benefits in annuity form payable to *S*; $200,000 worth of life insurance proceeds
payable to "the trustee named in my will"; and $200,000 of assets held by *D* and *S* as
joint tenants.

mented under the equitable-distribution system applied in both the common-law and community-property states when a marriage ends in divorce. When a marriage ends in death, that theory is also already implemented under the community-property system and under the system promulgated in the Uniform Marital Property Act. In the common law states, however, elective-share law has not caught up to the partnership theory of marriage.

The general effect of implementing the partnership theory in elective-share law is to increase the entitlement of a surviving spouse in a long-term marriage in cases in where the marital assets were disproportionately titled in the decedent's name; and to decrease or even eliminate the entitlement of a surviving spouse in a long-term marriage in cases in which the marital assets were more or less equally titled or disproportionately titled in the surviving spouse's name. A further general effect is to decrease or even eliminate the entitlement of a surviving spouse in a short-term, later-in-life marriage in which neither spouse contributed much, if anything, to the acquisition of the other's wealth, except that a special supplemental elective-share amount is provided in cases in which the surviving spouse would otherwise be left without sufficient funds for support.

§2-202. *Elective Share.*

(a) [Elective-Share Amount.] The surviving spouse of a decedent who dies domiciled in this State has a right of election, under the limitations and conditions stated in this Part, to take an elective-share amount equal to the value of the elective-share percentage of the augmented estate, determined by the length of time the spouse and the decedent were married to each other, in accordance with the following schedule:

If the decedent and the spouse were married to each other:	*The elective-share percentage is:*
Less than 1 year	Supplemental Amount Only.
1 year but less than 2 years	3% of the augmented estate.
2 years but less than 3 years	6% of the augmented estate.
3 years but less than 4 years	9% of the augmented estate.
4 years but less than 5 years	12% of the augmented estate.
5 years but less than 6 years	15% of the augmented estate.
6 years but less than 7 years	18% of the augmented estate.
7 years but less than 8 years	21% of the augmented estate.
8 years but less than 9 years	24% of the augmented estate.
9 years but less than 10 years	27% of the augmented estate.
10 years but less than 11 years	30% of the augmented estate.
11 years but less than 12 years	34% of the augmented estate.

12 years but less than 13 years	38% of the augmented estate.
13 years but less than 14 years	42% of the augmented estate.
14 years but less than 15 years	46% of the augmented estate.
15 years or more	50% of the augmented estate.

(b) [Supplemental Elective-Share Amount.] If the sum of the amounts described in Sections 2-207, 2-209(a)(1), and that part of the elective-share amount payable from the decedent's probate estate and nonprobate transfers to others under Section 2-209(b) and (c) is less than [$50,000], the surviving spouse is entitled to a supplemental elective-share amount equal to [$50,000], minus the sum of the amounts described in those sections. The supplemental elective-share amount is payable from the decedent's probate estate and from recipients of the decedent's nonprobate transfers to others in the order of priority set forth in Section 2-209(b) and (c).

(c) [Effect of Election on Statutory Benefits.] If the right of election is exercised by or on behalf of the surviving spouse, the surviving spouse's homestead allowance, exempt property, and family allowance, if any, are not charged against but are in addition to the elective-share and supplemental elective-share amounts.

(d) [Non-Domiciliary.] The right, if any, of the surviving spouse of a decedent who dies domiciled outside this State to take an elective share in property in this State is governed by the law of the decedent's domicile at death.

§2-203. *Composition of the Augmented Estate.* Subject to Section 2-208, the value of the augmented estate, to the extent provided in Sections 2-204, 2-205, 2-206, and 2-207, consists of the sum of the values of all property, whether real or personal; movable or immovable, tangible or intangible, wherever situated, that constitute the decedent's net probate estate, the decedent's nonprobate transfers to others, the decedent's nonprobate transfers to the surviving spouse, and the surviving spouse's property and nonprobate transfers to others.

§2-204. *Decedent's Net Probate Estate.* The value of the augmented estate includes the value of the decedent's probate estate, reduced by funeral and administration expenses, homestead allowance, family allowances, exempt property, and enforceable claims.

§2-205. *Decedent's Nonprobate Transfers to Others.* The value of the augmented estate includes the value of the decedent's nonprobate transfers to others, not included under Section 2-204, of any of the following types, in the amount provided respectively for each type of transfer:

(1) Property owned or owned in substance by the decedent immediately before death that passed outside probate at the decedent's death. Property included under this category consists of:

(i) Property over which the decedent alone, immediately before death, held a presently exercisable general power of appointment. The amount included is the value of the property subject to the power, to the extent the property passed at the decedent's death, by exercise, release, lapse, in default, or otherwise, to or for the benefit of any person other than the decedent's estate or surviving spouse.

(ii) The decedent's fractional interest in property held by the decedent in joint tenancy with the right of survivorship. The amount included is the value of the decedent's fractional interest, to the extent the fractional interest passed by right of survivorship at the decedent's death to a surviving joint tenant other than the decedent's surviving spouse.

(iii) The decedent's ownership interest in property or accounts held in POD, TOD, or co-ownership registration with the right of survivorship. The amount included is the value of the decedent's ownership interest, to the extent the decedent's ownership interest passed at the decedent's death to or for the benefit of any person other than the decedent's estate or surviving spouse.

(iv) Proceeds of insurance, including accidental death benefits, on the life of the decedent, if the decedent owned the insurance policy immediately before death or if and to the extent the decedent alone and immediately before death held a presently exercisable general power of appointment over the policy or its proceeds. The amount included is the value of the proceeds, to the extent they were payable at the decedent's death to or for the benefit of any person other than the decedent's estate or surviving spouse.

(2) Property transferred in any of the following forms by the decedent during marriage:

(i) Any irrevocable transfer in which the decedent retained the right to the possession or enjoyment of, or to the income from, the property if and to the extent the decedent's right terminated at or continued beyond the decedent's death. The amount included is the value of the fraction of the property to which the decedent's right related, to the extent the fraction of the property passed outside probate to or for the benefit of any person other than the decedent's estate or surviving spouse.

(ii) Any transfer in which the decedent created a power over income or property, exercisable by the decedent alone or in conjunction with any other person, or exercisable by a nonadverse party, to or for the benefit of the decedent, creditors of the decedent, the decedent's estate, or creditors of the decedent's estate. The amount included with respect to a power over property is the value of the property subject to the power, and the amount included with respect to a power over income is the value of the property that produces or produced the income, to the extent the power in either case was exercisable at the decedent's death to or for the benefit of any person other than the decedent's surviving spouse or to the extent the property passed at the decedent's death, by exercise, release, lapse, in default, or otherwise, to or for the benefit of any person other than the decedent's estate or surviving spouse. If the power is a power over both income and property and the preceding sentence produces different amounts, the amount included is the greater amount.

(3) Property that passed during marriage and during the two-year period next preceding the decedent's death as a result of a transfer by the decedent if the transfer was of any of the following types:

(i) Any property that passed as a result of the termination of a right or interest in, or power over, property that would have been included in the augmented estate under paragraph (1)(i), (ii), or (iii), or under paragraph (2), if the right, interest, or power had not terminated until the decedent's death. The amount included is the value of the property that would have been included under those paragraphs if the property were valued at the time the right, interest, or power terminated, and is included only to the extent the property passed upon termination to or for the benefit of any person other than the decedent or the decedent's estate, spouse, or surviving spouse. As used in this subparagraph, "termination," with respect to a right or interest in property, occurs when the right or interest terminated by the terms of the governing instrument or the decedent transferred or relinquished the right or interest, and, with respect to a power over property, occurs when the power terminated by exercise, release, lapse, default, or otherwise, but, with respect to a power described in paragraph (1)(i), "termination" occurs when the power terminated by exercise or release, but not otherwise.

(ii) Any transfer of or relating to an insurance policy on the life of the decedent if the proceeds would have been included in the augmented estate under paragraph (1)(iv) had the transfer not occurred. The amount included is the value of the insurance proceeds to the extent the proceeds were payable at the decedent's death to or for the benefit of any person other than the decedent's estate or surviving spouse.

(iii) Any transfer of property, to the extent not otherwise included in the augmented estate, made to or for the benefit of a person other than the decedent's surviving spouse. The amount included is the value of the transferred property to the extent the aggregate transfers to any one donee in either of the two years exceeded $10,000.

§2-206. *Decedent's Nonprobate Transfers to the Surviving Spouse.* Excluding property passing to the surviving spouse under the federal Social Security system, the value of the augmented estate includes the value of the decedent's nonprobate transfers to the decedent's surviving spouse, which consist of all property that passed outside probate at the decedent's death from the decedent to the surviving spouse by reason of the decedent's death, including:

(1) the decedent's fractional interest in property held as a joint tenant with the right of survivorship, to the extent that the decedent's fractional interest passed to the surviving spouse as surviving joint tenant,

(2) the decedent's ownership interest in property or accounts held in co-ownership registration with the right of survivorship, to the extent the decedent's ownership interest passed to the surviving spouse as surviving co-owner, and

(3) all other property that would have been included in the augmented estate under Section 2-205(1) or (2) had it passed to or for the benefit of a person other than the decedent's spouse, surviving spouse, the decedent, or the decedent's creditors, estate, or estate creditors.

§2-207.   *Surviving Spouse's Property and Nonprobate*
          Transfers to Others.

(a) [Included Property.] Except to the extent included in the augmented estate under Section 2-204 or 2-206, the value of the augmented estate includes the value of:

(1) property that was owned by the decedent's surviving spouse at the decedent's death, including:

(i) the surviving spouse's fractional interest in property held in joint tenancy with the right of survivorship,

(ii) the surviving spouse's ownership interest in property or accounts held in co-ownership registration with the right of survivorship, and

(iii) property that passed to the surviving spouse by reason of the decedent's death, but not including the spouse's right to homestead allowance, family allowance, exempt property, or payments under the federal Social Security system; and

(2) property that would have been included in the surviving spouse's nonprobate transfers to others, other than the spouse's fractional and ownership interests included under subsection (a)(1)(i) or (ii), had the spouse been the decedent.

(b) [Time of Valuation.] Property included under this section is valued at the decedent's death, taking the fact that the decedent predeceased the spouse into account, but, for purposes of subsection (a)(1)(i) and (ii), the values of the spouse's fractional and ownership interests are determined immediately before the decedent's death if the decedent was then a joint tenant or a co-owner of the property or accounts. For purposes of subsection (a)(2), proceeds of insurance that would have been included in the spouse's nonprobate transfers to others under Section 2-205(1)(iv) are not valued as if he [or she] were deceased.

(c) [Reduction for Enforceable Claims.] The value of property included under this section is reduced by enforceable claims against the surviving spouse.

§2-208. *Exclusions, Valuation, and Overlapping Application.*

(a) [Exclusions.] The value of any property is excluded from the decedent's nonprobate transfers to others (i) to the extent the decedent received adequate and full consideration in money or money's worth for a transfer of the property or (ii) if the property was transferred with the written joinder of, or if the transfer was consented to in writing by, the surviving spouse.

(b) [Valuation.] The value of property:

(1) included in the augmented estate under Section 2-205, 2-206, or 2-207 is reduced in each category by enforceable claims against the included property; and

(2) includes the commuted value of any present or future interest and the commuted value of amounts payable under any trust, life insurance settlement option, annuity contract, public or private pension, disability compensation, death benefit or retirement plan, or any similar arrangement, exclusive of the federal Social Security system.

(c) [Overlapping Application; No Double Inclusion.] In case of overlapping application to the same property of the paragraphs or subparagraphs of Section 2-205, 2-206, or 2-207, the property is included in the augmented estate under the provision yielding the greatest value, and under only one overlapping provision if they all yield the same value.

§2-209. *Sources from Which Elective Share Payable.*

(a) [Elective-Share Amount Only.] In a proceeding for an elective share, the following are applied first to satisfy the elective-share amount and to reduce or eliminate any contributions due from the decedent's probate estate and recipients of the decedent's nonprobate transfers to others:

(1) amounts included in the augmented estate under Section 2-204 which pass or have passed to the surviving spouse by testate or intestate succession and amounts included in the augmented estate under Section 2-206; and

(2) amounts included in the augmented estate under Section 2-207 up to the applicable percentage thereof. For the purposes of this subsection, the "applicable percentage" is twice the elective-share percentage set forth in the schedule in Section 2-202(a) appropriate to the length of time the spouse and the decedent were married to each other.

(b) [Unsatisfied Balance of Elective-Share Amount; Supplemental Elective-Share Amount.] If, after the application of subsection (a), the elective-share amount is not fully satisfied or the surviving spouse is entitled to a supplemental elective-share amount, amounts included in the decedent's probate estate and in the decedent's nonprobate transfers to others, other than amounts included under Section 2-205(3)(i) or (iii), are applied first to satisfy the unsatisfied balance of the elective-share amount or the supplemental elective-share amount. The decedent's probate estate and that portion of the decedent's nonprobate transfers to others are so applied that liability for the unsatisfied balance of the elective-share amount or for the supplemental elective-share amount is equitably apportioned among the recipients of the decedent's probate estate and of that portion of the decedent's nonprobate transfers to others in proportion to the value of their interests therein.

(c) [Unsatisfied Balance of Elective-Share and Supplemental Elective-Share Amounts.] If, after the application of subsections (a) and (b), the elective-share or supplemental elective-share amount is not fully satisfied, the remaining portion of the decedent's nonprobate transfers to others is so applied that liability for the unsatisfied balance of the elective-share or supplemental elective-share amount is equitably apportioned among the recipients of the remaining portion of the decedent's nonprobate transfers to others in proportion to the value of their interests therein.

Whether or not one approves of the terms of Uniform Probate Code §§2-203 to 2-209, at least their general policy and underlying objectives are rather obvious. Is the policy of §2-202(a) similarly apparent? Compare the equal "sharing" of marital earnings in the spousal "partner-ship" concept implicit in a community property system, regardless of the actual division of labor between the spouses. Also see the Uniform Marital Property Act (1983). What was the policy basis for setting the elective share in §2-201(a) of the original (1969) UPC at one-third, a fraction that has been and remains fairly typical of forced share statutes across the country? See Susan N. Gary, Marital Partnership Theory and the Elective Share: Federal Estate Tax Law Provides a Solution, 49 U. Miami L. Rev. 567 (1995). Contrast the "reasonable provision" ap-proach of the English legislation discussed in section E of this chapter.

3. Effect of Spouse's Election

A variety of problems may arise when an election is required, particu-larly if the will in question fails to make a complete disposition of the decedent's estate, or under any circumstances if the spouse elects *against* the will.

Assume that *W*'s net estate consisted of Blackacre, Whiteacre, and $50,000 in securities and that her will devised Blackacre to her husband *H* and Whiteacre to her brother *B* but contained no residuary clause. Assume further that *H* elects to accept Blackacre under *W*'s will. *H* now claims half of the securities as intestate property. Will he succeed in your state? Compare Ness v. Lunde, 394 Ill. 286, 68 N.E.2d 458 (1946) (the will provided: "In lieu of dower, homestead, widow's award and of any and all rights or interest she might have or claim in my estate, as heir, widow, or otherwise, I make the following provision for my wife . . ." but failed to dispose of all the testator's realty; the wife elected to take under the will, but the court held she was also entitled to a share of the intestate property) and Waring v. Loring, 399 Mass. 419, 504 N.E.2d 644 (1987) with Trafton v. Trafton, 96 N.H. 188, 72 A.2d 457 (1950), in which the widow failed to elect before her death and was thus deemed to take under the will; the statute provided: "Every devise or bequest [to the spouse] shall be holden to be in lieu of the rights which [the spouse] has by law . . . , unless it shall appear by will that such was not the intention"; the court held that the widow's estate was not entitled to share in the intestate property.

PROBLEM

3-Q. *H*'s will left $60,000 to an orphanage and the residue to his son, *S*, and his daughter, *D*, in equal shares. *H*'s wife, *W*, elects to take her forced share, which is one-third of *H*'s net estate of $150,000.

(a) How should the remaining $100,000 be distributed as among *S*, *D*, and the orphanage in the absence of a statute in point? Under the statute in your state? Cf. T. Atkinson, Wills §136 (2 ed. 1953), which states:

> "Abatement" is the reduction of legacies on account of the insufficiency of the estate to pay testator's debts and other legacies. Intestate property should be first applied for these purposes. In absence of testamentary indication as to order of abatement, legacies ordinarily abate in the following order: (1) residuary legacies, (2) general legacies, (3) specific and demonstrative legacies, which give way together ratably.

See also Uniform Probate Code §2-209. In the absence of a statutory provision on point, the general order of abatement has usually been followed. Assuming no statute governing the matter but that the state has a pretermitted heir statute like the Illinois statute on page 127, infra, how would you decide this case? See generally Traynor, Statutes Revolving in Common-Law Orbits. 17 Cath. U.L. Rev. 401 (1968); Williams, Statutes as Sources of Law Beyond Their Terms in Common-Law Cases, 50 Geo. Wash. L. Rev. 554 (1982).

(b) It is common for a will to make provision for the most important objects of the testator's bounty by way of the residuary clause. What does this suggest about drafting? About judicial and legislative actions? Cf. Leach, Lessons from the Depression in Drafting Wills and Trusts, 27 Vt. B.A. Rep. 109 (1933).

————————————

In Sellick v. Sellick, 207 Mich. 194, 173 N.W. 609 (1919), the testator devised $25,000 to his wife for life, then to defendants. He devised the residue to plaintiff. His wife elected to take a forced share, and plaintiff argued that if the remainder is accelerated, the defendants will get more than they would have taken had testator's wife not elected. Meanwhile, the plaintiff gets less because the residuary devise abates first. Agreeing that this was unfair, the court ordered the $25,000 sequestered, providing that the interest be paid to plaintiff to compensate for the abatement, with distribution to the defendants upon the death of the widow. What result under the UPC?

PROBLEM

3-D. H and W reside in a UPC jurisdiction. After a twenty-year marriage, H dies with a net estate of $500,000. Since W did not work outside the home, she has no assets in her name. H devised all to X. What result? What if, shortly before H died, W inherited $500,000 from her mother? What if, instead, H inherited $500,000 from his mother shortly before he died? Contrast the result if H had $500,000 saved from wages earned during marriage, $500,000 inherited from his mother, and W has no assets, and then *H* and *W* divorce. Assume the equitable distribution statute provides for an equal distribution of "marital property."

4. Attempts to Defeat Spouse's Statutory Rights

Statutory rights in the nature of dower, as distinguished from forced heirship provisions, give rise to inchoate interests in lands owned during coverture and cannot be defeated by conveyance after marriage without the spouse's consent. Persons who wish to deprive their spouses of dower rights may attempt to do so by conveyances *prior to marriage*. When such a transfer of land is found to have been intended to "defraud" the prospective spouse, it is generally held not to defeat the latter's rights, even though land disposed of before marriage is normally not subject to dower.

Greater difficulty is encountered where the surviving spouse has a statutory forced share in the decedent's estate at death. These rights are generally subject to inter vivos transfers. Nevertheless, transfers that appear to be will substitutes have been the subject of considerable litigation with varied results.

cannot convey in order to defraud

PROBLEM

3-E. Five years ago, following twenty years of marital strife, *H* began making gifts to his brother and sister. This year, at age 78, *H* died in the hospital following a sudden illness. His will left everything to his sister. His wife, *W*, elects to assert her statutory rights. Consider what *W*'s rights may be under the law of your state with regard to the following transfers by *H*; consider also the effects of these transfers under other typical forms of legislation protecting the surviving spouse.

(a) Four years before his death, *H* gave his sister, *S*, $50,000 in cash and securities, openly declaring his intent to leave as little as possible for his wife.

(b) Two years before his death, accompanied by similar declarations, *H* deeded Blackacre (worth $100,000) to his brother, *B*, in return for *B*'s cancellation of a note secured by a mortgage on Blackacre. The note ($40,000) represented the unpaid balance of a loan *B* had made to enable *H* to purchase Blackacre ten years earlier.

(c) In the hospital several days before his death, *H*, being aware that death was near, had the beneficiary designation on his insurance policies changed from *W* to *B*. Immediately thereafter *H* sent for *S* and made a gift to her of a large savings account, saying, "I won't be needing this any more."

Even in states that have not enacted the UPC, case law may bring the nonprobate asset within the reach of the surviving spouse.

non UPC states

Gillette v. Madden, 280 A.D. 161, 162, 112 N.Y.S.2d 543, 544 (1952), stated: "A married man has the right to make any disposition of his property he chooses even though he is motivated by a purpose to destroy an estate to which the survivor of the marriage might make claim under statute law. A purpose to defeat such a right by divestiture of the estate is not treated as a fraud invalidating the transfer." But see In re Montague's Estate, 403 Pa. 558, 170 A.2d 103 (1961) (transfers made by husband were invalid as attempted testamentary transfers where he retained the right to control property during his lifetime and through his will).

In Allender v. Allender, 199 Md. 541, 550-551, 87 A.2d 608, 611-612 (1952), it is stated:

> The doctrine of fraud on marital rights represents an effort to balance the social and practical undesirability of restricting the free alienation of personal property against the desire to protect the legal share of a spouse. It has always been recognized that a husband, in the absence of statutory regulation like that in the case of dower, has an unqualified right to give away his personal property during his lifetime, even though the effect is to deprive the wife of her statutory share. But if the gift is not absolute and unconditional and the donor retains dominion and control over the property during his lifetime, the courts have held that the gift is colorable and may be set aside. . . .
>
> *non-absolute gift*
>
> In the instant case it is clear that the donor retained no legal control over the devolution of the joint interest [with right of survivorship] at his death and no power to revoke or undo what he had done, a factor stressed in many of the cases. It is not necessary to decide whether the mere retention of a life estate would of itself amount to a violation of marital rights. In the instant case the donor retained nothing but a joint interest, and we think [this] does not render the transactions so colorable or illusory as to justify the setting aside of the transfers.
>
> Without relying solely on the test of degree, we may say that we think the fact that the joint interest . . . of the decedent and his children was by law severable . . . was not such a reservation of domination or title to the Key stock as amounted to a violation of the widow's rights.

Related problems involving revocable trusts are covered in Chapter 9 section C, infra.

5. Marital Property Reform in Common Law States

As noted above, much of the most recent impetus for elective share reform in common law states comes from the adoption of equitable distribution, a partnership-based regime that applies when the mar-

riage ends in divorce. The Uniform Marriage and Divorce Act
(UMDA), enacted in nine states, is illustrative and addresses spousal
property rights on separation and dissolution, as well as addressing the
formation of marriages and the support and custody of children. Section 306 provides that "In a proceeding for dissolution of marriage
. . . the terms of the separation agreement [except those pertaining to
children] are binding on the court unless it finds . . . that the separation
agreement is unconscionable." Section 307(A) (Alternative A) provides that "the court, without regard to marital misconduct, shall finally equitably apportion between the parties the property and assets
belonging to either or both."

Section 308 provides that "the court may grant a maintenance order
for either spouse only if it finds that the spouse seeking maintenance
(1) lacks sufficient property to provide for reasonable needs; and (2) is
unable to support himself." It adds that maintenance "shall be in
amounts and for periods of time the court deems just . . . considering
all the relevant factors," which specifically include "the financial resources of the party seeking maintenance, including marital property
apportioned to him." The UMDA does not affect property rights during an ongoing marriage or on death.

granting of maintenance order

The Uniform Marital Property Act (UMPA), enacted in Wisconsin,
does deal with property rights during the marriage and at death as well
as on dissolution during life. It purports to be a comprehensive regime
similar to a community property system.

See J. Oldham, Should the Surviving Spouse's Forced Share Be Retained?, 38 Case W. Res. L. Rev. 223 (1987). The English Inheritance
(Provision for Family and Dependents) Act 1975, §3 provides that in
determining provisions for the surviving spouse, the court shall "have
regard to the provision which the applicant might reasonably have expected to receive if on the day on which the deceased died the marriage, instead of being terminated by death, had been terminated by
a decree of divorce."

D. Protection of Issue from Disinheritance

The statutory law of nearly all states includes provisions intended to
diminish the risk of inadvertent disinheritance of descendants. These
"pretermitted heir statutes" do not create forced shares for the protected issue. Only one state has a form of forced heirship for descendants. La. Civ. Code, art. 1493; cf. Cal. Civ. Code §205 (if a dependent
child would become a charge of the county, the county may assert a
claim against the estate for the child's support). Thus, as a general rule,
a child may be disinherited if the intention to do so is expressed and
if the entire estate is otherwise disposed of. As a practical matter, the

exclusion of a child may invite a successful contest of a will. For an argument that children *should* be protected, see Ronald Chester, Should American Children Be Protected Against Disinheritance?, 32 Real Prop. Prob. & Tr. J. 405 (1997).

Pretermitted heir statutes are designed to avoid unintentional failure of a testator's natural and probable intention. The typical statute gives an intestate share to the child who is born after the will is executed, unless anticipated and clearly disinherited in the will or otherwise provided for. Unfortunately, this type of statute may defeat or distort intention and form books usually include casually drawn and questionably effective clauses intended to avoid them.

In studying the following material, consider what kind of statute is best suited to accomplish the purpose of avoiding unintentional disinheritance and what kinds may breed litigation or even defeat intent. In examining your local statute, it is important to look for certain details in which these statutes differ from state to state. For example, consider who may be a pretermitted heir.[6] Does your statute apply to all descendants who would take by intestacy, or just to children? Even if the statute merely refers to children, by judicial decision the issue of a deceased child may be allowed the protection of the statute as representatives of the child. Does the statute apply to such persons whenever born or only to those born after execution of the will? Consider also the conditions under which the statute does not operate. Must an intent to disinherit appear on the face of the will? Does a nontestamentary provision that is less than a full advancement of the intestate share prevent the statute's operation? Under many statutes one or more of these questions will not be clearly answered, in which case judicial decisions must be consulted.

PROBLEMS

3-F   A's will provides: "I leave everything to my wife." At the time the will was executed, A and W had two children, X and Y. After the will was executed, a third child, Z, was born. At A's death, are any of the children entitled take as pretermitted heirs in your jurisdiction? Under the statute set out below? Under the UPC §2-302 (below)?

3-G.   A's will provides: "I leave everything I own to my wife, W; I intentionally leave nothing to any other persons who may be my heirs." After the execution of the will, a child, C, was born to A and W. Thereafter A died, and his will has been admitted to probate. Does C take as a pretermitted heir under the statute of your state? Under the statute

---

6. See Estate of Frizzel, 156 So. 2d 558 (Fla. Dist. Ct. App. 1963), analyzing conflicting authorities and deciding that the pretermitted heir statute protected a child adopted after the will was executed.

set out below? How would you argue for *W*? For *C*? If *W* offers to prove
by testimony and other evidence that *A* actually intended to leave everything to her and assumed she would later make provision for any children if she thought appropriate, how would you argue for and against
admission of the evidence under these statutes?

Is it a good idea to insert a provision such as that quoted from *A*'s
will as a routine matter in drawing wills? Explain.

ILLINOIS REVISED STATUTES

Chapter 110 1/2, §4-10. Unless provision is made in the will for a child
of the testator born after the will is executed or unless it appears by
the will that it was the intention of the testator to disinherit the child,
the child is entitled to receive the portion of the estate to which he
would be entitled if the testator had died intestate, and all legacies shall
abate proportionately therefore.

ESTATE OF GLOMSET
547 P.2d 951 (Okla. 1976)

BARNES, JUSTICE.

[John Larson Glomset, Sr., and his wife, Margie, executed joint and
reciprocal wills leaving their estates to each other, or to their son, John
Larson Glomset, Jr., if both spouses should die in a common disaster.
John Glomset, Sr. died, survived by his spouse. His 40-year-old daughter, Carolyn Gay Ghan, sought a declaratory judgment that she was a
pretermitted heir and thus entitled to share in the estate. The trial
court granted the declaratory judgment, finding no affirmative intention to disinherit Ghan evident on the face of the will.]

Appellant . . . disputes the Trial Court's finding that Appellee is a
pretermitted heir under the provisions of 84 O.S. §132.

Title 84 O.S. §132 provides as follows:

When any testator omits to provide in his will for any of his children,
or for the issue of any deceased child *unless it appears that such omission
was intentional,* such child, or the issue of such child, must have the same
share in the estate of the testator, as if he had died intestate, and succeeds
thereto as provided for in preceding section. (Emphasis added.)

We must first determine if the intent of the deceased must be determined from the will itself, or if extrinsic evidence is admissible. . . . In
deciding if extrinsic evidence is admissible, we must determine whether
or not an intention to disinherit Appellee affirmatively appeared from
the four corners of the will. We have previously held that if there are

no uncertainties appearing on the face of the will, extrinsic evidence is not admissible. (Citations omitted.)

There are no uncertainties on the face of the will in this case. The testator admittedly failed to mention his daughter, Appellee Carolyn Gay Ghan, and also failed to indicate any reason for his failure to mention her. Thus . . . we must find that Appellee is a pretermitted heir and entitled to inherit her proportionate share of her deceased father's estate.

Appellant has failed to set forth a compelling reason why the interpretation of 84 O.S. §132 should be changed at this time to permit introduction of extrinsic evidence to show intent of the testator where no ambiguity appears on the face of the will.

The writ of certiorari petitioned for is granted, the decision of the Court of Appeals is vacated, and the judgment of the Trial Court is affirmed.

HODGES, VICE CHIEF JUSTICE (dissenting).

The majority opinion holds the will is unambiguous on its face and, therefore, extrinsic evidence is inadmissible to determine the intention of the testator. I believe this perpetuates a misinterpretation of the applicable statute, 84 O.S.1971, §132. . . .

Under comparable statutes providing an omitted child or issue of a deceased child should be entitled to a portion of the testator's estate, "unless it appears that such omission was intentional," . . . the majority of jurisdictions . . . have consistently held . . . that extrinsic evidence was admissible to prove that the testator intended to disinherit an omitted child. The pretermitted heir statute raises the presumption that children are not intentionally omitted from a will. However, the presumption is rebuttable by extrinsic evidence and parol testimony.

The purpose and legislative intent of the statute is to protect children unintentionally omitted from the will. It is not to be construed to alter the testamentary intent of the testator by including children he intentionally excluded from his estate. . . .

Assuming arguendo, the majority view is correct, I further believe the will is ambiguous on its face, and that the testator's intention to disinherit appears from the will itself. . . .

Extrinsic evidence should have been admissible because by omitting the daughter from the will she thereby is entitled to her statutory share, while the son who was mentioned in the will receives nothing. Thus on the face of the will an uncertainty is created and extrinsic evidence should be allowed. This extrinsic evidence which was offered, but rejected by the trial court, definitely shows the testator intentionally omitted the daughter. She would not visit her father or even allow her child to visit him. They had not seen each other for some time because of their strained relationship.

I believe a construction which permits a child not mentioned in the will to participate in the distribution of the estate while the other child who is mentioned and designated the contingent beneficiary takes nothing, is a tortured interpretation of the will and the Oklahoma Statutes regarding testamentary intent, and reaches a result totally unintended and uncontemplated by the testator or the statute.

The cause should be remanded to the trial court for determination of the factual question of whether the omission of the daughter was intentional.

I, therefore, respectfully dissent.

What result if *Glomset* had been governed by UPC §2-302 (below)?

UNIFORM PROBATE CODE

§2-302.   *Omitted Children.*

(a) Except as provided in subsection (b), if a testator fails to provide in his [or her] will for any of his [or her] children born or adopted after the execution of the will, the omitted after-born or after-adopted child receives a share in the estate as follows:

(1) If the testator had no child living when he [or she] executed the will, an omitted after-born or after-adopted child receives a share in the estate equal in value to that which the child would have received had the testator died intestate, unless the will devised all or substantially all of the estate to the other parent of the omitted child and that other parent survives the testator and is entitled to take under the will.

(2) If the testator had one or more children living when he [or she] executed the will, and the will devised property or an interest in property to one or more of the then-living children, an omitted after-born or after-adopted child is entitled to share in the testator's estate as follows:

(i) The portion of the testator's estate in which the omitted after-born or after-adopted child is entitled to share is limited to devises made to the testator's then-living children under the will.

(ii) The omitted after-born or after-adopted child is entitled to receive the share of the testator's estate, as limited in subparagraph (i), that the child would have received had the testator included all omitted after-born and after-adopted children with the children to whom devises were made under the will and had given an equal share of the estate to each child.

(iii) To the extent feasible, the interest granted an omitted after-born or after-adopted child under this section must be of the same character, whether equitable or legal, present or future, as that devised to the testator's then-living children under the will.

(iv) In satisfying a share provided by this paragraph, devises to the testator's children who were living when the will was executed abate ratably. In abating the devises of the then-living children, the court shall preserve to the maximum extent possible the character of the testamentary plan adopted by the testator.

(b) Neither subsection (a)(1) nor subsection (a)(2) applies if:

(1) it appears from the will that the omission was intentional; or

(2) the testator provided for the omitted after-born or after-adopted child by transfer outside the will and the intent that the transfer be in lieu of a testamentary provision is shown by the testator's statements or is reasonably inferred from the amount of the transfer or other evidence.

(c) If at the time of execution of the will the testator fails to provide in his [or her] will for a living child solely because he [or she] believes the child to be dead, the child is entitled to share in the estate as if the child were an omitted after-born or after-adopted child.

(d) In satisfying a share provided by subsection (a)(1), devises made by the will abate under Section 3-902.

————————————

The Pretermitted Spouse. A number of states, because forced share protection is lacking or, as is often the case, significantly less than a spouse's intestate share, have pretermitted spouse statutes. This type of legislation protects spouses from the effects of wills executed prior to the marriage by granting the survivor an intestate share (or some modification of that share) of the deceased spouse's estate. These statutes do not apply if the will shows (or possibly if extrinsic evidence discloses) that it was executed in contemplation of the marriage or with an intention to exclude the subsequent spouse. Nor do they apply if the will, or maybe some other arrangement, makes provision for the testator's spouse — and cases usually require that the provision be for the survivor "as a spouse." If the jurisdiction has a forced share statute that gives the spouse an intestate share, do you see the perceived need for a pretermitted spouse statute?

These statutes have many of the problems of pretermitted heir statutes. For example, when does a general anticontest or nonpretermission clause show the requisite intention to exclude the subsequent spouse or to limit the spouse's rights to those already provided (e.g., as friend) in the will? See generally Note, Premarital Wills and Pretermitted Children: West Virginia Law v. Revised Uniform Probate Code, 93 W. Va. L. Rev. 197 (1990).

UNIFORM PROBATE CODE

§2-301. *Entitlement of Spouse; Premarital Will.*

(a) If a testator's surviving spouse married the testator after the testator executed his [or her] will, the surviving spouse is entitled to receive, as an intestate share, no less than the value of the share of the estate he [or she] would have received if the testator had died intestate as to that portion of the testator's estate, if any, that neither is devised to a child of the testator who was born before the testator married the surviving spouse and who is not a child of the surviving spouse nor is devised to a descendant of such a child or passes under Sections 2-603 or 2-604 to such a child or to a descendant of such a child, unless:

(1) it appears from the will or other evidence that the will was made in contemplation of the testator's marriage to the surviving spouse;

(2) the will expresses the intention that it is to be effective notwithstanding any subsequent marriage; or

(3) the testator provided for the spouse by transfer outside the will and the intent that the transfer be in lieu of a testamentary provision is shown by the testator's statements or is reasonably inferred from the amount of the transfer or other evidence.

(b) In satisfying the share provided by this section, devises made by the will to the testator's surviving spouse, if any, are applied first, and other devises, other than a devise to a child of the testator who was born before the testator married the surviving spouse and who is not a child of the surviving spouse or a devise or substitute gift under Sections 2-603 or 2-604 to a descendant of such a child, abate as provided in Section 3-902.

The following case was decided under the pre-1990 UPC version of §2-301 (entitled "Omitted Spouse"). Would it be decided the same under revised §2-301 (above)?

HERBACH v. HERBACH
230 Mich. App. 276, 583 N.W.2d 541 (1998)

REILLY, J.

[Walter Herbach executed his last will and testament in 1982, leaving $50,000 to his "friend" Eileen. Walter and Eileen subsequently married and were married at the time of his death. Walter's son Barry, the personal representative for the estate, opposed Eileen's petition to take as a pretermitted spouse. The probate court ruled that although Eileen was named in the will, she could take as a pretermitted spouse as long as she was not named in the will in contemplation of marriage.]

[W]e agree with respondent's contention that because petitioner was named in the will, she is precluded as a matter of law from taking as a pretermitted spouse. . . .

The application of Michigan's pretermitted spouse statute to a surviving spouse named in the will, but not named in contemplation of marriage, is an issue of first impression in Michigan. The statute provides, in pertinent part:

> If a testator fails to provide by will for his surviving spouse who married the testator after the execution of the will, the omitted spouse shall receive the same share of the estate the omitted spouse would have received if the decedent did not leave a will, unless it appears from the will that the omission was intentional, or unless the testator provided for the spouse by transfers outside the will and the intent that the transfers were in lieu of a testamentary provision is shown by declarations of the testator, by the amount of the transfers, or by other evidence. . . .

In this case, it is undisputed that petitioner . . . was not left out of the will or left unmentioned in the will. Accordingly, under the plain language of the pretermitted spouse statute, petitioner is not eligible to take a share because she was not "omitted" from the testator's will.

Some appellate courts addressing similar provisions in other jurisdictions have allowed surviving spouses to recover against antenuptial wills in cases where they were named in the will in some capacity other than as a spouse. . . . To reach this result, however, these courts have been forced to read a "contemplation of marriage" requirement into their respective pretermitted spouse statutes. . . . Other foreign courts have interpreted similar pretermitted spouse statutes more narrowly. . . . These courts have reasoned that, because the "contemplation of marriage" requirement figured prominently in the common law, its omission from a subsequent statute on the subject should be deemed intentional. . . . We are persuaded that the reasoning of these latter courts is more in accordance with our principles of statutory construction.

. . . If the Legislature sought to include surviving spouses named in the will in some capacity other than spouse within the purview of the pretermitted spouse statute, it could have done so by including a "contemplation of marriage" requirement in the plain language of the statute. Finally, we note that Michigan's elective share provision, which does not require omission from the testator's will, is available to offer some protection to surviving spouses like petitioner.

PROBLEM

3-H.   *B* executes a will devising all to his friend, *Z*. Then *B* marries *A*. Fifteen years later, *B* dies survived by *A* but no parents or descendants. *B* had never changed his will. *Z* also survived *B*, whose probate estate consists of $500,000. *A* also has $500,000 in her name. What result in a UPC jurisdiction? What if *A* elects against the will?

entitled to intestate share   *entitled to intestate share*

E.   *Extent and Limits of Testamentary Power: Other Aspects*

Despite the unusual breadth of testamentary freedom typical of the states in this country, a testator's authority is subject to limitations, qualifications, and uncertainties that vary from jurisdiction to jurisdiction and that go beyond the widespread substantive and procedural safeguards we have just examined. Even today, relatively novel issues, evolutionary developments, and distinct changes of policy are observable. In this section, we look at several such aspects of the limits of our powers of testation — special prohibitions, disabilities, and the nature of personal and economic rights that may or may not be exercised by wills. It also might be worthwhile to point out briefly that many of the world's societies tolerate far less freedom of testation and particularly object to "substitutions," thus refusing to recognize future interests and trusts as they are known and taken for granted in this country. Even the common law world's acceptance of these forms of "dead hand control" is not unlimited — hence rules regulating "perpetuities" (see Chapter 20), public policy restrictions on trust purposes and conditions (see Chapter 9 and Chapter 15), and the like.

Restrictions on charitable dispositions. In a shrinking minority of states testamentary gifts to charity are subject to some limitation. Each statute must be studied to determine the type of limitation involved and the circumstances under which it operates. Some statutes, to protect the family, limit the amount that can be left to charity. Others invalidate charitable bequests and devises by a will executed within a specified period prior to death, perhaps to lessen the possible consequences of a dying person's fear of the hereafter. Still others embody both of these forms of limitation.

Typically these statutes apply only if the testator is survived by certain designated near relatives, and sometimes only if an objecting relative would take but for the charitable gift. See, e.g., Estate of Eckart, 39 N.Y.2d 493, 348 N.E.2d 905 (1976) (statute since repealed). In some states this has led to drafting practices that have — successfully — protected "prohibited" charitable bequests by providing substitute bequests to friends or others outside the protected class in the event the charitable bequest is invalidated.

SHRINERS' HOSPITAL v. HESTER
23 Ohio St. 3d 198, 492 N.E.2d 153 (1986)

SWEENEY, J. . . .

We believe that the protection of a testator's issue from disinheritance, as a result of the testator's unsound judgment or the undue influence of third parties upon the testator, is a legitimate state objective. Our [equal protection] analysis narrows, therefore, to the question of whether R.C. 2107.06 is rationally related to the accomplishment of that objective.

It is apparent that R.C. 2107.06 will accomplish its objective in some cases — i.e., those in which the testator, having acted under the belief that his death was near, executed a will within the six months prior to his death, making bequests therein for . . . charitable purposes on the basis of unsound judgment or as the result of undue influence. Unfortunately, a large number of cases falling within the scope of R.C. 2107.06 involve the estates of testators who did *not* execute their last will under the belief that their death was near. Furthermore, out of the remaining cases impacted by the statute in which the testator did believe that he was near death, it is reasonable to assume that few involved bequests that were based upon unsound judgment or the result of undue influence. . . .

Thus, by operation of R.C. 2107.06, a select class of beneficiaries is deprived of testamentary bequests, even though in the vast majority of cases such bequests are entirely legitimate and not within the scope of the statute's objective. Additionally, R.C. 2107.06 effectively creates an irrebuttable presumption that a testator . . . acted with unsound judgment or under undue influence. Such " 'irrebuttable presumptions have long been disfavored under the Due Process Clauses of the Fifth and Fourteenth Amendments,' especially when they are 'not necessarily or universally true in fact, and when the state has reasonable alternative means of making the crucial determination.' ". . .

The imprecise nature of R.C. 2107.06 is further borne out by its failure to address inter-vivos death-bed transfers that are made to the prejudice of the grantor's issue and bequests made by terminally ill testators *more* than six months before their death. . . .

Based upon all of the foregoing, we cannot conclude that former R.C. 2107.06 is *rationally related* to the accomplishment of a legitimate state objective.

Extramarital Relationships. A few states still have statutes that bar or limit testamentary gifts to participants in adulterous relationships with testators. These restrictions may or may not depend on whether certain family members or favored relatives would take the challenged disposition. See Ray v. Tate, 252 S.E.2d 568 (S.C. 1979), involving a statute invalidating bequests in excess of 25 percent of an estate to one with whom a testator "lived in adultery." Cf. E. Kandoian, Cohabitation, Common Law Marriage and the Possibility of a Shared Moral Life, 75 Geo. L.J. 1829 (1987).

A news story in The Advocate, Jan. 7, 1986, at 15, 16, reported on a New Orleans court battle between, inter alia, a son adopted at age 41 by the decedent in the same year decedent executed a will in that son's favor, and Danny, a lover to whom decedent purportedly left his estate by subsequent handwritten will. The judge ruled the latter will valid but that Danny was entitled only to 10 percent of decedent's personal property, the remaining estate going to the son under a statute limiting what persons living in "open concubinage" can leave to each other if the testator leaves issue. After noting the decision's "devastating impact on every gay couple in Louisiana," Danny's lawyer was quoted as stating that this ruling, based on a statute rooted "in the Puritan ethic of trying to make sure that everybody lives monogamous lives, . . . makes no sense in this situation because . . . there is no rational basis for punishing parties who are not married" when, under the state's law, "they could not be married if they wanted to."

"Rights of Publicity" as Estate Assets. "Unlike the right of privacy, which has been recognized as a personal right in that it protects a person's 'right to be let alone,' the right of publicity has been recognized as a property right, in that '. . . a celebrity has a legitimate proprietary interest in his public personality.'" Southeast Bank v. Lawrence, 483 N.Y.S.2d 218, 221 (App. Div. 1984). The opinion continues: "Some cases have held that, in order for the right of publicity to descend, the celebrity must have exploited that right during his or her lifetime. . . . Although we find that [Tennessee] Williams exploited his right of publicity when he was alive, we hold that there was no prerequisite" in New York that he have done so in order "to preserve [it for his] heirs." Id. at 222. "A number of courts have recognized the common law right of publicity," and the Appellate Division saw "no logical reason to terminate this right upon death of the person protected. . . , presumably [the reason] this right has been deemed a 'property right.'" Id. at 223. The New York Court of Appeals opinion follows.

SOUTHEAST BANK v. LAWRENCE
66 N.Y. 2d 910, 489 N.E.2d 744 (1985)

MEMORANDUM [OPINION]. . . .

Plaintiff, a Florida-based bank acting as personal representative of the estate of the late playwright Tennessee Williams, a Florida domiciliary at the time of his death, commenced this action to enjoin defendants . . . from naming [their Manhattan] theatre the "Tennessee Williams." . . .

Special Term granted plaintiff's motion for a preliminary injunction and [was] affirmed by the Appellate Division. . . . We now reverse.

The parties have assumed that the substantive law of New York is dispositive of the appeal and have addressed Florida law only tangentially. Both Special Term and the Appellate Division . . . have overlooked the applicable choice of law principle, followed by both New York and Florida, that questions concerning personal property rights are to be determined by reference to the substantive law of the decedent's domicile.

Under Florida law, only one to whom a license has been issued during decedent's lifetime and the decedent's surviving spouse and children possess a descendible right of publicity, which is extremely limited and which Florida courts have refused to extend beyond the contours of the statute. Since Tennessee Williams did not have a surviving spouse or child and did not issue a license during his lifetime, plaintiff possesses no enforceable property right. In light of this holding, we do not pass upon the question of whether a common-law descendible right of publicity exists in this State. . . .

Testamentary Guardianships. Typical state legislation authorizes the will of the last surviving parent of a minor child to designate or nominate a guardian of the person (or whatever the local terminology may be) for the child. The effect of such a nomination varies from state to state, and, in some jurisdictions, appointing judges are required only to give the nomination consideration along with other factors relevant to their determination of a child's "best interests." On the other hand, in many states a guardian (or appropriate fiduciary) for the estate or property of a minor beneficiary may be named by any testator for property passing under the will, and this nominee is entitled to serve in the absence of some legally disqualifying characteristic.

PROBLEM

3-I.   *M* was granted custody of her child, *C*, on her divorce six years ago from *C*'s father, *F*. For the last four years *M* and *C* have lived with *M*'s widowed sister, *S*, and her two children, sharing expenses and financial, household, and some parental responsibilities. *M* has come to you to have a will drawn, and she tells you that one of her greatest fears is that, if she were to die, *C* (now eight years of age) "would be returned to *F*." *M* believes it would be ideal for *C* to remain in *S*'s home with

S and her children. What advice would you give to *M* under the laws of your state? What further facts do you need to ascertain as relevant to this question? Is there anything *M* might do now to improve the chances of attaining her desired result in the event of her death while *C* is still a minor? What are your duties in this matter?

UNIFORM PROBATE CODE

§5-202.   [*Parental Appointment of Guardian for Minor.*]

(a) The parent of an unmarried minor may appoint a guardian for the minor by will, or other writing signed by the parent and attested by at least 2 witnesses.

(b) Subject to the right of the minor under Section 5-203, if both parents are dead or incapacitated or the surviving parent has no parental rights or has been adjudged to be incapacitated, a parental appointment becomes effective when the guardian's acceptance is filed in the Court in which a nominating instrument is probated, or, in the case of a non-testamentary nominating instrument, in the Court at the place where the minor resides or is present. If both parents are dead, an effective appointment by the parent who died later has priority.

(c) A parental appointment effected by filing the guardian's acceptance under a will probated in the state of the testator's domicile is effective in this State.

(d) Upon acceptance of appointment, the guardian shall give written notice of acceptance to the minor and to the person having the minor's care or the minor's nearest adult relative.

In Louisiana, LSA-C.C. art. 257 provides: "The right of appointing a tutor . . . belongs exclusively to the father or mother dying last. . . . This is called tutorship by will, because generally it is given by testament but it may likewise be given by [declaration] before a notary and two witnesses." But LSA-C.C. art. 258 provides: "If the parents are divorced or judicially separated, only the one to whom the court has entrusted care and custody of the children has a right to appoint a tutor for them as provided in the preceding article." On problems that arose when a custodial parent died without exercising her power under article 253, see Tutorship of Stanfield, 404 So. 2d 522 (La. App. 1981).

In the absence of a rare statutory provision like article 258, above, consider the implications of general doctrine concerning parental custody as expressed in Matter of Adoption of L., 61 N.Y.2d 420, 425, 462 N.E.2d 1165, 1168-1169 (1984): "It has long been the law of this State that a parent has 'a right to the care and custody of a child superior to that of all others, unless he or she has abandoned that right or is proved unfit to assume the duties and privileges of parenthood.' . . . The state may not deprive a natural parent of her child's custody merely because a court or social agency believes . . . it has found someone better to raise the child. So long as the parental rights have not been forfeited . . . the question of best interests is not reached. For once it is found that the parent is fit, and has neither abandoned, surrendered, nor otherwise forfeited parental rights, the inquiry ends.''

Contrast In re Adoption of Markham, 414 N.E.2d 1351 (Ill. App. 1981), following the death of the mother (the custodial parent under a divorce decree), the appellate court granted "permanent custody and control" to the child's paternal aunt and uncle but refused to authorize adoption by them. The contesting father was not found to be "an unfit person" or to have forfeited his rights to visitation and to prevent an adoption, but the court reversed the trial court's finding in favor of the father on the custody issue because it had failed to recognize the children's best interests, particularly based on the important continuity of environment offered by the aunt and uncle. The court also granted the father "reasonable visitation privileges . . . to foster the love and affection which should exist between parent and children." But cf. In re Custody of Peterson, 491 N.E.2d 1150 (Ill. 1986), severely restricting the circumstances under which a nonparent may petition for custody if a parent is alive.

See also the Report of the Governor's Commission on the Family, 4 J. Calif. Assembly 8061 (1969 Reg. Session), on the basis of which Cal. Civil Code $4600 was enacted:

[I]n the occasional case where the child's interests would be served best by giving custody to a non-parent — a stepparent or relative for example — the court can not presently achieve this without an affirmative finding that the [parent or] parents are wholly unfit. This doctrine is designed to secure the rights of the parents, which is surely a fit goal. Unfortunately, it sometimes loses sight, we believe, of the right of the child to an award of custody which will promote the stability of his life and best permit him to grow up as a happy and productive member of society.

We have no intention of undermining parents' rights to the custody of their children, and we believe that the primacy of those rights must be preserved. We are convinced, however, that no useful purpose can be served by forcing a formalized finding of unfitness. The cases in which the child's best interest would require a custodial award to a third person may be rare, but are nonetheless serious. To take the most common example, if the custodial parent dies and the Court should specifically find that the child's welfare would be best served by awarding custody to the stepparent, with whom the child has been living and with whom he has formed a warm and stable relationship, should not the Court be able to so order without having to find a long-absent or minimally-interested parent judicially unfit? We believe that it should. . . .

However, before custody can be awarded to one other than a parent, the court must specifically find that an award of custody to a parent would be detrimental to the child, and that the award to a non-parent is required to serve the best interests of the child. What is "detrimental" has not been set forth [in the proposed statute] with particularity. It is a nearly impossible task to devise detailed standards which will leave the courts sufficient flexibility to make the proper judgment in all circumstances.

F. Testamentary Restrictions: Some Reflections and Comparisons

PROVISION FOR DEPENDENTS: THE ENGLISH INHERITANCE ACT OF 1938
Notes and Legislation, 53 Harv. L. Rev. 465, 466-467 (1940)

. . . The British statute of 1938 [Inheritance (Family Provision) Act, 1938, 1 & 2 Geo. VI, c. 45], based upon earlier legislation in the Dominions, attempts to solve the problem of providing a scheme sufficiently elastic to allow disinheritance of the undeserving, yet sufficiently rigid to prevent an unjust testator from disinheriting the worthy in another fashion. Instead of the characteristic civil-law provision for a fixed portion beyond the power of a testator to disturb, and a provision for disinheritance of heirs for specified offenses, the English act gives probate courts the power to order reasonable provision for maintenance out of the income of the estate of any testator who does not make reasonable provision for his or her spouse, unmarried or disabled daughters, and minor or disabled sons. If the testator leaves property of less than £2000, recourse may be had to the principal. The income is to stop on remarriage of the spouse, the marriage of daughters, the majority of sons, and the end of disability of infirm children. The court is to look to the nature of the property in the estate, the claims of other dependents, the reasons for the testator's failure to provide, and the conduct of the dependents towards the testator. Where a testator bequeaths at least two-thirds of the income of the net estate to his surviving spouse, and the only dependents are the latter's children, no order can be made. . . .

Again, pioneering and imaginative English legislation! As a result of the Inheritance (Provision for Family and Dependents) Act, 1975, any child of the decedent may apply for maintenance. The court is also empowered to award maintenance to one who was treated by the decedent as a child of the decedent, or to a person who was in fact "maintained" by the decedent. See Re Beaumont, [1980] 1 All Eng. Rep. (Ch.) 266. There is even some provision for unremarried former spouses. Gratuitous transfers made by the decedent to defeat the maintenance provisions can in effect be revoked. In addition, the current statute no longer precludes a maintenance order where the spouse received "not less than two-thirds of the income of the net estate" and the only other dependents are the surviving spouse's children. Finally, the "periodical payments" are no longer payable only from income; resort to principal is no longer dependent on the testator's estate being under £2,000. If the court "sees fit," it can order "maintenance, in whole or in part, by way of a lump sum payment."

The Oregon Probate Code provides that the court shall make "necessary and reasonable provision" from the estate for the support for the decedent's spouse and dependent children, in a manner that is not detailed. See Note, Protection of the Surviving Spouse Under the Oregon Probate Code, 57 Or. L. Rev. 135 (1977). The provisions for support may be by periodic payments to continue for no more than two years or by outright transfers of real or personal property. In some cases, the entire estate may be set aside for the support of the widow and dependent children. Or. Rev. Stat. §§114.015-114.085 (1938). Cf. Maine Legislation as construed in In re Perkins, 141 Me. 137, 141, 39 A.2d 855, 857 (1944).

NUSSBAUM, LIBERTY OF TESTATION
23 A.B.A. J. 183-186 (1937)

> The transmission from generation to generation of vast fortunes by will, inheritance, or gift is not consistent with the ideals and sentiments of the American people. The desire to provide security for one's self and one's family is natural and wholesome, but it is adequately served by a reasonable inheritance. Great accumulations of wealth cannot be justified on the basis of personal and family security. In the last analysis such accumulations amount to the perpetuation of great and undesirable concentration of control in a relatively few individuals over the employment and welfare of many, many others. Such inherited economic power is as inconsistent with the ideals of this generation as inherited political power was inconsistent with the ideals of the generation which established our Government.

This is the language used by President Roosevelt in his message to Congress of June 19, 1935. The immediate objective of the sentences quoted was the recommendation, by the President, of a progressive inheritance tax. But the legal philosophy behind it is of a broader scope. It touches upon basic principles of Anglo-American inheritance law which permit, to a much greater extent than does foreign law, the undivided transfer of the decedent's estate to a single individual heir. . . .

Associating liberty of testation with the spirit of pioneering seems to be a plausible hypothesis. This liberty indeed is quite in line with "rugged individualism." And it is equally true that liberty of testation at the same time favors the maintenance of aristocracy and is particularly valuable to an industrial aristocracy of the American type. The Roman aristocracy performed its social duties by military services, the English by political ones, the American by granting large gifts and legacies for humanitarian, educational and other "charitable" purposes. . . .

The question arises whether the common law countries will in the long run continue to maintain unrestricted liberty of testation. There are distinct symptoms to the contrary within the English empire. . . .

As to the United States there has not yet appeared a similar distinct and general counteraction against liberty of testation. But there are indications of a slow, almost unconscious change in the mind of the community. . . . A certain preference for the spouse over the children might be in harmony with prevailing human sentiment, as appears from the great majority of wills. Yet the contrast between the amplitude of the spouse's protection on the one hand and the entire absence of the children's protection on the other hand may be regarded as unsatisfactory in the long run. Thus, from various sources pressure is going to be brought upon the time-honoured Anglo-American system for the institution of something like a legitime. Such an evolution might be considered as a weakening of the pioneer spirit. This process, however, seems to be inevitable due to the fact that the territorial prerequisites of American pioneering no longer exist. Rugged individualism probably is doomed. The fight for the maintenance of familial property will have to be conducted upon different fronts.

G.   Living Wills and Elder Law

Over the last few decades or so, a body of law and practice has emerged related to estate planning and the protection of clients and their families. *Elder law* deals with legal needs of older persons, particularly health care decisionmaking and property management. It is the result of the aging of the American population, and medical advances that extend "life" at increasing social and personal economic costs. Instruments associated with elder law — the living will and the durable power of attorney — are now part of the package of documents prepared by most estate planning attorneys, and are important for younger as well as older clients.

1. Health Care Decision Making

Although the potential human life span has not yet dramatically changed, the number of persons reaching their life expectancies has been significantly increasing. As associated illnesses increase, the emphasis in planning often shifts from the risk of an early death to planning for a life that lasts longer and becomes more costly than may have been foreseen.

The term *advance directive* or *medical directive* is usually used in a broad sense to describe any instrument expressing in some fashion the person's desires relating to medical treatment. The term is sometimes used in a narrower sense as an instrument expressing the person's wishes regarding specific types of medical treatment in several representative situations.

The advance directive may take the form of a *living will*, a somewhat misleading term. This is an instrument by which one may direct (or attempt to direct) health care providers not to use extraordinary means to prolong one's life in the event of terminal illness. The concept did not take hold until after the celebrated case of In re Karen Quinlan, 70 N.J. 10, 355 A.2d 647, cert. denied sub nom Garger v. New Jersey, 429 U.S. 922 (1976), which ultimately found no criminal liability in withdrawing mechanical ventilation (a respirator) from a young woman in a persistent vegetative state.

Quinlan's family and guardian were allowed to make the decision to withdraw treatment on a theory of substituted judgment (see infra). It was predicted that she would quickly die if removed from the respirator, but in fact she lived nine more years until dying from an infection.

In response to ethical and patient-autonomy concerns raised by *Quinlan*, many states have enacted living will statutes. Associated issues reached the Supreme Court in Cruzan v. Director, Missouri Department of Health, 497 U.S. 261 (1990). Nancy Cruzan had been in a persistent vegetative state for six years as the result of an automobile accident. Her parents requested the state hospital to terminate artificial nutrition and hydration in the belief that this was in accordance with her wishes and best interests. The hospital employees refused and litigation followed. The probate court authorized the termination but the state supreme court reversed, reasoning that, absent compliance with the Missouri living will statute, clear and convincing evidence of Nancy's preferences was required but had not been presented at trial. 760 S.W.2d 408 (Mo. banc 1988). On certiorari, the United States Supreme Court affirmed, holding that the state need not follow the directions of close family members but could constitutionally require clear and convincing evidence of the patient's preference. In subsequent proceedings in Missouri, the probate court found additional evidence sufficiently clear and convincing to support a finding that the patient did not want to live like a vegetable and ordered tubal feeding terminated. The Supreme Court's five-three decision generated several opinions, leaving most issues to the states to resolve, although analysis of the opinions suggests that a majority of the Court viewed a patient's right of "liberty" as imposing some obligation on the states to honor reliable writings executed by patients in anticipation of incapacity.

Following the *Cruzan* case, most states broadened their living will statutes to allow removal of mechanical ventilation from a person in a persistent vegetative state. The moral for drafters is to be sensitive to the coverage of living will statutes. One size does not fit all; individualized drafting may better reflect a client's wishes than a statutory form.

Another kind of advance directive is a *durable power of attorney for health care.* A power of attorney is an agency relationship, in which one person (the principal) grants another person (the agent or attorney-in-fact) the authority to make health care decisions for him. The traditional rule of agency law is that the death or incapacity of the principal automatically terminates the authority of the agent, whether or not the agent has notice of the death or incapacity. Obviously this usual rule would render health care powers of attorney almost useless, for it is the event of incapacity that creates the need for the attorney-in-fact to make decisions. Thus was born the *durable* power of attorney, which becomes or remains effective if the principal loses capacity. For a power of attorney to be durable, statutes typically require that it contain words to the effect that it shall not be affected by subsequent incapacity.

An instrument occasionally considered by the elderly is an *advance instruction for mental health treatment,* used primarily to express preferences regarding treatment but sometimes also to appoint an attorney-in-fact to make mental health decisions. The instrument was designed for persons who have been in and out of mental health treatment and are therefore familiar with potential treatments, including electroconvulsive treatment, but also may be used by others who suffer from senile dementia or other mental conditions. About a dozen states now provide for these instructions.

Other less-used but important health-related documents include an *instrument of anatomical gift* and a *personal statement.* There is a persistent problem of an undersupply of organs for transplantation. Gifts of organs and tissue are facilitated by the Uniform Anatomical Gift Act (1968, revised in 1987), now adopted in every state. A simple wallet card may suffice, but lawyers sometimes fail to raise this possibility with their clients. A *personal statement* is simply an expression, based on no particular statutory regime, of personal desires with respect to one or more aspects of medical treatment.

One effect of the heightened sensitivity to advance directive issues after the *Cruzan* case was the enactment by Congress of the Patient Self-Determination Act (1990), 42 U.S.C. §1396A. It requires that all hospitals and health care providers receiving federal aid (Medicare, Medicaid and the like, thus most health care institutions) provide upon admissions written information to adult patients about their rights under state law to make decisions about medical care.

An instrument may combine aspects of a living will and a durable power of attorney for health care, and perhaps even some other concepts. See the Uniform Health-Care Decisions Act (1993), infra. There is evidence that advance directives, at least living wills, are not always followed by health care providers. Most statutes provide protection to the health care provider who relies on the directive but no penalty for one who ignores it.

What if there is no directive? Some states have *family consent statutes*, also known as surrogate decisionmaking statutes, that track the living will statute. They provide that if a terminally ill person has not yet executed a living will or a durable power of attorney for health care and has no chance of recovery, he may be removed from medical treatment if the attending physician and the designated family members concur in the decision to do so. The patient may avoid the statute by a document executed while competent.

In the absence of an applicable statute, several courts have authorized patients' or (if the patient is disabled) family members' instructions to be implemented in these matters. Cf. Matter of Guardianship of L.W., 482 N.W.2d 60 (Wis. 1992) (guardian may consent to withdrawal of life-sustaining treatment for patient in persistent vegetative state). Applicable statutes or cases must be carefully examined for details, limitations, and formal and substantive requirements. In the absence of satisfactory evidence of the patient's actual desires, some courts have used a *substituted judgment* approach, whereby a proxy (e.g., a guardian or family member) is to determine what the patient would have wanted to be done under the circumstances. Other courts have used a *best interests* approach, under which the proxy decides what is in the patient's best interests.

Several states have enacted the Uniform Health-Care Decisions Act (1993), designed to replace existing living will, health care power of attorney, and family consent statutes. It acknowledges the right of a competent individual to decide all aspects of health care in all circumstances, including an unrestricted right to decline or discontinue health care even if death may ensue. Any or all health care decisions may be delegated to an agent. Absent an agent or guardian, the Act provides comprehensive authority for family and close friends (a "surrogate") to make health care decisions. It also offers a comprehensive optional form. The Act permits immediately effective powers, but absent an express provision the authority of an agent commences only upon a determination of incapacity.

The Act minimizes execution requirements. An instruction may be either written or oral. A power of attorney for health care must be written and signed, but need not be witnessed or acknowledged (although good practice suggests witnessing or acknowledgments). The Act validates out-of-state directives that conform to its minimal execution requirements.

Advance directives may be revoked in any manner that communicates that intent, but designation of an agent may be revoked only by a signed writing or by personally informing the health care provider. Divorce or separation revokes any designation of the spouse as agent. Copies of advance directives have the same effect as originals, and the later of conflicting directives controls.

The Act elaborately seeks to ensure that an individual's decisions will be effective. An agent or surrogate must make health care decisions in accordance with the individual's known instructions, and otherwise in accordance with her best interest and any personal values known to the agent or surrogate. Unless otherwise authorized by court order, guardians must comply with the ward's instructions or agent's decisions. In addition, health care providers (subject to risk of financial sanctions) must comply with the instructions of the patient or health care agent unless medically ineffective or contrary to generally accepted health care standards. The provider may also refuse to comply for reasons of conscience, but then must assist in transferring the patient to a provider that is willing to comply. Unless related to the principal, an owner, operator, or employee of a residential health care institution at which the principal is recieving care is disqualified from acting as agent or surrogate. Individuals with a direct interest in the patient's care may petition a court to enjoin or order the carrying out of a health care decision or to grant other equitable relief.[7]

7. In the first case interpreting the Act, Protection & Advocacy Sys., Inc. v. Presbyterian Healthcare Servs., 989 P.2d 890 (N.M. App. 1999), a 51-year-old man with moderate mental retardation had suffered a stroke, was hospitalized, and was kept alive by artificial nutrition and hydration; he appeared to be unconscious and unable to communicate, After a few weeks, his mother (his court-appointed limited guardian for twenty years) was appointed as his surrogate under the Act. She decided to terminate nutrition and hydration. A not-for-profit corporation (P&A), authorized by federal law to pursue legal remedies on behalf of developmentally disabled persons, sought to intervene in opposition to the decision. The court found that the mother's instruction was a "health care decision" within the language of the Act and within the surrogate's authority, observing that the Act reflects concerns about excessive judicial involvement and focuses primarily on decisionmaking procedures rather than on the content of decisions. The court held that P&A lacked standing to intervene under the Act. (The patient apparently died before the artificial nutrition and hydration were withdrawn.)

The new Act provides a useful roadmap for reviewing your state's law on health care decisions. Consider the following under the law of your state:

(1) In the absence of a health care directive, may the family make ordinary or extraordinary health care decisions for an incapacitated person?

(2) May a competent principal make the authority of the health care agent immediately effective?

(3) If there is a statutory form of health care power of attorney, must the principal use or follow that form?

(4) Must the signed statutory form be witnessed? Notarized?

(5) Must an attorney-in-fact or surrogate be designated in writing?

(6) May an advance directive be revoked orally?

(7) Are health care providers liable if they do not comply with an advance directive?

(8) In the event of conflict between a guardian and a health care agent, whose decision controls?

(9) Are any persons barred from acting as agent or surrogate?

(10) Are out-of-state directives recognized?

(11) If a patient is neither terminally ill nor in a persistent vegetative state, may a living will or health care agent authorize termination of life-sustaining treatment?

What is death? The usual definition is the irreversible cessation of circulatory and respiratory functions, but UCP §1-107 permits an earlier finding of death upon "irreversible cessation of all functions of the entire brain, including the brain stem" (i.e., brain dead). See also similar definition in 1980 Uniform Determination of Death Act. This definition permits the removal of organs for transplanation while circulatory and respiratory functions are being maintained.

Physician-assisted death. In recent years, the right-to-die focus has shifted to physician-assisted death for the terminally ill. So far two Supreme Court decisions have rejected due process and equal protection challenges to state laws banning physician-assisted death. Washington v. Glucksberg, 521 U.S. 702 (1997); Vacco v. Quill, 521 U.S. 793 (1997). How does one distinguish withdrawal of artificial life support from assisted death?[8]

---

8. On most of these matters, see generally 1 F. Collin, J. Lombard, Jr., A. Moses & H. Spitler, Durable Powers of Attorney and Health Care Directives (3d ed. 1994); E. Scoles, Acceleration of Death of the Terminally Ill with Physician Assistance, 5 Elder Law J. 213 (1997); C. Pratt, Efforts to Legalize Physician Assisted Suicide in New York, Washington and Oregon, 77 Ore. L. Rev. 1027 (1998).

2. Property Management

Special property issues facing the elderly include financing health care, considering Medicare, Medicaid, and long-term care insurance; management of property through conservatorship,[9] custodianship, agency, or trust; adequacy of income, whether from Social Security, Supplemental Security Income (SSI), veteran's benefits, or employee benefit plans; and meeting housing needs, such as in continuing care communities or by subsidized housing or reverse mortgages. Age discrimination, neglect, or elder abuse may factor into the equation. The focus here is on the most common document, the durable power of attorney, the utility of which is not confined to the elderly. Subsequent materials will consider conservatorships, custodianships, and trusts (Chapter 9) and transfers to qualify for Medicaid (Chapter 13).

The power of attorney concepts for property are similar to those described above for health care powers. Since the power of attorney is an agency relationship, it is customarily made *durable* so the attorney-in-fact's authority will survive the principal's incapacity. Uniform Probate Code §§5-501 to 5-505 include the 1979 Uniform Durable Power of Attorney Act. Section 5-501 sanctions the durable power concept and emphasizes that the power does not have to become effective immediately; §5-502 provides that the durable power is not affected by lapse of time, disability, or incapacity. Under §5-503 the agent is accountable to a subsequently appointed conservator, but the conservator's appointment does not revoke the power of attorney. Section 5-504 changes the common law rule by providing that death of the principal does not revoke the authority until the agent receives notice of the death; and §5-505 attempts to solve the problem of third parties who make unreasonable demands for proof of the continuing validity of powers, providing for proof of continuance by affidavit. All states have statutes authorizing durable powers for property management. A freestanding Uniform Statutory Form Power of Attorney Act (1988) provides a fill-in-the-blanks durable power. Many states have similar fill-in-the-blanks or short-form power statutes, which spell out through statutory detail the effects of the various choices of agents' powers.

---

9. A person who is appointed by a court to manage the estate of an incapacitated (i.e., incompetent) person is variously known as a *guardian of the estate* or a *guardian of the property* or, in Uniform Probate Code and Uniform Trust Code terminology, a *conservator*. As you will see in Chapter 9 on trusts, guardianship is not a good alternative for property management. Recall from the discussion of testamentary guardianships earlier in this chapter that a person who is appointed by a court or will to make decisions regarding the care, health, and welfare of an incapacitated person is a *guardian of the person*. A *general guardian* is a person who is appointed to manage both the estate and person of the incapacitated person. A parent is the *natural guardian* of the minor child's person, but absent court appointment has no legal authority over the minor child's estate.

Property powers of attorney may be created either to take effect immediately or to take effect upon some event in the future, typically the principal's incapacity (*springing* power). Drafters differ in their approach to springing powers. Some prefer to spell out the triggering event for the power, such as the principal's incapacity, which may inadvertently require a judicial determination of incapacity (which few would desire), unless third persons (e.g., physicians or family) are designated to determine incapacity. Others prefer to draft a *presently effective* power and place it in the hands of a trusted advisor (e.g., the attorney) for delivery to the agent at the appropriate time. If you were the attorney, would you want this responsibility?

Although you have yet to study the trust relationship, when you reach that material (Chapter 9) you should compare it, especially the revocable trust, to the power of attorney relationship. What is the effect of the death of the trustee or agent before the creator? Is the law governing the fiduciary's powers and duties well developed? Does each relationship provide adequate safeguards against abuse? Despite anecdotal reports of abuse by agents under durable powers, limited experience and data so far reveal little of the nature and extent of these problems. See C. Dessin, Acting as Agent Under a Financial Durable Power of Attorney: An Unscripted Role, 75 Neb. L. Rev. 574 (1996).

The typical statutory form or lawyer drawn durable power grants the attorney-in-fact broad powers. Nevertheless, some third parties are reluctant to deal with agents and may have exacting requirements about the kind of language needed to do what the agent seeks to do, and about the freshness of the instrument. Only a few statutes attempt to compel third parties to honor durable powers. Bar committees and thus legislatures have also been reluctant to deal with the possible duty of an attorney-in-fact to act in the event of the principal's incapacity. If action is taken, certainly the agent must act with due care, but is there a duty to act at all? Though it seems evident that *some* affirmative duty should exist — even if only to notify interested persons of the need for a substitute agent or conservator — there remains considerable doubt on this matter. Because statutory authority and legal duties are generally default law, yielding to the express terms of the power, the lawyer should anticipate these matters and, in other respects, tailor the instrument to the client's needs and objectives.

For lawyers whose clients are reluctant to proceed with the creation of fully funded revocable inter vivos trusts, a *standby trust* offer a means of dealing with the lack of well-defined power and duties of attorneys-in-fact. Under this arrangement a revocable trust instrument is executed, but it receives nominal or no funding. The client also executes a durable power for property, granting the agent authority to transfer the client's assets to the trustee. Later the client or, if the client loses capacity, the agent, can fund the trust. The trustee will then manage the property for the benefit of the client and other beneficiaries, with all the certainty and safeguards of traditional trust law. The arrangement is normally backed by a pour-over will (see section D of Chapter 12) that leaves any assets remaining in the settlor's name to the trustee of a standby or other revocable trust to be combined and coordinated with the postdeath plan.

Aside from the possible creation of a funded or standby revocable trust, counsel should consider the extent to which an attorney-in-fact under a durable power should, or can, be authorized to perform estate planning for an incompetent principal. The Restatement (Third) of Property: Wills and Other Donative Transfers §8.1, cmt. *i* (Preliminary Draft no. 7, 1999) states: "The agent (attorney-in-fact) may make inter vivos donative transfers of the mentally incompetent person's property to the extent allowed by the terms of the power of attorney. Unless authorized by statute, it is not legally possible, however, for the power of attorney to authorize the agent to make a will for the mentally incompetent person." Why not? If not, may an attorney-in-fact establish, or be expressly authorized to establish, a revocable trust as a will substitute? To modify an *existing* revocable trust? To create or modify other will substitutes? See flexibility and rationale provided in Restatement (Third) of Trusts §11(5), cmt. *f,* and Reporter's Notes thereto.

The case that follows is representative of issues and illustrative of evolving principles in an important area of estate planning, especially for dying individuals who are under legal disability. Counterpart issues arise under modern conservatorship legislation, durable power of attorney statutes, and evolving common law principles.

MATTER OF JONES
379 Mass. 826, 401 N.E.2d 351 (1980)

ABRAMS, J. . . .

This case is before us on the reservation and report by a Probate Court judge of certain questions of law arising from a petition by a conservator for approval of an estate plan for his ward under G.L. c. 201 §38.[10] . . .

---

10. General Laws c. 201 §38, as amended through St. 1976, c. 515 §§25-26, reads as follows : . . .

> The probate court, upon the petition of a conservator or guardian, other than the guardian of a minor, and after such notice to all other persons interested as it directs, may authorize such conservator or guardian to take such action, or to apply such funds as are not required for the ward's own maintenance and support, in such fashion as the court shall approve being in keeping with the ward's wishes so far as they can be ascertained and as designed to minimize inso-

The proposed estate plan principally consists of the creation of two inter vivos trusts: one, a revocable trust, providing for distributions to or for the ward during her lifetime from income or principal as necessary or advisable for her heath and comfortable support, with reminders [sic] to certain charitable organizations; the other, an irrevocable charitable remainder trust which provides for an annual payment to or for the ward, during her lifetime, of an amount equal to nine percent of the fair market value of the trust assets, determined annually, with remainders to certain charitable organizations.

As we read the judge's reservation and report, three basic questions are presented: (1) whether the creation of revocable and irrevocable trusts specifying the ultimate distribution of trust assets to other than the estate of the ward is the same as making a will; (2) whether G.L. c. 201, §38, as amended through St. 1976, c. 515, §§25-26, authorizes making a will; and (3) whether the proposed estate plan could be approved in a proceeding in which the Commonwealth's representation may have been neutralized by a conflict of interest, and in which the ward's next of kin were represented by a guardian ad litem for unborn and unascertained heirs. Although not reported by the judge, the parties have also asked whether an estate plan which is found to be in accordance "with the ward's wishes so far as they can be ascertained, although speculative" complies with the requirements of G.L. c. 201, §38.

We hold that the proposed estate plan is not a testamentary disposition and is authorized by the statute. Furthermore, we find no infirmities arising from representation of the next of kin by the guardian ad

---

far as possible current or prospective state or federal income, estate and inheritance taxes, and to provide for gifts to such charities, relatives and friends as would be likely recipients of donations from the ward.

Such action or application of funds may include but shall not be limited to the making of gifts, to the conveyance or release of the ward's contingent and expectant interests in property including marital property rights and any right of survivorship incident to joint tenancy or tenancy by the entirety, to the exercise or release of his powers as donee of a power of appointment, the making of contracts, the creation of revocable or irrevocable trusts of property of the ward's estate which may extend beyond his disability or life, the exercise of options of the ward to purchase securities or other property, the exercise of his rights to elect options and to change beneficiaries under insurance and annuity policies, and the surrendering of policies for their cash value, the exercise of his right to an elective share in the estate of his deceased spouse, and the renunciation or disclaimer of any interest acquired by testate or intestate succession or by inter-vivos transfer. . . .

Gifts may be for the benefit of prospective legatees, devisees or heirs apparent of the ward or may be made to individuals or charities in which the ward is believed to have an interest. The conservator or guardian shall . . . not, however, be required to include as a beneficiary any person whom he has reason to believe would be excluded by the ward.

litem or of the Commonwealth by the Attorney General. Finally, we uphold the judge's finding that the estate plan complied with the statutory criteria. . . .

Wanda W. Jones is [90 years old,] mentally incompetent and unlikely to recover sufficient mental capacity to execute a will. [In about 1959,] the conservator became the ward's attorney [and] alleges that to the best of his knowledge, the ward has no husband, issue or other kindred. On her death, [it appears] her estate would pass by escheat to the Commonwealth. The conservator believes his ward never made a will.

In 1968, the conservator drafted a will for the ward under which virtually all her estate would pass to various charities, but she never executed the will. Although the ward refused to sign the will, she never repudiated the dispositive provisions. The ward claimed that she had consulted with unidentified advisors who told her that the will was not properly drafted. There was no evidence as to the ward's competency at the time she refused to sign the will. Although the will was presented to the ward for signature only once, the conservator reminded her of it on several occasions, the last being either in 1974 or 1975. The conservator also testified that the ward made small annual gifts, shown in her tax returns, to the charities named in the draft will; however, no individual charitable gift exceeded seventy-five dollars.

Prior to the hearing on the petition, the judge ordered that notice be given to the Attorney General of the Commonwealth and the Department of Mental Health, and both filed acknowledgments of notice. The Attorney General's acknowledgment stated that the Attorney General assented to the allowance of the petition. Pursuant to the court order, a notice of the proceedings was also publishd in a major Boston newspaper once a week for three successive weeks. . . .

The court below appointed a guardian ad litem for the ward. The guardian ad litem's report opposed the allowance of the petition in so far as the petition proposed that ninety percent of the ward's property be transferred to the irrevocable trust and only ten percent to the revocable trust. The guardian ad litem for the ward recommended that fifty percent of the ward's assets should be transferred to the revocable trust in order to assure the availability of sufficient funds; including principal, for the ward's needs. With that modification, the guardian ad litem for the ward recommended approval of the estate plan. . . .

The court also appointed a guardian ad litem to represent the interests of the unascertained heirs. He filed a report opposing . . . the petition. . . .

The [probate] judge made the following findings. First, the proposed estate plan, modifed as recommended by the guardian ad litem of the ward, includes adequate provision for the ward's own maintenance and support. Second, the estate plan is in keeping with the ward's wishes, so far as they can be ascertained, although speculative, and provides gifts to such charities, relatives and friends as would be likely recipients of donations from the ward. Third, the estate plan is designed to minimize in so far as possible current and prospective State and Federal income, estate, and gift taxes.

The judge indicated that the plan might be substantially similar to making a will, and therefore not authorized by the statute, G.L. c. 201, §38. We do not think the proposed estate plan is objectionable for that reason.

In Strange v. Powers, 358 Mass. 126, 260 N.E.2d 704 (1970), we held that the prior version of §38 did not empower the court to approve the making of a will because that would involve "an unduly broad construction of the term 'estate plan.'" Id. at 133, 260 N.E.2d at 710. We think that the amendment to §38 still does not permit a conservator to execute a will on behalf of his ward. The 1976 amendment to §38 was largely drawn from §5-408(3) of the Uniform Probate Code, which specifically prohibits the conservator from making a will. . . .

. . . [O]ur case law does not support the view that the creation of an inter vivos trust is "the making of a will." . . .

The fact that a certain disposition of property, here the creation of revocable and irrevocable trusts with charitable remainders, is virtually a substitute for a will is unobjectionable. . . .

The amendment to §38 grants the ward through a conservator most of the powers that the ward would have if the ward were of full capacity. "[T]he purpose is to carry out the ward's wishes so far as they can be ascertained, and not solely for tax minimization. . . ." Young, Probate Reform, 18 Boston B.J. No. 3, 7, 19 (1974). . . . There is no reason not to allow the ward to use inter vivos trusts in estate planning. Given the legislative policy to carry out "the ward's wishes so far as they can be ascertained," the arguments of the guardian ad litem for unborn and unascertained heirs to the effect that authorization of the estate plan in question will undermine the well-established laws of this Commonwealth governing devolution and descent of property are not persuasive. . . .

The guardian ad litem for persons unborn and unascertained complains that the notice by publication ordered by the court is constitutionally inadequate. We disagree.

Due process permits notice by publication, for "[t]hose beneficiaries . . . whose interests or whereabouts could not with due diligence be ascertained." Mullane v. Central Hanover Bank & Trust Co., 339 U.S. 306, 317 (1950). Notice by publication is prohibited "with respect to a person whose name and address are known or very easily ascertainable." Schroeder v. City of N.Y., 371 U.S. 208, 212-213 (1962). . . .

The record is clear that the conservator had no actual knowledge of the existence of any heirs, and furthermore, that he possessed no information which, if pursued, might have led to the discovery of kindred. . . .

Finally, it is by no means clear that the heirs' participation in the proceedings would affect the outcome. General Laws, c. 201, §38, authorizes the conservator to exclude "as beneficiary any person whom he has reason to believe would be excluded by the ward." Thus, the interest of any person whose existence was unknown to the ward or whose existence she denied in conversations with family and friends is very attenuated. There is no evidence that the ward ever intended to benefit her next of kin.

Under similar provisions of North Carolina law, the North Carolina Supreme Court said persons who had a contingent or potential financial interest in the death of the incompetent are limited "to present [ing] to the court facts which will assist the court in determining whether the action proposed by the trustee is detrimental to the estate of the incompetent or whether the incompetent, if then competent, would probably not act as the trustee proposes to act." In re Kenan, 262 N.C. 627, 638 (1964). In the case at bar, the judge had appointed a guardian ad litem for persons unborn and unascertained, who very ably represented their interests. As a result, it is hard to imagine what further arguments could be presented on their behalf. . . .

The remaining question briefed by the parties is whether an estate plan which is found to accord "with the ward's wishes, so far as they can be ascertained, although speculative" complies with the requirements of G.L. c. 201, §38. . . . In a petition under §38, the conservator is not required to prove that a proposed estate plan conforms with absolute certainty to the ward's wishes. . . .

The guardian ad litem for unascertained heirs argues that the estate plan sought to be established is substantially based on the terms of a will the ward refused to sign. While this is true, the evidence indicated that the will was drafted according to her instructions, instructions which were never changed. The ward continued to make modest annual gifts to the same charitable institutions named in the will. Where the record is not clear as to the ward's wishes, §38 creates a presumption that the ward would favor a reduction in estate taxes and a distribution of her estate to achieve that goal. "[T]here is [no] evidence of any settled intention of the incompetent, formed while sane, to the contrary." Estate of Christiansen, 248 Cal. App. 2d 398, 423, 56 Cal. Rptr. 505, 521 (1967). . . .

Since specific questions were reserved and reported, we remand the case to the Probate Court for consideration of the proposed estate plan in light of this opinion.

The power of the agent under a durable power to make lifetime gifts for estate planning purposes deserves careful attention. As you will see later, there are often significant federal transfer tax advantages to making lifetime gifts, provided the principal is not thereby impoverished. The IRS has upset some of the gifts, however, by claiming that under state law the authority to make gifts under a durable power must be express, and that nothing in the instrument grants such authority. As a result, many states have amended their durable power statutes to specifically grant agents the power to make gifts. This power must be carefully considered, for example, to prevent the agent from abusing it. Statutory forms may require the principal to indicate whether the power is to include gifts to the agent; or they may limit the gifts by annual amount or to those made "in accordance with the principal's personal history of making or joining in the making of lifetime gifts." E.g., N.C. Gen. Stat. §32A-2(14) & (15). See generally F. Collin, J. Lombard, Jr., A. Moses & H. Spitler, Durable Powers of Attorney and Health Care Directives (3d ed. 1994); D. English, The UPC and the New Durable Powers, 27 Real Prop. Prob. & Tr. J. 333 (1992).

3. Professional Responsibility

PROBLEM

3-J. For many years, L represented E, who is now elderly, and advised her on estate planning and other matters. Observing that E's recent behavior has seemed erratic and inconsistent with her prior behavior, L is concerned that E may be incompetent and unable to manage her affairs. L learned that E had recently undergone a medical examination, contacted her physician, and obtained his opinion of E's competency, and concludes that E is incompetent and needs the assistance of a guardian and conservator. Did the physician or L breach any duty in exchanging information? May L disclose the medical information to E's family or seek the appointment of a guardian and conservator for E? Must L seek the appointment? May L disclose the medical information to the court?

AMERICAN BAR ASSOCIATION, MODEL RULES OF PROFESSIONAL CONDUCT
(1983)

Rule 1.14[11]   *Client Under a Disability.*

(a) When a client's ability to make adequately considered decisions in connection with the representation is impaired, whether because of

---

11. ABA Model Rule 1.6 (set out in Chapter 8, section G, infra) imposes a duty of confidentiality except as "impliedly authorized to carry out the representation" (with other exceptions of no relevance here).

minority, mental disability or for some other reason, the lawyer shall, as far as reasonably possible, maintain a normal client-lawyer relationship with the client.

(b) A lawyer may seek the appointment of a guardian or take other protective action with respect to a client only when the lawyer reasonably believes that the client cannot adequately act in the client's own interest.

Comment

The normal client-lawyer relationship is based on the assumption that the client, when properly advised and assisted, is capable of making decisions about important matters. When the client is a minor or suffers from a mental disorder or disability, however, maintaining the ordinary client-lawyer relationship may not be possible in all respects. In particular, an incapacitated person may have no power to make legally binding decisions. Nevertheless, a client lacking legal competence often has the ability to understand, deliberate upon, and reach conclusions about matters affecting the client's own well-being. Furthermore, to an increasing extent the law recognizes intermediate degrees of competence. For example, children as young as five or six years of age, and certainly those of ten or twelve, are regarded as having opinions that are entitled to weight in legal proceedings concerning their custody. So also, it is recognized that some persons of advanced age can be quite capable of handling routine financial matters while needing special legal protection concerning major transactions.

The fact that a client suffers a disability does not diminish the lawyer's obligation to treat the client with attention and respect. If the person has no guardian or legal representative, the lawyer often must act as de facto guardian. Even if the person does have a legal representative, the lawyer should as far as possible accord the represented person the status of client, particularly in maintaining communication.

If a legal representative has already been appointed for the client, the lawyer should ordinarily look to the representative for decisions on behalf of the client. If a legal representative has not been appointed, the lawyer should see to such an appointment where it would serve the client's best interests. Thus, if a disabled client has substantial property that should be sold for the client's benefit, effective completion of the transaction ordinarily requires appointment of a legal representative. In many circumstances, however, appointment of a legal representative may be expensive or traumatic for the client. Evaluation of these considerations is a matter of professional judgment on the lawyer's part.

If the lawyer represents the guardian as distinct from the ward, and is aware that the guardian is acting adversely to the ward's interest, the lawyer may have an obligation to prevent or rectify the guardian's misconduct. See Rule 1.2(d).

AMERICAN BAR ASSOCIATION, FORMAL OPINION 96-404
(1996)

. . . Because the relationship of client and lawyer is one of principal and agent, principles of agency law might operate to suspend or terminate the lawyer's authority to act when a client becomes incompetent, and the client's disability may prevent the lawyer from fulfilling the lawyer's obligations to the client unless a guardian is appointed or some other protective action is taken to aid the lawyer in the effective representation of the client. . . .

When a client is unable to act adequately in his own interest, a lawyer may take appropriate protective action including seeking the appointment of a guardian. The laywer may consult with diagnosticians and others, including family members, in assessing the client's capacity and for guidance about the appropriate protective action. The action taken should be the least restrictive of the client's autonomy that will yet adequately protect the client in connection with the representation. Withdrawal from representation of a client who becomes incompetent is disfavored, even if ethically permissible under the circumstances. The lawyer may recommend or support the appointment of a particular person or other entity as guardian, even if the person or entity will likely hire the lawyer to represent it in the guardianship, provided the lawyer has made reasonable inquiry as to the suggested guardian's fitness, discloses the self-interest in the matter and obtains the court's permission to proceed. In all aspects of the proceeding, the lawyer's duty of candor to the court requires disclosure of pertinent facts, including the client's view of the proceedings.

CALIFORNIA FORMAL OPINION 1989-112
(1989)

The Committee has been asked to opine on the ethical propriety of an attorney instituting conservatorship proceedings on behalf of a client but against that client's express wishes. For purposes of this discussion, it is assumed that the client's behavior patterns and dealings with his attorney over a significant period of time have convinced the attorney that the client requires a conservator. It is also assumed that other lawyers in the community would have a reasonable basis for concluding the same. . . .

It is the opinion of the Committee that instituting a conservatorship on these facts is barred . . . and furthermore creates a conflict that may not be waivable. The attorney must maintain the client's confidence and trust, even though the attorney will be torn between a duty to pursue the client's desires (including protecting his secrets) and a duty to represent his interest, which may best be served by instituting a conservatorship. While the attorney will not fall below the level of competence required by simply continuing the representation for which he or she was retained and avoiding filing a conservatorship for the client, withdrawal may be appropriate or even mandatory if the client's conduct impedes the attorney's ability to effectively carry out the duties for which he or she was retained.

Note also ABA Informal Opinion 89-1530 (1989), in which the committee concluded that, in order for the lawyer to function under Model Rule 1.14, "disclosure by the lawyer of information relating to the representation to the extent necessary to serve the best interests of the client reasonably believed to be disabled is impliedly authorized within the meaning of Model Role 1.6. Thus the inquirer may consult a physician concerning the suspected disability."

See also American College of Trust and Estate Counsel Foundation, ACTEC Commentaries on the Model Rules of Professional Conduct 216-231 (3d ed. 1999); Fordham Law Review, Proceedings of the Conference on Ethical Issues in Representing Older Clients, 62 Fordham L. Rev. 961-1583 (1994); Powell & Link, The Sense of a Client: Confidentiality Issues in Representing the Elderly, id. at 1197, 1233-1238; Restatement (Third) of the Law Governing Lawyers §35 & cmt. *e*, §43 cmt. *e*, §113 & §119 cmt. *f* (Proposed Final Draft No. 1, 1996). Compare the general rule of agency law that the insanity or incompetence of a principal terminates an agent's authority.

4

Execution of Wills

Although the original English Statute of Wills, 32 Hen. VIII, c. 1, was enacted in 1540, modern developments date from the English Statute of Frauds, 29 Car. II. c. 3 (1677), which prescribed certain formal requirements for wills disposing of land. It also imposed formalities on wills disposing of personalty, but these did not include a requirement of an attested writing. Over a century and a half later the English Wills Act, 7 Wm. IV & I Vict., c. 26 (1837), was enacted and set out formalities required for writings disposing of personal as well as real property on death. Legislation in all of the states of the United States followed the general pattern of the Statute of Frauds except that all American statutes, like the English Wills Act, treat real and personal property alike so far as attested wills are concerned. Certain formal details of the Wills Act also have commonly been put into wills acts in this country. Wholly new formalities have occasionally been introduced by American acts; for example, a requirement of publication is found in some statutes, requiring the testator to declare to the witnesses that the instrument is the testator's will.

STATUTE OF FRAUDS
29 Car. II, c. 3, §V (1677)

[A]ll devises and bequests of any lands or tenements, devisable either by force of the statute of wills, or by this statute, or by force of the custom of Kent, or the custom of any borough, or any other particular custom, shall be in writing, and signed by the party so devising the same, or by some other person in his presence and by his express directions, and shall be attested and subscribed in the presence of the said devisor by three or four credible witnesses, or else they shall be utterly void of non effect. . . .

WILLS ACT
7 Wm. IV & 1 Vict., c. 26, §IX (1837)

[N]o will shall be valid unless it shall be in Writing and Executed in manner hereinafter mentioned; (that is to say) it shall be signed at the

Foot or End thereof by the Testator, or by some other Person in his Presence and by his Direction; and such signature shall be made or acknowledged by the Testator in the Presence of Two or More Witnesses present at the same Time, and such Witnesses shall attest and shall subscribe the Will in the Presence of the Testator, but no Form of Attestation shall be necessary. . . .

MODEL PROBATE CODE

§47. *Execution.*   The execution of a will, other than a holographic or nuncupative will, must be by the signature of the testator and of at least two witnesses as follows:

(a) *Testator.* The testator shall signify to the attesting witnesses that the instrument is his will and either

(1) Himself sign, or

(2) Acknowledge his signature already made, or

(3) At his direction and in his presence have someone else sign his name for him, and

(4) In any of the above cases the act must be done in the presence of two or more attesting witnesses.

(b) *Witnesses.* The attesting witnesses must sign

(1) In the presence of the testator, and

(2) In the presence of each other.

UNIFORM PROBATE CODE

§2-502.   *Execution; Witnessed Wills; Holographic Wills.*

(a) Except as provided in subsection (b) and in Sections 2-503, 2-506, and 2-513, a will must be:

(1) in writing;

(2) signed by the testator or in the testator's name by some other individual in the testator's conscious presence and by the testator's direction; and

(3) signed by at least two individuals, each of whom signed within a reasonable time after he [or she] witnessed either the signing of the will as described in paragraph (2) or the testator's acknowledgment of that signature or acknowledgment of the will.

(b) A will that does not comply with subsection (a) is valid as a holographic will, whether or not witnessed, if the signature and material portions of the document are in the testator's handwriting.

(c) Intent that the document constitute the testator's will can be established by extrinsic evidence, including, for holographic wills, portions of the document that are not in the testator's handwriting.

§2-503. *Harmless Error.* Although a document or writing added upon a document was not executed in compliance with Section 2-502, the document or writing is treated as if it had been executed in compliance with that section if the proponent of the document or writing establishes by clear and convincing evidence that the decedent intended the document or writing to constitute (i) the decedent's will, (ii) a partial or complete revocation of the will, (iii) an addition to or an alteration of the will, or (iv) a partial or complete revival of his or her formerly revoked will or of a formerly revoked portion of the will.

alterations thereof

§2-504. *Self-Proved Will.*

(a) A will may be simultaneously executed, attested, and made self-proved, by acknowledgment thereof by the testator and affidavits of the witnesses, each made before an officer authorized to administer oaths under the laws of the state in which execution occurs and evidenced by the officer's certificate, under official seal, in substantially the following form: [omitted] . . .

(b) An attested will may be made self-proved at any time after its execution by the acknowledgment thereof by the testator and the affidavits of the witnesses, each made before an officer authorized to administer oaths under the laws of the state in which the acknowledgment occurs and evidenced by the officer's certificate, under the official seal, attached or annexed to the will in substantially the following form: [omitted] . . .

(c) A signature affixed to a self-proving affidavit attached to a will is considered a signature affixed to the will, if necessary to prove the will's due execution.

§2-506. *Choice of Law as to Execution.* A written will is valid if executed in compliance with Section 2-502 or 2-503 or if its execution complies with the law at the time of execution of the place where the will is executed, or of the law of the place where at the time of execution or at the time of death the testator is domiciled, has a place of abode, or is a national.

GULLIVER AND TILSON, CLASSIFICATION OF GRATUITOUS TRANSFERS
51 Yale L.J. 1, 2-5 (1941)

[U]nder a legal system recognizing the individualistic institution of private property and granting to the owner the power to determine his successors in ownership, the general philosophy of the courts should favor giving effect to an intentional exercise of that power. This is commonplace enough, but it needs constant emphasis, for it may be obscured or neglected in inordinate preoccupation with detail or dialectic. A court absorbed in purely doctrinal arguments may lose sight of the important and desirable objective of sanctioning what the transferor wanted to do, even though it is convinced that he wanted to do it.

If this objective is primary, the requirements of execution, which concern only the form of the transfer — what the transferor or others must do to make it legally effective — seem justifiable only as implements for its accomplishment, and should be so interpreted by the courts in these cases. They surely should not be revered as ends in themselves, enthroning formality over frustrated intent. Why do these requirements exist and what functions may they usefully perform? . . . The fact that our judicial agencies are remote from the actual or fictitious occurrences relied on by the various claimants to the property, and so must accept second hand information, perhaps ambiguous, perhaps innocently misleading, perhaps deliberately falsified, seems to furnish the chief justification for requirements of transfer beyond evidence of oral statements of intent.

In the first place, the court needs to be convinced that the statements of the transferor were deliberately intended to effectuate a transfer. People are often careless in conversation and in informal writings. Even if the witnesses are entirely truthful and accurate, what is the court to conclude from testimony showing only that a father once stated that he wanted to give certain bonds to his son, John? Does this remark indicate finality of intention to transfer, or rambling meditation about some possible future disposition? Perhaps he meant that he would like to give the bonds to John later if John turned out to be a respectable and industrious citizen, or perhaps that he would like to give them to John but could not because of his greater obligations to some other person. Possibly, the remark was inadvertent, or made in jest. Or suppose that the evidence shows, without more, that a writing containing dispositive language was found among the papers of the deceased at the time of his death? Does this demonstrate a deliberate transfer, or was it merely a tentative draft of some contemplated instrument, or perhaps random scribbling? Neither case would amount to an effective transfer, under the generally prevailing law. The court is far removed from the context of the statements, and the situation is so charged with uncertainty that even a judgment of probabilities is hazardous. Casual language, whether oral or written, is not intended to be legally operative, however appropriate its purely verbal content may be for that purpose. Dispositive effect should not be given to statements which were not intended to have that effect. The formalities of transfer therefore generally require the performance of some ceremonial for the purpose of impressing the transferor with the significance of his statements and thus justifying the court in reaching the conclusion, if the ceremonial is performed, that they were deliberately intended to be operative. This purpose of the requirements of transfer may conveniently be termed their ritual function.

Secondly, the requirements of transfer may increase the reliability of the proof presented to the court. The extent to which the quantity and effect of available evidence should be restricted by qualitative standards is, of course, a controversial matter. Perhaps any and all evidence should be freely admitted in reliance on such safeguards as cross-examination, the oath, the proficiency of handwriting experts, and the discriminating judgment of courts and juries. On the other hand, the inaccuracies of oral testimony owing to lapse of memory, misinterpretation of the statements of others, and the more or less unconscious coloring of recollection in the light of the personal interest of the witness or of those with whom he is friendly, are very prevalent; and the possibilities of perjury and forgery cannot be disregarded. These difficulties are entitled to especially serious consideration in prescribing requirements for gratuitous transfers, because the issue of the validity of the transfer is almost always raised after the alleged transferor is dead, and therefore the main actor is usually unavailable to testify, or to clarify or contradict other evidence concerning his all-important intention. At any rate, whatever the ideal solution may be, it seems quite clear that the existing requirements of transfer emphasize the purpose of supplying satisfactory evidence to the court. This purpose may conveniently be termed their evidentiary function.

Thirdly, some of the requirements of the statutes of wills have the stated prophylactic purpose of safeguarding the testator, at the time of the execution of the will, against undue influence or other forms of imposition. As indicated below, the value of this objective and the extent of its accomplishment are both doubtful. It may conveniently be termed the protective function.

The Functions of the Statutes of Wills . . .

Ritual Function. Compliance with the total combination of requirements for the execution of formal attested wills has a marked ritual value, since the general ceremonial precludes the possibility that the testator was acting in a casual or haphazard fashion. The ritual function is also specifically emphasized in individual requirements. . . . [For example, the] signature tends to show that the instrument was finally adopted by the testator as his will and to militate against the inference that the writing was merely a preliminary draft. . . .

Evidentiary Function. . . . [O]ral testimony [tends to be] even less trustworthy than it is in cases where there is some likelihood of the adverse party being an available witness and where the statute of limitations compels relative promptness in litigation. . . . [Thus, the] requirement that this type of will be attested obviously has great evidentiary significance. . . . Of course, this purpose is not accomplished in every case, since all of the attesting witnesses may become unavailable to testify because of death or some other reason, and their unavailability will not defeat the probate of a will. . . .

Protective Function. Some of the requirements of the statutes of wills have the objective . . . of protecting the testator against imposition at the time of execution. . . . [But] any requirement of transfer should have a clearly demonstrable affirmative value since it always presents the possibility of invalidating perfectly genuine and equitable transfers that fail to comply with it. . . . Why should there be a differentiation between inter vivos and testamentary transfers in this respect? The purely legal elements of the two categories suggest no justification. . . .

See also Lon L. Fuller, Consideration and Form, 41 Colum. L. Rev. 799 (1941); Lloyd Bonfield, Reforming the Requirements for Due Execution of Wills: Some Guidance From the Past, 70 Tul. L. Rev. 1893 (1996).

A. *The Formal Requirements of Attested Wills*

Although a lawyer must know the formal requirements for executing a will in his or her state, this is by no means sufficient. A will may come before the courts of other states and be judged on the basis of the requirements of a foreign law. To avoid invalidity, or at least costly litigation, an attorney drafting a will should assume that it may be offered for probate anywhere. Some states have less liberal rules on foreign execution than those prescribed in Uniform Probate Code §2-506, supra. The traditional rule, now modified in about half the states by validating statutes like UPC §2-506, has been that the validity of a will was judged by the law of the situs as to immovables and by the law of the decedent's domicile at death as to movables. A lawyer should develop a simple set of execution procedures that will satisfy the laws of all states. For an eight-step procedure that assures "maximum acceptability" in all the states see Restatement (Second) of Property: Donative Transfers §33.1, cmt *c*. (1992). See also section 5 below. The Uniform International Wills Act, promulgated in 1977 to facilitate implementation in this country of the Washington Convention of 1973, has been adopted in a number of states; compliance with special form and execution requirements, which must be certified by a qualified attorney or other "authorized person," assures validity as to form in all countries joining the convention. See Kearney, The International Wills Convention, 18 Intl. Law. 613 (1984). The Hague Convention on the Law Applicable to Succession to the Estates of Deceased Persons (1988) provides a choice of law guide for international estates in signatory nations.

Courts generally require at least substantial compliance with each of the formalities prescribed by statute, but they do not impose additional formal requirements, nor do they object to unnecessary formalities.

1.   Requirement of a Writing

The requirement of a writing may be satisfied by typing or by any reasonably permanent writing. Valid wills have been written in foreign languages, handwritten in pencil, and even scratched on hard surfaces.

2.   Testator's Signature and Acknowledgment

The universal requirement that a formal will contain the testator's signature is accompanied in nearly all statutes by express provision allowing someone else to sign for him. The proxy signing by another person must be in the presence of the testator, and generally it must be at his "request" or "direction." In a number of states it is provided that the person so signing for the testator shall also sign his own name, but some of these statutes make it clear that failure to do so does not render the will invalid.

By judicial decision or statutory provision a signature is generally sufficient if it is the complete act intended by the testator to serve as his signature. Thus, a will may validly be "signed" by initials, mark, or nickname; and partial and even typewritten names have been held to satisfy the requirement, although certainly a lawyer should not encourage his client to become a test case.

Many American statutes follow the English Statute of Frauds in not specifying where the signature of the testator is to be placed on the will, but many others, following the English Wills Act, do require that the will be "subscribed," signed "at the end," or so signed "as to make it manifest that the name is intended as a signature."

Statutes vary on the relationship of the witnessing process to the testator's act of authentication. Some require the testator to sign in the presence of the witnesses. As an alternative to his signing in their presence, many statutes allow the testator to acknowledge his signature to the witnesses, and still others provide that he may simply acknowledge in their presence that the instrument is his will. Some statutes require that the witnesses sign in the presence of the testator. What, do you suppose, is the reason for this requirement? The law of some states requires the act (signing or acknowledgment) to be done in the presence of all of the witnesses at one time, rather than permitting it to be done before each witness separately. A substantial minority of states require "publication" by the testator, although most states impose no such requirement. Publication is the testator's declaration to the witnesses that the instrument is his will; this does not require that the contents of the will be disclosed.

As might be expected, numerous problems arise in connection with the requirements relating to the testator's signature. In re Winter's Will, 277 A.D. 24, 98 N.Y.S.2d 312 (1950), is illustrative, invalidating a will because the testator's signature was followed by a clause appointing executors. New York Estates, Powers and Trust Law §3-2.1 still requires wills to be signed at the end but now provides that matter following the testator's signature at execution shall not invalidate matter preceding the signature, unless "in the discretion of the surrogate [the will without the omitted matter] is so incomplete as not to be readily comprehensible [or] would subvert the testator's general plan for the disposition or administration of his estate." See also Clark v. National Bank of Commerce, 802 S.W.2d 452 (Ark. 1991) (addition was "nondispositive," so document was "signed at the end").

Potter v. Ritchardson, 360 Mo. 661, 230 S.W.2d 672 (1950), noted in 16 Mo. L. Rev. 79 (1951), involved the question of whether a statute that does not expressly require signing at the end is satisfied by a signature elsewhere in the instrument. The court referred to the classic rule in Lemayne v. Stanley, 3 Lev. 1 (1691), that where a statute "does not appoint where a will shall be signed, . . . a signing in any part is sufficient." The court stated "that the ultimate fact is whether a testator's name was written with an intention . . . to make the document effective as his will; that the location of the name is an evidentiary fact relating to that intent; and that the name was not 'subscribed' is not conclusive that the required intent was not present." 360 Mo. at 668, 230 S.W.2d at 676.

In re Pulvermacher's Will, 305 N.Y. 378, 113 N.E.2d 525 (1953), involved a statute requiring a testator to "declare the instrument . . . to be his last will and testament" at the time he signs or acknowledges it. The witnesses emphatically testified that they were not informed, nor did they know, that the instrument was intended to be a will and that they could not read any part of the instrument as it was placed before them. The court, in denying the instrument probate, stated: "While 'no particular form of words' is necessary, the courts have held the minimum statutory prescription to be some kind of communication that the instrument . . . is testamentary in character. . . . 'It must appear that, as between the testator and the witnesses there was some meeting of the minds' . . . derived, one court has written, 'from some unequivocal act or saying of the testator.' " The court added that "[t]he reason for requiring publication is twofold: first, to furnish proof that the testator is under no misapprehension . . . as to the nature and identity of the instrument, and second, to impress upon the witnesses the fact that, since the document is a will, they are expected 'to remember what occurred at its execution and be ready to vouch for its validity in court'" and that ["i]f the result appears to be harsh . . . such consequence is compelled by legislative pronouncement." 305 N.Y. at 383, 385, 113 N.E.2d at 526, 528. Would the *Pulvermacher* case have been decided differently if the witnesses had known from another source, such as the testator's lawyer, that the instrument was intended as a will?

3. Attestation by Witnesses

Formal or attested wills must be witnessed by two or more persons in every state except Vermont, which requires three. In Vermont and many other states, however, a written will that was signed by the testator is valid if it complies with the law of the place of execution or if it complies with the law of the place where the testator is domiciled at the time of death. Most of these validating (or "borrowing") statutes have provisions similar to UPC §2-506.

Whether by express statutory provision or by judicial interpretation of the attestation requirement, witnesses are required to sign the will in all but one state. In that state apparently a will may be "proved" by the witnesses without their having signed it. Estate of Dawson, 277 Pa. 168, 120 A. 828 (1923). The signatures of witnesses may have to be "subscribed," but in many states a will is valid regardless of the location of the signatures. Some statutes also require that the witnesses be "requested" to act as such by the testator. A witness is occasionally directed by statute to write the witness's place of residence, but failure to do so is not fatal to the validity of the will.

The attestation requirement strongly suggests that the witnesses not sign the will until after the testator has performed the act of authentication to which they are to attest. It has frequently been held, however, that the order of signing is not critical as long as the testator and the witnesses all sign as a part of a "single transaction." The opposite conclusion has also been reached. Clearly, if an essential witness signs first and the testator signs on another occasion, the attestation is fatally defective.

Litigation has often resulted from the common requirement that the witnesses sign "in the presence" of the testator or from the occasional

requirement that they sign in the presence of each other.[1] For an argument that witnesses should not be required at all, see James Lindgren,
Abolishing the Attestation Requirement for Wills, 68 N.C. L. Rev. 541
(1990).

CUNNINGHAM v. CUNNINGHAM
80 Minn. 180, 83 N.W. 58 (1900)

[The applicable statute required attested wills to be "in writing, and *statute*
signed at the end thereof, by the testator . . . and attested and subscribed in his presence, by two or more competent witnesses."]

COLLINS, J.

[T]he only question in issue on this appeal is whether the alleged
will was attested and subscribed in the presence of the testator, Cun- *issue*
ningham, by the two persons whose names were attached as witnesses.
The testator had been confined to his room for some time. It was a
small bedroom with a doorway which led into a large room upon the
north, the head of his bed being near the partition between the two.
There was no door, but a curtain had been hung in the doorway, which
was drawn to the west side at the time in question. Three days before
the signing the testator sent for his attending physician, Dr. Adams, to
come to his house, and draw his will. At the same time he sent for Dr.
Dugan to be present as a witness. The draft of a will made by Dr. Adams
as dictated by Cunningham was unsatisfactory, and both of the physicians went away. They were again summoned November 12, 1899, and
went to the house in the forenoon. Dr. Adams drew a new will as instructed by Cunningham, the latter remaining in his bed. When the
document was fully written, both men stepped to the bedside, and Dr.

---

1. The statute in Estate of Peters, 107 N.J. 263, 526 A.2d 1005 (1987), simply required
that a will be "signed by at least two persons who witnessed either (a) the signing or
(b) the testator's acknowledgment of" the signing of the will. The atypically flexible
opinion stated:

> There may indeed be cases in which the affixation of witnesses' signatures
> after the testator's death would be reasonable, particularly if the witnesses were
> somehow precluded from signing before the testator died. This case, however,
> does not present such a situation. Even if one accepts the testimony that the
> emotional trauma of the moment prevented the witnesses from signing the will
> while the testator was hospitalized, there is simply no adequate explanation of
> the failure to have obtained their signatures in the extended fifteen-month inter-
> val prior to his death. If the Legislature's retention of the signing requirement
> is to be at all effectual, signing must occur within a reasonable time of observation
> to assure that the signature attests to what was actually observed, and not to what
> is vaguely remembered.

Compare revised UPC §2-502(a)(3), supra.

Adams read it to the sick man. Having heard it read through, Cunningham pronounced it satisfactory, and then signed it. When so signing he sat on the edge of the bed, and used as a place for the paper a large book which was lying upon a chair. Drs. Adams and Dugan were then requested to sign as witnesses. For this purpose they stepped to a table in the sitting room, which stood about 10 feet from where Cunningham sat, and there affixed their signatures. The time occupied in so signing did not exceed two minutes, and immediately thereafter Dr. Adams returned to the bedside with the paper. Dr. Dugan stepped to the doorway, about three feet from Cunningham, and then Adams showed the signatures of the witnesses to him as he sat on the edge of the bed. Cunningham took the paper, looked it over, and said, in effect, that it was all right. From where he sat he could not see the table which was used by the witnesses when signing. He could have seen it by moving two or three feet. While they were signing he leaned forward, and inquired if the instrument needed a revenue stamp, to which Dr. Adams replied that he did not know, the reply being audible to Cunningham. These are the salient and controlling facts found by the court below, on which it based an ultimate finding that the instrument so witnessed was attested and subscribed in the presence of the testator, and then affirmed the order of the probate court admitting it to probate as the last will and testament of the deceased.

The appellants (contestants below) insist that the attestation and subscription by the witnesses was insufficient, because Mr. Cunningham did not and could not see the witnesses subscribe their names from where he sat, and their contention has an abundance of authority in support of it from jurisdictions in which statutes copied from the English law on the subject, and exactly like our own, are in force. The rule laid down in these authorities is that the attesting and subscribing by the witnesses must take place within the testator's range of vision, so that he may see the act of subscribing, if he wishes, without a material change in his position; and that he must be mentally observant of the act while in progress. . . . In brief, the courts have, almost without exception, construed a statute requiring an attestation of a will to be in the "presence" of the testator to mean that there must not only be a consciousness on the part of the latter as to the act of the witnesses while it is being performed, but a contiguity of persons, with an opportunity for the testator to see the actual subscribing of the names of the witnesses, if he chooses, without any material change of position on his part. And yet. . . it has been held almost universally that an attestation in the same room with the testator is good, without regard to intervening objects which might or did intercept the view; and also that an attestation outside the room or place where the testator sat or lay is valid if actually within his range of vision. And no court seems to have doubted that a man unable to see at all could properly make a will under the statute, if the witnesses attested within his "conscious" presence, whatever that means. . . . Take the case at bar. The testator sat on the edge of his bed when the witnesses signed at the table in the adjoining room, a few feet distant, and within easy sound of his voice. If he could have seen them by leaning forward, the authorities in favor of upholding the will are abundant. Physically he was capable of stepping two or three feet forward, and from this point the witnesses would have been within his range of vision. It is extremely difficult to distinguish between the two cases, and yet it has been done again and again in applying the rule. . . . To say that this was not a sufficient attestation within a statute which requires such attestation to be in the "presence" of the testator, simply because the witnesses actually signed a few feet out of the range of his vision, is to be extremely technical without the slightest reason for being so. The signing was within the sound of the testator's voice; he knew what was being done; the act occupied not more than two minutes; the witnesses returned at once to the testator; their signatures were pointed out to him; he took the instrument into his own hands, looked it over, and pronounced it satisfactory. The whole affair, from the time he signed the will himself down to and including his expression of approval, was a single and entire transaction; and no narrow construction of this statute, even if it has met the approval of the courts, should be allowed to stand in the way of right and justice, or be permitted to defeat a testator's disposition of his own property. . . .

In Matter of Will of Jefferson, 349 So. 2d 1032 (Miss. 1977), the intended will was signed by the testator and then by his lawyer, as an attesting witness, who thereafter returned alone to his office and requested his partner to serve as a second witness. After telephoning the testator and receiving confirmation that the instrument was his will, the partner subscribed as requested. The chancellor concluded "that the telephone call constituted presence" and admitted the will to probate. On appeal, the court reversed for the partner's failure to attest "in the presence of the testator" and observed that the purposes of the presence requirement include avoidance of "imposition or fraud on either the testator or the witnesses by substitution of another will in place of that signed by the testator; and that the witnesses will be reasonably satisfied that the testator is of sound and disposing mind and capable of making a will."

Many cases have rejected the so-called conscious presence test, requiring that the decedent be able to see the writing by the witness if the decedent had looked. In re Beggan's Will, 68 N.J. Eq. 572, 59 A. 874 (1905), involved facts generally similar to *Cunningham*. Because of the conflicting evidence on the question of actual visibility had the testator turned in the proper direction, which the court considered to be the test, the evidence failed to rebut the presumption that a signing is out of the decedent's presence if it occurs in a room other than that where the decedent was at the time. Denial of probate was affirmed.

denial of probate affirmed

PROBLEM

4-A. John Deaux was survived by his son and daughter. He left a net estate of $60,000. The following is his will:

> I, John Deaux, hereby make my last will. I bequeath $40,000 to my daughter, Doris, and leave the residue of my estate to my son, Sidney. I appoint Beth Green as my executor.
>
> *John Deaux*
>
> *Henry White*, Witness [daughter Doris's husband]
> ~~Robert Black~~, Witness [a neighbor]
> *Beth Green*, Witness [nominated as executor]

Is the will valid? If so, how much do Doris and Sidney receive? Consider these questions under Model Probate Code §46(b), below, under your local statute, and under the Uniform Probate Code. Would it matter if Black had predeceased Deaux? If Black had not been a witness?

American statutes generally require witnesses to be "competent," while in a number of states the term *credible* is used. In general these requirements are the same regardless of the terminology used, since a witness need not actually be worthy of belief but must be competent to testify in court.

Courts have generally construed the requirement of competence as relating to the time of execution, and this rule has been codified in nearly half the states. Thus, if an essential witness is competent when the will is executed but subsequently becomes incompetent, the will is valid. In support of this position it has been observed that witnesses who are competent at the time of execution serve the statutory purpose of preventing fraud at that critical time and also that to relate the requirement of competence to the time of probate would prevent the proving of a will whenever an essential witness "should become insane, infamous, or otherwise disqualified, which would be opposed to the current of the authorities; for I take it to be well settled that in such cases the handwriting of the witnesses may be proved, and the will be thereupon allowed." Bruce v. Shuler, 108 Va. 670, 673-674, 62 S.E. 973, 975 (1908), quoting Hawes v. Humphrey, 26 Mass. 350 (1830).

At common law an interested party was incompetent as a witness, and therefore a legatee was not competent to serve as an attesting witness. If an essential witness to a will had an economic interest in it, probate was denied. Generally today, however, interested parties are competent to testify in court. Does this change in procedural law alter the meaning of *competence,* or does this requirement still have the meaning it had under the Statute of Frauds or under the state legislation when it was enacted? Different conclusions have been reached. The usual rule is represented by Hudson v. Flood, 28 Del. (5 Boyce) 450, 94 A. 760 (1915), where the wills statute required "two or more credible witnesses" and the evidence statute provided that no person was incompetent to "testify in a civil action" because he is "interested" in the litigation. The court concluded that, absent specific language dealing with wills, under the enabling act "persons taking an interest under a will are competent witnesses to prove its execution." A dissenting opinion argued that the Wills Act is unaffected by a change in the procedural law and that a beneficiary is still not a "credible" attesting witness.

In many states today this question has been resolved by legislation requiring "disinterested" witnesses. Under a few of these statutes, probate may still be denied if an essential witness would benefit from the will. Under some others, the gift to the interested witness is void but the will can be probated. Others are basically like Model Probate Code §46(b): "No will is invalidated because attested by an interested witness; but an interested witness shall, unless the will is also attested by two disinterested witnesses forfeit so much of the provisions therein made for him as in the aggregate exceeds in value, as of the date of the testator's death, what he would have received had the testator died intestate." See also Estate of Morea, 645 N.Y.S.2d 1022 (1996). (Do you see why some variations of the Model Probate Code language refer to "what he would have received but for the will in question"?)

Uniform Probate Code §2-505 does not require witnesses to be disinterested and eliminates the forfeiture of benefits by interested witnesses, concluding that sufficient other safeguards exist in this area to permit doing away with penalties for the rare, innocent use of beneficiary-witnesses in home-drawn wills. See Hairelson v. Estate of Franks, 720 N.E.2d 989 (Ohio App. 1998), applying Ohio's validating (or "borrowing") rule to uphold *in its entirety* a will executed in Florida, where (unlike Ohio) the no-forfeiture rule applies to interested witnesses. Yale, Witnessing Wills and Losing Legacies, 100 Law Q. Rev. 453 (1984), notes that the English Wills Act provides that "the witness who subscribes a will (and his or her spouse) loses any benefit conferred by that will," and the article adds: "The attestation is good but the legacy is bad. . . . In Ross v. Caunters [1980] Ch. 297, the solicitor who forgot found himself making good the lost legacy." In criticizing the rule, the author quotes the comment to UPC §2-505, above, which states that a substantial gift to a witness "would itself be a suspicious circumstance, and the gift could be challenged on grounds of undue influence."

A rare American statute that, like the English act, goes so far as to void not only a gift to an essential witness but also one to the spouse of such a witness was held constitutional in Dorfman v. Allen, 386 Mass. 136, 434 N.E.2d 1012 (1982), as a reasonable means of achieving the objectives of lessening the likelihood of perjury by a subscribing witness and of protecting the testator from undue pressure or influence. See also N.C. Gen. Stat. §31-10.

PROBLEMS

4-B. *D* died with a will that was witnessed by *A* and *X*. The will devises $100,000 to *A*, $100,000 to *B*, and residue to *C*. *A*, *B*, and *C* are *D*'s only issue, and *X* is a friend. All four survive *D*, whose wife predeceased him. The applicable statute simply voids gifts to interested witnesses. What disposition of *D*'s $500,000 estate?

4-C. The will of *D*, a widow, was witnessed by her friend, *F*, and her only children, *A* and *B*. The will provides: "Blackacre to *A* and all my personal property to *B*." *A*, who has two children, disclaims his devise. The statute provides: "A gift to an interested witness is void unless there are at least two other disinterested witnesses." What result? See Estate of Parsons, 163 Cal. Rptr. 70 (Cal. App. 1980).

4. Testamentary Intent

Probably the most fundamental requisite of a valid will is testamentary intent. There is normally a rather forceful inference that an instrument that has been executed with proper formalities, appearing on its face to be a will, was executed with the intent that it operate as a will. Some courts have refused to receive evidence of a contrary intent, while others have permitted such an instrument to be denied probate if shown by clear and convincing evidence to have been executed as a joke or otherwise without testamentary intent.

If it appears by the terms of an instrument that the decedent intended it to operate as his will only under certain circumstances, this intent will be given effect. A few statutes specifically authorize conditional wills. Ordinarily, intent to condition cannot be shown by extrinsic evidence. Even the terms of the will itself are generally interpreted as a mere statement of motive rather than condition if they admit of such interpretation. See, e.g., Estate of Taylor, 119 Cal. App. 2d 574, 259 P.2d 1014 (1953), in which the words "in case Davie Jones gets me out in the South Pacific" were held not to condition the will but only to explain why it was made.

PROBLEM

4-D. About a year before her death *D* filled out a standard deed form by which she might convey her farm, Blackacre, to her son, *S*. *D* had two friends sign next to her signature as witnesses, but it is conceded by all that she did not deliver the instrument to *S* and that there was no effective gift. *S* offers the instrument for probate as *D*'s will, *D* being otherwise intestate. Can *S* succeed under your local statute? Under any of the common statutes prescribing the formal requirements of an attested will? See, e.g., In re Estate of Ike, 7 Ohio App. 3d 87, 454 N.E.2d 577 (1982) (excluding extrinsic evidence of testamentary intent where none is shown by the document in question). *Intent,* *not*

5. Attestation Clauses and Procedures for Execution

Although not required by the law of any state, it is desirable to include an attestation clause, certified by the witnesses and reciting the events of execution and other facts to which it is desired that the witnesses attest:

SPECIMEN ATTESTATION CLAUSE

The foregoing instrument (consisting of seven pages including this one) was on July 1, 1999, signed and declared to be his last will by John C. Doe in our joint presence; we, at his request and in his presence and in the presence of each other, subscribe our names as witnesses to the execution of this will, declaring our belief that he is of sound mind and memory and under no constraint or undue influence whatsoever.

_____ residing at _____
_____ residing at _____
_____ residing at _____

Compliance with the formalities recited in this clause would result in a valid execution of an attested will in any state, and the inclusion of an attestation clause generally creates a presumption of the events recited, at least if the signatures of the witnesses are identified. Although the presumption is, of course, a rebuttable one, the clause is useful for many purposes, as the following problem may suggest. The clause also serves as a guide for execution, facilitating compliance with required formalities that might otherwise be overlooked. Statutes that provide for self-proved wills go beyond the recognition of attestation clauses and use affidavits to preserve evidence. See UPC §2-504, supra.

PROBLEM

4-E. At *D*'s death a document is offered for probate as her will. Below her signature are the signatures of three witnesses. In the following situations, consider the will's admissibility to probate if it does and then if it does not contain an attestation clause.

(a) All witnesses to the execution predecease *D*, but their signatures are identified. *admissible is attestation cl.*

(b) One of the witnesses surviving *D* is *X*, a long-time secretary of *D*'s lawyer. She recognizes her own signature but understandably cannot recall this particular execution, its circumstances, or the identity of *D*.

(c) The only other surviving witness is *Y*, who also identifies his signature but denies that he actually saw or heard *D* sign or acknowledge the will or signature, and *Y* testifies that *D* lacked testamentary capacity. Compare Estate of Velie, 183 N.E.2d 515 (Ill. 1962) with Fitch v. Maesch, 690 N.E.2d 350 (Ind. App. 1998).

MATTER OF ESTATE OF COLLINS
60 N.Y.2d 466, 458 N.E.2d 797 (1983)

KAYE, J. . . .

Appellant [offered for probate a 1977 will containing] a printed form attestation clause, beneath which appeared the signatures of two witnesses, Mary Pedaci and Richard H. Skellen. . . .

Appellant produced five witnesses: the two attesting witnesses, a physician [who testified to the good mental and physical condition of the testatrix, his patient] and two persons supporting the authenticity of [her] signature on the will. Mary Pedaci testified that, in January, 1977, she was the assistant manager of the Ransomville branch of Marine Midland Bank. Shown the 1977 will, she identified both her signature and that of Richard Skellen, but had no recollection of the circumstances surrounding the execution of the will. Richard Skellen, the branch manager, testified that he recalled signing his name to the document, that both of the attesting witnesses "were right there," and that he had in his mind "an older lady." Skellen, who had witnessed a number of wills previously, further recalled that he had read the heading on the instrument, "Will and Testament." Otherwise he had no recollection of the event. . . .

Respondents moved to dismiss appellant's petition to probate the 1977 will on the ground that he had not presented prima facie proof of due execution. The court denied the motion, holding that the formalities of due execution can be established despite the imperfect memory of both attesting witnesses. Relying on the attestation clause, the genuineness of the three signatures, and the testimony of the physician, the court found that the 1977 will had been duly executed. The Appellate Division, 91 A.D.2d 1167, 459 N.Y.S.2d 132, reversed and dismissed appellant's petition, holding that [N.Y. Surr. Ct. Proc. Act

§1405] (subd. 3) requires that at least one of the attesting witnesses confirm that the testatrix signed the instrument and intended it to be her will.

This appeal focuses on the import of SCPA 1405 (subd. 3), which ... provides: "Where an attesting witness has forgotten the occurrence or testifies against the execution of the will and at least 1 other attesting witness has been examined the will may be admitted to probate upon the testimony of the other witness or witnesses and such other facts as would be sufficient to prove the will." The issue of first impression which is presented is whether, given SCPA 1405 (subd. 3), a will may be admitted to probate where *both* attesting witnesses do not recollect the events surrounding execution of the will but the court is otherwise satisfied from all of the evidence that the will was properly executed. We conclude that the Legislature by this section did not intend the radical departure from prior statutory and decisional law urged upon us by respondents, and that a will may be admitted to probate even if both attesting witnesses cannot recall the will execution. . . .

For more than a century, the courts have consistently interpreted [predecessor] section 142 of the Surrogate's Court Act and its forbears to permit probate even where the attesting witnesses did not recall the event or testified against the will. "If the attestation clause is full and the signatures genuine and the circumstances corroborative of due execution, and no evidence disproving a compliance in any particular, the presumption may be lawfully indulged that all the provisions of the statute were complied with, although the witnesses are unable to recollect the execution or what took place at the time." (Matter of Kellum, 52 N.Y. 517, 519). . . .

To be sure, the testimony of the attesting witnesses is entitled to great weight. . . . A failure of their recollection intensifies the care and vigilance that must be exercised in examining the remaining evidence. . . .

Here, given the evidence, we cannot say that the Surrogate erred as a matter of law in admitting the will to probate. Accordingly, the order of the Appellate Division should be reversed and the case remitted to that court for a determination of whether the evidence is sufficient to prove the will.

B. *Unattested Wills*

There are several forms of wills that do not involve the formal safeguard of attested wills and that are likely to be used by persons unfamiliar with the law, particularly in haste or in ignorance. Of course, such wills have at least one basic requirement in common with attested wills: testamentary intent. Even where unattested wills are not authorized, they may be admitted to probate under validating statutes if certain minimum requirements are met, typically a writing signed by the testator.

1. Holographic Wills

entirely in testator's handwriting

The statutes of most states authorize holographic wills, which are entirely in the handwriting of the testator. See generally Richard H. Helmholz, The Origin of Holographic Wills in English Law, 15 Legal History 97 (1994). These statutes require no witnesses, although a few states still impose special requirements concerning the place of keeping or the method of proving such wills, and a number still require holographic wills to be dated. Why this last requirement, which does not exist in any state for attested wills?

no will dated

Although all holographic wills must be signed, only a few states require signing at the end. Even where attested wills must be subscribed, a signature anywhere on a holographic will is generally sufficient if it adequately appears that the testator's name was written with an intent that it serve as a signature.

name written w/ intent = signature

PROBLEMS

For purposes of the following recurring types of holographic will problems, assume a representative statute providing: "A holographic will is one that is entirely written, dated, and signed by the hand of the testator himself, and is subject to no other formality and need not be witnessed." Consider also how these problems might be resolved under the UPC and under your local statute if holographic wills are authorized.

4-F. Can the instrument below be probated as the will of Abner Hatfield, who wrote all of it by hand except the italicized portions, which were printed parts of a will form?

LAST WILL AND TESTAMENT

Know all Men by These Presents: That I, Abner Hatfield *of* Piney Creek, *North Carolina, do make and publish this as my Last Will and Testament, in manner and form following.*

(1) To Ginny McCoy $5,000.
(2) My house and grounds to Clem Hatfield, because part of it's his anyway.
(3) To Maw all the rest of what's mine.

Signed this 13 day of June 1973, Abner Hatfield

Contrast In re Will of Parsons, 207 N.C. 584, 178 S.E. 78 (1934), and Succession of Burke, 365 So. 2d 858 (La. App. 1978), with Estate of Thorn, 183 Cal. 512, 192 P. 19 (1920). In Estate of Brenner, 76 Cal. App. 4th 1298, 91 Cal. Rptr. 2d 149 (1999), an instrument was upheld as a valid holographic will even though most of its distributive provisions were in a photocopy of an earlier, handwritten, three-page list of dispositions; about a year before he died the testator made alterations in the list, wrote "This is my will" and "my [prior] will . . . is void." and added his name, all handwritten in ink on the photocopy. (The state does not require a date.) The court noted that the trial judge's contrary view was "not implausible" but concluded that the document, circumstances, and "uncontroverted extrinsic evidence" satisfied all statutory policies concerning the testator's intent and the document's authenticity.

4-G. The following handwritten paper is offered for probate. Should it be admitted? *not signed*

3-10-90

I, Mary Jones, declare it to be my will that on my death all of my property shall go to my husband.

4-H. In In re Estate of Richardson, 94 Cal. 63, 29 P. 484 (1892), the following handwritten letter was offered for probate by the deceased's sister, Nina.[2] Should it have been probated?

Los Angeles, Cal.
October 1, 1890

Nina:

I wrote you yesterday, hastily; answer my letter at once; I want to know everything about mother, and all about you, — your children. I have reached the point of perfect independence, pecuniarily. My health is probably ruined, and I want to anticipate possibilities. You and your chil-

---

2. A recent entry in the collection of regularly troublesome letter-will cases, typically presenting only issues of testamentary intent, is Estate of Kuralt, 981 P.2d 771 (Mont. 1999), involving a handwritten letter from the renowned journalist Charles Kuralt to his "intimate companion . . . for nearly 30 years," apparently wholly unknown to his wife and family who were the beneficiaries of his will, already probated in New York. Sixteen days before his death, Kuralt wrote (on the day of his unexpected hospitalization) in relevant part: "Something is terribly wrong with me and they can't figure out what. . . . I'll keep you informed. [¶] I'll have the lawyer visit the hospital to insure you inherit the rest of the place in MT if it comes to that." The Montana Supreme Court concluded that "the district Court improperly resolved a disputed issue of material fact on a summary judgment motion," after having allowed extrinsic evidence on the question of testamentary intent, "when it should have instead deferred the determination of that issue to the trier of fact at trial." Despite the trial judge's conclusion that the letter itself was not intended to serve as a will (i.e., codicil) because Kuralt "was contemplating a separate testamentary instrument not yet in existence," or maybe even a nontestamentary "sale" arrangement of which there was evidence, the supreme court stated that "it is far from certain that [another instrument] is the result Mr. Kuralt meant by the letter."

[Handwritten margin notes: "intent to serve as a will..."; "no intent to serve as sign b/c signed brother"; "not signature or initials or nickname"; "not intent of signature"]

dren get everything. Your boy I want given the best of educations. I would like him to go to Harvard. I would like to have him a lawyer. Don't bring him up a prejudiced southerner, but teach honor, — make it dearer than life, and he must, with the blood in his veins, be a man. Write me. As soon as I possibly can, I will be in Savannah.

Brother

In 1981 a cassette recording was admitted to probate as a holographic will in Alameda County, California, without contest and based on testimony identifying the decedent's voice. Cf. Jodi Granite Nash, A Videowill: Safe and Sure, 70 A.B.A. J. 86, 87 (Oct. 1984):

> Lawyers diligently and awkwardly compile evidence of due execution where a contest is anticipated. . . . [These procedures are often] unnecessarily difficult. One neat, compact, videocassette can contain not only the testator's dispositive scheme but also all the evidence required for it to be probated. . . . There have not yet been any cases reported of a videotape being offered for probate as a will, although the value of videotaping a will execution ceremony as supplementary evidence is being recognized. . . . It is time for the law to take the next logical step. The videotape will (or "videowill") can easily fulfill the statutory requirements, protect the testator and preserve evidence better than a written will.

The article makes an interesting case for new legislation taking this "next logical step" — but certainly not for setting the client up as a test case under existing statutes.

ESTATE OF REED
672 P.2d 829 (Wyo. 1983)

BROWN, J. . . .

The issue here is whether a tape recorded statement made by a deceased person can be admitted to probate as a will. We agree with the trial court that it cannot. . . .

[Handwritten margin note: "tape recorded stmt cannot be probated"]

According to appellant the major difference in magnetic tape recording and hand print is that in the former writing is done through voice print while the latter is done through hand print. Appellant reasons, therefore, that in this age of advanced electronics and circuitry the tape recorder should be a method of "writing" which conforms with the holographic will statute. . . .

Where the language of a statute is plain and unambiguous and conveys a clear and definite meaning, . . . the court has no right to look for and impose another meaning. . . . We are not aware of any definition of "handwriting" [or] any authority . . . that "handwriting" includes voice prints. It seems to be stating the obvious that a voice print is not handwriting; therefore, the requirement that a holographic will be "entirely in the handwriting of the testator" has not been met in this case.

Appellant directs our attention to §2-6-105, W.S. 1977 [and to cases to the effect that] "the intention of the testator as expressed in his will controls the legal effect of his disposition. . . ."

Section 2-6-105, supra, and the cases cited by appellant are pertinent to construction of language within a valid will. . . . We can not consider the testator's intent to justify the probate of a recorded statement that is not a valid will. An otherwise deficient will can not be made valid by showing the intent of the testator. . . .

Our attention is directed to Darley v. Ward, 28 Cal. 3d 257, 168 Cal. Rptr. 481, 617 P.2d 1113, 1115 (1980), where the court stated: "Tape recordings, properly authenticated, are admissable as 'writings.' " . . . Darley was not a will or probate case. . . .

There is [also] no indication that the definition of "handwritings" contained in Rule 1001(1) [Wyoming Rules of Evidence] was designed to change the plain meaning of handwriting in the holographic will statute. Were we to expand or modify the meaning of handwriting as required in the holographic will statute to include a tape recording, we would judicially amend the statute. This we refuse to do.

Affirmed.

2.   Oral Wills

Oral wills are of two basic types: the nuncupative will, under which a person in peril of death may dispose of limited amounts of personal property; and soldiers' and sailors' wills, which also are typically restricted to personal property and sometimes to limited amounts thereof. A number of states make some provision for the probate of oral wills of one or both of these varieties.

Nuncupative wills generally must be made during the testator's last illness, before a certain number of witnesses at least one of whom was requested to bear witness to the will, and in the testator's home or place of death. In addition, some requirement usually exists regarding the time within which the will must be probated and regarding prompt reduction of the will to writing.

The typical requirements that soldiers be "in actual military service" and that sailors be "at sea" have been, as might be expected, sources of litigation in soldiers' and sailors' wills. See Page on Wills §§20.13 et seq. (Bowe-Parker rev. 1970).

C.   *Commentary and Comparison*

JOHN H. LANGBEIN, THE CRUMBLING OF THE WILLS ACT: AUSTRALIANS POINT THE WAY
65 A.B.A. J. 1192, 1193-1195 (1979)

. . . In dealing with . . . botched wills, Anglo-American courts have produced one of the cruelest chapters that survives in the common law. Purely technical violations that could in no way cast doubt on the authenticity or finality of wills are held to invalidate the offending instrument. . . .

Because this rule of strict compliance with wills act formalities produces results so harsh, sympathetic courts have . . . enabled themselves to find literal compliance in cases that in fact show defective compliance. . . .

Not surprisingly, this state of affairs has provoked discontent. Recent law school casebooks in the field have prodded students to ask whether the purposes of wills acts compel the result inflicted under the rule of literal compliance. The Uniform Probate Code of 1969 has made a contribution toward reducing the dimensions of the problem — at least, in those states that have enacted it — by reducing the number and complexity of formalities. . . . Signature and attestation are still required, but the rules about placement of signatures and presence of witnesses have been abolished. . . .

Finally, the rule of literal compliance came under direct attack. Within a period of a few months in 1974-1975, literature appeared in England, Australia, and the United States calling for the development of a purposive standard for evaluating defectively executed wills. . . .

[In 1974], the official Law Reform Committee of South Australia took up the theme. . . . "It would seem to us that in all cases where there is a technical failure to comply with the wills act, there should be a power given to the court or a judge to declare that the will in question is a good and valid testamentary document if he is satisfied that the document does in fact represent the last will and testament of the testator." . . .

My position was summed up in the title [of my article at 88 Harv. L. Rev. 489 (1975)]: there should be a rule of "Substantial Compliance with the Wills Act" that would permit the proponents of a defectively executed will to prove that the particular defect was harmless to the purposes of the wills act. Drawing on a rich literature devoted to identifying the functions of the Wills Act formalities, I made the following points:

1. The Wills Act is meant to assure the implementation of the decedent's testamentary intention at a time when, by definition, he can no longer be on hand to express himself. The requirement of written

terms forces the testator to leave permanent evidence of the substance of his wishes. Signature and attestation provide evidence of the genuineness of the instrument, and they caution the testator about the seriousness and finality of his act. The attestation ceremony also has a protective function: disinterested observers are supposed to prevent crooks from deceiving or coercing the testator into making a disposition that does not represent his true intentions. Taken together, these evidentiary, cautionary and protective functions serve another end, the channeling function: when the formalities are complied with, they make testation routine, eliminate contest, reduce probate costs and court time, and facilitate good estate planning.

2. When, however, there has been a mechanical blunder, it does not follow that the purposes of the wills act have been disserved. For example, if the statute calls for signature "at the end" in order to prevent subsequent interpolation, it does not follow that in every case of misplaced signature such an event has occurred.

3. Accordingly, we could obtain all of the benefits of the wills act formal system and yet avoid so much of the hardship if the presumption of invalidity applied to defectively executed wills were reduced from a conclusive to a rebuttable one. The proponents of a defectively executed will should be allowed to prove what they are now entitled to presume in cases of due execution — that the will in question expresses the decedent's true testamentary intent. They should be allowed to prove that the defect is harmless to the purposes of the formality. In the example just given of a misplaced signature, the proponents would bear the burden of proving (on an ordinary preponderance-of-proof standard) that subsequent interpolation had not occurred.

4. Although the substantial compliance rule is a litigation doctrine, it should not be feared as a potential litigation breeder. Precisely because it is a litigation rule, it would have no place in professional estate planning. Nor would the substantial compliance doctrine attract the reliance of amateurs. Every incentive for due execution would remain, for no testator sets out to throw his estate into litigation.

Other factors would operate to diminish the incidence and the difficulty of the litigation that would arise under the substantial compliance rule. By no means would every defectively executed instrument result in a contest. On many issues the proponents' burden of proof would be so onerous that they would forgo the trouble and expense of hopeless litigation. On certain other issues the proponents' burden would be so easy to discharge that potential contestants would not bother to litigate. . . . Indeed, it seems plausible that the substantial compliance doctrine might actually decrease the levels of probate litigation. In numerous situations, such as the "at-the-end" cases, the literal compliance rule has produced a large and contradictory case law. . . . By substituting a purposive analysis for a formal one, the substantial compliance doctrine would make the standard more predictable, and contestants would lose their incentive to prove harmless defects.

5. An equivalent substantial compliance doctrine has been working smoothly for decades in the functionally identical sphere of the major will substitute, life insurance, in those situations in which there are technical violations of the testament-like formalities for change-of-beneficiary designations. . . .

Section 9 of the Wills Act Amendment Act (No. 2), which came into effect in January, 1976, amends the South Australian Wills Act to provide:

> A document purporting to embody the testamentary intentions of a deceased person shall, notwithstanding that it has not been executed with the formalities required by this Act, be deemed to be a will of the deceased person if the [court] . . . is satisfied that there can be no reasonable doubt that the deceased intended the document to constitute his will. . . .

[T]he first important lesson of the South Australian experiment appears to be — as proponents of the substantial compliance doctrine predicted — that the probate process functions well without the strict compliance rule. Future case loads may mount as potential schemers and contestants explore their new license, but the experience to date certainly is to the contrary. . . .

––––––––––––

See also John H. Langbein, Excusing Harmless Errors in the Execution of Wills: A Report on Australia's Tranquil Revolution in Probate Law, 87 Colum. L. Rev. 1 (1987); James Lindgren, The Fall of Formalism, 55 Alb. L. Rev. 1009 (1992); Bruce H. Mann, Formalities and Formalism in the Uniform Probate Code, 142 U. Pa. L. Rev. 1033 (1994); and Will of Ranney, 124 N.J. 1, 589 A.2d 1339 (1991), adopting a "substantial compliance" approach based on UPC §2-503 and on the American Law Institute's 1990 tentative approval of Restatement (Second) of Property §33.1 cmt. *g*. For a view that we need to retain the stricter rules, see Melanie B. Leslie, the Myth of Testamentary Freedom, 38 Ariz. L. Rev. 235 (1996).

RESTATEMENT (THIRD) OF PROPERTY

§3.3 *Excusing Harmless Errors*.   A harmless error in executing a will may be excused if the proponent establishes by clear and convincing evidence that the decedent adopted the document as his or her will.

The Reporter's Note 2 to this section mentions an actual case that would be decided differently under this rule:

> [Theodore W.] Dwight, the founder of the modern Columbia Law School, had neglected to make a will until he was near death. After giving instructions for the preparation of his will, he had the draft brought to his bedside on the morning of June 18, 1892. Witnesses were present as the will execution began. Professor Dwight had written "Theodore W. Dwi" and a part of the letter "g" when he suddenly fell back and died. The harmless error doctrine was not recognized at this time, and Dwight's will was not enforced.

The Dispensing Power. Adopting an approach more liberal than the "substantial compliance" rule its title suggests, this Restatement rule, intended for judicial adoption, allows a court to dispense with one or more formalities if the proponent meets the required burden of proof. Compare UPC §2-503, which expresses no limit on the nature or extent of the formal shortcomings a court might excuse, but its comment states: "The larger the departure from Section 2-502 formality, the harder it will be to satisfy the court that the instrument reflects the testator's intent." Many commentators favor the dispensing power, but there are some detractors. See L. Bonfield, Reforming the Requirements for Due Execution of Wills: Some Guidance From the Past, 70 Tul. L. Rev. 1893 (1996).

SUCCESSIONS OF EDDY
664 So. 2d 853 (La. App. 1995)

YELVERTON, J.

The trial court invalidated the testament of Frances Lee Tison Eddy because it was not signed on the first page containing all of the dispositive provisions. Mary Beth Marler, the executrix named in the will, appealed. We affirm.

Frances Lee Tison Eddy died in Grant Parish on January 14, 1994. A will dated February 23, 1993, was presented for probate by the named executrix. The will was ordered filed and executed. On May 18, 1994, Richard Tison, nephew of the deceased, filed a petition to annul the probated will, alleging that it did not meet the formal requirements of La. R.S. 9:2442 for a statutory will. Tison alleged that the deceased had left an earlier will dated January 4, 1993, which should be probated. The two wills differed in the naming of the executor and in the dispositive provisions.

The purported will under attack was prepared on an "E-Z Legal Form" which was apparently bought from a store. It consisted of a single piece of paper with printing on the back and front. There were spaces on the front for naming the "personal.representative" and the "guardian," and about half the front page was reserved for listing the "bequests." The attestation clause and places for all of the signatures were on the back.

The will was declared invalid by the trial judge on the sole ground that the front side of the single sheet did not bear the signature of the testatrix. La. R.S. 9:2442(B)(1) requires that the testator "sign his name at the end of the will and on each separate page of the instrument." The deceased signed it on the back, but not on the front. The front contained all the dispositions; the back contained only the deceased's signature and the attestation clause.

In 1980, the statute was amended to require that the testator sign "on each other separate page of the instrument." Before this amendment, it had required that the testator sign "on each other separate sheet of the instrument." The legislative history is silent as to the reason for change from page to sheet.

In deciding what constitutes a "page," the trial judge in our case decided that each side of the purported will constituted a separate page. He relied on the case of Land v. Succession of Newsom, 193 So. 2d 411 (La. App. 2d Cir. 1966), writ denied, 195 So. 2d 145 (La. 1967). We agree with this definition.

On appeal the executrix makes the argument that La. R.S. 9:2442 does not require a signature on each "page" of a will, but rather requires a signature on each "separate page" of a will. She cites Succession of Hoyt, 303 So. 2d 189 (La. App. 1st Cir. 1974) to show the importance of such a distinction.

Hoyt involved a two-page will signed only on the second page. The court of appeal affirmed the trial court judgment invalidating the will, reciting that the purpose of the requirement that the testator sign his name on each separate sheet is "to prevent fraud by the substitution of one typewritten page for another after the execution of the will by the testator." Id. at 189. Thus, the appellant contends that the danger the rule is designed to prevent — the substitution of another piece of paper — is not present in this case.

We cannot agree that a single sheet of paper with parts of the will on both sides eliminates the danger. A primary purpose of our statute authorizing the statutory will is to afford another and simplified means of making a testament whereby the authenticity of the act can be readily ascertained and fraudulent alteration of it will be most difficult. Succession of Morgan, 242 So. 2d 551 (La. 1970). In our present case, the entire will is contained on the front and back of a single piece of paper. Although it may be impossible to substitute one side of the paper for another as the appellant urges, it is entirely possible that the name of the executrix and the dispositive provisions could have been typed in on the front, or additional provisions added, after her signature was placed on the back side. Thus, the appellant's argument is without merit.

A liberal construction of the statutory will law requires us to maintain the validity of a will as long as it is in substantial compliance with the statute. Succession of Guezuraga, 512 So. 2d 366 (La. 1987). In deciding what constitutes substantial compliance, we must look to the purpose of the formal requirements — to guard against fraud. Id. To assure us that the testament is an accurate reflection of the testatrix' wishes, of paramount importance is her affirmance by a signature beneath the dispositive provisions of her testament, for the dispositive provisions are what primarily concern her. Id. Guezuraga involved a two-page will where all of the dispositive provisions were contained on the first page but not the second. The testator signed on the first page but not on the second. The testator signed the dispositive provisions of the will. The supreme court held that there was substantial compliance with the required formality of signing at the end of the will and on each separate page of the instrument.

In the present case, the purported will is prepared on a single piece of paper with the front and back each constituting a separate page. The testatrix failed to sign "each other separate page of the will" as required by La. R.S. 9:2442. However, we do not find the will invalid for only that reason. The statute also requires that the testator "shall sign his name at the end of the will" which, according to Guezuraga, is the place where the testamentary dispositions and the naming of the executor terminate. Here, all of the dispositions and the naming of the executor appear on the front page, and the testatrix did not sign the front page at all. She only signed the back page which contained only the attestation clause. We therefore hold that the testatrix's failure to sign her name at the "end of the will" was fatal to the validity of this statutory will.

The judgment of the trial court is affirmed. All costs of these proceedings are to be borne by the executrix, Mary Beth Marler.

Affirmed.

Was there any evidence suggesting wrongdoing or overreaching by the beneficiaries of the later instrument? Compare Stevens v. Casdorph, 508 S.E.2d 610 (W. Va. 1998), in which a dissent calls the will's rejection an "abandonment of common sense . . . in favor of technicalities." The case is described as a "textbook example" of the need for the UPC's dispensing power in R. D. Volkmer, New Fiduciary Decisions, 26 Est. Plan. 191 (May 1999).

5

Integration, Extrinsic Evidence, and Related Matters

Growing out of the requirements of execution are a variety of problems relating to the admissibility to probate of independent documents or separate sheets of paper not themselves displaying the signs of execution. What other writings or external facts are sufficiently "safeguarded" to be carried through the probate process by the protective formalities performed on an attested or holographic page? What are the *consequences* of permitting the "blessing" of one document's formal execution to be extended to another instrument, sometimes one that had itself been previously executed? To what extent may extrinsic evidence be introduced to clarify the meaning, or even to alter the effect, of a formally executed will? The principal problems involving the above questions are considered in this chapter: integration of separate pages into a single executed will; republication by codicil, which brings separate testamentary instruments together as a unit for at least some purposes; foreign documents being referred to and thereby incorporated into an executed instrument; independent facts that in some way affect the operation of a will; and the use of extrinsic evidence in interpreting or attacking the provisions of a will.

A.   Integration of Wills

A will usually consists of several pages, all of which are admitted to probate as a single testamentary instrument. Occasionally a court is confronted with the question of whether several sheets of paper are to be probated together as the decedent's will. It must decide whether the pages were present at the time of execution and were then intended to be a part of the will. Integration problems are especially likely in the case of holographic wills. If a particular paper was not present at the execution or was not then intended to be part of the will, it cannot be integrated into the will for purposes of probate.

Typically the pages of a will are admitted to probate on the basis of a presumption of intent and presence resulting from their being physically fastened together. Consequently the average will presents no

186

problem of integration. Lawyers often have their clients, and sometimes the witnesses, initial each consecutively numbered page for identification. Even in the case of unattached sheets of paper, integration may be predicated on the inference that naturally arises from the internal coherence of the provisions. Thus, a sentence may be begun at the bottom of one sheet and completed at the top of another, and the sheets may reveal a sensible pattern of disposition throughout. In such cases, then, it may readily be shown from the face of the alleged will that the separate sheets are to be integrated as a single instrument.

A more difficult problem is presented when separate sheets are offered for probate as a single will without physical attachment or coherent connection between the pages. Can the court rely on extrinsic evidence offered to prove that all of the pages were intended to be part of the will and were present at the execution? If so, how convincing must that extrinsic evidence be? Should courts be more liberal in the case of a holographic document?

In the leading case of Cole v. Webb, 220 Ky. 817, 295 S.W. 1035 (1927), two detached sheets of paper were offered for probate. The first contained dispositive provisions and named an executor, not leaving enough room for subscription and attestation. At the top of the other sheet was an attestation clause followed by the signatures of the testatrix and witnesses. Two attesting witnesses and a reputable attorney who prepared the alleged will identified the two sheets as those present before the testatrix at execution and intended as her will. On the basis of this uncontradicted testimony, the court admitted the papers to probate, observing that, by the weight of authority in this country, extrinsic evidence as well as internal coherence could support the integration of unattached sheets with one bearing the indicia of formal execution. But cf. the excerpt from *Seiter* quoted in the second *Maginn* opinion below.

PROBLEM

5-A. On *D*'s death an envelope was found in his desk. On the envelope was written "Will of *D*," and in it were ten unattached, typewritten sheets of paper folded together lengthwise and numbered from 1 to 10 in what appears to be the same ink as that used for the testator's signature on the last page. These sheets were not all typed on the same typewriter, and on each of the first nine sheets was typed but a single, self-contained provision, the ninth being a disposition of the residue of the estate. Page 10 was signed by *D* and three witnesses, each of whom, after identifying his own signature and *D*'s, now offers to testify (1) that he observed the facts of a proper execution and the signing of the sheet numbered 10 and (2) that a stack of papers like the one in question was before *D* at the time and was declared by *D* to be his will. No specific identification of pages 1 through 9 is possible. How would you argue for and against the admission of the testimony of these witnesses? If this evidence is admitted, how would you argue against the probate of these papers? In connection with this problem, consider the *Maginn* cases, infra; if these were the only integration cases in your jurisdiction, how would you argue in behalf of the proponents of the alleged will? Would a statutory provision like UPC §2-503 be helpful?

Should it matter in the decision of this problem that, instead of being typed, the pages in question were all written in the handwriting of *D* but with different colored ink appearing on different pages? See In re Sleeper, 129 Me. 194, 151 A. 150 (1930), noted at 40 Yale L.J. 144 (1930). ๛

MAGINN'S ESTATE
278 Pa. 89, 122 A. 264, 30 A.L.R. 418 (1923)

KEPHART, J. . . . .

In the present case we have seven loose pages [found in an envelope], fastened by a sliding clip, physically laid together as a will. The testator's name appeared on the [top] page in signature, with those of the subscribing witnesses. The other pages followed. [The bottom sheet appeared to be an intended first page, beginning the will.] One might take any of the pages, after what may be called the proper first page, and omit it from the collection, and the balance would make a complete will. Or one might substitute, interpolate, or entirely withdraw pages, without in the least destroying the symmetry of the remaining papers. Held together as they were, the leaves could be slipped out without leaving the slightest mark on them. There was absolutely nothing in them, no relation or recital, by which to indicate they were connected one to the other, except possibly two of the smaller nondispositive papers, and they in very minor matters. Standing alone, the pages contained no words of a testamentary character, except the last, and the same pages could be used in any other will, and it would be just as logical. . . .

To sustain as a will this collection of papers not only opens the door to fraud of the most aggravated character, but strikes down every protection thrown about a decedent's estate. It would encourage heirs or persons evilly inclined to employ every available means to get possession of a will and (acting under our decision, if these papers are found as a will) proceed to adjust it to their satisfaction. As stated by Mr. Chief Justice Mitchell in Swire's Estate, 225 Pa. 188, 191, 192, 73 A. 1110, 1111, reviewing Heise v. Heise, 31 Pa. 246, and other cases:

"Nor should we lose sight of the mischiefs which existed at the time when it (the statute) was enacted; mischiefs which it was designed to remedy. Among these, none was more serious than the facility with which unfinished papers, mere inchoate expressions of intention, were admitted to probate as valid wills of decedents. Letters, memoranda, mere notes unsigned, which were entirely consistent with a half formed purpose, and which may have been thrown aside, and never intended to be operative, were rescued from their abandonment, proven as wills, and allowed to prevail as dispositions of property which there was much reason to believe the decedent never intended. It was to remedy this mischief that the act of 1893 provided that every will should be signed at the 'end thereof,' that thus, by his signature in that place, the testator should show that his testamentary purpose was consummated, and that the instrument was complete." . . . The purposes of the act of 1893 were accuracy in the transmission of the testator's wishes, the authentication of the instrument transmitting them, the identification of the testator, and certainty as to his completed testamentary purpose. . . .

As stated at the beginning of this opinion, it might have been testator's intention to write some sort of a will, but he has not complied with the law. As all the pages between the beginning and the end may have been, so far as we know, written after attestation, and as they are not connected by their internal sense, the papers cannot be sustained as a will. . . .

[handwritten margin notes: "no compliance w/ law", "no internal connection", "∴ No will"]

MAGINN'S ESTATE
281 Pa. 514, 127 A. 79 (1924)

WALLING, J.

This appeal is from a decree of the orphans' court setting aside the probate of three separate typewritten sheets or pages as the last will of the late Daniel Maginn of Pittsburgh. The three pages so rejected are a part of seven, the probate of which was set aside by this court in Maginn's Estate, 278 Pa. 89. . . .

To entitle separate loose sheets of paper to be probated as a will they must be identified by their internal sense. As stated in Seiter's Estate, 265 Pa. 202, 108 A. 614:

A will may be made on separate pieces of paper, but when so made they must be connected by their internal sense, by coherence or adaptation of parts, to constitute a will. The order of connection must appear upon the face of the will, it cannot be established by extrinsic evidence; and it must be a will executed as directed by the act of assembly. . . .

Here appellant's case fails, for there is no internal sense connecting the first sheet with the second, or the second with the third, or the first with the third. There is no reference or recital to indicate they are connected the one with the other. The sheets are not numbered, and it is reasonably certain the second of the three sheets did not originally join the third, for, as found after Maginn's death, four sheets came between them. How then can the three, having no internal connection be probated as a will? At best they express but a fragment of the testamentary intent, while one omitted page entirely modifies a $5,000 bequest contained in those probated. The three pages do not disclose the testator's completed testamentary purpose. . . . The will on its face would be just as complete with the second page omitted and that page would fit just as well in any other will. . . . *mangof*

It would be unsafe to probate a single page of a will, which on its face disclosed other pages, as the one might be modified by the others. For example, a clause appointing executors might be modified by another requiring them to give bond or serve without compensation.

Undoubtedly there may be a case where certain provisions of a will are valid and others invalid, in which the former may be probated and the latter not (40 Cyc. 1080); but here . . . it was purely arbitrary to drop out some and offer the others for probate. To permit this to be done would expose estates to all the perils which our former decision is intended to guard against. . . .

The decree is affirmed, and appeal dismissed, at the costs of the estate.

KEPHART, J. (dissenting).

Without undue discussion, it is my opinion that at least the first and last pages offered for probate were so connected by their internal sense as to express and constitute the last will of Daniel Maginn. For this reason I would probate these two pages.

SCHAFFER, J. I join in this dissent.

B.   Republication by Codicil

Typically, a codicil is executed for the purpose of adding to or modifying an existing will without entirely revoking it. Thus, a codicil is normally a supplement to a will. The codicil itself must be executed with the statutory formalities of a will. A codicil may, rather than merely supplementing an effective will, serve to revive a revoked will or to republish a will. The revival of revoked wills is considered in Chapter 6, and the effect of a codicil on a defective instrument or on a defective addition to a will is considered as an aspect of incorporation by reference later in this chapter. The latter is properly a problem of incorporation by reference rather than one of republication, despite the tendency of courts to confuse them.

The effect of a codicil on the operation of a valid and subsisting will should be considered in light of the English law under the Statute of Wills, 1540, under which a will operated only on lands owned at its execution. Land acquired after execution of a will would not pass thereunder, but if a codicil were subsequently executed it was said to "republish" the will as of the date of the codicil. Thus, the will would speak as of the date of the codicil, and a residuary clause or a clause devising "all of my lands" would operate on land acquired between the execution of the will and the codicil.

Today, wills are clearly ambulatory in character in that they operate on the testator's property as it exists at his death without regard to when it was acquired. Thus, wills are said to speak as of the date of death. On the other hand, in *interpreting* a will, it is generally to be read as of the date of execution. Therefore, although a will speaks at the date of death, the meaning of what is spoken is generally judged on the basis of conditions existing at the time of execution. Under the doctrine of republication, a codicil is seen as updating the will, which is normally deemed to have been executed anew at the date of the codicil. For many purposes, then, a will and its codicils are a testamentary unit brought together or "republished" under the latest execution. This process of updating may affect the interpretation or even the validity of portions of the will or prior codicils.

How literally is republication to be taken? Mechanical application of such a concept would be destructive of intention in certain cases, although in other contexts the effect of republication would be salutary. As you examine the problems that follow, consider the proper limits of the doctrine of republication by codicil and §3.4 of the Restatement (Third) of Property, which states: "A will is treated as if it were executed when its most recent codicil was executed, whether or not the codicil expressly republishes the prior will, unless the effect of so treating it would be inconsistent with the testator's intent."

PROBLEMS

5-B. *T* and his brother, *B*, were the sole and equal shareholders of B&T Company. When *T* executed his will five years ago, his daughter, *D,* was already a successful physician, and his son, *S,* was finishing college with the intention of going to work for the B&T Company. *T*'s will provided: "All of the stock I now own in B&T Company I leave to *S*." A bequest of $100,000 was made to *D,* and the residue of the estate was left to *T*'s wife, *W. B* was named executor.

Two years ago *B* died, and *T* purchased the entire interest of *B*'s estate in B&T Company for $130,000. About three months ago, *T* was hospitalized. Realizing that a new executor should be named to replace *B, T* executed a codicil naming *X* Bank & Trust Company executor and died two weeks later leaving a net estate of $500,000. To what is *S* entitled?

5-C. Assume that, in addition to the facts in the above problem, *T*'s original will contained a bequest of $25,000 to *Y* church. Assume further that in the three years before *T*'s death a child, *C*, had been born to *T* and *W*. The relevant statutes include a restriction against all charitable bequests in wills executed within one month of death and a pretermitted heir provision protecting issue born after the execution of a will. How should the estate be distributed? On the pretermitted heir issue, see Azcunce v. Estate of Azcunce, 586 So. 2d 1216 (Fla. App. 1991), and ensuing action by unsuccessful "pretermission" claimant and personal representative against the drafting attorneys for malpractice (recovering only fees paid by testator) in Espinosa v. Sparber, Shevin, Shapo, Rosen & Heilbronner, 586 So. 2d 1221 (Fla. App. 1991). See also republication preventing pretermission claims of both spouse and adopted child in Estate of Wells, 983 P. 2d 279 (Kan. App. 1999).

C. Incorporation by Reference

Papers that cannot be "integrated" into a will because they were not present at the execution may, in most states, be given effect as a part of the will of a testator under the doctrine of incorporation by reference under appropriate circumstances. A few states refuse to permit incorporation by reference on the general ground that the incorporated instrument lacks the required formal safeguards against fraud.

The requirements for incorporating unexecuted writings by reference are thought to replace the safeguards of execution. These requirements are generally stated by the courts to be, in substance:

1. The extrinsic writing must in fact be in existence when the will is executed;
2. The will must refer to it as being in existence when the will is executed;
3. The intent to incorporate must appear in the will; and
4. The extrinsic writing must be identified with reasonable certainty and must conform to the description in the will.

How strictly these requirements are adhered to is quite a different question. The attitudes of courts have varied from case to case, even within a single jurisdiction. For example, In re Estate of Young, 123 Cal. 337, 342, 55 P. 1011, 1012 (1899), states that before "an extrinsic document may be so incorporated, the description of it in the will itself must be so clear, explicit, and unambiguous as to leave its identity free from doubt." With this, compare Clark v. Greenhalge, infra.

PROBLEM

5-D. On August 8, 1990, Howard Elliston executed a typewritten instrument purporting to be a will bequeathing all of his estate equally to Jones and Smith. However, at probate it has been proven that the execution of the instrument was fatally defective. Also offered for probate is a valid holographic instrument, which appears as follows:

> Codicil to My Last Will and Testament. I hereby bequeath $10,000 to the Eastside Orphanage and $2,000 to my housekeeper, Nellie Wolf.
>
> Howard Elliston
> Campville, Sept. 18, 1992

Can anything be done in behalf of Jones and Smith, who are not Elliston's heirs at law? Cf. Estate of Erbach, 41 Wis. 2d 335, 164 N.W.2d 238 (1969). But cf. Estate of Norton, 330 N.C. 378, 410 S.E.2d 484 (1991).

UNIFORM PROBATE CODE

§2-510. *Incorporation by Reference.* A writing in existence when a will is executed may be incorporated by reference if the language of the will manifests this intent and describes the writing sufficiently to permit its identification.

Section 3.6 of Restatement (Third) Property is substantially the same.

CLARK v. GREENHALGE
411 Mass. 410, 582 N.E.2d 949 (1991)

[Helen Nesmith's 1977 will named her cousin, F. T. Greenhalge, as executor and as recipient of all her tangible personal property, except that he is to "distribute such of the tangible property to and among such persons as I may designate by a memorandum left by me and known to him, or in accordance with my known wishes." With Greenhalge's assistance, Nesmith had earlier drafted a dated document, entitled "MEMORANDUM," listing 49 specific bequests of her tangible personal property. In 1976 she had modified that list by interlineations, additions, and deletions. Ms. Nesmith also made a later series of entries in a notebook under the title "List to be given, Helen Nesmith 1979." In 1980 she executed two codicils to her 1977 will, amending certain bequests, deleting others, and ratifying the will in all other respects. Following her death in 1986, Greenhalge, as executor, distributed Ms. Nesmith's property in accordance with the will and codicils and the 1972 memorandum as amended in 1976. He refused, however, to comply with a 1979 provision in the notebook purporting to bequeath a valuable painting to Virginia Clark, who commenced an action seeking to compel him to do so.]

NOLAN, J. . . .

The probate judge found that . . . [the] notebook qualified as a "memorandum" . . . within the meaning of Article Fifth of Helen Nesmith's will . . . [and that it] was in existence at the time of the execution of the 1980 codicils, which ratified the language of Article Fifth in its entirety. Based on these findings, the judge ruled that the notebook was incorporated by reference into the terms of the will . . . [and] awarded the painting to Ms. Clark. . . .

A properly executed will may incorporate by reference into its provisions any "document or paper not so executed . . . if it was in existence at the time of the execution of the will, and is identified by clear and satisfactory proof as the paper referred to therein." . . . The parties agree that the document entitled "memorandum," dated 1972 and amended in 1976, was . . . incorporated by reference into the terms of the will. . . .

The parties do not agree, however, as to whether the documentation contained in the notebook, dated 1979, similarly was incorporated into the will. . . . First, Greenhalge contends that the judge wrongly concluded that the notebook could be considered a "memorandum" within the meaning of Article Fifth, because it is not specifically identified as a "memorandum." Such a literal interpretation of the language and meaning of Article Fifth is not appropriate.

"The 'cardinal rule of the interpretation of wills, to which all other rules must bend, is that the intention of the testator shall prevail, provided it is consistent with the rules of law.'" The intention of the testator is ascertained through consideration of the [language of the will] . . . as well as the circumstances existing at the time of the execution of the will. . . . The circumstances existing at the time of the execution of a codicil to a will are equally relevant, because the codicil serves to ratify the language in the will which has not been altered or affected by the terms of the codicil.

. . . The appellant argues, however, that the notebook cannot take effect . . . because the language of article Fifth limits its application to "a" memorandum, or the 1972 memorandum. We reject this strict construction of Article Fifth. The language of Article Fifth does not preclude the existence of more than one memorandum which serves the intended purpose of that article. . . . To construe narrowly Article Fifth and to exclude the possibility that Helen Nesmith drafted the notebook contents as "a memorandum" under that article, would undermine our long-standing policy of interpreting wills in a manner which best carries out the known wishes of the testatrix. . . . [The testimony of witnesses also] supports the conclusion that Helen Nesmith intended that the bequests in her notebook be accorded the same power and effect as those contained in the 1972 memorandum. . . .

The appellant also contends that . . . the evidence established, at most, that [Nesmith] intended to bequeath the painting to Clark, and not that she intended to incorporate the notebook into her will. . . . The judge found that Helen Nesmith drafted the notebook contents with the expectation that Greenhalge would distribute the property accordingly. . . . It is clear that the judge fairly construed the evidence in reaching the determination that Helen Nesmith intended the notebook to serve as a memorandum of her wishes as contemplated under Article Fifth of her will. . . .

Judgment affirmed.

Was the notebook in the above case actually "in existence" at the time the will was executed? The court's implicit conclusion that it was is not novel. See, e.g., Simon v. Grayson, 15 Cal. 2d 531, 102 P.2d 1081 (1940), which involved a letter that was not in existence when the will was executed and bore a date subsequent to that of the will. The court noted, however, that "the letter was in existence at the time the codicil to the will was executed" and that "the execution of a codicil has the effect of republishing the will" so that the "letter was an 'existing document' within the incorporation rule [if it] can be satisfactorily identified as the one referred to in the will." See also Smith v. Weitzel, 338 S.W.2d 628 (Tenn. App. 1960).

Compare, however, Kellom v. Beverstock, 100 N.H. 329, 126 A.2d 127 (1956), where the court refused to apply the doctrine of incorporation by reference because "words of futurity" were used in referring to a list made up before the execution of a codicil but after the execution of the will, which stated: "I shall leave a list of [property], indicating to whom I wish to leave those items." And see the English statement of the rule: "[A] document will not be incorporated if the will refers to it in future terms, e.g., 'as I shall direct in a small memorandum' . . . even though the document is in fact in existence at the time of the will." Tiley, A Casebook on Equity and Succession 414-415 (1968).

Does an unincorporated writing become a "physical" part of the incorporating instrument by analogy to integration? Courts are not in agreement whether the incorporated document is itself to be probated, thereby becoming a part of the public record, possibly contrary to the purpose of its incorporation. Courts also disagree whether a nonholographic writing can be incorporated into a holographic will. The modern trend seems to be against treating the incorporated writing as a physical part of the will. See, e.g., Johnson v. Johnson, 279 P.2d 928 (Okla. 1954) (finding incorporation of nonholographic writings into holographic will to be valid).

The primary present-day interest in incorporation by reference is in the area of "pouring over" from a will into an inter vivos trust. This subject is taken up in a subsequent chapter. Section D of this chapter is also relevant for purposes of the later study of "pour-overs."

D.   Reference to Facts of Independent Significance

It is common — in fact generally accepted without question — that certain details of a will are to be supplied by looking outside the will. Descriptions of persons or property often require resort to extrinsic facts. When these facts are peculiarly within the control of the testator it is possible that a reference to them may be challenged as permitting unexecuted completion or variation of his will. Under many circumstances reference to extrinsic facts is not only quite safe, but borders on sheer necessity if wills are to have an ambulatory character. Today no one would question the formal sufficiency of a disposition of the residue of an estate in equal shares to the testator's children who survive him. Yet the content of the "residue" depends on events, including acts of the testator, that occur unaccompanied by testamentary formalities after the will has been executed. The same is true of determining the testator's surviving children in the above disposition.

[handwritten margin note: reliance — Quite safe & necessary]

Basically, the identity of persons and property may be determined by reference to events and to acts of the testator and others, provided these events and acts have "independent significance." It is generally required that such events or acts have a *substantial significance apart from their impact on the will;* that is, that they be the kind of thing that would occur without regard to their effect on the will. Of course, many cases will be difficult to resolve by this basic rule.

[handwritten margin note: Independent significance]

In First National Bank v. Klein, 285 Ala. 505, 234 So. 2d 42 (1970), the testatrix left property to her son, providing that, if he predeceased her, the property should go to the beneficiaries of "his last will." Recognizing that incorporation by reference was not appropriate when the testatrix referred to any will the son might leave, the court upheld the disposition on the ground that the effect of the son's will on his own estate gave it a substantial significance independent of the will of the testatrix. The court also noted that the fact that another will was involved was an adequate safeguard for the mother's bequest.

PROBLEM

5-E. What is the effect of the following provisions?
"I bequeath $5,000 to

(a)   "each person who may be a son-in-law or daughter-in-law of mine at my death."
(b)   "the person who is my housekeeper at my death."
(c)   "each of the persons listed on the paper I shall place with this will."

"I bequeath to *X*

(a) "all of the household furnishings in my apartment at my death."
(b) "the contents of my personal checking account."
(c) "all of the securities in my safe-deposit box."
(d) "the contents of the top drawer of my desk, and I bequeath the contents of the bottom drawer to *Y*."

UNIFORM PROBATE CODE

§2-512. *Events of Independent Significance.* A will may dispose of property by reference to acts and events that have significance apart from their effect upon the dispositions made by the will, whether they occur before or after the execution of the will or before or after the testator's death. The execution or revocation of another individual's will is such an event.

See also Restatement (Third) of Property §3.7: "The meaning of a dispositive or other provision in a will may be supplied or affected by an external circumstance referred to in the will, unless the external circumstance has no significance apart from its effect upon the will."

PROBLEM

5-F. The temptation is great, especially for persons not trained in the law, to try to dispose of tools, kitchen utensils, personal effects, and the family floor clock to friends and relatives by casual promises or informally drawn and revised lists. How might you handle the problem of elderly clients who cannot make up their minds about the division of their personal effects, even after you have drawn their wills? Assume these personally meaningful items have little monetary value — probably less than the time expected of you in keeping the wills up to date. The list of items and recipients is a long one. The clients telephone you frequently, possibly several times during a particularly thoughtful month, to make changes. What do you suggest? Do you approve of the novel provision of Uniform Probate Code §2-513?

UNIFORM PROBATE CODE

§2-513. *Separate Writing Identifying Devise of Certain Types of Tangible Personal Property.* Whether or not the provisions relating to holographic wills apply, a will may refer to a written statement or list to dispose of items of tangible personal property not otherwise specifically disposed of by the will, other than money. To be admissible under this section as evidence of the intended disposition, the writing must be signed by the testator and must describe the items and the devisees with reasonable certainty. The writing may be referred to as one to be in existence at the time of the testator's death; it may be prepared before or after the execution of the will; it may be altered by the testator after its preparation; and it may be a writing that has no significance apart from its effect on the dispositions made by the will.

E. Extrinsic Evidence

1. Introduction to Interpretation

The Restatement of Property, in §241, comment *c*, rejects the traditional distinction between *interpretation* and *construction*. Nevertheless, the distinction is often made and is often useful, even though it is unrealistic to view the two as separate or isolated processes. See Chapter 10, section A. "Interpretation . . . seems to be used to denote the process of ascertaining the meaning of language used through a search for the intent of the parties to the instrument. Interpretation, therefore, is essentially a factual, as distinguished from a legal, concept. A rule of construction is defined as a rule that attaches a given legal consequence to the words employed 'unless a contrary intent is shown by admissible evidence.'" Note, Choice-of-Law Rules for the Construction and Interpretation of Written Instruments, 72 Harv. L. Rev. 1154, 1155 (1959). Thus, it is sometimes said that construction supplies an attributed meaning where interpretation has failed to discover an intended meaning through examination of admissible evidence.

A variety of "rules" are regularly encountered in statutes and judicial opinions purporting to govern the process of interpretation. We start with the often repeated principle that the ultimate object of the process is to discover the intent of the testator and that all rules of construction yield to that intent when it can be discovered. This quest for intention, however, must be considered in light of other widely recognized principles. It is often stated, for example, that courts are seeking the meaning of what is said in the will rather than the subjective intent of the testator. Consider the often quoted dictum of Judge Learned Hand in Boal v. Metropolitan Museum of Art, 292 F. 303, 304 (S.D.N.Y. 1923): "[I]t is the court's duty to find out the legal effect of documents and to construe the language of the testator, without regard to his unexpressed intent. . . . I have to do with a situation quite outside of anything which the testator had in contemplation, and it is therefore obvious that any solution is bound to be verbal and indeed formal. Yet while it is idle to speculate upon what he personally would have done had he been able to look ahead, courts have always permitted themselves, within limits, to impute to testators an intent which they could not foresee." Is there no basis for attributed meaning other than "idle speculation"?

Before studying specific problem areas, examine the following representative quotations and keep them in mind as you study the problems and cases in the rest of this chapter.

"A testator's intent, unless unlawful, shall prevail; that intent shall be ascertained from a consideration of (a) all the language contained in his will, and (b) his scheme of distribution, and (c) the circumstances surrounding him at the time he made his will, and (d) the existing facts; and (e) canons of construction will be resorted to only if the language of the will is ambiguous or conflicting or the testator's intent is for any reason uncertain." In re Estate of Carter, 435 Pa. 492, 496, 257 A.2d 843, 845 (1969). *[handwritten margin: lang.; scheme of distribution, circumstance, existing facts; construction]*

"The will must be considered in its entirety to determine the testator's intent and, to the extent possible, that construction should be adopted which will give effect to all language employed; no technical rule of construction, however, will be permitted to interfere with ascertaining the testator's real intention." Landmark Trust Co. v. Aitken, 224 Ill. App. 3d 843, 851-852, 587 N.E.2d 1076, 1082 (1992). Compare In re Will of Gulbenkian, 9 N.Y.2d 363, 370, 174 N.E.2d 481, 483, 214 N.Y.S. 2d 379,382 (1961) (citations omitted): "[W]e may . . . glean the testator's dominant purpose 'from a sympathetic reading of the will *as an entirety* and in view of all the facts and circumstances under which the provisions of the will were framed' . . . and this purpose must prevail regardless of the fact that a literal interpretation might yield an inconsistent meaning because of the language and format employed."

"In determining the testator's intention, if no uncertainty or ambiguity exists, his meaning must be ascertained from the language of his will: it is not what the Court thinks he might or would have said in the existing circumstances, or even what the Court thinks he meant to say, but what is the meaning of his words." In re Estate of Ginter, 398 Pa. 440, 441, 158 A.2d 789, 792 (1960). "In determining the true intent and meaning of the testator we must look first to the will, and if the language therein is ambiguous we may look to surrounding facts and circumstances." Schubel v. Bonacker, 331 S.W.2d 552, 556 (Mo. 1960).

"[W]here a will is clear, definite and free from ambiguity, its provisions cannot be limited, extended or explained by resort to parol testimony." In re Bridge's Estate, 41 Wash. 2d 916, 925, 253 P.2d 394, 399 (1953). "Extrinsic evidence is not admissible to determine the intent of the testator as expressed in his will unless there is a latent ambiguity. Such evidence is not admissible to determine the intent of the testator where the ambiguity is patent and not latent. A patent ambiguity is one which appears upon the face of the instrument. It must be removed *[handwritten margin: patent ambiguity]* by construction according to settled legal principles and not by evidence, and the intention of the testator is to be determined from the four corners of the will itself. . . . [If] 'nothing appears within its four corners to resolve or clarify the ambiguity, the words must be given their generally accepted literal and grammatical meaning.' " Jacobsen v. Farnham, 155 Neb. 776, 780-781, 53 N.W.2d 917, 920 (1952) (citations omitted). Most commentators today reject the distinction between latent and patent ambiguities. See, e.g., Restatement (Third) of Property §11.1 (Tentative Draft No. 1, 1995), comment *a.*

Similarly, with respect to the terms of inter vivos trusts, it has been stated: "Long-settled rules of construction preclude an attempt to divine a settlor's intention by looking first to extrinsic evidence. . . . Rather, the trust instrument is to be construed as written and the settlor's intention determined solely from the unambiguous language of the instrument itself. . . . It is only where the court determines the words of the trust instrument to be ambiguous that it may properly resort to extrinsic evidence. . . . The rationale underlying this basic rule of construction is that the words used in the instrument itself are the best evidence of the intention of the drafter of the document." Mercury Bay Boating v. San Diego Yacht Club, 76 N.Y.2d 256, 267, 557 N.E.2d 87, 93 (1990).

But as early as the original Restatement of Property, §242, after noting that "intent . . . is normally determined by the language employed . . . , read as an entirety and in the light of the circumstances of its formulation," comment *c* stated: "The necessity for the reading of a deed or will as a whole, does not, however, justify a construction which relies solely on its language and excludes evidence as to the circumstances of its formulation. Such an exclusion is often the result of the so-called 'single plain meaning rule,' which unduly stresses the controlling force of the ordinary meaning of the words employed. This rule, in so far as it causes such exclusion, is disapproved, since language is so colored by the circumstances of its formulation that the exclusion of otherwise admissible evidence as to such circumstances is never justified."

4 William J. Bowe & Douglas H. Parker, Page on the Law of Wills §32.9 (1961) (emphasis added): "With the exception of cases in which language is used which seems intelligible and consistent, but which applies equally to two or more persons or things [called 'equivocations'], evidence of a *testator's direct declarations* of intent [is] inadmissible to show testator's actual intention, apart from . . . language which is used by him in the will itself." In re Estate of Fries, 221 Cal. App. 2d 725, 730, 34 Cal. Rptr. 749, 753 (1963): "[But this] proscription does not apply to oral declarations of a testator which are offered for the purpose of showing his state of mind with respect to the meaning of particular language used by him in a will which is ambiguous." See

also Estate of Taff, 63 Cal. App. 3d 319, 325-326, 133 Cal. Rptr. 737, 741 (1976), in which a statute authorized various uncertainties of meaning to be clarified by extrinsic evidence, expressly "excluding the oral declarations of the testator as to his intentions." Yet the court noted that "it has long been held that oral declarations made by a testator to the scrivener of the will are admissible to resolve a latent ambiguity" because this statutory prohibition applies to mere incidental fugitive utterances or declarations of intent as distinguished from specific instructions as to testamentary disposition.

When it was argued in the *Taff* case, supra, that another section and case law "require a trial court to interpret technical words used in a will drawn by an attorney in their technical sense" and that "technical words in a will are to be taken in their technical sense, unless the context clearly indicates a contrary intention, or unless it satisfactorily appears that the will was drawn solely by the testator, and that he was unacquainted with such technical sense," the court responded that the "presumption of technical meaning . . . is subordinate to the dominant purpose of finding and effecting the intent of the testator; the presumption is an aid to be used in ascertaining that intent, not a tool by which the court frustrates the testator's objectives." Compare: "[N]ontechnical words are to be taken in their ordinary, proper, and grammatical sense unless it clearly appears that the testator intended to use them in another sense and that sense can be ascertained . . . that technical words are to be given their correct meaning unless the contrary appears from the context . . . , although in determining whether such words were used in their technical sense the knowledge and skill of the draftsman in the use of such terms may be considered." Grace v. Continental Trust Co., 169 Md. 653, 657, 182 A. 573, 575 (1936).

"[A] construction of a will leading to partial intestacy is not favored and will not be adopted unless plainly required by the language." Holmes v. Welch, 314 Mass. 106, 109, 49 N.E.2d 461, 463 (1943).

"Where a will contains provisions which are apparently inconsistent or repugnant, every effort must be made so as to construe the instrument as to harmonize the conflicting words, phrases, or clauses." Wigglesworth v. Smith, 311 Ky. 366, 370, 224 S.W.2d 177, 179 (1949). "[W]hen there is an irreconcilable conflict between two clauses of a will pertaining to the same subject matter, the latter clause will prevail. . . ." In re Estate of Smith, 75 So. 2d 686, 688 (Fla. 1954). However, "[w]here an estate or interest is given in one clause of a will in clear and decisive terms, the interest so given cannot be taken away or cut down by . . . any subsequent words that are not as clear and decisive as the words of the clause giving the interest or estate." Springer v. Vickers, 259 Ala. 465, 469, 66 So. 2d 740, 744 (1953).

In re Helfman's Estate, 193 Cal. App. 2d 652, 655, 14 Cal. Rptr. 482, 484 (1961): "[W]here no extrinsic evidence is introduced or where

[handwritten margin note: conflict — latter clause prevails]

there is no conflict in such evidence, the construction of an uncertain provision in a will is a question of law . . . and it is the duty of an appellate court to make the final determination in accordance with the applicable principles of law. . . . While respondent suggests application of the rule that unless a different intention finds expression in the will it should be construed as applying to and disposing of the estate in its condition at the time of the death of the testator, it is also true that a testator's intent is to be determined as of the date of the execution of the instrument. Thus both rules must be applied together. The court in applying the will as of the date of the testator's death, attempts to ascertain the intent of the testator by the language of the will as understood by the testator at the time he wrote it, related to the circumstances then present."

For a comprehensive analysis of some related issues, see Henderson, Mistake and Fraud in Wills, 47 B.U.L. Rev. 309, 461 (1967).

RESTATEMENT (THIRD) OF PROPERTY: DONATIVE TRANSFERS
(Tentative Draft approved 1995)

§11.1 *Ambiguity Defined.* An ambiguity in a donative document is an uncertainty in meaning that is revealed by the text or by extrinsic evidence other than direct evidence of intention contradicting the plain meaning of the text.

§11.2 (a) *Resolving Ambiguities in Accordance with the Donor's Intention.* An ambiguity to which no rule of construction or constructional preference applies is resolved by construing the text of the donative instrument in accordance with the donor's intention, to the extent that the donor's intention is established by a preponderance of the evidence.

§12.1 *Reforming Donative Documents to Correct Mistakes.* A donative document, though unambiguous, may be reformed to conform the text to the donor's intention if the following are established by clear and convincing evidence:

    (1) that a mistake of fact or law, whether in expression or inducement, affected specific terms of the document; and

    (2) what the donor's intention was.

Direct evidence of intention contradicting the plain meaning of the text as well as other evidence of intention may be considered in determining whether elements (1) and (2) have been established by clear and convincing evidence.

PROBLEM

5-G. *T*'s will bequeaths: "(1) All of my property to my wife, *W,* without bond to do with as she pleases, to sell or transfer any or all of it. (2) If there is anything left at her death it is to go equally to my brother *B* and sister *S.*"

What are the rights of *W* in *T*'s property, and how would you argue the case for her? What might *B* and *S* claim, and how would you argue their case? See the quotations from Wigglesworth v. Smith, In re Estate of Smith, and Springer v. Vickers, supra. On this much-litigated question, contrast Gardner v. Worrell, 201 Va. 355, 111 S.E.2d 285 (1959) (finding interests like those of *B* and *S* repugnant to and ineffective to cut down an "absolute" interest comparable to *W*'s), and In re Wilson's Estate, 367 Mich. 143, 116 N.W.2d 215 (1962) (holding first bequest absolute), with Frederick v. Frederick, 355 Mass. 662, 247 N.E.2d 361 (1969) (upholding remainder), and Johnson v. Waldrop, 256 S.C. 372, 182 S.E.2d 730 (1971) (finding life estate and power to consume, followed by a valid remainder). A classic in the area is Fox v. Snow, 6 N.J. 12, 76 A.2d 877 (1950) (holding remainder impermissible), with a widely noted dissenting opinion by Chief Justice Vanderbilt. See Chapter 20.

Sadly enough, many ambiguous wills are drafted by attorneys. In Estate of Massey, 317 N.J. Super. 302, 308, 721 A.2d 1033, 1036 (1998), an attorney drafted a will that devised property to *A* "and/or" her daughter, *B.* The court said: "There is no end to the mischief caused by such inarticulate, if not illiterate, drafting. It seems to this court that the use of 'and/or' in a will bespeaks negligence on the part of the drafter."

One disappointed beneficiary opted for a remedy that was more drastic than suing the lawyer for malpractice. "Johnson City, Tenn. — A single word apparently cost 81-year-old lawyer John D. Goodin his life. Goodin left out the word 'stock' from a woman's will and her ex-husband, Walter Shell, believed that the omission cost him up to $100,000. On Thursday, police say, an enraged Shell went to Goodin's law office and shot him to death. . . . Shell and his daughters equally divided $12,000 from an insurance policy. Mrs. Shell also left him a car and lawn mower. The revised will also stipulated Shell was to receive 'all monies' after the legal costs for the estate were paid. His daughters . . . claim[ed] that since the word 'stock' was not included, Shell was not entitled to any of the $100,000 in shares their mother owned. A judge agreed. . . ." Angela K. Brown, Mistake in Will Instigates Killings, *Associated Press,* March 19, 1999.

2. Mistake: Misdescription and Omission

It is generally accepted doctrine that mistakes resulting in an omission are without remedy because a court will neither probate what is not in the will nor reform the will to supply what has been omitted. A constructive trust might conceivably be imposed in a particularly appealing case, but at present in most states the only real hope of the omitted beneficiary is through *construction*. Although it has also been said that an omitted provision cannot be supplied by construction, this statement goes too far. For example, there is the common case of the implied remainder to the issue of *A* where property is devised "to *A* for life and if he dies without issue, to *B*." See Lewis M. Simes, Future Interests §100 (2d ed. 1966). If it is possible to "imply" a provision solely from what is in the will, authority exists under which a court might provide the remedy and call it construction. Cf. W. Barton Leach, Perpetuities: Cy Pres on the March, in Perspectives of Law: Essays for Austin W. Scott 215 (1964). Contrast, for example, two cases decided the same day and reported almost simultaneously from the Surrogate's Court, New York County: In re Calabi's Estate, 196 N.Y.S.2d 443 (1959) (refusing even to admit evidence of the purpose of trusts *C* and *D* where the residue of the estate was to be divided into four lettered trusts but with terms supplied only for trusts *A* and *B*); In re Dorson's Estate, 196 N.Y.S.2d 344 (1959) (inadvertent omission of several lines of a will remedied by "construction" where the terms of residuary trusts Fund *A* and *B* were identical but for three lines of dispositive provisions omitted regarding Fund *B*).

Far more common are mistakes in the description of property or persons. In studying the following material, consider *under what circumstances* and then *by what evidence* such mistakes may be shown. Keep in mind (1) the "established proposition" that a description that accurately applies to persons or property cannot be shown to have been intended to apply to persons or property not accurately described and (2) the common dicta — occasionally codified — that even when extrinsic evidence may be admitted, the testator's own oral, direct declarations of intention are not admissible for most purposes.

PROBLEMS

5-H. Mrs. A. L. Gilkey's holographic will has been admitted to probate and appears as follows:

> My brother-in-law T. O. Gilkey owns a half interest in all of my livestock, and at my death I will him all of my interests in them, and also all my personal property. This is my will. T. O. Gilkey executor without bond. 8-17-90.
>
> (Sig.) *Mrs. A. L. Gilkey*

Mrs. Gilkey, a widow, left an estate consisting of a modest farm, machinery, livestock, some cash, and personal effects. Her sole heir at law was her sister, Bertha Chambers. T. O. Gilkey claims all the property of Mrs. Gilkey, including the farm. Bertha believes that the farm goes to her. How would you argue on behalf of each? Cf. Gilkey v. Chambers, 146 Tex. 355, 207 S.W.2d 70 (1947). For an extreme case holding "monies" to include real estate, see In re Estate of Breckenridge, 56 Ill. App. 3d 128, 371 N.E.2d 1286 (1978). See also Sandy v. Mouhot, 1 Ohio St. 3d 143, 146, 438 N.E.2d 117, 119 (1982), holding "all of my personal property and household goods" to include *intangible* personal property even though the will also contained a residuary clause referring to "the rest, residue and remainder of my property, real, personal, and mixed." In Estate of Walker, 609 So. 2d 623 (Fla. App. 1992), a gift of all of testator's "personal property" did not encompass intangibles, with the dissent arguing that clear language is not made ambiguous merely because (as emphasized by the majority) a residuary clause would have little effect.

5-I. Effie Smith's will, executed five years before her death, has just been admitted to probate. The provision in dispute is Article II, which reads: "I bequeath to Al Jones my 100 shares of General Dynamics stock, as an expression of the very great appreciation I feel for the kindness shown to me by Al and his wife since the death of my husband seven years ago. They have been like son and daughter to me."

The residue of her estate was left "to my beloved son, John," who has been a successful lawyer in a distant state since graduating from law school thirty years ago. Jones was named executor.

Jones has come to you for assistance. He calls your attention to the fact that General Dynamics stock is now selling for about $60 a share and that he is certain Effie meant to leave him 100 shares of General Ceramics stock.

Jones tells you that when he returned from military service he wanted to start a ceramics business. His neighbor, George Smith (Effie Smith's husband), seeing a promising future for Jones and wishing to help him, bought 100 shares of the $100 par value stock in General Ceramics, a corporation formed by Jones. In order to acquire control of the business, Jones had borrowed money from other sources to buy the other 101 shares that his corporation was to issue. Today the General Ceramics stock has a value of about $500 a share. Jones insists that Effie intended to leave him this General Ceramics stock, which she had inherited from her husband.

Effie's net estate is valued at slightly over $175,000. Included in her estate are the 100 shares of General Ceramics (inventoried at $50,000), a house valued at $75,000, some personal effects, and about $45,000 in listed securities, among which are included 120 shares of General Dynamics (inventoried at $7,200).

Jones tells you that Effie, who died at age 78, had been somewhat senile in her late years, although no one questions her testamentary capacity or suggests the existence of undue influence. He also states that Effie had lived on a pension and had paid almost no attention to business or investment matters either before or after George's death, relying almost completely on her accountant and Jones to handle her affairs since her husband's death. George Smith's will is brought to your attention by Jones; it provided that, if Effie (who took everything under the will) had failed to survive George, the General Ceramics stock would go to Jones, while everything else was to go to George's son, John. Effie's accountant also tells you that Effie had stated she intended to leave Jones "all the bonds I own in his [Jones's] company." At no time did Effie actually own any *bonds* of General Ceramics.

How would you argue and try to prove the case in behalf of Jones? What additional facts would you want to determine in your investigation, and why? Would you advise him to accept John Smith's settlement offer of $30,000? Why? As to the manner in which the expenses of construction proceedings would be borne, see 4 Page on Wills §31.13 (Bowe-Parker 1961).

BRECKHEIMER v. KRAFT
133 Ill. App. 2d 410, 273 N.E.2d 468 (1971)

[Clara Johnson's will, executed in April 1965, nine days before her death, bequeathed her residuary estate equally to her "nephew Raymond Schneikert and Mabel Schneikert his wife." At the time the will was executed, Raymond's wife's name was Evelyn, and his former wife, then named Mabel Reihs, had remarried. Relatives of Clara claimed the residue on the ground that the residuary bequest was invalid for misnomer, Raymond and Evelyn claimed the residue, and Mabel claimed half of the residue.]

DEMPSEY, J. . . .

Since the ambiguity is disclosed by extrinsic evidence it may be removed by such evidence. To assist the court in ascertaining what the language in the will means, it is proper in such an inquiry to take into consideration the facts and circumstances surrounding the testator at the time the will was executed and his relation with his family and the beneficiaries named in the will. . . .

At the hearing Mabel Reihs testified that . . . [f]rom 1952 until 1964 she neither saw nor corresponded with Mrs. Johnson and did not know of her death until two years after she passed away. . . . Evelyn Schneikert testified that she . . . [first met Mrs. Johnson] in 1964. In their subsequent correspondence Mrs. Johnson addressed her as "Dear Evelyn";

she never referred to her as Mabel. They also spoke over the telephone. . . .

Mrs. Johnson's pastor and the attorney who drew her will also testified. . . . They said that the will was prepared at the hospital. After satisfying himself as to her competency, the attorney inquired who was to receive her estate and she informed him she wanted an old friend to have a thousand dollars and the balance was to go to her nephew and his wife. The attorney asked the nephew's name and she replied "Raymond Schneikert." The attorney then requested the wife's name. Mrs. Johnson thought a second or two and said "Mabel." . . .

From this evidence and the language of the will, the trial court concluded that Mr. S. Johnson intended to bequeath the remainder of her estate to Raymond Schneikert and "his present wife." . . . If a bequest is made to the wife of a certain person, and there is nothing in the will indicating the contrary, the term "wife" will apply to the person who answers that description on the date of the will. . . . There was no one who answered to the name "Mabel Schneikert" but there was a person who answered the description "his wife, of Plymouth, Wisconsin." Alternatively, if the name "Schneikert" is ignored and only the name "Mabel" considered, the description, and the surrounding circumstances as well, point to Evelyn as the intended legatee.

. . . A mistake in description may be corrected by rejecting that which* is shown to be false, but no words may be inserted in place of those stricken and no words may be supplied. . . .

Complaint is made that the court erred in admitting, over objection, the testimony of the pastor and attorney and further erred in permitting them to testify concerning questions asked of, and answers made by, Mrs. Johnson. Declarations of a testatrix as to what she intended are not admissible in interpreting a will. Neither witness, however, testified to any declaration by Mrs. Johnson that differed from the words in her will; in fact, what she told them was identical to the language found in the instrument. Where there is no ambiguity in a will, the testimony of the draftsman is inadmissible to show the testator's intention. But the rule excluding the draftsman's testimony does not supersede the rule that parol evidence is admissible to explain a latent ambiguity. The testimony of the draftsman or a witness to a will is not in a special class, distinguishable from other permissible parol evidence. . . .

The judgment of the Circuit Court is affirmed.

Breckheimer is a classic misdescription case. Consider how it would differ if Raymond's divorce from Mabel and his remarriage to Evelyn had occurred *after* the will was executed.

SIEGLEY v. SIMPSON
73 Wash. 69, 131 P. 479 (1913)

[M. J. Heney's will left $6,000 to "my good friend Richard H. Simpson." The legacy was claimed by Richard H. Simpson and Hamilton Ross Simpson. The lower court held for Hamilton Ross, and Richard H. has appealed, arguing that parol evidence was not admissible to oppose his claim.]

MOUNT, J. . . .

"It is well settled that parol evidence is not admissible to add to, vary, or contradict the words of a written will, not only because the will itself is the best evidence of the testator's intention, but also because wills are required by the statute of frauds to be in writing." 30 Am. & Eng. Ency. Law (2d ed.) p. 673.

It may be stated generally that, where the beneficiary under a will is not designated with precision, parol evidence is admissible to show who was intended. Thus, where a latent ambiguity results from the fact that the description of the legatee or devisee is perfectly answered by two or more persons, or is applicable in part to two or more persons, parol evidence to identify the person intended is admissible. But where there is no ambiguity, and the object of the testator's bounty is sufficiently designated by plain language, so that it is clear who was intended, the construction is for the court, and parol evidence is inadmissible, although it might be thereby shown that the testator's intention was entirely different from that expressed in the will.

30 Am. & Eng. Ency. Law (2d ed.) pp. 682-3. . . .

"In cases of equivocation, as where the will or a provision thereof applies equally as well to two or more objects or persons, evidence of statements or declarations made by the testator at the time of the execution or about the time of the execution of his will is admissible for the purpose of identifying the person. . . ." 40 Cyc. 1435. Necessarily extrinsic evidence is admissible to prove the identity of the beneficiary named in a will, especially when two or more persons are claiming to be beneficially named; not for the purpose of varying the terms of the will, but to determine the person meant by the testator. . . .

In Woman's Foreign Missionary Society v. Mitchell, 93 Md. 199, 48 A. 737, 53 L.R.A. 711, the court said: "It is the identity of the individual, natural or artificial, that is material, and not the *name*, for that is simply one of the numerous means by which the identity is ascertained. The *identity* being established, the *name* is of no importance." In Hockensmith v. Slusher, 26 Mo. 237, the court said: "The general rule is that parol evidence cannot be admitted to supply or contradict, enlarge or vary the words of a will, nor to explain the intention of the testator, except in two specified cases: (1) Where there is a latent ambiguity, arising *dehors* the will, as to the person or subject meant to be described; and (2) to rebut a resulting trust." See, also, Reformed Presbyterian Church v. McMillan, 31 Wash. 643, 72 P. 502.

[margin note: exceptions to PE inadmissibility]

In this case if there had been two different persons by the name of Richard H. Simpson, and who in other respects answered the description in the will, and these two persons were claiming as legatees, clearly extrinsic evidence would be admissible to determine the identity of the person named in the will. For the same reason and upon the same principle, where there are two persons each claiming to be the beneficiary because they are each described in the will, the court must decide, from extrinsic evidence if need be, which is the person intended. And that is what was done in this case. The evidence is plain that by the words "I give . . . unto my friend Richard H. Simpson the sum of six thousand dollars," the testator referred to his friend Hamilton Ross Simpson, the respondent here, for the latter was his employee, and had been so for several years in Alaska and assisted the testator in railway work, where the testator accumulated his estate. Hamilton Ross Simpson was the testator's personal associate much of the time in Alaska, and the testator had told different persons that he had made provision for him in his will. The testator, while he was intimate with H. R. Simpson, the respondent, did not in fact know his given name or the order of his initials, and always addressed him as "Mr. Simpson" or "Bill" or "Rotary Bill," as he was commonly known on account of his ability to handle a railroad rotary snowplow. Richard H. Simpson, the appellant, was not a friend of the testator, had met him only once in twenty years, and then merely spoke to him as they passed by. These and other facts not necessary to recount, led the trial court to conclude that the testator used the name Richard H. Simpson when he referred to and really intended the person and name of Hamilton Ross Simpson as his beneficiary. Under the rule as above stated, where the beneficiary is not precisely described, extrinsic evidence was proper, and we are satisfied that the trial court correctly interpreted the intent of the testator and the meaning of the will.

[margin note: relying on true latent ambiguity]

The judgment is therefore affirmed.

CROW, C.J., and PARKER and GOSE, J.J., concur.

CHADWICK, J.

A most familiar rule of interpretation of wills is that effect should be given to every word contained therein. The testator, Heney, undertook to designate an object of his bounty. He did not do it by name alone. He said, "I give to my friend." The word "friend" is a word of weight and meaning. In the light of all the evidence, it fits Hamilton Ross Simpson, and it does not fit Richard H. Simpson. The record shows, as is said in the majority opinion, that Richard H. Simpson was never the friend of the testator. It is not shown that he was more than a casual acquaintance, and there is no independent evidence of that fact. Hamilton Ross Simpson was Heney's friend. . . . This creates an uncertainty or ambiguity, and parol testimony is admissible to clear the doubt. . . . If there had been no qualifying word, there might be no room for construction; but when it is shown that Mr. Heney had but one friend Simpson, and that friend was known to him as "H.R." or "R.H.," and by no familiar name other than "Bill," I have no hesitancy in holding that this case falls without the general rule quoted in the majority opinion.

MATTER OF SNIDE
52 N.Y.2d 193, 418 N.E.2d 656 (1981)

WACHTLER, J. . . .

This case involves the admissibility of a will to probate. The facts are simply stated and are not in dispute. Harvey Snide, the decedent, and his wife, Rose Snide, intending to execute mutual wills at a common execution ceremony, each executed by mistake the will intended for the other. . . .

Harvey Snide is survived by his widow [the sole beneficiary of his will] and three children, two of whom have reached the age of majority. These elder children have executed waivers and have consented to the admission of the instrument to probate. The minor child, however, is represented by a guardian ad litem who refuses to make such a concession. . . .

The gist of the objectant's argument is that Harvey Snide lacked the required testamentary intent because he never intended to execute the document he actually signed. This argument is not novel, and in the few American cases on point it has been the basis for the denial of probate. However, cases from other common-law jurisdictions have taken a different view of the matter and we think the view they espouse is more sound. . . .

. . . [W]e decline the formalistic view that this intent attaches irrevocably to the document prepared, rather than the testamentary scheme it reflects. . . .

Moreover, the significance of the only variance between the two instruments is fully explained by consideration of the documents together, as well as in the undisputed surrounding circumstances. Under such facts it would indeed be ironic — if not perverse — to state that because what has occurred is so obvious, and what was intended so clear, we must act to nullify rather than sustain this testamentary scheme. . . .

. . .There is absolutely no danger of fraud, and the refusal to read these wills together would serve merely to unnecessarily expand formalism, without any corresponding benefit. On these narrow facts we decline this unjust course.

Nor can we share the fears of the dissent that our holding will be the first step in the exercise of judicial imagination relating to the reformation of wills. . . .

[REVERSED, four to three.]

JONES, J. (dissenting).

I . . . am of the conviction that the willingness of the majority in an appealing case to depart from what has been consistent precedent in the courts of the United States and England will prove troublesome in the future. This is indeed an instance of the old adage that hard cases make bad law. . . .

On the basis of commendably thorough world-wide research, counsel for appellant has uncovered a total of 17 available reported cases involving mutual wills mistakenly signed by the wrong testator. . . . Relief was granted in the six cases from the British Commonwealth. In these cases it appears that the court has been moved by the transparency of the obvious error and the egregious frustration of undisputed intention which would ensue from failure to correct that error.

. . . I fear an inability to contain the logical consequences of this decision in the future. Thus, why should the result be any different where, although the two wills are markedly different in content, it is equally clear that there has been an erroneous contemporaneous cross-signing by the two would-be testators, or where the scrivener has prepared several drafts for a single client and it is established beyond all doubt that the wrong draft has been mistakenly signed? Nor need imagination stop there. . . .

KNUPP v. DISTRICT OF COLUMBIA
578 A.2d 702 (D.C. App. 1990)

NEWMAN, Associate Judge:

. . . The facts of this case show that the testator, a District of Columbia resident, executed a will from his hospital bed in March 1986 and died approximately one month thereafter. . . . Nowhere does [the will] name a residual beneficiary.

The will was drafted by Milton W. Schober, the attorney referred to in the eighth paragraph of the will and the drafter of the testator's two prior wills. In his two prior wills, the testator left significant bequests to his personal friend, Richard L. Knupp ("Knupp"). Appellant alleges that in this will testator also intended Knupp to benefit. Allegedly, approximately one month prior to his death, the testator told Schober to draft a new will which would leave specific dollar amounts to several named beneficiaries and which would leave the bulk of the estate to Knupp, as residual beneficiary. Schober drafted the new will and the testator signed it. The will, however, did not name the residual legatee. Schober submitted an affidavit to the trial court admitting that he mistakenly failed to designate a residual beneficiary in the will even though the testator had instructed him to name Knupp. Schober also provided the trial court with notes he took of his conversations with the testator to prove that the testator intended Knupp to be the residual legatee.

In an order dated November 16, Judge Barnes found that the will was ambiguous on its face and that the court should consider extrinsic evidence to determine the testator's intent. In a supplemental order, though, Judge Barnes ruled that as a matter of law, specific extrinsic evidence concerning the names of omitted legatees must be excluded. . . . The general rule in construing a will in the District of Columbia is that the testator's intent is the guiding principle. . . . If the intent is clear from the language of the will, the inquiry ends there. . . . However, "if the language 'upon its face and without explanation, is doubtful or meaningless' . . . a court may examine extrinsic evidence in order to understand the will." Wyman [v. Roesner, 439 A.2d 516, 520 (D.C. Ct. App. 1981)] (quoting Baker v. National Savings & Trust, 86 U.S. App. D.C. 161, 162, 181 F.2d 273, 274 (1950)); accord Starkey v. District of Columbia, 377 A.2d 382, 383 (D.C. 1977). . . .

. . . [T]here must be some ambiguity in order for a court to consider extinsic evidence. . . .

See also 7th Ga. Regiment, supra, 55 App. D.C. at 158, 3 F.2d at 203 ("[A]mbiguity may arise when a will names a person as the object of a gift, or a thing as the subject of it, and there are two persons or things that equally well answer such name or description. In such a case, it is apparent that extrinsic evidence is not only useful, but indispensable to a proper interpretation of the will."); Mitchell v. Merriam, 88 U.S. App. D.C. 213, 188 F.2d 42 (1950) (where testatrix devised property to "my nephew Edward A. Mitchell" and testatrix had both a nephew and a grandnephew named Edward A. Mitchell, the court allowed in extrinsic evidence to show which of the two individuals the testatrix was referring to in her will); In re Miller's Estate, 127 F. Supp. 23 (D.D.C. 1955) (where testatrix's will stated "I give and bequeath to my cousin, Sue McCook . . . any monies that are left after my just debts are paid," extrinsic evidence was allowed in order to determine whether testatrix intended the word "monies" to be restricted to cash and money on deposit in bank accounts or whether the word should be understood in the colloquial sense as meaning all personal property).

Any ambiguity in the will under consideration in this case is not of the sort that can be corrected by the consideration of extrinsic evidence. There is no language in the will that could lead a court to infer that the testator intended Knupp to be the recipient of the residual estate; thus, it was proper for the court not to admit the extrinsic evidence. . . .

For the aforementioned reasons, the decision is hereby affirmed.

Would relief have been available in *Knupp* under Restatement (Third) of Property: Wills and Other Donative Transfers §12.1?

If the mistakenly omitted devisee in *Knupp* later sues the lawyer for malpractice and the jurisdiction has abolished the traditional "privity" barrier to recovery, is there less need for a reformation doctrine for wills? Has the lawyer breached the duty of care? If adequate proof of the testator's intent is lacking, can it be established that the lawyer was negligent? Compare Williams v. Bryan Cave, et al., 774 S.W. 2d 847 (Mo. App. 1989) with Succession of Killingsworth, 292 So. 2d 536 (La. 1973). See also Arnold v. Carmichael, 524 So. 2d 464 (Fla. App. 1988), review denied, 531 So. 2d 1352 (will lacked residuary clause); In re Estate of Barker, 448 So. 2d 28 (Fla. App. 1984) (court earlier refused to reform same will).

PROBLEM

5-J. *T*'s will devised her estate in trust for three charities, one designated (as she instructed her lawyer) "Society for the Prevention of Cruelty to Animals (Local or National)." There is no such organization, although a number of societies with slightly different names claim the devise. Following litigation and settlement of these claims, a class action on behalf of the interested humane societies against the attorney alleged that the will had been negligently drawn, and that as a result the various societies had been damaged by having to hire legal counsel and participate in lengthy litigation. What result? See Ventura County Humane Society v. Holloway, 115 Cal. Rptr. 464 (Cal. App. 1984). See also W. McGovern, The Increasing Malpractice Liability of Will Drafters, Trusts & Estates 10 (Dec. 1994); and B. Ross, How to Do Right by Not Doing Wrong: Legal Malpractice and Ethical Considerations in Estate Planning and Administration, 28 U. Miami Inst. on Est. Pl. ¶¶800.802.2 (1994).

In Connecticut Junior Republic v. Sharon Hospital, 188 Conn. 1, 448 A.2d 190 (1982), the lawyer mistakenly put the wrong devisees in the residuary clause, and the court applied the traditional rule excluding extrinsic evidence of a mistake by a scrivener of a will. The case was overruled in Erickson v. Erickson, 246 Conn. 359, 716 A.2d 92 (1998), substantially adopting Justice Peters' dissenting opinion in *Connecticut Junior Republic,* which stated in part:

I take as a point of departure the established proposition that a will cannot validly be probated if it was executed by a testator in reliance on erroneous beliefs induced by fraud, duress, or undue influence. . . . I can see no reason of logic or of policy to treat the mistake case differently from the fraud or undue influence case. In each instance, extrinsic evidence is required to demonstrate that a will, despite its formally proper execution, substantially misrepresents the true intent of the testator.

The majority would disallow extrinsic evidence of a scrivener's error for two principal reasons: the existing Connecticut case law, and the risk of subverting the policy of the Statute of Wills. I find neither reason persuasive. The existing case law is . . . of ancient vintage. I agree that antiquity does not automatically disqualify common law precedents that continue to serve modern needs. But I find our case law less persuasive than does the majority. . . .

The risk of subversion of the intent of a testator, who cannot personally defend his testamentary bequest, is without doubt a serious concern. Balanced against that concern is the risk of blindly enforcing a testamentary disposition that substantially misstates the testator's true intent. We have long ago resolved this balance in favor of admitting extrinsic evidence when the testator's intent is undermined by fraud, undue influence or incapacity. . . . Under the modern law of misrepresentation, innocent misrepresentation is treated as generally equivalent to fraud in terms of its legal consequences. . . . The Statute of Wills does not compel enforcement of testamentary dispositions that a testator never intended to make. . . .

Objection to the admission of extrinsic evidence in this case must therefore find support outside the direct commandments of the Statute of Wills. Two such objections have been advanced. . . .

The first . . . states that whatever error the scrivener may have made was validated and ratified by the testator's act in signing his will. . . . While signing the will creates a strong presumption that the will accurately represents the intentions of the testator, that presumption is a rebuttable one.

The second objection is a fear that allowing extrinsic evidence of mistake will give rise to a proliferation of groundless will contests. There is no doubt that our increasingly fact-based jurisprudence serves to expose many apparently final dispositions to the . . . risk of unjustified judicial intervention. . . . In the law of wills, the risk is limited by the narrowness of the exception that this case would warrant. I would today do no more than permit the opponent of a will to introduce extrinsic evidence of the error of a scrivener, and would require proof . . . by clear and convincing evidence. . . .

In sum, I see no greater risk of juridical error in the case of a scrivener's error than in the case of fraud or undue influence. I find it difficult to draw a clear line of demarcation between a scrivener's mistake and an innocent misrepresentation. . . . Wills that do not reflect the true intent of the testator should be refused probate.

———————————

Does Restatement (Third) of Property §12.1 above (page 202), go further?

ESTATE OF KREMLICK
417 Mich. 237, 331 N.W.2d 228 (1983)

[Part of the residue of the testator's estate was left to "the Michigan Cancer Society." In a per curiam opinion the court of appeals upheld that Society's claim to the devise, finding no ambiguity. Further appeal was taken to the Michigan Supreme Court by the American Cancer Society, Michigan Division.]

PER CURIAM. . . .

We agree with the Court of Appeals that the designation "Michigan Cancer Society" is not a patent ambiguity. Determining the presence of a latent ambiguity, however, is more difficult. This Court has held that in interpreting contracts where an ambiguity *may exist,* extrinsic evidence is admissible: (1) to prove the existence of ambiguity; (2) to indicate the actual intent of the parties; and (3) to indicate the actual intent of the parties as an aid in construction. . . .

(margin note: extrinsic evid. is admissible to prove)

These rules are equally applicable to interpreting wills. Thus, not only may extrinsic evidence be used to clarify the meaning of a latent ambiguity, but it may be used to demonstrate that an ambiguity exists in the first place and to establish intent.

In this case, appellants produced an affidavit from the executrix of Mr. Kremlick's estate in which she asserted that the intended beneficiary was the American Cancer Society, Michigan Division, instead of the Michigan Cancer Society, an affiliate of the Michigan Cancer Foundation. The executrix stated that she had discussed the provisions of Mr. Kremlick's will with him on many occasions and that he frequently had mentioned that the American Cancer Society was to be a beneficiary. Appellants also sought to establish that Mr. Kremlick previously had made substantial direct contributions to the American Cancer Society, that the Society had helped his wife when she was dying of cancer, and that at the time of her death he requested memorials to the American Cancer Society.

This is the very kind of information that may be used both to establish an ambiguity and to help resolve it. Appellants should have been given the opportunity to do that. . . .

————————

In California and New Jersey, some noteworthy cases have been decided — possibly more noteworthy in their willingness to attempt to articulate openly what is being done than in the actual novelty of their use of evidence.

The California developments were largely fostered by Estate of Russell, 69 Cal. 2d 200, 70 Cal. Rptr. 561, 444 P.2d 353 (1968), which emphasized that whether or not a will is "ambiguous" cannot always be determined "until the surrounding circumstances are first considered." The court also noted, however, that if "in light of such extrinsic evidence" the terms of the will are not "reasonably susceptible of two or more meanings," evidence is not admissible to show "an intention *different* from that expressed by the words" — that is, to show a meaning of which the words are not "reasonably susceptible."

In New Jersey a greater departure from the traditional dicta has been acknowledged, as summarized in Engle v. Siegel, 74 N.J. 287, 290-291, 377 A.2d 892, 893-894 (1977): "The generally accepted method of determining testamentary intent was once described by this Court [as recently as 1953] in these words, 'It is elementary . . . that the controlling consideration is the effect of the words as actually written rather than the actual intention of the testator independently of the written words . . . [not] what he was minded to say, but rather the meaning of the terms chosen. . . .' This statement can no longer be said accurately to express the law of our State. . . . [Under] what has come to be known as the doctrine of probable intent . . . a court not only examines 'the entire will' but also studies 'competent extrinsic evidence'; it attributes to the testator 'common human impulses' and seeks to find what he would *subjectively* have desired had he in fact actually addressed the contingency which has arisen."

3. Mistake in the Inducement

Mistakes that give rise to problems of interpretation and mistakes concerning the document executed or its contents have just been considered. Quite different is the situation in which all or part of a will is contested on the ground that it is the product of a mistake in the inducement — that is, that although the document was as intended, the motivation underlying the will or provision in question was based on a mistaken belief.

UNION PLANTERS NATIONAL BANK v. INMAN
588 S.W.2d 757 (Tenn. App. 1979)

[The decedent's 1965 will, after a charitable bequest, would have left about a quarter of his estate outright to his wife and the residue equally to his three children. The will in question, executed in 1971, contained similar provisions except that the shares of the wife and children were left in trust rather than outright. The wife was given a power to appoint the remainder of her trust by will, the remainder interest in the children's trust was eventually to go to decedent's grandchildren, and both

trusts contained spendthrift provisions (see Chapter 14, infra) to protect the beneficiaries from creditors. The 1971 will was contested by
two of the children, who alleged that the decedent's lawyer falsely led
the decedent to believe that one son was heavily in debt and another
"had large exposure through real estate ventures" and encouraged
the decedent to include the trust arrangements in his will as a protection against the sons' creditors (with trusts also for the wife and daughter in order not to single out and embarrass the sons). It was further
alleged that the first son had paid off his debts before the 1971 will
was planned and that, but for the attorney's misrepresentations, the
decedent would not have changed his 1965 will. The evidence in the
case could not support the contestants' allegations of fraud and undue
influence, but there was conflicting evidence as to the financial circumstances of the sons. The trial judge, however, found "no genuine issue
as to a material fact" and granted proponent's motion for summary
judgment.]

EWELL, J. . . .

Taking the facts before us in the light most favorable to the contestants, we find that, at most, this is a case where the draftsman of the
will was mistakenly informed as to the financial condition of a son of
the testator and in the course of his conference with the testator related
to him erroneous information. . . . In the final analysis the only substantial insistence of the contestants is that a portion of the testator's will
is invalid because it was made under a mistake and misapprehension
of the facts as they existed at the time of the execution of the will. The
Supreme Court of this State in the case of Anderson v. Anderson, 220
Tenn. 496, 419 S.W.2d 166 (1967) affirmed the 1917 case of Bowerman
v. Burris, 138 Tenn. 220, 197 S.W. 490 and quoted the following statement therefrom: "Moreover, if the evidence [of mistake] could be at
all effective, under our system, two points would have to be established:
Firstly, that the testator was laboring under a mistake as to the fact;
and, secondly, that if the truth had been known he would have made
a different disposition, *and we think these facts should appear in the will
itself.*" (emphasis supplied.)

We have been unable to find a Tennessee case wherein the mistake
and misapprehension was brought about by statement of counsel. . . .
The Missouri case of Elam v. Phariss, 289 Mo. 209, 232 S.W. 693 (1921)
is based upon facts not substantially dissimilar to the case before us.
In that case the Supreme Court of Missouri quoted with approval language from the case of Couch v. Easthan, 27 W. Va. 796, 55 Am.
Rep. 346 as follows: "The mistake which will avail to set aside a will is
a mistake as to what it contains, or as to the paper itself, not a mistake
either of law or fact in the mind of the testator, as to the effect of what
he actually and intentionally did."

We find the foregoing to be the majority view, and the Tennessee
cases of *Bowerman,* supra and *Anderson,* supra are not inconsistent there-

with. In this case it does not appear within the will itself that Inman
was laboring under a mistake as to the facts and that if the erroneous
statements had not been made by Martin, he would have made a different disposition. . . .

[A]ffirmed. . . .

The frequently cited case of Bowerman v. Burris, quoted in the opinion above, involved a will allegedly executed under a mistaken belief
that the testator's only son was dead. The court held that evidence of
the testator's belief "was not competent" and observed that it would
be "contrary to sound policy to admit evidence of conversations . . .
as to his purposes or his reasons for making a disposition." To do so
"would open the door wide to fraud" when the testator "cannot give
his version of the matter." The court then stated the requirement that
the will itself must disclose both the mistaken belief and that a different
disposition would have been made if the truth were known. Would
Bowerman have been differently decided if the will had begun: "Because
my only son is dead, I therefore leave my estate as follows:"? Cf. Uniform Probate Code §2-302(c).

Would the result of *Bowerman* be different if, prior to execution of
the will and knowing the contrary to be true, one of the devisees had
told the testator that his son was dead?

An even stronger stand against reformation of a will based on mistake
in the inducement can be found in Carpenter v. Tinney, 420 S.W.2d 241,
244 (Tex. Civ. App. 1967), stating: "Generally a mistake of fact or law,
in the absence of fraud or undue influence, will not defeat the probate
of a will, even though the testator might have made a different will if
there had been no such mistake inducing the testator to make the will.
. . . It is also the general rule that courts have no right to vary or modify
the terms of a will or to reform it even on grounds of mistake. . . . It has
been held that if the testator labors under no mistake in identity of the
document executed, a mistake of fact or law, there being no fraud or
undue influence, will not defeat probate of a will."

PROBLEMS

5-K. *T*'s will, executed shortly before death, left his estate in equal
shares to *A* and *B*, two of his three children. The will also declared *T*'s
desire to treat all of his children alike and that he had "advanced" his
son, *C*, an amount roughly equal to his share of the estate. *C* offers
testimony intended to prove that *T* was mistaken and that he had not
made any such "advancement." How would you argue for admission

of this evidence? Against it? If you were the court, would you grant *C* relief? Cf. Estate of Baum, 4 Utah 2d 375, 294 P.2d 711 (1956).

5-L. The arguments and decision — the whole "feel" of the case — might be different in the above set of facts if *C* offered in evidence a large, uncleared check to him from his father. Why? If your decision with this evidence would differ from your decision without it, can you articulate a principled basis for these results for the guidance of other courts in other cases that might be somewhat analogous?

F. Further Explanation, Comments, and Comparison

V. EMMERICH, ESTATE PRACTICE IN THE UNITED STATES AND EUROPE
10-11 (1950)

In Anglo-American law, documents must be explicit, detailed and unequivocal. Courts will not make [wills]. This and often antiquated legal diction have led to a very technical legal language and more lengthy and complicated documents than found in continental practice.

The German Code contains in article 242 the rule that contracts are construed according to the requirements of good faith. Judicial practice has given most extended application to this rule. German legal documents of the twentieth century, especially wills, show the tendency to shortness and simple wording, sometimes in an exaggerated degree. Courts are not reluctant to construe ambiguous provisions, to fill in gaps and even to amend or change provisions according to the good faith rule.

The situation in the French and Western-Eurpean countries is intermediate between the Anglo-American and Germanic one. A rule like that of article 242 of the German Civil Code has not been formulated and [is] even sometimes denied by the courts, but their practice was often a similar one. Legal documents are also here generally simpler and shorter than in the Anglo-American countries, even if not to the same degree as in Germany.

POWER, WILLS: A PRIMER OF INTERPRETATION AND CONSTRUCTION
51 Iowa L. Rev. 75, 76-87, 103-106 (1965)

Directions as to the disposition of property after death will be given effect only to the extent they are expressed in a valid will. To the extent that testamentary directions are clearly and unambiguously expressed they will be given effect even if [someone seeks to show] that the words of the will do not express the testator's wishes. These two propositions suggest the truism that there are many instances of mistake for which there is no relief. . . .

In the nature of things it is always necessary to look outside the will in order to identify persons and property described in it. Though the use of extrinsic evidence in the existing system extends substantially beyond this, "the policies embodied in the . . . Statute of Wills, and the necessities implicit in an orderly and expeditious administration of justice, requires that inquiries as to the meaning of language be kept within reasonable limits." . . . The view which is gaining acceptance today is that . . . the "rule" against disturbing a clear meaning does not render extrinsic evidence inadmissible to show that the apparently clear words are in fact ambiguous and to show further that the words were intended to and do identify some less well described person or thing.[1]

. . . [T]he testator is not bound to usual linguistic conventions, and a seemingly incomprehensible word or symbol may often be readily explained by evidence of the testator's peculiar usages. . . .[But consider the following] frequently quoted words . . . :

> [I]t . . . is more important that the probate of the wills of dead people be effectively shielded from the attacks of a multitude of fictitious mistakes than that it be purged of wills containing a few real ones. The latter a testator may, by due care, avoid in his lifetime. Against the former he would be helpless.

Words and other graphic symbols are the only means of communicating complicated ideas. It is a worthy, even vital, objective for the law to preserve the instrumentality which enables such communication. . . . To the extent that words are said to mean something other than that

---

1. . . . [In] Estate of Gibbs, 14 Wis. 2d 490, 111 N.W.2d 413 (1961), the testator apparently intended his employee, Robert W. Krause of 2325 North Sherman Boulevard, Milwaukee, but erroneously designated him (probably as a result of picking the wrong name from the telephone directory) as Robert J. Krause of 4708 North 46th Street, where there lived a person named Robert J. Krause, a stranger to the testator so far as the evidence revealed. The Court, taking the view that there was no ambiguity, still permitted the intended beneficiary to take, saying (at 499, 111 N.W.2d at 418):

> We conclude that details of identification, particularly such matters as middle initials, street addresses, and the like, which are highly susceptible to mistake, particularly in metropolitan areas, should not be accorded such sanctity as to frustrate an otherwise clearly demonstrable intent. Where such details of identification are involved, courts should receive evidence tending to show that a mistake has been made and should disregard the details when the proof establishes to the highest degree of certainty that a mistake was, in fact, made.

which is established by conventional usage, absent an acceptable basis for finding an unconventional usage, communication of complicated ideas becomes uncertain and hence more difficult. . . . It is never claimed today that there exist infallible guides to determine a meaning, but that is not to say that basic sources of ascribing meaning may be ignored unless the context or circumstances permit. Neither can a sound interpretive process entail a commitment to inflexible adherence to a plain meaning, for, as Ogden and Richards have pointed out, words have meaning only as they are connected with objects and ideas through the writer's or reader's (or speaker's or hearer's) mental apparatus. An artificial limitation on the meaning to be derived from those arbitrary symbols, words, is as inimical to effective communication as is finding that words can mean something they do not ordinarily mean in the absence of an explanatory context or circumstance. . . .

A predictable result of a general discretion to repair would be a great increase in the incidence of litigation. . . . Judicial remaking of wills, whether avowed or under the guise of interpretation and construction, involves abandonment of the rationale of the Statute of Wills. The will, a unilateral act, has no existence apart from the writing which the testator executes. He is the only person whose intention is relevant, and his intention is relevant only to the extent it finds expression in the will. The fact that the owner of property has died (and consequently his unavailability as a witness) creates opportunity for fraud, and explains the limitations on relief for mistakes, epitomized in the frequent statement that equity will not reform a will. . . . Such limitations, which include restrictions on the sort of evidence which is admissible to show the meaning of the testator's words, are logical ramifications of the requirement of the Statute of Wills that testamentary dispositions be expressed in a witnessed writing and of the concomitant judicial reluctance or refusal to vary a clear meaning. It is tempting to think that judges are so skilled that they can best function freed from the restrictions of an elaborate system; that broad principles of justice and morality will alone suffice. . . . Though no one doubts that disharmony of the law and popular expectations in some particular often signals a need for change, a source of further reflection . . . is Ihering's discussion of the disadvantages of form (2 Ihering, Geisi des Romischen Rechts 480 (7th ed. 1923)):

> I begin with [the disadvantages of form] because without being sought out they are at once apparent to the unsophisticated, while the advantages of form require a conscious effort of research, and, I must add, demand for their discovery a juristic eye. It stands with formalism as with so many other arrangements — everyone feels its pinch, no one its benefits, because the latter are purely negative in nature, that is to say, consist in avoiding evil. A single case in which the disadvantages of form are

presented in dramatic form to the public (as for example when a testament is declared void for a defect in form . . .) causes more talk than the thousands of cases in which the course of events was a normal one, and form fulfilled its beneficial purpose. Small wonder that the judgment of the uninformed is so adverse to formalism.

What predictability the law has achieved in this area, based on standardization of the meaning of symbols, should not be forfeited to get the "right" result in an occasional hardship case, with the concomitant invitation to ill-founded claims and litigation. It is not sound to maintain that a system of rules can or should achieve the fair result or "justice" in every case. The law has achieved all that can be expected if it has sought to channel transactions into forms which people can reasonably be expected to utilize with high probability of attaining the desired legal result, and which must therefore be as free as possible of traps that reasonably acting people might fall victim to. . . . Perhaps it is [not sufficiently] recognized that the will fails when it produces litigation even if the testator's wishes are not ultimately frustrated. . . . Occasional failures, hopefully statistically rare, are the inevitable concomitant of any function subject to human fallibility, and in the case of wills this price is not unreasonable for the easily overlooked benefits of formalities.

JOHN H. LANGBEIN & LAWRENCE W. WAGGONER, REFORMATION OF WILLS ON THE GROUND OF MISTAKE: CHANGE OF DIRECTION IN AMERICAN LAW?
130 U. Pa. L. Rev. 521, 522, 577-580, 590 (1982)

. . . . The impulse to relieve against mistake is strongly felt in modern courts. . . . Yet because the black letter law has seemed so hostile, courts have often given remedy in specious or unreasoned theories of decision. We think that with the no-extrinsic-evidence rule now undergoing abrogation and with the Wills Act formal requirements understood to be not an obstacle, a principled reformation doctrine can be formulated that will strike the proper balance between the concerns that underlie the old no-reformation rule and the factors that have made that rule ever more unpalatable.

. . . The three elements of the [reformation] doctrine are already to be observed in the various situations where courts have been able to remedy mistake without affronting older notions of the force of the Wills Act. These elements . . . we label the (1) materiality, (2) particularity, and (3) burden-of-proof requirements. Each is directly responsive to the evidentiary concerns that were so prominent in discussions of the old no-reformation rule.

... [C]ases can be found in which materiality is lacking even though the mistake be proved, [as in an] old Rhode Island case . . . where the court found it "very apparent . . . that the testatrix would have made the same will had she known" that she was mistaken. . . .

... [T]he reformation doctrine will confine relief to situations where the alleged mistake involves a fact or event of particularity — for example, . . . the scrivener's misunderstanding of the import of the term "heirs"; . . . the scrivener's failure to provide a lapse clause appropriate to the testators' wishes; in *Snide* the mistaken execution of the spouse's will pursuant to the lawyer's direction.

The essential safeguard for a reformation doctrine in the law of wills is a standard of proof effective to deal with the evidentiary concerns to which the former no-reformation rule was addressed. Although that rule has been found too harsh, it did respond to the difficulty and the danger of proving that a testator now dead made a mistake in his duly executed will. . . . [A] modern reformation doctrine for wills must follow the law of non-probate transfers by placing upon the proponent of a mistake claim the burden of proving it by evidence of exceptional quality. The clear-and-convincing-evidence standard is pitched above the ordinary preponderance-of-the-evidence test characteristic of most civil litigation, but below the beyond-reasonable-doubt rule of the criminal law. . . .

[Do] statutory gap-filling rules take precedence over reformation in a well-proven case of mistake[?] The answer is no. . . . Because reformation puts the language back in the will, there is no gap for the gap-filling statutes to fill. Reformation is based upon the testator's actual intent and his actual language, whereas a statutory rule of construction is a device of subsidiary rank. . . .

So long as it is human to err, instances of mistaken terms in wills are inevitable. The impulse to remedy these errors in order to prevent unjust enrichment is also deeply rooted in our sense of justice, which is why the simplistic rule forbidding relief against mistake is dissolving. . . . We think that a principled reformation doctrine has all the advantages over the patchwork of inconsistency and injustice that characterizes the present law. . . .

6

Revocation and Revival

Revocation may occur by operation of law, by some physical act performed on the will with intent to revoke, or expressly or impliedly by a subsequent instrument meeting the statutory requirements. A will may be revoked in whole or in part. All states recognize that wills are revocable, this being an aspect of a will's ambulatory character. A will that has been revoked may be restored to testamentary life or "revived" under various circumstances. Also, under the doctrine of dependent relative revocation, a will that was assumed to have been revoked may be held not to have lost its validity.

Problems of revocation and revival often turn on the precise wording of a statute or on fine distinctions tediously drawn by courts. Sometimes cases turn on the elusive intention of the testator, either in executing an instrument or in performing some act. However, it must always be kept in mind that both the requirement of an authorized act or instrument of revocation and the requirement of an accompanying intent to revoke must be satisfied. In addition to providing for revocation by subsequent, formally executed writings, most American statutes have employed some or all of the terms of the English Statute of Frauds (authorizing revocation by "burning, canceling, tearing, or obliterating"), while a few statutes resemble somewhat the English Wills Act ("burning, tearing, or otherwise destroying"). In any close case it is necessary to consult the exact statutory language describing the methods of revocation.

In a sense, a revocation may occur by *ademption* (or *ademption by extinction*) when property specifically bequeathed or devised is not a part of the estate at the testator's death, or by *satisfaction* (or *ademption by satisfaction*) when a legatee receives an inter vivos gift of all or part of the legacy provided in the will. These matters are discussed elsewhere as problems of distribution rather than problems of revocation.

UNIFORM PROBATE CODE

§2-507.   *Revocation by Writing or by Act.*

(a) A will or any part thereof is revoked:
   (1) by executing a subsequent will that revokes the previous will or part expressly or by inconsistency; or

(2) by performing a revocatory act on the will, if the testator performed the act with the intent and for the purpose of revoking the will or part or if another individual performed the act in the testator's conscious presence and by the testator's direction. For purposes of this paragraph, "revocatory act on the will" includes burning, tearing, canceling, obliterating, or destroying the will or any part of it. A burning, tearing, or canceling is a "revocatory act on the will," whether or not the burn, tear, or cancellation touched any of the words on the will.

(b) If a subsequent will does not expressly revoke a previous will, the execution of the subsequent will wholly revokes the previous will by inconsistency if the testator intended the subsequent will to replace rather than supplement the previous will.

(c) The testator is presumed to have intended a subsequent will to replace rather than supplement a previous will if the subsequent will makes a complete disposition of the testator's estate. If this presumption arises and is not rebutted by clear and convincing evidence, the previous will is revoked; only the subsequent will is operative on the testator's death.

(d) The testator is presumed to have intended a subsequent will to supplement rather than replace a previous will if the subsequent will does not make a complete disposition of the testator's estate. If this presumption arises and is not rebutted by clear and convincing evidence, the subsequent will revokes the previous will only to the extent the subsequent will is inconsistent with the previous will; each will is fully operative on the testator's death to the extent they are not inconsistent.

A. *Revocation by Physical Act*

Because revocation almost universally may be accomplished by an appropriate physical act, and because of what seems a natural temptation of laypersons to use such methods, litigation often is required to determine whether an apparent attempt to revoke satisfies the local statute. Obviously, physical acts performed on the will may be vulnerable to questions of (1) whether the necessary present intention to revoke accompanied the alleged act of revocation and (2) whether the act in question was done by the testator (or by another at the direction and in the presence of the testator, as is generally authorized by statute). Often, though, it is the sufficiency of the act itself that is questioned under the statute. Is a large cross-mark on one of the pages or on the cover of the will sufficient? Is a will "burned" if its edges are singed? What of a notation on the face or the back of the will? What if some or even all dispositive provisions, or the testator's signature, are lined out? The cases are numerous and the results are varied. Decisions are often highly technical in their interpretation of the statutory requirements. The common "cancellation" requirement generally has been held to require defacing of the writing,[1] not just of blank portions of the will (but see UPC §2-507(a)(2) above), while a slight "tearing" or "burning" may be sufficient if accompanied by the requisite intention.

Partial revocations are also a recurrent source of difficulty. Although some courts have refused to recognize partial revocations by physical act,[2] statutory language (such as "no will or any part thereof may be revoked except . . .") is frequently construed to permit such revocations, and some courts have allowed partial revocation in the absence of any such statutory suggestion. Where a will can be revoked in part, difficulties arise when a testator fails to make clear whether the intent was to revoke the entire will or only the mutilated provisions. Of course, the form of the act frequently leaves little doubt, such as where a particular bequest is distinctly and thoroughly lined out.

A few statutes expressly provide that revocation of a will also revokes all codicils thereto. Even in the absence of such a statutory provision it is generally held that, if so intended, a physical act performed upon the will also revokes its codicils. However, revocation of a codicil does not normally revoke a will.

While intensive study of dubious attempts to revoke is of little value except with reference to a particular problem about to be litigated, the materials following the problem below illustrate the possible attitudes of courts in these situations.

PROBLEM

6-A.   Three years ago Thomas properly executed a will dividing his estate among his wife and cousins. Ten days ago he told his lawyer, Addison, that he wanted to increase his wife's share and perhaps leave her the entire estate. Addison set an appointment to review the will, but before that date arrived he received a telephone call from Thomas in a distant state where Thomas was hospitalized after becoming ill while traveling. After learning that his wife would take all of his intestate property, Thomas told Addison that he wanted to revoke his will

---

1. In Estate of Dickson, 590 So. 2d 471 (Fla. App. 1991), the testator sufficiently "defaced" the will to revoke it when he wrote "void" over the notarial in the self-proving affidavit to the will, and his entire handwritten statement on open parts of the document was admissible to establish the necessary accompanying intent to revoke by the act of defacement.

2. Cf. In re Minsinger's Estate, 228 Or. 218, 364 P.2d 615 (1961) (holding that drawing a line through parts of the will but leaving those provisions legible was ineffective as a partial revocation).

and directed Addison to get it from the file. Jane, Addison's secretary, brought the will and then picked up an extension phone in the office as the following conversation ensued:

Thomas: Addy, do you have the will?
Addison: Yes, Tom; Jane has just brought it to me.
Thomas: Jane, are you there?
Jane: Yes, and we have the will I witnessed three years ago.
Thomas: Addy, tear it up. I want to revoke it. See that he does what I say, Jane.
Jane: I will. He's tearing it in two.
Thomas: I hear him tearing it. It is done, Addy?
Addison: Yes, all done.
Thomas: Good, I want to die without a will.

This morning, Addison received a word from the hospital that Thomas had died during the night. Addison retrieved the fragments of the torn will from the wastebasket and put them in an envelope in Thomas's file with a memorandum of these facts. Will Thomas's estate be administered testate or intestate under the Uniform Probate Code? Why? Under the law of your state? See Matter of Will of Jefferson, 349 So. 2d 1032 (Miss. 1977).

THOMPSON v. ROYALL
163 Va. 492, 175 S.E. 748 (1934)

[Mrs. Kroll executed a will and a few days later a codicil amending the will. Soon thereafter, in the presence of two friends, she requested her lawyer to destroy both documents, but at his suggestion she decided to preserve them for future reference. The following was then written on the back of the manuscript cover of the will by the lawyer and signed by Mrs. Kroll: "This will is null and void and to be only held by H. P. Brittain, instead of being destroyed, as a memorandum for another will if I desire to make same. This 19 Sept. 1932. s/M. Lou Bowen Kroll." A similar notation was made on the back of the sheet on which the codicil was written. Two weeks later Mrs. Kroll died. This is an appeal from the order admitting the will and codicil to probate. The applicable statute provides: "No will or codicil, or any part thereof, shall be revoked, unless . . . by a subsequent will or codicil, or by some writing declaring an intention to revoke the same, and executed in the manner in which a will is required to be executed, or by the testator, or some person in his presence and by his direction, cutting, tearing, burning, obliterating, canceling, or destroying the same, or the signature thereto, with the intent to revoke."]

HUDGKINS, J. . . .

The notations, dated September 19, 1932, are not wholly in the handwriting of the testatrix, nor are her signatures thereto attached attested by subscribing witnesses; hence under the statute they are ineffectual as "some writing declaring an intention to revoke." The faces of the two instruments bear no physical evidence of any cutting, tearing, burning, obliterating, canceling, or destroying. The only contention made by appellants is, that the notation written in the presence, and with the approval, of Mrs. Kroll, on the back of the manuscript cover in the one instance, and on the back of the sheet containing the codicil in the other, constitute "canceling" within the meaning of the statute.

Both parties concede that to effect revocation of a duly executed will, in any of the methods prescribed by statute, two things are necessary: (1) The doing of one of the acts specified, (2) accompanied by the intent to revoke — the animo revocandi. Proof of either, without proof of the other, is insufficient. Malone v. Hobbs, 1 Rob. (40 Va.) 346, 39 Am. Dec. 263; 2 Minor Ins. 925.

The proof established the intention to revoke. The entire controversy is confined to the acts used in carrying out that purpose. . . .

The [relevant authorities] hold that revocation of a will by cancellation within the meaning of the statute contemplates marks or lines across the written parts of the instrument, or a physical defacement, or some mutilation of the writing itself, with the intent to revoke. If written words are used for the purpose, they must be so placed as to physically affect the written portion of the will, not merely on blank parts of the paper on which the will is written. If the writing intended to be the act of canceling does not mutilate, or erase, or deface, or otherwise physically come in contact with any part of written words of the will, it cannot be given any greater weight than a similar writing on a separate sheet of paper, which identifies the will referred to, just as definitely as does the writing on the back. . . .

For the reasons stated, the judgment of the trial court is affirmed.

What are the responsibilities and liabilities of the attorney for the testatrix in such a case as this? See Lucas v. Hamm, 56 Cal. 2d 583, 364 P.2d 685, 15 Cal. Rptr. 821 (1961); McAbee v. Edwards, 340 So. 2d 1167 (Fla. App. 1976); Ward v. Arnold, 52 Wash. 2d 581, 328 P.2d 164 (1958); Ogle v. Fuiten, 112 Ill. App. 3d 1048, 445 N.E.2d 1344 (1983). But see Barcelo v. Elliott, 923 S.W.2d 575 (Tex. 1996). See generally G. Johnston, Avoiding Legal Malpractice in Estate Planning, 43 U.S.C. Inst. on Fed. Tax 17.1 (1991).

KELLY v. DONALDSON
456 So. 2d 30 (Ala. 1984)

[Proponent offered her deceased aunt's will for probate, and decedent's sister and various nieces and nephews contested, alleging (inter alia) revocation. Proponent was the sole beneficiary of the will, and the sole evidence in support of the will was her testimony, including testimony that the decedent executed the lawyer-drawn will in duplicate originals, retained one copy, and gave the other to proponent. After the decedent's death her retained copy could not be found by the proponent. From a jury verdict in favor of the proponent, contestants appeal.]

BEATTY, J. . . .

We affirm. . . .

In Summerhill v. Craft, 425 So. 2d 1055, 1057 (Ala. 1982), this Court stated: "If a testatrix keeps one of two duplicate original wills and gives the other to another person, and no will is found in her possession at her death, 'the presumption arises that [s]he destroyed it for the purpose of revocation.' Stiles v. Brown, 380 So. 2d 792, 796 (Ala. 1980)." *[rebuttable presumption]* While this presumption is rebuttable, the burden of rebutting the presumption rests with the proponent of the will.

Evidence offered by the proponent which merely shows "that a will contestant had access to the will after the testatrix's death is not enough to overcome the presumption [of revocation]." *Summerhill,* 425 So. 2d at 1057. In Lovell v. Lovell, 272 Ala. 409, 412, 132 So. 2d 382, 384 (1961), it was held that the presumption was not overcome by evidence showing that a contestant not only had opportunity to destroy the will, but also told the proponent, who had a copy of the will, "that she would have 'to find the original will and it has got to be signed and the date has got to be right.'" Here, however, the proponent's testimony, taken as a whole, tends to show much more than the evidence in *Lovell.* Her account of the disordered condition of the house and her testimony that Minnie had several times reaffirmed the existence of the will, the last time being less than a month before her death, are factors to be considered. Cf. *Stiles,* supra (presumption rebutted by fact that attorney told testator he must, to revoke the will, destroy both the copy retained by the attorney and the copy taken by the testator, and with the fact that the testator never attempted to destroy the copy retained by the attorney, coupled with the fact that a contestant had access to the will after the testator's death).

Where, as here, the proponent's evidence is contradicted by evidence presented by the contestants, this Court cannot find that as a matter of law the proponent has "over[come] the presumption of revocation raised by the failure to find [the testatrix's] copy of the will." *Summerhill,* 425 So. 2d at 1057. However, a jury question on this issue was clearly presented, see *Summerhill,* supra, and the proponent's testimony, if believed, was sufficient to support the verdict. Cf. New York Life Ins. Co. v. Turner, 213 Ala. 286, 288, 104 So. 643, 644 (1925) ("When a presumption [in a civil case] is to be overcome, the jury, giving due weight to the presumption in the light of judgment and experience, and in connection with the whole evidence, must be reasonably satisfied."). . . .

Affirmed.

When a will is traced to the testator's possession but cannot be found at death, it is generally said that there is a presumption, and sometimes "a strong presumption," that the will was destroyed with the intent to revoke. See generally T. Atkinson, Wills §86 (2d ed. 1953); Estate of Haynes, 25 Ohio St. 3d 101, 495 N.E.2d 23 (1986). In a few states such facts merely permit an *inference* of revocation. Cope v. Lynch, 132 Ind. App. 673, 176 N.E.2d 897 (1961). See Estate of Mitchell v. Chapman, 623 So. 2d 274 (Miss. 1993), holding that clear and convincing evidence is necessary to rebut this presumption of revocation. The testator's oral declarations and acts up to the date of death are generally admissible to rebut the presumption or counter the inference. Mimms v. Hunt, 458 S.W.2d 759 (Ky. App. 1970).

Assuming the presumption of revocation is rebutted, a lost or destroyed will may be probated in most states on satisfactory proof of its contents. Some statutes appear to severely restrict the probate of lost or destroyed wills, and in these states the requirements for an effective revocation may conflict with statutory provisions governing probate of lost or destroyed wills. The latter may, for example, provide that a "lost or destroyed will" can be probated *only* if "the will was in existence at the time of the testator's death, or was fraudulently destroyed in his lifetime."

Destruction of a copy of a will does not revoke the will, at least without application of a dispensing power.[3] If the testator does not have

---

3. An important case to consider, especially under the increasing recognition of substantial compliance doctrines or reformation for mistakes, is Estate of Tolin, 622 So. 2d 988 (Fla. 1993), in which the testator tore up a photocopy of the executed codicil to his will; after his death, the original will and codicil (retained by the drafting lawyer) were both offered for, and admitted to, probate because the destruction of the copy was not a legally effective revocation. Evidence showed, however, that a retired lawyer friend told the testator (who had expressed his desire to revoke the codicil) that this could be done by simply tearing up the instrument — which the friend thought was the original rather than just a good copy. Therefore, there being no proper remedy at probate (cf. enforcement of mutual will contracts in the next chapter), the court imposed a constructive trust (see Chapter 9) on the takers under the codicil to avoid unjust enrichment and to confer the benefits intended for the devisee under the will.

possession of the original, revocation may be accomplished by subsequent instrument.

It generally is agreed that it is not a good idea to *execute* extra copies of wills. Duplicate originals invite litigation. If the testator keeps both of them, and one has been crossed out, can the other one be probated? In Etgen v. Corboy, 230 Va. 413, 337 S.E.2d 286 (1985), the testator retained duplicate originals of his will and made markings on one of them. The court found that, while state law allowed testators to partially revoke wills by physical acts, no revocation occurred where only one of the two duplicate originals that were in the testator's possession had been marked upon. In Jones v. Mason, 99 So. 2d 46 (La. 1958), only one of the multiple originals of the testator's will could be found among his possessions after his death. The court held that the presumption that he destroyed his will with the intent to revoke it, which is applied when a will that was in the testator's possession cannot be found after his death, does not apply where only one of the multiple originals that were in his possession is missing. *Jones* was extended in Succession of Altazan, 682 So. 2d 1320 (La. App. 1996), where the testator had possession of her original will and some unexecuted copies. After the testator's death, the original will could not be found, but the copies were found. The court found the presumption of destruction with intent to revoke overcome.

B.   Revocation by Subsequent Instrument

PROBLEM

6-B.   *T* executed a holographic will in which he devised his personal residence to *A*, $10,000 to *B*, and the residue to *C*. Later *T* duly executed holographic instrument # 2 in which he devised a farm to *D*, $5,000 to *B* and the residue to *C*. (Neither document has a title or other heading.) Who takes what in a UPC jurisdiction? In a non-UPC jurisdiction? Explain. What result in a UPC jurisdiction if document # 2 did not include the residuary clause?   2-507 a(1)(b-2)   p. 225

A will may be revoked by a subsequent will or codicil. Although a few courts require that, in order effectively to revoke a prior will, the revoking instrument must make disposition of the testator's estate, typically a writing executed with the prescribed testamentary formalities is a sufficient revocation if it merely declares the prior will revoked.

When the testator's intent is to revoke prior wills, this should be clearly expressed in the will. If this is not the intent, the codicil should so state, refer to the other wills and codicils, and indicate its intended effect on their provisions (partial revocation also being permissible). In the latter case the instrument should be given the label of codicil, but merely designating a later instrument a "Last Will and Testament" is not conclusive that it is intended to revoke prior instruments.

The primary problem created by subsequent testamentary instruments is whether or to what extent revocation occurs when the intent of the testator regarding prior instruments is not expressed. A later instrument controls over an earlier one, and the earlier will is generally said to be revoked in whole or in part by implication to the extent the instruments are inconsistent; it might, however, be more accurate in partial inconsistency situations to say that the later provision "supersedes" the earlier, at least for as long as the latter remains in effect. In a number of jurisdictions, statutes derived from early New York legislation provide essentially that "a will is not revoked by a subsequent will unless the latter contains an express revocation or terms wholly inconsistent with terms of the prior will" and that the prior will otherwise "remains effective so far as consistent with the provisions of the subsequent will." The difficulty, of course, is in determining what constitutes an inconsistency and the extent thereof. Contrast UPC §2-507.

C. Revocation by Operation of Law

Statutes prescribing the methods of revocation often fail to mention revocation by operation of law. Such statutes, even though purporting to make the recited methods exclusive, are often construed not to preclude revocation by operation of law; that is, the exclusive provisions of the statute may be deemed to refer only to revocation by the testator and thus to permit a court to hold a will revoked by operation of law under certain circumstances.

Unless otherwise provided by statute, divorce alone is generally not sufficient to revoke a will or even the provisions for the divorced spouse. If the divorce is accompanied by a property settlement, however, it is commonly provided by statute, or held by courts in the absence of a statute, that all provisions for the divorced spouse in a preexisting will are revoked. Some states have refused to recognize revocation even in this situation, either because of a general refusal to recognize revocation by operation of law (based on strict interpretation of statutes prescribing the exclusive methods of revocation) or because of a statutory provision dealing with revocation by operation of law without mention of this situation. A growing number of statutes now expressly provide that divorce revokes all provisions for the spouse in a preexisting will. Some cases hold that in that event the affected property passes as if the former spouse had failed to survive the testator. E.g., Jones v. Brown, 219 Va. 599, 248 S.E.2d 812 (1978). But see, e.g.,

Davis v. Davis, 24 Ohio Misc. 17, 258 N.E.2d 277 (1970). Uniform Probate Code §2-804 revokes provision for a spouse or relative of a spouse in the event of subsequent divorce or annulment and declares that the property passes as if the former spouse or relative disclaimed. It also declares that revocation results from no change of circumstances other than divorce, annulment, or homicide. See also Restatement (Third) of Property §4.1(b): "The dissolution of the testator's marriage is a change in circumstance that presumptively revokes any provision in the testator's will in favor of his or her former spouse. Neither marriage nor marriage followed by birth of issue is a change in circumstance that revokes a will or any part of a will."

To what extent do policies underlying revocation by operation of law on divorce also apply to will substitutes, such as joint tenancies and revocable trusts? (This question should be considered as you study Chapter 8 and Chapter 11, section C.1, especially problem 11-H.) Except as provided by the governing instrument, contract or court orders, 1990 Uniform Probate Code §2-804 revokes any revocable disposition previously made to the divorced spouse or relative of the divorced spouse and severs the spouses' interests in joint and survivorship property. Illinois Revised Statutes, c. 148, §301, provides that unless the governing instrument and judgment "expressly provide otherwise, judicial termination of the marriage of the settlor of a trust revokes every provision which is revocable by the settlor pertaining to the settlor's former spouse in a trust instrument or amendment thereto, executed by the settlor before the entry" of that judgment and that the trust is to be administered as if the former spouse had died.

The other situation that in some states may cause a revocation by operation of law is the subsequent marriage of the testator followed by birth of issue. This method of revocation existed at common law in England and was often recognized in this country by statute or common law, based on a presumed intent resulting from a fundamental change in the testator's situation. Modern states, however, generally deal with these problems solely through the pretermitted heir and omitted spouse statutes discussed in Chapter 3, section D.

A case reaching an unwarranted result under a statute that has since been repealed is In re Estate of Spencer, 591 P.2d 611 (Haw. 1979). There the testator devised his estate to a woman to whom he was engaged. Later they married. When he died, his children from a prior marriage successfully challenged the probate of his will on the ground that his marriage had revoked it! In Ericson v. Ericson, 246 Conn. 359, 716 A.2d 92 (1998), the testator devised the residue of his estate to the woman he was to marry two days after executing the will. He died eight years later, and his children from a prior marriage challenged the will under Connecticut's statute providing that marriage revoked the will unless the will indicated that it was executed in contemplation of marriage. The lower court avoided revocation by construing the will as necessarily being executed in contemplation of a marriage that was to take place two days later. Although rejecting this reasoning and acknowledging that the statute applied, the appellate court found the statute overcome by the scrivener's testimony indicating that the testator thought the will would remain effective after marriage. This case expressly overruled an analogous case adhering to the traditional rule that extrinsic evidence is inadmissible to contradict an unambiguous will. Marriage, divorce, separation, or a property settlement between spouses is an occasion for an estate planing review. What is the responsibility of counsel in these situations?

In In re Estate of Rayman, 495 N.W.2d 241 (Minn. App. 1993), *T* divorced *W,* and then executed a will devising property "to my former wife, [*W*]." Then *T* remarried *W* and again divorced her. Would *T* want the gift revoked if *W* survived him?

D. Reestablishing Revoked or Apparently Revoked Wills

A lawyer may be called on to salvage the apparent intent of a decedent by attempting to probate a "revoked" will. The lawyer may find it necessary to urge that a *revoked will* has been revived, or may have to contend that a will is not revoked even though the testator has, with *actual* intent to revoke, performed upon it one of the physical acts of revocation authorized by statute or despite the valid execution of a subsequent writing declaring or implying that the will is revoked.

1. Revival of Revoked Wills

Assuming that a second will (no. 2) has revoked an earlier will (no. 1) either expressly or by implication, and that will no. 1 has not been destroyed, what methods are available for the testator to revoke will no. 2 and also revive will no. 1 so that it would be operative at death? It would be appropriate and desirable to draft and execute a new will following the terms of will no. 1. Instead, the testator might formally execute another instrument expressly revoking will no. 2, while expressly incorporating will no. 1 by reference, declaring his intent to republish it, or setting out its provisions anew. All too often, however, a testator yields to the natural temptation merely to revoke will no. 2, usually by some physical act, intending will no. 1 to be effective. The problem then created is whether the prior, revoked will has been revived by this revocation of the subsequent will. Because this action is equally consistent with an intention to be intestate, the uncertainties of speculating about the testator's intent and the dangers of accepting available evidence of that intent are apparent.

The early English law furnishes a valuable background for considering the various American rules on revival. Under the English common law will no. 1 was revived automatically by the revocation of will no. 2, regardless of the testator's intent, on the theory that a will is ambulatory and therefore has no effect until the testator's death. Consequently, will no. 2 "never actually revoked" will no. 1. The English ecclesiastical courts took a quite different view. In their conception of the process through which wills and revocations operated, revocation took effect immediately when the revoking instrument was executed; nevertheless, the revoked will would be revived if the testator so intended when the subsequent will was revoked. English legislation (the Wills Act, 1837) resolves the matter by requiring reexecution to restore the effectiveness of a previously revoked will.

The American courts and legislatures have adopted a variety of views on the question of revival. Numerous courts have considered the revocation of will no. 2 to revive will no. 1, regardless of the testator's intent, following the English common law view; a few of these cases have indicated that this rule applies only when will no. 2 had revoked will no. 1 by inconsistency and that this rule would be inapplicable if will no. 1 had been expressly revoked. Many other courts have followed a form of the ecclesiastical rule that revival depends on the testator's intent. These courts have been liberal in regard to the types of evidence to be considered in establishing the intent to revive. Some decisions indicate no presumption as to this intention. Others presume the intent to revive did not exist, placing the burden of proof on those asserting such intent, while still others presume the existence of an intent to revive unless the contrary is shown. Finally, by statute in a great number of American jurisdictions (as in England since the Wills Act, 1837), and by judicial decision in a few states, the rule is that will no. 1 cannot be revived by the mere revocation of will no. 2; depending upon construction of the statute, republication of will no. 1 may be necessary to revive the first will.

In a number of states there are statutes patterned after early New York legislation stating: "If, after making a will, the testator makes a second will, the destruction or other revocation of the second will does not revive the first will unless it appears by the terms of such revocation that the testator intended to revive and give effect to the first will, or unless the first will is duly republished." Consider also the statute of your state and the provisions of the Uniform Probate Code below. Courts may disagree about whether this type of statute applies to a partial revocation of will no. 1, and about what constitutes a revocation of a will by total inconsistency. Under statutes based on original UPC

§2-509 (now superseded), will no. 1 is revived by revocation of will no. 2 only (1) if the intent to do so "appears from the terms of" a subsequent revoking instrument or (2) if, in a revocation of will no. 2 by a physical act, the intent to review will no 1 "is evident" from the circumstances or from the testator's contemporaneous or subsequent declarations.

Under any of the basic positions indicated above, a court might distinguish (1) *express* revocation of the earlier will by the later will from (2) an implied revocation of the earlier will *by inconsistency;* and in particular a court may distinguish complete revocation by either of these two methods from (3) a *partial* revocation of the earlier will by inconsistency of some of these provisions with the terms of the subsequent instrument, or possibly even by express revocation of only certain provisions of the earlier will.

PROBLEMS

6-C.   Ten years ago *T* executed a will devising Blackacre to *A* and giving the residue to *B*. Five years later *T* executed a new will expressly revoking the old one and giving his entire estate to *B*. A year ago *T* burned the second will. On *T*'s death how does his estate pass, assuming his nearest relative is *B*? Does it matter if evidence is offered that *T* declared to *W*, as he burned the later will: "Now *A* can have Blackacre"? How would the case be decided under a statute of the type derived from the early New York statute quoted in the text, supra?

6-D.   Ten years ago *T* executed a will devising Blackacre to *A* and leaving the residue to *B*. Five years later *T* executed an instrument entitled "Codicil to My Will," devising Blackacre to *C* but not otherwise mentioning the prior will. Last year *T* burned the codicil and thereafter died. Result? What would be the result of destroying the later instrument if it had contained no heading and no reference to the earlier will, but had simply devised Blackacre to *C* and left the residue to *B*? See Estate of Schnoor, 4 Cal. 2d 590, 51 P.2d 424 (1935).

6-E.   *T* executed Will # 1 that devised Blackacre to *A*, residue to *B*. Later *T* executed Will # 2 devising Blackacre to *C*, residue to *B*. Later *T* tore up Will # 2. Assuming there is no evidence of any other facts, is Will # 1 revived under the current UPC? Under Restatement (Third) of Property §4.2(a), stating: "A will that was revoked by a later will is revived if the testator: (i) reexecuted the previously revoked will; (ii) executed a codicil indicating an intent to revive the previously revoked will; or (iii) revoked the revoking will by act intending to revive the previously revoked will; or, (iv) revoked the revoking will by another, later will whose terms indicate an intent to revive the previously revoked will."?

UNIFORM PROBATE CODE

§2-509. *Revival of Revoked Will.*

(a) If a subsequent will that wholly revoked a previous will is thereafter revoked by a revocatory act under Section 2-507 (a)(2), the previous will is revived if it is evident from the circumstances of the revocation of the subsequent will or from the testator's contemporary or subsequent declarations that the testator intended the previous will to take effect as executed.

(b) If a subsequent will that partly revoked a previous will is thereafter revoked by a revocatory act under Section 2-507 (a)(2), a revoked part of the previous will is revived unless it is evident from the testator's contemporary or subsequent declarations that the testator did not intend the revoked part to take effect as executed.

(c) If a subsequent will that revoked a previous will in whole or in part is thereafter revoked by another, later, will, the previous will remains revoked in whole or in part, unless it or its revoked part is revived. The previous will or its revoked part is revived to the extent it appears from the terms of the later will that the testator intended the previous will to take effect.

2. Dependent Relative Revocation

In studying the following cases and text, give particular attention to when, for what purposes, and to what extent extrinsic evidence may and should be admitted for the purpose of establishing a mistake and then to establish the "probable intent" on which the application of the doctrine of dependent relative revocation (DRR) is generally predicated.

DRR has been described as "a fictional process which consists of disregarding revocation brought about by mistake on the ground that the revocation was conditional." T. Atkinson, Wills §88 (2d ed. 1953). See Palmer, Dependent Relative Revocation and Its Relation to Relief for Mistake, 69 Mich. L. Rev. 989 (1971), to the effect that the doctrine is neither applicable to all mistakes nor limited to mistake situations, but asserting that it should be confined to cases in which the "conditional" intent relates to another plan of disposition that fails.

The doctrine can best be introduced by a simple example of its operation. Assume that *T* had executed a valid will. Thereafter she had another instrument drawn and executed, intending and believing it to be her will. *T* canceled the old will, but on her death the new instrument is determined to be invalid. Assuming it is concluded that *T* would not have revoked the prior will but for her belief that the second will rendered it useless, a court would normally apply the doctrine to permit probate of the first will. In fact, once the mistake is established, a few courts might apply the doctrine mechanically, even without a finding that *T* would have preferred the first will over intestacy. The preferred approach is to compare the second instrument with the first will and then with the intestate result. If the first will more closely resembles the second than does intestacy, apply DRR and probate the first will. If intestacy more closely resembles the second will, do not apply DRR but let the property pass intestate. This approach is illustrated in Kroll v. Nehmer, 348 Md. 616, 705 A.2d 716 (Md. App. 1998) (not applying DRR).

Although decisions are too few to be certain, a purist would say (with supporting authority) that the doctrine does not apply to the case of a testator whose will was revoked by cancellation with the intent to execute another very soon but who died without doing so. Of course, refusal to apply the doctrine can be explained on the ground that the testator did not act under a "mistake." Even if this result is sound, however, does the doctrine always require a mistake as distinguished from an expectation or hope that does not materialize? As you read, consider whether you find any case authority that supports the view of Palmer, supra, that it does not.

How is the mistake, and then the basis for a legally attributed intention, to be proved when extrinsic evidence is not generally allowed to impair the integrity of testamentary transactions? The answer often given is that the evidence is admissible in cases of apparent revocation by physical act because such acts performed on wills are inherently ambiguous and that parol evidence is therefore necessary to show the character of an alleged act of revocation. Then, courts have generally been willing to go a step further and receive extrinsic evidence to clarify the nature of the intent, or more precisely to show a motivating mistake on which that intent is based. This is so even though courts usually refuse to correct, or even to receive evidence of, a mistake in the inducement of a will.

Although some courts have flatly refused to apply the doctrine of a dependent relative revocation when confronted by an express revocation contained in a will — a distinction rejected in most modern decisions — the true source of difficulty in such cases may be the problem of introducing extrinsic evidence when a testamentary instrument is clear and unambiguous on its face. Should parol evidence be admitted to contradict or to qualify a formal writing declaring or clearly implying the revocation of a prior will?

Restatement (Third) of Property §4.3 provides: "(a) A partial or complete revocation of a will is presumptively ineffective if the testator made the revocation: (1) in connection with an attempt to achieve a dispositive objective that fails under applicable law, or (2) because of a false assumption of law, or because of a false belief about an objective fact, that is either recited in the revoking instrument or established by clear and convincing evidence.'' Under subsection (b) the presumption established in (a) ''is rebutted if allowing the revocation to remain in effect would be more consistent with the testator's probable intention.''

PROBLEM

6-F.   What result would you expect in the following situations?

(a) Erroneously believing a favorite nephew to be dead, *T* destroys her will, which would have left everything to that nephew.

(b) Under the same erroneous belief, *T* executes a second will expressly revoking the first and leaving everything ''in equal shares to all of my nieces and nephews who survive me.''

(c) Under the same erroneous belief, *T* executes a second will reciting: ''Because my nephew, *N*, is dead, I hereby revoke my prior will and bequeath and devise my property in equal shares to all my nieces and nephews who survive me.''

In re KAUFMAN'S ESTATE
25 Cal. 2d 854, 155 P.2d 831 (1945)

TRAYNOR, J.

On March 18, 1940, Samuel B. Kaufman executed a will in New York. He subsequently moved to California where he executed a new will on April 30, 1941, containing the clause ''I, Samuel B. Kaufman, do hereby make and declare this to be my Last Will and Testament, revoking all former wills.'' Both wills named identical persons for identical cash bequests and the Second Church of Christ, Scientist, of New York City, as residuary legatee. The 1941 will named a new executor. . . . The testator died on May 2, 1941. On petition of one of the executors, the 1941 will was admitted to probate. [The charitable bequest in the 1941 will violated a then-existing statutory prohibition against charitable bequests executed within thirty day of death, so] [a]ppellant thereafter filed a petition to have the 1940 will admitted to probate, to which respondent filed a contest. The present appeal is taken from the judgment denying the 1940 will admission to probate.

The respondent contends that there is substantial evidence to support the finding of the trial court that it was the intention of the testator in executing the 1941 will to revoke the 1940 will unconditionally. The appellant contends that the 1940 will should be admitted to probate under the doctrine of dependent relative revocation, on the ground that the testator did not intend to destroy the testamentary effect of the 1940 will unless the 1941 will would become wholly effective. . . .

Under the doctrine of dependent relative revocation, an earlier will, revoked only to give effect to a later one on the supposition that the later one will become effective, remains in effect to the extent that the latter proves ineffective. The doctrine is designed to carry out the probable intention of the testator when there is no reason to suppose that he intended to revoke his earlier will if the later will became inoperative. The doctrine has been invoked in California and is sustained by the weight of authority. . . .

The doctrine is clearly applicable to the facts of the present case. . . . Since the second will was virtually identical with the first in the disposition of the testator's estate, it is clear that the first will was revoked only because the second duplicated its purpose and the testator would have preferred the first will to intestacy as to a substantial part of his estate. . . . [A] testator who repeats his purpose intends to confirm and not revoke it, and does not intend to have the new will operate as a revocation independently of its operation as a will. . . .

The trial court's finding that the testator intended to revoke the 1940 will unconditionally is not supported by the evidence. All the testimony, including the testimony of Trust Officer Seaman and of Attorney Fogel and his secretary, shows that the testator wanted no change in his will except for the naming of a California executor. Any conclusion as to the testator's intention must be considered in the light of his knowledge at the time he executed the will. The testator was not advised that he might provide in his 1941 will that the revocation of the charitable bequest by the revocation clause in the 1941 will was dependent upon the legal effectiveness of the 1941 will to carry out his bequest, nor was he advised that the same result would follow under the doctrine of dependent relative revocation. . . . It does not follow from the fact that he was advised that the new will would not be effective unless he lived for thirty days that he intended that the charitable bequest should fail if he died within that period. To so hold would be to read into the charitable bequest an intentional condition precedent that the testator should live for more than thirty days. There is no evidence that the testator had any such intention.

The judgment is reversed with directions to admit the 1940 will to probate with the 1941 will. . . .

Newman v. Newman, 199 N.E.2d 904 (Ohio Prob. Ct. 1964), discussed but refused to follow *Kaufman* in the analogous situation. See also Crosby v. Alton Ochsner Medical Foundation, 276 So. 2d 661 (Miss. 1973).

Note the use of oral testimony in the *Kaufman* case. Was it essential to the result? Although such evidence is admissible under the modern view, some courts would refuse to receive it. Should a court that is more strict about extrinsic evidence consider the prior will for what it may suggest concerning what the testator probably would have desired?

With the above case, contrast the following: *T*'s will left the residue of his estate to charity *A*, but his provision is invalid as in *Kaufman;* a prior will, executed before the statutory period, had provided for the residue to go to charity *B*, the other provisions being identical to those of the later will. If the court will "admit extrinsic evidence only if a will is ambiguous," how would one argue for consideration of the prior will? Would the two wills alone satisfy a court that *T* would prefer to leave his property to charity *B* rather than die intestate, as they might have under *Kaufman* facts? If not, what arguments are there for considering other evidence? What evidence would be persuasive? If the earlier will is admitted in evidence but its proponents can produce no other evidence from which to deduce what *T* would have wished if he had known of the defect in the second will, how would this case be decided? Consider the case that follows.

WOLF v. BOLLINGER
62 Ill. 368 (1872)

SHELDON, J. . . .

On the 2d day of February, 1868, Jacob Bizer duly executed his last will and testament, wherein Catharine Bollinger, the appellee, was made the devisee of a certain forty acres of land. A few weeks afterward, the testator sent for Frederick T. Krafft, the executor named in the will, and informed him that he wished to alter the will so that Christina Wolf, the appellant, should take the forty acres instead of Catharine Bollinger; and at his instance, Krafft canceled the name of Catharine Bollinger in the will, by drawing lines through it with a pen, leaving the name still legible, and interlined over it the name of Christina Wolf, so as to make the will read as a devise of the forty acres to her. . . . After the death of Jacob Bizer, the will, in its altered condition, was admitted to the probate. . . .

We come now to the main question in this case — the effect of this alteration of the will. . . . for want of [proper execution, the interlineations] did not operate as a disposing will as to Christina Wolf. Had the alteration any legal effects as to Catharine Bollinger?

Before the alteration, the will contained a valid devise to her of this forty acres of land. It is the rule that a valid will, once existing, must continue in force, unless revoked in the mode prescribed by statute; which, by the fifteenth section of our Chapter of Wills, is as follows:

controlling statute

No will, testament, or codicil shall be revoked, otherwise than by burning, canceling, tearing, or obliterating the same by the testator himself, or in his presence, by his direction and consent, or by some other will, testament or codicil. . . .

The only mode of revocation of this devise to Catharine Bollinger, that can be claimed in this case, is by cancellation or obliteration. Lines were drawn with a pen through her name as devisee, leaving it still legible, and the name of Christina Wolf was interlined above it. It has been often determined, in the construction of similar statutes, that the mere acts named, of cancellation or obliteration, will not constitute a valid revocation, unless done with the intent to revoke. And although every act of canceling imports prima facie that it is done with the intent to revoke, it is but a presumption, which may be repelled by accompanying circumstances.

The intent of the testator, as expressed by himself, when he directed the cancellation to be made, was, "that Christina Wolf should inherit the forty acres instead of Catharine Bollinger." The cancellation was not made with the intent to revoke the devise to the complainant simply, but with intent to substitute in her stead the defendant, Christina Wolf, as a devisee. The cancellation of the name of Catharine Bollinger was but as a means toward the effecting of the end of such substitution; and the ultimate object of substitution having failed of accomplishment, the canceling, which was done only in the view of, and in order to effect, that object, should be esteemed for nothing, and be considered, not as having been made absolutely, but only conditionally, upon the attempted substitution being made effectual. To give it effect under the circumstances, would seem to be to thwart the intention of the testator, and make him intestate as to this piece of land, when he manifested the contrary intent by his will. It can by no means be said to have been the intent of the testator, that in case Christina Wolf was not substituted as devisee, Catharine Bollinger should not take the devise, or that as between the latter and his heirs-at-law, he preferred that they should have the land. The original intention of the will certainly was to make her a devisee; it appears to have been changed no further than in order to effect the substitution of another devisee in her place; that purpose having failed to become perfected, the original intention to devise to Catharine Bollinger must be considered as remaining unchanged.

It is believed to be the doctrine, as laid down in Redfield on Wills, 314, 325, 327, and well settled by the authorities, that where the testator makes an alteration in his will, by erasure and interlineation, or in any other mode, without authenticating such alteration by a new attestation in the presence of witnesses, or other form required by the statute, it is presumed that the erasure was intended to be dependent upon the

Redfield presumption

alteration going into effect as a substitute; and such alteration not being so made as to take effect, the will, therefore, stands in legal force, the same as it did before, so far as it is legible after the attempted alteration. . . .

The award of costs against Christina Wolf, which is complained of, was a matter of discretion with the court, with the exercise of which we see no reason for interference.

Perceiving no error in the record, the decree of the court below is affirmed.

Is it apparent in the above case, even in light of the evidence of the testator's statement to Krafft, that the revocation of the devise to Catharine Bollinger was dependent on the validity of the devise to Christina Wolf? Would the decedent have desired the result reached by the court? Should this matter? Or does this particular court, when such a mistake appears, simply presume the fictitious intent to condition the revocation, at least if the contrary is not shown? Would it proceed differently if the revocation were by writing rather than by act?

Contrast (1) the obvious propriety of applying the doctrine of dependent relative revocation when the requisite intent is convincingly apparent in the alleged act of revocation performed upon the face of the will, as in the following invalid alteration:

$15,000
I bequeath $10,000 to my niece, Joan.

with (2) the *Wolf* case and with (3) the following:

$ 2,000
I bequeath $10,000 to my niece, Joan.

In the latter case would the testator prefer the larger legacy to stand rather than permit the legacy to fail? See Ruel v. Hardy, 90 N.H. 240, 6 A.2d 753 (1939), which acknowledged that the doctrine is based on probable intent — that is, on what the testator would have preferred if informed of the available choices. The court held that, although a presumption existed in favor of the doctrine's application, the nature and amount of the attempted change in the gift was sufficient to rebut the presumption absent other evidence of the decedent's intent. Thus, the court found the doctrine inapplicable under the evidence before it, while also indicating that "pertinent oral declarations" of the testator and other extrinsic evidence should be received in such cases.

PROBLEM

6-G.   *T* executed Will # 1 that devised one-third of her estate to *A*, one-fourth to *B*, and five-twelfths to *C*. If *T* died intestate, *A*, *B*, and *C* would get one-third each. *T* executed Will # 2, expressly revoking Will # 1 and devising half to *A* and half to *B*. Later, *T* tore up Will # 2, saying that she preferred Will # 1 after all. *T* died. The jurisdiction has a "no revival" statute that provides that a revoked will can only be revived by being re-executed, but also has an appellate court decision, in another context, following §4.3 of the Restatement (Third) of Property (above). Should Will # 2 be probated?

DRR and the UPC. It has been said that dependent relative revocation is the law of the "second best" and is unnecessary under the UPC, which allows for the "first best." Do you see why this might be so? Consider two typical DRR fact patterns:

1) *T* tears up his second will with the intention of reviving the first will. Extrinsic evidence is available to establish that the first will represents his true intent.

2) *T* crosses out her first will and executes a second, but defective execution prevents probate of the second will. There is extrinsic evidence showing that the second will represents her true intent.

7

Will Contracts

A surprising amount of litigation results from the attempts of persons to contract with regard to the disposition of property on the death of one or both of the parties. The problems are complicated in some cases by failure of the parties to reduce their "agreement" to writing or by failure to make the writing clear. Further complications sometimes result from confused intermingling of contract law with the law of wills in litigating these problems.

Two types of will contracts are particularly common. One arises from the situation in which one person, usually an elderly person, wishes to induce another to provide care and agrees to compensate the latter by bequeathing all or part of the promisor's estate. The other arises when two people — typically husband and wife — wish the survivor to receive the property of the first to die and then wish to assure by contract that on the survivor's death the property will pass in a certain fashion. Such arrangements are often thought useful where the natural objects of the bounty of each party are different persons.

UNIFORM PROBATE CODE

§2-514. *Contracts Concerning Succession.*   A contract to make a will or devise, or not to revoke a will or devise, or to die intestate, if executed after the effective date of this Article, may be established only by (i) provisions of a will stating material provisions of the contract, (ii) an express reference in a will to a contract and extrinsic evidence proving the terms of the contract, or (iii) a writing signed by the decedent evidencing the contract. The execution of a joint will or mutual wills does not create a presumption of a contract not to revoke the will or wills.

A.   Contract to Bequeath or Devise

Assuming the usual requirements for a valid contract and any special statutory requirements are met, a contract to make, not to make, or

245

not to revoke a will, or to bequeath or devise certain property, is valid. It is valid as a contract, however, and not as a will. The contract cannot be probated, for example, if the will is not made; nor can a revoked will be probated even if its revocation was in violation of a contract. Also, a contract generally cannot be used to oppose probate of an inconsistent will because the remedy for breach is not at probate. (Probate proceedings, however, should not be totally ignored. See Chapter 17 concerning timely filing of claims against estates.) If not performed, an enforceable promise gives rise to a cause of action against the estate or beneficiaries of the promisor.

The problems of enforcement are essentially those of enforcing any contract of a deceased person. Occasionally, however, the contract action is brought against the decedent before his or her death. In Wright v. Trask, 329 S.C. 170, 495 S.E.2d 222 (S.C. App. 1997), the testator promised to devise his ranch to his grandson, the plaintiff, in exchange for plaintiff's agreement to dedicate his life to managing the ranch. Years later, the grandfather amended his will to disinherit the grandson, who brought suit while his grandfather was still alive. The court held that he was entitled to specific performance of the contract. See also Battuello v. Battuello, 64 Cal. App. 4th 842, 75 Cal. Rptr. 2d 548 (1998). Assuming that the promisee discovers the breach in time, what are the advantages of bringing the action while the promisor is alive?

Contracts to make wills need not be executed with the formalities of wills, but there is frequently a requirement that such contracts be in writing. This requirement in some states stems from a statute specifically applicable to contracts to make wills. In other states, the typical statute of frauds provisions require a writing for many situations. For example, a contract to devise land is almost universally held to come within the statute; and generally when a contract relates to both real and personal property, it is held that the statute applies to the entire promise. Where land is not involved in the promise, there is a difference of opinion whether the provision of the statute of frauds relating to sale of goods is applicable, but usually the specific requirements of this provision will be found satisfied as a result of the promisee's performance even if the provision is deemed applicable. The section of the statute of frauds relating to contracts not to be performed within a year does not apply because the promise *may* be fully performed within that period.

If the promisor fails to perform and dies, the promisee *may* bring an action at law for damages. As an alternative, the promisee generally may obtain equitable relief under such labels as specific performance, quasi-specific performance, relief in the nature of specific performance, or constructive trust. In such cases — with the remedy generally sought in equity — the question of adequacy of the remedy at law is often not raised and is rarely given careful discussion. For the bases of equitable jurisdiction, see B. Sparks, Contracts to Make Wills 146-151 (1956). A third possible remedy is quantum meruit for the value of the services rendered or the support or other consideration furnished. This remedy is generally important as a means of obtaining relief when the requirement of a writing is found applicable and is neither satisfied nor removed on any of the usual grounds. However, the presumption that the services of a relative are gratuitous presents difficulties for a plaintiff in such a proceeding. The niceties of the contracts and remedies problems need not be examined here, but the intricacies of local procedural rules should be considered in bringing an action on a breached will contract. The fundamental problems inherent in contracts to bequeath and devise should become apparent as the chapter is studied.

The problem that follows raises some of the commonly encountered difficulties in the context of a typical situation for which will contracts are employed. Consider this problem in light of your local statutes and your general knowledge from other sources.

PROBLEM

7-A.   A has come to you for advice and relates the following facts to you. Ten years ago *T*, *A*'s 68-year-old mother, requested *A* and her husband, *H*, to live in *T*'s home and to look after her when she was plagued by illness and loneliness. In return *T* promised orally to leave her house and at least half of the rest of her estate to *A*. As soon thereafter as *A* and *H* could terminate the lease on their apartment, they moved into *T*'s home. They resided with her until she died two months ago and cared for her through this difficult period at considerable inconvenience to themselves. Just after *A* and *H* moved into *T*'s house, *T* executed a will that read in relevant part: "As an expression of my gratitude to my daughter, *A*, I leave her my home and personal effects and one-half of the rest of my property. The rest I leave equally to my other children *B*, *C*, and *D*." For about the last year of *T*'s life she was irritable and felt that, because she was deaf and unable to get around well, she was neither needed nor appreciated by her children. When she died the only traces of her will were the torn pieces of it in her desk drawer, with a notation on one piece reading "canceled." No one wishes to question *T*'s mental capacity to revoke or to make a will right up to the date of her death, but *A* asks whether she can take more than the $44,000 worth of property that she has determined would constitute her intestate share of *T*'s estate. (a) What are *A*'s rights? How should she proceed? (b) Would her case be different if she had not been related to *T*? (c) Would it matter if, instead of the above promise, *T* had merely said: "I shall reward you in my will"? See Restaino v. Vannah, 483 N.E.2d 847 (Mass. App. 1985).

B. Joint and Mutual Wills

A joint will is a single instrument executed by two persons as the will of each. Mutual wills are separate wills of different persons, containing similar or reciprocal provisions.

At one time joint wills were invalid. Today it is generally accepted that such a will is valid unless it appears that the will is to operate only on the death of the survivor of the cotestators. A valid joint will, then, operates and is probated on the death of each cotestator as if there were two separate documents.

Joint or mutual wills are revocable in the same manner as other wills. Sometimes, however, such wills are executed pursuant to a contract in which it is agreed that the property of the testators will be disposed of according to the present wills or that the wills will not be revoked. Here it is essential, in order to avoid the confusion found in some cases, to distinguish between the wills and the contract. Properly analyzed, wills executed pursuant to a contract are revocable, but the *power* to revoke and alter a will is not the *right* to do so and does not preclude liability on the *contract*. Thus, it is generally recognized that in the probate of a will the court is not concerned with whether the will is executed pursuant to or in violation of a contract.

Because rights would be created by a contract, the existence or non-existence of an underlying obligation is important in these will cases. Major problems therefore arise in determining whether a contract exists and in determining its terms, particularly with respect to the rights of the survivor. Essentially the problems of proving the contract are the same as in other types of contracts.

Mutual or joint will contracts are commonly employed in two types of cases. One is where a husband and wife have had no children, and each promises to leave everything to the survivor, who in turn promises to leave the property in agreed shares to certain collateral relatives of each. The other is where a husband or wife or both had children by a previous marriage, and the contract is arranged to assure that, on the survivor's death, certain provisions will be made for the children of the first spouse to die. Of course, these are not the only cases in which it might be tempting to contract for the execution and nonrevocation of mutual or joint wills. The usual advice of those who have studied the multitude of problems created by contractual wills is not to use them; but before this advice can be followed without disservice to one's client, one must decide what alternative arrangements are available to accomplish the desired purpose and to eliminate the risks inherent in the uncertain order of the clients' deaths. As the problems and cases hereafter are studied, consider (1) how the wills and the alleged contracts could have been used and drafted without creating the issues in question and (2) what other arrangement you might have suggested to accomplish the apparent purposes of the parties. Also, we might simply note that contractual wills may give rise to a number of serious tax problems that should not be disregarded, particularly where the estates of the parties are substantial.

B. SPARKS, CONTRACTS TO MAKE WILLS
27-28 (1956)

The clear weight of authority, and certainly the sounder view, is that the mere presence of either joint or mutual wills does not raise any presumption that they were executed in pursuance of a contract. Nor is this rule altered by evidence that the parties had "agreed" to the making of such wills. Of course they had so agreed. The mere presence of such wills reveals that the parties must have talked the matter over and must have arrived at an understanding or agreement concerning their testamentary dispositions. Such discussions and such understandings between persons of close affinities, especially between husbands and wives, are not unusual and the fact that they have taken place is no indication that there has been any thought of a binding contract.

CUMMINGS v. SHERMAN
16 Wash. 2d 88, 132 P.2d 998 (1943)

[Homer and Phoebe Shinn executed mutual wills in 1931. Homer died later that year, willing his residuary estate to Phoebe "with full and exclusive right of disposition," providing that had she not survived, half the residue would go to her relatives and half to his. The will was admitted to probate and Phoebe acted as executrix. Before her death in 1934, however, she had executed a new will, which was admitted to probate. This will made no provision for Homer's relatives (respondents), who sought and were awarded half of Phoebe's estate based on a contract by the Shinns to make and revoke the 1931 wills. Some of Phoebe's relatives appeal.]

SIMPSON, J. . . .

Allen v. Dillard, Wash., 129 P.2d 813, 817, . . . stated "contracts to make mutual wills are recognized under our law as valid and . . . may be specifically enforced. . . . Because, however, of the great opportunity for fraud, and because of reluctance on the part of courts to render ineffective a subsequent will of a testator, the contract to make mutual wills must be established by clear and convincing evidence."

The question first to be decided is whether or not the testimony introduced in this case was sufficient to prove the making of the oral contract under the rule to which we have just referred.

The proof of the oral agreement was supplied by Fred J. Cunningham, a member of the Spokane bar. Mr. Cunningham stated that he drew the wills in 1931 at the request of Mr. and Mrs. Shinn. His testimony relative to the oral agreement is as follows:

Q. Now, the first time that they consulted you together, state what the conversation was . . . in regard to executing wills. . . .

The Witness: They came in by appointment, and Mr. Shinn stated that they had now reached an agreement as to making wills, or the substance of the statement, and he asked that I explain to Mrs. Shinn the difference between mutual wills and individual wills, which I attempted to do.

By Mr. Grant: Q. State what you said to them in response to that question.

A. As I recall, I stated that if they wanted to deal with their own share, each one's own share of the community property, they could make individual wills which could be changed at any time they wanted to, up until their death. If they wanted to deal with their community property by some agreement between them as to the character of their wills, and they entered into such wills, then when one of the parties died and that will was probated, their rights became fixed and the survivor could not change the will, at his option, in any way to violate their agreement. Then, as I recall, I asked Mr. Shinn what the substance of their agreement was as to their wills, and he said that they wanted to make identical wills. . . .

They stated briefly, that they wanted [the residue to go to the] survivor, with the right to use that property in any way they saw fit during their lifetime, and that any residue left should be willed or divided between the parties, and each one's share should go to each one's named relatives. Then I asked her if she had talked this over with him, and if that was her understanding, in general, of this arrangement for the disposal of their property, and she said it was.

Then he produced a roll of papers, documents, most of which I had seen before. They were typewritten copies of a draft of a will or wills, and there were a number of pencil notations and different writings that apparently he had made, and some other notes that I had given him at different times in our conversation before. I asked her if she was familiar with these, and she said, "Well, I think I am with most of them. We have talked this over enough" or some expression of that kind.

Then I went over those briefly, and . . . asked them if that was their understanding, and they both said it was.

In speaking of the 1931 will, Mr. Cunningham testified further:

In one of these sections of this draft there was some provision to the effect that they might each make wills — that the survivor might make wills, or something like that, but in making these wills, or in making a will they would have to observe the provisions or the spirit of this will, and he had pencil marks through that, and I asked him about that, and he said, "Well, now, we hope this is a final arrangement as to our property, and I don't want any suggestion that if I live the longest that I will make any will changing our property arrangement here, and if I should die first, I don't want my wife to feel, or to be encouraged to make such a will."

I remember at that time that Mrs. Shinn stated that, "Well, we have been worrying over this —" I can't remember her language, but it was to this effect, that "we have been worrying over this for several months, and I don't want — I think that we should have it settled, and these arrangements — that is satisfactory with me. I don't want to make any more wills, or I don't expect to change my will, when I make it," or words to that effect.

Appellants argue that the trial court was in error in allowing Mr. Cunningham to testify concerning the statements made by Mr. and Mrs. Shinn for the reason that the conversations were prohibited under Rem. Rev. Stat. §1214, which reads: . . .

> 2. An attorney or counselor shall not, without the consent of his client, be examined as to any communication made by the client to him, or his advice given thereon in the course of the professional employment.

They also cite many authorities supporting this statute which is common to most jurisdictions. There are, however, many situations in which the statute does not and cannot apply.

The general rule is stated in 28 R.C.L. 566 §156 as follows:

> When two or more clients employ the same attorney in the same matter, communications made by them in relation thereto are not privileged . . . in any controversy between them or their personal representatives or successors in interest.

70 C.J. 438, §587, says:

> It is generally considered that the rule of privilege does not apply in litigation, after the client's death, between parties, all of whom claim under the client; and, so, where the controversy is to determine who shall take by succession the property of a deceased person and both parties claim under him, neither can set up a claim of privilege against the other as regards the communications of deceased with his attorney. . . .

In the present case, the statements concerning which Mr. Cunningham testified were made when both Mr. and Mrs. Shinn were present. The statements of the attorney which brought forth the ideas of the makers of the wills were given them in the presence of both. That advice given to them collectively concerned their community property rights and their obligations should they make mutual wills. The court did not err in admitting the testimony of Mr. Cunningham.

The next objection urged by appellants is that the facts and circumstances surrounding the making of prior wills by the Shinns demonstrated that they did not intend to make mutual wills in 1931. In support of this contention, counsel bring to our attention excerpts from wills made by Mr. and Mrs. Shinn in 1929 [which recited the terms of a contract limiting the rights of the survivor]. . . .

From the difference in the provisions of the 1929 and 1931 wills, it is argued that the 1929 wills were mutual and identical as shown by their contents and that having used different language in the 1931 wills it must be assumed that the 1931 wills did not express an intention on the part of the testators to make mutual identical wills.

We are unable to agree with this reasoning. The manifest intent in all of the wills was to see to it that each spouse should have his or her chosen individuals receive certain interests in the community property after the death of the makers of the wills.

Appellants next urge that the decree in the Homer J. Shinn estate forecloses the claims now made. They argue that the decree is an adjudication that Phoebe Shinn took the entire estate without restriction and that it cannot be contended she took a mere life estate with the right to use it during her lifetime. . . . The . . . decree [states]: . . .

> 4. That Phoebe Shinn is entitled to receive, and there is hereby distributed to her the entire residue of said estate. . . .

In the instant case the probate court neither attempted to interpret the provisions of the will pertaining to the mutual obligations of the parties nor to adjudicate respondents' equitable rights under the contract between the Shinns. . . .

Nor do we consider the distribution to Mrs. Shinn to be anything more than a distribution in accordance with the words and terms of the will and in no way inconsistent to respondents' claims. This is not a construction of the will, Martin v. Barger, 62 Wash. 672, 114 P. 505, and the failure to mention the restriction of disposition after death did not vest absolute title. . . .

Appellants take the position that the contract between Mr. and Mrs. Shinn was void since it was not drawn in conformity with Rem. Rev. Stat. §6894. . . .

> This court has definitely held that an agreement to make mutual wills is within the statute of frauds, if real property is involved, or real and personal property. We have also held that the making of mutual wills is not sufficient part performance to take the agreement without the statute of frauds, in the absence of any other consideration. We have also

definitely fixed the quantum of proof required to establish such a contract.

Allen v. Dillard, Wash., 129 P.2d 813, 820.

The oral contract made by Mr. and Mrs. Shinn was within the provisions of the above statute and in itself unenforceable. However, mutual wills were made by the Shinns in conformity with their oral agreement. Thereafter, Mrs. Shinn probated her husband's estate and took his estate given to her by his will executed in 1931. The actions of the parties were sufficient part performance to take the contract from the statute of frauds.

Upon the death of Mr. Shinn, Mrs. Shinn filed his will for probate and accepted the benefits . . . of the contract and will, and could not thereafter free herself of her obligation. . . .

The judgment is affirmed.

What ethical problems do you see for the attorney advising the husband and wife in these cases?

A few decisions have held the mere execution of joint or mutual wills to be part performance, removing the contract from the statute of frauds, e.g., In re Fischer's Estate, 196 Wash. 41, 81 P.2d 836 (1938); and a few others have held that such wills constitute sufficient memorandum to satisfy the statute, even without reciting the existence of a contract, e.g., Estate of Beeruk, 429 Pa. 415, 241 A.2d 755 (1968). These positions have generally been rejected, however. More, of course, occurred than mere execution of the wills in Cummings v. Sherman, and the part performance doctrine has been widely applied to like facts. On the basis of your understanding of the part performance doctrine, is there anything questionable about its application to these facts? Another rationale for the same solution to the recurrent problem of mutual wills executed pursuant to an alleged oral contract is found in Notten v. Mensing, 3 Cal. 2d 469, 473-474, 45 P.2d 198, 200-201 (1935):

> In this state . . . oral agreements to leave property by will . . . are unenforceable. [Cases] hold that the execution of a will in accordance with the oral agreement, which does not expressly refer to the contract, does not constitute a note or memorandum sufficient to satisfy the statute of frauds. The same cases also indicate that the execution of mutual wills, the death of one of the makers, and the acceptance of the benefits under such a will by the other, does not constitute a sufficient part performance to take the case out of the statute of frauds. This is contrary to the rule in some states.

However, the fact that the instant case does not come within one of
the above two exceptions to the operation of the statute of frauds is not
sufficient to dispose of the issues raised. There is a long line of authorities
in this state to the effect that under the proper circumstances a party
may be estopped to plead the statute of frauds. . . . [When] two parties
execute reciprocal wills pursuant to an oral agreement, and one of the
parties dies before either will is revoked, and the other party accepts the
benefit of the decedent's will, and then revokes, a constructive fraud
sufficient to raise an estoppel has been practiced on the decedent and
on the beneficiaries of the oral agreement.

Some courts have been willing to imply a contract merely from the
jointness or similarity of the wills of spouses, with little or no extrinsic
evidence of contractual intention. See, e.g., Pruitt v. Moss, 271 S.C.
305, 247 S.E.2d 324 (1978), Fisher v. Capp, 597 S.W.2d 393 (Tex. Civ.
App. 1980), and Estate of Maloney v. Carsten, 178 Ind. App. 191, 381
N.E.2d 1263 (1978), all involving joint wills; and Woelke v. Calfee, 45
Or. App. 459, 608 P.2d 606 (1980), involving separate wills. See also
the novel cases of Northern Trust Co. v. Tarre, 404 N.E.2d 882 (Ill.
App. 1980), and Reznik v. McKee, 216 Kan. 659, 534 P.2d 243 (1975),
involving revocable inter vivos trusts that were held to become irrevocable and unamendable after the first spouse's death based on findings
of unwritten agreements. Is it a good idea to find contractual obligations by implication in this area of the law?

On the matter of remedies, Levis v. Hammond, 251 Iowa 567, 573-
576, 100 N.W.2d 638, 642-644 (1960), states:

[A] suit for specific performance against the survivor of an agreement
to make mutual wills [requires] good consideration for the agreement,
acceptance by the survivor of the property under the will of the first to
die and reasonableness of the agreement. . . .

Although the mutual promises may have amounted to technical consideration . . . there was a great inequality of consideration moving from
the two makers. Thus the agreement was not sufficiently fair and reasonable to entitle plaintiff to the relief asked. . . .

A suit for specific performance of an agreement is always addressed
to the sound judicial discretion of the chancellor, guided by the general
principles of equity. Relief is not a matter of absolute right but is granted
or withheld according to the circumstances of each case.

Compare Rauch v. Rauch, 445 N.E.2d 77, 81 (Ill. App. 1983) ("on
the death of the first testator" there is, in effect, "a life estate in the
surviving testator, and the third-party beneficiaries receive a gift over")
and Halper v. Froula, 148 Cal. App. 3d 1000, 1005, 196 Cal. Rptr. 727,
730 (1983) (although survivor "had the right to use the [property] for

her comfort and support during her lifetime, giving away the property is not a proper use and enjoyment . . . by the life tenant'').

PROBLEM

7-B.   *H* and *W* entered into a written contract calling for irrevocable mutual wills under which the first to die was to leave his or her entire estate to the survivor, and the survivor was to leave everything to certain relatives of each. Wills were executed accordingly. *H* died recently, but by a later will he left *W* only her minimum statutory rights, and he devised the rest to his brother, *B*. *W* consults you to determine her rights. She informs you that shortly before his death, *H* told her he was going to change his will, and he did so despite her protests. What advice would you give *W*?

Incidentally, what if *H* had died leaving his will in the agreed form and, promptly after his death, *W* wished to assert her statutory one-third forced share by electing against his will? Cf. Estate of Edington, 489 N.E.2d 612 (Ind. App. 1986). Can she do so? Would it matter if *W* had advised *H* of her intentions while he was still competent a week or so before his death? Consider, as you study the rest of this chapter, why and under what circumstances she might wish to elect against *H*'s will.

———————

In considering the above problem, note the frequently cited case of Stone v. Hoskins, [1905] L.R.P. 194, 197, the holding of which is adequately reflected in its concluding dictum:

> If these two people had made wills which were standing at the death of the first to die, and the survivor had taken a benefit by that death, the view is perfectly well founded that the survivor cannot depart from the arrangement on his part, because . . . the will of that party and the arrangement have become irrevocable; but that case is entirely different from the present, where the first to die has not stood by the bargain and her "mutual" will has in consequence not become irrevocable. The only object of notice is to enable the other party to the bargain to alter his or her will also, but the survivor in the present case is not in any way prejudiced. He has notice as from the death. . . . [He] must, I think, fail to obtain the declaration which he seeks.

Dicta of similar effect are abundant in American cases, but it is usually observed also that for one of the parties to "revoke" during their joint lifetimes notice must be given to the other. Is it not a peculiar notion of contract that revocation of the promised will is permitted without liability — that is, in effect, a "rescission" without the *assent* of the other party? If the purported "agreement" is considered merely an offer of a unilateral contract, why must notice be given before the promisor's death rather than before performance by the promisee? Or is this in reality a problem of construing the contract and finding it to include an implied right to revoke by either party on notice to the other during their joint lives? If so, one must ask whether the contract in question allows of this construction when such a provision is not expressed. Today, possibly an implied power to "revoke" by giving timely notice can be justified by the widespread belief of lawyers, based on dicta in many cases, that Stone v. Hoskins represents the law of their states, especially if it can be shown that the parties were so advised by their lawyer. Where the precise question is presented, however, as in Problem 7-B, supra, the above-mentioned dicta have not necessarily been followed. See Estate of Johnson, 781 S.W.2d 390 (Tex. App. 1989); Brown v. Webster, 90 Neb. 591, 134 N.W. 185 (1912); In re Fischer's Estate, 196 Wash. 41, 81 P.2d 836 (1938); Note, 48 Calif. L. Rev. 858, 862-63 (1960). For a more recent look at the English view and at Stone v. Hoskins, see Rickett, Extending Equity's Reach Through the Mutual Wills Doctrine, 54 Mod. L. Rev. 581 (1991).

PROBLEMS

7-C.   *H* and *W* owned Blackacre as joint tenants. They contracted to execute a joint will under which the survivor would be entitled to a life estate in all of the property of both parties, with remainder on the death of the survivor to *A* and *B* equally. The parties executed a joint will reciting the terms of this agreement, adding that "the survivor shall not sell, encumber or give away any of the property without the consent of *A* and *B*." On *W*'s death five years ago, her will was admitted to probate. Several months ago *H* executed a deed purporting to convey Blackacre to *X* for a fair consideration. *H* has invested the proceeds in a speculative venture and has suffered a great loss. *A* and *B* ask you what their rights are. How would you advise them? Is there anything *A* and *B* could have done to have prevented this problem?

7-D.   In 1980 *H* and *W* executed a written contract not to revoke their mutual wills. *H* died in 1985 leaving everything he owned to *W*, as agreed, and now *W* has just died. In accordance with the contract, her will provides for the estate to pass one-half to *H*'s nephew, *A*, and one-sixth to each of *W*'s nieces and nephews, *X*, *Y*, and *Z*. However, *A* predeceased *W*, although he was alive at *H*'s death. A typical statute in the state provides that if a named beneficiary dies before the testator his interest fails, except that if the bequest or devise is to "kindred" of the testator and if the beneficiary is also survived by issue, the bequest or devise passes to the issue of the beneficiary. *A*'s will left his entire estate to *B*, his widow. *A* is also survived by a child, *C*. *X*, *Y*, and

Z are *W*'s sole heirs at law and claim the entire estate. Based on the materials that follow in this chapter, how would you argue their case? *C*'s? *B*'s? See Ruchert v. Boyd, 56 Wash. 2d 266, 352 P.2d 216 (1960); Rauch v. Rauch, 445 N.E.2d 77 (Ill. App. 1983). Contrast Keasey v. Engles, 259 Mich. 178, 242 N.W. 878 (1932), with Chadwick v. Bristow, 146 Tex. 481, 208 S.W.2d 888 (1948).

LAWRENCE v. ASHBA
115 Ind. App. 485, 59 N.E.2d 568 (1945)

[handwritten: 3 sons by 1st marriage]

DRAPER, C. J.

The appellees, who are the three sons by her first marriage of Sarah E. Lawrence, deceased, brought this action . . . for the specific performance of a contract; for an accounting; to set aside the conveyance of real estate; and for a judgment declaring a [constructive] trust. . . .

It appears that the father of appellees died in 1905 and in 1907 their mother married the appellant William T. Lawrence, who never had any children. In 1942 Mrs. Lawrence died. On July 1, 1937, Mr. and Mrs. Lawrence held some real estate by the entireties which they had been able to acquire largely as the result of her industry and thrift and a pension received by her because of the fact that the father of appellees was a Civil War veteran. On that day they each made a will. Items II and III of the will of Mrs. Lawrence read as follows:

> Item II. I will, bequeath and devise all my property, both personal and real, to my husband William T. Lawrence, absolutely and in fee simple.
> Item III. In the event my husband, William T. Lawrence, should predecease me, I then will, bequeath and devise all my property, both personal and real, to John J. Ashba, James A. Ashba and Charles R. Ashba, share and share alike.

The same clauses, but substituting the name of Sarah Lawrence for that of William T. Lawrence, appeared in the will of William T. Lawrence. There was no other [significant] difference in the wills. . . .

After making these wills they disposed of the real estate then held by them and acquired other real estate, taking title thereto by the entireties, and that real estate was so held when she died, and is the real estate involved in this case.

A few hours after her death William T. Lawrence, alone and unaccompanied by anyone, emptied their safety deposit box and by inference it appears he took therefrom cash and other personal property of considerable value, all of which he still retains. On October 13, 1942, her will was probated and he was appointed executor.

He married again on September 20, 1942, and eight days later made and caused to be made, conveyances intended to vest title to the real estate in his then wife, the appellant Iva B. Lawrence, said conveyances being intended to prevent appellees from ever acquiring the properties. Thereafter Mr. Lawrence stated to others that he had everything fixed and the boys wouldn't get a cent. There is no contention that Iva B. Lawrence furnished any consideration for the conveyances to her, or that she took without notice.

A will is generally ambulatory until the death of the testator, and mutual and reciprocal wills, unless founded on or embodying a binding contract, may be revoked at pleasure. 69 C.J. 1299, §2719.

The burden of proving that mutual and reciprocal wills were made pursuant to a valid and enforceable contract is upon those who assert such to be true, and the evidence thereof must be full and satisfactory. Indeed, the rule requires the agreement to be established by evidence clear, definite, convincing, unequivocal and satisfactory, and to be valid and enforceable the contract must be fair and just, definite and certain in its terms and as to the subject matter, and based upon a sufficient consideration.

The mere fact that the wills under consideration contain identical provisions and that they were drawn by the same scrivener, executed at the same time and before the same witnesses, with full knowledge on the part of each testator of the contents of both wills, and were clearly made for the accomplishment of a common purpose, is not sufficient evidence of a contract to make wills to remain unrevoked at the deaths of the testators, although such circumstances are to be regarded as some evidence that they were made pursuant to an agreement. But where the contract does not appear in the language of the wills, and so the wills, unaided, are not sufficient to show the contract, the agreement may be proven by the testimony of witnesses who know the facts, by admissions of the parties and by the acts and conduct of the parties and other circumstances surrounding the making of the wills.

With these rules in mind we examine the evidence. It reveals that at the time of the making of the wills Mr. and Mrs. Lawrence called at a lawyer's office. It was there discussed that the funds that had gone into their property held as tenants by the entireties had in a major part been the funds of Mrs. Lawrence before she married Mr. Lawrence. There was conversation that they might want to sell that property and invest in other property. They seemed in accord and harmony and wanted to execute such deeds, wills or other instruments as would effectuate their intentions, which were that their property should be held intact as long as each of them lived, and when both were gone, they wanted the property to go to the three boys. Both agreed to make disposition of their property in that fashion. No request was made that a provision be included in the wills making them irrevocable during the lifetime of both or after the death of either. They left it to the lawyer to prepare whatever papers were necessary to carry out their wishes and accomplish their purpose, and he prepared the wills above mentioned, he said, in conformity with their desires.

Before the death of Mrs. Lawrence she and Mr. Lawrence told one of the witnesses that they had made a will; that

> it was to be a joint will while if she outlived him everything should be hers for lifetime then it was to be the boys'; and if he outlived her why it should be the same way; her life earnings were in there and most of the money was hers and they decided that it was for the boys when they were gone.

The evidence above recited was in no way contradicted by either of the appellants or any other witness, nor in any manner questioned or impeached.

In our opinion this evidence, taken with the fact that the wills contain substantially identical provisions, were drawn by the same lawyer and were executed at the same time before the same witnesses with full knowledge by each testator of the contents of the other's will, was sufficient to meet the requirements of the rule and sustain a finding that the wills were mutual and reciprocal wills made pursuant to a valid and enforceable contract.

It is true the parties did not request that a provision be included making the wills irrevocable, but they did not in any respect suggest or dictate the kind of terms of the instruments to be used to accomplish their purpose. They apparently knew nothing of such things and so left everything to the lawyer. It is apparent however that their minds did meet on a particular testamentary disposition of the property to accomplish a particular purpose, and that they intended the wills made pursuant thereto to remain unrevoked at their death. The mutual agreement of the makers of the wills was sufficient consideration to bind the promisors. Equity will enforce such an agreement when well and fairly founded, and will not suffer one of the contracting parties to defraud and defeat his obligation, but will fasten a trust upon the property involved.

We agree with appellants that upon the death of a wife the husband takes all of their real estate held by entireties regardless of any attempt by the wife to make any disposition of it by testamentary devise [citations omitted], and so in this case it must be held that he took title to the real estate by operation of law and not as any result of the will. But we do not agree that the contract under consideration could not operate upon real estate so acquired by Mr. Lawrence. . . . Mr. Lawrence did not agree to leave to the appellees only the property he would take under the will of his wife. His agreement was that if his wife died before he did, he would leave to appellees *all* of his property.

Intent of parties

[I]t seems clear the parties intended that the survivor should have the use and benefit of the property for life, he to have the right to dispose of any or all of the corpus of the estate for his reasonable needs in the event the income should be inadequate for that purpose, but he could not dispose of it to defraud and defeat his obligation.

No question concerning the statute of frauds was raised in this case. . . .

Judgment affirmed.

A serious problem with contracts not to revoke is that circumstances change in unforeseen ways, and the enforcement of the contract may not effectuate the intent of either testator. This is particularly likely to happen when there is a long time span between the deaths of the decedents. For example, in Schaad v. Lorenz, 69 Or. App. 16, 688 P.2d 1342 (1984), husband (*H*) and wife (*W*) executed a joint will in 1946 that devised all to the survivor for life, then half to the named relatives of each. The will expressed an agreement not to revoke. *H* died in 1950 with an estate of $30,000. In 1972 *W* executed an new will that disinherited one of *her* relatives. *W* died in 1981 (31 years after *H*'s death) with a probate estate of $280,000. The court held that *W* was bound by the contract. Can this danger be handled by construction or by implying reasonable provisions in so cryptic a contract, relying on the parties' obvious purposes or on the deceased party's concerns?

brought by husband's children

MATTER OF ESTATE OF JUD
238 Kan. 268, 710 P.2d 1241 (1985)

[John and Jean Jud each had two children by a prior marriage and executed a contractual joint will by which, on the death of the survivor, "we mutually give . . . the entire residue of our property" equally to the four children. On the husband's death, his children brought this action and appeal certain unfavorable determinations by the lower court.]

HERD, J. . . .

The first issue on appeal is whether the contractual provisions of the joint and mutual will apply to property acquired by Jean Jud after the death of John Jud. . . .

effective dates

The contract is effective from the date of execution, while the wills are effective from the date of death of each testator. This means that once the will is executed by both parties it becomes a binding contract

after I dies= irrevocable

incapable of unilateral revocation and, after the death of one of the parties, it is irrevocable. . . .

[A] joint, mutual and contractual will speaks to the property of each testator at the time of his or her respective death and includes all after-acquired property of the survivor unless a different intention appears from the will. . . .

Appellants next argue the trial court erred in holding . . . the contractual will . . . did not sever the joint tenancies, under which ownership the Juds held much of their property. In light of our holding in the foregoing issue . . . this issue is moot. . . .

trial ct was incorrect

The trial court ruled Mrs. Jud's interest cannot be termed that of a "life tenant." We find this holding to be incorrect. . . . Accordingly our [earlier cases] relating to the duties of a life tenant to the remainderman are applicable here. . . .

Appellants argue Mrs. Jud, as a "trustee" of the residue of the estate, should be required to file periodic accountings of her administration of the trust or post a bond to protect the remainderman . . . since the bulk of the Jud's estate is composed of cash and personal property. . . . In the absence of an express provision in the will [so requiring], the survivor is not required to furnish bond and an accounting absent a showing of bad faith or waste. The issue is without merit. . . .

[A]ffirmed in part and reversed in part. . . .

On the line between gifts that are and are not permissible by the survivor in such cases, Dickinson v. Lane, 193 N.Y. 18, 25, 85 N.E. 818, 820 (1908), states: "That line is to be drawn where the courts always draw it when they can, along the boundary of good faith. . . . [The plaintiff's] theory is that any gift, or at least any substantial gift . . . was unauthorized and void. We do not so read the contract. Any gift made with actual intent to defraud would be void. . . . The gift may be so large that, independent of intent or motive, fraud upon the contract would be imputed, or arise constructively by operation of law. Reasonable gifts were impliedly authorized. Unreasonable gifts were not. . . . [T]he question is one of degree, and depends upon the proportion that the value of the gift bears to the amounts of the donor's estate."

The surviving spouse who remarries sometimes places property in joint tenancy with the second spouse despite the binding promise to leave the property by will to others. In such a case the transfer may be set aside, or the property in the hands of the joint owners or the survivor may be impressed with a constructive trust for the contract beneficiaries. See Estate of Chayka, 47 Wis. 2d 102, 176 N.W.2d 561 (1970). But cf. Blackmon v. Estate of Battcock, 78 N.Y.2d 735, 587 N.E.2d 280 (1991).

Elective share of survivor's subsequent spouse. Where the person whose property is subject to such a contractual obligation subsequently marries, does the right of the third-party beneficiary also prevail over the forced heirship rights of the new spouse? Should it matter whether the spouse knows or does not know of the previous agreement? The position of the promisor who has taken under the will of the promisee is often described as a constructive trustee or analogized for a variety of purposes to the position of a life tenant with a limited power to consume principal. What bearing do such analogies or descriptions have on the rights of the survivor's subsequent spouse?

This problem arises with some frequency, and the cases are split. See, e.g., Estate of Beeruk, 429 Pa. 415, 241 A.2d 755 (1968), subordinating the widow's forced share to the rights of the contract beneficiaries who took as "creditors," not as mere legatees. Also favoring the contract beneficiaries is Gregory v. Estate of H.T. Gregory, 315 Ark. 187, 866 S.W.2d 379 (Ark. 1993), where the court agreed with the reasoning in Rubenstein v. Mueller, 19 N.Y.2d 228, 233, 225 N.E.2d 540, 542-543 (1967), in which the majority opinion stated:

> There is unanimity of opinion in this court that [Mueller's] final will was ineffective to alter the testamentary arrangement provided for in the joint will, but we are divided over the question of whether the decedent's earlier covenant with his first wife [takes] precedence over the claim of the widow to [an elective forced share]. . . . [W]e are of the opinion that the named beneficiaries under the joint will are entitled to prevail, and a constructive trust in their favor was properly impressed upon the widow under the later will.
>
> As to the property received by Mueller under the joint will there can be no question but that upon his acceptance of such benefits under that instrument a trust was impressed in favor of the beneficiaries. . . . As to such property Mueller really took but an interest during his life with a power to use or otherwise dispose of principal, and the named beneficiaries took the interest which remained. Under such circumstances he had no property interest in these assets against which the widow's right of election could operate.

The dissenting opinion stated: "The husband, after the death of the first wife. . . , had complete title [and] could have given the property away or consumed it without any fiduciary accountability. . . . [P]laintiff had no [enforceable] interest [in] such property during his lifetime, and at his death [plaintiff had only a contract right] subject to the right of election of the surviving wife." Id. at 236, 225 N.E.2d at 545. Can this be squared with the quotation from the same court's earlier Dickson v. Lane decision, and with other authorities you have read? Consider whether a family allowance might have higher priority.

Among the cases protecting the subsequent spouse in such situations is Patecky v. Friend, 220 Or. 612, 350 P.2d 170 (1960), where *H* had contracted with *W* that the survivor would leave everything to their only child, *C*. Mutual wills were executed pursuant to the contract, and *W* died. *H* accepted the benefits of her will and later remarried. On death he left the bulk of his estate to his second wife, Lillian. *C* sued in equity to enforce the contract and was awarded the entire estate. On appeal, the court modified the decree, stating: "There is no evidence that Lillian, prior to [*H*'s] death, had knowledge of the contract between [*H* and *W*], nor of their wills. . . . Specific performance of a contract is not a matter of right in equity." Id. at 624, 350 P.2d at 175. Under the circumstances, the court deemed it equitable to allow Lillian only her statutory rights as widow, with *C* entitled to the rest of the estate by contract. See also Shimp v. Huff, 315 Md. 624, 556 A.2d 252 (1989), and Via v. Putnam, 656 So.2d 460 (Fla. App. 1995), in which the courts found the elective share policy to outweigh the interests of contract beneficiaries.

Compare Hudson v. Hudson, 701 So. 2d 13 (Ala. App. 1997), holding that a divorce decree, requiring the husband to execute a will in favor of his former wife and their children, resulted in an equitable conversion leaving no inheritable legal interest from which the second spouse could take a forced share. But cf. McKinnon v. White, 698 P.2d 94 (Wash. App. 1985), protecting the children of a second marriage from a divorce-settlement contract calling for the father's estate to be left to the children of the first marriage.

For a discussion of the issues raised in these cases, see C. L. Dessin, The Troubled Relationship of Will Contracts and Spousal Protection: Time for an Amicable Separation, 45 Cath. U.L. Rev. 435 (1996).

8

Will Substitutes and Introduction to Estate Planning

Although we are inclined to think of the will as the primary means of providing for postmortem disposition of property, there are several well-developed and commonly used alternatives by which similar results can be reached. These include such devices as gifts causa mortis, joint and survivorship interests, bonds or accounts payable on death to another, life insurance, and employee benefit plans. One of the important alternative means of disposition is the inter vivos trust, which is treated in detail subsequently. All of these alternatives are useful to the estate planner but none, alone, will fit every client's needs. Indeed, scarcely will one alone satisfy the needs of any one person. Consequently, the lawyer must be familiar with all forms of gratuitous transfers; yet all are subject to abuse and offer traps for the unwary and unadvised. See J. Langbein, The Twentieth-Century Revolution in Family Wealth Transmission, 86 Mich. L. Rev. 722 (1988).

Because most will substitutes (also called nonprobate transfers) are somewhat familiar to you from other courses, this chapter attempts mainly to orient your thinking toward the problems and uses of these devices in estates practice. Note how the issues in the cases differ: some ask whether, granted that the requirements of a valid life insurance contract (or whatever) are met, this is so close to a will that wills act requirements should be met (e.g., the *Rainey* case, page 268 infra); others focus on whether the requirements of an effective transfer or survivorship form (joint tenancy or whatever) are met (e.g., the *Wilson* case, page 275 infra) and, at least initially, do not raise issues about wills act requirements. Also, as each case or problem is studied, consider why the particular arrangement in question was used and how the parties' needs might better have been served. Finally, as this chapter and the next are read, including the materials on taxation, consider the following fairly common situation and questions.

Suppose *W* and *H* are retired and live on fairly generous pensions and income from investments. They own their home in joint tenancy, and their bank accounts are joint as well. Their life insurance is payable to one another or to their children outright, their investments are represented by joint stock certificates or payable-on-death bonds, and their car is rented. Their combined taxable estates could approximate $1 million, and the probate estate of the first to die would essentially consist of the change in the decedent's possession, some personal effects, household furniture, and the like. If debts and taxes are paid, along with funeral and last illness expenses, by the survivor, what need is there for probate — or at least for more than the summary proceedings allowed for "small estates" as defined by local probate law? On the other hand, are there other costs and risks in setting up an estate in this fashion, and in assuming that all significant assets should be handled in similar ways?

Nonprobate Transfers and "Subsidiary Wills Rules." Wills have been around for a long time, and, consequently, many subsidiary wills rules have evolved. For example, in Chapter 6, we considered the rule — often statutory — that divorce revokes a devise to an ex-spouse and the rule that a will can revoke all prior wills. Chapter 3 dealt with the surviving spouse's right to elect against the will. Later we will consider the lapse rule that requires a beneficiary to survive the testator and antilapse statutes that often substitute issue for predeceased devisees. To what extent should these, and other rules, apply to will substitutes? This is one of the most challenging issues of the law related to decedents' estates and trusts today. If these rules reflect probable intent or sound policy for wills, they probably do for most will substitute contexts. In reversing the position of prior Restatements with respect to revocable trusts, the Restatement (Third) of Trusts §25(2) states that such trusts are subject to substantive restrictions on testation and ordinarily to rules of construction and some other substantive principles applicable to testamentary dispositions.

The Uniform Probate Code applies some of the subsidiary wills rules to will substitutes. For example, §2-804 revokes provisions for an ex-spouse in any revocable instrument, including beneficiary designations in life insurance policies and pay-on-death accounts, but many states have not enacted this provision. Thus, in Cook v. Equitable Life Assurance Society, 428 N.E.2d 110 (Ind. App. 1981), in which the testator attempted by will to change the beneficiary named in his life insurance policy from his first wife to his second wife and son, the court held that neither the divorce nor the will changed the beneficiary designation. Some states have statutes providing that divorce revokes some, but not all, will substitute provisions. See 15 Okl. St. Ann. §178. More recently, Parsonese v. Midland National Insurance Co., 550 Pa. 423, 706 A.2d 814 (1998), held that the retrospective application of a "divorce-revokes" statute to a life insurance policy was an unconstitutional impairment of contractual obligations. Other courts have agreed. See Aetna

Life Insurance Co. v. Shilling, 616 N.E.2d 893 (Ohio 1993); Whirlpool Corp. v. Ritter, 929 F.2d 1318 (8th Cir. 1991). As you encounter various will substitutes in this chapter and later, consider which subsidiary wills rules (especially statutory rules) should apply to which will substitutes.

A.   Survivorship Rights via Contract and Joint Ownership

1.   Life Insurance, Annuities, and Related Arrangements

It is well settled that the usual selection of a beneficiary to receive the proceeds of a life insurance policy on the death of the insured is not a testamentary disposition. Thus, when the insured dies, the proceeds are payable directly to the designated beneficiary under the policy, if living, and are not subject to administration as assets of the insured's estate. Proceeds payable to a named beneficiary normally are not subject to the terms of the insured's will, even if inconsistent with the policy, because the terms of the contract are controlling. Generally these proceeds pass free of the claims of the deceased insured's creditors and are not part of the estate for purposes of the forced share of a surviving spouse. (But see the 1990 UPC set out in Chapter 3.) These results are not affected by the fact that the insured has paid the premiums and has retained incidents of ownership such as the rights to surrender, assign, and borrow against the policy, and the usual right during life to change the beneficiaries and select among the optional modes of settlement. Can you see any reasons why the insured might find it desirable to designate the insured's *estate* as the recipient of the insurance? Aside from tax considerations[1] can you see the disadvantages? Can you see any alternatives, then, for accomplishing the purposes for which one might make the proceeds payable to the estate?

In addition to the right to designate beneficiaries, life insurance policies offer the insured or other policy owner the right to select either a lump sum payment or one of a fairly standard set of optional modes of settlement for the beneficiaries. If a settlement option has not been selected, so that at the death of the insured the payee is entitled to receive the proceeds in a lump sum, the privilege will remain open to the payee to select one of the options. These typical options are: (1) an

---

1. Payment to the estate has state inheritance tax disadvantages in many states, but insurance proceeds are included in the insured's gross estate on death for purposes of the federal estate tax even though payable to a named beneficiary if the insured retained any of the *incidents of ownership* in the policies. I.R.C. §2042(2).

interest option, under which the company retains the proceeds, paying interest periodically to the beneficiary (often accompanied by withdrawal privileges and sometimes by the later right to choose a different option); (2) a *fixed period option,* under which amounts are paid at regular intervals over a set period of years (the amount of the installment being based on interest plus liquidation of principal); (3) a *fixed amount option,* with periodic payments (comprised of interest and principal) in the fixed amount being paid until the proceeds are exhausted; and (4) a variety of *life income options,* with installments paid over the beneficiary's lifetime on the basis of a straight life annuity, a joint and survivor annuity, a life annuity with a term certain (i.e., with a minimum number of payments), or a refund annuity. The considerations pertinent to the selection of a form of settlement are varied and sometimes complex, ranging from tax factors (e.g., the Internal Revenue Code §101(d)(1)(B) exclusion) to a beneficiary's need of a guaranteed income for life, and including also considerations of estate liquidity and flexibility of expenditures and investments. As we shall see later, proceeds are sometimes made payable to trustees.

A significant modern development is the growth of pension and employee benefit programs, most of which provide some form of death benefits that pass outside estate administration procedures. Most widespread of these, of course, is the federal social security system, but there are an infinite number and variety of other public and private programs. See Dunham, Sixty Different Succession Laws in Illinois, 46 Ill. B.J. 741 (1958) (finding forty different state programs, plus twenty under federal statutes, all operating in one state). Under many programs, survivor provisions offer little dispositive flexibility. Social security death benefits are paid in a prescribed pattern only for an overage or disabled spouse, underage (age 18, or 21 if a full-time student) or disabled children, and parents under some circumstances. Other plans may confine payments to the employee's immediate family or certain near relatives, with limited freedom, if any, to select beneficiaries or modes of settlement — and then generally not by will. The rights under such public and private plans may constitute the primary wealth of a given client, so the lawyer must consider them carefully in planning a client's affairs and integrate them as much as possible into the overall scheme of disposition.

In addition, a client may dispose of some wealth through the purchase of annuities, and lawyers are sometimes called on to advise in such matters. Detailed study of these and the other diverse arrangements is beyond the scope of this course, but they are regularly an aspect of estate situations and occasionally a source of litigation. The following case and problems are illustrative of questions that are central to this course and arise in various forms.

KANSAS CITY LIFE INSURANCE CO. v. RAINEY
353 Mo. 477, 182 S.W.2d 624 (1944)

DOUGLAS, J.

In 1925 Jessie A. Rainey became Herbert F. Hall's secretary and continued as such until his death. In 1931 Hall, aged 72, purchased an "Investment Annuity Policy" from the Kansas City Life Insurance Company for $50,000, the income payable to him, the principal payable to his wife at his death. After his wife died he named Miss Rainey beneficiary in the policy. Hall died in 1941. . . .

After Hall's death Miss Rainey . . . claimed the [insurance] proceeds . . . from the insurance company. The executor of Hall's estate also claimed the proceeds. . . .

The question for decision is whether the policy is invalid as a testamentary disposition not in the form prescribed by the statute of wills.

The executor concedes a life insurance policy is generally considered as not testamentary in character. But he argues this policy is not an insurance policy because there is no element of risk involved. Hall paid the company $50,000 and received quarterly interest for four percent under the term annuity. The insurance company, upon Hall's death, was obligated to pay out only the same amount it originally received, namely $50,000. . . . Thus, the executor asserts the policy is merely a certificate of deposit to take effect upon Hall's death and is testamentary in character. . . .

An insurance policy is a contract. A policy payable to a third person is a contract for the benefit of the third person.

The policy we are considering is a contract between Hall and the insurance company for the benefit of Miss Rainey. This is true regardless of the element of risk. It still would be a contract for the benefit of a third person if made with a bank, a corporation of any other sort, or an individual. In the policy Miss Rainey is a third-party donee-beneficiary. Restatement of Contracts, §133. She is entitled to enforce the contract even though she is a stranger to both the contract and to the consideration. 12 Am. Jur. Contracts, §277.

The policy is not testamentary because it became effective before Hall's death. It was a contract made and in force during Hall's lifetime. Hence there would be no reason to surround it with formalities which safeguard a will. See Krell v. Codman, 154 Mass. 454, 28 N.E. 578, 14 L.R.A. 860, 26 Am. St. Rep. 260.

The policy became effective upon its execution and the payment of the consideration of $50,000, all done during Hall's lifetime. The payment of the consideration was an immediate disposition of the $50,000. The money became the property of the insurance company. Upon Hall's death the money to be paid to the beneficiary constituted no part of Hall's estate. So far as Miss Rainey is concerned, any disposition as to her was effected at the time she was designated as beneficiary. Her enjoyment of the fund was merely postponed until Hall's death, subject to the right of revocation retained by Hall.

The mere fact a note, bond or other instrument for the payment of money is not payable until or after death is not sufficient to make such an instrument testamentary in character and invalid for that reason.

The reservation of the right by Hall to change the beneficiary or to cash in the policy does not make it testamentary. These are but methods of revocation. We see no reason why there should be any distinction between the effect of reserving a right of revocation as was done in the policy and reserving one in a living trust. . . .

The [judgment is] affirmed.

PROBLEM

8-A.   *H* owned a life insurance policy in the amount of $50,000, and under the policy his wife of twenty years, *W*, was designated to receive the full amount on his death. *H* also owned land and securities valued at $200,000. On *H*'s death without issue, his will was admitted to probate. The will made specific reference to the above-mentioned insurance and directed that *W* should receive one-half of the proceeds of the policy and that *B*, *H*'s brother, should receive the other half of the proceeds. The will further provided that all of *H*'s lands, securities, and other property were to be held by *T* Trust Company in trust to pay *W* the income and as much principal as required for her generous support, and on her death to pay the remaining principal to *B* or his issue then living by right of representation. What are *B*'s rights? Assuming *W* has no independently owned assets, as *W*'s lawyer what would you advise her? See Hartwig v. Schiefer, 147 Ind. 64, 46 N.E. 75 (1897); 5 Page on Wills §47.10 (Bowe-Parker, 1962). Cf. In re Estate of Smith, 108 Cal. 115, 40 P. 1037 (1895) (community property involved); Thurlow v. Thurlow, 317 Mass. 126, 56 N.E.2d 902 (1944) (joint tenancy property involved); Kentucky Trust Co. v. Kessel, 464 S.W.2d 275 (Ky. App. 1971) (tenancy by entirety involved). See the novel Washington statute (below), which became effective July 1, 1999. Why do you suppose other "blockbuster will" proposals have consistently been rejected or aborted? Should they be?

[handwritten margin notes: — ½ ins. proceeds -b/c writing requirement to change is met]

REVISED CODE OF WASHINGTON

§11.11.020.   *Disposition of nonprobate assets under will.*

(1) Subject to community property rights, upon the death of an owner the owner's interest in any nonprobate asset specifically referred

to in the owner's will belongs to the testamentary beneficiary named to receive the nonprobate asset, notwithstanding the rights of any beneficiary designated before the date of the will.

(2) A general residuary gift in an owner's will, or a will making general disposition of all of the owner's property, does not entitle the devisees or legatees to receive nonprobate assets of the owner.

(3) A disposition in a will of the owner's interest in "all nonprobate assets" or of all of a category of nonprobate asset under RCW 11.11.010(7), such as "all of my payable on death bank accounts" or similar language, is deemed to be a disposition of all the nonprobate assets the beneficiaries of which are designated before the date of the will.

(4) If the owner designates a beneficiary for a nonprobate asset after the date of the will, the will does not govern the disposition of that nonprobate asset. If the owner revokes the later beneficiary designation, the prior will does not govern the disposition of the nonprobate asset. A beneficiary designation with respect to an asset that renews without the signature of the owner is deemed to have been made on the date on which the account was first opened.

2.   Other Contract Rights and Joint Ownership

Under the joint tenancy form of ownership, on the death of one of the owners the property passes to the surviving owner or owners without administration and without regard to the deceased owner's will. The same is true of property held by husband and wife as tenants by the entirety, but it is not true of tenancy in common. The latter lacks the right of survivorship, which is the salient characteristic of the other two forms. Presumably you are acquainted with these forms of ownership, at least as they apply to real property, and this chapter does not examine extensively the nature of the various forms of concurrent ownership. These forms of ownership are in widespread use, particularly in the case of land owned by husband and wife. Of course, the joint tenancy form, unlike tenancy by the entirety, may be used by persons who are not husband and wife, and in most of the states that recognize one or both of these forms of ownership, they are available for personal as well as real property.

Because in most cases the client will not have given serious thought to the form in which title to property is held, the lawyer who is consulted for estate planning will find it necessary to go over such matters with the client. Certainly the lawyer cannot adequately plan a will without knowing the form in which the client's property is held, because, for example, wills do not operate on property subject to a right of survivorship. Furthermore, tax considerations may enter into the choice of ownership form. The creation or severance of a joint tenancy may have gift tax consequences, and such decisions also involve income tax and estate tax factors that should not be ignored.

At this point, consider what purposes are served by joint ownership with right of survivorship. Also consider what problems may arise from the careless creation of joint rights with regard to various properties, such as bank accounts and securities and valuables kept in safe-deposit boxes. In a great number of states these problems are affected by varying forms of legislation. A lawyer should become familiar with the terms of local statutes and the case law thereunder. Uncertainty may also be created by various arrangements providing for payment to one person on the death of another. (Cf. Bielat v. Bielat, 721 N.E.2d 28 (Ohio 2000), recently upholding the constitutionality of a statute retroactively validating pay-on-death beneficiary designations; no impairment of "vested" rights.) The following cases are illustrative of the handling of recurrent controversies.

FRANKLIN v. ANNA NATIONAL BANK
488 N.E.2d 1117 (Ill. App. 1986)

[Mrs. Franklin, as executor, commenced this action against defendant bank, alleging that funds in a joint savings account were property of the estate. The bank interpleaded Mrs. Goddard, who claimed the funds as surviving joint owner.]

WELCH, J. . . .

[T]he circuit court entered judgment for Mrs. Goodard. Mrs. Franklin appeals. We reverse. . . .

Decedent had eye surgery [and] was losing his eye sight in 1978. [His sister-in-law] Mrs. Goddard moved to Union County to help decedent and live with him. [Soon thereafter they went together] to the bank, according to Mrs. Goddard, to have his money put in both their names so she could get money when they needed it, "and he wanted me to have this money if I outlived him."

A bank employee prepared a signature card [and both decedent and] Mrs. Goddard signed it. . . . The front of the card states that one signature is required for withdrawals. The back of the card states that all funds deposited are owned by the signatories as joint tenants with right of survivorship.

Mrs. Goddard testified that she did not deposit any of the money in the savings account [and she] made no withdrawals. . . . According to Mrs. Goddard, on the day she signed the signature card decedent "asked me . . . if I needed any more money at that time and I said, no, and I said, just leave it in here and I will get it out whenever I need it." . . . Asked whether she ever had the passbook . . . in her possession, Mrs. Goddard answered "Only while I was at [decedent's]. It was there.". . .

The instrument creating a joint tenancy account presumably speaks the whole truth. In order to go behind the terms of the agreement, the one claiming adversely thereto has the burden of establishing by clear and convincing evidence that a gift was not intended. Each case involving a joint tenancy account must be evaluated on its own facts and circumstances. The form of the agreement is not conclusive. . . . The decision of the donor, made subsequent to the creation of the joint tenancy, that he did not want the proceeds to pass to the survivor, would not, in itself, be sufficient to sever the tenancy. However, it is proper to consider events occurring after creation of the joint account in determining whether the donor actually intended [at the time of creating the account] to transfer his interest in the account at his death to the surviving joint tenant.

We must examine the instant facts in light of the above principles: [Testimony indicated that] just nine months after adding Mrs. Goddard's name to [the account] decedent attempted to remove Mrs. Goddard's name and substitute Mrs. Franklin's. The second of decedent's hand written letters to the bank [indicates his concern] that he might lose his sight and be unable to transact his own banking business. These facts show that decedent made Mrs. Goddard . . . a signatory for his own convenience . . . and not with intent to effect a present gift. It does not appear that Mrs. Goddard ever exercised any authority or control over the joint account. While decedent's statement that he wanted Mrs. Goddard to have the money in the account if she outlived him suggests decedent's donative intent, literally decedent's statement is inconsistent with intent to donate any interest during the decedent's lifetime. Mrs. Goddard does not argue that there was a valid testamentary disposition in her favor, nor do we so find on the instant facts. . . .

[D]ecedent's attempts to change the account show his consistent view of the account as his own. The surrounding circumstances show decedent's concern for his health and his . . . use of Mrs. Goddard . . . to assure his access to his funds. The money in account 3816 should have been found to be the property of the estate. . . .

Where donative intent and survivorship rights are presumed in cases of this type, some courts treat the presumption as a weak one. In general, litigation of this type is appallingly abundant. In Johnson v. Herrin, 272 S.C. 224, 250 S.E.2d 334 (1978), the presumption of gift was found rebutted by the terms of a roughly contemporaneous will under which the testamentary scheme would have been rendered meaningless if a gift of the account funds had been intended. Four joint accounts were found to have been created for convenience only and with no donative intent in In re Estate of Fisher, 443 Pa. 419, 279 A.2d 754 (1971), where a court footnote says there is no reason for banks not to provide alternative forms, one of which is clearly marked for "convenience" only. A quite different approach was adopted in a leading recent case, Wright v. Bloom, 69 Ohio St. 3d 596, 635 N.E.2d 31 (1994), discussed and followed in the *Robinson* case below.

ROBINSON v. DELFINO
710 A.2d 154 (R.I. 1998)

[Decedent had placed funds in bank accounts in her name and defendants' names jointly with the right of survivorship. After the decedent died (intestate), defendants withdrew the funds. The administrator of the estate sued to recover the funds. The trial judge, relying primarily on Nocero v. Lembo (cited below), ordered the funds returned. The defendants appealed.]

BOURCIER, J.

. . . In Nocera v. Lembo, 121 R.I. 216, 397 A.2d 524 (1979), we said that the form of a joint bank account constituted only prima facie evidence that the creator of the account intended an inter vivos gift. . . .

We conclude that the law heretofore applied to joint bank accounts both in this jurisdiction and elsewhere has been both unpredictable and inconsistent, often frustrating the public's common understanding of what it always believed that a joint bank account was intended to accomplish. Accordingly, the time has now arrived for us to revisit our previous holdings in contested joint bank account cases, some of which date back into the last century.

Courts throughout this country have approached the analysis of joint bank accounts in a variety of ways. Some courts have historically used the common law gift theory when analyzing the legal effect of a joint bank account as we recognized in *Nocera*. . . . The gift theory requires the court to consider the depositor's intent and the question of whether a gift was in fact intended and accomplished by the depositor.

Other courts have used the [trust law] theory requir[ing] that before a survivorship interest in a joint bank account is granted, there must be a finding by the court that the depositor intended to convey an equitable interest in the funds in the joint account.

Still other courts have applied a joint tenancy analysis. . . while other states have avoided the joint tenancy requirement of the four unities, however, by enacting legislation that obviates the need for one or more of them. . . .

The contract theory has also been utilized by some courts . . . to avoid completely any application or consequence of the statute of wills. . . .

Finally, some courts have interpreted the bank protection statutes of their respective states to imply that the named survivor of a joint bank account acquires a present vested property interest in that account. . . .

The most recent trend among courts confronted with the ownership issue in joint bank accounts, however, and the trend that we conclude is most in conformity with the way the majority of the public actually perceive joint bank accounts, is that which finally recognizes that joint bank accounts cannot be uniformly understood or analyzed under any of the pre-existing common law methods. . . . As a result of that recognition courts have begun to treat joint bank accounts differently from gifts, trusts, joint tenancies, or contracts and have concluded that the form of the joint bank account is itself the conclusive proof of the depositor's intent to transfer a vested possessory interest in the ownership of the joint account money. The most cogent discussion of that new treatment of joint bank accounts has been framed by the Ohio court in Wright [v. Bloom]. . . . "Recent cases have created a morass of unpredictability, often occasioned by ambiguous and conflicting results. Presently, the depositor cannot rest assured as to whether the funds remaining in the account at his death will immediately pass to the survivor. Identical survivorship language expressly set forth in one joint and survivorship account agreement may be adjudged sufficient to pass ownership to the survivor while found to be insufficient in another." *Wright*, 635 N.E.2d at 33.

The Ohio court in *Wright* cogently reasoned from what courts in jurisdictions other than Ohio had concluded, namely, that extrinsic evidence of a depositor's intent should not be permitted to defeat survivorship rights in a joint bank account. . . . The Ohio court then proceeded to hold that "the opening of an account in joint and survivorship form shall, in the absence of fraud, duress, undue influence or lack of mental capacity on the part of the depositor, be conclusive evidence of the depositor's intention to transfer to the survivor the balance remaining in the account at the depositor's death.". . .

[To continue] to permit the introduction of all manner of extrinsic evidence to analyze the depositor's subjective intent, as has been permitted in our previous joint bank account cases, we believe persistently ignores the fact that the absolute common understanding of the vast majority of people establishing joint bank accounts nowadays is that they create immediate possessory as well as survivorship rights. . . . A surviving named joint account holder should be entitled to obtain funds remaining on deposit in a joint account without the necessity of first having to travel through several court systems and to have lawyers, trial judges, juries, and appellate judges perform post mortem cerebral autopsies and examinations in order to determine and second-guess what the subjective intent of the deceased joint owner of the account was at the time the account was created. . . . Accordingly, we conclude that the opening of a joint bank account wherein survivorship rights are specifically provided for is conclusive evidence of the intention to transfer to the survivor an immediate in praesenti joint beneficial possessory ownership right in the balance of the account remaining after the death of the depositor, absent evidence of fraud, undue influence, duress, or lack of mental capacity. Likewise, if a joint bank account does not provide for survivorship rights, that absence will be conclusive evidence of an intent not to transfer any right of ownership to the survivor, absent evidence of mistake or fraud. . . . For all the foregoing reasons the defendants' appeals are sustained and the order of the trial justice is reversed.

Do you understand what the court means in its statement that the opening of a joint bank account is conclusive evidence of the depositor's intention to create in the survivor "an immediate in praesenti joint beneficial possessory ownership right in the balance of the account remaining after the death of the depositor"? Do you believe that there is some "absolute common understanding of the vast majority of people establishing joint bank accounts nowadays"? Compare UPC §6-212 infra. See also §6-204(a) and (b) and the comment to §6-212.

Compare Estate of Wilson, 404 Ill. 207, 88 N.E.2d 662 (1949), involving a controversy over money and bearer bonds found at decedent's death in a bank safe-deposit box. The card for the box showed the decedent and his wife as "joint tenants with right of survivorship and not as tenants in common." The assets in question had been decedent's property initially, and his will left his estate half to his wife and half to his children of a prior marriage. In denying the spouse's right to the assets by survivorship, the court's opinion referred both to "reason and logic" and to decisions "of other jurisdictions . . . that renting a lockbox in a bank in the name of two or more persons, as joint tenants with right of survivorship, does not on the death of one vest the personal property in the box in the survivor." In Steinhauser v. Repko, 277 N.E.2d 73 (Ohio App. 1971), a printed safe-deposit box form (signed by the decedent and his sister-in-law, *declaring the contents* held "as joint tenants with right of survivorship") entitled the sister-in-law as survivor to cash that originally belonged to decedent but was found in the box after his death.

Analogous problems frequently arise with regard to land and securities ostensibly held in joint tenancy. This is especially true in those community property states that permit free conversion of community property to separate or joint ownership, and vice versa. Where a deed or stock certificate reads in joint tenancy form but has a community property source, what is the true ownership form? Was the instrument taken in apparent joint tenancy form "purely for the convenience of the parties" without adequate understanding or was there an "intent" to convert? Often the apparent or record form is presumed to reflect the intention of the parties but is rebuttable, even by oral evidence of their contrary, informal understanding. The results affect tax consequences as well as the rights of claimants. Related issues arise elsewhere and with regard to separate property, usually aggravated by problems of gift, estate, and income taxation. Furthermore, for estate planning or other reasons, parties often desire or are counseled to sever joint tenancies, and questions arise concerning the intentions of the parties or the legal effectiveness of steps taken to convert to another form of ownership. Oversight, neglect, and even misunderstanding of the law (with respect to the rights of the parties to act unilaterally or techniques for exercising those rights) are surprisingly common in the work of lawyers in this area of vital matters that should be relatively simple from a planning viewpoint.

RIDDLE v. HARMON
102 Cal. App. 3d 524, 162 Cal. Rptr. 530 (1980)

POCHE, J.

We must decide whether Frances Riddle, now deceased, unilaterally terminated a joint tenancy by conveying her interest from herself as joint tenant to herself as tenant in common. The trial court determined, via summary judgment quieting title to her widower, that she did not. The facts follow.

Mr. and Mrs. Riddle purchased a parcel of real estate, taking title as joint tenants. Several months before her death, Mrs. Riddle retained an attorney to plan her estate. After reviewing pertinent documents, he advised her that the property was held in joint tenancy and that, upon her death, the property would pass to her husband. Distressed upon learning this, she requested that the joint tenancy be terminated so that she could dispose of her interest by will. As a result, the attorney prepared a grant deed whereby Mrs. Riddle granted to herself an undivided one-half interest in the subject property. . . .

This court is now asked to reexamine whether a strawman is required to terminate a joint tenancy.

Twelve years ago, in Clark v. Carter (1968) 265 Cal. App. 2d 291, 295, 70 Cal. Rptr. 923, the Court of Appeal considered the same question and found the strawman to be in-dispensable. . . . That "two-to-transfer" notion stems from the English common law feoffment ceremony with livery of seisin. (Swenson and Degnan, Severance of Joint Tenancies (1954) 38 Minn. L. Rev. 466, 467.) If the ceremony took place upon the land being conveyed, the grantor (feoffor) would hand a symbol of the land, such as a lump of earth or a twig, to the grantee (feoffee). In order to complete the investiture of seisin it was necessary that the feoffor completely relinquish possession of the land to the feoffee. It is apparent from the requirement of livery of seisin that one could not enfeoff oneself — that is, one could not be both grantor and grantee in a single transaction. Handing oneself a dirt clod is ungainly. Just as livery of seisin has become obsolete, so should ancient vestiges of that ceremony give way to modern conveyancing realities. . . .

The most familiar technique for unilateral termination is the use of an intermediary "strawman." . . .

Another creative method of terminating a joint tenancy appears in Reiss v. Reiss (1941) 45 Cal. App. 2d 740, 114 P.2d 718. There a trust [with a right of reconveyance] was used. . . .

In view of the rituals that are available to unilaterally terminate a joint tenancy, there is little virtue in steadfastly adhering to cumbersome feudal law requirements.

> It is revolting to have no better reason for a rule of law than that so it was laid down in the time of Henry IV. It is still more revolting if the grounds upon which it was laid down have vanished long since, and the rule simply persists from blind imitation of the past.

(Justice Oliver Wendell Holmes, Collected Legal Papers 187 (1920)). Common sense as well as legal efficiency dictate that a joint tenant should be able to accomplish directly what he or she could otherwise achieve indirectly by use of elaborate legal fictions. . . .

We discard the archaic rule that one cannot enfeoff oneself, which, if applied, would defeat the clear intention of the grantor. There is no question but that the decedent here could have accomplished her objective — termination of the joint tenancy — by one of a variety of circuitous processes. We reject the rationale of the Clark case because it rests on a common law notion whose reason for existence vanished about the time that grant deeds and title companies replaced colorful dirt clod ceremonies as the way to transfer title to real property. One joint tenant may unilaterally sever the joint tenancy without the use of an intermediary device.

The judgment is reversed.

Riddle was followed in Minonk State Bank v. Grassman, 95 Ill. 2d 392, 447 N.E.2d 822 (1983).

Contrast Veterans' Agent v. Rinaldi, 483 N.E.2d 829 (Mass. App. 1985), in which the decedent applied for state benefits as the dependent father of a veteran and, on approval of his application, allowed a lien under the benefits statute to be executed and filed at the registry of deeds on real property then held with his wife as tenants by the entirety. On his death, his wife "became the sole owner of the property 'free and clear of [his] debts'. . . . [Because she] did not receive any of the benefits that gave rise to the lien and was the surviving tenant . . . the lien was extinguished." The court distinguished an earlier decision where the survivor had received benefits; it also noted in a footnote that the present case is stronger than one involving a joint tenancy because each tenant by the entirety "has an indefeasible right of survivorship in the entire tenancy which can not be defeated by any act taken individually by either spouse during his or her lifetime." Id. at 831.

Government bonds are frequently held in the names of "*A* or *B*" or "*A* payable on death to *B*." Do you — do the parties — know the rights of *A* and *B* during their joint lives under each of these forms? Or *B*'s rights if *A* dies? Treasury Regulations and recent decisions provide that after *A*'s death payment is to be made to *B*. Where the purchaser's intention is to the contrary, however, it is still possible to conclude that the regulations permitting payment to *B* are for the convenience and protection of the government but do not necessarily establish the rights as between *A* and *B*. See Byer v. Byer, 180 Kan. 258, 303 P.2d 137 (1956); Decker v. Fowler, 199 Wash. 549, 92 P.2d 254 (1939). But cf. United States v. Chandler, 410 U.S. 257 (1973).

In re Estate of Tonsic, 13 Ohio App. 2d 195, 235 N.E.2d 239 (1968), involved several "P.O.D." bank accounts (i.e., accounts in the name of the depositor, payable on death to another). The court upheld the P.O.D. provisions on the basis of legislation that had been enacted several years earlier, the opinion stating (at 196-197, 235 N.E.2d at 240-241) that but for the statute

> we would have had no difficulty in determining that this attempt to transfer title to the money in the bank was completely ineffective, either [as] an attempted testamentary transfer, or as a gift inter vivos or causa mortis that was incomplete. A gift . . . requires that the donor, during his lifetime, divest himself of all dominion of the gift and invest the donee therewith. There was no present right on the part of the donees to withdraw any money from the bank, and, in that respect, the accounts cannot be considered joint and survivorship accounts.
>
> The contract . . . between the bank and the depositor . . . is clearly a testamentary disposition [but] the statute herein expressly exempts such a gift from the statute on wills.

For a consideration of the bank's responsibility to the parties when a P.O.D. provision is invalid, see Blais v. Colebrook Guaranty Savings Bank, 107 N.H. 300, 220 A.2d 763 (1966).

In the case that follows, was the court confused by the intermingling of gift and contract concepts? If another court would decide the case *differently*, should it distinguish its facts from a situation in which the creditor attempted to create rights in others merely by written direction to the debtor to pay the debt to them if the creditor should die before receiving payment? What if the creditor executed a writing, a "deed of gift," and delivered it to the intended assignees? What if the delivered writing purports to give only payments not made before her death? Are the informal personal arrangements in *McCarthy* distinguishable from analogous, formal, institutionalized arrangements?

McCARTHY v. PIERET
281 N.Y. 407, 24 N.E.2d 102 (1939)

[Defendant Pieret executed a bond and mortgage to Mrs. Jackman, who later entered into an extension agreement whereby the due date of the payment was extended to March 7, 1940. Her extension agreement provided that in the event of her death before that date, the interest and principal payments were to be made to certain designated relatives. After Mrs. Jackman's death, the right to future payments was claimed by her husband as her administrator and also by the designated relatives.]

CRANE, C.J.

. . . The judgments below have held this extension agreement to be a valid disposition in the nature of a gift, and not an attempted testamentary disposition in violation of section 21 of the Decedent Estate Law (Consol. Laws, ch. 13). It is not always easy to determine whether a transaction is a gift or is testamentary in character. It depends upon the intention of the donor.

. . . [W]e must, I think, draw the inference that the mortgagee never intended to transfer a vested interest in the mortgage to the [designated relatives]. Neither did she divest herself of all control or interest in the mortgage. After March 7, 1940, the principal and interest were to be paid to her if she were alive. . . . She could have satisfied the mortgage and taken the principal at any time during her life. Had the mortgagor desired to pay the mortgage he could have paid it to the mortgagee. Surely if this had been done these collateral relatives would have had no interest by reason of the extension. Their rights, at best, only arose on the death of the mortgagee prior to March 7, 1940. . . . The mortgagee never intended to divest herself of all rights and control in and over this mortgage until her death. . . .

I do not say that the passing of property at death may not be provided for by contract or by deed, but the donor in such cases divests himself of all interest and vests it in the beneficiary. . . . He retains no further control over the transaction but, for a consideration or else because of relationship, establishes a present enforceable interest, postponed in enjoyment perhaps until death. . . .

[J]udgment . . . reversed. . . .

The *McCarthy* case was severely criticized in Mutual Benefit Life Insurance Co. v. Ellis, 125 F.2d 127 (2d Cir. 1942) and in Note, 53 Harv. L. Rev. 1060 (1940). Compare, almost thirty years later, Matter of Estate of Hillowitz, 238 N.E.2d 723 (N.Y. 1968):

> . . . A partnership agreement which provides that, upon the death of one partner, his interest shall pass to the surviving partner or partners, resting as it does in contract, is unquestionably valid and may not be defeated by labeling it a testamentary disposition. We are unable to perceive a difference in principle between an agreement of this character and one, such as that before us, providing for a deceased partner's widow, rather than a surviving partner, to succeed to the decedent's interest in the partnership.
>
> These partnership undertakings are, in effect, nothing more or less than third-party beneficiary contracts, performable at death. Like many similar instruments, contractual in nature, which provide for the disposition of property after death, they need not conform to the requirements of the statute of wills. . . . This type of third-party beneficiary contract is not invalid as an attempted testamentary disposition.
>
> The executors may derive little satisfaction from McCarthy v. Pieret [supra]. . . . [I]t is our considered judgment that the decision should be limited to its facts. . . . [and that] the case is clearly distinguishable from the one now before us. . . .
>
> The order of the Appellate Division should be reversed, with costs in this court and in the Appellate Division, and the order of the Surrogate's Court reinstated.

If *A* deposits her funds in a joint and survivorship account with *B*, what are *A*'s rights, and *B*'s, while they are both alive? See typical view offered for codification in UPC §6-211(b) below.

UNIFORM PROBATE CODE

§6-101. *Nonprobate Transfers on Death*

(a) A provision for a nonprobate transfer on death in an insurance policy, contract of employment, bond, mortgage, promissory note, certificated or uncertificated security, account agreement, custodial agreement, deposit agreement, compensation plan, pension plan, individual retirement plan, employee benefit plan, trust, conveyance, deed of gift, marital property agreement, or other written instrument of a similar nature is nontestamentary. This subsection includes a written provision that:

(1) money or other benefits due to, controlled by, or owned by a decedent before death must be paid after the decedent's death to a person whom the decedent designates either in the instrument or in a separate writing, including a will, executed either before or at the same time as the instrument, or later;

(2) money due or to become due under the instrument ceases to be payable in the event of death of the promisee or the promisor before payment or demand; or

(3) any property controlled by or owned by the decedent before death which is the subject of the instrument passes to a person the decedent designates either in the instrument or in a separate writing, including a will, executed either before or at the same time as the instrument, or later.

(b) This section does not limit rights of creditors under other laws of this State.

§6-211.   *Ownership [of Multi-party Accounts]*
         During Lifetime. . . .

(b) During the lifetime of all parties, an account belongs to the parties in proportion to the net contribution of each [defined in (a)] to the sums on deposit, unless there is clear and convincing evidence of a different intent. As between parties married to each other, in the absence of proof otherwise, the net contribution of each is presumed to be an equal amount.

(c) A beneficiary in an account having a POD designation has no right to sums on deposit during the lifetime of any party.

(d) An agent in an account with an agency designation has no beneficial right to sums on deposit.

§6-212.   *Rights at Death.*

(a) Except as otherwise provided in this part, on death of a party sums on deposit in a multiple-party account belong to the surviving party or parties. If two or more parties survive and one is the surviving spouse of the decedent, the amount to which the decedent, immediately before death, was beneficially entitled under Section 6-211 belongs to the surviving spouse. If two or more parties survive and none is the surviving spouse of the decedent, the amount to which the decedent, immediately before death, was beneficially entitled under Section 6-211 belongs to the surviving parties in equal shares, and augments the proportion to which each survivor, immediately before the decedent's death, was beneficially entitled under Section 6-211, and the right of survivorship continues between the surviving parties.

(b) In an account with a POD designation:

(1) On death of one of two or more parties, the rights in sums on deposit are governed by subsection (a).

(2) On death of the sole party or the last survivor of two or more parties, sums on deposit belong to the surviving beneficiary or beneficiaries. If two or more beneficiaries survive, sums on deposit belong to them in equal and undivided shares, and there is no right of survivorship in the event of death of a beneficiary thereafter. If no beneficiary survives, sums on deposit belong to the estate of the last surviving party.

(c) Sums on deposit in a single-party account without a POD designation, or in a multiple-party account that, by the terms of the account, is without right of survivorship, are not affected by death of a party, but the amount to which the decedent, immediately before death, was beneficially entitled under Section 6-211 is transferred as part of the decedent's estate. A POD designation in a multiple-party account without right of survivorship is ineffective. For purposes of this section, designation of an account as a tenancy in common establishes that the account is without right of survivorship.

(d) The ownership right of a surviving party or beneficiary, or of the decedent's estate, in sums on deposit is subject to requests for payment made by a party before the party's death, whether paid by the financial institution before or after death, or unpaid. The surviving party or beneficiary, or the decedent's estate, is liable to the payee of an unpaid request for payment. The liability is limited to a proportionate share of the amount transferred under this section, to the extent necessary to discharge the request for payment.

§6-213.   *Alteration of Rights.*

(a) Rights at death under Section 6-212 are determined by the type of account at the death of a party. The type of account may be altered by written notice given by a party to the financial institution to change the type of account or to stop or vary payment under the terms of the account. The notice must be signed by a party and received by the financial institution during the party's lifetime.

(b) A right of survivorship arising from the express terms of the account, Section 6-212, or a POD designation, may not be altered by will.

§6-214. *Accounts and Transfers Nontestamentary.* Except as provided in Part 2 of Article II (elective share of surviving spouse) or as a consequence of, and to the extent directed by, Section 6-215, a transfer resulting from the application of Section 6-212 is effective by reason of the terms of the account involved and this part and is not testamentary or subject to Articles I through IV (estate administration).

§6-215. *Rights of Creditors and Others.*

(a) If other assets of the estate are insufficient, a transfer resulting from a right of survivorship or POD designation under this part is not effective against the estate of a deceased party to the extent needed to pay claims against the estate and statutory allowances to the surviving spouse and children.

(b) A surviving party or beneficiary who receives payment from an account after death of a party is liable to account to the personal representative of the decedent for a proportionate share of the amount received to the extent necessary to discharge the claims and allowances described in subsection (a) remaining unpaid after application of the decedent's estate. A proceeding to assert the liability may not be commenced unless the personal representative has received a written demand by the surviving spouse, a creditor, a child, or a person acting for a child of the decedent. The proceeding must be commenced within one year after death of the decedent.

(c) A surviving party or beneficiary against whom a proceeding to account is brought may join as a party to the proceeding a surviving party or beneficiary of any other account of the decedent.

(d) Sums recovered by the personal representative must be administered as part of the decedent's estate. This section does not affect the protection from claims of the personal representative or estate of a deceased party provided in Section 6-226 for a financial institution that makes payment in accordance with the terms of the account.

§6-216. *Community Property and Tenancy by the Entireties.*

(a) A deposit of community property in an account does not alter the community character of the property or community rights in the property, but a right of survivorship between parties married to each other arising from the express terms of the account on Section 6-212 may not be altered by will.

(b) This part does not affect the law governing tenancy by the entireties.

B.   Inter Vivos Gifts of Personal Property

Attempts to make gifts without competent legal advice, and especially as substitutes for testamentary dispositions, are a constant source of litigation, and may also result in failure of a would-be donor's intention. Although the subject of gifts is usually given more substantial treatment in basic property law courses, the materials that follow present some fundamental issues and principles for your review.

1.   Gifts, Gifts Causa Mortis, and the Requirement of Delivery

PHILIP MECHEM, THE REQUIREMENT OF DELIVERY IN GIFTS OF CHATTELS . . .
21 Ill. L. Rev. 341, 341-342, 348-350 (1926)

It is well settled that delivery is essential to the validity of a parol gift of a chattel. This rule appears to be as old as the common law. . . .

It would be inaccurate in the extreme, however, to say that it is well settled just *what* amounts to delivery of a chattel. Courts have differed widely on that problem and an unfortunate confusion of the authorities has resulted. The doctrine of "constructive" or "symbolical" delivery, so-called, has been largely invoked, without, however, any very exact or analytical attempts being made to define just what is meant by such delivery, or just what acts or facts may constitute it. In some cases the doctrine has been so liberally and undiscriminatingly applied as practically to nullify the general rule. In others, narrow and technical distinctions have been drawn, tending to make the rule the cause of unnecessary hardship.

Considering the great and growing importance of the subject, it has seemed desirable to attempt some analysis of the situation. Obviously the focal point of attack must be this: exactly what is delivery, why is it required, and why (if at all) *should* it be required? An apparently plausible first step might be to define delivery in the abstract, as well as may be, in terms of possession. This would prove, in fact, fruitless, for two reasons, first, because it may be shown that in many cases the rule is satisfied by a "delivery" which involves no change of possession and, second, because the only sound and useful approach to a problem such as this is the pragmatic approach, i.e., the approach which defines a thing in terms of its functions. . . .

In the first place, the delivery makes vivid and concrete to the donor the significance of the act he is doing. Any one can realize the psychological difference between a man's saying he gives something, yet retaining it, and saying he gives it and seeing it pass irrevocably out of his control. The *wrench* of delivery . . . is an important element to the protection of the donor . . .

Secondly, the act of manual tradition is as unequivocal to actual witnesses of the transaction as to the donor himself. . . .

[Finally], the fact of delivery gives the donee, subsequently to the act, at least prima facie evidence in favor of the alleged gift . . . The evidence is of course at best presumptive, yet better than none . . . It is easier to fabricate a story than to abstract the property.

. . . The considerations just enumerated seem to . . . justify the rule and to furnish criteria for its proper application. . . . The policy that has led to the Statutes of Frauds and of Wills seems here to demand with added force that some kind of safeguards be set against fraudulent claims of gift. It is important to notice that the safeguard here advocated is neither arbitrary nor unreasonable. It arises automatically from the nature of the transaction. Cases where it is not spontaneously complied with are the exception and not the rule. . . .

Comment *a* Restatement (Second) of Property §31.1 states: "The delivery of personal property by the owner to another person is an act that calls for an explanation. The legal consequences of that act depend on the explanation. To disallow the explanation would be to force some arbitrary conclusion in all such cases. . . . If the explanation is legally admissible evidence of intent and justifies the conclusion that the owner . . . intended to give the ownership to another person, the gift is accomplished. . . ."

A *gift causa mortis* is a gift made in apprehension of death from an existing threat. Technically an inter vivos transfer (but considered a will substitute), it gives the donee a present possessory interest that is revocable and automatically divested if the donor survives the impending peril. Cf. Restatement (Second) of Property §31.3 providing that "failure to revoke within a reasonable time after the donor is no longer in apprehension of imminent death eliminates the right of revocation." It is recognized at common law and also by statute in some jurisdictions. See Cal. Civ. Code §5702. Why does the law distinguish this particular kind of transfer? Compare the gift causa mortis with the oral will which is recognized on a limited basis in some states. See Chapter 4. What safeguards are there against fraud or misunderstanding in these types of donative transfers?

2. Gifts to Minors

Parents and grandparents often wish to make gifts to minors. Generally, a minor's ownership of property that requires any amount of management supervision or business dealings will create a variety of problems, resulting in the necessity of obtaining formal appointment of a legal guardian or conservator of the minor's estate. For a variety of reasons a donor may find a guardianship or conservatorship arrangement unattractive. (See Chapter 9, section C.) The trust is, of course, an alternative and is taken up in subsequent chapters. For some purposes, especially where large amounts or special complications are involved, the flexible trust device will prove highly desirable. Often, however, the cost and nuisance of establishing a formal trust cause the donor to seek something less elaborate. Frequently, then, informal and purely oral trusts are employed, although the donor and "trustee" may not be aware of the significance or responsibilities of the arrangement — or even realize they are creating a trust.

In quest of another solution and to make readily available certain advantages under the federal gift tax law, all states have now enacted legislation based on the Uniform Gifts to Minors Act, the Model Gifts of Securities to Minors Act, or the more recent Uniform Transfers to Minors Act. Provided a qualified form of property is given in a qualified manner, donors today may conveniently use these statutes to create a statutory form of "canned" trust, commonly referred to as a *custodianship*. All that is required is that the act be invoked by a clear reference to it. Usually the property is simply registered or transferred, for example, to "[name] as custodian for [name] under the [state] Uniform Transfers to Minors Act." There is no need to prepare a complex document or to specify the details of the arrangement, for the statutory custodianship carries with it what amounts to a full set of beneficial provisions and managerial powers akin to an express private trust for the period of the donee's minority. The income and principal may be expended for the donee's benefit during minority; then the unexpended property is paid to the donee or to the donee's estate if he dies before coming of age.

The earlier versions of these acts usually were limited to inter vivos gifts of money and securities and could not be used for testamentary giving. The 1983 Uniform Transfers to Minors Act, however, applies to all types of property and all forms of transfers, including those under powers of appointment, life insurance and pension beneficiary designations, and the like. Although these statutes usually call for the custodianship to terminate at the age of majority, some statutes continue it until age 21. One state, however, has provided greater flexibility in this matter; California Probate Code §§3900-3925 allow testators and, for the most part, other transferors to set a termination age as high as age 25 by simply inserting additional words indicating, for example, that the custodianship is "for [name] until age 25."

The Uniform Custodial Trust Act, promulgated in 1987, has been enacted in about one-third of the states. Under this act, the type of "canned" trust found in the Transfers to Minors Act is adapted to the needs of older adults. A simple designation in an instrument of transfer or registration creates a revocable custodial trust that becomes a discretionary trust on the beneficiary's incompetence, with the assets passing to the named successor on the beneficiary's death.

C. Testamentary Nature of Deeds

NOBLE v. TIPTON
219 Ill. 182, 76 N.E. 151 (1905)

[John Noble died in 1904, survived by three sons and six daughters. His will, executed in 1898, disposed of all of his estate except the home farm, as the land in controversy was known. The will stated that the farm had previously been deeded to his son, Thomas. In 1897 a deed to this farm was executed, attested by two witnesses, and acknowledged. In 1898 John Noble placed the will, the deed in question, and another deed in the hands of a custodian, who put the documents in an envelope on the outside of which is written: "The deeds within to be delivered to grantees after death of grantor. . . . All of said property to be held subject to the order of John Noble." Thomas managed the farm and borrowed $3,000 from his father to make valuable improvements. They resided together on the farm until the latter's death. In a suit initiated by two of the daughters, the court below declared the deed null and void for want of delivery and ordered partition of the farm as intestate property. Thomas appealed.]

CARTWRIGHT, C.J. . . .

A delivery is essential to the validity of a deed, and to constitute a delivery the grantor must part with control over it and retain no right to reclaim or recall it. (Hawes v. Hawes, 177 Ill. 409; Spacy v. Ritter, 214 Ill. 206.) This deed was not delivered but was held by the custodian subject to the order of the grantor, who did not part with all control over it but retained the right to reclaim or recall it. The deed was intended as a testamentary disposition of the farm to take effect at the death of the grantor, and such a disposition can only be effected by an instrument in writing executed in conformity with the Statute of Wills. The instrument was not operative as a deed.

Counsel for appellant contends that if the deed was not operative as a conveyance the property was devised by the following clause of the will:

> *Fifth* — The remainder of my estate, both real and personal, excepting the home farm, containing 503 1/2 acres, which I have heretofore deeded to my son Thomas Noble, I give, devise and bequeath to my sons Robert Noble, Thomas Noble and John W. Noble, share and share alike.

By previous provisions of the will he had disposed of his household goods and furniture and farm implements and made certain bequests to his children. The argument is that the testator could not be presumed to intend to die intestate as to any part of his property, and that by the will he evinced an intention to devise the farm to his son Thomas, who would therefore take it by implication under the will. The rule on that subject is that, where a recital in a will is to the effect that the testator has devised something in another part of the will when in fact he has not done so, the erroneous recital may operate as a devise by implication of the same property, for the reason that it shows an intention to devise the property by the will; but where the recital is to the effect that the testator has by some other instrument given to a certain person named in the recital, property, when in fact he has not done so, such a recital does not disclose an intention to give by the will . . . and the courts cannot give that recital the effect of a devise. Nor does the recital aid in establishing that there had been a valid delivery of the deed so as to make it operative as such. Lange v. Cullinan, 205 Ill. 365.

The deed did not operate as a conveyance of the property, and whether it must fail as a testamentary disposition of the farm is a question not involved under the pleadings in this case. . . . At any rate, the instrument could not be effective as a devise until admitted to probate, and the county court has exclusive jurisdiction for that purpose. (Beatty v. Clegg, 214 Ill. 34.) Where a disposition of property made by a written instrument is not to take effect until the death of the maker it is testamentary in character, and will remain subject to revocation or change during his life. (Massey v. Huntington, 118 Ill. 80.) And it is sufficient for the decision of this case that the deed was not delivered and did not take effect in the lifetime of the grantor.

Noble v. Fickes, 230 Ill. 594, 82 N.E. 950 (1907), 21 Harv. L. Rev. 451, affirmed the subsequent denial of probate of the instrument that was in issue as a deed in Noble v. Tipton, the opinion (at 606-607, 82 N.E. at 953-954) stating:

Upon the general proposition that a valid will may be made in the form of an ordinary deed of bargain and sale, we entertain not the slightest doubt, where the formalities of the statute are properly observed, and it clearly appears on the face of the instrument that it is not to take effect until the death of the maker. The inherent difficulty with the instrument involved in this case is that there is nothing in the writing itself which imparts to it a testamentary character. To give it this character a resort must be had to extrinsic facts depending on parol evidence . . . [But our] statute requires wills to be in writing. If an unambiguous deed, which on its face purports to convey a present interest, can be converted into a will by proving an animo testandi in the maker by parol evidence, the effect is not only to change the legal character of the instrument, but to engraft upon it one of the essentials of a will by parol, in the face of our statute, which requires all wills to be in writing.

This case is clearly distinguishable . . . [from] the case between these parties decided in 219 Ill. 182, where the question at issue was whether a deed had been delivered. Delivery is largely a question of intention and may be shown by any competent evidence. Evidence on that point does not contradict or vary the terms of the instrument, but bears on the question whether the instrument, in fact, ever had a legal existence. It would be a strange result if the same evidence which destroyed the instrument as a deed should bring it to life as a will.

Our conclusion is that it would be an unsafe rule to hold that an unde-livered deed, which by chance happened to be attested by two witnesses, could be converted into a will by parol evidence.

A dissenting opinion stated: "We do not see how it can consistently be said that the instrument amounts to a testamentary disposition of the property described in it, and yet that it is not a testament, although it was executed with all the formalities required in the case of a will." Id. at 607-608, 82 N.E. at 954.

TENNANT v. JOHN TENNANT MEMORIAL HOME
167 Cal. 570, 140 P. 242 (1914)

SHAW, J.

On the seventh day of May, 1901, Margaret Tennant executed to the defendant, John Tennant Memorial Home, a deed purporting to grant and convey to it certain real property, "subject to the exceptions and reservations" thereinafter mentioned. Afterwards she died, and her heirs began and are prosecuting this action to quiet their title to the land and recover possession thereof, claiming that said deed is void. The administrator of her estate intervened and filed a complaint asking the same relief on behalf of her estate. The court below gave judgment for the defendant, from which the plaintiffs and the intervener appeal.

The exceptions and reservations mentioned in the opening clause of the deed are inserted therein immediately following the description of the property. They are as follows:

Excepting, however, and reserving to said grantor the exclusive posses-sion and the use and enjoyment in her own right, of the rents, issues and profits of said lots and each of them for and during the term of her natural life.

And further reserving to the said grantor the right to revoke this deed as to the said property above described or as to any portion thereof, and further reserving to her, the said grantor, the right during her natural life to sell any of the above described property, and to sign and execute deeds therefor in her own individual name and to convey by any such deed a full, perfect and absolute title to the purchaser thereof, and with right to use the proceeds arising from such sale or sales to her own use, without any liability for her or her estate to account therefor. In case of such revocation being made, it shall be made and can only be made in writing, duly acknowledged and recorded.

Margaret Tennant did not exercise, or attempt to exercise, the power to revoke the deed, nor the power to sell and convey the property, or any part thereof. The decision of the case depends on the validity of the deed. If it is valid, the judgment below was correct; if invalid, the judgment must be reversed. . . .

The effect of the reservation of a life estate is that the deed conveys a future interest, only to the grantee. . . . The main contention of the appellants is that the deed in question is not a present grant of property, so far as the remainder is concerned, but is an instrument testamentary in character and therefore invalid as a disposition of the property, because it is not executed with the formalities necessary to the execution of a will. . . .

[T]he fact that in this case there is also reserved a power to revoke the deed and to sell the remainder, is of no consequence in the argument upon the question whether it is or is not testamentary. The power of revocation being valid, its exercise would at once revest the title in the grantor and she would then have absolute power to dispose of it by deed or otherwise. The power of sale reserved is therefore of no consequence, since it was necessarily included in the power to revoke. The reservation of the power to revoke did not operate to destroy, or in anywise restrict the effect of the deed as a present conveyance of a future vested interest. It merely afforded a means whereby such vested future estate could be defeated and divested before it ripened into an estate in possession. . . .

Another argument presented in favor of the proposition that this deed is testamentary in nature is founded upon the circumstance that the disposition which the grantor thereby made of the property conveyed was substantially the same as she might have made by a will, so far as her enjoyment of the property and her control over the fee is concerned. This circumstance does not determine the effect of the deed and has but little bearing on the question. An instrument is declared to be testamentary in nature only when, and because, it appears from its terms that the intention of the maker thereof was that it should not be operative as a conveyance or disposition of the property, or of any interest, present or future, therein, until his death. This is always essential. If the instrument, according to its proper legal effect under the rules of conveyancing, passes at the time of its execution a present interest or title in the property to a third person, although it may be only an interest in a future estate and may be subject to defeat on the happening or nonoccurrence of a future event, it is a present conveyance and not a will. . . .

The judgment is affirmed.

D. *Claims of Creditors*

PROBLEM

8-B.   After working for a large manufacturer for years, *D,* a widow, opened her own business. To finance it, she used her savings and borrowed $100,000 from her uncle *U,* paying him the agreed interest for over ten years. During this time, as the business prospered, she invested most of her surplus income through her stockbroker, *B,* under an agreement the pertinent part of which provides an account title of "*D* or *S,* joint with right of survivorship" and that: all funds are held pending investment or distribution subject to and payable on order of *D;* all shares shall be purchased in name of "*D* or *S* or the survivor of them," with the certificates delivered to or held subject to order of *D;* and on death of either party the balance of the account after brokerage charges shall be paid to the survivor. *D* died unexpectedly as the result of an accident. It appears that, about five years ago, she had given most of her business assets to *S,* her son; her probate estate is insolvent. *S,* as executor and sole devisee of *D*'s will, did not inventory the $650,000 worth of securities held by *B* under the above agreement. *S* declines to pay any more than $20,000 on *D*'s unsecured $100,000 note to *U,* as the probate assets will allow only a 20 percent payment on creditor's claims. Surprised and hurt, *U* has consulted you. How would you advise him under the law of your state? Under the UPC?

RICHARD W. EFFLAND, RIGHTS OF CREDITORS IN NONPROBATE ASSETS
48 Mo. L. Rev. 431 (1983)

. . . Increasingly, a major portion of decedents' wealth is being transmitted to others not through the probate process but through a variety of devices which have acquired the label "nontestamentary." Some of these devices, like joint tenancy and gifts causa mortis, have long been legally accepted. Others, like revocable living trusts . . . and contractual benefits payable on death to designated beneficiaries, are developments of relatively recent origin.

At the outset, one must wonder why creditor groups have not been vocal about the drain of available assets from the probate estate. One possible explanation is that concern for creditors is misplaced. Contract creditors rely on security arrangements; retail organizations protect themselves by purchasing insurance against the risk of death of debtors or are content to write losses off on income tax returns; tort creditors sue primarily for the amount of insurance coverage. Interesting is the fact that during the preparation of the Uniform Probate Code (the Code) no credit organization voiced any comments on proposed claims procedures with the single exception of the American Association of Trial Lawyers, which was concerned only with tort liability. With regard to nonprobate assets, joint tenancy has long been a device that defeats unsecured creditors of the joint tenant who dies first; yet the one state which had legislation to protect such creditors has repealed the statute. Of course, one major creditor at death, the United States Government, has enacted its own procedure to reach taxable will substitutes if the probate estate is insufficient to pay estate taxes.

Institutional creditors therefore are likely to be able to protect themselves. It is the individual creditor who may be hurt most and who has no organization to speak on his behalf. The cases that are likely to occur with increasing frequency involve the divorced wife or child who has a claim by reason of a property settlement, separation agreement, or divorce decree. . . .

Still another explanation for the lack of creditor interest may be that in the majority of decedents' estates there are sufficient probate assets to meet claims of unsecured creditors. Only if the probate estate is inadequate for creditors is there a problem. A system that permits nonprobate assets to pass free of creditor claims therefore may be tolerable to creditors. Unfortunately, we have no empirical data to assess the validity of this explanation. . . .

. . . [Estate administration] serves other purposes than assuring succession to the persons intended by the decedent. Protecting the family against disinheritance is one; providing a convenient forum for creditors is another. Removing assets from the probate estate by will substitutes has posed a problem for the surviving spouse in those states where marital rights at death are defined in terms of an elective share in the probate estate. Significantly, the trend toward transmitting wealth by will substitutes led first to frequent litigation . . . and later in many states to legislation defining the share in terms of both the probate estate and the nonprobate assets passing by will substitutes. Lack of extensive creditor litigation may therefore mean that there is no corresponding need for creditor protection.

One subsidiary problem relates to the effect of nonclaim statutes on the right of creditors to pursue nonprobate assets. For example, section

3-803 of the Uniform Probate Code bars unpresented claims "against the estate, the personal representative, and the heirs and devisees of the decedent." There is no bar against the takers of nonprobate assets unless the courts would extend the statute by analogy. Some practicing lawyers therefore recommend against use of will substitutes where potential claims may be outstanding after death, as use of probate serves to cut off such claims if they are not presented in the administration of the estate and thus insulates the probate assets when distributed to the successors. . . .

There are two options. One is to do nothing and leave the law in its present uncertain and unsatisfactory state, in hope that courts will eventually work out a theory along the lines suggested in this Article: that effect should be given to the realities of nonprobate arrangements rather than to technical property doctrine; that realistically these arrangements shift economic benefits at death and a transfer therefore takes effect at that time; and that any such transfer is necessarily fraudulent as to creditors if the probate estate is insufficient to meet their claims.

The other option is to construct and enact a statutory solution along the lines of section 6-107 [now 6-215, supra] of the Uniform Probate Code [relating to multiparty accounts], with a delineation of nonprobate assets which should be available to the personal representative to satisfy presented claims if estate assets are insufficient. This would require appointment of a personal representative even if there are no probate assets to administer. In this latter case the lack of probate assets to pay administration expenses means that these in turn must be recovered from nonprobate assets. The statute should include either some system for equitable apportionment among recipients of nonprobate assets or a statutory scheme like abatement to determine the order in which nonprobate assets can be reached.

Joint tenancies pose special problems, because the original contribution for the purchase of the property may have come from the decedent, from the surviving joint tenant, or partly from each. Whether to treat the transfer at death as a transfer of a half interest or of the interest attributable to the decedent's contribution is the same issue involved in estate taxation. There is much to be said for the simple rule that a transfer at death involves in reality a half interest (or the appropriate fraction if there are more than two joint tenants) regardless of contribution, because that is the interest the creditor could reach immediately prior to the death of the debtor, unless the joint tenancy itself was a fraudulent conveyance. . . .

On Professor Effland's suggestion for treating the shift of economic benefits at death as a fraudulent conveyance if the estate thereby becomes insolvent, see In re Granwell, 20 N.Y.2d 91, 228 N.E.2d 779 (1967). See generally Thomas R. Andrews, Creditors' Rights Against Nonprobate Assets in Washington: Time for Reform, 65 Wash. L. Rev. 73 (1990).

E. Wills, Will Substitutes, and Will Supplements: A Peek at Integrated Planning

At this point it should be useful to think in an overall way about the role of will substitutes and their effect on the role of wills in typical family situations. This is also a good time to look ahead to the trust and anticipate where it fits in. All of these things, along with tax considerations, especially in larger estates, are elements of an integrated process called estate planning. This process involves not only the drawing of wills, or even of wills and trusts; it involves decisions about ownership forms and about rights under the wide variety of wealth items the nature of which has been suggested in part at the outset of this chapter. The process also involves client education through proper interviewing — education about the client's own estate and about how personal and family objectives relate to it.

A lawyer does not merely ascertain a client's intention and then use legal craftsmanship to implement that intention. The lawyer must help the client to develop that intent in the light of all the relevant considerations. The client must be led both to broaden and sharpen the nucleus of an idea that is initially brought to the lawyer and yet to develop a plan that is the client's own. When the planning and execution process is complete, the client should understand the will reasonably well, the properties and property arrangements involved, and the reasons for the estate's being planned as it is. This understanding can be of great help to a client in avoiding subsequent mistakes that might undo the estate planning that has been done. It will also enable the client to understand what the lawyer has done and to know when it is important to return for further counsel.

The following excerpt should help to accomplish this pulling together, and maybe some putting in perspective as well, particularly for those who mistakenly think of estate planning — either favorably or unfavorably — as merely dealing with the tax concerns of the wealthy.

SHAFFER, NONESTATE PLANNING
106 Tr. & Est. 319-322 (1967)

This article proposes and explains a will form for the young and promising but presently impecunious, Calvin Knox. He is called a "junior executive" by appliance dealers, and his property is called an "estate" by his flatterers. He is really a middle-class, white-collar worker, and what he really has is a nonestate of children and debts. . . .

He is married and the father of two preschool children. Employed as an engineer for an automobile body manufacturer, Mr. Knox earns $9,200 annually before taxes, and expects his salary to increase. His employer provides a retirement plan and hospital and life insurance — the latter in the face amount of $10,000. He also has privately obtained life insurance in additional face amounts totaling $30,000. He has as much as $1,800 in his checking account, a disappearing equity in an automobile, some beat-up furniture, and a fishing rod or two. He and his wife and children are in good health. He owns no real property but will probably "buy" a residential site within the next few years. . . .

Distilling what is found in bar-association pamphlets on wills, the writer sees three reasons for Calvin John Knox to have a will. First, the intestacy statute may give some of his property to his children. This reason is the weakest of the three and is inserted mainly to give a cumulative effect to the others. It is true that a good many intestacy statutes would give one-half or more to his children, thus invoking cumbersome, expensive guardianship protection against victimization by their mother. However, Knox has all his cash in a survivorship account, and if he buys residential real estate, it will probably be held by survivorship also. Almost all of the cash available to support his family after his death will be life insurance payable to his wife. What probate property there is will probably be eliminated by the widow's allowance or taken under a small estate procedure. Knox's children stand to inherit a half interest in his automobile and fishing rods, if he does not make a will.

The second reason for a will assumes that Knox will not predecease his wife, or that they will die at about the same time. If Knox dies intestate, his and his wife's property will be available to their children, but it will undoubtedly be placed in guardianship. Included will be all Knox's life insurance, either by inheritance from Knox's wife or through secondary beneficiary designations on the policies. A guardianship is cumbersome, expensive, inflexible, and unnecessary, whereas a trust arrangement is less expensive, more flexible, and more likely to work if Knox's children are being cared for out of state. It is amenable to the settlor's express restrictions and directions. Knox, therefore, needs a will if he wants to see that his small wealth is used to maximum efficiency for his orphaned children. . . .

The trust arrangement, however, will not entirely eliminate a need for guardianship; it will only confine the guardianship to its proper and necessary ambit — the physical care of the children. If Knox and his wife die at about the same time, somebody will have to take the children, and that somebody will be best advised to do so pursuant to appointment as guardian of their persons. The third reason for a will, then, is that Knox can designate in it who this guardian is to be. The great value of this argument is not that it causes Knox to make a will, but that it causes him to consider who is available to take care of his children and to discuss it with the persons he and his wife choose to be guardians.

When the first of these three reasons, which is the least potent, is discounted, it is apparent that the reasons for Knox to make a will bear almost no resemblance to the reasons for a person with a quarter of a million dollars to make a will. This project, in other words, is not a compact version of a "big" will. Knox is no patriarch dispensing his largesse evenly or capriciously to waiting relatives and friends. Disposition is the least of his problems. After his death, he must provide exactly what he is providing now — bare support for his children. It is not a matter of "estate planning," but a matter of planning without an estate, of doing what he can to relieve a thoroughly horrible situation for his family. . . .

Knox will need . . . to appoint a guardian for his children, to establish a trust for property management, and to add whatever he leaves in his probate estate to that trust. [His will need not be used] to establish the family-support trust. [It is now generally safe to use] unfunded, contingent life-insurance trusts which do not go into operation until the insured dies and the insurance proceeds are collected by the trustee. Bank trust departments in most communities will accept these trusts without fee during the settlor-insured's life. The wills of both parents can be made to "pour-over" into them. They are easily amended and are probably more flexible than testamentary trusts. Moreover, they go into operation immediately, so that insurance and any other funds made payable to them — even survivor benefits under employer-provided retirement plans — are available to the family without the delay and expense of probate. Assuming state law favors this sort of disposition and that the trust and will involved are drawn in reference to the tenor of state law, employing a "pour over insurance trust" is a useful primary device for providing a family-support trust. It does not, of course, eliminate the need for a will.

The payment of life insurance proceeds to testamentary trustees is an even more attractive alternative, eliminating the need for an inter vivos trustee and concentrating all economic resources in the testamentary trust. The insurance proceeds themselves, and the retirement-plan benefits, would not be subject to probate. In most cases, the only delay the device would entail is the delay before testamentary trustees are qualified to serve.

But the payment of insurance to testamentary trustees is a less fully sanctioned and less common alternative, carrying several risks with it. . . .

Joint ownership is another alternative, one that probably does not even need to be reduced to advice since Knox already holds his cash in survivorship. He may or may not own his automobile that way, but any residential real estate he obtains will probably be held by survivorship.

Many of the experts in "estate planning" would apparently urge Knox's lawyer to advise Knox to dissolve these survivorship arrangements in favor of sole ownership or tenancies in common; however, these commentators obviously are not writing for people like Knox. There seems to be no convincing reason against survivorship ownership for two people who are harmoniously married and who have no federal estate-tax problems. The device may even carry with it substantial state death-tax advantages, as well as some amount of immunity from the creditors of either spouse.

Knox should keep his bank account as it is, although a look at the signature card and an inquiry into the circumstances of its execution to make certain that it is what it appears to be is advisable. He should probably buy his residential real estate by the entirety or in joint tenancy, purchase his car in joint tenancy, and hold his securities if he ever buys any in joint tenancy.

Survivorship ownership, insurance designations in favor of his wife and contingently to the trust, and the widow's allowance or small-estate statute will probably avoid probate in the traditional sense, if Knox's wife survives him. His will is a formality in that case. If his wife does not survive him, or if they die at about the same time, the will becomes essential — and that reflection implies, of course, that his wife ought to have the same sort of will he has. What is suggested for Knox (and his wife) is a children-centered will. The "poor man's will" of survivorship ownership and life insurance will just about take care of everything else. . . .

F. An Introduction to Taxation and Tax Planning of Decedents' Estates, Trusts, Gifts, and Will Substitutes

Now that you are familiar with much of the law governing wills and will substitutes, including various property ownership forms, and are ready to undertake a fairly detailed study of the law of trusts and fiduciary administration, it is useful to become somewhat acquainted with some of the more important areas of tax law affecting probate and trust practice and estate planning. Often tax considerations lead us into the more complex and challenging forms of estate planning, and particularly planning and drafting problems that involve the use of trusts. The material in the next few pages is not intended to describe our estate and gift tax system or related income tax matters in detail or to explain tax planning techniques at a level of any sophistication. This brief summary of law and basic planning concepts attempts merely to present an overview of the federal system for taxing donative transfers, of selected features of the income tax, and of the tax system's influence on counseling with respect to the ownership and disposition of family wealth.

1. Estate, Gift, and Related Transfer Taxes

A gift tax and estate tax, now supplemented by a generation-skipping transfer tax, make up the federal transfer tax system, applying to donative transfers of wealth during life and at death. An *estate tax* is an excise tax levied on the privilege of *transferring* property at death, with tax liability being measured essentially by the size of the decedent's estate. As we shall later see, the federal estate and gift taxes were integrated by 1976 changes that made them cumulative and subject to a common scale of graduated rates, with a *unified credit* equivalent to an exemption (designated *applicable exclusion amount*) of about $175,000. As a result of the Economic Recovery Tax Act of 1981, the unified credit was increased in stages so that the effective exemption level rose gradually to $600,000. In 1997 Congress increased the exemption in a series of steps,[2] scheduled to top out at $1 million for persons dying in 2006 (indexed for inflation in multiples of $10,000 after 2007).

In contrast to the federal system, many state death taxes take the form of an *inheritance tax,* imposed on the privilege of *receiving* property from a decedent. The tax is geared to the inheritance of each recipient, with a structure of exemptions and rates that vary with the closeness of the recipient's relationship to the decedent. For example, an inheritance or devise received by a spouse or lineal descendant or lineal ancestor (typically styled a "Class A" beneficiary) might qualify for an exemption of $600,000, with remaining amounts taxed at rates graduated from 1 percent to 12 percent. Receipts by aunts and uncles and their descendants (typically "Class B" beneficiaries) might receive no exemption, with rates graduated from 4 percent to 16 percent. Receipts by all others ("Class C" beneficiaries) might receive no exemption, with rates graduated from 8 percent to 17 percent. Most states levy a *pick-up* (or "slack" or "sponge") tax, which is a tax equal to the maximum credit allowed for state death taxes against the federal estate tax. (Do you see why a pick-up tax in effect costs nothing to the taxpayers of the state?) Where a state has both an inheritance tax and a pick-up tax, the tax levied is the greater of the two. A few states have an estate tax

2. $675,000 (year of death or gift 2000, 2001), $700,000 (2002, 2003), $850,000 (2004), and $950,000 (2005).

that may incorporate some features of the federal estate tax, but with lower rates. Usually state death taxes are not a significant concern in planning estates, but in an unusual case (e.g., no near relatives and an estate of less than the federal exclusion amount) they may be a factor.

Subject to limited but significant exceptions, the estate tax on a particular estate is unaffected by who takes the decedent's property, how many beneficiaries there are, and in what shares or forms those people take. The important exceptions include provisions to exempt qualified charitable dispositions and qualified interspousal transfers (the so-called marital deduction, which is now unlimited in amount). Under the estate tax format, the individual beneficiaries are not the taxpayers; they do not separately report the amounts of their individual inheritances as they would under an inheritance tax system of the type employed by about half of the states. Thus, an estate tax looks at, and taxes, the amount the decedent is transferring rather than the amount the successor is inheriting. Our federal law is not concerned with the relationship of a beneficiary to the decedent, unless the recipient is the decedent's or donor's spouse.

a.   The Integrated or Unified Tax Structure

Historically the federal system for taxing family wealth transfers in this country has been a dual structure consisting of independent gift and estate taxes, each with its own separate exemption and rate structure. Gifts were cumulated over the donor's lifetime for purposes of the gift tax, but the amount of gifts had no effect on the size of the taxable estate at death or on the rates applicable to that estate. Consequently, lifetime giving offered enormous tax advantages. Taxpayers who were similarly situated would end up with significantly different overall tax burdens depending on whether substantial gift programs had been undertaken during life or whether the individual's wealth was retained and transferred at death. The Tax Reform Act of 1976 integrated the estate and gift taxes into what is commonly called a *unified transfer tax* under our present Internal Revenue Code (I.R.C.), although in form the statutes still appear as two taxes in separate chapters of the Code. The dual system's greatest avoidance opportunities were closed, but substantial incentives for carefully planned inter vivos giving remain. (The operation of the present unified system is described in subsection e at page 308 infra.)

b.   Taxable Transfers: Gifts

The federal gift tax is intended to reach gratuitous transmission of wealth during the donor's lifetime. In order to avoid subjective questions concerning donative intent, the tax applies to all transfers of property "for less than adequate and full consideration in money or money's worth." Judicially developed exceptions exclude from gift taxation (a) legitimate, arm's-length business transactions and (b) transfers that are "incomplete" in the sense that the donor retains power to revoke the transfer or to modify the rights of the beneficiaries. The tax is imposed not on the donee but on the donor, who must report all included transfers annually. (A gift, devise or inheritance is not income to the recipient.) A few states also have gift taxes, typically at rates that are not a significant estate planning concern.

The federal gift tax contains an important exemption that excludes many modest gifts from the transfers that must be reported by a donor. Each year a donor is entitled to an *annual exclusion* of $10,000 for gifts (unless disqualified as a gift of a *future interest*) to each donee, without limitation as to the number of donees. Only to the extent that more than the excludable amount is given to a single donee in any one year must the gift be reported by the donor. This annual exclusion is enhanced by a *gift-splitting privilege* that allows a gift of separate property by a married person to be treated as if it had been made one-half by each spouse — an accommodation to differences in laws of our community and non-community property states. The annual exclusion is indexed for inflation beginning with the 1999 tax year. The Code also allows an unlimited exclusion for tuition and medical expenses paid directly to the provider on behalf of an individual.

c.   Taxable Transfers: The Gross Estate at Death

The first step in applying the federal estate tax is to construct the *gross estate,* which is defined to include not only property owned by a decedent and passing at death to others but also to include ownership equivalents and a variety of property ownership forms or arrangements that serve as will substitutes.

Property Owned at Death (I.R.C. §2033). A general section provides for inclusion in the gross estate of all "property owned at death." It has traditionally been said that this section includes all probate assets — that is, all property of the decedent that is subject to estate administration. With increasing variations in the detail of the probate requirements of the various states, however, the inclusions under this section can more precisely be described as encompassing all property of the decedent that is subject to disposition by will or, in the absence of testamentary disposition, by the laws of intestate succession, even including property that is subject to some testamentary restriction by reason of the elective share of a surviving spouse. This means that this basic section includes all separate property owned by a decedent (including the decedent's interest in any property held with others in undivided interests as tenants in common) and, if applicable, the decedent's one-half interest in community property, the other half of which is excluded as property of the surviving spouse. The section thus encompasses a broad array of property, whether real or personal, tangible or intangible.

If *D* owned a future interest (such as a trust remainder) that did not fail by reason of his death, or if he owned an interest of limited duration (such as a right to property for a fixed term, say ten years) that did not terminate at his death, these property interests are included in *D*'s gross estate for tax purposes. Interests that expire at his death, however, leaving nothing to pass from *D* to others (such as a legal life estate or his equitable interest as life beneficiary of a trust) are not transmissible property interests included under this basic section.

This latter point concerning interests that are terminable at death is a very important one, as we shall see, for it becomes the focus of our planning efforts when clients wish to provide beneficiaries with the benefit and enjoyment of property but at the same time wish to avoid having that property eventually included in the beneficiaries' gross estates at death. In 1997 Congress added §2033A (now renumbered as §2057) to provide a family-owned business exclusion from the gross estate. This much-ballyhooed political provision is subject to numerous restrictions and limitations that usually render it insignificant.

Powers as Virtual Ownership (I.R.C. §2041). A special section of the estate tax law attempts to deal with situations in which a person holds, by virtue of a power to demand or consume property (usually trust property) or a power to dispose of the property, authority that might be considered the economic or substantial equivalent of either ownership or of free testamentary disposition. Property that is subject to such a power, referred to as a *general power of appointment,* is included in the gross estate of the decedent under many circumstances. Also, the exercise or release of such a power during life will usually constitute a taxable transfer for gift tax purposes. The Code defines general powers as powers by which the power holder may appoint "to himself, his creditors, his estate or the creditors of his estate." The lapse (expiration) of a general power during the holder's life is usually treated as a taxable release of the power, but only to the extent that it exceeds the greater of $5,000 or 5 percent of the value of the property subject to the power. This means that a drafter may give a donee a power to withdraw annually $5,000 or 5 percent of the trust property (often simply called a *5 or 5 power*), with no adverse estate or gift tax consequences to the donee except, ordinarily, in the year of death.

On the other hand, even broad powers by which the decedent may benefit only others are generally not a basis for inclusion in the gross estate, nor are powers held by others (such as a trustee) to benefit the decedent. An understanding of these concepts is vitally important because lawyers and their clients work with powers that are not "general," as well as interests that are terminable at death (see §2033 above), to establish trusts and other arrangements that confer protection, enjoyment, and often very broad benefits, without the adverse estate or gift tax consequences that outright ownership would have for the beneficiaries or their estates.

An Aside on Terminable Interests and Planning. Let us for a moment pursue the concluding observations in the preceding discussions in order to illustrate the significance of these rules and associated planning principles in the dispositions of relatively wealthy property owners. To summarize, the basic point is that, as long as the interests that are conferred on a beneficiary end at death, and as long as the powers of that beneficiary to take the property during life or to dispose of it at death are so limited in the beneficiary's hands (or in the hands of others) as not to constitute general powers of appointment, the beneficiary may be given extensive benefits — not far different from the advantages of ownership in many situations — without the property being subjected to tax at the beneficiary's death.

If *W* dies leaving an estate of $1 million and the transfer of that estate is in large measure subjected to tax at her death, it is understandable that she would wish the remaining (after tax) amounts of the same property not again to be subjected to taxation at the death of *H*, her widower. If she left all her property outright to him, as many clients are inclined to do in the absence of persuasive tax considerations, that property would be taxed at *H*'s death for the second time in a single generation — and at the upper brackets on top of *H*'s own property. Our system does provide a temporary credit for successive taxation, but that credit declines 20 percent every two years and expires after ten.

The end result is likely to be that *W* will ask her lawyer just how much benefit and authority she can confer on her husband without this adverse result — that is, without the properties being later included in *H*'s gross estate when he dies. She will learn from a competent lawyer that she can place this property in trust with an independent trustee (such as a bank) who will pay the income to *H* for as long as he lives and who is authorized to pay him very liberal additional amounts of principal for whatever purposes the trustee deems appropriate. In addition, *H* may have the right to demand certain additional amounts of principal under some exceptions to the general power of appointment rule, as long as the amounts he can take under this power are limited in certain ways, the most important of which is called "an ascertainable standard relating to his health, education, support, and maintenance." He may also be given a "5 or 5" power. Beyond this he may be given, within generous limits, power to decide who is to take the property on his death; thus, he may have almost full power to dispose of the property at death, as long as he is precluded from appointing to his estate or to its creditors and as long as he personally could not (but for the previously mentioned exceptions) have appointed to himself during his lifetime. In fact, with minor reductions in the trustee's authority, *W* could allow *H* to serve as trustee and to manage all of the property himself.

At this point your reaction may be like that of most tax policymakers — that this all sounds rather silly but that, so far at least, it is not really particularly disturbing in terms of its policy implications. This is because an important objective of our transfer tax system is that significant wealth be taxed under such a system once each generation but not more frequently than that; and it probably should not be taxed twice in the one generation of *W* and *H*. In fact, an understandable reaction might be simply that is is most unfortunate that we even have to use the trust under our system to avoid double taxation in a single generation; the taxes should be designed to work this out without the necessity of a trust. Proposals to bring about such a result have been made from time to time, and, as we shall see later, by reason of the marital deduction qualifying property can be left outright from the first spouse to the second with only a single tax in their generation. But this is only to the extent that the marital deduction exempts such property from tax at the first death, essentially on the condition that it be subject to tax at the second death. Nevertheless, a great deal of our estate planning (that is, beyond planning for the marital deduction) is designed to avoid unnecessary estate taxation through trusts as just described.

When the benefit-conferring, tax-avoiding trust concept is extended beyond the surviving spouse to its use in provisions for the lifetimes of the testator's children and subsequent generations, many in Congress and others concerned with tax policy feel quite differently and are quite troubled over the use of trusts by the wealthy as a means of continuous tax avoidance. Not only is there concern over the revenue loss but also over the inequitably disparate treatment of people who share substantially comparable economic circumstances, some through outright enjoyment and others with virtually equivalent enjoyment through the trust device.

The Generation-Skipping Transfer Tax (I.R.C. ch. 13). This concern eventually led to the second (recall our earlier discussion of unification of the gift and estate taxes) major revision of the transfer tax system in the 1976 Tax Reform Act. That legislation enacted, as a new Chapter 13 of the Code, a generation-skipping transfer tax. Then, the Internal Revenue Code of 1986 effectively replaced this much-criticized statute with a revised tax. As revised in 1986, Chapter 13 preserved many of the principles and provisions of the 1976 tax but also made fundamental changes.

Without descending into the considerable complexities of the 1976 legislation, it provided in essence (but subject to important qualifications) for property held in trust or trust equivalents to be taxed at the death of a younger-generation beneficiary in much the same manner and rates as if that beneficiary had owned the property. Thus, originally, the tax was usually imposed at the marginal rates of an appropriate deceased life beneficiary. Under the 1986 legislation, however, the revised tax is imposed at a single rate: the same rate as the maximum federal estate tax rate, now 55 percent. The tax is usually payable from the trust property.

The original statute taxed only termination of enjoyment, usually treating the enjoyed property much as if it had been owned by the deceased beneficiary; if enjoyment terminated by distribution or otherwise during life, the termination was treated much like a gift by the beneficiary. The tax also did not (and still ordinarily does not) apply if the beneficiary was of the same generation as (or of an older generation than) the person who established the trust. Thus, in our earlier planning example, the tax would not apply to a trust that *W* established for the present benefit only of *H,* or of only her parents or brothers and sisters. You can see, then, that the 1976 statute was intended merely to limit the extent to which trusts could be used to avoid taxes while conferring economic rights on persons belonging to generations below that of the transferor. To illustrate with a basic, typical example, if *A* deeds to child *B* for life, remainder to *B*'s child (*A*'s grandchild) *C,* the 1976 tax usually applied in much the same manner as if *B* had owned the property and left it to *C.* In short, a tax was not imposed if a generation was totally skipped but only if a generation was partially skipped, in the sense that one or more members of that younger generation enjoyed the property (through benefits or powers) before the property or its enjoyment passed to a subsequent generation.

The current tax is no longer this narrow; and, as we have seen, its rates are no longer tied to a beneficiary. The 1986 tax potentially applies as well to total (or *direct*) skips — most obviously when a testator leaves property directly to grandchildren, completely bypassing the children. An important exception provides that, if a child of the transferor (or of the transferor's spouse) is dead at the time the transfer is made by the donor or decedent, the child's issue move up a generation, so that a direct transfer to grandchildren in that line will not constitute a generation-skipping transfer.

Even with respect to what are clearly defined as generation-skipping transfers under this act, however, there are limited but potentially significant advantages to be achieved through the use of trusts and other generation-skipping transfers. Most significantly, the 1986 flat-rate tax is subject to an exemption of $1 million per transferor (inflation-indexed in 1997 in multiples of $10,000), with spouses allowed to "split" inter vivos transfers so that a nondonor spouse may elect to be treated as having made half of any gift made by the donor spouse.

All in all, the terminable interest trust arrangements discussed earlier continue to be of widespread importance from a tax-planning viewpoint. Chapter 13 does not impair the utility of (but may require care in drafting) trusts for the benefit even of spouses or others of the transferor's generation or higher. Trusts are also of continued importance in tax planning for children and others of younger generations to the extent of $1 million per transferor and under some circumstances even beyond that amount.

Lifetime Transfers Included as Will Substitutes (I.R.C. §§2035-2038). Let us now turn our attention to a second major category of rules concerning the contents of a decedent's gross estate. This category includes a variety of inter vivos transfers the decedent had made under circumstances in which it might be fair to say that the lifetime disposition or arrangement served as a will substitute, or more or less as a rough substitute for retaining the property until death.

One such rule (I.R.C. §2035) has traditionally required, in ways that have varied from time to time, inclusion in the decedent's gross estate of most property transferred within three years of death. This rule became less important and was modified following the unification of the transfer taxes in 1976 and finally, in 1981, was virtually abolished, with continued application only to transfers involving life insurance and several other highly specialized situations.

A second set of rules (I.R.C. §§2036-2038), in effect, says to a transferor, "If you do not wish the property you are transferring to be included in your gross estate at death, you had better make the transfer with almost no strings attached." More specifically, these rules say that property is to be included in the gross estate despite the decedent's transfer of it during life if the decedent retained for life either (a) significant rights to receive economic benefits from that property (usually by way of trust) or (b) significant rights to determine what persons (even persons other than the transferor) are to receive the present or future benefits of that property, or in what way. Note that lifetime benefits and nongeneral powers that would have been harmless for *other* beneficiaries (see above discussion of terminable interest planning) are, under this special set of rules, a source of tax dangers only to those who create trusts or similar arrangements during life.

Joint Tenancies, Life Insurance, and Annuities (I.R.C. §§2039-2040, 2042). Finally, the Code contains a set of rules designed to deal with certain common types of property or property ownership forms that are not adequately covered by the basic provisions applicable to property owned at death and general powers of appointment.

A special section (I.R.C. §2040) deals specifically with joint tenancies, tenancies by the entirety, and counterparts thereof. It provides for some or all of such properties to be included in the estates of decedents under most circumstances, often including more than the actual interest owned by the decedent during life. Essentially, this section provides a contribution-tracing test that directs inclusion in the gross estate of a portion of the property (even all of it) that corresponds to the portion of the consideration furnished by the decedent in purchasing (and improving) the property. An exception applies to survivorship arrangements exclusively between spouses: Under this simplified rule, enacted in 1981, half the property is included in the gross estate of the spouse who is the first to die, regardless of the source of the consideration. Incidentally, to the surprise of many taxpayers, the creation of joint tenancies and the like often (but not always) results in the making of taxable gifts.

A second section (I.R.C. §2042) deals specifically with insurance on the life of the decedent. (Insurance policies owned by a decedent on the life of *another* are covered by the basic section encompassing property owned at death.) The proceeds of insurance on the life of the decedent are included in the decedent's estate either (a) if those proceeds are payable to the decedent's estate or (b) if any of the "incidents of ownership" in the policy were held by the decedent at the time of death, even though the proceeds are payable directly to named beneficiaries. Incidents of ownership include such rights as the power to choose or change the beneficiaries, to select settlement options, to turn in a policy and receive its cash value, or to obtain loans from the insurance company against the policy.

Still another section (I.R.C. §2039) deals with annuities, pensions, and employee benefits that offer some form of postdeath payment or payments. It therefore may apply to such popular arrangements as Individual Retirement Accounts (IRAs), Keogh plans, 401(k) plans, and 403(b) plans. (Due to the spectacular performance of the stock market in recent years, the assets in many of these plans have significant value; persons who do not think of themselves as wealthy may find that, under the Internal Revenue Code, they are.) This section often provides for inclusion of all or part of these benefits in the estate of a decedent. For many years this section contained a general and then limited exemption for payments under "qualified" (and certain counterpart) plans. Legislation in 1982, effective generally for decedents dying in 1983 or later, abolished this exemption entirely, so that a portion or all of the survivor or other death benefits under retirement plans are includible in the gross estate if the basic requirements of §2039 are met. The notion is that the purpose of retirement plans is to provide funds for retirement, not a pool of wealth to give to the retiree's successors. In addition, when the benefits from a tax-deferred plan pass to the decedent's successors, they are treated as income in respect of a decedent under §691 of the Code and may trigger substantial income taxes. Without careful tax planning, the double-hit of estate and income taxes may consume most of the fund.

d.   Deductions from Includible Transfers by Gift or at Death

In calculating the taxable gifts of a donor and the taxable estate of a decedent, the included transfers are reduced by allowable deductions. These fall into two major categories: (a) deductions for the purpose of arriving at what might be called a decedent's *net* transferable wealth — that is, deductions for such items as debts, expenses of estate administration, and casualty losses (I.R.C. §§2053-2054); and (b) deductions for qualified transfers to privileged recipients — that is, transfers eligible for the charitable and marital deductions. The first category can present a number of troublesome problems for practitioners but merit no more than this casual mention for our present purposes. The deductions in category (b), however, justify closer examination.

The Charitable Deduction (I.R.C. §§2055, 2522). Although their income tax counterpart is subject to specific percentage limitations, the federal estate and gift tax charitable deductions are unlimited in amount or percentage of the estate. One can leave an entire multimillion dollar estate tax free to or in trust for organizations or purposes that qualify as charitable under Internal Revenue Code definitions. In order to be deductible, gifts, bequests, or devises to charity must be outright or in other qualifying form. Illustrative of forms that pose both policy issues for the system and planning problems for the profession are "split interest" gifts, such as a transfer in trust for the life benefit of a private individual with remainder thereafter to charity. Is the value of the charitable remainder deductible? Traditionally, this type of issue has revolved around general questions of whether the interest is sufficiently certain and susceptible of reliable valuation to justify a particular deduction. Today these split interest issues are governed by detailed rules and requirements specified in the Code. Deductions can be lost for minor noncompliance with these provisions.

The Marital Deduction (I.R.C. §§2056, 2523). The most important and troublesome of the deductions is the marital deduction. In planning, lawyers are concerned initially with how much of the allowable marital deduction, if any, the client should utilize and then with the forms of interspousal transfers that should be used to qualify for that intended deduction.

Traditionally the maximum allowable deduction (designed originally to offer separate property a treatment similar to the split inherent in community property) was an amount equal to approximately one-half the value of the separate property in the decedent's gross estate and, for gift tax purposes, half the amount of a gift of separate property. Following a short-lived modification of this limit in 1976, the present law was enacted in 1981, allowing an unlimited marital deduction. Thus, if the client chooses, the entire tax (if any) for the spouses' generation can be paid at the survivor's death.

From a planning viewpoint, it is necessary to consider what amount of deduction is likely to be most advantageous for each particular client, recognizing that deductibility requires that the property pass to the surviving spouse in a form susceptible to estate or gift taxation on the spouse's later death or on later disposition of the property inter vivos. There are two main objectives in the use of the marital deduction: (a) estate splitting (under a graduated tax, two estates of equal size being taxed less overall than one large estate and one small) and (b) tax deferral. The two objectives reinforce each other up to the point at which deductible transfers could be expected to cause the spouses' estates to reach the same marginal tax brackets, but they conflict to the extent one is considering deductible transfers in excess of that level.

The marital deduction also involves a rigorously drawn, interpreted, and enforced set of rules specifying the form of disposition — that is, the types of interests — that qualify for the deduction. Present policy generally requires that deductible property pass in the form of "nonterminable interests" so that the property will not escape gift or estate taxation again when the survivor's ownership ends during life or at death. Inheritances or gifts received outright and unconditionally by the surviving spouse obviously qualify, but a variety of highly technical and often treacherous rules determine what other transfers (such as in trust) will qualify as exceptions to the terminable interest rule. Prior to 1982 these special qualifying forms required that the survivor have complete power to dispose of the marital deduction property during life or at death, or both. The typical arrangement was a trust in which the survivor received income for life (or a legal life estate) and a general testamentary power of appointment. Legislation enacted in 1981, however, now allows certain *qualified terminable interest property* (so-called QTIP trusts or properties) to qualify for the deduction on the election of the donor, if alive, or of the transferor's personal representative. This popular device requires only a life interest. Detailed examination of these requirements and their problems is not worthwhile for our purposes here; suffice it to say that the planning or evaluation of possible marital deduction dispositions requires the careful attention of qualified counsel.

e.   Computing the Tax

The Tax Base. Traditionally the federal estate and gift taxes have each had a separate and independent tax base. Reportable gifts — essentially those in excess of $10,000 per donee per year — have been and still are reported annually or more frequently over the lifetime of the donor, but on a cumulative basis so that in any given year all of the recognized gifts over the donor's lifetime are reported and a tax is paid on the difference between the tax for the total of these gifts and the tax for the gifts of prior years. In other words, the tax for each year is computed at marginal rates where the prior year's tax left off. Actual gift tax liability did not begin under pre-1976 law until the total of reportable gifts exceeded the donor's lifetime gift exemption of $30,000. Then, at death, the pre-1976 estate tax was separately applied without regard to the donor's past record of gift tax liability. The estate tax had its own separate (and higher) rate structure and an indepen-dent $60,000 exemption, after which the graduated rate table was ap-plied beginning with the bottom brackets regardless of prior giving.

The essence of the unification of the two taxes under the current law, as revised in 1976, is that all transfers, both during life and at death, are cumulated and taxed on a single scale. The gift tax functions in essentially the same manner as before, but transfers at death are now treated rather like one large, last round of gifts to be reported and added on top of all lifetime gifts. The estate is taxed beginning at the marginal rate where the last gift tax return had left off. Thus, the estate tax return reports not only the taxable estate but also the taxable gifts over a lifetime and computes the tax on the aggregate amount, and the resulting transfer tax liability figure is reduced by the total amount of tax attributable to all prior gifts over the decedent's lifetime, with the difference being the estate tax liability.

Amounts Exempted. The current law provides for a single *unified credit* to offset against one's transfer tax liability, either the gift tax or the estate tax or partially against each. Actually, it is easiest to understand the workings of this credit by thinking of it as equivalent to an exemp-tion (replacing the old separate gift and estate exemptions) in the amount of $675,000 in 2000, with scheduled increases thereafter. This means that no gift tax will be paid until *reportable* gifts over a lifetime exceed the amount that is effectively exempted by the unified credit. If any of this "exemption" remains unused at death, it, in effect, re-duces the decedent's estate that is subject to taxation.

Rates. With technical qualifications that are not significant for our purposes, the effective rate structure for the transfer tax system begins at 37 percent. (The actual rate table begins with rates below that, but for practical purposes the lower brackets are eliminated by the unified credit, which, with that in mind, we are then able to call an exemption.) Rates reach a maximum of 55 percent at the level of $3 million of reportable gift and estate transfers. (In 1987 Congress established a 5 percent surcharge on estates over $10 million in order to recover the unified credit and the benefits of the graduated rates below the top rate. Once these are recovered, the rate returns to 55 percent. The surcharge does not affect the GST rate.)

2.   Selected Aspects of Federal Income Taxation

Income tax considerations are important in nearly all estate situations, even those for which estate and gift taxation is of little or no significance. Of particular importance for purposes of the subject matter of this course are rules affecting the income tax basis of estate and gift property and the income taxation of estates, trusts, beneficiaries, and settlors.

a.   Tax Basis of Property Acquired from a Decedent or Donor (I.R.C. §§1014, 1015)

For purposes of computing taxable gain or loss on the sale of inherited property and, if applicable, determining its depreciation base for income tax purposes, the property's basis is its value on the estate tax valuation date — that is, the date of the decedent's death or (if available and elected) the alternate valuation date, which is generally six months later. This may result in either a *stepped-up* or *stepped-down basis,* depending on whether the adjusted basis in the hands of the decedent had been lower or higher than the estate tax value. With two potentially important exceptions, this so-called new basis applies to all property interests includible in the decedent's gross estate, whether or not a tax return was actually required for the particular estate. One exception is for community property, with respect to which the interest of the survivor as well as that of the decedent receives a new basis on the death of the first to die; the other is that assets that are classified as "income in respect of a decedent" (I.R.C. §691) receive no new basis at death.

In the case of property received by gift, the donee's federal income tax basis is the donor's basis adjusted for part of the gift taxes, if any, paid on the gift. For purposes of subsequently reporting a *loss,* however, the basis of the donee (other than the donor's spouse) is limited to the fair market value of the property at the time of the gift.

These basis rules can be quite significant from a planning perspective. For example, in selecting the subject matter of inter vivos giving programs, they tend to encourage lawyers to counsel donors to retain low-basis properties (in order to obtain a new basis at death) and to give their children, grandchildren, and other younger donees high-basis assets but generally not assets that have a basis in excess of value. (The latter can be sold in order to realize a loss that would be wasted either by giving the property away or by retaining it until death.) Basis considerations, along with other factors, also influence how spouses should hold title to their properties. There tends, for example, to be a rule of thumb in community property states that appreciated properties should be held in community form (to maximize the basis step up) and that potential loss properties be held as tenants in common (to minimize the step down of basis), at least in the latter case if it is desirable to avoid the survivorship feature of joint tenancy. Do you see, from the estate tax discussion above, why joint tenancy is usually to be avoided in tax planned estates?

b. Income Taxation of Estates, Trusts, and Beneficiaries (I.R.C. Subchapter J)

Decedents' estates and trusts are treated as separate tax entities for purposes of reporting and paying income taxes. Estates are allowed an exemption of $600, and trusts either $300 or $100 depending on the circumstances; their taxable income is computed like that of an individual with some exceptions, most importantly (a) the absence of a *zero bracket amount* and (b) the allowance of a special deduction for income that is taxable to beneficiaries or grantors. The applicable tax rates are on a dramatically compressed bracket structure compared to the rates applicable to individuals. For example, the beginning estate or trust rate of 15 percent increases to 28 percent at taxable income over $1,500 and reaches the top bracket of 39.6 percent at taxable income of $7,500. By way of comparison, for married individuals filing jointly the 28 percent bracket is not reached until taxable income of $36,900, and the 39.6 percent bracket is not reached until taxable income of $250,000.

The Grantor Rules (I.R.C. §§671-677). In the case of an inter vivos trust, the first question that must be determined is whether the settlor continues to be taxable on any or all of the trust's income. Rather strict *grantor rules* make the settlor accountable for trust income under certain circumstances, even if that income is in fact accumulated in the trust or distributed to others. With limited exceptions, under these rules the settlor is treated as substantial owner of the trust property and is taxable on its income if the settlor (and sometimes even another close to the settlor) retains either (1) certain beneficial rights under the trust or (2) certain significant powers over its administration or over the interests of the beneficiaries. The specially privileged *Clifford* (or short-term) *trust* was eliminated by the 1986 reform package.

Taxing Estates and Trusts and Their Beneficiaries (I.R.C. §663). In the case of a decedent's estate, a testamentary trust, or a living trust under which the income is not taxable to the settlor, the focus of concern is the allocation of tax accountability as between the estate or trust and its various beneficiaries. The fundamental rule is that income is to be reported by a beneficiary to whom it is actually or constructively (that is, "required to be") distributed. Then the estate or trust is taxable as a separate entity on the remaining income — on the income from estate or trust property less the deduction for income distributions. That is, the entity is taxed on income that is accumulated currently and that is not taxable to a beneficiary (or settlor).

The "Draw-out" and Proration Principles. When is a payment by an executor or trustee deemed to be a distribution of *income?* The answer is important but regrettably complex. It involves what might be called the *draw-out principle,* which applies to all interests that are not sheltered by the limited "§663(a)(1) exceptions" for testamentary gifts of specific property (such as a devise of Blackacre to *X*) or of specific sums (such as a legacy of $5,000 to *Y*). Thus, its main application is to residuary and intestate interests. Under this principle, all distributions from a decedent's estate or trust are treated as distributions of *income* as long as the *distributable net income* of the entire[2] estate or trust has not been exhausted. (Distributable net income, or DNI, is a concept roughly corresponding to current ordinary income and generally excludes, for example, capital gain income.) Thus, regardless of accounting rules under applicable state trust law, for tax purposes distributions are generally deemed to draw out (and the distributees are required to report) income only, unless the distributions for the year exceed the DNI of that year. Principal is deemed to come out only to the extent DNI has been exhausted. In any year during which distributions do exceed DNI, the allocation of income (of all classes) and principal is generally governed by a system of proration, again regardless of the fiduciary's accounting for these items; subject to limited exceptions, all distributees in a given year share pro rata in the income and principal distributions of the year.

The Throwback Rule (I.R.C. §§665-668). In order that trust beneficiaries not be insulated permanently from tax liability by the trust device, the so-called *throwback rule* was enacted in 1965 and, in one form or another, was a part of our tax law until 1997. (It has no application to decedents' estates.) Under this highly complicated rule, trust distributions that exceeded the current year's DNI were deemed to be distribu-

---

2. In the case of *trusts,* however, if the trust consists of "substantially separate and independent shares" these are treated as separate trusts solely for purposes of the draw-out principle (not, for example, for purposes of taxing accumulations in the trust). In other trusts and in all decedents' estates, the draw-out principle applies to distributees without being limited to what one might think of as the particular distributee's share of the income — there being no general concept for tax purposes of distinct shares of DNI or of accumulations. For the essentials of income taxation of estates and trusts, see Sherman, All You Really Need to Know About Subchapter J You Learned from This Article, 63 Mo. L. Rev. 1 (1998).

tions of prior years' accumulated income rather than principal until all income accumulations in the trust had been exhausted. The income that was deemed to be paid out by such *accumulation distributions* was then, in some manner that varied from time to time under changing legislation, taxed to the distributee(s) with a credit being allowed for taxes already paid by the trust. In 1997 the throwback rule was abolished for distributions made in taxable years beginning after August 5, 1997. With the negligible tax savings available through accumulations after the 1986 compression in trust income tax brackets, the rule (which was at best sporadically enforced) was hardly worth the cost and complexity to government and taxpayer alike. With some exceptions, the throwback rule still applies to trusts created before March 1, 1984.

To summarize briefly the allocation of income as between a trust and its distributees: regardless of trust accounting for distributions under local law, for income tax purposes current income (DNI) comes out first, and principal comes out last; but any time more than DNI is thus deemed to have been distributed, the distributed items are allocated ratably among the distributees (except under special *tier system* rules that can be ignored for present purposes).

The *grantor rules* of the income tax, together with the analogous yet significantly different will-substitute rules of the estate tax (I.R.C. §§2035-2038), make the use of irrevocable inter vivos trusts a very complicated, if nevertheless an often attractive, part of substantial giving programs undertaken during life. Of more widespread importance, however, are the implications of the rules allocating income tax accountability between estates or trusts and their beneficiaries, and among the various beneficiaries. In estate administration, the applicable principles (including the lack of throwback and separate share rules for estates) significantly influence the use and timing of preliminary distributions and the preparation for and handling of final distribution, with sometimes extraordinary opportunities or risks being involved. In the planning of trusts, the rules are exploited through the use of discretionary trusts that may accumulate or pay out income and that are often designed to allow the trustee in making distributions to "sprinkle" income among a rather flexible class of beneficiaries — such as the testator's surviving spouse, children, and other descendants. This enables the testator to provide for a spouse or adult children, or some combination of both, in ways that are potentially generous but that (a) avoid burdening well-to-do primary beneficiaries with income of which they have no need and on which they would merely pay tax at unnecessarily high rates and (b) allow either distributions to low-bracket beneficiaries in the family (such as grandchildren) or limited accumulations in the trust. Even the traditional benefits of distributions to grandchildren or others under age 14 are undermined now by the 1986 enactment of the so-called kiddie tax, often causing unearned income of children to be taxed at the marginal rates of their parents.

3. Some Concluding Observations

Students at this point may well have come to suspect that the portions of the federal tax system discussed here are more complex and costly to live with than necessary, and more vulnerable than desirable to exploitation by competent counsel.[3] A good case can certainly be made for that proposition, and a substantial part of the reason is simply legislative neglect. Some of the complexity, of course, reflects the presence of some problems of inherent conceptual and practical difficulty. Regardless of the cause, the complexities and burdens of the tax law in this field make both planning and administration hazardous — and create risks of professional oversight and error that have strikingly boosted the cost of malpractice insurance, for which the client public as well as practitioners are paying. Yet, taxation is a fact of life in this and most other fields. This discussion should at least provide you with some sense of the nature of our transfer taxes and of some closely related aspects of income taxation, and also an awareness of some fascinating even if challenging planning problems and opportunities. As you proceed into the study of trust law, this background may help you to appreciate that the trust device is significantly responsible for many of the complexities of our income and transfer taxes. Nevertheless, the trust is also valued as one of the most flexible tools American lawyers have to meet the personal and family needs of clients and to protect clients and their beneficiaries from unnecessary taxes.

An entertaining bestseller on financial planning challenges the estate planner's usual assumption that people should want to conserve assets for gift to the next generation. See S. Pollan & M. Levine, Die Broke (1997).

---

3. The federal estate and gift taxes do not raise large revenues, accounting for about 1 percent of federal tax receipts. Only about 2 percent of all decedents' estates actually pay any estate tax. A significant investment of time and money is made to minimize or avoid the taxes, an investment that might be devoted to more productive uses. Of course, the question of abolition of the federal estate and gift taxes is fraught with social, political and ideological symbols and concerns. In recent years, bills to abolish the federal transfer taxes have passed the House of Representatives but ultimately yielded to senatorial or presidential opposition. For a law and economics perspective on the gift and estate taxes, see R. Posner, Economic Analysis of Law 505-507 (4th ed. 1992). Judge Posner concludes that "Because the estate tax raises so little revenue, the motives for it must be sought elsewhere than in notions of efficient taxation or even in the power of interest groups to get the government to channel wealth toward them."

G.   Professional Responsibility in Estate Planning

1.   Ethical Considerations

PROBLEM

8-C.   *L* has represented *H* for many years, in both business and personal matters, dating from *H*'s marriage. *H* operates a profitable business and has become wealthy. His wife, *W*, has substantial inherited assets of her own. They also hold substantial property as joint tenants. Their marriage is the first for each; they have two teenage children. In recent years *L* has done estate planning for both spouses, and they recently executed new wills. *H*'s will provides a family trust to take advantage of the federal estate tax exclusion amount, with the residue of his estate to a QTIP trust for *W* for life, remainder to their issue. *W*'s will contains a similar family trust but leaves the residue of her estate outright to *H* if he survives her.

L, H, and *W* have always shared relevant information but have never discussed the scope or details of *L*'s representation. Several months after *H* and *W* executed new wills, *H* revealed to *L* that he had just executed a holographic codicil (as permitted by the state involved) to devise a substantial sum to a woman with whom *H* was having an extramarital affair. *H* asks *L* to advise him regarding *W*'s elective share rights in the event she survives him. What should he do? May he advise *H* concerning *W*'s elective share? May he disclose the information about the codicil to *W*? *Must* he? May *L* remain silent about the information and advise *W* that he no longer represents her but continues to represent *H*? Is there anything *L* could or should have done at the outset of his representation of *H* and *W*?

A. v. B. v. HILL WALLACK
158 N.J. 51, 726 A.2d 924 (1999)

Pollock, J.

This appeal presents the issue whether a law firm [Hill Wallack] may disclose confidential information of one co-client to another co-client. Specifically, in this paternity action, the mother's former law firm, which contemporaneously represented the father and his wife in planning their estates [in which they devised their respective estates to each other] seeks to disclose to the wife the existence of the father's illegitimate child. . . . The devises created the possibility that the other spouse's issue, whether legitimate or illegitimate, ultimately would acquire the decedent's property.

. . . Because of a clerical error, the firm's computer check did not reveal the conflict of interest inherent in its representation of the mother against the husband. On learning of the conflict, the firm withdrew from representation of the mother in the paternity action. . . .

In the Family Part, the husband, represented by new counsel, [Fox Rothschild], requested restraints against Hill Wallack to prevent the firm from disclosing to his wife the existence of the child. The Family Part denied the requested restraints. The Appellate Division reversed and remanded "for the entry of an order imposing preliminary restraints and for further consideration."

Hill Wallack then filed motions in this Court seeking [and receiving] leave to appeal. . . . In October 1997, the husband and wife retained Hill Wallack [and] each signed a letter captioned "Waiver of Conflict of Interest." In explaining the possible conflicts of interest, the letter recited that the effect of a testamentary transfer by one spouse to the other would permit the transferee to dispose of the property as he or she desired. The firm's letter also explained that information provided by one spouse could become available to the other. Although the letter did not contain an express waiver of the confidentiality of any such information, each spouse consented to and waived any conflicts arising from the firm's joint representation. . . .

. . . Under N.J.S.A. 3B: 1-2, 3-48, the term "issue" includes both legitimate and illegitimate children. When the wife executed her will, therefore, she did not know that the husband's illegitimate child ultimately may inherit her property.

Hill Wallack . . . then wrote to the husband stating that it believed that it had an ethical obligation to disclose to the wife the existence, but not the identity, of his illegitimate child. Additionally, the firm stated that it was obligated to inform the wife "that her current estate plan may devise a portion of her assets through her spouse to that child." The firm suggested that the husband so inform his wife and stated that if he did not do so, it would. Because of the restraints imposed by the Appellate Division, however, the firm has not disclosed the information to the wife.

This appeal concerns the conflict between two fundamental obligations of lawyers: the duty of confidentiality, Rules of Professional Conduct (RPC) 1.6(a), and the duty to inform clients of material facts, RPC 1.4(b). The conflict arises from a law firm's joint representation of two clients whose interests initially were, but no longer are, compatible.

Crucial to the attorney-client relationship is the attorney's obligation not to reveal confidential information learned in the course of representation. Thus, RPC 1.6(a) states that "[a] lawyer shall not reveal information relating to representation of a client unless the client consents after consultation, except for disclosures that are impliedly authorized in order to carry out the representation." Generally, "the principle of attorney-client confidentiality imposes a sacred trust on the attorney not to disclose the client's confidential communication." . . .

A lawyer's obligation to communicate to one client all information needed to make an informed decision qualifies the firm's duty to maintain the confidentiality of a co-client's information. RPC 1.4(b), which reflects a lawyer's duty to keep clients informed, requires that "[a] lawyer shall explain a matter to the extent reasonably necessary to permit the client to make informed decisions regarding the representation." . . . In limited situations, moreover, an attorney is permitted or required to disclose confidential information. Hill Wallack argues that RPC 1.6 mandates, or at least permits, the firm to disclose to the wife the existence of the husband's illegitimate child. RPC 1.6(b) requires that a lawyer disclose "information relating to representation of a client" to the proper authorities if the lawyer "reasonably believes" that such disclosure is necessary to prevent the client "from committing a criminal, illegal or fraudulent act that the lawyer reasonably believes is likely to result in death or substantial bodily harm or substantial injury to the financial interest or property of another." RPC 1.6(b)(1). Despite Hill Wallack's claim that RPC 1.6(b) applies, the facts do not justify mandatory disclosure. The possible inheritance of the wife's estate by the husband's illegitimate child is too remote to constitute "substantial injury to the financial interest or property of another" within the meaning of RPC 1.6(b).

By comparison, in limited circumstances RPC 1.6(c) permits a lawyer to disclose a confidential communication. RPC 1.6(c) permits, but does not require, a lawyer to reveal confidential information to the extent the lawyer reasonably believes necessary "to rectify the consequences of a client's criminal, illegal or fraudulent act in furtherance of which the lawyer's services had been used." RPC 1.6(c)(1). Although RPC 1.6(c) does not define a "fraudulent act," the term takes on meaning from our construction of the word "fraud," found in the analogous "crime or fraud" exception to the attorney-client privilege. . . . When construing the "crime or fraud" exception to the attorney-client privilege, "our courts have generally given the term 'fraud' an expansive reading." . . .

We likewise construe broadly the term "fraudulent act" within the meaning of RPC 1.6(c). So construed, the husband's deliberate omission of the existence of his illegitimate child constitutes a fraud on his wife. When discussing their respective estates with the firm, the husband and wife reasonably could expect that each would disclose information material to the distribution of their estates, including the existence of children who are contingent residuary beneficiaries. The husband breached that duty. Under the reciprocal wills, the existence of the husband's illegitimate child could affect the distribution of the wife's estate, if she predeceased him. Additionally, the husband's child support payments and other financial responsibilities owed to the illegitimate child could deplete that part of his estate that otherwise would pass to his wife.

From another perspective, it would be "fundamentally unfair" for the husband to reap the "joint planning advantages of access to information and certainty of outcome," while denying those same advantages to his wife. . . . In effect, the husband has used the law firm's services to defraud his wife in the preparation of her estate.

The New Jersey RPCs are based substantially on the American Bar Association Model Rules of Professional Conduct ("the Model Rules"). RPC 1.6, however, exceeds the Model Rules in authorizing the disclosure of confidential information. A brief review of the history of the Model Rules and of RPC 1.6 confirms New Jersey's more expansive commitment to the disclosure of confidential client information.

In 1977, the American Bar Association appointed a Commission on Evaluation of Professional Standards, chaired by the late Robert J. Kutak. The Commission, generally known as the "Kutak Commission," originally proposed a rule that permitted a lawyer to disclose confidential information in circumstances comparable to those permitted by RPC 1.6. The House of Delegates of the American Bar Association, however, rejected the Kutak Commission's recommendation. As adopted by the American Bar Association, Model Rule 1.6(b) permits a lawyer to reveal confidential information only "to the extent the lawyer reasonably believes necessary to prevent the client from committing a criminal act that the lawyer believes is likely to result in imminent death or substantial bodily harm." Unlike RPC 1.6, Model Rule 1.6 does not except information relating to the commission of a fraudulent act or that relating to a client's act that is likely to result in substantial financial injury. In no situation, moreover, does Model Rule 1.6 require disclosure. Thus, the Model Rules provide for narrower disclosure than that authorized by RPC 1.6.

In 1982, this Court appointed a committee to consider the Model Rules. The committee, chaired by the Honorable Dickinson R. Debevoise, became known as the "Debevoise Committee." It determined that the original provisions proposed by the Kutak Commission more closely reflected the existing ethics rules in New Jersey. Thus, the Committee concluded that Model Rule 1.6 would "narrow radically the circumstances in which New Jersey attorneys either may or must disclose the information of their clients' criminal or fraudulent behavior." . . . When adopting the RPCs, this Court substantially followed the recommendation of the Debevoise Committee. Described as an "openly-radical experiment," Geoffrey C. Hazard, Jr. & W. William Hodes, 2 The Law of Lawyering §AP4:104 (1998), RPC 1.6 "contained the most far-reaching disclosure requirements of any attorney code of conduct in the country," Leslie C. Levin, Testing the Radical Experiment: A Study of Lawyer Response to Clients Who Intend to Harm Others, 47 Rutgers L. Rev. 81, 92 (1994).

Under RPC 1.6, the facts support disclosure to the wife. The law firm did not learn of the husband's illegitimate child in a confidential communication from him. Indeed, he concealed that information from both his wife and the firm. The law firm learned about the husband's child through its representation of the mother in her paternity action against the husband. Accordingly, the husband's expectation of nondisclosure of the information may be less than if he had communicated the information to the firm in confidence.

In addition, the husband and wife signed letters captioned "Waiver of Conflict of Interest." . . . Even in the absence of . . . explicit authorization, the spirit of the letters supports the firm's decision to disclose to the wife the existence of the husband's illegitimate child. . . . The forthcoming Restatement (Third) of The Law Governing Lawyers §112 comment 1 (Proposed Final Draft No. 1, 1996) ("the Restatement") suggests, for example, that if the attorney and the co-clients have reached a prior, explicit agreement concerning the sharing of confidential information, that agreement controls whether the attorney should disclose the confidential information of one co-client to another. . . .

As the preceding authorities suggest, an attorney, on commencing joint representation of co-clients, should agree explicitly with the clients on the sharing of confidential information. In such a "disclosure agreement," the co-clients can agree that any confidential information concerning one co-client, whether obtained from a co-client himself or herself or from another source, will be shared with the other co-client. Similarly, the co-clients can agree that unilateral confidences or other confidential information will be kept confidential by the attorney. Such a prior agreement will clarify the expectations of the clients and the lawyer and diminish the need for future litigation. In the absence of an agreement to share confidential information with co-clients, the Restatement reposes the resolution of the lawyer's competing duties within the lawyer's discretion. . . . Additionally, the Restatement advises that the lawyer, when withdrawing from representation of the co-clients, may inform the affected co-client that the attorney has learned of information adversely affecting that client's interests that the communicating co-client refuses to permit the lawyer to disclose. Ibid.

In the context of estate planning, the Restatement also suggests that a lawyer's disclosure of confidential information communicated by one spouse is appropriate only if the other spouse's failure to learn of the information would be materially detrimental to that other spouse or frustrate the spouse's intended testamentary arrangement. Id. §112 comment 1, illustrations 2, 3. The Restatement provides two analogous illustrations in which a lawyer has been jointly retained by a husband and wife to prepare reciprocal wills. The first illustration states:

> Lawyer has been retained by Husband and Wife to prepare wills pursuant to an arrangement under which each spouse agrees to leave most of their property to the other. Shortly after the wills are executed, Husband (unknown to Wife) asks Lawyer to prepare an inter vivos trust for an illegitimate child whose existence Husband has kept secret from Wife for many years and about whom Husband had not previously informed Lawyer. Husband states that Wife would be distraught at learning of Husband's infidelity and of Husband's years of silence and that disclosure of the information could destroy their marriage. Husband directs Lawyer not to inform Wife. The inter vivos trust that Husband proposes to create would not materially affect Wife's own estate plan or her expected receipt of property under Husband's will, because Husband proposes to use property designated in Husband's will for a personally favored charity. In view of the lack of material effect on Wife, Lawyer may assist Husband to establish and fund the inter vivos trust and refrain from disclosing Husband's information to Wife. [Id. §112 comment 1, illustration 2.]

In authorizing non-disclosure, the Restatement explains that an attorney should refrain from disclosing the existence of the illegitimate child to the wife because the trust "would not materially affect Wife's own estate plan or her expected receipt of property under Husband's will." Ibid.

The other illustration states:

> Same facts as [the prior Illustration], except that Husband's proposed inter vivos trust would significantly deplete Husband's estate, to Wife's material detriment and in frustration of the Spouses' intended testamentary arrangements. If Husband will neither inform Wife nor permit Lawyer to do so, Lawyer must withdraw from representing both Husband and Wife. In the light of all relevant circumstances, Lawyer may exercise discretion whether to inform Wife either that circumstances, which Lawyer has been asked not to reveal, indicate that she should revoke her recent will or to inform Wife of some or all the details of the information that Husband has recently provided so that Wife may protect her interests. Alternatively, Lawyer may inform Wife only that Lawyer is withdrawing because Husband will not permit disclosure of information that Lawyer has learned from Husband. [Id. §112 comment 1, illustration 3.]

Because the money placed in the trust would be deducted from the portion of the husband's estate left to his wife, the Restatement concludes that the lawyer may exercise discretion to inform the wife of the husband's plans. Ibid. . . .

Similarly, the American College of Trust and Estate Counsel (ACTEC) also favors a discretionary rule. It recommends that the "lawyer should have a reasonable degree of discretion in determining how to respond to any particular case." American College of Trust and Estate Counsel, supra, at 68. The ACTEC suggests that the lawyer first attempt to convince the client to inform the co-client. Ibid. When urging the client to disclose the information, the lawyer should remind the client of the implicit understanding that all information will be shared by both clients. The lawyer also should explain to the client the potential legal consequences of non-disclosure, including invalidation of the wills. Ibid. Furthermore, the lawyer may mention that failure to communicate the information could subject the lawyer to a malpractice claim or disciplinary action. Ibid.

The ACTEC reasons that if unsuccessful in persuading the client to disclose the information, the lawyer should consider several factors in deciding whether to reveal the confidential information to the co-client, including: (1) duties of impartiality and loyalty to the clients; (2) any express or implied agreement among the lawyer and the joint clients that information communicated by either client to the lawyer regarding the subject of the representation would be shared with the other client; (3) the reasonable expectations of the clients; and (4) the nature of the confidence and the harm that may result if the confidence is, or is not, disclosed. Id. at 68-69.

The Section of Real Property, Probate and Trust Law of the American Bar Association, in a report prepared by its Special Study Committee on Professional Responsibility, reached a similar conclusion. . . .

The Professional Ethics Committees of New York and Florida, however, have concluded that disclosure to a co-client is prohibited. New York State Bar Ass'n Comm. on Professional Ethics, Op. 555 (1984); Florida State Bar Ass'n Comm. on Professional Ethics, Op. 95-4 (1997). . . .

The Florida Ethics Committee addressed a similar situation:

Lawyer has represented Husband and Wife for many years in a range of personal matters, including estate planning. Husband and Wife have substantial individual assets, and they also own substantial jointly-held property. Recently, Lawyer prepared new updated wills that Husband and Wife signed. Like their previous wills, their new wills primarily benefit the survivor of them for his or her life, with beneficial disposition at the death of the survivor being made equally to their children. . . . Several months after the execution of the new wills, Husband confers separately with Lawyer. Husband reveals to Lawyer that he has just executed a codicil (prepared by another law firm) that makes substantial beneficial disposition to a woman with whom Husband has been having an extramarital relationship. [Id.]

Reasoning that the lawyer's duty of confidentiality takes precedence over the duty to communicate all relevant information to a client, the

Florida Ethics Committee concluded that the lawyer did not have discretion to reveal the information. In support of that conclusion, the Florida committee reasoned that joint clients do not necessarily expect that everything relating to the joint representation communicated by one co-client will be shared with the other co-client.

In several material respects, however, the present appeal differs from the hypothetical cases considered by the New York and Florida committees. Most significantly, the New York and Florida disciplinary rules, unlike RPC 1.6, do not except disclosure needed "to rectify the consequences of a client's . . . fraudulent act in the furtherance of which the lawyer's services had been used." RPC 1.6(c). . . . Second, Hill Wallack learned of the husband's paternity from a third party, not from the husband himself. Thus, the husband did not communicate anything to the law firm with the expectation that the communication would be kept confidential. Finally, the husband and wife, unlike the co-clients considered by the New York and Florida Committees, signed an agreement suggesting their intent to share all information with each other.

Because Hill Wallack wishes to make the disclosure, we need not reach the issue whether the lawyer's obligation to disclose is discretionary or mandatory. In conclusion, Hill Wallack may inform the wife of the existence of the husband's illegitimate child. . . . The law firm learned of the husband's paternity of the child through the mother's disclosure before the institution of the paternity suit. It does not seek to disclose the identity of the mother or the child. Given the wife's need for the information and the law firm's right to disclose it, the disclosure of the child's existence to the wife constitutes an exceptional case with "compelling reason clearly and convincingly shown."

The judgment of the Appellate Division is reversed and the matter is remanded to the Family Part.[4]

---

4. *Sources of Guidance.* The opinion in *Hill Wallack* reviews sources on professional responsibility in trusts and estates practice. See also P. Haskell, Preface to Wills, Trusts & Administration, ch. 14 (2d ed. 1994); R. Link, Professional Responsibility of the Estate Planning (part 1) and Estate Administration (part 2) Lawyer: The Effect of the Model Rules of Professional Conduct, 22 Real Prop., Prob., & Trust J. 1 (1987) and 26 id. 1 (1991); Committee Reports, 22 Real Prop., Prob., & Trust J. 763, 765, 803, 825 (ABA, 1994); M. Moore & A. Hilker, Representing Both Spouses: The New Section Recommendations, 7 Prob. & Prop. 26 (July/Aug. 1993); ACTEC Commentaries on the Model Rules of Professional Conduct (J. Price & B. Ross, 3d ed. 1999); Special Issue: Ethical Issues in Representing Older Clients, 62 Fordham L. Rev. 961-1583 (1994); Restatement (3d) of the Law Governing Lawyers §§112, 117, 211 (approved by ALI but not yet published in final form); Symposium: "Should the Family Be Represented as an Entity?": Reexamining the Family Values of Legal Ethics, 22 Seattle U. L. Rev. 1-173 (1998); Russell & Bicks, Joint Representation of Spouses in Estate Planning: The Saga of Advisory Opinion 95-4, 72 Fla. B.J. 1 (Mar. 1998).

What result in *Hill Wallack* under ABA Model Rule 1.6 (below)?

AMERICAN BAR ASSOCIATION, MODEL RULES OF PROFESSIONAL CONDUCT
(1983)

Rule 1.2 *Scope of Representation*

(a) A lawyer shall abide by a client's decisions concerning the objectives of representation, subject to paragraphs (c), (d) and (e), and shall consult with the client as to the means by which they are to be pursued. . . .

(c) A lawyer may limit the objectives of the representation if the client consents after consultation. . . .

(d) A lawyer shall not counsel a client to engage, or assist a client, in conduct that the lawyer knows is criminal or fraudulent, but a lawyer may discuss the legal consequences of any proposed course of conduct with a client and may counsel or assist a client to make a good faith effort to determine the validity, scope, meaning or application of the law. . . .

Rule 1.4 *Communication*

(a) A lawyer shall keep a client reasonably informed about the status of a matter and promptly comply with reasonable requests for information.

(b) A lawyer shall explain a matter to the extent reasonably necessary to permit the client to make informed decisions regarding the representation.

Rule 1.6 *Confidentiality of Information*

(a) A lawyer shall not reveal information relating to representation of a client unless the client consents after consultation, except for disclosures that are impliedly authorized in order to carry out the representation, and except as stated in paragraph (b).

(b) A lawyer may reveal such information to the extent the lawyer reasonably believes necessary:

(1) to prevent the client from committing a criminal act that the lawyer believes is likely to result in imminent death or substantial bodily harm; or

(2) to establish a claim or defense on behalf of the lawyer in a controversy between the lawyer and the client, to establish a defense to a criminal charge or civil claim against the lawyer based upon

conduct in which the client was involved, or to respond to allegations in any proceeding concerning the lawyer's representation of the client.

Rule 1.7   *Conflict of Interest: General Rule*

(a) A lawyer shall not represent a client if the representation of that client will be directly adverse to another client, unless:

(1) the lawyer reasonably believes the representation will not adversely affect the relationship with the other client; and

(2) each client consents after consultation.

(b) A lawyer shall not represent a client if the representation of that client may be materially limited by the lawyer's responsibilities to another client or to a third person, or by the lawyer's own interests, unless:

(1) the lawyer reasonably believes the representation will not be adversely affected; and

(2) the client consents after consultation. When representation of multiple clients in a single matter is undertaken, the consultation shall include explanation of the implications of the common representation and the advantages and risks involved.

Comment

Loyalty to a Client

Conflict questions may also arise in estate planning and estate administration. A lawyer may be called upon to prepare wills for several family members, such as husband and wife, and, depending upon the circumstances, a conflict of interest may arise. In estate administration the identity of the client may be unclear under the law of a particular jurisdiction. Under one view, the client is the fiduciary; under another view the client is the estate or trust, including its beneficiaries. The lawyer should make clear the relationship to the parties involved.

Rule 1.9   *Conflict of Interest: Former Client*

(a) A lawyer who has formerly represented a client in a matter shall not thereafter represent another person in the same or a substantially related matter in which that person's interests are materially adverse to the interests of the former client unless the former client consents after consultation.

(b) A lawyer shall not knowingly represent a person in the same or a substantially related matter in which a firm with which the lawyer formerly was associated had previously represented a client.

(1) whose interests are materially adverse to that person; and

(2) about whom the lawyer had acquired information protected by Rules 1.6 and 1.9(c) that is material to the matter; unless the former client consents after consultation.

(c) A lawyer who has formerly represented a client in a matter or whose present or former firm has formerly represented a client in a matter shall not thereafter:

(1) use information relating to the representation to the disadvantage of the former client except as Rule 1.6 or Rule 3.3 would permit or require with respect to a client, or when the information has become generally known; or

(2) reveal information relating to the representation except as Rule 1.6 or Rule 3.3 would permit or require with respect to a client.

Rule 1.16   *Declining or Terminating Representation*

(a) Except as stated in paragraph (c), a lawyer shall not represent a client or, where representation has commenced, shall withdraw from the representation of a client if:

(1) the representation will result in violation of the rules of professional conduct or other law; . . .

(b) except as stated in paragraph (c), a lawyer may withdraw from representing a client if withdrawal can be accomplished without material adverse effect on the interests of the client, or if:

(1) the client persists in a course of action involving the lawyer's services that the lawyer reasonably believes is criminal or fraudulent;

(2) the client has used the lawyer's services to perpetrate a crime or fraud;

(3) a client insists upon pursuing an objective that the lawyer considers repugnant or imprudent; . . . or

(6) other good cause for withdrawal exists. . . .

(d) Upon termination of representation, a lawyer shall take steps to the extent reasonably practicable to protect a client's interests, such as giving reasonable notice to the client, allowing time for employment of other counsel, surrendering papers and property to which the client is entitled and refunding any advance payment of fee that has not been earned. . . .

Rule 2.2   *Intermediary*

(a) A lawyer may act as intermediary between clients if:

(1) the lawyer consults with each client concerning the implications of the common representation, including the advantages and risks involved, and the effect on the attorney-client privileges, and obtains each client's consent to the common representation;

(2) the lawyer reasonably believes that the matter can be resolved on terms compatible with the clients' best interests, that each client will be able to make adequately informed decisions in the matter and that there is little risk of material prejudice to the interests

of any of the clients if the contemplated resolution is unsuccessful; and

(3) the lawyer reasonably believes that the common representation can be undertaken impartially and without improper effect on other responsibilities the lawyer has to any of the clients.

(b) While acting as intermediary, the lawyer shall consult with each client concerning the decisions to be made and the considerations relevant in making them, so that each client can make adequately informed decisions.

(c) A lawyer shall withdraw as intermediary if any of the clients so requests, or if any of the conditions stated in paragraph (a) is no longer satisfied. Upon withdrawal, the lawyer shall not continue to represent any of the clients in the matter that was the subject of the intermediation.

Comment

A lawyer acts as intermediary under this Rule when the lawyer represents two or more parties with potentially conflicting interests. A key factor in defining the relationship is whether the parties share responsibility for the lawyer's fee, but the common representation may be inferred from other circumstances. Because confusion can arise as to the lawyer's role where each party is not separately represented, it is important that the lawyer make clear the relationship.

AMERICAN COLLEGE OF TRUST AND ESTATE COUNSEL FOUNDATION, ACTEC COMMENTARIES ON THE MODEL RULES OF PROFESSIONAL CONDUCT
1 (3d ed. 1999)

Basic Themes of Commentaries. The main themes of the Commentaries are: (1) the relative freedom that lawyers and clients have to write their own charter with respect to a representation in the trusts and estates field; (2) the generally nonadversarial nature of the trusts and estates practice; (3) the utility and propriety, in this area of law, of representing multiple clients, whose interests may differ but are not necessarily adversarial; and (4) the opportunity, with full disclosure, to moderate or eliminate many problems that might otherwise arise under the MRPC. The Commentaries additionally reflect the role that the trusts and estates lawyer has traditionally played as the lawyer for members of a family. In that role a trusts and estates lawyer frequently represents the fiduciary of a trust or estate and one or more of the beneficiaries. In drafting the Commentaries we have attempted to express views that are consistent with the spirit of the MRPC as evidenced in the following passage: "The Rules of Professional Conduct are rules of reason. They should be interpreted with reference to the purposes of legal representation and of the law itself." MRPC, Scope.

AMERICAN COLLEGE OF TRUST AND ESTATE COUNSEL FOUNDATION, ENGAGEMENT LETTERS: A GUIDE FOR PRACTITIONERS
9-10 (1999)

JOINT SPOUSAL REPRESENTATION ENGAGEMENT LETTER

(date)

Dear (clients):

You have asked me to [describe scope of representation]. I have agreed to do this work and will bill for it on the following basis: [Describe arrangements pertaining to fees, billing, etc.]. If I am asked to perform tasks not described in this letter, an additional engagement letter may be required for that work.

It is common for a husband and wife to employ the same lawyer to assist them in planning their estates. You have taken this approach by asking me to represent both of you in your planning. It is important that you understand that because I will be representing both of you, you are considered my client, collectively. Accordingly, matters that one of you might discuss with me may be disclosed to the other of you. Ethical considerations prohibit me from agreeing with either of you to withhold information from the other. In this representation, I will not give legal advice to either of you or make any changes in any of your estate planning documents without your mutual knowledge and consent. Of course, anything either of you discusses with me is privileged from disclosure to third parties.

[CHOOSE ONE OF THE FOLLOWING]

#1   If a conflict of interest arises between you during the course of your planning or if the two of you have a difference of opinion, I can point out the pros and cons of your respective positions or differing opinions. However, ethical considerations prohibit me, as the lawyer for both of you, from advocating one of your positions over the other. Furthermore, I would not be able to advocate one of your positions versus the other if there is a dispute at any time as to your respective property rights or interests or as to other legal issues between you. If actual conflicts of interest do arise between you of such a nature that in my judgment it is impossible for me to perform my ethical obligations to both of you, it would become necessary for me to withdraw as your joint lawyer.

#2   If a conflict of interest arises between you during the course of
your planning or if the two of you have a difference of opinion
concerning the proposed plan for disposition of your property
or on any other subject, I can point out the pros and cons of
your respective positions or differing opinions. However, ethical
considerations prohibit me, as the lawyer for both of you, from
advocating one of your positions over the other. Furthermore, I
would not be able to advocate one of your positions versus the
other if there is a dispute at any time as to your respective property
rights or interests or as to other legal issues between you.

If actual conflicts of interest do arise between you of such a nature
that in my judgment it is impossible for me to perform my ethical obligations to both of you, it would become necessary for me to cease acting
as your joint attorney. Since [Bob] is a client of long standing, I may
elect to/would continue to represent him and in that event [Mary]
would have to retain another lawyer to represent her. However, I would
not be able to continue to represent [Bob] if prior to my undertaking
separate representation I learn that [Bob] has breached any understanding with [Mary] or has advised me that he intends to do so (such as
changing his estate plan to her detriment) unless [Mary] is fully informed of the breach or the intended breach and fully understands your
current circumstances. By signing her consent to this letter, [Mary]
agrees to my continued representation of [Bob] should a conflict arise
between you, subject to the conditions set forth in this letter.

[OPTIONAL]

Once documentation is executed to put into place the planning that
you have hired me to implement, my engagement will be concluded and
our attorney-client relationship will terminate. If you need my services
in the future, please feel free to contact me and renew our relationship.
In the meantime, I will not take any further action with reference to
your affairs unless and until I hear otherwise from you.

After considering the foregoing, if you consent to my representing
both of you jointly, I request that you sign and return the enclosed copy
of this letter. If you have any questions about anything discussed in this
letter, please let me know. In addition, you should feel free to consult
with another lawyer about the effect of signing this letter.

Very truly yours,

CONSENT

We have read the foregoing letter and understand its contents. We
consent to having you represent both of us on the terms and conditions

set forth. We agree that you may, in your discretion, share with both of us any information regarding the representation that you receive from either of us or any other source.

Dated:_____   _____
                                     [Spouse]

Dated:_____   _____
                                     [Spouse]

If the husband and wife and lawyer in *Hill Wallack* had signed the ACTEC joint spousal representation letter, would it have permitted the lawyer to disclose the paternity claim to the wife? Would it have required disclosure? Or would it not have covered the issue?

The ACTEC Guide also includes a "Concurrent Separate Spousal Representation Letter," preceded with the boldface warning: "Conflicts of interest and confidentiality are of paramount concern if a lawyer undertakes concurrent separate representation of spouses. Such representation should only be undertaken after careful consideration of all possible conflicts of interest." Why the warning for that model but not for the joint representation letter? See, e.g., Restatement (Third) of the Law Governing Lawyers §211 cmt. *c* (Proposed Final Draft No. 1, 1996).

The California Rules of Professional Conduct require an engagement letter. Cal. Rules of Professional Conduct Rule 3-310(C) and Id. Official Discussion (1999). See generally Ross, I Do, I Don't & I Won't: The Ethics of Engagement Letters, 31 Miami Inst. on Est. Pl. ch. 8 (1997).

Similar issues can arise where the lawyer represents more than one generation of the same family or two or more principals in a business, although the relevant considerations may vary somewhat.

Sanctions. Violation of ethical rules may have various consequences, some obvious and some not so obvious. Discipline ranging from private reprimand to disbarment is one possibility. Loss of fees is another where, for example, the attorney has represented persons with conflicting interests. Hardball litigators increasingly seek to disqualify opposing counsel, and ethical violations may provide the excuse. On whether violation of an ethical duty sounds in malpractice see section 2 infra. See generally Manley, The Impact of Ethical Rules on Estate Planning, SD36 ALI-ABA 275 (1999); Restatement (Third) of the Law Governing Lawyers §201 cmt. *f* (Proposed Final Draft No. 1, 1996).

2. Malpractice

PROBLEM

8-C.   *S* and *D* inform you that their father, *F*, has just died, leaving a recent will devising his entire estate in trust for *W* (the stepmother of *S* and *D*) for life, remainder essentially to *S* and *D* or their respective issue. Apparently, however, the probate estate consists only of trivial amounts of personal property, while substantial amounts of land and securities are held in the names of *F* and *W* as joint tenants. *S* and *D* tell you that, in the presence of two hospital staff members, *F* told them that he had just made a will that was in the custody of his lawyer. He further told them his will would assure that *W* had what she needed for as long as she lives and that thereafter they "would receive everything." How would you advise them concerning the courses of action that might be available to them?

Suppose that *S* and *D* bring a disciplinary complaint against the lawyer, resulting in a state bar decision of censure for incompetence. *S* and *D* then bring a civil suit against the lawyer for damages, plead the decision of censure, and move for judgment on the pleadings on the issue of standard of care. What ruling?

Suppose instead that *F* executed his will four years ago and that his statements were made at that time. After executing his will, *F* had no contact with the lawyer. Assume that no disciplinary complaint was brought. The jurisdiction has a three-year statute of limitations on tort actions and a five-year statute of limitations on contract actions. *S* and *D* bring suit against the attorney for malpractice four years after *F*'s death. What result?

LORRAINE v. GROVER, CIMENT, WEINSTEIN
467 So. 2d 315 (Fla. App. 1985)

NESBITT, J. . . .

Prior to his death, Johnson shared his residence with his mother . . . and his minor son. [His] will contained a provision which left his mother a life estate in the residence with the remainder going to his sons. In the probate proceedings, however, it was determined that the residence was Johnson's homestead and consequently was not subject to devise. See Art. X, §4, Fla. Const.; §732.401-.4015, Fla. Stat. (1981). It therefore passed directly to Johnson's children [because his spouse pre-deceased him]. . . .

The plaintiff, Johnson's mother, instituted the suit against Weinstein, his law firm, and their insurer. The complaint alleges that due to Weinstein's negligence and lack of skill in drafting the will, the devise of the life estate in the residence to the plaintiff failed. Upon motion, the trial court entered a summary final judgment in favor of the defendants. This appeal followed.

Generally, in a negligence action against an attorney, the plaintiff must prove: (1) the attorney's employment by the plaintiff (privity); (2) the attorney's neglect of a reasonable duty owed to the plaintiff; and (3) that such negligence resulted in and was the proximate cause of loss to the plaintiff. Florida courts have recognized, however, that an attorney preparing a will has a duty not only to the testator-client, but also to the testator's intended beneficiaries. In limited circumstances, therefore, an intended beneficiary under a will may maintain a legal malpractice action against the attorney who prepared the will, if through the attorney's negligence a devise to that beneficiary fails. Although it is generally stated that the action can be grounded in theories of either tort (negligence) or contract (third-party beneficiary), the contractual theory is "conceptually superfluous since the crux of the action must lie in tort in any case; there can be no recovery without negligence." In effect, [Florida cases] have established a limited exception in the area of will drafting to the requirement of the first element (the privity requirement) in a legal malpractice action.

On this appeal, the plaintiff argues that Weinstein was negligent in not advising Johnson of the prohibition against devising homestead property and of possible alternatives. As the plaintiff suggests, it may have been possible to structure a conveyance to avoid the constitutional provision by having Johnson make an inter vivos transfer of a vested interest in the residence to her. It is also possible that Johnson might have wanted to devise some other comparable property interest to his mother if he had known of the constitutional prohibition or that the devise might fail. . . .

With regard to the first possibility, there is no indication in the record of any desire on the part of Johnson to make a transfer of any interest in the residence prior to his death. Even if such a desire did exist, however, any alleged negligence attributable to Weinstein's failure to advise Johnson concerning the possibility of an inter vivos transfer falls outside the limited exception . . . to the privity requirement in legal malpractice actions. Generally, an attorney is not liable to third parties for negligence or misadvice given to a client concerning an inter vivos transfer of property. . . .

The holding in DeMaris [v. Asti, 426 So. 2d 1153], encompasses two concepts. First, for an action to fall within the exception, the testamentary intent that has allegedly been frustrated must be "expressed in the will." Second, the beneficiary's loss must be a "direct result of," or proximately caused by the attorney's alleged negligence.

In the present case, there is no indication that Johnson wished or intended any alternative property interest to pass to his mother under the will if the devise of the life estate in the residence failed. An intent to devise a comparable interest in other property upon the failure of the primary devise cannot reasonably be extrapolated from any of the provisions in Johnson's will. Furthermore, a disappointed beneficiary may not prove, by evidence extrinsic to the will, that the testator's testamentary intent was other than that expressed in the will. *DeMaris*. . . .

. . . Johnson's testamentary intent was not frustrated by Weinstein's professional negligence, but rather by Florida's constitution and statutes. Summary judgment for the defendants was therefore proper since any alleged negligence on the part of Weinstein in drafting the will could not have been the cause of the plaintiff's claimed loss.

Upon the foregoing analysis, the summary final judgment is affirmed.

PEARSON, J., dissenting.

As I understand it, . . . the majority declares the attorney to be immune from liability so long as, robot-like, he puts down on paper what the testator tells him to put down. And, according to the majority, if some law which was known or should have been known to the attorney prevents the testator's correctly recorded wishes from being carried out, it is the law, not the attorney, which has frustrated the testamentary intent.

I think it utterly indefensible to say that an attorney's failure to advise a testator that his desired devise is a nullity is any less negligent than an attorney's faulty draftsmanship or improper execution of a will. . . . The liability of an attorney to an intended beneficiary under a will exists because:

> [w]hen an attorney undertakes to fulfill the testamentary instructions of his client, he realistically and in fact assumes a relationship not only with the client but also with the client's intended beneficiaries. The attorney's actions and omissions will affect the success of the client's testamentary scheme; and thus the possibility of thwarting the testator's wishes immediately becomes foreseeable. Equally foreseeable is the possibility of injury to an intended beneficiary. In some ways, the beneficiary's interests loom greater than those of the client. After the latter's death, a failure in his testamentary scheme works no practical effect except to deprive his intended beneficiaries of the intended bequests. Indeed, the executor of an estate has no standing to bring an action for the amount of the bequest against an attorney who negligently prepared the estate plan, since in the normal case the estate is not injured by such negligence except to the extent of the fees paid; only the beneficiaries suffer the real loss.
> . . . [U]nless the beneficiary could recover against the attorney in such a case, no one could do so and the social policy of preventing future harm would be frustrated.

Heyer v. Flaig, 70 Cal. 2d 223, 228, 74 Cal. Rptr. 225, 228-29, 449 P.2d 161, 164-65 (1969).

Not until today has any court suggested that an attorney's liability to an intended beneficiary of a will is limited to cases in which the attorney forgets or ignores the testator's specific instruction. Certainly, no important public policy is served by distinguishing between the negligence of an attorney who fails to do what the client has told him to do, and the negligence of an attorney who does what the client has told him to do in a negligent manner, or, as here, does what the client has told him to do, but fails to advise the client that what the client wants done cannot legally be done. Indeed, these latter forms of negligence are, as they should be, unhesitatingly recognized as actionable when brought by intended beneficiaries. See . . . Lucas v. Hamm, 56 Cal. 2d 583, 15 Cal. Rptr. 821, 364 P.2d 685 (1961) (doctrine of privity no bar to cause of action against attorney by intended beneficiaries under will where testamentary trust created therein was declared invalid as violating rule against perpetuities; cause of action [failed], however, because confusion surrounding rule against perpetuities prevents finding of negligence); . . . Bucquet v. Livingston, 57 Cal. App. 2d 914, 129 Cal. Rptr. 514 (1976) (beneficiaries of inter-vivos trust have cause of action against attorney who failed to advise settlor that provision giving power of revocation to settlor's wife rendered nonmarital half of trust includable in wife's estate resulting in adverse tax consequences and ultimate financial loss to beneficiaries); McAbee v. Edwards, 340 So. 2d 1167 (daughter, intended sole beneficiary of estate, has cause of action against attorney who allegedly misadvised testator that it was unnecessary to change will in order to pretermit husband, whom testator married after will was executed).

I am equally, if not more, disturbed by the majority's conclusion that because there is no expression in the will as to what is to happen upon the failure of the "primary" devise "expressed in the will," that therefore Mr. Johnson had no intent to provide for his mother if a life estate in the homestead could not be devised. The majority's insistence that the appellant is an intended beneficiary of the will only if she could receive a life estate in the homestead is unfounded. Plainly, Mr. Johnson's intent to make his mother a substantial beneficiary of his estate is discernible from the will, and the reason, of course, that the will contains no secondary or alternative devise to the mother is that the testator allegedly was never informed that any was necessary. . . .

The only possible justification for the requirement that the testamentary intent be "expressed in the will," see DeMaris v. Asti, 426 So. 2d 1153, 1154 (Fla. 3d DCA 1983), is to guard against the onslaught of fraudulent claims. But where, as here, the . . . will on its face shows an intent by the testator to provide shelter or its equivalent for his mother during her lifetime in the event of his death, the envisioned horribles are of no concern, and there is thus no justification whatsoever to preclude the mother's action.

Although it may be said that to permit a finding of liability in this case is to contribute to the progressive "assault upon the citadel of privity," it seems to me that to absolve the attorney is to take a giant step backwards. . . .

Standard of Care and Proof of Negligence. See further Horne v. Peckham, 158 Cal. Rptr. 714 (Cal. App. 1979); Smith v. Lewis, 530 P.2d 589 (Cal. 1975); Restatement (Third) of the Law Governing Lawyers §74 (Tentative Draft No. 8, 1997).

Privity. Despite the majority rule recognized in *Lorraine,* a significant minority view continues to recognize the lack-of-privity defense. Cases are collected in Ross, How to Do Right by Not Doing Wrong: Legal and Malpractice Considerations in Estate Planning and Administration, 28 Miami Inst. On Est. Plan. ¶¶800, 802.1 (1994). See also Hazard, Triangular Lawyer Relationships: An Exploratory Analysis, 1 Geo. J. Legal Ethics 15 (1987); Symposium, the Lawyer's Duties and Liabilities to Third Parties, 37 So. Tex. L. Rev. 957 (1996). The Restatement (Third) of the Law Governing Lawyers abandons the privity lens and imposes a duty of care to a non-client when the lawyer "knows that a client intends as one of the primary objectives of the representation that the lawyer's services benefit the non-client"; absence of the duty "would make enforcement of those obligations unlikely." Restatement (Third) of the Law Governing Lawyers §73(3) (Tentative Draft No. 8, 1997). See also id. illus. 2, 3 and 4.

Tort or Contract. Lucas v. Hamm, cited in *Lorraine,* said that the disappointed beneficiary could sue the negligent planner either in tort on a negligence theory or in contract as a third party beneficiary on a theory of breach of an implied duty to use reasonable care and skill. Subsequent California holdings established a tort/negligence theory of recovery. See Ross, supra at ¶801.1. Does it make any difference which theory is used? Compare Restatement (Third) of the Law Governing Lawyers §71 cmt. *c* & Reporter's Note at 7 (Tentative Draft No. 8, 1997).

Statute of Limitations. According to Heyer v. Flaig, quoted in the dissenting opinion in *Lorraine,* the statute of limitations in a testamentary malpractice action starts to run from the date of the testator's death because the intended beneficiary acquires no legal entitlement and has no standing to sue as an injured party until that time. See also Restatement (Third) of the Law Governing Lawyers §76 cmt. *g* (Tentative Draft No. 8, 1997). On the other hand, Hargett v. Holland, 337 N.C. 651, 447 S.E.2d 784 (1994), involved a statute of repose barring actions for professional malpractice more than four years after the "last act of the defendant giving rise to the cause of action." The court held that the "last act" was the negligent misdrafting, not the lawyer's failure to correct the error before the testator died. See Byrne, Let Truth Be Their Devise: *Hargett v. Holland* and the Professional Malpractice Statute of Repose, 73 N.C.L. Rev. 2209 (1995).

Measure of Damages. What is the appropriate measure of damages in a negligent drafting case? If litigation is required to resolve an ambiguity in the instrument, would an award of the costs of litigation to the testator's estate be a more appropriate remedy than an award of the amount of the intended gift to the disappointed beneficiary? See W. McGovern, The Increasing Malpractice Liability of Will Drafters, Trusts & Estates, Dec. 1994, at 10, 14, 18, 22. Compare Restatement (Third) of the Law Governing Lawyers §75 cmts. *c* & *f* (Tentative Draft No. 8, 1997). Would an award for emotional distress, or punitive damages, be recoverable by a (very) disappointed beneficiary? See Id. §75 cmts. *g* and *h.*

On *Malpractice Generally,* see M. Begleiter, Attorney Malpractice in Estate Planning — You've Got to Know When to Hold Up, Know When to Fold Up, 38 U. Kan. L. Rev. 193 (1990); O'Malley, et al., Lawyer Liability in Trusts and Estates Practice SC13 ALI-ABA 177 (1977); J. Pennell, Professional Responsibility: Reforms Are Needed to Accommodate Estate Planning and Family Counseling, 25 Miami Inst. on Est. Pl. ch. 18 (1991).

Relationship of Ethics and Malpractice Rules. The *Scope* statement to the American Bar Association's Model Rules of Professional Conduct (1983) provides: "Violation of a Rule should not give rise to a cause of action nor should it create any presumption that a legal duty has been breached." It adds that the rules "are designed to provide guidance to lawyers and to provide a structure for regulating conduct through disciplinary agencies" and reiterates that they "are not designed as a basis for civil liability." The fundamental rule on *Competence,* Rule 1.1, asserts simply that "A lawyer shall provide competent representation to a client" and explains: "Competent representation requires the legal knowledge, skill, thoroughness and preparation reasonably necessary for the representation."

In marked contrast, the Restatement (Third) of the Law Governing Lawyers §74(2) provides that violation of a rule regulating the conduct of lawyers "may be considered by a trier of fact . . . to the extent that (i) the rule was designed for the protection of persons in the position of the claimant and (ii) proof of the content . . . of such a rule . . . is relevant to the claimant's claim." See also id. §74 cmt. *f,* illus. 3, and Foreword at xxii to xxvi (Proposed Final Draft No. 1, 1996). Compare Hizey v. Carpenter, 119 Wash. 2d 251, 830 P.2d 664 (1992); Lazy Seven Coal Sales, Inc. v. Stone & Hinds, P.C., 813 S.W.2d 400 (Tenn. 1991); Day v. Rosenthal, 170 Cal. App. 3d 1125, 217 Cal. Rptr. 89, cert. denied 106 S. Ct. 1267 (1986).

9

Introduction to Trusts: Their Nature, Classification, and Use

(handwritten margin notes: trust; trustee; beneficiary/cestui que trust; made while alive/by will)

The trust is a device, nearly unique to the Anglo-American legal system,[1] under which property is held by one or more persons for the benefit of others, the management powers and the beneficial interests being separated. The one who holds the property is referred to as the *trustee.* That person usually has legal title to the property interests held in the trust,[2] and as to third parties is considered the owner of the trust property for most purposes. A person for whose benefit the property is held is a *beneficiary* or *cestui que trust.* The trustee is said to be in a fiduciary relationship with the beneficiary. Under this relationship a very high standard of conduct is required of the trustee in handling the property for the beneficiary. A trust is usually created by a transfer of the property to the trustee from the owner, whom we call the *settlor, trustor,* or *grantor.* The transfer may be made while the settlor is alive (that is, an *inter vivos* or *living trust*) or it may be by will (that is, a *testamentary trust*). In some situations the owner of property may declare that henceforth the property is held in trust for another, and by so doing the owner or settlor becomes a trustee without a transfer to another. This is referred to as a *declaration of trust.*

A. Classification of Trusts

The trust with which this course is most concerned is the *express trust.* This is a trust created, either by declaration or through inter vivos or

1. Efforts are currently under way to provide international recognition of trusts under certain circumstances, especially by nations that do not have trusts as a part of their domestic law. In 1984 the fifteenth Session of the Hague Conference on Private International Law approved the Convention on the Law Applicable to Trusts and on Their Recognition, with thirty-three nations, including the United States, participating. (The first signatories were Italy, Luxembourg, and the Netherlands, July 1, 1985, and the United Kingdom of Great Britain and Northern Ireland on January 10, 1986.) See generally Trautman and Gaillard. The Hague Conference Adopts a Convention for Trusts, 124 Tr. & Est. 23 (1985).

2. As will subsequently be seen, equitable interests in property may be held in trust, and in that case legal title will not be in the trustee.

testamentary disposition, by the express and intended direction of the settlor. It is a most flexible and valuable device in that the beneficiaries may be relieved of management responsibilities and liabilities while yet receiving the benefits from the property held in the trust. In this deliberate separation of the managerial and beneficial aspects of the ownership of property, the trustee may be chosen for specialized managerial ability. This has advantages in many different areas, including some other than those we will presently study. For example, the business trust, the investment trust, and the trust deed as a security device all use trust concepts. See generally Langbein, The Secret life of the Trust: The Trust as an Instrument of Commerce, 107 Yale L.J. 165 (1997).

The purposes for which trusts may be created are many. The terms of the trust and the choice of trustees will be greatly affected by the purposes of the arrangement. We are concerned primarily with the usual family purposes of providing an income for life or for minority to immediate members of the family, particularly surviving spouses and children, while postponing distribution of principal to others at a later *in remainder* time — that is, in remainder. In this way a family may be assured means of support over an extended period of time. The main purpose of some trusts is to minimize estate and income taxation. Trusts are also created *charitable purposes* for charitable purposes whereby interests of the public in different endeavors are furthered through a nongovernmental device. The broad scope of charity includes the alleviation of poverty, support of religion or education, and, today, public recreation, as well as certain governmental matters. In short, most things of general interest and benefit to the public are broadly classified as charitable. We will see that there are some instances in which charitable trusts, their creation and administration, differ from the private trust with which we are most concerned. There are, of course, some limitations on the purposes for which a trust may be created. A trust will not be enforced, for example, if it is created to carry out a purpose that is contrary to law or so opposed to public policy that it should not receive the support of the government or of the public. Examples of illegal purposes include *illegal purposes* trusts for the operation of an illegal business or the operation of a business in an illegal fashion; and trusts in restraint of marriage are often contrary to public policy.

Trusts are not only classified in the manner noted above but also as regards the intention of the parties involved. The express trust, for example, is controlled by and is the product of the actual intention of the settlor. On the other hand, there are trusts that are said to arise by *operation of law*, without any expressed intention of the parties. For example, the resulting trust arises out of the inferred intention of the parties although unexpressed. Another so-called trust arising by operation of law is the *constructive trust*. This is a remedial or restitutionary device under which a person who has obtained the title to property by reason of fraud or overreaching or some other unlawful or improper means is considered as holding the property for the person who has been wrongfully deprived of its ownership. Here, obtaining property by fraud is a typical example; however, there are other instances in which the device is used. For example, we have seen that the murderer who receives property by reason of the victim's death may be required to hold the property on constructive trust for the persons to whom the property probably would have gone but for the wrongful action. Among other examples considered later in this course are situations in which a person obtains a device or bequest based on a promise to dispose of it in a particular fashion, and the owner dies relying on this promise.

Still another classification of trusts has to do with the nature of the trust administration and the functions of the trustee. If the trustee is solely to hold title to the property without any affirmative obligations, we say the trust is *passive*. On the other hand, if the trustee is under an affirmative duty to manage the property in some way for the benefit of the beneficiaries, then we say the trust is *active*. Nearly all of our attention will be directed toward the active trust that is created by an expression of intention and for a valid purpose.

1.   Trusts Arising by Operation of Law

a.   Resulting Trusts

The doctrine, antedating the Statute of Uses, 27 Hen. VIII, c. 10 (1536), that when *A* gratuitously conveyed to *B*, a resulting use for *A* presumptively arose, is virtually extinct today. With the enactment of the Statute of Uses, the application of such a rule would render the conveyance an idle act, although it did take some time for the law to recognize that the rule no longer made sense.

A variety of situations today, however, still produce resulting trusts. Basically, they may be grouped under two headings: (1) purchase money resulting trusts and (2) resulting trusts that arise because an express trust fails or makes an incomplete disposition of the trust property — that is, simply equitable reversionary interests. Much will be seen of the second of these types of resulting trusts as the course progresses, but in general it might be noted here that the presumption of a resulting trust in such cases is calculated to effectuate the probable wishes of settlors. The law presumes, if no particular indication of the contrary is found, that the settlor did not intend to confer a beneficial interest on the trustee. If for some reason an express trust fails, in whole or in part, the trustee holds the property or appropriate portions thereof subject to a duty to reconvey to the settlor or to the settlor's estate or successors in interest. So, too, if the property placed in an express trust is excessive for the trust purposes, it is presumed that the excess is to be returned to the settlor or the settlor's successor. Throughout this course you will observe that trusts are frequently attacked by persons whose claims are predicated on assertions of resulting trust.

The purchase money resulting trust also merits some explanation at this point because it sometimes appears in family transactions. It arises, presumptively, when one person pays the purchase price for property but title is taken in the name of another. The titleholder is presumed to hold the property on resulting trust for the person who furnished the consideration. In some states this presumption has been abolished with but limited exceptions. In the others there is an important exception to the resulting trust presumption in this type of situation. The presumption does not arise — or maybe it is rebutted absent other showings of intent — where the person taking title is a natural object of payor's bounty: the overriding inference then is one of gift.[3] One might question whether the real scope of this exception, by which a gift is presumed, is properly defined by the "natural object" standard. Some cases continue to apply the resulting trust presumption where the one taking title is the spouse or parent of the person who paid the purchase price. See generally V W. Fratcher, Scott on Trusts §442 (4th ed. 1989).

Facts or circumstances may overcome the presumption of a purchase money resulting trust, or the reverse presumption that the transaction was a gift because of the relationship of the parties. If an intent to make a gift can be proven, this intent controls. It is also permissible to show and give effect to an agreement that is contrary to the resulting trust presumption. For example, if A pays money to B, who conveys title to C, it may be shown that A's payment was arranged as a loan to C. C then does not hold title for A but is indebted to A.

Courts generally admit evidence of intent quite freely without discussion in these cases, in what might appear to be violations of rules excluding parol evidence. Why is a claim of resulting trust in land not precluded by the Statute of Frauds, which requires trusts of land to be proved by a signed writing? Why is parol evidence admissible in these cases to rebut or reinforce a presumption of resulting trust or gift, as the case may be?

3. In many states a gift has traditionally been presumed when a husband paid for property deeded to his wife, but a resulting trust was presumed when a wife furnished consideration for a deed in the husband's name. But see, e.g., Mims v. Mims, 305 N.C. 41, 286 S.E.2d 779 (1982), expressly overruling contrary cases and establishing a rebuttable presumption of gift in either case on a gender-neutral basis.

STATUTE OF FRAUDS
29 Car. II, c. 3 (1676)

VII. And be it further enacted by the authority aforesaid, that from and after the said four and twentieth day of June [1677] all declarations or creations of trusts or confidences of any lands, tenements or hereditaments, shall be manifested and proved by some writing, signed by the party who is by law enabled to declare such trust, or by his last will in writing, or else they shall be utterly void and of none effect.

VIII. Provided always, that where any conveyance shall be made of any lands or tenements by which a trust or confidence shall or may arise or result by the implication or construction of law, or be transferred or extinguished by an act or operation of law, then and in every such case, such trust or confidence shall be of the like force and effect as the same would have been if this statute had not been made; anything hereinbefore contained to the contrary notwithstanding.

b. Constructive Trusts

POPE v. GARRETT
147 Tex. 18, 211 S.W.2d 559 (1948)

[Suit by Claytonia Garrett against the heirs of Carrie Simons to impress a constructive trust on property that passed to the heirs by intestacy. It was alleged, and found by the jury, that "by physical force or by creating a disturbance" two of the heirs had prevented Carrie Simons, shortly before her death, from executing a will solely in favor of the plaintiff. The trial court entered judgment for the plaintiff as to the whole of the property. The Court of Civil Appeals reversed in part, holding that a trust should not be impressed on the interests of those heirs who had not participated in the wrongdoing.]

SMEDLEY, J. . . .

The case is a typical one for the intervention of equity to prevent a wrongdoer, who by his fraudulent or otherwise wrongful act has acquired title to property, from retaining and enjoying the beneficial interest therein, by impressing a constructive trust on the property in favor of the one who is truly and equitably entitled to the same. . . .

It has been said that "[t]he specific instances in which equity impresses a constructive trust are numberless — as numberless as the modes by which property may be obtained through bad faith and unconscientious acts." Pomeroy's Equity Jurisprudence, 5th Ed., Vol. 4, p. 97, Sec. 1045. . . .

Citing Hutchins v. Hutchins, 7 Hill, N. Y., 104, the defendants, Pope et al., make the contention that plaintiff, Claytonia Garrett, is not enti-

tled to any relief because she had no existing right in the property of
Carrie Simons and thus was deprived by the acts of the defendants of
nothing but an expectancy or hope to become a devisee. That case was
an action at law for damages, the plaintiff alleging that the defendants,
by false and fraudulent representations, induced his father to revoke
a will in his favor and to execute a new one by which he was excluded
from all participation in his father's estate. It was held that the plaintiff
had no cause of action for damages because, according to the allegations of his declaration, he had no interest in the property beyond a
mere maked possibility. Mr. Scott, citing the *Hutchins* case and two
other like decisions and several decisions to the contrary, recognizes
the conflict of authority on the question whether an action at law will
lie against the heir for tort, but expresses his opinion that clearly a
court of equity should prevent the heir from keeping the property
which he has acquired by the result of his wrongful conduct and that
the heir should be compelled to surrender the property to the intended legatee, since but for the wrong he would have received the
property, and this even though the intended legatee had no interest
in the property of the testator but only an expectancy. Scott on Trusts,
Vol. 3, pp. 2371, 2372, Sec. 489.4. This opinion is supported by the
authorities above cited and by many others.

The argument is often made that the imposition of the constructive
trust in a case like this contravenes or circumvents the statute of descent
and distribution, the statute of wills, the statute of frauds, or particularly a statute which prohibits the creation of a trust unless it is declared
by an instrument in writing. It is generally held, however, that the constructive trust is not within such statutes or is an exception to them. It
is the creature of equity. It does not arise out of the parol agreement
of the parties. It is imposed irrespective of and even contrary to the
intention of the parties. Resort is had to it in order that a statute enacted for the purpose of preventing fraud may not be used as an instrument for perpetrating or protecting a fraud.

In this case Claytonia Garrett does not acquire title through the will.
The trust does not owe its validity to the will. The statute of descent
and distribution is untouched. The legal title passed to the heirs of
Carrie Simons when she died intestate, but equity deals with the holder
of the legal title for the wrong done in preventing the execution of
the will and impresses a trust on the property in favor of the one who
is in good conscience entitled to it.

The second question is more difficult. Shall the trust in favor of Claytonia Garrett extend to the interests of the heirs who had no part in
the wrongful acts? From the viewpoint of those heirs, it seems that they
should be permitted to retain and enjoy the interests that vested in
them as heirs, no will having been executed, and they not being responsible for the failure of Carrie Simons to execute it. On the other hand,

extend trust
... no reward
for heirs who
wronged

from the viewpoint of Claytonia Garrett, it appears that a court of equity should extend the trust to all of the interests in the property in order that complete relief may be afforded her and that none of the heirs may profit as the result of the wrongful acts.

There are few decisions in point, and they are conflicting. . . .

The texts of Scott, Bogert and Perry seem to support [the view that a constructive trust] should be impressed even though the wrongful conduct because of which the title was acquired is that of a third person. Scott on Trusts, Vol. 3, pp. 2374–2376, Secs. 489.5, 489.6; Bogert's Trusts and Trustees, Vol. 3, p. 1467, Sec. 473; Perry on Trusts, 3d Ed., Vol. 1, pp. 260, 261, Sec. 211. The same is true of the Restatement. See illustrations 17 and 18, under Sec. 184, p. 754, Restatement of the Law of Restitution.

The policy against unjust enrichment argues in favor of the judgment rendered herein by the district court rather than that of the Court of Civil Appeals. But for the wrongful acts the innocent defendants would not have inherited interests in the property. Dean Roscoe Pound speaks of the constructive trust as a remedial institution and says that it is sometimes used "to develop a new field of equitable interposition, as in what we have come to think the typical case of constructive trust, namely, specific restitution of a received benefit in order to prevent unjust enrichment." 33 Harvard Law Review, pp. 420, 421. . . .

but for the
wrongful acts
innocent Δs
would not
have inherited in
interests in
the property

We realize that a constructive trust does not arise on every moral wrong and that it cannot correct every injustice. 54 Am. Jur., p. 169, Sec. 218. It must be used with caution, especially where as here proof of the wrongful act rests in parol, in order that it may not defeat the purposes of the statute of wills, the statute of descent and distribution, or the statute of frauds.

In the instant case the findings of the jury are well supported by the testimony of four disinterested, unimpeached witnesses, although their testimony is contradicted by that of two of the defendants. The will devising the property to the plaintiff, Claytonia Garrett, which Carrie Simons was prevented from executing, was introduced in evidence. In view of the authorities and equitable principles which have been cited and discussed, it is our opinion that the judgment of the district court should be affirmed in order that complete justice may be done.

dmt for π
constructive
trust should
be granted

The judgment of the Court of Civil Appeals is reversed and the judgment of the district court is affirmed.

See also Rogers v. Rogers, 63 N.Y.2d 582, 473 N.E.2d 226 (1984) (imposing a constructive trust on life insurance proceeds paid in violation of separation agreement, regardless of whether the designated recipient was innocent and without notice).

2. Active and Passive Trusts

STATUTE OF USES
27 Hen. VIII. c. 10 (1536)

That where any person or persons stand or be seised, or at any time hereafter shall happen to be seised, of . . . lands . . . to the use, confidence or trust of any person or persons, or of any body politick, . . . in every such case, all and every such person and persons, shall from henceforce stand and be seised . . . of . . . the same . . . lands . . . in such like estates as they had or shall have in use, trust or confidence. . . .

How, despite this statute, did the modern trust as we know it develop in England and in the American states that treat the Statute of Uses as a part of their common law? Obviously the statute does not execute all uses, and the typical trust of today must be an unexecuted use that is not within the scope of the statute for some reason. In drawing a trust instrument it is certainly not necessary to create a use on a use, or to transfer the property "to *T* to his own use to the use of *B*," the beneficiary, as in Doe v. Passingham, 6 B. & C. 305 (1827).

To what extent do procedures or the rights of interested parties vary depending on whether particular interests are legal or equitable?

Craig v. Kimsey, 370 Ill. 321, 324–325, 18 N.E.2d 895, 896 (1938), states:

> In construing the Statute of Uses three rules are applied whereby conveyances are excepted from its operation, viz: (1) Where a use was limited upon a use; (2) where a copyhold or leasehold estate or personal property was limited to uses; (3) where such powers or duties were imposed, with the estate, upon a donee to uses that it was necessary that he should continue to hold the legal title in order to perform his duty or execute the power. . . .
>
> It is true, as argued, that the [beneficiary] is permitted to collect the rents of the real estate and to have possession and control of the personal property. Nevertheless, the trust is far from passive. The duty is cast upon the trustees to determine if it is in the best interest of the [beneficiary] to sell the real estate and otherwise invest it. In such case it is their duty to sell, to determine whether the sale shall be public or private, to make the necessary conveyances and, in that event, to control and manage the property applying the income therefrom to the support and maintenance of the [beneficiary]. Where a trustee is required to make a conveyance he will take such title as will enable him to perform his duty and that, in this case, would be a fee simple.

HOOPER v. FELGNER
80 Md. 262, 30 A. 911 (1894)

ROBINSON, C.J. . . .

Where an estate is given to trustees and their heirs, upon trust to receive and pay the net income thereof to one for life, and, upon his death, in trust for all and singular his children and the issue of such children living at the death of the life tenant, the trust ceases upon the death of such life tenant, for the reason that it remains no longer an active trust. In such cases the statute of uses executes the use in those who are limited to take upon the expiration of the life estate, or, in other words, the statute transfers the use into possession, by converting the estate or interest of the cestui que trust into a legal estate, thereby determining the intermediate estate of the trustee. As to the real estate, it is clear, therefore, that . . . the trust was thereby at an end.

Now, as to the personal property, though it has been said that the object of the statute was to abolish all uses and trusts, yet, as the language of the statute was, "whenever any person is seised" etc., the English courts, by a strict construction, held that it did not apply to personal property, for the reason that one could not be said to be "seised" of a mere chattel interest. At the same time, however, it may be considered settled that a trust in regard to personal property will continue so long and no longer than the purposes of the trust require; and that, when all the objects of the trust have been accomplished, the person entitled to the beneficial use is regarded as the absolute owner, and as such entitled to the possession of the property. . . . Nor can we agree . . . that . . . the minority of one of the cestuis que trustent is any reason why the trust should continue until she is suijuris. . . . There can be no reason why the trust should continue merely to allow the trustees to receive the income, and pay it over to her guardians. . . .

RESTATEMENT (THIRD) OF TRUSTS
(Tent. Draft approved 1999)

§42. *Extent of Trustee's Title.* Unless a different intention is manifested, or the settlor owned only a lesser interest, the trustee takes an interest of unlimited duration in the trust property and not an interest limited to the duration of the trust.

Restatement (Second) of Trusts §88 had stated the same rule for personal property but limited the trustee of an interest in *land* to "such an estate, and only such an estate, as is necessary to enable him to perform the trust." Comment *a* to §42 (above) finds this latter limit "counterproductive and no longer justified."

B. Nature of Trusts

It might be helpful to look briefly at the American Law Institute's definition of a trust and then to see what things are said not to be trusts. To state what classes of relationships are not trusts is a relatively simple matter, but to decide whether a particular set of facts gives rise to one of these classes of nontrust relationships or to a trust is another matter. Yet the determination of whether an arrangement is a trust or something else may materially affect the substantive rights of the persons involved and the procedure by which those rights are enforced.

RESTATEMENT (THIRD) OF TRUSTS
(Tent. Draft approved 1996)

§2. *Definition of Trust.* A trust, as the term is used in this Restatement when not qualified by the word "resulting" or "constructive," is a fiduciary relationship with respect to property, arising as a result of a manifestation of an intention to create that relationship and subjecting the person who holds title to the property to duties to deal with it for the benefit of charity or for one or more persons, *the beneficiaries.* at least one of whom is not the sole trustee.

The Restatement then goes on to indicate, by way of distinction, what things are *not* trusts. It lists (§5): successive legal estates; decedents' estates; guardianships and conservatorships; receiverships and bankruptcy trusteeships; durable powers of attorney and other agencies; bailments and leases; relationships of corporate officers or directors to corporations and shareholders (with commentary and notes encompassing partnership and limited liability company relationships); conditions and equitable charges; contracts to convey and certain contracts for the benefit of third parties; assignments and partial assignments of choses in action; relationships of debtors to creditors; and mortgages, deeds of trust, pledges, liens, and other security arrangements. Various other devices using a "trust" label (e.g., voting trusts, business trusts, land trusts, and investment trusts) are primarily regulated by other bodies of law and excluded from Restatement coverage (cmt. *l*); but custodianships for minors under Uniform Transfers to Minors Acts, while not technically trusts, are referred to as "virtual trusts" and involve a relationship to which Restatement rules generally apply (cmt. *a*, and also see §1, cmt. *a*).

How does a court go about deciding cases in which the outcome is affected by its characterization of an unclear relationship as a trust or something else? Does it look for an "appropriate result" between the parties and then find that relationship which supports the desired result? Or does it look at the facts, somehow decide what relationship exists, and let the chips fall as they may? Throughout the course, as well as in the cases that follow, watch for ways in which these characterizations matter. Even in counseling, the choice of the type of relationship to be created may be affected by these differences — and, of course, in a lawyer-planned transaction no uncertainty should be left about the intended relationship.

PROBLEMS

9-A.   A mother purchased a $50,000 policy of insurance on her life, naming her son as the beneficiary of the proceeds if he survived her. The settlement option selected by the mother called for the insurer to pay the beneficiary interest at the rate of 5 percent on the face amount until he reached age 30, at which time he was to receive the $50,000. The mother died, survived by her son, who is now age 25 and in dire need of more than $2500 per year to pay the costs of his law school education. The son brings suit against the insurer, asking that so much of the policy amount be paid to him as the court deems necessary for his education. Is there a trust of the policy amount? Why or why not? What difference does it make? See McLaughlin v. Equitable Life Assurance Soc., 112 N.J. Eq. 344, 164 A. 579 (1933); Restatement (Third) of Trusts §5 cmt. a, illus. 2; and compare Chapter 13, section D.2.[4]

9-B.   SoftWear Corporation maintained an unincorporated welfare association (WelFare) to provide health insurance for its employees. WelFare was funded by dues that were automatically deducted from the paychecks of the employees. No funds were actually deposited in a separate account; rather, the matter was handled as a bookkeeping entry. As funds were needed to pay insurance premiums, SoftWear simply paid them from its general accounts. SoftWear became bankrupt, owing over $5 million to its many general creditors, plus showing on its books an obligation of about $1 million to WelFare. Is there a trust of the welfare association dues? Why or why not? What difference does it make? See McKee v. Paradise, 299 U.S. 119 (1936); Restatement (Third) of Trusts §5, cmt. k; and compare Chapter 9, section D.3.

---

4. It has been suggested that life insurers offer, as an additional settlement option, a trust with the insurance company acting as trustee of the proceeds of the policy. See Phillips, Toward a Trust Settlement Option, 24 Chartered Life Underwriters J. 38 (1970). Nothing seems to have come of this suggestion, although insurance companies have often been granted trust powers by corporate charter or enabling legislation.

Under the traditional and still prevalent concept, a trust is not a separate legal entity. This means, for example, that a trustee is to be sued individually; suit is not brought against the trust, or against the trustee in a representative (or fiduciary) capacity. A successful suit results in a judgment against the trustee personally, who is then left to seek reimbursement from the trust estate if the trustee had acted properly. Another result of the traditional concept is that a trustee's promissory note to the trust cannot be trust property; there being no "trust" entity, the debt can only be to the trustee — and one cannot be indebted to oneself! For illustrative recent cases struggling to cope with the traditional concept, see McBee v. Vandecnocke Revocable Trust, 1998 W.L. 201743 (Mo. App. 1998) (unpublished); and Mighty Oak Trust v. Nickel, 64 Cal. App. 4th 545, 75 Cal Rptr. 2d 312 (1998).

There seems to be no harm and considerable advantage in recognizing trusts as legal entities. Lawyers commonly speak and act as if they were, and income tax rules have long treated the trust as an entity separate from the trustee. E.g., Internal Revenue Code (Subchapter J) §§641-679. Also, the earlier Restatement position that a trustee's note could not be trust property is reversed in Restatement (Third) of Trusts §2, cmt. i, and §40, cmt. b. Most importantly, there is increasing statutory and other recognition of the trust as a legal entity, especially allowing third parties' suits against trustees in their representative capacities, normally resulting in a judgment, effectively, against the trust. See id. §2, cmts. a and i, and Reporter's Notes thereto (citing statutes); and Uniform Trust Code §1010.

C. Reasons for Using Trusts

Although trusts may be established for any of a great variety of reasons, certain particularly common reasons are mentioned at this point. Obviously the list is far from complete.

1. Testamentary Trusts

Property Management. Of potential importance in planning the testamentary affairs of virtually every individual is the problem of providing for the management of property that may be given to persons who are legally or practically unable to manage it for themselves. Most frequently this problem arises with regard to minor beneficiaries and persons who are elderly or inexperienced in business matters. Even where both spouses are able and willing to manage their own property and all children are adults, the client should be led to consider the possible need to provide property management for grandchildren in the event an adult child should predecease the client. Rarely are management problems wholly absent, but they may be met in a variety of ways. For example, a legally competent but inexperienced individual may employ investment counsel and agents, and the property of a minor or incompetent may be handled by a conservator or other legally appointed fiduciary, whatever the local terminology. Often, however, trust arrangements will be considered preferable by the client when the matter is fully discussed with a lawyer. Agencies traditionally terminate in the event of subsequent incompetency; and regardless of the availability of investment counsel, property in the hands of an elderly or inexperienced person is exposed to possible neglect or imprudence. For minors, guardianship is typically cumbersome, inflexible, and costly and complicated by uncertainty. By contrast the trustees make most of their decisions without the cost and delay of court proceedings for orders or instructions. Trust flexibility is almost as unlimited as the combined imaginations of settlor and lawyer; and unnecessary uncertainties can be removed by proper planning and drafting. In general, then, the trust device can be personally tailored — much like the rest of the will itself — while the guardianship device provided by law necessarily lacks this advantage — somewhat as does the law of intestacy.

Providing for Successive, Concurrent, and Limited Enjoyment. The trust offers numerous advantages over arrangements involving successive legal estates, such as the incessantly troublesome life estate and remainder situation. Normally the trust offers greater assurance of the protection of the future interest, and there is generally a greater certainty regarding the rights of the parties. Although the legal life tenant may be granted powers similar to those of a trustee, the drafting problems are increased by the very nature of successive legal estates and divided ownership, particularly where some of the remainder beneficiaries are underage or unascertained. Certain managerial powers inhere in the office of trustee, and considerable advantage follows from the mere fact that a trustee generally holds full legal title to the subject matter of the trust. Furthermore, greater flexibility and judicial assistance are usually available to deal with unanticipated situations and problems not covered by the terms of the trust. Particular difficulties are encountered with regard to successive legal interests in certain types of personal property, such as chattels that are normally consumed in their use. On the other hand, other types of personalty, such as art objects, may satisfactorily be the subject matter of legal life interests and remainders.

Trust flexibility also permits the rights of intended beneficiaries to be tailored to the precise wishes and concerns of the settlor. (Cf. M. Langley, Trust Me, Baby, Wall St. J. at A1 (Nov. 17, 1999).) The interest of beneficiaries can be limited or adjusted to changed circumstances, and contingent or other special provisions can be made for persons who are not primary beneficiaries of the property owner. Again, the trust for a surviving spouse and the trust for minor children provide ready examples — applicable even to the young family with only a life insurance estate. In these and other cases, dispositive flexibility, although often overlooked, is likely to be more important than management considerations. Assume a young client, *C,* who is married and has three small children. *C* would leave everything to his or her spouse, *S,* if *S* survives, except for a concern that, should *S* remarry, the property is likely to be left later to the second spouse or, in part at least, to the children of the second marriage. If *C* has sufficient insurance or other assets to make these concerns and a trust realistic, the trust can be used to provide for *S,* and even in a limited way (such as for emergencies) for *S*'s second family if *C* wishes, while still assuring that *C*'s property (or what remains) will eventually go to *C*'s own children or their families. We must also plan for the possibility that *S* will predecease *C* or that they will die of a common disaster while their children are still small. This requires an alternative plan for the benefit of orphaned minors, plus naming a personal guardian. The usual equal shares left outright to the children, by will or intestacy, will be held in three separate guardianship estates. Because of the inevitably different needs (such as medical and dental expenses) of the children over their different periods of minority, the results are apt to be very different from the type of equality envisaged by the parents. In fact, the share of one child may prove inadequate for that child's needs, while the other children receive tidy sums as they enter their adult lives. And the smaller the estate the more serious these problems tend to be. If *C* prefers, however, the trust offers a variety of other solutions. For example, a single family trust can provide flexibly for the needs of all the children, with the corpus to be divided equally among them when the youngest reaches maturity or some specified age. If *C* wishes, the trusts for *S* and the children can be designed to provide also for emergency needs of *C*'s parents or others, such as the family of the children's personal guardian, maybe on the condition that such payments will not jeopardize the security of the primary beneficiaries during their minorities. The foregoing are but suggestive of the many ways in which trusts can usefully be employed to permit concurrent and successive enjoyment of even limited family wealth.

Tax Purposes. Where substantial amounts are involved, as we observed in the material on taxation at the end of the previous chapter, trusts can be used to reduce or eliminate taxation of property later in the hands of the beneficiaries or in their estates.

First, trusts have been employed traditionally to prevent additional estate and inheritance taxation on the death of the testator's primary beneficiary or beneficiaries, while still conferring on them the protection and many of the benefits of the trust property. These opportunities under federal law were reduced but not eliminated by the enactment of the generation-skipping transfer tax first in 1976 and then in revised form in 1986. The trust's potential tax benefits to younger generation beneficiaries are still significant; and its benefits in planning for a surviving spouse and others not of "younger generations" were not impaired by that legislation. For example, *A* may leave her estate to *T* in trust to pay income to her husband, *H*, for life, and then to pay income to their child, *C*, for life, with the remainder to be distributed thereafter to *C*'s then living issue. Death taxation of the trust principal will be avoided on *H*'s death and can again be avoided (to the extent of up to $1 million of original corpus) on *C*'s death; this will be so, you may recall, even though *T* has broad authority to invade principal for the benefit of *H* and *C*, and even though *H* or *C* has power, subject to slight limitation, to decide how the property is to pass on the survivor's death (a nongeneral power of appointment).

Second, the testator may reduce the beneficiaries' income tax burdens by use of trusts. Even the trust just described offers some saving of income taxes because capital gains are normally taxable to the trust as a separate entity. Significant income tax savings can be achieved, however, through the proper use of discretionary trusts under which the trustee holds some power to select the recipients of the trust's income. Modest savings may also result from trusts that authorize distribution or accumulation of income in the trustee's discretion.

These and other tax-saving opportunities were alluded to in the prior chapter and can be studied thoroughly in other courses. The subsequent materials in this book do not cover tax law or tax aspects of estate planning specifically, but they do attempt to reflect new and special problems of trust law and fiduciary administration that are created by current tax laws or that arise out of tax-motivated behavior.

2. Inter Vivos Trusts

Living trusts may be subdivided, basically, into those that are revocable and those that are irrevocable. Which of these types will be used depends on the purposes the settlor has in mind. Some of the more common purposes of living trusts are indicated in the following paragraphs.

Avoidance of Probate. One of the important uses of the *revocable* trust is as a will substitute, to dispose of property without its being subjected to estate administration on the settlor's death. Estate administration involves delays, sometimes of several years, and significant expenses that are, in large measure, dependent on the size of the probate estate. These costs and delays may be reduced through the use of a revocable trust, although the ultimate distribution of a living trust may, in part at least, have to await completion of certain phases of estate proceedings, particularly the handling of tax matters. Also, trustee's fees will be incurred when a corporate or professional trustee is employed; however, a family member may be better able to cope as trustee with the problems of trust administration than as executor with those of a decedent's estate. The inter vivos trust also offers continuity, which may be important in the case of "sensitive" assets (such as a business interest) held in trust and for purpose of maintaining income flow to persons who would not qualify for a family allowance under local probate law. Like joint tenancy, trusts of property located outside the domicile are sometimes used to avoid ancillary estate administration proceedings. Living trusts also permit privacy to be preserved, in contrast to the public nature of proceedings in the administration of estates. All of the reasons for — and shortcomings of — using revocable trusts to avoid probate cannot be fully developed at this point, but as the course progresses the student should watch for the problems and opportunities inherent in such planning. It will also be important for you to become acquainted with the ways in which fees of executors and trustees, and their attorneys, are generally determined in your community, so that these matters may be seen in a realistic context. (See generally Chapter 17, section B.)

Property Management. Revocable living trusts are often superior to agency arrangements as methods of obtaining qualified supervision and handling of one's property. A revocable trust may be appropriate for one who is preoccupied with other affairs, unskilled in property management, fearful of senility, or merely likely to be absent at inconvenient times. In the event of legal incapacity, under traditional principles an agency terminates. Distasteful legal proceedings may be required to establish incompetency in order to vest managerial powers in an appropriate person, who then operates under the handicaps of the legal machinery provided for administering the estates of incompetents. (In recent years, the so-called durable power of attorney has been introduced through the Uniform Probate Code or its counterparts, allowing the agency relation to survive incompetency, if desired, but not death.) Under like situations, an inter vivos trust would normally continue uninterrupted in accordance with its presumably convenient provisions. In addition, living trusts offer a measure of protection against one's own imprudence, although interests retained by the settlor even in an irrevocable trust cannot be immunized from the claims of the settlor's creditors, at least under federal bankruptcy law.

Tax Purposes. Gifts, whether outright or in trust, are of advantage particularly to the wealthy as a means of shifting income from property to persons in lower tax brackets and as a means of removing assets from the taxable estate of the donor at death. The same reasons that encourage the use of a testamentary trust in lieu of outright bequests also encourage the use of gifts in trust as replacements for outright gifts inter vivos. In addition, gifts in trust may be made in a manner that will assure the accomplishment of certain objectives of the settlor, but here care must be exercised to avoid retention of interests or powers that may jeopardize the tax objectives. The use of trusts as means of making gifts also gives rise to special gift tax problems, but these tend to be relatively minor and can sometimes be avoided by proper planning. Generally, then, tax-motivated gifts may be made in a form more suitable to the donor's objectives through the use of trusts, especially in the case of gifts to minors; and occasionally trusts may be used for income tax advantages where the donor could not afford to make an outright gift. Because of the strict "grantor rules" of the income and estate tax laws (see pages 286 and 291-292, above), great care is required in the planning and drafting of inter vivos trusts that are intended to shift income tax burdens or to reduce the settlor's taxable estate at death or both. Inter vivos trusts that are tax motivated are necessarily *irrevocable*. Basically, wholly revocable trusts offer no tax advantages, and irrevocable inter vivos trusts are rarely used for any but tax reasons.

"Devious" Objectives. Trusts have, historically and in modern times, been used to circumvent or to attempt to circumvent legal policies. In the hands of resourceful lawyers and judges, the trust device has been an effective tool of avoidance — sometimes of outmoded rules, rigid concepts of technical disabilities, and sometimes of legitimate fiscal and social policies. It has been a constructive force for justice in individual cases and for innovation and progress in the law. As in feudal times, however, it continues to confound tax administrators and reformers. One of the most obvious illustrations of its role in policy avoidance is the use of revocable trusts to circumvent the forced heirship rights of a surviving spouse. A recent development is the use of offshore or even onshore trusts (in some states) to protect assets from divorcing spouses or general creditors or to evade the limitations of the Rule Against Perpetuities or other rules of social policy. These problems and others will be taken up in subsequent chapters.

D.   The Elements of a Trust

RESTATEMENT (THIRD) OF TRUSTS
(Tent. Draft approved 1996)

§13. *Intention to Create Trust.*   A trust is created only if the settlor properly manifests an intention to create a trust relationship.

§2. *Comment f. The elements of a trust.*   A trust involves three elements: (1) a trustee, who holds the trust property and is subject to duties to deal with it for the benefit of one or more others; (2) one or more beneficiaries, to whom and for whose benefit the trustee owes the duties with respect to the trust property; and (3) trust property, which is held by the trustee for the beneficiaries.

Although all three elements are present in a complete trust, either or both of elements (1) and (2) above may be temporarily absent without destroying the trust or preventing its creation.

See also Uniform Trust Code §402 (draft, Feb. 2000).

1.   Intention to Create a Trust

A manifestation of the settlor's intention to create a trust is essential to the existence of an express trust. Normally the creating instrument leaves no doubt about this intent, but an unfortunate amount of litigation is caused by precatory language in wills, particularly but not only those drawn without aid of a lawyer. Are such words intended to be binding and to create a trust, or are they mere suggestions for the legatee or devisee to follow or disregard as he wishes? Although the presence or absence of trust language is likely to be persuasive, the use of the word, "trust" does not *compel* a finding of intent to create a trust; nor does the failure to use the word *prevent* it.

PROBLEM

9-C.   *A*'s will bequeathed $50,000 "to my son, *B*, with the request that he use whatever he thinks appropriate to provide for the welfare of my sister, *C*."

(a) Does *B* take the money outright, or is he obligated to make provision for *C*? What other information would you want to know?

(b) Would the problem be different if *A* had left the money "with the request that *B* make such use of it for my family and friends as he thinks I would deem appropriate"? Why?

(c) How do these dispositions differ from a bequest by *A* to "*B* for life, remainder to such of *B*'s issue as *B* shall appoint by deed or will"; or a bequest to "*B* for life, remainder to such person or persons as *B* shall appoint by deed or will"?

COMFORD v. CANTRELL
177 Tenn. 553, 151 S.W.2d 1076 (1941)

GREEN, C.J. . . .

James G. Cantrell was the owner of valuable property on Fifth Avenue in Nashville which he devised to his wife. She was advised that she took an estate in fee under her husband's will and proceeded to dispose of the property by her will. Certain relatives of the husband, mentioned by his will in a connection that will hereafter appear, insist that Mrs. Cantrell took the property impressed with a trust in their favor at her death.

After certain provisions not here material, Cantrell's will continued:

> Third: I give, devise and bequeath all the rest, residue and remainder of my estate and property of whatsoever kind and nature, wherever situated, both real and personal, to which I am entitled, or which I may have the power to dispose of at my death, to my wife, Clara Augusta Cantrell, to be her absolute estate forever; but if said Clara Augusta Cantrell dies in my lifetime, I then bequeath the property described in the next succeeding paragraph to the persons and in accordance with the request therein contained.
>
> Fourth: It is my request that upon her death my said wife, Clara Augusta Cantrell, shall give, devise and bequeath my interest in the following described property in Nashville, Tennessee, to-wit; (Description follows)
>
> One quarter interest in my interest of the property described in the fourth section of this will to each of my brothers, Harvey W. Cantrell, Lee Cantrell and Julian W. Cantrell, or their heirs, and one quarter interest in my interest in said property to Charles E. Boisseau, Jr., and his sister Marguerite Boisseau, to be held by them jointly during the life of said Marguerite Boisseau, and at her death, the interest of said Marguerite Boisseau to revert to said Charles E. Boisseau or his heirs.

As observed by the chancellor, the testator used strong language in describing the character of the estate conferred upon his wife under his will. He said it was "to be her absolute estate forever." Absolute means without limitation or restriction. The word forever is almost invariably used in an instrument which creates an estate in fee simple. Forever is said to be an adjunct of a fee-simple estate. This will was obviously prepared by a lawyer and it is hard to conceive of words more clearly designed to pass a fee-simple estate than those quoted above.

Such being the will before us, we think the case falls under the authority of Smith v. Reynolds, 173 Tenn. 579, 121 S.W.2d 572, 574. In that case the court reviewed earlier decisions and re-affirmed the rule that a clear and certain devise of a fee, about which the testamentary intention was obvious, would not be cut down or lessened by subsequent words which are ambiguous or of doubtful meaning. Although the will said that the estate devised to his wife "is by my wish returned to my nearest blood kin" at her death, the court held that the wife took the fee, it having been clearly and without ambiguity given to her previously in the instrument. The court said that the testator did not use the word wish as a command. And further that a trust would not be declared on the basis of precatory words where the will showed an intention to leave property absolutely.

In Smith v. Reynolds the court noted the change in the trend of authority as to the force of precatory words. . . .

In 1 Bogert on Trusts and Trustees, §48, it is said:

> The words "request," "desire," and the like, do not naturally import a legal obligation. But the early view in England was that such words, when used in a will, were to be given an unnatural meaning, and were to be held to be courteous and softened means of creating duties enforceable by the courts. According to that opinion words of request prima facie created a trust. But since the beginning of the nineteenth century the English courts have changed their stand upon this question, and now hold that the natural significance of precatory words is not a trust, but that such an obligation may be shown by other portions of the instrument or by extrinsic circumstances. The American courts have adopted this natural construction of precatory expressions. . . .

Counsel for defendants rely on Daly v. Daly, 142 Tenn. 242, 218 S.W. 213, in which precatory words were treated as imperative. There, however, the court analyzed the whole will and showed that throughout the testator used such words as expressing a command rather than a mere desire. In Daly v. Daly our earlier cases were all set out and need not here be considered. In none of these cases was a trust held to exist where the recipient of the gift was to take it as an "absolute estate forever." These words are just incompatible with any other interest in the estate. . . .

[T]he decree of the chancellor must be affirmed.

The outcome of a case of this type will be influenced by a variety of factors. Courts tend to favor a "natural result" and are thus interested in the relationship and circumstances of the parties. The case for a trust would be strengthened by the fact that the bequest and suggestion are made to a fiduciary, such as the executor, or that clear and detailed instructions have been provided in the will. See generally G. Bogert, Trusts and Trustees §48 (rev. 2d ed. 1984). For one of the increasingly rare cases of a trust based on precatory language ("and I hereby request"), see Trustees of First Methodist Church v. Attorney General, 359 Mass. 658, 270 N.E.2d 905 (1971).

With these trust problems compare that of the nontrust "precatory remainder": A left his residuary estate to B, adding that "upon B's death, it is my desire that the property be divided among C, D, and E." See In re Wilson's Estate, 367 Mich. 143, 116 N.W.2d 215 (1962) (bequest to B absolute). See also Page v. Buchfinck, 202 Neb. 411, 275

N.W.2d 826 (1979) (bequest "upon the hope, desire and belief that ...."). Such cases pose other issues than that of intention. See Problem 5-G in Chapter 5. See also the classic dissent of Chief Justice Vanderbilt in Fox v. Snow, 6 N.J. 12, 76 A.2d 877 (1950) (no remainder due to so-called doctrine of repugnancy applied as a rule of law, not of intent).

Where a client wishes to leave property to another "with the suggestion, but without requiring" that he use it for a particular purpose, the lawyer should consider whether from a tax viewpoint it might be preferable to create a trust or otherwise to impose a legal duty on the recipient. Cf. Delaney v. Gardner, 204 F.2d 855 (1st Cir. 1953).

2. The Trustee

a. Necessity of Trustee

Because of the very nature of a trust, its operation requires that there be a trustee. It is a well-settled and basic principle, however, that once a trust is established it will not fail merely because of the trustee's death, incapacity, resignation, or removal. A successor will be appointed unless it quite clearly appears that the trust was to continue only so long as the designated trustee continues to act. Thus, the rule is stated: *A trust will not fail for want of a trustee.* See generally Restatement (Third) of Trusts §31.

Where the trustee named in a will predeceases the testator or disclaims, it is clear that a trustee will be appointed unless a contrary intention is manifested. In Hiles v. Garrison, 70 N.J. Eq. 605, 62 A. 865 (1906), the will left "all my property [to] be put in trust, and the income be divided between my brother, [my] sister, . . . and my wife." Once the court concluded that the intent to create a trust existed, it readily concluded that the failure to name a trustee "will not prevent the execution of the trust, for the court will always appoint a trustee wherever necessary to sustain the trust." 70 N.J. Eq. at 607, 62 A. at 865.

At the stage of trust creation, however, the absence of a trustee sometimes poses other complications because of its effect on the requirement, to be studied later, that a trust be created by a transfer of trust property. The preceding discussion involved wills, and an effective testamentary transfer requires only that the testator die with a will in force. Different issues arise when one attempts to create a trust by inter vivos transfer to a would-be trustee who is dead, undetermined, or legally incapable of taking title. In Frost v. Frost, 202 Mass. 100, 88 N.E. 446 (1909), the insured purported to assign his life insurance policies to "the trustees to be named in my will." The court found that the quoted language referred to the trustees under whatever will might finally be admitted to probate on the insured's death. The court then stated: "Upon the facts of this case these assignments never took effect within the lifetime of the assignor, for want of assignees, and never took effect after his death for want of proper attestation. There was therefore nothing upon which to base the contemplated trust, and it was never perfected." 202 Mass. at 103, 88 N.E. at 448. But cf. Wittmeier v. Heiligenstein, 308 Ill. 434, 139 N.E. 871 (1923), in Chapter 11, section A.

b. Successor and Substitute Trustees

On the death of one of several cotrustees, the surviving trustee or trustees normally hold title to the trust property by survivorship because cotrustees hold title as joint tenants unless otherwise provided by the terms of the trust. A successor to the deceased cotrustee generally will not be appointed unless the settlor manifested such an intention or unless the court considers the appointment to be in the interest of proper administration.

On the death of a sole trustee, in the absence of trust provision or one of the commonly enacted statutes to the contrary, the title to the trust property passes, subject to the trust, to the trustee's heirs, devisee, legatee, or personal representative, depending on the passage of title to individually owned property of the same type under state law. Such persons are not authorized to administer the trust, however, and the proper court will appoint a new trustee. The court order will vest title in the new trustee, or it will require the holder of the title to transfer the property if that is necessary under applicable law and the circumstances.

In the event of the death, resignation, or removal of a sole trustee, or when the position of one of several trustees becomes vacant and the appointment of a successor is appropriate, in the absence of a trust provision naming a successor, a new trustee will be appointed by the *[handwritten: new trustee is appointed by the ct]* appropriate court on the application of an interested person. In making such an appointment the court will usually consider the desires of the beneficiaries as well as the settlor's intent and the furtherance of sound administration. Frequently, however, trust instruments contain provisions naming successor trustees. Where this is the case, the terms of the trust will be followed in the absence of grounds for removal or grounds for refusing to confirm the appointment. Trust instruments sometimes provide procedures for the selection of successor trustees; for example, the trust may provide for the appointment of new trustees by the settlor of a living trust, by one or more adult beneficiaries, by a surviving trustee, or by some other person. Where a person is empowered to select a new trustee, it is generally said that courts will not disapprove a selection merely because it is one the court itself would not have made, but that such a selection is not entitled to the same respect as an appointment by the settlor. If a life beneficiary is given power, for any reason and with no express restriction, to remove the trustee and to appoint successors, should self-appointment by the beneficiary be permitted? The answer to this question may have significant tax implications, as well as posing questions of practical desirability: see, e.g., Treasury Regulations §20.2041-1(b)(1).

Other matters, involving qualification, appointment, and removal of trustees, are taken up in Chapter 17.

3. The Trust Property

trust fund?

"A trust requires a specific res, and where there is no specific res, there can be no trust." Cahill v. Monahan, 58 N.J. Super. 54, 66, 155 A.2d 282, 288 (1959).

ALI def. of trust

Note that the American Law Institute's definition of a trust, quoted supra page 345, describes a trust as a fiduciary relationship with respect to property. Also in the preceding chapter a pair of cases was encountered in which it was held that the arrangements in question were not trusts, and the holdings were at least aided by the fact that no specific res existed. In McKee v. Paradise, cited supra page 346, in circumstances similar to Problem 9-B the United States Supreme Court emphasized that no fund had been segregated for the purpose in question and that no identifiable trust fund or res had been established. McLaughlin v. Equitable Life Assurance Socs., cited supra page 346, involved an insurance contract in circumstances similar to Problem 9-A, with the standard result that retention of the proceeds by the company pursuant to a settlement option did not constitute a trust. This result is explained in IA W. Fratcher, Scott on Trusts §87.1 (4th ed. 1987), as follows:

> . . . If, as is almost universally the case, the insurance company is not required to and does not segregate the proceeds but merely undertakes to make the required payments out of its general funds, the company is not a trustee. There is certainly no trust in the technical sense of the term, for nothing is held by one person for another. It is immaterial that the agreement between the company and the insured person is called a trust agreement . . . if it is also agreed that the proceeds shall not be segregated from the other assets of the company. There is no trust . . . as long as the proceeds are not segregated.

Trust prop = any prop. interests

The trust property may consist of virtually any property interests, whether real or personal, tangible or intangible, legal or equitable. This would include such properties as patents and even the goodwill of a business. In general, then, any type of existing property interest that is transferable may be placed in trust, and even an interest that is not transferable can be held in trust. For example, where a tort claim is not assignable it cannot be *placed* in trust; but such a claim may comprise part of the subject matter of a trust and can be *held* in trust, as when it arises originally through tortious destruction of an asset held in the trust. Even property that is clearly transferable must be definite, or at least ascertainable, to be placed in trust. While the problem of trust property usually causes no difficulty when the intent presently to create a trust is clear, occasionally litigation arises in which there is a problem as to the identification of an "existing" property interest as the trust res.

PROBLEM

9-D. *A* is a prosperous business executive whose father, *F*, died some years ago. By *F*'s will most of his estate was placed in trust for *M*, *A*'s mother, for life, remainder to *A*. *M* also has a substantial estate of her own, which she plans to leave to *A*. *A* has decided that for tax reasons it will not be advisable to enlarge his estate or to increase his income. He therefore decided that his remainder interest in the trust created by *F*, and also anything he receives from *M*, should be placed in a trust for his issue. *A* then executed a deed purporting presently to transfer to *T*, as trustee, his remainder interest and any property he may receive from the estate of *M*. Is a trust created? If so, of what? If you had been advising *A*, what would you have recommended to accomplish his purpose?

Would your answer be different if, under *F*'s trust, the remainder had been to *A* if living at *M*'s death and otherwise to *C* Church?

Would your answer be different if *M* had died before *A*'s deed to *T* was executed and delivered?

4. The Beneficiaries

Except for charitable trusts and what are sometimes called "honorary trusts" (e.g., one for a pet or the care of a grave), a valid trust requires a beneficiary or beneficiaries who have a right to enforce it. Occasional cases present the question whether a particular instrument satisfies the requirement that there be definite beneficiaries, a requirement that is satisfied if there are beneficiaries who will be ascertainable within the mandates of applicable law relating to perpetuities.

If a person has capacity to hold title to property, he can be a trust beneficiary even though he lacks capacity to administer the property. In fact, the inability of a beneficiary to manage property is often the primary reason for creating a trust. In general, the ability to take and hold title to property is essential to the capacity to be a trust beneficiary. Nevertheless, it is generally held that an unincorporated association can be the beneficiary of a trust even where it is still not viewed as an entity and is unable to hold title to property under applicable state law. This is so even though the settlor intended to benefit the continuing association, rather than the individual members as of the date of the trust's creation, assuming applicable rules relating to perpetuities are not violated. The enforceability requirement is satisfied because suit may be brought by a member of the association, or by the association itself where it is treated as an entity in equity even if not at law. See generally II W. Fratcher, Scott on Trusts §§116–119 (4th ed. 1987); Restatement (Third) of Trusts §43, cmt. *d*. See also id. §43, cmt. *a*, that a "settlor of a trust may be the sole beneficiary or one of the beneficiaries of the trust" and that a trustee "may also be a trust beneficiary, provided the trust has at least one other beneficiary or another trustee."[5]

It is clear that a valid trust can be created under which some of the beneficiaries are unborn at the time. In fact, such trusts are not at all unusual. Can a valid trust be created in which none of the described beneficiaries are in existence at the time? Can a person create a trust solely for his unborn children? Contrast G. Bogert, Trusts and Trustees §163 (rev. 2d ed. 1979), with II W. Fratcher, Scott on Trusts §112.1 (4th ed. 1987). See Fratcher, Trustor as Sole Trustee and Only Ascertainable Beneficiary, 47 Mich. L. Rev. 907 (1949). How could such a trust be enforced? Consider the following case summaries.

In Morsman v. Commissioner of Internal Revenue, 90 F.2d 18 (8th Cir.), *cert. denied*, 302 U.S. 701 (1937), *A*, a bachelor, declared himself trustee of certain securities, providing that a trust company should succeed him as trustee within ten years. The terms of the declaration were that income was to be accumulated for five years and thereafter was to be paid to *A* for life and then for twenty years to his issue, at which time the principal was to be distributed to them; if *A* left no issue, the trust property was to pass to his widow, if any, and otherwise to his heirs. Soon after declaring himself trustee, *A* sold some of the securities at a profit and then turned the property over to the trust company, which reported the profit as income taxable to the trustee rather than to *A* individually. The court held the income taxable to *A* individually, on the theory that no trust had been created because there were no beneficiaries other than *A* himself. The court stated that if *A* had "sought to dissipate the property, there is no person in being who has

---

5. Conventional doctrine is that, if the sole trustee is the sole beneficiary, *merger* results and there is no trust. It is at least arguable that the maxim that equity does not allow a trust to fail merely for want of a trustee could be invoked to substitute or add a trustee different from the beneficiary, but there appears to be no authority to that effect.

such an interest that he may go into a court of equity and prevent the dissipation." The dissenting opinion pointed out that *A*'s brother, as a prospective heir, was a contingent beneficiary who could enforce the terms of the trust.

With *Morsman* compare Lane v. Taylor, 287 Ky. 116, 152 S.W.2d 271 (1941), in which *A* conveyed land to *B* in trust for *A* for life, and at *A*'s death, or in the event of an attempt to subject the land to *A*'s debts, the land was to go to *A*'s children. Thereafter *A*'s only child died, and all of his property passed to *A* and his wife, *W*. *A* and *W* purported to convey the land to *X*, who contracted to sell it to *Y*. *Y*, objecting to *X*'s title, declined to accept the deed tendered by *X* in fulfillment of the contract. In a suit by *X* against *Y* for declaratory relief, *X*'s title was held defective in that *A*, who was still living, might have children in the future.

In Moss v. Axford, 246 Mich. 288, 244 N.W. 425 (1929), Caroline Girard left her residuary estate to Henry Axford, her executor, "to pay the same to the person who has given me the best care in my declining years and who in his opinion is the most worthy of my said property. I make him the sole judge." Mrs. Girard's heirs contended that the intended trust was invalid because no beneficiary was designated in the will, but testimony "clearly established" that the person selected by Axford was proper if the intended disposition was valid. In sustaining the trust, the court stated:

> The purpose of Mrs. Girard was lawful and should be carried out, "unless there is such an uncertainty that the law is fairly baffled.". . . It is not necessary that a beneficiary be designated by name, or by a description which makes identification automatic. . . . Nor that the testator have in mind the particular individual upon whom his bounty may fall. . . . It is enough if the testator used language which is sufficiently clear to enable the court by extrinsic evidence to identify the beneficiary. . . .
>
> The ascertainment of testatrix's beneficiary by Mr. Axford was an imperative duty. The test and method were prescribed by the will. He was bound to exercise good faith . . . and the honesty of his decision would be reviewable in equity. . . . Upon his failure or inability to perform the duty, the court could from extraneous evidence ascertain and declare the beneficiary to fully carry out the intention of the testatrix. . . .

NICHOLS v. ALLEN
130 Mass. 211, 39 Am. Rep. 445 (1881)

[Testatrix bequeathed the residue of her estate to her executors and their successors "to be distributed to such persons, societies or institutions as they may think most deserving."]

GRAY, C.J.

Two general rules are well settled: 1st. When a gift or bequest is made in terms clearly manifesting an intention that it shall be taken in trust, and the trust is not sufficiently defined to be carried into effect, the donee or legatee takes the legal title only, and a trust results by implication of law to the donor and his representatives, or to the testator's residuary legatees or next of kin. . . . 2d. A trust which by its terms may be applied to objects which are not charitable in the legal sense, and to persons not defined, by name or by class, is too indefinite to be carried out. . . .

The terms of this bequest clearly manifest the intention of the testatrix to create a trust. The bequest contains no words tending to show that the executors are to take the property, or any part of it, absolutely or for their own benefit; and by our law no such intention is to be implied. . . . The bequest is not to the executors by name, but is to them and the survivor of them, and to their successors in the administration of the estate. . . .

The omission of the words "in trust" is unimportant where, as in the case before us, an intention is clearly manifested that the whole property shall be applied by the legatees for the benefit of others than themselves. . . .

Upon a review of the authorities, we find nothing in them to control the conclusion, based upon the intention which appears to us to be clearly manifested on the face of this will, that the executors take the estate, not beneficially, but in trust; and that the beneficiaries not being described by name or by class, the trust cannot be upheld unless its purposes are such as the law deems charitable.

The trust declared cannot be sustained as a charity. There is no restriction as to the objects of the trust, except that they must be "such persons, societies or institutions as they" (the trustees) "may consider most deserving." "Deserving" denotes worth or merit, without regard to condition or circumstances, and is in no sense of the word limited to persons in need of assistance, or to objects which come within the class of charitable uses. . . .

A gift to charitable or public purposes is good. Dolan v. Macdermot, L.R., 3 Ch. 676. But if the trustees are authorized to apply or distribute it to other purposes or persons, it is void. . . .

The conclusion of the whole matter is, that the testatrix having given the residue of her property to her executors in trust, and not having defined the trust sufficiently to enable the court to execute it, the plaintiff, being her next of kin, is entitled to the residue by way of resulting trust.

Demurrer overruled.

Do you see why the intended trust in the above case was not upheld on the ground that the beneficiaries, though not ascertained, *will become ascertainable* within the period of the Rule Against Perpetuities?

In the leading case of Morice v. Bishop of Durham, 10 Vex. 521 (Ch. 1805), the testatrix bequeathed her personal estate to the Bishop of Durham on trust to pay her debts and legacies and "to dispose of the ultimate residue to such objects of benevolence and liberality" as he "shall most approve of." Although the bishop disclaimed any beneficial interest and was ready to carry out the intended purposes of the testatrix, the trust failed for want of anyone to enforce it, its purpose being too broad to be enforceable as a charitable trust by the Attorney General. Lord Eldon held that the bishop should not be allowed to carry out the intended trust but held the property on a resulting trust for the next of kin of the testatrix.

An Aside on Powers of Appointment. Unlike the trust's requirement of definite beneficiaries, a valid power of appointment (see Chapter 10, section B) is personal to the power holder ("donee") and may have a definite class of beneficiaries or it may not. In fact, in general powers of appointment the "objects" (permissible appointees) are not limited. In marginal cases involving attempts to create trusts, courts distinguish powers from trusts and try to decide whether something is a trust or a power. Yet powers are not incompatible with trusts. The typical power of appointment is but a provision of a trust, intended to give flexibility to the trust and usually to provide a beneficiary of a limited beneficial interest some broader power to dispose of trust property or of some interest in it.

A fairly typical illustration is the following. *W* (the settlor of the trust and "donor" of the power) leaves her estate to *T* in trust to pay the income to *H* for life; on *H*'s death *T* is to distribute the principal to such of *H*'s issue as *H* may appoint by will, remainder in default of appointment to *H*'s then living issue by right of representation. *H* has a testamentary nongeneral ("special") power of appointment. (In addition to its managerial powers, *T* also may have a power over beneficial enjoyment, usually a power to invade principal for *H*'s benefit but sometimes broader; on such *fiduciary powers,* see Chapter 10, section A.2.) *H*'s power need not be exercised in a "fiduciary manner" and, in fact, may properly be left unexercised.

What if *W* had failed to specify takers in default of appointment and *H* died intestate or otherwise leaving the power unexercised? Here, even with a power of appointment, it becomes important to determine whether there is a definite class of objects. If not, subject to narrow exceptions, it will be held that *W* made an incomplete disposition of her property and that there is a reversion (or "resulting trust") under which the property belongs to her (not *H*'s) successors in interest. If, however, there *is* a definite class of objects, the property passes to that class. Most classes, such as *children,* then take in equal shares, although other definite classes, such as *issue* (and perhaps *relatives* where such terms are considered definite enough), may take in the pattern of local intestacy statutes. Thus, a remainder or gift in default of appointment is being *implied* in favor of the definite class. It is sometimes said that the gift was to the class, subject to *H*'s power to exclude some and to vary the shares. (Occasionally, to the unfortunate confusion of our terminology, it is said that the power is a *trust power*, or a *power in trust*, or the like.) In addition to the trust, therefore, it is worthwhile for present purposes (despite some judicial mixing of terms and concepts) to keep separately in mind: the fiduciary power; the power of appointment, either with an expressed gift in default or in favor of indefinite objects; and the power of appointment for which takers in default will be implied.

———————————

The case of Morice v. Bishop of Durham was criticized by Professor Ames in his classic article prompted by the failure of a provision of another famous will. See Ames, The Failure of the "*Tilden* Trust," 5 Harv. L. Rev. 389, 395-399 (1892):

> It may be said that there can be no trust without a definite cestui que trust. This must be admitted. . . . But it does not follow from this admission that such a gift is void. Even though there be no express trust, there is a plain duty imposed upon *A* [one in the position of the Bishop of Durham] to act, and his act runs counter to no principle of public policy. Why then seek to nullify his act? The only objection that has ever been urged against such a gift is that the court cannot compel *A* to act if he is unwilling. Is it not a monstrous non sequitur to say that therefore the court will not permit him to act when he is willing?
>
> It may be objected that a devise might in this way become "the mere equivalent of a general power of attorney"; but this objection seems purely rhetorical. Suppose a testator to give *A* a purely optional power of appointment in favor of any person in the world except himself, with a provision that in default of the exercise of the power the property shall go to the testator's representatives-or this provision may be omitted altogether, the effect being the same. Such a will is obviously nothing if not the mere equivalent of a general power of attorney. And yet the validity of the power would go unquestioned. If the power is exercised, the appointee takes. If it is not exercised, the testator's representative takes.
>
> Now vary the case by supposing that the testator imposes upon the donee of the power the *duty* to exercise it. Can the imposition of this duty furnish any reason for a different result? In fact, *A*, the donee of the power has in this case also the option of appointing or not, since, although he ought to appoint, no one can compel him to do so. Does it not seem a mockery of legal reasoning to say that the court will sanction the exercise of the power where the donee was under no obligation to act at all, but will not sanction the appointment when the donee was in honor bound to make it?

It is time enough for the court to interfere when *A* proves false to his duty and sets up for himself. Then, indeed, a court of equity ought to turn him into a constructive trustee for the donor or his representative. This contingent right of the heir or next of kin may be safely trusted to secure the performance of his duty by the trustee. And its existence is a full answer to the suggestion . . . in Morice v. Bishop of Durham . . . that the trustee could keep the property without accountability to anyone, if the beneficial interests were not given to the heir or next of kin immediately upon the testator's death. The position of the heir or next of kin is, in substance, the same as in the cases where property is given to them subject to a purely optional power of appointment in another to be exercised, if at all, within a reasonable time. . . .

Although Morice v. Bishop of Durham has never been directly impeached, either in England or this country, there are several groups of cases, undistinguishable from it in principle, in which equity judges have declined to interfere, at the suit of the next kin, to prevent the performance of a purely honorary trust.

Mussett v. Bingle [W.N. (1876) 170] is one illustration. The testator bequeathed £300 upon trust for the erection of a monument to his wife's first husband. It was objected that the trust was purely honorary [and it was not charitable]; that is, there was no beneficiary to compel its performance. But the trustees being willing to perform, Hall, V. C., sustained the bequest. . . . There are many American cases to the same effect. . . .

The most conspicuous illustration of the doctrine which is here advocated is to be found in the recent English case of Cooper-Dean v. Stevens [41 Ch. D. 552]. There was in that case a bequest of £750 for the maintenance of the testator's horses and dogs. It was urged by the residuary legatee, on the authority of Morice v. Bishop of Durham, that this trust must fail, although the trustees desired to perform it. But the trust was upheld.

A trust for a definite class, such as children, issue, or nieces and nephews, is valid. Trusts have been upheld for beneficiaries described only by such terms as *employees* and *family*, although there are also cases indicating that these designations are too indefinite to support a trust. "Family," of course, presents a question of construction, but one courts have generally have been willing to resolve. Some courts have been less willing to treat the word *relatives* as describing a sufficiently definite class to permit enforcement of a trust. Even this designation, however, has been upheld by other courts by construing the terms as applying only to next of kin.

In cases involving "class" designations that are arguably indefinite, the description of the potential beneficiaries is usually accompanied by a power in the trustee to select from among persons fitting the description. Assuming, however, that the class is ultimately found to be sufficiently definite to escape the rule of Nichols v. Allen, or even that the Ames theory of a valid but unenforceable power is adopted, certain additional problems are likely to arise.

A trustee, *T*, holds a power to distribute to such of a testator's "relatives" as he may select. *T* decides to make a distribution to a relative who is not among the testator's next of kin. Is such a selection permissible? It should be, and the few cases so indicate. For purpose of initial validity, the definiteness of the "class" here is sustained on the basis that "relatives" with no further method of ascertainment refers to next of kin. *T*'s power of selection, however, need not be so narrowly circumscribed.

Another problem might arise with regard to the same trust if *T* dies without having made a selection, or simply refuses to exercise the power of selection. In the absence of some standard to serve as a guide in the selection, or a fairly clear indication of intention that a successor trustee is to be appointed to exercise the power, the appropriate inference is that the power was personal to the settlor's chosen trustee. The court would then order distribution to beneficiaries and in shares determined as if the same class designation had been employed without a power of selection. Thus, the property might be distributed equally among the class members. In a situation involving the term *relatives*, distribution would be made to those relatives who are next of kin of the person in question; distribution would not, of course, be attempted among all relatives of all degrees. The shares of the kindred would be determined on the basis of the relevant rules of intestate succession. (If the class is indefinite, with Ames' *power* theory applied, the court would recognize a *resulting trust* at this point.)

Where the trustee has power to select beneficiaries from within a definite class, the required power to enjoin or redress a breach of trust resides in *any* of the class members, even though no individual rights to take have yet been established. See generally II W. Fratcher, Scott on Trusts §120 (4th ed. 1987).

PROBLEM

9-E.   Assume that the facts and opinion excerpts in the next paragraph represent the decision of an intermediate appellate court of your state. Assume further that Nichols v. Allen, supra, was decided years ago by the highest court of your state. On what bases might you seek, and how might you argue, to have the intermediate appellate decision reversed on appeal? After considering the possibilities, would you advise your client to pursue the matter? What arguments would you expect to be made for affirmance?

The intermediate appellate decision in question (based on Clark v. Campbell, 82 N.H. 281, 133 A. 166 (1926)) involves a bequest of personal property to named trustees "in trust to make disposal of such articles, by way of memento from me, to such of my friends as my trustees shall select. All of said property not so disposed of my trustees are directed to sell, the proceeds to become, and be disposed of as, a part of the residue of my estate." Citing Nichols v. Allen, the court held that the provision for selected "friends" fails for uncertainty of beneficiaries, stating: "Even if it be conceded that the doctrine requiring definite beneficiaries to enforce a trust is not a legal necessity, the fact that it has never been impeached affords strong evidence that in practical application it has been generally found just and reasonable and thus affords sufficient ground for our continued adherence to the rule." One contention presented was that the testator had no intention to create a trust of the personal property, the word *trustees* being merely descriptive of the persons earlier named as trustees, rather than defining the capacity in which they were to act. In dismissing this argument, the court stated, as a "sufficient answer," that "the language does not warrant this construction," adding that "the trustees' familiarity with the testator's property, wishes and friendships seems quite as consistent with a design to clothe them with a trusteeship as with an intention to make an absolute gift to them, with only a moral obligation imposed." The court further noted that the clause under consideration "provides for the disposal of the articles and imposes upon the trustees the duty of selling any balance thereof and adding the proceeds to the residue which they are to continue to hold and administer in their capacity as trustees, for ultimate distribution among 'such charitable institutions' as they shall designate." It was further sought to sustain the provision as one intended merely to create a *power*. The court responded: "The distinction apparently relied upon is that a power, unlike a trust, is not imperative and leaves the act to be done at the will of the donee of the power; but the clause in question, by its terms, imposes upon the trustees the imperative duty to dispose of the selected articles among the testator's friends. It is not an optional power, certainly, but one coupled with a trust, to which trust principles clearly apply." The opinion continued: "We must therefore conclude that this clause presents the case of an attempt to create a private trust and falls within the principle of Nichols v. Allen." Finally, the court concluded: "The *cestuis que trust* are designated as the testator's 'friends,' which, unlike 'relations,' has no accepted statutory or other controlling limit and no precise sense at all. It is a word of broad and varied application, and no specific evidence was offered that the testator used the word in any restricted sense."

A pronounced if somewhat unclear change of direction in England began with In re Baden's Deed Trust (McPhail v. Doulten), [1970] 2 All E.R. 228. Also, Ames' theory has influenced a few American decisions and several statutes (trustees being *allowed* but not *compelled* to carry out indefinite purposes). The clear weight of authority, however, still follows the rule of Nichols v. Allen. Nevertheless, as noted by Ames (above), the validity of "honorary (i.e., unenforceable) trusts" for limited types of definite, noncharitable purposes has become quite widely accepted. The trust for specific animals, too restrictive to be charitable, is a ready illustration. See Uniform Probate Code §2-907; Uniform Trust Code §405 (draft, Feb. 2000). Bequests for the care of graves have often been upheld by courts and are now usually provided for by statute, as are employee benefit trusts, without resort to the honorary trust doctrine. Absent specific statutory immunity, however, honorary trusts are limited and often invalidated by the rule against perpetuities. See generally Fratcher, Bequests for Purposes, 56 Iowa L. Rev. 773 (1971).

RESTATEMENT (THIRD) OF TRUSTS
(Tent. Draft approved 1999)

§46. *Members of an Indefinite Class as Beneficiaries*

(1) Except as stated in (2), where the owner of property transfers it upon intended trust for the members of an indefinite class of persons, no trust is created.

(2) If the transferee is directed to distribute the property to such members of the indefinite class as the transferee shall select, the transferee holds the property in trust with power but no duty to distribute the property to such class members as the transferee may select; to whatever extent the power (presumptively personal) is not exercised, the transferee will then hold for reversionary beneficiaries implied by law.

§47. *Trusts for Noncharitable Purposes.*

(1) If the owner of property transfers it in trust for indefinite or general purposes, not limited to charitable purposes, the transferee holds the property as trustee with the power but not the duty to distribute or apply the property for such purposes; if and to whatever extent the power (presumptively personal) is not exercised, the trustee holds the property for reversionary beneficiaries implied by law.

(2) If the owner of property transfers it in trust for a specific noncharitable purpose and no definite or ascertainable beneficiary is designated, unless the purpose is capricious, the transferee holds the property as trustee with power exercisable for a reasonable period of time, normally not to exceed 21 years, to apply the property to the designated purpose; if and to whatever extent the power is personal and not exercised, or the property exceeds what reasonably may be needed for the purpose, the trustee holds the property or the excess for reversionary beneficiaries implied by law.

The Restatement commentary develops many of the details of the above sections. For differences in scope and enforcement, compare Uniform Trust Code §402(a)(3) and (b) (draft, Feb. 2000) proposing to recognize the validity "of a trust for the care of an animal or other valid noncharitable purpose" and that a "power or direction to a trustee to select a beneficiary from an indefinite class is valid." Id. §406 (a) provides that a trust "for a particular noncharitable purpose . . . or for a noncharitable purpose to be selected by the trustee . . . may not be enforced for more than 21 years"; and subsections (c) and (b) provide, respectively, that such a trust "may be enforced by a person designated for that purpose in the terms of the trust or, if none, by a person appointed by the court" and that trust property "may not be applied to a use other than its intended use except to the extent the court determines that the value of the trust property exceeds the amount required" for that purpose, any excess to "be distributed to those who would take the trust property if the trust were to terminate on the date of the distribution."

5. Trust Purposes

Except in those few states in which statutes have attempted to enumerate the purposes for which trusts may be established, it is generally said, and in a sense it is true, that a trust may be created for any purpose that is not contrary to public policy. Thus, in some states it is provided by statute that a trust may be created "for any purpose or purposes for which a contract may be made" or for any purpose "which is not illegal."

This apparent liberality in describing trust purposes may be misleading. A purpose in the trust law may be "contrary to public policy" when it would not be in other contexts. The dead hand does not have all of the privileges of the living property owner. We have just seen (section 4, above) that, with limited exceptions (see Restatement (Third) of Trusts §§46, 47), an express trust must either be for a charitable purpose or for a private purpose with acceptably definite beneficiaries (id. §27). Furthermore, the individual property owner does not determine what is or is not charitable, and private purposes are not allowed to endure in perpetuity. See generally W. Fratcher, Bequests for Purposes, 56 Iowa L. Rev. 773 (1971). What may be thrift for an individual may be an unlawful accumulation in a trust following death or an inter vivos conveyance. Unlike the private property of the living, the property of a trust cannot be devoted even to a quite harmless capricious purpose,[6] nor has the dead hand the freedom of

---

6. Compare the matter of waste, which "a well-ordered society cannot tolerate," in Eyerman v. Mercantile Trust Co., 524 S.W.2d 210 (Mo. App. 1975), invalidating a testamentary direction that decedent's residence be razed; but another testator's direction to demolish her century-old family home and offer the property for sale to the city pursuant to an agreement with the city's urban renewal authority was sustained in Estate

the living in the use of wealth to influence the lives and behavior of others.

What is the effect of invalidity of a trust provision? Earlier cases drew some arcane distinctions. For example, an invalid condition *subsequent* might be stricken, leaving the trust or disposition otherwise in place, while an invalid condition *precedent* might cause the disposition to fail, leaving a resulting trust. The Restatement (Second) of Trusts rejected these distinctions, inferring that a settlor ordinarily would prefer the trust or disposition to be given effect without the offending provision. See id. Ch. 6, introductory note, and §65, cmts. *e, f.* Compare, however, the flexibility of reformation in Restatement (Third) §29, cmt. *d,* infra.

Both the Second and Third Restatements of Trusts invalidate provisions that are contrary to public policy. Restatement (Third) §29(b) is more specific than its predecessor and in some respects goes beyond existing case law in identifying policy limits on serious intrusions by settlors into the personal lives of their beneficiaries.

PROBLEM

9-F.   *A,* a wealthy client, has come to you to have his will planned and drawn. In the course of your interview he informs you that his daughter, *D,* has married a man, *X,* who is "a no-good bum." *D* and *X* "seem to be holding their marriage together well enough, but it has by no means been an easy life for her." *A* would like to see the marriage end. He wishes to leave half of his property to his son, *S,* and half in trust to pay *D* as much income as she may need as long as her marriage lasts. He wishes her to receive her share outright only if she divorces *X;* if she does not, *A* would like *D*'s trust to be distributed to *S* or *S*'s issue on *D*'s death. *A* asks if such a trust is valid. How would you advise him?

Can you draft a trust with the desired terms that will be upheld? How might you word the provisions? Would it be ethical for you to draft the desired trust in a way that would withstand attack if the cases that follow are decisions of courts in your state?

Would your responses differ under Ind. Ann. Code §30-4-2-12, which states that the terms of a trust "may not require the trustee to commit a criminal or tortious act or an act which is contrary to public policy" and adds: "A trust with terms which violate . . . this section is invalid unless the prohibited term is separable," in which case only that term fails "and the remainder of the trust is valid."

If the originally suggested trust is created and the provision encour-

---

of Beck, 676 N.Y.S.2d 838 (Surr. Ct. 1998), noting the irony that the authority had once sought to condemn the property and that maintaining the aging structure might burden the charitable residuary beneficiary of the will.

aging divorce is held invalid, what disposition will be made of the property involved? Would your response differ if Restatement (Third) of Trusts §29 is followed in your state?

FINEMAN v. CENTRAL NATIONAL BANK
161 N.E.2d 557 (Ohio Prob. Ct. 1959)

[Action for construction of the will of Saul I. Fineman and for a declaratory judgment. The relevant provisions of the will provide for the creation of a trust for the testator's daughter, Lillian, for her life and then provide for continuation of the trust for the purpose of making payments of $300 per month to testator's son, Roland, for as long as he remains married to his present wife, Ray. The trust is to terminate "at such time as my son, Roland, shall be divorced from his present wife, Ray Fineman, or at such time as his present wife shall be deceased"; and then, after paying $5,000 to a niece, distribution of the balance of the trust estate is to be made to Roland.]

MERRICK, J. . . .

It has been stipulated that there was no divorce action pending between the testator's son and his wife at the time of the making of this will, or at any time thereafter. The estate is substantial and the amount which might pass into the trust might exceed $100,000.

Any effort to interpret or construe the language of this will would necessarily lead to the conclusion that a divorce of the son from his wife would cause a vesting of a large sum of money in and for the taking by the son.

It has long been the established law in the State of Ohio, that a condition in a will by which an inducement is offered to a married person to obtain a divorce, or to live separate and apart from the other spouse, is contrary to public policy, and held to be invalid. Page on Wills, Lifetime Edition, Volume 3, page 812. . . .

Whether such provision in a will is void is to be determined by the circumstances existing at the time of its execution. The primary reason such a clause is void is that it is against public policy, because it places a reward, benefit or price upon divorce or domestic separation. Under some circumstances the surrounding facts might very well warrant a testator in placing such a contingency in his will. By carefully wording the language, it could be made apparent that the testator was making some provision or establishing some safeguard against the [possibility] of divorce. Certainly a man could provide that a certain allowance should be increased or a payment accelerated in the event that a daughter should be divorced and lose some means of support; or in the event a pending divorce case resulted in a final disposition that might be a handicap to the future support or well being of the devisee. The test seems to be whether the provision in the will provides a premium or reward in the event of divorce. If it appears from the whole will that it was the purpose of the testator to provide some support or maintenance for one who might suffer economically from the divorce, then no divorce has been encouraged and the clause would be valid. 40 Cyc. 1703.

A case in point is . . . Pickering v. Cleveland Trust Co., etc., 3 Ohio Law Abs. 243, [where] the court distinguishes between clauses rewarding separation or divorce and those affording protection and sustenance in the event of such an eventuality.

The plain language of the will in the instant case places a premium upon the marital separation. There being no language which could in any way change or modify this interpretation, the judgment of this Court is that the clause in question is void as against public policy. [Therefore] the remainder shall vest in Roland H. Fineman subject to the life interest of Lillian Fineman.

[The judgment was later modified by the Court of Appeals to require that Roland survive Lillian for the remainder to vest in him.]

Illustrative of cases upholding provisions that seem to encourage divorce is In re Estate of Donner, 263 N.J. Super. 539, 623 A. 2d 307 (1993) (trust terms and extrinsic evidence provided a "reasonable economic basis" for denying trust benefits until daughter reached age 65 unless her husband died or the couple divorced earlier; husband was under federal investigation and was regarded by settlor as a poor money manager, but undisputed evidence also suggested settlor strongly disliked husband). In Estate of Romero, 115 N.M. 85, 847 P.2d 319 (1993), the decedent's testamentary trust allowed his fianceé and his youthful sons to live in his former home, provided the fianceé remain unmarried and not cohabit with an unrelated male and that the sons' mother (testator's former wife) not also reside there. The court invalidated the condition regarding the sons but remanded for factual inquiry into the testator's motive regarding the fianceé.

How should a court treat a condition tending to *discourage* divorce, such as a forfeiture of rights by any child who obtains a divorce?

During life parents sometimes use their wealth to attempt to influence their children's lives, or make *outright devises* that will favor one child over another — or even disinherit a child — if certain aspects of the latter's lifestyle or behavior continue until the testator's death. Are these matters different in any significant way from using *trusts* for such purposes?

In re ESTATE OF HELLER
39 Wis. 2d 318, 159 N.W.2d 82 (1968)

[Lena Heller's will made no provision for her daughter, Katie Mau, "unless at the time of my death, she is married to and living with her husband, Willard Mau," in which case she "shall be included with my other daughters . . . and share equally with them." Katie divorced Willard before Lena's death.]

WILKIE, J. . . .

The trial court noted this was the first time he had been confronted with a question about a provision in a will "in which a legacy is conditioned on the continuance of a marriage." We find no Wisconsin cases on the validity of such a provision. . . .

The Restatement of the Law on Property surveys the law of testamentary provisions affecting marriage. It points out the following general rules.

(1) A condition rendering a gift contingent upon not marrying anyone is void unless clearly motivated by an intention to provide support until a marriage takes place. This invalidation results from the court's unwillingness to penalize a legatee for his failure to respect the socially undesirable attempt of the testator to use his property as a means of coercing abstention from marriage.

(2) Restraints limited as to person, group or time are valid unless the remaining sphere of permissible marriage is so small that a permitted marriage is not likely to occur. These partial restraints are valid upon the theory that guidance by parents or other donors with respect to a particular marriage is not unreasonable.

(3) Restraints on remarriage may be liberally imposed.

(4) Finally, attempts by testators to break up an already existing marriage, by conditioning a gift on divorce or separation, are invalid. If the dominant motive of the testator, however, is merely to provide support in the event of separation or marriage, the condition is valid.

Thus the Restatement does not deal directly with a situation such as that presented by the instant case. Appellant has not directed the court to any authority that has held a provision such as those before us invalid. Appellant's argument that the provision in Article V in effect discourages divorce, which has been declared to be good public policy (viz., public policy demands an end to intolerable marriages) regarding the marriage of Katie Mau, is not persuasive. The Restatement points out that the existence of statutes which permit divorce or separation of married persons is not an indication of public policy favoring provisions that encourage divorce. Likewise, statutes allowing divorce should not be indicative of a public policy that would attempt to prohibit restraints on the seeking of a divorce.

It is a familiar and well-settled principle of law that a will speaks as of the time of the death of the testator. Therefore, it would not be unreasonable to conclude that a will cannot contravene public policy until it begins to speak. Upon the death of the testatrix, there was nothing Katie Mau could do to increase or diminish the amount she was to receive under the will. Her portion (if any) was fixed absolutely as of the date of the death of the testatrix. It was Katie's status then that determined whether she was a beneficiary.

Katie Mau testified that until the death of her mother she was unaware of the questioned provision in the will. Therefore, irrespective of the true purpose of those provisions, it is difficult to understand how they could have had any restraining effect, one way or another, on Katie's marriage. Public policy regarding restraints on marriage should only be concerned with continuing inducements and not with a provision, as here, which could never truly be a restraint. A will written and executed is merely the expression of an intention to dispose of one's property in a certain way in the future, provided one does not have a change of mind. Only when death ensues, thus making a change of mind impossible, will these expressions of future intention bring rights into existence. When, as here, those rights become absolutely fixed at death, without a continuing inducement to either do or refrain from doing some act, it is difficult to imagine how a restraint in the true sense of the word could ever arise. . . .

Appellants contend that the Heller will attempts to penalize [Katie] for prosecuting a cause of action which a court found to be valid [and is therefore against public policy]. If appellant is correct then almost all conditional bequests would be void as against public policy because many donees are forced to forego the exercise of legal rights as a valid condition to taking under a will. The widow whose gift is conditioned on not remarrying is giving up a legal right in exchange for that gift. Yet, the widow's condition would not ordinarily be considered violative of public policy.

Judgment affirmed.

UNITED STATES NATIONAL BANK v. SNODGRASS
202 Or. 530, 275 P.2d 860 (1954)

[The trustee brought suit for a declaratory judgment to establish the validity and interpretation of a trust created by the will of C. A. Rinehart, who died in 1932. The terms of the trust provided that certain monthly payments were to be made to the testator's daughter, Merle, who was age 13 at the time of his death, until she reached age 25, then all of the income was to be paid to her until age 32, when the trustee was directed to distribute the trust estate to the daughter provided she has proved conclusively to my trustee . . . that she has not embraced, nor become a member of, the Catholic faith nor ever married to a man of such faith. In the event my daughter . . . becomes ineligible to receive the trust fund then I direct the principal of such trust fund to be divided as follows,

specifying certain other relatives who, along with the daughter, are made defendants in this action. It was stipulated that the daughter reached age 32 in 1951, that she had married a member of the Catholic faith, and that at the time she knew of the above provisions of her father's will. The lower court upheld the provisions of the will and decreed the forfeiture of the daughter's interest in the trust estate.]

WARNER, J. . . .

The appellant asserts that the court erred in holding as valid that provision of the will which disinherited her because of her marriage to a member of the Catholic faith before she was 32 years old. She leans heavily upon the proposition that such a provision violates public policy.

Mrs. Snodgrass did not join the Catholic church and therefore the clause restraining membership in that faith is not before us. Her loss, if any, accrues by reason of the restriction on her marriage to a Catholic within the time limitation. If the provision is valid, then the defendants-respondents take the entire corpus of the trust set up in the contested paragraph 7, and testator's daughter takes nothing.

The problem here is one of the validity of testamentary restraints upon marriage. While there is an abundance of law on the subject from other jurisdictions, the question and its solution are one of first impression in this court. . . .

Litigation springing from religious differences, tincturing, as here, every part and parcel of this appeal, tenders to any court problems of an extremely delicate nature. This very delicacy, together with the novelty of the legal questions in this jurisdiction, warrants pausing before proceeding further and reorienting our thinking in terms of the real legal problem which we must resolve. As a first step we rid ourselves of some erroneous definitions and the smug acceptance of conclusions arising from the too-frequent and inept employment of such terms as "religious freedom," "religious intolerance" and "religious bigotry." We also disassociate ourselves from the erstwhile disposition of many persons to treat any opposition to a religious faith as a prima facie manifestation of religious bigotry, requiring legal condemnation.

The testamentary pattern of Mr. Rinehart may offend the sense of fair play of some in what appears as an ungracious and determined effort to bend the will of another to an acceptance of the testator's concept of the superiority of his own viewpoint. . . .

While one may personally and loudly condemn a species of "intolerance" as socially outrageous, a court on the other hand must guard against being judicially intolerant of such an "intolerance," unless the court can say the act of intolerance is in a form not sanctioned by the law. We are mindful that there are many places where a bigot may safely express himself and manifest his intolerance of the viewpoint of others without fear of legal restraint or punishment. With certain limitations, one of those areas with a wide latitude of sufferance is found in the construction of the pattern of one's last will and testament. It is a field wherein neither this court nor any other court will question the correctness of a testator's religious views or prejudices. In re Lesser's Estate, 158 Misc. 895, 287 N.Y.S. 209, 216.

Our exalted religious freedom is buttressed by another freedom of coordinate importance. In condemning what may appear to one as words of offensive religious intolerance, we must not forget that the offending expression may enjoy the protection of another public policy — the freedom of speech. . . .

We therefore have no intention or disposition to disturb the provisions of Mr. Rinehart's will unless it can be demonstrated that they do violence to some legal rule or precept. Two general and cardinal propositions give direction and limitation to our consideration. One is the traditionally great freedom that the law confers on the individual with respect to the disposition of his property, both before and after death. The other is that greater freedom, the freedom of opinion and right to expression in political and religious matters, together with the incidental and corollary right to implement the attainment of the ultimate and favored objectives of the religious teaching and social or political philosophy to which an individual subscribes. We do not intend to imply hereby that the right to devise or bequeath property is in any way dependent upon or related to the constitutional guarantees of freedom of speech. . . .

Although the appellant rests her appeal primarily upon the premise that paragraph 7 of the will violates public policy, she brings to us no precise statute or judicial pronouncement in support of this contention; but before examining and demonstrating that the authorities cited by appellant are inapplicable, we think it is proper to observe here that it has long been a firmly-established policy in Oregon to give great latitude to a testator in the final disposition of his estate, notwithstanding that the right to make a testamentary disposition is not an inherent, natural or constitutional right but is purely a creation of statute and within legislative control. . . . No one has had the temerity to suggest that Mr. Rinehart in his lifetime could not have accomplished the equivalent of what he sought to accomplish by his will. It was within his power, with or without assigning any reason therefor, to have completely disinherited his daughter and left her in a state of impecunious circumstances. He could have gone even further and given all his fortune to some institution or persons with directions to propagandize his views adverse to any certain religion or creed for which he harbored antipathies. . . .

To sustain the contention that the contested provision of the will is against the public policy of the United States, the appellant depends upon the First and Fourteenth Amendments to the United States Constitution: 42 U.S.C.A. §§ 1981-83, relating to civil rights . . . ; and Shelley v. Kraemer, 334 U.S. 1.

The First Amendment prohibits Congress from making any law respecting the establishment of a religion. Everson v. Board of Education, 330 U.S. 1, 15. That amendment is a limitation upon the power of Congress. It has no effect upon the transactions of individual citizens and has been so interpreted. McIntire v. Wm. Penn Broadcasting Co. of Philadelphia, 3 Cir., 151 F:2d 597, 601, *certiorari denied*, 327 U.S. 779; In re Kempf's Will, 252 App. Div. 28, 297 N.Y.S. 307, 312, *affirmed*, 278 N.Y. 613, 16 N.E.2d 123. Neither does the Fourteenth Amendment relate to individual conduct. The strictures there found circumscribe state action in the particulars mentioned and in no way bear on a transaction of the character now before us. In re Civil Rights Cases, 1883, 109 U.S. 3. . . . Shelley v. Kraemer, supra, is authority only for the proposition that the enforcement by state courts of a covenant in a deed restricting the use and occupancy of real property to persons of the Caucasian race falls within the purview of the Fourteenth Amendment as a violation of the equal protection clause, but, said the court, "That Amendment [Fourteenth] erects no shield against merely private conduct, however discriminatory or wrongful." 334 U.S. 1.

It is not clear to us from appellant's argument whether she reads the offending provision of the will as an invasion of her constitutional right or religious freedom or views it as an unconstitutional act of discrimination; but whether one or the other, we are content that it does no violence to public policy resting upon different grounds from those here urged by appellant.

We are not unmindful that even though no positive law can be found in Oregon limiting a testator as appellant would have us do here, we should, nevertheless, look into the decisions of the courts of other states to discover, if we can, the prevailing rule applied elsewhere when a testator attempts to limit or restrain the marriage of a beneficiary in the manner that the late C. A. Rinehart attempted to do.

The general rule seems to be well settled that conditions and limitations in partial restraint of marriage will be upheld if they do not unreasonably restrict the freedom of the beneficiary's choice. In 35 Am. Jur. 357–358, Marriage, §256, we find:

. . . where the restraint is not general but is merely partial or temporary, or otherwise limited in effect, then the condition may or may not be void, according to whether it is considered reasonable or otherwise, and does not operate merely in terrorem. . . .

Among the restrictions which have been held reasonable are: Conditions to marry or not to marry . . . a person of a particular . . . religion. . . .

Of the same tenor is 1 Restatement, Trusts, 194, §62(g), reading so far as pertinent:

. . . such a provision is not invalid if it does not impose an undue restraint on marriage. Thus, a provision divesting the interest of the beneficiary if he or she should marry . . . a person of a particular religious faith or one of a different faith from that of the beneficiary, is not ordinarily invalid. . . .

We turn to an examination of the controverted provision and note that the condition is not one of complete restraint, in which character it might well be abhorrent to the law. It is merely partial and temporary and, as we shall show later, is not in terrorem. Mr. Rinehart's daughter is not thereby restrained from ever marrying a Catholic. This inhibition as a condition to taking under the will at the age of 32 lasts only 11 years, that is, from the legal marriageable age without parental consent (in this state, 21 years). After the age of 32 she is free to marry a Catholic or become a Catholic if she so pleases and have her estate, too. Moreover, the condition imposed does not restrict the beneficiary from enjoying marital status either before or after attaining the age of 32. Here, unfortunately, appellant would eat her cake and have it too. . . . So far as we are able to ascertain, only two states — Pennsylvania and Virginia — have invalidated testamentary provisions committing the beneficiary to adhere to the doctrines of a particular religion. This departure from the majority rule is reflected by Drace v. Klinedinst, 1922, 275 Pa. 266, 118 A. 907, 25 A.L.R. 1520; and Maddox v. Maddox's Admr., 1854, 11 Grat., Va., 804. . . . In the *Maddox* case the condition was that the testator's daughter should marry a member of the Society of Friends. There were only five or six marriageable males of that faith within the circle of her acquaintances, and under the circumstances peculiar to that case the court held that the condition was an unreasonable restraint on marriage.

The last contention of Mrs. Snodgrass requiring consideration is that the offending provision is in terrorem and therefore invalid. . . .

Generally, conditions in restraint of marriage are said to be in terrorem and therefore invalid when the subject of the gift is personal property and *there is no gift over,* but such a condition is not void as being in terrorem when there is a gift over. It is the absence of a gift over which supplies the quality of a coercive threat necessary to bring the condition under the in terrorem rule. 35 Am. Jur. 367, Marriage, §266. . . .

Affirmed. Neither party will recover costs.

BRAND, J., dissents.

If the validity of a restraint on marriage depends on the "reasonableness of its breadth and duration," how should a court treat provisions conditioned on the beneficiary's marrying someone "of Greek blood and descent and of Orthodox religion"? Keffalas Estate, 426 Pa. 432, 233 A.2d 248 (1967), upheld the condition, stating that probable effect, not subjective motivation, should determine the validity of a condition.

It is well accepted generally that a provision that tends to discourage marriage is valid as applied to the remarriage of a transferor's surviving spouse. Thus, is it common, and valid, for a testator's will to create a trust for a widow or widower, terminable in favor of the children if the spouse should remarry.

Georgia Code §19-3-6, entitled *Effect of restraint on marriage; when valid*, provides: "Marriage is encouraged by the law. Every effort to restrain or discourage marriage by contract, condition, limitation, or otherwise shall be invalid and void, provided that prohibitions against marriage to a particular person or persons or before a certain reasonable age or other prudential provisions looking only to the interest of the person to be benefited and not in general restraint of marriage will be allowed and held valid." Is this statute more restrictive than general case law?

RESTATEMENT (THIRD) OF TRUSTS
(Tent. Draft approved 1999)

§28. *General Rule Concerning Unlawful Purposes.* An intended trust or trust provision is invalid if its purpose or performance is unlawful.

Comment:

a. . . . An intended trust or a particular provision in the terms of a trust is invalid if: (1) it calls for the performance of a criminal or tortious act by the trustee; (2) its purpose is fraudulent; (3) the trust was created for an unlawful consideration; or (4) its enforcement would be contrary to public policy [§29]. This list is not necessarily exclusive.

§29. *Perpetuities and Provisions Against Public Policy.* Even though the performance of a trust or trust provision does not call for the commission of a criminal or tortious act by the trustee (§28), a provision in the terms of a trust is invalid if implementation of the provision would be

  (a) a violation of rules relating to perpetuities or
  (b) otherwise contrary to public policy.

Comment on Clause (b):

d. Rationale and nature of the rule.   The rules allowing and limiting the use of trusts, and the time-divided property ownership usually associated with deadhand control, reflect a compromise between free disposition of private property and other values. . . .

Thus, although one is free to give property to another or to withhold it, it does not follow that one may give in trust with whatever terms or conditions one may wish to attach. This is particularly so of provisions that the law views as exerting a socially undesirable influence on the exercise or nonexercise of fundamental rights that significantly affect the personal lives of beneficiaries and often of others as well. . . .

In cases of the types considered in the Comments that follow, however, simple and precise rules of validity or invalidity frequently cannot be stated . . . [Legitimate] concerns and objectives of settlors [may be weighed] against the objectionable effects or tendencies of conditions attached to beneficial interests. . . .

Consequences of invalidity.   Ordinarily, if a beneficial interest in a trust is to be conferred or is to terminate upon an invalid condition (whether, in form, precedent or subsequent), the interest becomes effective or continues as if the condition had not been imposed. A different result may be reached, however, to avoid distorting the settlor's underlying general plan for allocating his or her estate among family members. Furthermore, if the settlor provides for a certain disposition in case of a condition's invalidity, that direction will be respected unless it would have the effect of deterring a beneficiary from asserting the rule of this Clause (b) of this section.

In addition, a provision that is not to be upheld as written but is susceptible of adaptation to accommodate both public policy concerns and legitimate settlor objectives may be so modified by the court. The rule allowing reformation under the Comments that follow is rather like the use of equitable approximation in cases of violations of the rule against perpetuities (Comment *b*). [Also, compare reformation for mistake in Uniform Trust Code §411.]

Scope note.   The rule of Clause (b) of this section does not apply to outright dispositions conditioned on conduct prior to the death of the testator [or] the time a revocable trust becomes irrevocable. . . . Some of the personal relationships or freedoms considered [here] may be protected in some fashion by federal or state constitutions or statutes . . . [but the] rules and policies of the trust law [may] limit the purposes and terms of trusts in ways that are not based on constitutional or statutory safeguards.

e. Family relationships. A trust or a condition or other provision in the terms of a trust is ordinarily (see below) invalid if it tends to encourage disruption of a family relationship or to discourage formation or resumption of such a relationship. See also Restatement Second, Contracts §§189–191.

Thus, a trust provision normally may not terminate a beneficial interest if a beneficiary and spouse who are living apart should resume living together, or confer a beneficial interest upon a beneficiary if he or she obtains a divorce or legal separation. Similarly, a trust provision is ordinarily invalid if it would tend to induce termination of a long-established relationship of cohabitation without marriage.

In addition, a trust provision is ordinarily invalid if it tends to interfere with a beneficiary's freedom to marry by limiting the beneficiary's selection of a spouse or by unduly postponing the time of marriage. [Exceptions are then noted for remarriage of settlor's surviving spouse or, essentially, a son/daughter-in-law.] . . .

The policy against undermining family relationships applies as well to trust provisions that discourage a person from living with or caring for a parent or child or from social interaction with siblings.

Clause (b) of this section is generally concerned with the objective effects of a provision rather than with the settlor's underlying motive(s). Nevertheless, a subjective inquiry into the settlor's reasons for including a provision in a trust may be relevant. . . . In cases of these types a provision may fail in its original form but nevertheless be judicially reformed to accomplish the permissible objectives (possibly with fiduciary discretion over distributions) while removing or minimizing socially undesirable effects. Speculation about a settlor's motives and other difficulties inherent in these cases may be eased by this remedial flexibility under which an all-or-nothing decision is not required. . . .

f. Religious freedom. . . . A trust provision is ordinarily invalid if its enforcement would tend to restrain the religious freedom of the beneficiary by offering a financial inducement to embrace or reject a particular faith or set of beliefs concerning religion. . . .

g. Careers and conduct. It is not contrary to public policy for a trust provision to encourage a beneficiary to be a productive member of society or to pursue a particular career or form of training, as long as the effect of the provision is not punitive or so rewarding as to be coercive. Thus, a settlor may validly create a trust or include a provision solely to finance a beneficiary's higher education, or a particular type of education, or to facilitate pursuit of a particular type of career (such as religious or social service) by compensating for the financial sacrifices that tend to be associated with the career choice.

§30. *Impossibility and Indefiniteness.* A private trust, or a provision in the terms of the trust, may be unenforceable because of impossibility or indefiniteness.

R. POSNER, ECONOMIC ANALYSIS OF LAW
508, 512–513 (4th ed. 1992)

. . . The problem of a "dead hand" controlling resource use by the living arises when death does not result in a clean transfer to living persons that permits them to do with the money as they please. Since one motivation for accumulating a substantial estate may be to project influence beyond death . . . a policy of disregarding a testator's conditions would in some instances have much the same effect on the incentive to accumulate as would a heavy estate tax. Yet if conditions . . . were always obeyed, a frequent result would be that resources controlled by such conditions would be employed inefficiently. . . .

. . . Suppose a man leaves money to his son in trust, the trust to fail however if the son does not marry a woman of the Jewish faith by the time he is 25 years old. The judicial approach in such cases is to refuse to enforce the condition if it is unreasonable. In the case just put it might make a difference whether the son was 18 or 24 at the time of the bequest and how large the Jewish population was in the place where he lived. . . . Consider, however, the possibilities for modification that would exist if the gift were *inter vivos* rather than testamentary. As the deadline approached, the son might come to his father and persuade him that a diligent search had revealed no marriageable Jewish girl who would accept him. The father might be persuaded to grant an extension or otherwise relax the condition. But if he is dead, this kind of "recontracting" is impossible, and the presumption that the condition is a reasonable one fails. This argues for applying the *cy pres* approach[7] in private as well as charitable trust cases unless [expressly rejected by] the testator. . . .

The point just made may also explain why, although the owner of an art collection is perfectly free to destroy it during his lifetime, a court might consider a condition in his will ordering its destruction to be unreasonable. . . .

---

7. Under cy pres, studied in Chapter 15, if a specific *charitable* purpose becomes illegal, impossible or impracticable, the doctrine may allow the court to devote the trust property cy pres (as nearly as possible) to the settlor's more general charitable purpose. [EDS.]

10

Introduction to Future Interests and Powers of Appointment

A. Future Interests; Classification; Related Rules; Introduction to Construction

The materials in this casebook on the law of future interests are concerned essentially with future interest problems that arise in current estates and trusts practice — planning, drafting, litigation, and fiduciary administration. These materials deal primarily with the provisions of wills or trust agreements directing the disposition of principal on the termination of a trust. Nevertheless, an understanding of the common law system of estates in land and the historical background of the present-day law of future interests is an essential beginning.

1. Classification of Future Interests

A future interest is legally recognized and protected as an existing interest in the property that is subject to it. It is not an estate to be created in the future. It represents a presently existing right, whether certain or uncertain, to the possession or enjoyment of property in the future. Thus, a future interest "is looked upon as a portion of the total ownership of the land or other thing which is its subject matter." Simes, Future Interests §2 (2d ed. 1966).

Future interests may be classified in numerous ways, depending on the degree of refinement desired. Reversions, possibilities of reverter, and rights of entry for condition broken (also called powers of termination) are all future interests left in the transferor or his successors in interest. Future interests created in others, as transferees, are classified, initially at least, as remainders and executory interests. These same types of future interests, familiar as estates in land, can be created in personal property as well. A degree of uncertainty may remain in some states concerning the validity of attempts to create legal future interests in personal property, but at least successive equitable interests can be created in trust. In fact, most future interests today relate to securities held in trust, typically with full legal title in the trustee and the equitable ownership divided over time among the beneficiaries. Unfortunately, classification of future interests and the technical distinctions involved continue to be of significance, although the importance of classification is diminishing.

Possessory Interest	Possible Future Interest	
Created in Transferee	In Transferor (or his estate)	In Transferee
Fee Simple (A "to B and his heirs")	None Since Quia Emptores in 1290	None
Fee Simple Determinable or Fee Simple on a Special Limitation (A "to B and his heirs so long as . . ." or A "to B and his heirs until . . .")	Possibility of Reverter	Executory Interest
Fee Simple on a Condition Subsequent (A "to B and his heirs, but if . . ." or A "to B and his heirs, on the condition, however, that if . . .")	Right of Entry (also called Power of Termination or Right of Entry for Condition Broken)	Executory Interest
Fee Simple Subject to an Executory Limitation (A "to B and his heirs but if . . . then over to C")	None	Executory Interest
Fee Tail (A "to B and the heirs of his body")	Reversion	Vested Remainder Contingent Remainder Executory Interest
Life Estate (A "to B for life")	Reversion	Vested Remainder Contingent Remainder Executory Interest
Term of Years (A "to B for x years")	Reversion (also Fee Simple Subject to a Term of Years)	Vested Remainder (or Fee Simple Subject to a Term of Years)
None (A "to C to take effect at A's death" or "to C ten years after the date of the deed," or at any time in the future)	No future interest — A has present interest	Executory Interest

(Developed from chart prepared by Professor A.G. Gulliver)

a. Future Interests Retained by the Grantor

Rights of Entry. A power of termination, or right of entry for condition broken, results from a transfer that creates an estate subject to a condition subsequent. An example of the right of entry, which accompanies a fee simple subject to a condition subsequent, is a conveyance "to *A* and his heirs, *but if* the premises shall ever be used for commercial or industrial purposes, the grantor and his heirs may re-enter." This leaves the grantor with a right of entry for condition broken not incident to a reversion. However, the transferee's estate may be a life estate or, more commonly, a term of years, subject in either case to a condition subsequent. In these latter situations the right of entry is incident to a reversion.

Possibilities of Reverter. A possibility of reverter results from the creation of a fee simple determinable ("to *A* and his heirs *for so long as* . . .") or a fee simple that is subject to a condition that would cause the estate to expire, resulting in an automatic reverter (*O* conveys "to *A* and his heirs, but if *A* dies without issue, the property shall belong to *O* and his heirs." Unlike the right of entry, the possibility of reverter operates automatically and without action on the part of the grantor. Conceptually, the possibility of reverter is deemed not to cut short the fee simple determinable but to take effect in possession upon the natural expiration of the determinable fee by the latter's inherent limitation. By contrast, the right of entry divests the preceding estate upon the occurrence of the condition subsequent and the exercise of the right.

Reversions. All other interests left in a transferor or her successors in interest are reversions. A reversion results from the creation of one or more vested interests of lesser duration than that held by the grantor. A reversion cannot follow a vested interest in fee simple; even fee simple interests which are determinable or subject to conditions subsequent are not deemed to be of "lesser duration" than the fee simple absolute. A reversion can result, however, from the creation of a life estate, a fee tail, which is a "lesser estate," or from the creation of a contingent remainder. Because a reversion is an interest of which the grantor did not divest herself when she transferred a lesser interest than that which she had previously owned in the subject matter, all reversions are conceived of as being necessarily vested. A reversion can, of course, be subject to defeasance, such as when a life estate and a contingent remainder are granted ("to *A* for life, then to *B* if *B* survives *A*"). Once a transfer has been made leaving a reversion in the transferor or her successors, a subsequent transfer of that interest will not change its classification. The transferee of a reversion takes a reversion. The interest does not become a remainder.

Some Questions: What interests are created and retained if *A* conveys land "to *B* for so long as it is used for residential purposes, but if ever used for nonresidential purposes the grantor shall be entitled to possess and to hold the land in fee simple"? As you proceed through this chapter, consider what differences follow from the classification of these interests. Consider also the possible implications of the situation that might arise in fifty (or 100) years if all other parcels of land for a number of blocks on all sides of the property in question have gone over to commercial, light industrial, and municipal purposes.

Note on Legislation. Because possibilities of reverter and powers of termination are not subject to the rule against perpetuities, legislation restricting the duration and enforceability of these interests has been enacted in many states. See Cal. Civ. Code §885.030 (West Supp. 1996); Ky. Rev. Stat. §381.219 (Michie 1995); N.C. Gen. Stat. §41-32 (1996). Many of these statutes limit the duration of these interests to a period of time, usually thirty years, after which the antecedent interest becomes a fee simple absolute.

What different legal consequences flow from whether a possibility of reverter or power of termination is created?

b. Future Interests Created in Grantees

Remainders. A remainder is created in a person other than the transferor or his successors in interest, and it is always created simultaneously with one or more prior estates. The estate which precedes a remainder (the "particular estate") cannot be one of the fee simple estates, but a remainder can follow a fee tail[1] as well as a life estate or term of years. In addition, a remainder must be so limited at its creation that it *can* become a present interest immediately upon the expiration of the particular estate. By contrast, an executory interest either follows a fee simple interest or else is so created that it must vest, if it does so at all, by divesting a vested interest. Except where the doctrine of destructibility of contingent remainders is abolished, and there only where the doctrine would formerly have applied, a remainder cannot cut short — i.e., divest — a *present* estate, for this can be done for transferees only by executory interests. While cutting off vested *future* interests also is essentially a function of executory interests, a contingent remainder does have this effect when it divests a nonpossessory estate (a reversion) left in the grantor or his successors. Illustration: to *A* for life, *remainder to B if he survives A.* (You will recognize that some extremely fine distinctions are encompassed in tediously worded attempts to distinguish remainders from executory interests, and that they often fill the same purpose.)

---

1. See Section 2, Historical Background.

Remainders are further classified as vested and contingent:

a. Contingent remainders. A remainder is contingent when it is limited to an unborn or unascertained person or is subject to a condition *precedent* other than the termination of the preceding estates. Illustration: to *A* for life, *remainder to B if he survives A; remainder to C if B does not survive A.* *B*'s interest is a contingent remainder, so is *C*'s. This situation is said to create alternative contingent remainders. In some jurisdictions legal consequences may even depend upon further classification of contingent remainders. A remainder is not contingent because it is subject to a condition *subsequent.*

b. Vested remainders. Vested remainders are generally subdivided in three categories:

(1) Indefeasibly vested remainders are subject to no uncertainties. Illustration: to *A* for life, then to *B*. This future interest is subject to no uncertainties (except the disregarded one of when *A* will die). There is of course no certainty that *B* herself will be able to enjoy possession of the subject matter, but if she should die before *A*, the remainder interest is not affected; like other property of *B*'s, it will pass by her will or to her intestate successors.

(2) Vested remainders subject to partial divestment (or "subject to open") are certain of enjoyment in the future but uncertain as to amount, in that the size of the shares may be diminished and the number of shares increased. A remainder to a class which may increase becomes vested subject to partial divestment as soon as a member of the class qualifies, so that his interest vests. Illustration: to *A* for life *then to the children of A*. As soon as a child is born to *A*, the remainder vests in that child, subject to partial divestment (or subject to open) in order to admit afterborn children of *A*.

(3) A vested remainder subject to complete divestment is held by a born and ascertained person and is free from conditions precedent, but it is subject to being divested. Such a remainder may be a vested remainder in a trust which is subject to revocation or to invasion of principal, or it may take the form of a gift in default of appointment (i.e., a vested remainder subject to a power of appointment). For present purposes, however, this class of remainders and its problems can best be exemplified by a vested remainder subject to an executory interest. Illustration: to *A* for life, *then to B, but if B predeceases A*, then to *C*. *B*'s remainder is vested subject to a condition subsequent; *C* has an executory interest. Often the difference between a contingent remainder and a vested remainder subject to complete divestment involves no more than the formalistic and conceptual distinction between a condition precedent and a condition subsequent. Yet the distinction may be decisive of legal rights. It is often recited as a principle of construction that a vested rather than contingent construction is to be preferred, but this principle has been no solution to the problem of

conditions precedent and subsequent. The typical differences in form of expression, with the standard classifications of the interest, are indicated by the functional equivalents in the foregoing illustration and in that contained in paragraph a, above, involving alternative contingent remainders in *B* and *C*. Common sense would suggest that the interests of *B*, or of *C*, in each of these illustrations would be treated similarly, but it is not too early to caution about the limits of common sense and about the unfortunate burdens history has placed on the field of future interests.

Executory Interests. An executory interest is a future interest which, like a remainder, is created in a transferee but which cannot qualify as a remainder. An executory interest which divests an interest retained by the transferor is referred to as a "springing" executory interest, while one which divests or follows an interest created in a transferee is called a "shifting" executory interest. Executory interests are traditionally said to be non-vested until they become possessory, but a modern, and better, view would be that an executory interest can be vested if limited upon an event certain (e.g., "to *A* ten years from now").

A reference back to the description of remainders may be helpful in understanding what interests are classified as executory interests. Since a transferee's future interest following one of the fee simple estates cannot be a remainder, it is an executory interest. (This executory interest is the possibility of reverter's counterpart in a transferee.) At the time an interest is created, if it is so limited that it cannot possibly take effect in possession or enjoyment at the expiration of a particular estate, it also cannot be a remainder and is therefore an executory interest. Such an interest either divests an estate in the grantor or his successors, or it cuts short the prior estate of another grantee. Thus, it is the hallmark of an executory interest, except the type that follows a fee simple determinable, that when it vests it does so by divesting another interest (e.g., as a transferee's counterpart of a right of entry).

It is a blessing that this phase of the learning in our property law is diminishing in importance. See Dukeminier, Contingent Remainders and Executory Interests: A Requiem for the Distinction, 43 Minn. L. Rev. 13 (1958). On classification of future interests generally see Simes, Future Interests ch. 3 (2d ed. 1966); Bergin & Haskell, Preface to Estates in Land and Future Interests ch. 3 (2d ed. 1984).

PROBLEM

10-A.   Label the interests created in the following two transfers:

1. *O* conveys "to *A* for life, then to *B* if *B* attains age 25; and, if not, to *C*."
2. *O* conveys "to *A* for life, then to *B*, but if *B* fails to attain age 25, to *C*."

Although this appears to be a case of the law of future interests elevating form over substance, there are different practical consequences that follow. For example, assuming no doctrine of destructibility (see section E.2), what result if *A* dies when *B* is 21? Who is entitled to possession during the next four years?

Note here the possible implications of classification on this basis. There are others, as you will see. Should there be? Many questions of "why" concerning rules of estates in land cannot be answered in the satisfactory sense of what value there is in the particular rule; at least a rational, if not satisfying, historical *explanation* can usually be given, but occasionally even this is more than you will get.

2.   Historical Background

For purposes of this course it seems unnecessary to go back into much of the material studied in first-year property concerning the feudal systems of land holding and conveyancing, the Statutes Quia Emptores and De Donis, and the like. However, a limited review of some points may be helpful. Under the feudal system the lord was entitled to such "services" as were individually arranged with the tenant and to certain standard "incidents." The latter included *relief* (a predecessor of modern inheritance taxes), which was a payment to the lord by an heir when he succeeded to the land of his ancestor, first as a privilege usually granted by the lord and later as a matter of right. Also, seisin was an important concept, and livery of seisin was required in order to create or to transfer a present freehold. The freehold estates included not only the various types of fee simple estates but also life estates and fees tail. Only legal freehold interests in land became involved with seisin, which is often defined essentially as the possession of land under claim of freehold.

A review of the situation before the Statute of Uses and the Statute of Wills is important to an understanding of early English law. Only four classes of future interests were then recognized: reversions, possibilities of reverter, rights of entry, and remainders. The rules that *seisin could pass only by livery of seisin* and that *there could be no gap in seisin,* since a lord must always have someone to look to for the performance of the feudal obligations, were a source of certain technical restrictions upon the creation of future interests. From this it followed that *a freehold could not be created to commence in futuro.* Thus, executory interests of the springing variety did not exist. In a conveyance to *A for life, and then to B and his heirs from and after one year from the date of A's death,* *B*'s interest (which we would today label an executory interest) was invalid as an attempted freehold to commence in futuro. The concept of seisin also led to the destruction of contingent remainders under some circumstances. See section 5.b infra.

The early common law also forbade the creation of conditions in a stranger. This meant that no transferee could be granted an estate that would divest the estate of another transferee; i.e., it forbade what we now call shifting executory interests. The interest of C would have been void in a conveyance "to A for life, then to B and his heirs, but if B predeceases A, then to C and his heirs." Although the grantor could reserve to himself a right of entry for condition broken, for which re-entry may be said to have replaced livery of seisin as a means of cutting short the present estate, such a condition could not be created in a grantee. If a grantor attempted to convey "to A and his heirs, but if the land is ever used for other than agricultural purposes, then to B and his heirs," the intended estate in B was void. Since the divesting condition failed and A's estate contained no inherent limitation, such as would be found in a fee simple determinable, A's interest became absolute.

We turn now to an initial consideration of the Statute of Uses, 1536, 27 Hen. VIII, c. 10 and the Statute of Wills, 1540, 32 Hen. VIII, c. 1. The device of the *use* had become extensively used (1) as a means of enabling land to be, in effect, devised and (2) as a means of avoiding feudal incidents, destruction of contingent remainders, and other restrictions or rules affecting legal interests. In order to protect feudal revenues, and also to further the interests of the lawyers in parliament, who sought the return of land litigation from chancery to the law courts, the Statute of Uses was enacted. Shortly thereafter the Statute of Wills was enacted in order to restore the power of testation over land, which the Statute of Uses had placed in jeopardy.

In general, beyond the influence of these statutes in modernizing conveyancing, in facilitating testation, and in the development of the modern trust, these statutes permitted the creation of legal springing and shifting executory interests under appropriate circumstances. Executory interests were unknown at law, but these interests in uses were recognized and accepted in chancery, because seisin was not involved in the operation of equitable interests in land. The Statute of Uses provided, in essence, that where a person is seised of land to the use of another, the person having the use shall have a legal interest the same as that which he had in use. Since springing and shifting uses were already allowed and the *cestui que use* was to take a legal interest like that which he had in use, legal executory interests became accepted so long as they were created via the executed use, such as by bargain and sale or by feoffment to uses. Soon thereafter, the use procedure became unnecessary so far as executory devises were concerned. The Statute of Wills permitted the creation of executory interests without passing through the machinery of the use. Over the years following the Statute's enactment it developed that uses were not executed (a) where the feoffee to uses had active duties, (b) where the use was one on another use, and (c) where the seisin in land was not involved. Through the use, conveyancers were able to employ trustees to preserve contingent remainders that otherwise would be destructible (section 5.b infra).

Today, by statute or decision, executory interests can be created without resort to either the Statute of Wills or Statute of Uses and have been wholly accepted into the family of future interests.

The Fee Tail. You may recall from first-year property the struggle over the estate tail as a device for confining property to a given line of descent; the initial treatment of "to X and the heirs of his body" as a fee simple conditional (giving X a fee simple absolute upon birth of issue) resulted in the enactment of the Statute De Donis Conditionalibus in 1285, which recognized the fee tail. Then in Taltarum's Case, Y.B. 12 Edw. IV 19 (1472), the collusive lawsuit known as the "common recovery" allowed a tenant in tail to get "disentailed," spelling the demise of the fee tail in its pure form. In most states today, fee tail language creates a fee simple.

3.   Relations of Future Interests Owners with Possessory Owners and Others

a.   Protection of Future Interests

In general, the owners of future interests are entitled to legal protection of their rights of future enjoyment. Where the subject matter is held in trust, a certain amount of protection is inherent in the separation of the present beneficial interest from the legal title; problems of protecting equitable future interests remain, of course, but for the most part they are omitted from this chapter and left to be studied as an aspect of the law of trusts. This section is primarily concerned with problems arising from the creation of successive legal interests in real or personal property. Unfortunately, the instruments that create legal future interests often fail to cover adequately, if at all, the problems typified by those examined in this section.

b.   Waste, Powers of Consumption, and Related Matters

The owner of a future interest, as a person presently owning a portion of the total ownership of the subject matter, is generally able to prevent, or is entitled to be compensated for, damage to his rights. The nature of both the present interest and the future interest, as well as the type of remedy sought, are important issues. Consider, for example, the remedies available against a life tenant for waste. Can a reversioner or remainder beneficiary recover damages from him? The answer depends on the nature of the future interest, and whether it is certain that its owner will be entitled to the land in the future. The owner of an indefeasibly vested reversion or remainder can recover damages, but the owner of a contingent or defeasible future interest, suing for himself alone, cannot do so. This does not mean that uncertainty of future enjoyment leaves the future interest holder without any immediate remedy. He can generally have threatened waste enjoined, or he may be able to bring suit in behalf of the owners of all future interests to have damages awarded and impounded by the court until all uncertainties concerning the future interests are resolved. The principles applicable to waste are essentially applicable to remedies against third parties for similar injury to the land, although other questions may complicate the matter. For example, can the life tenant recover for all interests in the land, thereby precluding suit by the remainder beneficiary? Usually not. Assume now that the possessory interest is one of potentially infinite duration, such as a fee simple determinable or fee simple subject to a condition subsequent: Can the owner of the executory interest (or of the possibility of reverter or right of entry) enjoin waste, even though recovery of damages would be out of the question? You should see that such a person's right to an injunction raises issues not presented by the contingent remainder beneficiary's suit against a life tenant. Consider also what remedies should be available to the owner of an executory interest limited upon an event certain: With what group of future interests would you place her executory interest for these purposes?

The above generalizations would have to be modified if the owner of the present interest holds an absolute power by which he could extinguish the future interest for his own benefit at the time of the alleged waste. If, for example, a life tenant holds a power of revocation or a general power of appointment which is presently exercisable, the remainder beneficiaries could neither recover damages for waste nor enjoin threatened waste. The reasons for this should be apparent. Often the owner of the possessory interest is given, expressly or impliedly (as might be the case due to the wasting nature of the assets under some circumstances), a power to take or to consume the subject matter but the power is a qualified or limited one — or it may be unclear whether the power is absolute or limited and, if the latter, what its limits are. See Bell v. Killian, 93 So. 2d 769 (Ala. 1957); cf. Rock Island Bank v. Rhoads, 187 N.E. 139 (Ill. 1933). Questions concerning the meaning and effect of powers of consumption are to be compared with like questions concerning discretionary powers held by trustees to invade principal on behalf of the income beneficiaries of trusts.

COLBURN v. BURLINGAME
214 P. 226 (Cal. 1923)

KERRIGAN, J. . . . [T]he provision made for the defendant [was a life estate] with power to consume the principal of the estate . . . for her individual benefit and support. . . . [T]he provisions of the fourth paragraph of the will, giving the plaintiffs what is left of the estate upon the death of the defendant, make it quite clear that the testator intended to give to his wife only a life estate. It does not follow, however, that the plaintiffs are entitled . . . to enjoin the defendant from disposing of the corpus of the estate, and that she shall be compelled to furnish a bond to protect their rights as remaindermen. The averments of the complaint . . . are:

> IX. That . . . husband of [defendant], shortly after his marriage to her in the year 1920, gave up his employment in Chicago and has not since been employed, and that . . . [defendant] has and is contributing to the support and maintenance of [her] husband from the property of the [the] estate contrary to the last will and testament of [the] deceased, and to the detriment of the plaintiffs herein. . . .

We are of the opinion that, in view of the very broad language in which the bequest to the defendant is couched, this contention is untenable. The life estate of the defendant is in the whole of the property of the estate — "to have and to hold or use the whole or any part thereof in such manner as may in her judgment seem best for her own individual benefit and support without any hindrance on the part of any person or persons, wholly confiding in and believing my beloved wife will not allow said property to depreciate or go to waste."

It is seen that the right of the defendant to use the property is not confined to that necessary for her support; she may use it for her benefit — a term much broader than support; and she is made the judge of what is for her benefit; and she is to exercise that judgment without any hindrance on the part of any person or persons — a plain warning to these plaintiffs to keep hands off. For the preservation of the property the testator wholly confides in his wife. The defendant, it appears, has remarried, and for a time lived with her husband in Chicago. Having ample means — the value of the estate amounting to some $90,000 — the not unnatural desire arises in her to remove to California, or at least to live there during a part of the year. Should she leave her husband toiling and moiling in Chicago? Presumably she gave this question full consideration and concluded that it would be for her benefit that he should accompany her West. We can readily perceive that it might be much to her advantage that she should do so; and if in her opinion her life is made pleasanter or more to her liking by the freedom of her husband from the irksome demands of business, we perceive no reason why, under the wide discretion she enjoys as to what expenditures are for her benefit, the expense of their common life may not be included under this head.

We can imagine expenditures which would be neither for her support nor benefit, the indulgence in which would give to the remaindermen a right to protection by appropriate legal remedy; but until the defendant uses the funds of the estate for the purpose much more remotely connected with her individual benefit than contributing to the support of her husband, the plaintiffs must be content to leave the defendant in the undisturbed enjoyment of the estate bequeathed to her by the testator. . . .

Does this sort of construction seem appropriate in the will contract cases where the survivor's right to consumption is an issue?

Simes, Future Interests (2d ed. 1966) §53 states: "[T]he weight of authority . . . [holds] that a court of equity has the power to order a judicial sale of land affected with a future interest . . . where this is necessary for the preservation of all interests in the land." Simes further observes, "When this judicial power is exercised, the proceeds of the sale are held in a judicially created trust. The beneficiaries of the trust are the persons who held interests in the land, and their beneficial interests are of the same character as the legal interests which they formerly held in the land." One of the reasons lawyers advise the use of trusts rather than legal estates is that trust law generally implies that the trustee has a power of sale so that the best interest of the beneficiaries rather than "necessity" becomes the standard upon which property can be sold.

4.   Alienability of Future Interests

How would you classify the interests of B, C, and D if A creates an inter vivos trust reserving a right to the income for life and a power to amend or revoke the trust in whole or in part, and providing that on her death (without having amended or revoked) one half of the principal is to go "to B" while the other half is to go "to C or, if C is then dead, to D"? On the death of the owner, which of these interests will pass by will? By intestate succession? Which will pass by gift inter vivos? By sale? Which can be reached under state law by the owner's creditors? Which through bankruptcy proceedings? Be prepared to explain any of your answers that require qualification; and if there is a substantial division of authority on any of these matters, consider how you would argue for the various possible results if you found that the law of your state was unsettled.

a. Transmission on Death

When the owner of a legal or equitable future interest dies before the interest becomes possessory, his interest, whether vested or contingent, passes as an asset of his estate in the same manner as a present interest, provided, of course, that the interest does not terminate at the owner's death. (Questions of descendability and devisability are not to be confused with the recurrent constructional question of whether a condition of survivorship exists, but courts have not always kept the distinction clear.) If the owner dies intestate, the future interest passes to her heirs or next of kin. Similarly, a will operates upon future interests which are transmissible (i.e, essentially, not subject to a requirement of survival until the time of possession), just as it would upon other property of the testator. In a few states, an antiquated exception to these rules continues to exist in the case of rights of entry and possibilities of reverter, and they pass only by what might be called a special scheme of descent.

b. Voluntary Alienation Inter Vivos

Different rules prevail concerning certain aspects of the voluntary transfer of future interests inter vivos. From early times in England to the present day in the United States, *reversions* and *vested remainders* have been freely transferable inter vivos. This is so even when these vested interests are subject to complete divestment.

The principal difficulty is with contingent future interests — and hence, of course, frequently with artificial and technical distinctions between conditions precedent and subsequent. The present alienability problem can be traced back to the original inalienability of contingent future interests, resulting from early notions that such interests were not estates but mere "expectancies" or "possibilities" and that dealings in such speculative interests would stir up litigation and complicate titles. In most jurisdictions today, by statute or judicial decision, *contingent remainders* and *executory interests* are freely transferable inter vivos. A few states adhere to the early view that these interests are inalienable, while some distinguish between interests which are "contingent as to the person" who will take and those which are "contingent only as to event."

In most states today *possibilities of reverter* and *powers of termination* are probably freely alienable. A few states may still hold that a power of termination is destroyed by attempted transfer — a rule apparently calculated to do away with an obnoxious restriction on the use of property.

This discussion of the voluntary transferability of various future interests applies equally to legal and equitable interests, except insofar as modified by the doctrine of spendthrift trusts. Despite the invalidity of direct restraints on alienation as applied to legal interests, direct restraints on equitable future interests may be valid in states which recognize spendthrift trusts, depending on whether spendthrift restrictions are permitted with respect to interests in principal as well as income interest.

The preceding paragraphs refer to certain future interests as inalienable or, more precisely, as *not freely transferable*. This language requires explanation and qualification in order not to be misleading. Even "inalienable" future interests can be transferred by way of *release* to the owner of another interest in the property. (E.g., the owner of an executory interest can release it to the possessory owner whose interest it might divest.) Inalienable interests can also be alienated, in a sense, by two other methods. (1) An attempted transfer by warranty deed creates an *estoppel*, so that the property passes to the purported transferee if and when the interest vests. (Recall the doctrine of estoppel by deed, encountered in first year property.) (2) Equity will treat an attempted transfer of the interest for a fair consideration as an *equitable assignment* — a contract to convey, for which specific performance may be granted. "Transfers" by estoppel or equitable assignment were not inconsistent with early notions that contingent future interests were not existing estates, for these rules have long been applied to transactions involving the bare expectancy that an heir apparent has in the estate of a living relative.

See 3 Richard R. Powell, Real Property §21.02 (1998).

c.   Involuntary Alienation Inter Vivos

Next let us consider the more frequently troublesome problem of involuntary alienation, for which the rules of voluntary alienation are essential background. Vested interests, though subject to divestment, traditionally have been and are today subject to execution, creditor's bill, or other locally appropriate creditor process. Because they were inalienable voluntarily, contingent future interests have traditionally been immune to the claims of the owner's creditors. Where contingent interests are now freely transferable, the question arises whether these interests are now also subject to creditors' claims. Numerous courts have held that they are. (Where this is so, it generally does not matter whether the interest is legal or equitable, except insofar as procedure may be affected or unless a spendthrift trust is involved.) In some states contingent future interests continue to be unavailable to the owner's creditors. Where a particular type of future interest is still not freely alienable voluntarily, then, of course, this alone suffices to preclude forced sale for the satisfaction of creditors' claims. But some states that recognize the free voluntary transfer of contingent future interests hold them immune to creditor process today, principally because of the element of sacrifice involved in the forced sale of such unmarketable interests and, to a lesser extent, because such sale is said to interfere with the donor's intention. Yet these same courts adhere to the traditional rule that defeasibly vested interests may be reached to satisfy creditors. See Park v. Park, 541 N.E.2d 640 (Ohio Mun. Ct. 1988); but compare the sound, but quite different, approaches in Clarke v. Fay, 91 N.E. 328 (Mass. 1910) and Anglo Calif. Natl. Bank v. Kidd, 137 P.2d 460 (Cal. App. 1943).

The broad language of the Bankruptcy Reform Act of 1978, 11 U.S.C. §541(a)(1) (treating "all legal or equitable interests" of the debtor as part of the bankrupt's estate) should encompass contingent future interests that are exempt from creditors' claims under state law, except interests in spendthrift trusts. (See Chapter 14.)

See generally Halbach, Creditors' Rights in Future Interests, 43 Minn. L. Rev. 217 (1958).

5. Rules Restricting the Creation of Future Interests

a. The Repugnancy Doctrine

Although the rule of repugnancy is still a current problem, the primary objective of this section is to direct your attention to the very fundamental questions of applied jurisprudence raised by Fox v. Snow and especially by the widely noted dissent of the late Chief Justice Vanderbilt.

FOX v. SNOW
76 A.2d 877 (N.J. 1950)

PER CURIAM . . . The paragraph [in dispute] provided as follows: "Third: I give and bequeath unto my husband, William L. Green all of the money which I have on deposit at the Paterson Savings and Trust Company, New Jersey, however, any money which is in the said account at the time of my said husband's death, the said sum shall be held by my niece, Catherine King Fox, absolutely and forever."

. . . The husband . . . . [thereafter died intestate]. . . . The question presented is whether [the husband] became the absolute owner of the money on deposit, the gift over to the plaintiff, Catherine King Fox, being void, or whether the husband took a life estate only and the fee vested in the niece.

The bequest to the husband was in general terms with an absolute power of disposal. Under such circumstances the gift over of the part not disposed of is void. As determined by judge Grimshaw below, the husband . . . took an absolute ownership, an estate in fee, of the bank account. . . .

Appellants ask this Court to explicitly and expressly overrule the long established law of this State. This we decline to do. Such action would be fraught with great danger in this type of case where titles to property, held by bequests and devises, are involved. A change of the established law by judicial decision is retrospective. . . . On the other hand, a change in the settled law by statute is prospective only. . . .

The judgment of the Superior Court is affirmed.

VANDERBILT, C.J. (dissenting). I am constrained to dissent from the views of the majority of the court, first, because they apply to the case a technical rule of the law to defeat the plain intent of the testatrix without serving any public policy whatever in so doing and, secondly — and this seems to me to be even more important — because their opinion involves a view of the judicial process, which, if it had been followed consistently in the past, would have checked irrevocably centuries ago the growth of the common law to meet changing conditions and which, if pursued now, will spell the ultimate ossification and death of the common law by depriving it of one of its most essential attributes — its inherent capacity constantly to renew its vitality and usefulness by adapting itself gradually and piecemeal to meeting the demonstrated needs of the times. . . .

In Smith v. Bell, 31 U.S. 68 (1832), a case very much like the one now under consideration, Chief Justice Marshall . . . had this to say with respect to the intent of the testator, at p. 74:

> These words give the remainder of the estate, after his wife's decease, to the son, with as much clearness as the preceding words give the whole estate to his wife. . . . We are no more at liberty to disregard the last member of the sentence than the first. No rule is better settled than that the whole will is to be taken together, and is to be construed as to give effect, if it be possible, to the whole. . . . The limitation in remainder shows that, in the opinion of the testator, the previous words had given only an estate for life. This was the sense in which he used them.

Instead of following this obviously sound method of testamentary construction our courts have been misled by the complex and artificial rules of the old common law of real property into accepting a technical rule of testamentary construction which gained seeming but altogether undeserved immortality form the opinion of Chancellor Kent in Jackson v. Robins, 16 Johns. 537 (N.Y. Ct. App. 1819), wherein he categorically stated at p. 588:

> . . . we may lay it down as an incontrovertible rule, that where an estate is given to a person generally, indefinitely, with a power of disposition, it carries a fee: and the only exception to the rule is, where the testator gives to the first taker an estate for life only, by certain and express words, and annexes to it a power of disposal. In that particular and special case, the devisees for life will not take an estate in fee, notwithstanding the distinct and naked gift of a power of disposition of reversion. . . .

Stating that the rule is not a rule of construction to carry out the intention of the parties but that its aim and object is to defeat that intention, (John Chipman Gray in his Restraints on the Alienation of Property 67 (2d ed. 1895)) observed:

> The courts always recognize this fact; and that no considerations of public policy are involved is shown by its being perfectly easy to carry out the desired result by a slight change of phrase. If you give a man fee simple, you cannot provide that if he does not sell or devise it shall go to T, but if you give him a life estate with power to appoint by deed or will, and in default of appointment to T, the gift to T is perfectly good. In both cases the intention is clear and undisputed; when you defeat the intention in one case, you are defeating exactly the intention that is preserved in the other. . . .

The opinion of the majority of the court, like every other decision in this State on the subject, makes no attempt to justify the rule it perpetuates in reason or on the grounds of public policy. Despite the deleterious effects of the rule and the lack of any sound principle to support it, the majority maintains that it should not be overthrown, because it has been the long established law of this State and because overruling it "would be fraught with greater danger in this type of case where titles to property, held by bequests and devises, are involved" by reason of the retroactive effect of all judicial decisions. This view if it had been consistently applied in the past, would have prevented any change whatever in property law by judicial decisions. There would have been, e.g., no rule against perpetuities, no restraints on the alienation of property, no right to redeem mortgaged premises, no foreclosure of the equity of redemption, and so on endlessly. . . .

To hold, as the majority opinion implies, that the only way to overcome the unfortunate rule of law that plagues us here is by legislation, is to put the common law in a self-imposed straight-jacket. Such a the-

ory, if followed consistently, would inevitably lead to the ultimate codification of all of our law for sheer lack of capacity in the courts to adapt
the law to the needs of the living present. The doctrine of stare decisis
neither renders the courts impotent to correct their past errors nor
requires them to adhere blindly to rules that have lost their reasons
for being. The common law would be sapped of its life blood if stare
decisis were to become a god instead of a guide. The doctrine when
properly applied operates only to control change not to prevent it. . . .

The dangers that the majority fear, it is submitted, are more apparent
than real. The doctrine of stare decisis tends to produce certainty in
our law, but it is important to realize that certainty per se is but a means
to an end, and not an end in itself. Certainty is desirable only insofar
as it operates to produce the maximum good and the minimum harm
and thereby to advance justice. The courts have been reluctant to overthrow established rules when property rights are involved for the simple reason that persons in arranging their affairs have relied upon the
rules as established, though outmoded or erroneous, and so to abandon them would result sometimes in greater harm than to observe
them. The question whether the doctrine of stare decisis should be
adhered to in such cases is always a choice between relative evils. When
it appears that the evil resulting from a continuation of the accepted
rule must be productive of greater mischief to the community than
can possibly ensue from disregarding the previous adjudications on the
subject, courts have frequently and wisely departed from precedent. 14
Am. Jur., Courts §126.

What then, are the relative evils in the instant case? First, we should
consider the evils that will result from a perpetuation of the rule here
involved. It has already been demonstrated that the rule, in each and
every instance in which it is applied, results in a complete frustration
of the legitimate intention of the testator. It can only operate to take
property from one to whom the testator intended to give it and to
bestow it upon another. There is a further evil, moreover, resulting
from the very existence of the rule. As Professor Gray put it in his Restraints on the Alienation of Property 68 (2d ed. 1895) supra: "It is
often a question of the greatest difficulty to determine whether a testator has given a devisee a life estate with general power of appointment,
or whether he has given him a fee with an executory devise over in
case the first taker shall not dispose of his interest. If it were not for
this rule, that question would almost never become material. But now
that a testator's intention, if expressed in one form, cannot be carried
out, while it can be, if expressed in another, the question becomes of
vital importance, and consequently this arbitrary rule is responsible for
an enormous amount of litigation."

Bearing out this observation, an annotation in 75 A.L.R. 71-111 . . .
cites 386 cases . . . , and we cannot even hazard a guess as to the number

of additional cases, reported and unreported, in which the rule was involved. That a rule has been so productive of unnecessary litigation is in itself strong proof of its undesirability.

Having considered the evils flowing from continuing to follow the rule, let us now inquire into the evils, if any, which might result from its rejection. It is pertinent at this point to recall the words of Mr. Justice Cardozo minimizing the effect of overruling a decision: "The picture of the bewildered litigant lured into a course of action by the false light of a decision, only to meet ruin when the light is extinguished and the decision is overruled, is for the most part a figment of excited brains." The Nature of the Judicial Process (1921) 122. The rule in question by its very nature is never relied upon by those who are seeking to make a testamentary disposition of their property, for if the rule were known to a person at the time of the drawing of his will, its operation would and could be guarded against by the choice of words appropriate to accomplish the result desired. The rule is truly subversive of the testator's intent. It is relied upon only after the testator's decease by those who seek, solely on the basis of its technical and arbitrary requirements, to profit from the testator's ignorance. . . . Certainly it is not unjust or inequitable to deny such persons resort to this rule. There are three possible factual situations to be considered in weighing the retroactive effect of overturning this rule. First, where a will has already been the subject of legal proceedings, property rights determined by a judgement entered therein are beyond the reach of any change in the law. Such a judgement is res judicata. Second, where a will has been executed, but the testator is still living, or if dead, the clause similar to the one in question has not yet been construed by the courts, the "evil" caused by the overthrow of the rule will be to carry out the testator's intent. No existing will need be changed by a decision doing away with the old rule, since its overturning merely permits the expressed intent of the testator to be given effect. Third, where persons have not now, but in the future execute wills, no harm can result from overthrowing the rule. . . .

Isn't the case for Chief Justice Vanderbilt's approach to overruling even stronger when an unsound rule of construction (rather than a rule of law, as in this case) is involved? Such rules of construction — i.e., presumptions of intent — by their very nature yield to findings of contrary intent, thus leading to unnecessary litigation and unpredictable results when the rule is not sound. See Edward C. Halbach, Jr., Stare Decisis and Rules of Construction in Wills and Trusts, 52 Cal. L. Rev. 921 (1964).

Can you think of any other situations possibly more difficult to deal with than the "three possible factual situations" mentioned in the last paragraph of the dissent above? If so, how do you evaluate the possible arguments which might be based thereon in support of the majority opinion? Keep the pervasive questions raised by this case and this note in mind throughout the course. The repugnancy doctrine and its implications are stressed in Powell, Construction of Written Instruments, 14 Ind. L.J. 199 (1939).

In Bell v. Killian, 266 Ala. 12, 93 So. 2d 769 (1957), the testator left his estate "unto my wife" with an "absolute" power of sale and "empowered (her) to use said estate as she may deem fit for her maintenance, well-being, comfort and support." Thereafter, the unconsumed portions of the estate were to pass to the testator's brothers or their heirs. The appellants argued that the will created an absolute fee in the wife because of the cannon that "An absolute estate created in clear and decisive terms, cannot be taken away or cut down to a lesser estate or interest by subsequent words, which are not as clear and decisive." The court stated (citations omitted):

> While this is a recognized principle . . . we do not think it is applicable [to] the will before us for [it] does not create an absolute fee in clear and decisive terms. [A] general devise of this nature which fails to specifically define the extent of the estate created, does not necessarily import an absolute fee if subsequent provisions of the will indicate that the testator intended a lesser estate. . . . [W]hen the testator makes a general devise without defining the extent of the estate which he wishes to create, and he subsequently provides for a remainder in the same property, it seems only logical to assume that he intended to qualify or limit the initial gift. There is no repugnancy between such provision and none should be read into the will by the courts. [Therefore] the widow became a life tenant with [limited] power of disposition. . . .

See also Estate of Johnson, 387 N.W.2d 329 (Iowa 1986), where the court applied the repugnancy doctrine with the dissent arguing, "the trend is away from the strictures of the old repugnancy rule." Id. at 336.

b.   Destructibility of Contingent Remainders

PROBLEM

10-B.   Owner (*O*) conveyed a farm to his wife, *W*, for life, then to *S* if he attains 21. *W* died when *S* was 19. Explain the state of the title to the farm if the destructibility rule is in effect.

The Doctrine of Destructibility of Contingent Remainders originated in feudal notions concerning passage of seisin and its supposed
role (crude though it was) in preventing perpetuities. With the coming
of the Statute of Uses (1536), the Statute of Wills, and the common
law Rule Against Perpetuities, the doctrine should have vanished. It
was partially abolished in 1845 and completely in 1877 in England, but
the English case law lived on in a number of American jurisdictions.
Numerous legislatures have abolished the doctrine completely, and a
few have done so in part. Some courts have refused to recognize the
doctrine as a part of the common law, and this has long been the position of the American Law Institute. Restatement of Property §240
(1936). A few courts may still recognize the rule, however, and it remains significant in examining land titles in states in which it formerly
existed.

Under the destructibility rule, a contingent remainder is destroyed
if the prior estates of freehold terminate before the occurrence of the
contingency upon which the remainder is limited. Seisin reverts and
cannot later spring out of the grantor when the contingency is resolved.
Thus, a contingent remainder never takes effect unless it is vested or
vests at the termination of the supporting freeholds. If it vests in time,
the life tenant "carries the seisin" to the remainder beneficiary.

The operation of the rule can be illustrated by two types of cases in
which a contingency might not occur by the time the preceding estate
terminates. One is a transfer "to A for life, then to the heirs of B." If
A thereafter predeceases B, the remainder cannot vest and is destroyed
because B's heirs have not been determined. A second illustration is
a transfer "to A for life, then to such of A's children as reach the age
of 21." If A dies while all of his children are under 21, the remainder
is destroyed because the unsatisfied age contingency prevents it from
vesting. In each of these cases the transferor's reversion becomes possessory on A's death, and the subsequent occurrence of the condition
precedent does not serve to divest the reversion. Once the "gap" occurs and seisin reverts, the remainder can never take effect — it is
destroyed.

Keeping in mind that the doctrine of destructibility has to do with
limitations on the passing of seisin, its application is limited to cases
involving: (a) contingent remainders (thus exempting executory interests and vested remainders); (b) which are estates of *freehold;* (c) in *real
property* (thus having no application where the subject matter is a thing
other than land and not even where chattels real are involved); (d) the
remainder in question must be a *legal* estate (since the vesting of equitable interests does not involve seisin, which is in the trustee); and
(e) there must be no prior vested estate of freehold to support it.

There are two significant principles to be considered in connection
with requirement (a) above. On the one hand is the traditional prefer-

ence for construing an estate as a vested remainder subject to divestment rather than as a contingent remainder, serving to reduce the rule's application in cases where it is unclear whether a condition is precedent or subsequent. (E.g., an age requirement attached to a remainder might be construed as divesting the remainder beneficiary's estate if he dies before attaining the required age rather than as making attainment of the stated age a condition precedent to vesting.) On the other hand, there is the established corollary of destructibility that if the interest, viewed at its inception, could possibly take effect as a remainder, it *is* a remainder; thus, according to the rule of Purefoy v. Rogers, 2 Wms. & Saunders 380 (1670), a remainder cannot operate as an executory interest if (even after executory interests were allowed) the supporting freehold terminates before the remainder is ready to vest. In effect: "Executory interests can spring or shift but remainder interests cannot."

Where the doctrine of destructibility remains, a contingent remainder can also be destroyed artificially by merger of two consecutive, vested, legal estates which, after their creation, come together in a single owner. For example, assume the grantor conveys "to A for life, then to A's issue who survive him," and the grantor later dies leaving A as his sole heir. The grantor's reversion is inherited by A, whose life estate merges in his newly acquired reversion, which is the next vested estate of freehold. (Merger does not occur if the two consecutive vested estates are created in the same person simultaneously with the contingent remainder.) This form of destruction is expressly abolished as a part of most legislation abolishing destructibility. Another form of artificial destruction was recognized in the early common law. If the supporting freehold was eliminated by forfeiture, such as once resulted from attempted conveyance of the fee by a life tenant, the contingent remainder limited thereon was destroyed if it could not then vest. Destructibility can no longer occur in this fashion since forfeiture is no longer recognized. Although the modern rule against forfeiture is not dependent upon statute, the matter is often covered by legislation.

Even in jurisdictions in which remainders are destructible, the cases to which the doctrine can apply are relatively few. This is because most future interests today are created in securities held in trust. Either the fact that the subject matter is something other than land or the fact that a remainder is equitable (assuming it is not executed by the Statute of Uses) would be sufficient to prevent seisin from being involved, and hence to prevent the doctrine's operation.

Because the doctrine of destructibility did not apply to executory interests, Pells v. Brown. Cro. Jac. 590 (1620), their use could place property beyond the control of living persons. This created a need for some limit both on the resulting suspension of feudal obligation and on removing property from channels of commerce for excessively long periods of time. The Rule Against Perpetuities (Chapter 20) developed in response to this need.

After the abolition of the destructibility doctrine in modern times, the effect of contingent remainders and executory interests is much the same.

c. The Rule in Shelley's Case

The Rule in Shelley's Case existed at least as early as the fourteenth century, but it was not until several centuries later that the case for which the rule is named was decided. Lord Coke's report of the case enunciated the rule as he had stated it in argument, as counsel for the Defendant: "[I]t is a rule of law, when an ancestor by any gift or conveyance takes an estate of freehold, and in the same gift or convey-ance an estate is limited either mediately or immediately to his heirs in fee or in tail; that always in such cases, 'the heirs' are words of limita-tion of the estate, and not words of purchase." Shelley's Case, 1 Co. Rep. 93b, 104a (1581). A more precise but slightly modernized state-ment of the rule is: If a *single instrument* creates a freehold in a person and purports to create a *remainder,* mediately or immediately, in the heirs or heirs of the body of that person, and if the estates are *both legal* or *both equitable* (Do you see the relevance of the Statue of Uses?), that person also takes the remainder in fee simple or fee tail (or whatever the latter's present-day counterpart would be under applicable law). Shelley's Rule is a rule of law — or, as sometimes said, a rule of pol-icy — applicable only to land; as such it is applied regardless of intent if the circumstances are appropriate. An occasional case has held, how-ever, that the rule is merely one of construction; such a presumption of intent would be applicable to dispositions involving personal prop-erty as well as land.

Little is known of the origin of the rule or the reasons for it. It may have originated before contingent remainders were recognized, or it may have been intended to further the alienability of land; it may have been an attempt to effectuate the probable intent of grantors, in light of the early meaning of "heirs" and the then existing pattern of de-scent, coupled with the similarity of effect of a fee simple and a life estate with remainder to the life tenant's heirs. But the most probable reason for the rule was to preserve the valuable feudal incidents of descent (relief, wardship, and marriage) which did not accrue when land passed by purchase (i.e., treating "heirs" as language describing a person who is to take a remainder under the conveyance, whether by gift or for consideration). Thus, it functioned like a medieval gener-ation-skipping transfer tax, protecting the early version of an estate tax. See Chapter 8.

The Rule in Shelley's Case often upsets the obvious intent of the transferor. To the extent this relic of the English common law does, as sometimes asserted, tend to further alienability of property, it does so at the expense of intent and at a high price in litigation. A costly bit of litigation, in which Shelley's Rule was ultimately held not to apply (Orme v. Northern Trust Co., 25 Ill. 2d 151, 183 N.E.2d 505 (1962)), produced some $221,000 in attorney's fees (a significant amount at that time!). The rule also lacks the generality of application that rules of policy should have, because the scope of its application is so arbitrarily limited and readily susceptible of circumvention. It is, in effect, simply a punishment for bad drafting.

When the Rule in Shelley's Case operates, it does so only on the remainder. It does not, of itself, create a fee. Ultimately, therefore, whether the interest or interests taken by the person in question will be a fee simple or fee tail, rather than a life estate and remainder, depends upon whether merger applies. A conveyance to *A* for life, remainder to the heirs of *A*, produces a fee simple in *A* by merger. Merger does not apply so long as there remains an intervening indestructible estate. (E.g., to *A* for life, then to *B* for life, then to *A*'s heirs.) (Question: When would the intervening interest *not* be indestructible? Careful!) Nor does merger apply so long as the life tenant's remainder is contingent. (E.g., to *A* for life, and if *A* outlives *B* to the heirs of *A*.)

The Rule in Shelley's Case has now been rejected in nearly all states. A few courts have held the rule not to exist, concluding it had no place in the American common law; most states have abolished it by statute. See, e.g., Cal. Civ. Code §779 (abolishing it retroactively); the rule was abolished in England by Law of Property Act, 1925, 15 & 16 Geo. V, c. 20, §131. The significance of the rule would be readily apparent to a lawyer practicing in a jurisdiction in which it still prevails. Less obvious is its importance elsewhere. Since statutes abolishing the rule are generally not retroactive, interests created prior to the effective date of the legislation are unaffected.

Although the Rule in Shelley's Case itself is not a rule of construction, most of the litigation concerning the rule has involved construction to determine whether the language of the remainder is the equivalent of "heirs" or "heirs of the body" in the sense required by the particular court. If so, the rule is applied without regard to the virtually certain intent that the remainder belong to those heirs themselves rather than to the ancestor. A remainder to "children" is not a remainder to heirs or the equivalent, even though the children turn out to be the heirs. A remainder to the life tenant's "issue," however, may be held to invoke the rule if the term is deemed equivalent to "heirs of the body." Consider whether the Rule in Shelley's Case applies in the following situations:

1.   *A* devised to *B* for life, then to *C.* At the time of *A*'s death *C* was
     the sole child of *B,* an elderly widow, and at *B*'s death *C* was her
     sole heir at law.
2.   *A* devises to *B* for life, then to *B*'s heirs, share and share alike.
3.   *A* devises to *B* for life, then to *B*'s wife, *W,* for life if she survives
     B, then to those who would take *B*'s property by the laws of intes-
     tacy then in force.
4.   *A* and *B* reside in state *X. A* devises land situated in state *Y* to *B*
     for life, then to *B*'s heirs, to be determined according to the laws
     of state *X.*
5.   *A* devises to *B* for life, then to *C,* but if *C* predeceases *B,* to the
     heirs of *B.*

PROBLEM

10-C.   In 1970 *O* transferred Blackacre "to *A* for life, then to the
heirs of *A.*" In 1980 the legislature abolished the Rule in Shelley's Case.
In 2000 *A* died devising all of her estate to her friend, *F. A*'s surviving
relatives are her three children. Who owns Blackacre?

d.   The Doctrine of Worthier Title

PROBLEM

10-D.   *O* conveyed Blackacre "to *A* for life, remainder to my heirs."
Later *O* died devising all of her estate to her friend, *X. O* was survived
by two children, *B* and *C.* At *A*'s death, who is entitled to possession
of Blackacre?

The Doctrine of Worthier Title developed at early common law probably for reasons similar to those underlying the Rule in Shelley's Case.
The doctrine had both a testamentary and an inter vivos branch, the
former rarely being of any modern significance. The doctrine's operation was simple: a purported remainder to the heirs of the transferor
was void, leaving a reversion in the transferor. The result was that the
heirs took by inheritance if the transferor died intestate, rather than
taking "by purchase" (by the transfer that purported to grant them a
remainder). That's not so bad, but certain feudal dues were owed to
the feudal lord when an heir took by inheritance; hence, it was "worthier" from the lord's perspective.

This operated fairly well for a while, but later when property owners
regularly began to execute wills, the rule became intent defeating. Con-

sider the result if the transferor later died testate thinking his heirs were provided for, and left his entire estate to charity.

Doctor v. Hughes, 122 N.E. 221 (N.Y.1919), is the source of most modern American worthier title law. In that much-criticized case, Judge Cardozo turned the doctrine into a rule of construction rather than a rule of law. In other words, when the transferor says "then to my heirs," she is presumed to mean "then to myself." This presumption is rebuttable, so that language or circumstances may provide an argument that a remainder to the heirs was intended. A flood of litigation followed in New York and elsewhere, with unpredictable and unreconcilable results. The doctrine was abolished in New York in 1966. It is also abolished by statute in most other states, often by enacting §2-710 of the UPC.

Although many jurisdictions have abolished Worthier Title, some still retain it. Where it still exists, it can have adverse (surprise!) estate tax, as well as personal, consequences. On the other hand, it can allow a settlor to terminate a poorly planned trust that would otherwise be indestructible — a reason sometimes offered for its retention. Commentators critical of the rule argue that there are better ways to deal with trust termination problems. For example, see Hatch v. Riggs National Bank, 361 F.2d 559 (D.C. Cir. 1966), and Chapter 14.

6. Introduction to the Rule Against Perpetuities

THE DUKE OF NORFOLK'S CASE
3 Ch. Cas. 1, 26 (Chancery 1682)

[The Earl of Arundel and Surrey established a trust of a term of 200 years, in substance, for his second son, Henry, and the male heirs of his body, but if Thomas (the eldest son, who was mentally incompetent) should die without issue during Henry's lifetime so that the earldom descends to Henry, then in trust for Charles (the third son) in tail, with remainders in tail to the settlor's other sons, Edward, Francis, and Bernard. Thomas died without issue, and the earldom descended to Henry, as did also the dukedom of Norfolk.]

Lord Nottingham, Ch. . . . . [W]hether this be a good imitation to Charles in tail, is the question; for most certainly it is a void limitation to the other brothers in tail. . . .

The great matter objected is, it is against all the rules of law, and tends to a perpetuity.

If it tends to a perpetuity, there needs no more to be said, for the law has so long labored against any settlement, if it can be found to tend to a perpetuity.

Therefore, let us examine whether it do so, and let us see what a perpetuity is, and whether any rule of law is broken in this case.

A perpetuity is the settlement of an estate or an interest in tail, with such remainders expectant upon it, as are in no sort in the power of the tenant in tail in possession, to dock by any recovery or assignment, but such remainders must continue as perpetual clogs upon the estate; such do fight against God, for they pretend to such a stability in human affairs, as the nature of them admits not of, and they are against the reason and the policy of the law, and therefore not to be endured.

But on the other side, future interests, springing trusts, or trusts executory, remainders that are to emerge and arise upon contingencies, are quite out of the rules and reasons of perpetuities, nay, out of the reason upon which the policy of the law is founded in those cases, especially, if they be not of remote or long consideration; but such as by a natural and easy interpretation will speedily wear out, and so things come to their right channel again.

. . . [W]here no perpetuity is introduced, nor any inconveniency doth appear, there no rule of law is broken. . . .

Now where there is a perpetuity introduced, no cloud hanging over the estate but during a life, which is a common possibility where there is no inconvenience in the earth, and where the authorities of this court concur to make it good; to say, all is void, and to say it here, I declare it, I know not how to do it. . . .

Therefore my present thoughts are, that the trust of this term was well limited to Charles. . . .

[After reargument, Lord Nottingham added]

. . . You may limit, it seems, upon a contingency to happen in a life; what if it be limited, if such a one die without issue within twenty-one-years, or one hundred years, or while Westminster-Hall stands? Where will you stop if you do not stop here? I will tell you where I will stop: I will stop wherever any visible inconvenience doth appear, for the just bounds of a fee-simple upon a fee-simple are not yet determined, but the first inconvenience that ariseth upon it will regulate it. . . .

RESTATEMENT OF PROPERTY (1944)
Intr. Note to Div. IV, 2129-2133 (1944)

. . . Throughout this long period, beginning in the thirteenth century, the courts have repeatedly manifested strong belief in the importance to society of imposing restrictions upon attempted fetterings of property. . . .

The basis or justification for this assumption (that social welfare requires the imposition of restrictions upon the fettering of property) has never been adequately explored and has been seldom discussed. Insofar as this assumption lies at the root of the rule against perpetuities, some light as to its justification can be obtained by an examination of the purposes which are served by the rule against perpetuities.

In the first place, the rule against perpetuities provides an adjustment or balance between the desire of the current owner of property to prolong indefinitely into the future his control over the devolution and use thereof and the desire of the person who will in the future become the owner of the affected land or other thing, to be free from the dead hand. The maximum possible liberty for all is attainable only by means of substantial restrictions upon the actions of each. The emphasis in English society upon the perpetuation of landed families afforded a particular necessity for a judicial prevention of the undue cramping of the activities of the generations yet to come. Thus viewed, the regulation of the fettering of property is socially desirable because it embodies one of the compromises prerequisite to the maintenance of a going society controlled primarily by its living members.

In the second place, the rule against perpetuities contributes to the probable utilization of the wealth of society. This contribution is made in two different ways. By prohibiting certain categories of uncertain future interests, this rule minimizes the fear of loss of investment normally felt by the owner of a present interest subject to an outstanding future interest. To the extent that this feat is minimized, full development and full use of the affected thing, as well as the making of new investments therein, are encouraged. The rule against perpetuities facilitates the utilization of the wealth of society in still another way. This rule has been said by John Chipman Gray to have been adopted by the common law as a means "for forwarding the circulation of property" (Rule Against Perpetuities §2.1 (4th ed. 1942). This it does by prohibiting those categories of future interests which would make either impossible, or improbable, sales of land for long periods of time. By thus removing barriers to the transfer of property, the probability is increased that specific land or other tangible things will come into the ownership of a person who sees an available mode for its utilization. The contribution of the rule against perpetuities to the probable utilization of the wealth of society is greatest when the subject matter of the limitation is specific land or some other tangible thing. As to intangibles this socially desirable consequence of the rule is not so clear, since shares and bonds constitute an important bulk of intangibles, and, as to intangibles of these types, restrictions operative as to the shares or bonds would in no way hamper the utilization of its assets by the issuing corporation.

In the third place, the rule against perpetuities aids in the keeping of property responsive to the meeting of the exigencies of its current owners. The division of ownership into successive interests tends to lessen the sum realizable upon a sale of the separated interests, and thus diminishes the total purchasing power of the wealth represented by the thing in which such divided interests have been created. To whatever extent such diminution occurs, the responsiveness of these assets to the needs of their current owners is diminished. Regulation of the extent to which the division of ownership into successive interests can be carried serves to keep such diminution within reasonable bounds. In another quite different way the rule against perpetuities serves to keep property responsive to the needs of its current owners. When wealth takes the form of bonds or shares issued by a corporation, the assets represented by such bonds or shares are at least potentially productive in the business of the issuing corporation, regardless of how inalienable the bonds or shares may be in the hands of their owners. Similarly, when assets are transferred to a trustee who is given unqualified power to change the form of the trust res, no inalienability of any specific tangible thing can be said to be caused by the limitation of future interests under or after the trust. Nevertheless, it is well established law that the rule against perpetuities applies not only to limitations made concerning intangibles such as bonds and shares, but also to limitations of the beneficial interests under a trust where the trustee has unqualified power to change the trust res. Both of these situations have one common factor, namely, that a given quantum of wealth is sought to be committed to the satisfaction of specific and stated end. Such a commitment, for its duration, lessens the availability of these assets for the meeting of current newly arising exigencies. Law which is animated by the idea that the world and its wealth exist for the living cannot tolerate too long a commitment of this sort. Thus the rule against perpetuities, by regulating the future interests which can be created in these two situations, assists in keeping property reasonably free to answer the exigencies, as they arise, of the possessor and of his family. In these applications of the rule, it no longer is preventing lessened freedom of alienation. Its function has broadened to include the prevention of limitations which "freeze" or "tie up" or "fetter" property for too long a time, even though no specific thing has been made inalienable, even for a moment.

The keeping of property free to answer the exigencies of its possessor was a corollary of the English stress on individualism and rested upon the acceptance of a society organized upon a competitive theory. It is obvious that limitations unalterably effective over a long period of time would hamper the normal operation of the competitive struggle. Persons less fit, less keen in the social struggle, might be thereby enabled to retain property disproportionate to their skills in the competitive struggle. Hence the rule against perpetuities can be regarded as furthering the effective operation of the competitive system.

From this review of diverse purposes served by the rule against perpetuities, it is fair to conclude that the social interest in preserving property from excessive fettering rests partly upon the necessities of maintaining a going society controlled primarily by its living members, partly upon the social desirability of facilitating the utilization of wealth, partly upon the social desirability of keeping property responsive to the current exigencies of its current beneficial owners, and partly upon the competitive basis of modern society. . . .

In the absence of a statutory abrogation or modification, the common law rule against perpetuities is a part of the common law of each jurisdiction in the United States. An adoption of the common law of England on this subject does not restrict the law of the adopting jurisdiction to the rudimentary form of such rule on some date prior to its complete evolution. It is unimportant whether the local law includes a statutory adoption of the common law of England and it is also unimportant whether such statutory adoption, when present, specifies 1607 or 1776, or some other specific date, as the date as of which the English common law is adopted.

a. Summary of the Common Law Rule Against Perpetuities

J. GRAY, THE RULE AGAINST PERPETUITIES
(4th ed. 1942)

§201. No interest is good unless it must vest, if at all, not later than twenty-one years after some life in being at the creation of the interest.

As aptly stated by Leach and Tudor in 6 American Law of Property §24.7 (Casner ed. 1952): "Practically anything a testator is likely to desire can be done within the limits of the Rule Against Perpetuities. Wills fail because of inept work by lawyers, not because of excessive demands by testators." This fact, as well as the risk to the lawyer who mishandles a will, is demonstrated by the case of Lucas v. Hamm, 56 Cal. 2d 583, 15 Cal. Rptr. 821, 364 P.2d 685 (1961), in which the lawyer, after being held liable in the district court of appeals (11 Cal. Rptr. 727), was finally held not to be liable because the Rule is such a "technicality-ridden legal nightmare" that it would not be proper to hold, in the particular case, that the defendant "failed to use such skill, prudence, and diligence as lawyers of ordinary skill and capacity commonly exercise."

The Rule Against Perpetuities is not to be looked upon as an archaic doctrine or as a mere exercise for law students. The Rule is of relatively modern vintage, and its relevance to present-day estates practice should not be underestimated. Current estate planning involves the frequent use of long-term trust arrangements. Current tax law and other factors make the early vesting of remainder interests inadvisable, while the needs of flexibility invite the use of powers of appointment, which are notable as sources of concealed danger under the Rule. Reported litigation concerning perpetuities is an inadequate reflection of the frequency of violations. Many violations go unquestioned, and those that are raised rarely justify litigation since, construction aside, the Rule normally operates — as is so often said — with a mathematical certainty.

The Rule provides for the destruction of non-vested future interests that might under any possible circumstances vest later than the end of the period allowed. That is, at the moment of creation the interest must be absolutely certain either to vest or to fail according to the terms of the instrument within the permitted period, or the interest is destroyed. The Rule applies to both real and personal property and to equitable as well as legal interests. Thus, it invalidates offending beneficial interests in trust, even though the trustee may have the power in a fiduciary capacity to sell the trust assets.

b.   The Requirement of Vesting and Certainty

The Rule requires only that the future interest vest in interest and that the portion of the property or fund that so vests be determined. The interest need not vest in possession — i.e., it need not entitle the owner to immediate possession or to immediate payments of trust income or principal. For example, the Rule's requirements are satisfied as to all interests created by a devise "to my children for life, remainder in equal shares to my grandchildren for their respective lives, and on the death of each, the remainder of his or her share to X." Although the interests of the grandchildren may endure beyond the perpetuities period, all of their interests will have vested and the amounts of their shares will be known by the death of the testator's last surviving child (a "life in being" at the time of the devise); and although X's rights may not become possessory within the period of the rule, they are vested (in an ascertained person and free of conditions precedent) from the moment of the testator's death.

The emphasis upon vesting involves fine distinctions of a technical and often formalistic nature. One must, for example, distinguish between conditions precedent and conditions subsequent, for contingent remainders do not satisfy the vesting requirement whereas vested remainders subject to divestment do. Also, traditionally executory interests were not considered vested until they became possessory, and thus a conveyance "to X from and after 25 years from today" was void. (For the modern view, see section A.1.b above). On the other hand, it is settled that the common law Rule does not apply at all to possibilities of reverter or rights of entry; according to some authorities, this is because such interests are inherently vested, although others assert that these interests are contingent but nevertheless immune because they remain in the grantor or the grantor's successors in interest.

Gray's classic statement and most other statements of the Rule Against Perpetuities assert only that an interest must "vest" and say nothing about the taker's portion of the property or fund having to be known. In fact, it has been persuasively argued that there should be no such requirement; nevertheless, standard common law doctrine insists upon it, whether this is to be viewed as a special aspect of vesting for purposes of the Rule or as a separate though generally unstated additional requirement. The requirement is important in the case of class gifts, for, as a general rule, if it is possible for the interest of any single class member to vest beyond the period the entire class gift fails. Stated another way, for purposes of the Rule the rights of all class members stand or fall together as a part of a single future interest, even the rights of those who have already satisfied all requirements of the instrument and are free of any conditions precedent. Thus, although we have already seen that a remainder that is vested subject to divestment normally satisfies the Rule, a remainder in class gift form that is vested subject to partial divestment in order to provide for after-born or after-qualifying class members does not. A deed of land to be equally divided among "those of my grandchildren who attain age 50" (absent an immediate class-closing situation) is void even with respect to the intended rights of grandchildren who are alive at the time of the transfer and whose rights would therefore necessarily either vest or fail of its own terms within their own lifetimes.

Another well-recognized principle that may seem anomolous is a limited exception for charities. Under this exception, it is permissible for property rights to shift from one charity to another beyond the period. That is, if the property has become "vested in charity" within the period, a later gift over from one charity to another is permissible. A shift from a private to a charitable purpose, or vice versa, beyond the period is not permissible, however, and the interest that is to take effect on the excessively remote contingency would fail.

It is important to note that a future interest fails under the Rule if there is any possibility of remote vesting — that is, any possibility whatever that by the end of the period the question of vesting might not be resolved one way or the other according to the terms of the instrument. Thus, an attempt to create a future interest is void from the very outset unless it is absolutely certain at the time of the testator's death or at the time the deed is delivered that the interest will either vest or fail within the perpetuities period.

c. The Perpetuities Period

The permissible period of "lives in being and 21 years" is extended to encompass actual periods of gestation involved in the vesting of the interests in the beneficiaries. A child in gestation at the time of the transfer is, therefore, a life in being. Similarly, the 21-year period can be 21 years and additional months of gestation for a child who is unborn at the end of the measuring lives and who is required to reach age 21 in order to take.

A person may be a "life in being" for purposes of the Rule without being so designated in the instrument and without being beneficially interested in the property disposition. It is permissible, however, to designate specific measuring lives in the instrument, so long as the number selected is not so large as to be considered unreasonable or to make ascertainment of the relevant facts unreasonably difficult. (One noted case allowed a reference to the last survivor of all of Queen Victoria's descendants living at the testator's death; nevertheless, a large class or list of arbitrarily selected lives invites trouble, and apparently the use of animal lives is forbidden.) A careful reading of Gray's statement of the Rule will make it apparent that a measuring life cannot follow the 21-year period, but must precede it, inasmuch as the life must be in being at the start of the period. (For purposes of the Rule, the date of "the creation of the interest" in Gray's terms — i.e., the date when measuring lives must be in being and when the period begins to run — is the date of the testator's death in the case of a will and the date of the transfer in the case of a deed or inter vivos trust, except that if the transfer is wholly revocable it is the date on which the living trust or deed becomes irrevocable, usually the date of the transferor's death.)

When the measuring lives are not specified in the instrument, the court will refer to any "lives in being" that are relevant to, i.e., necessarily involved in, the eventual vesting of the interests in question. The court will not refer to lives that have no effect on the vesting of the interests either by having been expressly designated in the instrument in a special vesting provision or by naturally having some causal relationship to the time at which the vesting will occur. A ready example of the latter is a testamentary gift "to such of my grandchildren as attain age 21"; the bequest is valid because the children of the testator — all necessarily alive (or in gestation) at the testator's death — are eligible to serve as lives in being and they are relevant to the vesting in that it is not possible for a grandchild's interest to vest more than 21 years (and, again, any actual gestation period) after the last child's death. This disposition, however, would not have been valid had it been made irrevocably by deed during the transferor's lifetime or if it had been to grandchildren who attain age 25. Do you see why? And do you see why in each of these cases the disposition would be valid (and in all likelihood carried out exactly according to its original terms) if the instrument included a special cut-off or saving clause expressly designating measuring lives — i.e., specifying that if any interest does not vest earlier according to its own terms it shall vest in those beneficiaries (here, in the grandchildren) who are living 21 years after the death of the last of the transferor's descendants who were alive at the date of the transfer?

The Rule Against Perpetuities is treated in detail in the final chapter of this book, along with complementary common law rules, statutory substitutes or supplements, and modern reforms.

7.   Introduction to Construction and Drafting

a.   Generally

This section and the next chapter are concerned with construction of dispositive provisions involving future interests and, conversely, with their drafting. You should consider the functions of the interpretive process and of rules of construction; whether particular rules and the judicial treatment of these rules are satisfactory, including as a basis for counseling the various persons concerned with potential litigation. You should also consider how the drafter could better have handled the provision in question, for the recurring constructional problems you will study are the product of inadequate drafting. It is often said that most of future interests is a study of lawyers' mistakes. Wills and trusts frequently "fall apart" in the remainder provisions, and most of these failures are but variations of the recurring types of errors involved in these materials. It is risky business for an estate planner not to have some familiarity with these problems.

The term "construction" is often used to mean the same thing as "interpretation." Nevertheless, it may be worthwhile to distinguish rules of construction from those rules that govern the process of interpretation, which attempts to discover the actual intent of a transferor through the introduction and examination of all admissible evidence. Rules of construction are not rules for determining when a court may receive extrinsic evidence to clarify a writing or governing what evidence in particular is then admissible; they are presumptions by which an intention is attributed to a transferor who, in future interests cases at least, usually has failed to think or to formulate an actual intent about the particular question presented. In addition, the quest for an actual intent may be obstructed by the Statute of Frauds, wills acts, the parol evidence rule, rules of evidence, or sheer inadequacy of proof; consequently, even after examining the instrument in its entirety and all the circumstances and extrinsic evidence available, the court may have to proceed by construction just as if the specific issue had never occurred to the transferor, whether or not this is the case. Thus, it is often said that construction begins where interpretation fails to produce an answer. As the course proceeds, consider why this might be just a bit misleading.

2 POWELL, REAL PROPERTY
(1950)

¶316. . . . The construction of wills and deeds for the purpose of solving problems in the law of future interests is but a single facet of a much more pervasive process that permeates the law and operates in many non-legal areas of thought. The generalized task is the ascertainment and exposition of the meaning sought to be communicated by a writing. . . .

The identity of the central problem deserves more stress than it has had but a lawyer will also be well advised to take due note of the factors of difference as between different kinds of writings. A contract is a bilateral instrument. So also, commonly, is a deed which gives rise to a power of termination, or . . . or a trust settlement made in liquidation of a claim for alimony, or a will executed in accordance with a contract. . . . In all these bilateral instruments a conveyor is bound by the meaning which, reasonably, he should have anticipated that the conveyee would derive from the language and conduct employed. Construction, in such cases, must conform to objective criteria. In the majority of instances, however, future interests are created by donative unilateral instruments such as the conveyor's will or an inter vivos voluntary settlement. In such transactions, construction can, and should, be concerned primarily with the task of determining the disposition desired by the conveyor. This depends upon an ascertainment of the conveyor's subjective intent, insofar as he had one. . . . Similarly, private writings require a somewhat different handling from statutes affecting the public generally and from constitutions framed to serve the long continuing (and therefore changing) needs of a social unit. Perhaps the differences as between writings of different types are primarily differences in the problems which require solution, but there are also some differences in the rules of construction themselves.

The constructional process, as it applies to deeds and wills, has many ingredients. Its basic objective is the effectuation of the conveyor's dispositive plan. When, however, that plan is not inescapably clear, there is an area in which judicially made choices provide the needed supplement. The choices so made by courts can help greatly to establish drafting techniques which will increase predictability for future drafters. They can also weight the scales in favor of socially desirable results. Finally, they can minimize future controversy by providing *a* rule for cases in which either rule might be satisfactory but *a* rule is needed to end controversy. It is the author's belief that courts have been serving these supplementary objectives by their decisions on constructional problems for decades, if not for centuries. Many courts have freely said so. Some courts, however, continue to talk in terms of "ascertaining the conveyor's intent" when it is obvious that he had no intent on the problem at issue. This is regrettable as it tends to confuse the law and to create distrust of its honesty. The objectives of increasing future predictability, of promoting social welfare and of minimizing controversy are worthy ends for judicial effort and deserve recognition as constant ingredients in the constructional process. . . . The product of the process of construction is labelled the "judicially ascertained intent" of the conveyor. The inclusion in this product of a large ingredient of "attributed intent" is the inevitable consequence of the judicially evolved "constructional preferences" formulated in Section 243 [of the original Restatement of Property].

It is helpful to distinguish the process of construction from the ascertainment of the effect of an instrument. After the intent of the conveyor has been judicially ascertained, there remains the task of determining whether there is any rule of law which restricts, or prevents, the effectiveness of the desired disposition. Sometimes these two processes are kept wholly separate, so that construction is completed before the second task is undertaken. Sometimes this does not occur. A court "peeks" ahead to see which effect will flow from which construction, and returns to the task of construction with a new motivation in making its constructional decisions. This is both a common and a justifiable procedure. The law would be clarified, however, if courts more commonly made explicit this factor in their thinking.

Simes, Future Interests §88 (2d ed. 1966) characterizes rules of construction as follows: "(a) they are like rebuttable presumptions in that they are inoperative when a contrary intent is sufficiently expressed; (b) the presumptions involved in some rules of construction are stronger than in others, and, therefore, require more positive language of a contrary intent to rebut them; (c) a few rules of construction have little or no significance in deciding a case."

Specific rules of construction are to be distinguished from what might better be called constructional preferences. Compare introductory section to Part 21 (Construction Problems) of 5 American Law of Property §21.2 (Casner ed. 1952):

When the construction process goes into operation to give preciseness of meaning to language that is not clear and unequivocal, the basic search is for the intention of the transferor. By hypothesis, however, he has not manifested his intention with respect to the particular difficulty. Thus, the search for the intention of the transferor must of necessity be changed to a search for the intention it is reasonable to attribute to the average transferor with respect to the particular situation. A rule of construction which may be established as a guide to the interpretation of a donative transaction is nothing more than the formulation of the intention it is thought reasonable to attribute to a transferor in giving preciseness of meaning to language he has employed.

A rule of construction may be broad or narrow in its operation. A broad rule of construction is one that finds application in a variety of factual situations and a narrow rule of construction is one that is developed to meet a specialized factual situation. In the process of formulating a narrow rule of construction, an established broad rule of construction may be a significant or even predominant influence. For example, an established broad rule of construction is the preference for vested interests. With that preference in the background, the tendency will be to comply with it in formulating a narrow rule of construction if the circumstances permit.

Then in section 21.3, the following "broad" rules are listed; (a) preference for vested interests; (b) preference against partial intestacy; (c) preference in favor of maximum validity; (d) preference for the construction that produces the result which more nearly accords with the public interest; (e) preference for keeping property among blood relatives; (f) preference against disinheriting an heir; (g) preference in favor of the use of technical words in a technical sense.

Competing constructional preferences are properly to be weighed, if and as relevant, in formulating specific (or narrow) rules of construction, just as in other areas of law we are accustomed to weighing competing policies in arriving at specific legal rules.

b. Vested or Contingent Construction

The early common law placed great emphasis upon whether an interest was vested or contingent. While there are still situations in which the technically vested or contingent quality of a future interest is of substantive importance, this aspect of classification is of diminishing significance. In these materials, the term "vested" is used in the strict sense in which it is used by Gray in the quotation from his The Rule Against Perpetuities, infra; thus used, the term is not to be confused with other questionable usages, such as to denote freedom from a condition of survival. In reading opinions that use the term "vested," it is important for the reader's understanding to know how the term is being used and for what purposes the court is attempting to classify the interest in question.

At this point you might consider how many situations you have already encountered in which the technical vested or contingent character of an interest mattered. Later you will encounter others, in some of which counsel may have allowed courts to become confused into erroneously believing this classification question is relevant to other issues before it. More specifically, consider for what purposes it matters whether an obvious and admitted condition is classified as precedent rather than subsequent. The distinction, of course, is usually one of form, depending upon the language employed in the particular limitation. As you proceed, consider also whether there are other bases upon which courts might resolve the ultimate substantive issues for which the distinction is being used. Are vested-or-contingent construction cases an unnecessary waste of effort, tediously making difficult and meaningless classifications with no relevance to the real merits of the controversy? Is it possible for courts, through this elusive classification process, to "manipulate" the results of cases in which the outcome appears to depend on the distinction between conditions precedent and subsequent? If so, is this a good thing?

J. GRAY, THE RULE AGAINST PERPETUITIES
(4th ed. 1942)

§101. Since contingent remainders have been recognized, the line between them and vested remainders is drawn as follows: *A remainder is vested in A when, throughout its continuance, A, or A and his heirs, have the right to the immediate possession, whenever and however the preceding freehold estates may determine. A remainder is contingent if, in order for it to come into possession the fulfilment of some condition precedent other than the determination of the preceding freehold estates is necessary.*

§ 102. A remainder is nonetheless vested because it may terminate before the remainder-man comes into possession; thus if land be given to A for life, remainder to B for life, B may die before A, yet the remainder is vested, for during its continuance, namely, the life of B, it is ready to come into possession whenever and however A's estate determines. This result is not affected by the fact that the termination of the remainder is contingent; that is, that it is subject to a condition subsequent. For instance, if land is devised to A for life, remainder to B and his heirs, but if B dies unmarried, then to C and his heirs, B's remainder is vested, although it is possible that he may die unmarried in A's lifetime. [Emphasis added.]

"*To A for Life, then to A's Heirs*" — It is well accepted that this remainder is contingent, for *A* has no heirs while he is alive. But can you see how the notorious Moore v. Littel, 41 N.Y. 66 (1869), held the remainder "vested"? The opinion found identifiable persons "in being who would have an immediate right [of] possession . . . if the life estate should now cease," stating that contingencies that might "defeat the right [would] operate as conditions subsequent." Can one insist that this is wrong? How does the Gray excerpt, above, call for a different construction?

Can you see from Gray's definition how he and others conclude that "to L for life, then to R, but if R should die before L, then to X" gives *R* a vested remainder subject to divestment by an executory interest in *X*? But how can Gray and others further assert that, if the future interests had been "to R if living at L's death, and otherwise to X," *R*'s interest is contingent — i.e., *R* and *X* have alternative contingent remainders? Does all of this help you to understand why it is difficult to safely state more than that a remainder is vested when it is not subject to a "condition precedent"?

Compare Lewis M. Simes §91 (2d ed. 1966), which states: "Whether a limitation is construed as vested or contingent depends upon the form of the language," and thereafter adds:

> If a limitation is in favor of unborn or unascertained persons, it is obviously contingent. Moreover, even though a limitation is in favor of ascertained persons, if the only language of gift is language of condition, the court is likely to hold that a contingent interest has been created. Thus, if the limitation is "to such of the children of A as survive A," it would be contingent. But if it were "to the children of A, but if any child does not survive A, his share is to terminate," the interest of each living child would be vested subject to defeasance.

That section also states: "If the language is ambiguous, a vested construction is generally preferred," but continues by noting that the "rule favoring vesting and early vesting has recently been criticized, and courts have sometimes reached results inconsistent with it." It further observes: ". . . Probably this constructional preference was originally developed to avoid the destructibility rule and the rule making contingent interests inalienable. But perhaps it may still be justified in some situations on the ground that vested interests do not tie up titles as much as do contingent interests."

A somewhat modernized statement of the disposition in the classic Edwards v. Hammond, 83 Eng. Rep. 614 (C.P., 1683), would be: "Settlor S deeds to T in trust for S for life, remainder to C if C attains age 21, but if C dies before then to X." *S* died when *C* was 17. Asking, in effect, who is entitled to the income until *C* reaches 21 or dies, the court concluded that *C* is, because his interest is "vested," the age contingency being a condition subsequent. How do you explain this construction? Cf. In re DiBiasio, 705 A.2d 972 (R.I. 1998), in which *T* devised property in trust for his siblings for their lives, then to his nephew, *N*, "individually for his sole use free and clear of Trust." *N* predeceased the last surviving life tenant. *T*'s heirs argued that the quoted language indicated *T*'s "clear intent" to impose a survival requirement on *N*'s interest. The court disagreed, stating that in Rhode Island "the law favors the immediate vesting of remainders unless there is a clearly indicated intention to the contrary," and adding that this preference for a vested construction is "particularly strong when, as here, (1) the remaindermen are in existence at the death of the testator, (2) the remainder is a gift of the residue of the estate..., (3) the gift is to relatives of the testator, and (4) intestacy would otherwise result."

The difficulties and thus uncertainties of vested-or-contingent construction are aggravated because the presumptions, here based on form of expression, yield to findings of particular transferors' contrary intentions. (It is not unusual for "interpretation" to be used — or misused — to avoid rather than revise dubious substantive rules. Cf. United States v. 654.8 Acres of Land, 102 F. Supp. 937 (E.D. Tenn. 1952), escaping a deficiency inherent in the supposed Rule in Wild's Case, infra Chapter 11, section E.4, without identifying any evidence of contrary intent.) Furthermore, it generally appears that in modern times the hollow, supposed preference for early vesting has been replaced, in reality, by preferences for certain results, with the traditional preference recited and applied only when convenient. Combinations of decisions that are revealing in this respect can be found, even within the case law of individual jurisdictions, seemingly "cheating" on acknowledged rules of construction with no real indication of contrary intent. (Compare concluding observations in Powell excerpt in section A.7.a above.) Thus, if the question before a court is one of voluntary alienability or the Rule Against Perpetuities, the court may "find" that language fitting the standard form of condition precedent is a condition subsequent in order to find the interest vested. On the other hand, if the question is one of involuntary alienation, the court may well conclude that what ordinarily appears to be a condition subsequent constitutes a condition precedent, in order to find the interest contingent and apply the state's policy against creditor-forced "sacrifice sale." See Halbach, Vested and Contingent Remainders: A Premature Requiem for Distinctions Between Conditions Precedent and Subsequent, Perspectives of Law: Essays in Honor of Austin W. Scott 153 (1964), also suggesting that, for each situation purportedly governed by the traditional vested-contingent distinction, a preferable rule can be found that would better reflect the merits of the situation and would not turn on a constructional distinction that has proved so elusive and subject to manipulation.

For review and application, consider what interests are created by the following transfers:

(a)   To *A* for life, then to *B* if *B* attains age 21. (This should be easy.)

(b)   To *X* for life, then to *Y*, but if *Y* dies before *X*, to *Z*. (This should also be easy.)

(c)   To *A* for life, then to *B* if *B* attains age 21 [or "at age 21"] and if *B* dies before then, to *C* in fee.

(d)   To *X* if *X* attains age 21 [or "at age 21"] but in the event of *X*'s death before 21, to *Y* in fee.

(e)   To *X* for life, then to *X*'s children but if no child of *X* reaches age 21 to *Y*.

(f)   To *X* for life, then to such of *X*'s children as survive her, and if any child fails to do so that child's share shall go to *Y*.

(g)   To *X* for life, then to whomever *X* shall appoint by will, and in default of appointment, to *B*. See Doe d. Willis v. Martin, 100 Eng. Rep. 882 (K.B. 1790).

B.   *Introduction to Powers of Appointment*

1.   Generally

Restatement (Second) of Property: Donative Transfers §11.1 defines a power of appointment as the "authority, other than as an incident of the beneficial ownership of property, to designate recipients of beneficial interests in the property." A fairly typical example is *W*'s transfer to *T* in trust for *H* for life, then to or for "such of our issue as *H* may appoint by his will; if or to the extent *H* fails to appoint, remainder to our issue, per stirpes." *W* is the *donor*, and *H* the *donee* of a *testamentary special* (or "limited" or "nongeneral") power of appointment. The "issue," whose remainder is subject to divestment by the exercise of the power, are the *objects* (or "permissible appointees"), as well as the *takers in default* of *appointment*. (Possibilities that arise when the power is not exercised and the donor has failed to designate takers in default are considered in section B.3 below.)

Powers of appointment are classified in various ways, with some terminology used differently by different users or for different purposes. The original Restatement of Property stated that a power is *general* if, being testamentary, "it can exercised wholly in favor of the estate of donee" or, being exercisable inter vivos, "it can be exercised wholly in favor of the donee." (Id. §320.) A *nongeneral* power is often referred to as *special* when it is exercisable "only in favor of persons, not including the donee, who constitute a group not unreasonably large." (Id.) For federal transfer tax purposes, however (as you should recall), powers of appointment are defined to extend beyond conventional property usage to include such things as powers to modify or revoke, powers of withdrawal, and discretionary powers of trustees to distribute income or to invade principal; and a power is *general,* essentially, if "exercisable in favor of the [donee], his estate, his creditors or the creditors of his estate." (IRC §2041(b)(1).) The tax definition has been adopted (unfortunately, because of application difficulties in various property law contexts) in the Second Restatement (supra, §11.4) and in a few state probate or trust codes. An *inter vivos* power (i.e., one exercisable only "by deed" or exercisable by either deed or will) to appoint principal may either be *presently exercisable* or subject to some unfulfilled condition (e.g., donee attaining age 35). Often, however, a life beneficiary is given a power to appoint the remainder following his interest "by the last unrevoked instrument signed and delivered to the trustee during the donee's lifetime." Although such a power is essentially a substitute for one exercisable by will, it is illustrative of one for which there is no generally accepted terminology — e.g., is it exercisable "by deed" or is it "testamentary," or something else?

Relation Back. Under the so-called relation back doctrine a donee's appointment is viewed as a transfer by the donor (e.g., as filling out the terms of the settlor's trust), much as if a donee acts as a donor's agent, but without fiduciary duties. Although this doctrine has an element of fiction and is sometimes, for some purposes, not applied, it may well be influential in resolving specific issues. The doctrine is less likely to apply to general than limited powers, particularly if a general power is presently exercisable and thus the equivalent of ownership. As you proceed through this chapter and subsequent materials on powers, consider whether the doctrine is — or should be — applicable in the resolution of particular issues, and why or why not.

Role of Powers. Flexibility becomes a significant element of a satisfactory plan whenever a property owner wishes to make a present transfer providing for the devolution of the property over an extended period of time. Carefully tailored special powers of appointment are ideal for providing some of this flexibility by allowing adjustments to be made after the plan has become operative but without allowing diversion from the client's basic purpose. The donee of the power may thus appoint trust property or interests in it long after the donor's death, taking into account changed personal and economic circumstances the donor could not have foreseen. Through diverse powers of appointment, donors may also confer upon donees various advantages of ownership (such as the power, in effect, to devise the property) while avoiding various disadvantages of outright ownership. The disadvantages that might be avoided, aside from tax disadvantages (see Chapter 8), should be considered as you proceed through these materials.

2.   The Nature of Powers and Donee's Rights

In re ESTATE OF CURTIS
307 A.2d 251 (Pa. 1973)

O'BRIEN, J. . . . Cyrus H.K. Curtis died on June 7, 1933. . . . [His will] reads in part:

> Ninth, I give, devise and bequeath to my daughter, Mary Louise Curtis Bok, for her lifetime, my residence . . . and all other real estate belonging to me, situate in Montgomery County, Pennsylvania. . . . My said daughter shall have full power by will . . . to dispose of any or all of said property, but failing such disposition, upon her death, I give the same [to my issue, per stirpes]. . . .
> My said daughter shall have full power to sell any or all of said property real or personal. . . . The proceeds of such sale shall stand in place of the property and shall be turned over to my daughter without security.

In 1936, Mrs. Bok negotiated with the solicitor for the Board of Commissioners of Cheltenham Township [and deeded 43 acres of the above land to them in 1937] for the establishment of a public park in memory of Cyrus H.K. Curtis. . . . The park . . . has remained as such to date.

On January 23, 1943, Mrs. Bok released the general testamentary power of appointment given her in the testator's will. On January 4, 1970 Mrs. Bok died and appellees [the issue of Curtis] demanded that the township return the land in question to them. They allege that Mrs. Bok was not the owner in fee simple, but merely held a life estate, so that at her death they became the owners of the land under the terms of Cyrus H.K. Curtis's will.

The township refused this demand. Appellees then filed a petition in the Orphans' Court Division of Montgomery County [which] ruled that the land in question belonged to appellees and the township filed this appeal. . . .

The township first argues that Article Ninth of the testator's will, giving Mrs. Bok a life estate and general testamentary power of appointment, vested a fee simple in Mrs. Bok, making the transfer to appellants a conveyance of a fee simple determinable. We do not agree. . . . "[A] gift over in default of appointment . . . precludes an absolute ownership" [citation omitted]. . . .

[Omitted is the portion of the opinion rejecting the argument that Mrs. Bok held a full fee simple because of the Rule in Shelley's Case.]

. . . [W]e must now consider whether [Mrs. Bok's] actions constituted a sale under the power to sell given her by the will. Although [she] was given full power to sell and deliver good and sufficient deeds to a purchaser, she was required to substitute the proceeds of the sale for the land. The conveyance in question to the township did not, in fact, involve the transfer of any "proceeds" to Mrs. Bok.

The township asserts that, in exchange for the transfers, Mrs. Bok received the promise of the township to maintain the public park. . . . While the benefit that accrued to Mrs. Bok could be termed consideration, it clearly was not proceeds that could be substituted for the real estate. In addition, each of the deeds . . . and [a] letter reinforce the conclusion that the conveyances in question were gifts, rather than sales, as alleged by the township. . . .

Decree affirmed . . . [Dissenting opinion omitted.]

Could the park transaction have been structured to accomplish Mrs. Bok's objective? If so, could a court of equity have treated her misguided efforts as having that effect? Explain.

a.   Impermissible Appointments: Fraud and Contract

In Horne v. Title Insurance & Trust Co., 70 F. Supp. 91 (D.C. Cal. 1948), the bulk of the trust remainder was to go in equal shares to three named individuals subject to "the absolute right and power" of D (a childless widower), with a co-trustee's consent, to prescribe distribution "in different proportions from those provided." D later remarried and sought agreements for certain payments to provide for his wife, if she survived, from the three beneficiaries. Two agreed and one refused. D directed the shares of the former to be increased while drastically reducing the share of the latter, who sued after D's death for a declaratory judgment to restore the original shares. The plaintiff conceded that "a trustee holding an absolute power to appoint within a limited class may be even arbitrary or capricious in its exercise" but urged that "the power may not be exercised . . . with an intent to benefit a non-object of the power, as plaintiff maintains was done here." The court's opinion stated: "if a donee of a special power makes an appointment to an object of the power in consideration of a benefit conferred upon or promised to a non-object, the appointment is ineffective to whatever extent it was motivated by the purpose to benefit the non-object," citing Restatement of Property §353, and concluded: "Such an exercise of a special power is held to be a fraud upon the power and hence void."

WILL OF CARROLL
8 N.E.2d 864 (N.Y. 1937)

HUBBS, J. [Elsa, the second life beneficiary of a testamentary trust, was granted power to appoint "to or among her children or any other kindred who shall survive her." At her death, leaving no descendants, her will appointed $5,000 to her brother and $250,000 to her cousin, Paul Curtis, to whom her prior will would have appointed $50,000 and who had written to Elsa (in a letter prepared by her lawyer after executing her last will) "promis[ing]" to pay $100,000 of the $250,000 to Elsa's husband. The Surrogate found that the appointment constituted a fraud on the power and that Curtis' promise so permeated the appointment as to make it wholly void. The Appellate Division concluded that Curtis could retain $150,000, as separable from the $100,000 invalidly intended for Elsa's husband.]

. . . [I]t appears from the testimony of Curtis that [Elsa] had an understanding with him prior to the execution of the will and the writing constituted only a record of the actual prior agreement. The surrogate had the benefit of hearing the witnesses testify and of observing their conduct. He found nothing in their testimony to detract from the force of the letter signed by Curtis. Concededly, the attempted bequest for the benefit of the husband was not valid. . . . No one can say whether she would have left Curtis $100,000, $150,000, or a lesser or greater sum had it not been for the agreement to take care of her husband. Only by speculation can it be said that she would have left him $150,000 had it not been for that agreement. Had it not been for . . . the promise on the part of Curtis, no one can say but what she might have changed the will. Curtis was a party to the attempted fraud on the power. If the bequest to him be sustained to the extent of $150,000 on his own testimony, he suffers no penalty. It seems to us that on the facts, the conclusion of the surrogate was correct; that the entire bequest is involved in the intent to defeat the power and that it is impossible to separate and sustain the bequest to Curtis to the extent of $150,000.

The order of the Appellate Division should be modified in accordance with this opinion and, as so modified, affirmed, without costs.

Judgment accordingly.

Restatement (Second) Property: Donative Transfers §20.2 provides that an "appointment is ineffective to whatever extent it was motivated by" the purpose to benefit a non-object. Under that section what do you think the appropriate penalty is for Curtis' acquiescence? Should there be some punishment for Elsa's lawyer?

ESTATE OF BROWN
306 N.E.2d 781 (N.Y. 1973)

JONES, J. We hold . . . unenforceable the agreement made by this decedent to exercise two general testamentary powers of appointment in favor of his son.

The decedent was the donee of two separate powers of appointment — one over the assets of a trust under his mother's 1925 will, the other over the assets of an inter vivos trust he himself had created in 1927. Incident to the resolution of family differences, in 1944 he agreed to exercise his powers in part in favor of his son, James, respondent herein, and at the same time executed a will making appointments in accordance with that agreement. Some 20 years later, in 1964, the decedent executed a new will in which he appointed the assets of both trusts to his estate, with no benefits flowing to the son. On his death the 1964 will was admitted to probate. In the present proceeding the son seeks to enforce his father's 1944 agreement to exercise the powers in his favor.

Surrogate's Court, Queens County, held the agreement unenforceable as to the assets of both trusts under EPTL 10-5.2. The Appellate Division reversed in part, holding that the 1944 agreement was enforceable against the assets of the inter vivos trust, but agreeing that enforcement was barred as to the assets of the testamentary trust.

All of us agree that the agreement cannot be enforced as to the testamentary trust; a majority of us agree with the Surrogate that the agreement cannot be enforced as to the inter vivos trust either.

EPTL 10-5.3 provided: " . . . (a) The donee of a power of appointment which is not presently exercisable . . . cannot contract to make an appointment. Such a contract, if made, cannot be the basis of an action for specific performance or damages, but the promisee can obtain restitution of the value given by him for the promise unless the donee has exercised the power pursuant to the contract." . . .

We recognize that the statute may have been addressed primarily to powers of appointment created by a testator or a grantor other than the donee as to property of such testator or grantor. . . . We would be disposed [also] . . . to exclude from its operation inter vivos trusts of which the donee was also the grantor, if in addition . . . the grantor had an unlimited power to revoke the trust and thus had retained substantial dominion over the trust assets. In such instance . . . to say that where the grantor had power to *revoke* and thus to recapture the trust assets, he nevertheless could not agree to *appoint* the same assets, would be to exalt form over substance.

That is not, however, this case. . . . Under the terms of this trust instrument itself the grantor retained very limited and carefully circumscribed powers of invasion of principal, certainly no general power of revocation. . . . [The] decedent did not have such power of dominion over the assets of the 1927 inter vivos trust as in our view would support an argument that it would be excepted from the operative scope of EPTL 10-5.3. . . .

We accordingly hold that EPTL 10-5.3 is applicable to both testamentary and inter vivos trusts in this case and that this decedent's agreement to exercise his powers of appointment in the prescribed manner is unenforceable as to the assets of both trusts.

We further agree with the Surrogate that on the facts in this case respondent is not entitled to any restitution under the provisions of the last sentence of EPTL 10-5.3 [(a)].

Accordingly the order of the Appellate Division is reversed, the decree of Surrogate's Court is reinstated. . . .

GABRIELLI, J. (Dissenting) . . .

The definitive appraisal of the sort of thing sought to be guarded against is found in Farmer's Loan & Trust Co. v. Mortimer, 219 N.Y. 290, 114 N.E. 389. There, John Mortimer, the beneficiary of a trust created in his mother's will, was given a general power of appointment to be exercised in his own will. The donee procured a loan on his promise to exercise the power of appointment in favor of the creditor, and he made a will to that effect. Later, however, he made a new will in which he appointed in favor of his children. Judge Cardozo held the agreement with the creditor to be unenforceable. The exercise of the power, he said, was to represent the final judgment of the donee as asserted in his final will. "Up to the last moment of his life, he was to have the power to deal with the share as he thought best. [Citation omitted.] To permit him to bargain that right away would be to defeat the purpose of the donor. Her command was that her property should go to her son's issue unless at the end of his life it remained his will that it go elsewhere. It has not remained his will that it go elsewhere; and his earlier contract cannot nullify the expression of his final purpose." . . . [T]he subject-matter of the power is not the property of the promisor. It is the property of his mother. The promisor was not the legal owner of any legal estate. He was the beneficiary of a trust. ". . . *Those who take under this power have received nothing that was the property of John Mortimer.*" (219 N.Y., at p. 295, 114 N.E., at p. 390; emphasis supplied.)

In the instant case, of course, those who take under the power created in the inter vivos trust receive what is, was and always has been decedent's property. The rationale in *Mortimer,* from which EPTL 10-5.3 draws meaning, was constructed to protect the intent of the donor of the power against rash utilization of the power by the donee. . . .

It seems to us clear that in *Mortimer* Judge Cardozo's concern was [about] the holder of a power of appointment over property given him by another . . . [and that] the Legislature would have had no discernible reason for preventing a donor-donee from dealing with the power however he saw fit, especially when, as was actually accomplished in this case, he can appoint the corpus to his estate and actually effect a reversion. . . . Certainly remaindermen contingent upon default in the exercise of the power should have no say as to how the power is exercised by the donor-donee. Thus, it could not have been with their interests in mind that EPTL 10-5.3 was enacted. Rather, the statute was enacted to protect the interests of the settlor-donor. So, where the settlor-donor and donee are the same the statute should have no application. . . .

See also Charmichael v. Heggie, 506 S.E.2d 308 (S.C. App. 1998) (affirming decree invalidating, during donee's lifetime, her promise to make and not revoke a will exercising her testamentary general power in favor of her son in exchange for his caring for her in her old age). Should the promisee have a remedy against the donee's estate in a case like *Brown* or *Charmichael*? Should the promisee be allowed to keep the property if the donee performs the promise and exercises the power as agreed?

Can the donee of a presently exercisable nongeneral power of appointment enter into an enforceable contract to appoint property to an object of the nongeneral power?

PROBLEM

10-E.   *H* left his residuary estate in trust for *W* for life, remainder "to such of our issue and their spouses or surviving spouses as she may appoint by her will, and in default of appointment to our issue who survive her, by right of representation." In her late eighties and in deteriorating health, *W* became unable to care for herself and was considered by her physicians to be "at risk" without constant nursing supervision. *S*, the son of *H* and *W*, arranged for *W*'s placement in a nursing home — over her vehement protests about any relocation, whether to a care facility or into *S*'s home.[2] *S*, who lives about an hour's drive from *W*'s home and the nursing facility, worked closely with *W*'s physicians in making the arrangements, but *W* was furious and unforgiving about *S*'s actions. None of *W*'s family or friends doubts that *S*

---

2. Erica Goode of the New York Times reported on recent studies suggesting that "most incompetent people do not know they are incompetent" but "are usually supremely confident of their abilities — more confident, in fact, than people who do things well." She adds: "One reason . . . , researchers believe, is that the skills required for competence are often the same skills necessary to recognize competence." San Francisco Chronicle pp. 1, 11, Jan. 18, 2000.

acted unselfishly and in *W*'s best interest. *D*, the only other child of *H* and *W*, has tried unsuccessfully to explain *S*'s actions to her mother. At *W*'s death her recently executed will provides for the whole of her estate and the entire trust estate to go "to my daughter *D*, or if she should predecease me to her descendants, per stirpes, and if none survive then to *C* Charity; any rights or interests disclaimed by a beneficiary shall pass as if he or she had predeceased me, and in no event shall any of my property or the trust property go to or benefit my son, *S*, or his wife or descendants." *W* is survived by *S* and *D*, five adult grandchildren, and nine great-grandchildren ranging from several months to sixteen years of age. No one suggests that *W* lacked testamentary capacity when she executed her will. *S* says, "Well, I guess I'm just out of luck!" Is he right? (Do you find anything helpful in section A of Chapter 3?)

Release. Analogous to the contract issue is that of whether the donee of a power of appointment can release the power. Since the release of a power is tantamount to its exercise in favor of the takers in default, there has been some doubt concerning the release of powers that were not presently exercisable. Nevertheless, the general rule has developed that, absent express provision to the contrary, all powers of appointment, general or special, even though not presently exercisable, are releasable in whole or in part. The original Restatement adopted the position that testamentary special powers could not be released but Restatement (Second) of Property: Donative Transfers §§14.1 and 14.2 recognize that all powers of appointment are releasable. In recent years, largely prompted by tax considerations, legislation permitting release of powers has become widespread. Can a release sometimes accomplish what a contract cannot? Considerable uncertainty still remains concerning powers held in a fiduciary capacity.

b.   Creditors' Rights

PROBLEM

10-F.   *L* was life income beneficiary of a trust and donee of a power to appoint "the remainder at his death to such person(s) or entities as he may choose, without limitation, and in default of appointment by representation to his then living issue." On his death *L* left the residue of his estate, "including all property over which I hold a power of appointment," equally to his three children. At the time of death *L*'s own assets were worth about $100,000 but his otherwise modest debts included a $250,000 personal injury judgment recently entered against

him, for which he was not insured. The trust assets are worth about
$500,000. Can *L*'s creditors reach the trust property to satisfy their
claims? Explain. (What if *L*'s will had simply left "the residue of my
estate" to the children, with no reference to any power of appointment? Consider also the material in the next chapter.)

It is well accepted that the creditors of the donee of a nongeneral
power of appointment, inter vivos or testamentary, cannot reach the
appointive assets to satisfy their claims. Is this, or should it be, also true
of a general power? Federal bankruptcy law has long provided that the
bankruptcy estate includes property over which the bankrupt holds a
presently exercisable general power. See Bankruptcy Code of 1978
§541 and earlier Bankruptcy Act of 1898 §70(a). Should state law go
so far? Should it be so limited?

In Estate of Masson, 298 P.2d 619 (Cal. App. 1956), Paul Masson's
trust was to terminate on the death of his daughter (*D*), who held a
general testamentary power and appointed to "the American society,
which, in the discretion of my executors, does the best research [on
geriatric] diseases." On petition of the trustees the trial court instructed that the corpus was not to be paid to *D*'s executors (as they
claimed) for their use in satisfying the unpaid debts, taxes and expenses
of *D*'s estate. The court of appeals acknowledged "as the general rule
that . . . persons appointed by the donee take directly from the trustees
and not through the estate of the donee," but also noted that "the
donee of a general, i.e., unrestricted, power . . . may appoint the property to her estate." Thus, the question was whether *D* had done so.
The court found "the more reasonable construction" was that "she
intended the property to become a part of her estate" because she had
"conferred the discretion not upon individuals by name but upon her
executors, as executors." This, the court concluded, made the trust
property "a part of her estate" but "only for such portion of her debts
as cannot be paid from her personal estate."

Contrast In re Breault's Estate, 193 N.E.2d 824 (Ill. 1963), where the
deceased life beneficiary of a trust held a general testamentary power
of appointment and left a will disposing of his entire estate, including
any property "over which I have the power of disposition." The court's
opinion [citations omitted] states:

> . . . [W]e may start with firmly established principles of law governing
> the operation of powers of appointment. Repeated decisions have held
> that a power of appointment is not property and that the donor does
> not vest title to the property in the donee of the power; that the objects
> of an appointment take from the donor, not the donee of the power;
> that the property passing pursuant to the exercise of the power passes

under the instrument creating the power, just as though the appointment were read into the original instrument; and that property subject to the power passes as a part of the estate of the donor of the power.

There is, however, a recognized exception . . . that "property subject to a general power of appointment may pass as a part of the estate of the donee of the power if the donee shows an intention to take such property 'out of the instrument creating the power,' and 'to make it his own for all purposes.' " . . . [T]he intention of the donee to appoint to his own estate must be expressly stated or clearly implied. . . .

Some jurisdictions imply the intention where the testator masses, blends or merges, (as it is variously called,) his own personal property with the appointed property for all purposes, (viz., payment of debts, taxes, legacies, etc.,) and it is the contention of the appellees that this was accomplished here by the third paragraph of Oscar's will. However, we do not find this to be so. The only test we have found for determining whether there has been a blending of the two estates sufficient to imply appointment to the donee's estate is ". . . whether the testator has treated the two estates as one for all purposes and manifested an intent to commingle them generally." . . .

Considering the will in its entirety we do not find the requisite intent of the donee to make the property a part of his estate for all purposes. This being so, the appointee takes from the estate of the donor as in the normal case. . . .

University National Bank v. Rhoadarmers, 827 P.2d 561 (Colo. App. 1991), applied the "no-attachment rule" (i.e., that appointive assets are not "property" of the donee) to a "5 or 5" withdrawal power.

By a peculiar twist of the fraudulent conveyance concept, some courts have gone beyond the principles in the above cases and hold that the *exercise* of either a general power that is presently exercisable or one that is exercisable by will makes the appointive assets available to creditors, at least if other conditions for avoiding a fraudulent conveyance are met. Compare Restatement (Second) of Property: Donative Transfers §13.2: "Appointive assets covered by an unexercised general power of appointment, created by a person other than the donee, can be subjected to payment of claims of creditors of the donee, or claims against the donee's estate, but only to the extent provided by statute." Comment *a* explains: "Until the donee exercises the power, he has not accepted control over the appointive assets that gives the donee the equivalent of ownership." See also id. §§13.1, 13.4-.6. More recently, the Restatement (Third) of Trusts §56, Comment *b* (Tent. Draft approved 1999) has taken the position that, when the donee's own assets are insufficient, the donee's creditors may reach assets subject to a presently exercisable general power, whether or not exercised, and that creditors of a deceased donee's estate may reach even assets subject to an unexercised testamentary general power. For an interesting case allowing the deceased beneficiary-donee's creditors to reach appointive assets despite the fact that the objects (any "person or persons") expressly excluded payment to or appropriation for "any debts or liabilities" of the donee (cf. widely used, broad nongeneral power under IRC §§2041, 2514), see State Street Trust Co. v. Kissel, 19 N.E.2d 25 (Mass. 1925).

A number of statutes now allow creditors of the donee of a presently exercisable general power of appointment to reach the appointive assets whether or not the power is exercised (e.g., N.Y. EPTL §10-7.2), but not if the power is solely testamentary (id. §10-7.4). See also 1999 draft of Uniform Trust Code §505(b) (draft, Feb. 2000) (but exempting "5 or 5" withdrawal powers). A few statutes also allow creditors of a deceased donee's estate to reach assets subject to a testamentary general power. E.g., Cal. Civ. Code §1390.3. Compare UPC §2-202, including appointive property in the augmented estate of the donee of a general power for purposes of the surviving spouse's elective share (Chapter 3).

c. Other Matters

Lapse of Powers. A power of appointment cannot be exercised before it is created. Like other property rights, if a power is provided for in a will (of *A*, the donor) but the intended recipient (the donee, *B*) dies before the death of the testator (*A*), the intended power lapses and cannot be exercised by *B*'s will. If so intended by *A*, however, his desired disposition may be given effect in accordance with the terms of *B*'s will, although not as the exercise of a power. Do you see how this result can be reached? Also, compare the common provision in wills creating powers of appointment that, if the donee survives the donor, the power can be exercised by the donee's will even though executed before the donor's death.

Capacity of Donee. The donee of a power of appointment has capacity to exercise or release the power if she has capacity to transfer owned property (see Chapter 3, section A.1). It is arguable, however, that a donee who lacks this general capacity may exercise a power in reasonable circumstances if clearly authorized by the donor.

Formalities of Exercise. Unless otherwise required by the donor, the *formal* sufficiency of a donee's attempted appointment is ordinarily judged by the formal requirements for a valid transfer, by deed or by will, as the case may be, of an interest owned by the donee which is like that to be appointed. A related but more frequently encountered question, concerning *intention* to exercise a power when the donee's language is unclear, is considered in Chapter 11, section F.

11

Constructional Problems in Estate and Trust Distribution

An enormous amount of litigation occurs each year to determine the meaning of individual wills and trusts. Most of this litigation centers on the meaning of dispositive provisions, although the ensuing chapters also reveal the significance of interpretation and construction in the administration of trusts and decedents' estates. A natural starting point in studying the construction of dispositive provisions is to examine the problems created by such basic provisions as outright bequests and devises in simple wills. These matters are taken up at the start of this chapter. Subsequent discussion then moves on to examine recurring problems of trusts and other arrangements involving future interests and powers of appointment.

A. Distributive Problems: Changes in the Estate

Subsequent to the execution of a will but prior to the time an estate is distributed, many events may occur that affect the operation of the will and the rights of the beneficiaries. There may, of course, be births and deaths among the beneficiaries or within described classes after the will is executed. Significant problems of these types are taken up in section B of this chapter. There may also be changes in the assets of the estate, or there may be transactions between the testator and the legatees and devisees affecting estate assets or the beneficiaries' interests therein. These occurrences frequently create problems in the distribution of the estate and are the subject of section A of this chapter.

The traditional solution to certain distributive problems often requires bequests and devises to be classified. In deciding a particular question, a court may first find it necessary to determine whether a testamentary gift is specific, general, demonstrative, or residuary. Also, purely for convenience, it is useful to have accepted terminology by which reference can readily be made to common types of testamentary gifts.

Specific Devises. A specific devise is a gift of some particular thing or parcel of land. A devise of "the house and land at 185 4th Street" is specific. "My 100 shares of X Corporation stock" and "the grandfather clock in the living room" are also examples of specific devises (or, as some still say, bequests).

General Devises. A general devise is one that is payable out of the general estate rather than one requiring distribution of or payment from particular assets. The typical general devise is pecuniary, such as "$1,000 to A." Occasionally a general devise will be made in terms other than an amount of money. "One hundred shares of X Corporation stock" would be general if the testator is found to have intended his executor to use the general funds of the estate or, if necessary, to sell other assets in order to buy 100 shares of X stock for distribution to the devisee. Although it was once held that all devises of land were specific, it is now generally agreed that devises of land may be residuary or general under the same circumstances as devises of personal property.

Demonstrative Devises. A demonstrative devise is a gift, typically of an amount of money, payable primarily from a particular source and then from the general assets of the estate if that source fails or is inadequate. A gift of "$1,000 to A, payable out of my account in B Bank, and if this is insufficient then out of my other property," is demonstrative.

Residuary Disposition. A residuary disposition is a gift of whatever remains of the estate after the payment of all obligations and after all other devises have been satisfied. Thus it is a gift of "the residue of the estate."

How would you classify the following bequests and devises to A?

1. "I give all of my living room furniture to A."
2. "I give A any money X owes to me at my death."
3. "I give A $1,000 out of my account at X Bank."
4. "I give A $1,000 worth of my X Corporation stock."
5. "I give Blackacre to X and the rest of my land to A."
6. "I give A all of my personal property."
7. "I give A 100 shares of X Corporation stock." (Does it matter if the testator owned no X Corporation stock at his death? What if he owned 200 X Corporation shares when he executed the will? Or 200 when he died? What if he owned 100 when he died? Or 100 when he executed the will?)

1. Ademption

PROBLEM

11-A. *T* devised $50,000 to *A*, Blackacre to *B*, Greenacre to *C*, and the residue to *D*. After executing the will, *T* was declared incapacitated and a conservator was appointed. Thereafter, Blackacre was taken by eminent domain by the state highway commission, and the condemnation award of $200,000 was paid to the conservator and deposited in a savings account. By the time of *T*'s death five years later, the funds in this account were reduced to $25,000, the rest having been properly expended by the conservator for the support of *T*, whose incapacity continued until her death. The other assets of *T*'s estate consisted of Greenacre, listed securities worth $100,000, and $10,000 in a checking account. How is the estate to be distributed, assuming the jurisdiction in question has no legislation in point? What result in your state? What result under Restatement (Third) of Property §5.2 (infra p. 441) and §3-902 (infra, section 3)? Explain.

———————————

Ademption, sometimes referred to as *ademption by extinction*, occurs when the particular property devised is not a part of the testator's estate at the time of death, and the gift thereby fails. The doctrine of ademption applies only to specific devises. Thus, it is often necessary for this purpose to decide whether a particular testamentary gift is general or specific.

Early on (before 1786), the testator's intent was taken into consideration in England in determining if there had been an ademption. Then, in Ashburner v. MacGuire, 29 Eng. Rep. 62 (1786), Lord Thurlow enunciated the "in specie" test (also called the "identity" theory) which simply asks if the gift is specific and if the item is in the testator's estate. If the answers are "yes" (specific) and "no" (not in the estate), the gift is adeemed regardless of intent. This came to be known as the "modern" theory, and it still may represent the majority view in this country. See, e.g., Matter of Ireland, 257 N.Y. 155, 177 N.E. 405 (1931); McGee v. McGee, 413 A.2d 72 (R.I. 1980). The problem with taking intent into consideration, it is argued, is that it breeds litigation and is usually speculative.

Even under the "modern" view, some states have recognized exceptions for devised property that is sold or otherwise converted involuntarily, such as by a guardian. See, e.g., Hobin v. O'Donnell, 451 N.E.2d 30, 32 (Ill. App. 1983); Walsh v. Gillespie, 338 Mass. 278, 154 N.E.2d 906 (1959). Also, it has been held that the rule of ademption does not apply to a bequest of an automobile "where the decedent dies and the object of the specific legacy is simultaneously destroyed with his death," the legatee being entitled to the insurance proceeds received by the estate. In re Buda's Will, 21 Misc. 2d 931, 197 N.Y.S.2d 824 (1960). What would the legatee's rights be if the automobile had not been insured? Even where intent to adeem is said to be essential to an ademption by extinction, courts often require that the legatee, in order to take other property, find an identifiable replacement or trace proceeds to a fund that remains in the estate, thus not allowing resort to the general assets of the estate.

Because the "identity" theory tends to be harsh and intent-defeating, the more recent trend has been to move back to taking the testator's intent into consideration. See, e.g., Newbury v. McCammant, 182 N.W.2d 147, 149 (Iowa 1970); Wachovia Bank & Trust Co. v. Ketchum, 333 S.E.2d 542 (N.C. App. 1985); Estate of Austin, 169 Cal. Rptr. 648 (Cal. App. 1980). However, there still are some troublesome cases.

CHURCH v. MORGAN
685 N.E.2d 809 (Ohio App. 1996)

[Testator (Lacy) devised the money in a specific savings account to Spring Fleming and the residue of her estate to Ellene Lacy Cobbs. Lacy had been driven to the lawyer's office to sign the will by her friend and accountant, Samuel Church, who held a power of attorney and was named executor. On the drive home, Church (who was unaware of the specific provisions in the will) told Lacy that she would get a higher interest rate with certificates of deposit than with a savings account. So they drove to the bank, withdrew the money from the savings account, and purchased CDs. Church handled the transactions, but Lacy signed the documents because he did not have his power of attorney with him. Church testified that Lacy did not know from which accounts the money was taken, nor did she read any of the documents that she signed. Lacy died within three months. When Church saw the will, he was concerned that the devise to Fleming of about $90,000 (that had been in the savings account) was inadvertently adeemed. As executor, Church sued to construe. The trial court admitted evidence of the circumstances of the CD purchase and held that the devise was not adeemed because Lacy had devised the funds in the account and not the account itself. Cobbs appealed.]

HARSHA, J.

. . . Appellant's first assignment of error argues that the trial court improperly considered extrinsic evidence concerning the circumstances surrounding the $90,000 transfer from the savings account when it construed Lacy's will. For the reasons that follow, we reluctantly agree.

. . . Only when the express language of the will creates doubt as to its meaning may the court consider extrinsic evidence to determine the testator's intent. . . .

Unfortunately for Fleming, the words of Lacy's will clearly and unambiguously express her testamentary intent about the disposition of her estate. The second provision of her will enumerates several specific bequests to Ms. Fleming, testator's niece, one of which states, "I give, devise and bequeath to Spring Fleming all funds located in the following accounts: Savings Account # 72424, in my name at Belpre Savings Bank, of Belpre, Ohio.'' Since the express language contained within the four corners of this will creates no doubt as to its meaning, neither the lower court nor this court may consider any extrinsic evidence to determine Lacy's intent. At the time of testator's death, savings account No. 72424, in Lacy's name at Belpre Savings Bank in Belpre, Ohio, contained $4,108.25 plus interest. Pursuant to the express terms of the specific bequest cited above, appellee is thereby entitled to receive $4,108.25 plus interest from savings account No. 72424. . . .

[T]he executor has submitted extrinsic evidence that $90,000 was withdrawn from that account, literally within hours of the execution of the will, to fund a certificate of deposit at a higher rate of interest. Even though that extrinsic evidence might indicate that Lacy intended the $90,000 to remain part of Fleming's specific bequest, we are nevertheless bound to ignore that evidence and construe the terms of the will as written by the testator. To do otherwise would result in this court's rewriting the testator's will, an action which is clearly precluded by law. . . .

We admit that it is tempting in this case to substitute our interpretation of the testator's intent for the clear language of the will because the extrinsic evidence is capable of being construed to imply the intent to benefit Spring Fleming. However, we believe courts begin a treacherous descent upon a slippery slope when they start substituting their judgment in place of the express language of a will. The fact that the result in this case seems inequitable does not negate the potentially greater injury to jurisprudence were we to defer to our hearts rather than our minds.

Although this result may be inequitable, it is the only possible legal result given the record as it exists before us now. The express terms of the will are unambiguous. It is only by introducing the extrinsic evidence of the substantial transfer of funds on the day the will was executed that testator's intent may appear unclear. However, our independent examination of the will discloses no basis upon which to justify a consideration of the extrinsic evidence admitted by the lower court. This is especially true in light of the continued existence of account No. 72424 at the time of death.

Therefore, we hold that the will of Minnie Frances Lacy, on its face, clearly and unambiguously expresses her testamentary intentions. Any reference to the extrinsic evidence submitted by the executor in this case is unnecessary and cannot be permitted. As a result, the lower court erred in its admission and consideration of the extrinsic evidence in order to determine testator's intentions. Accordingly, certificate of deposit No. 53029825, which was not explicitly disposed of by the will, becomes part of the residue of testator's estate and must, by law, pass to the residuary beneficiary. . . .

Judgment reversed and cause remanded.

KLINE, JUDGE, dissenting.

I respectfully dissent. I agree that Minnie Frances Lacy executed an unambiguous last will and testament on February 27, 1995. However, she did not say in Item II of her last will that the funds must remain in the same specified CDs and savings accounts at the time of her death.

"The court's function in construing a will is to determine and apply the testator's intent as expressed in the language of the whole will, and read in light of the applicable law, and circumstances surrounding the will's execution.". . .

Courts must ascertain and give effect to the intent of the testator wherever legally possible. The express language of the last will and testament normally provides the court with the indicators of the testator's intentions. "However, other factors must be considered. [V]arious presumptions or rules of construction have historically been utilized by courts in this area of the law.". . .

" 'A will speaks from the time of execution as to its meaning and from the death of testator as to its effect and operation.' " . . . Pursuant to an established rule of construction, "a general description of property shows that testator intends the property as [it exists] at his death. A specific description of property so as to distinguish [it] from other property as [it exists] when the will is made, usually shows that testator makes his will with reference to the property as [it exists] at the time that the will is made." 4 Page on Wills (Bowe & Parker Rev.1961) 165, Section 30.26.

Applying the above rule of construction, I believe that the specific descriptions of the bequests in Item II of the will refer to the property as it existed at the exact time Lacy signed the document. Lacy bequeathed "all funds located in" the specified accounts at the time she executed her will. The $90,000 transferred from savings account No. 72424 is money that was funds located in that account at the time Lacy executed her will. Moreover, the $90,000 transferred out of the specified savings account does not pass pursuant to Item III because Lacy did not "acquire or become entitled to [the $90,000.00] after the execution of this Will."

. . . . Accordingly, I would overrule all three assignments of error and affirm the judgment of the trial court.

———

In another Ohio case, decided the same year, Testator's (*T*'s) cousin (*C*), operating under a power of attorney, sold *T*'s residence two months before *T*'s death. *C* knew that *T* had executed a will, but did not know its contents. When the will was admitted to probate, *C* discovered that *T* had devised the residence to her. The Ohio statute, modeled after pre-1990 UPC §2-608, provided for an exception to the ademption rule for property sold by a guardian. The court held that the guardian or conservator exception does not extend to a sale by an attorney-in-fact. Thus, *C* adeemed her own gift. Estate of Hegel, 76 Ohio St. 3d 476, 668 N.E.2d 474 (1996). The dissent argued that the decision gives a dangerous power to attorneys-in-fact: "At least in [*T*]'s case, [*C*] did what she believed was best for her charge, innocently depriving herself of her inheritance and providing an unintended windfall to the other heirs. But now, nothing prevents an attorney-in-fact from altering a will to his or her benefit." Id. at 478. Is this last statement true?

What result in *Church* and *Hegel* if Ohio followed Restatement (Third) §5.2, below, which is somewhat similar to current UPC §2-606?

RESTATEMENT (THIRD) OF PROPERTY: WILLS AND OTHER DONATIVE TRANSFERS

§5.2   *Failure ("ademption") of specific devises by extinction*

(a) If specifically devised property, in its original or in a changed form, is in the testator's estate at death, the devisee is entitled to the specifically devised property.

(b) If specifically devised property is not in the testator's estate at death, the devisee is entitled to any proceeds remaining unpaid at death of (i) any sale, (ii) any condemnation award, or (iii) any insurance on or other recovery for damage to or loss of the property.

(c) Subject to subsection (b), if specifically devised property is not in the testator's estate at death, the specific devise fails unless failure of the devise would be inconsistent with the testator's intent.

Comment *g* of §5.2 states that if an agent sells the specifically devised property during the testator's incapacity, failure of the devise is presumptively inconsistent with the testator's intent.

Avoiding Ademption. Assuming that under applicable law a specific gift cannot be saved from ademption on the basis of the testator's intent when the property was removed from the estate, several other possibilities remain. One of these possibilities is to salvage the gift through construction. Courts have often tended to classify a questionable devise as general rather than specific when confronted with a question of ademption. If such a classification is not permitted by the language of the gift, the court may construe the specific devise to refer to certain property which is found in the estate at death. As an example of this latter, a devise of "the automobile I now own" could, despite the usual tendency to relate the word "now" in a will to the time of execution, be held to refer to the automobile owned at the time of death to avoid ademption by a sale of the original and a later acquisition of a new automobile. See In re Cooper's Estate, 107 Cal. App. 2d 592, 237 P.2d 699 (1951) (avoiding issue of intent at the time of sale).

A second possibility, even where intent at the time of disposal is not relevant, is through application of the accepted principle that a mere change of form does not work an ademption. Of course, the problem then is to decide what changes constitute mere changes of form. Consider the materials that follow.

PROBLEM

11-B.   *T*'s will, executed five years ago, reads: "I give to *A* my checking accounts in X Bank and in Y Bank. I give *B* any interest I may have in the estate of my deceased sister, *S*. The residue of my estate I devise to *C*." After executing this will:

(a) *T* closed out both of the above-mentioned bank accounts two years ago and with the same funds opened a checking account (with a deposit of $5,000) in Z Bank and a savings account (with a $10,000 deposit) in the S-L Savings & Loan Association. Cf. In re Estate of Hall, 60 N.J. Super. 597, 160 A.2d 49 (1960); Baybank Harvard Trust Co. v. Grant, 23 Mass. App. 653, 504 N.E.2d 1072 (1987).

(b) Also two years ago, *T* received a preliminary distribution of $6,000 in cash and two months later a final distribution of $5,346 cash, together representing his full rights in the estate of *S*; *T* endorsed each check over to Z Bank, on each occasion purchasing a certificate of deposit in the amount of $5,000 and having the excess ($1,000 and $346 respectively) deposited in his checking account in that bank. See In re Estate of Brown, 252 N.E.2d 142 (Ind. App. 1969).

T died a year ago. Who is entitled to the two $5,000 certificates of deposit and the Z and S-L accounts, then containing $6,500 and $10,450, respectively? Does it matter whether an intent test is applied in the state in which the questions arise? Consider UPC §2-606. Are there additional facts you need to determine?

FIRST NATIONAL BANK v. PERKINS INSTITUTE
275 Mass. 498, 176 N.E. 532 (1931)

CARROLL, J.

This is a petition for instructions by the executor of the will of Amelia G. Dywer who died July 4, 1928. In the sixteenth clause of her will the testatrix gave to her nephew, John Baker, hereinafter referred to as the legatee, "all of my stock in the Standard Oil Company of New York and the Standard Oil Company of New Jersey." Instructions are sought as to the disposition of $7,000 in principal amount of the debentures of the Standard Oil Company of New Jersey, which the legatee contends passed to him under this clause of the will, and the other respondents contend belong to them under the residuary clause.

It was agreed that at the time of the execution of the will the testatrix owned one hundred ten shares of the seven percent preferred stock of the Standard Oil Company of New Jersey; that this stock was callable at $115 a share and accrued dividend and was called for payment by vote of the directors on November 15, 1926. To meet this call debentures totalling $120,000,000 were to be issued; these debentures were sold to bankers in New York. The bankers agreed to give the holders of the stock a preferential right to subscribe for these debentures. The testatrix sent to the bankers her one hundred ten shares of stock, subscribing for a sufficient number of debentures to absorb the stock. The issue of the debentures was oversubscribed; accordingly, there was allowed to Mrs. Dyer seven of these debentures in payment for sixty-two shares of stock. The remainder of her stock was redeemed by the New Jersey company. At the time of her death Mrs. Dyer owned the $7,000 of debentures.

There was no stock of the Standard Oil Company of New Jersey in the estate of the testatrix when she died. Her stock in that company had been taken up by the payment in cash from the New Jersey company, and the debentures which had been purchased by the bankers and transferred to her by these bankers in exchange for sixty-two of her shares. The debentures came to her, not from the New Jersey company but from the bankers who were the owners of them. In these circumstances the legacy of the stock of the Standard Oil Company of New Jersey was adeemed. The legacy of the specific thing had been disposed of by the testatrix before her death. The case cannot be distinguished from Moffatt v. Heon, 242 Mass. 201, where it was held that the specific legacy of a mortgage which was paid before the death of the testator had been adeemed. In that case the authorities are reviewed and this quotation from Tomlinson v. Bury, 145 Mass. 346, 348, appears at pages 203-204:

> If the testator subsequently parts with the property, even if he exchanges it for other property or purchases other property with the proceeds, the legatee has no claim on the estate for the value of his legacy. The legacy is adeemed by the act of the testator.

The legatee relies on Pope v. Hinckley, 209 Mass. 323. In that case the . . . exchange was not made during the lifetime of the testator, but was made by his executors shortly after his death. . . .

We do not think it necessary to discuss the cases from other jurisdictions, cited by the legatee. In many of them the facts are different from those in the case at bar; in so far as the decisions appear to be contrary to the conclusion we have reached, we must decline to follow them. We do not decide what would have been the rights of the legatee if the testatrix, in substitution of her stock in the New Jersey company, had received the debentures directly from the company. That question does not arise and we make no intimation regarding it. . . .

The decree is affirmed.

In re MANDELLE'S ESTATE
252 Mich. 375, 233 N.W. 230 (1930)

WIEST, C.J.

Mary S. Mandelle, possessed of a large estate, died testate, August 17, 1928. In her will, executed September 10, 1923, among many other bequests, she made the following:

> In recognition of his faithful and kindly medical services to me and his contribution to science and humanity, which I wish to facilitate, I give to Charles Jack Hunt, of Mt. Vernon, New York, his heirs and assigns forever, twelve hundred (1,200) shares, par value, of the capital stock of Parke, Davis & Company, a corporation, etc., of Detroit, Michigan.

At that time testatrix owned 3,744 shares of the stock of that company of the par value of $25 each. In February, 1927, the stockholders of Parke, Davis & Company reframed its capital structure in form only, and authorized the exchange of the $25 par value shares for no par value shares in the ratio of one par value share for five no par value shares, and in March, 1927, testatrix exchanged the mentioned par value shares, owned by her, for the no par value shares in accord with the designated ratio, and, at her death, held the no par shares only. The executors of her estate, being in doubt whether Dr. Hunt was entitled to 6,000 shares of the no par stock (the number of shares equivalent to the 1,200 shares of par value stock), or to only 1,200 shares of the no par stock, petitioned the probate court for instruction. The probate court held that the bequest to Dr. Hunt called for 6,000 shares of the no par stock, together with dividends received upon the 6,000 shares by the executors after the death of testatrix. The residuary legatees appealed to the circuit court, and, upon affirmance there of the probate order, prosecute review here.

Attorneys for the legatee contend that the legacy is specific, while attorneys for the residuary legatees say it is general, and attorneys for the executors think it demonstrative.

If the legacy is general, then the legatee takes 1,200 shares of the no par stock and may not participate in any accruals thereon during the course of administration. If the legacy is specific, then the legatee takes 6,000 shares of the no par stock, with all accruals since the death of the testatrix.

Appellants argue that the will speaks as of the date of death of testatrix. It is not expressive of the whole subject to say that a will speaks as of the date of the death of the maker. It is more accurate to say that a will is not operative until the death of the maker, and then speaks the intention of the maker at the time of its execution. It has been held that: "As to specific legacies, the will speaks as of the time of its execution."

The legacy is either specific or general. It is not a demonstrative legacy. Briefly stated, a demonstrative legacy is a pecuniary gift with a particular fund or source of means pointed out for its satisfaction. We think testatrix intended something more, in specifying the shares of stock bequeathed, than to point them out as a mere yardstick with which to measure a pecuniary gift. Upon the question of whether the legacy is specific or general, there exist certain general rules all, however, recognizing that the intention of the maker, found in any part of the will or reasonably deducible from the instrument, considered as a whole, must govern construction.

It is said, in behalf of appellants, that specific legacies are not favored. The main reasons for this is the peril of ademption, and not that the courts frown thereon. Our attention has been directed to many English and American cases. Without reviewing the cases, we will state our conclusions, together with applicable authority.

It was stated in Burnett v. Heinrichs, 95 N.J. Eq. 112 (122 A. 681):

> But the language of the bequest is not controlling. The entire instrument is to be examined, and if, upon the whole, it clearly appears that the testator intended to dispose of his stock, the legacy will be regarded as specific. If in the clause the testator has referred to the stock as "my" or "now in my possession" or "now owned by me," or like words of identification, the bequest would have been specific according to all accepted authority. And if similar expressions are found in the rest of the will, referable to and inclusive of the bequest, it is specific.

In the forty-second paragraph of the will testatrix declared:

 It is my express wish and desire that all of the above legacies and trust funds shall, as far as possible, be paid in stocks and bonds or other property which I may own at the time of my death. . . .

This expression of purpose is referable to every provision in the will and to the bequest to Dr. Hunt, and discloses that in making the bequest to Dr. Hunt she intended to give shares of stock then owned by her. . . .

We think the will, considered as a whole, shows it was the intention of testatrix to constitute her bequest in favor of Dr. Hunt a specific legacy. We think the provisions of the will individualized the shares of stock bequeathed to Dr. Hunt as stock then owned by testatrix. This brings us to the question of whether there was an ademption by reason of exchange of par value shares of stock for no value shares. The stock was changed in name and form only and at all times remained substantially the same thing.

There was no ademption accomplished by taking five shares of no par stock for each share of par value stock. Testatrix did not initiate the change in form of the shares of stock; the change occurred in consequence of corporate action which she could not control. Johns Hopkins University v. Uhrig, 145 Md. 114 (125 A. 606). Dividends, subsequent to death of a testator, on specific legacies of shares of stock follow the stock. Tifft v. Porter, 8 N.Y. 516; Dryden v. Owings, 49 Md. 356.

The judgment is affirmed, with costs against appellants.

Suppose a testator devises 1,000 shares of X Corp. stock to *A* and the residue of his estate to *B*. After the will was executed, but before *T*'s death, X Corp. declared a two-for-one stock split. Does *A* get the additional shares of X Corp. stock? Would it matter if the share distributions were designated as stock dividends? This problem of "increase," somewhat of an inverse of ademption, is considered in depth along with its trust counterpart in Chapter 19 infra. p. 1021-3

2.   Satisfaction

The doctrine of satisfaction or *ademption by satisfaction,* as it is sometimes called, is analogous to the doctrine of advancement in intestate estates (Chapter 2). T. Atkinson, Wills §133 (2d ed. 1953) states that a general or residuary devise may be satisfied in whole or in part by testator's inter vivos gift to the devisee, adding that when "the testator stands in loco parentis to the [devisee], the gift is presumed to be intended as satisfaction of the [devise]. By the prevailing view the doctrine of satisfaction does not apply to devises of land." Later in the same section Atkinson adds that when the "thing given is not of the same nature as the thing [devised], a presumption arises that an ademption by satisfaction was not intended." In some states statutes provide that "advancements or gifts are not to be taken as ademptions of general [devises], unless such intention is expressed by the testator in writing." Cf. Uniform Probate Code §2-609.

MATTER OF ESTATE OF WOLFF
349 N.W.2d 33 (S.D. 1984)

WOLLMAN, J.

This is an appeal from a decree of distribution . . . which held that there had been an ademption of certain devises of land in decedent's will. We affirm.

Jacob Wolff, Sr., (decedent) accumulated approximately 2,800 acres of farm land in Perkins County in South Dakota. When decedent and his wife moved to California in 1950, his three sons Jacob Jr., Arthur and Erwinn remained on the farmland. Jacob Jr., who had been farming 762 acres known as the "home place" with Erwinn, left South Dakota in 1957.

In 1971 decedent executed a will which provided that in the event his wife should predecease him, his estate should pass to his sons "equally, share and share alike." In 1972, decedent and his wife deeded 1,000.16 acres of the Perkins County land to Arthur for consideration of "one dollar and other good and valuable consideration." In 1973, decedent and his wife deeded 1,040 acres of the Perkins County land to Erwinn for the same consideration. The tracts of land deeded to Erwinn and Arthur and the remaining 762 acres were of approximately the same value.

Prior to deeding the two tracts of land to Erwinn and Arthur, decedent, who was born to immigrant parents and was not proficient in English, wrote the following to Jacob Jr. in a letter dated September 14, 1972:

> I had sent Arthur and Erwinn the Deed for their land. So from now on they did not have to send anymore rent from the land that is Deeded to them and about your land, I don't know yet. See how it is turning out. Erwinn can buy it or rent for cash, from now on. Or what did you think? I thought if Erwinn buys it I can make the Deed to him. If he rents for cash I make the Deed to you. It is 760 acres of land. All the land on the Southside of the road Sec3 — Sec4 — Sec5 — Sec9 — and Sec10. So he buy it, I deed it to him. If he rent it, he got to rent it for cash. But if you want it to deed it to you, I will do it? Say it the [way] you like it best.

Decedent's wife died in 1974, and Erwinn moved to California to live with decedent. Arthur's son, Lynn then took possession of the home place.

Decedent died in 1980 at the age of eighty-six. His will was admitted to probate in California, and with the exception of the land in Perkins County, South Dakota, decedent's estate was distributed in equal shares to his three sons pursuant to the California probate decree. The will was later admitted to probate in South Dakota. The circuit court concluded that decedent's delivery of the warranty deeds to Erwinn and Arthur, when considered in light of decedent's September 14, 1972, letter to Jacob Jr., constituted an ademption of their share of the South Dakota property.

"Ademption" is the term that describes either the act which makes inoperative a devise or bequest of specific property by the sale or extinction of the property during the testator's lifetime or, as is applicable to the case at hand, the satisfaction of a devise or bequest by money payment or delivery or conveyance of property to a beneficiary prior to the testator's death. . . .

The statutes regarding ademption are exclusive, and we therefore need not address common law rules and principles. . . .

Although there is authority that ademption applies only to specific legacies . . . SDCL 29-6-14 allows for ademptions of general legacies if an intention to adeem is expressed by the testator in writing.

The doctrine of ademption applies to both bequests of personalty and devises of realty. . . .

Arthur and Erwinn contend that the requirement in SDCL 29-6-14 that the testator express his intention to adeem was not satisfied by decedent's September 14, 1972, letter. In interpreting a statute similar to SDCL 29-6-14, the Supreme Court of California held:

> It is the established rule that no special form, nor even the signature of the decedent, is required to constitute a charge of the advancement in writing as prescribed by such statutes. It will be sufficient if it appears that the writing was done by the decedent and shows the intent to charge the money or property given as an advancement rather than as a gift or loan. Unsigned statements in the form of a charge entered in a book or on leaves inserted at the back of a book of miscellaneous accounts, the circumstances being such as to exclude the idea that it was charged as a debt, have been held sufficient.

In re Estate of Hayne, 165 Cal. 568, 573, 133 P. 277, 279 (1913). . . .

In the letter to Jacob Jr., decedent writes of sending Arthur and Erwinn the deed for "their land," and then refers to the remaining property as "your land." The land deeded to Arthur and Erwinn is contiguous with the respective tracts already owned by them. Moreover, after taking into account the disparity in the per acre value assigned to the several tracts, the land deeded to Arthur and Erwinn had a value closely approximating the value of the remaining 760 acres claimed by Jacob Jr. Given these facts, we conclude that the circuit court did not err in determining that the letter satisfied the writing requirement contained in SDCL 29-6-14. . . .

Decedent provided in his will that should a beneficiary contest the validity of the will, such beneficiary would forfeit his share of the estate.

Arthur and Erwinn maintain that by opposing their petition for the sale of the 762 acres of South Dakota land and by raising the issue of ademption, Jacob Jr. was disputing the validity of decedent's will. We disagree. Jacob Jr. was not claiming the will was invalid, but rather was correctly asserting that a portion of the devise under the will had been satisfied.

Any issues or sub-issues not discussed in this opinion have been considered and have been found to be without merit.

The decree is affirmed. . . .

WEST v. COOGLER
427 So. 2d 813 (Fla. Dist. Ct. App. 1983)

COWART, Judge.

This case involves an "advancement" to one beneficiary of a trust. On July 30, 1962, Margaret F. Coogler, as settlor, conveyed 160 acres to her daughter, appellant Jane West, in Trust for the use and benefit of the settlor during her lifetime with remainder in trust for the use and benefit of her four children: [Jane, Vivian, William, and Theodore]. The deed of trust provided that the trust expired 20 years from its date and that if any of the four children died prior to the expiration of the trust that child's interest would pass in equal shares to the surviving beneficiaries. Upon termination the corpus was to be distributed equally to the surviving beneficiaries. This was a spendthrift trust precluding any alienation of any interest therein by any beneficiary. This deed of trust was not recorded until March 3, 1964, and between the date of its execution and its recording . . . Margaret F. Coogler deeded her son Vivian . . . and his wife Clara, a quarter (40 acres) of the property included in the trust deed. On January 4, 1967, Vivian V. Coogler, Jr., deeded the forty acre tract he obtained from his mother to a third party. . . . In 1968 one of the four children, Theodore . . . , died and in 1969 the mother died. . . .

In 1979 Vivian V. Coogler, Jr., brought this action for declaratory decree and accounting, claiming a one-third interest in the corpus of the trust, being the 120 acres remaining of the 160 acres. . . .

In a strict technical sense, the legal definition of an "advancement" is an inter vivos gift made by a parent to a child with intent that such gift represents a part or the whole of the donor's estate that the donee would inherit on the death of the donor. However, the concept of an advancement rests on an ancient equitable doctrine that applies with equal force and logic to the inter vivos trust in this case . . . the assumed desire of a parent to equalize his estate among his heirs, not only as to property owned at death but as to all property that went from him to his children, so that one child will not be preferred to another in the final settlement of his estate. . . . [T]here is no apparent reason why it should not be applied to advances made by a settlor in the unusual case, as here. . . . Whether a particular transfer is an advancement or not is [a question] of intent and the relevant intent is that of the person making the gift. . . . Therefore, whether or not Vivian . . . knew of the trust at the time he received the 40 acres from his mother is irrelevant and immaterial. . . . [He] admitted that he paid his mother nothing for the 40 acres. In addition to a presumption, the testimony of Jane . . . as to her mother's intent was made without objection and is uncontradicted. As to why the mother gave the 1964 deed of 40 acres to Vivian . . . , in her deposition Jane [reported that the settlor had said that Vivian] "was pressuring her and she felt he needed it at that time instead of later." . . .

Therefore we hold that the conveyance of 40 acres by the settlor to Vivian . . . constituted an advancement and that for the purposes of distribution the 40 acres should be grouped, hotchpot, with the remaining trust corpus and treated as an advancement and, in this case, charged, not by valuation but in kind as 40 acres against the interest of Vivian . . . in the trust corpus. The effect of this is that Vivian . . . will share with Jane . . . and William . . . the share that their brother Theodore . . . would have received had he survived. . . .

3. Abatement

Any time a testator's property, after payment of claims against the estate, is insufficient to satisfy all bequests and devises, it is obvious that the shares of some or all beneficiaries under the will must be reduced ("abated"). In addition to losses in asset values and payment of debts, expenses of administration, and taxes, the testator's estate may be diminished by the assertion of statutory rights in contravention of the will by a surviving spouse or a pretermitted heir. These latter sources of abatement are normally unanticipated and particularly drastic in their impact on a testator's scheme. Consequently they pose special problems and may suggest departure from the usual rules for abatement. In the case of a spouse's election against a will, there may also be questions of sequestration or of acceleration of remainders, or both, caused by renunciation of a testate interest. These problems are raised and considered briefly in Chapter 3.

Although questions of abatement are controlled by the "testator's intent," typically nothing appears or may be inferred from the will regarding an actual intention. For cases in which no intention is discoverable, a presumed order of abatement for payment of debts is prescribed by decisional law or by statute. Property that would pass intestate is first taken for payment of debts before any testamentary gifts will be reduced. Generally, however, there will be no intestate property, unless there is no residuary clause or unless all or a part of the residuary provision fails for some reason. When there is no intestate property, it is apparent from the very nature of a residuary bequest that it should abate before general or specific bequests in the absence of manifestation of contrary intent or an inconsistent plan in the will. Beyond this, the order of abatement, whether prescribed by statute or common law rule, is more or less arbitrary but purportedly based on the probable intent of testators. "Modern" views on abatement are typified by the provisions of Uniform Probate Code §3-902 (except for abatement caused by the share of a pretermitted heir, for which the statutory trend favors ratable abatement of all testate interests, essentially in the manner provided in UPC §2-209(b) for a spouse's election).

UNIFORM PROBATE CODE

§3-902.   [*Distribution; Order in Which Assets Appropriated; Abatement*].

(a) Except as provided in subsection (b) and except as provided in connection with the share of the surviving spouse who elects to take an elective share, shares of distributees abate, without any preference or priority as between real and personal property, in the following order: (1) property not disposed of by the will; (2) residuary devises; (3) general devises; (4) specific devises. For purposes of abatement, a general devise charged on any specific property or fund is a specific devise to the extent of the value of the property on which it is charged, and upon the failure or insufficiency of the property on which it is charged, a general devise to the extent of the failure or insufficiency. Abatement within each classification is in proportion to the amounts of property each of the beneficiaries would have received if full distribution of the property had been made in accordance with the terms of the will.

(b) If the will expresses an order of abatement, or if the testamentary plan or the express or implied purpose of the devise would be defeated, by the order of abatement stated in subsection (a), the shares of the distributees abate as may be found necessary to give effect to the intention of the testator.

(c) If the subject of a preferred devise is sold or used incident to administration, abatement shall be achieved by appropriate adjustments in, or contribution from, other interests in the remaining assets.

Some statutes have eliminated the typical priority of specific gifts over general.

The older view, still prevailing in a few states, is that all devises of personal property abate before devises of real property. Some cases have avoided the effects of this position by finding that legacies were intended to be charges on lands not specifically devised, if the legacies exceeded the testator's personal estate at the time the will was executed.

Whatever the order of abatement, within a given class of equal priority the gifts generally abate ratably. By statute or decision in some states, however, within a given class, relatives may be preferred over strangers. Also, testamentary provisions for near relatives may be given a more general priority on the basis of probable intent on a case by case basis. Some cases recognize a priority for a spouse who is deemed to take a testamentary share as a "purchaser" by relinquishing statutory rights. This rule has even been applied to give a spouse's residuary interest priority over all other bequests. Nolte v. Nolte, 247 Iowa 868, 76 N.W.2d 881 (1956).

An interesting case dealing with a significant tax-related problem is Osborn v. Osborn, 334 S.W.2d 48 (Mo. 1960). In that case the testator made various specific and general gifts to his son and others and then provided that his wife should receive the amount required to take the maximum marital deduction then allowed under the federal estate tax law, with the residue to the testator's son. When the estate proved inadequate to pay the marital deduction devise and all of the other specific and general devises, the court held that the widow's share was to be paid in full and that only the other devises were to be abated, whether "characterized as 'specific' or not," since the testator's intent to take advantage of the maximum marital deduction rendered inoperative the normal order of abatement.

4. Miscellaneous Matters

a. Exoneration

T. Atkinson, Wills §137 (2d ed. 1953), summarizes exoneration as follows: "In absence of statute or of testamentary directions to the contrary, mortgages and other liens upon the decedent's realty and upon the subject-matter of his specific bequests must be exonerated out of the general personal assets of the estate." The rule varies from state to state and hardly justifies further discussion here other than to note (1) that the intent to require or not to require exoneration of encumbered property is a matter to be taken up with a client in the planning of a will, and (2) that the modern judicial and statutory tendency has been to narrow the application of the inferred right of exoneration.

A number of modern statutes, based on Model Probate Code §189, or more recently on UPC §2-607, abolish this right unless the will provides otherwise, and the UPC makes it clear that a general directive to pay debts does not create a right of exoneration. The comment to the Model Code section observes that the basis of the common law rule — that the personal estate has been benefited by the creation of the debt — generally "has no foundation in fact." See generally Estate of Brown, 240 Cal. App. 2d 818, 820, 50 Cal. Rptr. 78, 80 (1966).

b.   Right of Retainer

Uniform Probate Code §3-903 provides: "The amount of a non-contingent indebtedness of a successor to the estate if due, or its present value if not due, shall be offset against the successor's interest; but the successor has the benefit of any defense which would be available to him in a direct proceeding for recovery of the debt." Contrary to this last clause, some decisions hold as a matter of common law that the right of retainer applies even to debts barred by a statute of limitations or discharged in bankruptcy.

B.   *Introduction to Class Gifts*

1.   What Is a Gift to a Class?

Defining class gifts is no easy matter. One of the best-known definitions is Gray's: "A class is a number of persons having a common characteristic. By a gift to a class is meant a gift to persons, the share of each of whom is determined by the number of the class." Gray, The Rule Against Perpetuities §369 n.1 (4th ed. 1942). According to Simes, Future Interests §101 (2d ed. 1966): "[A] testamentary gift to a number of persons constitutes a class gift if (a) the terms of the will construed in light of the surrounding circumstances show that the testator was group minded; and (b) the group can increase or decrease in membership after the execution of the will." Unfortunately, class gift terminology tends to be used without appreciation of its legal consequences, simply because it is naturally descriptive of intended beneficiaries.

[margin annotation: class gift]

COOLEY, WHAT CONSTITUTES A GIFT TO A CLASS
49 Harv. L. Rev. 903, 930 (1936)

When should courts hold that a particular will contains a gift to a class? When the testator appears to have been so interested in the welfare of a group to whom he is giving something that, had he thought of it, he would have wanted those members who survived him to take it all in preference to having part of it lapse. In each case the question properly is whether it seems from the sort of disposition the testator made and from the attending circumstance that he was, so to speak, "group minded." There is evidence that this is the criterion upon which the majority of courts operate in disposing of these cases. Their statement of what they are doing, however is quite different.

2.   Class Closing: The Question of Class Increase

The Rule of Convenience. In determining the time within which a person must be born in order to be included in a class for purpose of a class gift — i.e., for purposes of determining the maximum membership of a class — courts frequently must resort to the so-called rule of convenience or, as it is often called in England, the rule in Andrews v. Partington, 3 Bro. C.C. 401 (1791). As the following materials are examined, consider: (a) in which types of cases this problem of class closing arises and in which types of cases it is of little practical importance; (b) what justification there is for the rule of convenience and whether this justification is convincing; and (c) whether there are any techniques by which the class-closing problem can be provided for by the drafter, who should certainly consider the matter in appropriate cases.

GULLIVER, CASES ON FUTURE INTERESTS
84-85 (1959)

The Closing of the Class. The statement that a class "closes" at a certain time means that nobody born after that time can share, except that here, as elsewhere, a child who is later born alive is considered as in being from the date of conception It is important to realize that nothing else than this is meant by the statement that a class is closed. It does not as such mean that a person has to be alive at the time to take, since the estate of a person then dead may be entitled to a share; nor does it insure that those living at the time will take, since their interests may still be subject to some condition that has not been fulfilled.

[T]he closing of the class depends theoretically upon the intention of the transferor, but such intention is only rarely expressed. Because of the necessity of deciding this matter without any specific guide from the instrument, the courts have adopted a rule of construction which is fundamentally a rule of convenience to expedite the distribution and enjoyment of the property. Any such rule can be translated into one that carries out "intent" on the theory that it may be assumed that the transferor would desire such expedition of distribution and enjoyment.

This rule is that, if no contrary intent is expressed, *the class will close at the time when any member of the class is entitled to immediate possession and enjoyment of his share.* This rule, in the case of personalty, permits immediate distribution of at least a minimum share to the member who first qualifies; and, in the case of realty, it tends to make the title more marketable by identifying the personnel of potential parties in interest and eliminating claims by people who might be born thereafter.

The following examples of a gift "to the children of *B*" will illustrate the operation of this rule, it being assumed in all cases that *B* is still alive, since, if he were dead, the class would have been physiologically closed at his death.

(1) In the case of an outright gift "*to the children of B,*" the beneficiaries will be entitled to enjoyment immediately on the operative date of the instrument (death of testator in case of a will; date of delivery in case of a deed), and the class will therefore close at that time. Suppose a legacy of $100,000 to the children of *B,* and that, at the death of the testator, *B* has two children, *X* and *Y.* Since the class is then closed, no children of *B* born thereafter will share, and immediate distribution of $50,000 apiece will be made to *X* and *Y.* If the class were kept open until the death of *B,* it would be impossible to determine even the minimum share of *X* and *Y,* since it would be impossible to predict how many more children *B* might have. This would make any distribution whatever to *X* and *Y* unsafe, without some such cumbersome and perhaps expensive procedure as the fiduciary's taking refunding bonds from them, and would prejudice *X* and *Y* by making it impossible for them to predict even the minimum amount of their interests. No careful fiduciary would take a chance on guessing that *B* would not have more than five children and thus distributing $20,000 apiece to *X* and *Y,* since, if the class were kept open, there might ultimately be ten children of *B* entitled to share, reducing each share to $10,000, and making it necessary for the fiduciary to try to get back from *X* and *Y* the excess of $10,000 apiece, which they might by then have dissipated. To avoid these difficulties, then, the courts have held that, in the absence of any contrary intent, the class closed at the death of the testator.

(2) In the case of a gift "*to X for life, and after his death to the children of B,*" the class will close on the termination of the life estate, since that is the time when the remaindermen will be entitled to possession and enjoyment. As pointed out above, the statement that the class closes on the termination of the life estate merely means that no children of *B* born thereafter will share. It does not mean that only those who are alive at the end of the life estate will share. Whether the estate of a member of a class who died before the end of the life estate is entitled to share is not in any way controlled by the class-closing rule, but depends on whether the language of the gift made survival to the end of the life estate a condition. With the above language, for exam-

[handwritten margin note: no children after B. born can take. class closes at X's death]

ple, the estate of a child of *B* who predeceased *X* would be entitled to a share, since there is nothing in the language to require survival. If, however, the gift had been "and after his death to the children of *B* then living," the interest of any child of *B* who predeceased *X* would be extinguished at that child's death.

In case (1) in the quoted discussion from Gulliver, above, what result would you expect if a third child, *Z*, were conceived and born to *B* during administration of the testator's estate? See Landwehr's Estate, 147 Pa. 121, 23 At. 348 (1892). What would the result be if *B* had no children at the time of the testator's death?

Should the rule of convenience apply where the instrument refers to class members "now living or hereafter born"? See Re Werhner's Settlement Trusts, 1 All Eng. Rep. 184 (1961) (where the court repeated the observation that the rule is "obviously convenient to those who take under it . . . but the irony of the rule is no doubt more apparent to those who are by its application excluded from taking what the testator intended them to take").

Is there any reason to apply the rule to a will in which the testator devises "$10,000 to each of my nieces and nephews"?

When does the class close if $100,000 is devised "in equal shares to the children of *B*, to be paid to each as he or she becomes 21," assuming that the oldest of *B*'s children dies at age 19, when the next child is 16?

PROBLEMS

11-C. *T*, a childless widower, died some years ago leaving his sizeable residuary estate in trust "for *L* for life, remainder to be divided among such of my nephews and nieces as reach age 21." *L* has recently died and the trustee has retained you to advise him of the following claimants' rights in the fund:

[handwritten margin note: Question on whether ste reached 21 b/f L dies]

a.   The executor of a niece, *A*, who was alive when the will was executed, later attained age 21, but predeceased *T*. *[handwritten: entitled]*
b.   A nephew, *B*, who was born after execution of the will and reached 21 after *T*'s death but before *L*'s. *[handwritten: Entitled (closes when L dies)]*
c.   The executor of a niece, *C*, who was living at *T*'s death and thereafter reached 21 but died before *L*. *[handwritten: reached 21 b/f L died]*
d.   A nephew, *D*, born between the death of *T* and *L* but not yet 21. *[handwritten: no, if no]*
e.   A nephew, *E*, born shortly after *L*'s death. *[handwritten: no class   21 b/f L]*

What is your advice and your reasons for it? *[handwritten: closes when L dies]*

11-D. *T* died leaving his modest residuary estate "to my grandchildren, Cheryl and Rudolph, and any child hereafter born to my son, or the survivor or survivors of them equally share and share alike, provided however that should either of my grandchildren be a minor at the time of my decease then I devise to my trustee the share of the minor child to invest and to pay the income to that grandchild during his or her minority. I further direct that my trustee may in his sole discretion pay the income and such additional sums from principal as he sees fit to my grandchild or to others for his or her use for support, general welfare, education and emergency expenses without necessity for the appointment of a guardian for the minor grandchild and the receipt of the grandchild or other for his or her use shall be good and sufficient discharge to my trustee."

On the date of his will, T had two living grandchildren, Rudolph and Cheryl, ages 5 and 3. Prior to T's death two years later, a third grandchild, Kenneth, was born. All three grandchildren, along with their father are still living. To date no other grandchildren have been born. Rudolph, now 17 years of age, has requested an "advance" on his share of the trust fund for educational expenses. The trustee petitions for instructions from the court as to whether he may make such payments and, if so, the maximum amount or portion he may expend. T's son is now 40 years of age, and his wife is 38. What instructions would you expect the court to issue? Explain.

— he may use his discretion

C. Survival Requirements

1. Lapse

When a devisee dies between the execution of a will and the death of the testator,[1] the bequest or devise lapses — that is, it fails — in the

---

1. Lapse is a rule of law and, as noted in the text above, relates to the date of the testator's death. It is thus to be distinguished from the constructional question of whether a future interest beneficiary is required to be alive at a date later than the effective date of the transfer — that is, whether the remainder beneficiary, C, must be alive at the date of distribution (the death of the life beneficiary, B) where A devises to T in trust for B for life, remainder to C. The general reluctance to imply a survival requirement, and the reasons for and limits of this reluctance, are considered in section C.2 infra.

Although not strictly a lapse problem (cf. simultaneous and near simultaneous deaths in section B.1 of Chapter 2), wills sometimes expressly require devisees to outlive the testator by a stated period or until completion of estate administration. An interesting but not unique case recently faced a situation in which the devisee, required to be alive at estate "distribution," died before that time but only because of undue delay (partly caused by court delays) in closing and distributing the estate; the court held that "unreasonable delay" could not defeat the devisee's rights and that her successors in interest were entitled to the devise. Estate of Justesen, 77 Cal. App. 4th 352, 91 Cal. Rptr. 2d 574 1999).

absence of testamentary or statutory provision to the contrary. If the named beneficiary is dead when a will is executed, the provision for him is void at common law. Void or lapsed gifts generally pass under the residuary provision, unless, of course, it is the residuary gift or a part thereof that fails, in which case the property goes to the other devisees or passes by intestacy. The distinction between void and lapsed gifts is of no consequence in most cases. Occasionally, however, an antilapse statute has been held not to apply to void gifts when the statute does not cover the point.

Nearly all states have enacted antilapse statutes, intended to give effect to what legislatures have thought to be the probable intention of the average testator. The terms of most current statutes (often without the UPC's 120-hour survival requirement) are illustrated by original UPC §2-605, which (before the 1990 comprehensive revision, below) provided:

> If a devisee who is a grandparent or a lineal descendant of a grandparent of the testator is dead at the time of execution of the will, fails to survive the testator, or is treated as if he predeceased the testator, the issue of the deceased devisee who survive the testator by 120 hours take in place of the deceased devisee and if they are all of the same degree of kinship to the devisee they take equally, but if of unequal degree then those of more remote degree take by representation. One who would have been a devisee under a class gift if he had survived the testator is treated as a devisee for purposes of this section whether his death occurred before or after the execution of the will.

Antilapse statutes vary regarding the devisees to whom they can apply. A few statutes limit their coverage to descendants of the testator, while several are so broad as to include all devisees. Most of the statutes extend coverage to certain described relatives or to all persons described as *kindred or relations* of the testator. These latter terms are held not to include a spouse. Would you expect the word "relative" to include a stepchild? See the typical, negative answer in Kimball v. Story, 108 Mass. 382 (1871); cf. Oliver v. Bank One, 60 Ohio St. 3d 32, 573 N.E.2d 55 (1991) (bequest to brother-in-law). A few statutes, however, now expressly extend their protection to issue of a spouse, and at least one recent statute applies to devises to "kindred of a surviving, deceased, or former spouse of the [testator]." Cal Prob. Code §21110(c).

Nearly all antilapse statutes apply to the shares of the described devisees only if they leave issue alive at the testator's death. Absent some manifestation of contrary intention, the issue are then substituted for the named beneficiary. In one state, the property passes as if the "legatee had died . . . owning the property." Md. Ann. Est. & Tr. Code

§4-403 (1991). Thus, in Rowe v. Rowe, 720 A.2d 1225 (Md. App. 1998), testator's predeceased son's wife, who was the successor to the son's estate, was substituted for him under the lapse statute. How, if at all, is Maryland's lapse statute different from simply rejecting the basic lapse rule that requires the devisee to survive the testator?

Lapse statutes yield to contrary intent, and the most frequently litigated issue in lapse cases is the question whether the will indicates such a contrary intent. See Problems 11-F and 11-G below. What if the testator expressly disinherits the person who would be substituted by the lapse statute? Should it apply? See Estate of Scott, 659 So. 2d 361 (Fla. App. 1995).

Occasionally lapse is avoided when a court, or the lawyer, does not understand the difference between "words of purchase" and "words of limitation." For example, in Estate of Calden, 712 A.2d 522 (Me. 1998), testator devised property to her stepson, X, and his heirs. When X predeceased testator, the court held that technical words should be given their technical meaning, and, thus, X's wife and children take as his "heirs." Is this right? Or a court might admittedly construe "and her heirs" to mean "or her heirs" in order to avoid lapse in a situation where the lapse statute does not apply. See, e.g., Estate of Griffen, 543 P.2d 245 (Wash. 1975).

See generally Susan F. French, Antilapse Statutes Are Blunt Instruments: A Blueprint for Reform, 37 Hast. L.J. 335 (1985); Patricia J. Roberts, Lapse Statutes: Recurring Construction Problems, 37 Emory L.J. 325 (1988).

PROBLEMS

11-E. *T* has recently died. His will left $50,000 to his son, *S*, and the residue to his daughter, *D*. *S* predeceased *T*, leaving a wife, *W*, a child, *C*, and several unpaid creditors. *W* and *C* come to consult you. What would you tell them? *check st. antilapse statutes*

11-F. *T* devised Blackacre "to *A* if *A* survives me. Everything else to *B*." *A* and *B* are sisters of *T*. *A* predeceased *T*. *A* has a child, *X*, who survived *T*. *B* also survived *T*. Who takes Blackacre under the UPC? Would it make any difference if *A* and *B* are children of *T*, and *X* had not yet been born when the will was executed? Compare Allen v. Talley, 949 S.W.2d 59 (Tex. App. 1997) (to "my living brothers and sisters") and Rumberg v. Rumberg, 1998 WL 896334 (Ohio App. 7 Dist.), disc. rev. den., 5 Ohio St. 3d 1467, 709 N.E.2d 173 (1999) ("if they survive me"), both finding contrary intent precluding application of the lapse statute, with In re Estate of Bulger, 586 N.E.2d 673 (Ill. App. 1991) ("to my children . . . or to the survivor or survivors of them" insufficient to overcome antilapse statute provision for issue of child who predeceased testator) and Estate of Fitzpatrick, 406 N.W.2d 483 (Mich. App. 1987).

11-G.   *T*'s will leaves her entire estate "equally to my brothers, *A* and *B*, or to the survivor." Under the laws of your state, what would the result be if *B* survived *T* but *A* predeceased her leaving a child, *C*, who survived *T*? What if both *B* and then *A* predeceased *T*, who was survived only by *C*? See Estate of Ulrikson, 290 N.W.2d 757 (1980). Cf. Cal. Prob. Code §21110(b); UPC §2-603(b)(3) and (4), below.[2]

11-H.   *D*, a widow, died intestate, leaving a modest estate. She did, however, have two large life insurance policies, each payable primarily to her husband if he survived her (which he did not); alternatively, one policy was payable "to my children equally" and the other was payable "in equal shares to my children who survive me." Many years after this "estate planning" was completed by her life insurance agent, *D*'s two grandchildren were born to son, *S*, who died some years later in an automobile accident. *D* has just died, survived by two daughters and the grandchildren. On behalf of the grandchildren and at the suggestion of *D*'s insurance agent, *S*'s widow has come to you in the hope that the grandchildren are entitled not only to one-third of *D*'s probate estate but also to a third of the insurance proceeds.

(a) How would you advise her under the antilapse statute of your state? Under the Uniform Probate Code? Cf. Dollar Savings & Trust Co. v. Turner, 39 Ohio St. 3d 182, 529 N.E.2d 1261 (1988), and In re Button's Estate, 79 Wash. 2d 849, 490 P.2d 731 (1971) for unusual extensions of antilapse statutes to revocable inter vivos trusts.

(b) Alternatively, might a claim by the grandchildren have a better chance under the pretermitted heir statute of your state or one like UPC §2-302?

Cf. West v. Coogler, supra this chapter; Miller v. First Natl. Bank & Trust Co., 637 P.2d 75 (Okla. 1981) (pour-over will incorporated receptacle trust by reference, subjecting it to statute invalidating *will* provisions in favor of an ex-spouse following divorce); and Clymer v. Mayo, 473 N.E.2d 1084 (Mass. 1985) (like *Miller,* applied statute revoking will provision for ex-spouse to inter vivos trust). More common is the view

---

2 . Compare Estate of Taylor, 6 Cal. 2d 855, 428 P.2d 301, 59 Cal. Rptr. 437 (1967), in which the will left decedent's residuary estate to a named beneficiary but provided that if she "predeceases the distribution of my estate" the residue was to go to others. The named beneficiary died during administration, and the trial court found that the executor was aware of her illness and unduly delayed administration of the estate. The California Supreme Court affirmed the lower court's ruling that "vesting cannot be postponed by unreasonable delay in preparing an estate for distribution" and that the beneficiary's interest "vest[ed] at the time distribution should have been made," noting that the decision was in accord with the rule in England and other states, protects testator intentions, and promotes prompt distribution of estates, while finding no merit in the contention that the holding will lead to undesirable uncertainty in the settlement of estates.

expressed in Williams v. Gatling, 542 N.E.2d 121 (Ill. App. 1989), in which the administrator of a divorced man's estate sought to recover life insurance and employee stock ownership plan proceeds, of which the decedent's former wife was named beneficiary. The administrator had urged the court to rule "that divorce automatically revokes the designation of beneficiary" in a manner similar to an Illinois statute applicable to devises to a former spouse in a will executed before the divorce. The court responded: "[W]e are not persuaded by any argument that we should extend . . . the Probate Act to . . . a contract," adding that "[s]uch an argument is properly directed, instead, to the legislature."

UNIFORM PROBATE CODE

§2-603.   *Antilapse; Deceased Devisee; Class Gifts.*

(a) [Definitions.] In this section:

(1) "Alternative devise" means a devise that is expressly created by the will and, under the terms of the will, can take effect instead of another devise on the happening of one or more events, including survival of the testator or failure to survive the testator, whether an event is expressed in condition-precedent, condition-subsequent, or any other form. A residuary clause constitutes an alternative devise with respect to a nonresiduary devise only if the will specifically provides that, upon lapse or failure, the nonresiduary devise, or nonresiduary devises in general, pass under the residuary clause.

[Other definitions omitted.]

(b) [Substitute Gift.] If a devisee fails to survive the testator and is a grandparent, a descendant of a grandparent, or a stepchild of either the testator or the donor of a power of appointment exercised by the testator's will, the following apply:

(1) Except as provided in paragraph (4), if the devise is not in the form of a class gift and the deceased devisee leaves surviving descendants, a substitute gift is created in the devisee's surviving descendants. They take by representation the property to which the devisee would have been entitled had the devisee survived the testator.

(2) Except as provided in paragraph (4), if the devise is in the form of a class gift, other than a devise to "issue," "descendants," "heirs of the body," "heirs," "next of kin," "relatives," or "family," or a class described by language of similar import, a substitute gift is created in the surviving descendants of any deceased devisee. The property to which the devisees would have been entitled had all of them survived the testator passes to the surviving devisees and the

surviving descendants of the deceased devisees. Each surviving devisee takes the share to which he [or she] would have been entitled had the deceased devisees survived the testator. Each deceased devisee's surviving descendants who are substituted for the deceased devisee take by representation the share to which the deceased devisee would have been entitled had the deceased devisee survived the testator. For the purposes of this paragraph, "deceased devisee" means a class member who failed to survive the testator and left one or more surviving descendants.

(3) For the purposes of Section 2-601, words of survivorship, such as in a devise to an individual "if he survives me," or in a devise to "my surviving children," are not, in the absence of additional evidence, a sufficient indication of an intent contrary to the application of this section.

(4) If the will creates an alternative devise with respect to a devise for which a substitute gift is created by paragraph (1) or (2), the substitute gift is superseded by the alternative devise only if an expressly designated devisee of the alternative devise is entitled to take under the will.

(5) Unless the language creating a power of appointment expressly excludes the substitution of the descendants of an appointee for the appointee, a surviving descendant of a deceased appointee of a power of appointment can be substituted for the appointee under this section, whether or not the descendant is an object of the power.

(c) [More Than One Substitute Gift; Which One Takes.] If, under subsection (b), substitute gifts are created and not superseded with respect to more than one devise and the devises are alternative devises, one to the other, the determination of which of the substitute gifts takes effect is resolved as follows:

(1) Except as provided in paragraph (2), the devised property passes under the primary substitute gift.

(2) If there is a younger-generation devise, the devised property passes under the younger-generation substitute gift and not under the primary substitute gift.

(3) In this subsection:

(i) "Primary devise" means the devise that would have taken effect had all the deceased devisees of the alternative devises who left surviving descendants survived the testator.

(ii) "Primary substitute gift" means the substitute gift created with respect to the primary devise.

(iii) "Younger-generation devise" means a devise that (A) is to a descendant of a devisee of the primary devise, (B) is an alternative devise with respect to the primary devise, (C) is a devise for which a substitute gift is created, and (D) would have taken effect

had all the deceased devisees who left surviving descendants survived the testator except the deceased devisee or devisees of the
primary devise.

(iv) "Younger-generation substitute gift" means the substitute gift created with respect to the younger-generation devise.

For an explanation of §2-603, the breadth of its application and its
possible justification, see Edward C. Halbach, Jr. & Lawrence W. Waggoner, The UPC's New Survivorship and Antilapse Provisions, 55 Alb.
L. Rev. 1091 (1992). The most controversial aspect of §2-603 is its position in section (b)(3) that words of survivorship alone do not constitute
contrary intent. Thus, even if a devise to a child is worded "to *C* if she
survives me," *C*'s issue would be substituted for her if she predeceased
the testator in a jurisdiction that has enacted §2-603. Do you think this
effectuates probable intent? Commentators are not in agreement. For
a criticism of §2-603, see Mark L. Ascher, The 1990 Uniform Probate
Code: Older and Better, or More Like the Internal Revenue Code?, 77
Minn. L. Rev. 639 (1993). For a defense, see Mary L. Fellows, Traveling
the Road of Probate Reform: Finding the Way to Your Will (A Response
to Professor Ascher), 77 Minn. L. Rev. 659 (1993). For the concern that
§2-603 may create a malpractice trap, see Martin D. Begleiter, Article II
of the Uniform Probate Code and the Malpractice Revolution, 59
Tenn. L. Rev. 101 (1991). On the other hand, isn't there a trap for
clients in the type of inadequate drafting that the statute targets?
Would a careful, informed lawyer rely on cryptic language that has
been a cause of litigation and has not produced consistent results?

PROBLEM

11-I.   *T*'s will devised "the residue of my estate in equal shares to
A, *B*, and *C*." After execution of the will but before *T*'s death, *C* died
leaving no issue. *A*, *B*, and *C* were all nephews of *T* but are not his next
of kin. What happens to the share that would have been *C*'s had he
survived *T*? Consider the cases that follow. to other devisees or intestacy

Would your answer be affected: (a) if *T*'s residuary devise had read
"one-third to *A*, one-third to *B*, and one-third to *C*"? (b) if the devise
had been "to my nephews, *A*, *B*, and *C*, in equal shares"? (c) if the
devise had been simply "to my nephews equally"?

In re MURPHY'S ESTATE
157 Cal. 63, 106 P. 230 (1910)

[Denis Murphy's will provided for the residue of his estate to be
"equally divided among the four children of my late sister Catherine
residue to deceased sis' children

C. Flynn, deceased; that is to say: I give [the residue] to Timothy J. Flynn, William D. Flynn, Mary Jane Logan and Kate I. Prendergast." William D. Flynn died without issue before the testator's death. In petitioning for distribution of the estate, the executors alleged that the residue was left to the sister's children as members of a class and that the whole residue should be divided among the three remaining children as the sole surviving members of the class. Certain other nieces and nephews of the testator, claiming to be among his heirs at law, answered that the testator died intestate as to the portion of his estate left to William D. Flynn and that they were entitled to participate in the distribution thereof. The court found that the intention was to devise the residue to the children of the sister as a class, and the contesting heirs appealed.]

LORIGAN, J. . . .

It must be conceded upon this appeal that under the testamentary clause in question the devise to William D. Flynn lapsed upon his death without leaving lineal descendants, before the testator (Civ. Code, §1343), and that as to the portion of the estate devised to him the testator died intestate, unless from the clause in the will creating the devise in which he was to participate, considered by itself, it is apparent that the testator intended the devise of the residue of his estate to go to the children of his sister Catherine as a class, or that such intention appears from extraneous evidence properly admissible to disclose it. While the lower court reached the conclusion that the devise in question was to a class consisting of the children of the deceased sister of testator who might survive him, we are of the opinion, in the light of the established rules of construction and authorities, that this conclusion was not justified either from the express terms of the devise itself or aided by extrinsic evidence. . . .

It is not contended by the respondents that the clause . . . [creates a] joint tenancy, nor do they predicate their right to take the whole devise as survivors by reason of any expressly created joint tenancy. They base their claim solely on the ground that the devise, while not in terms creating a joint tenancy, still is a devise to a class — the children of the deceased sister of testator — and that under a well-recognized rule of law, where a devise is made to a class, the death of one of the class prior to the death of the testator does not have the effect of causing the legacy to lapse, but those of the class who survive the testator take the whole devise. The rule contended for by respondents is correct, but we cannot agree with them, or the trial court, in the conclusion that either the terms of the devise disclose an intention on the part of the testator to devise to a class, or that, accepting the extraneous testimony admitted as bearing on his intention, it discloses any such intention. As to a gift to a class, the rule is stated as follows: "In legal contemplation a gift to a class is a gift of an aggregate sum to a body of persons uncertain in number at the time of the gift, to be ascertained at a future time, who are all to take in equal or some other definite proportions, the share of each being dependent for its amount upon the ultimate number." Jarman on Wills (6th Ed.) §232. . . . Tested under this rule, there is nothing in the devise which would indicate that the intention of the testator was that the devisees should take as a class, or in any other way than as individuals, and under our Code provision as tenants in common. There is nothing on the face of the devise indicating any uncertainty in the number of persons who were to take the property, or that they were to be ascertained at a future time, or that the share of the residuary estate which the devisees were ultimately to have was to be determined as to the amount by the number of those who would survive the testator. All the persons who are to take were specifically named and the share of each was designated. In fact, it is not only quite apparent that under the rule relied on this devise cannot be said to contain any of the elements which should characterize a gift to a class, but the plain impression which one would receive by reading the clause is that the testator intended to give to each individual an equal portion of his estate. It is true that the testator uses language in the clause of his will which would, if it stood alone, amount to a devise to a class. This would be the result if the devise had been to "the four children of my late sister Catherine" without further words. But here the terms of the bequest — the designation of the number of the children, followed by a repeated and express devise to them by name and in an equal share — cannot be ignored so as to make the other words in the will constitute a class.

And in determining whether a devise is to a class or to individuals great importance is attached in the solution of the question to the fact that the gift is to the devisees nominatim and that the particular share they shall each receive is mentioned, and, when this appears, the bequest is held to constitute a gift and devise individually as tenants in common, and not as a devise to a class. . . . But, assuming, however, that the language used in the clause in question is capable of two different legal meanings resulting from the testator devising his estate to the four children of his late sister, followed by other words of express devise to each of the children by name and in equal proportions, still this mention of them by name and a devise to them in equal shares will control the description of them as children of his deceased sister. If words, which, standing alone, would be effectual to create a class, are followed by equally operative words of devise to devisees by name and in definite proportions, the law infers from the designation by name and mention of the share each is to take that the devisees are to take individually and as tenants in common, and that the descriptive portion of the clause (children of a deceased sister) is intended merely as matter of identification. . . .

It is not pretended that there are any other provisions of the will bearing on the subject, and the only circumstances appearing from the extrinsic evidence are that the testator had lived with his sister . . . ; that he had a deep affection for these four children and took great interest in them and in their welfare; also, that he had other nieces and nephews not mentioned in his will. . . . All that this evidence discloses is just what the clause of the will does. It furnishes a reason generally why the testator devised his estate to these four devisees in preference to his other nieces and nephews. . . . Giving this evidence the greatest force that can be claimed for it, it discloses at most that the intention of the testator was just as compatible with the devise to these children individually as to them as a class. [Therefore] we are still remitted to the application of the general rule that when in a devise a class and individuals are both mentioned, and nothing appears from other clauses of the will or extraneous evidence requiring a different construction, the devise will be construed as one to devisees individually and not to them collectively — to them as tenants in common and not to them as survivors of a class.

Nor is the claim of respondents that the devise should be held to be one to a class strengthened by invoking the canon of construction that such an interpretation should be given to a will as will prevent intestacy as to any portion of the testator's estate. . . . [A] canon of interpretation applicable to prevent intestacy cannot be invoked to set aside plain rules of law declaring the legal meaning and effect to be given to language used in such a devise as is here under consideration. . . .

Under the law, that clause must be construed as a devise to the devisees individually and as tenants in common. By it each devisee was given one-fourth of the residue of the testator's estate, and, had all lived, each would have been entitled to that proportion on distribution. One of the devisees, William D. Flynn, having died prior to the testator, the devise of one-fourth of the residue of the estate to him lapsed. No provision being made in the will otherwise disposing of this portion of his estate, the testator died intestate as to it and it vested in his heirs at law, and should have been distributed to them and not to the surviving devisees as a class.

The decree of distribution is reversed.

In the *Murphy* case, assume that the property of the testator minus other bequests and devises amounted to $100,000 before debts and expenses. Assume further that the debts of the estate were $5,000 and that the expense of administration (including such of the costs of litigating the above case as were charged to the estate) were $15,000. How much would each of the three surviving residuary legatees be entitled to take under the will and how much would actually pass intestate?

Similar to *Murphy* is Brown v. Leadley, 81 Ill. App. 3d 504, 401 N.E.2d 599 (1980) ("to my children, to wit: [four names], in equal shares" held not a class gift). Contrast with *Murphy* (which is now superseded by Cal. Prob. Code §6148) the opinion and note case that follow; in particular, note the judicial method involved in these two opinions.

In re SLACK TRUST
126 Vt. 37, 220 A.2d 472 (1966)

BARNEY, J.

A residuary legatee predeceased the testator, John T. Slack, without issue. On distribution of the estate the share of the deceased residuary legatee, Ruth Merritt Waite, was decreed to the remaining residuary legatees, or their representatives or estates, as part of the residue of the estate. The widow and certain heirs challenged this distribution, asserting that a lapsed residual legacy should pass as intestate property.

Almost every jurisdiction that has dealt with the problem has announced its allegiance to the rule declaring that a lapsed legacy of part of the residue shall pass as intestate property. Other than its large numeral following, this rule admittedly has little to recommend it. Indeed, some of the more devastating criticisms of the rule have come from courts who declare "stare decisis" to be their only ground for following it. In Oliver v. Wells, 254 N.Y. 451, 457-458, 176 N.E. 676, Justice Cordozo characterized it "[as] a technical rule, reluctantly enforced by courts when tokens are not at hand to suggest an opposite intention.". . . In re Dunster, (1909) 1 Ch 103, suggests that the rule defeats the testator's intent in almost every case in which it is applied. As might be expected, the rule has been generally criticized in law reviews and treatises. . . .

The policy supporting the rule is not easy to determine. . . . How [a contrary rule would be] substantially different from increasing the share [of residuary legatees] by allowing lapsed specific bequests to pass under the residuary clause is difficult to see. Yet, this is an accepted rule. . . . And to say that because a lapsed legacy is already in the residue it cannot "fall into" the residue but must "fall out" of the will is confusing simile for substance. . . .

This approach is supported by a cardinal principle reiterated in our own cases that intestacy will not be presumed. . . . The majority rule overrides this major consideration. As a consequence, the courts that operate under this rule constantly strain to supply exceptions in order that its application will be unnecessary. This certainly suggests that, as a rule, it is founded on a very shaky premise. It seems far sounder to operate under a rule which is acceptable according to its terms, rather than its exceptions. . . .

It should be borne in mind that this is a rule of construction only, adopted because it appears to comport most closely with the presumed intent of the testator in the usual case. It is at all times subject to contrary expressions of intent in the instrument by a testator. . . . Until this case, this court had not ruled on the issue. . . . However, by this case, we do now adopt the rule that lapsed residuary legacies become part of the residue and pass with the balance of it, being content to let a general residuary clause perform its "dragnet" function unless a contrary disposition is demonstrably applicable, which is not this case.

In fact, not only is there no contrary intent on the part of this testator discoverable, but the presumption against intestacy is reinforced by the provisions of his will. One provision specifically excludes a particular relative who would be entitled to take under intestate succession, and the language establishing the trust of the residue broadly defines it as "all the residue of my estate of every kind and nature." Although such "tokens" are unnecessary to the application of the rule as we adopt it, they confirm the presumption that here, as in the usual case, this rule in fact truly carries out the testator's intent.

Since the adoption of this rule fully confirms the judgment and decree rendered below, other questions need not be considered.

Judgment affirmed. Let the result be certified.

See also Corbett v. Skaggs, 11 Kan. 380, 382-384, 207 P. 819, 820-822 (1922). In holding that the lapsed portion of the residue passes to the other residuary legatees, the court stated:

> It is a rule of the English common law . . . that, on the death before the testator, of one of several residuary legatees (who do not take . . . as members of a class) his share goes, not to the others, but to whoever would have inherited the property in case no will had been made. . . . In one state the court has held to the contrary [and in] two states the rule has been abrogated by statute. . . . The rule has been severely criticized even by judges and textwriters, who have felt constrained to follow it. . . .
>
> The rule thus established does not commend itself to sound reasoning, and is a sacrifice of the settled presumption that a testator does not mean to die intestate as to a portion of his estate, and also of his plain actual intent. . . . If the question were new in this state, speaking for myself I should not hesitate to reject the English rule as wrong in principle and subversive of the great canon of construction, the carrying out of the intent of the testator.

Gray's Estate, 146 Pa. 67, 74, 75, 23 A. 205, 206.

[Although there are facts from which an intention contrary to the usual rule can be inferred, we] prefer to rest our decision on the general principle [rather] than upon exceptional features of the particular case.

We regard the rule that lapsed shares of decreased residuary legatees shall be treated as intestate property as in direct conflict with the one . . . that the actual purpose of the testator . . . must be given effect. . . . The statement sometimes made in support of the [usual rule in other states] — that the share of a deceased residuary legatee cannot fall into the residue, because it is itself a part of their residue — appears rather to play upon words than to point out any real difficulty.

UNIFORM PROBATE CODE

§2-604. *Failure of Testamentary Provision.*

(a) Except as provided in Section 2-603, a devise, other than a residuary devise, that fails for any reason becomes a part of the residue.

(b) Except as provided in Section 2-603, if the residue is devised to two or more persons, the share of a residuary devisee that fails for any reason passes to the other residuary devisee, or to other residuary devisees in proportion to the interest of each in the remaining part of the residue.

PROBLEM

11-J. *S* bequeathed the residue of her estate "to my brothers equally." *S* had four brothers: *B*, who survived her; *X*, who was dead when *S*'s will was executed; and *Y* and *Z*, both of whom died after *S* made her will but before her death. *Z* left no issue. The entire residuary estate is claimed by *B*, while a nephew (the only descendant of *X*) and a niece (*Y*'s only issue) claim, respectively, one-third and one-half of the estate.

(a) Explain the basis for each of these claims under the applicable statute, which provides:

If a devisee or legatee dies during the lifetime of the testator, the testamentary disposition to him lapses, unless an intention appears from the will to substitute another in his place; but, when property is devised or bequeathed to blood kindred of the testator and when such devisee or legatee dies before the testator, leaving lineal descendants, or is dead at the time the will is executed leaving lineal descendants who survive the testator, such legacy or devise does not lapse but such descendants take the property in the same manner as the devisee or legatee would have done had he survived the testator.

(b) How would you argue on behalf of each of the claimants in an appeal before the highest court of your state if the excerpt below is the opinion of the intermediate appeal court (adapted from Drafts v. Drafts, 114 So. 2d 473 (Fla. App. 1959))?

> At common law if a testamentary gift is to a class and a member of the class dies before the death of the testator, his interest goes to the surviving members of the class unless the testator has expressed a contrary intention. Unquestionably our statute applies to testamentary gifts to named beneficiaries. However, the question is whether it applies to testamentary gifts to a class as well. A majority of states hold that a non-lapse statute does not apply to a member of a class who was dead at the execution of the will, based upon the common-law principle that a gift to a beneficiary who is dead when the will is executed is void, and no question of lapse arises. On the other hand, a majority of states hold that, in the absence of express provision on the point, non-lapse statutes apply to class members who die after the execution of the will but prior to the death of the testator, on the premise that the gift will pass to those the testator would most likely have wished substituted for the deceased class member. States which hold to a contrary view do so on the basis that a gift to members of a class cannot lapse so long as any member of the class survives the testator.
>
> In this jurisdiction, statutes in derogation of the common law must be strictly construed. But even strictly construing our antilapse statute [above], it seems to us that the legislature intended that statute to be applied to class gifts to blood relatives, at least those alive when the will was executed.
>
> A more difficult question is whether the statute should be applied to one who was deceased when the will was executed — a gift which, at common law, was void, and hence no question of lapse was presented. The antilapse statute, being directly in derogation of this principle of the common law, must be strictly construed. There is nothing in the will to suggest that the testatrix wanted to provide for her then-deceased brother or his descendants. It would be more logical to infer, when a testator provides for a class of his relatives, that he intends to include only his living relatives. We therefore align ourselves with the courts which have held that antilapse statutes do not apply in favor of members of a class who died before the execution of the will in question.
>
> For the foregoing reasons we affirm the Chancellor's holding excluding the child of the testatrix's brother (X) who was deceased at the time of the execution of her will; but we reverse the holding excluding the child of her brother (Y) who died before her but after she executed her will.

A dissenting opinion (also adapted from *Drafts*) states:

> Non-lapse statutes are enacted solely to prevent lapse of testamentary gifts, but a gift to a class is legally incapable of lapsing so long as any member of the class survives the testator. It is for this reason that non-lapse statutes have been held not to apply to class gifts unless made so

by clear and unambiguous statutory language. A testator is free to amend his will to include descendants of a deceased class member if he cares to do so. Failure to do so should be construed as evidencing a testamentary intent to confine class gifts to those who survive the testator. To hold otherwise would require that we read into the statute language which cannot be found there. To do this would constitute judicial legislation of the rankest sort, a practice in which I am not willing to indulge.

GIANOLI v. GABACCIA
82 Nev. 108, 412 P.2d 439 (1966)

[John Data's will devised $5,000 "to each of my brothers and sisters" and left the residue of his estate "to my nephews and nieces, share and share alike." At the time the will was executed, one brother and one sister were dead; subsequently but prior to Data's death, two other brothers and another sister died. Only one sister survived Data. In petitioning for distribution, the personal representative proposed distributing $5,000 to the sister and $5,000 to the issue of each of the two brothers and one sister who were alive when Data executed his will, based on NRS 133.200, providing: "When any estate shall be devised or bequeathed to any child or other relation of the testator and the devisee or legatee shall die before the testator, leaving lineal descendants, such descendants, in the absence of a provision in the will to the contrary, shall take the estate so given by the will in the same manner as the devisee or legatee would have done if he had survived the testator."]

[handwritten margin note: taken in same manner as legatee if had survived]

ZENOFF, D.J. . . .

The lower court [found that] the will was ambiguous and that NRS 133.200 did not apply. We disagree. . . .

There is nothing in either [the $5,000 bequests or the residuary clause] of Data's will which creates . . . an ambiguity. We therefore are restricted to the writing alone. . . .

We first consider the two brothers and sister of Data who were alive at the time of the will's execution but predeceased Data. At common law, their bequests would be said to "lapse" and thereby fail. Presuming this result contrary to a testator's intent, Nevada, as almost all other states, enacted an "anti-lapse statute.". . . Data's brothers and sisters come within this protection "in the absence of a provision in the will to the contrary." NRS 133.200.

[handwritten margin note: alive but predeceased — fail @ c.l.]

It is argued that the second paragraph refers to the brothers and sisters as a "class" and our anti-lapse statute should not apply to "class" gifts. We agree with the overwhelming weight of authority that an anti-lapse statute does apply to class gifts. . . .

[handwritten margin note: anti lapse stat. does not apply to class gifts]

Next, it is argued that Data intended for the anti-lapse statute not to apply. Such intent, of course, would control, "but to render the statute inoperative a contrary intent on the part of the testator must be plainly indicated." Nowhere is such a "plain intent" expressed within Data's will; nor did he even state "I give . . . to each of my surviving brothers and sisters. . . ." The fact that in the third paragraph he bequeathed his residue to his nieces and nephews "share and share alike" does not influence who takes "through an entirely separate channel, . . . an entirely different right" under the second paragraph.

Finally, we consider the status of the brother and sister who predeceased the execution of Data's will. At common law, their bequest would fail as "void." Our anti-lapse statute only speaks of a testamentary beneficiary who "shall die before the testator;" there is no specification as to how long "before," nor is there any express reference within the statute to "lapse" or "void" bequests or their distinction. However, "[i]t seems obvious that the [anti-lapse statute] was motivated by the purpose to protect the kindred of the testator and by a belief that a more fair and equitable result would be assured if a defeated legacy were disposed of by law to the lineal descendants of the legatees or devisees selected by the testator." Accepting this rationale, as have the majority of courts, we see little reason to not equally apply it to void as well as lapsed bequests and devises. . . .

Reversed. . . .

PROBLEM

11-K.   *D* had four children, one of whom (*C*) died two months before the execution of *D*'s will, leaving a son, *G*, who survived *D*. *G* seeks a construction of *D*'s will and claims the right to participate in the distribution of her estate. *D*'s will provides in relevant part:

> I hereby give, devise and bequeath all the rest, remainder, and residue of my estate and hereby direct that the same be divided into as many equal parts as I shall have children surviving me; and I hereby give one of such equal parts to each of my children surviving me, share and share alike; with the exception that, in apportioning the share that would go to my beloved child J, the sum of $40,000 be deducted therefrom, my reason being that both he and his family are well provided for.
>
> In the event that any child or children of mine shall predecease me, then it is my wish and I hereby direct that the share or shares that he or they would have become entitled to, had they survived me, shall go to the child or children of such deceased child or children, per stirpes and not per capita.

How would you argue in support of *G*'s claim to a share of the residue or of $40,000? How would you expect his claim to be resisted by *D*'s three surviving children? What result would you expect? Why? Cf. In re Eisner's Estate, 34 Misc. 2d 662, 228 N.Y.S.2d 29 (1962).

2. Survivorship Problems of Future Interests

Conditions of survival present some of the most frequently litigated questions in the law of future interests today. Consequently, this subject is important from the point of view of drafting as well as construction. The question in most of these cases is whether the interest of a beneficiary who is living at or after the effective date of a will or deed is subject to a requirement that the beneficiary also be living at some subsequent date. This question is to be distinguished from the problem of lapse (section 1 above), which has to do with the death of a beneficiary before the testator dies, i.e., before the effective date of a will. The question must also be distinguished from the question of vesting, discussed in the previous chapter. Questions of vesting and survivorship are often related, but whether a future interest is vested or contingent does not (or at least ought not) resolve the question of whether survival is impliedly required. Conversely, the fact that survival is impliedly required does not necessarily make an interest contingent. Unfortunately, courts have not always kept this distinction clear either in the language of their opinions or in actually deciding cases. As 3 Powell, Real Property §27.01 n.8 (1998) points out, even if a court "has concluded that the interest is 'vested,' it is then necessary to decide whether this 'vested' interest is defeasible by nonsurvival," and adds: "Words and mental energy would be saved, and the clarity of the law would be enhanced, by an immediate consideration of what is commonly the decisive question, i.e., the presence or absence of a requirement of survival." Of course, the widely asserted preference for vested construction or for early vesting may be deemed relevant, and this preference is often said to include a preference for early indefeasibility.

a. Implied Conditions of Survival

(i) Future Interests to Named Individuals

Easiest cases first. *A transfers to B for life, remainder to C.* This is the most obvious illustration of what is generally called an indefeasibly vested remainder. If *C* is living at the effective date of the instrument, his interest is not thereafter defeated by his death; if *C* dies before *B*, the remainder passes by will or intestacy as an asset of *C*'s estate. See, e.g., Estate of Lista, 18 Pa. Fid. Rep. 2d 333 (Phila. 1998). It is equally well settled that an indefeasibly vested remainder results when several individuals are named as remainder beneficiaries following a life interest, as in a devise to *A* for life, then in equal shares to *B* and *C*. If *B* predeceases *A*, *B*'s right to half the principal on *A*'s death is property that passes through *B*'s estate.

The results of these cases are not generally altered by the mere fact that so-called words of futurity are used in creating the remainder interests. (For example, "to my wife for life, and *upon her death I give* the property to my son, *S.*") Where the only language of gift is that, on the life beneficiary's death, the trustee is to divide the corpus and pay it over to *X, Y,* and *Z,* it is arguable that the only language in favor of *X, Y,* and *Z* is that requiring an act that cannot occur until a future time; therefore, the argument continues, no gift occurs until that time, and the named remainder beneficiary must then be alive to receive it. This is the so-called divide-and-pay-over rule. This rule has been widely criticized and generally discarded in this country, it being apparent that the testator's choice of such wording reveals nothing of actual intent. Even where the divide-and-pay-over rule is recognized, one of its acknowledged exceptions virtually eliminates it as a factor in most types of cases. The leading divide-and-pay-over case of Matter of Crane, 164 N.Y. 71, 76, 58 N.E. 47, 49 (1900), concedes that if payment is postponed "for the purpose of letting in an intermediate estate, then the interest should be deemed vested."

PROBLEM

11-L.   *T*'s will provided: "I bequeath $25,000 to each of my three grandchildren, *A, B,* and *C* as they attain age twenty-five; until then my executor shall hold and invest the $75,000 and pay or apply in his discretion such amounts of income as needed for their support and education." The residue of *T*'s estate was left to her second husband, *H. A, B,* and *C* were ages 21, 19, and 16, respectively, at *T*'s death. Two years later, while the estate was in administration, *A* and *C* died together in an accident. Both were intestate. *C*'s father, *F* (*T*'s son-in-law), as *C*'s administrator and on his own behalf, claims the $25,000 that was to have gone to *C,* plus a share of the income accumulated since *T*'s death. *A*'s widow, *W,* as his administrator, claims (one-third for herself and two-thirds for their children) a like share that would have gone to *A* had he lived. *H* claims not only these amounts but also the entire $75,000 fund with its income. *B* also claims the entire fund. What arguments and result would you anticipate and why?

CLOBBERIE'S CASE
2 Vent. 342, 86 Eng. Rep. 476 (Ch. 1677)

In one Clobberie's case it was held, that where one bequeathed a sum of money to a woman at her age of twenty-one years, or day of marriage, to be paid unto her with interest, and she died before either, that the money should go to her executor; and was so decreed by my LORD CHANCELLOR FINCH.

But he said, if money were bequeathed to one at his age of twenty-one years; if he dies before that age the money is lost.

On the other hand, if money be given to one, to be paid at the age of twenty-one years; though, if the party dies before, it shall go to the executors.

———————

Clobberie's Case has been influential in the development of the basic distinction in such cases between (1) gifts to A "at" or "if he reaches" or "when he reaches" a specified age and (2) those which are to A "to be paid at" or "payable at" a stated age. In the former types of cases a requirement of survival to that age often tends to be inferred, absent some suggestion of contrary intent, whereas the language in the latter types of cases tends to have the opposite effect. See 5 American Law of Property §§21.17, 21.18 (Casner ed. 1952). It is generally recognized that if A is entitled to the income in the interim between the effective date of the instrument and the specified age, this fact tends strongly to suggest that there is no implied requirement of survival and normally overcomes whatever opposite inference might have resulted from language such as "at" or "when A reaches" a designated age.

Coddington v. Stone, 9 S.E.2d 420 (N.C. 1940), involved a trust in which the trustee had discretion to make payments for the maintenance and education of the testator's three children until the youngest attains age 21, when the trust estate is to be divided into three parts and distributed to the children. The effect of the court's finding of no survival requirement was that the share of a then deceased son was subject to an inheritance tax when he died before age 21. (Do you see other probably undesired consequences of this construction?) The opinion (*passim*, citations omitted) observes:

> . . . We must assume from the record that [the testator] was acquainted with the vicissitudes of life. . . . Yet he made no provision or disposition of his property or limitation over in the event of the death of any of the named beneficiaries, or all of them, before the date appointed for the division and delivery of the trust estate. At that time Charles, had he lived, would have been twenty-five years old and Dabney twenty-three. Had any of the sons died before that date, leaving a wife or children, these would have been left unprovided for if the estate did not vest at the death of the testator. . . .
>
> Of further significance is the fact that the executor-trustee is also . . . given the power to use such part of the income of the trust as might be necessary for the maintenance and education of the named beneficiaries during the suspensive period when the estate was left in the hands of [the trustees] for its preservation and administration in the interest of the minor beneficiaries. . . .

It is true here that the whole income of the large estate was not required by the will to be devoted to the needs of the beneficiaries. Had it been so, under the vast majority of decided cases, it would have been conclusive. The best considered cases, however, regard the same presumption in favor of the immediate vesting to exist where only a portion of the income of the estate is intermediately given to the beneficiary. . . .

Closely connected with the common sense reasoning which negatives any intention of the testator to leave the disposition of his property incomplete is the rule against intestacy. . . . The presumption is against partial intestacy as well as against complete intestacy; . . .

Proceeding upon the same line of experience, as well as of policy, the law favors the early vesting of property interests. . . .

We do not regard as importantly bearing on the time of the vesting the expression in the will that when the property is delivered "each of my sons shall thereupon become the absolute owner thereof and the said Bank shall be discharged from any further duties as Trustee," since this language is not inconsistent with the intention to vest the property on the death of the testator. . . .

As to the quality of the estate which thus vests, it must be noted that the beneficiaries are named as individuals, not as a class, and the "roll call" principle does not apply. . . .

Compare Old Colony Trust Co. v. Tufts, 168 N.E.2d 86 (Mass. 1960), where the court said: "The individual residuary legatees were specifically named. Thus the usual rule of construction would require treating them as individuals. They were not made members of a class, who, respectively, must be living at the termination of each trust in order to share in the remainder. . . ."

In Summers v. Summers, 699 N.E.2d 958 (Ohio App. 1997), the testator (*T*) devised her property in trust for the benefit of her child, Ben, "until my child attains age 25, at which time the income and principal shall be distributed and paid over to him and the Trust shall terminate." Ben died at age 20. In holding that the property passed by intestacy to Ben's father, whom *T* had divorced, the court applied the common law preference for vesting. The court was influenced by what might have happened rather than what actually happened:

[*T*] was aware that if Ben died intestate . . . [and] if Ben had married or had a child prior to his death, [the property] would have passed to them. [*T*] did not express an intent to avoid this result. . . . Where the language of a will is clear, words cannot be added or changed, even if the consequences seem harsh to some. The theory that [*T*] would have drafted her will differently had she foreseen the circumstances existing at her death does not justify altering the manifest meaning of the will.

Do you agree that the language of the will was clear? Is the court's decision sound?

(ii) Class Gifts: The Question of Decrease in Membership

PROBLEMS

11-M.   Settlor, *S*, devised to *T* in trust for *W* for life, remainder then to be distributed "to our children." At *S*'s death, there were three children, *B*, *C*, and *D*. *B* predeceased *W*, leaving his estate to his child, *E*. Then *W* died. Who is entitled to receive distribution of the trust property?

11-N.   *S* devised to *T* in trust for *A* for life, "then to *A*'s issue." At *S*'s death, *A* had three children, *X*, *Y*, and *Z*. *X* predeceased *A*, survived by a child, *C*; *X* was also survived by her husband, *H*, to whom she left her entire estate. Then *A* died. *Y*, *Z*, *C*, and *H* all survive *A*. Who is entitled to the trust estate?

ESTATE OF STANFORD
49 Cal. 2d 120, 315 P.2d 681 (1957)

[Jane Stanford died in 1905, leaving $2,000,000 in trust for various purposes and her residuary estate to Stanford University. The income of a portion of the trust was to be paid to her niece, Amy Hansen, for life, remainder to Amy's "child or children." Walter, Amy's only child at the time, died in 1918 leaving his estate to Ruth Barton. In 1924 Amy adopted her adult niece and the niece's two minor children, all of whom survived Amy's death in 1954. The lower court ordered Amy's trust share distributed to the three adopted children; Ruth and Stanford University appealed. The university contended unsuccessfully (opinion omitted here) that the adoptees were not eligible to take the remainder. The portions of the majority and minority opinions below deal with Ruth's contention that Walter's interest vested in him at Mrs. Stanford's death and that his share of the remainder passed to her even though he predeceased the life beneficiary.]

CARTER, J. . . . In construing the language of a bequest, such as we have here, the primary common law rule in favor of early vesting of title in remaindermen and the preference for vested rather than contingent remainders is firmly established in this state. . . . And it has been said by noted authors on the subject, with the citation of numerous authorities, that: "A remainder limited without words of condition to a class of persons, such as 'children,' one or more of whom is in existence and ascertained, is vested, though subject to be divested in part by the coming into existence or ascertainment of other members of the class. This is the typical vested remainder subject to open. . . . [S]tated another way: The mere fact that the entire membership of the class cannot be determined until some later time when the interest becomes possessory does not mean that there is a condition precedent that the existing members of the class must survive until that time in order to partake of present ownership. *Only rarely does a court reach a contrary result.*" (Emphasis added; Simes and Smith, The Law of Future Interests (1956), §146; see [also] Rest., Property, §§256, 257, 260.) And: ". . . the cases indicate clearly that the mere fact that takers of a postponed gift are described by a class designation such as children, grandchildren, nieces, nephews, and the like, does not give rise to any implied condition of survival. [Simes & Smith §578] . . . [The result is that all] stirpes are represented." (*Id.*, §654.) . . . Estate of Norris 78 Cal. App. 2d 152, . . . [stated] at page 161: "The law is well settled that vested remainders can be created in a class the membership of which is not complete. . . . [T]hat factor would not indicate that the remainders were contingent. . . . In 2 Restatement of the Law of Property, section 157, it is provided that: 'A remainder can be (a) indefeasibly vested; or (b) vested subject to open . . . [or] (c) vested subject to complete defeasance.' As an illustration of clause (b) the Restatement states: '*A* . . . transfers Blackacre to *B* for life, remainder to the children of *B*. *B* has a child *C*. *C* has a remainder vested subject to open and let in other children born to *B*.' " . . .

. . . [T]he foregoing construction finds support in the will as a whole. . . . The manner in which the assets were disposed of reflects some intent to benefit the Lathrops [Mrs. Stanford's family] on a per stirpes basis in accordance with the then existing facts with respect to survivorship and existence of issue. . . .

. . . [Upon a sibling's death before distribution,] under a contingent construction . . . the share of the remainder going to that branch of the family would totally or partially fall into the residue, even though [the sibling] left issue. . . .

. . . [I]t appears that the testatrix would not have wished to treat unequally descendants . . . having the same relationship to [her]. Yet, if she were held to have intended a condition of survival with respect to the remainders following the life interests of Jennie Lawton and Amy Hansen, such a situation could easily have arisen. . . .

. . . [S]o far as the testatrix knew, it was possible that Walter would be the only child that Amy Hansen would ever have and that Walter would predecease his mother, leaving children of his own. In such an event, if the testatrix made the remainder following Amy's life interest contingent on survival of Amy, Walter's children could not benefit from it, either through intestate succession or under a will. . . . Ruth Barton is, of course, in the same position as children of Walter would have been, had they been the claimants here.

In short, the testatrix' intent in framing the will must be determined in the light of the eventualities which, so far as she was in a position to know, were possible, rather than in light of what actually developed after her death, and, so viewed, a contingent construction of the words . . . would seem to be out of harmony with the equal treatment of relatives which she appears to have had in mind. . . .

ASHBURN, J. PRO TEM., Dissenting. . . .

Significant and outstanding facts about this will and its codicil are concern for blood relatives and for the University which testatrix and her husband had founded. Aside from said employees and specified charitable institutions there is no word indicative of a desire to share her fortune with strangers to the blood. . . .

. . . Restatement [of Property §296(2)] (page 1607) says: "From the fact that a class can increase in membership until a certain future date no inference should be made that only such members of the class as survived to such future date become distributees." The first rule (opening for new members) is undoubtedly settled as a matter of law. But the effect of decrease in membership of a class has not crystallized into an inflexible rule of substantive law. . . . In the present state of the authorities the effect of a decrease in class membership presents primarily a question of the testator's intent. . . .

Simes & Smith, on the Law of Future Interests (2d ed.) . . . Section 652, page 103: ". . . [T]he question is whether there is any requirement of survival to a particular point of time. In many of the cases, the question is frequently discussed in terms of whether the gift is vested or contingent. . . . We have already seen, however, that analysis in such terms tends to obscure the real issue, since it is possible for a vested interest to be subject to a requirement of survival in a form of a condition subsequent, and it is also possible to have a contingent interest which is transmissible and which does not terminate with the death of the owner thereof." . . .

Mrs. Stanford's will plainly shows that she wanted the University to have anything that would not pass to the persons and in the manner specified in that instrument. . . . To infer that testatrix intended Walter to substitute some stranger as a recipient of a third of a million dollars of her property is to my mind too legalistic. There is not a scintilla of evidence that Mrs. Stanford actually intended any stranger to take any part of the Hansen trust through any device or in any circumstances whatever.

. . . That the [trial court] ruling may have been based upon the faulty view that Walter had only a contingent estate, in the sense of one to a condition precedent, does not affect the soundness of the decision. . . .

———————————

Consider whether different considerations are present and different principles should apply where the class of remainder beneficiaries is described in terms of "issue" or "descendants." Where property is conveyed to or in trust *for* A *for life, then to the issue of* A, it has readily been recognized that A's descendants must survive her in order to take. Thus, it is usually presumed that the "issue" or "descendants" are required to survive their named ancestor. The survivorship problem may be more difficult — but should the result be different? — in cases in which the issue in question are not those of a life beneficiary at whose death distribution is to be made, that is, where distribution is later than the ancestor's death.

ALTMAN v. RIDER
191 S.W.2d 577 (Ky. App. 1956)

CULLEN, Commissioner. [The testator died in 1926, leaving his entire estate to his daughter for life, the property to be liquidated at her death, with a portion of the proceeds to be distributed to the "descendants" of Wolf Bodenheimer, who died in 1894, having years earlier befriended the testator when the latter was a child in Germany.] . . .

All parties agree that the question is one of determining the intent of the testator. Any clear indications of specific intent being absent, the parties suggest the application of various rules for supplying the intent. The briefs discuss the law of class gifts, vested or contingent remainders, and per capita or per stirpes distributions.

We think perhaps the problem may be solved without our becoming involved in the intricacies of the law of property, if we merely attempt to project what the testator expected to happen. It is clear he expected that, upon his daughter's death, sums of money would be distributed to certain living individuals. He had no contemplation of such things as vested or contingent estates or class gifts — he simply wanted some people in Wolf Bodenheimer's bloodline to get some money when his daughter died. Since he obviously intended a physical distribution to living people, it must be concluded that there was an implied condition of survivorship. Accordingly, we must hold that only persons in existence at the termination of the life estate were to take under the will. . . .

. . . [W]e think it must be concluded that Samuel intended the distribution to be made in accordance with the degree of relationship of the takers to Bodenheimer, or in other words, per stirpes. . . .

Restatement (Second) of Property (Donative Transfers) §28.2 states: "If a gift is made to a class described as the 'issue' or 'descendants' of a designated person, or by a similar multigenerational class gift term, in the absence of additional language or circumstances that indicate otherwise," a class member "must survive to the date of distribution in order to share in the gift. . . ." Contrast id. §27.3 on gifts to classes "described as 'children,' 'grandchildren,' . . . or by [other] class gift terms that describe a one-generation class," stating that a potential class member who dies "after the dispositive instrument takes effect but before such class member is entitled to distribution . . . is not excluded from the class" unless the contrary is indicated by additional language or circumstances or by applicable statute."

(iii) Future Interests Complicated by Conditions Unrelated to Survival

FIRST NATIONAL BANK v. TENNEY
138 N.E.2d 15 (Ohio 1956)

[Mary Monfort transferred certain property to a trust company in trust to pay the income to herself for life, remainder "to trustor's sister, Adelaide M. Iredell." The settlor reserved the power "during her life, to amend, alter, revoke, or terminate" the trust.]

BELL, J. . . . [A]ppellants contend that since the named remainderman was not living at the time of the death of the life beneficiary a resulting trust arose in favor of the heirs of the trustor.

. . . [We are] confronted with a determination of the rights of the parties hereto in the light of events subsequent to the creation of the trust. Is the power of revocation reserved by the trustor to be treated as a limitation on the gift of the remainder or is it a condition subsequent? Or, in other words, did the remainderman take a contingent remainder, conditioned upon her survival [of] the life beneficiary and upon nonrevocation of the trust, or did she take a vested remainder subject to be divested by revocation? . . .

Simes and Smith, in The Law of Future Interests (2 ed.), Section 113, say: "It is thus possible to indicate a number of typical situations which may create remainders subject to complete defeasance. . . . Fifth, any remainder which, by the exercise of some power is subject to being defeated. This would include a power of appointment, or a power given to a trustee to invade the corpus of the trust for the benefit of some person or persons." We think they might well have added "or a power of revocation reserved to the trustor."

And one of the examples of such a defeasible remainder is given by Simes and Smith as follows: "If land be conveyed to *T*, trustee, for the benefit of *A* for life, and then for the benefit of *B* and his heirs, provided that *T* may expend all of the corpus of the estate for the benefit of *A*, the remainder of *B* is vested subject to complete defeasance."

Applying the facts of this case to the above example, it would read: "If property be conveyed to *T*, trustee, for the benefit of *A* for life, and then for the benefit of *B*, provided that *A* reserves the power to revoke the trust at any time during her lifetime, the remainder of *B* is vested subject to complete defeasance by *A* exercising the right of revocation."

Such a result appears to this court to be sound. The law favors the vesting of estates at the earliest possible moment and it is well settled in Ohio that a testamentary remainder after a life estate vests in the remainderman at the death of the testator unless the intention to postpone the vesting to some future time is clearly expressed. . . .

It has been suggested that, since Adelaide M. Iredell was not living at the time of the death of the trustor, there was no one in being who could take under the trust, and that, therefore, the property remaining in the hands of the trustee must go back to the heirs of the trustor.

Section 2131.04, [Ohio] Revised Code, provides: "Remainders, whether vested or contingent, executory interests, and other expectant estates are descendable, devisable and alienable in the same manner as estates in possession."

This section is a codification of the common law rule which set out as follows, in 33 Am. Jur. 614, Section 149: "A vested remainder is an actual estate and, by the rules of the common law, is susceptible of . . . sale or conveyance, devise, or inheritance. This rule applies to a vested remainder subject to be divested, and title in such case passes subject to the condition subsequent."

This court has specifically held in Millison v. Drake, 123 Ohio St. 249, 174 N.E. 776, that a vested remainder subject to be divested is alienable.

. . . [W]e hold that Adelaide M. Iredell took a vested interest subject to defeasance by the exercise of the power of revocation. By her will, that interest was bequeathed to Virginia Tenney, who then took the remainder subject to the same condition as was imposed upon it in the hands of Adelaide M. Iredell. If Mary E. Monfort had exercised her power of revocation, Virginia Tenney would have lost her interest. Inasmuch as the power was not exercised, Virginia Tenney's interest became indefeasible upon the death of Mary E. Monfort.

Judgment affirmed.

PROBLEMS

11-O.   Settlor, *S*, devised to *T* in trust for *L* for life, "then to *R*, but if *R* predeceases *L*, to *C*." *R* and *C* both predeceased *L*. Who is entitled to the property at *L*'s death?

11-P.   *S* devised to *T* in trust for his daughter, *D*, for life, "then to *D*'s issue, if any; if none, to her brothers." *D* and two brothers, *E* and *F*, survived *S*. *E* later died intestate survived by two children. Who is to receive the trust property upon the death of *D*, who never had children?

11-Q.   *S* devised to *T* in trust for *A* for life, "then to *A*'s children, the children of any deceased child to take that child's share." At *S*'s death, *A* had three children, *X*, *Y*, and *Z*. *X* predeceased *A*, survived by two children, *M* and *N*; but *M* also predeceased *A*, leaving a child, *C*, but devising all of her estate to her husband, *H*. *A* dies, survived by *Y*, *Z*, *N*, *C* and *H*. Who takes the trust property?

RUSHING v. MANN
910 S.W.2d 672 (Ark. 1995)

NEWBERN, JUSTICE.

[Andrew Comer died in 1951, devising certain land to a niece for life, then to Lester Mann for his life, and "then unto his bodily heirs, or if no bodily heirs, then to Claude Mann in fee simple." Claude predeceased Lester, who later died without issue three years before the niece's death. The Chancellor awarded the land by summary judgment to the heirs of Claude Mann, finding that his interest was a "vested fee simple remainder subject to defeasance." As the defeasance did not occur, the Mann heirs prevailed over the heirs of Andrew Comer, who contend that Claude's interest was a contingent remainder alternative to the one devised to Lester's bodily heirs]. . . . They say the land [reverts] to them . . . because neither contingent remainder vested. We agree with their argument and reverse. . . .

A remainder which is dependent upon a contingency which may not arise or which is granted to a person not in existence and who may not come into existence is contingent. . . . Thus, neither Claude Mann nor the bodily heirs of Lester Mann can be said to have had a vested remainder. . . . [T]he question becomes whether Claude Mann's heirs have an interest which vested despite the fact that Claude Mann did not survive the [niece]. . . .

The . . . Mann heirs [cite] Cox v. Danehower, 211 Ark. 696, 202 S.W.2d 200 (1947), and Bell v. Gentry, 141 Ark. 484, 218 S.W. 194 (1920). In the Bell case, the devise of the testator was to his widow for life or until her remarriage and upon her decease or remarriage to "my children and their bodily heirs in the following manner: . . ." Thereafter the testator named his two children and specified the lands each was to receive. We held that, upon the death of the widow, each child took the land specified in fee, the remainder having been fixed "when the remainder was cast." In an obiter dictum we said, "Had they [the children] or either of them died in the lifetime of their mother, their bodily heirs would have taken the fee; and these bodily heirs would have taken [in their own right] as devisees under the will. . . ."

Cox v. Danehower is at least ostensibly distinguishable [from the present case] on the basis that, as in Bell v. Gentry, the [bodily] heirs were "special" and in esse rather than "general" heirs [of a designated remainder beneficiary]. We distinguished the Fletcher case and the Cox case in [a later case] on the basis of the specific language of the grants.

While it was appropriate for the Chancellor to look to the four corners of the will . . . [he] properly declined to consider testimony about the intent of the testator.

Our holding is that Claude Mann's contingent remainder ceased to exist when he predeceased Elizabeth Swanson. . . . Reversed and remanded.

At least the court in *Tenney* got the result right. Based on its dicta, however, would it have fared any better than *Rushing* if faced with the *Rushing* facts? An earlier case of *Rushing*-like confusion, In re Coots' Estate, 234 N.W. 141 (Mich. 1931), was overturned by legislation in the year of the decision. Compare the influential decision in Tapley v. Dill, 217 S.W.2d 369 (Mo. 1949), involving a similar disposition. The opinion began by noting that "upon testator's death," his son, Joe Tapley, "took an alternative or substitutional contingent remainder" and continued:

> The word "vested" is used in different senses in the discussions of future interests. . . . The real issue is whether survivorship of the particular estate was a condition precedent (sic) to Joe Tapley's estate. Cases have considered contingent remainders subject to an implied condition of the donee surviving the particular estate although not so conditioned, seemingly because subject to a condition precedent. This is not logically sound. . . .
>
> Joe Tapley's will devised his interests in this real estate to Mary H. Tapley, his widow, appellant here. . . .
>
> Taking the will within its four corners and aided by applicable rules of construction it is evident, we think, that testator desired Joe to have half of his estate outright and that [by separate trusts] his grandchildren Harry and Mary should have the use and benefit of the other half . . . for their natural lives; and the corpus of said trust estates should vest in the heirs of the body of said respective life beneficiaries or of their survivor if there be any such heirs of the body, and if not testator intended that his son, Joe, take the [rest] of his estate [even though he failed to survive until distribution of the trust]. . . .

Other cases illustrating the usual result, refusing to imply a condition of survival merely because of another condition precedent, include Estate of Ferry, 361 P.2d 900 (Cal. 1961), and Daniel v. Donohue, 333 P.2d 1109 (Ore. 1959) (involving contingent remainder to a class). See also Restatement (Second) of Property: Donative Transfers §27.3 (an interest does not fail because a class member dies before distribution, as long as "such death does not make impossible the fulfillment of a condition, unless additional language or circumstances indicate otherwise, or an applicable statute provides otherwise").

Fortunately, the frequent tendency of other courts to confuse survival requirements with questions of whether interests are vested or contingent has generally and increasingly been confined to dicta and not carried over into their holdings. A few courts have implied a survival requirement when the future interest was to a *class,* in addition to being subject to a condition precedent, even though one of these factors alone would seemingly not have required such a condition to be implied. See, e.g., Drury v. Drury, 11 N.E. 140 (Ill. 1916), which held that the interest "was not only subject to the contingency of the life tenant dying without issue, but also to the contingency [*implied* by the court] of being a member of the class when ascertained." See also Lawson v. Lawson, 148 S.E.2d 546 (N.C. 1966), where *T* devised to his daughter, *D,* for life, then to her children; if none, to her brothers and sisters. The court held that because the remainder to *D*'s brothers and sisters was contingent, there had to be a "roll call" at *D*'s death. (The court seemed unaware of the significance of the fact that the "roll call" language was picked up from an earlier case involving an *express* condition of survival.) The dead folks couldn't answer the roll call in *Lawson,* so *T*'s grandchildren who were the children of the deceased siblings were unable to share in the property, while the surviving siblings, and ultimately their families, received everything.

If a court actually takes the view that all contingent remainders are also contingent on survival, it may recognize the inappropriateness of the distorted results that would follow from the order of deaths; it therefore may convince itself that what clearly appears to be a condition precedent is "merely" a condition subsequent, thus qualifying for the magic label "vested." It can thereby avoid concluding that the interest is subject to a condition of survival, holding the interest descendible. See In re Patterson's Estate, 93 A. 608 (Pa. 1915). At least one court, uncomfortable with the idea of future interests otherwise contingent being free of conditions of survival, then defined the interest as a "vested interest in a contingent remainder"! See Hays v. Cole, 73 So. 2d 258 (Miss. 1954).

b. Express Conditions of Survivorship

(i) Time to Which Survival Is Required

PROBLEMS

11-R.   Settlor, *S,* devised to *T* in trust for *L* for life, remainder to "*L*'s surviving children." *L* is *S*'s child and has two children, *C* and *D. C* predeceases *L* leaving a child, *X,* who survives *L*. Who takes at *L*'s death?

11-S.   *S* devised in trust for *A* for life, "then to my brother, *B*, but if he predeceases *A*, to *B*'s surviving children." *B* thereafter dies leaving two children, *X* and *Y*. Then *X* dies intestate survived by a spouse and children. Then *A* dies. Who takes? See In re Colman's Will, 33 N.W. 2d 237 (Wis. 1949), holding that "surviving" refers to surviving the death of the one whose death triggers the substitution — here, *B*, so that *X*'s interest does not fail. But cf. Matter of Gustafson Trust, 547 N.E.2d 1152 (N.Y. 1989) (4-to-3 opinion; dissent would have interpreted "children" to mean *B*'s "issue" to give effect to *S*'s "paramount intent"). Can you redraft the disposition to the children to make the time of survival clear? Is clarity on this point enough? What result do you suppose *S* would have wanted if properly interviewed?

The language of an instrument often makes it clear that some requirement of survivorship is being imposed upon the remainder beneficiaries but leaves its precise meaning uncertain. Most frequently the ambiguities take the form of uncertainty regarding the time to which the requirement relates. The typical form of the problem is as follows: *H* devises in trust for his wife, *W*, for life, "then to my surviving children." Question: are the children required only to be "surviving" when *H* dies or also at the later date of *W*'s death? If a child survived *H* but predeceased *W*, does his share of the remainder pass by his will or by intestacy, or is his interest defeated? It is generally accepted that, had the remainder been to "my then surviving children," the requirement would refer to the date of distribution, but where the language "my surviving children" is used, the cases are not in agreement. Restatement of Property §251 (1940) provides: "In a limitation purporting to create a remainder or an executory interest, a description of the intended takers as persons 'who survive,' or who are 'living,' or by other language of the same import, but which fails to designate the time to which such takers must survive, tends to establish the time of the termination of all preceding interests as the time to which survival is required."

This Restatement rule has generally been said to give the natural meaning to the transferor's words or to conform to the likely expectations of transferors in using such language. The minority rule referring the words of survivorship to the death of the testator has been said to be "an extreme application of the constructional preference for early indefeasibility." 3 Powell, Real Property §27.03[2] (1998). Is this all that can be said in behalf of the minority position, or for decisions in which courts that have adopted the majority rule have found it rebutted by finding that the particular settlor had a contrary intent? In re Nass' Estate, 182 A. 401, 403 (Pa. 1936), stated [citations omitted]:

Our rule of construction applied to survivorship has been held to refer to the time of death of the testator unless a contrary intent appears in the will. The rule is not without sound reason, for its general effect is to distribute the property among all of testator's descendants rather than to slant off into one line. . . . It is apparent that in this case any other construction would work an inequality which would not carry out what was presumably testator's scheme. . . . If testator's intent be considered otherwise, it results in giving the entire fund to one child, Julia, whose life has been prolonged beyond the lives of the other children, and would tend to prefer her and her heirs over the heirs of other children. . . .[3]

A case about twenty years later, In re Pleasanton's Estate, 131 A.2d 795 (N.J. Super. 1957), involved an interesting problem for consideration. In holding that a remainder to "my surviving child or children" went to those who survived the life tenant, the opinion stated [citations omitted]:

It has been repeatedly held in this State [New Jersey] consonant with the majority state rule and the modern English view, that where a life estate is given by will, remainder over at death of the life tenant to the "surviving children" of the testator, "surviving" denotes those who survive at the death of the life tenant, not those who survive the testator, unless the words are plainly used in the latter sense. . . .

But it is [argued] that since this will was made by a person then resident in Pennsylvania and presumably drafted by a lawyer cognizant of the judicial decisions of that commonwealth we ought to undertake the construction of this will on the basis of . . . the Pennsylvania law, and that such an approach would require the conclusion that survivorship is to be decided as of the time of testator's death. . . .

3. Cf. Dissent in *Gustafson* case cited in Problem 11-S above. The concern judges might have in cases of this general type is aptly illustrated by the dissent in another 4-to-3 New York decision twenty-eight years earlier in Matter of Welles' Will, 173 N.E.2d 876 (N.Y. 1961) (remainder to "all my grandchildren then living"), arguing for an interpretation that would include great-grandchildren because there was nothing in the will "to neutralize the presumed intent of the testator to avoid disinheritance" of a line of descent or to overcome the "testamentary scheme which favored a stirpital plan," and adding that the testator "did not intend, we are sure," the "discrimination" that a literal construction would produce merely because "the heads of those two branches failed to outlive a centenarian."

Whatever one's view of the majority and minority positions described in the text, supra, it may be interesting (or painful) to see the extremes to which a result-oriented court can go to interpret language that it labels "ambiguous." Comerica Bank v. United States, 93 F.3d 225 (6th Cir. 1996), found, under its purported understanding of Michigan's preference for early vesting, that a substitute gift to others if "any of the Settlor's grandchildren shall die before receipt of the corpus of the trust" was not sufficient to require survival beyond the settlor's death to the time of distribution, reversing a district court that had the temerity to take the words of the trust seriously and thereby deny the grandchildren the benefit of a special privilege then available under the federal generation-skipping transfer tax.

> But . . . the rule, being one designed solely to aid construction, must be given no greater probative weight in the search for actual intent than it rationally deserves. . . . The particular subject is one to which draftsmen are more apt to use language with an eye towards its effectiveness in expressing their intent as a matter of English rather than in terms of legal technology. We think . . . that if the scrivener actually intended these dispositions over to go to children surviving at the time of the testator's death, . . . and his thought adverted to the problem of clear expression of that intent, he would have set his mind to the use of words apt therefor as a matter of English rather than rely upon the so-called Pennsylvania rule of construction even if he was familiar with it.

Sometimes other wording is tantamount to an express condition of survival, and is so treated. Typical is a transfer in trust for *L* for life, remainder "to *R* or her issue" or "to my children or their issue." Do you see why, unlike the above remainder "to my surviving children," courts have had no difficulty agreeing on the appropriate rule, presuming that *R* or "my children" in these two provisions must survive to the point of distribution? Furthermore, this language is ordinarily construed as imposing a *general* (i.e., unrestricted) condition of survival upon the interests of the children, so that the initial interest fails whether or not *R* or a child leaves issue surviving. See Restatement of Property §252. Under this rule of construction, the word "or" imposes the survival requirement only on the interest that precedes it in the statement of the disposition; the word does not apply to the interest stated after it. You should see why this matters if such a future interest disposition (generally referred to as alternative contingent remainders) is modified to call for distribution on termination of the trust "to *R* or her *children*" or "to my children or their *children*." If you do not see why, consider what would happen under these various dispositions if a child of R, or one of the transferor's grandchildren, should also predecease the life beneficiary.

Further aggravations arise in a remainder to named nephews "or their survivors" (e.g., Lawyer v. Munro, 118 So. 2d 654 (Fla. App. 1960)) or to "my children or their heirs" (see, e.g., Taylor v. Taylor, 92 N.W. 71 (Iowa 1902)). On the latter, see section D of this chapter, below.

(ii)   Death "With [or "Without] Issue"

Frequent references in deeds, wills and trust instruments to a beneficiary's death "without issue" or "with issue" invite a variety of constructional problems. Consider, for example, the issues raised by the following prototypical dispositions:

(a) *H* devises to *T* in trust for *W* for life, "remainder to my daughter *D*, but if D should die *without* issue, then to my sons, *X* and *Y*."

(b) *W* devises in trust for *H* for life, "then to my daughter, *D*, but if she dies *leaving* issue, to her issue."

One of the problems presented by these dispositions, asking whether the interests of *X* and *Y* in (a) or of *D*'s issue in (b) are subject to implied requirements of survival, was considered in earlier parts of this chapter. Other questions are considered here.

Time Reference: The "Death When" Ambiguity. Under early English common law, a deed "to *B*" but if he should die without issue, then to *C*" referred to an *indefinite* (or "remote") failure of *B*'s issue — i.e., the expiration of *B*'s line of descent at any time, even long after his death. (Remember the fee tail and related problems from your property course?) Another early interpretation might have treated the expression as meaning "die without ever having had issue." Modern construction in the United States would treat this language in a deed as referring to a *definite* failure of *B*'s issue, meaning the failure of his issue at a particular time, ordinarily the time of his death. The foregoing constructions treat the interests of *B* and *C* as *successive* interests. On the other hand, a *devise* directly "to *B*, but if he should die without issue, then to *C*" presents the possibility of a *substitutional* construction under which *C*'s interest takes effect only if *B* should die before the testator leaving no issue surviving *B*. (Or is it surviving the testator?) The more frequent construction, however, is again that the will refers to the failure of *B*'s issue at his death whenever that may occur. (Do you see why a devise "to *X*, but if he should die, then to *Y*," is usually given the substitutional construction, as if the testator had said "if he should die before me," so that *X*'s title is absolute if he outlives the testator?)

Now let us consider the possibilities if the person in question has a future interest, as in dispositions (a) and (b) in the opening paragraphs of subsection (ii), above. To what time did *H* or *W* refer in providing a gift over upon their daughter *D*'s death without issue or with issue, respectively? The often-cited case of Pyne v. Pyne, 154 F.2d 297 (D.C. Cir. 1946), examined the early and modern alternatives, treating as serious alternatives *D*'s death with or without issue, as the case may be, before the death of the *life beneficiary* (i.e., before the time of distribution), before the death of the *testator,* or at the time of D *'s death,* whenever that might occur. *Pyne,* like nearly all cases of this type, concluded that the presumed answer to the "death when" question is before the *time for distribution* — i.e., prior to the surviving spouse's death. (Why do you suppose there is such a consensus here, as contrasted with the "surviving when" question in subsection b(i) above?)

Even under this typical construction, still another possible issue might be presented in the event *D* should die after the testator, leaving a young child who then also dies before the life beneficiary. Has *D* died "without issue" (or "with issue") before the surviving spouse within the meaning of these wills? What do you think the settlor had in mind, or would have intended? Does it matter, given that a future interest to "issue" carries with it an *implied* condition of survivorship (subsection a(ii) of this chapter)? Read on.

Scope of Survival Requirement: Restricted or General. Other significant questions are presented by the types of dispositions described and discussed above, and by some comparable dispositions.

PROBLEM

11-T.   In addition to (a) and (b) set out at the start of subsection (ii), consider the following two trusts created by the will of *S*:

1.   A trust for *L* for life, "remainder to *X* and *Y*, but if either *X* or *Y* should predecease *L* leaving descendants, his or her share shall go to his or her descendants who survive *L*."
2.   The second trust is also for *L* for life, but then provides for the remainder "to go to *L*'s children, the issue of any deceased child to take that child's share." At the time, *L* had two children, *C* and *D*.

X (in the first case) and *C* (in the second) died shortly after *S* without ever having had issue. Then *D* (in the second case) dies, leaving a child, *G* (*L*'s grandchild). Who is entitled to the property of these trusts when *L* later dies?

What happens if the specific conditions that are expressly stated in these various cases do not cover the situations that materialize? In other words, in disposition (a) above, what is the result if *D* predeceases *W* *leaving* issue alive at *W*'s death? In disposition (b), what result if *D* predeceases *H* *without* issue surviving? Courts have generally refused to imply gifts to issue in cases like (a) because to do so would amount "to writing or re-writing the will for the testator," but compare the generally recognized exception in section D.3 later in this chapter.

In re Krooss, 99 N.E.2d 222 (N.Y. 1951), involved a disposition "to my wife for life, remainder to my children share and share alike; in the event that either of my children should die before my wife leaving descendants, then such descendants shall take the share their parent would have taken if then living." Before the wife's death one of the children died, never having had issue. Her executor (her husband) later claimed a share of the remainder when the life beneficiary died. The court stated:

Over the years, the courts have uniformly held that language such as that used by the testator here, or language substantially identical, creates a vested remainder in fee subject to being divested by the remainderman's failure to survive the life beneficiary, *if, but only if* such remainderman leaves issue or descendants surviving. . . .

Leading commentators, after reviewing the cases, have expressed themselves in similar fashion. See 2 Powell on Real Property §330 (1950): "Supplanting limitations differ, in that some provide a taker who is to become the substitute whenever the prior taker fails to survive, while others provide a taker who is to become the substitute only under some circumstances. In cases of the second type, the constructional preference for an early indefeasibility causes the requirement of survival to be strictly construed, and to operate only under the exact circumstances stipulated. . . . Similarly, in a gift 'to my wife *B* for life, then to my children and to the issue of those of my children who may be dead,' the interest of a child of the testator who dies without surviving issue is indefeasible."

. . . In a word, not [the daughter's] failure under *all* circumstances to survive was specified as a condition defeating her estate, but *only* her death before her mother if she left descendants.

Accordingly, the deceased daughter's share of the trust was an asset of her estate as claimed by her executor husband. See also Restatement of Property §254. Cf. Estate of Houston, 201 A.2d 592 (Pa. 1964) (under facts comparable to the second trust in Problem 11-T, above). Contrast, however, the result in Robertson v. Robertson, 48 N.E.2d 29 (Mass. 1943) (remainder essentially "to X, Y and Z or to the issue of any that may be dead"); and see Restatement of Property §252 and the situations discussed in the last two paragraphs of subsection b(i) above.

In Turner v. Adams, 855 S.W.2d 735 (Tex. App. 1993), a testator devised property to her husband for life, remainder to her nieces and nephews, adding "In the event of the death of any of my nieces and nephews leaving a child or children surviving them, then the surviving child or children of each such deceased nephew or niece shall receive the share to which such deceased nephew or niece would have been entitled, if living." One of the nephews predeceased the life tenant without issue. In holding that the nephew's share passed not to his estate but to the other class members (i.e., the other nieces and nephews), the court said: "[W]here, as here, the death of a class member occurs after the effective date of the instrument but prior to distribution, that class member's interest passes through his estate, unless the will provides otherwise," citing Restatement (Second) of Property: Donative Transfers §27.3. The court added: "In the instant case the survivorship clause provides otherwise" and "must have been inserted to prevent against a class member's interests passing to their [sic] estate in the event they died prior to distribution."

The *Turner* opinion also quoted Comment *e* of §27.3 of the Second Restatement, which states: "Because of the undesirability of having the gift pass through the deceased member's estate and because the provision for substitution of issue is a sufficient indication of the donor's intent that he did not wish such a result, it should be presumed, in the absence of contrary indication, that the donor who provides for substitution of issue intends that the share of other class members be enlarged if a class member fails to survive to the date of distribution and leaves no issue who so survive."

Turner does not follow the traditional and still usual view represented by *Krooss*. The Second Restatement favors this departure from traditional doctrine as represented by the original Restatement. If a court does not believe a general departure from the traditional rule is appropriate, is there any way that *Turner* can be distinguished from *Krooss* (and *Houston*, also cited above)? If a court does agree with the *Turner* view, what results should it reach when the remainder is "to my children, but if any predecease the life beneficiary without issue, then to the shares of my other children," if a child dies leaving issue who survive to the time of distribution? Can you imagine why a settlor who makes express provision for a gift over upon one set of circumstances (i.e., upon death *either* "with" *or* "without" issue), but not upon the other, would wish not to have the interest fail upon the other (unmentioned) set of circumstances? If so, one might have some sympathy for the traditional view when the drafter has performed inadequately. How might an alert lawyer have done a better job for such a client?

On problems of survivorship generally and related problems of drafting, see Halbach, Future Interests: Express and Implied Conditions of Survival, Part I, 49 Cal. L. Rev. 297 (1961), and Part II. 49 Cal. L. Rev. 431 (1961). Also see Susan F. French, Imposing a General Survival Requirement on Beneficiaries of Future Interests: Solving the Problems Caused by the Death of a Beneficiary Before the Time Set for Distribution, 27 Ariz. L. Rev. 801 (1985); Laura E. Cunningham, The Hazards of Tinkering with the Common Law of Future Interests: The California Experience, 48 Hastings L.J. 667 (1997).

PROBLEM

11-U.   *T*'s will left his residuary estate in four equal shares, to be held in separate trusts for each of his four grandchildren, *A, B, C,* and *D*. Each trust provided that income payments were to be made to the designated grandchild and that he or she was to "receive one half of the principal at age 30 and the rest at age 35; but in the event such child should die before age 35, the remaining principal shall go to his or her descendants, if any, and if none then that share to be added to the trusts of my other grandchildren." *D*, the youngest, died childless and unmarried at age 33. The trusts of two of the other grandchildren have terminated. *A,* the oldest, received the final installment of her share 16 years ago but is now dead; she left a widower and three children, all of whom are still alive. *B* received final payment of his quarter of *T*'s estate on termination of his trust 13 years ago and is still alive. *C* died four years ago at age 31, leaving a widow and two children, *X* and *Y,* but *X* is now dead. *C*'s trust has not yet been terminated.

The trustee has consulted you, asking what to do with the remaining portions (worth about $130,000 each) of the last two trusts (*C*'s and *D*'s). What advice would you give? Can you design and draft this dispositive plan so that it is simple but clear? (This effort can help you to pull together much of the preceding material in this chapter.)

c. The 1990 UPC — A Change in Direction

Despite the common law's continuing, understandable reluctance to imply survival requirements for future interests given to named individuals or single-generation classes, commentators point out that well-drafted instruments expressly require survival to the point of distribution. With that in mind, Uniform Probate Code §2-707 was promulgated in 1990 to impose such a survival requirement in trust situations and to provide a substitute gift to the deceased beneficiary's issue analogous to the anti-lapse provision in §2-605. The rule has its critics, and this change has been rejected in several states that have enacted other provisions of the 1990 UPC.

UNIFORM PROBATE CODE

§2-707. *Survivorship with Respect to Future Interests Under Terms of Trust; Substitute Takers.*

(a) [Definitions.] In this section:

(1) "Alternative future interest" means an expressly created future interest that can take effect in possession or enjoyment instead of another future interest on the happening of one or more events. . . . A residuary clause in a will does not create an alternative future interest with respect to a future interest created in a nonresiduary devise in the will. . . .

[(2) through (7) omitted]

(b) [Survivorship Required; Substitute Gift.] A future interest under the terms of a trust is contingent on the beneficiary's surviving the distribution date. If a beneficiary of a future interest under the terms of a trust fails to survive the distribution date, the following apply:

(1) Except as provided in paragraph (4), if the future interest is not in the form of a class gift and the deceased beneficiary leaves surviving descendants, a substitute gift is created in the beneficiary's surviving descendants. They take by representation the property to which the beneficiary would have been entitled had the beneficiary survived the distribution date.

(2) Except as provided in paragraph (4), if the future interest is in the form of a class gift, other than a future interest to "issue," "descendants," "heirs of the body," "heirs," "next of kin," "relatives," or "family," or a class described by language of similar import, a substitute gift is created in the surviving descendants of any deceased beneficiary. The property to which the beneficiaries would have been entitled had all of them survived the distribution date passes to the surviving beneficiaries and the surviving descendants of the deceased beneficiaries [by representation]. . . .

(3) . . . [W]ords of survivorship attached to a future interest are not, in the absence of additional evidence, a sufficient indication of an intent contrary to the application of this section. . . .

(4) If a governing instrument creates an alternative future interest with respect to a future interest for which a substitute gift is created by paragraph (1) or (2), the substitute gift is superseded by the alternative future interest only if an expressly designated beneficiary of the alternative future interest is entitled to take in possession or enjoyment.

[Subsections (c), (d) and (e) omitted. These subsections cover possible situations in which multiple substitute gifts are provided by the statute and situations in which, after applying the preceding subsections, there is no surviving taker either under a testamentary trust (in which case the property passes to settlor's residuary devisees or would-be heirs by deferred determination) or under an exercised power of appointment.]

PROBLEM

11-V. In the following dispositions, who would receive the trust property at L's death under the UPC? Without the UPC? Which result do you think is more likely to effectuate probable intent? (Except as otherwise indicated in the facts below, all potential claimants survive L.)

1. A residuary devise in trust for L for life, "remainder to R." R predeceases L survived by a spouse (R's sole devisee) and a child.
2. The same facts except that the remainder is "to R, but if R predeceases L, to X."

3. The same facts as in 2, except that *X* also predeceases *L*, survived by a spouse (*X*'s sole devisee) and a child. Hint: Subsection (c), which is omitted here, contains a "break-the-tie" section like §2-603(c), infra p. 264. (Would your answer for this disposition differ if *X* had been one of the settlor's two children and if the other child survived *L*?)

4. A specific devise in trust for *L* for life, "remainder to *R* if *R* survives *L*." The will also devised the settlor's residuary estate to *X*.

D. *Meaning of Class Terms*

1. Problems of Definition and Shares

Chapter 2 examines at length the critically important issue of whether class terminology encompasses adopted and nonmarital children, including the particular difficulties presented in the future interest context. That chapter also contains a discussion of different systems of distribution, such as per capita and per stirpes; in the drafting of future interest provisions, the terms "issue" and "descendants," for example, should always be accompanied by some reference to the intended distribution system; the distribution system should then be pinned down by reference to a particular statute or to definitions set out in the instrument — e.g., ". . . to my issue living at *L*'s death, such issue to take by right of representation as hereafter defined in Article XII."

Although words are usually to be given their primary (or proper) meaning, courts occasionally depart from this principle based on evidence of a transferor's accustomed usage or because the context sometimes indicates confused usage, even by lawyers. Thus, "heirs" may be construed to mean "children" or "descendants," or the term "children" may be treated as having been intended to mean "issue" or otherwise to include grandchildren or great grandchildren. See, e.g., the discussion of the *Gustafson* and *Welles* cases (footnote 3 of this chapter) in which divided courts struggled with whether, respectively, "children" should be interpreted to mean "issue" and whether "grandchildren" should be so interpreted as to include great-grandchildren. Other issues about "heirs" and the like are explored immediately below.

2. Dispositions to "Heirs" and "Next of Kin"

A shamefully frequent source of litigation and uncertainty, even in lawyer-drawn wills, is the term "heirs," or its equivalent, used as a shorthand means of describing the takers of a future interest, especially following other future interest provisions in case those other provisions fail. Some insist that such terms should never be used to describe a remainder class, because of the number of problems inherent in their use. Others believe that such terms can be useful but that they must be employed carefully and only with a full understanding and complete coverage of the many questions involved. Neither of these seemingly defensible assertions, however, can be said materially to have affected the practices of lawyers in drafting wills and trust agreements.

If the gift is to the settlor's "heirs," there still may be a problem with the Doctrine of Worthier Title. (On "heirs" problems under the Rule in Shelley's Case, as well as Worthier Title, see Chapter 10.) Even assuming "heirs," "next of kin," or other language describing a person's *intestate* successors is used as language of purchase rather than of limitation, many problems remain. For example, if a remainder is given to "the heirs of *A*," is *A*'s surviving spouse included in the class of remainder beneficiaries — i.e., does a surviving spouse take his or her share as an "heir," or does the spouse take as a special "statutory successor" under local law? Cases differ on this point, depending on the jurisdiction involved.

If a testator died in State *X*, devising a remainder to the "heirs" of another, who died in State *Y*, what state's law determines the identity and shares of the heirs? Compare the recurring problem in Harris Trust & Savings Bank v. Jackson, 106 N.E.2d 188 (Ill. 1952):

> We come thus to the question whether the scope of the phrase "lawful heirs" is to be determined [by the law in effect] at the death of the testator, six months before the 1923 [statutory] amendment became effective, or at the time of Arthur Jackson's death in 1933. It seems clear that the testator, having employed the phrase in its technical sense, was saying, in effect, "Now let the law take its course." Had he desired a particular group as defined by the statute then in effect to be the recipients of the gift over, he could easily have so specified. The reasonable inference is that, absent a contrary intent of the testator as shown by additional language or circumstances, the law of intestacy in force at the death of the named ancestor, here Arthur Jackson, was intended. . . .

What are the arguments for a contrary result? What should a drafter provide with respect to each of the issues raised in this paragraph?

The most litigated of all questions about the meaning of "heirs" concerns when the heirs are to be ascertained — at the date of the death of the person whose heirs are in question (the strictly proper and technical sense of the term), at the date of possession (an artificial class of heirs), or at some other time. When the designated ancestor is the life beneficiary, a remainder to his heirs does not pose this particular problem. Whenever the date of distribution to the "heirs" or "next of kin" is later than the designated ancestor's death, however, trouble is invited. The following is a typical situation of this variety:

A devised "to *B* for life, then to my [*A*'s] heirs." Are the remainder beneficiaries those described by the applicable statute of intestate succession as applied to the family circumstances at the date of *A*'s death, so that from that time on those persons hold indefeasibly vested remainders? Or are they those persons who *would* be *A*'s heirs if the statute were applied to persons living at the date of possession (*B*'s death)? It may even be concluded that *A*'s heirs are determined at his death, but that those persons must, by implication, survive until *B*'s death.[4] The well-established basic rule of construction in nearly all jurisdictions (absent contrary legislation) is that the remainder beneficiaries (the heirs) are to be determined at the death of the named ancestor (*A*, in our example) and that, if not otherwise conditioned, their interests vest indefeasibly at that time.

This general presumption of intent is subject to a few commonly recognized "exceptions," and there are also those hard-to-predict cases in which the presumption is held rebutted or inapplicable under the circumstances without benefit of an admitted or generalized exception. One clear-cut exception that has received general acceptance is that if the designated ancestor has predeceased the testator, the heirs will be determined as of the date of the testator's death. Thus if *A* devises directly to the heirs of *B*, who predeceased *A*, an artificial class of heirs of *B* will be determined by applying the intestacy statute to persons alive when *A* dies. Because the lapse doctrine precludes any of *B*'s heirs who predecease *A* from taking under his will, the rule attributes to *A* an intent to defer the determination of *B*'s heirs, leaving the class flexible until *A*'s death in this situation. What other situations justify a departure from the usual rule of early ascertainment of heirs? What if *T* devised "to *A* for life, then to my heirs," and *A* was *T*'s sole heir? What if *A* was one of three heirs?

It is obvious from the very existence of the general rule that the mere fact that distribution is postponed beyond the ancestor's death is not sufficient indication of contrary intention to justify deferring the ascertainment of the heirs in a state that adheres to that rule.

PROBLEM

11-W.   All of *T*'s property was traceable to an inheritance from her father, *F*. On *T*'s death, leaving no issue, she left her estate in trust "to pay the income to *L* for life; on *L*'s death the principal is to go to his issue, but in the event of *L*'s death without issue surviving him, then to the heirs of *F*." Ten years after *T*'s death, *L* died without issue. All

---

4. The strange results of this rule are illustrated by the case of Continental Ill. Natl. Bank & Trust Co. v. Eliel, 161 N.E.2d 107 (Ill. 1959).

parties agree that the gift over to the "heirs" takes effect; the only problem is that of construing it.

At *F*'s death years ago, his estate passed intestate to his sole heirs at law, who were his four children, *Q, R, S,* and *T.* At *T*'s death only *Q* and *R* were still living, *S* having died intestate leaving as his only heir a child *CS.* By the time of *L*'s death *Q* had also died intestate leaving as his sole heir a child, *CQ.*

In the construction proceedings below *R* claimed the entire principal of the trust, *CQ* claimed half (or at least one-third) of the principal, and *CS* also claimed a right to half (or at least a one-third share) of the principal. The trial court held that *R* was entitled to the entire trust estate. (a) Can you see how the lower court could have reached this decision?[5] (b) On what basis might this decision be reversed on appeal and one of the more favorable results contended for by *CQ* be reached? (c) On what basis might the court reach the results contended for by *CS*?

The court had to resolve many of the above-mentioned issues in In re Dodge Testamentary Trust, 330 N.W.2d 72 (Mich. Ct. App. 1982). In a lawyer-drawn will, John F. Dodge (the automobile manufacturer, who should have been able to afford competent legal work) devised the residue of his estate in trust for the benefit of his children. Upon the death of all of his children, the corpus was to be distributed "to the heirs of his children [*A, B, C,* and *D*]." Dodge died in 1920 in Michigan, where *A* and *C* also died. *A* and *C* died in 1938 and 1971, respectively. *B* died in 1962 in Florida; and *D* died in Michigan in 1980. The court had to decide: (1) whether "heirs" means "issue" or "children" or intestate succcessors; (2) whether the various groups of heirs are to be ascertained at distribution (*D*'s death) or upon the death of each child; (3) whether to apply the intestacy statute as it existed at Dodge's death or as it read at the death of each child or at the death of *D*; (4) whether Florida or Michigan law determines *B*'s heirs; and (5) whether there should be an initial division into four equal shares. This was a case of lawyers making business for lawyers. Restatement (Second) of Property: Donative Transfers §29.4 reaffirms the essentially standard rule of construction as follows: "If a gift is made to a class described as the 'heirs' of a designated person, or by a similar class gift term, and a particular statute governing the intestate takers of property is to be used to determine the persons who come within the primary meaning of the class gift, in the absence of additional language or circumstances that indicate otherwise, such statute is applied as of the designated person's death." The commentary, however, recognizes several specific exceptions based on prevailing case law. For

---

5. See text supra at note 4.

example, if *O* transfers a present interest to the heirs of *A*, who is alive, the heirs are determined as if *A* died at the time of the gift. Id., Comment *c;* and cf. Comment *d* (future interest to heirs of a person who is still alive at the time for distribution). The most important of these crystallized exceptions is described in Comment *f:* If *T* devises "to *A* for life, then to my heirs," and *A* is *T*'s *sole* heir, *T*'s heirs are ascertained as if *T* had died at the time of *A*'s death, thus excluding *A*.

But compare Old Colony Trust Co. v. Stephens, 190 N.E.2d 110 (Mass. 1963):

> There is inevitably some incongruity in giving four beneficiaries equitable life interests in trust property and then giving them, as [his only] "heirs at law," vested legal remainder interests. A testator, who thought through his will carefully, might hesitate to make such a gift. In several cases, however, this type of incongruity has not been regarded as sufficient to lead this court to interpret the word "heirs" as not carrying its usual meaning. [Citations omitted.]
>
> We recognize that the considerations outlined above, viewed in the aggregate, furnish some support for the contention that the testator meant the ultimate remainder interest to go to his heirs at the termination of the trust. Nevertheless, after weighing these considerations, the actual intention of the testator remains a matter of conjecture. Accordingly, we apply the usual rule of construction. The circumstances which would support a determination of the heirs at the death of the surviving life beneficiary to not appear to us to be as persuasive as those discussed [other cases]. . . .

Similarly, in Estate of Easter, 148 P.2d 601 (Cal. 1944), involving a remainder to the settlor's "heirs at law" when the life beneficiary (settlor's widow) was *one* of *multiple* heirs, the court refused to recognize a generalized exception (although the state had earlier recognized the *sole* heir-life beneficiary exception as a special rule of construction); nevertheless, the court went on to conclude, from the particular wording involved, that the particular settlor's intention was "that the interest of the heirs should vest at the time of the termination of the trust," adding that any other interpretation would "ignore any usual meaning of the words 'shall go to invest in the heirs at law.' " A dissent argued that "rules of construction are essential" here, as they are "for deeds or negotiable instruments," and should generally be respected because "[w]ithout them counsel could not advise their clients with any reasonable certainty, for the meaning of a will could not be ascertained until it had been passed upon by a court of last resort." See also the finding that an artificial, deferred class of heirs was appropriate under the circumstances of the case, despite recognizing the usual rule of construction, in Harris Trust & Savings Bank v. Beach, 513 N.E.2d 833 (Ill. 1987) (which also ordered distribution to be made to the heirs per stirpes despite settlor's use of the words "equally" and "share and share alike").

UNIFORM PROBATE CODE

§2-711. *Interests in "Heirs" and Like.*   If an applicable statute or a governing instrument calls for a present or future distribution to . . . a designated individual's "heirs," "heirs at law," "next of kin," "relatives," or "family," or language of similar import, the property passes to those persons, including the state, and in such shares as would succeed to the designated individual's intestate estate under the intestate succession law of the designated individual's domicile if the designated individual died when the disposition is to take effect in possession or enjoyment. If the designated individual's surviving spouse is living but is remarried at the time the disposition is to take effect in possession or enjoyment, the surviving spouse is not an heir of the designated individual.

E.   Incomplete Dispositions and Other Drafting Defects

Incomplete dispositions are the frequent product of drafting oversight and unforeseen circumstances. We are here concerned with more than mere ambiguities. We are concerned with omissions in the instrument and with the methods by which courts might fill these "gaps." Methods commonly employed include: (1) acceleration of subsequent interests or, occasionally, extension of prior interests; (2) supplying a gift by implication (or possibly by statute, as in Cal. Civil Code §733); and (3) accumulating income not disposed of for the eventual taker of the succeeding interest. If none of these methods is appropriate, a court may ultimately have to accept that the disposition is only a partial one, resulting in a reversionary interest — i.e., usually, in a resulting trust for the settlor or his successors in interest.

What follows is a review of some recurring types of incomplete dispositions and other uncertainties. It suggests the types of solutions available and frequent drafting problems to be avoided.

1.   Failure of an Interest

The interest of a beneficiary may fail for various reasons other than mere failure to draft for the disposition of all interests in the property. Prominent examples are: (1) *invalidity,* possibly due to the Rule Against Perpetuities or illegality of purpose, or because a beneficiary (e.g., a life tenant) served as an essential witness to a will; (2) *lapse,* when a beneficiary predeceases the testator and no antilapse statute applies; or (3) *renunciation,* often either tax motivated or the result of a surviving spouse's election to take against a will.

When an interest is invalid under the Rule Against Perpetuities, the result depends on the nature of the other interests in the disposition. Normally a reversionary interest results, but a *prior* interest may be enlarged if the invalid interest is an executory interest and the prior interest contains no inherent limitation. Brown v. Baptist Church, 91 N.E.2d 922 (Mass. 1950).

If a prior interest fails, such as by renunciation, *subsequent* interests may be accelerated if no other disposition is provided and the remainder beneficiaries are "ready to take." The possibility of some types of renunciations should be anticipated in drafting. For example, tax-motivated disclaimers often can and should be anticipated by making appropriate provision for them in the planning. On the other hand, when a forced share election is made by a spouse who is given a life interest in a testamentary trust, the problem often must be resolved by sequestering the life interest to compensate those from whom the statutory share was taken. See Chapter 3 and Sellick v. Sellick, 173 N.W. 609 (Mich. 1919). This result is readily accomplished by acceleration of remainders when all beneficiaries from whom the spousal share was taken were remainder beneficiaries — e.g., a residuary estate left in trust for the electing spouse for life, remainder equally to the testator's children.

A decision whether or not to accelerate depends primarily on whether the remainder beneficiaries are deemed "ready to take" under the transferor's plan for the disposition of the property. The court will probably consider whether it is *practical* to accelerate, especially if the remainder beneficiaries are minors. Generally, to accelerate there must be no clear, separate, unfulfilled condition to the remainder beneficiaries taking. While judicial opinions sometimes say that vested remainders are subject to acceleration and that contingent remainders are not, it is really the existence and nature of a condition that will be determinative; whether the condition is technically precedent or subsequent is not an appropriate factor in deciding whether acceleration is consistent with the settlor's purposes. Future interests should not be accelerated when to do so would shift the beneficiaries in any way that *materially* distorts the transferor's scheme of disposition, as might be the case in a premature closing of a class under the rule of convenience. For example, if a remainder is to go to the children of a life beneficiary, acceleration following her renunciation might exclude her afterborn children, when, as drafted, all children necessarily would have been included since none could be conceived after the life beneficiary's death. Acceleration might therefore be "unfair" and violate the settlor's intention.

If a remainder is conditioned on the beneficiaries' survival "until termination of the preceding estate," does this requirement refer to normal termination, or might it relate as well to premature termination? This depends on a judicial evaluation of the settlor's purpose in requiring survival. A view frequently adopted is that the survival requirement is satisfied if the remainder beneficiary survives the life *interest,* which ends when the life beneficiary disclaims. (This is likely to be appropriate when the trust and the survival requirement are parts of a primarily tax-motivated estate plan.) Some courts, however, have viewed a survival requirement as indicative of an intention that would prevent acceleration. See, e.g., Linkous v. Candler, 508 S.E.2d 657 (Ga. 1998). Can a court ever accelerate a remainder to the "heirs" of a life beneficiary who has no need for the trust income and decides to disclaim her interest?

PROBLEM

11-X.   *T* devised his estate as follows: one-third to his grandchildren; one-third to his son *S* for life, then to his (*T*'s) grandchildren; and one-third to his daughter *D* for life then to his grandchildren. At *T*'s death, when *S* has three children and *B* none, *A* disclaims. What result? See Pate v. Ford, 376 S.E.2d 775 (S.C. 1989).

2.   Gifts Over on Date Later Than End of Prior Interest

One common "gap" in dispositions is illustrated by a conveyance "to A for life, then to A's children who reach 21, and if none do, then to B." If A dies while some or all of his children are under age 21, who is entitled to possession of the property in the meantime? The possible solutions, of course, are numerous.

A more common omission is found in a trust providing for distribution of "the income for life equally to my children, and on the death of the survivor the principal to my issue." When child A dies in the lifetime of the other children, we are not told what is to happen to A's "share" of the income. Would the problem be different if the remainder gift had been to "my issue on the termination of the life estates"? Or if the remainder had been of "the principal and accumulated income"? The problem, as originally stated, may be resolved in any of the following ways: (1) On A's death his share of the income (or of principal) might be distributed to A's issue (as in Dewire v. Haveles, 534 N.E.2d 782 (Mass. 1989)); (2) A's share of the income (or principal) might go by some form of representation to the *settlor's* issue (Estate of Robinson, 262 Cal. App. 3d 32 (1968), influenced by statute); (3) under the doctrine of *cross remainders,* A's share of income might go to the other life beneficiaries, thus paying the income for the duration of the trust to the children surviving from time to time (Westervelt v. First Interstate Bank, 551 N.E.2d 1180 (Ind. App. 1990)); (4) each child might be entitled to share in the income for the life of the survivor of the children (i.e., a life interest *pur autre vie*), so that *A*'s share of income for the remaining trust period would pass by the terms of his will or by intestacy (Briggs v. Briggs, 950 S.W.2d 710 (Tenn. App. 1997)); (5) there might be a reversion (i.e., a resulting trust) of *A*'s income share (Union & New Haven Trust Co. v. Selleck, 24 A.2d 485 (Conn. 1942)); or (6) *A*'s share of income (and that of each child as he or she dies) might be accumulated for distribution with the principal to the remainder beneficiaries on termination (Jones v. Heritage Pullman Bank & Trust Co., 518 N.E.2d 831 (Ill. App. 1987), appeal denied, 526 N.E.2d 831 (Ill. 1988)). If any solution to such problems appears traditionally to have been preferred, it is that of implying cross remainders in the income (3 above), assuming the words of the particular disposition will bear that construction. See Restatement (Second) of Trusts §143(2), following original Restatement of Property §115; but recently approved (1999) tentative draft of Restatement (Third) of Trusts §49, Comment *c* (see especially Illustration 3) adopts alternative (1) above (income share to *A*'s issue, if any living).

3. Implied Gifts to Issue

Whenever a gift assumes the existence of issue and there are in fact no issue, some provision must be made for disposition of the property on this failure of remainder beneficiaries. Thus, if a conveyance is made "to *A* for life, then to *A*'s issue," and *A* dies leaving no issue, the property reverts to the grantor or his successors in interest.

Compare, however, the following common type of disposition for which the courts usually supply a gift by implication: in trust for *L* for life, "and if *L* should die without issue, to *B*." What happens if *L*, who has only a life interest, should die *with* issue surviving her? There is abundant American and English authority supporting the proposition that there is a gift by implication to the issue of *L* in such a case. Do you see why this situation is to be distinguished from a disposition in trust for *L* for life, "then to *R*, but if *R* should die without issue, then to *X*"? We have seen (section B.2.b, above) that if *R* dies survived by issue, he generally has an interest that passes by his will or by intestacy (i.e., *R* has a vested remainder subject to divestment *only* on his death *without* issue), absent a statute like UPC §707 (in section 2.c above).

Except for the implied gift to issue in the initial situation in the above paragraph, courts traditionally have been very reluctant to imply dispositions, especially in cases involving wills. In recent years this reluctance appears to be diminishing in other trust and future interest contexts (see Matter of Bieley, 69 N.E.2d 1119 (N.Y. 1998)), much as the reluctance to cure mistakes is diminishing under the influence of Restatement (Third) of Property: Donative Transfers §12.1 (Tentative Draft No. 1, approved 1995) and cases such as Brinker v. Wobaco Trust Ltd., 610 S.W.2d 160 (Tex. Civ. App. 1980).

PROBLEMS

11-Y.   The settlor left his residuary estate in trust "to pay the income equally to my two nieces; if either should die leaving issue, the issue should take the corpus of the share of the niece so dying; if either should die without leaving issue, the share is to go to my surviving niece." One niece died leaving issue and a spouse; soon thereafter the other died leaving no spouse or issue. How is the trust estate to be distributed?

11-Z.   *T* devised Blackacre in fee simple to her son, *S*, "when he shall attain age 25, but if he should die before age 25 without leaving children surviving him, I give Blackacre to *C* Church in fee simple absolute." *S* survived *T* but died at age 23, leaving a child surviving. Who is entitled to Blackacre?

4. Combined Gifts: Rule in Wild's Case and Related Problems

Surprisingly frequent are cases in which, essentially, property is left "equally to *A* and the children of *B*" or "to *A* and her children." Wild's Case, 6 Co. Rep. 16b (1599), addressed the latter type of gift and, in dictum, set out two resolutions. The modern derivations of these resolutions are: (1) if *A* has no children at the time of the devise, *A* takes a life estate, and the children a remainder; but (2) if *A* has children at the time, *A* and the children take as tenants in common. Consider the effect of the second resolution if *A* is young, with a small child or two, at the time of the devise. (See reaction in United States v. 654.8 Acres of Land, 102 F. Supp. 937 (E.D. Tenn. 1952), to the prospect of the class closing prematurely under the rule of convenience in section B.2, above.) The first Restatement followed these resolutions, but under Restatement (Second) of Property: Donative Transfers §28.3 the language presumptively calls for the life estate and remainder result, whether or not there are children at the time of the devise.

In the above devise "to *A* and the children of *B*," even in the typical case in which *B* is deceased and the class closing problem is therefore avoided, there are other uncertainties. Does *A* take half, with *B*'s children sharing the other half, or does *A* take the same share as each child of *B*? (Would it help if the devise said "to *A* and the children of *B* in equal shares"?) If *B* has three children, the prevailing view is that the gift is one to a "class" and that *A* and the children each therefore take one-fourth. Does this seem right? (What if *A* and *B* were the testator's children, or his brother or sister?) Also, if *A* and *B* are unrelated to *T*, what would the result be if the intended share of one of *B*'s children lapsed?

How many issues are raised by a devise "to *A* for life, then equally to the heirs of *B* and *C*"?

The mistakes discussed in this section E are easily made. The fault is generally in the drafting, although some of the oversights may be excusable, as in certain of the renunciation cases. Once the drafter has failed, however, a court may be able to do little more than guess at a suitable solution. In doing so the judicial object is always to find the elusive (or hypothetical) "intent of the testator." Because of the infinite variety of factual situations and forms of expression, many such cases are decided without the development of a generalized principle of construction. In a few cases — like the gift by implication to the issue in section 3 above — the result is fairly certain and subject to generalization. Of course, omissions and ambiguities will never be wholly eliminated, but one can hope that, by recognizing the more common of them, they will occur less frequently.

F. *Constructional Problems in the Creation and Execution of Powers*

1. Intention to Exercise

BEALS v. STATE STREET BANK & TRUST CO.
326 N.E.2d 896 (Mass. 1975)

WILKINS, J. . . . Arthur Hunnewell died . . . in 1904, leaving his wife and four daughters. His will placed the residue of his property in a trust, the income of which was to be paid to his wife during her life. At the death of his wife the trust was to be divided in portions, one for each then surviving daughter and one for the then surviving issue of any deceased daughter. Mrs. Hunnewell died in 1930. One of the four daughters predeceased her mother, leaving no issue. The trust was divided, therefore, in three portions at the death of Mrs. Hunnewell. The will directed that the income of each portion held for a surviving daughter should be paid to her during her life and on her death the principal of such portion should "be paid and disposed of as she may direct and appoint by her last Will and Testament duly probated." In default of appointment, the will directed that a daughter's share should be distributed to "the persons who would be entitled to such estate under the laws then governing the distribution of intestate estates."

This petition concerns the distribution of the trust portion held for the testator's daughter Isabella. . . .

In February, 1944, Isabella, who was then a resident of New York, executed and caused to be filed in the Registry of Probate for Norfolk County an instrument which partially released her [pre-1941] general power of appointment under the will of her father [apparently for tax reasons]. . . . "to the extent that such power empowers me to appoint to any one other than one or more of the . . . descendants me surviving of Arthur Hunnewell."

On December 14, 1968, Isabella, who survived her husband, died without issue, still a resident of New York, leaving a will dated May 21, 1965. . . . Isabella did not expressly exercise her power of appointment under her father's will. The residuary clause of her will provided in effect for the distribution of all 'the rest, residue and remainder of my property' to the issue per stirpes of her sister Margaret Blake, who had predeceased Isabella. The Blake issue would take one-half of Isabella's trust share, as takers in default of appointment, in all events. If, however, Isabella's will should be treated as effectively exercising her power of appointment under her father's will, the Blake issue would take the entire trust share, and the executors of the will of Isabella's sister Jane (who survived Isabella and has since died) would not receive that one-half of the trust share which would go to Jane in default of appointment.

In support of their argument that Isabella's will did not exercise the power of appointment under her father's will, the executors of Jane's estate contend that (1) Massachusetts substantive law governs all questions relating to the power of appointment, including the interpretation of Isabella's will; (2) the power should be treated as a special power of appointment because of its partial release by Isabella; and (3) because Isabella's will neither expresses nor implies any intention to exercise the power, the applicable rule of construction in this Commonwealth is that a general residuary clause does not exercise a special power of appointment. The Blake issue, in support of their argument that the power was exercised, contend that (1) Isabella's will manifests an intention to exercise the power and that no rule of construction need be applied; (2) the law of New York should govern the question whether Isabella's will exercised the power and, if it does, by statute New York has adopted a rule that a special power of appointment is exercised by a testamentary disposition of all of the donee's property; and (3) if Massachusetts law does apply, and the will is silent on the subject of the exercise of the power, the principles underlying our rule of construction that a residuary clause exercises a general power of appointment are applicable in these circumstances.

1. We turn first to a consideration of the question whether Isabella's will should be construed according to the law of this Commonwealth or the law of New York. There are strong, logical reasons for turning to the law of the donee's domicile at the time of death to determine whether a donee's will has exercised a testamentary power of appointment over movables. See Restatement 2d: Conflict of Laws, §275, comment *c* (1971); Scott, Trusts, §642, p. 4065 (3d ed. 1967); Scoles, Goodrich's Conflict of Laws, §§175-177, p. 346 (4th ed. 1964). Most courts in this country which have considered the question, however, interpret the donee's will under the law governing the administration of the trust, which is usually the law of the donor's domicile. . . .

If the question were before us now for the first time, we might well adopt a choice of law rule which would turn to the substantive law of the donee's domicile, for the purpose of determining whether the donee's will exercised a power of appointment. However, in a field where much depends on certainty and consistency as to the applicable rules of law, we think that we should adhere to our well-established rule. Thus, in interpreting the will of a donee to determine whether a power of appointment was exercised, we apply the substantive law of the jurisdiction whose law governs the administration of the trust.

2. Considering the arguments of the parties, we conclude that there is no indication in Isabella's will of an intention to exercise or not to exercise the power of appointment given to her under her father's will. A detailed analysis of the various competing contentions would not add to our jurisprudence. In the absence of an intention disclosed by her will construed in light of circumstances known to her when she executed it, we must adopt some Massachusetts rule of construction to resolve the issue before us. The question is what rule of construction. We are unaware of any decided case which, in this context, has dealt with a testamentary general power, reduced to a special power by action of the donee.

3. We conclude that the residuary clause of Isabella's will should be presumed to have exercised the power of appointment. We reach this result by a consideration of the reasons underlying the canons of construction applicable to general and special testamentary powers of appointment. Considered in this way, we believe that a presumption of exercise is more appropriate in the circumstances of this case than a presumption of nonexercise.

When this court first decided not to extend to a special power of appointment the rule of construction that a general residuary clause executes a general testamentary power (unless a contrary intent is shown by the will), we noted significant distinctions between a general power and a special power. Fiduciary Trust Co. v. First Natl. Bank, supra, 344 Mass. at 6-10, 181 N.E.2d 6. A general power was said to be a close approximation to a property interest, a "virtually unlimited power of disposition," while a special power of appointment lacked this quality. We observed that a layman having a general testamentary power over property might not be expected to distinguish between the appointive property and that which he owns outright, and thus he can reasonably be presumed to regard this appointive property as his own. On the other hand, the donee of a special power would not reasonably regard such appointive property as his own: "[h]e would more likely consider himself to be, as the donor of the power intended, merely the person chosen by the donor to decide who of the possible appointees should share in the property (if the power is exclusive), and the respective shares of the appointees."

Considering the power of appointment given to Isabella and her treatment of that power during her life, the rationale for the canon of construction applicable to general powers of appointment should be applied in this case. This power was a general testamentary power at its inception. During her life, as a result of her bequest, Isabella had the use and enjoyment of the major portion of the property initially placed in her trust share. Prior use and enjoyment of the appointive property is a factor properly considered as weighing in favor of the exercise of a power of appointment by a will. Fiduciary Trust Co. v. First Natl. Bank, supra, at 10, 181 N.E.2d 6. Isabella voluntarily limited the power by selecting the possible appointees. In thus relinquishing the right to add the trust assets to her estate, she was treating the property as her own. Moreover, the gift under her residuary clause was consistent with the terms of the reduced power which she retained. In these circumstances, the partial release of a general power does not obviate the application of that rule of construction which presumes that a general residuary clause exercises a general power of appointment.

So ordered.

QUIRICO, J. (with whom TAURO, CHIEF JUSTICE, joins), concurring in the result:

I concur in the court's conclusion . . . However, I would reach that result without regard to whether the power of appointment was, either when it was created or when it was exercised, a general power of appointment or a special power of appointment, and without perpetuating the distinction made between the two types of powers in our decision in Fiduciary Trust Co. v. First Natl. Bank, 344 Mass. 1, 6-10, 181 N.E.2d 6-8 (1962). I would hold that the 'settled canon of construction that a general residuary clause will [exercise the general power]'. . . which has been a part of the case law of this Commonwealth at least since our decision in Amory v. Meredith, 7 Allen 397 (1863), applies equally to the execution of a special power of appointment, provided, of course, that (a) the residuary clause includes any beneficiary within the scope of the special power of appointment, (b) the instrument creating the special power does not prohibit its exercise by a general residuary clause, and (c) the residuary clause includes no disclaimer of intent to exercise the special power. . . .

The basic judicial objective in this and similar cases is to ascertain the testamentary intent of the donee of the power. I am unable to accept the proposition that a testator who subscribes to a will which includes a residuary clause in substantially the common form, broadly covering "all the rest, residue and remainder of my property" does not thereby express quite clearly an intention to dispose of all of the property and estate which can be the subject of testamentary disposition by him. Neither am I able to accept the proposition that such language, reasonably construed, permits any inference that the testator intended, by the use of such broad language, to exercise a general power of appointment but not a special one. . . .

. . . [U]nnecessary "refinements and subtleties" inevitably breed litigation. . . . We should, if possible, develop and apply rules of law which will eliminate the occasion for such litigation. One step in that direction would be to hold that a general residuary clause in a will is equally competent to execute a special power of appointment as it is to exercise a general power. . . .

In Bank of New York v. Black, 139 A.2d 393 (N.J. 1958), the donor of a general testamentary power died domiciled in New Jersey; the donee later died in Virginia, where by statute a general residuary clause presumptively exercises a general power. Rejecting the argument that it should overrule prior decisions and adopt the minority (Massachusetts) rule, the court purported to adhere to the majority common law views (i) that the law of the donor's domicile controls and (ii) that a general residuary clause "will not ordinarily suffice to exercise a power of appointment," but it found this donee's intention to appoint implied from the particular facts of the case, stating:

> Respondents [the default takers] direct us to the classic statement of Mr. Justice Story that: "Three classes of cases have been held to be sufficient demonstrations of an intended execution of a power: (1) Where there has been some reference in the will, or other instrument, to the power; (2) or a reference to the property . . . on which it is to be executed; (3) or, where the provision in the will or other instrument, executed by the donee of the power, would otherwise be ineffectual, or a mere nullity; in other words, it would have no operation, except as an

execution of the power." Blagge v. Miles, 3 Fed. Cas. Pages 559, 566, No. 1, 479, (1 Cir. 1841).

They argue that the case sub judice does not fall within any of the three categories enumerated in *Blagge*... [but the] fallacy of this reasoning lies in its assumed premise that Mr. Justice Story was attempting to describe all of the instances in which an intent to exercise could be found. The ... basic endeavor is to ascertain the testator's intent. ...

Mary and her mother [the donee] were as close as human affection and esteem could bind them, and one searches in vain for a cause why, under these circumstances, without explanation, the mother, at the infirm age of 82 years, ... should intentionally deprive her of the only sizable inheritance involved.

Essential justice does not permit "a discernible intention of the testator" to be defeated. The quantum of proof may be supplied by logical inferences if they are sufficiently persuasive to carry the necessary conviction. We accordingly, from the whole record, conclude that [the donee] intended to and did appoint the trust fund to her daughter.

For extensive treatment of choice of law matters and powers of appointment, see Eugene Scoles & Peter Hay, Conflict of Laws §21.8 et seq. (2d ed. 1992).

Uniform Probate Code §2-608 adheres to the usual view that, absent other provision in the creating instrument, a "general residuary clause in a will, or a ... general disposition of all of the testator's property" does not express the testator's intention to exercise a power unless (i) the power is general *and* the donor has provided no gift in default of appointment or (ii) the testator's will "manifests an intention to include the property subject to the power." See also Restatement (Second) of Property: Donative Transfers §17.3.

Under contrary statutes the question becomes the inverse of that in the New Jersey case (above): Under what circumstances is a general residuary clause to be interpreted *as not exercising* the power, contrary to the statutory presumption. For a case concluding, despite such a statute, that the power was not exercised because the residuary trust under the donee's will would have violated the Rule Against Perpetuities as to the appointive assets (due to the relation-back principle) but not as to the donee's own property, see Matter of Huntington's Estate, 170 N.Y.S.2d (Surr. 1957).

What policies are reflected in these different approaches? Which approach is preferable? Do different considerations attend special rather than general powers?

Specific Reference Requirements. Common drafting practices and numerous statutes now seek to protect against inadvertent or casual exercise of powers of appointment by expressly requiring testamentary exercise to be by specific reference in the donee's will. UPC §2-704 provides that if the instrument creating the power "expressly requires that the power be exercised by a reference, an express reference, or a specific reference" to the power "or its source," the donor's presumed intention is "to prevent an inadvertent exercise of the power." Under such statutory or document provisions, questions frequently arise whether the reference must be to the particular power or whether an express reference to powers to appointment generally will suffice. See, e.g., Clinton County Natl. Bank & Trust Co. v. First Natl. Bank, 403 N.E.2d 968 (Ohio 1980) (property "I may own or have power to dispose of at my death" not specific reference). See also Motes/Henes Trust v. Motes, 761 S.W.2d 938 (Ark. 1988); Schwartz v. BayBank Merrimack Valley, 456 N.E.2d 1141 (Mass. App. 1983) (donor-imposed requirement of specific reference not satisfied by general residuary clause despite pecuniary bequests in excess of donee's assets). Obviously, the donor or statute should be clear on this point. It is also obvious that a decision to exercise a power or not must be expressed with care and precision. This means that the donee's lawyer must interview thoroughly and examine relevant documents (especially trusts of which the client is a beneficiary) to understand not only the requirements for effective exercise but also the scope (objects, etc.) of the power. Without continuing care, however, specificity and respect for the power's limitations may not always be enough.

ESTATE OF HAMILTON
593 N.Y.S.2d 372 (App. Div. 1993)

[Anita Hamilton died in 1989, 15 days after the death of her husband ("decedent"), paragraph "Fourth" of whose 1982 will (like two earlier wills) granted her power to appoint the principal of a trust fund "in such manner [as she] may by her last Will and Testament direct," the power to be "exercisable only by specific reference to said power" in her will. In default of appointment the remaining principal would pass to decedent's two daughters. Mrs. Hamilton's 1967 will stated: "By this paragraph . . . I do specifically exercise the power of appointment given to me by paragraph 'Sixth' of the Last Will and Testament of my husband dated the 26th day of August, 1966, in favor of my son ["Ricketson," decedent's stepson] or to his issue him surviving, to the extent of seven-eights of the fund over which I have the power of appointment, and I give . . . to Sue M. Ricketson, wife of my son, one-eight (1/8th) of [that] fund. . . . By these provisions, I do specifically exercise the power of appointment given to me by the Will of my said husband."]

CREW, Justice. . . . Decedent's and Hamilton's respective wills were subsequently admitted to probate. [The Surrogate's Court concluded that Hamilton did not exercise her power and that the remainder of the fund passed in default to Decedent's two daughters; Ricketson appealed.] We affirm. EPTL 10-6.1 sets forth . . . , in part, that "[i]f the donor has expressly directed that no instrument shall be effective to exercise the power unless it contains a specific reference to the power, an instrument not containing such reference does not validly exercise the power" . . . This particular provision . . . was apparently designed to allow the donor to prevent the blind exercise of the power. . . .

Here, . . . Hamilton had to make "specific reference to said power." . . . This she did not do. The only power referenced by Hamilton in her will was the power of appointment granted her under decedent's 1966 will which . . . had been revoked by decedent's subsequent execution of a new will in 1975 and again in 1982. . . . Thus, Hamilton's sole reference was to a power that had ceased to exist.

. . . [W]e cannot infer from Hamilton's exercise of the appointive power conferred under decedent's 1966 will that she similarly intended to exercise any such power existing under decedent's 1982 will. In any event, Hamilton's intent in this regard is irrelevant for decedent "made it crystal clear" that the power of appointment granted by his 1982 will was exercisable only by Hamilton's specific reference thereto in her last will and testament. . . . We similarly reject Ricketson's assertion that Hamilton's exercise of the power of appointment conferred by decedent's 1966 will "reasonably approximates" the manner in which decedent directed the power be exercised under his 1982 will. . . .

Would the result of the above case have been different if the donee's will had not referred to the donor's by date? In any event, was there doubt about the donor's purpose or the donee's intent in either of the probated wills? Would the result have been different under UPC §2-704?

2. Limits on Types of Appointments

Exclusive vs. Nonexclusive Powers. When a donee has a special power "to appoint among his children," an issue may arise whether the property may be appointed to one or more of the children to the exclusion of others. If the power granted permits the donee to exclude any of the objects of the power, the power is said to be *exclusive.* If the power is viewed as requiring that each member of the designated class receive a share, it is classified as *nonexclusive,* i.e., none may be excluded. When a power is nonexclusive, the further question arises what minimum amount will satisfy the requirements of the power.

The English courts early developed the doctrine of the "illusory" appointment, which invalidated an exercise if less than a "substantial" amount was appointed to each object of a nonexclusive power. The ensuing litigation over what qualified as "substantial" led to the doctrine's abolition by statute. Some American states have enacted statutes similar to the English act, and many American courts have also rejected the doctrine.

The scrivener's obligation to avoid these uncertainties, as appropriate to the client's objectives, seems clear. How would you respond to the donor-client who wishes "each of the [objects] to get something" under a power you are drawing?

FERRELL-FRENCH v. FERRELL
691 So. 2d 500 (Fla. 1997)

KLEIN, JUDGE. [The donor's will gave her husband a power by will to divide trust assets "among my descendants in such manner and in such unequal proportions as he shall see fit." He exercised the power and excluded a daughter, who filed suit.]

Both sides agree that this case involves a special power of appointment because the donor of the power designated a specific class, her descendants, as the objects of the power. . . . What they disagree on, however, is whether the power is exclusive, i.e., whether the donee . . . could exclude persons in the class. . . .

Although there is a dearth of authority in Florida on the question . . . , the modern trend is that unless the donor manifests a contrary intent, a special power of appointment is exclusive, allowing the donee to exercise it in favor of any of the objects to the exclusion of others. . . .

This trend developed as the result of the experience of the courts in having to deal with powers of appointment which were non-exclusive. . . . [The] "substantial but not illusory" . . . rule . . . put the burden on the donee of the power to try to figure out how little could be directed to a nonfavored member of the class. If a court later determined that amount to be illusory, the entire power of appointment would fail. . . .

The Restatement (Second) of Property §21.1 (1986) provides:

> The donee of a power of appointment in exercising the power may exclude one or more of the objects from receiving an interest in the appointive assets unless the donor specifies the share of the appointive assets from which an object may not be excluded. If the donor does not specify any such share, the power is exclusive.

As comment "a" to the Restatement (Second) explains, the primary purpose of a power of appointment is to give flexibility to meet changing conditions, and the less the donee of the power is restricted in the selection of the objects who will benefit, the greater the flexibility.

We hold that a power of appointment is exclusive, unless the donor expressly manifests a contrary intent. Applying that principle here, and finding no intent manifested by the language in the testator's will to restrict the power of appointment so that it is non-exclusive, we conclude that appellant could properly be excluded. . . .

Appointing Less Than Absolute Interests. Among the important constructional matters for the donor's lawyer to resolve in drafting a power of appointment is the question of what types of interests the donee is permitted to appoint. If the donor's instrument is silent on this question, it may have to be resolved by litigation; or at least the donee might feel constrained to appoint shares outright rather than risk invalidity of an otherwise preferred disposition.

It seems reasonably clear that the donee of any *general* power, testamentary or inter vivos, may appoint the property in any desired combination of possessory and future estates, outright or in trust, and subject to any conditions and limitations that would be valid with respect to a transfer of the donee's own property. The law governing *special* powers now appears in nearly all states to be comparable: no prohibition will be implied against such appointments, provided persons who are not objects of the power are not benefited. Not all courts have been in agreement on these matters, however. For example, Loring v. Karri-Davies, 357 N.E.2d 11 (Mass. 1976), changed the rule prospectively to allow the donee of a nongeneral power to appoint interests in trust for the objects of the power.

By the better view, the donee of a general power, even though purely testamentary, may also create other powers of appointment in exercising his power. Even here there is some uncertainty, and there is substantial disagreement as to the validity of executing a special power in this manner. Restatement (Second) of Property: Donative Transfers §19.4 provides that, unless the donor provides otherwise, the donee of even a nongeneral power can create a general power in an object of the original power.

Again, in order to remove doubt, these are matters to be clarified by the instrument creating the power. If this is not done, these are matters about which the donee will have to be cautious. See generally Halbach, The Use of Powers of Appointment in Estate Planning, 45 Iowa L. Rev. 691, 710-718 (1960). Of course, any appointment of limited interests must comply with applicable rules regulating perpetuities.

3. Failure to Appoint and Ineffective Appointments

Objects and Takers in Default. The drafting of nongeneral (particularly special) powers of appointment requires careful consideration and attention to assure that the objects of the power are described adequately and clearly. Care is also required in providing for the possibility of non-exercise or defective exercise.

A common pitfall is that of unintentionally designating the permissible appointees so narrowly as to interfere with the purpose of the donor. In studying Daniel v. Brown, infra, consider whether this may have been the root of the problem. In creating the power the client must consider various changes in circumstances that might occur thereafter. The class of objects ought not to be so described as to exclude, by oversight, the spouse or issue of a member of the primary class of objects who dies after the power comes into being. A needy son-in-law or daughter-in-law or a parentless grandchild is a natural object of a settlor's bounty and should not unintentionally be excluded by conferring upon the donee a narrow special power to appoint only "to her children." This is the kind of power a client may initially suggest, never having contemplated the contingencies to which the lawyer should direct attention.

Numerous questions may arise in connection with the creation and exercise of powers of appointment, particularly the tax-popular non-general power. Differing views among the courts of various states and the likelihood of relevant contacts with several states further complicate these problems with choice-of-law questions. Harrison F. Durand & Charles L. Herterich, Conflict of Laws and the Exercise of Powers of Appointment, 42 Cornell L.Q. 185 (1957). Since most of these matters are normally controlled by the donor's intention, they should be recognized in advance and eliminated by provision in the will or trust instrument creating the power.

PROBLEM

11-AA. *W* held a power under her husband's testamentary trust to appoint the remainder by will "to such of [the husband's] relatives as she may select." No disposition in default of appointment was specified. On her death, *W*'s will appointed "the corpus of the trust under my late husband's will in equal shares to his brother *B*, his uncle *U*, his fourth cousin *C*, and to *A*, the adopted daughter of his late sister, *S*." *W* left the residue of her own estate to her mother, *M*. By the time of *W*'s death, both *B* and *U* were dead, the latter leaving a widow, two children, and a will. *B* left no spouse, issue, or will. *C* and *A* are alive and anxious to receive shares of the trust estate, as are two remaining sisters — now the nearest surviving relatives of the settlor, who was very fond of these sisters even though *W* was not. What arguments would each claimant advance? Who would you expect to prevail? Why?

DANIEL v. BROWN
159 S.E. 209 (Va. 1931)

[Joseph S. Jackson devised property to his wife, Jane, for life, with a testamentary power to appoint to Joseph's nieces and nephews. She appointed to three of his nieces and nephews and to the issue of any of the three who may predecease her, as all three did. Only one of them had a child, Josephine, who survived Jane.]

HUDGINS, J. . . . This controversy is between the [remaining] nieces and nephews of Joseph S. Jackson and the grandniece, Josephine J. Brown. [The trial judge decreed that Josephine took one-third of the property as issue of one of Jane's appointees, aided by Va. Code §§5226 and 5238; that the devises to the other appointees failed by reason of their deaths in Jane's lifetime; and that as to this two-thirds interest Joseph S. Jackson died intestate.]

It is admitted that the fourth clause of the will of Jane C. Jackson is invalid because she was limited in her appointment to the nieces and nephews of her husband, and this clause attempts to leave the property to the issue of the nieces and nephews named by her . . . , in the event that any of them should predecease her.

The appellee contends, however, and the trial court so held, that although the donee of the power was restricted in her selection to the nieces and nephews of her husband, yet the statute enabled her to do indirectly what she could not do directly, i.e., select from the class deceased members to be the beneficiaries, and by the provisions of sections 5226 and 5238 the issue of such deceased parties would be entitled to the property.

Section 5226, among other things, provides that an appointment by will, or by a writing in the nature of a will, in the exercise of a power, is a will. . . .

Section 5238 provides that if a devisee or legatee dies before the testator, leaving issue who survive the testator, such issue shall take the estate devised or bequeathed as the devisee or legatee would have done if they had survived the testator, "unless a different disposition thereof be made, or required, by the will."

If the property disposed of, or attempted to be disposed of, by the third clause of the will of Jane C. Jackson was her own and she had not made the provision set forth in the fourth clause, section 5238 would have prevented the lapse of that devise in so far as the parties named left issue. Without the statute, the fourth clause of her will would have accomplished the same result. But the property here did not belong to Jane C. Jackson; she was given a specified power to transfer this property in a specific manner, i.e., by will, to a certain class, i.e., the nieces and nephews of her husband. The two wills must be construed together. The sole authority that Jane C. Jackson had to dispose of this property was derived from the third clause of her husband's will, wherein she was expressly authorized to leave it to "such of my nieces and nephews . . . as she may choose."

A stream can rise no higher than its source, and the source of the authority here denies to Jane C. Jackson the power to leave this property to anyone except the nieces and nephews of her husband. Clearly, Joseph S. Jackson provided a different disposition than to leave his property to the issue of his nieces and nephews; by the very requirements of his will grandnieces and grandnephews were eliminated. If the power had been general in the donee to select the objects of the bounty and the donee of the power had exercised her discretion and the devisees named by her had died prior to her death, then section 5238 would have prevented the lapse of such devises in favor of the issue. This was the holding in the case of Thompson v. Pew, 214 Mass. 520, 102 N.E. 122.

This section does not enlarge the power of appointment; the limitations of such power are fixed by the instrument creating it. Hence the trial court was in error in holding that Josephine J. Brown, a grandniece, was entitled to one-third of the real estate, as issue of her father.

There being no valid exercise of the power, the court is confronted with two possible courses of action. One is to hold that there was no valid devise of this land after the life estate, and in the absence of a residuary clause it would pass under the statute of descent to the heirs at law, in which event the property would have to be divided per stirpes, as there were a brother, sister and the children of a deceased sister living at the time of the testator's death. Such is not the testamentary disposition of his property which the testator evidently had in mind.

The other course is to hold that the will disposes of all the property owned by the testator at the time of his death. When a party executes a will the presumption is reasonable and natural that such party intends to dispose of his entire estate.

. . . No provision was made in case there was a failure to exercise the power. The court is unable to say which of the nephews and nieces the donee of the power would have selected, and if the devise of the remainder should fail it must fail for this reason. For aid in the solution of this problem we turn to the authorities. . . .

[I]t has been uniformly held in Virginia that where the language of the will confers a non-exclusive power of disposal among a certain class, the members of that class take a vested remainder, or, as it is sometimes put, if the gift is in express terms to the class, with power in another to determine the proportion or share that each member of the class shall take, then there is a vested remainder in all members of the class. . . .

[I]f the donee refuses or neglects to execute the power, the courts have held that the power is coupled with a trust, or is a power which implies a trust, for the benefit of other parties. Equity will not allow a trust to fail for want of a trustee, or be defeated by the refusal or neglect of the trustee to execute the power. Of course, if it be a mere naked power, purely discretionary with the donee, equity will not compel or control his discretion or exercise it in his place. These principles are well established. The trouble arises in determining when a power is coupled with a trust or when it is purely discretionary with the trustee.

Lord Elden said in Brown v. Higgs, 8 Ves. 574, that if the power be one which it is the duty of the party to execute, made his duty by the terms of the will, and his interest is extensive enough to enable him to discharge it, he is the trustee for the exercise of the power and does not have discretion whether he will exercise it or not, and if he fails the courts will not disappoint the interests of those for whose benefit he is called upon to exercise it. Lord Hardwicke, in Godolphin v. Godolphin, 1 Ves. (Sr.) 23, said that such powers ought to be called trusts rather than powers. When the form of the gift is such that it can be construed as a trust the power becomes imperative and must be executed. . . .

Perry, in his admirable work on Trusts and Trustees (7th ed.), Vol. 1, section 250, quoting from Lord Cottenham, in Burrough v. Philcox, 5 My. & Cr. 72, states the general rule thus:

> "When there appears a general intention in favor of a class, and a particular intention in favor of individuals of a class to be selected by another person, and the particular intention fails from that selection not being made, the court will carry into effect the general intention in favor of the class. When such an intention appears, the case arises, as stated by Lord Eldon in Brown v. Higgs, of the power being so given as to make it the duty of the donee to execute it; and, in such case, the court will not permit the objects of the power to suffer by the negligence or conduct of the donee, but fastens upon the property a trust for their benefit."

Jarman on Wills, 549, states that under such circumstances the gift to the class is implied, and that the testator could not have intended the objects of the power to be disappointed of his bounty by the failure of the donee to exercise such power in their favor.

Applying the general principle to the facts in the instant case, the court will not permit the devise of the remainder to fail because of its inability to say which members of the class the donee of the power would have selected. The will gives it no guide by which it can distinguish or prefer one member of the class over another. Under such circumstances, equity will decree an equal distribution of the property among all of the nephews and nieces.

This case presents another point which has given the court some difficulty; that is, when does the gift take effect, at the death of the testator or at the death of the donee of the power? Between the death of the testator, Joseph S. Jackson, and the death of the donee, Jane C. Jackson, several of the nieces and nephews died, one leaving issue. Whether or not any nephews or nieces were born during that time does not appear. The donee could execute this power only by will. She was limited in her selection to the members of a certain class who were to take only at her death. If all the objects of the power had died in the lifetime of the donee there could have been no valid appointment by the donee. Inasmuch, therefore, as the donee was confined in her appointment by the will to the nieces and nephews living at the time the appointment should take effect, the court is likewise so confined. Perry on Trusts and Trustees, Vol. 1, section 258, states "that when it appears that the donee is to have his whole life to make the selection or distribution, or if the donee is to have the use of the fund for his life, then the court will distribute it to the parties entitled living at the death of the donee," and cites a great number of English cases supporting the text. To the same effect, see Minor on Real Property, section 1330, and Jarman on Wills, 551.

It is admitted that the donee could not select grandnieces and grandnephews under the power given her. It would be inconsistent to hold that they could take in default of appointment when no appointment could be made to them direct. Suppose that the property had been given to Jane C. Jackson for life and at her death "with power in *B* to give to such of my nieces and nephews and in such proportions as *B* may choose." Is there any question of the fact that in such a case *B*, if living at the death of Jane C. Jackson, would have been confined in his selection to the nieces and nephews living at that time? Does it make any difference that the power is given the owner of the life estate? We think not. It follows that the court in enforcing the trust will be confined to the nieces and nephews living at the death of Jane C. Jackson.

Reversed.

———————————

The court speaks both of an implied gift in default of appointment and of what it calls (in somewhat fictional and contradictory terms) a power held in trust. Do these two concepts necessarily suggest the same result? If not, with which one was the court's holding more consistent? Restatement (Third) of Trusts §46, Comment *c* (Tent. Draft approved

1999) rejects the power-in-trust concept and adopts the concept of implied gift in default of appointment. In imposing a requirement that an appointee must survive to the effective date of the appointment (contrast Chapter 10 section B.2.c, but see section C.1 supra), UPC §2-605 and Restatement (Second) of Property: Donative Transfers §18.6 apply antilapse provisions even when the substitute takers are omitted from the expressed class of objects of a nongeneral power. Without such broad antilapse provisions, is the requirement that objects or takers in default (expressed or implied) survive the donee sound (cf. section C.2 supra) or desirable?

LEWIS M. SIMES & ALLAN F. SMITH, THE LAW OF FUTURE INTERESTS
(2d ed. 1956)

§1033. *State of Authorities on Remedies for Non-Execution of Special Powers.* To what extent is the power in trust theory sustained by the decisions? . . . [T]he language of the court . . . is not always such as to indicate undeniably that the court is imposing a trust, nor is the term "constructive trust" used. Most of the cases leave us somewhat in doubt as to the precise theory on which the property is being distributed in lieu of an appointment. Quite often the language is of such a character as to make it impossible to tell whether the court is talking about a gift by implication or a trust. . . .

. . . In some, the language is that of implied gift; in some, that of powers in trust; and, in others, the two ideas are confused. . . .

It is believed that so far no reported case, either American or English, has been decided which tests absolutely the question whether the court is applying a trust theory or an implied gift theory. . . .

Whether the power in trust theory or the gift in default theory is accepted, two final observations as to the state of the law should be made. First, the rule that the objects of a special power take equally when there is no express gift in default and no appointment has been made, applies whether the power is exclusive or non-exclusive.

Second, in one situation, involving the failure to exercise a power such as is here described as a power in trust, the class of objects who take is narrower than that to which the donee might have made an appointment. Suppose A devises the residue of his estate to T on trust to pay the income to B for his life and then to transfer the trust estate to such of B's relations as he shall appoint by deed or will. This is construed to mean that B has a power to appoint to any person of his blood and not merely to heirs or next of kin. For he must execute the instrument of appointment in his lifetime, even though it is a will, and he cannot know at that time who will be his heirs or next of kin. But if he dies without exercising the power, it is held that the property will be distributed equally to those of his blood who would take on his death intestate. This is a sensible solution, for, obviously, it would be impracticable for the court to distribute this property to all persons of the blood of B. Moreover, the solution arrived at by the courts probably approximates more nearly what the donor would have desired than any other distribution.

See also Loring v. Marshall, 485 N.E.2d 1315 (Mass. 1985), implying a gift in default of appointment to the objects of a special power, and citing Restatement (Second) of Property: Donative Transfers §24.2, which states:

> To the extent the donor of a non-general power has not specified in the instrument creating the power who is to take unappointed property, the unappointed property passes
> (1) To the objects of the power (including those who are substituted objects under an antilapse statute) living at the time of the expiration of the power as if they had been specified in the instrument creating the power to take unappointed property, if —
>   (a) The objects are a defined limited class and
>   (b) The donor has not manifested an intent that the objects shall receive the appointive property only so far as the donee elects to appoint it to them; or
> (2) To the donor or the donor's estate, if subsection (1) is not applicable.

Doctrines of Capture and Selective Allocation. The doctrines of "capture" and "marshalling" (selective allocation of appointive and donee-owned assets) traditionally have been applied only to general powers of appointment. As you read on, consider whether, in appropriate (even if rare) circumstances, there are any policy or theoretical obstacles to the application of appropriately adapted versions of these doctrines to special and other nongeneral powers, such as the common tax-motivated power to appoint to "any persons or entities except the donee, her estate or the creditors of either."

PROBLEM

11-BB.   *H*'s first wife, *W*, died fifteen years ago and left part of her estate to her children and the rest in a marital deduction trust for *H* for life, with the principal remaining at his death to go "to such persons or entities, without limitation, as *H* may appoint by his will and in default of appointment to *C* Charity." *H* has just died; his will provides: "All property I own or over which I have power of appointment I leave as follows: one-half to my [second] spouse, *S;* the other half [in trust for] *S* for life, and at her death to such of my issue as *S* may appoint by will." *S,* however, predeceased *H;* she was childless. *H*'s closest surviving relatives are the children of his marriage to *W;* they claim the assets owned by *H* as intestate property and "are sure Dad would have wanted us to have" the appointive property as well. Do they have a case that is worth your time and their money? Explain. (Would their case be different if they were children of *H* and *S?* If the power of appointment intended for *S* had been general? If there had been an expressed gift in default to *H*'s issue?) How would the claimant's right be affected (in each situation) if *H*'s debts exceeded his individual assets?

LEWIS M. SIMES, FUTURE INTERESTS
(2d ed. 1966)

§69.   *Implied Execution Where Express Appointment Fails — Doctrine of Capture.* . . . When the express exercise of a power of appointment is void or ineffective, the appointed property ordinarily goes to the takers in default exactly as if there had been no attempt to exercise the power. . . .

Sometimes, however, the language of the instrument containing the ineffective appointment has been construed to contain an implied appointment in the alternative to the donee's estate. This has been referred to as the doctrine of capture. This doctrine is in no sense a legal remedy for the failure of an appointment. The instrument is construed as if it said: "I make an express appointment as here indicated, but, in any event, whether that is valid or not, I appoint the property to my own estate."

Suppose the language of execution of a general power consists in a so-called blending provision. For example, A, having a general power to appoint by will, prefaces the dispositive portions of his will with the following clause: "I hereby give, devise and bequeath all property which I own at the time of my death, or in which I have any interest, or over which I have any power of appointment, as follows." Then follow general and residuary devises of property without any further reference to any power of appointment. Suppose, also, one or more of these dispositive provisions fail, by reason of lapse or because of some rule of law such as the rule against perpetuities. The failure of such provisions will not cause the property to pass to the taker in default. For the donee has exercised the power in favor of his own estate. Hence, whether the specific dispositive provisions can take effect or not, it is implied that the donee intended to appoint the property to his own estate, so that it can pass to his heirs or next of kin in the absence of an effective provision in the will to the contrary, or can be used to pay his debts and the costs of administration.

Suppose there is no general blending provision in the donee's will, but the donee specifically exercises a general power by appointing the property to a trustee upon trusts which fail by reason of lapse, the Rule Against Perpetuities or some other rule of law. Is there a resulting trust to the donee's estate, or should the property go to the taker in default? In Talbot v. Riggs [287 Mass. 144, 191 N.E. 360 (1934)], testator, having a general power to appoint by will, attempted to exercise it by an express appointment in his will to a trustee "in trust to use the income thereof for the benefit and assistance of any legitimate descendant of my parents . . . who shall, for the time being, need the same for support, education or comfort, as long as any such descendant shall continue to be," and on failure of all such descendants, to a designated charity. The court held that the dispositions for descendants and for charity were void under the Rule Against Perpetuities, and that the property should be turned over to the administrator of the estate of the donee as property of his estate. The view of the court was that the appointment to a trustee took the property away from the heirs and next of kin of the donor for all purposes, even though all beneficial interests under the trust failed. In other words, it was held that the donee made an implied appointment to his own estate. . . .

PROBLEMS

11-CC.   *L* was the life beneficiary of a trust with remainder "to whomever *L* shall appoint by will." *L*'s will provided: "I devise $150,000 to my friend, *F*, and the rest of my property, including any property over which I have a power of appointment, to my friend, *G*." In addition to the appointive property, worth $250,000, *A*'s own assets are worth $100,000, and the debts and expenses of his estate amount to $50,000. How should the $350,000 be applied or distributed?

11-DD.   The trust is the same as above except that the remainder is to go "to such of *L*'s issue as *L* shall appoint by will, in default of appointment to *C* Church." *L* devised all of his property, "including any property over which I have a power of appointment, in equal one-third shares, to my son, *S*, my daughter, *D*, and my friend, *F*." In addition to the appointive property, worth $500,000, *L* has a net personal estate of $100,000. How should the $600,000 be distributed?

LEWIS M. SIMES, FUTURE INTERESTS
(2d ed. 1966)

§70. *Marshalling Owned and Appointed Property.* . . . The donee of a general power may exercise it by a blending clause in his will, so that the property is appointed to his estate generally. For example, he may provide, "I hereby give, devise and bequeath all my property and all property over which I have any power of appointment as follows." How is the appointed property allocated to the various dispositive provisions of the will and to creditors? Ordinarily we assume that owned property is to be used to pay creditors and costs of administration, and that the appointed property is allocated ratably with the remainder of the owned property to the various dispositions of the will. In some instances, however, a particular dispositive provision of the will may be void as to appointed property, but valid as to owned property. Thus, suppose *A* devises securities worth $100,000 in trust to pay the income to *B* for life and then to distribute the estate to such persons as *B* shall appoint by will. *B* executes a will in which he exercises the power in favor of his entire estate by such a blending clause as follows: "I give the residue of my estate to such of *C*'s children as survive him." *C* was unborn at the time the power was created and, therefore, the residuary clause is void under the Rule Against Perpetuities to the extent that it purports to dispose of appointed property, but as to owned property it is valid. Assuming that the claims of *B*'s creditors and the costs of administration amount to $50,000, and that his will contains general legacies in the amount of $50,000, the court will allocate the appointed property to creditors, costs of administration and general legacies. Thus, only owned property will fall into the residuary trust, and the appointment will be valid. . . .

For cases in which the court selectively allocated owned and appointed assets, see Dollar Savings & Trust Co. v. First Natl. Bank, 285 N.E.2d 768 (Ohio 1972); Estate of Burnham, 347 N.Y.S.2d 995 (Surr. Ct. 1973); In re Wall's Trust, 177 N.Y.S.2d 284 (Sup. Ct. 1958). The principle of selective allocation is stated in Restatement (Second) of Property: Donative Transfers §§22.1 and 22.2.

12

Creation of Trusts

Most present-day trusts are testamentary trusts created by will. Inter vivos or living trusts are also quite common, usually being created by a transfer from the settlor during lifetime to another person or corporation as trustee. Sometimes the settlor may create a trust by procuring a transfer from a third party to the trustee or by the exercise of a power of appointment. In each of these cases it can be seen that the trust comes about as the result of some kind of *transfer,* whether by will, deed, or some other method by which a transfer of the property can be effectuated.

All trusts are not created by transfer, at least not in the normal sense of that word. A trust of specific property can be created by a present declaration of trust by the owner of that property. Thus, for example, "one may create a trust in securities standing on one's name by a simple declaration to that effect, without the necessity of any further act of transfer or delivery." Bourgeois v. Hurley, 392 N.E.2d 1061, 1065 (Mass. App. 1980). To one who already owns the property, an act of transfer would often seem unnecessary or even "unnatural" and is apparently viewed as an inappropriate requirement for such cases. The owner-settlor's manifestation of *present* intention to create a trust therefore suffices, and the normal transfer requirement is excused. Or, we might say, there *is* a "transfer" of the property, from the owner as an *individual* to the owner as *trustee* (or we might see it as a transfer of *equitable* title from the settlor to the beneficiaries), with simply the requirement of "delivery" being excused as an unwarranted formality under the circumstances. Regardless of how creation of a trust by declaration is conceptualized, the declaration normally must satisfy any formal requirements for the transfer of an interest in the particular property; thus, for example, if land is involved the local statute of frauds requirement of a writing would apply to the declaration; but such a requirement would typically not apply to a declaration creating a trust of personal property. The law does, however, insist strictly on a manifestation of present intent, so that an owner's gratuitous promise or expression of future intention will not suffice. It seems particularly worth noting here (though also true of other methods of creating trusts) that a trust can be created without notice to or acceptance by any beneficiary or trustee.

Just as valid and enforceable nontrust rights can be created by contract, enforceable rights may be created in intended trust beneficiaries by a person's *binding* promise to establish a trust, either by transfer or declaration. Here, the requirements of contract law must be met. Again, however, the trust concepts may not be clear. We might say that the promissory right is a property interest (a chose in action) presently held in trust; or we might view the situation as one in which there is no trust now but merely an enforceable obligation of the promissor to make a transfer in the future, with the trust coming into being at that later time. Analogous uncertainties of concept arise in connection with the creation of life insurance trusts, especially if (as usual) the policies are not actually assigned to the trustee.

Among the major problems relating to the creation of inter vivos trusts by transfer are questions concerning the effectiveness of the alleged transfer. These are problems of compliance with the formalities required for impressing the essential elements of the trust on the transferred property and problems of whether the creation of a given trust is subject to the formal requirements and substantive restrictions governing inter vivos transfer or to those applicable to testamentary dispositions.

Because an effective transfer (at least of equitable interests) is required to create a trust, a preliminary requirement is that the settlor have capacity to make a valid transfer. The capacity to create a trust is generally the same as the capacity required to make a similar transfer of the property free of trust. Despite careless dicta in many cases, the law is finally beginning to clarify and refine rules concerning the standards of capacity for creating, amending, and revoking inter vivos trusts. Reflecting the widespread use of revocable trusts as will substitutes, and the similarity of the settlor's rights and interests in the property to those of a living testator, the appropriate test for the validity of such a living trust is the capacity to make a will (see Chapter 3). See Restatement (Third) of Trusts §11 (2) (Tent. Draft approved 1996). See also Uniform Trust Code §601 (draft, Feb. 2000). For irrevocable inter vivos trusts, a *gift* standard (adding to the will standard the ability to understand the transfer's impact on the future financial security of the settlor and dependents) is appropriate for trusts that are donative, while a *contract* standard is appropriate for nondonative dispositions, such as trusts created incident to a divorce or commercial transaction. See Restatement, supra §11 (3) and cmt. *c*. A related issue, whether a personal fiduciary (e.g., an agent acting under an express provision of a durable power of attorney or a conservator exercising substituted judgment with court approval) may engage in estate planning on behalf of a legally incapacitated person, was considered in Chapter 3, section G.2. The Restatement (supra, §11 (5) and cmt. *f*) recognizes this authority to establish, modify, or revoke trusts except as prohibited by statute.

A. *Trusts Created by Will*

When a testator intends to transfer property by will to another person or to a corporation to be held in trust, there must be compliance with the applicable wills act. The intended express trust fails if the trust intent and the essential terms of the trust are not manifested by means satisfying the statutory requirements. This is so even though the property is effectively transferred by a valid will. Two questions basically are presented: what constitutes sufficient compliance with the requirements of the wills acts, and what happens when an intended trust fails to satisfy these requirements?

The appropriate practice, of course, is for the will itself clearly to evidence the trust intention and the other terms needed to create the trust: ordinarily the trustee, the trust property, the beneficiaries, and — even if inferred from the beneficiaries' interests — the trust purposes. See Restatement (Third) of Trusts §17(2). Short of that, an apparent failure in expression should not be fatal if the will satisfies the requirements of the doctrine of incorporation by reference or the doctrine of facts of independent significance. Illustrative of the latter is Moss v. Axford, supra page 361 (for "the person who has given me the best care in my declining years"). Some drafters may not be so skillful — or lucky.

PROBLEM

12-A. *A*'s will provided for certain legacies and left "the residue of my estate to my executor to pay the sums in her hands in her sole discretion to the persons I have previously indicated to her. I nominate *B* as my executor." *B*, who is also the attorney who drew the will, testified that, before calling in two witnesses and having the will executed, she had received oral instructions from *A* relating to the disposition of the residue. What result? Should the court allow *B* to testify to the nature of her instructions? See In re Liginger's Estate, 14 Wis. 2d 577, 111 N.W.2d 407 (1961). If the heirs of *A* succeed in obtaining the residuary property by way of resulting trust, is *B* liable to the intended beneficiaries for her handling of this matter? See Ogle v. Fuitan, 112 Ill. App. 3d 1048, 445 N.E.2d 1344 (1983); Committee on Professional Ethics v. Behnke, 276 N.W.2d 838 (Iowa 1979), *appeal dismissed*, 444 U.S. 805 (1979).

In Wagner v. Clauson, 399 Ill. 403, 78 N.E.2d 203 (1948), the testatrix left the residue of her estate "to Katherine Clauson, as trustee, for the purpose of converting into cash and making distribution thereof in accordance with a memorandum of instructions prepared by me and delivered to her . . . so that only Katherine Clauson and the distributee shall know of its disposition.'' At the death of the testatrix a sealed envelope and the will were found together in a safe-deposit box. The envelope contained an unattested letter written by the testatrix and bearing a date several days later than the date the will was executed. Evidence disclosed that Clauson had placed both the will and the envelope in the safe-deposit box at the request of the testatrix but knew nothing of the contents of the envelope until after probate of the will. The intended trust was held invalid because the requirements for incorporation by reference were not met. (See Chapter 5.) The court held that, the intended express trust failing, there was a resulting trust for the heirs of the testatrix because it was apparent from the will that Clauson was not to take beneficially but as trustee.

How could the testatrix in Wagner v. Clauson have accomplished the purpose of secrecy expressed in her will? Would the result have been different if Clauson had promised to hold the property for the intended purpose?

Cases are abundant in which a bequest or devise, absolute on its face, is made to someone who has either expressly or impliedly agreed to administer the property for a specific purpose or to transfer it inter vivos or by will to another person. This is the so-called secret trust. Frequently the promise of the legatee or devisee is oral. The disposition may even be induced by the acquiescence implied from the legatee's silence when informed of the intended purpose of the bequest. What is the result of such cases? A few courts have taken the position that, unless actual fraud, duress, undue influence, or confidential relationship is shown, the recipient of an absolute bequest or devise takes the property free of obligation. The clear weight of authority, however, is represented by the statement in Olsen v. First National Bank, 76 S.D. 605, 611, 83 N.W.2d 842, 846 (1957):

> The general proposition is well settled that where a testator devises his property in reliance upon an agreement or understanding with a devisee or legatee that the latter hold it in trust, the devisee or legatee holds the property upon a constructive trust for the person for whom he agreed to hold it. Restatement, Trusts, §55; see also Annotations in 66 A.L.R. 156 and 155 A.L.R. 106. The principle rests on the basis that though the acquiring of the property was not wrongful the testator having relied on the agreements and made a disposition of his property accordingly the devisee or legatee would be unjustly enriched if he were permitted to retain the property. It is immaterial whether the agreement was made at the time of or after execution of the will. An agreement which induces the testator to refrain from revoking his will is as effective as an agreement which induced him to make a will. See comments, Restatement, Trusts, §55 and Restatement, Restitution, §186. The trust in other words arises not from the will, but from operation of equities. The

will takes effect as written and proved, but to prevent injustice the court imposes a constructive trust to compel the devisee or legatee to apply the property obtained in accordance with his promise and good conscience.

See generally G.G. Bogert & G.T. Bogert, Trusts and Trustees §§498-501 (rev. 2d ed. 1977); IA W. Fratcher, Scott on Trusts §§55.1-55.5 (4th ed. 1987); Levine and Holton, Enforcement of Secret and Semi-Secret Trusts, 5 Probate L.J. 7 (1985). Rarely is the rationale of this rule thoroughly discussed in the cases. Most courts consider the problem one of the wills acts, but some opinions treat the problem as one of contract law involving the statute of frauds. Which is it, or is it both? Should it matter whether the subject matter is land? Why, if the legatee is not to be unjustly enriched, is it not preferable to restore the property to the testator's estate? Compare the secret trust situation with the following often cited case involving what might be called a "semi-secret trust."

RESTATEMENT (THIRD) OF TRUSTS
(Tent. Draft approved 1996)

§18. *Secret Trusts*

(1) Where a testator devises or bequeaths property to a person in reliance on the devisee's or legatee's expressed or implied agreement to hold the property upon a particular trust, no express trust is created, but the devisee or legatee holds the property upon a constructive trust for the agreed purposes and persons. . . .

OLLIFFE v. WELLS
130 Mass. 221 (1881)

[Bill in equity by the heirs of Ellen Donovan, whose duly probated will left the residue of her estate "to the Rev. Eleazer M.P. Wells . . . to distribute the same in such manner as in his discretion shall appear best to carry out the wishes which I have expressed to him or may express to him." The bill sought distribution of the residue to the heirs, alleging that the bequest to Wells had failed. The defendant Wells, who had been appointed executor, answered, and all parties stipulated, that the testatrix had, before and after executing her will, expressed her intention and directed that Wells dispose of the residue for charitable purposes benefiting the aged, poor, and infirm. The answer also stated that Wells had agreed and desired to carry out these directions, but he died while the case was pending.]

GRAY, C.J.

Upon the face of this will the residuary bequest to the defendant gives him no beneficial interest. It expressly requires him to distribute all the property bequeathed to him, giving him no discretion upon the question whether he shall or shall not distribute it, or shall or shall not carry out the intentions of the testatrix, but allowing him a discretionary authority as to the manner only in which the property shall be distributed pursuant to her intentions. The will declares a trust too indefinite to be carried out, and the next of kin of the testatrix must take by way of resulting trust, unless the facts agreed show such a trust for the benefit of others as the court can execute. Nichols v. Allen, [130 Mass.] 211. . . .

It has been held in England and in other States, although the question has never arisen in this Commonwealth, that, if a person procures an absolute devise or bequest to himself by orally promising the testator that he will convey the property to or hold it for the benefit of third persons, and afterward refuses to perform his promise, a trust arises out of the confidence reposed in him by the testator and of his own fraud, which a court of equity, upon clear and satisfactory proof of the facts, will enforce against him at the suit of such third persons.

Upon like grounds, it has been held in England that, if a testator devises or bequeaths property to his executors upon trusts not defined in the will, but which, as he states in the will, he has communicated to them before its execution, such trusts, if for lawful purposes, may be proved by the admission of the executors, or by oral evidence, and enforced against them [and also] against the heirs or next of kin of the testator. . . . But these cases appear to us to have overlooked or disregarded a fundamental distinction.

Where a trust not declared in the will is established by a court of chancery against the devisee, it is by reason of the obligation resting upon the conscience of the devisee, and not as a valid testamentary disposition by the deceased. . . . Where the bequest is outright upon its face, the setting up of a trust, while it diminishes the right of the devisee, does not impair any right of the heirs or next of kin, in any aspect of the case; for if the trust were not set up, the whole property would go to the devisee by force of the devise; if the trust set up is a lawful one, it enures to the benefit of the cestuis que trust; and if the trust set up is unlawful, the heirs or next of kin take by way of resulting trust. . . .

Where the bequest is declared upon its face to be upon such trusts as the testator has otherwise signified to the devisee, it is equally clear that the devisee takes no beneficial interest; and, as between him and the beneficiaries intended, there is as much ground for establishing the trust as if the bequest to him were absolute on its face. But as between the devisee and the heirs or next of kin, the case stands differently. They are not excluded by the will itself. The will upon its face showing that the devisee takes the legal title only and not the beneficial interest, and the trust not being sufficiently defined by the will to take effect, the equitable interest goes, by way of resulting trust, to the heirs or next of kin, as property of the deceased, not disposed of by his will. . . . They cannot be deprived of that equitable interest, which accrues to them directly from the deceased, by any conduct of the devisee; nor by any intention of the deceased, unless signified in those forms which the law makes essential to every testamentary disposition. A trust not sufficiently declared on the face of the will cannot therefore be set up by extrinsic evidence to defeat the rights of the heirs at law or next of kin. . . .

Decree for the plaintiffs.

Where secret trusts are given effect by constructive trust, the trust is generally not considered testamentary, and it comes about through intervention of equity, not via probate. The fact that secret trusts generally escape the purely formal restrictions applicable to trusts created by will, however, does not mean that these trusts can also be used to escape substantive restrictions on testamentary freedom, such as limitations on charitable giving. See IA W. Fratcher, Scott on Trusts §55.6 (4th ed. 1987).

B. Inter Vivos Trusts

1. The Requirement of a Present Transfer or Declaration

Except in the case of a present declaration of trust or a binding promise made to a person as trustee, the creation of a trust requires a transfer. The trust and the equitable interests thereunder are created by a transfer, just as the rights of donees, legatees, and devisees are the result of a transfer either by inter vivos gift or by will. The problems of transfer in the creation of trusts are the same as in the transfers free of trust.

Essentially, the *transfer* requirement in testamentary trusts poses no difficulties other than those that relate to the validity of the will itself. If the will is valid, the required transfer will take place when the settlor dies.

The typical living trust situation, in which *A* transfers to *B* in trust for the designated beneficiaries, requires a *present transfer*. Clearly a mere promise by *A* to create a trust does not give rise to a trust unless the promise is enforceable. On the other hand, if a completed transfer in trust has been made in a manner sufficient to transfer like property free of trust, the result is enforceable without further consideration. The interests are created by gift in such cases. The typical inter vivos trust is the product of a donative transfer for the benefit of the transferor or family members. Consequently, if such a trust is to be established, a completed transfer must be shown. Present doctrine in this area is discussed and criticized in Love, Imperfect Gifts as Declarations of Trust: An Unapologetic Anomaly, 67 Ky. L. Rev. 309 (1979).

A declaration of trust is also enforceable even though gratuitous. Again, however, the declaration must be intended to be presently effective. It cannot be a mere unenforceable promise to hold in trust.

PROBLEMS

12-B.   *O,* the owner of a bond, orally expressed her intention to transfer it to *T* in trust for *L* for life, remainder to *R,* but attempted no delivery of the bond. Has a trust been created? See Restatement (Third) of Trusts §16, cmt. *b,* illus. 1. Assume, instead, that *O* executed a writing purporting to transfer the bond to *T* as trustee for *L* for life, remainder to *R,* and later handed the deed to his stockbroker *S,* asking her to act as his agent to make delivery to *T. O* thereafter died in an automobile accident before *S* has opportunity to make delivery to *T.* Has a trust been created? If not, do *L* and *R* have any remedy? Cf. Restatement, supra, cmt. *c,* illus. 7.

12-C.   *O* tells his niece, *N,* that he wants her to have a specified bond that he owns when she graduates from college next month. *O* sets the bond aside in his desk but dies before *N*'s graduation. The evidence regarding *O*'s actual statement to *N* is conflicting: one witness thinks *O* said, "I have decided to give you this bond when you graduate this month"; but another reports that *O* said, "I am holding this bond for you, to be turned over to you on your graduation next month." Does it matter whose version is believed? If the evidence of *O*'s intent is marginal, which interpretation should the law prefer? See Restatement, supra, §16(2) and id., cmt. *d* and illus. 9.

12-D.   *A* executed a deed of Blackacre to *T* as trustee for *B* for life, remainder to *R.* Before the deed was delivered, *T* died. *A* then talked to *X* about becoming trustee and gave *X* a photocopy of the deed that had been intended for *T. X* later wrote *A* that she would act as trustee. *A* wrote back immediately stating that he was having the deed redrawn with the same terms; *A* enclosed his personal promissory note for $25,000 payable on demand to *X* or order, stating in the letter that he also wanted the trust to start out with some cash. Nothing further was done by either *A* or *X* until *A*'s death three weeks later. Copies of this correspondence, along with a deed to *X* in terms identical to the deed to *T*, are found in a folder in *A*'s desk. On the front of the folder is written "My trust for *B* and *R*." Is there a trust? Would a trust be created if the deed to *X* had been executed and mailed by *A* but received by *X* after *A*'s death? In this latter situation, would it matter if *X* promptly renounced and declined to act as trustee? See generally Restatement (Third) of Trusts §16.

Ex parte PYE
18 Ves. Jr. 140 (Ch. 1811)

[Petitioner Pye was administrator d.b.n. of the estate of the testator, William Mowbray, who had by letter authorized Christopher Dubost in Paris to purchase in France an annuity for the benefit of testator's mistress, Marie. This Dubost did, but because Marie was married and deranged, the annuity was purchased in the testator's name; therefore, the testator sent Dubost a power of attorney authorizing him to transfer the annuity to Marie. The testator died in June 1809, but Dubost did not learn of the death until November 1809 and in the meantime exercised the power of attorney to transfer the annuity to Marie. Pursuant to procedures for ascertaining foreign law, a Master was appointed, and he reported, inter alia, that by French law, the exercise of a power of attorney in ignorance of the principal's death is valid.]

The first petition prayed that so much of the Report as certifies the French annuity to be no part of the testator's personal estate may be set aside; and that it may be declared, that the annuity is part of his personal estate. . . . [The following is argued] in support of the first Petition. The French annuity being purchased in the testator's name, and no third person interposed as a trustee, the interest could not be transferred from him without certain acts, which were not done at the time of his death. It was therefore competent to him during his life to change his purpose, and to make some other provision for this lady by funds in this country; conceiving perhaps, that she might return here. . . .

The other question involves . . . whether the power of attorney amounts here to a declaration of trust? It is clear that this Court will not assist a volunteer yet, if the act is completed, though voluntary, the Court will act upon it. It has been decided, that upon an agreement to transfer stock this Court will not interpose; but if the party had declared himself to be the trustee of that stock, it becomes the property of the cestui que trust without more; and the Court will act upon it. (18 Ves. 99.)

THE LORD CHANCELLOR [ELDON]. These petitions call for the decision of points of more importance and difficulty that I should wish to decide in this way, if the case was not pressed upon the Court. With regard to the French annuity, the Master has stated his opinion as to the French law perhaps without sufficient authority, or sufficient inquiry into the effect of it, as applicable to the precise circumstances of this case; but it is not necessary to pursue that; as upon the documents before me it does appear, that, though in one sense this may be represented as the testator's personal estate, yet he has committed to writing what seems to me a sufficient declaration, that he held this part of the estate in trust for the annuitant.

[First petition dismissed.]

FARMERS' LOAN & TRUST CO. v. WINTHROP
238 N.Y. 477, 144 N.E. 686 (1924)

CARDOZO, J.

On February 3, 1920, Helen C. Bostwick executed her deed of trust to the Farmers' Loan and Trust Company as trustee. It is described as the 1920 deed, to distinguish it from an earlier one, made in 1918, which is the subject of another action. By the later of the two deeds she gave to her trustee $5,000, "the said sum, and all other property hereafter delivered to said trustee as hereinafter provided," to be held upon the trusts and limitations therein set forth. The income was to be paid to her own use during life, and the principal on her death was to be divided into two parts — one for the benefit of the children of a deceased son, Albert; and the other for the benefit of a daughter, Fannie, and the children of said daughter. The donor reserved "the right, at any time and from time to time during the continuance of the trusts, . . . to deliver to said trustee additional property to be held by it" thereunder. She reserved also a power of revocation.

At the date of the execution of this deed, a proceeding was pending in the Surrogate's Court for the settlement of the accounts of the United States Trust Company as trustee of a trust under the will of Jabez A. Bostwick. The effect of the decree, when entered, would be to transfer to Mrs. Bostwick money, shares of stock, and other property of the value of upwards of $2,300,000. The plan was that this property, when ready to be transferred, should be delivered to the trustee, and held subject to the trust. On February 3, 1920, simultaneously with the execution of the trust deed, three other documents, intended to effectuate this plan, were signed by the donor. One is a power of attorney whereby she authorized the Farmers' Loan & Trust Company as her attorney "to collect and receive any and all cash, shares of stock and other property" to which she might "be entitled under any decree or order made or entered" in the proceeding above mentioned. A second is a power of attorney authorizing the Farmers' Loan & Trust Company to transfer and sell any and all shares of stock then or thereafter standing in her name. A third is a letter to the Farmers' Loan & Trust Company, in which she states that she hands to the company the powers of attorney just described, and in which she gives instructions in respect of the action to be taken thereunder:

> My desire is and I hereby authorize you to receive from the United States Trust Company of New York all securities and property coming to me under the decree or order on the settlement of its account and to transfer such securities and property to yourself as trustee under agreement of trust bearing even date herewith executed by me to you.

The decree in the accounting proceeding [in Jabez Bostwick's estate] was entered March 16, 1920. It established the right of Helen C. Bostwick to the payment or transfer of shares of stock and other property of the market value (then or shortly thereafter) of $2,327,353.70. On April 27, 1920, a representative of the Farmers' Loan & Trust Company presented the power of attorney to the United States Trust Company and stated that he was authorized to receive such securities as were ready for delivery. Shares of stock having a market value of $856,880 were handed to him then and there. No question is made that these became subject to the provisions of the deed of trust. The controversy arises in respect of the rest of the securities, $1,470,473.70 in value, which were retained in the custody of the United States Trust Company, apparently for the reason that they were not yet ready for delivery. During the night of April 27, 1920, Helen C. Bostwick died. She left a will, appointing the Farmers' Loan & Trust Company executor, and disposing of an estate of the value of over $20,000,000. The securities retained as we have seen, in the custody of the United States Trust Company, were delivered on or about July 13, 1920, to the executor under the will. Conflicting claims of ownership are made by the legatees under the will and the remaindermen under the deed.

We think with the majority of the Appellate Division, that the gift remained inchoate at the death of the donor. There is no occasion to deny that in the setting of other circumstances a power of attorney, authorizing a donee to reduce to possession the subject of a gift, may be significant as evidence of a symbolical delivery. We assume, without deciding, that such effect will be allowed if, apart from the power, there is established an intention that the title of the donor shall be presently divested and presently transferred. The assumption ignores difficulties not to be underestimated . . . , but we pass them over for the purpose of the argument, and treat them as surmounted. Even so, the basic obstacle remains that there is here no expression of a purpose to effectuate a present gift. The power of attorney, standing by itself, results, as all concede, in the creation of a revocable agency.

If some more was intended, if what was meant was a gift that was to be operative at once, the expression of the meaning will have to be found elsewhere, in the deed of trust or in the letter. Neither in the one, however, nor in the other, can such a purpose be discerned. Deed and letter alike are framed on the assumption that the gift is executory and future, and this though the addition of a few words would have established it beyond cavil as executed and present. In the deed there is a present transfer of $5,000 and no more. This wrought, there is merely the reservation of a privilege to augment to the subject-matter of the trust by deliveries thereafter. The absence of words of present assignment is emphasized when we consider with what simplicity an assignment could have been stated. All that was needed was to expand the description by a phrase:

> The right, title, and interest of the grantor in the securities and other property due or to become due from the United States Trust Company as trustee under the will.

The deed and the other documents, we must remember, were not separated in time. They were parts of a single plan, and were executed together. In these circumstances, a present transfer, if intended, would naturally have found its place in the description of the deed itself. If omitted for some reason there, the least we should expect would be to find it in the letter. Again words of present transfer are conspicuously absent. What we have instead is a request, or at best a mandate, incompetent without more to divest title, or transfer it, serving no other purpose than a memorandum of instructions from principal to agent as a guide to future action. Deed and documents were prepared by counsel learned in the law. With industrious iteration, they rejected the familiar formulas that would have given unmistakable expression to the transfer of a present title. With like iteration, they chose the words and methods appropriate to a gift that was conceived of as executory and future. We must take the transfer as they made it. The very facility with which they could have made it something else is a warning that we are not at liberty, under the guise of construction, to make it other than it is. Matter of Van Alstyne, 207 N.Y. 298, 309, 310, 100 N.E. 802. They were willing to leave open what they might readily have closed. Death overtook the signer before the gap was filled.

Viewed thus as a gift, the transaction was inchoate. An intention may be assumed, and indeed is not disputed, that what was incomplete at the moment should be completed in the future. The difficulty is that the intention was never carried out. Mrs. Bostwick remained free (apart from any power of revocation reserved in the deed of trust) to revoke the executory mandate, and keep the property as her own. Very likely different forms and instrumentalities would have been utilized, if she or her counsel had supposed that death was to come so swiftly. We might say as much if she had left in her desk a letter or memorandum expressing her resolutions for the morrow. With appropriate forms and instrumentalities available, she chose what the course of events has proved to be the wrong one. The court is without power to substitute another.

The transaction, failing as a gift, because inchoate or incomplete, is not to be sustained as the declaration of a trust. The donor had no intention of becoming a trustee herself. The donee never got title, and so could not hold it for another.

There was no equitable assignment. Equity does not enforce a voluntary promise to make a gift thereafter. . . .

WITTMEIER v. HEILIGENSTEIN
308 Ill. 434, 139 N.E. 871 (1923)

CARTER, J.

Certain issues in this case were decided in Heiligenstein v. Schlotterbeck, 300 Ill. 206, 133 N.E. 188. The issue here relates to rights claimed to arise under an invalid deed executed by Josephine Wittmeier to the St. Clare's Roman Catholic Church of Altamont seeking to convey to that church a 60-acre farm and part of two lots in Altamont. The deed was for the consideration of $1, and contained a provision that the church —

> shall pay to Charles Wittmeier the sum of $50 per month, beginning one month after my death, for and during his life, and shall pay the doctor's and hospital bill, if any, and upon his death provide him with a Christian burial and pay his funeral expenses and inter his body on the lot owned by me in the cemetery at Altamont, Illinois.

Wittmeier was married to Josephine in 1880, but they separated in 1895, and she subsequently obtained a divorce.

We have already held in Heiligenstein v. Schlotterbeck, supra, that the deed made to the St. Clare's Roman Catholic Church of Altamont is void because an unincorporated religious society is incapable, in law, of taking by deed. . . .

The single issue here involved is whether the deed to the St. Clare's Church, void for want of a lawful grantee, can have the effect of impressing a trust upon the property in favor of Charles Wittmeier. Although void as a deed, does the instrument create a valid trust? Had the church been competent to take the property, words were used ade-

quate to establish his rights. Does the incapacity of the church to take
the property destroy the rights sought to be created in favor of Wittmeier? It is held by the standard works on trusts that no particular form
of words to create a trust need be used in the instrument; that the word
"trust" need not be used. It is a rule of equitable construction that
there is no magic in particular words. Any expression which shows unequivocally the intention to create a trust will have that effect. . . .

The inability of the trustee to take will not invalidate a deed, where
the settlor and the cestui que trust are both competent, and the property is of such a nature that it can be legally placed in trust.

Clearly, Josephine Wittmeier did everything necessary under the law
to create a trust in favor of Charles Wittmeier except to choose a competent grantee. The deed was executed by the grantor with the intention to part with the title, subject to provision made for Charles. There
were words sufficient to accomplish her purpose. There was a beneficiary capable of taking but no lawful grantee. The void deed did not
transfer title to the property from Josephine, and title remained in her,
notwithstanding the deed, from the date of its execution, August 21,
1919, until the date of her death, August 25, 1919. If the void deed
impresses a trust upon the property in the hands of her heirs, it must
have had the effect to impress a trust from the date of its execution.
It is true as often said, that equity does not allow a trust to fail for want
of a lawful grantee; and this statement applies, even though the grantor
fails in one of her purposes — that of devoting the property to religious
uses.

Somewhat related to the issue here involved was that in Childs v.
Waite, 102 Me. 451, 67 A. 311, which involved a will leaving certain
property to a school district for the purpose of building and supporting
a church. The school district had no legal power to act, and it was held
not to succeed to the title of the trust fund; but the court ordered the
appointment of a trustee. In that case, however, the property was to
be devoted to a single purpose, and the preservation of the trust completely carried out that purpose. While this is not exactly the situation
here, the principle involved in that case is identical with the one involved here. . . .

In the present case the purpose of the grantor is clearly manifested
and the trust in favor of Charles Wittmeier clearly created. The trust
is fully and finally declared in the instrument creating it. With a competent grantee of the deed, no further act was necessary to give it effect.
Massey v. Huntington, 118 Ill. 80, 7 N.E. 269. Viewing the trust as we
think it should be properly held here, we do not discuss the issue of the
consideration of the trust. The grantor intended the deed to establish a
trust in favor of Wittmeier. Although the deed did not, in fact, transfer
title from her, we think it sufficient to impress the trust upon the property in the hands of the grantor and of the heirs to whom it descended.

We are of the opinion that the incapacity of the church to take the property does not defeat the purpose of the grantor, and that the heirs take the property impressed with a trust in favor of Wittmeier. The fact that the grantor had two purposes in mind, one of which must fail, is no reason why the other should fail, when it is expressed with sufficient definiteness and can be legally carried out.

It is suggested it would be possible to take the view that Josephine Wittmeier, while making her purpose clear, did not make it effective, because of the incompetent grantee, and that therefore the property descends to her heirs, free from all obligations sought to be impressed upon it in favor of Charles Wittmeier, as in Meyer v. Holle, 83 Tex. 623, 19 S.W. 154; but such a conclusion, in our judgment, by weight of authority, is not required, and would unreasonably and unnecessarily defeat the purpose of the grantor. . . .

Reversed and remanded.

See also Hebrew University Association v. Nye, 26 Conn. Supp. 342, 223 A.2d 397 (1966), on remand from 148 Conn. 223, 169 A.2d 641 (1961), where the widow of a distinguished Hebrew scholar, Abraham Yahuda, publicly described her husband's scholarly library and announced gift of it to the Hebrew University. She began cataloging the collection, giving the University a list of most of the contents, and the University began a fundraising campaign to build a new library showing the Yahuda room in its plans, removing the room from possible designation by other contributors. The widow died before the books were actually shipped (thus there was no actual delivery), but the transfer was sustained on three theories: (1) a gift inter vivos based on a constructive or symbolic delivery; (2) a constructive trust based on a contract theory, because of the University's actions in reliance on the widow's promise to make the gift; and (3) a constructive trust arising out of an ineffective gift made by one who died believing an effective gift had been made. Note, however, that the 1961 decision rejected the theory that the widow's public statements could be construed as a declaration of trust of the books, since her intention was to make a gift, not to declare herself trustee.

In Estate of Heggstad, 16 Cal. App. 4th 943, 20 Cal. Rptr. 2d 433 (1993), the settlor executed an instrument declaring himself trustee of assets described in "Schedule A," which was attached to the declaration. The assets included an interest in real property for which the settlor did not execute a separate deed conveying the property to himself as trustee. About a month later the settlor married *W* and thereafter died testate without having made a new will or codicil to provide for her. *W* claimed a share of the settlor's estate under California's pretermitted spouse statute. The issue before the court was whether the real property mentioned in Schedule A was part of the intended trust or still part of the probate estate to which *W*'s claim would apply. The court held that the declaration of trust and accompanying schedule were sufficient to create a valid trust of the real property and other listed assets.

A similar issue may arise where a property owner enters into a written trust agreement with a third party as trustee but executes no instruments of transfer other than a recitation in the trust agreement expressing a present or accomplished transfer of assets identified in the agreement itself or by reference to an attachment. Assuming the delivery requirement is satisfied, is the writing sufficient to constitute a deed of transfer? Because a deed to land or a deed of gift need not take any particular form, there is no reason why a writing effectively expressing the intention to transfer identified assets to a trustee or other transferee should not be given effect. Compare Estate of Binder, 386 N.W.2d 910 (N.D. 1986) (trust of land created, without deed, by intention and other elements shown in divorce settlement); Ballard v. McCoy, 247 Va. 513, 433 S.E.2d 146 (1994) (signed trust agreement with appended list of assets found insufficient to create a trust by transfer, but apparently only because the agreement specified the alleged settlor's intention that the trust should come into being only when the "property" was later "delivered" by the settlor to the trustee).

For both the declaration of trust and the transfer in trust situations, see common law and statutory acceptance in Restatement (Third) of Trusts §10, cmt. *e*, and §16, cmt. *b* (Tent. Draft approved 1996) and Uniform Trust Code §401(b) (draft, Feb. 2000) ("a trust instrument may subject identified property to a self-declared trust or [may] transfer to a trustee property identified in the trust instrument"). Commentary in both the Restatement and the UTC, however, warn that appropriate practice is for a settlor to re-register securities in the name of the trustee, to execute and record deeds to the trustee, and the like. These steps may be important, for example, for protection against bona fide purchasers or for obtaining title insurance, but locally appropriate steps can be taken even after a settlor's death as long as the transfer has been accomplished and the trust created. (Perfecting of title under recording acts is rarely made a requirement for the effectiveness of the transfer itself; the distinction is important in the unfortunately frequent cases in which unexpected death, oversight, or mere procrastination prevent the timely taking of steps that are at least practically useful and may even leave uncertainty in some states concerning the validity of the transfer itself.)

Restatement (Third) of Trusts §16(1) (Tent. Draft approved 1996), entitled *Ineffective Inter Vivos Transfers,* states that no express trust is created when "a property owner undertakes to make a donative [transfer] to another as trustee [but] fails during life to complete the contemplated transfer," but adds that "in some circumstances" the trust intention "may be given effect by constructive trust in order to prevent unjust enrichment of the . . . successors in interest" of a would-be settlor who has died or become incompetent and therefore cannot try again to create the apparently desired trust. (Comment *c* explains that the property owner in such a case may have "taken all the steps that would be required of the owner personally in order to implement the transfer in the intended manner," such as via an agent, so that "the acts and circumstances . . . satisfy the underlying legal policy of determining, by objective and reliable evidence, that the property owner had arrived at a definite, considered intention to create a trust either immediately or soon thereafter.") Id. §16(2) states that, if an intended outright inter vivos gift fails for lack of the required transfer, the "gift intention will not be given effect by treating it as a declaration of trust"; but the commentary (cmt. *d*) notes and examines the practical difficulty of drawing a line between an intended outright gift and a declarant's intention to act as trustee. Compare Love, Imperfect Gifts as Declarations of Trust: An Unapologetic Anomaly, 67 Ky. L.J. (1979).

② Formalities: Requirement of a Writing

Assuming a valid transfer of the intended trust property has been made, or that a declaration of trust is involved, does it matter that the existence and terms of the trust agreement are not evidenced by a writing? The statutory setting in which this question may arise will vary from state to state. Consideration must be given to rules such as the parol evidence rule, and in most states the question will require a consideration of a statute of frauds provision relating to trusts of land.

RESTATEMENT (THIRD) OF TRUSTS
(Tent. Draft approved 1996)

§21.   *The Parol Evidence Rule*

(1) In the absence of fraud, duress, undue influence, mistake, or other ground for reformation or rescission, if the owner of property

    (a) transfers it inter vivos to another person by a writing that states that the transferee is to take the property for the transferee's own benefit, extrinsic evidence may not be used to show that the transferee was intended to hold the property in trust; or

(b) transfers it inter vivos to another person by a writing that states that the transferee is to hold the property upon a particular trust, extrinsic evidence may not be used to show that the transferee was intended to hold the property upon a different trust or to take it beneficially; or

(c) by a writing declares that the property owner holds the property upon a particular trust, extrinsic evidence may not be used to show that the owner intended to hold the property upon a different trust or to hold it free of trust.

(2) If the owner of property transfers it inter vivos to another person by a writing that does not state either that the transferee is to take the property for the transferor's own benefit or that the transferee is to hold it upon a particular trust, except as excluded by a Statute of Frauds or other statute, extrinsic evidence may be used to show that the transferee was to hold the property in trust for either the transferor or one or more third parties, or for some combination of the transferor, the transferee, and one or more third parties.

The above section of the Restatement is particularly significant in cases where there is no statutory requirement of a writing for the creation of trusts or where (as in most states) the statute of frauds is inapplicable because the subject matter is not an interest in land. In parol evidence cases, despite the absence of grounds for reformation or rescission in equity, extrinsic evidence may be admitted (1) in the process of interpreting ambiguous language in the instrument, and (2), by the majority view, for the purpose of proving a trust where the deed or bill of sale transferring legal title is silent as to the possible existence of a trust. This latter rule, adopted in §21(2) of the Restatement, is rationalized on the basis that proof of a trust purpose does not vary but merely supplements the writing. To establish a trust by parol the proof is generally required to satisfy some such standard as that of "clear and convincing evidence." Indeed, Uniform Trust Code §403 (draft, Feb. 2000) generally provides that "the creation of an oral trust may be established only by clear and convincing evidence." Some cases have at least purported to distinguish between oral trusts for the grantor and those for third persons where the instrument is silent, and to exclude extrinsic evidence only in the former.

In holding that the existence of an oral partnership agreement need not be established by clear and convincing evidence, the court in Weiner v. Fleischman, 54 Cal.3d 476, 489, 286 Cal. Rptr. 40, 47-48, 816 P.2d 892, 899-900 (1991), distinguished "other areas of the law where courts have traditionally required clear and convincing evidence." The court observed: (1) "Oral agreements to make wills are disfavored

because such claims arise after the testator . . . is deceased . . .";
(2) "Allegations that deeds absolute . . . are subject to a trust . . . have
also been historically disfavored because society and the courts have a
reluctance to tamper with duly executed instruments and documents
of legal title"; and (3) "Finally, the higher burden of proof required
to prove oral trusts of personal property is derived from the special
care that courts have historically shown in recognizing the creation of
trusts . . . because of special concerns that the terms of the trusts specify
the information needed for courts to deal with the trust, such as the
identification of the trust property and purpose, the beneficiaries and
trustees, and any special administrative provisions."

STATUTE OF FRAUDS
29 Car. II. c. 3 (1677)

VII. . . . [A]ll declarations or creations of trusts or confidences of
any lands, tenements or hereditaments, shall be manifested and proved
by some writing, signed by the party who is by law enabled to declare
such trust, or by his last will in writing, or else they shall be utterly void
and of none effect.

VIII. [Exempts resulting and constructive trusts. See page 340,
supra.]

IX. And be it further enacted, that all grants and assignments, of
any trust or confidence shall likewise be in writing, signed by the party
granting or assigning the same, or by such last will or devise, or else
shall likewise be wholly void and of none effect.

Although many American statutes of frauds similarly state that oral
trusts of land are "void," they are generally interpreted as meaning
only that the trust is *unenforceable* over the objection of the *trustee*. This
is reaffirmed in Restatement (Third) of Trusts §24, infra. (See also id.,
cmt. *a.*)

A statute of frauds becomes involved whenever the statute's requirement of a writing is expressly made applicable to trusts of interests in
land. It also becomes a factor, even in the absence of such an express
reference to trusts, whenever the general writing requirement applicable to contracts and conveyances concerning interests in land has been
held to apply to trusts of interests in land. Interests in land generally
include leaseholds but not debts secured by a mortgage. A few statutes
require a writing to establish trusts of personalty.

Except in cases to which these various statutes apply, oral trusts are enforceable, assuming the parol evidence rule does not preclude proof of them.

The Restatement Third, supra (at §22(1)), states that, for the creation of an enforceable express trust "of property for which a Statute of Frauds requires a writing," the writing must "be signed as provided in §23 and must (a) manifest the trust intention and (b) reasonably identify the trust property, the beneficiaries and the purposes of the trust," adding (§22(2)) that the required writing "(a) may consist of several writings, (b) need not be intended as the expression of a trust, and (c) continues to satisfy the Statute . . . even though later lost or destroyed." Section 23(1) (*Signing Requirement: When and by Whom?*) states that where a property owner declares "that he or she holds upon a trust for which the Statute of Frauds requires a writing, a writing evidencing the trust as provided in §22 is sufficient . . . if it is signed by the declarant (a) before or at the time of the declaration, or (b) after the time of the declaration but before the declarant has transferred the property"; and id. §23(2) states that, in the case of a transfer *to another,* "a writing evidencing the trust as provided in §22 is sufficient to satisfy the Statute if it is signed (a) by the transferor before or at the time of the transfer or (b) by the transferee (i) before or at the time of the transfer or (ii) after the transfer was made to the transferee but before the transferee has transferred the property to a third person." See also IA W. Fratcher, Scott on Trusts §§47-49 (4th ed. 1987).

PROBLEM

12-E. Several months before his recent death, *A* conveyed the Blackacre Apartments (real property valued at about $200,000) to his brother *B,* a real estate broker. The deed was in the form of a standard warranty deed, reciting merely that it was "for a valuable consideration" and making no reference to the existence or nonexistence of a trust. *A*'s daughter, *D,* has come to consult you about this conveyance. *D* states that *B* had orally agreed to serve as trustee for *A* and then on *A*'s death to distribute the trust estate to *D. D* further reveals that, in *D*'s presence before the conveyance, *A* had told *B* that he did not wish to be bothered with investment management because he wished to be free to travel, now that his wife had died and he was alone; furthermore, at his age (68), *A* thought that following the stock market would be too burdensome and he could not continue to supervise the apartments. *D* recalls that *A* and *B* had talked generally about the possibility of the apartments being sold and the proceeds being invested in stocks and mortgages or deeds of trust, since *B* was often able to find good investment opportunities of these types. Then *A* persuaded *B* to act as a trustee, not just as his agent, and *B* agreed. *B* had not made any payments to *A* and now claims the apartments as his own, refusing to transfer the property to *D*. *A* left no will and very little other property. He is survived by *D* and by *X* and *Y*, *A*'s two sons, both of whom are successful businessmen.

(a) As you study the three cases and related materials in the next two subsections, consider what additional information you need to determine, what facts you might seek to establish, and in general how you might go about preparing a case for *D* under a typical statute patterned after the English statute of frauds.

(b) If the fairly representative case of Gregory v. Bowlsby, infra, were the latest decision by the highest court of your state, and if you were *B*'s lawyer, how would you argue the *law* in support of your case? How would the cases for *D* and *B* differ under the statute of frauds in your state? Where there is no applicable statute of frauds?

(c) If you were appointed to a bar association committee for the purpose of considering statutory amendments or new legislation to deal with the constantly troublesome problems of this type, what would you propose?

a. Oral Trust for the Settlor

GREGORY v. BOWLSBY
115 Iowa 327, 88 N.W. 822 (1902)

[Plaintiffs' petition, which the court recognized "must be treated as presenting the facts," stated: that plaintiffs' father, defendant Benjamin Bowlsby, requested them to deed him their interest in land left by their deceased mother, in order that he might use the land to better advantage; that he orally promised to hold the land, not to sell or dispose of it, and to allow it to descend to the plaintiffs at his death; that plaintiffs executed deeds to defendant reciting a consideration of $1; that by reason of relations existing between them and their father, they relied on his statements without legal advice; that neither the defendant nor his attorney, who was present at the time, advised them that the promises could not be enforced; that defendant paid no consideration for the conveyance, which was induced by his representations; that the defendant made the promises solely to defraud the plaintiffs and without intention to perform; and that he gratuitously conveyed a one-third interest in the land to the co-defendant, his second wife, who knew of the defendant's agreement. The petition asks that the deeds be canceled, that plaintiffs be adjudged owners of interests in the land, and that an accounting be had of rents and profits. Demurrer was sustained on the ground that the alleged agreement was within the statute of frauds.]

DEEMER, J. . . .

That plaintiffs, in the first instance, are seeking to establish an express trust is too clear for argument; and it is equally clear that such a trust cannot rest in parol. . . . As the deed was absolute on its face, and recited the payment of a valuable consideration, plaintiffs will not be permitted to establish a trust by showing that there was in fact no consideration but the parol agreement to hold the title in trust.

As an express trust cannot be shown by parol, and as there was no resulting trust, we have one question left, and that is, was there such a fraud perpetrated by defendant Benjamin Bowlsby as entitles plaintiffs to the relief asked? That relief is not a reformation of the contract, but its cancellation; not a judgment at law as for fraud, but a decree quieting title, and for an accounting. If there is any cause of action stated, it is for the declaration and establishment of a constructive trust, growing out of the alleged fraud of the defendants. While some facts are recited for the purpose of showing fiduciary relations between the parties, we apprehend they are insufficient for that purpose. A father bears no such confidential or fiduciary relations to his adult children as to bring transactions between them relating to the lands of either under suspicion. He may deal with them as with strangers, and no presumption of fraud or undue influence obtains. It is charged, however, that, with intent to cheat and defraud, defendant made the representations charged, fully intending at the time he made them not to carry them out, but to obtain the title to the land, and thus defraud the grantors. Does this make such a case of fraud as that a court will declare a constructive trust in the land in favor of the grantors? This instrument was in the exact form agreed upon by the parties, and there was no promise to execute defeasances or other instruments to witness the trust. The sole claim is that defendant made the promises and agreements with intent to cheat and defraud the plaintiffs. Mere denial that there was a parol agreement as claimed will not constitute a fraud. If it did, the statute would be useless. Nor will a refusal to perform the contract be sufficient to create a constructive trust. But the statute was not enacted as a means for perpetrating a fraud; and, if fraud in the original transaction is clearly shown, the grant[ee] will be held to be a trustee ex maleficio. If, then, there was a fraudulent intent in procuring the deed without intention to hold the land as agreed, and pursuant to that intent the grantee disposed of the property, or otherwise repudiated his agreement, equity will take from the wrongdoer the fruit of his deceit by declaring a constructive trust. Mere breach of or denial of the oral agreement does not, as we have said, constitute a fraud. . . . [A]s said by Mr. Pomeroy, in his work on Equity Jurisprudence (section 1055): "There must be an element of positive fraud accompanying the promise, and by means of which the acquisition of the legal title is wrongfully consummated." Breach of the agreement may, of course,

be considered, but it is not alone sufficient. There must be also some
clear and explicit evidence of fraud or imposition at the time of the
making of the conveyance to constitute the purchaser a trustee ex maleficio. The instant case, however, does not present the question of the
quantity of proof required, for, as has been stated, it was decided upon
a demurrer to the petition, which pleads fraud in the inception of the
transaction, and specifically alleges that the deed was made through
defendant's agency, and upon his promise and representations, with
the specific intent to cheat and defraud. Our observations regarding
the character of the evidence required will perhaps prevent misapprehension of the role in the future. The authorities are not harmonious
on the questions discussed, although the points of difference seem to
relate more to the quantum of proof in addition to the mere breach
of promise than to the rule itself. . . .

We think the petition on its face recites facts showing a constructive
trust, and that the demurrer should have been overruled. Reversed.

Section 182 of the Restatement of Restitution provides:

> Where the owner of an interest in land transfers it inter vivos to an-
> other upon an oral trust in favor of the transferor or upon an oral agree-
> ment to reconvey the land to the transferor, and the trust or agreement
> is unenforceable because of the Statute of Frauds, and the transferee
> refuses to perform the trust or agreement, he holds the interest upon
> a constructive trust for the transferor, if
>
> (a) the transfer was procured by fraud, misrepresentation, duress,
> undue influence or mistake of such a character that the transferor is
> entitled to restitution, or
>
> (b) the transferee at the time of the transfer was in a confidential
> relation to the transferor, or
>
> (c) the transfer was made as security for an indebtedness of the
> transferor.
>
> Caveat: The Institute takes no position on the question whether the
> transferee holds upon a constructive trust for the transferor an interest
> in land transferred to him inter vivos, where he orally agreed with the
> transferor to hold it in trust for the transferor or to reconvey it to the
> transferor, except under the circumstances stated in this Section.

It is stated in IA W. Fratcher, Scott on Trusts §44 (4th ed. 1987): "By
the weight of authority in the United States, however, the transferee
of land upon an oral trust or contract [for the settlor] is allowed to
retain the land." A considerable number of the cases cited for this
proposition, however, actually involved a failure to prove the existence
of the alleged oral agreement adequately rather than a holding that

the plaintiff's evidence of an agreement was inadmissible or that his pleadings failed to state a claim upon which relief could be granted.

Stewart v. Hooks, 372 Pa. 542, 546, 94 A.2d 756, 758 (1953), discussing the confidential relationship exception, states:

> We likewise find little merit in plaintiff's argument that a confidential relationship is here established [by the testimony of a witness] . . . that plaintiff "said he had confidence in her [the grantee] and he knew everything would be done as he wanted it." . . . Confidence of this character is obviously present in every case where title is transferred upon an oral promise to reconvey. The Statute of Frauds would wholly fail to render unenforceable such an oral promise if it could be circumvented merely by having the transferor say to the transferee in the presence of a third party: "I have confidence that you will reconvey this property when I ask you to do so."

See also the concurring opinion of Allen, J., in Horsley v. Hrenchir, 146 Kan. 767, 771-772, 73 P.2d 1010, 1012-1013 (1937), which states:

> [I]f it is shown there was a confidential relationship between the parties . . . the court will compel restitution by raising a constructive trust. The same is true if the transfer was secured by fraud, duress or mistake. If it is possible to show the oral agreement in such cases, no valid reason has been given why the statute of frauds should forbid showing the oral trust to prevent unjust enrichment. . . .
>
> By a long line of cases it seems settled in this state that the transferee can keep the property. One reason given is that deeds would no longer be valuable as muniments of title. . . . The reason given seems unsubstantial, for it would prevent enforcing restitution when a transfer of land was procured by fraud, misrepresentation, mistake, duress, undue influence, or where the transfer was made as a security transaction. But in any view of the question it must be conceded that the rule followed in this case is too firmly established to be departed from at this late day.

An Aside on Precedent and the Role of Courts. Consider whether the attitude reflected in the concluding sentence of the quotation immediately above represents a workable view of the judicial function or a satisfactory approach to precedent in this particular type of case. What reasons are there *in general* for adhering to precedent? Which of these reasons would prevent a court in the type of case under consideration here from reconsidering the rule it has laid down in prior decisions? Note that this is a different question from the ultimate question of which of several possible rules is preferable on the merits. Consider what reasons there might be — in general, and then in this type of case — for not reaching the issue of the substantive merits of the possible rules.

The opinion that follows is representative of what was referred to in Restatement (Second) of Trusts §44, comment *a,* as "a growing body of authority" and is reflected in the general rule of Restatement (Third) of Trusts §24(3) (Tent. Draft approved 1996).

ORELLA v. JOHNSON
38 Cal. 2d 693, 242 P.2d 5 (1952)

[Appeal from a judgment for defendants entered after the granting of a motion for nonsuit. In 1933 plaintiff borrowed $1,000 from the defendant, May (his stepdaughter), to pay off a mortgage on his home, known as the Harder Road place. In 1938 he and his wife conveyed the land to May, who sold it for $3,900 in 1941 and retained $1,400 in payment of the debt and interest thereon. $1,800 of the remaining $2,500 was used to purchase a new home, the Winton Road place, for plaintiff, with title again taken in May's name. In 1943 this property was sold for $4,500, of which $2,300 was used to buy land in Santa Cruz, also in May's name. After his wife's death, plaintiff asked May to convey the land to him, and she refused. Plaintiff then brought suit to impress a constructive trust on the Santa Cruz property and to obtain an accounting of amounts realized by May on the previous sales, alleging that the 1938 conveyance was made on the understanding that May would reconvey the land on request. The trial court excluded evidence offered to prove a conversation between plaintiff and his wife in which his wife presented him with "a proposition May wants me to put to you" and as a result of which the deed was executed.]

TRAYNOR, J. . . .

If a grantor conveys property to another in reliance on the oral promise of the latter to hold the property in trust for the grantor or a third person and the grantee subsequently repudiates the trust, it is settled that a constructive trust may be enforced against the grantee if the conveyance was induced by fraud or if there was a confidential relationship between the parties. Such trusts are enforced under the provisions of section 2224 of the Civil Code that "One who gains a thing by fraud . . . is . . . an involuntary trustee of the thing gained, for the benefit of the person who would otherwise have had it." It is either the actual fraud that induced the conveyance, or the constructive fraud arising from the confidential relationship coupled with the breach of the oral promise, that brings the provisions of the section into play. Since under this section the trust is in favor of the person who, but for the fraud, "would otherwise have had" the property, the effect of its application when the grantee refuses to perform his oral promise, is to enforce the trust in favor of the intended beneficiary.

Whether or not there is a confidential relationship or whether or not the original transfer was induced by fraud, the fact remains that the grantee will be unjustly enriched, if he is allowed to repudiate his promise and retain the property. Accordingly, the view has been forcefully advocated that although the grantee cannot be compelled to perform his promise in view of the statute of frauds, unjust enrichment should be prevented by compelling him to make specific restitution to the grantor. See, I Scott on Trusts §44, p. 248, and authorities cited. This view is supported by the rule that a purchaser under an invalid oral contract to buy land may recover the amount he has paid if the seller refuses to perform the contract, see Moresco v. Foppiano, 7 Cal. 2d 242, 247, 60 P.2d 430; Rest., Restitution, §108(d), and the rule that a person who renders services under an invalid oral contract to devise property may secure quantum meruit for the value of those services. Zellner v. Wassman, 184 Cal. 80, 88, 193 P. 84. Although there are cases where recovery has been denied despite an apparent unjust enrichment, in none of them was the question raised or considered of the availability of the remedy of specific restitution as distinct from the remedy of a constructive trust based on the abuse of a confidential relationship. In cases where the question has been considered, however, the right to relief has been recognized. Accordingly, it is unnecessary to decide whether there was a confidential relationship in this case. The nonsuit must be reversed if there is evidence, either that plaintiff conveyed his property in reliance on an oral promise to reconvey it to him, or that the conveyance was induced by fraud. . . .

The judgment is reversed.

b. Oral Trusts for Persons Other Than the Transferor

The preceding cases dealt with transfers by A to B on oral trust for A. How are the results affected by the fact that the deed is from A to B on oral trust for C? Can B retain the property? If not, should a constructive trust be imposed for C, the intended beneficiary? Or would it be appropriate to impose a constructive trust for the transferor, A?

JONES v. GACHOT
217 Ark. 462, 230 S.W.2d 937 (1950)

McFADDIN, J.

This is a suit seeking to impress a trust on real property.

In 1932 Mrs. Felice Field executed a regular warranty deed to L. C. Gachot and J. F. Gachot (her nephews), conveying certain lands in Pulaski County. There was nothing in the deed to indicate, or even suggest, that the grantees received the title in any way except as the owners thereof. Under an agreement with J. F. Gachot, L. C. Gachot went into possession of the property here involved and so remained until his death in 1948. Then, in 1949, this suit was filed alleging (and evidence was offered to that effect) that when Mrs. Felice Field made the deed to L. C. Gachot and J. F. Gachot in 1932, the said grantees agreed with the grantor to hold the property as trustees for themselves and their brothers and sisters. Such agreement is the trust that is sought to be impressed on the property against the widow and heirs of L. C. Gachot. The Chancery Court rejected the evidence as to the alleged trust agreement and dismissed the complaint for want of equity; and this appeal ensued.

At the outset, appellants concede that an *express trust* cannot be established by oral evidence. But appellants contend that the trust here sought to be imposed is not an express trust but a *constructive trust* and they cite, inter alia, Section 45 of the Restatement of the Law of Trusts:

> Where the owner of an interest in land transfers it inter vivos to another in trust for a third person, but no memorandum properly evidencing the intention to create a trust is signed, and the transferee refuses to perform the trust, the transferee holds the interest upon a constructive trust for the third person, if, but only if,
>
> (a) — the transferee by fraud, duress or undue influence prevented the transferor from creating an enforceable interest in the third person, or
>
> (b) — the transferee at the time of the transfer was in a confidential relation to the transferor, or
>
> (c) — the transfer was made by the transferor in contemplation of death.

It is conceded that sub-paragraph (a) does not apply to this case; but it is earnestly insisted that a trust should be decreed in the case at bar under either sub-paragraph (b) or sub-paragraph (c).

In the briefs no Arkansas case is cited as going to show that such sub-paragraphs (b) and (c) are recognized by holdings in the State. But even if the rules stated in sub-paragraphs (b) and (c) prevail in Arkansas (which it is unnecessary to decide), nevertheless the proof in the case at bar is entirely insufficient to justify the application of either of these sub-paragraphs. As to sub-paragraph (b), there was no more of a "confidential relation" existing between the grantor, Mrs. Field, and the grantee, L. C. Gachot, than exists between any other aunt and nephew; there was a kinship, but not a confidential relationship; he did not importune her to make the deed; they were not living in the same home; she consulted an attorney who prepared the deed for her. As to sub-paragraph (c), there was no more "contemplation of death" on the part of Mrs. Field, the grantor, when she made the deed in question than there is such contemplation by any person of advanced years: she was both physically and mentally active at the time she had the attorney prepare the deed; she was not in extremis; she lived fourteen months after its delivery.

A study of the evidence in the case at bar reflects that this suit — filed after the death of L. C. Gachot — is an effort to establish an express trust by oral evidence, and is within the interdiction of Sec. 38-106, Ark. Stats. 1947. . . .

LEFLAR, J.

I concur in the conclusion that the evidence in this case was insufficient to establish a constructive trust in appellants' favor. But I wish to make it clear that, our statute prohibiting express oral trusts in lands, Ark. Stats. §38-106, does not in any wise inhibit the establishment of constructive trusts. The next following section in the statute of frauds, §38-107, provides:

> Where any conveyance shall be made of any lands or tenements, by which a trust or confidence may arise or result by implication of law, such trust or confidence shall not be affected by anything contained in this act.

The great weight of American authority recognizes the validity of constructive trusts under the circumstances set out in the Restatement of Trusts, §45, as quoted in the majority opinion. Unless constructive trusts are enforced in those circumstances the statute of frauds will be made an instrument for achieving fraud, by vesting in nominal grantees the title to lands for which they have paid nothing and to which in equity and good conscience they are not entitled. Under §38-107 it is clear that this was never the intent of the statute of frauds.

Whether the constructive trust in such circumstances should run in favor of the ones for whom the oral trust was declared, as the Restatement suggests, thus effectuating it as though it were an express trust, or should run in favor of the grantor or his successors, on the theory that the parties should be restored as nearly as possible to the position they were in prior to the making of the deed, is another matter. Certainly, the latter disposition of the property would be more nearly in keeping with the law of constructive trusts generally. See 3 Bogert, The Law of Trusts, p. 215; 1 Scott, The Law of Trusts, p. 269. This form of relief, however, was not sought in the present case.

In Person v. Pagnotta, 541 P.2d 483 (Or. 1975), the grantor, elderly and seriously ill, executed and delivered a deed to a close friend, expressly reserving a life estate. The transfer was based on the grantee's oral promise to transfer the land to the grantee's daughter at the grantor's death, which appeared imminent. Later the grantor's conservator sued to recover the land on the theory of a resulting trust based on the failure of the intended trust under the statute of frauds. Recovery was denied because a valid constructive trust of the remainder was created for the grantee's daughter, with the grantee as constructive trustee.

Like section 45(a) and (b) of the prior Restatement, quoted in Jones v. Gachot, Restatement (Third) of Trusts §24(2) (Tent. Draft approved 1996) recognizes the fraud, undue influence, duress, and confidential relationship bases for constructive trust relief to implement the transferor's objectives, but id. §24(3) goes further. It not only calls for a constructive (or resulting) trust to restore the property to the transferor in other cases (to avoid unjust enrichment of the *transferee*), whether the intended trust was for the transferor or for others, but it also provides that in the latter type of cases a constructive trust is to be imposed to go forward with the agreed objectives if "the transferor is incompetent or dead and a constructive trust for the intended beneficiaries and purposes is necessary as a means of preventing unjust enrichment of the *successors in interest of the transferor*" (emphasis added). See also id. §24(4) for a counterpart rule for declarations of trust.

Instead of being absolute on its face, a deed may recite simply that a transfer is "in trust" or that the transferee takes "as trustee," without stating the terms of the trust. If clear evidence is available that by oral agreement the land was to be held in trust for X, can the trust be enforced? The limited number of cases in point hold that it cannot. Because it is clear from the deed itself that the transferee takes title in trust, and because the intended trust fails if the transferee refuses to perform the agreement, the transferee holds the property on a *resulting* trust for the transferor. There is no need to allow a constructive trust to avoid an unjust enrichment. (Restatement (Third) of Trusts §24, cmt. *g*, calls for a *constructive* trust to go forward with the intended trust in such a case.) On the other hand, if the grantee under such a deed chooses, an enforceable written trust agreement can apparently be executed or the agreed oral trust can be carried out. Just as in cases where the deed is absolute on its face, the intended trust will fail only if the grantee, or the grantee's successor in interest, asserts the defense of the statute of frauds.

3. Special Problems of Revocable Trusts

During life one may execute and deliver a deed of certain property to another, or declare oneself trustee of certain property, and even though the existence and terms of a trust are so specified as to comply fully with the requirements of the statute of frauds, it is still possible that the trust will be deemed illusory and thus "testamentary" in character and then be held invalid for failure to comply with the statutory formalities prescribed for wills. At this point we are concerned with determining what circumstances may lead to such a result. In particular we are concerned with determining what trust provisions might be a source of danger in this regard, and you should consider carefully what steps might be taken to eliminate this hazard. Compare the cases in Chapter 8, section C, particularly Noble v. Tipton, 219 Ill. 182, 76 N.E. 151 (1905).

William Nicholls established a living trust in which he reserved for life the right to receive $230 a month and also such amounts as the trustee "may deem necessary for his benefit." The remainder was to pass to such persons as Nicholls might appoint or, in default of appointment, to his next of kin under Massachusetts law. He also reserved the power to alter, amend, or revoke the trust. Nicholls's business adviser, one Neville, was given power to control the trustee's investments. Following Nicholls's death, the lower court instructed the trustee to distribute the remainder in accordance with the provisions of the trust, rather than to certain legatees whose bequests under Nicholls's will could not be paid due to insufficiency of other assets. The legatees contended that Nicholls retained full dominion over the property, that the provisions of the instrument were testamentary in nature and created a mere agency, and consequently that the intended disposition of the remainder failed for non-compliance with the formal requirements of the wills act. In rejecting these contentions and affirming the decree below, the court, in National Shawmut Bank v. Joy, 315 Mass. 457, 474-476, 53 N.E.2d 113, 124-125 (1944), stated that the power to appoint and the power to revoke, in addition to an interest for life, did not render the remainder disposition incomplete or testamentary. The court added:

> The same is true, a fortiori, of a reservation of the lesser powers to alter or amend the trust, or to withdraw principal from it, either with or without the consent of the trustee. Obviously an exercise of the power to revoke would enable the settlor to establish a new trust changed as he might desire. There is no reason why he may not reserve the right to take a short cut by altering or amending the original trust instrument. . . .
>
> But the legatees contend that by reserving power to alter, amend or revoke the trust the settlor made it possible for him as a practical matter to dominate Neville, and that the power to control the investments was in effect reserved to Nicholls himself. We assume without deciding that this contention is true. It does not follow that the gift over to the statutory next of kin is therefore testamentary and void. We need not decide whether the trust would have been invalid had the trustees been reduced to passive impotence, or something near it. A reservation by a settlor of the power to control investments does not impair the validity of a trust.

PROBLEM

12-F.   Nine years ago *S* entered into a trust agreement with the *T* Trust Company under which he delivered to the trust company securities then worth $80,000 and certain life insurance policies in the face amount of $100,000 on his life. The beneficiary designated in each policy was the *T* Trust Company. *S* expressly reserved the power to change the beneficiaries of the policies and to amend or revoke the trust. The agreement provided that the trust company, as trustee, acknowledged receipt of the securities and the policies and that it agreed to accumulate the income from the securities and on the death of *S* to collect the proceeds and hold all of the properties in trust to be paid in equal shares — that is, one-fifth to *W*, his wife of 25 years, and one-fifth to each of his four children as they severally attained age 21 — if, but only if, *W* took under his will. In the event that *W* renounced his will, the properties were to be paid in equal shares to his four children.

S died last month. The value of the securities in the inter vivos trust is now $170,000. His will, which has just been filed for probate, disposes of his net probate estate, consisting of $100,000 in securities and $50,000 in realty, in five equal shares to his wife and his four children. *T* Trust Company is executor and is directed to hold the shares of minor children in trust until they reach their majority. Only two of the children are minors, one age 15 and the other age 17.

(a) Under the law of your state, what approach would you expect *W* to take in claiming a maximum share in these assets and how would you support her claims? How would your answers be affected if the Uniform Probate Code applies?

(b) As attorney for the children, how would you attempt to resist *W*'s claims?

(c) Outline the opinion you would give to support the decision you think would be appropriate in this case. Would your conclusion differ if the trust had been created nine days rather than nine years before *S*'s death?

(d) How would you advise a client in *S*'s position during his lifetime?

(e) Is this an area in which applicable policies could be given greater effect by statute? If so, what provisions would you suggest? Consider the Uniform Probate Code.

INVESTORS STOCK FUND, INC. v. ROBERTS
179 F. Supp. 185 (D. Mont. 1959), *aff'd,*
286 F.2d 647 (9th Cir. 1961)

[Interpleader action filed by Investors Stock Fund, Inc. against Franklin H. Roberts, as "beneficiary" (actually, remainder beneficiary) under a declaration of trust executed by George W. Roberts, and against Loretto Lohman Roberts, as widow and sole heir of George W. Roberts, seeking a determination of the rights and conflicting claims of the defendants in certain stock. Loretto Roberts and Franklin Roberts each moved for summary judgment.]

MURRAY, C.J. . . .

Two questions are presented by the motions for summary judgment: . . .

Is the Decree of Distribution in the Estate of George W. Roberts, Deceased, Conclusive as to the Ownership of the Stock? Loretto Lohman Roberts' first contention is that, regardless of the validity or invalidity of the declaration of trust made by George W. Roberts, the ownership of the stock in question was conclusively determined by the decree in the George W. Roberts' estate distributing said stock to her as the widow and sole heir at law of George W. Roberts, deceased, and that . . . the decree of distribution of the probate court is res judicata in this action.

. . . [R]egardless of the sufficiency or insufficiency of the notice to Franklin H. Roberts, and regardless of whether or not the probate court was aware at the time it made the decree of distribution of the fact that the stock certificate was issued in the name of George W. Roberts, as trustee for Franklin H. Roberts, it is clear under Montana law, as well as the law generally, that the probate court in the Roberts estate was without jurisdiction to try the title to the stock in question as between Franklin H. Roberts, on the one hand, and either the Estate of George W. Roberts, deceased, or Loretto Lohman Roberts, as the widow and sole heir of George W. Roberts, deceased, on the other. . . .

Is the "Declaration of Trust-Revocable" Executed by George W. Roberts in His Lifetime Valid as a Trust? The [next] contention of plaintiff is that the instrument is ineffective as . . . a trust . . . because it was merely an attempt on the part of George W. Roberts to make a testamentary disposition of the stock to Franklin H. Roberts without complying with the Montana statutes on wills. . . .

The contention . . . is based on two premises: first, it is claimed that by virtue of the declaration of trust George W. Roberts parted with none of the rights or incidents of ownership of the stock, and in reality retained complete ownership, both legal and equitable, and all of the rights and incidents of such ownership; and, second, that by virtue of the declaration of trust Franklin H. Roberts, the alleged beneficiary, acquired no interest of any kind in the stock.

This being a diversity case, it is governed by Montana law. However, the problems presented here have never been passed upon by the Montana Supreme Court, so recourse must be had to the law of trusts generally as announced by text writers and courts of other jurisdictions in an attempt to determine how the Montana Supreme Court would view the matter. . . .

. . . While it is true that there can be no trust when the full legal and equitable ownership vests in a single person, it is also true that a person may occupy two capacities with regard to a trust. Thus, the settlor of a trust may make himself trustee thereof (Restatement of Trusts, Sec. 100), or the settlor may likewise be a beneficiary of the trust (Restatement of Trusts, Sec. 114). . . .

By the declaration of trust George W. Roberts declared that he held said stock in trust for Franklin H. Roberts. That a valid trust may be created in this manner is clear (Restatement of Trusts, Secs. 17 and 28; 54 Am. Jr. "Trusts," Sec. 61, p. 69). In declaring the trust, George W. Roberts reserved to himself *in his capacity as settlor or trustor* the following rights with respect to the trust property.

1. The right to receive during his lifetime all cash dividends.
2. The right at any time to change the beneficiary of the trust, or to revoke the trust by written notice to Investors Stock Fund, Inc., in such form as that Company prescribed, and regain the entire ownership of the property, and
3. Upon the sale or redemption of the stock by the trustee, the right to retain the proceeds of such sale or redemption.

Likewise the trust was to terminate upon the death of the beneficiary.

Under the declaration of trust, George W. Roberts, *in his capacity as trustee,* had the right to vote, sell, redeem, exchange, or otherwise deal in or with the stock, but in the event of sale or redemption, the trust was to terminate as to the stock sold or redeemed, and the proceeds of the stock sold or redeemed were to become the property of George W. Roberts as settlor.

By this distribution of the rights incidental to ownership of the stock in question between George W. Roberts, in his capacity as settlor, and George W. Roberts, in his capacity as trustee, George W. Roberts as settlor effectively relinquished some of the incidents of complete ownership of the stock. While he was free to sell or redeem the stock and apply the proceeds to his own use under the trust, his right to vote, exchange or deal with the stock in any manner otherwise than by sale or redemption was subject to the obligation which the law imposes on trustees. . . . As an absolute owner of the stock, George W. Roberts would be free to exchange the $5,000 worth of stock for a $10 hat, if he chose, but as trustee he would not be free to make such an exchange without first revoking the trust. And if George W. Roberts died after having committed any violation of his duties as trustee without revoking the trust, the beneficiary could hold his estate liable for any loss resulting to the trust fund as a result of such violations. . . .

On the other hand, immediately upon the execution of the declaration of trust, Franklin H. Roberts became vested with an equitable interest in the stock. This interest consisted essentially in a right to the performance of the trust, that is the right to have the trustee perform the duties imposed upon him by law, and eventually to succeed to complete ownership of the stock. That this interest was not to vest in enjoyment until the future, and was contingent in character, does not make it any less a vested interest. . . .

Much of the attack of the plaintiff upon the validity of the trust is necessarily based upon the erroneous proposition that the reserved power of revocation invalidates the trust. It seems clear to the Court that were the power of revocation not contained in the declaration of trust, there would be no question of its validity. Yet the right to reserve the power to revoke and still establish a valid trust is so well established in the law of trusts, that it cannot be questioned. Such right is indeed recognized by statute in Montana. Section 86-602, R.C.M. 1947, provides:

> A trust cannot be revoked by the trustor after its acceptance, actual or presumed, by the trustee and beneficiaries, except by the consent of all the beneficiaries, *unless the declaration of trust reserves a power of revocation to the trustor,* and in that case the power must be strictly pursued.

Likewise, the reservation of the right to revoke by George W. Roberts, coupled with the reservation of the cash dividends, and the reservation of the right to the proceeds of any of the stock sold or redeemed do not render the trust testamentary in character. . . .

In Cleveland Trust Co. v. White, 134 Ohio St. 1, 15 N.E.2d 627, 118 A.L.R. 475 at page[s] 478 and 479, the Court said:

> By the weight of authority, a trust, otherwise effective, is not rendered nugatory because the settlor reserves to himself the following rights and powers: (1) The use of the property and the income therefrom for life; (2) the supervision and direction of investments and reinvestments; (3) the amendment or modification of the trust agreement; (4) the revocation of the trust in whole or in part; (5) the consumption of the principal.

Finally, it is elementary that the creation of a trust is primarily dependent upon the intention of the settlor, and his manifestation of such intention. . . . By declaring that he held the stock in question for his brother, Franklin H. Roberts, George W. Roberts clearly manifested his intention to create a trust, and there is nothing elsewhere in the declaration of trust or in the record of this case to refute that manifestation of his intention. And . . . there is nothing in the law which requires the Court to thwart that intention by holding the trust invalid.

The Court is fortified in this opinion by the fact that "Declarations of Trust-Revocable," identical with the one involved here, were considered by the Supreme Courts of the States of Illinois and North Carolina, in the face of attacks similar to those made here, and were held to be valid, in the cases of Farkas v. Williams, 5 Ill. 2d 417, 125 N.E.2d

600, and Ridge v. Bright, 244 N.C. 345, 93 S.E.2d 607. Not only were the instruments in those cases identical word for word with the instrument here involved, but the subject of the trust was stock of the same company as in this case. . . .

The Court is therefore of the opinion that the "Declaration of Trust-Revocable," executed by George W. Roberts, created a valid inter vivos trust, and upon the death of George W. Roberts the 375.094 shares of Investors Stock Fund, Inc., represented by Certificate No. 1738, became the absolute property of the beneficiary, Franklin H. Roberts. . . .

Do you find convincing the court's assertion in Investors Stock Fund v. Roberts that the settlor-trustee took on real, immediate fiduciary responsibilities for the disregard of which he or his personal representative would be liable?

Although it is now generally accepted without question that revocable inter vivos trusts can serve as will substitutes without compliance with the wills act,[1] litigation continues in abundance. The question of "illusory" or "testamentary" character therefore remains a significant one to be understood and handled by lawyers in both planning and litigation contexts. The question is no doubt confused by the unfortunate tendency of courts (as in *Roberts*, above) to use the term "vested" when they mean to refer to interests that are legally recognized as presently existing property rights, which do not depend on whether they are, for example, vested or contingent, and which in any event begs the very question at issue. Most importantly, it is evident today in nearly all states that the question before the court is not whether revocable trusts *can* be used as will substitutes but generally whether in a given situation the transferor really intended a trust or something less — whether the transferor's actions and intentions were such that the law should take the alleged trust disposition seriously. Nearly all "trusts" that have "failed" in recent cases have been the result of informal and casual, if not sloppy, handling (sometimes by lawyers) leaving the transferor's understanding of the transaction or true intentions in the matter in substantial doubt. In some of these instances, as in the preceding case, the alleged settlor and trustee were the same person, although this situation does not readily lend itself to an "agency" explanation either. Usually, however, in reported cases finding no trust, the clouded role of "trustee" or "agent" is played by a family member or

---

1. Perhaps the ultimate case of a thin trust was the recent Roberts v. Roberts, 419 Mass. 685, 646 N.E.2d 1061 (1995), which involved a "nominee trust," an entity created for the purpose of holding title to property with the trustees having only perfunctory duties. The court sustained the trust against the assertion that it was invalid for want of execution with wills act formalities.

other trusted individual, with whom either oral or written communications are understandably ambiguous. Yet an occasional case is still encountered in which a formal arrangement, even one with a corporate fiduciary, falls on the wrong side of the vague line between trust and agency. The portion of the Ohio opinion reproduced below serves as a warning and suggests some of the danger signals, even though this portion of the opinion may only be dictum because of the result of another but omitted issue in the case.

OSBORN v. OSBORN
10 Ohio Misc. 171, 226 N.E.2d 814 (1966)

CORRIGAN, J. . . .

[T]he mere designation of "trustee" does not elevate a custodian or an agent to that status. In that event, the death of the so-called settlor or donor revokes the agency and the property of the decedent passes either under a will or pursuant to the intestate laws. The question for determination then is whether you are dealing with a trust or merely an agency.

[The Henry C. Osborn Trust, established in 1920 with the Cleveland Trust Company as trustee, also referred to as] the No. 1 Trust, must be viewed in the light of the facts and surrounding circumstances. In the instant case the mere retention of the income rights in the No. 1 Trust by Mr. Osborn together with the right to amend or revoke did not equal such control or dominion which would vitiate the trust. In serving its proper function an inter vivos trust provides management during the settlor's life, expeditiously disposes of the property at his death, limits costs of administration and widespread publicity on the probate of a will. During his lifetime he can observe how the trustee manages the trust, participate to some degree in the management, modify or even revoke the trust entirely. If the law is to recognize these rights of the settlor and sanction inter vivos trusts, the courts are charged with the responsibility of determining whether or not the trust is, in fact, a true trust.

After hearing all the testimony on this issue and reviewing the scores upon scores of exhibits received into the evidence, the court concludes that the Henry C. Osborn Trust fails to meet the requirements of a true trust, "both in the manner of administration by the bank and in the pervasive dominion and control which Mr. Osborn continually exercised, solely for his own personal advantage." Without attempting to list all the instances of domination and practically exclusive control of the bulk of the corpus of the trust, we will refer to some of the facts supporting this conclusion. As was suggested by counsel for plaintiff it served more as a combination bank account and safety deposit box for his benefit. Not only were all of his securities included, but an insurance policy issued by the Cleveland Automobile Club to its members and qualifying shares in various private clubs. His Cleveland home was carried as an asset of the trust, but he paid no rent and when it was of no more use to him as a home he took it back and used it to cut his income tax by a charitable deduction. Trust assets were used as collateral on personal loans and to pay his personal expenses, although he dutifully completed the revocation forms from a supply he kept available. A loan arrangement worked out with the bank provided him with a device to raise cash without incurring substantial tax liability and to defer sales until after his death when no capital gains tax would be payable, with the interest in the interim used as a tax deduction.

Although the trust agreement called for nothing more than obtaining "whenever practicable" his approval of the trustee's investment determinations, he made the decisions and continually rejected the trustee's demands for trust diversification. According to a former vice-president who handled the matters for the trust and Mr. Osborn, he could not think of an instance in which the bank ever changed a decision or refused a request by Mr. Osborn, after discussing the matter with him. Further all the indicia of ownership of the stocks which were issued in his name were sent to him, not the trustee. With one exception, Mr. Osborn's income and personal property tax returns show this income as received directly by him rather than through the trust. . . .

Several exhibits revealed:

> While cash additions and withdrawals were often large in amount (in the years 1956 through 1960, the cash revocations alone total over $580,000), they include amounts as low as $12.19 (addition) and $10.94 (withdrawal). The number and scope of these "additions" and "revocations" transactions reveal a use of the account not unlike the use one would make of an ordinary commercial bank account or a custodianship.

Without further enlarging this memorandum with additional details, we believe the evidence reflects that the arrangement between the bank and Mr. Osborn was so completely dominated by him that although it was referred to as a trust it remained an agency account. While conceding that [a contrary] argument might be advanced [on the basis of certain facts], the court looking at the total picture believes that such a working arrangement was a custodial account and in the nature of a testamentary disposition and certainly did not meet the true concept of a trust.

With the increasing popularity of the revocable living or inter vivos trust in modern estate planning, it should be made clear that the phraseology used in the trust instrument is meaningless, if the so-called settlor or donor actually remains in virtual control and the so-called trustee for fear of losing the business acquiesces in his every act and wish.. Where the trustee continually yields and makes adjustments in an attempt to keep a semblance of a true trust, a mere agency or custodianship is bound to result.

By way of summary, then, under the current law of Ohio, a person can observe the operation of one's estate plan and provide for the consolidation of the entire estate in a trust program, but the trust must meet the test of a true trust in order to maintain its non-testamentary character. The trust instrument executed by Henry C. Osborn in 1920 and modified over the years meets the test as to form [if] there had been full compliance with the terms and spirit of the No. 1 Trust. . . . However, due to the complete dominance of Henry C. Osborn and the meek acquiescence of the bank the trust in question was not a trust in fact. . . .

RESTATEMENT (THIRD) OF TRUSTS
(Tent. Draft approved 1996)

§25.   *Validity and Effect of Revocable Inter Vivos Trust*

(1) A trust that is created by the settlor's declaration of trust, by his or her inter vivos transfer to another, or by beneficiary designation or other payment under a life insurance policy, employee benefit or retirement arrangement, or other contract is not rendered testamentary merely because the settlor retains extensive rights such as beneficial interest for life, powers to revoke and modify the trust, and the right to serve as or control the trustee, or because the trust is funded in whole or in part or comes into existence at or after the death of the settlor, or because the trust is intended to serve as a substitute for a will.

(2) A trust that is not testamentary is not subject to the formal requirements of [wills acts] or to procedures for the administration of a decedent's estate; nevertheless, a revocable inter vivos trust is ordinarily subject to substantive restrictions on testation and to rules of construction and other rules applicable to testamentary dispositions, and in other respects the property of such a trust is ordinarily treated as if it were owned by the settlor.

4.   Tentative ("Totten" or Bank Account) Trusts

PROBLEM

12-G.   Five years ago, *X*, a single person, deposited $25,000 in a savings account opened in her own name "in trust for *Y*." Shortly thereafter she wrote to *Y*, stating at one point: "Incidentally, several days ago I put $25,000 in trust for you." A year later *X* withdrew $8,000 from the account, and six months ago she executed a will bequeathing $10,000 to *A*, $10,000 to *B*, and the residue of her estate to *C*. At the time of her death last month *X*'s assets consisted solely of marketable securities worth $12,000, a personal checking account containing about $600, and her interest, if any, in the savings account mentioned above (the balance of which was then slightly over $19,000, including interest). What are the rights of *A*, *B*, *C*, and *Y* in these assets? What other facts would you seek to determine?

It is not uncommon for a person to deposit funds in a bank or savings and loan association in the depositor's own name as trustee for another without specifying the real intent or the terms of a trust. Thus *A* may deposit money in a savings account in the name of "*A* in trust for *B*." What are the consequences of this act? Is a trust created? If so, is the trust revocable or irrevocable, and what are its other terms? We are dealing with what has come to be known as a tentative or *Totten* or bank account trust.

In the leading case of Matter of Totten, 179 N.Y. 112, 120, 125-126, 71 N.E. 748, 750, 752 (1904), Judge Vann's opinion states:

> [W]hen it became common practice for persons to make deposits in that form, in order to evade restrictions upon the amount one could deposit in his own name and for other reasons, the courts . . . sought to avoid unjust results by adapting the law to the customs of the people. A brief review of the cases will show how the subject has gradually developed so as to accord with the methods of the multitude of persons who make deposits in these banks. . . .
>
> It is necessary for us to settle the conflict [in opinions from different appellate divisions] by laying down such a rule as will best promote the interests of all the people in the state. . . . A deposit by one person of his own money, in his own name as trustee for another, standing alone, does not establish an irrevocable trust during the lifetime of the depositor. It is a tentative trust merely, revocable at will, until the depositor dies or completes the gift in his lifetime by some unequivocal act or declaration, such as delivery of the pass book or notice to the beneficiary. In case the depositor dies before the beneficiary without revocation, or some decisive act or declaration of disaffirmance, the presumption arises that an absolute trust was created as to the balance on hand at the death of the depositor.

Evidence is admissible to show the actual intent of the depositor, and if his intention is discovered it will be given effect. "The evidence bearing upon the intent of the depositor, aside from the deposit itself, may be divided into three classes, namely: (a) Express statements of intent; (b) acts or omissions of the depositor with respect to the deposit or the supposed beneficiary, aside from express statements; (c) the circumstances of the depositor." G. Bogert, Trusts §20 (3d ed. 1952).

From the form of the deposit alone any of several inferences might be drawn. Some cases infer no intent to create a trust. Some others infer that an irrevocable trust is created. By the weight of authority the inference is that stated in Matter of Totten, supra. See also Uniform Probate Code §§6-201 to 6-216.

In Abbale v. Lopez, 511 So. 2d 340 (Fla. App. 1987), *H* deposited his funds in a bank account in the names of *H* and *W* (his wife) "in trust for *B*." When *H* died, the court concluded that this deposit had created a *Totten* trust with cotrustees, that the trust continued with *W* as sole trustee, but that she had no power to revoke. Does this seem like an appropriate interpretation? Contrast Hillyer v. Hillyer, 499 N.E.2d 569 (Ill. App. 1986). Should the result be different (and, if so, how) if both *H* and *W* had contributed to the account, such as if the deposited funds had been their community property or partly the property of each? See Restatement (Third) of Trusts §26, cmt. *c* (omitted in excerpt below). Doctrinal issues for tentative trusts are reasonably well settled in most states. Continuing difficulties generally involve questions of fact and interpretation in individual cases. See id., cmt. *a* reporter's note.

RESTATEMENT (THIRD) OF TRUSTS
(Tent. Draft approved 1999)

§26. . . . *Comments:*

c. Revocation and termination of tentative trust. A tentative trust can properly be revoked by the depositor at any time during life by a manifestation of intention to do so. No particular formalities are necessary to manifest that intention.[2]

Thus, the trust is terminated by withdrawal of all the funds or by transferring them to a different account. If any part of the deposit is withdrawn during the depositor's lifetime, this operates as a revocation of the trust to the extent of the withdrawal; and the beneficiary will be

---

2. The Reporter's Note to §26, Comment *c* of the Restatement (Third) goes on to explain:

> Although tentative trusts under the "Totten trust" doctrine are a form of revocable trust, the rules . . . are not necessarily the same as for other revocable trust situations. Differences in treatment are the result of the special relationships involved, the absence of a fiduciary relationship, and the special types of needs or purposes that tend to be served by savings account trusts. Thus, for example, revocation of a tentative trust may be much more informal or casual. . . .

entitled only to the amount remaining on deposit at the death of the depositor. . . .

In the absence of a statute to the contrary [see UPC §§6-201, 6-213] a tentative trust may be revoked in whole or in part by the depositor's will, either by express provision or by necessary implication. The conservator of a depositor who becomes incompetent may, with such court permission as may be required by law, withdraw some or all of the tentative trust funds as necessary for the welfare of the depositor and appropriate members of his or her family. . . .

d. Creditors' rights, family protection, and rules of will construction. The creditors of a person who establishes a tentative trust can reach the funds on deposit, as may the personal representative of a deceased depositor if assets otherwise available in the estate administration are insufficient to pay debts and funeral, last illness, and administration expenses.

The tentative trust, like other revocable inter vivos trusts, is subject to restrictions on testamentary disposition and also to pretermitted heir and omitted spouse protections. . . .

In re ESTATE OF KRYCUN
24 N.Y.2d 710, 249 N.E.2d 753 (1969)

Scileppi, J. . . .

In the case at bar, the testatrix had six separate bank accounts, four of which were in the *Totten* Trust form and two in her name alone. The language in paragraph SEVENTH of the will relied upon by the respondents states: "I give and bequeath any and all funds on deposit to my credit, in any bank or trust company or similar financial institution." The majority of the Appellate Division held that this language, in itself, was "clear and absolute to show the intention of the testatrix to revoke any prior trust bank accounts and to have such proceeds become part of the assets of the estate." We do not agree.

If the money on deposit in the four trust accounts comprised all or most of the assets of the estate or if the trust accounts were the only bank accounts in the decedent's name, that would be a strong indication that the testatrix intended to revoke the *Totten* Trusts. Such, however, was not the case. The money on deposit in the trust accounts only comprised a little more than one third of the total estate, and as indicated earlier the testatrix had two bank accounts in her name alone. We conclude, therefore, that the language in paragraph SEVENTH, in itself, under the facts of this case, is insufficient to overcome the presumption of nonrevocation. In such a case it is necessary to scrutinize the surrounding circumstances and the will as a whole, very carefully, in determining the true intention of the testatrix. It is our opinion that the posting of interest to the trust accounts up to the date of death [and] the language in paragraph THIRTEENTH of the will which contemplated "property passing outside [the] Will" ... manifest an intention on the part of the testatrix not to revoke. . . .

manifested intent not to revoke

See also Litsey v. First Federal Savings and Loan Assn., 243 So. 2d 239 (Fla. App. 1971). The abatement of legacies where funds do not permit payment in full is considered in Chapter 20.

5. Life Insurance Trusts

The use of life insurance trusts (typically a form of revocable inter vivos trust) is an important and common feature of estate planning. Where trusts are to be employed for any of the reasons already considered with regard to estates generally (see Chapter 9, section C), there are a variety of reasons for using insurance trusts for any life insurance owned by the client rather than simply having the proceeds made payable to the estate for inclusion in a testamentary trust. Among the major reasons are (1) avoidance of the costs and delays that would result from insurance proceeds being administered as part of the insured's estate; (2) the fact that such trusts are inter vivos trusts rather than testamentary trusts where retained jurisdiction in the probate court is provided for the latter by statute or practice and where the particular circumstances render such retained jurisdiction undesirable; and (3) avoidance of unnecessary state inheritance taxation under fairly common state rules taxing insurance proceeds payable to the estate of the insured but exempting proceeds payable to named beneficiaries. Inasmuch as the various insurance options also avoid probate and qualify for the typical inheritance tax exemption, what advantages do you see in an insurance trust over the selection of an annuity or interest option under the policy?

Life insurance trusts are generally created in either of two ways. Frequently, the owner of the insurance policy will designate the trustee as the beneficiary under the policy, normally designating that payee as trustee but occasionally without mention of the fiduciary capacity in the policy; the settlor and trustee will also execute a trust agreement. Under this method the trustee is usually given custody of the policy for convenience. The second method is to assign the insurance policies to the trustee pursuant to a trust agreement. Under each method the trust may be either funded or unfunded. The funded insurance trust involves also a transfer of other property to the trustee, with the income from the property used by the trustee to pay the premiums on the policies. Insurance trusts are often made wholly revocable, with the insured (or other owner of the policy) reserving all rights under the policies; this is common even where the policies are assigned to the trustee. Thus, the settlor of such a revocable trust would have the right to change the beneficiary designation or to surrender or borrow against the policies.

The life insurance trust techniques are often useful for other kinds of nonprobate transfers such as distributions from employee benefit plans, other pension arrangements, and individual retirement accounts (IRAs). These techniques are similar in concept, validity, and nontestamentary character to the life insurance trust. See, e.g., California Probate Code §6321, infra.

PROBLEM

12-H.   Your client, *H,* who has $100,000 worth of insurance and very little else, wishes to make his insurance payable to *W,* his wife, if she survives him; but if *W* does not survive him, *H* wants the proceeds to be payable to his sister, *S,* to hold in trust for *H*'s minor children. What steps would you take to bring about the desired result, and what beneficiary designations would be written into the policies? Does this arrangement pose any special problems regarding the validity of the trust as a nontestamentary disposition? If so, can you recommend any step that might be taken at the planning stage to protect against such a challenge? On what theory or theories might you argue to sustain such a trust if a challenge materializes?

GURNETT v. MUTUAL LIFE INSURANCE CO.
356 Ill. 612, 191 N.E. 250 (1934)

[Knowlton Ames and the Central Trust Company entered into a trust agreement in 1930. The agreement stated that Ames deposited with the trust company insurance policies (acquired between 1906 and 1927) insuring his life for a total of $1 million and making it beneficiary of all the policies. The agreement further provided that Ames would continue to pay the premiums and that he retained all rights under the policies, including the right to change the beneficiary, to borrow against the policies, and to surrender any policy for its cash value. He also reserved powers to revoke and amend the trust and twice exercised the latter power. During Ames's lifetime the trustee's only duty was to return the policies to Ames on his demand; on his death the trustee was to collect and administer the proceeds as provided in the trust instrument. Following Ames's death in 1931, complainants, creditors of his estate, brought suit against the insurance companies, the trustee, the executors of Ames's will, and his heirs at law. They sought to have the trust agreement declared void and to have the trustee ordered to hold the proceeds of the life insurance policies under a resulting trust in favor of Ames's estate. Complainants alleged, inter alia, that the rest of Ames's estate was insufficient to pay the claims of creditors, that Ames had not assigned the policies to the trustee but had treated them as his sole property, including borrowing on several of them, even after the date of the agreement, that there was no actual corpus of the trust and no transfer of property during Ames's lifetime, and that the intended trust fails with the proceeds rightfully belonging to the executors via resulting trust. Fraud was not alleged. The chancellor found a valid trust and entered a decree dismissing complainants' bill.]

DE YOUNG, J. . . .

A life insurance policy is property and may constitute the subject-matter of a trust. . . . The designated beneficiary of the policy may, by the provisions of collateral trust agreement, be named as the trustee. . . . When the beneficiary promises the insured to pay either the whole or a portion of the proceeds of the policy to a third person, the proceeds will be impressed with a trust to the extent of the promise made. . . .

The date of the death of the insured merely fixed the time when the obligation of the insurers to pay and the right of the beneficiary to receive the proceeds of the policies became enforceable. . . . The trust agreement and the change of beneficiaries, however, became effective during the lifetime of the settlor. The continuing right to receive the proceeds of an insurance policy is not impaired by the unexercised right or privilege of the insured to designate another beneficiary. The designation of a beneficiary in a policy of life insurance creates an inchoate gift of the proceeds of the policy, which, if not revoked by the insured in his lifetime, vests in the beneficiary at the time of the former's death. A policy of life insurance is not deemed an asset of the estate of the insured unless it is made payable to him, his executors or administrators. The mere fact that the insured may change the beneficiary does not make the policy or its proceeds a part of his estate. Neither the policies nor their proceeds constituted a part of the estate of Knowlton L. Ames, deceased. Since his death, the trust agreement is merely evidence of the trustee's contract under which it must collect the policies and hold the proceeds for the purposes of the trust. . . .

. . . [I]n the case of Hirsh v. Auer, 146 N.Y. 13, 40 N.E. 397, 398, [the court stated:]

> The fact that the trust dealt with a contingent interest of the insured in the certificate of insurance is of no moment. That interest became vested

at the death of the insured, and, the beneficiary having collected the insurance money, the trust, under the agreement creating and acknowledging it, attached to the fund. A trust of this character is not to be distinguished from assignments of contingent interests, which courts of equity recognize as valid.

The reservation of the power to revoke an entire trust does not invalidate the agreement presently creating it or render it testamentary. The plaintiffs in error concede the validity of the provision reserving power to the settlor to terminate the trust agreement in whole or in part. Naming new beneficiaries in one or more of the policies would have produced precisely the same effect as the termination of the trust with respect to such policies. The power to designate another beneficiary in an insurance policy is a privilege personal to the insured. The powers and privileges reserved do not affect the obligations of the insurers to pay the proceeds of the policies to the trustee upon the death of the insured. . . .

The judgment of the Appellate Court is affirmed. . . .

The above case is illustrative of the consistent response of courts to the assertion that insurance trusts are testamentary. See also Gordon v. Portland Trust Bank, 201 Or. 648, 653-655, 271 P.2d 653, 655 (1954), 2 U.C.L.A. L. Rev. 151:

The older rule which gave a vested interest to the beneficiary does not, of course, square with the modern notions of life policies. . . . But the courts are by no means in accord on the issue. Many hold that the beneficiary takes a vested interest subject to divestment upon change of beneficiary in accordance with the provisions of the policy. . . . Where this view obtains, there is no problem concerning the testamentary aspect of the transaction, for the vested right of the beneficiary is without doubt a proper subject for a trust. . . .

Under the general view that the beneficiary has no more than an expectancy, it is more difficult to find the necessary res for a present trust. Rather, the transaction appears to be a contract . . . to create a trust at the insured's death. The courts, however, have not felt constrained to arrive at this conclusion, and the cases are legion which have upheld the usual form of unfunded insurance trust even where the court had previously announced that the beneficiary has no more than a mere expectancy. In some of the earlier cases, the rationale appeared to be that, since a life insurance policy payable to an ordinary third-party beneficiary is not testamentary, then neither is one wherein the third-party beneficiary is also trustee, for in both cases the legal title to the proceeds is in the beneficiary according to the doctrine of the third party beneficiary as it has developed in the law of contracts. In the insurance trust device, the trustee-beneficiary takes a divided interest in the property, but this is specifically a trust problem and has no bearing on the testamentary character of the device. . . . We observe, therefore, that both under the old view, where the beneficiary is considered the owner, and under the new view where he has only an expectancy, the result is the same, for even in the new view, the third-party beneficiary has a present right to fulfillment of the insurer's promise to pay. There is no inconsistency in this position.

PROBLEM

12-I. John died nine days after changing the beneficiary of his $50,000 life insurance policy from his wife to the Peoples Bank "to be held in Trust," but without specifying the trust terms in the beneficiary designation. Six days before his death, he executed a will bequeathing his estate, without mention of the insurance, to Peoples Bank in trust for his wife for life, remainder to their children. An apparent suicide note in the decedent's handwriting stated that Peoples Bank "will have control of all the property and insurance money for the family." Peoples Bank, as executor and trustee, petitioned for instructions with respect to the insurance proceeds, which it had collected as beneficiary under the policy. Claims against the decedent's estate exceeded $51,000; the estate was worth less than $1,000 without the insurance proceeds, the bulk of the family assets being jointly held land that passed to decedent's widow by right of survivorship. From an order that the insurance proceeds were to be held by the bank in an inter vivos trust under the terms set out in the will, one of the estate creditors appealed. What arguments would you expect by the various parties? What result would you anticipate? Why? See Pavy v. Peoples Bank & Trust Co., 195 N.E.2d 862 (Ind. App. 1964).

Even in those decisions in which, because of some defect in the intended trust arrangement or some peculiar facts of the case, an intended insurance trust has been found to be illusory or otherwise held invalid, the opinions have usually recognized the general validity of insurance trusts. See, e.g., Bickers v. Shenandoah Valley National Bank, 197 Va. 145, 88 S.E.2d 889 (1955), noted in 54 Mich. L. Rev. 880, 31 N.Y.U. L. Rev. 967, 42 Va. L. Rev. 256.

Where the beneficiary under an insurance policy has orally agreed to hold the proceeds for a particular purpose or on a particular trust, the trust is generally enforceable. Shaull v. United States, 161 F.2d 891 (D.C. Cir. 1947) (oral promise by brother to hold for children of insured); Fahrney v. Wilson, 180 Cal. App. 2d 694, 4 Cal. Rptr. 670 (1960) (oral promise by widow to pay insured's debts); Cooney v. Montana, 347 Mass. 29, 196 N.E.2d 202 (1964). In Ballard v. Lance, 6 N.C.

App. 24, 169 S.E.2d 199 (1969), an oral trust of flight insurance was sustained although the insured's intention and instructions were conveyed to someone other than the trustee to whom the policies were made payable. Under a few statutes of frauds, however, these oral agreements or directions may be difficult to sustain. See, e.g., Desnoyers v. Metropolitan Life Insurance Co., 108 R.I. 100, 272 A.2d 683 (1971) (intended trust of insurance failed because trusts of personalty must be in writing); but see Blanco v. Valez, 295 N.Y. 224, 66 N.E.2d 171 (1946) (enforcing oral promise).

With these various insurance trusts, compare the situation in which the insured wishes the proceeds to be held in trust by a testamentary trustee. Frost v. Frost, 202 Mass. 100, 88 N.E. 446 (1909), involved a purported *assignment* of life insurance policies to "the trustees to be named in my will." The intended trust failed for want of a completed transfer, no delivery of the policies having been made to the "trustees" who remained unascertained during the insured's lifetime. Do you see why this trust was not upheld on the theories of the *Gurnett* and *Gordon* cases, supra?

Statutes permitting designation of testamentary trustees as beneficiaries of life insurance policies have been enacted in a growing number of states. The principal provision of one of these statutes is set out below. Would this statute have changed the result of the *Frost* case? See generally discussion in Schlesinger, Paying Insurance to Testamentary Trustees, 104 Tr. & Est. 1095 (1965), and compare discussion of "pour-over trusts" infra this chapter.

CALIFORNIA PROBATE CODE

§6321. *Designation of trustee as beneficiary, payee, or owner.* An instrument [broadly defined to include various life insurance contracts, employee benefit plans, self-employed retirement plans, IRAs, multiple-party accounts, and other provisions for nonprobate transfer] may designate as a primary or contingent beneficiary, payee, or owner a trustee named or to be named in the will of the person entitled to designate the beneficiary, payee, or owner. The designation shall be made in accordance with the provisions of the contract or plan or, in the absence of such provisions, in a manner approved by the insurer if an insurance, annuity, or endowment contract is involved, and by the trustee, custodian, or person or entity administering the contract or plan, if any. The designation may be made before or after the execution of the designator's will and is not required to comply with the formalities for execution of a will.

Insurance trusts pose a peculiar conceptual problem. Does the trust come into existence when the trust agreement and beneficiary designation are executed, or does it arise on the death of the insured by operation of two contracts? See the quotation from Gordon v. Portland Trust Bank, supra. Does it matter whether the policies are assigned or whether the trustee is merely designated as beneficiary of the policies? The effective date of the trust can be a crucial issue in cases involving the rule against perpetuities. Properly analyzed, however, this latter question does not arise where the insurance trust remains wholly revocable until the insured's death because the period of the rule against perpetuities does not begin to run until the trust becomes irrevocable. Cook v. Horn, 214 Ga. 289, 104 S.E.2d 461 (1958).

C. Will Substitutes and Policies Restricting Testation

We have seen that, for the most part, even thin inter vivos trusts that are used as will substitutes survive quite well against the charge that they circumvent the *formal* requirements imposed on testation. We now turn to cases in which trusts that have the character of will substitutes are employed to circumvent — or at least may have the effect of circumventing — what might be called *substantive* policies governing testamentary disposition. As earlier observed, the history of the trust's development reveals its frequent use to avoid undesired consequences of legal ownership. One of the trust's particular contributions has been avoiding outmoded rules and technical restrictions in advance of legal reform; equity does not necessarily follow the law.

Modern tax law reveals the efforts that are being made to prevent the use of trusts to circumvent tax policy. Express provisions of the federal estate tax law now treat property as belonging to the settlor when it has been placed in a trust that has the nature of a will substitute. (See Chapter 8, section E, supra.) For example, sections 2036 and 2038 of the Internal Revenue Code of 1954 require inclusion in a decedent's taxable estate of certain property that had been transferred with retention of various rights, benefits, or powers. On the other hand, statutes restricting bequests and devises to charity are generally held not to invalidate trusts for charitable purposes, despite the settlor's retention of a life interest and a power of revocation. IA W. Fratcher, Scott on Trusts §57.5 (4th ed. 1987). This is consistent with the generally accepted policy of narrowly construing such statutes.

1. Elective Share of Surviving Spouse

Another area of problems involves the use of living trusts to circumvent statutes intended to prevent disinheritance of a surviving spouse. The American cases have historically taken the position that "if it is provided by statute that the wife of a testator shall be entitled to a certain portion of his estate of which she cannot be deprived by will, a married man can nevertheless transfer his property inter vivos in trust and his widow will not be entitled on his death to a share of the property so transferred, even though he reserves a life estate and power to revoke or modify the trust." 1 Restatement (Second) of Trusts §57, cmt. *d*. This statement is predicated on the basic rule that, in the absence of contrary statute, a person may defeat a spouse's forced share by giving away property during life. The statement does not apply, of course, when even an outright gift of the property would not defeat the spouse's right, such as in the case of land subject to dower.

A modest but increasing number of cases have reached results contrary to the traditional position reflected in the Restatement (Second) of Trusts. See changed position in Restatement (Third) of Trusts §25(2) and cmt. *d*. The diversity of the views adopted by various courts and the uncertainty created by some of the opinions can be sources of considerable difficulty. See generally W. MacDonald, Fraud on the Widow's Share 67 et seq. (1960).

NEWMAN v. DORE
275 N.Y. 371, 9 N.E.2d 966 (1937)

LEHMAN, J.

The Decedent Estate Law . . . does not limit or affect disposition of property inter vivos. In terms and in intent it applies only to decedents' estates. Property which did not belong to a decedent at his death and which does not become part of his estate does not come within its scope. . . .

[B]y section 18 of the revised Decedent Estate Law . . . "a personal right of election is given to the surviving spouse to take his or her share of the estate as in intestacy, subject to the limitations, conditions and exceptions contained in this section." These limitations and exceptions include a case where "the testator has devised or bequeathed in trust an amount equal to or greater than the intestate share, with income thereof payable to the surviving spouse for life. . . ."

Ferdinand Straus died on July 1, 1934, leaving a last will and testament dated May 5, 1934, which contained a provision for a trust for his wife for her life of one-third of the decedent's property both real and personal. In such case the statute did not give the wife a right of election to take her share of the estate as in intestacy. She receives the income for life from a trust fund of the amount of the intestate share, . . . [which] includes no property which does not form part of the estate at the decedent's death. The testator on June 28, 1934, three days before his death, executed trust agreements by which, in form at least, he transferred to trustees all his real and personal property. If the agreements effectively divested the settlor of title to his property then the decedent left no estate and the widow takes nothing. The widow has challenged the validity of the transfer to the trustees. The beneficiary named in the trust agreement has brought this action to compel the trustees to carry out its terms. The trial court has found that the "trust agreements were made, executed and delivered by said Ferdinand Straus for the purpose of evading and circumventing the laws of the State of New York, and particularly sections 18 and 83 of the Decedent Estate Law." Undoubtedly the settlor's purpose . . . could not [be accomplished] by testamentary disposition of his property. The problem in this case is whether he has accomplished that result by creating a trust during his lifetime.

The validity of the attempted transfer depends upon whether "the laws of the State of New York and particularly sections 18 and 83 of the Decedent Estate Law" prohibit or permit such transfer. . . . [A] "purpose of evading and circumventing" the law [cannot] carry any legal consequences. . . . "The fact that it desired to evade the law, as it is called, is immaterial, because the very meaning of a line in the law is that you intentionally may go as close to it as you can if you do not pass it." Superior Oil Co. v. State of Mississippi, 280 U.S. 390, 395. . . .

 Under the trust agreements executed a few days before the death of the settlor, he reserved the enjoyment of the entire income as long as he should live, and a right to revoke the trust at his will, and in general the powers granted to the trustees were in terms made "subject to the settlor's control during his life," and could be exercised "in such manner only as the settlor shall from time to time direct in writing." Thus, by the trust agreement which transferred to the trustees the settlor's entire property, the settlor reserved substantially the same rights to enjoy and control the disposition of the property as he previously had possessed, and the inference is inescapable that the trust agreements were executed by the settlor, as the court has found, "with the intention and for the purpose of diminishing his estate and thereby to reduce in amount the share" of his wife in his estate upon his death and as a "contrivance to deprive . . . his widow of any rights in and to his property upon his death." They had no other purpose and substantially they had no other effect. Does the statute intend that such a transfer shall be available as a means of defeating the contingent expectant estate of a spouse?

In a few states where a wife has a similar contingent expectant interest or estate in the property of her husband, it has been held that her rights may not be defeated by any transfer made during life with intent to deprive the wife of property, which under the law would otherwise pass to her. In those states it is the intent to defeat the wife's contingent rights which creates the invalidity and it seems that an absolute transfer of all his property by a married man during his life, if made with other purpose and intent than to cut off an unloved wife, is valid even though its effect is to deprive the wife of any share in the property of her husband at his death. . . .

Motive or intent is an unsatisfactory test of the validity of a transfer of property. In most jurisdictions it has been rejected, sometimes for the reason that it would cast doubt upon the validity of all transfers made by a married man, outside of the regular course of business; sometimes because it is difficult to find a satisfactory logical foundation for it. Intent may, at times, be relevant in determining whether an act is fraudulent, but there can be no fraud where no right of any person is invaded. "The great weight of authority is that the intent to defeat a claim which otherwise a wife might have is not enough to defeat the deed." Leonard v. Leonard, 181 Mass. 458, 462. . . . Since the law gives the wife only an expectant interest in the property of her husband which becomes part of his estate, and since the law does not restrict transfers of property by the husband during his life, it would seem that the only sound test of the validity of a challenged transfer is whether it is real or illusory. That is the test applied in Leonard v. Leonard, supra. The test has been formulated in different ways, but in most jurisdictions the test applied is essentially the test of whether the husband has in good faith divested himself of ownership of his property or has made an illusory transfer. . . . In Pennsylvania the courts have sustained the validity of the trusts even where a husband reserved to himself the income for life, power of revocation, and a considerable measure of control. In other jurisdictions transfers in trust have been upheld regardless of their purpose where a husband retained a right to enjoy the income during his life. . . . In some of these cases the settlor retained, also, a power of revocation. In no jurisdiction has a transfer in trust been upheld where the conveyance is intended only to cover up the fact that the husband is retaining full control of the property though in form he has parted with it. Though a person may use means lawfully available to him to keep out-side of the scope of a statute, a false appearance of legality, however attained, will not avail him. Reality, not appearance, should determine legal rights.

In this case the decedent, as we have said, retained not only the income for life and power to revoke the trust, but also the right to control the trustees. We need not now determine whether such a trust is, for any purpose, a valid present trust. It has been said that, "where the settlor transfers property in trust and reserves not only . . . a power to revoke and modify the trust but also such power to control the trustee as to the details of the administration of the trust that the trustee is the agent of the settlor, the disposition so far as it is intended to take effect after his death is testamentary. . . . " American Law Institute, Restatement of the Law of Trusts, §57, subd. 2. We do not now consider whether the rule so stated is in accord with the law of this state or whether in this case the reserved power of control is so great that the trustee is in fact "the agent of the settlor." We assume, without deciding, that except for the provisions of section 18 of the Decedent Estate Law the trust would be valid. Perhaps "from the technical point of view such a conveyance does not quite take back all that it gives, but practically it does." That is enough to render it an unlawful invasion of the expectant interest of the wife. Leonard v. Leonard, supra; Brownell v. Briggs, 173 Mass. 529, 54 N.E. 251.

Judged by the substance, not by the form, the testator's conveyance is illusory, intended only as a mask for the effective retention by the settlor of the property which in form he had conveyed. We do not attempt now to formulate any general test of how far a settlor must divest himself of his interest in the trust property to render the conveyance more than illusory. Question of whether reservation of the income or of a power of revocation, or both, might even without reservation of the power of control be sufficient to show that the transfer was not intended in good faith to divest the settlor of his property must await decision until such question arises. In this case it is clear that the settlor never intended to divest himself of his property. He was unwilling to do so even when death was near.

The judgment should be affirmed, with costs. . . .

In Matter of Halpern, 303 N.Y. 33, 100 N.E.2d 120 (1951), the executrix, the testator's widow and the sole beneficiary of his will, sought to have included in his otherwise insignificant estate certain savings accounts (tentative trusts) created by the testator in his name as trustee for a grandchild. In modifying the surrogate's decision that the trusts were illusory, the Appellate Division held that the tentative trusts failed only to the extent required to satisfy the widow's statutory share computed as though the accounts were included in the estate. The executrix appealed but the grandchild did not. The Court of Appeals, however, stated:

We hold that respondent's legal position is correct, and that these *Totten* trusts were, on this record, valid, effective and not illusory. It is, perhaps, regrettable that any husband resorts to such transfers to keep his money from his wife. But *Totten* trusts, if real and not merely colorable or pretended, are valid transfers with legally fixed effects. . . .

The Appellate Division, reasoning . . . from its conclusion that these trusts were illusory because destructive of section 18 benefits, decided that only so much thereof should be set aside as was required to put the widow in the section 18 position. . . . We see no power in the courts to divide up such a *Totten* trust and call part of it illusory and the other part good. The only test is that quoted above, from Newman v. Dors, . . . and the results of its applications would necessarily be either total validity or total invalidity, as to any one transfer.

303 N.Y. at 37-40, 100 N.E.2d at 122-123.

A review of the New York experience and legislation expanding the spouse's protection can be found in Amend, The Surviving Spouse and the Estates, Powers and Trust Law, 33 Brooklyn L. Rev. 530 (1967).

SULLIVAN v. BURKIN
390 Mass. 864, 460 N.E.2d 572 (1984)

[Mary Sullivan elected against the will of her husband, Ernest, and sought unsuccessfully in the probate court to have included in his estate for that purpose the assets of a revocable inter vivos trust of which he was settlor, sole trustee, and income beneficiary with a right to principal on demand. The Sullivans had been separated for many years before the husband's death.]

WILKINS, J. . . .

[T]he wife's claim was simply that the inter vivos trust was an invalid testamentary disposition. . . . If [that were so] the trust assets would be a part of the husband's probate estate [and] we would not have to consider any special consequences of the wife's election. . . .

We conclude, however, that the trust was not testamentary in character and that the husband effectively created a valid inter vivos trust. . . . We [further] conclude that, in this case, we should adhere to the principles expressed in Kerwin v. Donaghy, [59 N.E.2d 299 (1945)], that deny the surviving spouse any claim against the assets of a valid inter vivos trust created by the deceased spouse, even where the deceased spouse alone retained substantial rights and powers under the trust instruments. For the future, however, as to any inter vivos trust created or amended after the date of this opinion, we announce that the estate of a decedent, for the purposes of G.L. c. 191, §15, shall include the value of assets held in an inter vivos trust created by the deceased spouse as to which the deceased spouse alone retained the power during his or her life to direct the disposition of those trust assets for his or her benefit, as, for example, by the exercise of a power of appointment or by revocation of the trust. Such a power would be a general power of appointment for Federal estate tax purposes (I.R.C. §2041(b)(1) [1983]) and a "general power" as defined in the Restatement (Second) of Property §11.4(1) (Tent. Draft No. 5, 1982).

We consider first whether the inter vivos trust was invalid because it was testamentary. . . . We believe that the law of the Commonwealth is correctly represented by the statement in Restatement (Second) of Trusts §57, comment *h* (1959), that a trust is

> not testamentary and invalid for failure to comply with the requirements of the Statute of Wills merely because the settlor-trustee reserves a beneficial life interest and power to revoke and modify the trust. The fact that as trustee he controls the administration of the trust does not invalidate it.

We come then to the question whether, even if the trust was not testamentary on general principles, the widow has special interests which should be recognized.

. . . In considering this issue at the May, 1982, annual meeting of the American Law Institute the members divided almost evenly on whether a settlor's surviving spouse should have rights, apart from specific statutory rights, with respect to the assets of an inter vivos trust over which the settlor retained a general power of appointment. See Proceedings of the American Law Institute, May, 1982, pp. 59-117; Restatement (Second) of Property — Donative Transfers, Supplement to Tent. Draft No. 5 at 28 (1982).[3] . . .

In this Commonwealth a husband has an absolute right to dispose of any or all of his personal property in his lifetime, without the knowledge or consent of his wife, with the result that it will not form part

---

3. The reporter, Professor A. James Casner, recommended the following statement:

> §13.7   *Spousal Rights in Appointive Assets on Death of Donee.* The spouse of the donee of a power of appointment is entitled to treat appointive assets as owned assets of the donee on the donee's death, only to the extent provided by statute.

Restatement (Second) of Property — Donative Transfers, Tent. Draft No. 5 at pp. 108-109 (1982). This statement is consistent with the principles expressed in Kerwin v. Donaghy, supra. By a vote of 63 to 60, the members rejected the substitution of the following statement under §13.7, recommended by an adviser to the project, Justice Rava S. Dreben of the Massachusetts Appeals Court:

> Appointive assets are treated as owned assets of a deceased donee in determining the rights of a surviving spouse in the owned assets of the donee if, and only if, the deceased spouse was both the donor and donee of a general power that was exercisable by the donee alone, unless the controlling statute provides otherwise.

Restatement (Second) of Property — Donative Transfers, Supplement to Tent. Draft No. 5 at pp. 6 and 28 (1982).

of his estate for her to share under the statute of distributions (G.L.
[Ter. Ed.] c. 190, §§1, 2), under his will, or by virtue of a waiver of his
will. That is true even though his sole purpose was to disinherit her.
In the *Kerwin* case, we applied the rule to deny a surviving spouse the
right to reach assets the deceased spouse had placed in an inter vivos
trust of which the settlor's daughter by a previous marriage was trustee
and over whose assets he had a general power of appointment. The
rule of Kerwin v. Donaghy has been adhered to in this Commonwealth
for almost forty years and was adumbrated even earlier. The bar has
been entitled reasonably to rely on that rule in advising clients. In the
area of property law, the retroactive invalidation of an established principle is to be undertaken with great caution. . . . We conclude that,
whether or not Ernest G. Sullivan established the inter vivos trust in
order to defeat his wife's right to take her statutory share in the assets
placed in the trust and even though he had a general power of appointment over the trust assets, Mary A. Sullivan obtained no right to share
in the assets of that trust when she made her election under G.L. c.
191, §15.

We announce for the future that, as to any inter vivos trust created
or amended after the date of this opinion, we shall no longer follow
the rule announced in Kerwin v. Donaghy. There have been significant
changes since 1945 in public policy considerations bearing on the right
of one spouse to treat his or her property as he or she wishes during
marriage. The interests of one spouse in the property of the other have
been substantially increased upon the dissolution of a marriage by divorce. We believe that, when a marriage is terminated by the death of
one spouse, the rights of the surviving spouse should not be so restricted as they are by the rule in Kerwin v. Donaghy. It is neither equitable nor logical to extend to a divorced spouse greater rights in the
assets of an inter vivos trust created and controlled by the other spouse
than are extended to a spouse who remains married until the death
of his or her spouse.

The rule we now favor would treat as part of "the estate of the deceased" for the purposes of G.L. c. 191, §15, assets of an inter vivos
trust created during the marriage by the deceased spouse over which
he or she alone had a general power of appointment, exercisable by
deed or by will. This objective test would involve no consideration of
the motive or intention of the spouse in creating the trust. We would
not need to engage in a determination of "whether the [spouse] has
in good faith divested himself [or herself] of ownership of his [or her]
property or has made an illusory transfer" (Newman v. Dore, 275 N.Y.
371, 379, 9 N.E.2d 966 [1937]) or with the factual question whether the
spouse "intended to surrender complete dominion over the property"
(Staples v. King, 433 A.2d 407, 411 [Me. 1981]). Nor would we have

to participate in the rather unsatisfactory process of determining whether the inter vivos trust was, on some standard, "colorable," "fraudulent," or "illusory."

What we have announced as a rule for the future hardly resolves all the problems that may arise. There may be a different rule if some or all of the trust assets were conveyed to such a trust by a third person. Cf. Theodore v. Theodore, 356 Mass. 297, 249 N.E.2d 3 (1969). We have not, of course, dealt with a case in which the power of appointment is held jointly with another person. If the surviving spouse assented to the creation of the inter vivos trust, perhaps the rule we announce would not apply. We have not discussed which assets should be used to satisfy a surviving spouse's claim. We have not discussed the question whether a surviving spouse's interest in the intestate estate of a deceased spouse should reflect the value of assets held in an inter vivos trust created by the intestate spouse over which he or she had a general power of appointment. That situation and the one before us, however, do not seem readily distinguishable. See Schnakenberg v. Schnakenberg, 262 A.D. 234, 236-237, 28 N.Y.S.2d 841 (N.Y. 1941). A general power of appointment over assets in a trust created by a third person is said to present a different situation. Restatement (Second) of Property — Donative Transfers, Supplement to Tent. Draft No. 5, reporter's note to §13.7 at 29 (1982). Nor have we dealt with other assets not passing by will, such as a trust created before the marriage or insurance policies over which a deceased spouse had control. Id. at 30, 38.

The question of the rights of a surviving spouse in the estate of a deceased spouse, using the word "estate" in its broad sense, is one that can best be handled by legislation. See Uniform Probate Code, §§2-201, 2-202, 8 U.L.A. 74-75 (1983). See also Uniform Marital Property Act, §18 (Natl. Conference of Commrs. on Uniform State Laws, July, 1983), which adopts the concept of community property as to "marital property." But, until it is, the answers to these problems will "be determined in the usual way through the decisional process." Tucker v. Badoian, 376 Mass. 907, 918-919, 384 N.E.2d 1195 (1978) (Kaplan, J., concurring).

We affirm the judgment of the Probate Court dismissing the plaintiff's complaint.

So ordered.

See also Moore v. Jones, 44 N.C. App. 578, 261 S.E.2d 289 (1980), holding a revocable trust agreement "ineffective" to impair the surviving spouse's statutory rights. Except to that extent, the court upheld the trust and directed that it otherwise be carried out, as far as practicable, in accordance with its terms. The court expressly declined to find the trust illusory or to base its decision on fraud or intention to impair the spouse's rights; in the court's view, the record would not support such an interpretation.

For a decision relying on the "illusory trust" basis for recognizing the spouse's right in "*Totten* trust" property, see Johnson v. LaGrange State Bank, 73 Ill. 2d 342, 383 N.E.2d 185 (1978).

An interesting approach to the allocation of the legislative and judicial responsibilities in this matter is reflected in In re Jeruzal's Estate, 269 Minn. 183, 194-196, 130 N.W.2d 473, 481-482 (1964), noted in Note, 34 U Cin. L. Rev. 179 (1965), in which it is stated:

> [I]t appears that in Minnesota a motive to deprive one's spouse of the statutory inheritance by inter vivos transfer generally is irrelevant, the only test being whether the transaction is real. This principle, if extended to *Totten* trusts, would lead to the adoption of the New York rule enunciated in the *Halpern* case. . . . We are not satisfied that [a] rule should be adopted [under which] the trust is either good against the spouse or void altogether. We would prefer the Restatement [(Second) of Trusts §58, comment *e*] rule, by which the beneficiaries receive what the decedent intended them to have except so far as [*Totten*] trust funds are necessary to satisfy statutory interests of the spouse after the general assets of the estate have been exhausted. However, in view of the widespread use of *Totten* trusts in the area of testamentary disposition we do not feel free to adopt the Restatement rule without first giving the legislature an opportunity to provide for it by statute as was done in Pennsylvania. . . .
>
> However, this court will feel free to follow the Restatement rule hereafter if the legislature declines to act on this matter. The *Totten* trust itself is a judicial creation, [and it] is therefore our duty to subject this judicially-created doctrine to such limitations as are necessary to prevent the defeat of substantive statutory policies. . . . The statutory policy against allowing the widow to be left destitute should not be subordinated to the policy of giving broad effect to savings account trusts, however desirable the latter may be. We cannot overlook the danger that lies in the general use of *Totten* trusts as they may affect the surviving spouse. Actually, a depositor accomplishes nothing by a *Totten* trust which he could not accomplish by will. Only the procedure, not the substance, is changed. . . . We feel that the Restatement rule . . . provides a satisfactory balance of the two policies here involved. . . .
>
> This conclusion does not limit the effect of any of our earlier decisions on the extent to which marital rights may be defeated by the use of trusts. *Totten* trusts are a special case not necessarily subject to rules governing trusts generally.

Legislative solutions to this conflict are gradually emerging. In a number of states statutes have been enacted specifically to protect the forced share of a surviving spouse against revocable trusts and certain other will substitutes. Pennsylvania enacted one of the earliest of these, and after the *Jeruzal* case Minnesota enacted legislation patterned after Pennsylvania's. (Subsequently, with the adoption of versions of the Uniform Probate Code in these states, both statutes have been revised or replaced.) Since the New York decisions, supra, N.Y. Estates, Powers & Trusts Law §5-1.1(b) was enacted. It excludes life insurance and employee benefits, based on the experience of Pennsylvania, which had initially included life insurance but which eight years later dropped it (and still continues to exclude insurance and "broad-based" employee benefit plans) from the coverage of the legislation. Pa. Stat. Ann. tit. 20, §2203(b). A similar approach, also excluding insurance, annuities, and pensions, is now found in California Probate Code §§101, 102, protecting a surviving spouse's forced right to half of a decedent's foreign-acquired marital ("quasi-community") property from gratuitous transfers in which the decedent retained income, control, or right of survivorship. Federal law, however, mandates provision (unless waived) for surviving spouses of participants in pension plans governed by the Employee Retirement Income Security Act (ERISA), 29 U.S.C.A. §§1001 et seq. (1974), as amended by the Retirement Equity Act, 98 Stat. 1426 (1984). Compare the comprehensive provisions of the "augmented estate" in Uniform Probate Code §§2-201 to 2-207, set out in Chapter 3, supra.

A remarkable case of statutory interpretation is Seifert v. Southern Nat'l Bank, 409 S.E.2d 337 (S.C. 1991). The holding and associated history are well-described in the Reporter's Note to Restatement (Third) of Property (Wills and Other Donative Transfers) §10.1, at 167-168 (Preliminary Draft No. 7, 1999):

> [T]he Supreme Court of South Carolina held that "where a spouse seeks to avoid payment of the elective share by creating a trust over which he or she exercises substantial control, the trust may be declared invalid as illusory, and the trust assets will be included in the decedent's estate for calculation of the elective share." In a footnote, the court said that "[s]ubstantial control means that a settlor has retained such extensive powers over the assets of the trust that he has until death the same rights in the assets after creation of the trust that he had before its creation." The *Seifert* decision is especially important because the South Carolina legislature had amended the elective share statute so that it expressly applied to the decedent's "probate estate" rather than to the decedent's "estate," and because the legislature had rejected the Original UPC's augmented estate concept. The Reporter's Comment to S.C. Code Ann. §62-2-2-202 stated:
>
> > This section rejects the "augmented estate" concept promulgated by the drafters of the Uniform Probate Code as unnecessarily com-

[handwritten margin note: Movement is to protect surviving spouse]

plex. The spouse's protection relates to all real and personal assets owned by the decedent at death but does not take into account the use of various will substitutes which permit an owner to transfer ownership at death without use of a will.

The court nevertheless said: "Since nothing in [the elective-share statute] prohibits the proceeds of a trust, once declared invalid or illusory from being included in the probate estate, we hold that the proceeds of the trust should be included in Husband's estate for the purpose of calculating Widow's elective share." After *Seifert* was decided, the legislature enacted a statute providing that "a judicial decision finding that a trust is illusory shall only have the effect of treating the trust assets as part of the probate estate for purposes of the elective share." S.C. Code Ann. §62-7-112. The same approach — making the assets of a revocable trust available for purposes of the statutory election without entirely invalidating the trust — was taken by the court in Taliaferro v. Taliaferro, 843 P.2d 240 (Kan. 1992). The Kansas legislature subsequently enacted the Revised UPC augmented estate.

PROBLEM

12-J. Your client, *W*, resides in state *X*, which has enacted legislation providing: "A conveyance of assets by a person who retains a power of revocation over the principal thereof shall, for purposes of the forced share election of his or her surviving spouse, be treated as a testamentary disposition." *H*, her husband, died six weeks ago. His probate estate consists of property, mostly land in state *X*, valued at $200,000. *H*'s will has been admitted to probate and provides for the property to be divided equally between *W* and *H*'s only child, *D*, a daughter by a previous marriage.

About a year before his death *H* established an inter vivos trust in state *Y*, with the *T* Trust Company of that state as trustee, although *H* then resided in state *X*. Under this trust *H* reserved the income for life and a power of revocation, providing for the principal to go on *H*'s death to *D*, who lives in state *Z*. This trust consists of securities valued at $250,000.

W wants to establish whatever rights she may have in *H*'s estate and in the trust estate. How would you proceed to obtain as much of the property as you think possible? What type of evidence would you seek to present, and how would you argue the case in *W*'s behalf? What other factual and legal information do you need to know? Your research reveals that the Restatement rule, noted supra page 396, represents the law of the state *Y* and was recently quoted in an opinion of the *Y* Supreme Court. Consider the case that follows. Would the result differ if State *X* is a state of the United States but States *Y* and *Z* are foreign countries? Consider The Hague Convention discussion, infra.

NATIONAL SHAWMUT BANK v. CUMMING
325 Mass. 457, 91 N.E.2d 337 (1950)

WILKINS, J.

The plaintiff bank is the surviving trustee under a declaration of trust, dated August 25, 1944, in which the bank and the settlor, William Gray Cumming, of Barre, Vermont, were named as trustees. The settlor died on August 19, 1947. The defendants are the settlor's widow, Cora Mann Cumming, and the mother, brother, and three sisters of the settlor, and constitute all the surviving life beneficiaries under the trust instrument. This bill in equity seeks (1) the removal of a cloud upon the plaintiff's title as trustee to the trust property, as well as upon the beneficial interests of the defendants, the said cloud consisting of a claim asserted by the widow that the trust is invalid; and (2) a binding declaration of the rights of the parties under the trust instrument. G.L. (Ter. Ed.) c. 231A, inserted by St. 1945, c. 582, §1. The answers of the defendants other than the widow admit the allegations of the bill and join in the prayers for relief. The widow's answer sets up that the trust was created in bad faith with intent to defraud her of rights under Vermont law after waiver of the will, and that the validity of the trust is to be determined by the laws of the State of Vermont. The widow (hereinafter called the defendant) appealed from a final decree adjudging that the trust is valid, and that she has no claim to the trust property except as a beneficiary under the trust instrument. The judge filed "Findings, ruling and order for decree." The evidence is reported.

We summarize certain facts found by the judge or by ourselves.

The trust agreement provided that the income, and such amounts of the principal as the settlor might direct in writing, should be paid to him for life; and that after his death the income should be paid equally to his widow, his mother, two brothers (one of whom predeceased him), and three sisters, the principal, if necessary, to be used to insure the receipt of $150 monthly by each beneficiary. Upon the death of the settlor and the last survivor of the life beneficiaries, the trust was to terminate and distribution be made to the nieces and nephews of the settlor then living and to the living issue of each deceased niece or nephew by right of representation. The settlor reserved the power to amend, to revoke in whole or in part, and to withdraw principal. The last paragraph reads, "This instrument shall be construed and the provisions thereof interpreted under and in accordance with the laws of the Commonwealth of Massachusetts." Extensive powers of management were reserved to the trustees, but by an amendment of September 26, 1945, the settlor "delegated" his powers as cotrustee to the plaintiff.

The settlor died domiciled in Vermont at the age of fifty-seven. On January 5, 1925, when in Florida, he married the defendant. It was his first marriage. She was "several years" his senior and a widow with three children. The settlor, who until then had lived with his mother, was an eldest son who had assumed the obligation of the head of the family. He took these obligations very seriously, and strong family ties continued throughout his life. . . .

The settlor and the defendant "had not gotten along well," and the "rupture became more pronounced in December, 1944 . . . ."

The judge stated:

> I find that the settlor meticulously and designedly arranged his holdings and his business affairs so that his mother, wife, brothers and sisters would share the income, or principal, if necessary, equally after his death. That he knew that but for this arrangement his widow would have been entitled under the laws of Vermont to $4,000 and one half of his estate. But I do not find that in doing what he did . . . he was actuated by bad faith, or that he sought to accomplish something which he under all the circumstances considered to be unjust or unfair to his wife. I do not find that he set up the trust, with the fraudulent intent of preventing his wife from obtaining her distributive share of his property. I find and rule that the trust is valid. I find that the settlor intended that the trust be administered in Boston by the National Shawmut Bank as trustee. . . .

If the settlor had been domiciled in this Commonwealth and had transfered here personal property here to a trustee here for administration here, the transfer would have been valid even if his sole purpose had been to deprive his wife of any portion of it. Kerwin v. Donaghy, 317 Mass. 559, 571, 59 N.E.2d 299. The Vermont law we understand to be otherwise and to invalidate a transfer made there by one domiciled there of personal property there, if made with an actual, as distinguished from an implied, fraudulent intent to disinherit his spouse. In re O'Rourke's Estate, 106 Vt. 327, 331, 175 A. 4.

The plaintiff contends that the validity of the trust is to be determined by the law of this Commonwealth, and, in the alternative, that should the question be determined by Vermont law, the trust would still be valid on the judge's findings. The defendant, on the other hand, contends that the trust is not valid under either Vermont or Massachusetts law." This argument is founded upon alleged illegality according to the law of Vermont and an assertion that our courts must look to the law of the State of domicil, which determines the right of succession to the settlor's personal property here. Reliance is placed upon . . . Phelan v. Conron, 323 Mass. 247, 253, 81 N.E.2d 525. See G.L. (Ter. Ed.) c. 199, §1.2; Restatement: Conflict of Laws, §301, comment b. . . .

One answer to the defendant's contention is that, wholly apart from what may be the law of Vermont, it was not shown that the trust was created to defraud the wife of statutory rights in Vermont. The judge was not plainly wrong in not making such a finding. There was no evidence which compelled it. The findings which he did make, including the finding that the settlor knew that but for the trust arrangement his wife would be entitled to $4,000 and one half of his estate, meaning, of course, at its then valuation, are not tantamount to findings that the trust was created, or added to, with intent to defraud her, nor are the findings inconsistent with one another.

Another independent and insuperable difficulty is that before death the settlor had effectively disposed of the trust property, which had its situs in this Commonwealth and was not subject here to any equity in favor of a wife or to any similar limitation upon his power of disposition. He had expressed an intent in the trust instrument that it should be construed and interpreted according to the laws of this Commonwealth.

The elements entering into the decision as to the law of which State determines the validity of the trust are, on the one hand in Vermont, the settlor's domicil, and, on the other hand in Massachusetts, the presence of the property or its evidences, the completion of the trust agreement by final execution by the trustee, the domicil and the place of business of the trustee, and the settlor's intent that the trust should be administered by the trustee here. The general tendency of authorities elsewhere is away from the adoption of the law of the settlor's domicil where the property, the domicil and place of business of the trustee, and the place of administration intended by the settlor are in another State. The situation is unchanged by the fact that the one seeking to set aside the transaction is the widow of the settlor. We are of the opinion that the question of validity is to be determined by the law of this Commonwealth. There was no error under our law in adjudging the trust to be valid when created, or in omitting to adjudge it to be invalid at the time of the additions to principal made in 1945.

We are not sure whether any contention is made that the trust instrument is illusory on its face apart from alleged fraud toward the widow. The trust is not illusory. . . .

Decree affirmed.

Choice of Law. In addition to its relevance to the spouse's elective share, a case like National Shawmut Bank v. Cumming may provide a powerful choice of law tool for the estate planner. Notice the factors that led the court to choose Massachusetts law. Are these within the estate planner's control? Under *Cumming* can the settlor *choose* the law of a favorable jurisdiction, whether to avoid a spouse's elective share, creditors, the Rule Against Perpetuities or other restrictive rules? See generally VA W. Fratcher, Scott on Trusts ch. 14 (4th ed. 1989) and particularly the UTC, below. Does it matter whether the trust property is land, and if so, how might the planner deal with the matter?

UNIFORM TRUST CODE
(Draft, Feb. 2000)

§108.   *Choice of Law*

(a) A trust not created by will is validly created if its creation complies with the law of this State, the law of the place where the instrument was executed, or the law of the place where, at the time of creation, the settlor was domiciled, had a place of abode, or was a national, or a trustee was domiciled or had a place of business, or any trust property was located.

(b) The meaning and effect of the terms of a trust are determined by:

(1) the law of the State designated in those terms unless the designation of that State's law is contrary to a significant public policy of the State most significantly related to the matter at issue; or

(2) in the absence of a controlling designation in the terms of the trust, the law of the State most significantly related to the matter at issue.

§109.   *Principal Place of Administration. . . .*

(b) The trustee is under a continuing duty to administer a trust at a place appropriate to its purposes, its administration, and the interests of the beneficiaries. Without precluding the right of the court to order, approve, or disapprove a transfer, a trustee, in fulfilling this duty, may transfer a trust's principal place of administration to another State or country. The trustee must notify the qualified beneficiaries [defined in §103(14)] of the proposed transfer not less than 60 days before initiating the transfer.

(c) In connection with a transfer of a trust's principal place of administration, the trustee may transfer some or all of the trust property to a successor trustee designated in the terms of the trust or appointed pursuant to Section 704 [on methods of filling vacancies and appointing successor trustees].

PROBLEM

12-K.   (a) *X* created a testamentary trust of land located in her state of domicile; the trustee's domicile is in the same state. She provided in the will that the law of another state shall govern the construction of the trust. Which state's law governs construction? See Uniform Trust Code, supra, and compare Uniform Probate Code §2-703.

(b) A settlor creates an otherwise valid irrevocable trust but provides that no beneficiary shall receive any distribution to which the beneficiary is otherwise entitled unless the beneficiary regularly votes a straight Democratic ticket. The settlor, the trustee, and the beneficiaries are residents of State X in which the voting restriction is contrary to public policy, but the settlor specifies that the validity of the trust is governed by the law of State Y where the restriction is valid. Under the Uniform Trust Code, which state's law governs the trust restriction?

(c) A settlor creates an irrevocable trust in her domicile of State A and provides that the law of State A shall govern the construction of the trust. The corporate trustee and the beneficiaries are also domiciled in State A. The trust provides for the retention of a significant amount of income in the trust. Later the legislature in State A doubles the rate of income taxation for trusts from 5 percent to 10 percent. Under the Uniform Trust Code, may the trustee transfer the trust to its affiliated corporate trustee in State B, which taxes trust income at 4 percent?

Cumming is relevant to choosing the law of a foreign country, not just a different American state. See, for example, the discussion in Chapter 13, pages 660-663, of asset protection trusts that use a foreign situs to attempt to insulate property from the claims of creditors or others.

The concept of the trust, growing out of the feudal English use, is unique to Anglo-American jurisprudence. In an effort to clarify the status of the trust in civil law and other non-common law countries, the Hague Convention on the Law Applicable to Trusts and on Their Recognition was promulgated in 1985 by the Hague Conference on Private International Law, an organization of over 30 member states including the United States. The Conference attempts to formulate treaties aimed at creating unity in the laws of civil and common law countries. The Senate has not yet ratified the Trusts Convention. Only a few countries have signed the Convention. Article 6 provides that a trust shall be governed by the law chosen by the settlor, and Article 7 provides that where no applicable law has been chosen, a trust shall be governed by the law with which it is most closely connected. In ascertaining the closest connection, particular reference is made to the place of administration designated by the settlor, the situs of the trust assets, the place of residence or business of the trustee, and the objects of the trust and the places where they are to be fulfilled. Under Article 15 the Convention does not override laws protecting minors, incompetents, spouses, creditors and the like. For an analysis of the problems with the Hague Convention, see J. Schoenblum, The Hague Convention on Trusts: Much Ado About Very Little, 3 J. Int'l Tr. & Corp. Plan. 5 (1994).

Three years after the trust project, the Hague Convention on the Law Applicable to Succession to the Estates of Deceased Persons was unanimously approved by the Conference. Its goal was to create predictable rules for determining the applicable law incident to settling the estates of decedents who die leaving assets in different countries.

The Convention does not apply to will substitutes (Article 1). The main agreements achieved by the Convention on Succession were partial acceptance by civil law countries of the common law preference for a modified domicile rule ("habitual residence" in the words of Article 3), together with limited recognition for testamentary choice of law, which is generally not recognized in civil law countries (see Articles 5 and 6), while common law countries accepted the civil law preference for unity in choice of law and the law of nationality (see Article 7). Only six countries have signed the Convention, and the United States has yet to ratify it. See D. Trautman & E. Gaillard, The Hague Conference Adopts a Convention for Trusts, Trusts & Estates Feb. 1985, at 23; J. Schoenblum, Choice of Law and Succession to Wealth: A Critical Analysis of the Ramifications of the Hague Convention on Succession to Decedents' Estates, 32 Va. J. Int'l L. 83 (1991); E. Scoles, The Hague Convention on Succession, 42 Am. J. Comp. L. 85 (Winter 1994).

2. Other Claimants

PROBLEM

12-L.   A litigation partner in your firm has asked for your advice on a case. He wants to know whether any of the potential claimants has rights against the trust property (in a "typical" non-UPC jurisdiction). The settlor, *S*, properly declared herself trustee of most of her substantial property, reserving the right to all income for life and a power of revocation. Upon *S*'s death, the income was to be paid to *H-1* for life, remainder to charity. *S* later executed a will purporting to devise all her property to charity, but her probate estate at death is insolvent. The claimants, asserting interests in or claims against the trust, are the following:

> *C-1,* a nonmarital child born to *S* after declaring the trust but before making the will
> *H-1,* *S*'s spouse at the time of the declaration of trust but later divorced by her
> *H-2,* a spouse whom *S* married before making her will
> *C-2,* a child born to *S* and *H-2* after the making of the will
> *X,* to whom *S* was heavily indebted at the time of her death
> *F,* the funeral home that provided *S*'s burial services
> *R,* the charity named as remainder beneficiary of the trust

Disregard the elective share, but consider any other theories that the surviving spouse or the other claimants might pursue. Authority is sparse on many of these issues. Consider relevant policies, including administrative convenience. Compare Restatement (Third) of Trusts §26, cmt. *d.*

There is a divergence of views on whether creditors of the settlor, under otherwise appropriate circumstances, can avail themselves of the settlor's power to revoke a trust. Can the creditors reach this power and exercise it, terminating the trust and even restoring the interests of other beneficiaries to the settlor to the extent needed to satisfy his debts? The right of creditors in bankruptcy is clear; the Federal Bankruptcy Act (11 U.S.C. §541) excludes from the bankruptcy estate only those powers that are exercisable "solely for the benefit of [persons or entities] other than the debtor." Bankruptcy, however, is available only during the debtor's lifetime. Under state law, absent a statute comparable to the bankruptcy provision, traditional case law generally supports the anomalous combination of rules set out in the Restatement (Second) of Trusts. Comment *c* of §156 states that if the settlor reserves "not only a life interest but also a general power to appoint the remainder by deed or by will or by deed alone or by will alone, his creditors can reach the principal of the trust as well as the income." But §330, comment *o*, states: "Unless it is otherwise provided by statute a power of revocation reserved by the settlor cannot be reached by his creditors [who] cannot compel him to revoke the trust for their benefit." Does this combination of rules make sense? Is there any conceivable reason why creditors should fare better when the settlor retains the right to receive corpus only in the trustee's discretion (Restatement (Second) of Trusts §156, comment *e*, recognizing that the rights of creditors are measured by the maximum amount the settlor might receive) than when the trust property can be taken by revocation at the whim of the settlor?

Should states adopt the position that revocable trust assets are subject to the claims of the settlor's creditors? If so, should these assets also be reachable by creditors after the settlor's death? See Restatement (Third) of Trusts §25(2), supra, and especially id., cmt. *e*.

STATE STREET BANK & TRUST CO. v. REISER
389 N.E.2d 768 (Mass. App. 1979)

KASS, J.

State Street Bank and Trust Company (the bank) seeks to reach the assets of an inter vivos trust in order to pay a debt to the bank owed by the estate of the settlor of the trust. . . .

Wilfred A. Dunnebier created an inter vivos trust on September 30, 1971, with power to amend or revoke the trust and the right during his lifetime to direct the disposition of principal and income. He conveyed to the trust the capital stock of five closely held corporations. Immediately following execution of this trust, Dunnebier executed a will under which he left his residuary estate to the trust he had established.

About thirteen months later Dunnebier applied to the bank for a $75,000 working capital loan. A bank officer met with Dunnebier, examined a financial statement furnished by him and visited several single family home subdivisions which Dunnebier, or corporations he controlled, had built or were in the process of building. During their conversations, Dunnebier told the bank officer that he had controlling interests in the corporations which owned the most significant assets appearing on the financial statement. On the basis of what he saw of Dunnebier's work, recommendations from another bank, Dunnebier's borrowing history with the bank, and the general cut of Dunnebier's jib, the bank officer decided to make an unsecured loan to Dunnebier for the $75,000 he had asked for. To evidence this loan, Dunnebier, on November 1, 1972, signed a personal demand note to the order of the bank. The probate judge found that Dunnebier did not intend to defraud the bank or misrepresent his financial position by failing to call attention to the fact that he had placed the stock of his corporations in the trust.

Approximately four months after he borrowed this money Dunnebier died in an accident. His estate has insufficient assets to pay the entire indebtedness due to the bank.

Under Article Fourteen of his inter vivos trust, Dunnebier's trustees ". . . may in their sole discretion pay from the principal and income of this Trust Estate any and all debts and expenses of administration of the Settlor's estate." The bank urges that, since the inter vivos trust was part of an estate plan in which the simultaneously executed will was an integrated document, the instruction in Dunnebier's will that his executor pay his debts should be read into the trust instrument. This must have been Dunnebier's intent, goes the argument. . . . [W]e find the trust agreement manifests no such intent by Dunnebier. Article Fourteen speaks of the sole discretion of the trustees. Subparagraphs A and B of Article Five, by contrast, direct the trustees unconditionally to pay two $15,000 legacies provided for in Dunnebier's will if his estate has insufficient funds to do so. It is apparent that when Dunnebier wanted his trustees unqualifiedly to discharge his estate's obligations, he knew how to direct them. As to those matters which Dunnebier, as settlor, left to the sole discretion of his trustees, we are not free to substitute our judgment for theirs. . . .

During the lifetime of the settlor, to be sure, the bank would have had access to the assets of the trust. When a person creates for his own benefit a trust for support or a discretionary trust, his creditors can reach the maximum amount which the trustee, under the terms of the trust, could pay to him or apply for his benefit. Ware v. Gulda, 331 Mass. 68, 70, 117 N.E.2d 137 (1954). . . . Under the terms of Dunnebier's trust, all the income and principal were at his disposal while he lived.

We then face the question whether Dunnebier's death broke the vital chain. His powers to amend or revoke the trust, or to direct payments from it, obviously died with him, and the remainder interests of the beneficiaries of the trust became vested. . . .

Traditionally the courts of this Commonwealth have always given full effect to inter vivos trusts, notwithstanding retention of powers to amend and revoke during life, even though this resulted in disinheritance of a spouse or children and nullified the policy which allows a spouse to waive the will and claim a statutory share, G.L. c. 191, §15. It might then be argued that a creditor ought to stand in no better position where, as here, the trust device was not employed in fraud of creditors.

There has developed, however, another thread of decisions which takes cognizance of, and gives effect to, the power which a person exercises in life over property. When a person has a general power of appointment, exercisable by will or by deed, and exercises that power, any property so appointed is, in equity, considered part of his assets and becomes available to his creditors in preference to the claims of his voluntary appointees or legatees. These decisions rest on the theory that as to property which a person could appoint to himself or his executors, the property could have been devoted to the payment of debts and, therefore, creditors have an equitable right to reach that property. It taxes the imagination to invent reasons why the same analysis and policy should not apply to trust property over which the settlor retains dominion at least as great as a power of appointment. . . .

Frequently, as Dunnebier did in the instant case, the settlor retains all the substantial incidents of ownership because access to the trust property is necessary or desirable as a matter of sound financial planning. Psychologically, the settlor thinks of the trust property as "his," as Dunnebier did when he took the bank's officer to visit the real estate owned by the corporation whose stock he had put in trust. See Fiduciary Trust Co. v. First Natl. Bank, 344 Mass. 1, 9, 181 N.E.2d 6 (1962). In other circumstances, persons place property in trust in order to obtain expert management of their assets, while retaining the power to invade principal and to amend and revoke the trust. It is excessive obeisance to the form in which property is held to prevent creditors from reaching property placed in trust under such terms. . . .

The Internal Revenue Code institutionalizes the concepts that a settlor of a trust who retains administrative powers, power to revoke or power to control beneficial enjoyment "owns" that trust property and provides that it shall be included in the settlor's personal estate. I.R.C. §§2038 and 2041.

We hold, therefore, that where a person places property in trust and reserves the right to amend and revoke, or to direct disposition of principal and income, the settlor's creditors may, following the death of the settlor, reach in satisfaction of the settlor's debts to them, to the extent not satisfied by the settlor's estate, those assets owned by the trust over which the settlor had such control at the time of his death as would have enabled the settlor to use the trust assets for his own benefit. Assets which pour over into such a trust as a consequence of the settlor's death or after the settlor's death, over which the settlor did not have control during his life, are not subject to the reach of creditors since, as to those assets, the equitable principles do not apply which place assets subject to creditors' disposal.

The judgment is reversed. . . .

See also Johnson v. Commercial Bank, 284 Or. 675, 679, 588 P.2d 1096, 1100 (1978):

> Defendants argue, correctly, that "creditors can reach the trust only to the extent of the settlor's interest." . . . But this principle argued by defendants is not on point. Defendants cite a case where the settlor gave himself a life estate with remainder to specified persons and did not retain the power to revoke. We agree that creditors could not reach the remainder interests under such facts because such conveyances give the remaindermen present vested interests in the property that cannot be defeated by any act of the settlor. Such remainder interests are present gifts that are no more subject to the claims of creditors than are any other gifts. See A. Scott, The Law of Trusts §156 at 1192 (3d ed. 1967); E. Griswold, Spendthrift Trusts §544 (2d ed. 1947). In the case at bar, Elmer did not divest himself of the remainder interests; they were subject to complete defeasance at any time during his life if he chose to exercise his right to revoke.

D. Pour-over Trusts

RESTATEMENT (THIRD) OF TRUSTS
(Tent. Draft approved 1996)

§19. *"Pour-over" Dispositions by Will*

Where a will contains a testamentary disposition for the purpose of adding property to an irrevocable or revocable inter vivos trust, or for the purpose of funding a trust pursuant to the terms of an instrument of trust executed but not funded during the testator's lifetime, the intended disposition is effective if and as

    (a) Provided by statute; or

    (b) Validated by incorporation by reference or by the doctrine of facts of independent significance; or

(c) The trust instrument, together with the will, either

(i) satisfies an applicable rule of substantial compliance, harmless error, or judicial dispensation, or

(ii) otherwise satisfies the policies underlying the formal safeguards of the applicable Wills Act.

UNIFORM PROBATE CODE

§2-511.   *Testamentary Additions to Trusts.*

(a) A will may validly devise property to the trustee of a trust established or to be established (i) during the testator's lifetime by the testator, by the testator and some other person, or by some other person, including a funded or unfunded life insurance trust, although the settlor has reserved any or all rights of ownership of the insurance contracts, or (ii) at the testator's death by the testator's devise to the trustee, if the trust is identified in the testator's will and its terms are set forth in a written instrument, other than a will, executed before, concurrently with, or after the execution of the testator's will or in another individual's will if that other individual has predeceased the testator, regardless of the existence, size, or character of the corpus of the trust. The devise is not invalid because the trust is amendable or revocable, or because the trust was amended after the execution of the will or the testator's death.

(b) Unless the testator's will provides otherwise, property devised to a trust described in subsection (a) is not held under a testamentary trust of the testator, but it becomes a part of the trust to which it is devised, and must be administered and disposed of in accordance with the provisions of the governing instrument setting forth the terms of the trust, including any amendments thereto made before or after the testator's death.

(c) Unless the testator's will provides otherwise, a revocation or termination of the trust before the testator's death causes the devise to lapse.

PROBLEM

12-M.   *A* entered into an unfunded life insurance trust agreement on January 20, 1972, designating *T* Trust Company as beneficiary under several policies insuring *A*'s life for a total of $50,000. The trust agreement reserved to *A* the power to amend or revoke the trust. Shortly thereafter *A* executed his will leaving the residue of his estate, amounting to about $100,000, "to the *T* Trust Company as trustee of that life insurance trust executed on January 20, 1972, of which I am the settlor, this property to be added to and administered as a part of said trust as it exists at the date of my death." Subsequent to the execution of this will, *A* amended the trust agreement. Although both the original trust agreement and the amendment were in writing, neither was executed with testamentary formalities. According to the original terms of the agreement, on *A*'s death the trustee was to invest the trust estate and to pay the income in equal shares to *A*'s son *S* and daughter *D*, and on the death of each, the child's issue were to receive outright the share of corpus from which the child had been receiving the income. The amendment removed *S* and his issue as beneficiaries, providing instead that the entire trust estate should be held for *D* for life, remainder to her issue. *A* has just died, survived by *S* and *D* and several children of each.

(a) What rights might *S* assert and how might his case be argued? What arguments can be made by the lawyer for *D* and her children, seeking to uphold the intended disposition of *A*'s estate and the insurance proceeds? Cf. State ex rel. Citizens National Bank v. Superior Court, 236 Ind. 135, 138 N.E.2d 900 (1956). Under what theory, if any, do *S*'s issue have a claim to some interest in the estate of *A*? Consider the cases and notes that follow. How would the case be affected if it arose under the law of your state? Under the Uniform Probate Code?

(b) In the absence of legislation authorizing testamentary additions to trusts, how would you have planned the will and trust for a client who wished to create a revocable and amendable trust and, at death, to provide for unified administration of the assets of the trust and those passing by will? What reasons might there be for "pouring over," other than the objective of unified administration?

———

In Atwood v. Rhode Island Hospital Trust Co., 275 Fed. 513 (1st Cir. 1921), the settlor created an amendable inter vivos trust and later executed a will providing for the residue of his estate to go to the "Rhode Island Hospital Trust Co., to be held, managed and disposed of as a part of the principal of the estate and property held by it in [the inter vivos trust] in the same manner as though the [residue] had been deposited by me as a part of said trust estate." He thereafter twice amended the remainder provisions of the trust. In invalidating this attempted pour-over, the court stated that the

> plan disclosed in the will and the inter vivos trust together is obnoxious to the statute of wills. . . . "A testator cannot by his will prospectively create for himself a power to dispose of his property by an instrument not duly executed as a will or codicil." . . .
>
> Manifestly, then, the real disposition of this residuary estate is made, not by the will, but by the shifting provisions in the trust instrument. No

amount of discussion could make plainer the absolute destruction by such plans of the safeguarding provisions in the statute of wills. . . .

It seems equally clear to us that this case does not fall within the rule which permits a testator to determine to some degree the objects of his testamentary bounty by his own subsequent conduct, as, for instance, in the cases of gifts to servants in the employ of a testator at his decease, or to surviving partners, or to the persons or institutions caring for the testator in his last sickness. . . . There is a great practical as well as legal difference between such relationships — arising "in the ordinary course of his affairs or in the management of his property" — and a relationship which arises solely out of the bounty-giving volition of the testator.

See also President & Directors of Manhattan Co. v. Janowitz, 260 App. Div. 174, 179, 21 N.Y.S.2d 232, 236-237 (1940):

Here, while the original trust indenture and the first two supplemental indentures were in existence at the time the will was executed, the third supplemental indenture did not become effectual until after the will was executed, and the fourth supplemental indenture did not come into existence until approximately two months after the will was executed. . . . [T]he settlor reserved the right to alter and revoke the trust indenture and in fact modified it both prior and subsequent to the execution of his will. Therefore, the disposition . . . was not made by the will "but by the shifting provisions in the trust instrument." [Citing *Atwood*.] To permit the incorporation of the trust indenture, as amended, would allow the testator to alter his will by an instrument not published and attested as required by the statute of wills. The statute may not be so circumvented. Moreover, if the property is to pass under the original and three supplemental indentures, as the court below has decreed, then the purpose and intention of the testator is frustrated because he intended that his property should be disposed of as provided in the original and four supplemental indentures. As stated by Professor Scott: ". . . [I]t would seem that the testamentary disposition should fail altogether, since the doctrine permits incorporation only of an instrument existing at the time of the execution of the will, and it would defeat the purpose of the testator to have the property pass according to the original terms of the inter vivos instrument."

Nor may article "Third" be upheld on the ground that the trust indenture and its amendments were facts of independent significance. . . . The reservation of the power to amend the trust indenture and its repeated exercise eliminated all independent significance that might be attached to the trust indenture.

Compare Clark v. Citizens National Bank, 38 N.J. Super. 69, 118 A.2d 108 (1955). On March 1, 1952, Clark, ill and confined to his home, executed two instruments, a will and an amendable inter vivos trust agreement. The will bequeathed the residue of Clark's estate to a named bank "subject to the terms and provisions of a certain agreement of trust entered into between the said Citizens National Bank and myself, and bearing even date herewith, including such amendments to and modifications of the same, if any, as may hereafter and during my life be made." There was no evidence showing the order of Clark's signing of the two instruments, but the court treated the trust as having been signed first since "it is to be presumed that the prescribed order has been followed." It was established, however, that the trust property had not been delivered to the bank or the trust accepted by the bank until Monday, March 3, 1952. After the will was admitted to probate, the attempted pour-over was challenged. The court held the residuary bequest invalid because (1) "one of the essential elements [of incorporation by reference] is lacking, i.e., the existence of a valid trust on the date of the execution of the will" and (2) "the trust instrument has no independent significance." In what respect is the court's statement about incorporation by reference fallacious? Would it have mattered if the trust had not been amendable?

Contrast Koeninger v. Toledo Trust Co., 49 Ohio App. 490, 197 N.E. 419 (1934), in which a preexisting inter vivos trust was amended subsequent to the execution of the will; the amendment was effective to modify the disposition of the original trust estate, but held under the doctrine of incorporation by reference the testamentary assets were to be held in trust according to the terms of the trust as they existed at the time the will was executed, unaffected by the subsequent amendment.

Today, the vast majority of states have pour-over legislation akin to Uniform Probate Code §2-511, supra, but the judicially recognized issues and concepts are still important to understand for marginal cases and analogous problem areas.

CANAL NATIONAL BANK v. CHAPMAN
157 Me. 309, 171 A.2d 919 (1961)

WILLIAMSON, C.J.

On report. This is an action by the Canal National Bank of Portland, executor under the will of Marion P. Harmon for construction of a "pour over" provision in the will. The issue is whether the property under paragraph Sixth of the will passes into an inter vivos trust as amended subsequent to the execution of the will, or passes into an inter vivos trust as it existed when the will was executed or passes by intestacy.

The facts are not in dispute. The testatrix, who is also the settlor of the trust, executed her will on September 24, 1948, and died on January 31, 1960. Paragraph Sixth of the will reads:

Sixth: I hereby give, bequeath and devise all and any other rights and credits, cash on hand, monies in banks or on deposit, any notes, obligations and securities of any and all kinds to the Canal National Bank of Portland as well as any shares in any loan and building associations, the same to be added to and made a part of the Trust Fund created by me under a Trust Agreement with said Bank dated August 24, 1934, as well as any Supplemental Agreement or amendments thereof, in which Agreement provisions are made for additions to said fund.

The trust agreement of August 24, 1934 between the settlor and the plaintiff bank as trustee was a revocable and amendable inter vivos or living trust. At the time of the execution of the will the trust had been amended in 1942 and again on the day of the execution of the will in 1948.

On September 23, 1955, the trust was again amended with changes in the ultimate disposition of the trust property after the death of the settlor. The amendment was signed and sealed by the settlor and the trustee before one witness. In short, the amendment was not made with the formalities required for the execution of a will under the Statute of Wills (e.g., "subscribed in his presence by 3 credible attesting witnesses" — R.S. c. 169, §1).

It is unquestioned that the property held in the trust has been of substantial value since its inception in 1934, and likewise that property of substantial value passes under paragraph Sixth of the will. Indeed, in argument, without objection, it was indicated that at the death of the testatrix the trust amounted roughly to $120,000 and the estate to $93,000.

> The cardinal rule to be applied in the construction of a will is that the intention of the testator when clearly expressed in the will must be given effect, provided it be consistent with legal rules. . . . The intention of the testator is that which existed at the time of the execution of the will.

First Portland Natl. Bank v. Kaler-Vaill et al., 155 Me. 50, 57, 58, 151, A.2d 708, 712.

The testatrix beyond doubt intended under paragraph Sixth to add property to the trust as it existed at her death. We can think of no sound reason why the testatrix would have intended in 1948 that property should be added to the trust as it then existed, and not to the trust as it might later be amended. One trust and only one trust was intended, and this was the trust created by her in 1934 and continuing after her decease.

The doctrine of incorporation by reference is not applicable under the circumstances. First: The 1955 amendment to the trust was not in existence in 1948 when the will was executed. By definition, therefore, it could not have been incorporated by reference in the will. First Portland Natl. Bank v. Kaler-Vaill et al., supra; In re Sleeper (Littlefield),

129 Me. 194, 151 A. 150, 171 A.L.R. 518. Second: The testatrix intended, as we have discussed above, to add property not to the trust existing by virtue of the 1934 agreement as amended when the will was executed, but to the trust existing on her death in 1960. Lastly, the testatrix intended to create not a testamentary trust, but to add property to an existing continuing non-testamentary trust, revocable and amendable in her lifetime.

Our decision is reached through the operation of the doctrine of the facts of independent significance. Here we have in the inter vivos trust as amended after the execution of the will such a fact. The 1934 trust as amended in 1955 is itself of unquestioned validity. The case arises as we have seen not with reference to the validity of the trust, but with reference to the validity of the provision of the will for "pouring over" assets from the estate to the trust.

The trust from 1934 until the death of the testatrix at no time was a mere shell without the body of a trust. The trust with substantial assets has had since 1934 and continues to have an active independent life of its own. We are not concerned here, for example, with a trust with nominal or no assets in the settlor's lifetime which in substance is created by will. There is not the slightest suggestion that the trust will wither away unless nourished by the gift under paragraph Sixth. On the separate entity of the inter vivos trust see Swetland v. Swetland, 102 N.J. Eq. 294, 140 A. 279; In re York's Estate, 95 N.H. 435, 65 A.2d 282, 8 A.L.R.2d 611; Matter of Rausch's Will (In re Locke), 258 N.Y. 327, 179 N.E. 755, 80 A.L.R. 98, which, however, do not involve amendments after the will.

There are situations not uncommon in the settlement of estates which bear a strong analogy to the case before us. In Lear v. Manser, 114 Me. 342, 96 A. 240, we held valid a gift in trust "to such person or persons, or to such institution as shall care for me in my last sickness." The identification of the beneficiary was considered sufficiently certain and capable of proof.

The "receptacle cases" so-called, are also in point. In Merrill v. Winchester, 120 Me. 203, at page 216, 113 A. 261, at page 267, the following provision was sustained:

> To said Clossen C. Hanson I give in trust for himself and wife and children as may suit the needs and wishes of each, the libraries in my house in rooms below and above and all books, magazines, papers, etc. and all articles of personal property in said house not herein otherwise disposed of; and also all personal property of every kind in my stable and buildings, not heretofore mentioned.

In Gaff v. Cornwallis, 219 Mass. 226, 106 N.E. 860, the Court upheld the gift of the contents of a drawer. The opportunity, for example, of adding or removing books from libraries or contents from a drawer after the execution of a will is obvious.

In each of the cases noted there is a fact of independent significance, that is to say, a fact of significance apart from its effect upon the disposition of property under the will. The "pour over," the future identification, the "receptacle" are alike in this respect.

The "pour over" problem has not been decided specifically by our Court. . . .

In Second Bank-State Street Trust Co. v. Pinion, Mass., 170 N.E.2d 350, decided in 1960, a "pour over" from an estate to an amendable, revocable inter vivos trust amended after the execution of the will was upheld. The court said, at page 352:

> We agree with modern legal thought that a subsequent amendment is effective because of the applicability of the established equitable doctrine that subsequent acts of independent significance do not require attestation under the statute of wills. . . .

We find no solid ground for refusing to give effect to the intention of the testatrix. The trust is adequately identified in the will. The provisions of the trust for amendment were duly carried out. The amendments and indeed the trust as amended are facts of independent significance. The "pour over" under paragraph Sixth from estate to trust as it existed at the death of the testatrix is valid and the executor should make distribution to itself as trustee thereunder.

The entry will be remanded for judgment in accordance with this opinion. Cost and reasonable counsel fees to be determined by the single justice to be paid from the estate.

Note on "Court" and "Noncourt" Trusts — Retained Jurisdiction in the Probate Court. In some states, statutes provide that testamentary trusts (then called *court trusts*) are subject to continuing jurisdiction in the court of probate, whereas in most of these same states trusts that are created inter vivos are not. The latter then remain subject to the traditional jurisdiction of equity courts. A few of these probate statutes apply to inter vivos trusts as well, or provide that living trusts become subject to continuing jurisdiction of the probate court once the court's jurisdiction is invoked by one of the parties. The retained jurisdiction is likely to entail required periodic accountings in court and judicial supervision and control. These are often considered to be burdensome and costly, especially for nonprofessional trustees. The often unreleasable attachment to the court of probate may prove to be a particular nuisance when administration of the trust in another state is desirable, and court-trust status often precludes the appointment of a foreign (that is, out-of-state) corporate fiduciary as trustee. By contrast, *noncourt trusts* are subject to no continuing jurisdiction of court, but justiciable matters are generally brought to a convenient court of equity that has a basis for jurisdiction. Court trusts are sometimes favored by settlors and their lawyers because they offer trustees and beneficiaries broader and more expeditious access to court, whereas noncourt trusts are often preferred for their greater administrative flexibility, simplicity, and freedom. The preference in any given case will depend on such things as the nature of the property to be administered and the expected location of the beneficiaries. Pour-overs may be resorted to as a means of attempting to manipulate the court or noncourt character of trusts and thus court jurisdiction where arbitrary distinctions are drawn between testamentary and living trusts. Sometimes the inverse of the pour-overs in the above cases is used (often referred to as a "pour up" or "uphill pour over"), the objective being to add the assets of an inter vivos trust (sometimes an insurance trust) to a testamentary trust after the latter has been established. Article 7 of the Uniform Probate Code seeks to eliminate these distinctions between trusts created by will and those created inter vivos, providing for interstate mobility and offering ready access to a single court for all trusts without the disadvantages of continuing jurisdiction.

PROBLEM

12-N. *A* created a revocable living trust on June 10, 1985, with *T* Trust Company as trustee. In 1986 *A* executed a will leaving the residue of his estate "to *T* Trust Company, as trustee of the trust created by me on June 10, 1985, to be held and administered in accordance with the provisions of said trust." In 1990 *A* revoked the living trust but made no changes in his will. *A* has just died. What is the effect of the residuary bequest? How would you argue the case for *A*'s next of kin? For the beneficiaries designated in the original trust instrument? What facts would be relevant for purposes of guiding your investigation? See Fifty-Third Union Trust Co. v. Wilensky, 79 Ohio App. 73, 70 N.E.2d 920 (1946); but cf. Bank of Delaware v. Bank of Delaware, 39 Del. Ch. 187, 161 A.2d 430 (1960).

If *A*'s will had provided that if his wife, *W*, should predecease him the residue of his estate was to pass "to the trustee under the will of my wife, executed on this date, upon the terms therein provided," what is the result if at *A*'s death *W* had changed her will and predeceased him? See Marshall v. Northern Trust Co., 22 Ill. 2d 391, 176 N.E.2d 807 (1961); cf. In re Brandenburg's Will, 13 Wis. 2d 217, 108 N.W.2d 374 (1961).

E. Some Further Observations

The Uniform Custodial Trust Act (1987) provides for the creation of a complete, revocable, discretionary trust by a simple designation or registration in statutory form. The Act has been enacted in over a dozen states. The Prefatory Note to this Act states:

> This Uniform Act provides for the creation of a statutory custodial trust for adults to be governed by the provisions of the Act whenever property is delivered to another "as custodial trustee under the (Enacting state) Uniform Custodial Trust Act." . . . The Custodial Trust Act is designed to provide a statutory standby inter vivos trust for individuals who typically are not very affluent or sophisticated, and possibly represented by attorneys engaged in general rather than specialized estate practice. The most frequent use of this trust would be in response to the commonly occurring need of elderly individuals to provide for the future management of assets in the event of incapacity. The statute will also be available for accomplishing distribution of funds by judgment debtors and others to incapacitated persons for whom a conservator has not been appointed. Since this Act allows any person, competent to transfer property, to create custodial trusts for the benefit of themselves or others, with the beneficial interest in custodial trust property in the beneficiary and not in the custodial trustee, its potential for use is extensive. . . .
>
> This Act follows the approach taken by the Uniform Transfers to Minors Act and allows any kind of property, real or personal, tangible or intangible, to be made the subject of a transfer to a custodial trustee for the benefit of a beneficiary. However, the most typical transaction envisioned would involve a person who would transfer intangible property, such as securities or bank accounts, to a custodial trustee but with retention by the transferor of direction over the property. Later, this direction could be relinquished, or it could be lost upon incapacity. The objective of the statute is to provide a simple trust that is uncomplicated in its creation, administration, and termination. . . . A simple transfer document, examples of which are set forth in the Act, and a receipt from the custodian, also in the Act, would provide for identification of beneficiaries or distributees upon death of the beneficiary. Protection is extended to third parties dealing with the custodian. . . .

See G. W. Beyer, Simplification of Intervivos Trust Instruments, 32 S. Tex. L. Rev. 203 (1991). Also compare the widespread use of statutory trusts in England since 1925 in certain intestate situations and for family provision. See Chapters 2 and 3. Consider the possible pros and cons of attempting to develop more general legislation offering several alternative forms of statutory trusts that could be easily invoked, if one wished to do so instead of having one's own trust tailor-made, by a simple reference in a will or other instrument of transfer to the desired statutory trust option. See generally E. Halbach, Probate and Estate Planning: Reducing Need and Cost Through Change in the Law (Ch. 11), in Death, Taxes and Family Property 169-174 (American Assembly 1977); G. W. Beyer, Statutory Will Methodologies, 94 Dick. L. Rev. 231 (1990).

To date statutory wills have followed either of two basic models: a fill in the blanks model and an incorporation by reference model. The fill in the blanks model is simpler in concept, but it is not foolproof. For example, like other wills, it must be properly executed. On the other hand, statutory lists of executors' or trustees' owners designed for incorporation by reference have proved useful. See, e.g., N.C. Gen. Stat. §§32-26, 32-27.

As you reflect on this chapter's major problem areas involving (1) oral promises and the statute of frauds, (2) the possible testamentary character of revocable inter vivos trusts, and (3) the validity of pour-over transactions, consider how the handling of these problems by the courts does or does not reflect the considerations and policies discussed in the excerpts from the Gulliver and Tillson article in the introduction to Chapter 4 and the Mechem article in Chapter 8.

Unauthorized Practice and the Creation of Trusts. In the planning, drafting, and creation of trusts, especially inter vivos trusts, questions arise in various forms about the possible unauthorized practice of law both by lawyers and by others with the participation of lawyers. On the former generally, see Cleveland Bar Ass'n v. Moore, 87 Ohio St. 3d 583, 722 N.E.2d 514 (2000), holding that "a lawyer admitted to practice in another state, but not . . . in Ohio, who counsels Ohio clients on Ohio law and drafts legal documents for them is engaged in the unauthorized practice of law in Ohio."

In some jurisdictions nonlawyer organizations ("trust mills") have aggressively marketed revocable living trusts as the solution to everyone's estate planning needs, typically through free seminars or by telemarketing followed by in-person solicitation. Lawyers often become involved in these marketing efforts or in the delivery of the estate planning products. Clients/customers are often provided with prepackaged forms that are neither well-drafted nor appropriate to the situations of the individuals. They may be charged fees of several thousand dollars, and sometimes are sold unsuitable annuities or other financial products. Illinois has passed a statute providing that the drafting of a living trust by a nonlawyer is an unlawful business practice (Ill. Comp. Stat. ch. 815, §505/2BB). There have been successful actions against the purveyors of these arrangements for unauthorized practice (e.g., The Florida Bar v. American Senior Citizens Alliance, Inc., 689 So. 2d 255 (Fla. 1997)), and participating lawyers have been disciplined for aiding in unauthorized practice or engaging in conflict of interest transactions (e.g., Committee on Professional Ethics v. Baker, 492 N.W.2d 695 (Iowa 1992)). See also Butler County Bar Ass'n v. Bradley, 76 Ohio St. 3d 1, 665 N.E.2d 1089 (1996), involving a client who attended a seminar, decided to create a living trust, and contacted an insurance agent (with whom she had frequent prior financial discussions) who recommended respondent-lawyer to prepare the trust. Concluding from the disciplinary board's report that the client's "estate planning information was transmitted to respondent by a non-lawyer and that the non-lawyer set the initial fee before either the client or the non-lawyer consulted with respondent," the *per curium* opinion stated that an attorney "should avoid even the perception that his or her work can be influenced or controlled by a party other than the client" and agreed "with the board that a public reprimand is warranted . . . [with costs] taxed to the respondent." Typically, however, unauthorized practice committees, state enforcement agencies, and their equivalents operate on limited budgets with limited staff, resulting in sporadic enforcement of underdeveloped principles.

Some of the most recent activities raising these unauthorized practice questions involve not so much problems of incompetence and exploitation but rather issues about lawyers' independence, conflicts of interest, duty of confidentiality, and compliance with general professional standards. Several major American accounting firms have moved aggressively in other countries to offer one-stop shopping for a range of professional services, including legal services as well as traditional accounting and tax work, and have more recently imported this model into the United States. In addition to hiring recent law graduates, these firms are reported to have lured experienced, highly skilled estate planning and tax attorneys to their staffs. A forthcoming ACTEC Task Force 2000 report and the ongoing work of the ABA Commission on Multidisciplinary Practice are worth continued watching, probably not so much for efforts to exclude others from traditional areas of law practice but more to further "the public interest without sacrificing or compromising lawyer independence and the legal profession's loyalty to clients."

13

The Nature of the Beneficiaries' Interests

This chapter deals with the rights of a beneficiary to enforce the interest the settlor intended to confer, as the court determines the settlor's intent from the terms of the trust interpreted in light of the relevant circumstances. This chapter also concerns certain of the characteristics of various beneficial interests, including transferability and susceptibility to the claims of a beneficiary's creditors.

A. Enforceability of Beneficial Interests

1. General Principles

A beneficiary can compel the trustee to carry out the terms of the trust and to administer the trust in accordance with fiduciary standards. Problems of administration and management of trust property are taken up in subsequent chapters. At this point we are concerned with the trustee's duties and the beneficiaries' rights as they relate to the dispositive provisions of the trust. Certain closely related matters, such as the determination of what receipts and disbursements are allocable to principal and income, are also deferred.

Arising from the recognition that a beneficiary's rights can be enforced not only against the trustee but can also be asserted against third parties is the conceptual question: What is the true nature of a beneficial interest under a trust? Is the beneficiary an equitable owner of the trust property, or does the cestui que trust have something more akin to a personal claim against the trustee? One leading scholar expressed the "considered judgment . . . that the traditional and historically sound view (namely, that the beneficiary of a trust has only a chose in action plus collateral and supplementary protections against interferences by third persons) is still pragmatically the preferable modern rule." 4 R. Powell, Real Property §515 (1967). But see Restatement (Second) of Trusts §130; Restatement (Third) of Trusts §49 (Tent. Draft approved 1999), Reporter's Notes; and Scott, The Importance of the Trust, 39 U. Colo. L. Rev. 177-179 (1967) (concluding that "[al]though the trustee has the legal title, the beneficiaries are the equitable owners"). Chemical Bank New York Trust Co. v. Steamship Westhampton, 358 F.2d 574, 584 (4th Cir. 1965), states:

> Scholars have long debated whether the beneficiary of a trust has a property interest in the trust res or merely a personal right against the trustee. The courts have had less trouble with this question. The Supreme Court has held that beneficiaries of a trust have an interest in the property to which the trustee holds legal title.[1]

In the common situation in which a beneficiary is entitled to the income from the trust estate, or from a portion thereof, the trustee can be compelled to make the income payments at reasonable intervals where payment dates are not fixed by the terms of the trust. The trustee is liable for interest on amounts unreasonably withheld. If there is an overpayment or payment to the wrong person, the trustee is liable to the proper beneficiary, even though the trustee acted in good faith. Misinterpretation of the trust instrument and mistakes of law or fact, even though reasonable, are generally no defense. In order to be protected in the event of doubt, a trustee should apply to the proper court for instructions. If granted, such instructions will normally protect the trustee from liability. Where reasonable doubt exists as to who is entitled to a distribution, a delay is justifiable, and the trustee is not personally liable for interest on amounts reasonably withheld.

A trustee may generally withhold income reasonably required as a reserve for those anticipated expenses that, although extraordinary, would be chargeable to income. This is treated merely as an aspect of determining the proper net income of a period. On the other hand, where a beneficiary is entitled to the income, a trustee may not retain any of the net income merely because it is not needed by the beneficiary; nor can the trustee distribute principal that is ultimately to be paid to another because the income is inadequate for the needs of the income beneficiary, assuming no provision authorizing such payments.

If a beneficiary who is entitled to income is legally incapacitated, such as by minority or judicial determination, may the trustee apply the income directly for the beneficiary's benefit? Well-drafted trusts typically so authorize or include a "facility of payment clause."[2] If the

---

1. A contrary view nevertheless continues to be asserted occasionally, as in In re George Trust, 986 P.2d 427, 431 (Mont. 1999): "[T]he trustee has the entire or complete interest and estate in the trust property. Thus, . . . the beneficiaries of an express trust in real property do not have either a legal or an equitable estate or interest in the trust property; they may only enforce the performance of the trust."

2. Uniform Trust Code §816(22) (draft, Feb. 2000) provides a statutory facility of payment clause, granting trustees power to pay amounts distributable to a beneficiary who is (or the trustee reasonably believes is) under legal disability in any of the following ways: (1) to the beneficiary; (2) by applying funds for the beneficiary's benefit; (3) to the beneficiary's conservator, if any, or guardian; (4) to the beneficiary's custodian

trust is silent, the Restatement (Third) of Trusts (supra) states that a direction to distribute income or other amounts impliedly authorizes the trustee to apply the funds for the benefit of the beneficiary. It further implies that, if the trustee has good-faith doubt concerning the beneficiary's practical or legal capacity to handle funds, the trustee may retain and manage them as a separate fund for the beneficiary, subject to proper demand by or on behalf of the beneficiary. Id. §49, cmt. *c* and Illus. 2.

2. Discretionary Distributions

Much of the essential character of the trust relationship and of the rights of beneficiaries is revealed by the issues posed by trusts in which some of the beneficial interests are subject to the discretion of the trustee. It has become common, particularly in recent years, for the trustee to be given the power to decide certain matters relating to the benefits to be received by the beneficiaries. Most well-drawn trusts include a provision for invasion of principal for the needs of the income beneficiary, who is often the primary object of the settlor's bounty. Sometimes a life beneficiary is not given the right to income but is entitled only to such payments as are required for a certain purpose, typically support. Trusts occasionally provide that the income, or part of the income, is to be distributed among a group of beneficiaries in amounts to be decided by the trustee. Modern tax law often encourages the use of discretionary powers to determine the distributive rights of beneficiaries. As the rights of beneficiaries and the problems of their enforcement are studied, consider the significance of these problems in the interviewing of clients and in the planning and drafting of trust provisions. See generally Halbach, Problems of Discretion in Discretionary Trusts, 61 Colum. L. Rev. 1425 (1961).

See Judge Learned Hand's widely quoted dictum in Stix v. Commissioner of Internal Revenue, 152 F.2d 562, 563 (2d Cir. 1945):

> [N]o language however strong, will entirely remove any power held in trust from the reach of a court of equity. After allowance has been made for every possible factor which could rationally enter into the trustee's decision, if it appears that he has utterly disregarded the interests of the beneficiary, the Court will intervene. Indeed, were that not true, the power would not be held in trust at all; the language would be no more than a precatory admonition.

---

under the Uniform Transfers to Minors Act or Uniform Custodial Trust Act; or (5) to an adult relative or other person having legal or physical care or custody of the beneficiary.

PROBLEM

13-A.   You have been asked to review the draft of a will by which
H, if survived by his wife, *W,* wishes to create a trust for *W*'s life with
remainder on her death to certain of *H*'s collateral relatives, there being no issue. The draft presently provides in relevant part:

> a. The Trustee shall pay the net income annually to my wife.
> b. In addition to such income, the Trustee may pay to my wife such
> amount of the principal of the trust as the Trustee in its absolute discre-
> tion deems appropriate.

[handwritten: he doesn't have to give her any.]

What problems do you see in paragraph *b?* If those problems become
issues in litigation, how would you expect them to be handled by a
court? In particular, what types of changes would you suggest be made
in this provision for invasion of principal before the will is executed?
Consider the materials that follow and what additional information you
need to know about *H*'s purposes and the circumstances of *H* and *W*
in order to make specific changes of the types you would suggest.

[handwritten: - absolute is strong word it would say I intended he uses it so trustee can do as he pleases]

ROWE v. ROWE
219 Or. 599, 347 P.2d 968 (1959)

[handwritten left margin: w/out std]

[Suit for declaratory judgment to construe the provisions of two similar testamentary trusts under which plaintiff is the surviving life beneficiary and the trustee and remainderman are defendants. The trusts,
created by the wills of Enoch and Nellie Peterson (who died in a common disaster), were for the primary benefit of Mrs. Peterson's parents.
Mrs. Peterson's cousin, as trustee, had power to distribute income and
principal to the two beneficiaries "entirely according to his own judgment and discretion." In five years or so since the trust was created its
income approximated $7,500 of which a total of $600 had been paid
out to the plaintiff and his now deceased wife.]

[handwritten left margin: power to distribute]

O'CONNELL, J. . . .

The provision in question was effective to create a discretionary trust.
Such a trust may be created even though there is no *specific* standard
to guide the trustee in exercising his authority. Stated differently, a
settlor may create a valid trust which vests in the trustee the discretion
to pay or apply only so much of the income or principal as the trustee
sees fit. 2 Scott on Trusts (2d ed.) §§128.3 and 155; 3 Bogert, Trusts
and Trustees, §560. The standard in such a case is not a specific one,
such as the beneficiaries' need, but is, rather, a general standard of
reasonableness in exercising the discretion granted to him. The standard is stated in 2 Scott on Trusts, §128.3, p. 936 as follows:

. . . If the settlor manifested an intention that the discretion of the trustee should be uncontrolled, the court will not interfere unless he acts dishonestly or from an improper motive.

The court will not interfere if the trustee acts within "the bounds of a reasonable judgment." 2 Scott on Trusts, §187, p. 1375. What these bounds are will vary with the terms and purposes of the trust and the circumstances of each case. Although there are some cases which seem to express a contrary view, there would appear to be no reason why a settlor could not, if he wished, vest in the trustee the authority to dispose of, or withhold, the income of a trust upon the basis of the trustee's own judgment unrelated to any standard. There is no policy precluding a person from vesting in another the uncontrolled authority to dispose of the property of the donor of the power. This is evident from the fact that the law has long recognized that a general power of appointment may be conferred upon a donee permitting him to dispose of the property to whomsoever he pleases and for reasons which are left entirely to his own choice. . . .

There is an abundance of authority recognizing the proposition that the trustee may be given a discretion so broad that he may refuse to make a disposition of the trust property for reasons which he is pleased to withhold. The rule is stated in 2 Scott on Trusts, §187.2, p. 1388, as follows: "By the terms of the trust the requirement of reasonableness in the exercise of a discretionary power by the trustee may be dispensed with." . . .

. . . In such a case the exercise by the trustee of his discretion will not be interfered with by the court, even though he acts beyond the bounds of a reasonable judgment, if he acts in good faith and does not act capriciously. . . .

Even though there is no standard by which it can be judged whether the trustee is acting reasonably or not, or though by the terms of the trust he is not required to act reasonably, the court will interfere where he acts dishonestly or in bad faith, or where he acts from an improper motive. . . .

We must decide, however, whether the language of the provision, read in light of the circumstances existing at the time of the creation of the trust, conferred upon the trustee a more restricted power.

When the specific purpose or purposes of the settlor can be ascertained the trustee's choice of action, if it is to constitute a reasonable judgment, must be within the limits set by the settlor's purpose. The difficulty in many if not in most of these cases is finding the purpose of the settlor with sufficient definiteness to be helpful in marking out the limits beyond which the trustee should not be permitted to go in dealing with the trust property. The settlor's specific design in framing a discretionary trust is normally unexpressed or vaguely outlined. In looking outside of the terms of the trust itself the court is permitted to consider the circumstances attendant upon the creation of the trust in attempting to determine the scope of the trustee's power, but frequently these circumstances are not particularly illuminating.

Ct. can consider

The instant case presents an example of this difficulty of finding the settlor's purpose in the creation of a particular trust. We receive no aid to construction from the language directing the trustee "to pay to and for the use and benefit" of the life beneficiaries. This language is . . . not equivalent to the words "for the maintenance and support." Huffman v. Chasteen, 1948, 307 Ky. 1, 209 S.W.2d 705. . . .

The beneficiaries were the natural objects of Nellie's bounty; but not of Enoch Peterson's bounty. As the will recites, the life tenants were at an advanced age in life, one being 74 and the other 75 years of age. At the time of the death of the settlors the life beneficiaries owned property the total value of which was not made clear by the testimony, but it was at least $24,000. There was no other evidence of the circumstances existing at the time of the making of the wills from which we might derive the trust purpose.

The trustee indicated in his testimony that he understood that he had the duty to pay income to the life beneficiaries in case of "need." He stated that he was guided in the exercise of his judgment by what was stated in the will and by what Enoch Peterson, one of the settlors, told him. Statements made by a testator at the time of the execution of his will generally are not admissible for the purpose of showing his intention with respect to the disposition of his property. There is an exception where the evidence is necessary to aid in interpreting an equivocation. Since the scope of the trustee's power under the trust before us was not clear his declaration of purpose in vesting discretion in the trustee may have been admissible to resolve the uncertainty. However, it is not necessary for us to pass upon this question. . . . [B]oth plaintiff and defendants have proceeded upon the assumption that trustee's power is limited to a determination of the needs of the life beneficiaries; it is assumed that the only question is whether the trustee properly interpreted the meaning of "needs" by limiting payments to such small amounts and to the few instances mentioned. The trustee understood that he was to pay over income to the beneficiaries only if they were in need in the sense that they lacked the essential things in life or were substantially inconvenienced by the lack of money. . . . The trustee explains that he made such limited payments because the life beneficiaries were getting along fairly well with the income they were receiving from other sources.

Plaintiff testified that he had "about eight or ten thousand" dollars in cash; a pension of $100 a month; social security of $87.90; a little income from property and investments. Plaintiff owned his own home free of encumbrances; he also owned a television set, an automobile (which was later destroyed, however), a Wurlitzer organ, and other items of furniture and equipment. With respect to house furnishings plaintiff testified that he and his present wife had "everything we need."

There is no question of the trustee's good faith in making his decision to limit the payments as he did. The only question presented is the reasonableness of his judgment. It is quite possible that we would have been more liberal in our treatment of the life beneficiaries had the power to decide been vested in us. But we have no right to substitute our judgment for that of the trustee. 3 Bogert, Trusts and Trustees §560; 2 Scott on Trusts §187. We are permitted to control the trustee only if we can say that no reasonable person vested with the power which was conferred upon the trustee in this case could have exercised that power in the manner in which it was exercised. We cannot say that the trustee's conduct in the instant case was unreasonable in this sense. . . .

It should be noted that the trust in question was created not only for the life beneficiaries but for the remaindermen as well. In vesting a broad discretion in the trustee it is possible that the settlors intended that the trustee should consider the needs of the remaindermen as well as the needs of the life beneficiaries. There is nothing in the record to show the needs of the remaindermen. . . . Irrespective of whether this was a consideration, we are without authority to interfere with the trustee's function under the circumstances of this case. . . .

[handwritten margin notes: "std", "Trustees conduct was not unreasonable", "hcw"]

What is the significance of a provision granting a trustee "absolute" or "sole and uncontrolled discretion"? Restatement (Second) of Trusts §187, comment *j* (1959), widely quoted by courts, states that words like these are not taken literally but "are ordinarily construed as merely dispensing with the standard of reasonableness," so that courts will not intervene where the trustee has merely "acted beyond the bounds of reasonable judgment" so long as the trustee acts "in a state of mind . . . contemplated by the settlor." Essentially consistent are Restatement (Third) of Trusts §50, cmt. *c* (Tent. Draft approved 1999), and Uniform Trust Code §814 (draft, Feb. 2000), which provides that, despite such language, the trustee must exercise the power "in good faith and with regard to the purposes of the trust and the interests of the beneficiaries." Can you suggest why an extended discretion of this type might be granted? Can you think of drafting alternatives for accomplishing the objectives you suggest? Is the language in the above case ("entirely according to his own judgment and discretion'') the equivalent of "absolute" or "sole and uncontrolled" discretion? Also, consider the difficulties that standardless discretionary powers like the one in the *Rowe* case present to the trustee and ultimately to a court. And consider what dangers this type of discretion poses in the hands of fiduciaries and, on review, even in the hands of judges. Compare K. Davis, Discretionary Justice: A Preliminary Inquiry v (1969):

> If all decisions involving justice to individual parties were lined up on a scale, with those governed by precise rules at the extreme left, those involving unfettered discretion at the extreme right, and those based on various mixtures of rules, principles, standards, and discretion in the middle, where on the scale might be the most serious and the most frequent injustice? I believe that officers and judges do reasonably well at the rules end of the scale, because rules make for evenhandedness, because creation of rules usually is relatively unemotional, and because decision-makers seldom err in the direction of excessive rigidity when individualization is needed. And probably injustice is almost as infrequent toward the middle of the scale, where principles or other guides keep discretion limited or controlled. I think the greatest and most frequent injustice occurs at the discretion end of the scale, where rules and principles provide little or no guidance, where emotions of deciding officers may affect what they do, where political or other favoritism may influence decision, and where the imperfections of human nature are often reflected in the choices made.

The issue before the court in the case that follows is today, as the Surrogate noted it was at the time of the decision, one of the most frequently litigated questions in the trust law. Yet it continues to be much neglected in drafting.

In re GATEHOUSE'S WILL
149 Misc. 648, 267 N.Y. Supp. 808 (Surr. Ct. 1933)

WINGATE, S.

The present proceeding raises again the frequently litigated question of testamentary interpretation, as to whether, on a gift for support and maintenance, the private resources of the beneficiary shall be taken into consideration in determining the amount properly payable to him for this purpose from the funds of the estate. An examination of reported cases on the subject indicates that this question is one of growing interest, since it has been raised almost as many times in the last decade as during the entire preceding period of New York legal history.

In the case at bar, the testator, by the "fourteenth" item of his will, gave the residue of his estate to his executors and trustees with directions:

> To pay the entire income therefrom to my wife, Kathryn H. Gatehouse, for and during her natural life, and should the income prove insufficient to maintain my wife in her accustomed style of living, then I direct my Trustees in their discretion to apply from the principal so much as may be necessary to maintain my wife in her accustomed style of living. I further direct my Trustees to pay from the principal all necessary expenses incurred for hospital or medical attention or other extraordinary expenses that may be necessary for the care and comfort of my wife. In the event of any unforeseen or unexpected emergency that will require additional funds for the necessary care of my wife, I authorize and direct my Trustees, or either of them, in their discretion, to make such payment as to them or either of them may seem best. It is my intention to amply provide for the care and comfort of my wife and the discretion given to my Trustees is to be used by them in a broad sense, and I hereby expressly relieve them or either of them from the necessity of accounting to any person except my wife for the exercise of their discretion. . . .

At the time of the executorial accounting in 1929, a question having arisen in respect to the annual sum necessary to maintain the beneficiary in her accustomed style of living, the matter was fully litigated, and such sum was fixed at $3,600 a year, which, in view of the income of the trust at that time, involved an annual invasion of principal to the extent of $740.

It has now been made to appear that the widow was remarried, with consequent obligation upon her present husband to support and maintain her, and it is contended that by reason of this fact, further payments for this purpose from the estate of her first husband are improper.

This position is contested by the cestui que trust for two reasons: First, on the ground that the terms of the will absolutely entitle her to support; and, secondly, that her second husband has fallen on evil days and is unable to maintain her. If her first contention were to be overruled, an issue of fact would be presented for trial on the second; but if the first position is sound, the second is immaterial.

Under ordinary circumstances, as has been pointed out on innumerable occasions, particular precedents are substantially valueless in testamentary interpretation. In the present instance, however, the paucity of possible variations in testamentary language in this regard arouses interest in previous adjudications respecting the subject. Of the . . . most frequently cited decisions of New York courts bearing on the question, seventeen have determined that the private sources of support of the beneficiary have no bearing upon his rights in a testamentary gift for that purpose, [while six] have reached contrary results. . . .

Holden v. Strong, 116 N.Y. 471, 22 N.E. 960, 961 . . . is, perhaps, the leading precedent in this state on the general subject. The testator there gave the residue of his estate in trust for his son, vesting the trustee with "full power and authority to use so much of the said trust fund, either interest or principal" as shall, in the "judgment and discretion" of said trustee "be necessary for the proper care, comfort and maintenance" of his son. In determining that the beneficiary was entitled to receive his entire support from the fund irrespective of his other means or sources of income, the court said at page 475 of 116 N.Y., 22 N.E. 960, 961:

> We do not understand that in order to receive the benefit of the provisions of the will it is necessary for him to remain idle and refrain from all personal exertion, neither does the fact that he is frugal and saving and has accumulated a fund which he has deposited in the bank deprive him of the right to the support provided for him.

An analysis of the foregoing precedents demonstrates that in all except two of their number the courts have carefully analyzed the donative language to determine precisely what was given by the will. . . .

As has many times been indicated, the purpose in the mind of the testator in the making of a gift is wholly immaterial so long as such purpose does not modify the terms of the gift itself, and the latter remains absolute and unqualified. A gift of "support and maintenance," if absolute, is therefore merely a gift of a sum of money, the amount of which is ascertainable by a calculation of the component effect of extraneous circumstances and contributing factors, and differs neither in nature nor in kind from an ordinary gift of income; the sole diversity arising from the difference of the factors which unite in determining the particular number of dollars which the donee thereof is entitled to receive.

It follows, therefore, that when an absolute gift is made of the sum which is compounded from the elements going into the computation of "support and maintenance," it assumes the nature of any other absolute gift and is not subject to defeat by an extraneous condition. No one would have the temerity to assert that because a legatee of a gold watch already possessed such an article, or because a life tenant, who was given the income of a $100,000 trust, had income of his own, the testamentary gift to the legatee would be defeated for this reason. The same considerations apply to an absolute gift of "support and maintenance," and the fact that the intended recipient may be able to supply his needs in this regard from other sources is wholly immaterial in any evaluation of his rights to the testamentary gift of the sum which would ordinarily be required for this purpose. . . .

In [four of the cases reviewed courts determined that] the income was given absolutely to the life tenant, but power to invade principal was expressly made subject to conditions; that in Matter of Briggs' Will [223 N.Y. 677, 119 N.E. 1032] was that such use be "necessary and proper"; in Matter of Niles' Will [122 Misc. 17, 202 N.Y. Supp. 475], "if necessary for his support and maintenance"; in Matter of Johnson's Will [123 Misc. 834, 207 N.Y. Supp. 66], in case he "needs it for care, support and maintenance"; and in Matter of Hogeboom's Will [219 App. Div. 131, 219 N.Y. Supp. 436], "he shall need it for support and maintenance." In all of these cases, an affirmative demonstration respecting the state of the financial affairs of the possible recipient was made an express condition precedent to any right to receive more than the income. . . .

Applying these principles to the case at bar, the testamentary direction made an absolute gift of all income to the wife. It also directed an invasion of principal to the extent necessary to maintain the wife "should the *income* prove insufficient" for that purpose, not as in Matter of Hogeboom's Will, and similar cases, if *she* needed it. Here is therefore an absolute gift of maintenance to the wife which is charged on the entire estate. She is entitled to receive it irrespective of her outside resources in like manner to the supposed donee of the watch who already possessed one. . . .

One of the respondents who may be entitled to receive a part of the remainder, if there is any, upon the death of the life tenant, has suggested that the allowance to the widow of $3,600 per year may be too high, in view of a change of living costs since the prior determination of this matter. This, if seriously asserted, obviously presents a question of fact for decision, the issue in respect to which the court would remit to a referee for hearing and report. Since the presumption of a continuance of conditions so recently determined carries with it a strong inference that the sum awarded is presently reasonable, the court would be inclined to grant an application to compel the nonresident remainderman to furnish security for costs in the event that she elects to litigate the question.

Proceed accordingly.

As illustrative of conflicting results and views, contrast Estate of Lindgren, 28 Mont. 86, 885 P.2d 1280 (1994), with its contemporary Nationsbank v. Estate of Grandy, 248 Va. 557, 458 S.E.2d 140 (1994). See also Martin v. Simmons First National Bank, 467 S.W.2d 165 (Ark. 1971), finding that the trustee was not to consider the life beneficiary's independent resources. Concerning the manner in which such issues are to be resolved, the court stated:

> Examination of the will can only lead to the conclusion that appellant was intended to be the primary object of Mrs. Nichol's bounty. . . . This preference standing alone, however, is not of sufficient significance to control the construction of the clause. . . .

Whenever there is uncertainty as to the intention of a testator which cannot be clearly ascertained when the words of his will are considered in their ordinary sense, the court must read the language employed by the testator in the light of the circumstances existing when the will was written and, in order to put itself in the place of the testator as nearly as possible, may consider all surrounding facts and circumstances known to him, including the condition, nature and extent of the testator's property, his relations with his family and other beneficiaries named, the motives which may reasonably be supposed to influence him, the subject matter of the gift, the financial condition of the beneficiary and other such matters. . . .

Restatement (Second) of Trusts §128, comment *e*, states: "It is a question of interpretation whether the beneficiary is entitled to support out of the trust fund even though he has other resources. The inference is that he is so entitled." Accord, Godfrey v. Chandley, 811 P.2d 1248 (Kan. 1991). The opposite inference is adopted by Restatement (Third) of Trusts §50, cmt. *e* (Tent. Draft approved 1999), but with several specific qualifications plus recognition of "some [trustee] discretion in the matter." Guaranty Trust Co. v. New York City Cancer Commission, 145 Conn. 542, 144 A.2d 535 (1958) (trustee must consider all other means of support). Under the facts and language involved in Sibson v. First National Bank, 64 N.J. Super. 225, 165 A.2d 800 (App. Div. 1960), it was held that the trustee was to consider the beneficiary's outside income but was not to require her to consume the principal of her independent estate.

Boston Safe Deposit & Trust Co. v. Boynton, 443 N.E.2d 1344 (Mass. App. 1983), involved a petition brought by a trustee to be instructed whether, in exercising its discretionary power to invade principal, the beneficiary's independent resources were to be considered. The declaration of trust provided that the settlor's widow was to receive the net income quarterly "and in addition if such net income should be insufficient to provide for her comfortable maintenance, support and medical care, the trustee in its sole discretion may from time to time use such part of the principal as it deems necessary therefore." The court noted that whether "Mrs. Boynton's separate resources are to be considered . . . is a 'question of interpretation' of the intent" of the settlor and that the Massachusetts Supreme Judicial Court has stated "that where such terms as 'when in need' or 'if necessary' are used, other resources of the life beneficiary are to be considered." The court further noted that "the circumstances of the parties at the time the instrument was drawn shed light on the meaning of the clause." The trust was executed in connection with an antenuptial agreement that

set forth the parties' intent to retain the right to leave their property to their respective children and to waive their rights in the other's estate.

> We do not think it consistent with that intent to ignore the outside re-sources of Mrs. Boynton in determining when principal is "necessary" for her support, or to permit Mrs. Boynton, when in need of income for herself, voluntarily to dispose of productive assets so as to deplete her husband's estate and the shares of his children in order to increase the amounts to be received by her own.

The court did not consider whether real estate given by Mrs. Boynton to her children was "impressed with a trust for her benefit" but decided "only that the trustee is required, under the terms of the trust, to consider Mrs. Boynton's other resources, including the resources distributed to her children, in determining whether and to what extent she is entitled to receive payments from the principal of the trust."

Should it matter whether the trustee's power is expressed in terms of "absolute discretion"? See First National Bank v. Howard, 149 Tex. 130, 136, 229 S.W.2d 781, 785 (1950) (such discretion does not apply to the question of whether to consider other resources). But see Offutt v. Offutt, 204 Md. 101, 102 A.2d 554 (1954).

Meaning of Standards. What benefits are included in a provision for the welfare or the support of a beneficiary? It is generally implied that "support" is to be in the manner to which the beneficiary was accustomed at the time the trust was created. This "station in life" test implies more than bare necessities, so that a beneficiary who has been accustomed to a wealthy lifestyle would be entitled to more than a person accustomed to a lesser standard of living. Does accustomed support include the support and education of the beneficiary's family? See Robison v. Elston Bank & Trust Co., 113 Ind. App. 633, 654, 48 N.E.2d 181, 189 (1943):

> The needs of a married man include . . . the needs of his family living with him and entitled to his support. It would not be consistent with his welfare for his family to be in want, and it is hardly probable that the testator intended to provide for his needs and let his wife and children go without.

Does the support of a minor beneficiary include the support of that minor's parent or guardian in the event of need? Where the testator desires to create a trust for minor grandchildren if a child should predecease, provision for the possible needs of a widowed daughter-in-law or son-in-law ought not to be omitted by inadvertence. The nature and extent of the benefits intended for the various distributees should be given careful consideration in the drafting of discretionary trusts. The discretionary power conferred on the trustee to determine the amount and purpose of distributions is likely to be the most significant provision of such a trust, particularly in a trust for minor children or grandchildren.

When discretionary interests are conferred on each of multiple beneficiaries under a single trust (providing, for example, for discretionary
distributions among the settlor's spouse and descendants), are inequalities in distributions during the trust period to be taken into account
in determining the shares of the beneficiaries or their descendants on
termination? See New England Merchants National Bank v. Morin, 449
N.E.2d 682 (Mass. App. 1983); Hartford National Bank v. Turner, 21
Conn. Supp. 437, 156 A.2d 800 (Super. Ct. 1959) (disregarding prior
inequalities). Restatement (Third) of Trusts (supra) §50, cmt. *e*, states
that in trusts of this type there is an inference that beneficiaries at the
top of a line of descendants are favored over their own issue (though
with flexibility to take account of differences in their needs and objectives), and that among multiple lines of descent the various lines are
entitled to impartial (which does not necessarily mean equal) treatment.

Public Benefits as Other Resources.   When public benefits are potentially available to trust beneficiaries, are these benefits among the kinds
of resources that trustees may have a duty to consider in exercising
discretionary powers over distributions? Given the growth in entitlement programs and increasing settlor sensitivity to the needs of disabled or elderly beneficiaries, it is not surprising that the interplay
between public benefits and discretionary trusts has become a subject
of keen attention. The *Phillips* and *Roberts* cases illustrate the issues and
tensions surrounding what are often called "special (or supplemental)
needs" trusts. The Restatement (Third) of Trusts §50, cmt. *e* states that
"the presumption is that the trustee's discretion should be exercised
in a manner that will avoid either disqualifying the beneficiary for other
benefits or expending trust funds for purposes for which public funds
would otherwise be available."

DEPARTMENT OF MENTAL HEALTH v. PHILLIPS
114 Ill. 2d 85, 500 N.E.2d 29 (1986)

WARD, J. . . .
[This court has] found it "proper and fitting" that a patient, his
estate or relatives should reimburse the State as they are able, or to
[the extent required by statute], thereby lessening the burden on the
public. . . . This court has held that the income yielded by trust assets

is part of a recipient's estate against which the Department may bring
a claim . . . , and later rejected the contention that only the income
and not the principal is subject to service charges. . . . [Courts in this
state and] in other jurisdictions have held that a spendthrift trust [sec-
tion B.2 infra] established for the benefit of an incompetent is subject

to reimbursement proceedings brought under statute by public agencies. . . . We are aware that there are decisions to the contrary. . . .

Here [the trust instrument] authorizes the trustee to expend as much of the trust assets "as the trustee deems necessary or advisable for the beneficiary's education (including a college or professional education), maintenance, medical care, support, general welfare and comfortable living." It is not clear from this provision whether the settlor intended to establish a fund to provide services for Steven supplemental to the care provided by the State, or whether her intent was simply to provide for Steven's support regardless of whether or not Steven is in a public institution. The circumstances surrounding the execution of the trust instrument, however, support the conclusion that the settlor's intent was to provide that which the Department was unwilling or unable to furnish.

Sue Phillips executed the trust instruments shortly after Steven reached his 18th birthday. . . . Thus it is clear that at the time the trust instrument was executed, [she] was under no legal obligation . . . to reimburse the Department for services. . . . It is also significant that the trust assets would be exhausted if the Department were to prevail in its claim against the trust.

. . . [O]ur construction of the trust preserves the settlor's intent to create a fund for Steven's education, maintenance, medical care, support, general welfare and comfortable living beyond that which the State is willing or able to provide. . . .

MATTER OF ROBERTS
61 N.Y.2d 782, 461 N.E.2d 300 (1984)

MEMORANDUM [Opinion of the Court]. . . .

In 1957, the grantor created a trust providing in part that the income be applied, as the trustees saw fit, for the support and maintenance of her daughter, and permitting the trustees "in their absolute discretion" to apply all or part of the corpus for the daughter's support and maintenance. After the grantor's death, the daughter was hospitalized at Kings County Hospital for a considerable period at public expense. Appellant [City Health and Hospital Corporation] obtained a judgment against the daughter of $111,000 for the unpaid charges and seeks to satisfy this judgment from the trust principal, now valued at approximately $45,000.

Special Term declined to order the trustees to expend the trust funds in partial satisfaction of appellant's judgment. It found, both from the terms of the trust indenture and from the surrounding circumstances, that the grantor did not intend to exhaust the trust principal to provide for her daughter's hospitalization; knowing of her daughter's disability, the grantor nonetheless made no amendment of the pertinent trust provisions, which gave the trustees discretion to determine what funds would be used for her welfare and provided for remaindermen. . . . The Appellate Division unanimously affirmed, and the affirmed findings have support in the record. The trustees did not abuse their discretion as a matter of law by refusing to pay over the trust corpus to appellant.

See extensive and thoughtful discussion in Frolik, Discretionary Trusts for a Disabled Beneficiary: A Solution or a Trap for the Unwary?, 46 U. Pitt. L. Rev. 335 (1985), discussing the social and personal utility of discretionary trusts but pointing out the danger that the existence of such a trust may disqualify a disabled beneficiary from state or federal assistance. See also Clifton B. Kruse, Jr., Third Party and Self-Created Trusts — Planning for the Elderly and Disabled Client (2d ed., Amer. Bar Assn. 1998) (also indicating that a view that public policy prevents recognition of special needs trusts is more difficult to justify in the Medicaid arena following the Omnibus Budget Reconciliation Act of 1993, 42 USC §1396p, on "Disability Trusts").

Moloshok v. Blum, 109 Misc. 2d 660, 441 N.Y.S.2d 331 (Sup. Ct. 1981), involved a proceeding to annul and reverse the determination of the New York State Department of Social Services (respondent Blum) and to direct respondent to make certain payments for nursing care services without reduction for payments that petitioner could receive under a trust. "Respondent Blum contends that the petitioner may not be considered a person who requires public assistance until she has made a bona fide effort to seek an invasion of the corpus of the trust," but, the court concludes, "[a]ssets denied to petitioner within the authorized discretion of the trustees cannot be considered assets available to her" for these purposes. The opinion states:

> The testamentary trust gives absolute discretion to the trustees and further states that they "shall not be held accountable to any court or to any person for the exercise or non-exercise of this completely discretionary power." Since the creator of the trust was the owner of the funds, their disposition must comply with his wishes. His direction that the discretion of the trustees be absolute cannot be invaded by the court nor by anyone else. The trustees' conduct in [retaining principal] cannot be held to be either illegal, arbitrary or capricious. Implicit in their designation is a fiduciary obligation to preserve the corpus for the remaindermen. . . .
>
> Furthermore, the discretion of the Court is limited under [special legislation enabling New York courts to authorize invasion of trust princi-

pal] by the phrase "unless otherwise provided in the disposing instrument." The disposing instrument herein does otherwise provide and specifically precludes an interference by the court with the complete discretionary power given to the trustee.

Compare the increasingly common practice of establishing discretionary trusts in arranging personal injury judgments or settlements, discussed in Berkness, Abusive Discretion: Discretionary and Supplemental Trusts Created in Settlement of Personal Injury Claims, 67 Wash. L. Rev. 437 (1992), arguing for *creditor* as well as government access on policy grounds and because the trusts are "self-settled," as has frequently been held, as in, e.g., Cricchio v. Pennisi, 90 N.Y.2d 296, 683 N.E.2d 301 (1997).

Medicaid. The costs of long-term care are a significant concern for an aging population. The Medi*care* program covers only skilled care, and with a 100-day limit. Medi*caid,* on the other hand, was designed by Congress to cover long-term unskilled (i.e., custodial) care, but only for the needy. May an elderly person deliberately impoverish himself by giving away or spending down assets in order to qualify for Medicaid, or may assets be placed in trust for the elderly person's benefit without being counted as assets that would disqualify the person for Medicaid? These were common tactics by the middle-class until Congress enacted the Omnibus Budget Reconciliation Act of 1993 ("OBRA '93"), which significantly restricted but did not wholly eliminate the techniques. Then in 1996 Congress attached a rider to the Health Insurance Portability and Accountability Act that would make it a federal crime under certain circumstances to knowingly and willfully dispose of assets (including by any transfer in trust) in order to become eligible for medical assistance under Medicaid. See 42 U.S.C. §1320a-7b(a)(6) (1996) (unpopularly known as the "Granny Goes to Jail Act"). Then Congress enacted Section 4734 of the Balanced Budget Act of 1997, which rewrote the subsection to make it a crime instead for anyone (e.g., a lawyer) for a fee to knowingly counsel an individual to dispose of assets in order to qualify for Medicaid. See 42 U.S.C. §1320a-7b(a)(6) (1997) (unpopularly known as the "Granny's Advisor Goes to Jail Act"). After much hue and cry, the subsection was held an unconstitutional infringement on First Amendment free speech. New York State Bar Assn v. Reno, 999 F. Supp. 710 (N.D.N.Y. 1998). After some conflicting signals, the Justice Department ultimately decided not to appeal the decision to the Second Circuit.

Planning opportunities remain. The *Young* case below, involving Medicaid eligibility of the settlor's adult child, illustrates the public policy debate. Even if trust beneficiaries prevail in principle in the debate, trust instruments must be carefully drawn to avoid an interpretation that would make the beneficial interest an "available resource" that would render the beneficiary ineligible for Medicaid. Of course, an occasional settlor might actually wish the trust assets to take the place of public benefits, rather than to supplement them, as in State ex rel. Secretary of SRS v. Jackson, 249 Kan. 635, 822 P.2d 1033 (1991).

YOUNG v. OHIO DEPARTMENT OF HUMAN SERVICES
76 Ohio St. 3d 547, 668 N.E.2d 908 (1996)

[Janet Lee Young was the life beneficiary of a $53,000 irrevocable trust created by her father. The trustee was directed to pay such amounts of the net income and, if necessary, the principal of the trust as "she deems necessary" for the benefit of Janet; provided, however, that the trustee "shall not make any distributions . . . which shall render [Janet] ineligible or cause a reduction in any benefit she may be entitled to receive, including . . . institutional care provided by Medicaid. . . . Distributions of income or principal to [Janet] shall be made liberally and generously, but not for the purpose of providing for anything which could otherwise be provided for her by governmental assistance." Janet entered a nursing facility, the trustee refused to pay the facility's bill, and Janet then applied for Medicaid benefits. Her application was denied by the Ohio Department of Human Services (ODHS) on the ground that the trust constituted a "countable resource" that exceeded the resource limitation for Medicaid eligibility.]

MOYER, CHIEF JUSTICE. . . .

The stated purpose of the Medicaid program is to provide assistance to financially needy citizens in their efforts to procure adequate health care. . . . In view of this objective, ODHS promulgated regulations, consistent with federal law, which limit the available resources an individual may have if he or she is to receive Medicaid. . . .

The language of the trust instrument clearly prohibits the trustee from making distributions which would result in a reduction in benefits or elimination of Young's Medicaid eligibility. The restriction, however, was held unenforceable by the trial court on the grounds that it was an attempt to force Medicaid to accept primary liability for Young's nursing facility expenses despite the existence of substantial personal financial resources. The trial court found the enforcement of such a provision to be against public policy and therefore found that term of the trust instrument to be unenforceable.

. . . In reversing the trial court, the court of appeals concluded that no public policy considerations rendered the trust provisions unenforceable.

ODHS argues that the court of appeals' holding must be reversed because it thwarts the fundamental purpose of Medicaid, which is to help those who are truly needy. ODHS also asserts that the appellate court's interpretation will, if upheld, permit all citizens to restrict the availability of their assets and defeat the Medicaid eligibility criteria, converting Medicaid from a safety net to an estate planning tool for the wealthy and middle income persons. Therefore, ODHS urges that the court of appeals be reversed and the trust provision held unenforceable as contrary to important public policy. We do not agree. . . .

It is axiomatic that a grantor may dispose of his or her property in any manner chosen so long as the disposition is not prohibited by law or public policy. Neither party to this dispute contends that George Albright was under any obligation to provide for the support of his adult child. Had Albright not chosen to establish the trust and name his daughter beneficiary, there would be no question as to her eligibility to receive Medicaid benefits.

Though the issue before us is one of first impression in Ohio, the majority rule from other jurisdictions appears to hold that if the purpose of a trust is to supplement rather than supplant Medicaid (or other government benefit programs), the instrument will be enforceable as drafted. . . .

ODHS would have us treat "supplement" as a controlling word without which the trust restriction may not be enforced. We reject such a rigid and formalistic rule. We find that ODHS's approach would not serve the ends of justice and is not required in this case by any special circumstances demanding that we raise form over function. We prefer a standard analysis that requires us to determine the intent of the settlor from the language of the instrument, rather than to attribute intent on the basis of a magic words rule.

The plain meaning of the restrictive language in the present case is that Albright intended to provide his daughter with a source of supplemental support that would not jeopardize her access to basic assistance from Medicaid. The absence of the word "supplement" is not determinative of the settlor's intent to supplement or supplant the beneficiary's Medicaid support.

Our resolution of this case, however, is guided most directly by the language of the administrative regulations themselves, as was the judgment of the court of appeals. Former Ohio Adm. Code 5101:1-39-271(E) stated: "If the individual/beneficiary's access to the trust principal is restricted, the principal is not a resource to the individual." Under former Ohio Adm. Code 5101:1-39-05(A)(8), a resource will not be counted unless the applicant has both a legal interest in the resource and the legal ability to use or dispose of the resource. Janet Young has neither.

First, Young's interest in the corpus of the trust is equitable rather than legal. . . . Second, the language of the trust gives the trustee sole discretion over distributions made to Young (limited by the proviso that the trustee may not make any distributions affecting Young's Medicaid eligibility). We conclude, therefore, that because Young has no control over the distributions that the trustee decides to make for her benefit, she does not have the ability to use or dispose of the resource. . . .

Finally, we decline, as did the court of appeals, the invitation to hold the Albright trust provision unenforceable on public policy grounds. We prefer to rely on the plain regulatory language in effect at the time this litigation arose.

The judgment of the court of appeals is affirmed [4-3]. . . .

PFEIFER, JUSTICE, concurring.

I concur because of the limited effect our decision today will have. The loophole exploited in this case has been closed by the recently adopted Ohio Adm. Code 5101:1-39-271(A)(2)(e). While the exclusionary clause in the Albright trust constituted a nifty piece of legal craftsmanship, it would make for unacceptable public policy were it applicable in many cases beyond this one. The world of Medicaid eligibility is rife with enough duplicity and treachery without this court allowing a further opportunity for abuse.

STRATTON, JUSTICE, dissenting.

I respectfully dissent from the majority opinion. Where a child has reached the age of majority and the obligation to support has ceased, I strongly believe it would be against public policy to allow a parent to create a trust where the trust income or trust corpus can go to the child at the discretion of the trustee, except when such distributions would render the child ineligible for medical assistance from the government. . . .

It would be a different scenario if such a child had already entered the nursing home and a grantor chose not to give any of his assets to that child. While certainly not commendable, a grantor is free to do with his inheritance as he sees fit, as long as it is not contrary to public policy. However, these assets had already transferred by trust to Janet Young and were to be "liberally and generously" used for her benefit, unless the government could pick up the tab. I would find that to allow a trust to distribute income or principal for virtually any purpose except for purposes that would eliminate or reduce Medicaid is against public policy because it shifts the beneficiary's financial responsibility to the taxpayers despite the fact the beneficiary has the financial means to pay for his or her own medical expenses. Medicaid is a safety net for those who are destitute, not insurance coverage for those who can pay their medical expenses like Young. Obviously, the limiting language of this trust is against public policy because it circumvents the purpose behind Medicaid. Where trust language is against public policy, the court has a duty to nullify such trust language. . . .

Another prominent public-benefits case, this one involving Medicaid eligibility of the settlor, is Cohen v. Commissioner, 423 Mass. 399, 668 N.E.2d 769 (1996). There the Supreme Judicial Court of Massachusetts considered discretionary trusts created by four different Medicaid applicants. The trusts had somewhat varying terms, but the court sustained the government's argument in all four trusts that if, in any circumstances any amount of money might be paid to a beneficiary (see *Creditors of Settlor-Beneficiary,* page 659 infra), the maximum amount was deemed to be available to the beneficiary within the meaning of the statute. Thus the settlor-beneficiaries were denied Medicaid reimbursement. The opinion includes a nice review of the moves and countermoves of settlors and the government in the Medicaid chess game.

An interesting case, although resorting to an artificial distinction that, not surprisingly, was (as it has been in other cases) the source of decisional difficulty, is Matter of Estate of Ferguson, 186 Mich. App. 409, 465 N.W.2d 357 (1990), reversed, 439 Mich. 963, 483 N.W.2d 353 (1992), involving sole and uncontrolled discretion for "best interest" of the beneficiary, with the wish that she reside in a group home and be provided with "all reasonable needs"; the intermediate appellate court had held that this was a "support" rather than "discretionary" trust and thus that its assets were available to pay for public mental services; the Supreme Court, however, reversed and remanded for a determination, via evidentiary hearing, whether a "discretionary" trust had been intended.

B.   Transfer of a Beneficiary's Interest

1.   In General

a.   Voluntary Assignment

As a general principle, and subject to exceptions we will study later in this chapter, the beneficiary's equitable interest in trust property can be transferred if and to the extent the beneficiary has capacity to transfer other property. Thus it can be sold or mortgaged; a gift can be made of it, absolutely or subject to another trust; if the interest is not so limited as to terminate on the beneficiary's death, it can be devised or bequeathed, and if this is not done, it will pass by intestacy. In a few jurisdictions special problems are presented by the fact that a beneficiary's interest is a contingent future interest, but these problems are the result of future interest rules that relate to the alienability of certain legal as well as equitable interests and are not peculiar to trusts.

The transfer of a beneficiary's interest need not be in writing except as required by statute. In most states the statute of frauds requires, or is interpreted as requiring, a writing for the assignment of a beneficiary's interest in a trust of land. In a few states a writing is not required although the trust property is land, while in a few other states a writing is required for a transfer of a beneficial interest in any trust, including trusts of personalty.

When a beneficiary's interest is assigned to another, the assignee acquires only the interest that the beneficiary owned. If *A* assigns to *B* her right to income for life, *B*'s right to the income ceases on *A*'s death; if *B* predeceases *A*, the right to income for *A*'s life continues and passes by *B*'s will or to *B*'s next of kin. Where *X* is entitled to receive the trust principal on *A*'s death if *X* is then living, a valid assignment of *X*'s interest to *Y* will entitle *Y* or his legatees, devisees, or heirs to the principal on *A*'s death if and only if *X* is then alive.

If the trustee has notice of the transfer of a beneficiary's interest, the trustee is liable to the transferee if payments are thereafter made to the original beneficiary. In the absence of notice of the transfer, however, a trustee is not liable for continued payments to the transferor.

When the interest of a beneficiary is assigned first to *A* and subsequently to *B*, which of the assignees prevails? A number of states have adopted the rule that *A* prevails over *B* even though *B* was the first to give notice of the assignment to the trustee. In other words, priority in the time of the assignment is controlling in these states. This view is reflected in Restatement (Second) of Trusts §163 and Restatement (Third) of Trusts §54 and cmt. *a* (Tent. Draft approved 1999). A number of states, however, have followed the leading English decision of Dearle v. Hall, 3 Russ. 1, 48 (1828), which concludes:

> [T]he Plaintiffs . . . , having neglected to give the trustees notice of their assignments, . . . could not come into this Court to avail themselves of the priority of their assignments in point of time, in order to defeat the right of a person who had acted as Hall had acted [having corresponded with one of the trustees], and who, if the prior assignment were to prevail against him, would necessarily sustain a great loss. . . .
>
> [I]t does not appear that the precise question has ever been determined. . . . But the case is not new in principle. . . . [O]n the assignment of a bond debt, the bond should be delivered, and notice given to the debtor; and . . . with respect to simple contract-debts, for which no securities are holden, such as book-debts for instance, notice of the assignment should be given to the debtor in order to take away from the debtor the right of making payment to the assignor, and to take away from the assignor the power and disposition over the thing assigned. In cases like the present, the act of giving the trustee notice, is, in a certain degree, taking possession of the fund. . . .

b.   Rights of Creditors of a Beneficiary

Subject to exceptions taken up in the succeeding portions of this chapter, the interest of a trust beneficiary may generally be reached by the beneficiary's creditors in satisfaction of a judgment. The procedure by which creditors subject a beneficiary's interest to their claims varies from state to state, often requiring that other available assets be exhausted before the creditor may resort to equitable process (such as a creditor's bill) to reach the debtor's equitable interests.

Except in the rare case in which a debtor is the sole beneficiary of a trust and can presently demand conveyance of the trust property, a creditor cannot reach the trust property itself. It is the beneficial interest of the debtor that is subjected to the claim. The basic remedy of the creditor is to have the beneficial interest sold and the proceeds of the sale applied to satisfy the claim. The buyer acquires the rights that the debtor owned as beneficiary, whether it be the right to receive periodic income payments or the right to share in the principal on termination. The element of sacrifice involved in a forced sale of such rights is likely to work a hardship on the beneficiary. Consequently, courts of equity generally refuse to order sale of an income interest, instead directing that the trustee pay the creditor the distributions to which the beneficiary is entitled, if it can be expected that this remedy will satisfy the debt within a reasonable time. If this milder remedy is inadequate or if the debtor's interest is a future interest, the court will normally direct a sale of the interest. The beneficiary can avoid this result if the needed funds can be raised by mortgaging the interest.

Statutes in several states exempt from the reach of creditors the amount of trust income required for the beneficiary's support, ordinarily interpreted as meaning in her accustomed standard of living. Restatement (Third) of Trusts (supra) §56, cmt. e, states that a court, in the absence of statute, may order the trustee to pay an attaching creditor less than all of the distributions to which the beneficiary would be entitled, leaving some for reasonable maintenance of the beneficiary and her family to the extent her other resources are insufficient. See also Uniform Trust Code §501 (Draft, Feb. 2000).

In numerous jurisdictions, certain future interests (particularly if subject to a condition precedent) are immune to creditors' claims, either because of their general inalienability under outmoded local property law or, more frequently today, because of the sacrifice involved in their forced sale. (See Chapter 10, section 4.c supra.) For present purposes (deferring questions of restraints on alienation), it is sufficient to note that the mere fact that the future interest is equitable rather than legal generally does not affect the rights of creditors.

c. Disclaimer by a Beneficiary

The principles governing renunciation (or "disclaimer") of a beneficiary's interest in a trust are fundamentally the same as those governing nonacceptance of gifts and disclaimer of rights under a will. Although acceptance of a bequest or devise is generally implied, a person need not accept and retain benefits conferred by will or by the law of descent and distribution. Whether a beneficiary can, by renouncing or disposing of the interest, avoid the usual consequences of property ownership, however, is not a simple matter.

Stoehr v. Miller, 296 Fed. 414, 425 (2d Cir. 1923), stated:

> ... [T]he creator of [a] trust cannot compel a third person to be the trustee against his consent, but his acceptance of the office is necessary to constitute him trustee and to vest the title in him. It is equally true that property cannot be forced upon a cestui que trust against his will. . . . If the cestui que trust when he learns of the trust accepts it his acceptance relates back to the date of the declaration [of trust]. If he repudiates it when he learns of it, his repudiation relates back in the same manner. . . .
>
> The record in this case discloses that the cestuis que trustent under the declaration herein involved renounced their rights . . . when they learned of [them]. . . . This court is not concerned with the motive which may have induced the renunciation . . . [even] if their renunciations had been made in order to defeat the seizure [by] the Alien Property Custodian. . . .

Coomes v. Finnegan, 233 Iowa 448, 451, 7 N.W.2d 729, 730 (1943), distinguished testate situations from the intestate situation before the court as follows:

> A testamentary trust, bequest or devise may, prior to any act of acceptance, be renounced by the beneficiary . . . and such renunciation when made will revert back to the death of the testator, and will displace the lien of any personal judgment against the beneficiary existing at that time or of any levy upon the property made subsequent thereto. Such a renunciation will prevent the [will] from having any effect to pass any title or interest, and since it relates back to the death of the testator, or the taking effect of the gift, there is nothing to which a lien or levy may attach. Renunciation [in a testate situation] is not an assignment.

The other aspect of this traditional common law concept of how disclaimers operate is stated in Hardenbergh v. Commissioner, 198 F.2d 63 (8th Cir. 1952), cert. denied, 344 U.S. 836 (finding a divesting "transfer" by a disclaimer): "[T]itle to the property of an intestate passes by force of the rules of law . . . and those so entitled by law have no power to prevent the vesting of title in themselves," while recogniz-

ing that the "rule is otherwise as to legatees or devisees under a will."
For a rare modern case finding that a *testate* beneficiary's renunciation
constituted a transfer under the state's law and thus a fraudulent conveyance, see Estate of Reed, 566 P.2d 587 (Wyo. 1977). Contrast Tomp-
kins State Bank v. Niles, 127 Ill. 2d 209, 537 N.E.2d 274 (1989), finding
no fraudulent conveyance under one of the many modern disclaimer
statutes that are intended to eliminate "transfer" treatment even in
intestate situations. Despite such legislation or common law concepts,
if the disclaimant purports to redirect the disclaimed interest to another, or otherwise expressly or impliedly accepts the interest or fails to
meet statutory requirements for an effective disclaimer, the ineffective
disclaimer constitutes a "release." A release is treated for many purposes as a *transfer* from the purported disclaimant to those who benefit
from the release. See Restatement (Third) of Trusts (supra) §50, cmt.
f. Also, despite statutory or common law disclaimer concepts, Medicaid
programs often define the "actions" that may cause ineligibility to include "waiving the right to receive an inheritance." Id., Reporter's
Notes; and see Estate of Cross, 75 Ohio St. 3d 530, 664 N.E.2d 905
(1996) (eligibility lost by failure to elect against spouse's will, thereby
giving up "available" assets). But see Estate of Kirk, 591 N.W.2d 630
(Iowa 1999) (disclaimer effective re Medicaid reimbursement claim).

For federal gift and estate tax purposes, the significance of the conceptual distinctions based on state law and much of the variation in
application of the federal taxes from state to state have been largely
removed by the enactment in 1976 of Internal Revenue Code §2518.
That section prescribes limitations of both timing and substance that
must be complied with if a disclaimer is to be "qualified" so as not to
constitute a "transfer" for tax purposes. The details of federal law differ from most state disclaimer statutes (see, e.g., Uniform Probate Code
§2-801). Thus, counseling and drafting must take account of both bodies of law. Tax objectives of disclaimers, or their favorable incidental
tax treatment even when not tax motivated, ordinarily will require compliance with the mandates of both state and federal doctrine.

PROBLEM

13-B.   A's will left the residue of her estate to *T* in trust for her son,
S, for life, remainder to his issue who survive him. The trust entitles *S*
to all of the income during his lifetime and also gives him an unrestricted power to demand one-fourth of the trust principal after attaining age 25 and one-third of the rest after age 35. *S* was 30 years of
age at A's death. Two months later, following lengthy discussion with
his lawyer, *S* filed a statement with the probate court declaring his acceptance of his income interest but purporting to renounce "any and

all other rights I may have under my mother's will, and specifically all power to withdraw portions of the trust principal, now or hereafter."

C, a creditor of *S*, has come to you for advice. She reports that, as a result of business reverses and heavy borrowing, *S* has been insolvent for some time and owes her $50,000. Your preliminary research reveals several possibly relevant code provisions in your state. One is a section exempting from creditors' claims "any right of a trust beneficiary to receive the income of a trust created by another person." The second provides that creditors may reach, inter alia, any property over which the debtor has at the time "a power of appointment presently exercisable for his own benefit." The annotation indicates that this "section reverses the usual American rule that such powers, unless exercised, cannot be reached by creditors except under the Federal Bankruptcy Act." The third is a series of sections adopting an early version of the Uniform Fraudulent Conveyances Act, including the typical, primary provision that "every conveyance . . . by a person who is insolvent or will thereby be rendered insolvent is fraudulent as to creditors without regard to his actual intent if made without fair consideration," and allows one in *C*'s position to set aside the conveyance to the extent necessary to satisfy a claim.[3]

How would you advise *C*? What other information would you wish to determine? Consider the cases and other material in this chapter that appear pertinent, and also whether the 1999 uniform act described infra would affect your answer.

First City National Bank v. Toombs, 431 S.W.2d 404 (Tex. Civ. App. 1968), in upholding a partial renunciation, states: "Perhaps the leading case upholding renunciation in part and acceptance in part is Brown v. Routzahn, 63 F.2d 914 (C.C.A. 6th 1933), *certiorari denied,* 290 U.S. 641, . . . where the Court said: 'where a testator makes two separate and distinct gifts one beneficial and the other burdensome, the donee may undoubtedly accept the beneficial gift and reject the other, but, where there is a single gift, including burdensome and beneficial properties as an aggregate, then unless a contrary intention appears from the will the donee cannot disclaim the burdensome gift and accept the beneficial one.'" The court in *Toombs* went on to find two "separate, distinct and independent gifts," neither involving "burdensome fea-

---

3. The North Carolina enactment of 1984 Uniform Fraudulent Transfer Act §4 (setting out another form of transfer covered by such statutes) adds to the statutory list of factors for determining whether a disclaimant acted with "intent" to "hinder, delay, or defraud" any present or future creditor: "(13) whether the debtor transferred his assets in the course of legitimate estate or tax planning." N.C. Gen. Stat. §39-23.4. Were legislators concerned that a disclaimer would otherwise be regarded as a fraudulent transfer? What is "legitimate" estate or tax planning?

tures" that might "result in loss or hardship" to other beneficiaries, and nothing in the will to suggest that acceptance of one gift required acceptance of both — "one a cash bequest . . . and the other an income interest for life in a trust." A forceful concurring opinion stated that the "right of partial renunciation should exist in all cases except where the testator indicates an intent that the beneficiary shall take all or none" or where the disclaimer "would impose a burden on other recipients of the testator's estate," adding that any "distinction between 'separate' and 'distinct' gifts . . . and a 'single aggregate gift' . . . can be productive of nothing other than judicial opinions replete with 'nice' differentiations placing misdirected emphasis on the literary style of the draftsman rather than on the practical effect of the attempted renunciation."

WILLIAM P. LAPIANA, UNIFORM DISCLAIMER OF PROPERTY INTERESTS
14 Prob. & Prop. 57-61 (Jan./Feb. 2000)

The National Conference of Commissioners on Uniform State Laws (NCCUSL) approved the Uniform Disclaimer of Property Interests Act (UDPIA) on July 29, 1999. The new disclaimer act replaces three uniform acts promulgated in 1978 . . . and will be incorporated into the Uniform Probate Code (UPC) to replace current UPC §2-801. . . .

UDPIA does not include a specific [or a "reasonable"] time limit for making any disclaimer and makes no reference to the nine month limit of [Internal Revenue] Code §2518. . . . [T]he basic concept underlying all disclaimers [is]: no one can be forced to accept a gift. The only bar to a disclaimer, therefore, should be acceptance of the offer. This recognizes that, in almost all jurisdictions, disclaimers can be used for more than tax planning. . . . UDPIA leaves the tax consequences of the refusal to tax law. . . .

UDPIA reads differently from current disclaimer statutes because it abandons the term "relation back" . . . [but still] makes disclaimers effective [as of] the time when the offer of the gift is irrevocable. For example, a disclaimer of a gift under a will is "effective" when the will [became] irrevocable at the death of the testator. In addition, §4(f) states that a disclaimer "is not a transfer, assignment, or release." . . .

UDPIA creates rules . . . also for the disclaimer of powers over property. The act includes sections devoted to the disclaimer of powers not held in a fiduciary capacity (powers of appointment) (§9) and of powers held in a fiduciary capacity (§11). Trustees may have tax motives for surrendering powers. For example, a trust for the primary benefit of a surviving spouse will not qualify for the marital deduction if the trustee has the power to invade principal for others. If the trustee effectively disclaims the power, the trust might then qualify. . . . Any disclaimer by a trustee must, of course, comport with the trustee's fiduciary duty. . . . UDPIA §5 [also] allows trustees to disclaim property that would otherwise be added to a trust. . . .

. . . [U]nless the instrument [creating the disclaimed interest] provides for the disposition of the disclaimed interest . . . or . . . of disclaimed interests in general (§6(b)(2)), the disclaimed interest passes as if the disclaimant had died immediately before the time of distribution of the interest under §6(b)(3)(A) [defined in §6(a)(1)] as "the time when the disclaimed interest would have taken effect in possession or enjoyment." . . . [Thus,] time of distribution of present interests created by will [or] intestate succession is the date of the decedent's death. . . . The time of distribution of a future interest is the time when it comes into possession. Previous uniform acts and UPC §2-801 [treated] a disclaimant . . . as predeceasing the creation of the future interest. Section 6(b)(3)(A) ensures . . . that a disclaimer cannot alter the representational scheme of a multigenerational gift or the intestacy statute. . . .

The concept of the disclaimer as a deemed death follows the approach that existing statutes take. Just as under those statutes, the result of a disclaimer of an interest created under a will is seldom in doubt under §6. Even if the will does not provide for the death of the disclaimant before the testator, the doctrine of lapse and anti-lapse statutes will give a clear answer. The law of lapse as it applies to non-testamentary instruments . . . is far less certain. In the absence of comprehensive lapse provisions like UPC §§ 2-606, 2-706 and 2-707, general principles may dictate the exact result of the disclaimer of an interest created in an instrument other than a will. Unfortunately, the exact application of those general principles to any particular situation may not be obvious. . . .

Section 6(b)(4) continues the approach taken in prior uniform acts and UPC §2-801 that provides for the acceleration of future interests on the making of a disclaimer. For example, Father's will creates a testamentary trust to pay income to his son *S* for life, and on his death to pay the remainder to *S*'s descendants then living, by representation. If *S* disclaims his life income interest in the trust, the remainder will immediately become possessory in *S*'s descendants determined as of Father's death, just as if *S* really had not survived. It is immaterial that the actual situation at *S*'s death might be different, with different descendants entitled to the remainder.

Section 9 deals with disclaimers by holders of powers of appointment. . . . A properly disclaimed power ceases to exist as of the time the disclaimer becomes effective. . . . If a holder disclaims a power before exercising it, the disclaimer takes effect at the time that the instrument creating the power became irrevocable and the disclaimer destroys the power. If the holder has exercised the power the disclaimer takes effect immediately after the last exercise of the power. The power ceases to exist from that time forward, unless the power is a presently exercisable general power of appointment. Once exercised, such a power cannot be disclaimed. . . .

Section 10 makes a disclaimer by an appointee take effect as of the time that the instrument by which the holder exercised the power becomes irrevocable. Disclaimers by objects and takers in default take effect as of the time the instrument creating the power becomes irrevocable. . . . The disclaimed interest will pass according to the explicit provisions of the instrument exercising or creating the power or under the default rule of §6(b)(3)(A), which deems the disclaimant to have predeceased the time of distribution. . . .

The delivery provisions of §12 are designed to ensure that the disclaimer reaches the person or entity having the responsibility to distribute the disclaimed interest. UDPIA does not require filing the disclaimer with a court unless there is no person or entity to whom delivery can be made. . . .

. . . Like existing statutes, [§13] recognizes that a waiver of the right to disclaim, as well as an assignment, conveyance, encumbrance, pledge, transfer or judicial sale of the interest sought to be disclaimed, will bar a disclaimer. . . . The section also includes three novel provisions. First, subsection (e) states that other law can bar or limit a disclaimer. This provision recognizes situations such as the cases holding that disclaimers [may be treated as] transfers in the context of Medicaid qualification or issues in dealing with federal tax liens.[4] . . . Second, subsection (f) provides that a disclaimer barred by §13 [i.e., a *release*] takes effect as a transfer of the interest disclaimed to those who would have taken the interest had the disclaimer not been barred. . . . Third, subsection (g) provides that any disclaimer that meets the requirements [of IRC] §2518 is a valid disclaimer under UDPIA. . . .

---

4. Shortly after this article was written, Drye v. United States, 120 S. Ct. 474 (1999), held that state disclaimer concepts yield to federal tax lien rules. Notice of the liens had been filed when the taxpayer acquired and properly disclaimed his rights as sole heir to his mother's estate, which would thereby pass to his daughter. Although acknowledging that under the state law the property could not be reached by disclaimant's creditors, and that state law determines his rights, the Court noted that federal law determines whether those rights are "property" and their federal tax treatment. The opinion distinguishes (i) the limited deference to disclaimers under the specific tax provisions of I.R.C. §2518 and (ii) the situation of a donee who "declines an inter vivos gift . . . leaving the donor to do . . . what she will" from that of an heir or devisee whose disclaimer "does not restore the status quo [but] inevitably exercises dominion over the property."

2. Restraints on Alienation: Spendthrift Trusts

PROBLEM

13-C. *A* conveyed Blackacre to *B* in fee simple absolute and the deed contained a sentence which stated: "Provided, however, that *B* shall not convey the same nor shall it be subject to his creditors until ten years from the date hereof." Can *B* sell or mortgage and give good title in five years? Can *B*'s creditors successfully attach the property? Could *A* have better accomplished his apparent objectives had he been fully advised? Would your response to the last question differ if the creditors were *B*'s wife and child seeking support?

BROADWAY BANK v. ADAMS
133 Mass. 170, 43 Am. 504 (1882)

MORTON, C.J.

The object of this bill in equity is to reach and apply in payment of the plaintiff's debt due from the defendant Adams the income of a trust fund created for his benefit by the will of his brother. The eleventh article of the will is as follows:

> I give the sum of $75,000 to my said executors and the survivors or survivor of them, in trust to invest the same in such manner as to them may seem prudent, and to pay the net income thereof, semi-annually, to my said brother Charles W. Adams, during his natural life, such payments to be made to him personally when convenient, otherwise, upon his order or receipt in writing; in either case free from the interference or control of his creditors; my intention being that the use of said income shall not be anticipated by assignment. . . .

There is no room for doubt as to the intention of the testator. It is clear, that if the trustee was to pay the income to the plaintiff under an order of the court, it would be in direct violation of the intention of the testator and of the provisions of his will. The court will not compel the trustee thus to do what the will forbids him to do, unless the provisions and intention of the testator are unlawful. . . .

It is true that the rule of the common law is, that a man cannot attach to a grant or transfer of property, otherwise absolute, the condition that it shall not be alienated; such condition being repugnant to the nature of the estate granted. Co. Litt. 223 a; Blackstone Bank v. Davis, 21 Pick. 42.

Lord Coke gives as the reason of the rule, that "it is absurd and repugnant to reason that he, that hath no possibility to have the land revert to him, should restrain his feoffee in fee simple of his power to

alien,'' and that this is ''against the height and puritie of a fee simple.''
By such a condition, the grantor undertakes to deprive the property
in the hands of the grantee of one of its legal incidents and attributes,
namely, its alienability, which is deemed to be against the public policy.
But the reasons of the rule do not apply in the case of a transfer of
property in trust. By the creation of a trust like one before us, the trust
property passes to the trustee with all its incidents and attributes unimpaired. He takes the whole legal title to the property, with the power of
alienation; the cestui que trust takes the whole legal title to the accrued
income at the moment it is paid over to him. Neither the principal nor
the income is at any time inalienable. . . .

[F]rom the time of Lord Eldon the rule has prevailed in the English
Court of Chancery . . . that when the income of a trust estate is given
to any person . . . for life, the equitable estate for life is alienable by,
and liable in equity to the debts of, the cestui que trust, and that this
quality is so inseparable from the estate that no provision, however
express, which does not operate as a cesser or limitation of the estate
itself, can protect it from his debts.

rule in English

The English rule has been adopted in several of the courts of this
country.

Other courts have rejected it, and have held that the founder of a
trust may secure the benefit of it to the object of his bounty, by providing that the income shall not be alienable by anticipation, nor subject
to be taken for his debts.

The precise point involved in the case at bar has not been adjudicated in this Commonwealth. . . . The founder of this trust was the
absolute owner of his property. He had the entire right to dispose of
it, either by an absolute gift to his brother, or by a gift with such restrictions or limitations, not repugnant to law, as he saw fit to impose. His
clear . . . intentions ought to be carried out, unless they were against
public policy. . . .

We are not able to see that it would violate any principles of sound
public policy to permit a testator to give to the object of his bounty
such a qualified interest in the income of a trust fund, and thus provide
against the improvidence or misfortune of the beneficiary. The only
ground upon which it can be held to be against public policy is, that
it defrauds the creditors of the beneficiary.

rule in Mass

It is argued that investing a man with apparent wealth tends to mislead creditors, and to induce them to give him credit. The answer is,
that creditors have no right to rely upon property thus held, and to
give him credit upon the basis of an estate, which by the instrument
creating it is declared to be inalienable by him, and not liable for his
debts. By the exercise of proper diligence they can ascertain the nature
and extent of his estate, especially in this Commonwealth, where all
wills and most deeds are spread upon the public records. There is the

same danger of their being misled by false appearances, and induced to give credit to the equitable life tenant when the will or deed of trust provides for a cesser or limitation over, in case of an attempted alienation, or of bankruptcy or attachment, and the argument would lead to the conclusion that the English rule is equally in violation of public policy. . . . Under our system, creditors may reach all the property of the debtor not exempted by law, but they cannot enlarge the gift of the founder of a trust, and take more than he has given.

The rule of public policy which subjects a debtor's property to the payment of his debts does not subject the property of a donor to the debts of his beneficiary, and does not give the creditor a right to complain, that in the exercise of his absolute right of disposition, the donor has not seen fit to give the property to the creditor, [but] has left it out of his reach.

Whether a man can settle his own property in trust for his own benefit, so as to exempt the income from alienation by him or attachment in advance by his creditors, is a different question, which we are not called upon to consider in this case. But we are of opinion that any other person, having the entire right to dispose of his property, may settle it in trust in favor of a beneficiary, and may provide that it shall not be alienated by him by anticipation, and shall not be subject to be seized by his creditors in advance of its payment to him. . . .

Bill dismissed.

G. BOGERT, TRUSTS
(6th ed. 1987)

§40. *Spendthrift Clauses.*   A spendthrift trust is one in which, either because of a direction of the settlor or because of a statute, the beneficiary is unable to transfer his right to future payments of income or principal and his creditors are unable to subject the beneficiary's interest to the payment of their claims. Such a trust does not involve any restraint on alienability or creditors' rights with respect to property after it is received by the beneficiary from the trustee, but rather is merely a restraint with regard to his rights to future payments under the trust.

An attempted transfer of his right to future income by the beneficiary of a spendthrift trust does not give the assignee a right to compel the trustee to pay income to him, but if the assignment has not been repudiated by the beneficiary, the trustee may treat it as an order to pay to the assignee and the trustee will be protected in making payments to the assignee until the order is revoked, unless the instrument directed payment into the hands of the beneficiary alone.

Spendthrift clauses are void, as creating an unlawful restraint on alienation and as against public policy, in England and a few American states. In the majority of the American states such clauses are valid, either to an unlimited extent or subject to some statutory restrictions. Where the spendthrift clause is declared invalid, the remainder of the trust is enforced.

SCOTT v. BANK ONE TRUST CO.
62 Ohio St. 3d 39, 577 N.E.2d 1077 (1991)

PER CURIAM.

. . . Since we may constitutionally answer certified questions, we shall now consider the . . . certified question. The federal court has asked us whether spendthrift trusts are enforceable under Ohio law. . . .

. . . Most states enforce such trusts, at least to some degree. . . . However, in Sherrow v. Brookover (1963), 174 Ohio St. 310, 189 N.E.2d 90, . . . we held that, absent legislative authorization, a restraint on the involuntary transfer of the beneficiary's continuing and enforceable rights in the trust property is invalid.

In a technical sense, it is arguable that the trust provision at issue here is not a true spendthrift provision. . . . Instead, it provides that Bank One shall distribute the trust property outright to McCombe unless he is, *inter alia,* insolvent ("the insolvency clause"), has filed a petition in bankruptcy ("the bankruptcy clause"), or would not personally enjoy the property ("the nonenjoyment clause"). When any of these things occurs, the trust becomes a discretionary trust. Only when all the conditions cease to exist will McCombe again be entitled, under the terms of the trust, to outright distribution of the trust property.

. . . Thus the nonenjoyment clause makes McCombe's future interest [sic] in the trust property worthless to anyone but McCombe.

Under such circumstances, it is unlikely that creditors would trouble to attach the future interest. . . . Even if they did, McCombe would simply receive distributions at the discretion of a trustee selected by his mother.

Enforcement of the Brewer trust as written would neatly circumvent *Sherrow* and allow McCombe to enjoy the property free of his creditors' claims. A rule so easily avoided would be no rule at all. We therefore agree with the federal court's characterization of the Brewer trust as a spendthrift trust. We must either apply *Sherrow* or overrule it. So we turn to the question raised by *Amici:* Should *Sherrow* be overruled?

. . . In evaluating *Sherrow*'s viability, we recognize that "the principle of *stare decisis* is necessary to an orderly and predictable system of law." . . . However, we are also mindful "that our adherence to former decisions [must] not be arbitrary, but founded on their continuing reason and logic." . . .

Amici raised several arguments in favor of overruling *Sherrow* and allowing spendthrift trusts. Most persuasively, they argue that a property owner should have the right to dispose of her property as she chooses. This is why most courts . . . have enforced spendthrift trusts. . . .

On the other hand, an owner's rights over her property are not absolute. We endorsed that notion in *Sherrow;* we do not shrink from it today. As Dean Griswold rightly says [see excerpt infra this chapter]: "The validity of spendthrift trusts is a matter of policy, not logic." . . .

However, as a matter of policy, it is desirable for property owners to have, within reasonable bounds, the freedom to do as they choose with their own property. This freedom is not absolute . . . [but] is a policy consideration to be balanced against other policy considerations. In a society that values freedom as greatly as ours, this consideration is far from trivial.

The most important argument against spendthrift trusts is that they are unfair to the beneficiary's creditors because they allow the beneficiary to enjoy the trust property without paying his debts. . . .

As a matter of logic, *Sherrow*'s reasoning [on this point] begs the question. Of course, we agree that McCombe's creditors may collect from any property he has, including whatever interest he has in the trust property. But McCombe *has* no greater interest in the trust property than the trust agreement gives him. And McCombe's interest in the trust property is contingent on his personal enjoyment of it. If his interest in the trust property passes to his creditors, he will not personally enjoy it; if he will not personally enjoy it, then he has no interest in it to transfer to his creditors.

More important *Sherrow*'s reasoning fails as a matter of policy. Suppose that Brewer had said to McCombe: "I will give you this property when you are out of debt, but not before. " No one would suggest that McCombe's creditors . . . could take the property from Brewer. . . . McCombe's creditors are no worse off than they would be if the Brewer trust is enforced. The results are identical: McCombe enjoys Brewer's property and the creditors get no share of it. . . .

Some have suggested that spendthrift trusts, like other restraints on alienation, are economically inefficient. . . . However, the overwhelming majority of states recognize such trusts, and we know of no evidence that spendthrift trusts have harmed those states' economies. . . .

We certainly cannot dispute the general proposition that "an individual [property] owner" may claim only such exemptions as the Revised Code allows him. But we think the *Sherrow* court drew the wrong conclusion from that proposition . . . [begging] the question of what the "individual [property] owner" *actually owns* as the beneficiary of his spendthrift trust. The beneficiary owns no greater interest in the trust property than the settlor has given him. In the case of a spendthrift trust, the settlor has not given the beneficiary an alienable interest. . . .

. . . The General Assembly undoubtedly could have outlawed spendthrift trusts, but it has not . . . [so] we must, as the *Sherrow* court did, make our best effort to balance the competing policies favoring and disfavoring spendthrift trusts.

We are no longer satisfied with the balance struck 28 years ago. The policy reasons against spendthrift trusts, which seemed so strong then, now look weak. The *Sherrow* court too easily dismissed the countervailing policy that the law should allow the property owner, within reason, to dispose of her property as she chooses. We can no longer sustain the *Sherrow* doctrine.

Accordingly we overrule *Sherrow* and hold that spendthrift trusts will be enforced in Ohio. . . .

———————

No particular language is required to create a spendthrift trust. If the terms of the trust manifest such an intention, the trust will be deemed a spendthrift trust.

Doubt remains in some states whether a spendthrift provision can validly apply to future rights in the principal of a trust, even where such provisions are valid as to income interests. The trend of modern decisions is to uphold spendthrift restraints on equitable future interests in corpus, assuming the intent (which is often narrowly construed) is made clear and also that the statute of uses does not execute the interest converting it to a legal future interest. An extension of the spendthrift trust doctrine to remainders is criticized in Niles, Matter of Vought's Will: A Tighter Grip by the Dead Hand, 45 N.Y.U.L. Rev. 421 (1970).

PROBLEMS

13-D.   *S* created an inter vivos trust with $100,000 in securities to pay *B* income for life, remainder to *B*'s children, *X*, *Y*, and *Z*. At the same time *S* executed a will leaving her residuary estate to this trust by a pour-over clause. *S* executed a later will leaving the residue to *X*, *Y*, and *Z*, and died soon thereafter. *B* filed a contest against *S*'s second will. On compromise settlement *X*, *Y*, and *Z* each received $25,000 in cash, and the $50,000 balance of the residue went into the trust. A few years ago *B* retired and transferred a $50,000 piece of realty to this same trust.

Four months ago *B* was involved in a boat collision while uninsured. Judgment for $100,000 was obtained against *B*, who owns outright about $50,000 in assets. What are the judgment creditor's chances against the trust? Why? What effect would a spendthrift clause have in *S*'s trust?

13-E.   *X* devised an apartment house to her son, *S*, $50,000 to her daughter, *D,* and the residue of her substantial estate to *T* as trustee to pay the income in equal shares to *S* and *D* for life, remainder on the survivor's death to *X*'s then living issue. A trust provision stated:

"The interests of the beneficiaries hereunder shall not be alienable nor subject to anticipation by assignment or claims of creditors." Both S and D were single and childless when X died. S accepted the trust income interest but filed a timely renunciation under state law, properly disclaiming the devise of the apartment building.

Fifteen years after X's death, S became involved in litigation concerning a partnership liability, and a judgment for $100,000 was obtained against him. The judgment creditor has retained you to initiate a garnishment proceeding to reach S's interest in the trust to satisfy the judgment. What arguments can you reasonably make on behalf of the creditor? What result would you anticipate? Why?

RESTATEMENT (THIRD) OF TRUSTS
(Tent. Draft approved 1999)

§58. *Spendthrift Trusts: Validity and General Effect*

(1) Except as stated in Subsection (2), and subject to the rules in Comment *b* (ownership equivalence) and §59, if the terms of a trust provide that a beneficial interest shall not be transferable by the beneficiary or subject to claims of the beneficiary's creditors, the restraint on voluntary and involuntary alienation of the interest is valid.

(2) A restraint on the voluntary and involuntary alienation of a beneficial interest retained by the settlor of a trust is invalid.[5]

---

5. Section 505(b) of the Uniform Trust Code provides that "the holder of a [presently exercisable] power of withdrawal is treated in the same manner as the settlor of a revocable trust to the extent of the property subject to the power" (also implying that the lapse or release of the power causes the donee to be treated to that extent as settlor of the trust) *except* for lapses to the extent of the "amount specified" in current or subsequently amended I.R.C. §§2041(b)(2) and 2541(e) (presently, the "5 or 5" power described in Chapter 8, section F.1.c). Except for the 5 or 5 exception, the provisions are consistent with Comments *b* and *f* of Restatement §58.

When, more generally, is a person the settlor of a trust? If *A* pays full consideration for *B*'s transfer to *T* in trust for *A* for life, remainder to *A*'s issue, it is clear that *A* is to be treated as settlor of the trust. Some cases are more difficult and authorities (except in analogous tax contexts) are rare. For example, is *W*'s election to take under *H*'s will, instead of asserting her elective share in his estate, sufficient to make her a "purchaser" (and thus settlor) of her interest in his testamentary trust? If the income beneficiary of a residuary trust is also a specific devisee and disclaims the devise so that the property falls into the residue, would a spendthrift restraint in the trust be effective to protect the enlarged portion of his income interest? Restatement (Third) of Trusts §58, cmt. *f,* takes the position that neither *W* nor the disclaimant is to be treated as the settlor. The Reporter's Note to that Comment, however, points out the difference between these cases and a forced election with respect to a surviving spouse's pre-existing, equal co-ownership rights in community property (discussed supra Chapter 3, section C, and cf. Chapter 8, Problem 8-F).

§59. *Spendthrift Trusts: Exceptions for Particular Types of Claims*

The interest of a beneficiary in a valid spendthrift trust can be reached in satisfaction of an enforceable claim against the beneficiary for

(a) support of a child, spouse, or former spouse; or

(b) services or supplies provided for necessities or for the protection of the beneficiary's interest in the trust.

General Comment: . . .

Governmental claims. It is implicit in the rule of this section, as a statement of [state] common law, that governmental claimants, and other claimants as well, may reach the interest of a beneficiary of a spendthrift trust to the extent provided by federal law or an applicable state statute. Governmental claims and claims under governmentally assisted programs are often granted this special status. . . .

Other exceptions. The exceptions to spendthrift immunity stated in this section are not exclusive, as special circumstances or evolving policy may justify recognition of others. . . .

The Uniform Trust Code (draft, Feb. 2000) provides that a spendthrift trust "is valid only if it restrains both voluntary and involuntarily alienation" (§502(a)) and is consistent with the above Restatement excerpts, except that the "necessities" portion of id. §59(b) is omitted (§503(a)).

A substantial number of cases have refused to recognize exception (*a*), relating to support and alimony, and in many states the law is unclear or changing. Recent legislation on this matter in various states, the policy influence of uniform acts, and the details of spendthrift trust legislation in a particular state must be carefully considered.

In re MATT
105 Ill. 2d 330, 473 N.E.2d 1310 (1985)

[Garnishment action against petitioner's former husband to enforce a $7,000 child-support judgment. Respondent is entitled to receive $3,600 per year as life beneficiary of a testamentary trust established by his mother, containing a spendthrift provision, which included language expressly referring to "claims for alimony or support of any spouse of such beneficiary." Because there was no reference to child support, the circuit court concluded that respondent's mother had no intent to protect the trust from his child-support obligations; the intermediate appellate court reversed on the ground that the applicable statute prohibits *any* garnishment of trust income.]

SIMON, J. . . .

The [garnishment] statute provides: "No court shall order the satisfaction of a judgment out of any property held in trust for the judgment debtor if such trust has, in good faith, been created [or funded] by . . . a person other than the judgment debtor." (Ill. Rev. Stat. 1983, ch. 110, par. 2-1403.) The respondent contends that because this trust was created in good faith by . . . a person other than the judgment debtor, the circuit court's order that the trust income be subject to a claim for the respondent's child-support arrearages was improper.

However, section 4.1 of the Non-Support Act (Ill. Rev. Stat. 1983, ch. 40, par. 1107.1) now provides for the withholding of "income," "regardless of source," for the purpose of securing collection of unpaid support obligations. . . .

Significantly, the same section of the statute provides: "Any other State or local laws which limit or exempt income or the amount or percentage of income that can be withheld shall not apply." . . . We read this provision to indicate the General Assembly's intention that section 4.1 prevail over all laws to the contrary, including section 2-1403 of the Code of Civil Procedure. . . .

In enacting section 4.1, together with corresponding provisions in the Illinois Marriage and Dissolution of Marriage Act, the Revised Uniform Reciprocal Enforcement of Support Act, and the Illinois Public Aid Code [citations omitted], the General Assembly established that it is the public policy of Illinois to ensure that support judgments are enforced by all available means. However, the accommodation that the General Assembly devised between that policy and the long-standing policy of protecting spendthrift trusts from invasion does not entail a serious infringement of the latter policy. Only the income and not the principal of such a trust is subject to garnishment, and then only when the obligor is delinquent in support payments. . . . Moreover, . . . it is only in circumstances in which the obligor cannot be located, as here, or takes no steps to avoid garnishment that the income from a spendthrift trust would become subject to withholding. . . .

Reversed and remanded.

The *Matt* case was limited by Miller v. Miller, 268 Ill. App. 3d 132, 643 N.E.2d 288 (1994), *appeal denied,* 159 Ill. 2d 570, 647 N.E.2d 1011 (1995), where the court interpreted a statutory amendment enacted two years after *Matt* as limiting garnishment of spendthrift trusts to child support but not the spouse's claim. The court was "not unmindful that, perhaps a more just application of [the statute] would be to overlay the *Matt* court's broad policy analysis . . . so as to enable collection of [spousal] maintenance arrearages, particularly where, as here, defendant has an 18-year history of avoiding his support obligations," but lamented that "such legislative task is not a function of this court." Id. at 32, 643 N.E.2d at 294-295.

Without aid of legislation, Council v. Owens, 770 S.W.2d 193 (Ark. App. 1989), concluded that public policy requires that spendthrift restraints not be given the effect of barring claims for arrearages in child support and alimony and held that the beneficiary's former spouse could reach trust income in the hands of a trustee who had no discretion to withhold the income from the beneficiary. Some cases, however, have refused to recognize an exception for support claims, and in many states the matter is unresolved.

SLIGH v. FIRST NATIONAL BANK
704 So. 2d 1020 (Miss. 1997)

[Will Sligh suffered paralysis as a result of an auto accident with Gene Lorance, an uninsured motorist who was operating a vehicle while intoxicated. Sligh and his wife sued for personal injury, property damage, and loss of consortium, and received a default judgment for $5,000,000 in compensatory and punitive damages. Lorance's only assets were his interests as a beneficiary of two trusts established by his mother. The trustee had "full and complete authority to expend all or any part of the income or corpus" for Lorance's benefit. The trust further provided that "[n]o part of this trust, either principal or income, shall be liable for the debts of [Lorance], nor shall the same be subject to seizure by any creditor of his." The Slighs alleged that Lorance's mother knew that he was an habitual drunkard, a reckless driver who had been in many accidents, and had been convicted on numerous occasions of driving under the influence. They further alleged that the trusts were established as part of an intentional plan to enable Lorance to continue his debauched lifestyle while shielding his interests in the trusts from his tort creditors. A short dissenting opinion is omitted.]

. . . [O]ne can identify three public policy considerations observed by this Court when enforcing spendthrift trust provisions: (1) the right of donors to dispose of their property as they wish; (2) the public interest in protecting spendthrift individuals from personal pauperism, so that they do not become public burdens; and (3) the responsibility of creditors to make themselves aware of their debtors' spendthrift trust protections. Upon consideration of these public policy concerns in the present context, we find that they do not weigh in favor of enforcing spendthrift trust provisions as against the claims of tort creditors or those found liable for gross negligence.

¶18. Regarding the responsibility of creditors when entering into transactions with spendthrift trust beneficiaries, Austin W. Scott stated in *The Law of Trusts:*

. . . Certainly, the situation of a tort creditor is quite different from that of a contract creditor. A man who is about to be knocked down by an automobile has no opportunity to investigate the credit of the driver of the automobile and has no opportunity to avoid being injured no matter what the resources of the driver may be.

. . . [I]t is plain to see that one of the main reasons for enforcing spendthrift trust provisions — the responsibility of creditors to be aware of the law and of the substance of such provisions — simply does not apply in the case of tort judgment creditors.

¶19. As for the public interest in protecting spendthrift individuals from personal pauperism, we believe that this interest is not as strong in the case of tort judgment creditors, where the inability to collect on their claims may well result in their own personal pauperism. While it is true that most contract creditors do not risk becoming insolvent if they do not collect on a particular claim, such is often not the case with tort judgment creditors, particularly those who have suffered such devastating and expensive injuries as did the Slighs. The public interest against individuals becoming public burdens would not be served by protecting a spendthrift tortfeasor from personal pauperism where such protection would result merely in the pauperism of his victim. If one must choose whom to reduce to personal pauperism in such a case, the spendthrift tortfeasor or the innocent tort judgment creditor, we are inclined to choose the party at fault, especially where that fault rises to the level of gross negligence or intentional conduct.

¶20. This limitation on the public interest in protecting individuals from personal pauperism is reflected in our federal bankruptcy laws, whose very purpose is to protect debtors from pauperism. Under the Federal Bankruptcy Act, debtors may not discharge their debts to tort victim creditors whose claims are based on "willful and malicious" injuries. 11 U.S.C.A. §523(a)(6) (West 1993). Thus, it has been recognized that the rights of intentional tort creditors are greater than the public interest in protecting debtors from personal pauperism.

¶21. Perhaps the most important policy consideration in favor of enforcing spendthrift trust provisions is the right of donors to dispose of their property as they wish. . . .

¶22. Clearly, the right of donors to place restrictions on the disposition of their property is not absolute, for as discussed above, there are several generally recognized exceptions to the spendthrift trust doctrine. Rather, a donor may dispose of his property as he sees fit so long as such disposition does not violate the law or public policy. We find that it is indeed against public policy to dispose of property in such a way that the beneficiary may enjoy the income from such property without fear that his interest may be attached to satisfy the claims of his gross negligence or intentional torts.

¶23. Our tort doctrine has evolved into two types of torts, ordinary torts and intentional torts. Public policy deems it so important to deter the commission of intentional torts or acts of gross negligence, that we allow victims of gross negligence or intentional torts to recover damages above and beyond what is necessary to compensate them for their injuries, i.e., punitive damages. However, the intended deterrent effect would be completely lost upon individuals whose interests are immune from the satisfaction of such claims.

¶24. The Slighs have alleged facts to the effect that Lorance's mother intended that her son should be able to commit acts of gross negligence or intentional torts without fear that his beneficial interests would be attached as a result thereof. However, in cases such as this where the donor has died, such facts may often be difficult, if not impossible, to prove. We hold that plaintiffs need not prove such facts but that such intent shall be presumed where a party has obtained a judgment based upon facts evidencing gross negligence or an intentional tort against the beneficiary of a spendthrift trust. . . .

¶25. The parties agree that the trusts' two remaindermen . . . have vested remainders. The trusts provide that First National Bank "shall have full and complete authority to expend *all or any part* of the income or corpus of said trust property for the benefit of myself and my said son." (Emphasis added.) Therefore, the interests . . . are vested remainders subject to complete defeasance in the event that all of the trust assets are expended to satisfy the interest of Lorance. Put another way, Lorance has a beneficial interest in *all* of the trust assets. Accordingly, we hold that all of the trust assets should be subject to the Slighs' claim, thereby defeating the interests of the two remaindermen. . . .

The view in *Sligh* was rejected by the Mississippi legislature; the Family Trust Preservation Act of 1998, Miss. Code Ann. §91-9-503, has no exceptions to spendthrift trust protection other than for self-settled trusts. Nevertheless, with little authority on point, *Sligh* may prove influential elsewhere. See Fox & Murphy, Are Spendthrift Trusts Vulnerable to a Beneficiary's Tort Creditors?, 137 Trusts & Estates 57 (Feb. 1998). Was the recovery in *Sligh* excessive in defeating the interests of the remainder beneficiaries?

Legislation. Statutes in some states have dealt with the problems of voluntary and involuntary alienation of a beneficiary's interest. They vary widely in their approaches.

Based on legislation dating back to 1830, N.Y. Est. Powers & Trusts Law §7-1.5 provides: "The right of a beneficiary of an express trust to receive the income from property and apply it to the use of or pay it to any person may not be transferred by assignment or otherwise, unless a power to transfer such right, or any part thereof, is conferred upon such beneficiary by the instrument creating or declaring the trust." (Recent amendments, patently motivated by income tax consider-ations, then follow providing limited exceptions permitting certain gra-tuitous, intrafamily assignments.) According to N.Y. EP&TL §7-3.4 (having the same early origin), in the absence of a valid direction for accumulation, the income of the above described trusts "in excess of the sum necessary for the education and support of the beneficiary is subject to the claims of his creditors in the same manner as other prop-erty which cannot be reached by execution." Unfortunately for the creditor, "support" under the New York statute (and others similar to it) has been construed to require application of a "station-in-life" or "accustomed-standard-of-living" test. This protection for the benefi-ciary has been partially impaired in New York, however, by various pro-visions of the Civil Practice Law and Rules.

In several other states, as in New York (but in some without the ex-ceptions), the interests of trust beneficiaries are made automatically unassignable, even without an express spendthrift provision. A second group of statutes merely provides that a trust beneficiary *may* be re-strained by the terms of the trust instrument from voluntarily disposing of a beneficial interest, occasionally limiting this authorization to inter-ests for life or for a term of years; this type of provision is likely to be accompanied by a section dealing with the rights of creditors under such trusts — often with limitations along the lines of N.Y. EP&TL §7-3.4, supra. In a number of states there are statutes dealing only with the rights of creditors, as in the *Matt* case, supra, usually permitting the beneficiary to assign his interest voluntarily unless the terms of the trust contain a valid spendthrift restriction.

Section 206(d)(1) of the Federal Employee Retirement Income Se-curity Act (ERISA) states: "Each pension plan shall provide that bene-fits provided under the plan may not be assigned or alienated." See also the associated Treasury Regulation §1.401(a)-13(b)(1) stating that "a trust will not be qualified unless the plan of which the trust is a part provides that benefits provided under the plan may not be anticipated, assigned (either at law or in equity), alienated or subject to attachment, garnishment, levy, execution or other legal or equitable process." The ERISA statutory spendthrift provision is given great force in Guidry v. Sheet Metal Workers Union Nat'l Pension Fund, 493 U.S. 365 (1990).

If *S* creates a trust to pay the income to *L* for life, remainder to *L*'s issue, and the terms of the trust state merely that *L*'s creditors cannot reach his interest in the trust, can *C*, a creditor of *L*, reach that interest if *L* is insolvent? Would *C*'s position be improved if *C* could force *L* into bankruptcy? See Eaton v. Boston Safe Deposit & Trust Co., 240 U.S. 427 (1916), and especially see Federal Bankruptcy Code §541(c)(2) ("a restriction on the transfer of a beneficial interest of the debtor in a trust that is enforceable under applicable nonbankruptcy law is enforceable in a case under this title"). Would *C*'s position be affected if the trust instrument contained no express restraint on alienation but applicable state law made *L*'s interest assignable voluntarily but not reachable by creditors? (The Bankruptcy Code allows the debtor to elect to exempt, inter alia, property that is "exempt" under applicable state or local law.) Cf. Young v. Handwork, 179 F.2d 70 (7th Cir. 1949), *cert. denied*, 339 U.S. 949 (1950).

It has become a widespread practice to insert spendthrift provisions routinely in wills and trust agreements. Is this a good practice? Consider when it might be disadvantageous to include such a clause.

PROBLEM

13-F.   *H,* a wealthy client who has just become a widower, has come to you for advice. His late wife's will leaves him a portion of her estate of well over $1 million to take advantage of the marital deduction under the federal estate tax. The residue of her estate is left in trust to pay *H* the income for life, remainder to her issue, with provision for invasion of principal for certain needs of *H* and the issue. The trust includes a spendthrift provision. Because *H* is also the life beneficiary of a large trust (also containing a spendthrift clause) under his father's will, he is certain he will not need the income from his wife's residuary trust and realizes that his income tax position will be most unfavorable for the rest of his life. How would you advise him in an effort to relieve his tax burdens?

Restraints on alienation of *legal* interests in property, even life estates, are generally invalid. Forfeiture restraints, however, have met with limited acceptance, particularly in relation to legal life estates. See generally 6 American Law of Property §§26.13-26.54 (J. Casner ed. 1952). For purposes of evaluating spendthrift trusts as a matter of policy, consider the extent to which there are material differences relevant to restraints on alienation between legal interests and the equitable interests of trust beneficiaries. To what extent, on the other hand, are the policy considerations substantially similar in the two cases? What other policy considerations ought to enter into legislative or judicial judgments as to whether and to what extent spendthrift trusts are to be permitted?

E. GRISWOLD, SPENDTHRIFT TRUSTS
(2d ed. 1947)

§32. *Gray's Futile Attack on Spendthrift Trusts*

The most careful and thoughtful text on the subject was of course John C. Gray's Restraints on the Alienation of Property which first appeared in 1883. Gray attacked the doctrine of spendthrift trusts, thoroughly and with not a little vehemence. The arguments which he set forth have never been completely answered, but, as so frequently happens with such arguments, they have had little influence in shaping the law. . . .

In the preface of the second edition of his book, Gray wrote what has become the classic statement of the opposition to spendthrift trusts. For reasons which seem hard to understand now, he found these to be an earmark of socialism. He argued that the judges who had aided in the introduction of spendthrift trusts must

> have been influenced, unconsciously it may well be, by those ideas which the experience of the last few years has shown to have been fermenting in the minds of the community; by that spirit, in short, of paternalism, which is the fundamental essence alike of spendthrift trusts and of socialism.

At this day, it seems easy to see that this argument went too far. We can readily agree with the observation of a recent writer [Manning, The Development of Restraints on Alienation Since Gray, 48 Harv. L. Rev. 373, 404 (1935)]

> That socialism should rise through a device designed to protect the fortunes of Pennsylvania manufacturers and Massachusetts shipping and textile overlords from the depredations of their extravagant, and none too competent, progeny now seems a curious idea indeed.

. . . [T]he reasoning advanced by the Court in Nichols v. Eaton [91 U.S. 716 (1875)] may be examined as typical of that adopted and followed in other cases. Apart from the authorities cited, all of which seem to have been distinguishable, the decision there was based on what was apparently regarded as a logically necessary conclusion. A person who owns property, it was said, may give it as he pleases, and may therefore "attach to that gift the incident of continued use, of uninterrupted benefit of the gift, during the life of the donee." A similar basis was expressed for the decision in Broadway Natl. Bank v. Adams. There, too, the court proceeded on grounds based on supposed logic. . . .

There is in all this a deference to the dead hand which is perhaps typical of the nineteenth century's attitude toward property. Closer examination, however, makes it clear that the conclusion so generally adopted is certainly not a logically necessary one, regardless of whatever other merit it may have. The difficulty is that the major premise — that the owner of property may dispose of it as he desires — is patently fallacious. . . .

[Section 553 summarizes a few limitations on the disposition of property: dower, forced heirship, and restrictions on charitable bequests; prohibitions against trusts that have indefinite beneficiaries or illegal purposes or that unreasonably restrain marriage or encourage divorce or neglect of duties; rules relating to perpetuities; and, most closely analogous, rules prohibiting restraints on alienation of legal interests.]

§554 [and §555].   *The Validity of Spendthrift Trusts*
                   Is a Matter of Policy, Not of Logic

It is apparent from the summary statement in the previous section that the bundle of rights known as ownership of property does not embrace an unqualified power of disposition in any way desired. There is no syllogistic basis for the spendthrift trust. If such trusts are valid it is not because the owner of property may dispose of it as he sees fit, but because the particular restriction in question is not contrary to public policy. The question therefore involves an examination of public policy. . . .

. . . This question, like many others in law, presents intangible elements in many fields, including, among others, ethics, economics, and psychology. In the past this question has generally been disposed of by assertion. And, indeed, it is difficult to dispose of it otherwise.

Spendthrift trusts have been attacked on the ground that the assurance of a guaranteed income destroys the initiative and the self-reliance of the beneficiary. Thus, it has been asserted that the commercial decline of New England has been caused in part by the spendthrift trust [Gerish, Commercial Structure of New England (1929) 65, 66]:

> Those with the initiative, foresight, and purpose to undertake new enterprises have been hampered in many instances by the "spendthrift trust." . . . The "spendthrift trust" has tended to develop a class of what has been termed "four percenters." . . .

But assertions like this will not withstand more critical examination. Spendthrift trusts are not confined to [New England]. . . . The reason for the decline in New England, if it exists, must be found elsewhere. Moreover, the argument in question, so far as it has validity, is directed against all trusts, not against spendthrift trusts alone. It is the trust, not the spendthrift provision, that tends to take property out of commerce.

The effect of spendthrift trusts on the commerce of the nation obviously does not lend itself to statistical analysis. Speculation is scarcely worthwhile when the answer depends upon so many unknown variables. . . .

An argument which is perhaps less difficult to evaluate is found in the unfairness of spendthrift trusts to creditors. It will not do to say that creditors should not extend credit to apparently opulent spendthrift beneficiaries because the restraints on their interests are a matter of public record which could be looked up. The argument is obviously not applicable to tort creditors. Moreover, many trusts, including nearly all of those created inter vivos, are not a matter of record. And finally, the argument is most unrealistic in holding creditors responsible for not doing what no one really expects a creditor to do. The fact remains that a decision allowing the beneficiary of a trust to refuse to pay bills for lodging and clothes though her trust income amounts to more than $171,000 a year [Congress Hotel Co. v. Martin, 312 Ill. 318, 143 N.E. 838, (1924)] must be shocking even to the most hardened conscience. And the same is true of the early New York case which so aroused Mr. Gray's wrath, where the beneficiary was allowed a larger exemption from the claims of his creditors because of his "high social standing," because "his associations are chiefly with men of leisure," and because he "is connected with a number of clubs."

There would seem, too, to be little reason why a matter of so great importance not only to the beneficiary but also to the public generally should be left to the control of individuals. Property in the hands of its owner is normally subject to his debts. The spendthrift trust allows the owner in transferring it to another to create an exemption from this general liability, an exemption which the settlor himself did not have. Exemptions of this sort should be regulated by the state, not by the wishes of individual testators. They should be open to all, not limited to a favored few. . . .

For a recent statutory suggestion, see Emanuel, Spendthrift Trusts: It's Time to Codify the Compromise, 72 Nebraska L. Rev. 179 (1993). See also Alexander, The Dead Hand and the Law of Trusts in the Nineteenth Century, 37 Stan. L. Rev. 1189 (1985); and Hirsch, Spendthrift Trusts and Public Policy: Economic and Cognitive Perspectives, 73 Wash. U.L.Q. 1 (1995).

3. Discretionary, Protective, and Related Trusts

PROBLEM

13-G. *S* left his estate to *T* in trust "to pay such amounts of income or principal, or both, to *L* as *T* may, in her absolute discretion, deem appropriate for *B*'s support, welfare and happiness," remainder to *L*'s issue. *L* is now insolvent. His major creditor, *C*, asks your advice concerning the availability of the trust assets, or any of *L*'s rights therein, to satisfy *C*'s claim. How would you advise *C*? Consider the materials that follow.

TODD'S EXECUTORS v. TODD
260 Ky. 611, 86 S.W.2d 168 (1935)

[Paulina Todd died in 1933. Her will left a portion of her estate to her executor in trust

> to use the income or principal in the support, maintenance and comfort of Romulus Todd during his life, and is to have an absolute discretion as to what part of either he shall use for said purpose or pay to said Romulus, and this discretion is not to be controlled by any other person and in no event is any portion of the principal or interest to be applied to any debt of said Romulus, and . . . this trust is to cease and the principal is to go to the remaindermen [Romulus's children], if the Court should adjudge that any part could be subjected to the claims of any creditor.

Iva Todd, who had divorced Romulus in 1923, asked for an attachment against the trust fund to satisfy her personal judgment against Romulus for unpaid alimony and child support. The three minor children of Iva and Romulus filed an intervening petition alleging that the interest of Romulus was subject to Iva's claim and that they were thus entitled to the principal of the trust estate.]

REES, J. . . .

[I]t was adjudged that Iva Todd was entitled to have her judgment for $3,420 paid out of the trust fund. The executors and Romulus Todd have appealed.

The question squarely presented is whether the provision of Paulina E. Todd's will creating a trust estate for the benefit of her son, Romulus Todd, is void and unenforceable as in violation of section 2355 of the Kentucky Statutes, which reads:

> Estates of every kind held or possessed in trust, shall be subject to the debts and charges of the persons to whose use, or for whose benefit, they shall be respectively held or possessed, as they would be subject if those persons owned the like interest in the property held or possessed as they own or shall own in the use or trust thereof.

This depends upon whether or not the will creates a beneficial interest that can be enforced by the cestui que trust. Where the trustee is authorized in his discretion to withhold all payments, the cestui has no absolute right which he can enforce or which can be reached by creditors. In Cecil's Trustees v. Robertson & Brother, 105 S.W. 926, 927, 32 Ky. Law Rep. 357, it was said:

> The rule is that, when the trustee has the discretion to withhold from the beneficiary all interest in the trust fund, then the fund may not be subjected to the debts of the beneficiary, but that, if the beneficiary may in equity compel the trustee to pay her a certain part of the estate or income, the creditors may do the same.

Where a testator provides in his will that property actually devised shall not be subject to the debts of the devisee, such provision is void, and where the income from certain property is devised to one for life, with the provision that if any court should ever hold it subject to the devisee's debts his interest therein should cease and the title should vest at once in the remaindermen, such provision is valid. . . .

The provision in the will of Paulina E. Todd falls in neither of these classifications. There is no misconstruing the intent of the testatrix in the instant case. The language of the will is direct and unambiguous. It was the manifest intent of the testatrix that the legal title and the absolute control of the property should pass to the trustees, and that they should be vested with absolute discretion in the matter of payments to the cestui out of the principal and income. No interest vested in the cestui. He has no rights which he can enforce. The property is given to the trustees to be applied in their discretion, uncontrolled by any other person, to the use of Romulus Todd, and no interest goes to him until the trustees have exercised this discretion. Section 2355 of the Statutes has no application where the cestui is without any interest in the trust estate which he can enforce. Davidson's Executors v. Kemper, 79 Ky. 5; Hackett's Trustee v. Hackett, 146 Ky. 408, 142 S.W. 673.

In Louisville Tobacco Warehouse Co. v. Thompson, 172 Ky. 350, 189 S.W. 245, 247, the provision of the will there under consideration was very similar to the provision of Paulina E. Todd's will heretofore quoted, and it was held that no interest was created which could be subjected to the debts of the beneficiary. After reviewing a number of cases, the court said:

> From the brief review we have given these cases, it becomes apparent that the rule is that, where the beneficiary whose interest is sought to be subjected is given an enforceable interest in the property devised, that interest may be subject to his debts. Such an interest is given when a specific sum is directed to be paid to him, and the payment of which sum he can legally enforce. It is likewise given when the language creat-

ing the interest is sufficient to give him an estate in the property devised, but when neither of these is given, and the sum which he is to receive is discretionary with the trustee, no interest is created which may be subjected to the payment of his debts.

Our conclusion is that the will under consideration gives to Romulus Todd no interest in his mother's estate which can be subjected to the payment of his debts. . . .

The judgment is reversed, with directions to enter a judgment in conformity with this opinion.

RESTATEMENT (SECOND) OF TRUSTS

§155.   *Discretionary Trusts.*

(1) Except as stated in §156 [where the settlor is a beneficiary], if by the terms of a trust it is provided that the trustee shall pay to or apply for a beneficiary only so much of the income and principal or either as the trustee in his uncontrolled discretion shall see fit to pay or apply, a transferee or creditor of the beneficiary cannot compel the trustee to pay any part of the income or principal.

(2) Unless a valid restraint on alienation has been imposed in accordance with the rules stated in §§152 and 153, if the trustee pays to or applies for the beneficiary any part of the income or principal with knowledge of the transfer or after he has been served with process in a proceeding by a creditor to reach it, he is liable to such transferee or creditor.

Comment: . . .

b. Discretionary trust distinguished from spendthrift trust. A trust containing such a provision as is stated in this Section is a "discretionary trust" and is to be distinguished from a spendthrift trust, and from a trust for support. In a discretionary trust it is the nature of the beneficiary's interest rather than a provision forbidding alienation which prevents the transfer of the beneficiary's interest. The rule stated in this Section is not dependent upon a prohibition of alienation by the settlor; but the transferee or creditor cannot compel the trustee to pay anything to him because the beneficiary could not compel payment to himself or application for his own benefit.

§154. *Trusts for Support.*   Except as stated in §§156 and 157, if by the terms of a trust it is provided that the trustee shall pay or apply only so much of the income and principal or either as is necessary for the education or support of the beneficiary, the beneficiary cannot transfer his interest and his creditors cannot reach it.

G. BOGERT, TRUSTS
(6th ed. 1987)

§43. *Blended Trusts.*   If a trust is for the benefit of described persons as a group and no member of the group is intended to have a right to any individual benefits separate and apart from the others, then no member has an alienable interest or one which his creditors can reach.

§44. *Protective Trusts.*   The phrase "protective trust" has been used in England to describe a trust of an ordinary type which, on attempted alienation of his interest by the cestui or attempted attachment by his creditors, becomes a discretionary trust to apply the income for the benefit of any one or more or all of the group consisting of the original beneficiary and his spouse and issue, or if he has no spouse or issue, for the original beneficiary and his prospective next of kin. . . .

Bogert's third edition (1952) pointed out that in England "the protective trust takes the place of the outlawed spendthrift trust," and stated that a protective trust "can be created in the United States but the validity of spendthrift or other similar trusts renders it of little use." Can you think of reasons for using protective trust provisions even where spendthrift trusts are valid?

MATTHEWS v. MATTHEWS
450 N.E.2d 278 (Ohio App. 1982)

[Action against the beneficiary of a trust to recover alimony and child support. The trustee was directed to pay to or for defendant Matthews such part of the income "as the trustee in his sole discretion shall deem necessary for his reasonable support, maintenance and health" and also to pay or apply principal for these purposes as the trustee "shall deem necessary and proper under the circumstances." The trial court found that there was nothing in the trust instrument indicating an intent by the settlor to provide for defendant's children and that no "vested interest existed because the trust was fully discretionary."]
MOYER, J. . . .
[D]efendant's ex-wife . . . attempted to reach defendant's interest in the trust to satisfy her judgment against defendant [but] Martin v. Martin [54 Ohio St. 2d 101, 374 N.E.2d 1384 (1978)], clearly holds that a former spouse may not attach the interest of a beneficiary of a discretionary trust. Defendants rely on *Martin* also for their argument that defendant Matthews' child may not attach [his] interest. . . .

The trial court erred in concluding that the trust was fully discretionary. The first branch of the syllabus in *Martin* reads as follows:

> A trust conferring upon the trustees power to distribute income and principal in their "absolute discretion," but which provides standards by which that discretion is to be exercised with reference to needs of the trust beneficiary for education, care, comfort or support, is neither a purely discretionary trust nor a strict support trust, and the trustees of such trust may be required to exercise their discretion to distribute income and principal for those needs. . . .

The trust before us, as the trust in *Martin,* is neither a purely discretionary trust, nor a strict support trust. It follows that, at least to the extent of his needs, defendant Matthews has an interest in . . . the income of the trust.

The next question is whether plaintiffs may claim an interest in the beneficiary's income interest in the trust. We find no decision of the Supreme Court that disposes of the issue. A review of the cases from other jurisdictions . . . causes us to conclude that there is no unanimous view of the law. [One view] is that the child may, in the absence of an express exclusion in the trust instrument, recover from the trust. The reasoning upon which this position is based is that beneficiary should not be allowed to enjoy his interest while neglecting to support his children. We believe this to be the better rule.

The trial court held that there was no indication that the settlor intended to provide for defendant Matthews' children. However, the trust document states that the trustee shall pay what he deems necessary for the beneficiary's "reasonable support, maintenance and health." Support of one's children is mandated by R.C. 3103.03. "Reasonable support" includes payment of all the beneficiary's normal, expected and legal responsibilities. It would have been unreasonable, had defendant Matthews lived with his child, for the trustee to have refused to pay defendant Matthews sufficient funds from the trust to support both himself and his child. We have been given no reason why "reasonable support" should have a different application simply because defendant lived apart from his daughter. . . . The final question is, from what fund the judgment should be satisfied. Plaintiffs claim that [the will] authorizes payment from the corpus of the trust . . . when the income from the trust is insufficient to provide for the beneficiary's needs. . . .

Assuming no significant change in the trust income, the judgment for child support could reasonably be expected to be paid from the trust income within 3 to 5 years. It would, therefore, be imprudent to order the trustee to invade the principal to satisfy said judgment. This amount constitutes over one-tenth of the entire principal, and the payment of such an amount might jeopardize the trust itself. Therefore, we hold that the trustee did not abuse its discretion by refusing to invade the corpus of the trust to pay the judgment. . . .

Judgment reversed and cause remanded.

MOYER, J. [reaffirming the reversal on reconsideration]. . . .

The general rule is that the income from a trust which is neither a purely discretionary nor a strict support trust and which contains no express exclusion therefrom of the beneficiary's children, may be attached for the purpose of paying for the support of the beneficiary's children. . . .

RESTATEMENT (THIRD) OF TRUSTS
(Tent. Draft approved 1999)

§50. *Enforcement and Construction of Discretionary Interests*

(1) A discretionary power conferred upon the trustee to determine the benefits of a trust beneficiary is subject to judicial control only to prevent misinterpretation or abuse of the discretion by the trustee.

(2) The benefits to which a beneficiary of a discretionary interest is entitled, and what may constitute an abuse of discretion by the trustee, depend on the terms of the discretion, including the proper construction of any accompanying standards, and on the settlor's purposes in granting the discretionary power and in creating the trust.

General Comment:

a. Scope of section. . . .

This section deals with situations in which trustees are granted discretion with respect to beneficiaries' rights to trust benefits. For these situations, the terminology "discretionary trust" or "discretionary interest" is used in this Restatement whether or not the terms of the trust provide standards (see Comments *d, e,* and *f*) to limit or guide the trustee's exercise of the discretionary power.

. . . A power's "discretionary" character may be implied from its being attached to a standard, such as a simple direction to pay "amounts appropriate to B's support."

§56. *Rights of Beneficiary's Creditors*

Except as stated in Chapter 12 [on spendthrift and discretionary trusts], creditors of a trust beneficiary, or of a deceased beneficiary's estate, can subject the interest of the beneficiary to the satisfaction of their claims, except insofar as a corresponding legal interest is exempt from creditors' claims.

Comment:
   a. Scope of section. . . .
   The rule of this section applies to all beneficial interests in a trust.
Thus, subject to the rules of Chapter 12 and applicable exemptions
(Comment *d*), creditors may reach a beneficiary's right to receive the
trust income or an annuity or unitrust payments. They may also attach a
beneficiary's right to discretionary distributions, subject to the practical
limitations described in §60. . . .

§60.   *Transfer or Attachment of Discretionary Interests*

   Subject to the rules stated in §§58 and 59 (on spendthrift trusts), if
the terms of a trust provide for a beneficiary to receive distributions
in the trustee's discretion, a transferee or creditor of the beneficiary
is entitled to receive or attach any distributions the trustee makes or
is required to make in the exercise of that discretion after the trustee
has knowledge of the transfer or attachment. The amounts a creditor
can reach may be limited to provide for the beneficiary's needs (Comment *c*), or the amounts may be increased where the beneficiary either
is the settlor (Comment *f*) or holds the discretionary power to determine his or her own distributions (Comment *g*).

Comment:
   a. Scope of the rule. The rule of this section allows a beneficiary's assignee to receive discretionary distributions to which the beneficiary
would otherwise be entitled, and allows creditors of the beneficiary to
attach his or her discretionary interest. The rule does not apply if the
beneficiary's interest is subject to a valid spendthrift restraint under
the rules of §58 unless the situation falls within an exception under
§59.
   This section recognizes special rules for discretionary interests retained by a settlor (compare §58(2)) and for trusts in which the beneficiary, as trustee or otherwise, holds the discretionary authority to
determine his or her own distributions (compare §58, Comment *c*).
These rules (in Comments *f* and *g*, respectively) expand the amount
such a beneficiary's creditors may reach.
   The rules stated in this section and its commentary apply to whatever
extent a beneficiary's interest is discretionary. Thus, if the beneficiary
is entitled to all of the trust's net income but only to principal in the
trustee's discretion, the section applies to the provision for invasion of
principal but not to the income interest. Also, the section prevents the
trustee not only from making payments to the beneficiary but also from
making "distributions" by applying funds directly for the beneficiary's
benefit contrary to the rights of the transferee or creditor. (On the
latter, see especially Comment *c*.)

"Discretionary interests" for purposes of this section include those encompassed by §50 (see especially id., Comment *a*). Thus, this section applies where trustees are granted discretionary authority over benefits, regardless of whether the trust terms provide simply for the beneficiary's support, provide other or additional standards, or express no standards to limit or guide the trustee's exercise of discretion. For purposes of this section, however, unlike §50 (see id., Comment *a*), discretionary interests also include powers by which beneficiaries who are *not* trustees may determine their own benefits pursuant to any form of standards but which are not equivalent to ownership under §58, Comment *c*. Thus, Comment *g* deals with nonfiduciary as well as fiduciary powers under which beneficiaries may distribute trust funds to themselves subject to some expressed or implied standard, often the "ascertainable" or "objective" standards dictated by Internal Revenue Code §2041 or cases under id. §2038.

Comment *a* [Reporter's Notes]: . . .

Purported distinction between "discretionary" and "support" trusts abandoned. This section (like §50) departs significantly from prior Restatements, and from some lines of cases that were largely influenced by the prior Restatement positions (and cf. Miss. Code Ann. §§91-9-505 and -507), in that this Restatement Third does not attempt to draw a bright line between "discretionary" interests (Restatement Second, Trusts §155) and "support" interests (id. §154) or other analogous interests ("personal" in §160 or "inseparable" in §161, or "class" or maybe "blended" in §155, Comment *d*). The so-called "support trust" is viewed here as a discretionary trust with a support standard. This in turn requires asking and examining all of the questions that follow from that view, such as how a particular standard, in context, is to be interpreted and whether a beneficiary's other resources are to be taken into account in making a fiduciary judgment about appropriate distributions to the beneficiary. See generally §50 and its commentary.

The Uniform Trust [Code] similarly provides a single rule and a single section (§504, draft 1998) for all discretionary trusts, including an interest or trust that is subject to a support standard.

Not only is the supposed distinction between support and discretionary trusts arbitrary and artificial, but the lines are also difficult — and costly — to attempt to draw. Attempting to do so tends to produce dubious categorizations and almost inevitably different results . . . from case to case for beneficiaries who appear, realistically, to be similarly situated as objects of similar settlor intentions. The price of the supposed distinction in litigation costs and to the general goal of equitable treatment seems particularly noticeable in those of the Medicaid and public benefit cases that have succumbed to this deceptively simple appearing distinction. See, e.g., . . . Lang v. Department of Public Welfare, 515 Pa. 428, 528 A.2d 1335 (1987) (trust "discretionary" despite terms "maintain" and "support"); . . . and generally cases and discussion in Reporter's Note to Comment *e* of §50. . . .

The fundamental deficiency of the traditional Restatement approach is revealed simply by recognizing the vast (yet much traveled) territory between support and discretionary provisions — territory simply omitted from coverage by the prior Restatements' definitions of support and discretionary trusts. . . . Discretionary trusts thus defined, in which "the beneficiary could not compel payment to [or] for his own benefit," would be unusual indeed not only in light of the rules stated in §50 of this Restatement but even under the rules of §187 of Restatement Second, Trusts itself, dealing with abuse of discretion and the requirement, even under an "absolute" discretion provision, to act in a manner consistent with the settlor's purposes. See also Uniform Trust Act (draft 1998) §801 and §815 ("Notwithstanding the breadth of discretion granted to a trustee, including the use of such terms as 'absolute,' 'sole,' or 'uncontrolled,' the trustee shall exercise a discretionary power in good faith and with regard to the purpose of the trust and the interest of the beneficiaries").

The fact of the matter is that there is a continuum of discretionary trusts, with the terms of distributive powers ranging from the most objective (or "ascertainable," IRC §2041) of standards (pure "support") to the most open ended (e.g., "happiness") or vague ("benefit") of standards, or even with no standards manifested at all (for which a court will probably apply "a general standard of reasonableness"). And these trusts use an unlimited variety of combinations of such terms or standards, . . . [all] subject to the same general principle that courts will interfere only to prevent abuse. . . .

Insofar as the settlor's purpose, in whatever manner expressed or implied, is to provide for the beneficiary's needs, and if it is an acceptable social policy that a beneficiary not be left without essential means of support and care (and education as appropriate), the rules of this section accommodate that objective (on a reasonable *need*, not a station-in-life, basis) regardless of how the discretionary trust might be worded and categorized (Comment *c*) and under a policy of general application when creditors are allowed to attach beneficial interests (see §56, Comment *e*, as well as §59, Comment *b*). Cf. . . . Uniform Trust Act (draft 1998) §504(b). . . .

Creditors of Settlor-Beneficiary. Greenwich Trust Co. v. Tyson, 129 Conn. 211, 222-225, 27 A.2d 166, 172-174 (1942), states:

> The trust before us is not a spendthrift trust but, by reason of the discretion reposed in the trustee as to the use of the income, it is a "dis-

cretionary" trust. If in such a trust the settlor is the sole person entitled to the income, that income can be reached by his creditors. Griswold, Spendthrift Trusts 481; Restatement, Trusts, §156(2). A provision in the trust instrument that the trustee might in his discretion withhold the income from the settlor and accumulate it would not in itself place the income beyond the reach of his creditors. . . . We are brought, then, to the question of the effect of the provision that the trustee in his "absolute discretion" might expend any part of the income for the support and maintenance of the wife of the settlor or the support, education and maintenance of a named son and of other children who might be born to him. . . .

The outstanding factor in the situation is that, under a trust where the trustee has absolute discretion to pay the income or expend it for the settlor's benefit, the trustee could, even though he had a like discretion to expend it for others, still pay it all to the settlor. Such a trust opens the way to the evasion by the settlor of his just debts, although he may still have the full enjoyment of the income from his property. To subject it to the claims of the settlor's creditors does not deprive others to whom the trustee might pay the income of anything to which they are entitled of right; they could not compel the trustee to use any of the income for them. The public policy which subjects to the demands of a settlor's creditors the income of a trust which the trustee in his discretion may pay to the settlor applies no less to a case where the trustee might in his discretion pay or use the income for others. The trial court was correct in holding that the plaintiff was entitled to reach the income if necessary to satisfy its judgment, but was in error in holding that its rights were limited to so much only of that income as the trustee in his discretion deemed not to be required for the support, maintenance or education of the settlor's wife and children.

The fact that the provisions of the trust agreement are ineffective to protect the income of the trust from the claims of Tyson's creditors does not invalidate the trust as a whole or in itself destroy the remainder interests created.

Asset Protection Trusts. One of the "hot" topics in estate planning today is the use of asset protection trusts (APTs), i.e., trusts whose primary purpose is the protection of trust assets from the claims of creditors or others. These trusts may be offshore (OAPTs), using such exotic locales as the Cook Islands off New Zealand, or they may be domestic (DAPTs), using such states as Alaska or Delaware. How widely used these trusts are, in fact, is hard to say, but the APT literature is full of articles and books, and there is even an *Asset Protection Journal.* Several American states have rushed to enact laws to facilitate DAPTs. What led to this interest and activity?

The early APTs appear to have been offshore ones, established either by persons in high-risk businesses or professions, e.g., surgeons, or by high-income persons seeking to avoid United States taxation. Wealthy persons may distrust the unpredictable American jury system, may fear huge punitive damage awards, and may despair of novel theories of liability encouraged by a contingent fee rather than a loser-pays system for attorney fees. Most high-income persons have always sought to minimize their taxes.

Over the last few decades Congress has acted to severely discourage the use of OAPTs for tax avoidance. There are burdensome reporting requirements, potential penalties, new definitions of foreign trusts, and new Code sections which, combined with a jaundiced Internal Revenue Service view of OAPTs, limit the usefulness of OAPTs for tax purposes. This leaves asset protection as the primary motivation.

How is an OAPT a significant impediment to creditors? Through a combination of factors: United States judgments may not be enforceable in offshore jurisdictions. The offshore legal system will require the creditor to retain a local attorney (who may be difficult to find because of ties to the trustee), and to pay hourly rates and abide by loser-pays rules. Offshore laws may be less creditor-friendly; they may, for example, even protect self-settled spendthrift trusts. There may be layers of ownership and trusteeship that are difficult to penetrate. Many OAPTs provide for a trust "protector" with broad discretion to change the trustee, the trust situs, or even the trust terms. Compare the discussion of trust protectors in Chapter 17 infra. Nevertheless, some commentators have predicted an onslaught of new litigation strategies to reach OAPTs.

Faced with a loss of trust business to offshore entities, in recent years some American states, following the lead of Alaska and Delaware, have significantly amended their laws to retain business from their own residents and even to attract business from other states. The changes from longstanding doctrine and policy have been remarkable. More than ten states have abolished in one fashion or another the Rule Against Perpetuities.[6]

Effective 1997 Alaska changed its law to specifically provide that properly established self-settled irrevocable trusts that are both spendthrift and discretionary are not subject to claims of the settlor's creditors. Delaware followed suit later that same year. (Contrast Greenwich Trust Co. v. Tyson, supra, and other materials in this Chapter 13.) Both states have safe harbors that allow the settlor to establish situs by selecting an individual or institution domiciled in the state and maintaining at least some features of the trust administration in the state. Compare National Shawmut Bank v. Cumming and the materials following it in

---

6. Alaska Stat. §§34.77.010-.995 also offers non-residents as well as residents an "opt-in" community property system, enabling surviving spouses to receive a full new basis for assets that would receive only a partial new basis if held in other forms of co-ownership. See I.R.C. §1014(b)(6).

Chapter 12, section C, supra. In Alaska there are exceptions to the effectiveness of self-settled spendthrift trusts where the transfer was fraudulent (recall the references to fraudulent transfers in this chapter, supra) or where the settlor was more than thirty days in arrears in child support at the time of the transfer. Delaware is somewhat more creditor-friendly. The transfer is not valid if it was a fraudulent transfer, and the trust is not effective against the claims for support or alimony of a spouse, former spouse, or child. It is also not effective against claimants who suffered death or personal injury caused by the settlor before the trust was created. Compare *Sligh* and the protections of certain favored claimants illustrated in this chapter. Both Alaska and Delaware require that fraudulent conveyance actions be brought within the later of four years of the transfer to the trust or one year after the transfer was or reasonably could have been discovered. By statute effective in 1998, Alaska recognized the effectiveness of no contest or in terrorem clauses, even if probable cause existed for instituting the proceedings (see Chapter 16).

Both the Alaska and Delaware law are designed to allow the settlor/ beneficiary to have the option of making a completed gift and removing the assets from those subject to estate tax, while at the same time having the possibility of getting the assets back under some circumstances. A successful Private Letter Ruling was obtained under Alaska law for gift tax purposes, but the Service declined to rule on the estate tax issue.

Alaska law provides that no action may be brought against a person involved in the preparation of a self-settled spendthrift trust for aiding a fraudulent transfer or participating in the trust transaction. If the APT disinherits a spouse or child, would the attorney be liable for tortious interference with inheritance? What litigation advantages would a plaintiff's lawyer seek in bringing an action for tortious interference with inheritance rather than some other theory? Are there ethical concerns for attorneys who assist in establishing APTs? Compare Townsend v. State Bar of California, 197 P.2d 326 (Cal. 1948) (discipline where lawyer advised client to convey property to defraud judgment creditor); McElhanon v. Hing, 728 P.2d 256, 264 (Ariz. App. 1985), *aff'd in part & rev'd in part on other grounds*, 728 P.2d 273 (Ariz. 1986) (lawyer's privilege to advise and act for client does not apply to participation in client's fraudulent conveyance); Restatement (Third) of the Law Governing Lawyers §§151, 157 (Tent. Draft No. 8, 1997); Model Rules of Professional Conduct 1.1(a); 1.2(d), 1.3; Manley, The Impact of Ethical Rules on Estate Planning, SD36 ALI-ABA 275 (1999).

As you no doubt have recognized, techniques associated with asset protection trusts touch on many aspects of estate and trust law, often in remarkable new ways. It is too early to predict whether these trusts are the wave of the future or a thunderstorm that will soon pass and be forgotten. Will the Congress be content to allow dynasty trusts with no Rule Against Perpetuities, given that the estate and gift taxes are predicated on a perpetuities rule that exposes assets to transfer tax every generation or so? What will happen when spouses attack APTs, seeking alimony (family maintenance) or elective share rights or an omitted spouse's share? What of the rights of a child to child support or a pretermitted heir's share? What about satisfaction of homestead, family allowances, and exempt property? What are the possible bases for effective court jurisdiction for all these types of actions? If APTs prove to be effective, can they be unwound? (Compare Chapter 14 on trust termination.)

There are few appellate decisions on any of these issues. There have been reports in the press of some trial-level cases. Most have been settled. Some of the courts have not been sympathetic to attempts to oust their jurisdiction and have asserted jurisdiction through an order imposing personal liability on the settlor or a finding that the trustee operated a subsidiary in the state. Cf. FTC v. Affordable Media, 179 F.3d 1228 (9th Cir. 1999) (settlors held in civil contempt); G. Rothschild & D. Rubin, Offshore Trusts-Onshore Litigation, Prob. & Prop. 29 (Nov./Dec. 1999). In the long run, protection of domestic APTs through possible application of the Full Faith and Credit Clause may make them more popular than offshore APTs.

Note, finally, the availability of more traditional techniques for asset protection. As noted previously, ERISA requires that qualified pension plans include a spendthrift clause. (What do you think the effect on popularity of qualified plans would be if, as at least one senator favors, spendthrift clause protection were capped at $1 million?) Most state laws protect IRAs. State law often protects other pension arrangements, as well as life insurance and annuities. Homestead is essentially an exemption from the claims of creditors; in Florida there is no limit on value, and it was reported a few years ago that a former major league baseball commissioner acquired a million dollar residence there just weeks before filing for bankruptcy. In states recognizing the tenancy by the entirety, often any real estate held in that form is exempt from the creditors of one of the spouses. Various business entities such as corporations and limited liability companies and various business strategies such as use of multiple entities, life insurance, and passive investments can operate to limit some risk.

See generally J. Eason, Home from the Islands: Domestic Asset Protection Trust Alternatives Impact Traditional Estate and Gift Planning Considerations, 52 Fla. L. Rev. 41 (2000); Manley, The Situs Wars: Recent Developments in the Struggle to Win Your Trust, 1999 ACTEC Annual Meeting Materials HT I-RLM 1-15 (Mar. 1999); Claypool, Asset Protection Overview: Techniques in the United States and Offshore, 24 ACTEC Notes 302 (1999); Symposium, The International Trust, 32 Vand. L. Rev. 1, 711-875 (1999).

14

Modification and Termination
of Trusts

In the typical case a trust is terminated according to its terms when its purpose has been fulfilled in due course. In the unusual case, a trust may terminate because the purposes of the trust become unlawful, impossible to achieve, or contrary to public policy. After the creation of a trust but before the time fixed for its regular termination, questions sometimes arise regarding possible modification or premature termination of the trust. This chapter deals with certain of the problems presented by such questions and also with express powers to modify or to terminate. (Whether creditors of the settlor can avail themselves of the settlor's power to revoke a trust was considered in Chapter 13, section C.2.)

A. Power of the Settlor to Modify or Revoke

Can the settlor, once an inter vivos trust has been created, terminate the trust, take away the rights given the beneficiaries, and recover the trust property? Essentially this depends on whether the trust is revocable. In a properly drawn trust agreement or declaration the question would be answered expressly. Sometimes, however, the question is not adequately covered by the terms of the trust — that is, either the provisions of the trust instrument or some other admissible evidence of the settlor's intent. In certain informal trusts a power of revocation may be implied, as in the case of tentative or *Totten* trusts. Occasionally it is asserted that the settlor intended to reserve a power to revoke the trust but omitted it by mistake.

 In most states the settled rule is that, in the absence of grounds for reformation or rescission, a trust created or declared by a written instrument is irrevocable unless a power of revocation is expressly reserved or may be implied from language contained in the instrument. Restatement (Second) of Trusts §330. In a few states there are statutory provisions reversing this standard common law rule. For example, California Probate Code §15400 provides that "[u]nless expressly made irrevocable by the trust instrument, the trust is revocable by the settlor." See also proposal in Uniform Trust Code §602(a) below.

A trust may be reformed or rescinded on the same grounds as a transfer free of trust. See Restatement (Third) of Trusts §12 (Tent. Draft approved 1996). Yet problems in the reformation of trusts, particularly on the ground of unilateral mistake, are made somewhat distinctive by the donative character of the typical trust, and the problems are shaped by the circumstances of a trust's planning and preparation. "The creation of a trust being substantially a unilateral transaction, the mistake of the settlor, not shared by the trustee or beneficiary, is sufficient to avoid the transfer if it induces a conveyance whose consequences the settlor does not understand or intend." Nossaman, Wyatt, and McDaniel, Trust Administration and Taxation, §21.12[4] (rev. 2d ed. 1990).

Coolidge v. Loring, 235 Mass. 220, 223-224, 126 N.E. 276, 277 (1920), states:

> [T]he mistaken "belief" of the settlors as set forth in the agreed facts affords no ground for relief. Misconception of the legal effect of the language in the instrument is not a "mistake of law" against which our courts afford a remedy. The parties are bound by the legal effect of what has really been agreed on, and cannot have the declaration set aside on the ground that they did not fully understand the legal effect of the language used, and that certain legal consequences which were not anticipated by the settlors flowed from its execution. . . . The language is entirely consistent with a view that the subject of . . . termination in the lifetime of the settlors did not occur to the parties at the time of the declaration of trust. . . . It is settled that an instrument will not be reformed on the ground of mistake, except upon "full, clear and decisive proof" of the mistake.

In Atkinson v. Atkinson, 157 Md. 648, 651-652, 147 A. 662, 663 (1929), involving a trust of all of the settlor's property, the court stated:

> The record convinces us that the grantor did not intend to relinquish control of his estate to that extent. His physical and mental debility . . . was sufficient to account for his apparent failure to comprehend clearly the real effect of the deed of trust and the true intent of his attorney's explanations. There was no consideration for the deed, and, as it appears not to be in accord with the grantor's actual purpose and understanding, we shall affirm the decree.

In a number of cases a settlor or donor has been allowed to rescind a trust or gift on the grounds of mistake as to the tax consequences of the transfer. See IV W. Fratcher, Scott on Trusts §333.4 (4th ed. 1989). For an example of reformation to salvage a deceased settlor's tax objectives (qualification for estate tax marital deduction), see Berman v. Sandler, 399 N.E.2d 17 (1980). See also the UTC section, below, seeking to encourage, and to some extent to reflect, development of the law in matters of reformation and modification.

UNIFORM TRUST CODE
(Draft, Feb. 2000)

§414. *Reformation to Correct Mistakes.* The court may reform the terms of a trust, even if unambiguous, to conform to the settlor's intention if the failure to conform was due to a mistake of fact or law, whether in expression or inducement, and the settlor's intent can be established by clear and convincing evidence.

§415. *Modification to Achieve Settlor's Tax Objectives.* To achieve the settlor's tax objectives, the court may modify the terms of a trust in a manner that is not contrary to the settlor's probable intention. The court may provide that a modification has retroactive effect.

The power to revoke is generally held to include the power to amend. See Heifetz v. Bank of America, 147 Cal. App. 2d 776, 305 P.2d 979 (1957); Annot., 62 A.L.R. 2d 1043 (1957). Is there any reason for not implying the power to amend from a power to revoke? An *unrestricted* power to amend includes the power to revoke the trust. Whether a power to amend is unrestricted depends on the terms of the trust (a phrase terms generally defined to mean the "intention of the settlor with respect to the trust provisions expressed in a manner [admissible] in judicial proceedings." Restatement (Third) of Trusts §4. See also Uniform Trust Code §103(20).[1] See generally on amendment and revocation IV W. Fratcher, Scott on Trusts §§331.1, 331.2 (4th ed. 1989).

As to the manner of revocation, ordinarily the revocation of a trust is accomplished by signing and delivering a written document to the trustee. Cases occasionally arise where the settlor has not followed the better practice. While it is said that if the settlor reserves a power to revoke in a particular manner, he can revoke only in that manner, the courts have not always insisted on a literal adherence to the trust requirements. In Barnette v. McNulty, 21 Ariz. App. 127, 516 P.2d 583 (1973), the court held that the methods of revocation in a trust drawn from Norman Dacey's book, *How to Avoid Probate!*, were not exclusive,

---

1. See also Durst v. United States, 559 F.2d 910 (3d Cir. 1977), relying on similar language of prior Restatement.

and the settlor's oral statements were a sufficient revocation. Cf. In re Estate and Trust of Pilafas, 172 Ariz. 207, 836 P.2d 420 (1992) (court refused to extend to missing revocable living trust the wills presumption of revocation by destruction where a will last seen in testator's possession could not be found after death).

In Connecticut General Life Insurance Co. v. First National Bank, 262 N.W.2d 403 (Minn. 1977), the court held that a will that purported "to supercede and cancel any wills or trusts established by me" was ineffective to revoke an inter vivos life insurance trust that reserved a power to revoke "by written instrument . . . delivered to any trustee . . . during [the settlor's] lifetime." The majority view seems to agree with *Connecticut General* on the issue of whether a will can revoke a revocable trust. See IV W. Fratcher, Scott on Trusts §330.8 (4th ed. 1989). The issue of revocation by will may also arise with respect to other will substitutes (see Chapter 8), including *Totten* trusts (see Chapter 11, section B.4). See IA Scott on Trusts, supra, §58.4 (1987). Courts must balance the need for certainty and predictability against evolving policies of carrying out intent despite lack of compliance with formalities; for example, a provision requiring notice to the trustee might be regarded as merely for the protection of the trustee. See IV Scott on Trusts, supra, §330.8 (1989).

What effect will adoption of the UTC provisions below have on these various matters?

UNIFORM TRUST CODE
(Draft, Feb. 2000)

§602. *Revocation or Amendment of Revocable Trust.*

(a) Unless the terms of a trust expressly provide that the trust is irrevocable, the settlor may revoke or amend the trust. This subsection does not affect a trust created under an instrument executed before [the effective date of this [Act]].

(b) If a revocable trust is created or funded by more than one settlor:

(1) to the extent the trust consists of community property, the trust may be revoked by either spouse acting alone but may be amended only by joint action of both spouses; and

(2) to the extent the trust consists of other property, each settlor may revoke or amend the trust as to the portion of the trust property attributable to that settlor's contribution.

(c) A trust that is revocable by the settlor may be revoked or amended:

(1) by substantially complying with a method prescribed by the terms of the trust; or

(2) unless the terms of the trust expressly make the prescribed method exclusive, by a later will or codicil that refers to the trust or which specifically devises property that would otherwise have passed according to the trust; or

(3) by any other method manifesting clear and convincing evidence of the settlor's intent.

(d) Upon revocation of a revocable trust, the trustee shall deliver the trust property as the settlor directs.

(e) A settlor's powers with respect to revocation, amendment, or distribution of trust property may be exercised by an agent under a power of attorney only to the extent expressly authorized by the terms of the trust or the power.

(f) A [conservator] may revoke or amend a revocable trust with the approval of the court supervising the [conservatorship]. A [guardian] may not revoke the settlor's revocable trust.

Comment . . .

While revocation of a trust is ordinarily accomplished by signing and delivering a written document to the trustee, other methods, such as by physical act or by oral statement coupled with a withdrawal of the property, may also demonstrate the necessary intent. These less formal methods, because they provide less reliable indicia of intent, are not to be encouraged. . . .

[Under §602(e) an] . . . express provision is required because most settlors usually intend the revocable trust, and not the power of attorney, to function as the settlor's principal property management device. . . .

Many States allow a conservator to exercise the settlor's power of revocation with the prior approval of the court supervising the conservatorship. See, e.g., Unif. Prob. Code §5-407. [UTC §103] allows a settlor to direct in the terms of the trust that this other law not apply. The fact that a conservator may be prohibited from revoking the trust does not mean that the conservator is prohibited from taking appropriate action to protect the settlor's interest if the settlor, now under conservatorship, is also a beneficiary of the trust. For example, the conservator could petition for removal of the trustee [see §706] acting on the settlor-beneficiary's behalf, . . . [or] bring an action to enforce the trust. . . .

Subsection (f) denies a guardian the right to revoke a revocable trust created by the ward. A "guardian," as defined in Section 102(5), does not have authority to manage property. Also, in most States statutory provisions authorizing a court to revise the ward's estate plan only apply to the person appointed to manage the ward's property, described as a "conservator" under this Act. . . .

B. Termination or Modification by the Trustee

The trustee has power to terminate or modify a trust only to the extent expressly or impliedly granted by the terms of the trust. Such a power is to be exercised in accordance with fiduciary standards and the intent of the settlor as manifested in the terms of the trust. The general principles encountered in the preceding chapter relating to trustees' discretionary powers over distributions are applicable to discretionary powers to terminate. See Watling v. Watling, 27 F.2d 193 (6th Cir. 1928).

Where the trustee is not expressly given a power to terminate the trust but is given discretion to invade principal, the latter power would presumably permit termination by distribution of all of the principal if reasonably required to carry out the settlor's purpose. See Boyden v. Stevens, 285 Mass. 176, 188 N.E. 741 (1934). But the trustee may not exercise a discretionary power of invasion to terminate a trust for reasons beyond the intended purpose of the power. See Kemp v. Paterson, 6 N.Y.2d 40, 159 N.E.2d 661 (1959), in which three dissenting judges thought that the purpose of saving taxes fell within the expressed standard relating to the beneficiary's "best interest."

It is not unusual that two or more trusts are established for the same family. May the trusts be combined in order to simplify administration or to achieve administrative economies? Conversely, division of a single trust into two or more trusts may be desirable to obtain maximum advantage of exemptions available under the federal generation-skipping tax or to accommodate different investment objectives or distributional requirements of the beneficiaries. See, e.g., BankBoston v. Marlow, 428 Mass. 283, 701 N.E.2d 304 (1998). Many state statutes allow for division of trusts under certain circumstances, and Uniform Trust Code §416 allows both combining and dividing to be done by trustees without court or beneficiary approval, although notice to certain beneficiaries is required; some trustees might be reluctant to act without court approval.

C. Termination and Modification by the Beneficiaries

99% = term. cases

PROBLEMS

14-A. *S* left the residue of his estate to *T* in trust "to pay the income to my wife, *W*, for life, remainder to such of my children as survive her." No spendthrift provision was included in the trust. *W*, age 65, and *S*'s only children, *A* and *B*, ages 40 and 35, jointly petition the court to terminate the trust and to convey the trust assets to them. What result?

Would the inclusion of a spendthrift clause alter the result? What if this spendthrift trust had been created inter vivos and S were still alive and gave his consent to the requested termination? (Careful!)

If there were no spendthrift clause, but the trust provided for the payment of income to W for life "in the trustee's discretion" or "as is appropriate for W's support," would either of these phrasings alter the result?

Would any of your answers change if the Uniform Trust Code provisions, infra pages 686-688, were in effect?

14-B.   Suppose in the spendthrift trust situation in Problem 14-A, W, A, and B request T to convey the trust assets to them in termination of the trust. T does so and they receipt for it. Later, W files suit to require T to reestablish the trust and to pay her the income until her death. What result?

Assume further while suit is pending, T pays W, A, and B $100 each for a release of all liability in settlement of the suit. What is the effect of this?

In the landmark case of Claflin v. Claflin, 149 Mass. 19, 20 N.E. 454 (1889), the settlor created a testamentary trust to pay his son $10,000 at age 21, $10,000 at age 25, and the balance of the principal at age 30. Following his twenty-first birthday the son sought to compel the trustees to pay the entire trust fund over to him. The court conceded that the son was the sole beneficiary and that all equitable interests in the property were indefeasibly vested in him; it also concluded that the trust was not a dry or passive trust and that all purposes of the trust had not been accomplished. The question then was whether, under such circumstances, the sole beneficiary could compel termination. The court stated, 149 Mass. at 23-24, 20 N.E. at 456:

> In the case at bar nothing has happened which the testator did not anticipate, and for which he has not made provision. It is plainly his will that neither the income nor any part of the principal should now be paid to the plaintiff. It is true that the plaintiff's interest is alienable by him, and can be taken by his creditors to pay his debts, but it does not follow that, because the testator has not imposed all possible restrictions, the restrictions which he has imposed should not be carried into effect.
>
> The decision in Broadway National Bank v. Adams, 133 Mass. 170, rests upon the doctrine that a testator has a right to dispose of his own property with such restrictions and limitations, not repugnant to law, as he sees fit, and that his intentions ought to be carried out, unless they contravene some positive rule of law, or are against public policy. The rule contended for by the plaintiff in that case was founded upon the same considerations as that contended for by the plaintiff in this, and the grounds on which this court declined to follow the English rule in

that case are applicable to this, and for the reasons there given we are unable to see that the directions of the testator to the trustees to pay the money to the plaintiff when he reaches the age of 25 and 30 years, and not before, are against public policy, or are so far inconsistent with the rights of property given to the plaintiff, that they should not be carried into effect. It cannot be said that these restrictions upon the plaintiff's possession and control of the property are altogether useless, for there is not the same danger that he will spend the property while it is in the hands of the trustees as there would be if it were in his own. . . . The existing situation is one which the testator manifestly had in mind, and made provision for. The strict execution of the trust has not become impossible; the restriction upon the plaintiff's possession and control is, we think, one that the testator had a right to make; other provisions for the plaintiff are contained in the will, apparently sufficient for his support; and we see no good reason why the intention of the testator should not be carried out.

Where, after the creation of a trust, one beneficiary or a third person acquires all of the beneficial interests, whether by assignment or by testate or intestate succession, premature termination is frequently appropriate. Thus, the *Claflin* opinion quoted and distinguished the earlier case of Sears v. Choate, 146 Mass. 395, 15 N.E. 786 (1888), as follows:

In Sears v. Choate it is said:

> Where property is given to certain persons for their benefit, and in such a manner that no other person has or can have any interest in it, they are in effect the absolute owners of it; and it is reasonable and just that they should have the control and disposal of it, unless some good cause appears to the contrary.

In that case the plaintiff was the absolute owner of the whole property, subject to an annuity of $10,000 payable to himself. The whole of the principal of the trust fund, and all the income not expressly made payable [via the annuity] to the plaintiff had become vested in him . . . by way of resulting trust, as property undisposed of by the will. Apparently the testator had not contemplated such a result, and had made no provision for it, and the court saw no reason why the trust should not be terminated and the property conveyed to the plaintiff.

149 Mass. at 22-23, 20 N.E. at 455-456.

A few American courts have followed the English rule under which the beneficiaries, if all consent and are sui juris, can modify or compel termination even though the purposes of the trust have not been accomplished. See the classic case, Saunders v. Vautier, 4 Beav. 115, *aff'd*, 41 Eng. Rep. 482 (Ch. 1841). In most states, however, some version of the so-called *Claflin* doctrine prevails. Do you see the consistency of the

English rules on termination and against enforcement of spendthrift clauses (Chapter 13)? Of *Claflin* and the general American acceptance of spendthrift restraints?

The *Claflin* doctrine, as it is interpreted and applied in many states, is summarized by the American Law Institute, Restatement (Second) of Trusts, as follows:

§337. *Consent of Beneficiaries.*

(1) Except as stated in Subsection (2), if all of the beneficiaries of a trust consent and none of them is under an incapacity, they can compel the termination of the trust.

(2) If the continuance of the trust is necessary to carry out a material purpose of the trust, the beneficiaries cannot compel its termination.

The doctrine is discussed in Speth v. Speth, 8 N.J. Super. 587, 592, 598, 74 A.2d 344, 347, 350 (1950), as follows:

The American cases recognize primarily the privilege of the donor to qualify his gift as he pleases within legal limits. . . . The English courts concentrate their predominant attention upon the situation of the beneficiary who being substantially the owner of the trust estate should be permitted in their judgment to deal with it as he wished. . . .

This retrospective exposition of the subject may well be concluded in the words of Chief Justice Vanderbilt. . . :

The English authorities are of no force here because of our fundamentally divergent view of the power of the settlor and the beneficiaries of a trust over the trust res. In England the beneficiaries of the trust may by united action terminate, notwithstanding the fact that to do so may nullify the intention of the settlor. In this State it is the intention of the settlor of the trust that governs and not the desires of the beneficiaries.

Consent of Settlor. Where the settlor of an inter vivos trust is alive and joins with all of the beneficiaries in seeking termination or modification, even under the *Claflin* doctrine the trust will be terminated or modified as requested without regard to the original purposes of the settlor.

There would seem to be no good reason for holding that the courts owe it to the settlor to carry out his intention once expressed, if neither he nor anyone else any longer desires to have it carried out. . . . It is true that in the United States the beneficiaries alone cannot terminate the trust if its purposes have not been accomplished. It is true that where some of the beneficiaries do not consent, the others, even with the consent of the settlor, cannot terminate the trust. But where the settlor and all of the beneficiaries are of full capacity and consent, there seems to be no good reason why they should not have power to make such disposition of the trust property, as they choose.

IV W. Fratcher, Scott on Trusts §338 (4th ed. 1989). Similarly, §339 of the Restatement (Second) of Trusts provides: "If the settlor is the sole beneficiary of a trust and is not under an incapacity, he can compel the termination of the trust, although the purposes of the trust have not been accomplished."

In particular applications of the *Claflin* doctrine the problems generally center about one or both of two issues:

1. Do the parties to the agreement or petition hold all of the potential beneficial interests?
2. Is there a "material purpose" of the trust that would be defeated by its premature termination or by the proposed modification?

Consent of All Beneficiaries. When modification or premature termination of a trust is sought by the beneficiaries, the court must initially determine who are the beneficiaries of the trust and whether each has capacity to give consent, for under the traditional general rule guardians ad litem or others cannot give this consent. (Contrast, however, Hatch v. Riggs National Bank, infra, as to representation by a guardian ad litem.) Determining all of the beneficiaries is not always an easy matter. Even when the meaning of the dispositive provisions of a trust instrument is clear, however, it will not be possible to obtain the consent of all beneficiaries in the typical modern trust. The presence of unborn, unascertained, or incompetent beneficiaries, even those holding contingent interests, will preclude obtaining the consent of all beneficiaries as required.

In re LEWIS' ESTATE
231 Pa. 60, 79 A. 921 (1911)

[Petition to compel termination of a testamentary trust. The trust provided for investment of the property and payment of the income to the settlor's widow for life and, in effect, for corpus thereafter to be distributed to the settlor's then-living descendants, per stirpes. Petitioners are the widow and the only living child of the settlor, his other two children having died without issue prior to the time of the petition. The trial court denied the petition.]

PER CURIAM.

The widow of the testator, for whose benefit he created the trust which she and their sole surviving child wish to have terminated, is still alive. Who will be the ultimate distributees of the fund under the will of her husband cannot be determined until her death, and the court below could not have made a decree determining the trust without the consent of all parties in interest. Such parties were not before it, for some who may ultimately participate in the fund may not yet be in existence.

Decree affirmed at appellants' costs.

[handwritten margin note: not all ben. Known — none yet in existance .: not term.]

For purposes of giving consent to termination or modification of a trust, should the donee of a power of appointment be treated as holding the interests that are subject to the power? Certainly the donee who holds only a special power of appointment is not so treated, but the donee who holds a *presently exercisable* general power *is* so treated. Do you see why? But what of the holder of a general power exercisable only by will? Assume that *A* is the life beneficiary of a trust and also holds a general testamentary power to appoint the trust property at death, remainder in default of appointment to *B*. If no substantial purpose of the settlor will be impaired by doing so, can the trust be terminated by *A* as a sole beneficiary? Cf. Restatement (Second) of Property §§16.1, 16.2 and Uniform Probate Code §1-108. Uniform Trust Code §302 (Draft, Feb. 2000) makes a substantial break with traditional doctrine by allowing the holder of a general testamentary power of appointment to represent and bind those whose interests are subject to the power, absent a conflict of interest. How does (should) this section apply here?

LEVY v. CROCKER-CITIZENS NATIONAL BANK
14 Cal. App. 3d 102, 94 Cal. Rptr. 1 (1971)

[The attorney for plaintiff's mother prepared the trust instruments here in question, and plaintiff executed them in 1956 shortly after his twenty-first birthday.] *[handwritten: atty for / settlor]*

GUSTAFSON, J. . . .

Plaintiff is the trustor and the beneficiary of the net income for his life. Upon his death, the corpus is to be distributed pursuant to his exercise of a testamentary general power of appointment, or, in default of such appointment, to his then surviving lawful issue per stirpes or, if he has no surviving issue, to the then surviving lawful issue of his mother.

Plaintiff's testimony concerning his intent and the circumstances existing at the time of his execution of the trust instruments was objected to by the trustee (the only defendant) on the ground that the trust instruments were clear and unambiguous thus precluding extrinsic evidence of the meaning of the words used. . . . [N]o matter how clear and unambiguous language may appear to the reader, extrinsic evidence is admissible for the purpose of ascertaining what was meant by the person using the words in question. The extrinsic evidence, however, may not show that what was meant by the words used was something to which, under all of the circumstances, the words are not reasonably susceptible. . . . Plaintiff's testimony would have been relevant in an action to rescind the trust instruments on the ground of mistake or undue influence. . . . But here the action was not to rescind the trust instruments on the ground of mistake or undue influence, but rather an action by the trustor, assuming the validity of the trust instruments, to terminate the trusts. Plaintiff's testimony that he did not know what was in the documents he signed is not evidence that he intended by the words used therein not to make a gift to anyone.

It is conceded that if a trustor is the sole beneficiary of a trust, he may revoke it even though by its terms the trust is irrevocable. (Rest. 2d Trusts §339.) If there are other beneficiaries, however, consent of all beneficiaries is generally necessary to revoke the trust. (Rest. 2d Trusts §340.) Putting aside for the moment the existence of a testamentary power of appointment in the trustor, [plaintiff argues that the surviving] issue of the trustor, whose existence and identity will not be known until the trustor dies, are [not] beneficiaries. . . . The only answer to plaintiff's argument is that the authorities binding on us compel a contrary result. . . .

We now consider the effect of the trustor's general power to appoint by will. If a trustor receives a general power to appoint by deed or will, by appointing to himself by deed he becomes the sole beneficiary and obviously can terminate the trust. Plaintiff argues, again quite persuasively, that he has a will, that in all likelihood he will not die intestate and that there is therefore little likelihood that anyone will take in default of exercise of the power of appointment. The existence of the power, plaintiff argues, manifests an intent not to make a gift to those who would take in default of the exercise of the power of appointment.

But again the authorities compel us to reject plaintiff's argument. . . . While it is true that in neither [of the leading California cases] did the court explain why the existence of the power did not alter the result which would have been reached had there been no power of appointment, we are nevertheless bound by the decisions in those cases. (See also Rest. 2d Trusts §127, Com. b.)

The judgment is affirmed.

HATCH v. RIGGS NATIONAL BANK
361 F.2d 559 (D.C. Cir. 1966)

[Appellant seeks modification of a trust she created in 1923, reserving the income (with a spendthrift restraint) for life and a general power to appoint corpus by will; the unappointed remainder on her death is to go to her next of kin. The instrument expressly declared the trust irrevocable.]

LEVENTHAL, C.J. . . .

Appellant does not claim that the declaration of trust itself authorizes her to revoke or modify the trust. In effect she invokes the doctrine of worthier title, which teaches that a grant of trust corpus to the heirs of the settlor creates a reversion in the settlor rather than a remainder in his heirs. She claims that since she is the sole beneficiary of the trust under this doctrine, and is also the settlor, she may revoke or modify under accepted principles of trust law.

The District Court, while sympathizing with appellant's desire to obtain an additional stipend of $5000 a year, out of corpus, "to accommodate recently incurred expenses, and to live more nearly in accordance with her refined but yet modest tastes," felt that denial of the requested relief was required by this court's decision in Liberty National Bank v. Hicks, 173 F.2d 631 (1948). Summary judgment was granted for appellees. We affirm. . . .

The abbreviated discussion in *Hicks* may be taken as an implied rejection of [the] doctrine of worthier title. . . . This appeal squarely raises the question, and we deem it appropriate that we rely not on the aura of *Hicks*, but on an express consideration of the applicability of the doctrine of worthier title.

The doctrine of worthier title had its origins in the feudal system which to a large extent molded the English common law which we inherited. In its common law form, the doctrine provided that a conveyance of land by a grantor with a limitation over to his own heirs resulted in a reversion in the grantor rather than creating a remainder interest in the heirs. It was a rule of law distinct from, though motivated largely by the same policies as, the Rule in Shelley's Case. Apparently the feudal overlord was entitled to certain valuable incidents when property held by one of his feoffees passed by "descent" to an heir rather than by "purchase" to a transferee. The doctrine of worthier title — whereby descent is deemed "worthier" than purchase — remained ensconced in English law, notwithstanding the passing of the feudal system, until abrogated by statute in 1833.

The doctrine has survived in many American jurisdictions, with respect to inter vivos conveyance of both land and personalty, as a common law "rule of construction" rather than a "rule of law." In Doctor v. Hughes, 225 N.Y. 305, 122 N.E. 221 (1919), Judge Cardozo's landmark opinion reviewed the common-law history of the doctrine and concluded that its modern relevance was a rule of construction, a rebuttable presumption that the grantor's likely intent, in referring to his own heirs, was to reserve a reversion in his estate rather than create a remainder interest in the heirs. Evidence might be introduced to show that the grantor really meant what he said when he spoke of creating a remainder in his heirs. . . .

The views of the critics of the doctrine, which we find persuasive against its adoption, and borne out by the experience of the New York courts in the series of cases which have followed Doctor v. Hughes, supra, may be summarized as follows. The common-law reasons for the doctrine are as obsolete as those behind the Rule in Shelley's Case. Retention of the doctrine as a rule of construction is pernicious in several respects.

First, it is questionable whether it accords with the intent of the average settlor. It is perhaps tempting to say that the settlor intended to create no beneficial interest in his heirs when he said "to myself for life, remainder to my heirs" when the question is revocation of the trust, or whether creditors of the settlor's heirs should be able to reach their interest. But the same result is far from appealing if the settlor-life beneficiary dies without revoking the trust and leaves a will which makes no provision for his heirs-at-law (whom he supposed to be taken care of by the trust). In short, while the dominant intent of most such trusts may well be to benefit the life tenant during his life, a subsidiary but nevertheless significant purpose of many such trusts may be to satisfy a natural desire to benefit one's heirs or next of kin. In the normal case an adult has a pretty good idea who his heirs will be at death, and probably means exactly what he says when he states in the trust instrument, "remainder to my heirs."

It is said that the cases in which such is the grantor's intent can be discerned by an examination into his intent; the presumption that a gift over to one's heirs creates a reversion can thereby be rebutted in appropriate cases. . . . After three decades of observing the New York courts administer the rule of construction announced in Doctor v. Hughes, supra, Professor Powell [Cases on Future Interests 88 n.14 (3d ed. 1961)] observed that

> there were literally scores of cases, many of which reached the Appellate Division, and no case involving a substantial sum could be fairly regarded as closed until its language and circumstances had been passed upon by the Court of Appeals. . . . This state of uncertainty was the product of changing an inflexible rule of law into a rule of construction.

An excellent example of this confusion is the effect to be given the fact that, as in the case at bar, the settlor has reserved the power to defeat the heirs' interest by appointing the taker of the remainder by will. One might think that the reservation of a power of appointment was an index intent which buttressed the presumption of a reversion by demonstrating that the settlor did not wish to create firm interests or expectations among his heirs, but intended to retain control over the property. Most courts, including the New York Court of Appeals in its most recent pronouncement on the subject, have disagreed, albeit over the voice of dissent. They have reasoned that the retention of the testamentary power of appointment confirms the intent to create a remainder in the heirs, since the settlor would not have retained the power had he not thought he was creating a remainder interest in the heirs.

We see no reason to plunge the District of Columbia into the ranks of those jurisdictions bogged in the morass of exploring, under the modern doctrine of worthier title, "the almost ephemeral qualities which go to prove the necessary intent." The alleged benefit of effectuating intent must be balanced against the resulting volume of litigation and the diversity and difficulty of decision. We are not persuaded that the policy of upholding the intention of creators of trusts is best effectuated by such a rule of construction with its accompanying uncertainty.

The rule we adopt, which treats the settlor's heirs like any other remaindermen, although possibly defeating the intention of some settlors, is overall, we think, an intent-effectuating rule. It contributes to certainty of written expression and conceptual integrity in the law of trusts. It allows heirs to take as remaindermen when so named, and promises less litigation, greater predictability, and easier drafting. These considerations are no small element of justice.

We hold, then, that the doctrine of worthier title is no part of the law of trusts in the District of Columbia, either as a rule of law or as a rule of construction. Any act or words of the settlor of a trust which would validly create a remainder interest in a named third party may create a valid remainder interest in the settlor's heirs. It follows that the District Court was correct in granting summary judgment for appellees in this case since appellant's action is based on the theory that she was the sole beneficiary and hence could revoke the "irrevocable" trust she had created. . . .

Appellant's invocation of worthier title was premised in part on the injustice alleged to result in many cases from holding such a trust irrevocable. The irrevocability was supposed to be riveted into the trust by the impossibility of obtaining consent to revocation from all the beneficiaries, since some of them are still unborn. Appellant's argument reflects a misunderstanding of the consequence of the judgment of the District Court.

It is hornbook law that any trust, no matter how "irrevocable" by its terms, may be revoked with the consent of the settlor and all beneficiaries.

The beneficiaries of the trust created by appellant are herself, as life tenant, and her heirs, as remaindermen. Her heirs, if determined as of the present time, are her two sisters. There is no assurance that they will in fact be the heirs who take the remainder under the trust; appellant might survive one or both. Yet their consent is necessary, we think, to revocation, since they are at least the persons who would be beneficiaries if the settlor died today.

In addition, it is necessary to protect the interests of those additional persons, both living and unborn, who may, depending on circumstances, be members of the class of heirs at the time the corpus is distributed. We think that upon an adequate showing, by the party petitioning to revoke or modify the trust, that those who are, so to speak, the heirs as of the present time consent to the modification, and that there is a reasonable possibility that the modification that has been proposed adequately protects the interest of those other persons who might be heirs at the time the corpus is to be distributed, that the District Court may appoint a guardian ad litem to represent the interests of those additional persons.

Although the question has not been previously discussed by this court we think basic principles of trust law are in accord with appointment of a guardian ad litem to represent interests of unborn or unascertained beneficiaries for purposes of consent to modification or revocation of a trust. This use of a guardian ad litem is not uncommon in other jurisdictions. In a number of states authority for [the appointment of guardians ad litem] is provided by statute. These statutes reflect a broad sentiment of the approaches that are consistent with the Anglo-American system of law and adopted to promote the objective of justice. Where it is at least debatable whether rulings must await express legislative authorization, this court must take into account the fact that the legislature for the District of Columbia is primarily concerned with awesome questions of national policy, and we should be more ready to accept our obligation as a court to refine and adapt the corpus of law without waiting for a legislative go-ahead. Here we are certainly in a field where it is not inappropriate for courts to act without statutory foundation. . . . "Courts of justice as an incident of their jurisdiction have inherent power to appoint guardians ad litem." [Quoting Mabry v. Scott, 51 Cal. App. 2d 245, 258, 124 P.2d 659, 665 (1942), set out hereafter in Chapter 15, section C.] The efficacy of a guardian ad litem appointed to protect the interest of unborn persons is no different whether he be appointed pursuant to statute or the court's inherent power. Given such protection, the equitable doctrine of representation embraces the flexibility, born of convenience and necessity, to act upon the interests of unborn contingent remaindermen to the same effect as if they had been sui juris and parties.

The use of guardians ad litem to represent interests of unborn and/or otherwise unascertainable beneficiaries of a trust seems to us wholly appropriate. Though the persons whose interests the guardian ad litem represents would be unascertainable as individuals, they are identifiable as a class and their interest, as such, recognizable.

The settlor seeking to revoke or modify the trust may supplement his appeal to equity with a quid pro quo offered to the heirs for their consent. In many cases it may well be consistent with or even in further-ance of the interest of the heirs to grant such consent. The case at bar provides a good example. Here the interest of all heirs is contingent, since appellant can defeat their remainder by exercising her testamen-tary power of appointment. If the modification agreed upon not only increased the annual income of the life tenant but also transferred assets in trust for the benefit of the heirs, without any power of alter-ation in the settlor, the heirs' remainder interest would be secure, and accordingly more valuable than it is now. The pattern of such a modifi-cation is clearly available where the remaindermen of a trust are spe-cific named persons, and, we think, should also be available where the remaindermen are recognizable as a class even though the members of the class are not now individually ascertainable.

Appellant, proceeding on a different theory, has not taken steps to obtain the consent of heirs. We think it important to make clear that, in rejecting the doctrine of worthier title, we do not mean to put set-tlors and life tenants of trusts in which the remaindermen are the set-tlor's heirs at an unwarranted disadvantage with respect to legitimate efforts to modify trust arrangements concluded largely for their own benefit. Our affirmance of the judgment for appellees is without preju-dice to a future submission by appellant on such a basis.

Affirmed.

The settlor-life beneficiary seized the court's invitation to modify this trust with consent of the living remaindermen and of a guardian ad litem acting for other possible remaindermen. The modification agree-ment was approved in Hatch v. Riggs National Bank, 284 F. Supp. 396 (D.D.C. 1968), which does not discuss the contents or merits of the modification agreement but is concerned solely with the issue of the court's inherent authority to appoint a guardian ad litem, this question having been raised again by the trustee out of concern that the opinion of the court of appeals on this point was purely dictum.

Judge Leventhal's opinion, first rejecting the doctrine of worthier title and then dealing with the dilemma arising from a desire to leave open to settlors the possibility of amendment in these appealing types of cases, actually skirts a significant issue, and a particularly important one for our purposes. The opinion asserts that basic principles of trust law support the use of guardians ad litem for the purpose of consenting to proposed modifications of trusts, yet the court's discussion then deals only with the more general issue of a court's power, without legislative authority, to appoint guardians ad litem for any purpose. One need not question the wisdom or propriety of finding such an inherent judicial power (although authorities are divided) in order to note that such a determination does not reach the most novel aspect of the opinion — that of then allowing a guardian ad litem to give *consent* to an *agreement* authorizing modification by action of the beneficiaries. It is a traditional function for guardians ad litem to represent and defend beneficiaries in *litigation* (such as where the rights of unborn beneficiaries are being litigated or, in the more immediate context, where the court is exercising its own power, independent of consent, to modify a trust, as discussed infra), and as an adjunct of this probably also to compromise litigation in order to protect the represented interests. This, however, is different from allowing the guardian ad litem to enter into a transaction — that is, to consent to a contract that involves, in effect, a transfer — which then newly *creates* a basis for altering the beneficiaries' interests. This latter, without any real discussion of the point in the opinion, eliminates the traditional requirement, recognized even where the use of guardians ad litem is well established, that all beneficiaries must be sui juris and must consent to modification or termination of the trust.

These comments are not at all intended to suggest that the thrust of Judge Leventhal's innovative and influential opinion is undesirable. In fact, it may be a very good judicially designed solution to the dilemma presented by the competing objectives of properly construing "heirs" provisions and yet of preserving flexibility of amendment for settlors in this type of case. Certainly the widespread abolition of worthier title by legislation speaks for itself, and the all too rare, clear-cut undertaking by a court to clean up the common law is both admirable and refreshing. A major concern of legislatures in considering abolition of worthier title has been the consent problem and the effect the recognition of an interest in unascertainable heirs would have on the ability of the settlor and other living persons to terminate or modify inter vivos trusts. Here too, though on a far lesser scale, some legislatures have acted. In order to facilitate revocation and amendment of living trusts by the beneficiaries, several statutes have provided, in some form, essentially that for those particular purposes the actions of the settlor and the other persons beneficially interested can bind interests created in a presently undeterminable class described as the settlor's heirs (or equivalent) or, under one statute, described solely by relationship to a consenting person. See N.Y. Est. Powers & Trusts Law §7-1.9 (originating as a response to the messy aftermath of Doctor v. Hughes, discussed supra in the *Hatch* case) and Wis. Stat. Ann. §701.13 (1969). See generally Han, Premature Termination of Non-Spendthrift Trusts: Reconciling a Dead Settlor's Intent With a Living Beneficiary's Needs,

3 Texas Wesleyan L. Rev. 191, 206-207 (1996). See also Uniform Trust Code §§301–305 (some of which are set out infra) and California Probate Code §15405, which provides:

> For the purposes of [modification of trusts], the consent of a beneficiary who lacks legal capacity, including a minor, or who is an unascertained or unborn person may be given in proceedings before the court by a guardian ad litem, if it would be appropriate to do so. In determining whether to give consent, the guardian ad litem may rely on general family benefit accruing to living members of the beneficiary's family as a basis for approving a modification or termination of the trust.

All of the foregoing is to be contrasted with the limited powers of courts under special circumstances to modify trusts without the consent of the beneficiaries, to be discussed in section D of this chapter. Nevertheless, the approach of the *Hatch* case should be kept in mind, particularly as section D.2 is studied, for it may be applicable to that type of situation in the District of Columbia and may be suggestive of an approach different from the traditional approach in other jurisdictions. For another recent case that is apparently unique but is significantly analogous to *Hatch*, see Estate of Lange, 75 N.J. 464, 383 A.2d 1130 (1978), set out infra at section D.1 of Chapter 17; that case involves estoppel, or waiver of trust beneficiaries' rights, by vicarious consent obtained through the doctrine of virtual representation, also a concept normally confined to the necessities of representation in court.

A Note on Representation. Observe that the representation issue can come up in a number of contexts. The General Comment to Article 3 of the Uniform Trust Code lists not only trust modification or termination but also notice of proposed trust combination or division, notice of temporary assumption of duties without accepting trusteeship, appointment of a successor trustee, notice of resignation of a trustee, notice of a trustee's report, and nonliability of a trustee upon consent of a beneficiary. The UTC representation principles may apply in any of these situations. Should there be a unitary approach to all questions of representation? We will revisit the representation issue in a number of contexts later in the book.

Material Purpose. What constitutes a "material purpose" of a trust for purposes of the second requirement that no significant objective of the settlor be defeated by a revocation or modification by the beneficiaries? How readily should such a purpose be inferred? See Rust v. Rust, 176 F.2d 66, 67 (D.C. Cir. 1949):

> To say that the beneficiaries cannot compel termination of a trust if its continuance is necessary to carry out a *material purpose* of the settlor is not to say they cannot do so if continuance is necessary to carry out his *intent* regarding duration of the trust. Such a proposition would go farther than our law in preferring the dead over the living. . . . The

"purpose" with which the rule is concerned is not the settlor's intent
but the aim, object or motive underlying his intent.

When the settlor creates a trust to protect one or more of the beneficiaries from their own improvidence, the beneficiaries cannot compel
termination of the trust where the *Claflin* doctrine prevails. It is often
difficult, however, to ascertain whether such a purpose exists.

It is accepted that even the unanimous consent of the beneficiaries
cannot compel termination of a spendthrift trust. This is sometimes
explained on the ground that termination would be a prohibited alienation or exchange of a beneficiary's trust interest. It is also explained
on the ground that the spendthrift provision demonstrates that protection from the beneficiary's own improvidence was a material purpose
of the settlor. The routine inclusion of spendthrift clauses by many
lawyers removes the possibility of total or partial termination by the
beneficiaries in a great number of trusts. For example, a life income
beneficiary might like (often for tax reasons) to assign part or all of
the income interest to the remainder beneficiaries (often the life beneficiary's children), but this assignment and the desired termination of
some or all of the trust will be frustrated by the spendthrift restraint.

BENNETT v. TOWER GROVE BANK & TRUST CO.
434 S.W.2d 560 (Mo. 1968)

WELBORN, C.

Action to terminate a testamentary trust for the reason that the life
beneficiary transferred her interest in the trust to the remaindermen.
The court below refused to decree termination and the remaindermen
and life tenant appeal.

[Under the will in question the respondent bank, as trustee, was to
pay a share of the trust income to testator's widow and a share to his
daughter, Lois Bennett, and on the death of either both shares to the
survivor; on the death of the survivor, the remainder was to go free of
trust to three named nephews. The trust provided for no invasion of
principal, no discretion over income payments, and no spendthrift restraints. The widow elected her statutory share against the will.]

Respondents do not question two preliminary propositions advanced
by appellants: First, that the renunciation by the widow resulted in an
acceleration of the trust and Lois Bennett became the sole life tenant.
Second, that the remainder interests of the three nephews are vested
interests. Conceding these propositions, the respondents assert that
termination of the trust would thwart the intention of the testator,
whose wishes must prevail without regard for the desires of the beneficiaries. The appellants, on the other hand, contend that, in the circum-

stances of this case, the only purpose of the trust was preservation of the corpus for the benefit of the remaindermen, and, therefore, when they acquired the outstanding life estate, the trust had no further purpose and should be terminated. . . .

Appellants acknowledge that [Peugnet v. Berthold, 183 Mo. 61, 81 S.W. 874 (1904)], is the only [Missouri] case in which the trust in question was terminated. They contend, however, that the three subsequent cases recognize the rule laid down by *Peugnet*, and that the cases represent exceptions to the *Peugnet* rule, not a repudiation of it. Respondents, on the other hand, contend that the *Peugnet* rule has been repudiated and that the three subsequent cases lay down the applicable rule which prevents termination of the trust in this case. . . .

Appellants would distinguish [the first case] Evans [v. Rankin, 329 Mo. 411, 44 S.W.2d 644 (1931)], because the trustee there had absolute discretion as to payment of any part of the income and corpus to the life tenant. Hamilton [v. Robinson, 236 Mo. App. 289, 151 S.W.2d 504 (1941)], is distinguished by reason of the express provision for continuation of the trust until the beneficiary reached the age of 28 years. Thomson [v. Union National Bank, 291 S.W.2d 178 (Mo. 1956), the most recent case], would be distinguished on the grounds that it involved a trust for support of the widow during her life.

The Restatement of Trusts, Second, adopts the rule that, if all of the beneficiaries of a trust consent and none is under an incapacity, they can compel termination of a trust, unless its continuance is necessary to carry out a material purpose of the trust. 2 Rest. of Trusts, Second §337, p. 158. Comment *f* to this section is as follows (Id., pp. 159-160):

> f. Successive beneficiaries — Purposes accomplished. The mere fact that the settlor has created a trust for successive beneficiaries does not of itself indicate that it was a material purpose of the trust to deprive the beneficiaries of the management of the trust property for the period of the trust. If a trust is created for successive beneficiaries, in the absence of circumstances indicating a further purpose, the inference is that the only purpose of the trust is to give the beneficial interest in the trust property to one beneficiary for a designated period and to preserve the principal for the other beneficiary, and if each of the beneficiaries is under no incapacity, and both of them consent to the termination of the trust, they can compel the termination of the trust. . . .

The Restatement recognizes that continuation is essential to carry out the material purpose of a trust when the enjoyment of the interest of the sole beneficiary is postponed (Id., Comment *j*, p. 163), the situation in *Hamilton*, trusts for support of a beneficiary (Id., Comment *m*, p. 165), the situation in *Evans*, and discretionary trusts (Id., Comment *n*, p. 165).

The respondents argue that the primary purpose of the trust here must have been to care for the testator's wife and daughter, not to preserve the corpus for his nephews. However, [absent] other circumstances to show the intention of the testator, we are of the opinion that the mere creation of the trust for successive beneficiaries did not indicate a purpose other than preservation of the corpus for the remaindermen and, therefore, the trust may be terminated by the action here taken. See IV Scott on Trusts, 3rd ed. §337.1, p. 2664.

Although it may not be possible to reconcile the language in all of our cases with the rules laid down by the Restatement, the actual results of such cases are consistent with such rules. As above noted, *Evans* and *Hamilton* clearly fit into situations recognized by the Restatement when continuation is necessary to effectuate an essential purpose of the trust. The *Thomson* case does not so clearly fit within such situations. However, the close restrictions upon investment which the testator there laid down evidenced a strong desire on the part of the testator to preserve the corpus of the estate during his widow's lifetime. Evidence of such intention is not to be found in this case. In our opinion, the rules laid down by the Restatement adequately protect the scheme of the testator in those cases where there is a genuine necessity for continuation of the trust, but the situation of continuing a trust for the benefit of the trustee is avoided.

The decree below is reversed. . . .

The *Hamilton* case mentioned in the above opinion involved a trust designed from the outset for a single beneficiary whose right to principal was postponed beyond age 21, as in the *Claflin* case, which additionally involved staggered principal payments. A later case (also with principal distributions staggered beyond age 21), however, departed from the normal refusal to terminate prematurely trusts established for longer than the minority of a sole beneficiary. Ambrose v. First National Bank, 482 P.2d 828 (Nev. 1971). This result, from which two of the five judges dissented, may best be explained as reflecting an attitude falling somewhere between the usual American rule and England's rule allowing termination by unanimous consent regardless of the settlor's purposes. The concluding paragraph of Justice Thompson's opinion (at 831) states:

> We are not persuaded that the doctrine of the leading American case of Claflin v. Claflin should rule the trust before us. . . . No reason is expressed in the trust instrument for delaying the daughter's enjoyment beyond the settlor's death. No provision is made therein for the daughter's support between the ages of 21 and 28. Should the daughter die during that period of time she would be denied enjoyment of the corpus.

All these factors together with a strong public policy against restraining one's use and disposition of property in which no other person has an interest leads us to conclude that termination should be decreed and the beneficiary spared the expense incident to the continued administration of the trust.

It should be observed that up to this point we have been dealing with the question of whether the beneficiaries can *compel* the trustee to convey the trust property to them. Assume now that we are dealing with a trust in which all of the beneficiaries seek but cannot compel termination due to an unaccomplished purpose of the trust. What if the trustee in such a case *does* convey the trust property either to a sole beneficiary or in accordance with an agreement entered into by all of the beneficiaries? If the funds are thereafter dissipated, can the trustee be held liable by a beneficiary, assuming the latter was under no incapacity when the consent was given? The cases quite consistently hold that the trustee cannot be held liable for so terminating a trust. The beneficiary is precluded by consent from recovering from the trustee for breach of trust.

Should the consenting beneficiary of a spendthrift trust be treated differently? Section 342, comment *f*, of the Restatement (Second) of Trusts has adopted the position that the beneficiary is estopped and cannot hold the trustee liable for terminating the trust. Because the few cases in point are divided, the comment adds: "In a State which rejects the rule here stated . . . if the trustee is compelled . . . to make restitution to the trust, he can recover the amount from the property of the beneficiary other than his interest under the trust."

UNIFORM TRUST CODE
(Draft, Feb. 2000)

§303. *Representation by Fiduciaries and Parents.*
To the extent there is no conflict of interest between the representative and the person represented with respect to a particular question or dispute:

(1) a [conservator] may represent and bind the estate the [conservator] controls;

(2) a [guardian] may represent and bind the ward if a [conservator] of the ward's estate has not been appointed;

(3) an agent having authority to do so may represent and bind the principal;

(4) a trustee may represent and bind the beneficiaries of the trust;

(5) a personal representative of a decedent's estate may represent and bind persons interested in the estate; and

(6) if a [conservator] or [guardian] has not been appointed, a parent may represent and bind the parent's minor or unborn child.

§304. *Representation by Person Having Substantially Identical Interest.* Unless otherwise represented, a minor, incapacitated, or unborn person, or a person whose identity or location is unknown and not reasonably ascertainable, may be represented by and bound by another having a substantially identical interest with respect to the particular question or dispute, but only to the extent there is no conflict of interest between the representative and the person represented.

[UTC §305 provides for court appointment of a representative (e.g., guardian ad litem) if other representation is lacking or "inadequate," and the representative, in making decisions, "may consider general family benefit accruing to the living members of the . . . family" of the person being represented.]

§410. *Modification or Termination of Irrevocable Trust by Consent.*

(a) An irrevocable trust may be terminated or modified upon the consent of all of the beneficiaries unless the termination or modification is inconsistent with a material purpose of the trust. The inclusion of a spendthrift provision in the terms of the trust is presumed not to constitute a material purpose of the trust.

(b) Whether or not continuance of the trust is necessary to achieve a material purpose of the trust, an irrevocable trust may be modified or terminated upon consent of the settlor and all beneficiaries. A settlor's power to consent to a trust's termination may be exercised by an agent under a power of attorney only to the extent the power of attorney or the terms of the trust expressly authorize the agent to do so, or by a [conservator] with the approval of the court supervising the [conservatorship] if the agent is not so authorized. . . .

(c) Upon termination of a trust pursuant to subsection (a) or (b), the trustee shall distribute the trust property as agreed by the beneficiaries.

(d) If a beneficiary does not consent to a proposed modification or termination of a trust by the other beneficiaries or . . . by the settlor and other beneficiaries, the court may approve the proposed modification or termination only if the court is satisfied that:

(1) if all beneficiaries had consented, the trust could have been terminated or modified under this section; and

(2) the interests of a beneficiary who does not consent will be adequately protected.

Comment . . .

Subsection (a) of this section is based on Section 337 of the Restatement (Second) of Trusts (1959), except that this subsection, unlike the Restatement, deals expressly with the effect of a spendthrift provision. While the inquiry on whether continuation of a trust is necessary to achieve a material purpose should focus on the material purpose or purposes of the particular settlor, the courts have tended to preclude termination based on whether the trust contains particular language without examining its context. . . . The insertion of a spendthrift provision, which is often added to instruments with little thought, has been a particular problem. Subsection (a) does not negate the possibility that continuation of a trust to assure spendthrift protection might have been a material purpose of the particular settlor. It instead negates the assumption that inserting such a clause is always a bar to termination or modification. Whether a spendthrift provision bars termination or modification of a particular trust is a question of fact to be determined based on the totality of the circumstances.

The authority to consent on behalf of another person . . . does not include the authority to consent over the other person's objection. See Section 302. . . . A consent obtained by virtual representation is valid only if there is no conflict of interest between the representative and the person represented. Given this limitation, virtual representation will rarely be available in a trust termination case, although its use will be frequent in cases involving trust modification, such as a grant to the trustee of additional powers. If virtual representation is unavailable, Section 306 of the Act permits the court to appoint a representative who may give the necessary consent.

Subsection (d), which is based on Restatement (Second) of Trusts §338(2) (1959), [allows] the court to fashion an appropriate order protecting the interests of the nonconsenting beneficiaries while at the same time permitting the remainder of the trust property to be distributed without restriction. The order of protection for the nonconsenting beneficiaries might include partial continuation of the trust, the purchase of an annuity, or the valuation and cashout of the interest.

Note that under the Uniform Trust Code definitions, a "conservator" is a person appointed by the court to administer the estate of a minor or incapacitated adult (§102(3)), while a "guardian" is a person appointed to make decisions regarding the person's support, care, education, health, and welfare (§102(5)). The UTC usage is followed in this casebook.

D. *Judicial Power to Modify or Terminate*

1. Equitable Deviation from Administrative Provisions of the Instrument

RESTATEMENT (SECOND) OF TRUSTS

§167. *Change of Circumstances.*

(1) The court will direct or permit the trustee to deviate from a term of the trust if owing to circumstances <u>not known to the settlor</u> and not anticipated by him <u>compliance would defeat or substantially impair the accomplishment of the purposes of the trust;</u> and in such case, if necessary to carry out the purposes of the trust, the court may direct or permit the trustee to do acts which are not authorized or are forbidden by the terms of the trust.

(2) Under the circumstances stated in Subsection (1), the trustee can properly deviate from the terms of the trust without first obtaining the permission of the court if there is an emergency, or if the trustee reasonably believes that there is an emergency, and before deviating he has no opportunity to apply to the court for permission to deviate.

(3) Under the circumstances stated in Subsection (1), the trustee is subject to liability for failure to apply to the court for permission to deviate from the terms of the trust, if he knew or should have known of the existence of those circumstances.

MATTER OF PULITZER
139 Misc. 575, 249 N.Y.S. 87 (Surr. Ct. 1931), *aff'd mem.,*
237 A.D. 808, 260 N.Y.S. 975 (1932)

FOLEY, S.

This is a proceeding for . . . instruction and determination of the court as to the propriety, price, manner, and time of sale of a substantial portion of the assets of the Press Publishing Company, the stock of which constitutes a material part of the assets of the trust here involved. . . . A serious and imperative emergency is claimed to exist, whereby, if such a sale is not made, a valuable asset of the trust estate may be in great part or wholly lost to the trust, the life tenants, and remaindermen. . . .

Joseph Pulitzer died in the year 1911. He left a will and four codicils which were admitted to probate by this court on November 29, 1911. The provisions directly pertinent to the issues here are contained in the first codicil, which is dated March 23, 1909. By its terms he gave the shares of the capital stock of the Press Publishing Company, which were owned by him, and his shares of the Pulitzer Publishing Company, of St. Louis, in trust for the life of each of the two youngest of his sons, Joseph Pulitzer, Jr., and Herbert Pulitzer. . . .

To distinguish it from the residuary trust, the particular trust here has been called the "Newspaper Trust." Its trustees are the testator's three sons, Ralph Pulitzer, Herbert Pulitzer, and Joseph Pulitzer, Jr. The Pulitzer Publishing Company publishes the St. Louis Post Dispatch. The Press Publishing Company publishes the New York World, the Sunday World, and the Evening World. The trustees of the so-called "Newspaper Trust" hold within the trust a very large majority of shares of the Press Publishing Company. The remaining shares are owned by the trustees individually. The paragraph particularly sought to be construed here, which deals with the powers of the trustees and the limitations thereon, is contained in article seventh of the codicil of March 23, 1909, and reads as follows:

> I further authorize and empower my Executors and Trustees to whom I have hereinbefore bequeathed my stock in the Pulitzer Publishing Company of St. Louis, at any time, and from time to time, to sell and dispose of said stock, or any part thereof, at public or private sale, at such prices and on such terms as they may think best, and to hold the proceeds of any stock sold in trust for the beneficiaries for whom such shares were held in lieu thereof, and upon the same trusts. This power of sale is not to be construed as in any respect mandatory, but purely discretionary. This power of sale, however, is limited to the said stock of the Pulitzer Publishing Company of St. Louis, and shall not be taken to authorize or empower the sale or disposition under any circumstances whatever, by the Trustees of any stock of the Press Publishing Company, publisher of "The World" newspaper. I particularly enjoin upon my sons and my descendents the duty of preserving, perfecting and perpetuating "The World" newspaper (to the maintenance and upbuilding of which I have sacrificed my health and strength) in the same spirit which I have striven to create and conduct it as a public institution, from motives higher than mere gain, it having been my desire that it should be at all times conducted in a spirit of independence and with a view to inculcating high standards and public spirit among the people and their official representatives, and it is my earnest wish that said newspaper shall hereafter be conducted upon the same principles.

There are fifteen remaindermen in existence. One of them is an adult; the other fourteen are infants. Because of a possible adversity of interest they are represented here by two separate special guardians. The adult life tenants and remaindermen join in requesting the relief sought by the trustees.

Counsel for the trustees contend that the express denial of a power of sale contained in the paragraph was modified and cut down, as a matter of testamentary intent, by Mr. Pulitzer in subsequent language. . . .

But I prefer to place my determination here upon broader grounds and upon the power of a court of equity, in emergencies, to protect the beneficiaries of a trust from serious loss, or a total destruction of a substantial asset of the corpus. The law, in the case of necessity, reads into the will an implied power of sale. . . .

The same rule applies to emergencies in trusts not only where there is an absence of power of sale in a will, but also where there is a prohibition against sale. It has been satisfactorily established by the evidence before me that the continuance of the publication of the newspapers, which are the principal assets of the Press Publishing Company, will in all probability lead to a serious impairment or the destruction of a larger part of the trust estate. The dominant purpose of Mr. Pulitzer must have been the maintenance of a fair income for his children and the ultimate reception of the unimpaired corpus by the remaindermen. Permanence of the trust and ultimate enjoyment by his grandchildren were intended. A man of his sagacity and business ability could not have intended that from mere vanity, the publication of the newspapers, with which his name and efforts had been associated, should be persisted in until the entire trust asset was destroyed or wrecked by bankruptcy or dissolution. His expectation was that his New York newspapers would flourish. Despite his optimism, he must have contemplated that they might become entirely unprofitable and their disposal would be required to avert a complete loss of the trust asset. The power of a court of equity, with its jurisdiction over trusts, to save the beneficiaries in such a situation has been repeatedly sustained in New York and other jurisdictions. . . .

The trustees here find themselves in a crisis where there is no self-help available to them. A judicial declaration is necessary, not only as to their general authority, but as to the effect of the words of Mr. Pulitzer contained in his will. The widest equity powers exist in the Surrogate's Court of this state by the grant of legislative authority contained in section 40 of the Surrogate's Court Act. Matter of Raymond v. Davis' Estate, 248 N.Y. 67, 71, 161 N.E. 421.

I accordingly hold, in this phase of the decision, that the terms of the will and codicils do not prohibit the trustees from disposing of any assets of the Press Publishing Company, that the trustees have general power and authority to act in the conveyance of the assets proposed to be sold, and that this court, in the exercise of its equitable jurisdiction, should authorize them by an appropriate direction in the decree to exercise such general authority. . . .

PAPIERNIK v. PAPIERNIK
45 Ohio St. 3d 337, 544 N.E.2d 664 (1989)

[The settlor established an inter vivos trust with a bank serving as trustee and with the settlor's wife, Elizabeth (now the life beneficiary), and R.B. Cohen (settlor's accountant) serving in the position of "trust advisors.'' Without the advisors' approval, the trustee could not sell, lease, exchange, or reinvest assets of the trust; and the advisors had joint authority to remove any trustee and appoint a successor, with each having the power and duty to appoint a successor if the other ceased to act. The trust advisors had no other responsibilities and could not require the trustee to sell or make specific investments. Certain remainder beneficiaries brought the present action seeking modification of the trust and injunctive relief against the trust advisors because of alleged abuses by the advisors. The Court of Common Pleas entered judgment removing the trust advisors and modifying the trust agreement by deleting the trust advisor positions.]

EVANS, J. . . .

Deviation from the administrative provisions of a trust will be permitted by a court of equity, if owing to circumstances not known to the grantor and not anticipated by him, compliance would defeat or substantially impair the accomplishment of the purposes of the trust. . . . Furthermore, the doctrine of deviation is to be applied with caution and only to the extent necessary to accomplish the purpose of the grantor. In this case, deviation by eliminating the position of trust advisor could serve to defeat the intent of the grantor . . . [and] goes well beyond that which is necessary to correct the circumstances which threaten the purpose of the trust. We therefore hold that it was error to delete the trust advisor provisions from the trust.

Finally, we consider the issue of the removal of both Elizabeth and Cohen from the position of trust advisor.

The record in this case clearly establishes that Elizabeth completely misunderstood the office of trust advisor and acted irrationally, irresponsibly and unsuitably in relation to the trust. . . . Instead of confining herself to the given duties, Elizabeth inserted herself into the management of the trust . . . to the extent that the continued existence of the trust [was] threatened. . . .

Elizabeth had a duty to limit her activities . . . to those duties assigned to a trust advisor.

The [remainder beneficiaries] argue that the role of trust advisor is akin to that of a fiduciary, but we believe it is unnecessary to make this determination to decide this case. The conduct of Elizabeth was unsuitable whether or not she was a fiduciary by virtue of her position of trust advisor. . . .

It is apparent that the trial court properly exercised its equity jurisdiction in removing Elizabeth as a trust advisor.

However, there is nothing in the record which justifies the removal of Cohen from office. . . .

We remand this cause to the trial court with instructions to restore the trust provisions which create the position of trust advisor and to restore Cohen to his position of trust advisor with an appropriate period of time to permit Cohen to fill the vacancy created by the removal of Elizabeth as trust advisor.

Judgment affirmed in part, reversed in part and cause remanded.

PROBLEM

14-C.   Assume that the opinion that immediately follows is an opinion just handed down by an intermediate appellate court in your state. The lawyer for whom you work has now been retained to handle the petitioners' appeal of that decision to the state's highest court. Following the *Stanton* opinion are a Minnesota case and a note about a Delaware case; these two recent decisions are among the most favorable authorities available to you. In order to begin preparations, study the subject opinion and the case and note case following it. Then consider and prepare to discuss the following questions:

Do you see why the desired modification could not be effectuated by *consent of all beneficiaries* under principles studied in the previous section? How might you nevertheless argue for modification based on consent?

According to the *Stanton* opinion, precisely what appears to be lacking in your case to permit *deviation under judicial power* according to the usual rule as stated in §167 of the Restatement, supra? How might the matters of inflation and trust purposes be handled in your brief and arguments so that the court can fit your case within the Restatement rule, assuming you can persuade the judges to want to decide your way but find them unwilling to depart from that widely accepted formulation of the applicable law?

Are there good reasons for adopting a less restrictive rule for deviation from trust investment provisions than the rule of the Restatement? If the court is so inclined, it will wish to spell out a principled course for lower courts to follow in future cases. In what terms might we suggest that such a rule be framed?

STANTON v. WELLS FARGO BANK & UNION TRUST CO.
150 Cal. App. 2d 763, 310 P.2d 1010 (1957)

[Petition by the life beneficiaries of a trust, created by will in 1931, to authorize the trustee to make investments pursuant to the statutory "prudent man rule" of the California Civil Code and to deviate from the terms of the trust, which specifically limit the trustee to investments

in bonds of the United States government, in bonds of the States of the United States, and municipalities thereof, and in such other bonds . . . as shall be rated "AA" by Moody's Investor's service, and then provide an alternative if Moody's service ceases to exist. Under the trust the income was payable to certain beneficiaries for life, and these beneficiaries held general testamentary powers to appoint the remainders following their respective life interests, and in default of appointment the remainder in each share was to pass to the descendants of the life beneficiary. From the decree of the superior court authorizing deviation, one of the trustees has appealed.]

PETERS, P.J. . . .

The main contention of respondent . . . is that if the trustees are compelled to adhere to the terms of the trust the settlor's intent and his main trust purpose would be frustrated. It is argued that all of the interested beneficiaries, including the living remaindermen, have consented to the deviation, and all will benefit by the proposed modification. Respondent refers specifically to the evidence showing a marked decline in the purchasing power of the dollar, and to the return on bonds as compared to the return on stocks. It is urged that since the settlor drafted this trust the following unanticipated events have occurred: The depression of the thirties; World War II and the cold war; the current defense program; the increase in income taxes; and the government controls on capital. In order to keep the record straight, it is obvious that respondent erroneously refers to the depression as an unanticipated event. The trust was drafted in the middle of the depression and undoubtedly the depression was one of the reasons that motivated the trustor to insert the provision in question.

The power to permit deviation from the terms of private trusts is analogous to the cy-pres doctrine applicable to charitable trusts. . . . A few generalizations can be made. Normally, of course, the trust instrument constitutes the measure of the trustee's powers. . . . Except in unusual or emergency situations the courts will limit the trustees to the powers conferred. But the courts will not permit the main purpose of a trust to fail by compelling slavish adherence to the administrative limitations of the trust instrument. Where the main purpose of the trust is threatened the courts will and should grant permission to deviate from restrictive administrative provisions. But the court should not permit a deviation simply because the beneficiaries request it where the main purpose of the trust is not threatened and no emergency exists or is threatened. It must be remembered that it is the theory of this rule that, by the exercise of this power, the court is not defeating the trust, but in fact is furthering it. The equity court is simply doing what the testator, presumably, would have done had he anticipated the changed conditions. In other words, the specific intent of the testator is disregarded in order to enforce his general intent.

In the instant case all persons interested in the trust except one trustee, and unlikely unborn contingent remaindermen request that the modification be made. This is a factor to be considered. Also, the requested modification concerns only the method of administration of the trust and does not affect any rights of the beneficiaries between themselves. This, too, is important. It should also be mentioned that the objecting trustee concedes that the existing restriction is ill advised. No doubt economic changes have occurred since 1931.

On the other hand, the considered conclusions of the settlor regarding what should constitute appropriate investments cannot be lightly disregarded. He had managed to preserve a large fortune during a terrible depression. He had seen stock investments wiped out overnight. He knew that in the past there had been recurring periods of inflation and deflation. He, the man who had accumulated this fortune, whose property it was, wanted to protect his niece and her children from such vicissitudes, and to provide them with an adequate income. He decided that this could best be done by limiting the trustee's reinvestment powers to the purchase of certain types of bonds. While the equity court has power in an emergency to disregard these directions, the express and considered wishes and desires of the settlor should not be cavalierly disregarded. In the instant case the judgment of the settlor, to date, has not proved devastatingly erroneous. . . . The distributable annual income was $88,890.66 in 1938, and by 1954 this had increased to $109,942.84. There is no evidence that any beneficiary is in want or that the distributable income is not sufficient to supply the reasonable needs of all beneficiaries. No emergency exists. The existing inflationary cycle has continued for some years. The government has adopted many economic measures to try to control and stop this inflationary trend. Some economists predict an era of deflation and others warn us of a depression. These matters are mentioned to indicate that, while the settlor might not have been omniscient, neither are the beneficiaries nor the courts, omniscient. No one can forecast, with any certainty, future events. Certainly, it is true that misguided restrictions imposed by a settlor should not be permitted to defeat his fundamental trust purpose, but it is equally true that the court should not try to guess what economic conditions may be in a few years by permitting deviations when no real emergency exists or is threatened. . . .

It is not the function of courts to remake the provisions of trust instruments. Generally, it is the duty of courts to enforce the provisions of the trust instrument. A court should not presume to remake a trust instrument even though the court believes that it could do a better job. The court's power to permit a deviation exists so that the settlor's main trust purpose will not fail, and to take care of grave emergencies. That is not this case. The trial court should not have permitted the deviation. . . .

The judgment appealed from is reversed.

BRAY and WOOD, J.J., concur.

How would the *Stanton* case be resolved under Uniform Trust Code §411 infra (end of section D.2)? What changes does §411 make from traditional doctrine? Would §411 be a good model for a *court* to use in reframing the common law doctrine of equitable deviation? What is the underlying rationale of the new Uniform Trust Code rules for modification and termination?

In re TRUSTEESHIP UNDER AGREEMENT WITH MAYO
259 Minn. 91, 105 N.W.2d 900 (1960)

[In 1917 and 1919 Dr. Charles H. Mayo created two trusts that remained revocable until his death in 1939. The trustees were authorized under both instruments to invest "in real estate mortgages, municipal bonds or any other form of income bearing property (but not real estate nor corporate stock)." This is an appeal by a number of the beneficiaries from the district court's denial of a petition to authorize deviation from the investment restrictions to permit investment in corporate stock. One trust containing assets worth approximately $1 million will last for at least another twenty-one years, while the other, with assets of about $186,000, will probably terminate somewhat sooner.]

DELL, C.J. . . .

In support of the petition, evidence was submitted that an inflationary period, which could not have been foreseen, had commenced shortly after the donor's death in 1939; that it had reduced the real value of the trust assets by more than 50 percent; that a further inflationary period of a permanent "creeping inflation," which the donor could not have foreseen, must be expected; . . . [and] that the provisions of the trust prohibiting investments in real estate and corporate stocks had caused such shrinkage. . . . Appellants state that even in the short period between March 1959 and November 1959 the Consumer Price Index of the Bureau of Labor Statistics has increased from 123.7 to 125.6, representing an increase of almost 2 percent in 8 months.

Petitioner urges that the donor's ultimate and dominant intention was to preserve the value of the trust corpus and that this will be circumvented unless the court authorizes the trustees to deviate from the investment provisions of the trusts and invest part of the funds in corporate stocks; that it is common practice of trustees of large trusts which have no restrictive investment provisions (including the First National Bank of Minneapolis, one of the trustees in both trusts here) to invest substantial proportions of trust assets in corporate stocks to protect such trusts against inflation, and . . . that if no deviation is permitted and the next 20 years parallel the last 20 years the ultimate beneficiaries of these trusts will be presented with assets having less than one-fourth of the value which they had at the time of the donor's death.

In opposition to the petition, the trustees refer to the donor's clear intention, as expressed in the trust instruments, that no part of the trust funds should be invested in real estate or corporate stocks, and urge that, since no emergency or change of circumstances which could not have been foreseen or experienced by the donor during his lifetime has been shown, no deviation from the donor's clearly expressed intention would be justified. They urge that the rule is well established that where prospective changes of conditions are substantially known to or anticipated by the settlor of a trust the courts will not grant a deviation from its provisions. They point out that the donor here had survived some 20 years after the creation of the trusts during a period in which there had been both a great inflation and a severe depression; that after creating such trusts he had observed the inflation of the post-World-War-I period, the stock market fever of the pre-1929 era, the market crash of 1929, and the subsequent depression and lowering of bond interest rates during the late 1930's; that despite these economic changes he had never altered the investment restrictions in these trusts; and that he was always aware of his right to amend the trust instruments. . . . Petitioner offered expert testimony favoring deviation and respondents' expert testimony was to the contrary. The lower court found in favor of respondents and these appeals followed.

1. The principles governing construction of trust instruments are well settled. One of the court's highest duties is to give effect to the donor's dominant intention as gathered from the instrument as a whole. Neither the court, a beneficiary, nor the legislature is competent to violate such intention. When the language of the instrument is clear, the intention of the donor must be ascertained therefrom. In determining such intention the court is not at liberty to disregard plain terms employed in the trust instrument.

2. With respect to trust provisions restricting investments in which a trustee may invest trust funds, the courts are especially concerned in giving full effect to the donor's intention. . . .

3. . . . The general principles governing deviation to which this court has adhered whenever the question has been presented are set forth in Restatement, Trusts (2 ed.) §167, comment c:

> Where by the terms of the trust the scope of investment which would otherwise be proper is restricted, the court will permit the trustee to deviate from the restriction, if, but only if, the accomplishment of the purposes of the trust would otherwise be defeated or substantially impaired. Thus the court will permit the investment if owing to changes since the creation of the trust, such as the fall in interest rates, the danger of inflation, and other circumstances, the accomplishment of the purposes of the trust would otherwise be defeated or substantially impaired. Where by the terms of the trust the trustee is not permitted to invest in shares of stock, the court will not permit such an investment merely because it would be advantageous to the beneficiaries to make it.

In applying the foregoing rule the courts have adopted certain rules for guidance. It is only in exceptional circumstances described as cases of emergency, urgency, or necessity that deviation from the intention of the donor, as evidenced by the trust instrument, has been authorized. In most of the cases where deviation was authorized, the fact that the donor could not have foreseen the changed circumstances played an important part. Even under such circumstances deviation will not be authorized unless it is reasonably certain that the purposes of the trust would otherwise be defeated or impaired in carrying out the donor's dominant intention.

4. In our opinion the evidence here, together with economic and financial conditions which may properly be judicially noticed, compels us to hold that unless deviation is ordered the dominant intention of the donor to prevent a loss of the principal of the two trusts will be frustrated. When the trusts were created and for many years prior thereto, the dollar, based upon the gold standard, remained at a substantially fixed value. [I]t was not until after the death of the donor that inflation commenced to make itself really known and felt. Since then it has gradually increased. . . .While the experts called by the respective parties disagreed as to when inflation, which they felt was then dormant, would start again and at what percentage it would proceed, there was no disagreement between them that further inflation ''in the foreseeable future'' could be expected. [F]rom the date of trial to November 1959 there was an increase of almost 2 percent in the cost of living index.

At the time these trusts were created it was common practice for businessmen, in protecting their families through the creation of trusts, to authorize investments to be made by their trustees only in high-grade bonds or first mortgages on good real estate. Many of the states then had statutes preventing trustees from investing in corporate stocks or real estate. Since that time many of the states, including Minnesota, have enacted statutes permitting trustees to invest in corporate stocks and real estate. In recent years most trust companies have encouraged donors, when naming the companies as trustees, to permit investment in common stocks as well as bonds and mortgages. And these trustees maintain competent and efficient employees, well acquainted with the various aspects of corporations having listed stocks, so as to enable them to make reasonably safe and proper corporate-stock purchases.

Throughout the trial considerable reference was made to the 1929 stockmarket crash as a reason why deviation should not be granted. There are many reasons, however, why the market action of that period is not a controlling factor today. [Omitted is the court's discussion of earlier practices, conditions, and abuses in business and in the stock market, plus various developments, curative measures, and regulations believed to make stock investments safer than previously.] Since 1932, because of heavy Federal expenditures, the national debt has grown . . . to approximately $290,000,000,000 at the present time. Inflation has been steadily increasing. None of this was foreseeable by an ordinarily prudent investor at the time these trusts were created, nor at the time of the donor's death in 1939, since these inflationary practices did not become noticeably fixed and established until after his death.

It appears without substantial dispute that if deviation is not permitted the accomplishment of the purposes of the trusts will be substantially impaired because of changed conditions due to inflation since the trusts were created; that unless deviation is allowed the assets of the trusts, within the next 20 years, will, in all likelihood, be worth less than one-fourth of the value they had at the time of the donor's death. To avoid this we conclude that in equity the trustees should have the right and be authorized to deviate from the restrictive provisions of the trusts by permitting them, when and as they deem it advisable, to invest a reasonable amount of the trust assets in corporate stocks of good, sound investment issues. Through an investment in bonds and mortgages of the type designed by the donor, plus corporate stocks of good, sound investment issues, in our opinion, the trusts will, so far as possible, be fortified against inflation, recession, depression, or decline in prices. Corporate trustees of the kind here are regularly managing trusts consisting of corporate stocks, bonds, and mortgages, on a successful basis. There appears to be no sound reason why they cannot do the same thing here.

Reversed and remanded for further proceedings in conformity with this opinion.

In Bank of Delaware v. Clark, 249 A.2d 442 (Del. Ch. 1968), the trustee, adult beneficiaries, and guardian ad litem all agreed that deviation from a provision restricting investments to mortgages on local land was "in the interest of the trust estate and the beneficiaries." Although Delaware courts have statutory power to authorize deviation, cases indicate that they are to do so "with extreme caution, and only when clearly required for the benefit of all interested and for the preservation of the corpus of the trust fund." The court found there had been a change of economic conditions and a sharp decline in the purchasing power of corpus since the creation of the trust. It also concluded that the settlor could not have anticipated these changes and that if he had "it is fair to say" he would not have restricted investments as he did. In authorizing deviation, the court said there was no need to consider cases from other states because it was satisfied that Delaware cases had adopted a different rule involving a "so-called substitution of judgment approach."

W. FRATCHER, FIDUCIARY ADMINISTRATION
IN ENGLAND
40 N.Y.U.L. Rev. 12, 35-36 (1965)

If there is reasonable doubt as to the construction or legal effect of the terms of a trust [in the United States and in England], the trustee may apply to the court for instructions, and they will protect him, and the persons dealing with him, against the beneficiaries. In the absence of statute, courts of equity have inherent power to authorize deviation from the terms of a trust if, because of circumstances not known to the settlor when the trust was created and not anticipated by him, failure to do so would defeat or substantially impair the accomplishment of the purposes of the trust. . . . This narrow doctrine . . . is of no assistance in the common case in which the circumstances are known or anticipated, but the draftsman of the trust is unaware of the necessity of inserting express powers to do acts required for prudent administration. Moreover, even if circumstances which the settlor did not anticipate occur, the doctrine is operative only when action is necessary to prevent defeat or substantial impairment of the trust purposes; it is not sufficient that it would make administration of the trust more efficient or economical or would be advantageous to the beneficiaries, as by increasing the trust income.

The English statutes greatly enhance the powers of the court to authorize deviations from the terms of trusts. The court may authorize any transaction affecting or concerning settled land, or any part thereof, which in the opinion of the court would be for the benefit of the settled land, or any part thereof, or [for the benefit of] the persons interested under the settlement, if it is one which could validly have been effected by an absolute owner. [Settled Land Act of 1925, 15 & 16 Geo. 5, c. 18 §64, as amended.] The court may empower a trustee of any other type of trust to make any investment or engage in any transaction not otherwise authorized by the terms of the trust or by law, which is in the opinion of the court expedient. [Trustee Act of 1925, 15 & 16 Geo. 5, c. 19 §57, as amended.] . . .

COLONIAL TRUST CO. v. BROWN
105 Conn. 261, 135 A. 555 (1926)

[Suit to construe a will establishing a trust that originally consisted of two parcels of land, referred to as the Exchange Place and the Homestead. The will restricted the height of buildings on the properties to three stories and limited all leases to periods of one year. The trustee was to pay certain long-term annuities and then to distribute the remainder "among the heirs of the blood" of the testator's father, per stirpes.]

MALTBIE, J. . . .

The Exchange Place property . . . is located in the heart of the financial and retail business district of Waterbury. . . . There is, and for a long time has been, upon it a group of several old buildings. They are costly to maintain, expenditures for this purpose during the last seven years absorbing more than fifty per cent of the gross rentals. . . . Tenants of the most desirable class cannot be secured for the property, and could not be, even if the properties were improved, unless leases for more than one year could be given. This reacts upon rental values and the character of the business done in the neighborhood and retards the normal development of the property in use and value. . . .

The Homestead property . . . cannot be improved, so long as the height of buildings upon it is restricted to three stories, or, if improved, cannot be rented so long as leases upon it are restricted to one year, so as to secure the best income return from it, and the effect of these restrictions is likely to be more serious in the future. . . .

The effect which would be caused by the restrictions as to height of buildings and length of leases to be given, inserted in the will, was apparent when the testator executed it and thereafter until his death was known to him. . . . [A]lthough the annuities provided in the will have been paid, there has been an accumulation of excess income. . . .

We are asked to advise whether the provision in the fourth article, restricting leases of the property to one year and forbidding any promises of longer leases, and that in the eleventh article, directing that no new buildings placed upon the Exchange Place property and the Homestead shall exceed three stories in height, are binding upon the trustee. In Holmes v. Connecticut Trust & Safe Deposit Co., 92 Conn. 507, 514, 103 Atl. 640, . . . we said:

> As a general rule, a testator has the right to impose such conditions as he pleases upon a beneficiary as conditions precedent to the vesting of an estate in him, or to the enjoyment of a trust estate by him as cestui que trust. He may not, however, impose one that is uncertain, unlawful or opposed to public policy.

So it may be said of the directions and restrictions which a testator may impose upon the management of property which he places in a trust, that they are obligatory upon the trustee unless they are uncertain, unlawful or opposed to public policy. Lewin on Trusts (12th Ed.) 90. In the instant case, the length of time during which the testator directed that the property should remain in the trust and the complete uncertainty as to the individuals to whom it would ultimately go, preclude any thought of an intent on his part to forbid the encumbering of the property by long leases or the burdening of it with large buildings, lest the beneficiaries be embarrassed in the development of it along such lines as they might themselves prefer. The only other purpose which can reasonably be attributed to him is to compel the trustee to follow his own peculiar ideas as to the proper and advantageous way to manage such properties. That the restrictions are opposed to the interests of the beneficiaries of the trust, that they are imprudent and unwise is made clear by the statement of agreed facts, but that is not all, for their effect is not confined to the beneficiaries. The Exchange Place property is located at a corner of the public square in the very center of the city of Waterbury, in the heart of the financial and retail business district, is as valuable as any land in the city, and is most favorably adapted for a large building containing stores and offices, and the Homestead is located in a region of changing character, so that its most valuable use cannot now be determined. . . . The effect of such conditions cannot but react disadvantageously upon neighboring properties, and to continue them, as the testator intended, for perhaps seventy-five years or even more, would carry a serious threat against the proper growth and development of the parts of the city in which the lands in question are situated. The restrictions militate too strongly against the interests of the beneficiaries and the public welfare to be sustained, particularly when it is remembered that they are designed to benefit no one, and are harmful to all persons interested, and we hold them invalid as against public policy. . . .

2. Deviation from Distributive Provisions

In re VAN DEUSEN'S ESTATE
30 Cal. 2d 285, 182 P.2d 565 (1947)

[The testatrix died in 1944, bequeathing her residuary estate in trust to pay the net income equally to her two daughters, Gladys and Hazel, for their joint lives and then all of the income to the survivor for life. On the death of the survivor the trust was to terminate, with the principal to go to the testatrix's descendants by right of representation. In 1945 the life beneficiaries petitioned the probate court to instruct the trustee to pay each of them $200 a month from income and, if necessary, from corpus. The petition alleged that the provision for the daughters was to provide enough income for their needs, that on the basis of a contemplated trust income of $400 a month when the will was executed the testatrix intended each daughter to receive at least $200 a month, that since the creation of the trust one daughter has come to require special medical care, and that the other daughter must rely on trust income for the necessities of life. The court granted the petition after determining that the trust income was now less than $250 a month and finding that the petitioners were the primary objects of the trust, that they were intended to receive $200 each month, and that the primary purpose of the trust could not be accomplished by strict adherence to its terms. From this order the trustee, who appeared at the hearing in opposition to the petition, has appealed.]

TRAYNOR, H. . . .

[T]he order appealed from is erroneous on its merits. The theory of the order, and the only basis for granting it after the decree of distribution, was to allow a modification or deviation from the trust to carry out the purpose of the testatrix in view of changed conditions. A court of equity may modify a trust on a proper showing of changed conditions occurring after the creation of a trust if the rights of all the beneficiaries may be protected. If it is assumed that a probate court has the same power under section 1120, the order appealed from is nevertheless erroneous, since it provides for an invasion of the corpus of the trust contrary to the express provisions of the decree of distribution without any attempt to protect the interests of the residuary beneficiaries in that corpus.

The only interest given respondents in either the will or the decree of distribution is the net income from the corpus. The grandchildren of the testatrix, children of the respondents, are entitled to distribution of the corpus on the death of the surviving respondent. To allow an invasion of the corpus without the consent of the residuary beneficiaries contrary to the provisions of the trust instrument is to take property from one without his consent and give it to another. (See 3 (pt. 1) Bogert, Trusts and Trustees, 504.) As stated in the Restatement of Trusts (168, comment *d*):

> The court will not permit or direct the application of the principal to the support or education of one beneficiary whereby the terms of the trust income only is to be so applied, if the result would be to deprive another beneficiary of property to which he is or may become entitled by the terms of the trust, whether the interest of such other beneficiary is vested or contingent, or unless such other beneficiary consents to such application.

(See also, Hughes v. Federal Trust Co., 119 N.J. Eq. 502, 504 [183 Atl. 299]; Scott on Trusts, §168.)

In Whittingham v. California Trust Co., 214 Cal. 128, 134 [4 P.2d 142], the claimant, a beneficiary of a testamentary trust, was the only person interested in the estate. It was held that a court of equity could modify the trust to allow distribution of part of the corpus to the beneficiary on a proper showing of the beneficiary's need therefor and of changed circumstances occurring since the execution of the will. In the present case, the respondent life beneficiaries are not the only persons interested in the trust, and the rights of the residuary beneficiaries must be protected. The respondents contend, however, that the probate court did not have to protect the interests of the residuary beneficiaries, and that the trustees had no right to attempt to do so, since the living residuary beneficiaries were all served with notice of the filing of the petition and two of them, who appeared through counsel, stated that they had no objection to increasing the payments to $150. This can hardly be considered consent by all the residuary beneficiaries to an invasion of the corpus of the trust to provide each of the life beneficiaries with at least $200 a month. . . .

Sympathy for the needs of the respondents does not empower the court to deprive the residuary beneficiaries of their interests in the corpus of the trust without their consent, nor does it enable the court to construe the nontestamentary declarations of the testatrix into an expression of her plan or purpose in providing for the trust some eleven years previous thereto. If the courts could increase the payments under testamentary trusts without the consent of all the beneficiaries merely because the income therefrom is not what it was at the time the will was executed and because at one time or another the testator expressed the desire to provide adequately for the beneficiaries, there would be no stability to any testamentary trust in this state.

The order is reversed.

See also Staley v. Ligon, 239 Md. 61, 210 A.2d 384, 388–389 (1965):

> Inasmuch as the testator clearly gave the widow . . . the net income of the estate and gave no right to corpus, express or implied, to anyone other than the grandchildren, the court was without power to order corpus to be given to the widow, for to do so would be to give one cestui part of a fund which the testator gave to another, without the consent of that other. This the decisions and the text writers say cannot be done. Hughes v. Federal Trust Co., 119 N.J. Eq. 502, 183 A. 299. . . . To the argument that the testatrix would want the life tenant to have this relief, the New Jersey Court said it had no doubt this might be true "but the fact remains that she gave [her daughter] only a life interest. I cannot rewrite the will." See also In re Cosgrave's Will, 225 Minn. 443, 31 N.W.2d 20, in which there is a full discussion of the reasons why corpus may not be invaded for the benefit of one who has only a life interest. In the Anno. "Invasion of Trust Principal," 1 A.L.R.2d 1328, 1333-1334, the editor summarizes the authorities thus:

>> [In] most jurisdictions the power of a court of equity to authorize an invasion or deviation from the terms of a trust in unforeseen circumstances not contemplated by the trustor is rightly exercised

only in matters of administration — such as the sale, mortgage, or pledge of trust property, the making of investments, the hastening of enjoyment, or the early termination of the trust contrary to the instrument — and is not in any case to be extended to an extinction or reduction of the interest of any of the beneficiaries.

It is surprising how often a fiduciary power to invade principal is apparently omitted by oversight or thoughtlessness in the drafting of trusts. Although a statement of Policies for the Acceptance of Trust Business by the Trust Division of the American Bankers Association indicates a reluctance to accept powers requiring the trustee to pass on the character and judgment of beneficiaries, the inclusion of powers to pay principal to meet the *needs* of beneficiaries is an important factor in making a trust instrument acceptable to corporate fiduciaries. See Sanders, An Examiner's Views on Estate Planning, 99 Tr. & Est. 485 (1960). Even when the income beneficiary is in grave need of additional funds, the *Van Deusen* and *Staley* cases are representative of the standard refusal of courts to authorize invasion of principal, absent one of the rare statutes to the contrary, if to do so would impair the interest of any nonconsenting beneficiary or potential beneficiary. See, e.g., Matter of Rotermund, 61 Misc. 2d 324, 305 N.Y.S.2d 413 (1969), where the life beneficiary's testamentary general power of appointment did not change this result. A virtually unique case openly reaching the opposite result is Petition of Wolcott, 95 N.H. 23, 56 A.2d 641 (1948), under most appealing circumstances and with the encouragement of those of the remaindermen who were adults, authorizing the trustee to do what the settlor "presumably would have authorized had he foreseen the emergency." Also compare the approach of Hatch v. Riggs National Bank in section C, supra. Occasionally courts "discover" an implied power to invade corpus, as in Longwith v. Riggs, 123 Ill. 258, 14 N.E. 840 (1887); and as noted in *Van Deusen*, supra, invasion is also permitted by deviation where the beneficiary is indefeasibly entitled to the principal later so that only an acceleration at no possible cost to others is involved.

In Probasco v. Clark, 58 Md. App. 683, 474 A.2d 221 (1984), the testator left his estate in trust to pay his son $300 per month for life with the principal to go to a church on the son's death. The estate was over $250,000 and produced substantially more than $300 per month. The church and trustee petitioned the court to terminate the trust after purchasing a $300 per month annuity for the son. Although the trial court granted the petition, the appellate court reversed and refused to terminate because the court could not rewrite the trust to permit the acceleration of the remainder over the objections of the son. Is this an appropriate application of Maryland's Staley v. Ligon, supra, and of the *Van Deusen* principles?

As we have already seen, in England statutes broaden considerably the power of courts to expand the administrative powers of trustees, and the Trustee Act of 1925, 15 Geo. 5, c. 19 §32, authorizes trustees in their discretion to advance limited amounts of capital to persons holding absolute or *contingent* future rights to it, as long (the courts have held) as the instrument does not manifest a contrary intention of the settlor. Nevertheless in Chapman v. Chapman [1954], A.C. 429 (H.L.), the House of Lords held that courts could not modify trusts in a way that would alter the interests of minor or unborn beneficiaries except in the limited ways set out in the Trustee Act. In response, Parliament enacted new legislation four years later.

The English Variation of Trusts Act of 1958, 6 & 7 Eliz. 2, c. 53, empowers courts to give assent on behalf of unborn, unascertained, infant and otherwise disabled beneficiaries to "any arrangement . . . varying or revoking . . . trusts, or enlarging the powers of trustees" provided the court is satisfied that "the carrying out thereof would be for the benefit of" the person on whose behalf the consent is given. The act does not, but for very limited exceptions, permit courts to alter the interests of nonconsenting beneficiaries who are sui juris.

A Pennsylvania statute, 20 Pa. Cons. Stat. Ann. §6102 (1982), provides that a court, regardless of any spendthrift provision, "in its discretion may terminate a trust in whole or in part, or make an allowance from principal to one or more beneficiaries" provided that the court "is satisfied that the original purpose of the conveyor cannot be carried out or is impractical of fulfillment and that the termination, partial termination, or allowance more nearly approximates the intention of the conveyor, and notice is given to all parties in interest or to their . . . fiduciaries." The former statute was more limited: the total maximum allowance was $25,000, and could be made only for income beneficiaries who fell within the categories of the settlor or the settlor's spouse, issue, and parents.

In 1965 the New York legislature enacted what is now N.Y. Est. Powers & Trusts Law §7-1.6, authorizing limited principal invasion for income beneficiaries who also have some interest in the principal of a trust created before June 1966. More important, however, as to trusts created thereafter, where the terms fail to authorize invasion of principal but do not manifest an intention to preclude it, the statute empowers a court in its discretion, after notice and hearing, to make an allowance from principal for the benefit of any income beneficiary who is in need of additional funds for support or education if the court finds that the allowance will further the settlor's intention. Neither an interest in principal nor the consent of affected beneficiaries is required. Consider California Probate Code §15409(a), which provides:

> On petition by a trustee or beneficiary, the court may modify the administrative or dispositive provisions of the trust or terminate the trust

if, owing to circumstances not known to the settlor and not anticipated by the settlor, the continuation of the trust under its terms would defeat or substantially impair the accomplishment of the purposes of the trust. In this case, if necessary to carry out the purposes of the trust, the court may order the trustee to do acts that are not authorized or are forbidden by the trust instrument.

In 1983 Missouri enacted a distributive deviation statute, Mo. Rev. Stat. §456.590.2, which provides that when all of the adult beneficiaries who are not disabled consent, the court may change the shares of beneficiaries or change the time or amount of payments or terminate the trust, upon a finding that the variation will benefit disabled, minor, unborn, or unascertained beneficiaries. Hamerstrom v. Commerce Bank, 808 S.W.2d 1991 (Mo. App. 1991), gave effect to the statute by holding that the beneficiaries whose consent was required were only those named or included in a named class, and not unnamed or unascertained potential survivors of the named beneficiaries.

UNIFORM TRUST CODE
(Draft, Feb. 2000)

§411. *Modification or Termination Because of Unanticipated Circumstances or Inability to Administer Trust Effectively.*

(a) The court may modify the administrative or dispositive terms of a trust or terminate the trust if:

(1) because of circumstances not anticipated by the settlor, modification or termination will substantially further the settlor's purposes in creating the trust; or

(2) the purposes of the trust have been fulfilled or have become illegal or impossible to fulfill.

(b) The court may modify the administrative terms of a trust if continuation of the trust on its existing terms would be impracticable, wasteful, or impair the trust's administration.

(c) Upon termination of a trust under this section, the trust property must be distributed in accordance with the settlor's purposes in creating the trust.

Comment . . .

Subsection (b) broadens the court's ability to modify the administrative terms of a trust. . . . Subsection (b) is also an application of the principle that a trust have a purpose which is for the benefit of its beneficiaries, both in its terms and in how it is administered. See Restatement (Third) of Trusts §27(2) & cmt. *b* (Tentative Draft No. 2,

1999). Although the settlor is granted considerable latitude in defining the purposes of the trust, the principle that a trust have a purpose which is for the benefit of its beneficiaries precludes unreasonable restrictions on the use of trust property. Owners may deal without restraint with their own property but not when impressed with a trust for the benefit of others. . . . Thus, attempts to impose unreasonable restrictions on the use of trust property, such as a provision severely impairing the use of real property, will fail. See, e.g., Colonial Trust v. Brown, 135 A. 555 (Conn. 1926). See also Restatement (Third) of Trusts §27 Reporter's Note to cmt. *b* (Tentative Draft No. 2, 1999).

Upon termination of a trust under this section, subsection (c) requires that the trust be distributed in accordance with the settlor's purposes in creating the trust. . . . Typically, such terminating distributions will be made to the qualified beneficiaries, perhaps in proportion to the actuarial value of their interests, although the section does not so prescribe. For the definition of qualified beneficiary, see Section 102(11).

How does Uniform Trust Code §411 differ from the conventional doctrine of equitable deviation? Could §411(a) be used to increase support of a beneficiary whose trust provision and other means have become insufficient to provide for support due to poor health or serious injury? Under §411(a) is it necessary that circumstances have changed since the creation of the trust?

The Code (§412) also includes a provision allowing termination of uneconomic trusts, providing: "(a) Except as otherwise provided by the terms of the trust, if the value of the property of a noncharitable trust is less than [$50,000], the trustee may terminate the trust." It adds: "(b) Upon termination . . . the trust property must be distributed in accordance with the settlor's purposes in creating the trust"; and "(c) The court may modify or terminate a noncharitable trust or remove the trustee and appoint a different trustee if it determines that the value of the trust property is insufficient to justify the cost of administration."

Compare related Uniform Trust Code §§414 and 415, supra page 666 allowing reformation and modification of trusts by the court, and §416, supra page 669, allowing combination and division of trusts by the trustee.

15

Charitable Trusts

Charitable trusts are accorded a number of special privileges by the law. On the other hand, to qualify for these privileges charitable trusts are in some respects subject to restrictions not applicable to other trusts. Thus, certain aspects of charitable trusts are taken up separately at this point. You have already encountered in Chapter 3 the subject of limitations on testamentary gifts to or for charity. Other restrictions and privileges that are more or less peculiar to charitable trusts are taken up in this chapter.

A. History of Charitable Trusts

The English Statute of Charitable Uses, 43 Eliz. c. 4 (1601), included a list of charitable purposes and provided a method of enforcing charitable trusts. Historical research now makes it clear, however, that charitable trusts for like purposes were enforced at common law in England long before the enactment of this statute. Where gifts to charitable "corporations" (which included religious associations and individuals) were restricted, transfers to individuals to the use of charities offered a means of circumventing the restrictions. For example, uses (then apparently honorary rather than enforceable) were employed to avoid mortmain statutes, prohibiting ownership of land by religious corporations, until the statutes were amended to prevent this circumvention.

When the enforcement procedures of the Statute of Charitable Uses were subsequently repealed, the attorney general undertook the primary burden of enforcing charitable trusts. The attorney general had apparently assumed responsibility for enforcing charitable trusts in a few cases prior to the statute.

In the United States the common law of charitable trusts in most states followed the English law, including enforcement by the attorney general. In several states, however, statutes specifying purposes for which trusts could be created did not include charitable purposes; and in a number of states legislation declared that only certain English statutes remained in force, either not mentioning the Statute of Charitable Uses or excluding it among others. How did such legislation affect charitable trusts? Both illustrative and influential were two United

States Supreme Court cases. In Trustees of Philadelphia Baptist Association v. Hart's Executor, 17 U.S. (4 Wheat.) 1 (1819), the opinion by Chief Justice Marshall concluded that charitable trusts were not enforceable under the common law in England but depended on the Statute of Charitable Uses, which was not a part of the law of the state (Virginia) involved in the case. Twenty-five years later, in Vidal v. Girard's Executors, 43 U.S. (2 How.) 127 (1844), it was decided that charitable trusts were not dependent on the Statute of Charitable Uses. The opinion of Justice Story points out that authoritative historic publications since 1819 establish the fact that charitable trusts were enforced in Chancery before the statute. Today, by statute if not by common law, charitable trusts are valid and enforceable in all the states.

B.   General Nature of Charitable Trusts

Note, in the materials that follow, not only the issues about what constitutes a charitable purpose but also the advantages that follow from a finding that a particular purpose is charitable.

Restatement (Second) of Trusts §368 states that charitable purposes include

(a) the relief of poverty; (b) the advancement of education; (c) the advancement of religion; (d) the promotion of health; (e) governmental or municipal purposes; (f) other purposes the accomplishment of which ·is beneficial to the community.

Uniform Trust Code §404(a) restates the same well-established categories, and subsection (b) goes on to provide: "If the purposes of a trust are charitable but the terms of the trust do not indicate a particular purpose or beneficiary, the trustee may select one or more charitable purposes or beneficiaries."

In re FRESHOUR'S ESTATE
185 Kan. 434, 345 P.2d 689 (1959)

[The testator's heirs challenged the clause of his will leaving a share of his residuary estate in trust "for the benefit of the Parish of St. Joseph's Catholic Church" and "for the benefit of the members of the First Methodist Church," both of Hays, Kansas. This is an appeal from the decision of the district court holding that the trusts were private trusts for the benefit of the individual members of the two churches and that they were therefore invalid for indefiniteness of beneficiaries and for violation of the Rule Against Perpetuities.]

SCHROEDER, J. . . .

A trust may be valid as a trust for the advancement of religion although in the terms of the trust it is not stated in specific terms that the purpose is religious. Thus, the fact that a legatee or devisee is a religious organization or a person holding a religious office *may indicate* that it is to be applied for religious purposes, although by the terms of the trust its application is not specifically so limited. Restatement of Law, Trusts, §371c, p. 1150. . . .

A charity is broadly defined as a gift for general public use. In the legal sense a charity may be more fully defined as a gift to be applied consistently with existing laws for the benefit of an indefinite number of persons, *either by bringing their minds or hearts under the influence of education or religion,* by relieving their bodies from disease, suffering or constraint, by assisting them to establish themselves in life, or by erecting or maintaining public buildings, or works or otherwise lessening the burdens of government.

It is essential to a valid charitable gift that it be for a purpose recognized in law as charitable. To constitute a charitable use or purpose, it must be a public as distinguished from a private one. It must be for the public use or benefit, and it must be for the benefit of an indefinite number of persons. However, this does not prevent the donor from selecting some particular class of the public and limiting his benefaction to that class, provided the class is composed of an indefinite number of persons rather than certain designated and named individuals.

The most important differences between private trusts and charitable trusts relate to the validity of the trust. There cannot be a private trust unless there is a beneficiary who is definitely ascertained at the time of the creation of the trust or definitely ascertainable within the rule against perpetuities (See, Restatement of Law, Trusts, §112, p. 288). On the other hand, a charitable trust can be created although there is no definite or definitely ascertainable beneficiary designated (See, Restatement of Law, Trusts, §364, p. 1136), and a charitable trust is not invalid although by the terms of the trust it is to continue for an indefinite or unlimited period (See, Restatement of Law, Trusts, §365, p. 1136). . . . As long as the property given in trust vests in the trustee immediately or within the period prescribed by the rule [against perpetuities], trusts for charitable uses are not obnoxious to the rule although they may continue forever and beneficial interests may arise under them at a remote time.

The law must find in the trust, if it is to achieve the status of being "charitable," some social advantages which more than offset the detriments which arise out of the special privileges accorded to that trust. 2A Bogert, The Law of Trusts and Trustees, §361, p. 3. While the human beings who are to obtain advantages from charitable trusts may be referred to as beneficiaries, the real beneficiary is the public and the human beings involved are merely the instrumentalities from whom the benefits flow. Whether a gift is or may be operative for the public benefit is a question to be answered by the court. . . .

In our opinion, the testator's use of the words "parish" and "members" in association with the organizations named in the will was intended to refer to the respective ecclesiastical societies, and we are confident he intended the word "members" to have the same connotation as the word "parish." . . . The words "parish" and "members" were simply used by the testator to limit the trustees in the use of the trust property to the respective congregations, rather than to permit the trustees to use it for the benefit of other localities. It was his intention to confine the trustees in activities of the two religious organizations to the area which they served.

It remains to inquire whether the respective bequests and devises are void because the testator designated no uses to which the property should be applied. . . . [A] gift to a church or a church society by name, without declaration or restriction as to the use to be made of the subject matter of the gift, must be deemed to be a gift for the promotion of the purposes for which the church was organized. Courts look with favor upon trusts for charitable purposes and construe language creating such trusts most favorable to their validity. . . .

The judgment of the trial court is reversed.

HIGHT v. UNITED STATES
256 F.2d 795 (2d Cir. 1958)

MOORE, C.J. . . .

The testatrix by will left all her residuary estate to "such charitable, benevolent, religious or educational institutions as my executors hereinafter named may determine." Despite the fact that all institutions which received legacies are conceded to be "so created and constituted that a legacy to any one of them is deductible under Federal law in determining the net estate subject to the Federal estate tax" (Stip. of Facts, par. 15), the Commissioner disallowed all such legacy deductions "upon the theory that the plaintiffs had power to appoint said remainder and residue exclusively to benevolent institutions that were not also charitable" (Id. par. 22).

The question to be determined is whether the word "benevolent" included with the words "charitable," "religious" or "educational" is sufficient to deprive this estate of the tax benefits bestowed by Congress upon public-minded citizens who desire to devote their estates to public purposes.

The word "benevolent" has no fixed meaning which is self-defining. Webster's New International Dictionary (1934 Ed.) defines it in part as "disposed to give to good objects; kind; charitable" thus giving it a place within the category of "charitable." . . .

Restatement of Trusts, section 398, comment *d,* singles out the phrase "charitable or benevolent" as an example of the application of the principle of ejusdem generis to uphold a charitable trust:

> Where by the terms of the trust a word is used which standing alone would be broader than charity, it may in view of the other terms of the trust be interpreted as limited to charity. Thus, where a testator devises or bequeaths property to be applied to "charitable or benevolent" purposes, the word "benevolent" may be interpreted as a synonym for "charitable," and not as including purposes which are not charitable, even though the word "benevolent" standing alone might be interpreted as including purposes which are not charitable. . . .

[Omitted is the court's review of evidence showing that the testatrix gave generously during her lifetime to institutions whose tax-exempt status she had verified in advance and that she had prepared for the guidance of her executor a list of suggested charities all of which were tax exempt.]

From these facts there can be no doubt that Mrs. Cochran during her lifetime gave ample proof of the type of institution which she selected for her benefactions. Her wishes were conveyed to her executors both orally and in writing. The executors understood these wishes and explicitly carried them out. . . .

[In an action for declaratory judgment brought by the executors of this will, the Supreme Court of Errors of Connecticut, in Cochran v. McLaughlin, 128 Conn. 638, 24 A.2d 836] specifically upheld the validity of the disposition of residuary estate, thereby indicating that the term "benevolent" was a sufficiently definite direction to her executors. The district court in the instant case distinguished the federal decisions allowing deductions where the devises were to "benevolent institutions" on the ground that the Connecticut court had precisely delineated the term "benevolent" so as to encompass "institutions whose principal function is to provide pleasure and cheer to their members." However, had the Connecticut court reached such a conclusion, it would have had no alternative but to find the trust incapable of being enforced, and would have been compelled to strike out the disposition of the entire residuary estate as void for uncertainty and indefiniteness. . . .

The judgment below is reversed and the case is remanded to the District Court for recomputation of the tax and entry of judgment in conformity with this opinion. . . .

Contrast Morice v. Bishop of Durham, 10 Ves. 521 (Ch. 1805), discussed supra Chapter 10, section D, holding "benevolence and liberality" noncharitable. In Hegeman's Executor v. Roome, 70 N.J. Eq. 562, 62 A. 392 (1905), a trust for "such religious, benevolent, or charitable objects as my husband may select" was held not valid as a charitable trust. The trend of judicial attitudes in this country, however, is better illustrated by a later New Jersey decision.

In Wilson v. Flowers, 58 N.J. 250, 277 A.2d 199 (1971), the issue was whether the testator intended *philanthropic* to be limited to charitable or to have its broader dictionary meaning. The next of kin urged (1) that the court adhere to its cases following the English rule that terms such as *benevolent* and *philanthropic* are broader than charitable, and (2) that even if such terms have come generally to mean charitable for these purposes, this testator's usage indicated a broader intention inasmuch as he gave the property to "such philanthropic causes as my trustee may select, *special consideration,* however, to be given to charitable, educational and scientific fields" (emphasis added). The court considered at length the admissibility of extrinsic evidence in such cases and approved the flexible use of a broad range of evidence showing the particular testator's intention. It then concluded:

> While "philanthropic" may be technically broader than "charitable," we think it has come to mean the same thing in modern usage. However, even if it has not, it is ambiguous enough to be construed as such. . . . And if there were any doubt, well established rules of construction would lead us to lean in favor of a construction which upheld the gift as charitable.

58 N.J. at 263-264, 277 A.2d at 206-207.

Dispositions in trust simply for "such charitable purposes as my trustee may select" and bequests to "such charitable institutions as my executor may select" are valid. E.g., Boyd v. Frost National Bank, 145 Tex. 206, 196 S.W.2d 497; Annot., 168 A.L.R. 1326 (1946); Rabinowitz v. Wollman, 174 Md. 6, 197 A. 566 (1939). See also Newick v. Mason, 581 A.2d 1269 (Me. 1990). So are bequests and intended trusts for "charity" or for some class of charity without naming a trustee, for trusts do not fail for want of trustees, which courts can appoint. See In re Jordan's Estate, 329 Pa. 427, 197 A. 150 (1938) ("to charity"); In re Vanderhoofven's Estate, 18 Cal. App. 3d 940, 96 Cal. Rptr. 260 (1971) ("to some Protestant school . . . of engineering").

In contrast to the broad purposes considered above, the purposes of a trust may be so restricted as to be challenged on the ground that the limited purpose is not charitable. If such a trust is too indefinite as to its beneficiaries or duration to be upheld as a private trust, it must fail if not found to be charitable. When is a specific purpose not charitable? "A trust is not a charitable trust if the persons who are to benefit are not a sufficiently large or indefinite class so that the community is interested in the enforcement of the trust." Restatement (Second) of Trusts §375. Thus, a trust for the care of unspecified stray animals is charitable, but the notorious trusts for the care of specific pets are not. (The latter, however, may be permitted as *honorary trusts,* as noted in Chapter 10, section D.) A trust for Masses for the soul of a particular person is now considered to be charitable; this is because the religious purpose is not limited to particular souls, according to Restatement §371, comment *g.* A trust to establish a museum to exhibit objects that the particular testator regarded as works of art but that have no artistic value will not be enforced. Restatement §374, comment *m.* When troublesome cases arise, how is it decided whether the required interest or benefit to the community is present? This is for the court, not the donor, to decide. But how is this to be done if we are to avoid personalized decision-making, which merely substitutes the values and attitudes of the individual judge or panel of judges on a given court at a given time for those of the donor, especially in particularly controversial areas?[1]

Certain types of trusts tend to pose difficult questions regarding what is of benefit to the community. A trust to disseminate beliefs that are judged to be so irrational or inconsequential as to be of no community interest is not valid. The mere fact that views are unpopular or have but a few adherents, however, is not sufficient to deprive a trust of the educational or religious purpose to which the special privileges of a charitable trust attach. Where is the line drawn in such cases? On which

---

1. With the Restatement references above on Masses and personal museums, compare two English cases that are illustrative of problems concerning the meaning of public benefit and how that benefit may be determined. In invalidating a gift for the "purposes of the Roman Catholic community known as the Carmelite Priory," Lord Simonds's opinion in Gilmore v. Coats [1949] A.C. 426, 444-446, states:

> It is said . . . that religious purposes are charitable, but that can only be true [of activities] tending directly or indirectly towards the instruction or edification of the public. . . . [A court does not] accept as proved whatever a particular church believes [for] the court can act only on proof. A gift to one or two or a hundred cloistered nuns in the belief that their prayers will benefit the world at large does not from that belief derive validity any more than does the belief of any other donor for any other purpose.

In the other case the quality of a testator's collection of his own and others' paintings, plus some antique furnishings, led one expert witness to express "surprise that so voracious a collector should not by hazard have picked up even one meritorious object," and Davies, L.J., to observe that in such cases the court must

> receive expert evidence on the question whether the display [is] for the advancement of education or otherwise of benefit to the public. For without such evidence the court would be unable to decide the question.

Re Pinion, [1965] 1 Ch. 98, 197 (C.A.).

side does spiritualism fall? See IVA W. Fratcher, Scott on Trusts §370.4 (4th ed. 1989); cf. Estate of Kidd, 106 Ariz. 554, 479 P.2d 697 (1971) (trust to provide funds for research to discover scientific proof of a soul which leaves the human body at death held to be charitable). And what of a trust the income of which is to be used as the trustee deems appropriate to further a specific radical or reactionary political philosophy? What of partisan political purposes, or advocacy of a particular change in the law (as distinct from general support of the work of a law revision commission)?

In Jackson v. Phillips, 96 Mass. (14 Allen) 539 (1867), a trust to "create a public sentiment that will put an end to negro slavery" was upheld, along with a trust "for the benefit of fugitive slaves who may escape from the slave-holding states." The very same case, however, held invalid another bequest to create a trust to promote women's suffrage because the purpose was "to change the laws." A later Massachusetts case also invalidated a trust to promote "women's rights," interpreted as meaning the right to vote and hold office, while upholding two other trusts in the same will to promote "the cause of temperance" and the "best interests of sewing girls in Boston." Bowditch v. Attorney General, 241 Mass. 168, 134 N.E. 796 (1922). In re Estate of Breeden, 208 Cal. App. 3d 981, 256 Cal. Rptr. 813 (1989), held that a trust for distribution "to persons, entities, and causes advancing the principles of socialism and those causes related to socialism" was a valid charitable trust.

RESTATEMENT (SECOND) OF TRUSTS

§374. . . . A trust for the promotion of purposes which are of a character sufficiently beneficial to the community to justify permitting property to be devoted forever to their accomplishment is charitable. Comment: . . .

j. *Change in existing law.* A trust may be charitable although the accomplishment of the purpose for which the trust is created involves a change in the existing law. If the purpose of the trust is to bring about changes in the law by illegal means, such as by revolution, bribery, illegal lobbying or bringing improper pressure to bear upon members of the legislature, the purpose is illegal. See §377. The mere fact, however, that the purpose is to bring about a change in the law, whether indirectly through the education of the electors so as to bring about a public sentiment in favor of the change, or through proper influences brought to bear upon the legislators, does not prevent that purpose from being legal and charitable. . . .

k. *Political purposes.* A trust to promote the success of a particular political party is not charitable. Thus, a trust of a large sum of money to use the income forever in the discretion of the chairman of a party committee to assist the party in the election of members of the party or otherwise to promote the interests of the party is not a charitable trust. There is no social interest in the community in the underwriting of one or another of the political parties. If, however, the promotion of a particular cause is charitable, the mere fact that one or another of the political parties advocates the cause, does not make the promotion of the cause non-charitable. Thus, a trust . . . to promote an economic doctrine, such as the desirability of free trade or of protective tariffs, is charitable although the political parties take different stands on these questions.

PROBLEMS

15-A.   George Bernard Shaw left the residue of his estate to trustees to use the income for 21 years to support the study of the advantages of a phonetic alphabet consisting of 40 letters (one for every sound and having but one sound per letter), to finance publication and free distribution to libraries of his play *Androcles and the Lion* in this alphabet, and to fund a campaign to promote the adoption of the proposed alphabet. How would you argue to uphold this intended trust in the United States? How would you argue against it?[2] See generally W. Fratcher, Bequests for Purposes, 56 Iowa L. Rev. 773 (1971).

15-B.   The will of Jack Robbins left property to named trustees, the income

> to be used for the support, education, and welfare of such minor Negro child or children as they may select whose father or mother or both have been convicted of a crime of a political nature. Wishing to preserve the right of dissent and being aware of the changing nature of attempts to restrict free expression and to circumscribe activity in unorthodox causes, I authorize my Trustees to decide what Negro child or children shall receive benefits under this trust.

What recognized charitable purpose is involved? Is this trust valid? In re Robbins' Estate, 57 Cal. 2d 718, 371 P.2d 573 (1962). Consider the material below.

---

2. A major asset of Shaw's estate eventually turned out to be the royalties from the musical *My Fair Lady,* based on his *Pygmalion,* in which a professor of phonetics was portrayed. Shaw's project was invalidated as noncharitable and not within the limited purposes for which honorary trusts are allowed. In re Shaw, [1957] 1 All F.R. 745 (Ch.), but the other charitable residuary beneficiaries, whose rights accelerated, have allowed these purposes to be pursued.

IVA W. FRATCHER, SCOTT ON TRUSTS
§377 (4th ed. 1989)

§377. *Illegal purposes.*   A trust cannot be created for a purpose that is illegal. The purpose is illegal if the trust property is to be used for an object that is in violation of the criminal law, or if the trust tends to induce the commission of crime, or if the accomplishment of the purpose is otherwise against public policy. Questions of public policy are not fixed and unchanging, but vary from time to time and from place to place. A trust fails for illegality if the accomplishment of the purposes of the trust is regarded as against public policy in the community in which the trust is created and at the time when it is created. Where a policy is articulated in a statute making certain conduct a criminal offense, then, of course, a trust is illegal if its performance involves such criminal conduct, or if it tends to encourage such conduct. . . .

A trust is illegal, even if it does not involve the performance of an illegal act by the trustees, if the natural result of the performance of the trust would be to induce the commission of crime. Thus a bequest to purchase the release of persons committed to prison for nonpayment of fines under the game laws was held illegal.

The trust that came before the United States Supreme Court in 1844 in Vidal v. Girard's Executors, mentioned in section A supra, returned to the Court in 1957. In 1776 a one-eyed sea captain named Stephen Girard began a shipping business in Philadelphia and died in 1831, a lonely man but one of the country's wealthiest tycoons. Most of his estate was bequeathed in trust to the mayor, aldermen, and citizens of Philadelphia to establish a "college" (an elementary and secondary school) for "poor male white orphan children." In Girard Will Case, 386 Pa. 548, 127 A.2d 287 (1956), the Pennsylvania Supreme Court upheld the trust, which was then administered by a statutory body created to accept and execute charitable trusts for the City of Philadelphia. The decision was reversed in Pennsylvania v. Board of Directors of City Trusts, 353 U.S. 230 (1957), on the ground that the refusal of admission to applicants because of their race by a state agency, though acting as a trustee, was discrimination forbidden by the fourteenth amendment. On remand the orphans' court removed the board and appointed thirteen private citizens as trustees. The Pennsylvania Supreme Court upheld the substitution of trustees and affirmed the decree of the orphans' court providing for execution of the trust according to its terms. In re Girard College Trusteeship, 391 Pa. 434, 138 A.2d 844, *appeal dismissed, cert. denied sub nom.* Pennsylvania v. Board of Directors of City Trusts, 357 U.S. 570 (1958). After the Supreme Court decided

Evans v. Newton, infra, Pennsylvania v. Brown, 392 F.2d 120 (3d Cir.), *cert. denied*, 391 U.S. 921 (1968), concluded that, in light of the "fairly comparable" facts and trusteeship histories of the college and of the park in Evans v. Newton, the latter decision "governs the issue before us" and required that applicants to Girard College be admitted without regard to race.

EVANS v. NEWTON
382 U.S. 296 (1966)

DOUGLAS, J., delivered the opinion of the Court.

In 1911 United States Senator Augustus O. Bacon executed a will that devised to the Mayor and Council of the City of Macon, Georgia, a tract of land which, after the death of the Senator's wife and daughters, was to be used as "a park and pleasure ground" for white people only, the Senator stating in the will that while he had only the kindest feeling for the Negroes he was of the opinion that "in their social relations the two races (white and negro) should be forever separate." The will provided that the park should be under the control of a Board of Managers of seven persons, all of whom were to be white. The city kept the park segregated for some years but in time let Negroes use it, taking the position that the park was a public facility which it could not constitutionally manage and maintain on a segregated basis.

Thereupon, individual members of the Board of Managers of the park brought this suit in a state court against the City of Macon and the trustees of certain residuary beneficiaries of Senator Bacon's estate, asking that the city be removed as trustee and the court appoint new trustees, to whom title to the park would be transferred. The city answered, alleging it could not legally enforce racial segregation in the park. The other defendants admitted the allegation and requested that the city be removed as trustee.

Several Negro citizens of Macon intervened, alleging that the racial limitation was contrary to the laws and public policy of the United States, and asking that the court refuse to appoint private trustees. Thereafter the city resigned as trustee and amended its answer accordingly. Moreover, other heirs of Senator Bacon intervened and they and the defendants other than the city asked for reversion of the trust property to the Bacon estate in the event that the prayer of the petition were denied.

The Georgia court accepted the resignation of the city as trustee and appointed three individuals as new trustees, finding it unnecessary to pass on the other claims of the heirs. On appeal by the Negro intervenors, the Supreme Court of Georgia affirmed, holding that Senator

Bacon had the right to give and bequeath his property to a limited class, that charitable trusts are subject to supervision of a court of equity, and that the power to appoint new trustees so that the purpose of the trust would not fail was clear. 220 Ga. 280, 138 S.E.2d 573. The case is here on a writ of certiorari. 380 U.S. 971.

There are two complementary principles to be reconciled in this case. One is the right of the individual to pick his own associates so as to express his preferences and dislikes, and to fashion his private life by joining such clubs and groups as he chooses. The other is the constitutional ban in the Equal Protection Clause of the Fourteenth Amendment against state-sponsored racial inequality, which of course bars a city from acting as trustee under a private will that serves the racial segregation cause. Pennsylvania v. Board of Trusts, 353 U.S. 230. A private golf club, however, restricted to either Negro or white membership is one expression of freedom of association. But a municipal golf course that serves only one race is state activity indicating a preference on a matter as to which the State must be neutral. . . . [W]hen private individuals or groups are endowed by the State with powers or functions governmental in nature, they become agencies or instrumentalities of the State and subject to its constitutional limitations.

Yet generalizations do not decide concrete cases. [T]he fact that government has engaged in a particular activity does not necessarily mean that an individual entrepreneur or manager of the same kind of undertaking suffers the same constitutional inhibitions. While a State may not segregate public schools so as to exclude one or more religious groups, those sects may maintain their own parochial educational systems. Pierce v. Society of Sisters, 268 U.S. 510.

If a testator wanted to leave a school or center for the use of one race only and in no way implicated the State in the supervision, control or management of that facility, we assume arguendo that no constitutional difficulty would be encountered.[3]

This park, however, is in a different posture. For years it was an integral part of the City of Macon's activities. From the pleadings we assume it was swept, manicured, watered, patrolled, and maintained by the city as a public facility for whites only, as well as granted tax exemption under Ga. Code Ann. §92-201. The momentum it acquired as a public facility is certainly not dissipated ipso facto by the appointment of "private" trustees. So far as this record shows, there has been no change in municipal maintenance and concern over this facility. Whether these

---

3. It is argued that this park was a product of Georgia's [statutory] policy to allow charitable trusts of public facilities to be segregated. . . . We do not, however, reach the question whether the state facilitated, through its legislative action, the establishment of segregated parks.

public characteristics will in time be dissipated is wholly conjectural. If the municipality remains entwined in the management or control of the park, it remains subject to the restraints of the Fourteenth Amendment. . . . We only hold that where the traditions of municipal control had become firmly established, we cannot take judicial notice that the mere substitution of trustees instantly transferred this park from the public to the private sector.

This conclusion is buttressed by the nature of the service rendered the community by a park. The service rendered even by a private park of this character is municipal in nature. It is open to every white person, there being no selective element other than race. Golf clubs, social centers, luncheon clubs, schools such as Tuskegee was at least in origin, and other like organizations in the private sector are often racially oriented. A park, on the other hand, is more like a fire department or police department that traditionally serves the community. . . . [A]nd state courts that aid private parties to perform that public function on a segregated basis implicate the State in conduct proscribed by the Fourteenth Amendment. . . .

Under the circumstances of this case, we cannot but conclude that the public character of this park requires that it be treated as a public institution subject to the command of the Fourteenth Amendment, regardless of who now has title under state law. . . .

Reversed.

WHITE, J. . . .

That the Fourteenth Amendment prohibits operation of the park on a segregated basis so long as the city is trustee is of course not disputed. . . . Whether the successor trustees may themselves operate the park on a segregated basis is the question. The majority holds that they may not, I agree, but for different reasons. . . .

[T]he record does not show continued involvement of the city in the operation of the park — the record is silent on this point. . . . That the city's own interest might lead it to extricate itself at once from operation of the park does not, of course, necessarily mean that it has done so [but what] the majority has done . . . is simply a disguised form of conjecture and, I submit, is an insufficient basis for decision of this case.

I would nevertheless hold that the racial condition in the trust may not be given effect by the new trustees because, in my view, it is incurably tainted by discriminatory state legislation validating such a condition under state law. The state legislation to which I refer is §69-504 and §69-505 of the Georgia Code, which were adopted in 1905, just six years before Senator Bacon's will was executed. . . .

As this legislation does not compel a trust settlor to condition his grant upon use only by a racially designated class, the State cannot be said to have directly coerced private discrimination. Nevertheless, if the validity of the racial condition in Senator Bacon's trust would have been in doubt but for the 1905 statute and if the statute removed such doubt only for racial restrictions, leaving the validity of non-racial restrictions still in question, the absence of coercive language in the legislation would not prevent application of the Fourteenth Amendment. For such a statute would depart from a policy of strict neutrality in matters of private discrimination by enlisting the State's assistance only in aid of racial discrimination and would so involve the State in the private choice as to convert the infected private discrimination into state action subject to the Fourteenth Amendment. . . .

Apart from §69-504 and §69-505, the Georgia statute governing the determination of permissible objects of charitable trusts is §108-203. This statute "almost copies the statute of 43d Elizabeth," Newson v. Starke, 46 Ga. 88, 92 (1872), and has the effect of fully adopting in Georgia the common law of charities. Jones v. Habersham, 107 U.S. 174, 180. We may therefore expect general charitable trust principles to be as fully applicable in Georgia as elsewhere in the several States. Under such principles, there is grave doubt concerning whether a charitable trust for a park could be limited to the use of less than the whole public. . . . Professor Scott states this principle as follows:

> As we have seen, a trust to promote the happiness or well-being of members of the community is charitable, although it is not a trust to relieve poverty, advance education, promote religion or protect health. In such a case, however, *the trust must be for the benefit of the members of the community generally* and not merely for the benefit of a class of persons.

IV Scott on Trusts §375.2, at 2715 (2d ed. 1956). (Emphasis added.) . . .

On the whole, therefore, I conclude that prior to the 1905 legislation it would have been extremely doubtful whether §108-203 authorized a trust for park purposes when a portion of the public was to be excluded from the park. . . .

BLACK, J., dissenting. . . .

[T]he narrow question of whether a city could resign such a trusteeship and whether a state court could appoint successor trustees depended entirely on state law. . . . [S]ince the Georgia courts decided no federal constitutional question, I agree with my Brother Harlan that the writ of certiorari should have been dismissed as improvidently granted. . . .

HARLAN, J., whom STEWART, J., joins, dissenting. . . .

In my view the writ should be dismissed as improvidently granted. . . . To infer from the Georgia Supreme Court's opinion, as the majority here does, a further holding that the new trustees are entitled to operate Baconsfield on a racially restricted basis, is to stretch for a constitutional issue. . . .

On the merits, which I reach only because the Court has done so, I do not think that the Fourteenth Amendment permits this Court in effect to frustrate the terms of Senator Bacon's will, now that the City of Macon is no longer connected, so far as the record shows, with the administration of Baconsfield. If the majority is in doubt that such is the case, it should remand for findings on that issue and not reverse. . . .

Quite evidently uneasy with its first ground of decision, the majority advances another which ultimately emerges as the real holding. This ground derives from what is asserted to be the "public character" of Baconsfield. . . .

More serious than the absence of any firm doctrinal support for this theory of state action are its potentialities for the future. [Despite similarities of parks and schools in terms of "public functions" involved,] the majority assumes that its decision leaves unaffected the traditional view that the Fourteenth Amendment does not compel private schools to adapt their admission policies to its requirements, but that such matters are left to the States acting within constitutional bounds. I find it difficult, however, to avoid the conclusion that this decision opens the door to reversal of these basic constitutional concepts, and, at least in logic, jeopardizes the existence of denominationally restricted schools while making of every college entrance rejection letter a potential Fourteenth Amendment question.

While this process of analogy might be spun out to reach privately owned orphanages, libraries, garbage collection companies, detective agencies, and a host of other functions commonly regarded as nongovernmental though paralleling fields of governmental activity, the example of schools is, I think, sufficient to indicate the pervasive potentialities of this "public function" theory of state action. . . .

———————————

Following the above decision, a Georgia trial court ruled that Senator Bacon's trust was not enforceable according to its terms and that the trust property reverted to his heirs, rejecting the arguments of certain Macon citizens and the Georgia Attorney General that the trust should continue and that the doctrine of cy pres, infra, should be applied to modify the trust terms by striking the racial restrictions. The court found the doctrine inapplicable because the park's segregated character was so essential a part of the testator's plan as to preclude finding the general charitable intent required to vary the terms of the trust instead of allowing the property to revert to the heirs. Evans v. Abney, 396 U.S. 435 (1969) (Justices Douglas and Brennan dissenting), affirmed the decision of the Georgia Supreme Court (224 Ga. 826, 165

S.E.2d 160 (1968)) affirming the trial court's ruling. Justice Black, writing for the Court, stated:

> We do not understand petitioners to be contending here that the Georgia judges were motivated either consciously or unconsciously by a desire to discriminate against Negroes. . . . What remains of petitioners' argument is the idea that the Georgia courts had a constitutional obligation in this case to resolve any doubt about the testator's intent in favor of preserving the trust. Thus stated, we see no merit in the argument. The only choice the Georgia courts either had or exercised in this regard was their judicial judgment in construing Bacon's will to determine his intent, and the Constitution imposes no requirement upon the Georgia courts to approach Bacon's will any differently than they would approach any will creating any charitable trust of any kind. Surely the Fourteenth Amendment is not violated where, as here, a state court operating in its judicial capacity applies its normal principles of construction to determine the testator's true intent in establishing a charitable trust and then reaches a conclusion with regard to that intent which, because of the operation of neutral and nondiscriminatory state trust laws, effectively denies everyone, whites as well as Negroes, the benefits of the trust.

396 U.S. at 447.

The opinion had earlier noted (id. at 445) that the case was distinguishable from Shelley v. Kraemer, 334 U.S. 1 (1948), in that here "the effect of the Georgia decision eliminated all discrimination against Negroes in the park by eliminating the park itself."

In comparable cases facing the choice between having trust property revert or eliminating racially discriminatory restrictions by cy pres, cases have usually found the requisite general charitable intent to reform the trust. E.g., Howard Savings Institution v. Trustees of Amherst College, 61 N.J. Super. 119, 160 A.2d 177 (1960). But not always. See La Fond v. City of Detroit, 357 Mich. 362, 98 N.W.2d 530 (1959). The racial restriction in a trust for the support and education of "poor white citizens of Kent County" was held invalid and cy pres was applied to delete the word *white* in In re Will of Potter, 275 A.2d 574 (Del. Ch. 1970), where again the finding of state action was based on peculiar facts of the case rather than deciding that charitable trusts inherently involve state action because of special functions and privileges or that state *trust* law requires that, in order to be charitable, trusts must not involve invidious racial discrimination.

In Ebitz v. Pioneer National Bank, 372 Mass. 207, 361 N.E.2d 225 (1977), a trust (with a bank trustee) to provide law scholarships to worthy "young men" was construed in a generic sense to include women, partly on the basis that "declared policy of the Commonwealth . . . regarding equal treatment of the sexes" should lead the court to resolve any ambiguity in that fashion rather than raise a question of the trust's validity.

MATTER OF ESTATE OF WILSON
59 N.Y.2d 461, 452 N.E.2d 1228 (1983)

[Companion cases involving testamentary trusts for college scholarships: the Wilson trust income to aid five "young men" who have graduated from a designated high school with certain academic achievements, to be certified by the superintendent of schools for that school district; and the Johnson trust income to be used for "bright and deserving young men" who have graduated from another high school, who meet certain need requirements, and who are selected by the principal and board of education of that school. Following complaints lodged with the Civil Rights Office of the U.S. Department of Education in each case, and certain investigations, negotiations, and agreements, both cases ended up in court. The Surrogate's Court in *Wilson* held that the school superintendent's cooperation with the trustee, a bank, violated neither federal statute or regulation nor the equal protection clause of the fourteenth amendment. The Appellate Division (Third Department), however, found administration of the trust according to its literal terms impossible because of the superintendent's agreement not to certify the students and exercised its cy pres power to reform the trust by striking the clause in the will providing for the school superintendent's certification, permitting candidates to apply directly to the trustee. In *Johnson,* the school district having agreed not to serve as trustee, the Surrogate replaced the school district with a private trustee. The Appellate Division (Second Department) held that a court's reformation by substitution of trustees would constitute state action and a violation of the fourteenth amendment's equal protection requirement; accordingly the Appellate Division exercised its cy pres power to reform the trust by eliminating the gender restriction.]

COOK, C.J. . . .

These appeals present the question whether the equal protection clause of the Fourteenth Amendment is violated when a court permits the administration of private charitable trusts according to the testator's intent to finance the education of male students and not female students. When a court applies trust law that neither encourages, nor affirmatively promotes, nor compels private discrimination but allows parties to engage in private selection in the devise or bequest of their property, that choice will not be attributable to the State and subjected to the Fourteenth Amendment's strictures. . . .

There can be no question that the trusts, established for the promotion of education, are for a charitable purpose within the meaning of the law. Charitable trusts are encouraged and favored by the law. . . . [U]nlike other trusts, a charitable trust will not necessarily fail when the settlor's specific charitable purpose or direction can no longer be accomplished. . . .

The court, of course, cannot invoke its cy pres power without first determining that the testator's specific charitable purpose is no longer capable of being performed by the trust. In establishing these trusts, the testators expressly and unequivocally intended that they provide for the education expenses of male students. It cannot be said that the accomplishment of the testator's specific expression of charitable intent is "impossible or impracticable." So long as the subject high schools graduate boys with the requisite qualifications, the testator's specific charitable intent can be fulfilled.

Nor are the trusts' particular limitation of beneficiaries by gender invalid and incapable of being accomplished as violative of public policy. It is true that the eradication in this State of gender-based discrimination is an important public policy. Indeed, the Legislature has barred gender-based discrimination in education, employment, housing, credit, and many other areas. . . . The restrictions in these trusts run contrary to this policy favoring equal opportunity and treatment of men and women. A provision in a charitable trust, however, that is central to the testator's or settlor's charitable purpose, and is not illegal, should not be invalidated on public grounds unless that provision, if given effect, would substantially mitigate the general charitable effect of the gift (see 4 Scott, Trusts [3d ed.], section 399.4).

Proscribing the enforcement of gender restrictions in private charitable trusts would operate with equal force towards trusts whose benefits are bestowed exclusively on women. "Reduction of the disparity in economic condition between men and women caused by the long history of discrimination against women has been recognized as . . . an important governmental objective" (Califano v. Webster, 430 U.S. 313, 317 . . .). There can be little doubt that important efforts in effecting this type of social change can be and are performed through private philanthropy. And, the private funding of programs for the advancement of women is substantial and growing. Indeed, one compilation of financial assistance offered primarily or exclusively to women lists 854 sources of fundings. Current thinking in private philanthropic institutions advocates that funding offered by such institutions and the opportunities within the institutions themselves be directly responsive to the needs of particular groups. It is evident, therefore, that the focusing of private philanthropy on certain classes within society may be consistent with public policy. Consequently, that the restrictions in the trust before this court may run contrary to public efforts promoting equality of opportunity for women does not justify imposing a per se rule that gender restrictions in private charitable trusts violate public policy.

Finally, this is not an instance in which the restriction of the trusts serves to frustrate a paramount charitable purpose. In Howard Sav. Inst. v. Peep, 34 N.J. 494, 170 A.2d 39, . . . [d]ue to the religious restrictions, the college declined to accept the bequest as contrary to its charter. The court found that the college was the principal beneficiary of the trust, so that removing the religious restriction and thereby allowing the college to accept the gift would permit administration of the trust in a manner most closely effectuating the testator's intent.

In contrast, the trusts subject to these appeals were not intended to directly benefit the school districts. Although the testators sought the school districts' participation, this was incidental to their primary intent of financing the college education of boys who attended the schools. Consequently, severance of the school districts' role in the trusts' administration will not frustrate any part of the testators' charitable purposes. Inasmuch as the specific charitable intent of the testators is not inherently "impossible or impracticable" of being achieved by the trusts, there is no occasion to exercise cy pres power.

Although not inherently so, these trusts are currently incapable of being administered as originally intended because of the school districts' unwillingness to cooperate. These impediments, however, may be remedied by an exercise of a court's general equitable power over all trusts to permit a deviation from the administrative terms of a trust and to appoint a successor trustee.

A testamentary trust will not fail for want of a trustee and, in the event a trustee is unwilling or unable to act, a court may replace the trustee with another. Accordingly, the proper means of continuing the Johnson Trust would be to replace the school district with someone able and willing to administer the trust according to its terms.

When an impasse is reached in the administration of a trust due to an incidental requirement of its terms, a court may effect, or permit the trustee to effect, a deviation from the trust's literal terms. This power differs from a court's cy pres power in that "[t]hrough exercise of its deviation power the court alters or amends administrative provisions in the trust instrument but does not alter the purpose of the charitable trust or change its dispositive provisions." The Wilson Trust provision that the school district certify a list of students is an incidental part of the trust's administrative requirements, which no longer can be satisfied in light of this district's refusal to cooperate. The same result intended by the testator may be accomplished by permitting the students to apply directly to the trustee. Therefore, a deviation from the Wilson Trust's administrative terms by eliminating the certification requirement would be the appropriate method of continuing the trust administration. . . .

It is argued before this court that the judicial facilitation of the continued administration of gender-restrictive charitable trusts violates the equal protection clause of the Fourteenth Amendment (see U.S. Const., 14th Amdt., section 1). The strictures of the equal protection clause are invoked when the State engages in invidious discrimination.

Indeed, the State itself cannot, consistent with the Fourteenth Amendment, award scholarships that are gender restrictive.

The Fourteenth Amendment, however, "erects no shield against merely private conduct, however discriminatory or wrongful." (Shelley v. Kraemer, 334 U.S. 1, 13; . . . Evans v. Abney, 396 U.S. 435, 445 . . .). Private discrimination may violate equal protection of the law when accompanied by State participation in, facilitation of, and, in some cases, acquiescence in the discrimination. Although there is no conclusive test to determine when state involvement in private discrimination will violate the Fourteenth Amendment, the general standard that has evolved is whether "the conduct allegedly causing the deprivation of a federal right [is] fairly attributable to the state." . . .

The Supreme Court has identified various situations in which the State may be deemed responsible for discriminatory conduct with private origins. . . .

"The court has never held, of course, that discrimination by an otherwise private entity would be violative of the Equal Protection Clause if the private entity receives any sort of benefit at all from the State, or if it is subject to state regulation in any degree whatever." Rather, "the State must have 'significantly involved itself with invidious discriminations' . . . in order for the discriminatory actions to fall within the ambit of the constitutional prohibition."

The state generally may not be held responsible for private discrimination solely on the basis that it permits the discrimination to occur. Nor is the state under an affirmative obligation to prevent purely private discrimination. Therefore, when the state regulates private dealings it may be responsible for private discrimination occurring in the regulated field only when enforcement of its regulation has the effect of compelling the private discrimination.

In Shelley v. Kraemer (supra), for example, the Supreme Court held that the equal protection clause was violated by judicial enforcement of a private covenant that prohibited the sale of affected properties "to people of Negro or Mongolian Race." When one of the properties was sold to a black family, the other property owners sought to enforce the covenant in State court and the family was ordered to move from the property. The Supreme Court noted

> that the restrictive agreement standing alone cannot be regarded as violative of any rights guaranteed to petitioners by the Fourteenth Amendment. So long as the purposes of those agreements are effectuated by voluntary adherence to their terms, it would appear clear that there has been no action by the State and the provisions of the Amendment have not been violated

(334 U.S. at p. 13). The court held, however, that it did not have before it cases

in which the States have merely abstained from action leaving private individuals free to impose such discriminations as they see fit. Rather, these are cases in which the states have made available to such individuals the full coercive power of the government to deny petitioners on the grounds of race or color the enjoyment of property rights

(id., at p. 19). It was not the neutral regulation of contracts permitting parties to enter discriminatory agreements that caused the discrimination to be attributable to the State. Instead it was that the State court's exercise of its judicial power directly effected a discriminatory act. . . .

More recently, the Supreme Court considered whether a State's regulation of private clubs licensed to serve liquor caused a club's restrictive membership policy to be attributable to the State (see Moose Lodge No. 107 v. Irvis, 407 U.S. 163, 92 S. Ct. 1965, 32 L. Ed. 2d 627). The court held that although the State extensively regulated these private clubs, it was not responsible for the private discrimination simply because the regulation permitted the discrimination to occur. . . .

A court's application of its equitable power to permit the continued administration of the trust involved in these appeals falls outside the ambit of the Fourteenth Amendment. Although the field of trusts is regulated by the State, the Legislature's failure to forbid private discriminatory trusts does not cause such trusts, when they arise, to be attributable to the State. It naturally follows that, when a court applies this trust law and determines that it permits the continued existence of private discriminatory trusts, the Fourteenth Amendment is not implicated.

In the present appeals, the coercive power of the State has never been enlisted to enforce private discrimination. . . . The court's power compelled no discrimination. That discrimination has been sealed in the private execution of the wills. Recourse to the courts was had here only for the purpose of facilitating the administration of the trust, not for enforcement of their discriminatory dispositive provisions.

This is not to say that a court's exercise of its power over trusts can never invoke the scrutiny of the Fourteenth Amendment. This court holds only that a trust's discriminatory terms are not fairly attributable to the State when a court applies trust principles that permit private discrimination but do not encourage, affirmatively promote, or compel it.

The testators' intention to involve the State in the administration of these trusts does not alter this result, notwithstanding that the effect of the court's action respecting the trusts was to eliminate this involvement. The court's power to replace a trustee who is unwilling to act as in *Johnson* or to permit a deviation from an incidental administrative term in the trust as in *Wilson* is a part of the law permitting this private conduct and extends to all trusts regardless of their purposes. It compels no discrimination. Moreover, the minimal State participation in the trust's administration prior to the time that they reached the courts for the constructions under review did not cause the trusts to take on an indelible public character.

In sum, the Fourteenth Amendment does not require the State to exercise the full extent of its power to eradicate private discrimination. It is only when the State itself discriminates, compels another to discriminate, or allows another to assume one of its functions and discriminate that such discrimination will implicate the Amendment.

Accordingly, in Matter of Wilson, the order of the Appellate Division should be affirmed. . . . In Matter of Johnson, the order of the Appellate Division should be reversed . . . and the decree of the Surrogate's Court . . . reinstated.

JASEN, JONES, WACHTLER, and SIMONS, J.J., concur with COOKE, C.J.

MEYER, J. (concurring in Matter of Wilson and dissenting in Matter of Johnson). . . .

In [the latter] the trustee is the Board of Education, a public body. The establishment of a public trust for a discriminatory purpose is constitutionally improper. . . . For the State to legitimize that impropriety by replacement of the trustee is unconstitutional State action. The only permissible corrective action is, as the Appellate Division held, excision of the discriminatory limitation.

Contrast In re Certain Scholarship Funds, 133 N.H. 227, 575 A.2d 1325 (1990), 90 A.L.R.4th 811, using the cy pres power, below, to remove gender restrictions rather than substituting private fiduciaries for state agencies as trustees.

Much of the focus in cases challenging discriminatory trusts has been on whether the trust restrictions violated the United States Constitution. Note, however, the possibility of arguing that the restrictions violate common law prohibitions on trust provisions that are contrary to public policy (see Chapter 10, section E, supra) or that certain dispositions simply do not meet the trust law standard for a charitable purpose. (Why might a litigant want to allege a federal constitutional right rather than relying on state constitutional or trust law principles, or on principles derived from state or federal legislation?) Conversely, even if a possibly discriminatory provision (or one significantly involving lobbying) is valid as a matter of trust law, it is possible that the charitable trust will be denied tax-exempt status by the Internal Revenue Service, making the provision less attractive to some donors. In Bob Jones University v. United States, 461 U.S. 574 (1983), the Supreme Court held that an educational institution that practiced racial discrimination did not qualify for tax-exempt status under the Internal Revenue Code.

C. Cy Pres

Among the peculiar advantages of the charitable trust is its potential indefinite existence. In considering the *Freshour* case at the outset of this chapter, you may have wondered what would happen to the trusts if the designated churches eventually ceased to exist. What *would* happen? You have, of course, just encountered a form of this problem immediately above.

PROBLEM

15-C. *A* died in 1965, leaving her residuary estate to the trustees of Blackstone University in trust "to use the income, or as much of the income or principal as the Trustees deem appropriate, for the sole purpose of acquiring books, periodicals, and other research materials devoted to the subject of Law and Anthropology for the library of the College of Law of Blackstone University." At the present time, mainly as a result of this trust, the Blackstone Law Library possesses a singularly outstanding collection on law and anthropology, but the income of the trust is no longer being expended. As the collection has developed, annual expenditures have declined, and the fund has begun to accumulate in increased amounts each year. The librarian and the appropriate university and law school committees agree that further duplication is unnecessary and that normal current acquisitions will require only a portion of the income. No one associated with the law library doubts that much better use can be made of much of the trust income. As counsel for the Trustees of the University, how would you advise on this matter and how might you proceed? What factual inquiries would you make? What possibilities and what obstacles do you see?

JACKSON v. PHILLIPS[4]
96 Mass. (14 Allen) 539 (1867)

[Bill for instructions as to the validity and effect of certain provisions of the will of Francis Jackson. The fourth article of the will named a board of trustees and bequeathed $10,000 to them in trust to be used

> for the preparation and circulation of books, newspapers, and delivery of speeches, lectures, and such other means, as, in their judgment, will create a public sentiment that will put an end to negro slavery in this country. . . . My desire is that they [the board of trustees] may become

4. Portions of this early influential case, which have been mentioned in section B, supra, are omitted here.

a permanent organization; and I hope and trust that they will receive the services and sympathy, the donations and bequests, of the friends of the slave.

The fifth article of the will bequeathed $2,000 to the same board of trustees in trust "for the benefit of fugitive slaves who may escape from the slave-holding states of this infamous Union from time to time." These dispositions were upheld as valid charitable trusts, but while the case was under advisement the thirteenth amendment was adopted.]

GRAY, J. . . .

By the thirteenth amendment of the Constitution of the United States, adopted since the earlier arguments of this case, it is declared that

neither slavery nor involuntary servitude, except as a punishment for crime whereof the party shall have been duly convicted, shall exist within the United States or any place subject to their jurisdiction.

The effect of this amendment upon the charitable bequests of Francis Jackson is the remaining question to be determined; and this requires a consideration of the nature and proper limits of the doctrine of cy pres.

It is contended for the heirs at law, that the power of the English chancellor, when a charitable trust cannot be administered according to its terms, to execute it so as to carry out the donor's intention as nearly as possible — cy pres — is derived from the royal prerogative or the St. of 43 Eliz., and is not an exercise of judicial authority; that, whether this power is prerogative or judicial, it cannot, or, if it can, should not, be exercised by this court; and that the doctrine of cy pres, even as administered in the English chancery, would not sustain these charitable bequests since slavery has been abolished.

Much confusion of ideas has arisen from the use of the term cy pres in the books to describe two distinct powers by the English chancellor in charity cases, the one under the sign manual of the crown, the other under the general jurisdiction in equity. . . .

The principal, if not the only, cases in which the disposition of a charity is held to be in the crown by sign manual, are of two classes: the first, of bequests to particular uses charitable in their nature, but illegal, as for a form of religion not tolerated by law; and the second, of gifts of property to charity generally, without any trust interposed, and in which either no appointment is provided for, or the power of appointment is delegated to persons who die without exercising it. . . .

[The first] is clearly a prerogative and not a judicial power, and could not be exercised by this court. . . .

The jurisdiction of the court of chancery to superintend the administration and decree the performance of gifts to trustees for charitable uses of a kind stated in the gift stands upon different grounds; and is part of its equity jurisdiction over trusts, which is shown by abundant evidence to have existed before the passage of the Statute of Charitable Uses. . . .

A charity, being a trust in the support and execution of which the whole public is concerned, and which is therefore allowed by the law to be perpetual, deserves and often requires the exercise of a larger discretion by the court of chancery than a mere private trust; for without a large discretionary power, in carrying out the general intent of the donor, to vary the details of administration, and even the mode of application, many charities would fail by change of circumstances and the happening of contingencies which no human foresight could provide against; and the probabilities of such failure would increase with the lapse of time and the remoteness of the heirs from the original donor who had in a clear and lawful manner manifested his will to divert his estate from his heirs for the benefit of public charities.

It is accordingly well settled by decisions of the highest authority, that when a gift is made to trustees for a charitable purpose, the general nature of which is pointed out, and which is lawful and valid at the time of the death of the testator, and no intention is expressed to limit it to a particular institution or mode of application, and afterwards, either by change of circumstances the scheme of the testator becomes impracticable, or by change of law becomes illegal, the fund, having once vested in the charity, does not go to the heirs at law as a resulting trust, but is to be applied by the court of chancery, in the exercise of its jurisdiction in equity, as near the testator's particular directions as possible, to carry out his general charitable intent. . . .

The intention of the testator is the guide, or, in the phrase of Lord Coke, the lodestone, of the court; and therefore, whenever a charitable gift can be administered according to his express directions, this court, like the court of chancery in England, is not at liberty to modify it upon considerations of policy or convenience. But there are several cases, where the charitable trust could not be executed as directed in the will, in which the testator's scheme has been varied by this court in such a way and to such an extent as could not be done in the case of a private trust. Thus bequests to a particular bible society by name, whether a corporation established by law or a voluntary association, which had ceased to exist before the death of the testator, have been sustained, and applied to the distribution of bibles through a trustee appointed by the court for the purpose. . . .

In all the cases cited at the argument, in which a charitable bequest, which might have been lawfully carried out under the circumstances existing at the death of the testator, has been held, upon a change of circumstances, to result to the heirs at law or residuary legatees, the gift was distinctly limited to particular persons or establishments. . . .

The charitable bequests of Francis Jackson cannot, in the opinion of the court, be regarded as so restricted in their objects, or so limited in point of time, as to have been terminated and destroyed by the abolition of slavery in the United States. They are to a board of trustees for whose continuance careful provision is made in the will, and which the testator expresses a wish may become a permanent organization and may receive the services and sympathy, the donations and bequests, of the friends of the slave. Their duration is not in terms limited, like that of the trust sought to be established in the sixth article of the will, by the accomplishment of the end specified. They take effect from the time of the testator's death, and might then have been lawfully applied in exact conformity with his expressed intentions. The retaining of the funds in the custody of the court while this case has been under advisement cannot affect the question. The gifts being lawful and charitable, and having once vested, the subsequent change of circumstances before the funds have been actually paid over is of no more weight than if they had been paid to the trustees and been administered by them for a century before slavery was extinguished.

Neither the immediate purpose of the testator — the moral education of the people; nor his ultimate object — to better the condition of the African race in this country; has been fully accomplished by the abolition of slavery. . . .

Slavery may be abolished; but to strengthen and confirm the sentiment which opposed it will continue to be useful and desirable so long as selfishness, cruelty, and the lust of dominion, and indifference to the rights of the weak, the poor and the ignorant, have a place in the hearts of men. Looking at the trust established by the fourth article of this will as one for the moral education of the people only, the case is within the principle of those, already cited, in which charities for the relief of leprosy and the plague were held not to end with the disappearance of those diseases. . . .

The mode in which the funds bequeathed by the fourth and fifth articles of the will may be best applied to carry out in a lawful manner the charitable intents and purposes of the testator as nearly as possible must be settled by a scheme to be framed by a master and confirmed by the court before the funds are paid over to the trustees. In doing this, the court does not take the charity out of the hands of the trustees, but only declares the law which must be their guide in its administration. Shelford on Mortmain, 651-654, Boyle on Charities, 214-218. The case is therefore to be referred to a master, with liberty to the attorney general and the trustees to submit schemes for his approval; and all further directions are reserved until the coming in of his report.

FREME v. MAHER
480 A.2d 783 (Me. 1984)

[The will in question, executed two years before decedent's death, left her entire estate to "Ricker Classical Institute and Ricker College . . . to be . . . held by it in trust . . . , the net income only to be used for such general purposes of said Institution as the Board of Trustees of said Institution may determine." Several months after decedent's death in 1978, Ricker College was adjudicated bankrupt in a Chapter 11 proceeding initiated in 1974. Ricker's physical plant was subsequently closed. On the executor's petition for directions, the superior court ordered the matter to be heard by a referee. The college trustees urged that they be permitted to hold the bequest in trust for college scholarships for Maine students. The referee found a general charitable intent and recommended that the cy pres power be exercised to allocate the estate in equal shares to Bates, Bowdoin, and Colby Colleges. The superior court agreed with the recommendation except that it scheduled a hearing to determine the propriety of selecting those three colleges; but it refused to enlarge the scope of the hearing to include consideration of the Ricker proposal, noting that the decedent intended to support "a functional school."]

ROBERTS, J. . . .

In In re Estate of Thompson, 414 A.2d 881, 886 (Me. 1980), we listed three prerequisites for the application of the cy pres doctrine. First, the gift must create a valid charitable trust. Second, the specific purpose of the trust must be impossible or impracticable to carry out. Third, the settlor must have had a general charitable intent. On appeal, the trustees of Ricker contend that resort to cy pres was unnecessary because the second prerequisite was not met. . . .

In addressing the second prerequisite to the application of cy pres, therefore, we focus on two issues. Does Ricker College, as it exists in its present form, qualify as the beneficiary? If it does, can it still carry out the general charitable purpose for which the trust was intended? Cy pres is often applied when a testamentary charitable trust has been established in favor of a corporation or institution that ceases to exist by the time of the testator's death. . . . We note that Ricker was a functioning institution at the time of Mrs. Knox's death, and that a bequest speaks as of the time of the testatrix's death. See Pushor v. Hilton, 123 Me. 225, 227, 122 A. 673, 673 (1923). Moreover, while Ricker College is bankrupt, no longer maintains a physical campus, and has no faculty or students, its corporate existence continues. The trustees retain the power to receive, to hold, and to disburse assets. As discussed at oral argument, there is no evidence that Ricker's corporate existence will in any way change or be dissolved in the future. In addition, the Knox will does not suggest a clear attachment to Ricker, the college, as opposed to Ricker, the corporation. See State v. Rand, 366 A.2d 183, 196 (Me. 1976). Instead, the bequest was made "unto Ricker Classical Institute and Ricker College, a corporation organized and existing under the laws of the State of Maine and maintaining an educational institution at Houlton. . . ." The Ricker corporation possesses the legal capability of accepting the Knox bequest. We conclude, therefore, that the trust does not fail, and the doctrine of cy pres need not be applied, based upon any want of a qualified, existing beneficiary.

Nevertheless, at oral argument the counsel for Bates, Bowdoin and Colby Colleges argued that Ricker's continuing corporate existence was not necessarily determinative. Instead, they contend, the issue is whether Ricker, in its present form, is capable of carrying out the purpose of the bequest. We agree with that posture of the issue. We emphasize that the Knox will sought to establish a trust fund at Ricker the income from which would be used for "such general purposes of said Institution as the Board of Trustees of said Institution may determine." The language of the will is determinative.

We note that the testamentary language refers to the "general purposes of said Institution," having referred earlier to "Ricker Classical Institute and Ricker College, *a corporation* organized and existing under the laws of the State of Maine and maintaining an educational institution at Houlton. . . ." (emphasis added). The referee interpreted the will's language to mean "general (college) purposes." He assumed, therefore, that "the demise of Ricker College as a functional education institution . . . made it impossible to make the trust operative in its precise terms." We disagree. We consider instead the relevant general purposes of Ricker to be among those enunciated by the Legislature at various times through Ricker's history: "to promote the cause of education," P. & S.L. 1847, ch. 10; . . . and to furnish "the opportunity for a college education at modest cost to great numbers of deserving youths of Aroostook County." P. & S.L. 1955, ch. 42.

The trustees' proposal to use the trust income to provide scholarships to Aroostook area students is fully consistent with these general purposes. The referee erred in concluding that the trustees could not, without a functioning college, carry out the testatrix's intent. . . . A resort to cy pres would tend to defeat, rather than further, the general charitable intent expressed in the Knox will, . . . and application of the doctrine under the circumstances of this case was therefore error as a matter of law. . . .

Remanded to the Superior Court for further proceedings consistent with the opinion herein.

RESTATEMENT (SECOND) OF TRUSTS

§399. . . . If property is given in trust to be applied to a particular charitable purpose, and it is or becomes impossible or impracticable or illegal to carry out the particular purpose, and if the settlor manifested a more general intention to devote the property to charitable purposes, the trust will not fail but the court will direct the application of the property to some charitable purpose which falls within the general charitable intention of the settlor.

§400. . . . If property is given upon trust to be applied to a particular charitable purpose, and the purpose is fully accomplished without exhausting the trust property, and if the settlor manifested a more general intention to devote the whole of the trust property to charitable purposes, there will not be a resulting trust of the surplus, but the court will direct the application of the surplus to some charitable purpose which falls within the general charitable intention of the settlor.

According to generally accepted principles, cy pres may be exercised even though it is possible to carry out the particular trust specified by the settlor if the court finds that it would be "impracticable" to do so, in the sense that the settlor's intention would not be fulfilled by adhering to his specified purpose. As long as the purpose specified by the settlor is both legal and practicable, however, that purpose must be carried out even though the court recognizes that another purpose would be more useful. The line, of course, can be a difficult one to draw. Statutes in several states seemingly provide a more liberal standard for the exercise of cy pres. See, e.g., Minn. Stat. Ann. §501B.31 (circumstances so changed since execution of the instrument as to render literal compliance "impracticable, *inexpedient* or impossible") and Wis. Stat. §701.10 (purpose is or becomes "*impractical,* unlawful or impossible," or administrative provision is or becomes "*impractical,* unlawful, *inconvenient* or *undesirable,*" or if size of trust is or becomes "uneconomic" or less than $50,000) (emphasis added). Some commentators have advocated a broadening of the cy pres doctrine. See, e.g., Sisson, Relaxing the Dead Hand's Grip: Charitable Efficiency and the Doctrine of Cy Pres, 70 Va. L. Rev. 635 (1988). Compare J. Macey, Private Trusts for the Provision of Private Goods, 37 Emory L. Rev. 295 (1988) (arguing that cy pres should be limited because the attempt to discern the settlor's intention involves risk of error and increased transaction costs).

If a particular charitable purpose fails or the funds for its accomplishment are excessive, a provision in the trust instrument for disposition of the property or the surplus will be controlling. Typically no such provision is made because the situation was not contemplated by the settlor. Consequently it is frequently difficult to determine whether a resulting trust arises for the settlor, or for the settlor's next of kin or residuary legatees, or whether the doctrine of cy pres is applicable. It is generally said that this depends on whether the settlor had a "general charitable purpose." The mere fact that the terms of the trust provide for application of the funds to a particular charitable purpose and no other, or that the funds are given upon condition that they be applied to a specified purpose, is not controlling.

In re Scott's Will, 8 N.Y.2d 419, 171 N.E.2d 326 (1960), involved a remainder "to St. Thomas' Church in the City of New York, for the purpose of erecting and maintaining . . . buildings for the care of persons suffering from tuberculosis to be called the Scott Memorial Home." At the termination of the life estates the testamentary trustee petitioned for a determination of the effect of this provision. The parties to the proceeding, including the attorney general, agreed that modern methods of treating tuberculosis no longer require special hospitals and that at current costs the funds were inadequate to erect and maintain an appropriate building. The Surrogate, later affirmed by the Appellate Division, had directed a modification of the terms of the disposition to provide a Scott Memorial Fund to be used "for the care of persons suffering from respiratory and thoracic diseases." The church appealed on the ground that the funds should be applied to the purposes of the church. The court of appeals decided that the testator's intention is a matter of law where it is to be determined from the terms of the will and undisputed surrounding circumstances and that it could review the Surrogate's exercise of cy pres. The court of appeals found the Surrogate's exercise improper but declined to substitute its judgment for that of the court below, remanding for the Surrogate to exercise the power with appropriate respect for all three of the basic purposes of the testator: a memorial building in his name, to be erected by St. Thomas's Church, for the aid of tuberculosis patients. Three judges dissented on the ground that the discretion inherent in the exercise of cy pres had not been abused by the lower court.

BURR v. BROOKS
75 Ill. App. 3d 80, 393 N.E.2d 1091 (1979)

GREEN, J. . . .

The dispute arises because the will provides [both for a primary charitable trust and] for an alternate charitable trust, and literal compliance with either the primary or alternate charitable trust is not possible or practical.

The City [which is interested in the primary trust purpose] seeks to avoid [arguing] a cy pres theory by asserting that its proposals should have been accepted under the doctrine of "equitable deviation." As with cy pres this doctrine is applicable when literal compliance with the terms of the trust endowment is impractical, illegal or impossible. This power is distinguishable from cy pres in that the former is applicable to all trusts and can be applied where the settlor manifests a specific as well as a general charitable intent. (15 Am. Jur. 2d Charities §§157 and 164 (1976).) The two doctrines are further distinguished by the statement in comment (a) to Restatement (Second) of Trusts §381 (1959) that equitable deviation concerns the administration of the trust while cy pres permits the application of the trust proceeds to purposes other than those provided for in the trust instrument.

A general rule has developed that the cy pres doctrine cannot be applied where the settlor provides for an alternate use of the trust corpus if the primary purpose fails or is refused, but it is clear that "equitable deviation" is permissible even though such an alternate use has been stated. . . .

The proposals of the City here are more . . . than merely a matter of administration as described in the comment to §381 of the Restatement. . . .

Accordingly, we are required to consider the general rule that a cy pres application of charitable trust funds may not be made if there is an alternate charitable gift. . . . [I]n all cases cited by the parties, the alternate trust was capable of being performed literally. Under those circumstances, the general rule makes sense. . . . [But] logic requires a different interpretation of the rule when a trust instrument (1) provides for a primary and alternate charitable gift *neither* of which can be carried out, and (2) also indicates a strong desire that the charitable interest of the document be followed. . . .

[Accordingly, the requested cy pres modification of the primary trust purpose is granted.]

UNIFORM TRUST CODE
(Draft, Feb. 2000)

§412. *Cy Pres.*

(a) Except as otherwise provided in subsection (b), if a particular charitable purpose becomes unlawful, impracticable, impossible to achieve, or wasteful:

    (1) the trust does not fail, in whole or in part;

    (2) the trust property does not revert to the settlor or the settlor's successors in interest; and

(3) the court may modify or terminate the trust by directing that the trust property be applied or distributed in whole or in part, in a manner consistent with the settlor's charitable purposes.

(b) The power of the court under subsection (a) to apply cy pres or to modify or terminate a charitable trust is subject to a contrary provision in the terms of the trust that would result in distribution of the trust property to a noncharitable beneficiary only if fewer than twenty-one years have elapsed since the date of the trust's creation.

PROBLEM

15-D. Some years ago an alumnus died devising a portfolio of securities "to the Dean of State University Law School in trust for the sole and exclusive purpose of providing scholarships for poor, white, male law students from Poverty County." The current dean has had the school's records searched and has learned that, on average, only two students from Poverty County have been enrolled in the law school at any given time, and that, on average, only one of them would qualify for the scholarships. As a result of appreciation in value and accumulation of unexpended income, the value of the trust fund now exceeds $10 million and the annual income is about $225,000. The dean asks your advice about the potential issues and the practical and legal alternatives involved. Would your advice be affected if Uniform Trust Code §412, above, were the governing law? Would your advice differ if a private university or a bank trustee were involved?

D. Supervision of Charitable Trusts

Although only the beneficiaries have the right to enforce a private trust, the indefiniteness of the beneficiaries of a typical charitable trust poses special problems. Suit to enforce a charitable trust is brought by or in the name of the attorney general, or, in a few states, by some local official such as the county attorney. This power of the attorney general exists even in the absence of a statute so providing.

The attorney general must typically be made a party to any action brought by another person or organization to enforce, construe, modify, or determine the validity of a charitable trust.

One who is entitled to a specific benefit, other than the general benefit of members of the community, may maintain a suit for enforcement of a charitable trust. A trustee may also enforce the trust against a cotrustee and may bring suit for instructions or to have the terms of the trust construed. A person who has no special interest in the performance of the trust — and this category includes the settlor or his representatives, according to the majority of decisions — cannot maintain a suit to enforce a charitable trust. Such a person can only hope to induce action by the attorney general. See Restatement (Second) of Trusts §391; Carl J. Herzog Foundation v. University of Bridgeport, 243 Conn. 1, 699 A.2d 995 (1997). But cf. Uniform Trust Code §706 (draft, Feb. 2000) authorizing the settlor of a trust to petition for the removal of a trustee.

Unfortunately, busy attorneys general and their staffs do not always satisfactorily discharge their general obligations concerning charitable trusts, nor do they always respond to legitimate pleas for action on the part of interested citizens. This presents practical difficulties of supervision of and performance by trustees and foundation boards. Perceived abuses by charitable donors and boards have led to various state law and post-1950 federal tax law restrictions on "unreasonable" accumulations. The 1969 Tax Reform Act and subsequent federal legislation have sought, with varying degrees of effectiveness, to address other political concerns about abuses of charitable trusts and their tax status.

In the way just mentioned and others, the procedures for enforcing and supervising charitable trusts are often uncertain or inadequate. In a number of states patchwork or comprehensive legislation is being enacted to clarify procedures and to improve enforcement of charitable trust law and nonprofit corporation codes. For example, versions of the Uniform Supervision of Trustees for Charitable Purposes Act have been enacted in four states, California, Illinois (in modified form), Michigan, and Oregon. This uniform act is somewhat similar to the New York legislation described in the Glasser excerpt below. Responding to press accounts of overly aggressive fundraising tactics and retention of excessive fees, a number of states have enacted statutes requiring various disclosures by professional fundraisers; some of these statutes have been held to be unconstitutional infringements of free speech. See IVA W. Fratcher, Scott on Trusts §349 (1997 Supp. to 4th Ed. 1987, and 1997 Supp. with M. Ascher). Also, in recent years legislation has been enacted in some states to facilitate compliance with the requirements of Internal Revenue Code §508(e) added by the Tax Reform Act of 1969. (In general, these latter statutes provide for distribution of income annually and set out prohibitions against self-dealing, excessive compensation, excess business holdings, and the making of certain investments and expenditures.)

At this point it is worthwhile at least to note the potentially serious risks facing clients (and lawyers, for that matter) who serve, often almost casually, as trustees or as members of boards of trustees or directors for charitable trusts, associations, foundations, and like institutions. Charitable entities — especially the smaller ones — are frequently operated, with the best of intentions, in an informal and excessively lax manner, with inadequate accounting procedures and inadequate attention to legal requirements and sound business practices. The absence of reliable public or private monitoring often makes it easy for part-time, civic-minded volunteers to participate unwittingly in breaches of trust. Essentially, the rules of fiduciary conduct and liability to be studied hereafter, primarily in the context of decedents' estates and private trusts, apply to uncompensated charitable trustees, whose outlook and behavior patterns often reflect little or no awareness of their obligations and risks.

GLASSER, TRUSTS, PERPETUITIES, ACCUMULATIONS AND POWERS UNDER THE ESTATES, POWERS AND TRUSTS LAW
33 Brooklyn L. Rev. 551, 562-563 (1967)

[N]ew legislation, which confers upon the attorney general broad supervisory powers over charities, has been incorporated into [New York's] EPTL as section 8-1.4. In broad outline, the new statute requires the attorney general to maintain a register of trustees containing such information as he deems appropriate. For the purpose of establishing and maintaining that register, the attorney general may conduct such investigations and examine such documents as he deems necessary. Every trustee is required to file with the attorney general the instrument from which he derives his title, powers and duties. The attorney general must be notified of any action or proceeding in which the disposition for charitable purposes may be affected. Trustees are required to file periodic written reports (for which filing fees are to be paid) disclosing the assets held and how they are administered. The failure of a trustee to register or file reports may justify his removal from office. The register, instruments and reports which are filed shall be available for public inspection, subject to stated exceptions. The attorney general may investigate the administration of such trusts and is given the power of subpoena and the power to administer oaths to facilitate any investigation he may make. He may also institute proceedings to secure compliance with the new law and to secure the proper administration of the trust.

A. SCOTT, TRUSTS, ABRIDGEMENT
(1960)

§348.1. *Charitable Corporations.* . . . Certainly many of the principles applicable to charitable trusts are applicable to charitable corporations. In both cases the Attorney General can maintain a suit to prevent a diversion of the property to other purposes than those for which it was given; and in both cases the doctrine of cy pres is applicable. . . .

It is not infrequently stated in the cases that a charitable corporation does not hold upon a charitable trust property conveyed or bequeathed to it. In fully as many cases, however, it is stated that a charitable corporation holds its property in trust. It is sometimes said that a charitable corporation holds property in trust if the property is to be used only for a particular charitable purpose or if only the income is to be used.

A charitable corporation certainly does not hold its property beneficially in the same sense in which an individual or noncharitable corporation can hold it beneficially, since in the case of a charitable corporation the Attorney General can maintain a suit to prevent a diversion of the property from the purposes for which it was given. Where property is conveyed to a charitable corporation, a provision restricting the use of the property to a particular purpose, or a provision that only the income of the property shall be used, is binding and enforceable at the suit of the Attorney General.

Where property is left by will to a charitable corporation, whether it may be used for the general purposes of the corporation or whether the devise or bequest is subject to restrictions as to its use, and the property is conveyed by the executor to the corporation, the corporation is not thereafter bound to account as if it were a testamentary trustee. The situation is quite different from that which arises where property is left by will to individual trustees, or to a trust company, charged with a duty to make the property productive and to pay the income to a charitable corporation.

E.   Community Foundations, Charitable Gift Funds, and Other Charitable Giving Arrangements

An often-useful alternative to a settlor-created charitable trust, corporation or foundation, particularly where modest amounts are involved, is a gift or devise to a *community foundation*, sometimes referred to as a community trust. Community foundations exist in most large and many medium-sized communities and are designed, inter alia, to avoid the problem of outmoded charitable purposes. The foundation itself is treated as a "public" charity for purposes of the Internal Revenue Code. A distribution committee chosen to represent the interests of the community administers the foundation and seeks to determine from time to time the most important charitable needs of the community, and applies the funds to those purposes. The donor may retain the right to advise the community foundation as to desired charitable recipients (a "donor-advised fund").

Another alternative, particularly for lifetime transfers, is a donation to a *charitable gift fund* established and administered by a mutual fund company. The first of these was the Fidelity Charitable Gift Fund, established in 1992 by Fidelity Investments of Boston and qualified with the IRS as a public charity. Donors to such funds receive an immediate tax deduction for their contributions, often giving low-basis stock to receive a deduction for those stocks' fair market value without capital gains tax on the excess value over the donor's basis. Donors are allowed to direct investment among a menu of mutual funds managed by the company. In a donor-advised fund, amounts may then be distributed from time to time to charities "suggested" by the donor, who cannot *control* the specific charitable distributees without running afoul of various tax law restrictions. Funds have been quite responsive to donor suggestions, however, and the right to advise the fund may be transferred during life or by will.

Because of the nature and success of this innovation, charitable gift funds have not been free from controversy. Community foundations have feared that these funds will siphon donations away from the foundations, given the marketing and investment expertise of mutual fund companies.[5] (Charitable gift funds are not purely eleemosynary, sometimes producing combined annual administration and management fees as high as two percent.) Questions have also been raised concerning the qualification of these funds as *public* charities, given the near-universal honoring (at least by some funds) of donor "advice" on distributees and the lack of assurance that recipients are qualified charities, or even about the possibility that distributions are being made in satisfaction of donor pledges (thus arguably resulting in debt-satisfaction income). Some funds have instituted controls to ameliorate these concerns, and the IRS has imposed stricter standards on subsequent mutual fund applicants for public charity status.

The financial benefits and simplicity of charitable gift funds suggest that they will continue to be significant players in the world of charitable giving. These funds also enable donors to enjoy many of the advantages of *private foundations* without the onerous regulations imposed on private foundations by the 1969 Tax Reform Act.[6] The success of these funds has led some to claim that they will democratize charitable giving, much as mutual funds have democratized investing. See generally S. Pinkerton, Estate Planning Making Teachers Smile: You Don't Have

5. At latest report, the Fidelity fund was receiving over $500 million per year in contributions, making it the third largest charity in the United States in terms of annual donations, and has a total corpus currently approaching $2 billion.

6. Responding to concerns about private foundation abuses of their tax status, Congress levied a 2 percent excise tax on investment income, required that the private foundation pay out at least 5 percent of the value of its assets per year, and required a detailed annual tax return, all combining to make private foundations expensive to create and administer. Nevertheless, see R. Silk, When Is a Private Foundation an Appropriate Strategy?, 27 Est. Plan. 87 (Feb. 2000).

to Be a Billionaire to Start a Foundation — or Its Equivalent — in
the Form of a Donor-Advised Fund, Forbes, June 14, 1999, at 334; M.
Langley, Give and Take: You Don't Have to Be a Rockefeller to Set up
Your Own Foundation, Wall St. J., Feb. 12, 1998, at A1 (this article
triggered controversy over the Fidelity Charitable Gift Fund).

A number of other currently used charitable arrangements are motivated, or at least their specifics dominated, by tax considerations. *Charitable gift annuities* are investment-donation hybrids set up by charities
that provide steady lifetime income to donors. *Pooled-income funds* are
also set up by charities to pool gifts of various donors, who receive
lifetime income based on the fund's performance. The popular *split-
interest charitable trusts* are of two types: charitable remainder trusts and
charitable lead trusts. In the *charitable remainder trust,* the donor retains
either the right annually to a specified amount (a charitable *annuity*
trust) or a specified percentage of the trust's worth valued annually (a
charitable *unitrust*), with remainder to charity after a specified period
or on the donor's death. A *charitable lead trust* is the inverse of the charitable remainder trust: the charity receives an annuity or unitrust stream
of payments for a specified number of years, with reversion or remainder to the donor or to the donor's successors or designated beneficiaries. Split-interest trusts are popular vehicles for gifts of retirement plan
benefits, given the almost confiscatory combination of income and estate taxes on qualified plan distributions that do not pass to a surviving
spouse and thereby qualify for the estate tax marital deduction.

F.   Some Further Observations

R. POSNER, ECONOMIC ANALYSIS OF LAW
508-511 (4th ed. 1992)

The character of the [dead hand and cy pres problems] is illustrated
by a controversy over a park donated to the City of Macon, Georgia by
[Senator] Augustus Bacon [see Evans v. Newton and notes thereafter,
section B, supra]. . . .

At first glance, the result may appear to vindicate the policy of enforcing testators' desires as revealed by the conditions in bequests. But on
closer examination this becomes doubtful. Senator Bacon may have
inserted the racial condition to induce the city to administer the park.
There is no indication that the dominant purpose of the gift was to
foster racial segregation rather than to provide a recreational facility
for the people of Macon. Bacon was a liberal person by the standards
of his time, and it is plausible therefore that if he could be consulted
on the matter today, when racial attitudes are different, he would pre-

fer that the park remain a park, albeit open to nonwhites, rather than that his distant heirs subdivide the property for residential or commercial use. . . .

As the case suggests, the dilemma of whether to enforce the testator's intent or to modify the terms of the will in accordance with changed conditions since his death is often a false one. A policy of rigid adherence to the letter of the donative instrument is likely to frustrate both the donor's purposes and the efficient use of resources. In the Macon case itself no serious efficiency issue was involved since . . . if the land was more valuable as a park than in an alternative use the city could always purchase it back from the heirs . . .

. . . [S]ince no one can foresee the future, a rational donor knows that his intentions might eventually be thwarted by unpredictable circumstances and may therefore be presumed to accept implicitly a rule permitting modification of the terms of the bequest in the event that an unforeseen change frustrates his original intention. The presumption is not absolute. Some rational donors, mistrustful of judicial capacity intelligently to alter the terms of the bequest in light of changed conditions, might prefer to assume the risks involved in rigid adherence to the original terms. Should their desire be honored? . . .

The *cy pres* doctrine is reasonably well designed to avoid frustration of the donor's intentions and could have been used in the Macon park case to justify disregarding the racial condition. True, the interest in efficiency, narrowly conceived, would be as well or better served by a rule providing that when enforcement of the conditions of a gift becomes either unlawful or uneconomical, the gift lapses and the property [reverts], thus vesting the property in a living owner free to apply it to its most valuable use. . . . But this approach may ultimately be an inefficient one because it would (1) reduce the incentive to accumulate wealth, by making it virtually impossible to create a perpetual charity with reasonably well-defined purposes, and (2) discourage the establishment of charitable trusts. If, however, the donor had specified in his will that under no conditions would he wish the terms of the gift altered — that in such a case he would prefer that the property go to the residuary legatees — would there be any economic justification for application of the *cy pres* doctrine? . . .

Even where no unforeseen contingencies occur, perpetual charitable gifts raise an economic issue. . . . A charitable foundation that enjoys a substantial income, in perpetuity, from its original endowment is an institution that does not compete in any product market or in the capital markets and that has no stockholders. Its board of trustees is self-perpetuating and is accountable to no one (except itself) for the performance of the enterprise. (Although state attorneys general have legal authority over the administration of charitable trusts, it is largely formal.) At the same time, neither the trustees nor the staff have the kind of property right in the foundation's assets or income that would generate a strong incentive for them to maximize value. Neither the carrot nor the stick is in play.

The incentives to efficient management of foundation assets could be strengthened by a rule requiring charitable foundations to distribute every gift received, principal and interest, including the original endowment, within a specified period of years. The foundation would not be required to wind up its operations within the period; it could continue indefinitely. But it would have to receive new gifts from time to time in order to avoid exhausting all of its funds. Since donors are unlikely to give money to an enterprise known to be slack, the necessity of returning periodically to the market for charitable donations would give trustees and managers of charitable foundations an incentive they now lack to conduct a tight operation. Foundations — mostly religious and educational — that market their services or depend on continuing charitable support, and are therefore already subject to some competitive constraints, could be exempted from the exhaustion rule. . . .

Compare Ross, Let's Not Fence in the Foundations, Fortune, June 1969, at 148, 166-172:

> One of the great virtues of foundations is the broad charter now permitted them in law. Their freedom is essential to their leavening role in society. They must be free to pioneer, to aid projects that lack majority support, indeed to aid unpopular causes. Without such freedom there would be little point in maintaining private philanthropy. . . .
>
> This plea for freedom embraces only the program area of foundations. But when it comes to the financial operations of foundations, there is a compelling case for tighter government regulations. In this area many abuses have occurred, particularly on the part of small foundations. The more blatant abuses can be reached by present law. . . . In general, however, the [pre-1969] Internal Revenue Code has been too permissive. It does not deal, for example, with the conflict between public and private interest that [sometimes] arises. . . .

Also compare Calkins, The Role of the Philanthropic Foundation, 11 Foundation News 1-13 (1970) (paper delivered shortly before the Tax Reform Act of 1969 was enacted):

> The philanthropic foundation during this century has been an important innovative force in the life of this country and throughout much of the free world. . . .
>
> The foundations which have had the greatest impact on American life are the large general and special purpose foundations which make over 60 percent of the grants. . . . Their object is not charity, or the alleviation

of distress by palliatives, but the correction of evils through discovery, knowledge, and innovation, through which important correctives may be achieved. They are not operated to maintain existing institutions, or to finance what others will finance, but to pioneer. . . . Thus their search is ceaseless for those who with financial help may achieve objectives of wide import and impact. . . .

In the Congressional haste . . . there is danger that the role of foundations in advancing the public good may be overlooked. It is well, therefore, to remind ourselves of some of the many achievements that foundations have helped to bring about. . . .

One of the greatest virtues of the American foundation system is that it reinforces and contributes to our pluralistic society. . . . To curb the creation of new foundations and to impose life terms on all would in time place innovation and innovators largely at the mercy of governmental financing. That the welfare of this country and mankind would be better served in this way, I leave to your judgment. My own view is that it would not.

16

Introduction to Fiduciary
Administration

During the administration of a decedent's estate or trust, the drafting skill of the estate planner is put to its most stringent test, for this is the period in which most of the provisions must be put into effect. In the case of a will, this is when the validity of the instrument is determined, and then its directions must be carried out while coping with administrative requirements. In the case of a trust, over the period of administration the trustee will encounter a number of specific problems, some inherently troublesome and others arising out of changed circumstances that can be anticipated only in a general way.

Even though the general purposes of estate and trust administration differ, there are so many common aspects of the fiduciary relationships that treating them together is desirable for purposes of comparison and contrast. As you begin now to study these matters you should review, quickly at least, that portion of Chapter 1, sections E3 and E4, that tells the story of an estate and trust administration. This should help place the portions of the course ahead into context; section E3 should be particularly helpful as background for your necessarily piecemeal study of the administration of decedent's estates.

A. Function and Necessity of Administration

In the estate of any decedent, intestate as well as testate, it is necessary to go through a liquidation process, that is, winding up the property and business affairs of the deceased. This process, whether formal or informal, is essentially one of collecting and conserving the assets of the deceased, paying from the assets all debts and charges thereon, and making the distribution that is proper. More specifically, formal estate administration involves publicizing the fact of the decedent's death; discovering and collecting assets; determining and paying the taxes, debts, and funeral expenses of the decedent, and the administration expenses of the estate; determining and making distribution to persons entitled to receive the property under the decedent's will or by operation of law; and, throughout this process, managing estate assets.

Many problems similar to those of decedent's estates arise in administering trust estates, but the basic purpose differs. Rather than being a liquidating process, the general purpose of trust administration is securing efficient management of assets to provide continuing benefit to the family. In a testamentary trust, administration of the trust begins with distribution to the trustee, generally after the full cycle of estate administration has been completed.

Because of the differences of function, the possible liability of a fiduciary who is named to serve both as executor and as trustee may depend on whether certain acts were performed in the former or the latter capacity. For example, if the fiduciary, without negligence, invests funds of the estate and a loss is incurred, liability may depend on whether there was authority to invest at all at the time. The capacity in which the fiduciary acted may be decisive, since a trustee's function is to make the estate productive by investment while an executor generally has no inherent power to invest. Assuming the power to invest is not expressly conferred on an executor by will or by statute, the fiduciary must prove (1) that the investment was made in the capacity of trustee, which normally must be preceded by some overt act such as the settling of accounts as executor in the probate court, or (2) that the power to invest is implied from the dual capacity or from other facts, such as that the estate will remain open for a considerable period of time. For an interesting case involving questions of these types, see Estate of Beach, 15 Cal. 3d 623, 542 P.2d 994 (1975).

Model Probate Code §133, which influenced the legislation in many states during the 1950s and 1960s, authorized the personal representative to make investments of the kind permitted to trustees, subject to "his primary duty to preserve the estate for prompt distribution." See also Uniform Probate Code §§3-711 and 3-715(5).

AN OUTLINE OF TYPICAL STEPS IN THE
SETTLEMENT OF ESTATES

Preliminary Steps

Meet with family.

Review funeral arrangements and obtain proof of death.

Obtain and review will or ascertain fact of intestacy.

Ascertain and safeguard assets, notify banks, review books and records, and inquire into insurance and business interests.

Meet with others than family members who are interested in the estate, confer with persons familiar with decedent's legal and financial affairs (such as the attorney who drew the will), and locate witnesses to will.

Open Estate Administration

Probate will, if any, and obtain letters testamentary or of administration.

Issue Notice to Creditors.

Collect and Inventory Estate Assets

Obtain transfer of bank accounts, store or protect personal effects and furnishings, and obtain custody of securities.

Collect income, debts, and any insurance payable to estate.

Ascertain out-of-state assets (and the possible need for ancillary administration) and interests in trusts or other estates.

Inspect real estate (check mortgages, taxes) and look into leases and business ventures (collection of rents, arrange management, supervision, and representation in these activities).

Determine asset values, and obtain appraisals.

Prepare and file inventory of estate assets (note distinctions between assets to be accounted for and nonprobate assets or will substitutes for tax returns).

Claims and Taxes

Receive, analyze, and allow or disallow claims, to be paid in order of priority.

Obtain information about and file tax returns (decedent's final and estate's fiduciary income tax returns, federal and state death tax returns, and, if applicable, final year's or even overdue gift tax returns); pay taxes in a timely manner; obtain releases or waivers; and handle audits and possible assessments or tax controversies.

Management of Estate Assets

Determine liquidity requirements (debts, family allowance, administration expenses, taxes, and legacies).

Analyze, safeguard, and manage investments, including securities (sale or retention in light of authority and responsibilities under will or local law and market necessities/opportunities), real estate (sale or supervision), and business interests (liquidation, sale or retention, and supervision in light of fiduciary authority and duties).

Fund cash needs through sales or otherwise (including possible borrowing from or sales to recipients of insurance proceeds, especially life insurance trusts).

Accounting and Distribution

Determine rights and needs of beneficiaries.

Prepare and submit accountings (receipts, disbursements, principal/ income allocations), interim and final, in or out of court, as appropriate.

Determine the need or desirability, and the nature and timing, of allowance payments and possible preliminary distributions (including their tax effects and whether they should be in cash or in kind) with respect to bequests and devises, including residuary and trust interests; make distributions during administration accordingly.

Plan and make final distributions; obtain receipts and releases.

In section C of Chapter 9 we considered some of the important reasons for having property administered under a trust. The materials that follow are concerned with some of the quite different reasons for having a decedent's estate formally administered.

Creditors. The law relating to the administration of decedent's estates has always reflected a strong policy to protect creditors of the decedent who have usually contributed, indirectly at least, to the assets of the estate. Although this policy that a decedent should be just before being generous gives creditors priority over gratuitous distributees, it does conflict with those policies calling for protection of the family and for prompt, secure distribution of assets to those next entitled. The resolution of these policy conflicts are reflected in nonclaim statutes, as well as in those (see Chapter 3, supra) providing homestead rights and family allowances.

UNIFORM PROBATE CODE

§3-801. *Notice to Creditors.*

(a) Unless notice has already been given under this section, a personal representative upon appointment [may] [shall] publish a notice to creditors once a week for three successive weeks in a newspaper of general circulation in the [county] announcing the appointment and the personal representative's address and notifying creditors of the estate to present their claims within four months after the date of the first publication of the notice or be forever barred.

(b) A personal representative may give written notice by mail or other delivery to a creditor, notifying the creditor to present his [or her] claim within four months after the published notice, if given as provided in subsection (a), or within 60 days after the mailing or other delivery of the notice, whichever is later, or be forever barred. Written notice must be the notice described in subsection (a) above or a similar notice.

(c) The personal representative is not liable to a creditor or to a successor of the decedent for giving or failing to give notice under this section.

§3-802. *Statutes of Limitations.*

(a) Unless an estate is insolvent, the personal representative, with the consent of all successors whose interests would be affected, may waive any defense of limitations available to the estate. If the defense is not waived, no claim barred by a statute of limitations at the time of the decedent's death may be allowed or paid.

(b) The running of a statute of limitations measured from an event other than death or the giving of notice to creditors is suspended for four months after the decedent's death, but resumes thereafter as to claims not barred by other sections.

(c) For purposes of a statute of limitations, the presentation of a claim pursuant to Section 3-804 is equivalent to commencement of a proceeding on the claim.

§3-803. *Limitations on Presentation of Claims.*

(a) All claims against a decedent's estate which arose before the death of the decedent, including claims of the state and any subdivision thereof, whether due or to become due, absolute or contingent, liquidated or unliquidated, founded on contract, tort, or other legal basis, if not barred earlier by another statute of limitations or non-claim statute, are barred against the estate, the personal representative, and the heirs and devisees of the decedent, unless presented within the earlier of the following:

(1) one year after the decedent's death; or

(2) the time provided by Section 3-801 (b) for creditors who are given actual notice, and within the time provided in 3-801 (a) for all creditors barred by publication.

(b) A claim described in subsection (a) which is barred by the non-claim statute of the decedent's domicile before the giving of notice to creditors in this State is barred in this State.

(c) All claims against a decedent's estate which arise at or after the death of the decedent, including claims of the state and any subdivision thereof, whether due or to become due, absolute or contingent, liquidated or unliquidated, founded on contract, tort, or other legal basis, are barred against the estate, the personal representative, and the heirs and devisees of the decedent, unless presented as follows:

(1) a claim based on a contract with the personal representative, within four months after performance by the personal representative is due; or

(2) any other claim, within the later of four months after it arises, or the time specified in subsection (a)(1).

(d) Nothing in this section affects or prevents:

(1) any proceeding to enforce any mortgage, pledge, or other lien upon property of the estate;

(2) to the limits of the insurance protection only, any proceeding to establish liability of the decedent or the personal representative for which he is protected by liability insurance; or

(3) collection of compensation for services rendered and reimbursement for expenses advanced by the personal representative or by the attorney or accountant for the personal representative of the estate.

Many nonclaim statutes do not apply, as the above does, to claims of the state and its subdivisions or to claims arising at or after death. Applicability to the state might be especially significant where the state seeks reimbursement from the estate for Medicaid payments or other old age assistance benefits. Subsequent sections spell out the methods of presenting (including by commencing an action within the claim period), allowing, paying, and compromising claims. Section 3-810 provides that unmatured, contingent, and unliquidated claims may be paid at their present (discounted) or other agreed value, or that provision for future payment may be made by retention of funds in trust or by the distributees' limited liability secured by lien or bond.

Section 3-805 specifies priorities among claimants of insolvent estates, giving the usual preferences to the expenses of administration, followed in order by funeral expenses, debts, and taxes preferred under federal law, last illness expenses, and then debts and taxes preferred under state laws.

Many statutes contain provisions allowing claimants who receive no notice "by reason of being out of the state" to present claims after the claim period but "before a decree of distribution is entered." Some offer other special and limited exceptions to the bar of the statute. See application of a statute exempting claims covered by liability insurance in Collier v. Connolley, 400 A.2d 1107 (Md. 1979), and application of a fairly broad statute allowing late filing without culpable neglect (while protecting recipients of prior distributions) in Hastoupis v. Gargas, 398 N.E.2d 745 (Mass. App. 1980).

Do due process requirements concerning the necessity and quality of notice apply to nonclaim statutes? See materials beginning with *Mullane* case infra.

PROBLEM

16-A.   *H* and his wife, *W*, executed mutual wills pursuant to a contract not to revoke. Under the wills and the agreement the property of the first of them to die was to pass to the survivor, and the survivor was to leave an estate as follows: one half was to go to *H*'s child, *C*, by a former marriage; the other one-half was to be divided between *S* and *D*, *W*'s two children by a prior marriage. *H* died leaving his estate to *W* as agreed. *H*'s net estate of $110,000 consisted of $50,000 cash in banks and a $60,000 parcel of real estate. On *W*'s later death eleven months ago her entire estate was left to *S* and *D* by the terms of a subsequent will. *W*'s estate is now about to be distributed in disregard of the contract. Inventoried in *W*'s net estate of $200,000 are the parcel of land she received from *H* and $10,000 in one of the bank accounts *H* had at death. Also in *W*'s estate were $70,000 in securities, a $20,000 piece of real estate, $10,000 worth of chattels, and $20,000 on deposit in another bank. *C* has not filed a claim in *W*'s estate and the statutory nonclaim period has expired. Can *C* now enforce his claim to half of the estate? How would you advise him to proceed and how would you argue his case? What arguments do you anticipate would be made in behalf of *S* and *D*? Compare O'Connor v. Immele, 77 N.D. 346, 43 N.W.2d 649 (1950), with Abrams v. Schlar, 27 Ill. App. 2d 237, 169 N.E.2d 583 (1960). Estate of Leavitt, 733 A.2d 348 (Me. 1999), rejected the frequent judicial exemption of "ownership" claims or constructive trust remedies, observing that "creative labeling" (as "an issue of title" rather than "a contractual claim") cannot relieve a claimant from the mandates of the Maine version of the UPC nonclaim statute.

Vanderpool v. Vanderpool, 48 Mont. 448, 453-455, 138 P. 772, 774 (1914), states:

> [T]he trial court proceeded upon the theory that if plaintiff was led into error in filing her claim, by the attorney for the estate, the estate itself is estopped to deny that the claim was presented as required by law. . . . The executor or administrator is in effect a trustee of the funds of the estate for the benefit of the creditors and heirs, and cannot waive any substantial right which materially affects their interest, and, for the same reason, cannot be estopped by his own conduct. He cannot, by failure to plead the statute of nonclaim. . . , preclude the heirs or other creditors of the estate from setting it up upon settlement of his accounts, and he renders himself personally liable for devastavit in case of payment of such a claim. While an equitable estoppel might be invoked as against an executor or administrator so far as his individual interest in the estate is concerned, it cannot operate to the prejudice of the heirs or other creditors. Even his misleading statements, his assurances or his conduct

which induces a creditor to omit compliance with the statute, will not operate to estop him from contesting the claim upon the ground of noncompliance. The reason for these rules ought to be manifest at once, and with reference to them there is substantial unanimity of opinion among the authorities. . . .

If [the claimant] has any cause of action which she can now assert, it must be one against Mr. Burleigh and not against this estate.

Thompson v. Owen, 249 Mass. 229, 144 N.E. 216 (1914), involved an action on a note that matured after the decedent's death. The executor gave notice of his appointment by posting and by publication in the local newspaper. After the executor's final accounting, the plaintiffs made application to the probate court to have the accounting reopened and to have assets retained to pay their claim, which had not been presented within the statutory period. Plaintiffs alleged that they had no knowledge of the debtor's death. The court stated:

> This. . . . is not a claim which "could not legally be presented to the Probate Court." Presentation of such claims at "any time before the estate is fully administered" is specifically provided for. . . . [A]s they neglected to do so, it follows that they cannot maintain a bill against the heirs, next of kin, devisees or legatees of the testator. Before the estate was fully administered they could have been given the relief afforded by §10 of the same chapter, if justice and equity so required. . . .
>
> It is strenuously urged by the plaintiffs that they are entitled to maintain the bill because they did not learn of the death of the decedent or of the appointment of the executor until after the estate had been fully administered; but there is no allegation that such want of information was due to any fraud or deception practised upon them. There is nothing in the statutes under which the bill is brought which gives the plaintiffs a remedy because of their failure seasonably to learn of the death of the decedent, or because they did not seasonably know of the taking out of administration.

249 Mass. at 233-234, 144 N.E. at 217-218.

Compare Estate of Pfaff, 41 Wis.2d 159, 163 N.W.2d 140 (1968), that an often routine will direction to pay "my just debts" required payment of just debts whether or not they were otherwise legally enforceable.

PROBLEM

16-B.   A friend and regular client of mine has just telephoned my secretary and has made an appointment to see me late this afternoon. Her mother, a widow, recently died. My client and her brother are the only children, and they are to receive everything under the will, which has not been probated. They would like to avoid probate proceedings and have worked out how they will divide the property, essentially equally as their mother's will provides.

My secretary's note says that my client stated: "Probate was a pointless nuisance, and a waste, when Dad died a few years ago." She also said that the estate was surely more than adequate to cover all her mother's debts and concluded:

> Even though I suppose I'll be told it's always possible we could be wrong, we have discussed the matter and will gladly take that risk. There's no one who might possibly question our right to the estate, and anyway we're prepared to run any risks of that sort as well. So, I'd like to know if there are any really good reasons for going through administration again.

We will no doubt be able to take care of tax returns without formal probate. Under these circumstances, are there any reasons why I should advise my client to go through formal proceedings? If so, what are they? In order to reach an informed judgment, what more will I need to know about the estate or other matters, and why? Consider the cases and notes in the rest of this section.

HEINZ v. VAWTER
221 Iowa 714, 266 N.W. 486 (1936)

[Millie Vawter died intestate and without issue in 1930, survived only by her husband, H. M. Vawter, and her father, Edward Heinz. No administration was had on her estate of about $11,300. Her husband took possession of her entire estate, paid all of her known debts and burial expenses aggregating about $1,900, and paid her father $2,000, for which Heinz signed a receipt "in full settlement of my distributive share as heir at law." Vawter retained the residue in satisfaction of his statutory rights. About four years later Heinz petitioned and was appointed to serve as administrator of his daughter's estate and brought suit against H. M. Vawter for the sum of $11,300 that it might be administered on. He alleges no fraud or overreaching.]

ANDERSON, J. . . .

[I]n the face of the facts as disclosed by the record in this case, there was no good reason for the appointment of an administrator. Under the statute the husband was entitled to $7,500.00 of the estate of his deceased wife. . . . [In paying his wife's debts and] making the payment to the father of $2,000 the husband used $114.57 of his own share of the estate, and the record further shows that some of the property of the deceased wife was turned over to the sisters of the deceased, to wit, a diamond ring and a fur coat; and a shotgun was turned over to the father, Edward Heinz; and that the father knew of the distribution, was present when it was made, and agreed and acquiesced therein. It appears conclusively by the record that at the time the father petitioned for his appointment as administrator of the estate of his daughter there was nothing to administer. All debts and expenses had been paid, and the entire estate disbursed and distributed. There was no expense whatever incident to the settlement of the estate by the husband. The father, having acknowledged the receipt in full of his distributive share in the estate, had no further interests therein. . . .

Where there are no debts and the property of an estate is such that it can be divided and the persons entitled thereto agree upon a division thereof, there is nothing either in law or reason to prevent them from settling and distributing the estate without the appointment of an administrator. . . .

Affirmed.

BROBST v. BROBST
190 Mich. 63, 155 N.W. 734 (1916)

[Action on a promissory note executed by the defendant payable to Almanda Adams, who died intestate in 1913. Plaintiff is a daughter of Mrs. Adams, whose other heirs assigned their interests in the note to the plaintiff. No administration was had of Mrs. Adams's estate. Uncontradicted testimony was given that there were no debts or claims against Mrs. Adams's estate, and judgment was given for the plaintiff. Exception by the defendant is on the ground that the plaintiff has not shown such title to the note as to authorize recovery by her on it.]

PERSON, J. . . .

It is unquestionably the law, as stated in Foote v. Foote, 61 Mich. 181, 28 N.W. 90, that:

> . . . When there are no creditors, the heirs or legatees may collect, if they can, the estate together, and make such distribution among themselves as they may agree to and carry into effect, without the intervention of any administrator; and the law favors such arrangements. . . .

And where there is no fraud or mistake, such an arrangement, particularly when carried into effect, will be binding upon the heirs and distributees; and, in the absence of creditors, they will be estopped from disturbing it by asking for the appointment of an administrator. Needham v. Gillett, 39 Mich. 574. The heirs themselves being bound by such settlement, and no creditors existing, there is no one with authority to question the distribution they may make; they are the equitable owners of the estate, and, in the absence of administration, there is no one to assert the legal title against them. It will be observed, however, that while this rule recognizes the right of the heirs and distributees to divide among themselves such property of the estate as may be in their possession, and such as they may be able to get into their possession, it does not recognize any authority upon their part, they not having the legal title, to enforce the payments of debts owing to the estate and unpaid.

Notwithstanding the right of heirs and distributees to make such arrangements among themselves, "It is well settled in this State that, on the decease of an intestate, the title (legal title) to his personal effects remains in abeyance until the appointment of an administrator, and then vests in him, in trust, in his official capacity, as of the time of the intestate's death, and he is entitled to the possession of such assets, and to manage the property for the purposes of his trust." Parks v. Norris, 101 Mich. 71, 59 N.W. 428. And, except under special circumstances, such administrator, or other personal representative, as holder of the legal title, is alone authorized to bring an action for the recovery of a debt due to the estate. . . .

If the heirs and distributees of an estate were entitled to receive and enforce payments of debts due the estate whenever it was believed that there were no creditors, then every debtor would be under the necessity of determining, at his peril, whether there were such creditors or not. And for a stranger to the estate to reach such a conclusion would ordinarily be no safe or assured matter. There might be debts depending upon a contingency that had not happened, or incurred in a fiduciary relation not falling within the bar of the statute of limitations. As was said in Powell v. Palmer, 45 Mo. App. 236:

> From the nature of the case, the proposition that there are no debts provable against the estate of a deceased person is therefore a negative proposition, which is not susceptible of absolute proof. No evidence which could be offered in support of such a proposition could go further than to reach a strong degree of probability. . . .

The judgment will be reversed, and a new trial granted.

In reversing the lower court's refusal to appoint an administrator on petition of a debtor who wished to pay his debt to the estate and receive discharge of the mortgage on his land, In re Collins' Estate, 102 Wash. 697, 698-700, 173 P. 1016, 1017 (1918), states:

> This court has held that a claim against an estate is not barred by lapse of time where no notice to creditors has been published as required by law. . . .
> So it is plain that there may be debts, and if there are. . . . such debts are not now barred, because no administrator has been appointed and

no notice to creditors has been published. . . . When the appellant pays
the note he is entitled to have the mortgage satisfied by one authorized
to do so, in order that he may not again be liable to pay the note or any
part thereof. . . . We are satisfied, therefore, that there is necessity for
the appointment of an administrator of this estate, in order that . . .
appellant's mortgage, when paid, may be legally satisfied.

In Matter of Estates of Thompson, 226 Kan. 437, 601 P.2d 1105
(1979), the parties did not find the will in question, but an executed
copy was in the files of the decedent's lawyer. The heirs and the sole
legatee under the will entered an agreement settling the rights to the
estate. Later the will was found, and the legatee petitioned for probate
and for a decree setting aside the settlement agreement on the basis
of mutual mistake. In enforcing the agreement and reversing the lower
court, the Kansas Supreme Court (at 442, 601 P.2d at 1109) stated that
"the parties clearly intended to resolve all disputes," and added:

> . . . They knew that a will had been written and executed. They were
> uncertain whether it had been revoked, destroyed, lost or merely mis-
> laid. . . . Appellee undoubtedly believed that an original will would not be
> found or he would not have agreed to the settlement. He was mistaken in
> his belief as to this uncertainty but relief will not be granted for a mistake
> in prophecy, opinion or in belief relative to an uncertain event. . . .
>
> [W]e have frequently stated that family settlement agreements are fa-
> vorites of the law and, when fairly made, are to be given liberal interpre-
> tation and should not be disturbed by those who entered into them or
> by those claiming under or through them. . . . In the instant case there is
> no claim of fraud, misrepresentation, concealment or other inequitable
> conduct. . . .

PROBLEM

16-C.   *T* died eighteen years ago survived by *D* as sole heir. No will
was found, and *D* went into possession of land owned by *T* at her death.
Eleven years after *T*'s death, *D* conveyed the land to *E* by warranty deed,
and two years later it was transferred by warranty deed to *P*. The following year a will was found and probated under which *T* devised the land
to *D* for life with remainder in fee to *D*'s children, *A* and *B*. Thereafter
P filed a bill to quiet title in him as an innocent purchaser free of any
claims of *A* and *B* and praying that their claims be removed as clouds
on his title. What are the arguments in behalf of *P*? What are the arguments for *A* and *B*? What result would you anticipate in absence of
statute? Under the laws of your state? (Consider the cases that follow.)
   Is there anything *P* might have done at the time of purchase to protect himself? Do the statutes of your state adequately meet the problems
raised under these and similar circumstances? If not, what statutory

provisions would you suggest to remedy the matter? See Uniform Probate Code §3-108 (limiting the time within which a will may be probated) and cf. §3-910 (protecting purchasers from distributees holding deeds from personal representatives). Consider Uniform Probate Code §3-312 (succession without administration).

MURPHREE v. GRIFFIS
215 Ala. 98, 109 So. 746 (1926)

[Action of ejectment, commenced in 1923. D. M. Murphree died in 1910 owning the land in question, which he devised to his widow. He left no children and was survived by his wife and by the plaintiffs, who are his heirs at law. In 1910 Murphree's widow conveyed the land to the defendant. The widow died in 1922. The will by which Murphree devised the land was not probated until 1925, when it was duly admitted to probate after notice to the heirs.]

MILLER, J. . . .

It is true, . . . "An instrument, testamentary in character, cannot be recognized as valid in any form until it has been admitted to probate." [But this is] not consistent with . . . Whorton v. Moragne, 62 Ala. 201, 207, in which this court said:

> At the common law, the authority and duty of an administrator extended only to personal assets. Lands descended immediately on the death of the ancestor to the heir, who was invested with the title and all its incidents. The title of an executor, if there was no devise of the lands to him, and no power over them conferred by the will of the testator, was also confined to the personal assets. Lands devised passed immediately on the death of the testator to the devisee. . . .

To prove [the widow's] title, it was necessary that the will should be probated; and, when duly probated, either before or after her death, it was evidence of her title, which was vested in her at the time of the testator's death, by this instrument. The title to his land of this devisee vested in her at the death of the testator; and not at the time of the probate of the will. The title cannot be kept in abeyance. The will and its probate are the proof of her title; and when probated it relates back to the death of the testator, so as to make valid whatever she had previously done with the land, which under the will, after probate, she could have lawfully done. . . .

[T]he title to the land sued for is in the defendant. . . .

Affirmed.

Where there is no statute limiting the time for probating a will, if a prior will has been admitted to probate and another will is thereafter discovered, what is the effect of a statute providing that a will that has been probated cannot be attacked or contested after a specified period of time, which has now expired? The cases are divided, but the prevalent view is that the probate of a second will is permissible as it is not a "contest" of the previously admitted will. Thus, it is reasoned, probate establishes the valid execution of the will but not that it was the *last* will of the testator. E.g., In re Bentley's Will, 175 Va. 456, 9 S.E.2d 308 (1940); 2 J. Woerner, The American Law of Administration §§217, 227 (3d ed. 1923). With certain exceptions, the view of *Bentley's Will* is rejected by the Uniform Probate Code. UPC §3-412(3)(iii) bars probate of any will that is offered more than one year after a formal testacy order or an order that the decedent left no will and determining heirs. UPC §3-108 places an ultimate three-year limit on a proceeding to probate a will. When a probate of a subsequent will revokes the order admitting a prior will to probate, bona fide purchasers from the devisees under the earlier will are generally protected if the time has expired within which the prior order could have been contested. See T. Atkinson, Wills §96 (2d ed. 1953).

SEIDEL v. SNIDER
241 Iowa 1227, 44 N.W.2d 687 (1950)

MANTZ, J.

Plaintiff's husband died intestate April 19, 1949, owning an [undivided] interest in common — not in joint tenancy in the premises involved here. The contract sought to be enforced is dated September 17, 1949, five months later. By it plaintiff, as vendor, agreed to furnish defendant, the purchaser, an abstract showing merchantable title of record. She later tendered one which showed various affidavits designed to serve in lieu of administration proceedings on her husband's estate, in order to show heirs, freedom from debts and the homestead character of the premises from date of their acquisition, November 17, 1944.

The one question presented is the sufficiency of such showing on the abstract to comply with the requirement of the contract as to "merchantable title," whether, within the five-year period allowed for administration, affidavits are competent to make of record for title purposes facts that are normally and properly shown by administration proceedings. . . .

Affidavits are not eligible to record except as provided by statute, Fagan v. Hook [134 Iowa 381, 388], 105 N.W. 155, 158. . . .

There is of course no law to compel resort to administration by the heirs and surviving spouse of an intestate decedent. The title to his property passes whether administered upon or not. Reichard v. Chicago, B & Q.R. Co., 231 Iowa 563, 578, 1 N.W.2d 721. The surviving spouse and heirs may agree among themselves to its distribution. Heinz v. Vawter, 221 Iowa 714, 716, 266 N.W. 486. But we are speaking here of the manner of making that devolution of title a matter of record so it may be properly reflected by an abstract.

Under the language of Code section 558.8 affidavits are recordable only to *explain* defects in the chain of title. To hold that affidavits are competent to be filed *in lieu* of administration proceedings during the time in which such proceedings can be instituted would make the statute a device to create defects rather than to explain them, to encourage omission of administration, thereby making defects to be "explained." That surely is not its purpose. Rather it is designed as a practical remedy for defects due to failure to follow orderly procedure when such procedure was available.

Our conclusion is somewhat based on judicial knowledge of the practice of lawyers to whom is usually entrusted the duty of examining abstracts and of advising clients as to the merchantability of title shown by them. That is perhaps the best index to the mental processes of purchasers of real estate as reasonably prudent men. Fortunately, at this point we have concrete justification for taking such judicial notice. The Title Standards Committee of our State Bar Association has adopted standards that would limit the use of affidavits in lieu of administration proceedings (in the case of decedents dying within the state) to cases where the affidavit shows:

(1) that the decedent died intestate at least five years prior [because there is a five-year limit on the commencement of original administration in Iowa]; (2) (applicable only to nonresident decedents); (3) that the estate of said decedent had not been administered upon; (4) that all debts and claims, including the expense of last sickness and burial, have been paid; (5) that the decedent was survived by the persons named in the affidavit, specifying their relationship to said decedent; and (6) such statements of the assets of decedent's estate, . . . and such statement of estate liabilities as to enable the title examiner to determine what further showing, if any, to require as to inheritance and estate taxes.

Iowa Land Title Examination Standards (1950), pages 47, 48 (problem 9.18). . . .

From all the foregoing it follows that plaintiff did not tender an abstract showing merchantable title of record and the decision of the trial court is accordingly reversed.

Reversed.

Although it is important to understand the purpose and necessity of putting a particular estate through administration under our existing law, awakened concern over the delivery and cost of legal services demands that we also ask what needs of society our present probate system serves. Can these requirements of our legal system be met by a fundamentally revised probate system, simplified and less costly to both society and the interested individuals? Indeed, can these functions be fulfilled, at least for normal estate situations, by a system that requires *no* fiduciary intervention and estate administration as we know it?

Most states now offer summary procedures for small estates. The Uniform Probate Code (§§3-1201 to 3-1204) provides examples of the two basic forms of collection by affidavit and summary distribution. The UPC affidavit limitation of $5,000 is surprisingly small. California, for example, allows up to $100,000 to be transferred by affidavit, Cal. Prob. Code §13100, and other statutory limits ranging up to that amount are common. Why might the UPC limit be so small, in view of the UPC's general thrust of minimizing judicial oversight? Both the UPC and California exclude realty from the assets collectible by affidavit. UPC §3-1201(a); Cal. Prob. Code §13115. The UPC rationalizes this exclusion on the ground that the Code's flexible system of administration makes it "unnecessary to frame complex provisions extending the affidavit procedures to land." UPC Art. III, Part 12, General Comment.

In addition to summary procedures, some states now offer other noteworthy opportunities for succession without administration. A limited opportunity of this type (applicable initially to community property and now to any property that passes outright to the surviving spouse) is authorized by California Probate Code §13650. The state of Washington has for many years had a statute allowing spouses to enter into an agreement with respect to the disposition of all or any part of their community property at death. Wash. Rev. Code §26.16.120. "The statute does not limit the parties to survivorship dispositions, nor in any other fashion (except for preserving the rights of creditors), and despite the lack of a definitive decision, the writer believes that any conceivable disposition not otherwise proscribed could be made, even cutting off the survivor entirely or vesting only a life interest in the survivor with remainders over, etc." Cross, The Community Property Law in Washington, 15 La. L. Rev. 640, 645 (1955). One study found that more married persons disposed of their property at death in this fashion than by any other method. Price, The Transmission of Property at Death in a Community Property Jurisdiction, 50 Wash. L. Rev. 277, 299 (1975). There is no apparent reason why such laws and practices need be confined to community property or to transfers between spouses. See UPC §6-101, which does not rely on the more traditional forms of will substitutes encountered in Chapters 8 and 12, supra.

The Uniform Probate Code was amended in 1982 to provide a procedure (not yet widely adopted in UPC states) for succession without administration; and The Uniform Succession Without Administration Act, a freestanding act for states not adopting the UPC, was promulgated in 1983.

UNIFORM PROBATE CODE

SUCCESSION WITHOUT ADMINISTRATION. *Prefatory Note.* This amendment to the Uniform Probate Code is an alternative to other methods of administering a decedent's estate. The Uniform Probate Code otherwise provides procedures for informal administration, formal administration and supervised administration. This amendment adds another alternative to the system of flexible administration provided by the Uniform Probate Code and permits the heirs of an intestate or residuary devisees of a testator to accept the estate assets without administration by assuming responsibility for discharging those obligations that normally would be discharged by the personal representative.

The concept of succession without administration is drawn from the civil law and is a variation of the method which is followed largely on the Continent in Europe, in Louisiana and in Quebec.

This proposed amendment contains cross-references to the procedures in the Uniform Probate Code and particularly implements the policies and concepts reflected in Sections 1-102, 3-101 [devolution of estate at death; restrictions] and 3-109 [successors' rights if no administration]. . . .

§3-312. *Universal Succession; In General.* The heirs of an intestate or the residuary devisees under a will, excluding minors and incapacitated, protected or unascertained persons, may become universal successors to the decedent's estate by assuming personal liability for (1) taxes, (2) debts of the decedent, (3) claims against the decedent or the estate, and (4) distributions due other heirs, devisees, and persons entitled to property of the decedent as provided in Sections 3-313 through 3-322.

§3-316. *Universal Succession; Universal Successors' Powers.* Upon the Registrar's issuance of a statement of universal succession: (1) Universal successors have full power of ownership to deal with the assets of the estate subject to the limitations and liabilities in this [Act]. The universal successors shall proceed expeditiously to settle and distribute the estate without adjudication but if necessary may invoke the jurisdiction of the court to resolve questions concerning the estate.

(2) Universal successors have the same powers as distributees from a personal representative under Section 3-908 and 3-909 and third persons with whom they deal are protected as provided in Section 3-910.

(3) For purposes of collecting assets in another state whose law does not provide for universal succession, universal successors have the same standing and power as personal representatives or distributees in this State.

§3-317. *Universal Succession; Universal Successors' Liability to Creditors, Other Heirs, Devisees and Persons Entitled to Decedent's Property; Liability of Other Persons Entitled to Property.*

(a) In the proportions and subject to the limits expressed in Section 3-321, universal successors assume all liabilities of the decedent that were not discharged by reason of death and liability for all taxes, claims against the decedent or the estate, and charges properly incurred after death for the preservation of the estate, to the extent those items, if duly presented, would be valid claims against the decedent's estate.

(b) In the proportions and subject to the limits expressed in Section 3-321, universal successors are personally liable to other heirs, devisees, and persons entitled to property of the decedent for the assets or amounts that would be due those heirs, were the estate administered, but no allowance having priority over devisees may be claimed for attorney's fees or charges for preservation of the estate in excess of reasonable amounts properly incurred.

(c) Universal successors are entitled to their interests in the estate as heirs or devisees subject to priority and abatement pursuant to Section 3-902 and to agreement pursuant to Section 3-912.

§3-321. *Universal Succession; Liability of Universal Successors for Claims, Expenses, Intestate Shares and Devises.* The liability of universal successors is subject to any defenses that would have been available to the decedent. Other than liability arising from fraud, conversion, or other wrongful conduct of a universal successor, the personal liability of each universal successor to any creditor, claimant, other heir, devisee, or person entitled to decedent's property may not exceed the proportion of the claim that the universal successor's share bears to the share of all heirs and residuary devisees.

§3-322. *Universal Succession; Remedies of Creditors, Other Heirs, Devisees or Persons Entitled to Decedent's Property.* In addition to remedies otherwise provided by law, any creditor, heir, devisee or person entitled to decedent's property qualified under Section 3-605, may demand bond of universal successors. If the demand for bond precedes the granting of an application for universal succession, it must be treated as an objection under Section 3-314(c) unless it is withdrawn, the claim satisfied, or the applicants post bond in an amount sufficient to protect the demandant. If the demand for bond follows the granting of an application for universal succession, the universal successors, within 10 days after notice of the demand, upon satisfying the claim or posting bond sufficient to protect the demandant, may disqualify the demandant from seeking administration of the estate.

See E. Scoles, Succession Without Administration: Past and Future, 48 Mo. L. Rev. 371 (1983), pointing out why universal succession is a natural evolution in American efforts to transmit assets from generation to generation with maximum economy of time and value. The article also points out the common functions served by traditional administration and by universal succession, namely identifying the appropriate collector of assets; protecting the collector from the risk of double liability; protecting creditors, tax collectors, and others; and identifying the new owners of the property. See also W. Fratcher, Probate Can Be Quick and Cheap: Trusts and Estates in England i, 48, 52, 55, 102-04 (1966) (available in almost identical form at 40 N.Y.U.L. Rev. 12 (1965)); and V. Emmerich, Estate Practice in the United States and Europe 7-8, 17-18, 38-41 (1950).

Nonprobate Assets (Will Substitutes). Recall from Chapter 8, that nonprobate assets pass without any formal administration usually pursuant to a contract theory, and otherwise via conventional property (trust or joint ownership) doctrine. As noted in Chapter 8, most wealth in the United States probably passes from one generation to another outside the probate system. As we progress through the material on fiduciary administration, continue to consider whether nonprobate transfers provide adequate security and, conversely, whether required probate procedures can be reduced or eliminated without loss of security.

As mentioned in previous chapters, the revocable living trust (RLT) has replaced the will as the principal estate planning document in some states for assets that otherwise might pass through probate. While there are often management or dispositive reasons for using the RLT (e.g., problems with durable powers of attorney as well as conservatorships), its popularity is often due to the lamentable state of local probate systems and the understandable desire, therefore, to avoid probate. Nevertheless, estate planners who use the RLT, particularly for wealthy clients, are somewhat chary of probate avoidance, lest some unknown and unbarred creditors belatedly appear and reach the trust assets. (See Chapter 13, supra.) Consider the lawyer's potential for malpractice liability for failing properly to advise on or manage such client risks; and consider the UTC solution, below, drawn from Cal. Prob. Code §16061.7 and Ill. Comp. Stat. 5/13-223 (Similar statutes have not been widely proposed or enacted, perhaps because traditional law specific to RLTs and particularly to other types of will substitutes often simply denies creditors any rights in the assets.).

UNIFORM TRUST CODE

(Draft, Feb. 2000)

§604.   *Limitation on Action Contesting Validity of Revocable Trust.*

(a) Unless the trustee has sent the person a notice shortening the period for bringing a contest as provided in subsection (b), a person may at anytime within [three] years after the settlor's death initiate a judicial proceeding to contest the validity of a trust that was revocable at the settlor's death.

(b) The trustee may shorten the period a person has to contest the validity of a trust that was revocable at the settlor's death by sending the person a copy of the trust instrument and a notice informing the person of the trust's existence and of the trustee's name and address. A person who is sent a notice and copy of the trust instrument must initiate a judicial proceeding to contest the validity of the trust within [120] days after the date the notice and copy of the trust instrument was sent, but in no event more than [three] years after the settlor's death.

(c) Upon the death of the settlor of a trust that was revocable at the settlor's death, the trustee may proceed to distribute the trust property in accordance with the terms of the trust. This distribution may be made without liability unless the trustee knows of a pending judicial proceeding contesting the validity of the trust, or is informed by a potential contestant of a possible judicial proceeding, followed by its filing within 60 days.

(d) Until a contest is barred under this section, a beneficiary of what later turns out to have been an invalid trust is liable to return any distribution received.

B.   *Opening Administration*

Before the administration of a decedent's estate can begin, there are certain preliminary matters that must be cared for by someone. The matter of making the funeral arrangements is usually handled by the family. The person making the arrangements should be aware that the court may not allow more than a reasonable amount in funeral expenses as a claim against the estate, and the balance, if any, may be the personal obligation of the one making the arrangements. Some states also give a priority for the payment of a fixed maximum amount for funeral expenses, and any balance must be presented as a general claim after administration expenses are paid. Although family members rarely object to any excessive expenses, creditors may object in the event the assets are insufficient for their claims.

Another of the matters that should be handled promptly after the death of a person is to suspend transactions in the name of the deceased, and sometimes to notify banks and brokerages to stop payment on checks outstanding. The powers of agents are terminated by the death of the principal, and in order to avoid the problem of transactions that may be completed after the death of the principal, prompt notification to persons who may have powers of attorney or other agencies may prevent costly litigation. If a check is a gift, the payee may not collect after the donor's death; however, if a check has been given in payment for goods or services, then the payee can come as a creditor and be paid the amount due.

Promptly after the death of the deceased there should be an investigation to discover any life insurance on the deceased so a claim for the proceeds can be filed. Life insurance has as one of its principal functions the provision of funds that will financially carry the family over the period of estate administration. Life insurance proceeds are usually payable promptly so the family can be in funds during this period in which the need is great.

One of the unpleasant but nevertheless important jobs at the outset of administering a decedent's estate is the process of going through the private papers of the deceased. The first reason for doing so is of course to find a will if any exists. It is important that this be done promptly because subsequent proceedings depend on whether a will is found. There is the practical problem of making certain the latest will has been found and protecting against the possibility of someone destroying or hiding it. Should the will be in the custody of some person, it is necessary to obtain the will and file it with the court. If the custodian should refuse to file it with the court, summary proceedings are available by which the filing may be obtained. The problem of going through the private papers can be a considerable task. Most persons accumulate a vast amount of relevant and irrelevant papers during their lifetime. These must be searched and classified in order to determine whether any have significance. It is often better to destroy nothing even though the papers seem to be insignificant. In several instances circulars or old envelopes with old notations on them have become important. It also avoids the possibility of any assertion that a will or other important paper was destroyed during the process of destroying what appeared to be waste paper. One of the places to be searched in this process is any safety-deposit box of the deceased. A court order may be necessary to open the box. It is often required by statute and advisable to have a public official, such as a representative of the taxing authority, as well as a bank representative present at the time the box is opened and searched in order to avoid any question of concealment of assets at a later date. An inventory should be taken of contents at the time of the initial opening and witnessed by those present.

Finally it is necessary to determine the appropriate court in which to file the petition for administration or for probate of the will if one is found. Once the court is chosen, it is necessary to proceed with probate and to petition for the appointment of the personal representative. Determining the place of administration or the court that has jurisdiction in administrative matters is not always easy. The concepts of in rem jurisdiction and in personam jurisdiction are particularly confused in decedent's estates. The in rem concept still prevails generally to determine where administration may or must be taken out; administration is required or excused by the law of the place where the assets are located. Even so, the principal or *domiciliary* administration is taken out in the state and county of the domicile of the deceased. Administration in other states is *ancillary*. Traditionally, under the in rem concept, the service of process by publication has been thought to be adequate, but since 1950 (after the *Mullane* case, discussed infra, section C), there has been increased recognition of the personal service requirement under both state and federal law.

In administration of trust estates the matter of jurisdiction is usually less complex. An inter vivos trust usually will not come to a court's attention until a party seeks judicial relief of some kind. Ordinarily jurisdiction of such matters is taken by a court of equity at the place where the trust is administered, which in most instances is where the trustee lives or does business. On the other hand, statutes in some states subject testamentary trusts to the probate court's jurisdiction by reason of statute, and then administration of a testamentary trust is in the state where principal administration of the decedent's estate occurred. See generally the note on court and noncourt trusts near the end of section D of Chapter 12. Also compare the approach of Uniform Probate Code, Article 7 (especially §§7-107, 7-103, and 7-203) discussed in that note.

UNIFORM PROBATE CODE

§3-201.   *Venue for Estate Proceedings; Location of Property.*

(a) Venue for the first informal or formal testacy or appointment proceedings after a decedent's death is:

(1) in the [county] where the decedent had his domicile at the time of his death; or

(2) if the decedent was not domiciled in this state, in any [county] where property of the decedent was located at the time of his death. . . .

C. *Estate and Trust Proceedings*

PROBLEM

16-D.   *D*, a retired executive, recently died and his son, *S*, comes to you for legal advice. *D*'s usual residence and most of his continuing business activities were in the state where you practice. He died while vacationing in a sunbelt state where he and his wife, *W*, owned a condominium as joint tenants; in recent years *D* and *W* had spent increasing amounts of their time at the condo. *D* was survived by *W*, *S*, and *G*, the child of a deceased daughter. *G* lives in another state halfway across the country. *D* left a will naming S as executor and dividing his property equally among *W*, *S*, and *G*. *W* now expects to live in the sunbelt condo and would like to sell the residence in this state. *H* owned a number of valuable paintings, some kept at the condo and others in the residence. At the time of his death he had deposits in the savings banks in this state and in the sunbelt state and had automobiles registered in both states. He had major shareholdings in a Delaware corporation and also in a company incorporated in this state; in addition, he was a partner in a business operated in this state, with local land, buildings, and equipment in the partnership name. There are two life insurance policies on *D*'s life, one payable to *W* and the other payable to his estate. Where would you open administration, and what procedures would you plan to follow? Do you see reason for any particular procedural concerns?

UNIFORM PROBATE CODE

Article 3. *General Comment.* The provisions of this Article describe the Flexible System of Administration of Decedents' Estates. Designed [for] both testate and intestate estates and to provide [interested persons] as little or as much by way of procedural safeguards as may be suitable under varying circumstances, this system is the heart of the Uniform Probate Code. . . .

(1) Post-mortem probate must occur to make a will effective, and appointment of a personal representative by a public official. . . . is required in order to create the duties and powers attending the office

of personal representative. Neither are compelled, however, but are left to be obtained by persons having an interest in the consequence of probate or appointment. . . .

(2) Two methods of securing probate of wills which include a nonadjudicative determination (informal probate) on the one hand, and a judicial determination after notice to all interested persons (formal probate) on the other, are provided.

(3) Two methods of securing appointment of a personal representative [informal and formal] are provided. . . .

(5) Probate of a will by informal or formal proceedings or an adjudication of intestacy may occur without any attendant requirement of appointment of a personal representative.

(6) One judicial, in rem, proceeding encompassing formal probate of any wills (or a determination after notice that the decedent left no will), appointment of a personal representative and complete settlement of an estate under continuing supervision of the Court (supervised administration) is provided for testators and persons interested in a decedent's estate, whether testate or not, who desire to use it.

(7) Unless supervised administration is sought [interested persons] may use an "in and out" relationship to the Court so that any question . . . may be resolved. . . . by adjudication after notice without necessarily subjecting the estate to the necessity of judicial orders in regard to other or further questions. . . .

(8) The status of a decedent in regard to whether he left a valid will or died intestate must be resolved by adjudication after notice in proceedings commenced within three years after his death. If not so resolved, any will probated informally becomes final, and if there is no such probate, the status of the decedent as intestate is finally determined, by a statute of limitations which bars probate and appointment unless requested within three years after death.

(9) Personal representatives appointed informally, or after notice, and whether supervised or not, have statutory powers enabling them to collect, protect, sell, distribute and otherwise handle all steps in administration without further order of the Court, except that supervised personal representatives may be subjected to special restrictions on powers as endorsed on their letters.

[(10) and (11) mention protections for purchasers and personal representatives to make nonadjudicated settlements safe and feasible.]

(12) Statutes of limitation bar creditors of the decedent who fail to present claims within four months after legal advertising of administration, and unsecured claims not barred by non-claim statutes are barred after three years from the decedent's death.

Overall, the system [is based on] the premise that the Court's role in regard to probate and administration. . . . is wholly passive until some interested person invokes its power to secure resolution of a matter. The state, through the Court, should provide remedies which are suitable and efficient to protect any and all rights regarding succession, but should refrain from intruding into family affairs unless relief is requested, and limit its relief to that sought.

The cases that follow involve certain procedural aspects of estate and trust administration proceedings and of related litigation that are likely to arise during the administration of a trust. These cases are concerned primarily with problems of jurisdiction and notice and with the representation and protection of the interest of minors, incompetents, and unascertained or unborn persons.

RILEY v. NEW YORK TRUST CO.
315 U.S. 343 (1941)

[Coca-Cola International Corporation, incorporated in Delaware, filed a bill of interpleader in a Delaware court against the Georgia executors (Riley and Spalding) of the will of Julia Hungerford and against the New York Administrator c.t.a. (New York Trust Co.) of the same decedent. Each claimed the right to receive transfer of the Coca-Cola stock now standing in the decedent's name. The outstanding certificates are now in the hands of the Georgia executors. The parties agreed that Delaware was the situs of the stock. The petitioners (Georgia executors) asserted that original domiciliary probate was obtained in Georgia, with the husband and all beneficiaries and heirs at law of the testatrix as actual parties by personal service; the respondent (administrator c.t.a.) was not a party. The Georgia record of probate included a finding that the testatrix was domiciled in Georgia. Petitioners offered to pay all Delaware taxes and charges on the stock and requested issuance of new certificates to them on the basis that the Georgia domicile had been conclusively established against "all persons," relying on the full faith and credit clause (art. IV, §1) of the federal Constitution. Respondent admitted that all parties entitled to oppose probate in Georgia were actually before the Georgia court but denied that the testatrix was domiciled in Georgia or that the Georgia judgment was binding on the respondent trust company; it averred that New York was the domicile of the testatrix at death, that there were New York creditors, and that New York had claims for estate and inheritance taxes. As domiciliary administrator c.t.a., respondent prayed issuance to it of the certificates for the stock in controversy. The Supreme Court of Delaware, reversing the trial court's finding of fact, determined that New York was the testatrix's domicile and denied that the full faith and credit clause required issuance of the certificates to the Georgia executors. Certiorari was granted to review the alleged error in denying full faith and credit to the Georgia judgment.]

REED, J., delivered the opinion of the Court. . . .

The constitutional effect of the Georgia decree on a claim in his own name in another state by a party to the Georgia proceedings is not here involved. The question we are to decide is whether this Georgia judgment on domicile conclusively establishes the right of the Georgia executors to demand delivery to them of personal assets of their testatrix which another state is willing to surrender to the domiciliary personal representative; when another representative, appointed by a third state, asserts a similar domiciliary right. For the purpose of this review, the conclusion of Delaware that the testatrix was in fact domiciled in New York is accepted. The answer to the question lies in the extent to which Article IV, §1, of the Constitution, . . . nevertheless controls Delaware's action.

This clause of the Constitution brings to our Union a useful means for ending litigation. Matters once decided between adverse parties in any state or territory are at rest. Were it not for this full faith and credit provision, so far as the Constitution controls the matter, adversaries could wage again their legal battles whenever they met in other jurisdictions. Each state could control its own courts but could not project the effect of its decisions beyond its own boundaries. Cf. Pennoyer v. Neff, 95 U.S. 714, 722. That clause compels that controversies be stilled, so that, where a state court has jurisdiction of the parties and subject matter, its judgment controls in other states to the same extent as it does in the state where rendered. . . . By the Constitutional provision for full faith and credit, the local doctrines of res judicata, speaking generally, become a part of national jurisprudence, and therefore federal questions cognizable here. . . .

The full faith and credit clause allows Delaware, in disposing of local assets, to determine the question of domicile anew for any interested party who is not bound by participation in the Georgia proceeding. . . . But, while allowing Delaware to determine domicile for itself where any interested party is not bound by the Georgia proceedings, the full faith and credit clause. . . . [does] require that Delaware shall give Georgia judgments such faith and credit "as they have by law or usage" in Georgia. . . .

We find nothing. . . , however, which would lead to the conclusion that, in Georgia, the New York administrator c.t.a., was in privity, so far as the. . . . estate is concerned, with any parties before the Georgia court. . . . Hence, if the Georgia judgment is to bind the New York administrator, it can be considered to do so only in rem.

By §113-602, Georgia Code of 1933, set up by petitioner as a basis for his contention as to the finality of the Georgia judgment in Delaware it is provided that the Court of Ordinary is given exclusive jurisdiction over the probate of wills and that "such probate is conclusive upon all parties notified, and all the legatees under the will who are represented in the executor." All the parties entitled to be heard in opposition to the probate, including Mr. Hungerford, were actually before the Court of Ordinary. It may be assumed that the judgment of probate and domicile is a judgment in rem and therefore, as "an act of the sovereign power," "its effects cannot be disputed" within the jurisdiction. But this does not bar litigation anew by a stranger, of facts upon which the decree in rem is based. Hence it cannot be said, we think, that because respondent would have no standing in Georgia to contest the probate of a will. . . . thereafter respondent could not file a claim in Delaware, dependent upon domiciliary representation of testatrix, for assets in the latter state. While the Georgia judgment is to have the same faith and credit in Delaware as it does in Georgia that requirement does not give the Georgia judgment extra-territorial effect upon assets in other states. So far as the assets in Georgia are concerned, the Georgia judgment of probate is in rem; so far as it affects personalty beyond the state, it is in personam and can bind only parties thereto to their privies. . . . Phrased somewhat differently, if the effect of a probate decree in Georgia in personam was to bar a stranger to the decree from later asserting his rights, such a holding would deny procedural due process.

It seems quite obvious that the administrator c.t.a. appears in Delaware as an agency of the State of New York, and not as the alter ego of the beneficiaries of the Hungerford estate. In its answer to the petitioners' statement of claim, it established its status by alleging that. . . . creditors residing in New York and the State of New York were interested in the estate, that its appointment as temporary administrator had been sought by the New York Tax Commissioners "to protect the claim of the State of New York to inheritance and succession taxes," [asserted] on the theory that the domicile was New York. . . .

Georgia and New York might each assert its right to administer the estates of its domiciliaries to protect its sovereign interests, and Delaware was free to decide for itself which claimant is entitled to receive the portion of Mrs. Hungerford's personalty within Delaware's borders.

Affirmed.

STONE, C.J.

I concur upon the single ground that the New York administrator was not bound by the Georgia judgment. He was not a party to the Georgia proceedings, nor was he represented by any of those who were parties. As administrator appointed under the New York statutes, he was charged with the duty of administering the estate of the decedent and paying inheritance taxes upon it. His interest so far as he owes duties to the state is therefore adverse to that of the husband and the next of kin, who alone were parties to the Georgia proceeding. To have bound him by representation of those so adverse in interest would have been a denial of due process. . . . A judgment so obtained is not entitled to full faith and credit with respect to those not parties. . . . Any other conclusion would foreclose New York from litigating its right to collect taxes lawfully due by simple expedient of a probate by the next of kin of the will of the decedent as the domiciled resident of another state, without notice to any representative of New York or opportunity to be heard.

It is unnecessary to consider the other questions discussed by the opinion.

FRANKFURTER and JACKSON, J.J., concur in this opinion.

UPC §3-202 solves the problem in Riley v. New York Trust Co. by providing a first in time rule: if conflicting claims of domicile are made in two different states, the determination of domicile made in the proceeding first commenced must be accepted as determinative in the other state. Of course, the other state may not be one that follows the UPC rule, although with proper exercise of jurisdiction (e.g., to the extent proper notice is given) the determination will be covered by the Full Faith and Credit Clause. An interesting case for comparison is Toledo Trust Co. v. Santa Barbara Foundation, 32 Ohio St. 3d 141, 512 N.E.2d 664 (1987).

Hanson v. Denckla, 357 U.S. 235 (1958), involved a controversy over the right to $400,000 of the corpus of a trust of securities established in Delaware. In 1935, while domiciled in Pennsylvania, the settlor established the trust in question with a Delaware trustee. She reserved the income to herself for life and a variety of powers, including powers of revocation, amendment, and appointment. In 1944 the settlor became domiciled in Florida. In 1949 she executed an inter vivos instrument appointing $400,000 of the corpus at her death to trusts previously established with another Delaware trustee and the balance to her executrix. The settlor died domiciled in Florida in 1952. The residuary legatee under her will sought a declaratory judgment in Florida, where the will was probated, holding the trust and inter vivos appointment of the remainder invalid as being testamentary in nature. The trustee and some of the beneficiaries were not served in Florida; the executrix and several of the beneficiaries were personally served in Florida. While the Florida case was pending, a suit was started in Delaware to determine the disposition of the assets under the trust. The Florida court held the trust and the appointment void, while the Delaware court held both the trust and the appointment valid. Delaware refused to give effect to the Florida decree on the basis that it had been rendered without jurisdiction. Certiorari was granted by the United States Supreme Court in both cases. The Supreme Court affirmed the Delaware decree, holding it valid, and reversed the Florida decree, holding that it was void. In holding that Florida had no jurisdiction either in rem or in personam, the majority opinion, written by Chief Justice Warren, stated:

> *In rem jurisdiction.* . . . The . . . assets that form the subject matter of this action were located in Delaware and not in Florida. . . .
>
> The Florida court held that the presence of the subject property was not essential to its jurisdiction. Authority over the probate and construction of its domiciliary's will, under which the assets might pass, was thought sufficient to confer the requisite jurisdiction. But jurisdiction cannot be predicated upon the contingent role of this Florida will. Whatever the efficacy of a so-called "in rem" jurisdiction over assets admittedly passing under a local will, a State acquires no in rem jurisdiction to adjudicate the validity of inter vivos disposition simply because its decision might augment an estate passing under a will probated in its courts. If such a basis of jurisdiction were sustained, probate courts would enjoy nationwide service of process to adjudicate interests in property with which neither the State nor the decedent could claim any affiliation. The settlor-decedent's Florida domicile is equally unavailing as a basis for jurisdiction over the trust assets. For the purpose of jurisdiction in rem the maxim that personalty has its situs at the domicile of its owner is a fiction of limited utility. . . . The fact that the owner is or was domiciled within the forum State is not a sufficient affiliation with the property upon which to base jurisdiction in rem. . . .
>
> *In personam jurisdiction.* Appellees' stronger argument is for in personam jurisdiction over the Delaware trustee. They urge that the circumstances of this case amount to sufficient affiliation with the State of Florida to empower its courts to exercise personal jurisdiction over this nonresident defendant. Principal reliance is placed upon McGee v. International Life Ins. Co., 355 U.S. 220 [and] International Shoe Co. v. State of Washington, 326 U.S. 310. But it is a mistake to assume that [these cases herald] the eventual demise of all restrictions on the personal jurisdiction of state courts. . . . However minimal the burden of defending in a foreign tribunal, a defendant may not be called upon to do so unless he has had the "minimal contacts" with the State that are a prerequisite to its exercise of power over him. . . .
>
> We fail to find such contacts in the circumstances of this case. The defendant trust company has no office in Florida, and transacts no business there. None of the trust assets has ever been held or administered in Florida, and the record discloses no solicitation of business in that State either in person or by mail. . . .
>
> The cause of action in this case is not one that arises out of an act done or transaction consummated in the forum State. In that respect, it differs from McGee v. International Life Ins. Co. . . . In contrast, this action involves the validity of an agreement that was . . . executed in Delaware by a trust company incorporated in that State and a settlor domiciled in Pennsylvania. The first relationship Florida had to the

agreement was years later when the settlor became domiciled there, and the trustee remitted the trust income to her in that State. From Florida Mrs. Donner carried on several bits of trust administration that may be compared to the mailing of premiums in *McGee*. But the record discloses no instance in which the *trustee* performed any acts in Florida that bear the same relationship to the agreement as the solicitation in *McGee*. . . . This case is also different from *McGee* in that there the State had enacted special legislation . . . to exercise what *McGee* called its "manifest interest" in providing effective redress for citizens who had been injured by nonresidents engaged in an activity that the State treats as exceptional and subjects to special regulation. . . .

The execution in Florida of the powers of appointment under which the beneficiaries and appointees claim does not give Florida a substantial connection with the contact on which this suit is based. It is the validity of the trust agreement, not the appointment, that is at issue here. . . . [W]e think it an insubstantial connection with the trust agreement for purposes of determining the question of personal jurisdiction over a nonresident defendant. The unilateral activity of those who claim some relationship with a nonresident defendant cannot satisfy the requirements of contact with the forum state. The application of that rule will vary with the quality and nature of the defendant's activity, but it is essential in each case that there be some act by which the defendant purposely avails itself of the privilege of conducting activities within the forum state, thus invoking the benefits and protections of its laws. International Shoe Co. v. State of Washington, 326 U.S. 310, 319. The settlor's execution in Florida of her power of appointment cannot remedy the absence of such an act in this case.

It is urged that because the settlor and most of the appointees and beneficiaries were domiciled in Florida the courts of that State should be able to exercise personal jurisdiction over the nonresident trustees. This is a non sequitur. With personal jurisdiction over the executor, legatees, and appointees, there is nothing in federal law to prevent Florida from adjudicating concerning the respective rights and liabilities of those parties. But Florida has not chosen to do so. As we understand its law, the trustee is an indispensable party over whom the court must acquire jurisdiction before it is empowered to enter judgment in a proceeding affecting the validity of a trust. It does not acquire that jurisdiction by being the "center of gravity" of the controversy, or the most convenient location for litigation. The issue is personal jurisdiction, not choice of law. It is resolved in this case by considering the acts of the trustee. As we have indicated, they are insufficient to sustain the jurisdiction. . . .

As we have noted earlier, the Florida Supreme Court has repeatedly held that a trustee is an indispensable party without whom a Florida court has no power to adjudicate controversies affecting the validity of a trust. For that reason the Florida judgment must be reversed not only as to the nonresident trustee but also as to appellants, over whom the Florida court admittedly had jurisdiction.

357 U.S. at 246-255. Justices Black and Douglas dissented.

L. SIMES, FUTURE INTERESTS
(2d ed. 1966)

§49. In some situations the person to whom a future interest in property is limited is not a necessary party to a proceeding involving the title to the property, but may be represented by some other person. A trustee may sometimes represent the beneficiaries of a trust, and a guardian ad litem may sometimes represent his ward. There is also a doctrine of representation based upon the fact that the representing person has an interest in the property which will be affected by the judgment or decree in the same way as the interest of the represented person or in a similar way. This kind of representation is commonly limited to cases where an unborn or unascertained person is represented.

MABRY v. SCOTT
51 Cal. App. 2d 245, 124 P.2d 659 (Dist. Ct. App.), *cert. denied,*
317 U.S. 670 (1942)

[In 1931 the defendant trust company executed an irrevocable declaration of trust acknowledging receipt of $1,350,000 to be held in trust. The living beneficiaries were the settlor, W. J. Garland, and his then wife Alzoa, and their four minor children. The trust was to terminate on the death of the last survivor of these six beneficiaries, and the corpus was to go to Mr. and Mrs. Garland's then living issue, and in default of issue to the living spouses of the four children, if any, and otherwise to the settlor's heirs. The trust, which bore the same date as a property settlement agreement between Mr. and Mrs. Garland, provided for payment of income essentially as follows: (1) $15,000 annually to Mrs. Garland; (2) any remaining income to the settlor; and (3) on various contingencies and on the death of Mr. and Mrs. Garland, part or all of the income was distributable to the four children. About four months after the creation of the trust, Alzoa Garland secured a divorce from the settlor. Thereafter she married M. L. Scott, and the settlor also remarried and had a minor child of that marriage. In 1936 the settlor brought suit to set aside the trust, alleging fraud and undue influence. The allegations were denied by all defendants, including the trustee and all beneficiaries appearing in person or by guardians ad litem. The plaintiff and his former wife, Alzoa, agreed on a compromise of the litigation: each of them was to receive $60,000 cash from principal, and 75 percent of the income was to be paid equally to them or their successors until termination of the trust, with 25 percent of the income to be divided among the children. With the exception of the trustee, all parties (including contingent remaindermen) personally or by guardians ad litem joined in a petition to the court to authorize and approve the proposed compromise. On the hearing of the petition the guardians ad litem recommended approval of the compromise, and the court entered judgment accordingly, ordering the agreed modification. The trustee argued below and on appeal that judgment deprived unborn remaindermen of property without due process of law in that their interests are impaired by the $120,000 reduction of corpus and the elimination of certain contingent rights to income.]

DRAPEAU, J. PRO TEM. . . .

When the litigation is between them, all beneficiaries of a trust are indispensable parties; without their presence the trial court has no jurisdiction to proceed.

The latest expression of the rule is by Mr. Chief Justice Gibson in the case of First National, etc., Bank v. Superior Court, 19 Cal. 2d 409, 417, 121 P.2d 729, 733:

> The law is settled in this state that, where one of several beneficiaries seeks to fix his share in a trust fund and where judgment in his favor would inevitably determine the amount available for others similarly situated, such other beneficiaries are indispensable parties. A judgment rendered in their absence and purporting to determine their rights is in excess of the court's jurisdiction.

But this rule of indispensable parties has one manifest exception. It is founded on the paramount duty of every court to see that justice be done. It takes effect when there are remaindermen not in being and when it is apparent that it is essential, in the interests of justice, to adjudicate rights of living persons.

This exception has been stated, approved, and applied by our courts in numerous cases in which future estates of unborn or unknown contingent remaindermen in real property and the relationship of such estates to rights of living persons have been under consideration. One of the best statements of it is to be found in section 182, chapter 12, Restatement of the Law, Property, Future Interests:

> Prerequisites for binding effect as against interest limited in favor of an unborn person. A judicial proceeding has binding effect as against the future interest limited in favor of a person who was unborn at the time of the commencement of such proceeding when the requirements stated in some one of the clauses of this section are satisfied, but not otherwise: (a) Such person was duly represented in such proceeding in accordance with one of the rules stated in sections 183 [involving virtual representation] and 186 [involving representation by a trustee]; (b) Such person was duly represented by a guardian ad litem appointed to protect the interests limited in favor of unborn persons. . . .

The reason behind the exception is a simple one of human relationships, implicit in the principle that human laws, and all other temporal things, are for the living; not for the dead or for those not yet in being, if to hold otherwise would result in injustice to living persons. Because parties are not in being, and therefore cannot be brought before the tribunal, is not sufficient reason for a court to stand by, helpless and impotent, when rights of living persons, in ordinary common sense ought to be adjudicated.

Were the unborn contingent remaindermen represented in the litigation? . . .

The trial court was correct in its determination that there was virtual representation of the unborn contingent remaindermen by the living children of Mr. and Mrs. Garland. There were no living members of this class of unborn contingent remaindermen. . . .

[In County of Los Angeles v. Winans, 13 Cal. App. 234, 244, 109 P. 640, 645 (1910)] it is said: "The interests of representative and represented must, however, be so identical that the motive and inducement to protect and preserve may be assumed to be the same in each." That case held that there was hostility of interest which precluded representation because a parent life tenant and a child remainderman had acted adversely to the interests of other child remaindermen who might later be born.

Appellant contends that by the compromise in the present case the living children secured a better participation in income than in the trust as originally drawn. Indeed a close reading of the trust agreement supports a theory of the appellant that the living children were to receive no income from the original trust until the death of their mother, or upon the nomination of their father, and that it is necessary to read the property settlement agreement into the trust to give any income to the children. But, assuming that by the compromise the living children received income not provided by the original trust, we are unable to agree with either minor premise or conclusion of appellant's suggested syllogism: that this caused them to profit at the expense of their unborn issue: and that there was thereby created hostility of interest as between the living children and their unborn issue which prevented virtual representation by the living children of the unborn contingent remaindermen.

The principal argument in support of this proposition is that . . . the living children consented to these changes in the trust agreement so that they might get the better participation in income provided by the compromise, and thereby deprived the contingent remaindermen of $120,000 which otherwise would eventually have gone to them, and of contingent income. To thus hold would involve conclusions of collusion and conspiracy which the facts of this case will not sustain. The decisive fact still remains that the remaindermen had no interest in the income: the living children had no interest in the corpus, except in the contingencies above stated. These contingencies are too remote to require a decision that the incentive on the part of the living children to protect and preserve the rights of their issue was destroyed. And computations are in the briefs which indicate that should any of these contingencies come to pass, neither income nor corpus will be depleted to the disadvantage of the remaindermen. Therefore, there was no adverse interest as between the living children and their issue which prevented the living children from representing the unborn contingent remaindermen. Under the doctrine of virtual representation the contingent remaindermen were represented and the court had jurisdiction over them and their interests in the trust. . . .

Under the pleadings, when the issues were joined in fraud, undue influence, failure of consideration, and mistake, the court had jurisdiction to hear and determine the controverted facts. If an affirmative finding could have been made as to any such facts, supported by competent testimony, the court had power to terminate the trust. Therefore it had the right and it was its duty to adjudicate this case, unless the action of all of the parties except the trustee in presenting the petition to approve the compromise, divested the court of jurisdiction. Obviously, there is here involved all of the aspects of the case, and the terms and conditions of the compromise.

In this connection there has been presented a most persuasive argument. It is that courts should always have in mind the rights of remaindermen not in being; that by affirming the judgment in this case, there may be sanctioned a method whereby trusts may be destroyed at will by combinations of living beneficiaries; that this may be done by pleadings framing issues giving jurisdiction to courts of equity to modify trusts, and then by securing judgments based on compromises giving to living beneficiaries property of unborn remaindermen.

The answer to this argument is equally persuasive. It is that courts may be safely entrusted with the protection of rights of unborn remaindermen. And it is in cases of this sort, in which there is jurisdiction in equity of the controversy, that such rights are protected by the courts themselves. In the present case we can confidently assume that this duty was performed by the trial court.

In actions for rescission, when a jurisdiction of equity attaches, it is the duty of equity to adjust all the differences arising from the cause of action presented and to leave nothing for further litigation. To aid it in the exercise of its jurisdiction to hear and determine this matter, the court appointed a guardian ad litem to represent and protect the interests of the contingent remaindermen. Courts of justice as an incident of their jurisdictions have inherent power to appoint guardians ad litem. . . .

There has been considerable argument in the briefs, and citation of authority, as to whether the trustee in this case represented the interests of the unborn contingent remaindermen. In view of there being virtual representation and equitable jurisdiction, it is not necessary to go into this question to any particular extent. There is strong authority for the statement that if it were necessary in order that justice might be done to living parties, the interests of contingent remaindermen in this trust estate could be represented by the trustee. . . .

The . . . judgment is affirmed.

MATTER OF WILL OF SANDERS
123 Misc. 2d 424, 474 N.Y.S.2d 215 (Surr. 1984)

RADIGAN, Surrogate.

In this executor's account proceeding the court is required to pass on the question of virtual representation (SCPA 315). Article TWENTI-ETH of the will provides for the establishment of a sprinkling trust of the entire residuary estate with income in the trustee's discretion payable to testatrix's son, Robert, and any of his issue, with principal invasion [on limited terms] for the benefit of the son [and] any child or grandchild of the son. . . . The trust is to terminate on the death of the son and his two children, Ian and Zara (grandchildren) with the principal and all accrued and accumulated income to be paid to the issue of the decedent's son living at the termination of the trust per stirpes.

Both Ian and Zara have children of their own (great grandchildren). It is these three great grandchildren upon whom service of process is sought to be disposed of on the ground that they are virtually represented by their parents, the decedent's grandchildren. Petitioner's argument is based upon the theory that the grandchildren and the great grandchildren have the requisite "same interests" under the virtual representation statute in this executor's accounting; that is, the maximization of the trust principal and therefore their interests are not in conflict. . . .

The interests of the grandchildren and the infant great grandchildren, both of whom are presently interested in income and principal as beneficiaries of the sprinkling trust, are identical as to those [sprinkling] interests. . . . In addition, . . . the three infant great grandchildren are the remaindermen as far as this application is concerned, subject to the trustee's limited power to invade principal.

The court must be ever mindful of its obligation to expedite the administration of estates and avoid unnecessary expenses including that of fees to be paid to guardians ad litem where possible. At the same time, the court, mindful of our litigious society, seeks to secure decrees from attack and not permit them to lie in waiting for an adult representee or for an incapacitated person to reach majority and with his disability unshackled to move to vacate same on the basis that they were not adequately represented. The court has an obligation to seek to insure finality of its decrees and to avoid a possible later attack based on lack of jurisdiction. Accordingly, a court must carefully evaluate the petitioner's request to use virtual representation, especially where any doubt may exist in the court's mind as to the adequacy of the representation. . . .

The Third Report 1984 P. 284 of the Temporary State Commission on Estates (The Bennett Commission) indicates that a present income interest is not the same and is in fact antagonistic to a future remainder interest. . . . [H]ere in an accounting proceeding . . . the income and principal interest can be adverse, especially under the terms of the will herein where the grandchildren may prefer to focus on their income interest [while] in the long term the great grandchildren would have more of an interest in the preservation of the corpus. The grandchildren and great grandchildren both have a potential to receive income and limited principal but the great-grandchildren are the only ultimate takers of the remainder and may therefore be benefited by a portfolio that consists of assets which have a growth potential rather than favoring a high yield potential which may be more beneficial to their parents. . . .

[N]ecessarily an accounting by an executor with a trust involved must include allocations of receipts and expenses between principal and interest which may create conflicts. Here the trust indeed was funded and there may be diversity of interests between the income beneficiaries and the remaindermen concerning the funding of the trust. While both income and principal interests ostensibly have the identical interest of maximizing the trust, they may have a diversity of interest as to the specific assets to be distributed to the trust in addition to potential diversity concerning allocation of receipts and expenditures.

The court must be concerned with whether or not the representees are being actively represented and not [merely] with whether or not they could be represented. . . . The court is not satisfied that the great grandchildren will be adequately represented [by the grandchildren] under the statute.

Accordingly, the court directs citation be served on the great grandchildren.

A statutory provision for virtual representation in appropriate cases and appointment of guardians ad litem can be found in §1-403 of the Uniform Probate Code. Paragraph 3 of that section and §1-401 prescribe methods for giving notice efficiently and in accordance with due process requirements. Also recall (Chapter 13, section C) the innovative Uniform Trust Code §§301-305 provisions for representation both by fiduciaries and under the doctrine of virtual representation (see especially §304), or, if necessary, by a guardian ad litem (court appointed "representative" under §305). Under the UTC, the same principles apply to all issues within the scope of the Code (e.g., trust termination and modification).

Mullane v. Central Hanover Bank & Trust Co., 339 U.S. 306 (1950), involved a petition for judicial settlement of accounts by the New York trustee of a common trust fund (a pooled investment fund primarily for small trusts). In compliance with New York banking law, the trustee gave notice only by newspaper publication, setting forth the name and address of the trustee and the fund, and a list of the participating trusts. The notice was challenged as inadequate. The first issue related to a conceptual matter encountered at the outset of Chapter 13, namely whether the interest of a trust beneficiary is a property interest or merely a personal right against the trustee. It was argued that the interest was merely a personal right, making the proceeding one in personam. Therefore, under Pennoyer v. Neff, 95 U.S. 714 (1877), the state court arguably was without jurisdiction over nonresidents without personal service. The Supreme Court rejected the argument, saying that the requirements of the Due Process Clause did not turn on such elusive distinctions, in fact refusing to decide — as irrelevant — whether the proceeding was in rem, in personam, or quasi-in rem. Rather, the interest of each state in providing means to close the accounts of trusts that existed under state law and were administered under the supervision of its courts was "so insistent and rooted in custom as to establish beyond all doubt the right of its courts to determine the interests of all claimants."

The next issue was whether newspaper publication was sufficient under the Due Process Clause. The Court said that due process required "notice reasonably calculated, under all the circumstances, to apprise interested parties of the pendency of the action and afford them an opportunity to present their objections." In *Mullane* the trustee had on its books the names and addresses of the income beneficiaries of the participating trusts, to whom it periodically remitted their shares of the income, and as to them the Court found "no tenable ground for dispensing with a serious effort to inform them personally of the accounting, at least by ordinary mail." The statutory notice by publication was therefore incompatible with the Fourteenth Amendment, except as to persons who were not ascertainable by reasonable efforts.

For decades after *Mullane*, probate lawyers wondered about the extent of its reach into estate and trust matters, where notice by publication is common. Answers came gradually, and the next case, Tulsa Professional Collection Services v. Pope, answered some, but not all, of their questions.

TULSA PROFESSIONAL COLLECTION
SERVICES v. POPE
485 U.S. 478 (1988)

Justice O'CONNOR delivered the opinion of the Court.

This case involves a provision of Oklahoma's probate laws requiring claims "arising upon a contract" generally to be presented to the executor or executrix of the estate within 2 months of the publication of a notice advising creditors of the commencement of probate proceedings. Okla. Stat., Tit. 58, §333 (1981). The question presented is whether this provision of notice solely by publication satisfies the Due Process Clause.

I

Oklahoma's probate code requires creditors to file claims against an estate within a specified time period, and generally bars untimely claims. Ibid. Such "nonclaim statutes" are almost universally included in state probate codes. See Uniform Probate Code §3-801, 8 U.L.A. 351 (1983); Falender, Notice to Creditors in Estate Proceedings: What Process is Due?, 63 N.C.L. Rev. 659, 667-668 (1985). Giving creditors a limited time in which to file claims against the estate serves the State's interest in facilitating the administration and expeditious closing of estates. See, e.g., State ex rel. Central State Griffin Memorial Hospital v. Reed, 493 P.2d 815, 818 (Okla. 1972). Nonclaim statutes come in two basic forms. Some provide a relatively short time period, generally 2 to 6 months, that begins to run after the commencement of probate proceedings. Others call for a longer period, generally 1 to 5 years, that runs from the decedent's death. See Falender, supra, at 664-672. Most States include both types of nonclaim statutes in their probate codes, typically providing that if probate proceedings are not commenced and the shorter period therefore never is triggered, then claims nonetheless may be barred by the longer period. See, e.g., Ark. Code Ann. §28-50-101(a), (d) (1987) (3 months if probate proceedings commenced; 5 years if not); Idaho Code §15-3-803(a)(1), (2) (1979) (4 months; 3 years); Mo. Rev. Stat. §473.360(1), (3) (1986) (6 months; 3 years). Most States also provide that creditors are to be notified of the requirement to file claims imposed by the nonclaim statutes solely by publication. See Uniform Probate Code §3-801, 8 U.L.A. 351 (1983); Falender, supra, at 660, n.7 (collecting statutes). Indeed, in most jurisdictions it is the publication of notice that triggers the nonclaim statute. The Uniform Probate Code, for example, provides that creditors have 4 months from publication in which to file claims. Uniform Probate Code §3-801, 8 U.L.A. 351 (1983). See also, e.g., Ariz. Rev. Stat. Ann. §14-3801 (1975); Fla. Stat. §733.701 (1987); Utah Code Ann. §75-3-801 (1978).

The specific nonclaim statute at issue in this case, Okla. Stat., Tit. 58, §333 (1981), provides for only a short time period and is best considered in the context of Oklahoma probate proceedings as a whole. . . .

Immediately after appointment, the executor or executrix is required to "give notice to the creditors of the deceased." §331. Proof of compliance with this requirement must be filed with the court. §332. This notice is to advise creditors that they must present their claims to the executor or executrix within 2 months of the date of the first publication. As for the method of notice, the statute requires only publication: "[S]uch notice must be published in some newspaper in [the] county once each week for two (2) consecutive weeks." §331. A creditor's failure to file a claim within the 2-month period generally bars it forever. §333. The nonclaim statute does provide certain exceptions, however. If the creditor is out of State, then a claim "may be presented at any time before a decree of distribution is entered." §333. Mortgages and debts not yet due are also excepted from the 2-month time limit.

This shorter type of nonclaim statute is the only one included in Oklahoma's probate code. Delays in commencement of probate proceedings are dealt with not through some independent, longer period running from the decedent's death, see, e.g., Ark. Code Ann. §28-50-101(d) (1987), but by shortening the notice period once proceedings have started. Section 331 provides that if the decedent has been dead for more than 5 years, then creditors have only 1 month after notice is published in which to file their claims. A similar 1-month period applies if the decedent was intestate. §331.

II

H. Everett Pope, Jr. was admitted to St. John Medical Center, a hospital in Tulsa, Oklahoma, in November 1978. On April 2, 1979, while still at the hospital, he died testate. His wife, appellee JoAnne Pope, initiated probate proceedings in the District Court of Tulsa County in accordance with the statutory scheme outlined above. The court entered an order setting a hearing. Record 8. After the hearing the court entered an order admitting the will to probate and, following the designation in the will, id., at 2, named appellee as the executrix of the estate. Id., at 12. Letters testamentary were issued, id., at 13, and the court ordered appellee to fulfill her statutory obligation by directing that she "immediately give notice to creditors." Id., at 14. Appellee published notice in the Tulsa Daily Legal News for 2 consecutive weeks beginning July 17, 1979. The notice advised creditors that they must file any claim they had against the estate within 2 months of the first publication of the notice. Id., at 16.

Appellant Tulsa Professional Collection Services, Inc., is a subsidiary of St. John Medical Center and the assignee of a claim for expenses connected with the decedent's long stay at that hospital. Neither appellant, nor its parent company, filed a claim with appellee within the 2-month time period following publication of notice. In October 1983, however, appellant filed an Application for Order Compelling Payment of Expenses of Last Illness. Id., at 28. In making this application, appellant relied on Okla. Stat., Tit. 58, §594 (1981), which indicates that an executrix "must pay . . . the expenses of the last sickness." Appellant argued that this specific statutory command made compliance with the 2-month deadline for filing claims unnecessary. The District Court of Tulsa County rejected this contention, ruling that even claims pursuant to §594 fell within the general requirements of the nonclaim statute. Accordingly, the court denied appellant's application. App. 3.

The District Court's reading of §594's relationship to the nonclaim statute was affirmed by the Oklahoma Court of Appeals. App. 7. Appellant then sought rehearing, arguing for the first time that the nonclaim statute's notice provisions violated due process. In a supplemental opinion on rehearing the Court of Appeals rejected the due process claim on the merits. Id., at 15.

Appellant next sought review in the Supreme Court of Oklahoma. That court granted certiorari and, after review of both the §594 and due process issues, affirmed the Court of Appeals' judgment. . . . We noted probable jurisdiction, 484 U.S. 813, 108 S. Ct. 62, 98 L. Ed. 2d 26 (1987), and now reverse and remand.

III

Mullane v. Central Hanover Bank & Trust Co., 339 U.S. 306, at 314, 70 S. Ct. 652, at 657 (1950), established that state action affecting property must generally be accompanied by notification of that action: "An elementary and fundamental requirement of due process in any proceeding which is to be accorded finality is notice reasonably calculated, under all the circumstances, to apprise interested parties of the pendency of the action and afford them an opportunity to present their objections." In the years since *Mullane* the Court has adhered to these principles, balancing the "interest of the State" and "the individual interest sought to be protected by the Fourteenth Amendment." Ibid. The focus is on the reasonableness of the balance, and, as *Mullane* itself made clear, whether a particular method of notice is reasonable depends on the particular circumstances. . . .

Applying these principles to the case at hand . . . [a]ppellant's interest is an unsecured claim, a cause of action against the estate for an unpaid bill. Little doubt remains that such an intangible interest is property protected by the Fourteenth Amendment. . . .

The Fourteenth Amendment protects this interest, however, only from a deprivation by state action. Private use of state sanctioned private remedies or procedures does not rise to the level of state action. . . . Nor is the State's involvement in the mere running of a general statute of limitation generally sufficient to implicate due process. See Texaco, Inc. v. Short, 454 U.S. 516, 102 S. Ct. 781, 70 L. Ed. 2d 738 (1982). . . . But when private parties make use of state procedures with the overt, significant assistance of state officials, state action may be found. . . . The question here is whether the State's involvement with the nonclaim statute is substantial enough to implicate the Due Process Clause.

Appellee argues that it is not, contending that Oklahoma's nonclaim statute is a self-executing statute of limitations. Relying on this characterization, appellee then points to *Short,* supra. Appellee's reading of *Short* is correct — due process does not require that potential plaintiffs be given notice of the impending expiration of a period of limitations — but in our view, appellee's premise is not. Oklahoma's nonclaim statute is not a self-executing statute of limitations.

It is true that nonclaim statutes generally possess some attributes of statutes of limitations. They provide a specific time period within which particular types of claims must be filed and they bar claims presented after expiration of that deadline. Many of the state court decisions upholding nonclaim statutes against due process challenges have relied upon these features and concluded that they are properly viewed as statutes of limitations. . . .

As we noted in *Short,* however, it is the "self-executing feature" of a statute of limitations that makes *Mullane* . . . inapposite. . . . The State's interest in a self-executing statute of limitations is in providing repose for potential defendants and in avoiding stale claims. The State has no role to play beyond enactment of the limitations period. . . .

Here, in contrast, there is significant state action. The probate court is intimately involved throughout, and without that involvement the time bar is never activated. The nonclaim statute becomes operative only after probate proceedings have been commenced in state court. The court must appoint the executor or executrix before notice, which triggers the time bar, can be given. Only after this court appointment is made does the statute provide for any notice; §331 directs the executor or executrix to publish notice "immediately" after appointment. . . . It is only after all of these actions take place that the time period begins to run, and in every one of these actions, the court is intimately involved. This involvement is so pervasive and substantial that it must be considered state action subject to the restrictions of the Fourteenth Amendment.

Where the legal proceedings themselves trigger the time bar, even if those proceedings do not necessarily resolve the claim on its merits, the time bar lacks the self-executing feature that *Short* indicated was necessary to remove any due process problem. Rather, in such circumstances, due process is directly implicated and actual notice generally is required. . . . Our conclusion that the Oklahoma nonclaim statute is not a self-executing statute of limitations makes it unnecessary to consider appellant's argument that a 2-month period is somehow unconstitutionally short. See Tr. of Oral Arg. 22 (advocating constitutional requirement that the States provide at least 1 year). We also have no occasion to consider the proper characterization of nonclaim statutes that run from the date of death, and which generally provide for longer time periods, ranging from 1 to 5 years. . . .

Nor can there be any doubt that the nonclaim statute may "adversely affect" a protected property interest. In appellant's case, such an adverse effect is all too clear. The entire purpose and effect of the nonclaim statute is to regulate the timeliness of such claims and to forever bar untimely claims, and by virtue of the statute, the probate proceedings themselves have completely extinguished appellant's claim.

In assessing the propriety of actual notice in this context consideration should be given to the practicalities of the situation and the effect that requiring actual notice may have on important state interests. . . . Creditors, who have a strong interest in maintaining the integrity of their relationship with their debtors, are particularly unlikely to benefit from publication notice. As a class, creditors may not be aware of a debtor's death or of the institution of probate proceedings. Moreover, the executor or executrix will often be, as is the case here, a party with a beneficial interest in the estate. This could diminish an executor's or executrix's inclination to call attention to the potential expiration of a creditor's claim. There is thus a substantial practical need for actual notice in this setting.

At the same time, the State undeniably has a legitimate interest in the expeditious resolution of probate proceedings. Death transforms the decedent's legal relationships and a State could reasonably conclude that swift settlement of estates is so important that it calls for very short time deadlines for filing claims. As noted, the almost uniform practice is to establish such short deadlines, and to provide only publication notice. . . . Providing actual notice to known or reasonably ascertainable creditors, however, is not inconsistent with the goals reflected in nonclaim statutes. Actual notice need not be inefficient or burdensome. We have repeatedly recognized that mail service is an inexpensive and efficient mechanism that is reasonably calculated to provide actual notice. . . . In addition, *Mullane* . . . disavowed any intent to require "impracticable and extended searches . . . in the name of due process." . . . [A]ll that the executor or executrix need do is make "reasonably diligent efforts" . . . to uncover the identities of creditors. For creditors who are not "reasonably ascertainable," publication notice can suffice. Nor is everyone who may conceivably have a claim properly considered a creditor entitled to actual notice. Here, as in *Mullane*, it is reasonable to dispense with actual notice to those with mere "conjectural" claims. . . .

On balance then, a requirement of actual notice to known or reasonably ascertainable creditors is not so cumbersome as to unduly hinder the dispatch with which probate proceedings are conducted. Notice by mail is already routinely provided at several points in the probate process. In Oklahoma, for example, §26 requires that "heirs, legatees, and devisees" be mailed notice of the initial hearing on the will. Accord Uniform Probate Code §3-403, 8 U.L.A. 274 (1983). Indeed, a few States already provide for actual notice in connection with short non-claim statutes. See, e.g., Calif. Prob. Code Ann. §§9050, 9100 (Supp. 1988); Nev. Rev. Stat. §§147.010, 155.010, 155.020 (1987); W. Va. Code §§44-2-2, 44-2-4 (1982). We do not believe that requiring adherence to such a standard will be so burdensome or impracticable as to warrant reliance on publication notice alone.

In analogous situations we have rejected similar arguments that a pressing need to proceed expeditiously justifies less than actual notice. . . . Probate proceedings are not so different in kind that a different result is required here.

Whether appellant's identity as a creditor was known or reasonably ascertainable by appellee cannot be answered on this record. Neither the Oklahoma Supreme Court nor the Court of Appeals nor the District Court considered the question. Appellee of course was aware that her husband endured a long stay at St. John Medical Center, but it is not clear that this awareness translates into a knowledge of appellant's claim. We therefore must remand the case for further proceedings to determine whether "reasonably diligent efforts" . . . would have identified appellant and uncovered its claim. If appellant's identity was known or "reasonably ascertainable," then termination of appellant's claim without actual notice violated due process.

IV

We hold that Oklahoma's nonclaim statute is not a self-executing statute of limitations. Rather, the statute operates in connection with Oklahoma's probate proceedings to "adversely affect" appellant's property interest. Thus, if appellant's identity as a creditor was known or "reasonably ascertainable," then the Due Process Clause requires that appellant be given "[n]otice by mail or other means as certain to ensure actual notice." . . . Accordingly, the judgment of the Oklahoma Supreme Court is reversed and the case is remanded for further proceedings not inconsistent with this opinion.

It is so ordered.

Justice BLACKMUN concurs in the result.

Chief Justice REHNQUIST, dissenting.

In Texaco, Inc. v. Short, 454 U.S. 516, 102 S. Ct. 781, 70 L. Ed. 2d 738 (1982), the Court upheld . . . an Indiana statute providing that severed mineral interests which had not been used for a period of 20 years lapsed and reverted . . . unless the mineral owner filed a statement of claim. . . .

Obviously there is a great difference between the 20-year time limit in the Indiana statute and the 2-month time limit in the Oklahoma statute, but the Court does not rest the constitutional distinction between the cases on this fact. Instead, the constitutional distinction is premised on the absence in *Texaco, Inc.,* of the "significant state action" present in this case. . . .

The "intimate involvement" of the Probate Court in the present case was entirely of an administrative nature. . . .

. . . Virtually meaningless state involvement, or lack of it, rather than the effect of the statute in question on the rights of the party whose claim is cut off, is held dispositive.

. . . [T]here is no reason to conclude that the perfunctory administrative involvement of the Oklahoma probate court triggers a greater level of due process protection. . . .

Uniform Probate Code §§3-801 et seq., supra pages 752-754, contain amendments made in response to the *Pope* case. Are they adequate, and are they valid? See Reutlinger, State Action, Due Process and the New Non-Claim Statutes: Can No Notice Be Good Notice When Bad Notice Is Not?, 24 Real Prop., Prob. & Tr. J. 433 (1990). Other concerns were earlier expressed about probate notice statutes (following a case that presaged *Pope*) in Wade, Notice and Due Process in Probate, 10 Probate Notes 356 (1985):

> Initially it seems clear that the typical state law provisions regarding notice to creditors . . . are constitutionally inadequate as to "known creditors." It is less clear, however, as to what is meant by "known creditors." In *Mennonite* [Board of Missions v. Adams, 462 U.S. 791 (1983),] the interest of the mortgage holder may not have been actually known to the taxing authority [but] the interest was of record and was reasonably ascertainable. Similarly, the personal representative may reasonably be required to examine the decedent's records for the existence of creditors. Does the constitution impose a duty to inquire further?

The article goes on to note that most statutes prescribing notice of hearings for probate of wills fail

> to provide for notice to persons whose interests would often be most seriously affected, that is the successors under the decedent's "next to

the last" will or other prior wills. Such prior wills may, in fact, be logged with the court or their existence may be known to the petitioner for probate. The rationale of *Mullane* would seem to require a notice at least to those apparent successors under the prior wills in order to give the court jurisdiction to enter a fully binding order of probate.

In re ESTATE OF THOMPSON
484 N.W.2d 258 (Minn. App. 1992)

LANSING, J.

Anchor Realty challenges (1) the trial court's determination that [personal representative] Doris Thompson conducted a reasonably diligent search for creditors . . . and (2) the court's refusal to allow a late claim against the estate. . . .

The Due Process Clause of the United States Constitution requires the personal representative of an estate to provide actual notice of probate proceedings to known or reasonably ascertainable creditors. Tulsa Professional Collection Servs., Inc. v. Pope, 485 U.S. 478, 489-90, 108 S. Ct. 1340, 1347, 99 L. Ed. 2d 565 (1988). Consistent with that requirement, the Minnesota probate statute [enacted in 1990] provides that within three months of publication of notice of probate proceedings, the personal representative must serve notice upon all known and identified creditors. Minn. Stat. §524.3-801(b)(2). Further, the personal representative may determine, in the personal representative's discretion, that it is or is not advisable to conduct a reasonably diligent search for creditors of the decedent who are either not known or not identified. If the personal representative determines that a reasonably diligent search is advisable, the personal representative shall conduct the search. Minn. Stat. §524.3-801(b)(1). Any creditors discovered in the search must then be served with notice. Minn. Stat. §524.3-801(c).

Due process does not require "impracticable and extended searches." *Pope,* 485 U.S. at 490. . . . Rather, the personal representative must make "reasonably diligent efforts." Id. (quoting Mennonite Bd. of Missions v. Adams, 462 U.S. 791, 798 n.4, 103 S. Ct. 2706, 2711 n.4, 77 L. Ed. 2d 180 (1983)). No Minnesota case law has defined the scope of a "reasonably diligent search" for creditors. See generally Thomas L. Waterbury, Notice to Decedents' Creditors, 73 Minn. L. Rev. 763 (1989).

If a reasonably diligent search for ascertainable creditors is interpreted to require an extensive search, the timely and efficient administration of estates will be impaired, while few additional creditors will be discovered. Id. at 782. A statute giving the personal representative discretion on whether to search suggests a corresponding duty to avoid an abuse of that discretion. Id. Thus, the personal representative must act with good faith and from proper motives, and within the bounds of reasonable judgment. Id. at 782-83 n.97. . . .

Doris Thompson retrieved her husband's records from his secretary and his attorney. She reviewed the records of stores currently owned by herself and her husband, talked to his business associates, the board of directors of his company, and the partners and shareholders in his current business transactions. She paid off or served the required notice on all creditors she knew about or discovered. Nowhere in her search did Thompson encounter information about the [claim in question].

Anchor contends that Thompson's search was not reasonably diligent because she did not speak with all the employees of the stores owned by her husband or with all former business associates, and because the law firm that represented the Thompsons examined only files kept under Robert Thompson's name and not files kept under the names of businesses in which Thompson was involved. Information about the [claim] was contained in the files of Midwest 10, Inc. and DARB Investors, but in a branch office of the firm.

Robert Thompson was involved in numerous business transactions over the course of many years. To require his personal representative to determine the status of every past business transaction and contact all past associates approaches the "extended search" that *Tulsa* rejects. Doris Thompson pursued all current, potentially productive sources of information known to her. She exercised her discretion and acted in good faith.

The trial court applied the statutory language to essentially undisputed facts, therefore, its conclusion was one of law and does not bind this court. . . . We agree with the trial court, however, that Doris Thompson's search was reasonably diligent.

A court may allow a claim to be filed against an estate after expiration of the statutory filing time if the creditor can show good cause. Minn. Stat. §524.3-803(c)(4)(ii). The trial court has broad discretion to determine whether good cause exists, and its finding will not be disturbed unless clearly erroneous. . . .

. . . This court had identified hardship, misunderstanding, and diligent but mistaken procedures as reasons for granting a petition to file a late claim. . . .

The trial court denied Anchor's petition to file a late claim because although Anchor did not delay filing a claim once it discovered Robert Thompson was deceased, it had done little to protect itself up to that time. . . .

Doris Thompson conducted a reasonably diligent search for creditors under the statute. The trial court did not abuse its discretion in refusing to allow the late claim.

Affirmed.

D. Ancillary Administration

Nearly all estates are administered at the domicile of the decedent, and this is known as the *principal* or *domiciliary administration*. But for various reasons, administration elsewhere may also be required. This nondomiciliary administration is called *ancillary administration*. The in rem jurisdictional concepts applicable in many instances in estate matters in the United States, together with the strong policy of protecting the decedent's creditors, have led to the general requirement that the assets of an estate be administered in each state in which they are found at the decedent's death. State death tax obligations often require a similar result. Thus, for example, in absence of statutory modification of this view by the situs, administration proceedings must be had in each state in which the deceased owned property at death. Because this requirement is not limited to land, it is important to distinguish the question of where administration must be had from the question of what state's law governs rights of succession to various assets. Although situs law has traditionally governed nearly all issues concerning succession to immovables, under an increasing number of modern statutes various issues may be controlled by domiciliary law, such as UPC §2-201 and California Probate Code §120 relating to the rights of surviving spouses, or by other law, such as the place of execution under UPC §2-506. Normally the law of the decedent's domicile will determine who are the successors to movables even though they are administered where located. Determining the location of tangible movable property (that is, chattels) is not difficult, but intangibles raise many questions. Nonnegotiable debts and causes of action are generally subject to administration wherever suit may be brought to collect them. Negotiable paper and documents of title, to the extent interests represented thereby have been chattelized in the paper, are generally subject to administration where the paper is found. Corporate shares may also be embodied in the share certificates under the law of the place of incorporation of the issuing company. (This is now so in all states as to negotiable securities.) If all assets owned by the decedent are not thus "located" at the domicile, additional ancillary proceedings may be necessary. See generally Scoles and Hay, Conflict of Laws ch. 22 (2d ed. 1992).

Because traditional doctrine treats the administration in different states as separate, the acts of one personal representative may not be binding on another. As a result, many problems arise concerning the effect of suits by and against different personal representatives. Unusual applications of the doctrine of res judicata are to be expected and call for exceedingly close analysis of the interests of the parties and the statutes of the states involved.

Creditors may file their claims in any jurisdiction where administration is open and usually may force administration where assets can be found. Once paid, however, the creditor's claim is discharged everywhere. As a notable exception to the separate administration concepts, an insolvent estate is generally administered as a unit by paying a creditor's dividend based on the ratio of all claims wherever filed to all assets wherever located. Illustrative of the ease with which traditional concepts requiring separate administrations can be overcome, even without statute, the insolvent estate cases point the way for much-needed reform in the handling of multistate estates by our judicial system.

After ancillary administration is completed, local creditors and tax collectors being satisfied, the movable property remaining normally may be and usually is sent to the principal (that is, domiciliary) personal representative for distribution with the other assets there. This is, however, within the discretion of the ancillary court, and in some circumstances distribution may be made directly in the ancillary proceedings to those persons entitled thereto by the law of the domicile. These and other exceptions or limitations on transfer to the domiciliary representative may result from provisions in the will or statute. E.g., Cal. Prob. Code §§12540, 1132; Ill. Prob. Act §7-6 (1988). Title to land is determined locally in ancillary administration and possession granted by that court according to the situs law.

In most instances initial administration should be opened in the state of the decedent's domicile to take advantage of the opportunities for avoiding multiple administrations. This rule of thumb may not, however, apply in many situations, and careful inter vivos and postmortem planning is necessary to avoid the costly and complex problems of multistate administration. These estate administration problems should be anticipated by the parties and their attorneys on such occasions as the incorporation of a business, the making of investments, and extending business operations into other states. Of course, the use of will substitutes should also be considered. Such matters are particularly important when a property owner retires or has an estate plan reviewed. These matters are explored in Scoles and Rheinstein, Conflict Avoidance in Succession Planning, II Law 4 Contemp. Probs. 499, 520 (1956).

Some states have noted the additional expense and trouble caused by needless ancillary administration and have provided statutory exceptions or modifications of the requirements of separate administrations. Provisions permitting summary probate of a foreign will (such as Wis. Stat. Ann. §868.01 (1971)) and provisions permitting a domiciliary personal representative to collect assets within the state without local appointment (such as Fla. Stat. §734.101 (1975)) are among the most significant. Such provisions often permit avoidance of ancillary administration by careful planning and prompt action.

The Uniform Probate Code offers a simplified, rational approach to multistate administration. Article 4 provides a comprehensive set of provisions to minimize the needs for as well as complexities of ancillary administration. In part this is done by expanding the recognition and authority of domiciliary representatives in nondomiciliary states that adopt the Code. Key provisions include §§4-201, 4-301, 4-302, and 4-401 of Article 4, plus §§2-506, 3-203(g), 3-602, 3-703, 3-815, and 3-816.

E. Probate and Contest of Wills

In a testate estate, probate of the will is a prelude to administration in most instances. *Probate* is here used in its restrictive sense to mean the judicial proof of the will. Two general types of probate are in common use in the United States. The first is probate in an informal ex parte proceeding, often referred to as *probate in common form,* in which no notice need be given at the initiation of the proceedings. This is a development from the early form of probate commonly used in England. Ex parte probate has the advantage of speed and economy, but because of lack of notice the decree admitting the will is subject to attack by one aggrieved. On the other hand, formal probate with notice to all interested parties — that is, *probate in solemn form* — is slow, allowing parties an opportunity to appear, and expensive, with costs of notice and a formal hearing; but is generally conclusive if not successfully appealed or contested within a limited time allowed by statute. The filing of a caveat to a will normally brings up the question of its validity, for trial after notice to interested parties prior to its admission to probate and thus would convert an ex parte proceeding to one in solemn form.

Both of these concepts of probate are employed in varying forms in the United States. Under each, the general theory is that probate is a proceeding in rem to establish the will and to administer certain assets. This reliance on a single proceeding to establish or disestablish the will as against all parties reduces litigation expense and permits maximum reliance on a single decree. However, characterizing the proceeding as in rem does not dispense with the procedural safeguards calculated to assure potential litigants a reasonable opportunity to be heard. Notice that is reasonably calculated under the circumstances to bring knowledge of the litigation to interested parties is required in all cases without regard to the classification employed. See Mullane v. Central Hanover Bank & Trust Co., 339 U.S. 306 (1950), and Tulsa Professional Collection Services v. Pope, 485 U.S. 478 (1988), section C, supra. Perhaps it is preferable not to classify the proceedings rigidly as in rem or in personam but rather to consider the needs that are to be served and the results achieved by any classification. In order to satisfy due process requirements, the tendency of modern legislation is to recognize, and thus increase, the requirements of notice in proceedings to establish wills; for example, it may be provided that the period beyond which ex parte probate may not be attacked must be commenced by the giving of notice after probate, after which a period is allowed within which the probate may be set aside, or that notice must be given before the hearing on admission to probate. You should consider whether the procedures prescribed by your local statute are adequate in light of the notice requirements under the *Mullane* doctrine.

The technicalities of *execution* were considered in Chapter 4; and substantive *grounds* of contest, usually consisting of the testator's failure to meet the requirements of testamentary capacity and its voluntary exercise, were considered in Chapter 3. Certain limitations on the rights of probate and contest, as well as procedural matters, are examined here.

1. Proving the Will

In the typical case, probate of a will is a simple matter. At the hearing on probate the sole question before the court is whether the propounded instrument is the authentic will of the decedent; the validity and meaning of its provisions are not in issue. Some duty of producing the will is generally imposed on any person having custody of it, and a person nominated to serve as executor or some other person interested in the will normally petitions for its probate. (In the absence of a will someone interested in the estate will usually petition for the issuance of letters of administration.) Local statutes prescribe in some detail the contents of the petition, the procedure for giving notice, and the time and method of hearing the petition.

Assuming no contest, the proponent of the will is generally required to offer evidence of jurisdictional facts, compliance with notice requirements, due execution, and often testamentary capacity. The nature of evidence required to prove these matters varies, but typically the requirements are slight when the will is uncontested. The modern trend is to reduce the burdens of proving wills in uncontested proceedings; thus, many states permit reliance on affidavits. For example, Uniform Probate Code §3-303 requires only the affidavit of the proponent in an informal probate proceeding. It is further provided in §§3-405 and 3-406 that proof by the affidavits of one or more of the attesting witnesses to due execution is adequate in a formal proceeding. The self-proved will, UPC §2-504, requires only the affidavit of the testator and the attesting witnesses for prima facie proof of due execution even in contested cases. UPC §3-406.

PROBLEM

16-E.   The proponents seek to probate a homemade will executed several years ago. It was signed by three witnesses. One witness has since died, one does not recall the execution, and the third, an illiterate, signed the will by mark. The former county health nurse also was present at the execution of the will but did not attest it. She is an intelligent, mature woman who was well acquainted with the testator and remembers the circumstances of the valid execution at the testator's home. As attorney for the proponents, in what order would you call the witnesses and how would you examine each? What would you do if all witnesses had predeceased the testator? If the will had been executed in your office, what would you have done to avoid the difficulties present in this problem?

Gillis v. Gillis, 96 Ga. 1, 15-17, 23 S.E. 107, 111-112 (1895), states:

The fact to be established is the proper execution of the will. If that is proved by competent testimony, it is sufficient, no matter from what quarter the testimony comes, provided the attesting witnesses are among those who bear testimony, or their absence is explained. . . . The law does not allow proof of the valid execution and attestation of a will to be defeated at the time of probate by the failure of the memory on the part of any of the subscribing witnesses. . . .

The main reason of the rule for calling all witnesses in a proceeding for probate in solemn form is to give the other party an opportunity of cross-examining them; and, while the law requires a will to be attested by three witnesses, it does not necessarily mean that all three must concur in their testimony to prove it on probate. To do this would make the validity of the will depend upon the memory and good faith of the witnesses, and not upon that reasonable proof the law demands in other cases. . . .

In re THURMAN'S ESTATE
13 Utah 2d 156, 369 P.2d 925 (1962)

CROKETT, J. . . .

The will bore an adequate attestation clause which recited full compliance with the requirements of our statute. . . .

Appellant asserts that notwithstanding those *written* recitals, the actual *testimony* adduced at the hearing left the proof of proper execution deficient in certain particulars: that it did not show affirmatively that [the testator] had declared the document was his will; nor that he requested the witnesses to act as such.

It has been held, and we think correctly, that under such circumstances the fact that the witness does not recall or relate [that] the full detail of the statutory formalities were complied with will not defeat the will. Where there is an attestation clause reciting observance of the statutory requirements for the execution of a will, and the genuineness

[handwritten margin note: faulty wit. recognition does not defeat will]

of the signatures is proved, a presumption arises that the recitals contained therein are true and that the will was duly executed. This is justified because it is reasonable to assume that persons acting in regard to something this important will do so seriously and deliberately; and that they therefore know the contents of what they signed. The presumption of due execution is of such strength that it will support a finding to that effect; and it can be overcome only by clear and convincing evidence to the contrary. There being no such evidence here, the finding that the will was valid is sustained. . . .

See also In re Estate of Koss, 84 Ill. App. 2d 59, 70, 228 N.E.2d 510, 515-516 (1967):

> It is settled law that execution of an instrument may be sufficiently proved where one attesting witness testified positively to the requisites of execution and the other witness does not recollect or denies compliance with the statutory requisites. . . .
>
> Where an attestation clause is in due form and the will bears the genuine signatures of the testatrix and of the witnesses this is prima facie evidence of the due execution of the will, which cannot usually be overcome by the testimony of a witness that there was not compliance with all of the statutory requisites. The testimony of a subscribing witness which seeks to impeach a will is to be viewed with suspicion and received with caution. . . .

Proof of Lost or Destroyed Wills. In In re Murray's Estate, 404 Pa. 120, 129, 171 A.2d 171, 175-176 (1961), the court stated:

> Certain proof is essential to establish a destroyed or suppressed will: (1) that testatrix duly and properly executed the original will; (2) that the contents of the executed will were substantially as appears on the copy of the will presented for probate; (3) that, when testatrix died, the will remained undestroyed or unrevoked by her. . . . The difficulty arises in proving the status of that will when decedent died. In determining such status, we must bear in mind that where a testatrix retains the custody and possession of her will and, after her death, the will cannot be found, a presumption arises, in the absence of proof to the contrary, that the will was revoked or destroyed by the testatrix. To overcome that presumption, the evidence must be positive, clear and satisfactory.

In re Estate of Gardner, 69 Wash. 2d 229, 236-237, 417 P.2d 948, 952-953 (1966), stated:

> The contents of [a lost] will need be clearly and distinctly proven [under our statute] by two witnesses who are not required to be the attesting

witnesses to the will. The two witnesses . . . must be able to testify to the provisions of the will from [their] own knowledge, and not from the declarations of another. . . . Auritt's Estate, 175 Wash. 303, 27 P.2d 913 (1933):

> [I]n establishing the terms and provisions of the will, it is not necessary that the witnesses testify to its exact language but only to the substantive provisions. The cases in this and other jurisdictions have used various terms as to the quantum of evidence needed to establish the provisions of the will [such as] "clear and satisfactory," [and] "to a reasonable certainty." . . .

But the court further observed that "the rule seems to be well settled that where one deliberately destroys or purposely induces another to destroy a written instrument of any kind, and the contents of such instrument subsequently become a matter of judicial inquiry between the spoliator and an innocent party, the latter will not be required to make strict proof of the contents."

Often the probate of lost and destroyed wills is governed by statute. The possible conflict between such statutes and rules governing the revocation of wills is treated in Chapter 6, section A, supra.

2.   Limitations on the Rights of Probate and Contest

Aside from statutes that may limit the time within which a will must be offered for probate (such as Uniform Probate Code §3-108) or within which a will must be contested, the law, the provisions of a will, or the acts of interested parties may limit or deter rights to petition for probate of a will or to contest it.

a.   Parties: The Requirement of Interest

In an effort to reduce litigation in the area of will contests, courts and legislatures have required the parties to the suit to show an "interest" in its outcome in order to have standing to sue. Although this standing requirement typically exists with reference to petitions for probate, the requirement is more often significant and more strictly interpreted in will contests. For example, one nominated as an executor may petition for probate but often is not allowed to contest a subsequent will. Also, a creditor of the decedent may petition for the opening of testate or intestate administration although denied any right to contest a will. As far as the right to contest is concerned, courts generally require the showing of a direct pecuniary interest in the denial or setting aside of probate. Thus, where the interests of a person are the same whether probate is granted or denied, that person has no right to contest. Is there any reason why the law should permit contest of a will by the decedent's creditors, as such, or by a pretermitted heir, who will take an intestate share by statute regardless of the will's validity?

Consider whether, if a person entitled to contest a particular will died without having contested it, the right to contest should survive and pass to the personal representative. What facts might influence your decision in a particular case, or is a fixed rule one way or the other appropriate? Compare the question of whether the right of a surviving spouse to renounce the will and receive a statutory share can be exercised by the personal representative in the event the spouse dies before making an election. See Chapter 3, section B, supra.

PROBLEMS

16-F.   *D* was a citizen of the United States domiciled in Maryland but spent much of his life abroad, mostly in Spain. He died recently in London.

Two years before his death, *D* executed a will in Spain in Spanish, leaving his substantial asset holdings in Spain to *R*, a stepchild (the child of his third wife, who predeceased him) and leaving all assets located elsewhere to his brother *B*, who lives in the United States. The next month *D* traveled to Maryland and, while there, executed a similar will in English also leaving the Spanish assets to *R* and all other property to *B*. Several months ago, back in Spain, *D* executed another will in Spanish, purporting to revoke "prior wills" and to devise all the Spanish assets to *B* but making no reference to assets in the United States.

In addition to *B* and *R*, *D* is survived by two children of his second marriage, which had been annulled in Spain prior to his third marriage. He had no children by his first marriage, which had ended in divorce in Maryland. The Maryland will has been admitted to probate in Maryland, and *B* was appointed executor. *D*'s two children now move to probate the third (that is, the last Spanish language) will in the same Maryland court. *B* objects on the grounds that the children lack standing because they are not legatees of the proposed will or any other will and are disinherited by the previously admitted Maryland will.

How would you support the children's petition for probate of the latest will? How would you expect the executor to resist it? What result would you expect? Why? See Lowenthal v. Rome, 57 Md. App. 728, 471 A.2d 1102 (1984).

16-G.   *H,* who died a number of years ago, created a testamentary trust for *W*, his wife by his second marriage, for life, remainder "to such persons or corporations as *W* may appoint by her last will and testament," and in default of appointment to *X,* a child of *H*'s first marriage. Recently *W* died leaving an instrument purporting to be her last will and to dispose of her property, including that over which she held a power of appointment, to *Z. X* is to take nothing under *W*'s will, but he believes he can prove that *W* lacked testamentary capacity when she executed her will. *X* is in no way related to *W. X* has come to you for advice. How would you advise *X* to proceed? How would you argue the case for *Z* on the question of interest? See Hogarth-Swann v. Weed, 274 Mass. 125, 174 N.E. 314 (1931).

Assuming it is decided that *X* has no interest permitting him to oppose probate of *W*'s will, is there any hope for *X*'s case? How would you proceed? How is *X*'s case affected by the "in rem character" of a probate decree and its "immunity from collateral attack"?

In re O'Brien's Estate, 13 Wash. 2d 581, 584-585, 591-593, 126 P.2d 49, 51-52 (1942), states that

> [T]here has been sharp disagreement as to whether or not an executor under a prior will or a previously appointed administrator is eligible [to contest a will]. . . .
>
> [Numerous cases have] held that an executor under an earlier will cannot caveat, or contest, a later will. . . .
>
> [However], . . . a trustee named in the earlier will could prosecute a contest. The basic reason for making the distinction seems to be that a testamentary trustee has a more substantial interest than an executor under an earlier will; that the trustee is clothed with title, and . . . "In fact a trustee is a legatee." . . . Some courts have gone so far as to hold that the administrator of an estate, who has been appointed and has qualified and assumed the duties of his office, cannot contest. . . .
>
> To contest a will, one must have a direct, pecuniary interest therein. An executor under a prior will has no interest other than the prospect of receiving compensation for his services, and that interest is not a direct, pecuniary one. . . . [I]n this state, the proposition that the executor receives only the value of his services is not merely a theory. It is a clearly defined statutory rule. . . .
>
> It is our conclusion that . . . both the weight of authority and the better reasoning favor the rule that a will contest cannot be initiated by an executor named in a prior will.

Nearly all authorities agree that the interest of general creditors of an heir or beneficiary under a prior will is not sufficient to permit them to contest a will. However, there is disagreement as to the right of a creditor whose judgment would give rise to a lien on the interest of an heir or a devisee under a prior will. See Lee v. Keech, 151 Md. 34, 133 A. 835 (1926), noted in 36 Yale L.J. 150 (1926).

In re LENT
142 N.J. Eq. 21, 59 A.2d 7 (1948)

[An instrument purporting to be Ella Lent's will, executed in 1946, was admitted to probate. It bequeathed two-thirds of her estate to charitable institutions and one-third to the respondent. In 1927 testatrix had executed a will leaving her entire estate to charity. Appellants, testatrix's next of kin, sought to contest the 1946 will and then to appeal from the adverse findings of the Orphans' Court. The Prerogative Court reasoned that if the 1946 will failed, the 1927 will would be effective and thus that appellants would have no standing to attack the 1946 will unless the 1927 will were also attacked. When no proof of the invalidity of the 1927 will was offered on the appointed day, the Prerogative Court dismissed the appeal. This is an appeal from that dismissal.]

DONGES, J. . . .

It seems clear that in a case of this kind, involving the validity of a will, the next of kin, those who would take an interest in the event of intestacy, do have a standing to attack any and all wills of a decedent. They may have a valid ground of attack upon the 1927 will, but they are in no position to attack that instrument unless and until it is offered for probate. With a decree of the Orphans' Court sustaining the 1946 will in effect, the 1927 instrument will most certainly not be offered for probate. The 1927 will could not have been attacked in this proceeding, as has been suggested, because, besides not having been offered for probate, the parties in interest, the beneficiaries and the executor, are not in court and could not be bound by a decree against their interests in a proceeding to which they were not parties. Therefore, it would seem that the only course which the appellants could pursue was to make their attack upon the will offered and if successful then make a further attack upon the earlier will when it was offered, as it would have to be.

The rule applied by the court below if carried to an extreme case would certainly work an injustice. Suppose, for instance, an insane man made a series of wills cutting off his family and benefitting strangers, even unscrupulous fortune seekers, could it be that upon the last of these wills being offered for probate, the man's immediate family, perhaps his minor children, would have no standing to attack it because of the existence of earlier wills under which they were not beneficiaries? No such rule of law applied and appellants were entitled to file a caveat and to appeal from the adverse decree. . . .

The decree is reversed and the case remanded in order that the Prerogative Court may pass on the merits of the appeal.

See also on the effect of an unprobated prior will on an heir's right of contest In re Powers' Estate, 362 Mich. 222, 106 N.W.2d 833 (1961), 15 Vand. L. Rev. 308 (1962).

b.   Anticontest Clauses

If any devisee, legatee, or beneficiary under this will shall contest it or any of its parts or provisions, any share or interest given to that person shall be revoked and augment proportionately the share of such of the beneficiaries hereunder as shall not have joined or participated in said contest.

Sample form from G. Stephenson, Drafting Wills and Trust Agreements: Dispositive Provisions §17.12 (1955).

BARRY v. AMERICAN SECURITY & TRUST CO.
77 U.S. App. D.C. 351, 135 F.2d 470 (1943)

[The will in question provided for forfeiture and a gift over of the interest of any person contesting its provisions. Appellant Samuel Barry and others filed an unsuccessful caveat to the will on the grounds of mental incapacity, fraud, and undue influence. The court held that their interests under the will were forfeited by this contest.]

PARKER, C.J. . . .

[V]erdict was directed for the propounders. So far as the record before us shows, there was not a scintilla of evidence to justify the allegations of the caveat. . . . Under these circumstances, the court below was unquestionably correct in holding that the interest of Barry under the will was forfeited by his filing of the caveat. Under the law applicable in the District of Columbia, the forfeiture provision contained in the will was valid and the filing of the caveat worked the forfeiture of the interest of the devisee filing it, irrespective of the question of good faith or probable cause for the litigation. Smithsonian Institution v. Meech, 169 U.S. 398. But even if good faith and probable cause could avoid the forfeiture, there is no evidence in the record before us upon which the court could base a finding of probable cause. . . . Even if probable cause were held to exist with respect to undue influence, this would not justify a contest based on a number of other grounds for which no cause whatever existed.

The validity of provisions for forfeiture in case of contest has been denied in bequests of personalty in the absence of a gift-over. This exception, even if valid, has no application here, as the devise is of an interest in realty and there is a gift-over to the residuary legatee in case of breach of condition. In some jurisdictions, it is held that a contest in good faith and upon probable cause will not work a forfeiture under such a provision. What we regard as the weight of authority, however, is to the contrary. A contest on the ground of forgery or subsequent revocation, neither of which is here involved, would seem to stand on different footing from the ordinary contest based on defective execution, mental incapacity or undue influence.

In the District of Columbia, the law is settled in accordance with the weight of authority, we think, by Smithsonian Institution v. Meech, supra, [in which] the Supreme Court stated the philosophy underlying the rule as follows [169 U.S. 398]:

> . . . [C]ontests are commenced wherein not infrequently are brought to light matters of private life that ought never to be made public, and in respect to which the voice of the testator cannot be heard either in explanation or denial; and, as a result, the manifest intention of the testator is thwarted. . . . And, when a testator declares in his will that his several bequests are made upon the condition that the legatees acquiesce in the provisions of his will, the courts wisely hold that no legatee shall without compliance with that condition, receive his bounty, or be put in a position to use it in the effort to thwart his expressed purposes.

We feel ourselves bound by this decision of the Supreme Court; but, even in its absence, we would follow the rule that it lays down as being supported by the weight of authority and as embodying the sounder reasoning. The view that the wishes of the testator should be disregarded with respect to the disposition of his property in the interest of greater freedom of litigation does not impress us as resting on a sound or logical basis. Studies which have been made show that only a very small percentage of will contests made on the grounds of defective execution, mental incapacity or undue influence are successful; and the public interest in freeing such contests from the restraining influence of conditions like that here involved seems of little importance compared with enforcing the will of the testator that those who share in his bounty shall not have been guilty of besmirching his reputation or parading the family skeletons after his death. But, as stated above, even if the rule avoiding forfeiture where contest is based on probable cause were recognized here, it would not avail appellant, since there was no probable cause shown for the contest.

For the reasons stated, the judgment appealed from will be affirmed. Affirmed.

MILLER, A.J. (concurring in part, dissenting in part).

I concur in the result and in the conclusion that no probable cause was shown for the contest. I join also in believing that the public interest will be better served if, in cases which involve no more of merit than is revealed by the present record, those who share the bounty of the testator should be strongly deterred from "besmirching his reputation or parading the family skeletons after his death." However, I doubt the wisdom of closing the door completely to contests calculated to reveal the use of fraud, coercion and undue influence in procuring the execution of wills. It seems to me that public policy may be well served by keeping the door a little open for some extreme situations, as where one person or a group of heirs conspire to shut out another; or, perhaps, to prevent the probate of an earlier will containing a bequest for charitable purposes. The object of an in terrorem clause may be to protect the family reputation, but it may be to silence a legatee who, otherwise, would be a material witness.

Where a legatee or devisee is fully competent, armed with adequate legal counsel, and financially able to hazard a contest, public policy may be satisfied by the assumption that fraud or undue influence will be challenged. Under such circumstances a successful contest may break the will and cause a distribution different from the one therein directed. But, while the rule as declared by the majority opinion would, perhaps, be consistent with public policy in such a case, it will not much affect the type of case which it is supposed to affect, or restrain the person whom it purports to restrain, namely, the litigious troublemaker. He will be most apt to take his chances on a successful contest. The person who *will be* discouraged and restrained is just the person whose right to litigate, the public policy should be most concerned to protect: poor, timid people; children, widows, incompetents. It is against the interests of such persons that the schemer, the confidence-man and the ruthless rascal are most apt to operate. If fraud, coercion and undue influence — rarely as they now may be used in procuring the execution of wills — can be covered up and made secure by the insertion of a forfeiture condition into a will, then, far from establishing a beneficient rule of public policy, we may, instead, be putting another weapon into the hands of the racketeer.

Text and other legal writers, generally, favor treating the forfeiture clause as invalid where probable cause for contest exists. The history of the contrary rule and the artificial distinctions which were written into it, do not much commend it for present day uses. . . .

Cf. American Bar Association, Model Rules of Professional Conduct, Rules 1.2, 4.1.

ESTATE OF LARSEN
162 Cal. App. 3d 134, 207 Cal. Rptr. 526 (1984)

STONE, Presiding Justice.

William Edwin Larsen appeals from a judgment forfeiting his interest in his mother's estate because he violated the in terrorem clause in her will. We affirm the judgment.

By will dated July 28, 1973, Mother Larsen specifically bequeathed one parcel of real property to her son Edwin and two parcels of real property to her daughter Alberta. The residue of her estate was to be divided equally between the siblings.

The will contains two provisions which are pertinent here: "Any apparent inequality in value of the properties in favor of my daughter [Alberta] is intended to equalize the gifts my children shall have received from me, in that my son has received substantial amounts from me during my lifetime," and "If any beneficiary under this Will in any manner, directly or indirectly, contests or attacks this Will or any of its provisions, any share or interest in my estate given to that contesting beneficiary under this Will is revoked and shall be disposed of in the same manner provided herein as if that contesting beneficiary had predeceased me without issue."

When his mother died in 1978 Edwin presented a creditor's claim to her estate seeking $41,786 for services to his mother during her lifetime and for travel expenses incurred by him in rendering those services. The creditor's claim expressly states: "All of the foregoing services were rendered in accordance with an oral agreement between claimant and decedent by which she agreed to devise certain property [plus half the rest of her estate] in exchange therefor and which was breached by decedent."

Alberta, the executrix, denied the claim. On January 24, 1979, Edwin filed a "Complaint for Services Rendered." . . .

Edwin informs us that "this case presents a single, straightforward issue of law: Is a beneficiary's suit on a creditor's claim for services to a decedent a 'contest' of or 'attack' upon the decedent's will, compelling forfeiture of the claimant's gifts under the will?" We disagree. "We recognize that while no-contest clauses 'are to be given effect according to the intent of the testator, yet it is also the rule . . . that such a provision — being by way of forfeiture and condition subsequent — is to be strictly construed and not extended beyond what was plainly the testator's intent.' . . . By the same token, however, we must not rewrite the testatrix's will in such a way as to immunize legal proceedings plainly intended to frustrate her unequivocally expressed intent from the reach of the no-contest clause." (Estate of Kazian (1976) 59 Cal. App. 3d 797, 802, 130 Cal. Rptr. 908.)

"Whether there has been a contest within the meaning of the language used in a no-contest clause is to be determined according to the circumstances in each case." . . . "The answer cannot be sought in a vacuum, but must be gleaned from a consideration of the purpose that the testatrix sought to attain by the provisions of her will." (Estate of Kazian, supra, 59 Cal. App. 3d at p. 802, 130 Cal. Rptr. 908.)

There may be instances where a beneficiary of a will who is also a legitimate creditor of the estate could file a creditor's claim without violating an in terrorem clause. However, the facts in this case support the implied finding that Edwin was using his creditor's claim to disguise his attack upon the will. . . .

Except for the parcels of real property and the small residue, the balance of her property passed to the children outside of probate by way of joint tenancy bank accounts. Thus, in order to satisfy Edwin's $41,786 creditor's claim, one of the parcels of real property would have to be sold. That would plainly frustrate Mother Larsen's testamentary intent. . . .

The in terrorem clause here prevents a beneficiary from "contesting or attacking" the provisions of the will "directly or indirectly." That clause is sufficiently broad to include what the probate court found to be Edwin's "indirect attack." . . .

Edwin himself fatally describes the nature of his suit for services rendered: "The claim is premised upon the fact that the will does not leave appellant the property he claims was promised him, and therefore that he did not receive the consideration for his services." This argument admits that, if the will had read the way Edwin had expected it to read, as opposed to the manner in which Mother Larsen intended that it read, there would have been no creditor's claim and no lawsuit. That is the definition of a "contest of" or "attack upon" a will.

We are mindful that equity abhors a forfeiture, and that forfeiture provisions should be strictly construed. . . . [But] loss of an inheritance due to the violation of an in terrorem clause is not a "forfeiture" in the strict sense of that term. An heir's "right" to take under a will is not absolute. Mother Larsen was entitled to dispose of her assets in whatever manner she chose. (Estate of Fritschi (1963) 60 Cal. 2d 367, 373, 33 Cal. Rptr. 264, 384 P.2d 656.) She chose to make her legacies subject to the condition that an heir not attack her intended testamentary disposition. Edwin did not abide by the condition.

The judgment is affirmed.

Just prior to the decision in the above case, Estate of Black, 160 Cal. App. 3d 582, 206 Cal. Rptr. 663 (1984), had decided "that petitioner, a beneficiary under the will and alleged unmarried partner of decedent, may seek a determination of claimed property rights arising during the couple's lengthy relationship [a so-called *Marvin* petition] without forfeiting, by operation of the will's no-contest clause, the specific gift of their residence." In re Estate of Wojtalewicz, 93 Ill. App. 3d 1061, 418 N.E.2d 418 (1981), the court refused to enforce a clause calling for forfeiture of the rights of a beneficiary who initiates a "proceeding to challenge or deny any of the provisions" of the will, concluding that enforcement would be contrary to public policy when the beneficiary opposed appointment of an executor who had failed for nearly a year to offer the will for probate. See also Estate of Watson, 177 Cal. App. 3d 569, 223 Cal. Rptr. 14 (1986), finding that the testator's daughter did not violate a no-contest clause by filing a claim against the estate of testator's spouse and an action for constructive trust against the heirs of the spouse. The daughter alleged, unsuccessfully, that testator's residuary devise to the spouse was based on the latter's oral agreement to devise that property at her death to the claimant daughter. Under a narrow but reasonable construction of her recently deceased father's will, this claim was not a contest of the will or an attempt "to impair or invalidate any of its provisions."

If a contest of a will in its entirety is successful, of course, the no-contest provision will fail along with the will. Furthermore, it is generally said by courts that no-contest clauses are to be narrowly construed for purposes of determining what conduct constitutes a contest under the provision. On each of these points, however, note the facts of Smithsonian Institution v. Meech, 169 U.S. 398 (1898), discussed in the *Barry* case, supra. In *Smithsonian* the will read, in relevant part: "These bequests are all made upon the condition that the legatees acquiesce in this will." Does this language explain the application of the forfeiture provision to a mere dispute (won by the legatee) over the ownership of property? Is that case, then, more like those involving the problems of election discussed in Chapter 3? On the question of what constitutes a "contest," note that the form quoted from Stephenson, supra, refers not only to contesting the will but also to contesting "any of its parts or provisions." Is this desirable?

How far should a court allow no-contest clauses to be extended? Commerce Trust Co. v. Weed, 318 S.W.2d 289 (Mo. 1958), required forfeiture of the interests of the *issue* of the testator's son because of a contest by the *son* under a provision that a contest should forfeit the interest of the issue as well as that of the son, whose own interest was slight. The court also rejected the probable cause exception.

The quotation from the *Smithsonian* case recited in the *Barry* case supra emphasizes, in support of provisions against contest, that "the voice of the testator cannot be heard either in explanation or denial." Should this not be a consideration in will contests generally? In studying the latter portions of this chapter, consider whether this is or should be a persuasive factor in the receipt of parol evidence. On the other hand, in questions of the validity of no-contest clauses, is it not equally true that the testator is unable to speak out against forgery, fraud, or undue influence? And is not a foresighted perpetrator of undue influence likely to include such a clause for protection and as a threat against those who would challenge the will?

Can a clause provide for a beneficiary to be disinherited for attempting to remove an executor? See Estate of Ferber, 66 Cal. App. 4th

244, 77 Cal. Rptr. 2d 774 (1998), a case in which the testator directed his attorneys to prepare the strongest possible no-contest clause. M. Begleiter, Anti-Contest Clauses: When You Care Enough to Send the Final Threat, 26 Ariz. St. L.J. 629 (1994), argues that courts should abandon the strict construction of no-contest clauses.

3.   Settlement Agreements

After the testator has died, the beneficiaries are able to transfer their interests in the estate and to contract with regard to those interests. Such actions are not viewed as defeating a testator's intent but as the beneficiary's exercise of property rights the testator has bestowed. Thus, threatened or pending controversy over the probate of a will is likely to be avoided by a settlement providing for probate of the will and for certain changes in the distribution of the estate. In such a case the problem is essentially a simple one of contract. The parties to such a contract would be bound, while others who are not parties would not be. (Difficulties may arise, however, as to the methods of enforcement if such a contract is dishonored.) On the other hand, certain modes of settlement may be undertaken that would interfere with the rights of others if special provision is not made to assure those rights. For example, either to prevent contest or for some other reason, the parties may agree not to probate the will in question but to administer the estate as if it were intestate, in which case provision must be made for the testamentary beneficiaries to look to the heirs for the satisfaction of their agreed rights.

PROBLEM

16-H.   The testator's will left his entire estate, valued at about $200,000, in trust to pay the income to A for life, with remainder to B. The heirs at law of the testator commenced an action to set aside the will. A, B, and the heirs subsequently entered into a compromise agreement providing for distribution of 40 percent of the estate to A, 30 percent to B, and 30 percent among the testator's heirs. All of the heirs and trust beneficiaries were sui juris and joined in the agreement, but the executor and trustee have opposed it. The latter argued that the court should refuse to approve the settlement on the grounds that the trust cannot be terminated on the consent of A and B because, under the usual American rule (the *Claflin* doctrine, discussed in Chapter 13), a material purpose of the settlor would thereby be defeated. See Adams v. Link, 145 Conn. 634, 145 A.2d 753 (1958). See also the note that follows. But see IV W. Fratcher, Scott on Trusts §337.6 (4th ed. 1989).

(a) How should the case be decided? Why?

(b) Assume that the court rejects the settlement agreement but that *A* and your client, *B*, still wish to compromise the issues in litigation, and the heirs are still willing to accept 30 percent of the estate in settlement. Can you suggest any solution? Would the presence of a spendthrift clause in the trust provisions of the will affect your proposed solution? Consider the possible utility of disclaimers.

In In re Estate of Swanson, 239 Iowa 294, 31 N.W.2d 385 (1948), probate of a will, under which the proponents were nominated as executors, was opposed by the decedent's widow and heirs on the basis of an agreement among themselves providing for settlement of the estate entirely as if it were intestate. In sustaining the position of the heirs, the court stated (at 300-303, 31 N.W.2d at 389-390):

> [I]t is generally held that the beneficiaries under a will may agree to disregard the instrument and have the estate distributed as intestate or in any other manner they see proper. . . .
>
> It is sometimes said family settlements are favored by courts. In upholding such settlements, courts have reasoned that beneficiaries under a will may, immediately after the distribution, divide the property as they see fit and there is no reason why they may not make such division before they receive the property. Also the beneficiaries are not compelled to accept provisions of the will. . . .
>
> There are two exceptions to, or limitations upon, the rule permitting family settlements: (1) Beneficiaries under a will cannot defeat a trust . . . (2) Such an agreement may not deprive one not a party thereto of his interest in the estate or prejudice the rights of non-consenting creditors.
>
> Neither of these exceptions is applicable here. The will creates no trust. . . . [O]ne who, like these proponents, has been nominated executor in a will but not appointed by the court cannot be called a trustee. . . . The nomination in the will may be disregarded by the court if the best interests of this estate so require.
>
> Unlike an heir, legatee or creditor of decedent, proponents had no interest in the estate of which they were deprived by the settlement agreement. That they would be compensated as executors, if appointed by the court, gave them no such interest. Such compensation would be only in return for services rendered.

In Altemeier v. Harris, 403 Ill. 345, 350-355, 86 N.E.2d 229, 233-235 (1949), the court stated:

> The appellants rely entirely upon the application of the family-settlement doctrine, which has been before this court on several occasions. . . .

Undoubtedly, the members of a family are not privileged to alter the terms and provisions of a will merely for the convenience of the family or for the sole purpose of securing greater individual financial advantages than those specified in the will and intended by the testator. However, the rule is well established that courts of equity favor the settlement of disputes among members of a family by agreement rather than by resort to law. Where there is a reasonable or substantial basis for the belief or assurance that prolonged and expensive litigation will result over the proceeds or distribution of an estate, that the estate will be materially depleted and that the family relationship will be torn asunder, the parties interested therein are warranted in preventing such bona fide family controversy by a settlement agreement. . . .

It is observed that in every one of the cases just cited, wherein the family-settlement doctrine is announced, no trust existed, and no contingent beneficiaries were interested, and no spendthrift provisions changed or set aside. . . .

Settled rules apply to the administration of trusts, and, where all of the persons are of age and sui juris and no principle of law is violated, the trust may generally be terminated if all of the cestuis que trustent consent. It has likewise been held by this court that where the trust makes provision for distribution to contingent beneficiaries, or upon uncertain contingencies, the trust may not be terminated even by the unanimous consent of all the beneficiaries, or the prospective beneficiaries, before the time fixed by the terms of the trust. . . . Likewise, the rule is clear that a spendthrift trust may not be destroyed or terminated by the unanimous consent of the beneficiaries. . . .

In view of the foregoing, we are of the opinion that the object and purpose of a trust created by a will cannot be varied or terminated unless the purpose of the trust is accomplished, nor can such a trust be terminated by unanimous consent where it contains spendthrift provisions or where contingent interests cannot be definitely ascertained. All three of these conditions exist in the instant case. . . .

A very few courts have refused to permit agreements among all beneficiaries to suppress probate of a will. They generally do so out of respect for the testator's wishes and particularly because of the fact that all possible interests (such as those of the creditors or devisees) cannot be accounted for with complete certainty. Can these objections be answered?

Under appropriate circumstances, other courts uphold settlements providing for the avoidance of the probate of a will. When trusts or successive legal estates have been provided for in the will, should it be required that such a settlement also satisfy all of the requirements for premature termination of a trust or for transfer of complete title to the property in which a legal life estate and remainder have been created? Can contingent future interests be extinguished by agreement not joined in by unborn or unknown remainder beneficiaries in the face of a will contest? If not, how can a settlement be arranged where the will creates interests in unborn persons? In a few states, statutes facilitate agreements of this sort, and the Uniform Probate Code suggests possible statutory solutions. In addition to the two following sections, see UPC §2-801, dealing with renunciation. On the problems posed by statutes dealing with these matters, see Schnebly, Extinguishment of Contingent Future Interests by Decree and Without Compensation, 44 Harv. L. Rev. 378 (1930).

UNIFORM PROBATE CODE

§3-912. *Private Agreements Among Successors to Decedent Binding on Personal Representative.*   Subject to the rights of creditors and taxing authorities, competent successors may agree among themselves to alter the interests, shares, or amounts to which they are entitled under the will of the decedent, or under the laws of intestacy, in any way that they provide in a written contract executed by all who are affected by its provisions. The personal representative shall abide by the terms of the agreement subject to his obligation to administer the estate for the benefit of creditors, to pay all taxes and costs of administration, and to carry out the responsibilities of his office for the benefit of any successors of the decedent who are not parties. Personal representatives of decedents' estates are not required to see to the performance of trusts if the trustee thereof is another person who is willing to accept the trust. Accordingly, trustees of a testamentary trust are successors for the purposes of this section. Nothing herein relieves trustees of any duties owed to beneficiaries of trusts.

§3-1101. *Effect of Approval of Agreements Involving Trusts, Inalienable Interests, or Interests of Third Persons.*   A compromise of any controversy as to admission to probate of any instrument offered for formal probate as the will of a decedent, the construction, validity, or effect of any probated will, the rights or interests in the estate of the decedent, of any successor, or the administration of the estate, if approved in a formal proceeding in the Court for that purpose, is binding on all the parties thereto including those unborn, unascertained or who could not be located. An approved compromise is binding even though it may affect a trust or an inalienable interest. A compromise does not impair the rights of creditors or of taxing authorities who are not parties to it.

17

The Fiduciary Office

This chapter is concerned with the fiduciary and with the essential nature of the office. The material in this chapter includes an examination of the basic standards and duties by which the conduct of a trustee or personal representative is judged. It also covers the rights and liabilities that accompany the fiduciary office.

A. Qualification, Selection, Appointment, and Removal of Fiduciaries

UNIFORM PROBATE CODE

§3-203. *Priority Among Persons Seeking Appointment as Personal Representative.*

(a) Whether the proceedings are formal or informal, persons who are not disqualified have priority for appointment in the following order:

(1) the person with priority as determined by a probated will including a person nominated by a power conferred in a will;

(2) the surviving spouse of the decedent who is a devisee [which term includes legatee in the UPC] of the decedent;

(3) other devisees of the decedent;

(4) the surviving spouse of the decedent;

(5) other heirs of the decedent;

(6) 45 days after the death of the decedent, any creditor. . . .

(c) A person entitled to letters under (2) through (5) of (a) above, and a person [18] and over who would be entitled to letters but for his age, may nominate a qualified person to act as personal representative. . . . When two or more persons share a priority, those of them who do not renounce must concur in nominating another to act for them, or in applying for appointment. . . .

(g) A personal representative appointed by a court of the decedent's domicile has priority over all other persons except where the decedent's will nominates different persons to be personal representative in this state and in the state of domicile. The domiciliary personal representative may nominate another, who shall have the same priority as the domiciliary personal representative. . . .

PROBLEM

17-A. The decedent died leaving as sole survivors and equal beneficiaries of his will his wife, *W,* and two adult children, *D* who lives in another state and *S* who lives in this state. The will named *D* as executor and provided that "my executor shall receive as compensation $6,000 per year." Consider the following matters under Uniform Probate Code §3-203 and the law of your state.

(a) *D* petitions for letters. May she be appointed?

(b) *D* declines and seeks to have a local bank appointed. What result?

(c) *D* declines and *W* seeks to have a local bank appointed. May *W* do this? What could *W* do to obtain assistance in business matters with which she is unfamiliar if she were appointed?

(d) *D* and *W* decline, but *W* nominates a local bank. *S* has no business experience but objects strenuously to the appointment of the bank because of a strong dislike for, and a prior disagreement with, the president of the bank.

(e) If *D, W,* or the bank is appointed, what compensation may each expect?

All states have statutes specifying persons entitled to appointment as personal representatives. (In such a statutory scheme, preference for males over females violates the right of equal protection. Reed v. Reed, 404 U.S. 71 (1971).) In a testate situation, the decedent's nominee is preferred, but in intestate situations or where a will does not nominate an executor, priorities for the selection of a personal representative are generally based on interest in the estate and relationship to the decedent. Some jurisdictions require that personal representatives be residents, while other statutes contain no such requirement; some others permit nonresident personal representatives subject to restrictions or distinguish between executors and administrators, imposing a residency requirement only for the latter.

In Estate of Svacina, 239 Wis. 436, 1 N.W.2d 780 (1942), it was argued that because the person nominated as executrix was indebted to the estate her appointment should be denied on the ground that her personal interests were antagonistic to those of the estate. In reversing the lower court's refusal to issue letters testamentary to the person named in the will, the court pointed out that the decedent's nominee *must* be confirmed unless precluded by mental incompetency or other legal disability, and that such a disqualification does not exist by reason of an indebtedness that was known to the testatrix at the time she made her will. The court noted that it "has ever been the policy of the law of this state that every citizen making a will has the right to select according to his own judgment the person or persons whom he would have execute it" and that "the court might well follow the maxim 'Whom the testator will trust so will the law.'" Cf. In re Estate of Moss, 183 Neb. 71, 157 N.W.2d 883 (1968).

In general, any natural person capable of taking title to property may take title to like property as a trustee. If a trustee has the capacity to take and to hold title but lacks the legal or practical capacity to *administer* the trust, the trustee may be removed in an appropriate proceeding and replaced by another trustee. For example, infants and insane persons can administer trust property only to the extent they can manage their own and therefore would normally not be suitable trustees because of their legal disabilities. Nonresident or noncitizen individuals who have capacity to administer their own property are generally eligible to act as trustees of testamentary as well as inter vivos trusts, although special requirements may be imposed on them, and a court may refuse to confirm a nonresident's appointment under a will or may remove a nonresident from office if unavailability is likely to impede the administration or enforcement of the trust. The fact that a designated trustee witnesses a will is not disqualifying, even in those states which bar interested witnesses, because the fiduciary role (even with compensation) does not constitute a "beneficial interest." On the matters in this paragraph generally, see Restatement (Third) of Trusts §32. (Tent. Draft approved 1999).

An unincorporated association may be a trustee only where it is recognized as a legal entity for purposes of taking and holding property for its own benefit. The defective appointment of an unincorporated association to act as trustee does not cause the trust to fail, however, since another trustee will be appointed. This assumes, of course, that the transfer on which the creation of the trust would depend has not been defective because of the association's inability to take the property. See Wittmeier v. Heiligenstein, 308 Ill. 434, 139 N.E. 871 (1923), supra Chapter 11. Much the same principles apply to partnerships as trustees, but if the transfer is deemed to be to the *partners* they can act as trustees. This solution does not pose the same practical difficulties as would be posed by treating the purported appointment of an unincorporated association as an appointment of the persons who comprise its shifting membership. See generally Restatement (Third) of Trusts §33.

A corporation may be a trustee, although its capacity to administer a trust is dependent on the corporate objectives and the powers conferred on it by law. Thus, in all states, corporations locally chartered to conduct a trust business, typically banks and trust companies, may be appointed to act as trustee, subject to whatever limitations and requirements are imposed by applicable state law. The field includes state banks and trust companies and national banks, which have the same privileges in the state in which they are located as a bank or trust company chartered there. Both legal and practical problems may arise when a foreign corporation is designated to serve as trustee. State law frequently excludes foreign corporations from carrying on trust business in the state or imposes severe burdens on foreign corporations seeking appointment. Many statutes permit a foreign corporation to act as trustee only if it qualifies to do business in the state; others will admit a foreign corporation to engage in trust activities if reciprocal privileges are extended by the company's state of incorporation. It is important for a lawyer to be aware of the problems posed by these statutes, particularly with regard to testamentary trusts for estates that will require estate administration in several jurisdictions. A settlor's desire to use a foreign corporation as trustee of an inter vivos trust is not likely to present problems of these types unless real property is involved. See generally Restatement (Third) of Trusts §33.

In recent years the constitutionality of state discrimination against nonresident individuals and foreign corporations has come into question in connection with both personal representative and trustee positions. Challenges have been based, inter alia, on the Privileges and Immunities Clause (which is said not to apply to corporations), the Equal Protection Clause, and on the testator's right to due process in freely selecting the trustee. See particularly cases arising in Florida: In re Estate of Greenberg, 390 So. 2d 40 (Fla. 1980), *appeal dismissed,* 450 U.S. 961; Fain v. Hall, 463 F. Supp. 661 (M.D. Fla. 1979); BT Investment Managers v. Lewis, 461 F. Supp. 1187 (N.D. Fla. 1978). A flexible system for the selection and substitution of trustees is provided in Article 7 of the Uniform Probate Code, including provisions for registration of trusts and for taking account of the mobility and multistate character of modern estates. See especially UPC §7-105, requiring a foreign corporation to qualify locally only if it maintains the principal place of administration of any trust within the state.

Selection of Trustees; Multiple Trustees. It is apparent from the above that the selection of a trustee involves the initial legal question of capacity to hold and administer trust property in the relevant state or states. The settlor should also be led to consider the practical problems of administration presented whenever the settlor owns land in a state other than where the intended trustee resides. The practicalities of trust administration and of the trustee's problems may require the creation of several trusts or the appointment of multiple trustees. Furthermore, the selection of trustees requires a consideration of the alleged advantages and disadvantages of corporate trustees, professional individual trustees, and beneficially interested or disinterested relatives. Where a relative is a possible candidate for the office of trustee, consideration should be given to any special knowledge that person may have of the settlor's property or business affairs and also to the possibility of such a person serving gratuitously.

One solution to difficult choices might be to appoint cotrustees (e.g., one a trust company and the other an individual), but the potential practical operating difficulties of this ready solution should be carefully considered. Is it appropriate to place on a family member, particularly a person of little business experience, all of the burdens and responsibilities of general trusteeship merely to provide a "family voice" in distributive or managerial decisions? Is an advisory role more appropriate? Can the same objectives be accomplished by a special power of appointment? If cotrusteeship is decided on, should the authority of each fiduciary be specified, or should one of them be given limited duties? Should the traditional unanimity of decision required of cotrustees of private trusts[1] be changed or qualified by the terms of the trust, or should broad delegation be authorized? Questions of this type should be kept in mind as the administration of trusts is studied.

Ordinarily cotrustees, like sole trustees, have a duty to participate in and perform all of the functions of the trusteeship. The role of trustee may be viewed as involving three different functions: investment, administration, and distribution. See J. Langbein, The Uniform Prudent Investor Act and the Future of Trust Investing, 81 Iowa L. Rev. 641, 665 (1996). There are signs that the prototypical model of the trusteeship is changing — a recognition that a person or institution that is good at one or two of the trustee functions is not necessarily good at all of them. As Professor Langbein writes, "No deep connection exists between, for example, being good at working with the beneficiaries on the distribution side, and being expert at investing trust funds or preparing fiduciary tax returns." Id. Practitioner Mark Edwards sees corporate trust departments evolving away from the role of full-service fiduciary to an

---

1. *Decision making by three or more trustees.* Absent a contrary provision in the terms of the trust, the traditional common law rule requires unanimity of action by trustees of private trusts, while a principle of majority rule applies to charitable trusts. Restatement (Second) of Trusts §§194, 383; cf. UPC §3-717 (unanimity rule for multiple personal representatives, with exceptions). There appears to be no compelling reason for the unanimity rule, and some statutes and many instruments provide for majority decisionmaking. Restatement (Third) of Trusts §39 (Tent. Draft approved 1999) and Uniform Trust Code §703 (draft, Feb. 2000) provide for majority control as the default rule for both charitable and private trusts. Dissenting trustees are protected from liability for acts authorized by the majority but have the normal fiduciary duty and right to keep informed, to participate in deliberations, and to take reasonable action to prevent a breach of trust by the majority. Restatement (Third) of Trusts §39, cmt. *a*; cf. UTC §703(g).

investment manager and custodian, resulting in increased use of individuals to perform discretionary distributive functions. See M. Edwards,
Trusts for the New Century: The Third Paradigm, 19th Annual Est.
Plan. & Fiduciary Law Seminar ch. 7, at 7-8 (N.C. Bar Ass'n Foundation
1998). Corporate trustees are increasingly willing to "unbundle" their
services and perform, for an appropriate fee, whatever functions another fiduciary, or sometimes the beneficiaries, may desire, or the settlor provides for.

Other methods for obtaining family input range from a right to be
consulted on some or all contemplated actions, to a veto power, to a
power to direct the actions of the trustee. Although there is only modest authority on directory powers, it appears (as reflected in Uniform
Trust Code §808) that the trustee has a duty to honor the directions
of one holding such a power unless the direction is "manifestly contrary" to the terms of the trust or is known by the trustee to violate a
fiduciary duty of the power holder, who is presumptively a fiduciary.

In addition, the "trust protector" model, drawn largely from Asset
Protection Trust practice (Chapter 12, section B.3) may become increasingly common in this country as a means of providing some measure of control to beneficiaries or third parties. "The protector may
be one of several trustees or a beneficiary, but often is neither, and
may be granted extensive authority or just a narrowly defined power
[such as] to change trustees or the situs of administration." E. Halbach,
Uniform Acts, Restatements, and Other Trends in American Trust Law
at Century's End, 25 ACTEC Notes 101, 119-120 (1999), which continues:

> Some protectors with broader authority are granted powers to clarify or
> modify trust terms for purposes such as: qualifying for or accomplishing
> some specific tax or non-tax objective(s); improving administration or
> otherwise promoting the settlor's general purposes or the beneficiaries'
> best interests; or adding or eliminating beneficiaries or rearranging their
> rights.
>
> The diverse types of protectors and the sheer variety of their uses and
> powers create serious difficulties in attempting to generalize about the
> nature of the protector's role and obligations. Under what circumstances
> and to what extent is a trust protector a fiduciary? . . . The present void
> in American trust doctrine aggravates the difficulty of interpretation and
> the issues of fiduciary responsibility . . . — not to mention the risk of
> unanticipated, adverse tax consequences. All of this leaves an immense
> challenge for estate planners. . . .
>
> And it leaves this writer merely able to speculate that in the United
> States: Absent some clear indication (possibly even circumstantial) of a
> settlor's contrary intent, the powers granted to a protector will be
> deemed to be held in a fiduciary capacity, even if not strictly that of
> trustee (compare powers granted to others to direct trustees, considered

in Uniform Trust Code §808 (draft, Feb. 2000)), with considerable breadth of freedom to act in the collective best interest of the beneficiaries, in good faith, and with a general duty of impartiality, and in a manner consistent with the settlor's purposes in creating the trust and the office of trust protector. One might further speculate that, presumptively at least, it would be appropriate to treat a trust protector who has broad, "sole and uncontrolled," and "binding" discretion essentially as the common law of trusts and statutory trust law would treat a *trustee* with a similarly "absolute" discretion. . . .

What accounts for the significant growth of the corporate trustee's role in modern trust activities? What factors enter into the choice between corporate and individual trustees? In McAvinchey, Worthy of Its Hire, 96 Tr. & Est. 976 (1957), a probate court judge mentions the corporate fiduciary's reliability, the reduced or eliminated bonding costs, specialization within the trust department, and impartiality. Lowndes, Corporate Trustees in the United States, 1958 J. Bus. L. 332, attributed the popularity of corporate trustees (1) to "the increasing complexity of trust administration owing to the complicated tax forms and reports which make a trustee's duties well nigh intolerable for an individual who is not equipped with the clerical facilities and experience to cope with them" and (2) to the trend today in which wealth "typically takes the form of stocks and securities of national and international enterprises . . . [requiring] the familiarity with national and international markets supposedly possessed by the large trust company." Porter, Professional Opinion of Trust Departments; 95 Tr. & Est. 439 (1956), reporting the results of a survey, indicated a 93 percent yes response to the question: "Is the permanence of a trust department, as opposed to an individual, an important factor in your recommendations?" Although evaluations of trust companies certainly vary widely from place to place, from time to time, and from person to person within a given location, it might be worth noting that Porter, supra, also reported certain common criticisms, including cold and indifferent attitude toward beneficiaries; conservatism in invasion of principal for beneficiaries' needs; shrinking from business decisions, particularly in going enterprises; the competence of a trust department too often depends on its size; and excessive fees, especially in small trusts. On this latter point, however, note that fee-setting practices vary; for example, in some parts of the country it has become the custom of trust companies to charge a minimum fee that suggests a de facto minimum corpus requirement of $500,000 or more.

Trustees: Acceptance, Appointment, Succession, Resignation, and Removal. The court that is responsible for the supervision of a trust has the power to remove and replace trustees. Often that will be a court of equity, but in any given state the supervisory power over trusts, particularly testamentary trusts, may be conferred by statute on some other court, such as the probate court.

RESTATEMENT (THIRD) OF TRUSTS

(Tent. Draft approved 1999)

(cross-referencing omitted; some paragraphing disregarded)

§35. *Acceptance or Renunciation of Trusteeship.*

(1) A designated trustee may accept the trusteeship either by words or by conduct.

(2) A designated trustee who has not accepted the trusteeship may decline it.

Comment:

a. . . . To be distinguished from the rejection of a trusteeship . . . is a disclaimer in the trustee's fiduciary capacity either of property that would otherwise be transferred to the trust or of specific powers that would otherwise accompany the trusteeship. A trust may be created despite the designated trustee's refusal to accept the trust, and a court can appoint a new trustee. . . .

b. Manifestation of intention to accept or decline. No particular formalities are necessary for a designated trustee to manifest a refusal to accept the trusteeship; similarly, unless otherwise provided by the terms of the trust, no particular formality is necessary to constitute an acceptance by the trustee of the fiduciary office. Thus, although trustees usually indicate acceptance by signing a trust agreement or other writing to that effect, an acceptance can be expressed orally or inferred from conduct.

It is a question of fact in each case whether the trustee has manifested an intention to accept or reject the trusteeship. Dealing with trust property in a manner that would be proper only by a trustee normally constitutes an acceptance, but merely protecting the property temporarily until a trustee is appointed does not.[2]

Failure to accept a trusteeship for a long period of time normally indicates an intention to reject it. If the trustee, before the creation of the trust, made a promise to accept the trust, such a promise does not preclude the trustee from declining; but under these circumstances a failure promptly to decline may constitute an acceptance. Even if one designated as trustee has not accepted the office, in some circumstances it may be appropriate to impose liability for delay in acting or

---

2. Uniform Trust Code §701(c)(2) allows a trustee to make an environmental inspection without being deemed to have accepted the trusteeship.

in declining the trusteeship if this conduct causes harm to beneficiaries who reasonably relied on the designated trustee to protect their interests. . . .

d. *Partial renunciation.* A person designated both as executor and trustee under a will may accept [one office and decline the other] unless the testator manifests a different intention. If two separate trusts are created . . . a person named as trustee may accept one and decline the other, unless this would be contrary to the purposes of the settlor or the sound administration of the trusts. . . .

§36. *Resignation of Trustee.* A trustee who has accepted the trust can properly resign:

    (a) in accordance with the terms of the trust;

    (b) with the consent of all beneficiaries; or

    (c) upon terms approved by a proper court

Comment:

a. *Terms of the trust.* The terms of a trust may allow a trustee to resign without court proceedings. For example, a trustee may be authorized to resign by notice to or with consent of certain designated beneficiaries. Where there are several trustees or a provision naming a successor trustee, unless the terms of the trust provide otherwise, a trustee may resign by written notice to the co-trustee(s) or to the person named as successor trustee. [Comment *b* also notes that *statutes* in some states facilitate informal resignation by allowing certain defined beneficiaries to act for all in accepting a trustee's resignation.]

Under any such provision, the trustee's resignation becomes effective only upon the acceptance of the trusteeship by a new trustee. Also, a trustee may not exercise a power of resignation or otherwise resign for the purpose of facilitating a breach of trust by the remaining cotrustee(s) or of escaping adverse circumstances without disclosing the breach or circumstances to the beneficiaries, settlor, or court, as the case may be. . . .

c. *Authorization of court.* It is within the discretion of the court to determine the conditions upon which a trustee's resignation becomes effective. The purpose of this discretion is not to force involuntary service by a trustee but to protect the interests of the beneficiaries and to assure continuity and efficiency in the administration of the trust. Of particular importance in this respect is the ability to find a suitable successor to the resigning trustee.

d. *Liability and duties of resigning trustee.* Resignation does not relieve the trustee from liability for breaches of trust committed prior to the time the resignation becomes effective. Normally the trustee has a duty to account to the beneficiaries, and this accounting may have the effect of determining any liability of the resigning trustee and of relieving the trustee of other liability. The trustee also has a duty to administer and preserve the trust property until a successor is properly appointed and assumes the duties of the trusteeship.

Trust provisions should normally nominate alternative and successor trustees and deal with the question whether, when co-trustees are nominated, one may be appointed or may continue to act alone in the event of the other's failure or inability to serve. Wills and trust instruments often provide *procedures* for appointing alternate or successor fiduciaries if the transferor does not wish to make additional nominations or if the list of nominees is exhausted. These procedures frequently authorize certain defined beneficiaries or prior fiduciaries to make appointments or nominations. In such cases, the attitude of In re Trust of Selsor, 13 Ohio App. 3d 164, 167, 468 N.E.2d 745, 748 (1983), is fairly typical. Finding the lower court's failure to follow the recommendation of a surviving trustee arbitrary, contrary to the terms of the trust, and an abuse of discretion, the opinion states:

> Where a will provides for the selection process of a successor trustee, the "intention of the testator as it affects the power of the Court to name a successor trustee is controlling." . . . Since the surviving testamentary trustee [was] given the authority to nominate the successor of a deceased trustee, full effect is to be given to the intent of the testator as expressed in the will. . . . "Under such circumstances it [is] the duty of the Probate Court to follow the recommendations of [the surviving trustee] as to who should be a cotrustee unless the person chosen as a cotrustee was incompetent to administer the trust or such appointment would be detrimental to the trust."

In the absence of special statutory provisions, the matter of a trustee's removal is left to the sound discretion of the court in an appropriate proceeding. This discretion is, of course, reviewable for abuse.

PROBLEM

17-B. *H* died six years ago. His will bequeathed to his son, *S,* $115,000 worth of stock representing *H*'s entire interest in a family corporation owned by *H* and *S.* The residue of *H*'s estate was valued at $260,000 and was left to *S* in trust to pay the income to *W, H*'s wife, for her life, remainder on *W*'s death to *D, H*'s only daughter. Under the terms of the trust *S,* as trustee, was authorized to distribute principal to *W* "in such amounts as may be deemed appropriate in the absolute discretion of the trustee."

Several months ago *D,* who had never married, died leaving her entire estate to her brother, *S.* The only property of any consequence owned by *D* was her vested remainder in the above described trust created by her father's will.

Since the establishment of the trust on distribution of *H*'s estate about a year after his death, *W* has received principal in amounts of between $4,000 and $11,000 each year. She is concerned that *S* will no longer be as generous with her and wishes to have *S* removed as trustee because the trust property consists of securities requiring no special managerial skills peculiar to *S.* How would you argue for *S*'s removal? How would you argue for his retention as trustee? Compare In re Borthwick's Estate, 102 N.H. 344, 156 A.2d 759 (1959) (the fact that the survivor of two cotrustees was a life beneficiary was to be taken into consideration in deciding whether to appoint a successor to replace the deceased cotrustee).

Was *S* in the above problem a wise choice as trustee? If *S* had been an intended remainder beneficiary at the time *H*'s will was drawn, how would you have advised *H* on the selection of the trustee? Why?

In re ESTATE OF BEICHNER
432 Pa. 150, 247 A.2d 779 (1968)

JONES, J.

This appeal challenges the propriety of a decree of the Orphans' Court of Beaver County removing an executrix of an estate and revoking letters testamentary granted to her. . . .

A testamentary executor or trustee is one whose choice was made by the person whose estate was to be administered and managed and represents an expression of trust and confidence in the person or persons so selected; an administrator appointed by the Register of Wills represents not the choice of the decedent nor are the person or persons appointed those in whom, necessarily, the decedent placed trust and confidence.

That an Orphans' Court possesses the power to remove an executor is clear beyond question. . . . [S]uch removal lies largely within the discretion of such courts, [but] an abuse of such discretion renders its exercise subject to appellate review. . . .

The removal of a personal representative chosen by the testator is a drastic action which should be undertaken only when the estate within the control of such personal representative is endangered. To justify the removal of a testamentary personal representative the proof of the cause for such removal must be clear. . . .

The only cause assigned for Mrs. Groom's removal by the court below was that animosity existed between Mrs. Groom and her stepmother, Mrs. Beichner, such cause being shown only by an admission in the pleadings. Such animosity may have arisen, as it too often and unfortunately does, because Mrs. Beichner was the second wife and Mrs. Groom a daughter of the first wife or it might have arisen through the fault of Mrs. Beichner or Mrs. Groom; nothing of record indicates *why* the animosity existed. Moreover, there is not a scintilla of evidence on this record that indicates that, assuming this animosity to exist, the estate is being mismanaged or wasted or that such animosity has jeopardized the estate or the interest therein of Mrs. Beichner. Animosity per se, absent any showing of any adverse effect on the estate or the rights of any beneficiary by reason of such animosity, does not constitute a ground for removal of an executor in whom the testator placed trust and confidence. . . .

We recognize that Mrs. Groom . . . had failed to file an inventory or a statement of debts and deductions or pay the transfer inheritance tax, failures which Mrs. Groom attempted to account for in her answer to the removal petition. Such failures could have been promptly rectified by action on the part of Mrs. Beichner's counsel had the executrices been cited to file an inventory, etc. For some unexplained reason such remedies were not resorted to.

On this record, absent a showing of any impact on the handling and management of this estate arising from any ill-feeling existing between Mrs. Groom and her stepmother or that Mrs. Beichner's interest in this estate has been jeopardized by such animosity, the court below should not have removed Mrs. Groom.

Decree reversed. Costs on Mrs. Beichner.

McDONALD v. O'DONNELL
56 App. D.C. 31, 8 F.2d 792 (1925)

[Appeal from a decree removing the appellant, McDonald, as sole trustee under the will of Michael O'Donnell, who died in 1910. The terms of the trust provided, among other things, for payments to the testator's widow of $25 monthly and such additional sums as the trustee deems necessary "for her needs, condition, and station in life."]

MARTIN, C.J. . . .

In November, 1920, the widow, Mary O'Donnell, filed a bill of complaint in the court below against said trustee, wherein, as amended, she charged that he had for a long time past continuously refused to pay her sufficient funds from said estate to maintain her in her station of life, although sufficient funds were available, thereby humiliating and embarrassing her, and imposing great hardship upon her; also that he had maintained an attitude of harshness, antagonism, and hostility towards her ever since about two years after the testator's death; and for these reasons she prayed that the defendant should be removed as trustee and a successor be appointed. . . . The court below granted the prayer of the bill, removed the appellant as trustee, and appointed a successor. . . .

It is unnecessary for us to discuss in detail the evidence contained in the record. We find nothing in it which reflects upon the integrity of the trustee, nor do we find grounds there for any condemnation of the discretion with which he has managed the trust in his dealings with third parties. But we are convinced from the record that the relations between the trustee and the testator's widow have become irreconcilably hostile, to such an extent and with such results as to defeat the true purpose which the testator had in mind when he created the trust.

It is clear, from a reading of the testator's will, that his wife and his adopted daughter [now deceased] were the principal objects of his bounty. . . . [The wife accepted the trust] in lieu of her legal dower in the estate. The duties of the trustee toward her, under the terms of the will and codicil, are intimate and personal. . . . The relations existing for a long time between them make the proper performance of such duties almost impossible under the circumstances.

It is true that the testator selected the appellant as trustee, but it should be remembered that the selection was made more than 15 years ago, and the relations of the parties have changed since that time. . . .

A trustee, who is beneficiary's son, may be removed, on application of beneficiary, because a state of mutual hostility has arisen between them since the creation of the trust, attributable in part to the fault of the trustee, and which would naturally pervert the feelings and judgment of the trustee, who is given full power to determine what allowance the beneficiary shall have, limited only by the duty of exercising a fair and reasonable discretion, although there is no distinct proof of misconduct in consequence of such hostility. . . .

We may say, moreover, that the decision of the trial court upon such a complaint should not be disturbed, except upon clear and convincing grounds.

The decree of the lower court is affirmed, with costs.

RESTATEMENT (THIRD) OF TRUSTS
(Tent. Draft approved 1999)
(cross-referencing omitted; some paragraphing disregarded)

§37. *Removal of Trustee.* A trustee may be removed
(a) in accordance with the terms of the trust; or
(b) for cause by a proper court.

Comment:

a. Refusal to appoint. If a statute requires testamentary trustees to
be appointed by a court, the court will refuse to appoint a person as
trustee under circumstances that would warrant the person's removal
as trustee. In similar circumstances, even if court appointment is not
required, while a settlor's estate is in administration, a court may replace a person designated by the settlor to serve as a testamentary
trustee.

Courts are less hesitant to reject a designated trustee's appointment
at the outset than to remove an acting trustee, because of the severity of
the action and the disruption in administration which the latter entails.

Trustees may be disqualified for reasons that predate the creation
of the trust. For example, a spouse named as a fiduciary in a will or
will substitute may be ineligible to serve if the settlor and the spouse
are later divorced. . . .

c. Terms of the trust. The settlor may remove the trustee if the power
to do so is reserved in the terms of the trust, or if the settlor has retained
the power to revoke the trust. Also, power to remove a trustee may be
conferred by the terms of the trust upon one or more beneficiaries or
others. . . . The tax consequences of the retention or grant of removal
powers are beyond the scope of this Restatement [but may require care
in drafting, as discussed in the Reporter's Notes]. . . .

e. Grounds for removal. The following are illustrative but not exhaustive, of possible grounds for a court to remove a trustee: lack of capacity
to administer the trust; unfitness, whether due to insolvency, diminution of physical vigor or mental acuity, substance abuse, want of skill,
or the inability to understand fiduciary standards and duties; acquisition of a conflicting interest; refusal or inability to give bond, if bond
is required; repeated or flagrant failure or delay in providing accountings or information to beneficiaries; the commission of a crime, particularly one involving dishonesty; gross or continued underperformance
of investments; changes in the place of trust administration [or] location of beneficiaries, or other developments causing a serious geo-
graphic inconvenience to the beneficiaries or to the administration of
the trust; unwarranted preference to the interests of one or more bene-

ficiaries; a pattern of indifference toward some or all of the beneficiaries; or unreasonable or corrupt failure to cooperate with a co-trustee. Not every breach of trust warrants removal of the trustee, but serious or repeated misconduct, even unconnected with the trust itself, may justify removal. . . .

Friction between trustee and beneficiaries. Friction between the trustee and some of the beneficiaries is not a sufficient ground for removing the trustee unless it interferes with the proper administration of the trust. . . . Serious friction between co-trustees may also warrant removal of one or both of them. . . .

f. Trustee named by settlor. The court will less readily remove a trustee named by the settlor than one appointed by a court. . . . Such deference, however, may no longer be justified if, after being designated, a corporate trustee undergoes a significant structural change, such as by merger, or any trustee significantly reduces the level or quality of service to the trust or its beneficiaries. Ordinarily, a court will not remove a trustee named by the settlor upon a ground that was known to the settlor at the time the trustee was designated, even though a court would not itself have appointed that person as trustee. . . . Thus, the fact that the trustee named by the settlor is one of the beneficiaries of the trust, or would otherwise have conflicting interests, is not a sufficient ground for removing the trustee or refusing to confirm the appointment. This is so even though the trustee has broad discretion in matters of distribution and investment. A trustee's removal may be warranted, however, by a conflict of interests that existed but was unknown to the settlor at the time of the designation, or that came into being at a later time. Furthermore, when a beneficiary serves as trustee or when other conflict-of-interest situations exist, the conduct of the trustee in the administration of the trust will be subject to careful scrutiny. . . .

g. Alternatives to removal of trustee. Courts may grant more limited relief to deal with cases in which removal is not necessary or appropriate. For example, conflict-of-interest problems may be ameliorated by the appointment of an additional trustee, or by the appointment of a trustee *ad litem* to handle a specific, sensitive transaction. Insolvency concerns might be dealt with by requiring a bond or other security for the proper administration of the trust. . . .

As indicated in the foregoing cases and excerpts, a beneficiary who is named to act as trustee is normally entitled to do so, although practical considerations may nevertheless make it preferable for a settlor not to designate a person who, as trustee, would be subject to conflicting

interests. The possible personal, administrative, and tax problems of
such arrangements should be taken into account. This is not at all to
suggest that beneficiaries[3] or other interested persons should not be
named as trustee in appropriate cases. In fact, it is quite common today
for such persons to act alone or as one of two or more cotrustees. In
trusts that are prompted by tax considerations, the use of a family member as trustee or cotrustee involves special tax risks and may require
that the family trustee's powers be carefully limited to avoid certain
income and estate tax hazards — particularly in cases of irrevocable
or inter vivos trusts that are intended to relieve a settlor of the normal
consequences of owning the property. In small trusts it may also be
desirable to appoint an interested person who will serve gratuitously
as trustee; and when some of the shares of, or assets used in connection
with, a closely held business are placed in trust, the settlor may wish
to have the surviving co-owner of the business serve as trustee, despite
the obvious possibility of conflicting interests. All of this does suggest,
however, that careful planning and drafting are required in such cases
and particularly that special administrative provisions will usually be
necessary.

Where the terms of a trust provide that the trustee may be removed
by one or more beneficiaries or some other person, the power may be
validly exercised without justification in the absence of some limitation,
such as removal "for good and sufficient cause," and as long as it is
not found that the exercise will jeopardize the interests and rights of
the beneficiaries. As indicated in the Restatement excerpt above, in
the absence of a provision authorizing removal by one or more of the
beneficiaries, they possess no such power over the trustee, except by
petitioning a court for removal or under circumstances (see Chapter
14) in which all beneficiaries could terminate the trust.

B.   Rights to Compensation and Indemnification

PROBLEM

17-C.   *D* died shortly after her retirement, leaving an estate existing
primarily of readily marketable securities listed on national exchanges.
The only parcel of real property, a condominium, was held in joint
tenancy with a child. Estate administration has proceeded smoothly
and the executor, Friendly Bank & Trust Co., has just filed with the

---

3. Of mainly academic interest is the rule that a trust is extinguished by *merger* if the
sole trustee is or becomes the sole beneficiary. It is generally recognized, however, that
merger does not result if a sole trustee is one of several beneficiaries, a sole beneficiary
is one of several trustees, or even if all of several beneficiaries are also the only trustees.
See IA W. Fratcher, Scott on Trusts §§99-99.5 (4th ed. 1987).

court its final accounts and its petition for approval and discharge, accompanied by a request for allowance of its executor fee, supported by its printed regular schedule of charges based on a percentage of the estate's gross value. You represent the residuary devisee, who is surprised and irritated at the size of the fee. Considering the cases and other materials below, what advice would you give?

Unless personal representatives and trustees accept appointment to serve gratuitously, they are entitled to compensation for their services. In many states the fee is left to the discretion of the court pursuant to a flexible standard. See, e.g., UPC and UTC excerpts below. Under these "reasonable compensation" standards, local courts have sometimes developed an informal schedule of fees as a guide. In some states a standard schedule of fees is set by statute. The 1991 California statutory schedule, infra, is illustrative of compensation for personal representatives. Consider also the policies reflected in the parallel provisions of §§10810-10814 for attorneys.

UNIFORM PROBATE CODE

§3-719. *Compensation of Personal Representative.* A personal representative is entitled to reasonable compensation for his services. If a will provides for compensation of the personal representative and there is no contract with the decedent regarding compensation, he may renounce the provision before qualifying and be entitled to reasonable compensation.[4] A personal representative also may renounce his right to all or any part of the compensation. . . .

UNIFORM TRUST CODE
(Draft, Feb. 2000)

§708. *Compensation of Trustee.*

(a) If the terms of a trust do not specify the trustee's compensation, a trustee is entitled to compensation that is reasonable under the circumstances.

---

4. In the absence of legislation, a typical view (applicable at least in the absence of unanticipated circumstances) is stated in Bailey v. Crosby, 226 Mass. 492, 494, 116 N.E. 238, 239 (1917): "The executor was not bound to accept the trust, but having done so he is entitled to receive only the compensation named in the will, whether that sum be more or less than a reasonable sum."

(b) If the terms of a trust specify the trustee's compensation, the trustee is entitled to be compensated as specified, but the court may allow more or less compensation if:

(1) the duties of the trustee are substantially different from those contemplated when the trust was created;

(2) the compensation specified by the terms of the trust would be unreasonably low or high.

CALIFORNIA PROBATE CODE

§10800.   *[Compensation of personal representative] based on value of estate.*

(a) Subject to the provisions of this part, for ordinary services the personal representative shall receive compensation based on the value of the estate accounted for by the personal representative, as follows:

(1) Four percent on the first fifteen thousand dollars ($15,000).

(2) Three percent on the next eighty-five thousand dollars ($85,000).

(3) Two percent on the next nine hundred thousand dollars ($900,000).

(4) One percent on the next nine million dollars ($9,000,000).

(5) One-half of one percent on the next fifteen million dollars ($15,000,000).

(6) For all above twenty-five million dollars ($25,000,000), a reasonable amount to be determined by the court.

(b) For the purposes of this section, the value of the estate accounted for by the personal representative is the total amount of the appraisal value of property in the inventory, plus gains over the appraisal value on sales, plus receipts, less losses from the appraisal value on sales, without reference to encumbrances or other obligations on estate property.

[Other sections of the California Probate Code allow the court to approve additional compensation for "extraordinary services" in an amount that is "just and reasonable" (§10801(a)); allow the personal representative to employ tax experts and pay them from estate funds (§10801(b)); allow the court, after notice and hearing, to authorize compensation greater than provided in the will if doing so is "to the advantage of the estate" and "in the best interest of the persons interested in the estate" (§10802); provide that an agreement between the personal representative and an heir or devisee for higher compensation than the statutory schedule is void (§10803); and direct the court to apportion the compensation among multiple personal representatives "according to the services actually rendered by each" (§10805).

Section 10804 provides: "Notwithstanding any provision in the decedent's will, a personal representative who is an attorney may receive the personal representative's compensation, but shall not receive compensation for services as the attorney for the personal representative unless the court specifically approves the right to the compensation in advance and finds that the arrangement is to the advantage, benefit, and best interests of the decedent's estate."]

§10810.   *Compensation [of estate attorney] for conducting ordinary proceedings.*

(a) Subject to the provisions of this part, for ordinary services the attorney for the personal representative shall receive compensation based on the value of the estate accounted for by the personal representative, as follows: [setting out the same same schedule as provided for personal representative in §10800, above.]

[Special provisions are set out in §§10811-10814 for additional, extraordinary, or contingent compensation for attorneys, for relief from attorney compensation specified in a will, for an attorney's agreement with a personal representative for higher than statutory compensation, and for apportionment of compensation among attorneys.]

ESTATE OF EFFRON
117 Cal. App. 3d 915, 173 Cal. Rptr. 93,
appeal dismissed, 454 U.S. 1070 (1981)

WIENER, A.J. . . .

[Appellants] challenged on theoretical and practical grounds both customary probate practices fostered by corporate fiduciaries and statutory attorney's fees: On a theoretical level, they claim as a matter of law statutory attorney's fees violate the antitrust laws and their application denies due process of law to those affected. As a practical matter, they question the ethical and legal propriety of what they allege to be the customary practice involving reciprocal back scratching between corporate fiduciaries and lawyers in which the lawyer drafting the will is always retained as counsel for the executor. In describing this scenario where the corporation's only purpose is to perpetuate corporate trust and probate business, they claim a conflict of interest is created causing a breach of the executor's duty, reflected here by the Bank's failure to negotiate a lesser fee for its lawyer than that allowed by statute and its failure to discharge counsel when Beneficiaries believed it was in their best interest to do so.

As we will explain, we conclude the system of statutory fees is valid, falling within the state action exemption to the Sherman Antitrust Act enunciated in Parker v. Brown (1943) 317 U.S. 341. We also decide the Bank did not breach its fiduciary responsibilities. We affirm the order. . . .

The Sherman Act of 1890, enacted to prevent undue restraints upon trade having a significant effect on competition, provides simply, "Every contract, combination in the form of trust or otherwise, or conspiracy in restraint of trade or commerce among the several States . . . is . . . illegal." (15 U.S.C. §1.) Lawyers can no longer take solace in the naive belief that, as members of a learned profession, they are exempt from the Act. "In the modern world it cannot be denied that the activities of lawyers play an important part in commercial intercourse, and that anticompetitive activities by lawyers may exert a restraint on commerce." (Goldfarb v. Virginia State Bar (1975) 421 U.S. 773, 788.) . . .

Within this framework, the applicability of the Sherman Act turns on our determination of whether statutory probate fees fall within the state action exemption of Parker v. Brown, supra.

> These decisions establish two standards for antitrust immunity. . . . First, the challenged restraint must be "one clearly articulated and affirmatively expressed as state policy"; second, the policy must be "actively supervised" by the State itself. [Citation.]

(Cal. Retail Liquor Dealers Assn. v. Midcal Alum., . . . 445 U.S. 97, 105 (1980).)

> It is clear that no exemption applies if the anticompetitive act is performed by a private association and is not compelled by the state (*Goldfarb*) or if the state merely approves anticompetitive conduct initiated by a private agency and the program does not effectuate any statewide policy (Cantor v. Detroit Edison Co., 428 U.S. 5 (1976).)

(Rice v. Alcoholic Bev., etc., Appeals Bd., . . . 21 Cal. 3d 431 at p. 444, 146 Cal. Rptr. 585, 579 P.2d 476 (1978).) . . .

The Legislature, after expending enormous energy on attorney's fees in probate proceedings, pointedly examining and reexamining the issue in various contexts, has determined the present statutory system of compensating lawyers is both cost effective and fair. Presumably, the public's interest is served where those bereaved are insulated from negotiating over a lawyer's fee during the traumatic post-death period.

Efficiency and economy are present in the use of judicial time which would otherwise be spent verifying fees and trying cases over questions of time, need, and reasonableness of the hourly rate charged. Theoretically, the present system also works in favor of smaller estates, for percentage fees are a financial incentive to lawyers to develop expertise and efficiency in the handling of those estates on a profitable basis, at lower fees than would otherwise be charged, thereby promoting greater access to competent legal services in such matters.

Our State Supreme Court also periodically reviews questions pertaining to the setting of attorneys' fees when it considers and approves State Bar Rules of Professional Conduct. Present rule 2-107 contains the factors which are to be considered in determining the reasonableness of a fee. The rules do not contain any prohibition against a lawyer charging a statutory fee nor do they suggest any ethical impropriety when he does so.

We do not wish to minimize the soundness of many of Beneficiaries' arguments criticizing the present system. One appellate court from another state, in describing legislative changes in probate, has referred to "the public outcry over antiquated and expensive probate laws" criticizing the percentage fee system as unnecessary and expensive. It commended the legislature for passing a law which authorizes payment to the attorney for the personal representative on a basis of numerous factors, only one of which is the monetary value of the estate. (See Matter of Estate of Painter (1977) 39 Colo. App. 506, 567 P.2d 820, 822.)

The caldron of public dissatisfaction over probate fees, which many view as having been forged through an amalgam of lawyer self-interest and lawyer mistrust, continually bubbles. A recent article in the Washington Post bemoaning a $1,908 hourly fee in a probate matter said, in part,

> Percentage fees . . . for settling estates . . . are generally a rip-off. Some lawyers, to be sure, can't stomach them; but most . . . think they are just dandy. There is little chance that this Legislature [Maryland], or any other, will do anything about this situation this year. But sooner or later lawyers are going to have to accept, or have imposed on them, the revolutionary idea that how much they charge a client should be related to how much work they do.

(Quoted in Los Angeles Daily Journal (Mar. 27, 1981) §1, p. 4.)

The fact that others, including legislatures from other states, have different views on the best system for compensating lawyers in probate matters does not mean this court may encroach upon the legislative prerogative where it has been lawfully exercised. We may not substitute our view for a legislative decision which legislators have made after the weighing of the relevant policy considerations. . . .

We also reject Beneficiaries' claim [that] the Bank's adherence to the statutory procedure and consequent failure to negotiate attorney's fee is private, anticompetitive conduct not mandated by the statute and thus constitutes a violation of the antitrust laws. This factual record, establishing what this Bank's practice is in hiring counsel for executors, is insufficient to establish a form of conspiracy falling within the purview of the Sherman Act. . . .

Beneficiaries say the Bank must be removed as executor because it breached its fiduciary duty when it did not fire the Rose firm upon their request. They claim the proper rule of law is that an executor, upon unanimous demand of an estate's beneficiaries, must discharge the attorneys for the executor, with or without cause, unless the executor will be subjected to some economic liability to third parties arising out of its duties as executor as a result of the discharge. . . .

An executor . . . is charged with the statutory duties of collecting, preserving and protecting the assets of the estate until distribution, subject to the continuing control of the probate court. . . . In the performance of those duties, the executor has the right to retain counsel whose fees for ordinary services, determined by statute, are treated as an expense of administration entitled to priority in payment of the decedent's debts. . . .

Beneficiaries argue the Bank's judgment over terminating the Rose firm was colored by its concern not to jeopardize its favorable trust business relationship with that firm. There is no doubt that economic self-interest is a factor which motivates a corporate fiduciary to retain the same lawyer who drafts the will. Nevertheless, where the testator's selection of the executor is free and voluntary, his wish may not be annulled except on a clear showing the best interests of the estate require it. (Estate of Sherman (1936) 5 Cal. 2d 730, 744, 56 P.2d 230.) The executor has the right to choose independent counsel to perform the necessary legal services on behalf of the estate. Presumably, the lawyer with familiarity of the decedent's property is a reasonable choice. Where lawyers' fees are governed by statute and require court approval, the element of the executor's self-interest standing alone does not create an absolute bar to retaining the same lawyer who drafted the will.

The order is affirmed.

ESTATE OF DAVIS
509 A.2d 1175 (Me. 1986)

WATHEN, J. [Case citations omitted.]

On a petition to review fees filed by personal representative Stuart E. Hayes, the Somerset County Probate Court approved a fee of $44,700 for services as personal representative of the estate of Linea A. Davis. Benjamin D. Harrington, Sr., and James B. Harrington, Jr., residual beneficiaries under the will of Linea Davis, appeal the Probate

Court's order, challenging the reasonableness of the fee, which Hayes admitted was based on a fixed percentage of the decedent's estate, under the Maine Probate Code. We conclude that the court erred in its determination of reasonableness, and accordingly, we vacate the Probate Court's order.

Hayes, an attorney, testified that he calculated his fee on a percentage basis. From decedent's gross estate, valued at $1,388,000, he deducted a total of $590,400 attributable to real and personal property situated in Florida, leasehold property located in Maine, and lifetime transfers made by the decedent. He then charged five percent of the remaining $797,600 value of the estate and five percent of $96,000 in income earned by the estate, for a total fee of $44,700.

Hayes testified that the handling of the Davis estate required performance of numerous tasks. The will listed many charities as beneficiaries but did not provide addresses for the various charitable legatees. Name changes increased the difficulty of locating some of the charities. In addition, payment to one individual beneficiary was impossible because she was incompetent and, as best Hayes could ascertain, did not have a representative to handle her affairs. The federal estate tax return had to be prepared under some time pressure due to delay in resolving a dispute between beneficiaries regarding the valuation of certain property. Hayes also testified that he encountered difficulty in obtaining information from various institutional trustees regarding four trusts created by decedent during her lifetime.

With regard to certain leasehold property held by the estate, Hayes testified that he had to negotiate the transfer of the leases to the beneficiaries and also described becoming embroiled in a dispute between beneficiaries as to whether the personal representative should undertake repairs on the leased property. Hayes was also responsible for overseeing the maintenance and subsequent sale of Florida real estate. Finally, Hayes testified that he timed certain distributions to minimize the beneficiaries' ultimate tax liability.

The record reveals that Hayes was familiar with the decedent's estate. He had acted as personal representative of the estate of decedent's husband in 1978. Thereafter, he prepared decedent's will in which he was named personal representative. Later, the decedent granted him a power of attorney to handle her financial affairs. . . .

The Probate Court made the following factual findings: Attorney Hayes is an experienced, able, and reputable practitioner of probate law. Personal representatives in the locality customarily charge five percent of the taxable estate for their services. Hayes and his staff spent approximately 250 hours working on the estate. The estate required considerable skill on the part of the personal representative and was handled in an efficient and competent manner. Finally, the court found that under the circumstances of this case, the fee charged constituted reasonable compensation for Hayes' services as personal representative.

The Harringtons argue that the Probate Court's decision must be vacated because the personal representative based his fee on a percentage of the estate, a practice the Legislature has sought to eliminate. We agree that with the enactment of the Maine Probate Code in 1981, the Legislature intended to abolish the prevailing practice in determining compensation for personal representatives as a percentage of the estate and to substitute a system based on reasonable compensation.

Prior to 1981, personal representatives were authorized by statute to charge up to five percent of the personal assets of an estate for their services. . . .

> One important, and highly undesirable, aspect of the . . . present Maine system is the tying of compensation to various percentages of the estate's value. It is precisely this kind of approach that has led to criticism of probate expense and has given rise to anti-trust problems when used as a general and pervasive standard for attorneys' fees throughout the bar. . . . Compensation should be based on the amount and value of the work done, under a variety of relevant circumstances.

Maine Probate Law Commission, Report of the Commission's Study and Recommendations Concerning Maine Probate Law 305 (October 1978). The Maine Probate Code, enacted in 1981, implemented the commission's recommendation regarding fees for personal representatives. Section 3-719 states that a personal representative "is entitled to reasonable compensation for his services." 18-A M.R.S.A. §3-719 (1981). Section 3-721 sets forth the following criteria for determining the reasonableness of a fee:

(1) The time and labor required, the novelty and difficulty of the questions involved, and the skill requisite to perform the service properly;

(2) The likelihood, if apparent to the personal representative, that the acceptance of the particular employment will preclude the person employed from other employment;

(3) The fee customarily charged in the locality for similar services;

(4) The amount involved and the results obtained;

(5) The time limitations imposed by the personal representative or by the circumstances;

(6) The experience, reputation and ability of the person performing the services.

18-A M.R.S.A. §3-721(b) (1981).[5]

The current provisions of the Probate Code, along with the legislative history surrounding their enactment, demonstrate that the Legislature intended to abolish the determination of fees for personal representatives on a percentage basis and to mandate that in all cases, such fees be governed by a standard of reasonable compensation. The clear expression of legislative intent is not dispositive of the present case, however, because the order of the Probate Court recites consideration of most[6] of the factors set forth in section 3-721 and ultimately finds the fee assessed to be reasonable. The determination of a reasonable fee is reviewed only for abuse of discretion, and the court's factual findings are final unless demonstrated to be clearly erroneous. . . .

Nevertheless, the court abused its discretion in concluding that a fee of $44,700 constitutes reasonable compensation for the services provided in this case.

Section 3-721 places complexity of the services required and the time and skill necessary to perform those services first among the factors to be considered in arriving at a reasonable fee. Courts in other jurisdictions with similar statutory provisions have emphasized that the reasonableness of a fee depends on the services actually performed rather than on the size of the estate.

Although the estate in this case cannot be described as simple, the personal representative himself testified that it involved no difficult negotiations or litigation and presented no novel legal questions. In cases such as this, when the services required are routine rather than extraordinary, the amount of time expended should be the predominant factor.

The Probate Court found that Hayes and his staff devoted 250 hours to handling the estate. Utilizing this figure, over half of which consists of secretarial and bookkeeping time, the fee amounts to an hourly rate of $180. If only the hours put in by attorney Hayes are considered, the hourly rate exceeds $400. It is evident that in finding such extraordinary hourly compensation to constitute a reasonable fee, the Probate

5. 18-A M.R.S.A. §3-719 is identical to sections 3-719 of the Uniform Probate Code. The formulation of the factors designated in 18-A M.R.S.A. §3-721(b) for determining the reasonableness of a fee, is not contained in the uniform act. Other states, however, have adopted similar additions to the Uniform Probate Code. See, e.g., Colo. Rev. Stats. §15-12-721 (1974); Fla. Stat. Ann. §733.617 (West Supp. 1986).

6. The Probate Court made no findings regarding the extent to which work on the estate precluded Hayes from accepting other employment, §3-721(b)(2), or as to time constraints involved in handling the estate, §3-721(b)(5). In his petition to review fees, Hayes admitted that work on this estate did not preclude his accepting other employment. The only evidence in the record as to time constraints was noted above with regard to filing of the federal estate tax return.

Court relied heavily on the local custom of charging a five percent fee for estate work. Given that sections 3-719 and 3-721 embody a legislative intent to abolish the percentage fee system, any continuing practice of charging percentage fees should carry little or no weight in evaluating the reasonableness of a fee under the new statutory scheme. The Probate Court's reliance on the local custom of percentage charges was improper.

Because we conclude that the Probate Court abused its discretion, we vacate the order and remand for further proceedings. . . .

AMERICAN BAR ASSOCIATION, STATEMENT OF PRINCIPLES REGARDING PROBATE PRACTICES AND EXPENSES
(1975)

2. Where, as is the usual case, the testator has made no prior arrangements for compensation, then (a) the commissions of the personal representative and the fee of the attorney for services in settlement of a decedent's estate should bear a reasonable relationship to the value of the services rendered by each and the responsibility assumed by each . . . ; and (b) the following factors, in particular, should be given significant weight in determining reasonable fees for the attorney and for the personal representative for their respective services in the settlement of the estate: (A) The extent of the responsibilities assumed and the results obtained. (B) The time and labor required, the novelty and difficulty of the questions involved, and the skill requisite to perform the services properly. (C) The sufficiency of assets properly available to pay for the services.

3. Rigid adherence to statutory or recommended commission or fee schedules, even when not illegal, is a frequent source of unfairness to beneficiaries of estates, to personal representatives or the attorney, as the case may be. Where such a schedule is consulted, it should (a) be considered to have been projected upon the assumption of the full and timely performance of the normal services involved in the proceeding and the full assumption of the responsibilities attached thereto, and (b) not be regarded automatically as either a maximum or a minimum, but only as a possible or suggested starting point to be considered in determining reasonable compensation, which, depending upon the circumstances, could be more or less than the amount (or amounts) indicated by the schedule.

4. Even if he is the sole personal representative an attorney may serve both as a personal representative of a decedent's estate and as counsel to the personal representative and may receive reasonable compensation for his aggregate services and responsibilities. . . .

6. When an attorney or personal representative, either by choice or by lack of experience, has certain of his normal duties performed by others, his compensation should, generally, be lower than otherwise to reflect the fact that certain services and responsibilities were not performed and assumed. . . .

7. When a personal representative or any attorney is required to render services with regard to nonprobate property, he should be reasonably compensated for such services and a determination should be made with respect to the amount to be charged and the property against which the charge should be made. . . .

Historically, a common practice among lawyers was to bill for estate planning services at "loss leader" rates, in the expectation of receiving a percentage fee for probating the client's estate. This practice has been questioned on various grounds and seems to be diminishing with intra-firm pressure to bill an increasingly transient client population at hourly rates, and as percentage fees continue to be criticized.

Recent attacks on fee requests have come from unexpected fronts. First, some local courts have challenged probate fees on their own motion, even when beneficiaries raised no objection. See J. Pennell, Ethics, Professionalism, and Malpractice Issues in Estate Planning and Administration, SC75 ALI-ABA 67, 129 (1998). Second, even if local courts have approved probate fees, the Internal Revenue Service may challenge the reasonableness of the fees for purposes of their estate tax deductibility under §2053. State court approval is not binding on the federal government under the principles of Commissioner v. Estate of Bosch, 387 U.S. 456 (1967).

Restatement (Third) of the Law Governing Lawyers §46 (Proposed Final Draft No. 1, 1996) supports the trend toward reasonable compensation. It provides that "[a] lawyer may not charge a fee larger than is reasonable in the circumstances or that is prohibited by law." Comment c notes the list of factors bearing on reasonableness that are found in Model Rule 1.5(a) and Model Code DR 2-106B, most of which are codified in the Maine statute quoted in Estate of Davis, supra. It further observes that "Other factors might also be relevant, such as the client's sophistication, the disclosures made to the client, and the client's ability to pay. . . . Relevant circumstances include whether . . . the client was a fiduciary whose beneficiary deserves special protection."

A trustee's right to a commission is generally expressed in terms of "reasonable compensation," either by statute or judicial decision. A few statutes still provide a fee schedule, but even in the absence of a statutory schedule local practice often tends to become more or less standardized. Uniform Probate Code §§3-721, 7-205 provide for judicial review of fiduciary compensation.

A representative fee schedule for a corporate trustee might look something like the following: 1 percent on the first $3 million of principal; 3/4 of 1 percent on the next $2 million; 1/2 of 1 percent on the next $5 million; and 3/8 of 1 percent on the balance. There might be a base fee of several thousand dollars annually, to which the schedule fees are added, or there might be a minimum annual fee of $5,000 or so, which is eliminated when the schedule produces an amount exceeding the minimum fee. If trusts of moderate size are invested in the fiduciary's common trust funds (recall the funds in the *Mullane* case discussed at page 785 in Chapter 16, supra), or in the increasingly popular "proprietary" mutual funds to which the bank provides advice or services and receives compensation (allowed by legislation in nearly all states as an exception to traditional principles of undivided loyalty, infra), the fiduciary typically charges a somewhat reduced rate. Increasing numbers of small banks are replacing their common trust funds by investment programs relying on independent mutual funds. Reduced fees in these cases are based upon greater efficiency in managing a trust's investments, and fees should also be reduced for compensation received from a proprietary mutual fund, so that total compensation from the trust and the mutual fund satisfies a "reasonableness" standard. Fees are likely to be increased for assets that are difficult to manage, such as a farm or closely held business. Some corporate trustees may charge or statutes may authorize an acceptance fee at the start of the trusteeship or a termination fee when the trust property is distributed, or both.

Like the Uniform Trust Code (supra), the Restatement (Third) of Trusts (Tent. Draft approved 1999) reinforces the trend to allow trustees *reasonable compensation* (§38(1)) and to recognize that courts have authority to depart from fee schedules prescribed by statute or trust instrument when circumstances show those fees to be distinctively excessive or inadequate (§38, cmts. *c* and *e*), while also suggesting flexibility with respect to compensation of multiple trustees and with respect to the effects of a trustee's employment of advisors (§38, cmts. *c* and *i*). Modern cases and legislation increasingly support a flexible approach in these matters. See generally Reporter's Notes to id. §38.

When compensation has been fixed by the terms of the trust, that provision normally controls, although changed circumstances or extraordinary services may lead a court to authorize different compensation. Sometimes when a trust company is appointed, the settlor will provide in the instrument for normal compensation in accordance with the trustee's standard fee schedule as it exists from time to time.

A. LORING, A TRUSTEE'S HANDBOOK
(1998 ed. C. Rounds & E. Hayes)

§3.5.2.3. *Right in Equity to Exoneration and Reimbursement.* Inasmuch as there is a rigid restriction against personal participation by the trustee in any of the profits and gains resulting from the administration of the trust estate, equity takes pains to hold the trustee harmless from personal liability for obligations properly incurred.

Inherent in the right of exoneration is the trustee's right to pay directly from the estate all of the expenses properly incurred as owner, including taxes, repairs, insurance, and other legitimate expenses of management, traveling expenses, the cost of justifiable litigation including attorneys' fees, and expenses of consulting counsel when there is reasonable cause. This right of exoneration is coupled with a right of reimbursement for sums paid from the trustee's own pocket for expenses properly incurred.

Where unauthorized expenses have been incurred in good faith, it has generally been held that the trustee is entitled to indemnification to the extent the trust estate has actually been benefited. Although this result is soundly grounded in unjust enrichment principles, there is some authority for the contrary result. Even though the estate is benefited, the trustee is not entitled to be reimbursed for an expense incurred in bad faith.

Ordinarily a trustee or personal representative may pay reasonable attorney fees for legal services incurred for the benefit of the estate, but not for those incurred for the benefit of the fiduciary personally. A related issue is whether, or under what circumstances, a beneficiary who is not acting in a fiduciary capacity may recover attorney fees from the estate. Much depends on the court's "sound" discretion, which, traditionally, has not been generously exercised. In Matter of Estate of Greatsinger, 67 N.Y.2d 177, 492 N.E.2d 751 (1986), the trial court awarded attorneys fees to remainder beneficiaries who had brought an unsuccessful will construction proceeding, the court's theory being that the suit benefited the estate by resolving a justifiable doubt as to the testator's intention. The decision was reversed on appeal on the ground that the remainder beneficiaries were acting in their own interest. On the other hand, Becht v. Miller, 279 Mich. 629, 273 N.W. 294 (1937), awarded attorney fees to a residuary legatee who challenged the personal representative's misconduct, although the amount of the lower court's fee award was reduced by about 75 percent on appeal.

C. General Fiduciary Duties and Standards

The functions of the fiduciary, and the standards and duties to which a fiduciary is held, reflect the nature of the interests that the fiduciary and beneficiary have in the property subjected to the relationship. The beneficiary has the beneficial interests and the fiduciary the management and administration of the property. Consequently we find that the fiduciary's functions are such as to enable and require the property to be managed for the exclusive benefit of those having the beneficial interest in it. The fiduciary owes the highest obligation to the beneficiaries to protect the property and to manage it solely in their interest, without regard to the fiduciary's own interests. As we consider the duties, powers, and liabilities of fiduciaries at different stages in these materials, it should be borne in mind that we are discussing different aspects of the fiduciary relationship.

There is some variation in the specific powers and liabilities of trustees as contrasted with those of personal representatives and with those of guardians, but usually these differences are but variations on the general theme of the fiduciary relationship. The law governing trustees is largely decisional, growing out of the practice of the early chancery courts. That governing personal representatives is largely statutory, though often also reflective of early chancery and common law practice. However, both common law and statutory techniques for the development of doctrine are important in these areas, as no statute is without some gap and no common law doctrine without some legislative embroidery.

Even though the various aspects of the fiduciary's functions are treated in greater detail later, it is worthwhile to consider them in general terms at the outset. The trustee has the duty to administer the property in the trust for the beneficiaries, and the personal representative has the duty to administer the property in the estate for the benefit of the creditors of the estate as well as the distributees. Both fiduciaries are obligated to observe the utmost loyalty to those with whom they are in a fiduciary relationship and to refrain from all manner of self-dealing whereby there may even be so much as temptation to place the interests of the beneficiaries second to the fiduciary's own. As we shall see, the law has hedged the relationship with many safeguards to prevent division of loyalties. Because the fiduciary is the one charged with the responsibility of making decisions in the administration of the estate, there has traditionally been a modestly qualified duty not to delegate this responsibility to others. The fiduciary is required to keep beneficiaries informed and to maintain records and render accounts to those interested in the estate in order to provide adequate information regarding the administration of the estate or trust. Appropriate to the obligation to preserve the property is the duty to keep the trust property separated from assets of the fiduciary and others in order that confusion of title may be avoided. We have already seen that the functions of a trustee require that the property be kept productive, while an executor or administrator, who is primarily involved in a liquidation process, ordinarily has no such affirmative duty. Should administration of a decedent's estate be unduly extended, however, the personal representative may very well be obligated to make the property productive in order to avoid unnecessary loss to the beneficiaries. In carrying out the many duties of administration, a fiduciary is required to use reasonable care and skill and to treat all of the beneficiaries impartially.

The details of an administrator's functions are governed by statute. Most of the powers, duties, and liabilities of executors and trustees are, for the most part at least, subject to the control of the testator or the settlor. The extent to which the usual procedures or obligations may be modified by appropriate directions in the will or trust instrument will be explored as particular problems are treated.

1. Prudence: The Standards of Care, Skill, and Caution

UNIFORM PROBATE CODE

§7-302. *Trustee's Standard of Care and Performance.* Except as otherwise provided by the terms of the trust, the trustee shall observe the standards in dealing with the trust assets that would be observed by a prudent man dealing with the property of another, and if the trustee has special skills or is named trustee on the basis of representations of special skills or expertise, he is under a duty to use those skills.

A fiduciary is required to exercise reasonable care, skill, and caution in the performance of the functions of the office. This set of standards is expressed in various ways. In later chapters we will see the possible effect of various formulations of the standard and its application in different aspects of estate and trust administration. Modern cases often quote the language of Professor Scott and the Restatement, which provide that a trustee is to exercise "such care and skill as a man of ordinary prudence would exercise in dealing with his own property." 1 Restatement (Second) of Trusts §174; IIA Fratcher, Scott on Trusts §174 (4th ed. 1987). The duty to act with prudence is not affected by whether the trustee receives compensation. (See comment to Uniform

Trust Code §804 (draft, Feb. 2000).) The element of caution implicit in the prudence standard has frequently been emphasized by stating that the test is not how one would act with regard to one's *own* property but how a prudent trustee would act in administering the property of *others* or how a trustee would act in *conserving* the property.

In re Mild's Estate, 25 N.J. 467, 136 A.2d 875 (1957), involved the surcharge of an administratrix for delegation of duties and failure to supervise the activities of her attorney. To the assertion that the administratrix was not capable of adhering to the usual standard of care and skill, the court responded (25 N.J. at 480-481, 136 A.2d at 882):

> This standard does not admit of variation to take into account the differing degrees of education or intellect possessed by a fiduciary. The standard of the "ordinary prudent person" is of necessity an ideal one and is not tailored to the imperfections of any particular person. Mr. Justice Holmes aptly stated the rule as follows:
>
>> The standards of the law are standards of general application. The law takes no account of the infinite varieties of temperament, intellect and education which make the internal character of an act so different in different men. . . .
>
> Holmes, The Common Law, p. 108 (1881).
>
> Mrs. Dorn's conduct must be measured by the standard of the mythical ordinary prudent administratrix, notwithstanding her natural limitations.

On the other hand, a fiduciary possessing greater than ordinary skill and more than ordinary facilities is under a duty to exercise the skill and to utilize the facilities at hand. Thus, in Liberty Title & Trust Co. v. Plews, 142 N.J. Eq. 493, 509, 60 A.2d 630, 642 (1948), it is stated:

> In the present case, the corporate trustee held itself out as an expert in the handling of estates and trust accounts. It also held itself out as having particular departments for investments and statistical information, and special skill in this respect. It had so advertised for a number of years. . . . It therefore represented itself as being possessed of greater knowledge and skill than the average man and, " . . . if the trustee possesses greater skill than a man of ordinary prudence, he is under a duty to exercise such skill as he has." . . . The manner in which investments were handled must be viewed and assayed in the light of such superior skill and ability.

See also comment to Uniform Trust Code §806 that the higher standard applies also to "a trustee of modest abilities who makes representations of great competence."

2. Duty of Loyalty

HALLGRING, THE UNIFORM TRUSTEES' POWERS ACT AND THE BASIC PRINCIPLES OF FIDUCIARY RESPONSIBILITY.
41 Wash. L. Rev. 801, 808-811 (1966)

The trustee may justify a self-dealing transaction only by showing (1) that the beneficiaries consented, (2) that their consent was given after full disclosure of all facts material to the transaction, and of the beneficiary's legal rights in the light of those facts, and (3) that the transaction was fair and reasonable. The "uncompromising rigidity"[7] of the rule requiring undivided loyalty is not an arid formalism. The courts have consistently held that this inflexibility is essential to its effective operation.

In refusing to make ready exceptions to the rule, the courts have recognized three principal considerations. I will discuss these briefly, in the belief that the reasons which gave rise to the present state of the law go far to commend its retention.

First, the courts have acknowledged that it is difficult, if not impossible for a person to act impartially in a matter in which he has an interest. Lord Loughborough said, in Whichcote v. Lawrence:[8] "Where a trustee has a prospect of advantage to himself, it is a great temptation to him to be negligent." A similar statement may be found in Thorp v. McCullum.[9] "Between two conflicting interests, it is easy to foresee, and all experience has shown, whose interests will be neglected and sacrificed." . . .

Just as no one may be a judge in his own cause, so a trustee can not be expected to utilize his best, most objective and disinterested judgment in situations where that judgment may run counter to his

---

7. I shall not be the first to depart from tradition by failing to quote Judge Cardozo's classic, if florid, statement of the principle of fiduciary loyalty in Meinhard v. Salmon, 249 N.Y. 458, 464, N.E. 545, 546 (1928):

> Many forms of conduct permissible in a workaday world for those acting at arm's length, are forbidden to those bound by fiduciary ties. A trustee is held to something stricter than the morals of the market place. Not honesty alone, but the punctilio of an honor the most sensitive, is then the standard of behavior. As to this there has developed a tradition that is unbending and inveterate. Uncompromising rigidity has been the attitude of courts of equity when petitioned to undermine the rule of undivided loyalty by the "disintegrating erosion" of particular exceptions. Only thus has the level of conduct for fiduciaries been kept at a level higher than that trodden by the crowd. It will not be consciously lowered by this court.

8. 3 Ves. Jr. 740, 750, 752 (1978).
9. 6 Ill. 614 (1844).

own interest. This observation, as earlier suggested, seems to be something of a constant in human affairs. It is not confined to the law of trusts, but has its analogies in the law of agency and of public officers.

It should be noted that the stricture against conflicting interest does not rest upon an imputation of dishonesty. That the most conscientious and judicious of men cannot be unmoved by the obtrusion of his own interest has long been recognized. It should, if anything, be more obvious in our own time in view of our increasing understanding of the importance of subconscious factors in human motivation. However upright the trustee, if the intrusion of personal advantage does not tip the scales of judgment against the interest of his beneficiary (perhaps without his conscious recognition), it will, by causing him to "lean over backwards" or in some still more subtle way, distort his objectivity. In any case, the beneficiary is deprived of that disinterested and impartial judgment to which he is entitled. The man of intelligent and refined sensitivity will be the first to recognize this, and to give wide berth to situations in which his freedom of judgment will be encumbered by a prospect of personal advantage.

Secondly, the courts have realized that fiduciary relationships lend themselves to exploitation. This is especially true in the case of the trust, in which the fiduciary aspect is peculiarly "intense." The trustee, by reason of his more-or-less complete control and day-to-day management of the trust property, often for long periods, has a large advantage over the beneficiary with respect to any matter in which their interests conflict. Normally, the trustee's position gives him superior knowledge of all the facts and circumstances relating to the trust property and its administration. Furthermore, the main purpose of his appointment is often to relieve the beneficiary of the cares of management, and to confer upon him the benefit of the trustee's superior skill and judgment. For these reasons, the success of the trust relationship will depend on the ability of the beneficiary to trust the trustee. The morals of the market place will not suffice. If the beneficiary must deal with the trustee at arm's length, look behind his representations, and supervise his conduct, the utility of the trust is greatly impaired. The only way to insure that the beneficiary can sleep at night in free and easy reliance on the loyalty of the trustee is to remove all serious temptations to disloyalty.

Finally, the courts have made much of the fact that disloyal conduct is hard to detect. Lord Loughborough, quoting Lord Hardwicke, said, in Whichcote v. Lawrence:[10]

> Where a trustee has a prospect of advantage to himself, it is a great temptation to him to be negligent; acting in a manner, that does not quite

10. 3 Ves. Jr. 740, 750, 752 (1798).

fix an imputation on him. His conduct may be so covered, that it may
be difficult to fix direct fraud upon him. . . .

The reasons why disloyalty will often go undetected are plain
enough. The trustee, by reason of his day-to-day management of the
trust estate, generally commands better information concerning its affairs than the beneficiary. Even a court, inquiring into his administration at a later date, cannot expect to match the trustee's knowledge.
Furthermore, many decisions of a trustee are matters of refined judgment and discretion. On such subjects as the value of trust property,
the wisdom of the retention or reinvestment of assets, and the needs
of the beneficiaries, judgments are rarely clear-cut. A wide variety of
determinations can generally be supported by plausible argument, and
rationalizations made after the fact will generally be unassailable. As
to these decisions of the trustee, undivided loyalty can be guaranteed
only by removing all factors which might give rise to a contrary motivation. This, of course, will not insure that the trustee's judgments are
infallible or even that they are the best of which he is capable; but it will
insure that they are not influenced by motives adverse to the interest of
the beneficiary.

See Matter of Rothko, 43 N.Y.2d 305, 372 N.E.2d 291, 401 N.Y.S.2d
449 (1977), and also Surrogate Midonick's opinion at 84 Misc. 2d 830,
379 N.Y.S.2d 923 (1975); R. Wellman, Punitive Surcharges Against Disloyal Fiduciaries — Is *Rothko* Right?, 77 Mich. L. Rev. 95 (1979).

PROBLEMS

17-D.   The testator left his residuary estate to three of his children
in trust in equal shares for the exclusive benefit of the testator's five
children. The trust included a parcel of valuable industrial real estate
that was subject to a mortgage. Four years after the testator's death,
the lessee of the property became insolvent and defaulted on the rent.
After evicting the tenant, the trustees were unable to obtain another
tenant because of a temporary business recession in the community.
The five children discussed the matter and decided to try to negotiate
an extension of the mortgage to avoid selling other assets of the trust.
The trustees were unable to secure an extension and the mortgagee
threatened foreclosure. Thereafter *S*, the spouse of one of the trustees,
purchased the mortgage from the mortgagee for $100 more than any
offer received by the mortgagee and granted an extension of six
months, which was acknowledged by the three trustees. One of the
other children was overseas at the time and was the only child who had
no knowledge of the purchase and extension of the mortgage by *S*. At

the end of the six months, the amount due on the mortgage remained unpaid. S foreclosed the mortgage and bought in the property at the public foreclosure sale. Five months later S sold the property to an industrial concern for a profit of $105,000.

The children, with the exception of S's spouse, sue to impress this $105,000 with the trust. How would you proceed if you represented the different parties involved? What result should the court reach?

How could the parties have protected themselves if they had secured counsel at the outset? Would the problem of protecting the transaction be complicated if the trust had provided for remainders to the testator's grandchildren and the issue of deceased grandchildren?

17-E.   D died leaving a large estate including real estate, securities, notes receivable, some limited partnership interests, and some valuable works of art. Her will directed payment of several pecuniary legacies, sale of certain assets, and distribution of the residue of her estate to her son T as trustee for certain family members and their descendants.

The estate has been in administration for about three years and First Bank, as executor, is preparing for final distribution, accounting, and discharge. T has retained you to advise him on the executor's accounting. The executor had regularly deposited estate cash receipts with its commercial banking department in a no-interest checking account entitled "First Bank as Executor of the Estate of D." It had drawn on this account for estate purposes, such as payment of debts and expenses, but maintained a minimum balance of $10,000 entitling it to free checking privileges. On the first of each month, First Bank transferred any amounts in the checking account over $10,000 to a 4 percent passbook savings account in its commercial department, using the same account title. When the balance in the passbook account exceeded $60,000, the executor invested $50,000 in six-month certificates of deposit in its commercial department, again designated by the same title. These CDs paid about 6 percent interest at maturity, after which the funds were reinvested in similar certificates. All accounts and certificates of deposit were insured by the Federal Deposit Insurance Corporation.

During the time the estate was in administration, the prime rate of interest at which the bank loaned to its best customers fluctuated between 8 percent and 9 percent. The bank also made other loans in its regular business at rates up to 14 percent.

The applicable state law includes Uniform Probate Code §3-715(5) authorizing a personal representative, "if funds are not needed to meet debts and expenses currently payable and are not immediately distributable," to "deposit or invest liquid assets of the estate, including moneys received from the sale of other assets, in federally insured interest-bearing accounts, readily marketable secured loan arrangements or other prudent investments which would be reasonable for use by trustees generally," and a Banking and Trust Code section entitled "Deposits by Corporate Fiduciaries" stating:

> Principal and income received and held by corporate fiduciaries awaiting investment or distribution may be invested temporarily in deposit accounts or other investment vehicles of such corporation, provided that it shall first set aside in its trust department obligations of the United States or securities wholly guaranteed, both as to principal and interest, by the United States having an aggregate market value, at all times, of at least 100% of the amount of such trust funds, unless such trust funds are insured by the Federal Deposit Insurance Corporation.

What advice would you give *T* in this situation? Why?

TRACY v. CENTRAL TRUST CO.
327 Pa. 77, 192 A. 869 (1937)

SCHAFFER, J.

In this proceeding in equity two of the three trustees of the Estate of David E. Tracy seek to compel the third one, Central Trust Company, to take back mortgages which it sold to the trust estate and properties obtained by foreclosure of some of them and to substitute therefor the money it received for them. The court below refused to grant the relief prayed for and dismissed the bill. From the decree so ordering we have this appeal by plaintiffs.

There is no dispute that defendant, having in its banking department and owning in its own right certain mortgages, sold them to the trust estate of David E. Tracy, of which it was one of the trustees and received from all of the trustees funds of the estate in payment therefor. The amount of the mortgages was $204,380.

The decedent under his will created a trust, the income from which is payable to his wife Gertrude H. Tracy for life and the principal in the main to named charities. The court below found as a fact, and there is no dispute of the finding, that plaintiffs participated in the purchases of the mortgages and knew that the trust company owned them. There is no question of bad faith on the part of defendant.

Appellants state the controlling question to be: Whether it is a breach of trust for a corporate trustee to sell to a trust estate, of which it is a cotrustee, mortgages originally taken and held by it for its own corporate purposes. While there are minor questions suggested and debated, an answer to the main one disposes of the controversy. It has long been an outstanding principle of the law of trusts that a trustee violates his duty to the trust estate if he sells to himself as trustee property which he individually owns. This principle has been crystallized in the Restatement, Trusts, sec. 170, comment *h,* (p. 435) thus: "The trustee violates his duty to the beneficiary if he sells to himself as trustee his individual property." We have always held to this principle: Painter v. Henderson, 7 Pa. 48; Everhart v. Searle, 71 Pa. 256. That the trustee acted in good faith makes no difference: Restatement, Trusts, Sec. 170, comment *h.* The doctrine applies, though the purchaser be one of several trustees: 26 R.C.L. 1327. And, covering the exact factual situation before us, in comment *i* of Sec. 170, (p. 436) of the Restatement, Trusts, it is stated: "A corporate trustee violates its duty to the beneficiary if it purchases property for the trust from one of its departments, as where it purchases for the trust securities owned by it in its securities or banking department." This rule is incorporated in our statutory law. "A bank and trust company shall not, directly or indirectly, purchase with funds held by it as fiduciary, or exchange for any real or personal property held by it as fiduciary, any asset of its commercial department": Act May 15, 1933, P.L. 624, Art. XI, Sec. 1111, 7 PS Secs. 819-1111.

The remedy for such a breach of trust is clear.

> If the trustee in breach of trust sells his individual property to himself as trustee and the price paid by him as trustee was more than the value of the property at the time of sale, the beneficiary can compel him to repay the difference; or, at his option, the beneficiary can set aside the purchase and compel the trustee to repay the amount of the purchase price with interest thereon, in which case the trustee will be entitled to receive from the trust estate the property and any income thereon actually received by the trust estate.

Restatement, Trusts, Sec. 206, comment *c* (p. 560).

A subordinate question arises out of the fact that plaintiffs, two of the trustees, participated in the purchases of the mortgages. This does not prevent relief.

> If there are several trustees, each trustee is under a duty to the beneficiary to participate in the administration of the trust and to use reasonable care to prevent a cotrustee from committing a breach of trust or to compel a cotrustee to redress a breach of trust.

Restatement, Trusts, Sec. 184.

> If there are several trustees, one or more of them can maintain a suit against another to compel him to perform his duties under the trust, or to enjoin him from committing a breach of trust, or to compel him to redress a breach of trust committed by him. A trustee is not precluded from maintaining such a suit by the fact that he himself participated in the breach of trust, since the suit is on behalf of the beneficiary.

Id., Sec. 200, comment *d* (p. 529). See also Abbott v. Reeves, Buck & Co., 49 Pa. 494.

Bill reinstated, with direction to enter a decree in accordance with this opinion. Costs to be paid by defendant.

In re ESTATE OF SWIECICKI
460 N.E.2d 91 (Ill. App. 1984)

HARRISON, P.J. . . .

During its tenure as guardian, the Bank invested [the minor ward's] money in two six-month certificates of deposit in itself. . . . During the times [the] money was not invested in these certificates, it was placed in a passbook savings account at the Bank. . . . By making commercial loans at an interest rate higher than that which it paid on its own certificates of deposit and savings accounts, the Bank made a profit on the estate's funds during its term as guardian. . . . The sole question presented by this appeal is whether [the Bank] must account to the estate for that profit. . . .

[W]e are compelled to conclude that the estate is entitled to the profit which the Bank made through the use of the estate's money. . . . [I]n the instant case, the Bank's financial motives and fiduciary responsibilities were incompatible. As "buyer" of [the ward's] money for its own use, the Bank had an interest in acquiring the money at the lowest possible rate, in order to insure the profitability of that acquisition. As "seller" of that same money for the purpose of earning interest income for the estate, the Bank as guardian was faced with the conflicting responsibility of considering only the interests of the estate in determining how to invest the estate funds. While it is not claimed and there is no evidence to suggest that the bank acted with anything less than good faith in carrying out its responsibilities as guardian, this fact does not preclude application of the rule prohibiting the trustee from dealing with the trust property on its own account. " . . . [T]he only safe rule is one which absolutely forbids a trustee to occupy two positions inconsistent with each other." Joliet Trust and Savings Bank v. Ingalls (1934) 276 Ill. App. 445, 451. In making the determination which we reach here, we are cognizant of the fact that courts in other jurisdictions have found no conflict of interest on facts similar to those presented in this case. These cases essentially treat the institutional trustee as two separate entities, one which acts as trustee and the other which acts as custodian of the estate. From this premise it is reasoned that the trustee is not actually buying trust property on its own account, or that money made by the institution through its handling of the trust fund constitutes a reasonable profit for the institution in its capacity as custodian, provided that the trust is paid at least the prevailing rate of interest on the fund. We find these cases unpersuasive, because we reject the premise underlying them. There is nothing to suggest that, in reality, the Bank here is anything other than one business entity, controlled by one board of directors and owned by a single set of stockholders. That the acquisition of money at a low rate and subsequent loaning of money at a higher rate inures to the benefit of the Bank as a whole is a fact undoubtedly within the understanding of both the trust and the commercial departments of the Bank. . . .

Nothing in the statute permitting a guardian to invest in obligations guaranteed by the United States indicates a legislative attempt to override the common law duty owed by the guardian, and we will not infer the existence of such an intention. . . .

Section 21-1.03 of the Probate Act . . . expressly permits the representative of a decedent's estate to invest in savings accounts or certificates of deposit in a state or national bank "even though the bank of deposit is the representative of the estate." [Section 21-2.06] of the [same] Act allowing the representative of a ward's estate to make similar investments, however, contains no provision permitting the representative to invest in itself. . . . [W]e will not presume in this case that the legislature intended to significantly alter the common law fiduciary rules pertaining to guardians without saying so. Nor do we believe that Section 3 of the Trust Companies Act . . ., discussed in the dissenting opinion, affects the result here. The funds in question were not "awaiting investment or distribution" as contemplated by Section 3. . . .

Reversed and remanded. . . .

JONES, J., dissenting. . . .

The majority's holding . . . is, I believe, contrary to legislative intent regarding a bank's investment of funds held in trust. Notwithstanding the general common law rule that a trustee shall not make any advantage to itself of a trust fund, the legislature of this state has specifically authorized the deposit of trust funds by a corporate trustee in its own banking department under certain conditions. Such a deposit of funds "awaiting investment or distribution" is proper . . . provided the deposit is protected by securities set aside for that purpose or is guaranteed by the Federal Deposit Insurance Corporation. . . .

In considering whether, under the general common law rule regarding a trustee's duty of complete loyalty to its cestui que trust, a bank may deposit funds in its own banking department, courts of other jurisdictions have reached different conclusions. Courts dealing with this question have noted the inherent conflict of interest that arises from a bank lending trust money to itself individually. Thus, it has been said, a corporate trustee may be tempted to leave large amounts of trust monies on deposit for an unnecessarily long time due to the convenience and profit derived from the use of such funds and may be tempted to make and continue such deposits despite knowledge by the bank's officers that the bank is in a precarious financial position.

The potential for self-dealing resulting from the temptation to consider the commercial activities of a bank in administrating [sic] its trusts (see 2 Scott, Trusts §170.23(A), at 100 (Supp. 1983)) has led in some instances to a flat prohibition against a corporate trustee depositing trust funds in its own account. Indeed, the American Law Institute, after much deliberation, adopted the position in its Restatement of Trusts that a bank or trust company that makes a general deposit of trust funds in its own banking department thereby commits a breach of trust, unless it is authorized to do so by the terms of the trust. This rule was continued in the Restatement (Second) of Trusts §170, comment *m* (1959). It is, however, common practice for banks and trust companies to deposit trust funds in their own institutions, and, despite the view of some courts that such transactions involve disloyalty, this practice is sanctioned by the weight of authority at common law. Bogert, Trusts and Trustees §598, at 488-89 (2d. ed. rev, 1980). . . .

A federal statute (12 U.S.C. §92a(d) (Supp. 1983)) makes similar provision [to that of the Illinois Trust Companies Act] for national banks operating in the state. See Comptroller of the Currency Regulation 9.10, 12 CFR §9.10 (1983). These statutes . . . provide an exception to the general rule prohibiting a trustee from dealing with trust property on its own account.

This exception can be justified on policy grounds as allowing "efficient temporary investment of funds held in a trust by a bank pending their ultimate disposition, while providing maximum security for those funds." (Humane Society of Austin v. Austin National Bank, 531 S.W.2d 574, 579.) The convenience for a corporate trustee of making such deposits in itself rather than in another institution is evident. . . . "Under the . . . statutory rule there is great security for the trust deposits, first through the insurance provided by the FDIC, and secondly, through the fund which is set apart in the trust department of the bank as security for all trust deposits." Bogert on Trusts and Trustees, §598, at 495 (2d. ed. rev. 1980).

While it may be objected that, despite these considerations of convenience and security, there remains the potential for self-dealing inherent in a bank's use of trust funds deposited in its own accounts, the statutes here referred to reflect a legislative recognition of the distinctive character of corporate trustees. . . . Such trust companies operate in a regulated environment under the supervision of banking authorities and are required to be examined, separately from an affiliated banking department, regarding their investment of funds and their actions generally. . . . In any event, the legislature of this state . . . has made a policy decision that the benefits to be afforded outweigh the potential for self-dealing inherent in such transactions. For this reason, the omission, referred to by the majority, of expressed statutory language permitting the representative of a ward's estate to invest in its own accounts must be disregarded as merely legislative oversight rather than as an expression of legislative intent.

Although the statutes here noted authorize the use of trust funds in the conduct of the trustee bank's business, these statutes do not relieve the bank of its fiduciary duty as trustee. . . . The deposit of trust funds in itself by a corporate trustee, then, must be consonant with principles of good faith and reasonableness in order to come within the cloak of immunity afforded by the statutes authorizing such deposits. . . .

In the absence of a basis for holding the bank liable for profits from the use of the minor's funds, the bank's payment of interest at the market rate leads to the same result as if the bank had taken the funds to any other institution and deposited them in similar accounts. Thus, the bank's actions here were proper, and the decision of the trial court approving the bank's final report and account should be affirmed.

MATTER OF ESTATE OF ALLISON
488 N.E.2d 1035 (Ill. App. 1986)

[Hazel Allison died in 1982, survived by five children. Her will nominates her son John as executor, and she left her residuary estate to three of her other children. The residue included the farm in question, which was apparently to be sold and the proceeds divided among the residuary distributees. Prior to her death, Hazel had executed a 50/50 crop share lease with Allison Farming Co., of which John was sole owner. The lease was terminable on certain notice by either party, and absent notice the year-to-year tenancy would automatically extend into the next year. On Hazel's death, John petitioned for and received letters testamentary, assuming, the court noted, "the awkward position of both landlord and tenant," but the will granted the executor "full power to engage in farming operations . . . to lease on shares . . . and to perform any other acts necessary or desirable in [his] discretion to operate such farm properties." The next spring (1983) the Department of Agriculture instituted the Payment in Kind (PIK) program allowing farmers to draw a certain amount of surplus commodities in exchange for their not planting those commodities; small cash diversion-payments were also part of the program. As executor, John enrolled in the program and, pursuant to the crop share agreement, divided the receipts (grain and cash) between the estate and Allison Farming Co. The receipts by the estate were reported in his first and second accounts, but neither mentioned Allison Farming's receipts from the PIK program. The residuary legatees would now have John account to the estate for all receipts from the PIK program. John's responses were: at the date of his mother's death the tenancy under the lease had continued automatically into 1983, so that "there were no dealings, therefore no self-dealing"; the will purportedly created and sanctioned his conflict of interest by allowing the executor to carry on farming operations; and there is no allegation that his decision to enroll in PIK was either in bad faith or contrary to the best interests of the estate. The trial court construed the lease and will together and concluded that it was Hazel's intention to allow such a conflict to exist.]

HEIPLE, P.J. . . .

The net effect of [prior cases] is to call John's actions as executor and de facto tenant into serious question. The first questionable act was the acceptance of the office of executor. He knew that the lease would automatically extend into the 1983 farming year when he became executor. At this point, he should have either refused the position or assigned the lease, [although] assignment might have disqualified the farms from the PIK program. . . . Turning to the decision to opt into the PIK program, it is undisputed that the decision was sound and that the estate was not harmed thereby. It is also the case that the profit realized by John from the set-aside would have occurred even if someone else had made the decision to participate. However, these circumstances are not entirely relevant. The profits earned by a fiduciary as the result of self-interested transactions belong to the beneficiaries. . . . Had John either petitioned the court for permission to enroll the farms in PIK or resigned and allowed a substitute executor to serve, then he could have received the tenant's share of the PIK bounty without adverse consequences. However, because he allowed himself to remain in a position to profit from a self-interested transaction, the profit must be accounted for and returned to the estate.

The argument that John raised before the trial court concerning the intent of the testatrix to create such a conflict is misplaced. While there is an exception to the general principles of fiduciary responsibility where the instruments creating the relationships sanction a conflict of interest, the exception does not govern here. . . .

Paragraph Six of the will makes it abundantly clear that John was to sell the farm as soon as reasonably possible and divide the proceeds among the residuary legatees. As such, the only conflict sanctioned by Hazel was a brief, limited period of John in the dual role of landlord and farm tenant. Unfortunately, the PIK program entered into the equation. It is impossible for Hazel to have foreseen the redistribution of profits and expenses occasioned by PIK when she executed her will. Thus, the windfall profit that John earned as a result of his decision as executor to enroll the farms in PIK constituted a self-interested transaction the kind of which Hazel did not sanction.

We reiterate that the decision to participate in PIK was a sound exercise of discretion and in the best interests of the estate. Moreover, John would have been entitled to this profit if a different executor had made the decision to participate. He also could have petitioned the court for instructions or sought prior approval from the legatees. However, because John used his fiduciary office to profit from a self-interested transaction with estate property, he must account to the estate.

John argues that he did not deal with himself because the lease was between the estate and his solely-owned corporation. We can not agree. The prohibition against self-dealing by a fiduciary cannot be avoided by use of the corporate persona. . . .

John further contends that the propriety of the PIK transactions was adjudicated as a result of the approval of the First Current Account and Report. Thus, objections to the second report are subject to the defenses of res judicata and collateral estoppel. The only transaction reported on the first accounting was the . . . payment to the estate. Nothing was mentioned regarding Allison Farming Company. . . . The record suggests that the trial court did not decide in approving the first account that the payments to the tenant were proper.

Accordingly, the order overruling the legatee's objection . . . is reversed and remanded for further proceedings consistent with this opinion. . . .

See also Amalgamated Clothing & Textile Workers, etc. v. Murdock, 861 F.2d 1406 (9th Cir. 1988). In Matter of Scarborough Properties Corp., 25 N.Y.2d 553, 558, 255 N.E.2d 761, 763-764 (1969), Chief Justice Fuld stated:

> The rule has long been established that a trustee "should not be allowed to become a purchaser of the trust property, because of the danger in such a case that the interests of the beneficiary might be prejudiced." However, there is little danger of such prejudice if the transaction is subjected to prior judicial scrutiny and given court approval. Accordingly, the rule against self-dealing has not been applied, and does not apply, to interdict the purchase of trust property by a trustee where the court, after conducting a full adversary hearing at which all interested parties are represented, approves and authorizes the sale.

Compare Estate of Halas, 568 N.E.2d 170, 178 (Ill. App. 1991) (citations omitted):

> The creator of the trust can waive the rule of undivided loyalty by expressly conferring upon the trustee the power to act in a dual capacity, or he can waive the rule by implication where he knowingly places the trustee in a position which might conflict with the interests of the beneficiaries.
> . . . Where a conflict of interest is approved or created by the testator, the fiduciary will not be held liable for his conduct unless the fiduciary

has acted dishonestly or in bad faith, or has abused his discretion. Further, where the will approves the conflict of interest, the burden of proof remains on the party challenging the fiduciary's conduct as there is no presumption against the fiduciary despite the divided loyalty.

With the exceptions for authorization by court or in the trust instrument, compare Uniform Probate Code §3-713 (personal representatives) and §5-421 (conservators). Estoppel, of course, may bar suit against a fiduciary by any beneficiary whose properly informed consent (or acquiescence or ratification) has been obtained. See, e.g., Uniform Trust Code §1009 (draft, Feb. 2000). See also id. §802(c) ("transaction involving . . . trust property" is not automatically voidable but "presumed to be affected by a conflict [of interest] if entered into by a trustee with" certain relatives or an "agent or attorney" of the trustee or with an enterprise in which the trustee (or one holding a significant ownership interest in the trustee) has "an interest that might affect the trustee's best judgment") and §802(h) (allowing court appointment of a "special fiduciary [cf. trustee ad litem] to make a decision" on a transaction involving a potential violation of the duty of loyalty).

UNIFORM PROBATE CODE

§1-108. *Acts by Holder of General Power.*   For the purpose of granting consent or approval with regard to the acts or accounts of a personal representative or trustee, including relief from liability or penalty for failure to post bond, to register a trust, or to perform other duties, and for purposes of consenting to modification or termination of a trust or to deviation from its terms, the sole holder or all co-holders of a presently exercisable general power of appointment, including one in the form of a power of amendment or revocation, are deemed to act for beneficiaries to the extent their interests (as objects, takers in default, or otherwise) are subject to the power.

CITY BANK FARMERS TRUST CO. v. CANNON
291 N.Y. 125, 51 N.E.2d 674 (1943)

[Appeal from Appellate Division order affirming a judgment settling plaintiff's accounts as trustees. The Appellate Division made findings of fact as follows:

1. Although the interest of the trustee, City Bank Farmers Trust Company, in its own stock, evidenced by the certificates of stock of The National City Bank of New York received by the trustee upon said Bank

and Trust Company becoming affiliated, was such as to place the trustee in a position of divided loyalty as a matter of law, there was no divided loyalty in fact.

2. Mary E. Cannon, the settlor and life beneficiary, had knowledge of the facts which placed City Bank Farmers Trust Company as trustee in a position of divided loyalty as a matter of law, and of her right to remedy the situation by revoking the trust or amending it so as to substitute another trustee, or requiring the trustee to sell the shares of stock of The National City Bank of New York, the ownership of which gave to the trustee a beneficial interest in shares of its own stock, but she consented to the City Bank Farmers Trust Company continuing to occupy the said position giving rise to divided loyalty as a matter of law.

The conclusions of law read:

1. The interest of the trustee, City Bank Farmers Trust Company, in its own stock . . . was such as to place the trustee in a position of divided loyalty, which would have constituted a breach of trust if the settlor had not consented to said Trust Company continuing to occupy such position.

2. The settlor had the power to revoke the trust or to amend it so as to remove the trustee or to require the trustee to sell the stock of The National City Bank of New York. Since the settlor had knowledge of the facts which, as a matter of law, placed the trustee in a position of divided loyalty, and of her right to remedy the situation, and she consented to the City Bank Farmers Trust Company continuing to occupy such position, said trustee was not guilty of a breach of trust in continuing as trustee and in continuing to hold such stock.

The appeal is from every part of the judgment that directly or by implication determines that the corporate trustee should not be surcharged for loss in the value of bank stock while the trustee was in a position of divided loyalty.]

THACHER, J.

The action was brought by City Bank Farmers Trust Company and two individuals, as trustees, under a deed of trust for the judicial approval and settlement of their accounts. The only questions presented on this appeal were raised by the guardian ad litem of the infant defendants interested in the trust who sought to surcharge the corporate trustee for loss on investments in National City Bank stock incurred after the Bank's affiliation with the trustee. None of the other defendants has objected to the accounts. . . .

The trustee was expressly authorized to retain securities "so long as it may seem proper" and also to sell the same from time to time in its discretion and to invest and reinvest the proceeds thereof and any other cash at any time in its hand as trustee in such securities as to it may seem wise without being limited to investments legally authorized for trust investments.

Included in the securities delivered to the trustee under the deed of trust were 300 shares of National City Bank stock of the par value of $100. During the years 1926, 1927 and 1928 the donor requested the trustee to increase this holding of National City Bank stock through the exercise of subscription rights and to this end made additions of cash and securities to the trust to be used in partial payment for the additional shares. The result of these transactions was that prior to the affiliation of the National City Bank with the trustee there were held in the trust 3,000 shares of the Bank stock having a par value of twenty dollars a share. There is no suggestion that these investments were improper when made. . . . It is, however, contended that by the affiliation of the Bank and the Trust Company the latter as trustee became the beneficial owner of its own stock, was thus placed in a position of divided loyalty and should be surcharged for retaining the Bank shares which were inseparable from beneficial ownership of its own shares. The affiliation was accomplished by increasing the capital stock of the Bank and exchanging the new shares for all of the shares of the Trust Company on a basis of five Bank shares for one Trust Company share. The Trust Company shares were placed in trust for all the shareholders of the Bank each of whom acquired a pro rata beneficial interest in all the shares of the Trust Company. . . . After affiliation the two companies had several common officers and directors. Earnings distributed as dividends by the trustee were paid to the shareholders of the Bank. . . . The trustee with the donor's approval and active participation turned in the old certificates of stock of National City Bank held in the trust and received for them new certificates exactly like the old ones except for an additional endorsement showing that ownership of the stock carried with it a proportionate beneficial interest in the stock of the trustee. Thus the trustee acquired as an asset of the trust a substantial beneficial interest in its own stock which could only be sold by selling its shares in the National City Bank with which it was so closely affiliated. The fact is established that Mrs. Cannon not only approved the investment but insisted that the shares be retained by the trustee and as long as she lived was opposed to a sale of these shares. In this opposition she was supported by the honest judgment of the trustee. Nor is there any doubt that the donor was fully cognizant of her full powers of revocation and modification.

The standard of loyalty in trust relations does not permit a trustee to create or to occupy a position in which he has interests to serve other than the interest of the trust estate. Undivided loyalty is the supreme test, unlimited and unconfined by the bounds of classified transactions. . . . Undivided loyalty did not exist after affiliation of the trustee and the Bank because of the ownership by the trust of the shares of the Bank. The officers of the trustee responsible for the administration of the trust were under a duty with unremitting loyalty to serve both the interest of the Trust Company and the interest of the trust estate. These were conflicting interests insofar as the trust investment in the National City Bank shares required a decision whether to hold or to sell the shares in a falling market. The sale of this large number of shares might have seriously affected the interests of the Trust Company by depressing the value of these shares in a rapidly deteriorating market. Consequently the trustee had conflicting interests to serve in deciding to sell or not to sell. We do not for a moment suggest that the trustee did not act in the utmost good faith. Both courts below so found. But that is not enough for when the trustee has a selfish interest which may be served, the law does not stop to inquire whether the trustee's action or failure to act has been unfairly influenced. It stops the inquiry when the relation is disclosed and sets aside the transaction or refuses to enforce it, and in a proper case, surcharges the trustee as for an unauthorized investment. It is only by rigid adherence to these principles that all temptation can be removed from one acting as a fiduciary to serve his own interest when in conflict with the obligations of his trust. The rule is designed to obliterate all divided loyalties which may creep into a fiduciary relationship and utterly to destroy their effect by making voidable any transactions in which they appear.

In continuing to act as trustee and retaining the shares, the respondent Trust Company violated the rule of undivided loyalty and is accountable for the loss on the shares unless the donor by approving the investment and its retention has estopped the guardian ad litem and the infant remaindermen he represents from objecting to the investment. A similar problem was presented in Central Hanover Bank & Trust Co. v. Russell (290 N.Y. 593 [1943]). There we held that a settlor of a trust, who retained a testamentary power of appointment over the remainder limited upon life estates of the settlor and of her sister, by joining with her sister in approving investments of funds of the trust in the stock of the corporate trustee precluded the appointees named in her will from objecting to the investments thus approved. In the *Russell* case, the power retained was a power to appoint by will. Here we are concerned with powers to change and to revoke the trust.

A settlor who reserves absolute power of modification and revocation possesses all the powers of ownership and for many purposes is treated as the absolute owner of the property held in trust. . . .

Since the settlor reserved the right to exercise all the powers of ownership insofar as the trust was concerned, we hold that her action in approving the exchange of National City Bank shares for shares carrying a beneficial interest in the shares of the corporate trustee and in opposing any sale of the new shares was an effective estoppel not only against her own objections but also against an objection by the recipients of her bounty to the acts of the trustee which she approved. . . .

The judgment should be affirmed, without costs.

Compare with the above case the situation in which a testator names a bank as executor and trustee under his will and the estate includes a block of the shares of the named bank. Although it is probably the duty of the bank to dispose of its own stock, this may cause problems. In a relatively small community the available market for such shares may be limited to — or at least significantly impaired by the absence of — persons who are already substantial shareholders, officers, and directors of the bank. What problems does this situation pose? Particularly consider the responsibility of the lawyer who draws a will for a person in the circumstances of such a testator.

As a matter of social and economic policy, concerns have been raised about the power lodged in large banks through their trust department holdings of billions of dollars of securities in private trust accounts and employee benefit funds. The trust departments could exercise control by voting corporate shares held in these accounts, or by decisions to buy or sell shares in a corporation. See Berle, "Our Problem of Financial Power?" Washington Post, Aug. 11, 1968; Staff Study, Senate Subcommittee on Reports, Accounting, and Management, Committee on Governmental Affairs, Voting Rights in Major Corporations, 59th Cong., 1st Sess. 1-4 (1978). See also P. Harbrecht, Pension Funds and Economic Power (1959); D. Kotz, Bank Control of Large Corporations in the United States (1978); Twentieth Century Fund, Abuse on Wall Street (Schotland ed. 1980).

Legislation that is relevant — or at least potentially relevant — to a trustee's voting of its own stock frequently takes one of two forms. The Ohio litigation reported in the two opinions that follow is affected by both of these types of statutes and ultimately becomes concerned with the common law on the question, with differing viewpoints on the latter being reflected in the two opinions.

One form of legislation is patterned after a federal statute providing that a national bank that holds its own stock as a sole trustee may not vote those shares in the election of its directors unless it is directed to do so by a beneficiary or settlor who is authorized to so direct by the terms of the trust, and where the bank is a cotrustee its shares may be voted by the *other* trustee or trustees. 48 Stat. 186 (1933), as amended by 80 Stat. 242 (1966), 12 U.S.C. §61. Comparable legislation now exists in some states. See Cal. Corp. Code §703; N.Y. Banking Law §6012. See also Ohio Rev. Code §1109.10(c), enacted after the start of the litigation below.

The other form of legislation, more general but arguably applicable, is illustrated by Ohio Rev. Code §1701.47(c), originally enacted prior to the litigation below. In relevant part, it provides: "No corporation shall directly or indirectly vote any shares issued by it." A similar prohibition was held inapplicable to shares held by a bank *in trust.* Graves v. Security Trust Co., 369 S.W.2d 114 (Ky. 1963).

CLEVELAND TRUST CO. v. EATON
11 Ohio Misc. 151, 229 N.E.2d 850 (Ct. App. 1967)

CORRIGAN, J.

Stated in its simplest form the issue facing this court is: May the present management of the Cleveland Trust Company at the stockholders meeting for the election of directors vote directly or through its nominee the shares of Cleveland Trust stock held by it in a fiduciary capacity? . . .

While there are some Ohio cases . . . dealing with this general problem, no court in this state has been called to rule upon the direct question of whether the prohibition of Section 1701.47(C), Revised Code [text, supra], against an Ohio corporation voting stock issued by it applies to a bank and trust corporation. . . . [We conclude] that the plaintiffs herein, the Cleveland Trust Company, are not entitled to vote Cleveland Trust stock held by the bank in a fiduciary capacity. . . .

The law is clear that self-dealing or breach of good faith on the part of a trustee can not be excused on the ground that the instrument creating the trust and making him trustee has given him broad authority and unlimited discretion in the administration of the trust . . . unless express authorization is contained in the instrument creating the trust or in a provision of law. . . . [Furthermore, it] is elementary that to bind a beneficiary in a breach of trust, by acquiescence, it must be made to appear not only that he was aware of all the material facts, but that he was also advised of his legal rights and failed thereafter to register objection. . . .

CLEVELAND TRUST CO. v. EATON
21 Ohio St. 2d 129, 256 N.E.2d 198 (1970)

[In 1968, after the above decision, Ohio Rev. Code §1109.10(c) and other sections applicable to trust companies were enacted; at the outset of this opinion the Supreme Court of Ohio determined that the present case was governed by pre-1968 law without §1701.47(c) — that is, by the common law.]

TAFT, C.J. . . .

[When a corporation owns its own shares, the] voting rights have been regarded in effect as corporate property [and might accordingly be allocated] to each stockholder in proportion to the amount of his ownership interest in the corporation. Because of the impracticability of doing this and because the same effect can be obtained by suppressing the exercise of voting rights with respect to such stock, the common law developed a rule preventing a corporation from exercising, in the election of directors, voting rights on those of its shares owned by it. . . .

[T]he reason for not allowing a bank to vote its own shares for directors does not exist where those shares are held by it as trustee for others. . . . If shares so held by the bank in trust cannot be voted, voting rights belonging to those beneficiaries are in effect given without consideration to the remaining shareholders.

We conclude therefore that any common-law rule, against a corporation in an election for its directors voting shares of stock owned by the corporation, does not apply to such corporations so voting its own shares held by it as a trustee for others. . . .

In our opinion, the mere fact that a corporate trustee might acquire some advantage from voting [those shares] does not require the conclusion that a trust should be deprived of the protection that the trustee can and should give to the trust by voting such shares so as to benefit the trust.

We recognize that, in voting shares held by it in trust, a bank may commit a breach of trust. . . . [W]here it does commit such a breach of trust it can be held accountable to the trust. . . .

Judgment reversed.

[Concurring and dissenting opinions omitted.]

———————

The novel by Arthur Hailey, The Moneychangers (Doubleday, 1975) is purportedly based on the Cleveland Trust situation and gives a dramatic picture of insider information and problems of self-dealing.

What if a bank's commercial department loans money to X Company to finance a takeover of Y Company, whose shares the bank's trust department holds? Also, may the bank, as trustee, vote its own shares held in trust accounts it administers? See Cal. Corp. Code §703(c); Ill. Comp. Stat. Ann. Ch. 805, §§5/7.40, 5/7.50; Kan. Stat. Ann. §17-6410; Tex. Prop. Code §113.055.

PROBLEM

17-F.   Your client owns half of the stock of an incorporated department store. The other half of the stock is owned by her brother. The building in which the store operates under a long-term lease is owned by the client and her brother as tenants in common. Your client's interests in the department store and the building are valued at about $400,000 and $500,000 respectively. The rest of the client's estate is comprised of listed securities. The client's situation calls for the use of a trust, and she would like to have the securities administered by the *T* Trust Company and to have her brother administer the business interest and the store building. The brother knows the business well, and your client has complete confidence in him; as a matter of fact, the client feels a great loyalty to her brother and would not want the management of his own interests to be hampered by the independent decisions of a trust company, particularly by sale to a person who would not be a satisfactory "partner" to the brother. Although it is likely that on the death of either sibling the building and stock of both may be sold, the properties will be difficult to sell without sacrifice, and continuation of the business for a number of years for profit or for an advantageous sale is likely to be necessary or at least desirable. What problems do you see in your client's wishes? What solutions would you recommend, and what drafting details would you want covered in the will?

Some states tacitly encourage lawyers to name themselves as fiduciaries in instruments they draw by permitting an attorney who acts as a fiduciary to receive additional compensation for performing legal services. For example, Wash. Rev. Code §11.48.210 (1990) provides that "[a]dditional compensation may be allowed for his services as attorney and for other services not required of a personal representative." See also N.C. Gen. Stat. §28A-23-4 (1989). Cf. Cal. Prob. Code §§10804, 15642. But cf. State v. Gulbankian, 54 Wis. 2d 599, 196 N.W.2d 730 (1972). Characterization of legal services as extraordinary services was criticized in the leading case of Estate of Parker, 200 Cal. 132, 139, 251 P. 907, 910 (1926), in which the court stated:

> It clearly is the duty of every executor, when engaging counsel to render professional services for the estate, to employ the best legal talent available for the stipulated compensation. But he would place himself in a position where there would be a clash between his own personal interest and his duty to employ the ablest counsel obtainable for the agreed compensation if, being himself a lawyer, he should undertake to perform that service himself with the intention of charging the estate therefor, or if, being a member of a law firm and sharing in the profits to be made, he should employ his firm to render the necessary professional

services. Again, it is the duty of every executor to oppose any charge which the attorney or attorneys employed by him might make against the estate for extraordinary legal services, if there be no substantial ground for the claim that the services were indeed extraordinary. But his personal interest would conflict with this duty, if the services were rendered by his own law firm and he is to share in the earnings. These examples will suffice to show how an executor might be tempted to look with too friendly an eye upon improper claims for legal services if we were to relax the salutary rule . . . merely because our Code provides that an executor may be allowed extra compensation for extraordinary service. . . .[11]

See also In re Estate of Schuldt, 428 N.W.2d 251 (S.D. 1988); C. Wolfram, Modern Legal Ethics §8.12.4 (1986).

AMERICAN BAR ASSOCIATION, MODEL CODE OF PROFESSIONAL RESPONSIBILITY
(1969)

Canon 5. *A Lawyer Should Exercise Independent Professional Judgment on Behalf of a Client.*

EC 5-6 A lawyer should not consciously influence a client to name him as executor, trustee, or lawyer in an instrument. In those cases where a client wishes to name his lawyer as such, care should be taken by the lawyer to avoid even the appearance of impropriety.

The 1983 Model Rules of Professional Conduct contain no direct counterpart to EC 5-6, above. A reporter's note to Model Rule 1.8 states

---

11. Cf. Williams v. Barton, [1927] 2 Ch. 9, 12 (Ch. D.), where the court stated with regard to the actions of a cotrustee who was a member of a firm of stockbrokers employed by the trust to value securities:

> From this it seems to me evident that the case falls within the mischief which is sought to be prevented by the rule [prohibiting a fiduciary from making a profit from opportunities arising out of his trusteeship]. The case is clearly one where his duty as trustee and his interest in an increased remuneration are in direct conflict. As a trustee it is his duty to give the estate the benefit of his unfettered advice in choosing the stockbrokers to act for the estate; as the recipient of half of the fees [received by his own firm] on work introduced by him his obvious interest is to choose or recommend [that firm] for the job.

As to whether the prohibition against profits arising from the trusteeship is different from or purely derivative from the prohibition against conflicts of interest, see McLean. The Theoretical Basis of the Trustee's Duty of Loyalty, 7 Alberta L. Rev. 218 (1970), which also provides a thorough review of Canadian authorities on the duty of loyalty.

that an appointment of the scrivener as a fiduciary "is not expressly prohibited . . . but is subject to the general conflict of interest provision in Rule 1.7 and the more specific requirements of paragraph (a) of this Rule." Would the requirements of ethical conduct differ depending on whether Rule 1.7 (set out at page 324 supra) or 1.8[12] applies? Does either fit the situation?

REPORT OF THE SPECIAL STUDY COMMITTEE ON PROFESSIONAL RESPONSIBILITY, PREPARATION OF WILLS AND TRUSTS THAT NAME THE DRAFTING LAWYER AS FIDUCIARY
28 Real Prop., Prob. & Tr. J. 803, 805-806 (1994)

A number of separate but related issues of professional responsibility must be considered, including: (1) the duty to provide a client with competent estate planning advice; (2) the duty to use independent judgment in advising the client; (3) the lawyer's ability to provide competent fiduciary service; (4) the general duty not to take advantage of a confidential or fiduciary relationship; (5) the avoidance of conflicts of interest with other clients; and (6) issues relating to fiduciary compensation, including the duty to charge no more than a reasonable fee.

Application of the Model Rules . . . to these issues may be summarized as follows: Lawyers, by virtue of the attorney-client relationship, stand in a fiduciary or confidential relationship with their clients. This relationship should not be abused. A lawyer may not allow personal interests to interfere with the exercise of independent judgment in connection with representation of a client. Seeking a fiduciary office that would benefit the personal or financial interests of a lawyer might interfere with this exercise of independent judgment. There also may

---

12. Model Rule 1.8, par. (a) states: "A lawyer shall not enter into a business transaction with a client or knowingly acquire an ownership, possessory, security or other pecuniary interest adverse to a client unless: (1) the transaction and terms on which the lawyer acquires the interest are fair and reasonable to the client and are fully disclosed and transmitted to the client in writing in a manner which can be reasonably understood by the client; (2) the client is given a reasonable opportunity to seek the advice of independent counsel in the transaction; and (3) the client consents in writing thereto."

Also, cf. Disciplinary Counsel v. Wherry, 87 Ohio St. 3d 584, 722 N.E.2d 515 (2000) (disbarment for lending funds from fiduciary account to another client without probate court permission and filing false reports with court); and earlier Disciplinary Counsel v. Glinas, 76 Ohio St. 3d 87, 666 N.E.2d 1083 (1996) (indefinite suspension for seeking excessive fees for representing executor, after preparing will and survivorship arrangements for the decedent (not a relative) under which attorney received significant benefits).

be a potential for conflicts of interest with other clients of the lawyer and a question whether the lawyer is competent to function properly as a fiduciary. Finally, service by a lawyer as personal representative or trustee may involve conflicts of interest if the lawyer may be compensated separately for legal services as well as for fiduciary services.

How should the lawyer respond if the client asks for advice on the selection of a fiduciary? If the client asks the lawyer to serve? Is it ever really possible for the lawyer to exercise "independent judgment" in drafting the specifics (e.g., the terms of discretionary powers over distributions) of a will or trust instrument when the lawyer is to serve as trustee? When an instrument names the lawyer as fiduciary, is it ethical — enforceable? — to include a normally permissible "exculpatory clause," used as boilerplate by some firms, exonerating the fiduciary from liability except for acts of gross negligence or willful misconduct? How should the lawyer respond if the client asks for a particular trust company to be named as fiduciary and the lawyer knows that company's policy is to retain the scrivener to represent it in its fiduciary capacity? May the lawyer suggest such a trust company, especially if the lawyer knows from personal experience that the company offers quality service and is particularly responsive to "friendly" scriveners? Would it be ethical to draft an instrument that directs the fiduciary to hire the scrivener as its counsel? If the attorney accepts appointment as fiduciary and, in that role, breaches the duty of loyalty, would malpractice breaches insurance cover the attorney's liability? Sources for guidance on these various matters include ACTEC Foundation, Engagement Letters: A Guide for the Practitioner 35-44 (1999); Report of Working Group on Lawyer as Fiduciary, 62 Fordham L. Rev. 1055-1061 (1994); Recommendations of the Conference, id. at 998-1001; Restatement (Third) of the Law Governing Lawyers §216 cmt. c & illus. 1-2 (Proposed Final Draft No. 1, 1996).

In re ESTATE OF DEARDOFF
10 Ohio St. 2d 108, 461 N.E.2d 1292 (1984)

[The testator directed his executrix to employ either of two named attorneys to represent his estate and that, if she failed to do so, she "shall be replaced" and the court shall appoint "a suitable person" who will do so. The named executrix declined to serve, and testator's alternative nominee sought to employ counsel of her choice. On this basis the designated attorneys objected to her appointment, but the probate court appointed her and the court of appeals affirmed.]

HOLMES, J. . . .

It cannot be questioned that an executor has the right to employ counsel to assist in the performance of various duties in the administration of an estate. The employment of counsel, however, is not mandatory as the executor may perform all such duties.

R.C. 2109.03 provides that upon court appointment, the fiduciary has discretion to select counsel who will represent him during the administration of the estate. Under this statutory scheme, it is important to note that the attorney represents the fiduciary, not the estate. In light of this fact, we believe that although he may well accede to the wishes of the testator, the fiduciary must have unfettered discretion to select an attorney, as said fiduciary may incur personal liability for the attorney's unlawful conduct concerning matters of the estate.

In addition, the attorney-client relationship is quite personal and usually involves confidential matters. The relationship demands complete faith and trust between the parties. Such a relationship thrust upon the client against his will would be ill-conceived and not conductive to an atmosphere of reciprocal confidence. This, in turn, would interfere with the administration of the estate.

We further note that today's decision is in line with the majority of jurisdictions which have addressed this issue. . . . Therefore, we hold that a provision of a will which designates an attorney to represent the executor in the administration of the estate may not be considered as a condition precedent to the appointment of the executor, but is merely precatory and not binding upon the fiduciary or the probate court. . . .

Judgment Affirmed.

PROBLEM

17-G.   *L* has been asked to represent *W* as executor and trustee under the will of her deceased husband, *H*. *L* had planned the estates of *W* and *H*, whose marriage was the second for both. *D* and *S*, adult children of *H*'s first marriage, survived him. The will establishes a tax-planned discretionary family trust, of which *W*, *D*, and *S* are the permissible distributees, with the remaining principal to be distributed on *W*'s death to *H*'s then living decendants. *H*'s residuary estate was left to a QTIP trust to pay the income to *W* for life, principal thereafter to *H*'s then living descendants. If *L* undertakes the representation, whom does he represent? *W* individually? *W* as executor and trustee? The estate and trust? The beneficiaries? Or some combination of these? If he represents *W* as executor and trustee, does he owe any duties to *D* and *S*? What conflicts (and expectations) confront him? What steps might he take to ameliorate possible conflicts? Would your answers be different if *D* or *S* had been named executor (or trustee) and sought *L*'s representation?

If *L* undertakes to represent *W* as executor, under what terms may he continue to represent her individually? If he discovers that *W* has misappropriated estate funds and misstated trust income in accounts filed with the court, what courses of action are open to him? Must he, or may he, remain silent? May he, or must he, disclose the misappropriation to the court? To *D* and *S*? If *L* chooses to remain silent, would he be liable for malpractice for failing to prevent *W*'s misappropriation, or for failing to take reasonable steps to obtain restoration of the funds? Or if *L* assisted *W* by preparing or falsifying her accounts?

AMERICAN BAR ASSOCIATION STANDING
COMMITTEE ON ETHICS, FORMAL OPINION 94-380
(1994)

The Committee has been asked to address the applicability of the Model Rules of Professional Conduct (1983, as amended) to lawyers representing the fiduciary in a trust or estate matter, with specific reference to whether there are exceptions to the Model Rules that apply only to lawyers practicing in this area. We find no such exceptions.

We address in this opinion the circumstances of a lawyer who has undertaken to represent only the fiduciary, and not the beneficiaries of the estate or trust for which the fiduciary has responsibility. We do not, therefore, deal with the conflict of interest issues that may arise when a lawyer undertakes simultaneously to represent both fiduciary and beneficiary with regard to the same subject matter. Of course, other conflict of interest issues under Model Rules 1.7 and 1.9 may arise if the lawyer previously represented or currently represents a beneficiary about other matters.

When the fiduciary is the lawyer's client all of the Model Rules prescribing a lawyer's duties to a client apply. The scope of the lawyer's representation is defined by and limited by Model Rule 1.2. The lawyer must diligently represent the fiduciary, *see* Model Rule 1.3, preserve in confidence communications between the lawyer and the fiduciary, *see* Model Rule 1.6, and be truthful in statements to others, *see* Model Rule 4.1(a). The fact that the fiduciary client has obligations toward the beneficiaries does not impose parallel obligations on the lawyer, or otherwise expand or supersede the lawyer's responsibilities under the Model Rules of Professional Conduct.

A lawyer's duty of confidentiality to a client is not lessened by the fact that the client is a fiduciary. Although the Model Rules prohibit the lawyer from actively participating in criminal or fraudulent activity or active concealment of a client's wrongdoing, they do not authorize the lawyer to breach confidences to prevent such wrongdoing. . . .

The Comment to Rule 1.6 succinctly explains its purpose:

> A fundamental principle in the client-lawyer relationship is that the lawyer maintain confidentiality of information relating to the representation. The client is thereby encouraged to communicate fully and frankly with the lawyer even as to embarrassing and legally damaging subject matter.

There are only three exceptions to the inviolability of confidences imparted to a lawyer by the client.

The first, in paragraph (a) of the Rule, is for disclosures that are impliedly authorized in order to carry out the representation of the client. Disclosure of client confidences is not impliedly authorized simply because the client owes duties to third parties. The Comment to Model Rule 1.6 describes the limited nature of this exception. It applies to relatively mundane matters such as admitting an undisputed fact or disclosing information during settlement negotiations. The exception does not negate the obligation of confidence simply because the client-fiduciary owes particular duties to beneficiaries. . . .

The second exception, in subparagraph (b)(1), authorizes only the disclosure of information necessary to prevent the client from committing a criminal act that the lawyer believes is likely to result in *imminent death or substantial bodily harm,* but not to prevent the client from committing any criminal or fraudulent act. . . .

The third exception, in subparagraph (b)(2), relates to controversies between a lawyer and his client and has nothing to do with the protection of beneficiaries. No other exception applies. . . .

. . . Although the Committee recognizes that some jurisdictions have lessened the protection of client confidence in order to provide greater protection to the interests of third parties, the Model Rules provide no additional exception to Rule 1.6's prohibition.

Although a lawyer may not disclose confidences of the fiduciary, if the fiduciary insists on continuing a course of fraudulent or criminal conduct the lawyer may be required to terminate the representation because the lawyer's services will be involved in that conduct, so as to invoke Rule 1.16(a)(1), or may have the option of a voluntary withdrawal under Rule 1.16(b)(1). If either of these provisions of Rule 1.16 applies, this will be not because the client is a fiduciary, but because the client is acting in the manner described by the Rule. . . .

Compare N.Y. Op. No. 649 (1993) (while the executor's attorney has a duty to represent the executor with undivided loyalty, the attorney is prohibited from taking any position antagonistic to the estate or inconsistent with the executor's duty to carry out the will). In Goldberg v. Frye, 217 Cal. App. 3d 1258, 266 Cal. Rptr. 483 (1990), devisees sued the attorney for the personal representative, claiming that the attorney was negligent in not advising them of the significance of estate proceedings for which they had received formal notice but which were resolved to their ultimate detriment. The court rejected the claim, stating at 1267, 1269, 166 Cal. Rptr. 488-490 [citations omitted]:

> Contrary to the allegations of the complaint, it is well established that the attorney for the administrator of an estate represents the administrator, and not the estate. A key element of any action for professional malpractice is the establishment of a duty by the professional to the claimant. Absent duty there can be no breach and no negligence. By assuming a duty to the administrator of an estate, an attorney undertakes to perform services which may benefit legatees of the estate, but he has no contractual privity with [them]. . . .
>
> Particularly in the case of services rendered for the fiduciary of a decedent's estate, we would apprehend great danger in finding stray duties in favor of beneficiaries. Typically in estate administration conflicting interests vie for recognition. The very purpose of the fiduciary is to serve the interests of the estate, not to promote the objectives of one group of legatees over the interests of conflicting claimants. The fiduciary's attorney, as his legal adviser, is faced with the same task of disposition of conflicts. It is of course the purpose and obligation of both the fiduciary and his attorney to serve the estate. In such capacity they are obligated to communicate with, and to arbitrate conflicting claims among, those interested in the estate. While the fiduciary in the performance of this service may be exposed to the potential of malpractice (and hence is subject to surcharge when his administration is completed), the attorney by definition represents only one party: the fiduciary. It would be very dangerous to conclude that the attorney, through performance of his service to the administrator and by way of communication to estate beneficiaries, subjects himself to claims of negligence from the beneficiaries. The beneficiaries are entitled to even-handed and fair administration by the fiduciary. They are not owed a duty directly by the fiduciary's attorney. . . .

See also Spinner v. Nutt, 631 N.E.2d 542 (Mass. 1994) (dismissing malpractice action by beneficiaries against the lawyers for the trustees; the court was concerned that a finding of duties in tort or contract to the beneficiaries might interfere with the attorney's task of advising the trustee, noting also that disciplinary rules require lawyers to preserve clients' secrets); Trask v. Butler, 872 P.2d 1050, 1085 (Wash. 1994) ("After analyzing our modified multifactor balancing test, we hold that a duty is not owed from an attorney hired by the personal representative of an estate to the estate or to the estate beneficiaries"). But see Fickett v. Superior Court, 27 Ariz. App. 793, 558 P.2d 988 (1976) (privity not required for the ward to pursue malpractice claim for negligence against lawyer for guardian), discussed in Johns, Fickett's Thicket: The Lawyer's Expanding Fiduciary and Ethical Boundaries When Serving Older Americans of Moderate Wealth, 32 Wake Forest L. Rev. 445 (1997). See also Elam v. Hyatt Legal Services, 44 Ohio St. 3d 175, 541 N.E.2d 616 (1989) (permitting, in a state that still allowed privity defense in estate planning malpractice, negligence suit against estate attorney by remainder beneficiaries, who contended they had lost their inheritance because attorney had recorded certificate of title to real estate in name of testator's husband alone, when property devised to husband for life only, with remainder to plaintiffs; the court said the remainder beneficiaries were in privity with the attorney because their interests were vested).

Restatement (Third) of the Law Governing Lawyers (Tentative Draft No. 8, 1997) §73 (*Duty of Care to Certain Non-Clients*) states: "For purposes of liability under §71 a lawyer owes a duty to use care within the meaning of §74: . . . (4) to a non-client when and to the extent that: (a) the lawyer's client is a trustee, guardian, executor, or fiduciary acting primarily to perform similar functions for the non-client; (b) circumstances known to the lawyer make it clear that appropriate action by the lawyer is necessary with respect to a matter within the scope of the representation to prevent or rectify the breach of a fiduciary duty owed by the client to the non-client, where (i) the breach is a crime or fraud or (ii) the lawyer has assisted or is assisting the breach; (c) the non-client is not reasonably able to protect its rights; and (d) such a duty would not significantly impair the performance of the lawyer's obligations to the client. . . ." See also id. §73, ill. 5-7, and §§151, 155, 157, 163; and id. (Proposed Final Draft no. 1, 1996) §§201, 212, 213, 216.

AMERICAN COLLEGE OF TRUST AND ESTATE COUNSEL FOUNDATION, ACTEC COMMENTARIES ON THE MODEL RULES OF PROFESSIONAL CONDUCT
3-6 (3d ed. 1999)

Lawyer for Fiduciary. Under the majority view, a lawyer who represents a fiduciary generally with respect to a fiduciary estate stands in a lawyer-client relationship with the fiduciary and not with respect to the fiduciary estate or the beneficiaries. In this connection note that a distinction should be drawn between the duties of a lawyer who represents a fiduciary in the fiduciary's representative capacity (a "general" representation) and the duties of a lawyer who represents the fiduciary individually (*i.e.,* not in a representative capacity). . . . [U]nder some circumstances a lawyer may properly represent the fiduciary and one or more of the beneficiaries. . . .

Duties to Beneficiaries. The lawyer who represents a fiduciary generally is not usually considered also to represent the beneficiaries. However, most courts have concluded that the lawyer owes some duties to them. Some courts subject the lawyer to the duties because the beneficiaries are characterized as the lawyer's "joint", "derivative" or "secondary" clients. Other courts do so because the lawyer stands in a fiduciary relationship with respect to the fiduciary, who, in turn, owes fiduciary duties to the beneficiaries. . . .

General Nature of Duties. Unfortunately, the duties that the lawyer for a fiduciary owes to the beneficiaries of the fiduciary estate have not been adequately identified, defined, or discussed. In general, the duties prohibit the lawyer from taking advantage of his or her position to the detriment of the fiduciary estate or its beneficiaries. . . . Indeed, in exceptional cases the lawyer for a fiduciary may be subject to the duties of the fiduciary. . . .

Good Faith, Fairness and Impartiality. The lawyer who represents a fiduciary generally is required to act in good faith and with fairness toward the beneficiaries. In addition, the lawyer should advise the fiduciary to act impartially with respect to the beneficiaries and to provide the beneficiaries with information regarding material matters affecting their interests in the fiduciary estate. Consistent with the provisions of the MRPC, especially MRPC 4.1 (Truthfulness in Statements to Others), the lawyer may not deliberately misinform or mislead the beneficiaries or withhold information from them. . . .

Affirmative Duties to Beneficiaries. . . . [I]n some circumstances the lawyer may owe some affirmative duties to the beneficiaries. Thus, the lawyer for a fiduciary may be required to take affirmative steps to protect the interests of the beneficiaries if the lawyer learns that the fiduciary is engaged in acts of self-dealing, is embezzling assets of the fiduciary estate, or is engaged in other wrongdoing. In some cases it may be appropriate for the lawyer to disclose the misconduct to the beneficiaries or to the court. If the local rules do not permit disclosure in such cases, it may be appropriate for the lawyer to resign with notice to the beneficiaries.

The existence of such affirmative duties is implicit in the nature of the representation, which involves the lawyer advising the fiduciary in a representative and not a personal capacity. Recognition of such duties is also supported by the fact that the fiduciary estate is almost invariably created by a testator or trustor for the exclusive benefit of the beneficiaries. In addition, the fiduciary and the lawyer are both compensated by the fiduciary estate. Finally, recognition of some affirmative duties is also appropriate because the lawyer for a fiduciary is typically in a superior position relative to the beneficiaries, who may repose trust and confidence in the lawyer. . . .

Recall Model Rule of Professional Conduct 1.2 (supra Chapter 8, section G.1) prohibiting a lawyer from participating in or assisting a client in the commission of a fraudulent or otherwise unlawful act. Also see traditional liability of third parties for participating knowingly in a breach of trust (infra section E).

Transactions Involving Beneficiaries Rather Than Trust Estate. The strict prohibition normally applicable to self-dealing does not prohibit a trustee personally from dealing with a beneficiary *as an individual.* In transactions with beneficiaries, however, trustees must act with the utmost fairness, with a presumption that any advantage obtained by the trustee was the result of improper conduct. The burden is on the trustee to prove that no advantage was taken of the trust and confidence inherent in the fiduciary relationship and that the beneficiary was fully informed of all relevant matters. If this burden is not sustained, the beneficiary has the choice of either affirming the transaction or avoiding it. Uniform Trust Code §802(d) (draft, Feb. 2000) is similar.

Impartiality. A trustee's duty of "loyalty" to multiple beneficiaries, with their diverse and almost inherently conflicting interests (in, e.g., investment decisions, principal-income accounting and discretionary distributions), is resolved by a duty of impartiality. Properly understood, impartiality would not seem to call for an *equal* balancing of diverse interests but a balancing in a manner consistent with the terms and purposes of the trust, including any ascertainable or inferred preferences of the settlor for some beneficiaries over others, such as the priority frequently intended for a surviving spouse over descendants or other holders of future interests. Essentially, the duty of impartiality forbids the trustee, "substantively," from injecting its *own* favoritism in making discretionary distributions or investment decisions, for example, and "procedurally," from consulting with or providing information to the life beneficiary to the exclusion of persons interested in the remainder. Thus, the concerns and wishes, and the personal, financial and tax circumstances, of the various beneficiaries are all to be taken into account in a manner consistent with the terms and objectives of the particular trust.

UNIFORM TRUST CODE
(Draft, Feb. 2000)

§803. *Impartiality.* If a trust has two or more beneficiaries, the trustee shall act impartially in investing, managing and distributing the trust property, giving due regard to the beneficiaries' respective interests.

3.   Duty to Provide Information and to Render Accounts

Trustees and personal representatives have a duty to keep and render accounts and to furnish beneficiaries information at reasonable times. This duty is commonly regulated by statute and local practice. Periodic accounting to the courts may still be required in some states, especially in the case of testamentary trusts, or may be ordered by a court elsewhere if need appears. In the absence of statute, the power to compel an accounting is an inherent aspect of the general jurisdiction of courts of equity over trusts. See also Uniform Probate Code §7-303.

UNIFORM TRUST CODE
(Draft, Feb. 2000)

§813.   *Duty to Inform and Report.*

(a) A trustee shall keep the qualified beneficiaries of the trust reasonably informed about the administration of the trust and, unless unreasonable under the circumstances, promptly respond to a beneficiary's request for information. [Subsections (b) and (c) entitle beneficiaries to a copy of the trust instrument, and specify certain other circumstances in which a trustee has a duty to provide information.] . . .

(d) A trustee shall send the qualified beneficiaries at least annually and at the termination of the trust a report of the trust property, liabilities, receipts, and disbursements, including the source and amount of the trustee's compensation and, if feasible, a listing of the trust assets with their respective market values. . . .

(e) A beneficiary, by a consent made in writing or by other record, [and not revoked,] may waive the right to a trustee's report or other information. . . .

(f) The terms of the trust may dispense with the requirements of this section only as to a beneficiary who is a settlor or has not attained 25 years of age.

(g) Except as otherwise provided by the terms of a trust, while the trust is revocable and the settlor has capacity to revoke the trust, the duties of the trustee under this section are owed exclusively to the settlor. . . .

Compare Restatement (Third) of Trusts §50 (Tent. Draft approved 1999), on *Enforcement and Construction of Discretionary Interests,* which

states in cmt. *b* (cross references omitted): "Relevant fiduciary principles include (i) the general duty to act, reasonably informed, with impartiality among the various beneficiaries and interests and (ii) the
duty to provide the beneficiaries with information concerning the trust
and its administration[, including and entitling] the beneficiaries (and
also the court) not only to accounting information but also to relevant
information concerning the bases upon which the trustee's discretionary judgments have been or will be made."

Significantly different but somewhat related to the general obligation of confidentiality applicable to attorneys for fiduciaries (part 2,
above) is the interplay between a fiduciary's duty of disclosure and the
attorney-client privilege. See, e.g., the leading case of Riggs National
Bank v. Zimmer, 355 A.2d 709 (Del. Ch. 1976), involving a successful
motion by beneficiaries to compel a trustee to produce legal memoranda prepared by its lawyers. In holding that the attorney-client privilege did not protect the trustee, the court stated:

> As a representative for the beneficiaries of the trust which he is admin-
> istering, the trustee is not the real client in the sense that he is personally
> being served. And, the beneficiaries are not simply incidental beneficia-
> ries who chance to gain from the professional services rendered. The
> very intention of the communication is to aid the beneficiaries. The trust-
> ees . . . cannot subordinate the fiduciary obligations owed to the benefi-
> ciaries to their private interests under the guise of attorney-client
> privilege. The policy of preserving the full disclosure necessary in the
> trustee-beneficiary relationship is . . . ultimately more important than
> the protection of the trustee's confidence in the attorney for the trust.

WELLS FARGO BANK V. SUPERIOR COURT
22 Cal. 4th 201, 91 Cal. Rptr. 2d 716, 990 P.2d 591 (2000)

WERDEGAR, J. [Most citations omitted.]

In this action for an accounting, the beneficiaries of a private express
trust seek to compel the trustee to disclose its privileged communications with attorneys. We conclude the trustee may assert the attorney-
client privilege against the beneficiaries [settlor's daughter and her
children, collectively "the Boltwoods," other beneficiaries not having
joined].

. . . Wells Fargo commenced this action by petitioning the probate
court to settle its accounts and to approve its resignation as cotrustee.
The Boltwoods filed objection to Wells Fargo's accounts and petitioned
for removal of Rosa Couch [settlor's widow and a trust beneficiary] as
cotrustee, and for surcharge and damages.

In the course of the litigation, the Boltwoods requested that Wells Fargo produce documents related to the trust. Wells Fargo produced documents reflecting confidential communications with its attorneys on the subject of trust administration [but not those involving] the Boltwoods' claims of misconduct. Wells Fargo's outside trust administration council, [O'Melveny], claimed the protection of the work product doctrine for other documents. . . . [T]he documents not produced include communications between Wells Fargo's employees and its attorneys, either inhouse or at O'Melveny, and work product of O'Melveny.

The Boltwoods moved to compel production. The superior court granted the motion and ordered Wells Fargo to produce the remaining documents within 30 days. . . .

. . . [T]here is no authority in California law for requiring a trustee to produce communications protected by the attorney-client privilege, regardless of their subject matter.

The Boltwoods contend Wells Fargo must produce privileged communications to fulfill its statutory and common law duties as a trustee to report to the beneficiaries about the trust and its administration. Wells Fargo's duties as a trustee, the Boltwoods argue, take precedence over its privilege. . . . The argument lacks merit. The privileges set out in the Evidence Code are legislative creations; the courts of this state have no power to expand them or to recognize implied exceptions. The Boltwoods' argument is nothing more than a plea for an implied exception.

. . . Probate Code section 16060 provides simply that "[t]he trustee has a duty to keep the beneficiaries of the trust *reasonably informed* of the trust and its administration" [emphasis by court]. Probate Code section 16061 in pertinent part says only that, "[e]xcept as provided in Section 16064, . . . the trustee shall provide the beneficiary with a *report of information* about the assets, liabilities, receipts, and disbursements of the trust, the acts of the trustee, and the particulars relating to the administration of the trust relevant to the beneficiary's interest, including the terms of the trust. . . ." [Court's emphasis] Certainly a trustee can keep the beneficiaries "reasonably informed" and provide "a report of information" without necessarily having to disclose privileged communications. The attorney-client privilege is commonly regarded as "fundamental to . . . the proper functioning of our judicial system" and thought to "promote broader public interests in the observance of law and administration of justice." If the Legislature had intended to restrict a privilege of this importance, it would likely have declared that intention unmistakably, rather than leaving it to courts to find the restriction by inference and guesswork in the interstices of the Probate Code. Nor does the Boltwoods' argument . . . that "the trustee's records as to the administration of the trust are deemed a part of the trust estate, and the right of the beneficiaries to an inspection of them stems from their common interest in the property along with the trustee" . . . [provide] the foundation for an implied exception. . . .

In most of the other jurisdictions in which this question has arisen, courts have given the trustee's reporting duties precedence over the attorney-client privilege. But those courts consider themselves free, in a way we do not, to create exceptions to the privilege. New York's attorney-client privilege, while statutory, is "not absolute [and may] yield to a strong public policy requiring disclosure." The law in Delaware evolved at a time when that state recognized the attorney-client privilege solely as matter of common law. . . . The federal courts, interpreting their own common law attorney-client privilege, have largely followed [the leading Delaware case].

Typical of the federal decisions is U.S. v. Mett [178 F.3d 1058, in which] the Ninth Circuit held that a trustee can invoke the federal common law attorney-client privilege against beneficiaries when the trustee "retains counsel in order to defend herself against the . . . beneficiaries," but not when the "trustee seeks an attorney's advice on a matter of administration and where the advice clearly does not implicate the trustee in any personal capacity." Neither of the two reasons the court gave for this conclusion has any validity under California law. . . . What courts in other jurisdictions give as common law privileges they may take away as exceptions. We, in contrast, do not enjoy the freedom to restrict California's statutory attorney-client privilege based on notions of policy or ad hoc justification. Furthermore, under California law, the attorney-client privilege "applies not only to communications made in anticipation of litigation, but also to legal advice when no litigation is threatened."

The Boltwoods argue that our recent decision in *Moeller* [v. Superior Court 16 Cal. 4th 1124, 947 P.2d 279 (1997)] compels a different result. It does not. In *Moeller*, we held that a successor trustee, unless the trust instrument otherwise provides, assumes the power to assert the attorney-client privilege as to confidential communications between an attorney and a predecessor trustee on the subject of trust administration, so long as the predecessor was acting in the official capacity of trustee rather than in a personal capacity. . . . In *Moeller* we did not suggest that anyone other than the current holder of the privilege might be entitled to inspect privileged communications. Nor did we create or recognize any exception to the privilege. Instead, . . . we merely identified the current holder of the privilege.

The Boltwoods also contend that, even if the trustee's communications with attorneys about its potential liability are privileged, a trustee still should enjoy no privilege as against the beneficiary for communications about trust administration. . . . Although in *Moeller* we did distinguish between communication about potential liability and communications about trust administration, . . . our purpose was to determine, as between a successor trustee and a predecessor, which trustee was the current holder of the privilege [and] we explained that ". . . [if] a predecessor seeks legal advice in its personal capacity out of a genuine concern for possible future charges of breach of fiduciary duty, the predecessor may be able to avoid disclosing the advice to a successor by hiring a separate lawyer and paying for the advice out of its personal funds." . . . Nor would the decision in Talbot v. Marshfield [Ch. 1865] 62 Eng. Rep. 728, justify a California court in limiting the trustee's attorney-client privilege to communications about the trustee's personal liability. We have already explained that courts interpreting the common law evidentiary privileges are free, in a way we are not, to recognize exceptions. *Talbot* . . . required the trustees of the testamentary trust to produce to the beneficiaries an opinion of counsel concerning trust administration that had been prepared before litigation between the trustee and the beneficiaries had commenced. The court did not, however, require the trustees to produce an opinion of counsel prepared after litigation had commenced advising the trustees how to defend themselves. . . .

[Omitted are portions of the opinion rejecting the argument that Wells Fargo had waived its privilege in disclosing some confidential communications on trust administration in the belief that it was required to do so and that, in the present circumstances, the trustees and beneficiaries had become joint clients.]

The Boltwoods contend they are entitled to inspect Wells Fargo's privileged communications with attorneys for the additional reason that the trust paid for the attorney's advice. . . . Payment of fees does not determine ownership of the attorney-client privilege. The . . . *trustee*, rather than the beneficiary, is the client of an attorney who gives legal advice to the trustee, whether on the subject of trust administration or of the trustee's own potential liability. . . . Under California law, a trustee may use trust funds to pay for legal advice regarding trust administration and may recover attorney fees and costs incurred in successfully defending against claims by beneficiaries. . . . [I]f the trustee's expenditures turn out to have been unauthorized, the beneficiaries may ask the probate court to surcharge the trustee. But this question of cost allocation does not affect ownership of the attorney-client privilege. [In a footnote, the court observes: "The better practice may be for a trustee to seek reimbursement after any litigation with the beneficiary concludes, initially retaining separate counsel with personal funds."]

[Omitted is the portion of the opinion upholding O'Melveny's assertion of its protection under the work product doctrine.]

Concurring and Dissenting Opinion by Mosk, J. . . .

I agree . . . that communications involving Wells Fargo's potential liability for misconduct were subject to the attorney-client privilege. But I am not persuaded by the majority's conclusion that Wells Fargo was also entitled to assert the privilege with regard to the attorney-client communications on the subject of trust administration, which it obtained on the behalf of the beneficiaries and at their expense.

In my view, the Probate Code required disclosure of those documents, consistent with the fiduciary duties of the trustee . . . to keep the beneficiaries reasonably informed . . . by providing complete and accurate information with regard to the administration of the trust. . . .

Unlike the majority's, my view of the requirement under Probate Code section 16060 is also consistent with the prevailing rule in most jurisdictions that the trustee's fiduciary duty of full disclosure to the trust beneficiary extends to *all* contents of the trustee's file concerning trust administration matters affecting the trust interests of the beneficiaries, including legal advice. Thus, Professor Scott [§173] summarizes the general law as follows: " . . . A beneficiary is entitled to inspect opinions of counsel procured by the trustee to guide him in the administration of the trust." . . . See also Bogert, The Law of Trusts and Trustees (2d rev. ed. 1983) §961 ("The beneficiary . . . has the right to obtain and review legal opinions given to the trustee to enable the trustee to carry out the trust, except for such opinions as the trustee has obtained on his own account to protect against charges of misconduct."); 1A Nossaman et al., Trust Administration and Taxation (1999) §27.27[1] . . . ; cf. Rest. 2d Trusts, §173 & com. (b) (as an exception to the duty of the trustee to furnish "complete and accurate information . . ." the trustee is "privileged to refrain from communicating to the beneficiaries opinions of counsel obtained by him at his own expense and for his own protection").

The doctrine is of long standing, finding its roots in the seminal [1865] decision in *Talbot v. Marshfield.* . . .

The majority concede that the overwhelming authority in point is in agreement. . . .

I disagree that the legislature intended by implication to exclude attorney communications from the scope of the duty to furnish information under Probate Code section 16060. It is doubtful that it would have created so detrimental an exception to the trustee's duty under the statute subsilentio. . . .

REPORT OF FIDUCIARY ACCOUNTING
STANDARDS COMMITTEE[13]
(1980)

"Fiduciary Accounting" does not have one commonly understood meaning. In a broad sense, it can mean the entire process whereby a fiduciary — normally a personal representative, trustee or guardian — communicates information on an on-going basis regarding his administration of a fund and periodically justifies his administration to the parties in interest and, perhaps, to a court. In another sense, it may be the process whereby a fiduciary — here more often a trustee — periodically keeps parties in interest currently informed of transactions and investment policies being followed.

In a narrower sense, to which this report is directed, a fiduciary accounting may refer to the statement prepared by a fiduciary at the close of his administration of a fund (or at some appropriate intermediate stage) to reflect transactions that have occurred and to be presented to the parties in interest as part of a process whereby the fiduciary seeks discharge from liability for the events disclosed. . . .

The fundamental objective of an account should be to provide essential and useful information in a meaningful form to the parties interested in the accounting process. It is also important that the account should be sufficiently simple to enable its preparation without unreasonable expense. . . .

Maximum clarity, full disclosure and complete description and explanation of all events to be disclosed appear to be standards that all would accept. But, in combination, they may present many difficulties. For example, clarity may be obscured by the detail that is required for a disclosure that omits nothing. Full explanation of all investment decisions might produce a massive document that few beneficiaries would read. On balance, a set of flexible principles keyed to the standard of good faith supports the utmost protection of the parties. . . .

Fiduciary accounts rarely will be identical. In addition to the predictable variables of the size and composition of the assets, the period covered and the position of those interested, the significance of particular issues in a controversy may be illuminated by special accounting treatment of some portion of a fund. This suggests that a fiduciary should have enough flexibility to state an account in the manner best adapted to the particular circumstances and discourages any effort to prescribe

13. A joint project (Robert Whitman, Reporter) of the American Bar Association, the American Bankers Association, the American College of Probate Counsel, the American Institute of Certified Public Accountants, the National Center for State Courts, the National College of Probate Judges, and the Uniform Probate Code Project.

a totally rigid format. Accordingly, the following principles are suggested as general standards for fiduciary accounting. . . .

    I.   Accounts should be stated in a manner that is understandable by persons who are not familiar with practices and terminology peculiar to the administration of estates and trusts. . . .

    II.   A fiduciary account shall begin with a concise summary of its purpose and content. . . .

    III.   A fiduciary account shall contain sufficient information to put the interested parties on notice as to all significant transactions affecting administration during the accounting period.

Commentary [on I-III]: The presentation of the information in an account shall allow an interested party to follow the progress of the fiduciary's administration of assets during the accounting period without reference to an inventory or earlier accounting that is not included in the current account.

An account is not complete if it does not itemize assets on hand at the beginning of the accounting period. . . .

    IV.   A fiduciary account shall include both carrying values — representing the values of assets at acquisition by the fiduciary — and current values at the beginning and end of the accounting period. . . .

    V.   Gains and losses incurred during the accounting period shall be shown separately in the same schedule. . . .

    VI.   The account shall show significant transactions that do not affect the amount for which the fiduciary is accountable. . . .

WOOD v. HONEYMAN
178 Or. 484, 169 P.2d 131 (1946)

[Appeal from decree finding that defendant, Honeyman, failed to account, removing him from the office of trustee, entering judgment against him for conversion of trust assets, and denying him compensation for his services as trustee. The trust instrument purported to relieve the trustee of all obligation to account.]

ROSSMAN, J. . . .

We believe that the principal contention which the appellants wish to submit under these two assignments of error is that the defendant was under no duty to account.

It must be apparent that when one becomes a trustee and thus undertakes to administer an estate for the benefit of another, he must maintain records of his transactions so complete and accurate that he can show by them his faithfulness to his trust. It is not enough for him to know that he is honestly performing his duty. Since, generally, the burden of proof rests upon him to prove his fidelity, he must be able to sustain his position by honest records. . . .

. . . The rule which authorizes the beneficiary to inspect the trust records is essential in order that the beneficiary may be assured that he is obtaining the income or other advantages which the settlor intended. . . .

The trust instrument . . . , however, contains the clause which says:

> The said trustee is hereby relieved from all obligations to account to the beneficiaries of this trust, or to any one, for any of the trust funds or income therefrom; the provisions above that receipts by the mother or custodian of said children shall fully acquit said trustee, and that having made payments to said mother or custodian, he shall not be further bound to see to the application of said trust funds or income, being merely for the guidance and protection of the trustee, and not obligatory on him, and he is hereby relieved from any duty of accounting whatsoever. . . .

Colonel Wood [the settlor] and those who signed the writing did not make a gift to the defendant of the $15,000 fund by signing that paper. The document refers to the defendant many times as trustee and repeatedly used the word "trust." Although the legal title to the fund was in the defendant, the beneficial interest was not in him but in the three beneficiaries. . . . The [trust terms] conferred upon the defendant wide discretion concerning the investment of the fund; the use of principal as well as of income; the amount to be distributed to each beneficiary; the periods, whether quarterly or semi-annually, when distributions should be made; and the time when the final distribution should take place. Yet, notwithstanding those facts, the fund was not his, but was entrusted to him in a capacity — a trust relationship — which is a favorite of our law. The law attaches such great social value to trusts of the kind now before us that virtually every duty owed by a trustee is enforcible by a decree of the chancellor. In the present instance, whether expressly set forth in the trust instrument or not, the defendant was required to distribute nothing to any one except to the three beneficiaries, to refrain from self-dealing, and to give to the beneficiaries, before the expiration of the trust, the entire amount of the principal and income, less lawful expenses. The settlors of the trust expected him to perform those duties, and the only way by which obedience could be enforced was by suit in equity. For a violation of any of those duties, a court of equity could remove the defendant from his office, deny him compensation for his services or enter judgment against him for any sum misspent. But remedies of that kind normally are not feasible unless an accounting has first been had. . . .

If a fiduciary can be rendered free from the duty of informing the beneficiary concerning matters of which he is entitled to know, and if he can also be made immune from liability resulting from his breach of the trust, equity has been rendered impotent. The present instance would be a humiliating example of the helplessness into which courts could be cast if a provision, placed in a trust instrument through a settlor's mistaken confidence in a trustee, could relieve the latter of a duty to account. Such a provision would be virtually a license to the trustee to convert the fund to his own use and thereby terminate the trust. When we mentioned mistaken confidence, we had in mind the words of the Wood Trust instrument: "I think Dave Honeyman would be an ideal trustee." It was that mistaken impression which caused Colonel Wood to write the provision which the defendant now seeks to employ as an impenetrable shield.

Bogert on Trusts and Trustees, §972, says:

> A settlor who attempts to create a trust without court accountability in the trustee is contradicting himself. A trust necessarily means rights in the cestui, enforcible, in equity. . . . If the court finds that the settlor really intended a trust, it would seem that accountability in chancery or other court must inevitably follow as an incident. Without an account the cestui must be in the dark as to whether there has been a breach of trust and so is prevented as a practical matter from holding the trustee liable for a breach. . . .

We come now to an expression of our own views. We are completely satisfied that no trust instrument can relieve a trustee from his duty to account in a court of equity. We are, however, prepared to adopt the point of view of the Restatement that a trust instrument may lawfully relieve a trustee from the necessity of keeping formal accounts. When such a provision is found in a trust instrument, a beneficiary can not expect to receive reports concerning the trust estate. But even when such a provision is made a part of the trust instrument, the trustee will, nevertheless, be required in a suit for an accounting to show that he faithfully performed his duty and will be liable to whatever remedies may be appropriate if he was unfaithful to his trust. Such being our views, it follows that, so far as the Educational Trust is concerned, the defendant was not required to maintain formal records and supply information to the beneficiaries concerning the condition of the corpus of the trust. The provision under consideration did not, however, relieve him from the accounting which the circuit court exacted of him. . . .

See also Shields v. Shields, 264 Ga. 559, 468 S.E.2d 436 (1994) (surviving spouse life tenant required to account for "quasi-trusteeship" despite will provision purporting to excuse accountability). It is not unusual for courts to hold or state that clauses excusing a trustee from any duty to account are void as contrary to public policy.

Informal Accountings. The trustee's duty to render accountings may be satisfied by privately settling his accounts with the beneficiaries. A beneficiary who participates in such a settlement may be estopped or subject to a defense of laches if questions later arise concerning the trustee's administration for the period covered. Often corporate trustees follow a practice of obtaining an instrument from the beneficiaries approving an informal accounting and discharging the trustee for the acts reported. In Matter of James, 173 Misc. 1042, 1045, 19 N.Y.S.2d 532, 535 (1940), the beneficiary had executed an instrument of this type after consultation with a lawyer, and the court said of such settlements:

> The law encourages the making of agreements for the release of fiduciaries and for the approval of their informal accounts principally because they avoid expense and delay. Except where fraud or imposition is shown, such agreements and releases are approved. . . . [The beneficiary] "may not be heard to say that the accounting trustee owed him . . . an affirmative duty to detail an open state of facts as to which he was content to waive inquiry."

The terms of trusts sometimes go further and provide that the trustee is to submit an accounting to a particular person, such as an adult beneficiary, and that approval of the account by that person discharges the trustee as to all beneficiaries. There is some doubt that such a provision is effective, but the American Law Institute takes the position that it is effective as long as the approval is given in good faith and the accounting makes proper disclosure of the trustee's acts. Restatement (Second) of Trusts §172, cmt. *d.* For further discussion of this matter and related problems, see Westfall, Nonjudicial Settlement of Trustees' Accounts, 71 Harv. L. Rev. 40 (1957). For a statutory authorization (and possibly a model for private authorizations in the terms of trusts) see Uniform Trust Code (draft, Feb. 2000) §110, together with §§301-305 (Art. 3 on *Representation by others*).

A trustee may also voluntarily render account in court. By periodic judicial settlements the trustee may wish to obtain a discharge from further liability for previous acts of administration and to receive compensation for those acts. In some states the practice of courts of equity may limit voluntary settlements in court to final accountings, in the absence of an actual controversy between trustee and beneficiary.

In re ENGER'S WILL
225 Minn. 229, 30 N.W.2d 694 (1948)

[Trustees appeal from a court order that had vacated prior orders as far as necessary to enable the beneficiaries to litigate claims against the trustees for alleged self-dealing. The court stated that the primary question raised was whether the prior order allowing the trustees' account was res judicata.]

PETERSON, J. . . .

An order made in proceedings under §501.35 allowing the annual account of a trustee has the legal effect of a final judgment. The statute, so far as here material, provides that a trustee may file and petition the court for the settlement and allowance of any account, whereupon the court shall set the matter for hearing and give notice thereof as therein provided; and that "[u]pon such hearing the court shall make such order as it deems appropriate, which order shall be final and conclusive as to all matters thereby determined and binding in rem upon the trust estate and upon the interests of all beneficiaries, . . . except that appeal to the supreme court may be taken from such order within 30 days from the entry thereof. . . ." The statute denominates an order allowing an account thereunder an "order," and, because that is true, we are bound by that characterization. But the statute also provides that the legal effect of such an order is that it is *final and conclusive* as to all matters thereby determined, the meaning of which we think is that the determinative effect of such order shall be the same as a final judgment. . . .

In a trustee's accounting, the "matters" involved include the transactions set forth in the trustee's account and the petition for the allowance thereof and the objections thereto, if any. The pleadings consist of the account and the petition on the one side and of the objections thereto on the other. . . . The issues are framed by the account and the petition and the objections thereto as the pleadings in an accounting proceeding. . . . Here, since there were no objections to the annual accounts, the matters determined by the orders allowing the annual accounts were those put in issue by the accounts and the petitions for the allowance thereof filed by the trustees. The proceedings having been by default, the court had jurisdiction to determine only the questions thus raised. . . .

Self-dealing by a trustee is not a matter involved in an accounting proceeding by a trustee where the account and the petition for the allowance thereof do not apprise the beneficiaries of the fact. It is the trustee's duty to disclose to the beneficiary fully, frankly, and without reservation all facts pertaining to the trust. In re Trusteeship under Will of Rosenfeldt, 185 Minn. 425, 430, 241 N.W. 573, 575. In the cited case our decision related to the trustee's duty of disclosure in extra-judicial transactions. The duty of disclosure does not end at the commencement of a legal proceeding, but continues to be just as obligatory therein as it was prior thereto. That being true, the duty rests on the trustee in accounting proceedings to make the fullest measure of disclosure. . . .

Because a beneficiary may rely upon the disclosures in the trustee's account and the petition for its allowance, a proceeding for the allowance of the account does not impose upon the beneficiary as an ordinary adversary the burden of making his own inquiry to ascertain the truth of the trustee's disclosures. The beneficiary may accept them as true. In this respect the rule is different from what it is in ordinary litigation, where the parties are not only adversary, but where there is no fiduciary relationship. . . .

Here, there is not one word in any of the petitions and accounts or in the proceedings for the allowance of the annual accounts apprising the beneficiaries of any self-dealing on the part of the trustees. On the contrary, all information with respect to the matter was concealed. Hence no issue was tendered by the trustees in any of the prior proceedings concerning any self-dealing. The self-dealing was not, therefore, a matter determined by any of the orders relied on as having that effect.

From what has been said it must be apparent that the orders allowing the trustees' annual accounts are not res judicata as to self-dealing by the trustees. Section 501.35, as the controlling statute, determines the extent to which such orders are res judicata. . . . The statute in express terms provides that such orders shall be final and conclusive as to all matters thereby determined. The effect of this provision is that if the matter was determined by the order the order is res judicata, and if the matter was not so determined the order is not res judicata. This is the rule independent of statute. . . . It has been held that where an investment is listed in the account, but the facts showing its illegality are not, the order is not res judicata as to the question of the illegality of the investment, because the mere listing of it fails to apprise the beneficiaries of the fact of illegality. . . .

Since the orders allowing the annual accounts of the trustees are not res judicata of the question whether the trustees are liable for self-dealing, it can make no possible difference whether they were vacated to permit litigation of the question. . . .

Affirmed so far as orders relate to orders allowing trustees' annual accounts and appeal dismissed as to other parts of the order.

PROBLEM

17-H.   *W*, a widow, devised her estate to *T* Trust Co. (*T*) in trust to distribute any or all or none of the income in *T*'s discretion to *W*'s adult children, *A, B,* and *C,* and on the survivor's death to distribute the trust property to such persons, including *A*'s estate, as *A* might appoint by will, in default of appointment to *F* Foundation. The will expressly relieved *T* of any duty to account to any of the beneficiaries; after *W*'s death *A* executed an instrument waiving *T*'s duty to account to him or to any remainder beneficiary. The trust property consisted of *W*'s interest in a closely held business, worth about $1 million, and a diversified portfolio of listed securities worth about $1.5 million. Despite the waivers, *T* rendered fairly detailed accounts to *A* and *B* listing such items as dividends and interest, proceeds from sales of securities, payments to purchase securities, trustee fees, taxes, distributions to beneficiaries, and trust holdings with cost basis and market values. Feeling that *C* (a lawyer) was a troublemaker, *T* refused his requests for similar detailed accountings and provided him only with minimal information that showed the trust income, distributions to each beneficiary, and the total value of the trust property. *A* and *B* also received more generous income distributions than *C, T*'s undisclosed reason being that *C*'s own income is much greater than *A*'s or *B*'s. Based on its analysis of market conditions, *T* sold for $1 million the trust's closely held business interest, which shortly thereafter increased in value to $1.5 million due to developments that could not have been foreseen at the time of the sale. *T* did not advise any of the beneficiaries in advance of contemplated sales or purchases of trust assets, nor did its accounts disclose its reasons for any sales or purchases. *T*'s accounts also did not disclose its method of computing fees, although it increased its fees twice when it published a new fee schedule, relying on a will provision stating that the trustee was entitled to charge "fees based on its fee schedule as published from time to time."

F Foundation suspects that *T*'s investments have been skewed toward production of income for the life beneficiaries, but *T* has refused *F*'s requests for copies of *T*'s accounts, for its reasons for buying or selling securities, and for a full copy of the trust provisions. *T* did, however, provide *F* with a copy of the following language from *W*'s will: "provided, that if *A* fails to exercise this power of appointment, then the trust property shall be distributed free of trust to *F* Foundation." *A* wants to know *T*'s reasons for selling the closely held business interest and for buying and selling certain securities. *B* wants an explanation of how *T* has been computing its fees. *C* wants a copy of the accounts *T* has provided to *A* and *B,* and wants an explanation of the greater distributions *T* has made to *A* and *B. F* wants an explanation of *T*'s investment policies, as well as a copy of the trust provisions in their entirety. For the time being *T* has refused all these requests but seeks your opinion as to its duties in these matters. What advice would you give?

4. Duty to Identify and Take Control of Assets and to Segregate Trust Property

Every fiduciary has an obligation to take control of the assets of the estate he is to administer and to keep a record of those assets and of his administration of them. In the inter vivos trust, the schedule of assets transferred to the trustee represents the starting point of the accounting procedure (supra). On the other hand, the assets constituting a decedent's estate are likely to be uncertain and the subject of conflicting claims of ownership. The accounting procedure is initiated by the filing of an inventory by the personal representative identifying property he considers to be assets of the decedent's estate. Nearly all states require the inventory to be filed promptly after the appointment of the personal representative. In all states it includes personalty, and in most real property is also required to be inventoried whether or not it is subject to administration in the hands of the personal representative.

UNIFORM PROBATE CODE

§3-706. *Duty of Personal Representative; Inventory and Appraisement.* Within 3 months after his appointment, a personal representative, who is not a special administrator or a successor to another representative who has previously discharged this duty, shall prepare and file or mail an inventory of property owned by the decedent at the time of his death, listing it with reasonable detail, and indicating as to each listed item, its fair market value as of the date of the decedent's death, and the type and amount of any encumbrance that may exist with reference to any item.

The personal representative shall send a copy of the inventory to interested persons who request it. He may also file the original of the inventory with the court.

[§3-707 authorizes hiring appraisers; §3-708 requires a supplementary inventory for revised valuations and after-discovered property.]

§3-709. *Duty of Personal Representative; Possession of Estate.* Except as otherwise provided by a decedent's will, every personal representative has a right to, and shall take possession or control of, the decedent's property, except that any real property or tangible personal property may be left with or surrendered to the person presumptively entitled thereto unless or until, in the judgment of the personal representative, possession of the property by him will be necessary for purposes of administration. The request by a personal representative for delivery of any property possessed by an heir or devisee is conclusive evidence, in any action against the heir or devisee for possession thereof, that the possession of the property by the personal representative is necessary for purposes of administration. The personal representative shall pay taxes on, and take all steps reasonably necessary for the management, protection and preservation of, the estate in his possession. He may maintain an action to recover possession of property or to determine the title thereto.

The trend of modern legislation is to provide for immediate vesting of *title* to personal as well as real property in beneficiaries; but most of these statutes provide that the beneficiaries' rights are subject to the personal representative's *right of possession* over some or all of the estate. In the absence of statute, the courts of most of the states continue to adhere to traditional concepts under which title to and possession of personal property pass to the personal representative of a decedent, whereas both title and right of possession in real property pass directly to devisees or heirs on the decedent's death.

MILLER v. PENDER
93 N.H. 1, 34 A.2d 663 (1943)

JOHNSON, J. [Bill in equity for an accounting by the defendant trustee] . . .

The securities invested in by the trustee were taken in his own name without any marks on them to show that they belonged to the trust estate. . . . Whether the reason for the trustee's action was as stated by the Court [in good faith and to facilitate transfer] or was simply neglect, the important point to decide is to what extent, if any, the trustee should be held liable.

Further facts found are as follows: that the trustee kept the original trust certificates apart from his own in a safe in his house; that he made notations of income and remittances on separate slips of paper from which with duplicate deposit slips it was possible for the accountant to trace the income and remittances of the trust fund; that the accountant was able to trace and learn the condition of the trust affairs and the administration of the trust.

It is the duty of a trustee to earmark assets of the trust as trust property. Certificates of stock should be issued in the name of the trustee as trustee.

Failure to do this, however, is not so contrary to public policy that it cannot be authorized by the trust instrument. . . .

A trustee guilty of a breach of trust in failing to have the securities properly tagged is liable for any loss occasioned by such breach. So if personal creditors of the trustee attach the trust securities, written in the name of the trustee personally and cause loss to the estate, the trustee is liable in damages.

In the present case, however, it has been found that the depreciation amounting to $7,666.44 was not due to the breach of trust in taking the securities in the name of George E. Pender individually, but was caused by general economic conditions. The securities would have had the same value and would have sustained the same losses if they had been properly earmarked.

According to Professor Scott the authorities have held that a trustee is liable for any loss that is only simultaneous with a breach of the duty to earmark and not at all caused by it.

> By the weight of authority it is held that the trustee is liable for any loss resulting from a fall in value of the shares, even though the loss did not result from the fact that the shares were taken in the name of the trustee individually. The courts seem to have felt that the practice is so dangerous that the trustee should be held liable for any loss which results from the purchase of the shares, even though he acted in good faith in making the purchase and in taking the title to the shares in his own name.

2 Scott, Trusts, s.205.1. See also s.179.3 of the same work. . . .

The purpose of the rule has been stated to be the prevention of any false claim on the part of the trustee or his estate as to the ownership of the securities of the trust or of the trustee. 3 Bogert, Trusts and Trustees, s.596. This reasoning of course applies only to the prevention of losses that cannot be known. Losses that are known can be dealt with according to the ordinary principles of causation. Losses due to commingling of trust property, whether intentional or not, or due to conversion can be properly compensated for by the usual rules of causation and damages. . . .

A similar rule with regard to earmarking deposits has been said to be a harsh one. 2 Scott, Trusts, s.205.1.

The rule requires the loss to be borne by the trustee as a penalty for the technical breach of the trust duty to earmark, since the loss is not caused by the breach but merely takes place during the time of the breach.

There is a tendency in the more recent cases involving investments in mortgages to adopt a more liberal view and to hold the trustee liable only for such loss as results from the failure to earmark and not for losses due to general economic conditions. . . .

Under the above circumstances a trustee should not be held liable according to Restatement, Trusts, s.179, commend *d.*

> If the trustee takes title to the trust property in his individual name in good faith, and no loss results from his so doing, he is not liable for breach of trust. Thus, if . . . the only objection to the transaction is that he took title in his own name, he is not liable merely because the property depreciates in value. The breach of trust in such a case is merely a technical breach of trust, and no loss has resulted therefrom. If, however, he took title in his own name in bad faith, intending to misappropriate the property, he is liable for the full amount of the mortgage and interest thereon. Even if he acted in good faith, if a loss resulted from the fact that he took title in his own name, as for example if his personal creditors were thereby enabled to reach the property free of trust, he would be liable for the loss. . . .

The practice of failing to earmark the securities of a trust has been said to be dangerous because of wrongful claims on the part of the trustee or his estate that cannot be known. A penalty may be needed to stop a dangerous practice, but the penalty should be in proportion to the culpability of the offense. It should not consist of a loss in no wise caused by the offense but one that merely occurs during the time of the offense. The State of New York has made it a misdemeanor for a testamentary trustee to engage in this practice. This is an appropriate way of curbing a dangerous practice. It is inequitable for a Court of Equity to substantially penalize a trustee acting in good faith for a neglect of duty that in no way caused the loss complained of when the administration of the trust estate can be accounted for in all essential details.

The rule of penalizing the trustee by making him an insurer against losses not caused by his conduct is inequitable and illogical. . . . Yet there is danger of false claims on the part of the trustee as to title when there are no losses in the trust estate. . . .

The trial Justice properly decreed that the defendant should pay the expense of the accountant. This was made necessary by the inadequacy of the trustee's accounts. [Case remanded for trial of now-relevant issue of whether trustee invested imprudently.]

Cf. Stokes v. Henson, 217 Cal. App. 3d 187, 265 Cal. Rptr. 836 (1990); Daniels and Martin, Myth and Reality in Punitive Damages, 75 Minn. L. Rev. 1 (1990).

Does the more lenient breach and damages rule accord sufficient weight to the deterrent policies underlying the general duty of loyalty (see Hallgring, The Uniform Trustees' Powers Act and the Basic Principles of Fiduciary Responsibility, supra section C.2), and to the mismatch between sophisticated trustees in control of the facts and unsophisticated beneficiaries who may have proof problems resulting from severe time lag and may even have been unborn or minors at the time of the act in question?

AMERICAN BAR ASSOCIATION, MODEL RULES OF PROFESSIONAL CONDUCT

Rule 1.15.   *Safekeeping Property.*

(a) A lawyer shall hold property of clients or third persons . . . separate from the lawyer's own property . . . [and] identified as such. . . . Complete records of such account funds and other property shall be kept by the lawyer and shall be preserved for a period of [five years] after termination of the representation.

(b) Upon receiving funds or other property in which a client or third person has an interest, a lawyer shall promptly notify the client or third person. Except as stated in this rule or otherwise permitted by law or by agreement with the client, a lawyer shall promptly deliver to the client or third person any funds or other property that the client or third person is entitled to receive and, upon request by the client or third person, shall promptly render a full accounting regarding such property.

(c) When in the course of representation a lawyer is in possession of property in which both the lawyer and another person claim interests, the property shall be kept separate by the lawyer until there is an accounting and severance of their interest. If a dispute arises concerning their respective interests, the portion in dispute shall be kept separate by the lawyer until the dispute is resolved.

Comment:

[1] A lawyer should hold property of others with the care required of a professional fiduciary. . . . All property . . . of clients or third persons should be kept separate from the lawyer's business and personal property and, if monies, in one or more trust accounts. Separate trust accounts may be warranted when administering estate monies or acting in similar fiduciary capacities. . . .

Wills and trust instruments sometimes provide for a relaxation of the requirements of keeping separate and earmarking the property of a trust or decedent's estate. In fact it is common practice to authorize trustees to hold trust property in the name of another as nominee. It may also be provided that the funds of various trusts may be commingled or that estate or trust property may be commingled with the fiduciary's own. Such provisions are generally given effect by courts so that commingling or failure to earmark will not constitute a breach of trust. The purpose of such provisions may include the economy of managing commingled funds and the simplicity of acquiring and transferring title to trust property.

Most of the states have now enacted legislation to simplify the transfer of securities by fiduciaries, generally in the form of the Uniform Act for Simplification of Fiduciary Security Transfers or provisions of the Uniform Stock Transfer Act or Uniform Commercial Code. Supportive rules have been adopted by the New York, American, and regional stock exchanges and by the National Association of Securities Dealers (over-the-counter market), so that securities registered in the names of "domestic individual" trustees, personal representatives, and guardians (or conservators) are effectively delivered when accompanied by a properly executed and guaranteed assignment or power.

In most of the states some legislation exists relating to the use of nominees, especially by banks and trust companies. For example, Uniform Probate Code §3-715(14) authorizes the personal representative to "hold a security in the name of a nominee or in other form without disclosure of the interest of the estate but the personal representative is liable for any act of the nominee in connection with the security so held."

UNIFORM TRUST CODE
(Draft, Feb. 2000)

§810. *Separation and Identification of Trust Property.*

(a) A trustee shall keep trust property separate from the trustee's own property.

(b) Except as otherwise provided in subsection (c), a trustee other than a regulated financial-service institution shall cause the trust property to be designated so that the interest of the trust, to the extent feasible, appears in records maintained by a party other than a trustee or beneficiary.

(c) As long as the trustee maintains records clearly indicating the respective interests, a trustee may invest as a whole the property of two or more separate trusts.

Comment . . . Except for a regulated financial-service institution, whose trust records are subject to regular state or federal audit, the interest of the trust must appear in the records of a third party, such as a bank or brokerage firm. Because of the serious risk of mistake or misappropriation even if disclosure is made to the beneficiaries, a noninstitutional trustee is not allowed to show the interest of the trust solely in the trustee's own internal records. Section 816(8), which allows a trustee to hold securities in nominee form, is not inconsistent with this requirement. While securities held in nominee form are not specifically registered in the name of the trustee, they are properly earmarked because the trustee's holdings are indicated in the records maintained by an independent party, such as in an account at a brokerage firm.

Earmarking is not practical for all types of assets. With respect to assets not subject to registration, such as tangible personal property and bearer bonds, arranging for the trust's ownership interest to be reflected on the records of a third-party custodian would be impracticable. For this reason, subsection (b) waives separate recordkeeping for these types of assets. Under subsection (a), however, the duty of the trustee not to mingle these or any other trust assets with the trustee's own remains absolute.

Subsection (c), following the lead of a number of state statutes, allows a trustee to make joint investments of the property of two or more trusts even though such joint investments, under traditional principles, would violate the duty to earmark. Such joint investments are often more economical than attempting to invest the funds of each trust separately. Also, because the trustee owes fiduciary duties to each trust, the risk of misappropriation or mistake is less than if the trust funds are invested jointly with those of the trustee or some other person.

5. Duty With Respect to Delegation

PROBLEM

17-I. The settlor, *S*, left his residuary estate to his daughter *X*, as trustee, to pay the income equally to herself and her brothers, *Y* and *Z*, for their lives, and thereafter to distribute the principal equally among *S*'s then surviving issue. *X* often took extensive trips in this country and abroad. Before one such trip to Europe, *X* entered into an "Agency Account Agreement" with the Fidelity Trust Company, which provided:

> The Fidelity Trust Company hereby acknowledges receipt of the assets listed in the attached inventory. The Trust Company hereby is appointed and becomes the agent and attorney-in-fact of *X*, trustee, and agrees to invest and reinvest the funds so received as authorized by said trustee

under the terms of the will of *S* deceased. The Trust Company further agrees to collect the rents, dividends, interest, and other income and after deducting proper charges including three percent of such income as agency fee to distribute the same in accordance with the will of *S*.

Fidelity has now acted under this agreement for a period of eleven years. For the first three years, it secured prior approval for all transactions concerning the estate. After that, *X* arranged to have Fidelity make a semiannual report to her, which she would review, approve and return. During the last three years *X* lived in France and did not return the semiannual reports but reviewed and accumulated them. After her return from France and after a conference with Fidelity, she signed a statement ratifying and approving all reports for the three-year period.

Many securities in the trust and the portfolio as a whole have depreciated in value over this eleven-year period, although the securities and the portfolio would have been proper for *X* herself to have acquired and held. *Y* and *Z* and several grandchildren seek to surcharge *X* and Fidelity for losses in value. As attorney for the complainants, on what would you base your claim of surcharge? If you represented the defendants, what position would you take? What result would you anticipate under the authorities (below), running from Meck v. Behrens through Restatement (Second) of Trusts §171? Would you expect a different result under the Restatement (Third) of Trusts and the Uniform Prudent Investor Act and Uniform Trust Code referred to thereafter?

If *S* had left the residue of his estate to *X* and the Fidelity Trust Company as cotrustees, what result would you expect, assuming again *X*'s frequent travels and an "Agreement Between Cotrustees" providing "the Fidelity Trust Company hereby is appointed and becomes the agent and attorney in fact of *X*, cotrustee, and agrees to invest and reinvest the trust funds as authorized by *X* and by Fidelity in its capacity as cotrustee"? See In re Mueller's Trust, 28 Wis. 2d 26, 46-47, 135 N.W.2d 854, 865-866 (1965).

Meck v. Behrens, 141 Wash. 676, 678-688, 252 P. 91, 94-96 (1927), states:

> It is undoubtedly the rule that, while a trustee may delegate to someone else a purely ministerial duty, he may not delegate to another his discretionary powers. 39 Cyc., at page 304, states:
>
> > It is a general rule that a trustee in whom there is vested discretionary powers involving personal confidence cannot delegate his powers and shift his responsibility to other persons. . . .
>
> The authorities seem to be practically harmonious in holding that when a trustee unlawfully delegates and surrenders his discretionary

powers to someone else, with reference to the control and management of the trust property, he becomes a guarantor and is responsible for any loss that may have resulted, whether or not such loss can be shown to be the result of the delegation of power; the theory being that it is against public policy for one to delegate powers which have been entrusted to him alone, and that the trustee who has placed the trust property in the hands of others will not, after the property has been lost, be heard to say that the delegation of power was not responsible for the loss and that, if he had performed his duties as the law required, the loss would also have occurred. . . .

We are fully conscious of the fact that we have not measured the amount of cross-appellant's rightful claim against appellants with any sort of mathematical accuracy. Indeed, it is impossible to do so from the much involved record before us. . . . Appellants are in no position to complain of want of exactness in measuring their liability.

See also McClure v. Middletown Trust Co., 95 Conn. 148, 153, 154, 110 A. 838, 840, 841 (1920):

While the trustee may not delegate his duties and powers to others, it is obvious that he must act frequently through agents or attorneys. This is not a delegation of his powers, for the trustee remains responsible for the reasonable diligence of his agent or attorney. He must select his agents with reasonable care and he must supervise their acts with the same care. . . . The necessities of the trust may require the services of an agent, on account of the complexity or extent of the business or the special expert knowledge required. . . . [Compare Restatement Second excerpt below.]

Contrast G. Bogert, Trusts §92 (6th ed. 1987), which states that a trustee may delegate the exercise of a power

where a reasonably prudent owner of property of the same type as the trust property who was acting for objectives similar to those of the trust would employ assistance. In the case of such highly important transactions as would be managed personally by a property owner following customary business practices, the trustee must personally make the decisions and perform the acts involved.

RESTATEMENT (SECOND) OF TRUSTS

§171. *Duty Not to Delegate.*   The trustee is under a duty to the beneficiary not to delegate to others the doing of acts which the trustee can reasonably be required personally to perform.

RESTATEMENT (THIRD) OF TRUSTS:
PRUDENT INVESTOR RULE
(1992)

§171. *Duty with Respect to Delegation.*   A trustee has a duty personally to perform the responsibilities of the trusteeship except as a prudent person might delegate those responsibilities to others. In deciding whether, to whom and in what manner to delegate fiduciary authority in the administration of a trust, and thereafter in supervising agents, the trustee is under a duty to the beneficiaries to exercise fiduciary discretion and to act as a prudent person would act in similar circumstances.

General Comment:
   a.   Fiduciary duty and discretion. . . .
   Decisions of trustees concerning delegation are matters of fiduciary judgment and discretion. Therefore these decisions may not be controlled by a court except to prevent abuse of that discretionary authority. . . .
   A trustee's discretionary authority in the matter of delegation may be abused by imprudent failure to delegate as well as by making an imprudent decision to delegate. Abuse of discretion may also be found in failure to exercise prudence in the degree or manner of delegation. Prudence thus requires the exercise of care, skill, and caution in the selection of agents and in negotiating and establishing the terms of delegation. Significant terms of a delegation include those involving the compensation of the agent, the duration and conditions of the delegation, and arrangements for monitoring or supervising the activities of agents.
   f.   Delegation of authority to do particular acts.   Although the administration of a trust may not be delegated in full . . . [d]elegation is not limited to the performance of ministerial acts. In appropriate circumstances delegation may extend, for example, to discretionary acts, to the selection of trust investments or the management of specialized investment programs, and to other activities of administration involving significant judgment. . . .

   Contrast Restatement Second, supra, cmt. *h,* which explicitly prohibited delegation of the "power to select investments."
   The Prudent Investor Rule, supra (§227(c)(2)), requires the trustee to "act with prudence in deciding whether and how to delegate authority" and in selecting, instructing and supervising agents. Uniform Prudent Investor Act (1994) §9(a) and Uniform Trust Code (draft, Feb.

2000) §807(a) are similar, with §9(b) and (c) and §807(b) and (c) adding that "[i]n performing a delegated function, an agent owes a duty to the trust to exercise reasonable care to comply with the terms of the delegation" and that a "trustee who complies with the requirements of subsection (a) is not liable to the beneficiaries or to the trust for the decisions or actions of the agent, to whom the function was delegated." (Do you see why these delegation rules apply to *agents* and why considerably more restrictive principles should apply to delegation among *cotrustees*? Cf. UTC §703 and comment thereto.)

The Uniform Probate Code allows personal representatives (§3-715) and conservators (§5-423(c)(24)), except as limited by will or court order, to "employ persons, including attorneys, auditors, investment advisors, or agents, even if they are associated with the [fiduciary], to advise or assist . . . in the performance of his administrative duties; act without independent investigation upon their recommendations; and instead of acting personally, employ one or more agents to perform any act of administration, whether or not discretionary."

D. *Liability of Fiduciaries*

1. Liability to Beneficiaries

In other parts of this chapter we have encountered the matter of a fiduciary's personal liability for failure to comply with the duties and standards appropriate to the office. The subject continues to arise in various contexts throughout these materials. This section deals simply with fundamentals of the fiduciary's potential liability to the beneficiaries.

A cause of action against a fiduciary may be brought by a beneficiary, and in the case of a decedent's estate also by a creditor of the estate; or it may be brought by a successor or cofiduciary. Typically, questions of liability arise on accounting or in actions to surcharge or remove a trustee or personal representative. In the usual case where the fiduciary has given bond with sureties for the performance of duties, recovery may be against the surety, a matter that depends on the construction of the bond and the cause of the fiduciary's liability. The judgment against a fiduciary usually is not a preferred claim but has the same status as general claims of the fiduciary's personal creditors, except where the beneficiary is granted a lien on certain property of the trustee or is able to trace particular trust property into the hands of the trustee. Codifying traditional remedies as set out in Restatement (Second) of Trusts §199, Uniform Trust Code §§1001, 1002 (draft, Feb. 2000) provide a broad range of remedies for breach of trust. The latter section allows the trustee to be charged with "the greater of: (1)

the amount required to restore the value of the trust property and its trust distributions to what they would have been had the breach not occurred; or (2) the profit that the trustee [personally] made by reason of the breach." Most breach-of-trust remedies are equitable, and as such jury trial is not available, nor, under typical doctrine, are punitive damages. Uniform Trust Code §1004 also expressly permits the court, "as justice and equity may require," to award reasonable attorney's fees and other litigation costs to any party, to be paid by another party or from the trust estate.

The measure of a fiduciary's liability may best be understood in the context of the various cases involving such liability, but as a general principle it has been stated that the "measure of damages is usually the difference between the values of the capital and income of the trust as they would have been if the trust had been performed and as they existed as a result of the wrongful conduct of the trustee." G. Bogert, Trusts §157 (6th ed. 1987). Although the above quotation may not so suggest, traditional doctrine refuses to allow, as too speculative, surcharge recoveries to reflect (with narrow exceptions) appreciation in value that reasonably could have been expected from an appropriate investment program. See, e.g., Matter of Estate of Janes, 90 N.Y.2d 41, 681 N.E.2d 332 (1997). A change of direction is called for, however, by Restatement (Third) of Trusts: The Prudent Investor Rule §§205, 208-211 (1992), providing for a trustee's liability for improper investment conduct to be based on a *total return,* positive or negative, measure of damages. Thus, inappropriate investment strategies are not insulated from liability merely because a trust's investment program has escaped loss of dollar value during periods of significantly rising markets. This approach was adopted in Estate of Wilde, 708 A.2d 273 (Me. 1998); and see Noggle v. Bank of America, 82 Cal. Rptr. 2d 829 (Cal. App. 1999). Also compare the language of Uniform Trust Code §1002 (1), quoted above.

The materials below are concerned with the basic principles governing the occasions of a fiduciary's liability and the measure of it.

CREED v. McALEER
275 Mass. 353, 175 N.E. 761 (1931)

[Because all remainder beneficiaries did not agree to the distribution of stock in kind on termination of the trust, the court ordered the stocks to be sold within a reasonable time. Appellants sought unsuccessfully below to charge the trustees for the difference between the peak price of the stocks following the life beneficiary's death and the price at which they were sold.]

PIERCE, J.

. . . The trustee is chargeable . . . with failure to sell such stocks at the peak price only if such failure was an abuse of "the sound discretion and good judgment of a prudent man dealing with his own permanent investments." . . . As a reasonable man, the trustee could await the outcome of the petition for partial distribution in kind. He could not be held to forecast the sudden drop in stock prices in October and November [and] is not chargeable with the difference between the market price of the stock at the life tenant's death and the price of such stock at the time of the actual sale. . . .

The Probate Court charge[d] the trustee with the [loss resulting from] the retention of [certain mining] stocks beyond a reasonable time after he received them. This charge in legal contemplation compensates the remaindermen for the failure of the trustee to convert [these stocks that were impermissible as trust investments]. . . .

There was a slight gain on the sale of the . . . mining stocks over the inventory value. There was a substantial gain over the inventory values in the sale of all stocks. The trustee contends that "the total gains should be taken into consideration in considering whether or not the trustee should be held for any losses." . . . The gain in each investment belongs to the trust estate. . . . A trustee cannot offset a loss for which he is liable by a gain belonging not to him but to his cestui. . . . The failure to [offset gain from the sale of the *same* stock on which losses were surcharged, however, was] an apparent oversight, and [that offset] should be allowed. . . .

FALL v. MILLER
462 N.E.2d 1059 (Ind. App. 1984)

[The decedent bequeathed certain corporate stock to Fall. During administration, although there was no necessity to sell the stock, the executrix petitioned the court (without Fall's knowledge or consent) to sell the stock, erroneously alleging that it was necessary to do so to pay debts and expenses of the estate. The petition was granted, and the executrix sold the stock. About eight months later her attorney acknowledged the mistake in a letter to Fall and promised to compensate him or replace the stock. Thereafter, without further disclosure, the executrix reacquired on the market equal shares of the same stock for less than the earlier sale price. In her final account she proposed to distribute the specific shares to Fall and to retain the profit in the residue, which was to be divided among herself and others. From an adverse ruling on his objections to that proposal, Fall appeals; the executrix argues that Fall is entitled to and did receive his distribution in kind, fully satisfying her fiduciary duty to him.]

NEAL, P.J.

. . . Executrix [concedes that she] had no right to sell the stock and it was a breach of her duty to do so. A personal representative is regarded as a trustee appointed by law for the benefit of and protection of creditors and distributees. . . .

There is a thread which runs through the law governing fiduciary relationships which forbids a person standing in a fiduciary capacity to another from profiting by dealing in the property of his beneficiary, and any profit realized must be disgorged in favor of that beneficiary. . . .

A legatee may either charge the personal representative with the value of the converted property, or elect to claim and pursue the property for which it has been exchanged. . . .

The Executrix held Fall's stock in a fiduciary capacity, and wrongly sold it, even if by mistake. Neither she nor anyone claiming through her should be permitted to retain the profits or fruits of the transaction. Fall, as equitable owner of the stock, subject only [if needed] to abatement for payment of debts, is entitled to his stock and all profits made by the Executrix in wrongfully dealing in it. One rationale for the rule is that the property which generated the profit belonged to Fall, and in equity and good conscience the property should belong to him. A more persuasive rationale is that if a fiduciary is not allowed to retain any gain or profit from wrongful, speculative or self-dealing transactions in his beneficiary's property and at the same time can be held liable for any loss incurred, an effective deterrent to such activity exists. Any other rule would encourage residuary legatees in control of the estate to speculate in estate assets. Policy forbids such conduct. . . .

Judgment reversed.

Is the so-called no-netting rule (that gains from one breach of trust may not be set off against losses from a *separate* breach), supra, inconsistent with modern portfolio theory? The suggestion that this is so might be considered — carefully — as the "prudent investor rule" is studied in Chapter 18.

When a fiduciary undertakes an act that is forbidden or not authorized, it is no defense that the action was taken in good faith and with reasonable care and skill. Thus, as must be apparent from earlier cases in this chapter, the trust is breached any time there is a violation of a duty imposed by law or by the terms of the trust, regardless of compliance with general standards of care and skill. The trustee must know or ascertain and then must obey the valid terms of the trust and the applicable rules of law. Although in most respects a fiduciary is not a guarantor of the success of actions undertaken in the course of estate or trust administration, under principles of strict liability, traditional doctrine (with a few modern cases contra) does not excuse a fiduciary for reasonable, honest mistakes concerning the nature and extent of the fiduciary's powers and duties, nor for payment of trust funds to one who is not the proper beneficiary. Cf. Uniform Trust Code §1006 (reasonable reliance on language of trust instrument).

If there is reasonable doubt as to the powers and duties of a trustee, for example, or as to the proper interpretation of administrative or distributive provisions of the instrument, it is generally recognized that application may be made to the appropriate court for instructions at the expense of the trust estate. A court will ordinarily refuse to instruct a trustee when reasonable doubt does not exist or where the question is one of business judgment or one that is within the discretion of the trustee. The trustee will be protected if an act is pursuant to court instructions, obtained in good faith and on full disclosure, with respect to beneficiaries who were parties to the proceeding.

A beneficiary who consents to or participates in a breach of trust cannot complain of it. Where powers or duties are uncertain or where contemplated actions are likely to exceed proper authority, a trustee may seek to obtain the approval of the beneficiaries. As a practical matter it is rarely possible under traditional doctrine to obtain consent of all beneficiaries, but those who are sui juris and give their informed consent to a particular act are estopped to object. This assumes that the trustee has concealed no material facts and has acted in a manner consistent with the fiduciary relationship to the beneficiary in obtaining the consent. Beneficiaries who do not or cannot give their consent are not bound by the act of those who do consent, in the absence of special circumstances such as where the consent of the settlor of a revocable trust binds all beneficiaries, as in City Bank v. Cannon, page 859 supra.

In re Estate of Lange, 75 N.J. 464, 383 A.2d 1130 (1978), involved an innovative but growing use of the doctrine of virtual representation to solve the usual difficulties of obtaining beneficiary consent. The testator devised the residue of his estate in trust for his widow for life, remainder on her death to his three adult children, if living, or if not "to their surviving issue, per stirpes." After the testator's death but before the widow's death one of the adult children died, survived by two adult sons. The estate needed to raise cash to pay estate taxes, but the co-executor widow objected to the sale of estate stock at unfavorable terms. One of the adult children suggested a loan to raise cash, with the stock as security. The attorney for the estate rendered his opinion that the loan was within the powers of the executors, and the transaction was carried out. Another adult child was co-executor with her mother and participated in obtaining the loan, although she informally objected to the loan. The third adult child acquiesced in the loan but later objected to its repayment. All three adult children signed boilerplate releases of the co-executors, and none of the adult beneficiaries objected to the loan in the informal and formal estate accountings. The estate stock ultimately declined precipitously in value, and the lower courts held that the loan was not within the powers of the executors. The next question was whether the various living adult beneficiaries had consented to the transaction. Although dealings between fiduciaries and beneficiaries are closely scrutinized for fairness, the court found approval "in the totality of the circumstances." That left the key question of whether the minor or unborn beneficiaries were bound, since the ultimate takers were the testator's issue who survived the widow, who was still alive. The court held that consent of the three adult children (and later the two adult sons of the deceased adult child) was binding on the minor or unborn remainder beneficiaries under the doctrine of virtual representation:

> The presumptive takers are persons who would be the actual takers of the future interest if the contingency occurred at the time of the commencement of the proceeding affecting the property in which the future interest exists. They are permitted to represent the entire class of potential takers, but only in the absence of any demonstrable conflict of interest or other hostility between the presumptive takers and the other members of the class sought to be represented. The assumption underlying the doctrine of virtual representation is the existence of a relationship between the presumptive takers and the class of potential takers sufficiently close to guarantee an identity of interest between the representatives and the class and thus to assure that the representation will be adequate. See Mabry v. Scott, [supra page 779]. See also Restatement, Property, §§180-185 (1936). Utilization of virtual representation enables the court to act upon the interests of unascertainable contingent remaindermen to the same effect as if they all had been sui juris and parties to the action without any infringement of their right to due process. See Mullane v. Central Hanover Bank & Trust Co., [supra page 785].

On vicarous consent more generally, see Hatch v. Riggs National Bank, supra page 675 (on use of guardian ad litem), and Uniform Trust Code art. 3, supra page 686.

As a general rule a fiduciary is not liable to the beneficiaries for the wrongful or negligent act of another if the fiduciary is not also personally at fault. Thus, an individual trustee is not liable to the beneficiaries for the acts of an agent in the absence of an improper delegation of authority, unless the trustee participated or acquiesced in the agent's wrongful act or neglected to compel the agent to make good a loss for which the agent was liable, or unless the trustee failed to use reasonable care in the selection, supervision, and retention of the agent. A corporate trustee, which necessarily acts through its employees, is generally liable for their negligence as the negligent act of the company itself.

One of several fiduciaries is normally not liable for the acts of a cofiduciary unless there has in some way been a failure in the former's own duties. Each cofiduciary, however, must participate in the administration of a decedent's estate or trust assuming at least that such participation is not excluded by the terms of the governing instrument. Thus, a trustee is under a duty "to use reasonable care to prevent a cotrustee from committing a breach of trust or to compel a cotrustee to redress a breach of trust." Restatement (Second) of Trusts §184. A fiduciary must not delegate duties to a cofiduciary, at least in the absence of circumstances that require it in the interest of proper administration. A cofiduciary who violates these duties is liable. When cofiduciaries are both liable, their liability is joint and several; and when neglect renders one liable for the wrongful act of the other, either may be required to make good the entire loss. In such a case the greater fault of one may create a right of indemnity in the other.

Normally a fiduciary is not liable for the acts of a predecessor in office. On the other hand, a fiduciary will generally be held liable for failing to compel redress of a breach of trust by the predecessor, and even for negligent failure to detect the predecessor's breach of trust. Therefore, in order to be safe, a trustee must require an accounting of the predecessor and inquire into the condition of the trust estate. In the absence of a valid provision excusing such inquiry, this admonition would apply whether the successor fiduciary is assuming the administration from another trustee or receiving distribution from an executor or administrator.

Exculpatory Clauses. It is common to find wills and trust agreements that purport to restrict or even eliminate the liability of a fiduciary. The extent to which a trustee or personal representative generally may be relieved by the terms of the instrument of normal liability for breach of duty is reflected in Fleener v. Omaha National Co., 131 Neb. 253, 257, 267 N.W. 462, 464-465 (1936):

> Appellants contend that, as the trust deed was drawn by the trustee, it ought to be construed against it. This would be true if the provisions of the trust deed were so worded as to require a construction, but where the language used is definite and unambiguous, its usual and ordinary meaning should be adopted by the court. We conclude therefore that the exculpatory provisions of the trust deed may be invoked by the trustee to relieve it of all liability except for gross negligence and wilful default. The proper rule is stated by a highly regarded authority as follows [quoting Restatement, Trusts §222]:
>
> (1) Except as stated in subsections (2) and (3), the trustee, by provisions in the terms of the trust, can be relieved of liability for breach of trust.

(2) A provision in the trust instrument is not effective to relieve the trustee of liability for breach of trust committed in bad faith or intentionally or with reckless indifference to the interest of the beneficiary, or of liability for any profit which the trustee has derived from a breach of trust.

(3) To the extent to which a provision relieving the trustee of liability for breaches of trust is inserted in the trust instrument as the result of an abuse by the trustee of a fiduciary or confidential relationship to the settlor, such provision is ineffective.

Uniform Trust Code §1009(a) is similar, with subsection (b) going further than some cases by providing that "An exculpatory term drafted by or on behalf of the trustee is presumed to have been inserted as a result of an abuse of a fiduciary or confidential relationship unless the trustee proves that the exculpatory term is fair under the circumstances and that its existence and contents were adequately communicated to the settlor."

Contrast Committee Report, Current Investment Questions and the Prudent Person Rule, 13 Real Prop., Prob. & Tr. J. 650, 669 (1978):

With respect to any employee benefit plan subject to ERISA, section 410(a) provides as follows:

Except as provided in sections 405(b)(1) and 405(d), any provision in an agreement or instrument which purports to relieve a fiduciary from responsibility or liability for any responsibility, obligation, or duty under this part shall be void as against public policy.

The first exception referred to permits the allocation of fiduciary duties among co-trustees, in which case a trustee to whom a given duty has not been allocated is not liable for a loss due to a breach on the part of the trustee to whom that duty has been allocated. The second exception provides that a trustee is not liable for the acts or omissions of a qualified investment manager who has been properly appointed to manage plan assets, unless the trustee knowingly participates in or knowingly conceals an act or omission of the investment manager which it knows constitutes a breach.

Section 410(b), however, does permit a fiduciary to purchase personal fiduciary liability insurance at his own expense, or at the plan's expense if the insurance policy permits recourse by the insurer against the fiduciary in the event of a breach by the fiduciary. To permit a plan to purchase such insurance with plan assets without a recourse provision would constitute a prohibited relief from personal liability for the fiduciary.

Statutes of Limitations and Laches. "[A]s between a trustee and cestui que trust the statute of limitations does not commence to run so long as the trust continues." Meck v. Behrens, 141 Wash. 676, 681, 252 P. 91, 93 (1927). Compare Developments in the Law — Statutes of Limitations, 63 Harv. L. Rev. 1177, 1214-1215 (1950):

> [Actions for breach of fiduciary duty] have been accorded . . . spe-
> cial treatment under statutes of limitations . . . because . . . the
> plaintiff will not ordinarily learn of the wrong for some time after the
> defendant's defalcation. This consideration is especially appropriate to
> the express formal trust, a relationship used frequently for the preser-
> vation and management of property for the young, infirm, or inexperi-
> enced, who are unlikely to have sufficient business acumen to determine
> when a breach has occurred. . . . Thus, the statute does not begin to
> run during the existence of the relationship unless the beneficiary
> knows, or reasonably should know, of the facts constituting the breach
> of duty.

The frequent judicial assertion that statutes of limitations have no
application to express trusts has been said to mean merely that the
statute does not begin to run until the beneficiary had actual or constructive notice of the trustee's breach or repudiation of the trust. G.
Bogert, Trusts §170 (6th ed. 1987). The more common view, however,
is that statutes of limitations of most states are not applicable to equitable claims but that the barring of a beneficiary's cause of action against
a trustee is a matter of laches, for which the length of time necessarily
depends upon the circumstances. Restatement (Second) of Trusts
§219, comments *a, b.* "The arbitrary operation of the statutes of limitations is very different from the operation of the equitable doctrine of
laches, which is a very flexible doctrine." III W. Fratcher, Scott on
Trusts §219 (4th ed. 1988). Compare Uniform Probate Code §7-307
(six-month limitation on proceedings against a trustee after a final account); Uniform Trust Code §1006(a) (barring claim for breach of
trust one year after beneficiary or representative of beneficiary is sent
"a report that adequately disclosed the facts constituting the claim"
and "informed the beneficiary of the time allowed") and §1006(b)
(adequate disclosure requires "sufficient information so that the beneficiary knows of the claim or reasonably should have inquired into its
existence").

2. Liability to Third Parties

PROBLEM

17-J.   *E,* as executor of an estate valued at $750,000, has continued
the hardware store business that the testator had operated as a sole
proprietorship. The assets of the business constitute in value slightly
more than half the estate. An employee, driving the store truck to make
a delivery, ran over a pedestrian, who has filed suit for $1 million. What
are the potential liabilities in the absence of statute? Under the UPC?
Would the issues differ if a cornice stone fell from a building held in

the estate, injuring a pedestrian on the sidewalk? If the building had been specifically devised to *X*?

The general concept of the fiduciary relationship is that the fiduciary is the owner of the property as far as third persons are concerned. In absence of statute, the fiduciary is *personally* liable on contracts relating to the property and its management and is the only person who can make contracts involving the administration of the trust or estate. Similarly, the fiduciary is subjected to personal liability for tax assessments and for torts arising out of the administration. The position of a trustee or personal representative must be distinguished from that of an agent, who has a principal to respond for his acts. Because of the harshness of the common law rule, the Uniform Probate Code §§3-808, 5-428, 7-306 provide for personal liability in contract only if the fiduciary fails to reveal the representative capacity to the third party and in tort only if the fiduciary is personally at fault. Uniform Trust Code §1010 is based on and similar to UPC §7-306. These provisions attempt to make an estate or trust a corporate-like entity as far as third parties are concerned. As we have already seen, even at common law if the administration is proper, the fiduciary is entitled to reimbursement from the estate for expenses and liabilities.

The normal contract liability of a fiduciary at common law can be eliminated or limited by the terms of the contract. In attempting to so limit liability, the fiduciary should be certain that the intended limitation is clearly expressed. See Torrey Pines Bank v. Hoffman, 231 Cal. App. 3d 308, 282 Cal. Rptr. 354 (1991) (trustee's contract prior to effective date of Cal. Prob. Code §18000, which adopted UPC principles). The traditional view is that the mere addition of the word *trustee* or *executor* to one's signature is not sufficient; nor is a provision of the trust instrument effective to preclude a trustee's personal liability, at least in the absence of knowledge by the third party or contractual reference to the instrument. An innocent third party does not lose recourse against the fiduciary where the contract limiting the latter's liability was improper so as not to bind the trust estate.

Legislation may eliminate the trap that mere addition of the word *trustee* or *executor* is insufficient to eliminate the fiduciary's contract liability. Under the UPC sections cited above a personal representative, conservator, or trustee is not personally liable if the contract "reveal[s] his representative capacity and identif[ies] the [estate] in the contract." Uniform Trust Code §1011 makes a subtle change in UPC wording by providing that a trustee is not personally liable "if the trustee in the contract discloses the fiduciary capacity." What result under the

UPC or the UTC if a trustee properly enters into a contract on behalf of a trust and simply signs it, "Jamal Smith, Trustee"?

For a careful discussion of the justification for the rule of personal liability of fiduciaries, see Johnston v. Long, 30 Cal. 2d 54, 181 P.2d 645 (1967), holding an executor personally liable for torts committed by employees of a business operated by the executor pursuant to authority granted by the California Probate Code (an overhead door fell on the plaintiff as he was entering a garage of an automobile agency). Writing for the majority, Justice Traynor pointed out that: (1) unlike a corporation, an estate is not a legal entity; (2) direct recovery against the estate would be unfair to the beneficiaries, as they might not be heard on the issue of the executor's personal fault; (3) the executor could be protected against personal liability by procuring insurance on behalf of the estate; and (4) procedurally, suit directly against the estate would be difficult or futile where administration had been completed or the estate assets had been distributed. In dissent, Justice Schauer expressed views now reflected in the UPC and UTC: "We should not [adopt a construction of Prob. Code §572 (which allows a court to authorize continuation of a decedent's business)] which seems so certain to produce multiplicity of suits, delays in final settlement of estates, and, at least occasionally, admittedly unjust actual responsibility, all stemming from the unrealistic concept that authorization to an executor to conduct a business in his official capacity does not carry with it authorization to sue or be sued *in the same capacity* in respect to . . . the very thing authorized."

Under traditional rules an action in tort or on a contract is brought and judgment is entered against the fiduciary in his individual capacity. Thus, to satisfy a judgment against a trustee, the creditor may look to the trustee's own assets. The trust assets may be reached only in equity through subrogation, and then the right of the creditor is dependent on the trustee's right of indemnification. See generally on these matters Cook v. Holland, 575 S.W.2d 468 (Ky. App. 1978). Rules relating to the personal liability of fiduciaries and the procedures to be followed by creditors have been modified by statute or judicial decision in some of the states.

In Kirchner v. Muller, 280 N.Y. 23, 28-29, 19 N.E.2d 665, 667-668 (1937), the court stated:

> The general rule as contended for by appellant is that for their torts trustees or executors are liable in their individual, and not in their representative, capacity. Judgments obtained against executors or trustees are collectible out of their private property, and not out of the trust or estate assets. Although the question appears to have arisen infrequently, the trustee or executor has been held entitled to reimbursement from the

estate where he was free from willful misconduct in the tort which occurred during his administration of the estate. A few States have gone so far as to hold that where a trustee or executor would be entitled to reimbursement, the injured third party may sue him in his representative capacity, on the ground that thereby circuity of action may be avoided. No New York authorities are found supporting this procedure. Such a procedure would involve a trial in the same action of both the tort liability and whether the nature of the tort was such as to entitle the trustees or executors to reimbursement, out of the estate, which might entail an undesirable clash of interests between the trustee in his individual capacity and in his representative capacity.

Compare Smith v. Rizzuto, 133 Neb. 655, 659-660, 276 N.W. 406, 408-409 (1937), in which it is stated:

> It is the general rule that a "trustee is subject to personal liability to third persons for torts committed in the course of the administration of the trust to the same extent that he would be liable if he held the property free of trust." . . . We therefore conclude that the petition states a cause of action against the defendant.
>
> The question immediately arises as to the nature of the liability and the right of the defendant to be indemnified from the trust estate. While "the trustee is personally liable to third persons for torts committed by him in the course of the administration of the trust, if the liability was incurred in the proper administration of the trust and the trustee was not personally at fault in incurring the liability, he is entitled to indemnity out of the trust estate." Restatement, Trusts, sec. 247, comment *a*. As to whether a trustee is personally liable for the amount of a judgment in excess of the amount that the trust estate is able to pay raises another question. We are constrained to the view that, if the liability arises from the mere fact that the fee title to the trust property is in the trustee, the liability of the trustee to third persons is limited to the extent to which the trust estate is sufficient to indemnify him where he is without fault and where he is not responsible for the insufficiency of the estate to make indemnity. See Restatement, Trusts, sec. 265.

The reference to the Restatement, in support of the last sentence quoted above, is to a section dealing with items such as property taxes and assessments.

Environmental Liability. A recent concern of fiduciaries has been liability based simply on the ownership of land, without regard to fault. Under the Comprehensive Environmental Response, Compensation, and Liability Act of 1980, 42 U.S.C. §§9601-9675 ("CERCLA" or "Superfund"), any "owner" of land on which toxic waste is found may be liable for the cost of cleaning up the waste, whether or not the "owner" was the source of the contamination. A fiduciary is deemed to be an "owner," but the key question for fiduciaries is whether the fiduciary is personally liable or is liable only to the extent of the estate assets. Litigation left the matter in doubt. See City of Phoenix v. Garbage Services Co., 827 F. Supp. 600 (D. Ariz. 1993). Congress eventually amended CERCLA in 1996 to limit liability to the assets held in a fiduciary capacity. See 42 U.S.C. §9607(n). The statute provided a number of safe harbors for the fiduciary, among them administering property which was contaminated before the fiduciary relationship began. Id. §9607(n)(4). Of course, the statute does not deal with possible fiduciary liability under other federal (or state) environmental legislation. See C.D. Fox, IV, and S. Zabel, Environmental Fiduciary Liability: The Mist Clears, 136 Trusts & Estates 30 (Jan. 1997). UTC §1010(b) specifically protects a trustee from personal liability for violations of environmental law unless the trustee was personally at fault, and §701(c)(2) allows a designated trustee to investigate trust property for environmental liability without being deemed to have accepted the trusteeship. UTC §816(14) provides comprehensive trustee powers to deal with possible environmental liability.

E.   Third Party Liability for Breach of Duty by a Fiduciary

In this section we are concerned with the extent to which obligations of the fiduciary affect persons who are not themselves parties to the fiduciary relationship. The other side of this problem is the question of when a beneficiary's interests may be impaired by the dealings of the trustee or personal representative with outsiders. We have previously considered the fiduciary's liability to third persons, as well as to the beneficiaries. We now turn to those situations in which a third person, allegedly at least, has interfered with the fiduciary relationship or has dealt with a fiduciary who has exceeded its powers or otherwise violated its duties.

A trustee "is in many respects like a buffer between the beneficiaries and the outer world." IV W. Fratcher, Scott on Trusts §279A (4th ed. 1989). In this role the fiduciary is entitled to bring actions against outsiders when required by the interests of the estate. In fact there normally is an obligation to do so. Thus, the burden of enforcing contract and tort claims against third parties falls on the fiduciary. For example, in seeking redress for a tortious interference with trust property, a trustee can sue the wrongdoer without joinder of the beneficiaries. Although in equity, and under modern codes at law, joinder of beneficiaries is permissible, this is not necessary unless a complete determination cannot be had without their being made parties. (This limitation is best illustrated by litigation involving controversies among beneficiaries or between beneficiaries and the trustee.) The beneficiary cannot ordinarily maintain an action against a third party. Exceptions are generally recognized (1) where the beneficiary had a possessory right that was interfered with and (2) where the trustee neglects or declines to act. In the latter case the interests of a beneficiary may be protected by bringing suit in equity against the trustee, joining the third party as codefendant; when required by jurisdictional considerations, beneficiaries have been allowed to bring suit directly against the third party alone. The foregoing generalizations assume situations in which the third person has acted independently of the fiduciary.

In the class of cases of particular concern in this section, the procedural aspects may be quite different from the cases referred to in the preceding paragraph. Here we deal with cases in which the alleged liability of the third party stems from a violation of duty by the fiduciary. In a sense, and quite realistically in certain situations, the "buffer" between the beneficiaries and the outside world has been lost. If the third party was a participant with the trustee in a breach of trust, ordinarily the beneficiary would be entitled to bring suit against the outside wrongdoer directly. Here the interference is with the fiduciary relationship. The better view is that an action could also be brought against the third person by the trustee, but a difference of opinion exists on this point, particularly where the trustees had acted in bad faith rather than by inadvertence. Where a cotrustee or a successor trustee is available to seek redress, the right of a beneficiary to bring suit is doubtful.

An example of possible third party liability arises where a bank honors checks drawn by a fiduciary on the fiduciary account in breach of duty, particularly where the checks are payable to the fiduciary personally. It would be impractical to expect the bank to assume the hazard of correctly reading in each check the purpose of the drawer, so the bank is generally not liable. Nevertheless, if the bank knows or has reason to know that a breach is being committed, or if the bank is a creditor of the fiduciary personally and receives payment of the debt by a check drawn on the fiduciary account, the bank is liable to the fiduciary estate. See Bischoff v. Yorkville Bank, 218 N.Y. 106, 112 N.E. 759 (1916); In re Estate of Dillon, 441 Pa. 206, 272 A.2d 161 (1971).

The Uniform Commercial Code embraces similar principles for negotiable instruments. Under §3-304(2) "[t]he purchaser has notice of a claim against the instrument when he has knowledge that a fiduciary has negotiated the instrument in payment of . . . his own debt . . . or otherwise in breach of duty." Under §3-304(4) mere "[k]nowledge . . . that a person negotiating the instrument is or was a fiduciary" does not give the purchaser notice of a claim.

Another issue for financial institutions has been the transfer of stocks and bonds held in fiduciary name. The common law view was that the corporation or its stock transfer agent was under a duty to inquire into the propriety of the change in registration from the fiduciary to a third party. If the transfer was in breach of duty, the corporation or its agent was liable if it made the transfer. As a result, corporations required voluminous documentation about the propriety of the transfer, and trading in stocks and bonds was impeded. The result was the Uniform Simplification of Fiduciary Security Transfers Act, which reduced the documentation required of the fiduciary and provided that if the corporation or its transfer agent obtained the specified documentation it was not under any further duty of inquiry or liable if the fiduciary had transferred wrongfully. Article 8 of the Uniform Commercial Code is similar (see §§8-304, 8-403). These statutes have been widely adopted.

Where a trustee transfers trust property in breach of trust to a purchaser who takes in good faith and without notice, the transferee takes free of the trust and is not liable to the beneficiaries. This is because the interest of the beneficiary is equitable. The result is not dependent upon principles of estoppel, although decisions are occasionally worded in this fashion. Today, of course, the result is facilitated by recording acts in the case of real property when the trust is not of record and by special legislation dealing with negotiable instruments and corporate stock, but the basic rule exists independently of statute. By the better view it applies to nonnegotiable choses in action as well as to chattels held in trust. See 4 A. Corbin, Contracts §900 (1951 & Supp. 1998).

The rule that a bona fide purchaser cuts off outstanding equities of which the purchaser has no notice is well settled. It is to be distinguished from the rule of common law, often carried to harsh extremes, that the legal owner prevails over a bona fide purchaser from a wrongdoer in the absence of grounds for estoppel, assuming that the subject matter is not of a negotiable character. The doctrine that a bona fide purchaser takes free of *equitable* interests is understandable only by recognizing that each of the claimants has roughly equal claim on the conscience of the court and that in such cases courts have traditionally refused to disturb the status quo. As a result the party having the legal title prevails. Thus, when the prior right was merely an equitable one, the innocent purchaser of the legal title prevailed. The equitable claimant is left with only his claim against the wrongdoer and can no longer obtain the property itself. See generally Brown, Personal Property §70 (3d ed. 1975); IV W. Fratcher, Scott on Trusts §284 (4th ed. 1989). The typical trust case is a ready demonstration that this result does not depend on estoppel, for rarely would grounds for estoppel exist with respect to the beneficiary — especially minors and unborn beneficiaries.

Because these results depend on the passage of legal title, the rule does not apply in favor of a bona fide purchaser who has paid consideration but has not yet received the legal title. IV W. Fratcher, Scott on Trusts §310 (4th ed. 1989). This limitation on the success of the bona

fide purchaser does not apply where there are grounds for estoppel
or where the purchaser can claim the protection of a recording act.

The result of the rules stated above is that the main area of difficulty
is in determining whether a particular purchaser from a trustee satisfies
the requirements of a bona fide purchaser. Certain aspects of this issue
are peculiar to situations involving dealings with fiduciaries who hold
legal title. Beyond the initial question of whether the purchaser had
notice of the *existence* of a trust, for example, there is the further issue of whether, assuming such notice, there was notice of the *breach* of
trust.

PROBLEM

17-K.   Your client, *C*, has entered into a contract to purchase Blackacre from *T*. A search of the record reveals only that *T* holds title to
Blackacre in the name of "*T* as trustee." At this point, how would you
advise *C* to proceed, assuming that she wishes to go through with her
purchase?

If *C* had completed this transaction before consulting you and the
beneficiaries seek to set aside the deed from *T*, who was not authorized
to sell Blackacre, what would *C*'s rights be? Would she be charged with
whatever knowledge a reasonable inquiry would have disclosed? What
would constitute a reasonable inquiry? What result under the Uniform
Trust Code, infra?

Suppose that you are still advising *C* and that she has not yet accepted
T's deed or paid the purchase price, and suppose that on examination
you find the trust instrument entirely silent on the question of whether
T has power to sell Blackacre. How would you advise *C* to proceed now?
For purposes of this and other questions in this problem, consider the
materials that follow and also consider, as you subsequently begin your
study of Chapter 18, whether the trustee has an implied power to sell
Blackacre.

FIRST NATIONAL BANK v. NATIONAL
BROADWAY BANK
156 N.Y. 459, 51 N.E. 398 (1898)

[Action to compel National Broadway Bank to transfer certain shares
of its stock to the plaintiff, which had made a loan to Philo Hotchkiss
by discounting the note of Hotchkiss & Co. The securities in question,
standing in Hotchkiss's name as trustee, were pledged as part of the
collateral for this note. Hotchkiss was at the time serving as trustee
under a trust created by W. H. Imlay for his daughter Georgiana
(Hotchkiss's wife) and her issue. At the time of the loan the plaintiff

also received a writing signed by Georgiana Hotchkiss authorizing her husband to borrow on "the stock standing in his name as trustee for my benefit, and owned by me." When Hotchkiss defaulted on the note, the plaintiff purchased the shares at a public auction held pursuant to the terms of the note. When the defendant bank refused to transfer the stock on its books and to issue a new certificate to the plaintiff, this action was instituted, the lower courts holding that the successor trustee to Hotchkiss was entitled to the stock and accrued dividends thereon because the plaintiff had constructive notice that the shares were the subject of a trust and that the pledge was contrary to its terms.]

GRAY, J. . . .

I do not understand the appellant as disputing the general rule, which imposes upon a party dealing with a trustee, in respect of the trust estate in his hands, the duty of inquiry as to the character of the trust, and a consequent responsibility for the property received, if it turns out that a reasonable inquiry would have disclosed that the property had been transferred in violation of the duty or power of the trustee. Nor does the appellant appear to dispute that the presence of the word "trustee" upon the stock certificate was, of itself, notice of the character of the property, and sufficient to put the plaintiff upon inquiry as to Hotchkiss' authority to pledge it. The argument is that [appellant's] . . . duty of inquiry was performed in a way that an ordinarily prudent and careful man would pursue in his own affairs. . . . [E]vidence is lacking to show what inquiry was made, or what the . . . information [might have] disclosed, at the time. The court therefore is more or less remitted to the presumptions which arise from the known facts of the transaction, and which it is bound to entertain in view of the settled rule of law. Any person who receives property knowing that it is the subject of a trust, and that it has been transferred in violation of the duty or power of the trustee, takes it subject to the right, not only of the cestui que trust, but also of the trustee, to reclaim possession of the property. Knowledge of the trustee's violation of the trust conditions will be chargeable to the person dealing with him, if the facts were such as, in reason, to put him upon inquiry, and to require him to make some investigation, as the result of which the true title and authority of the trustee might have been disclosed. He will then be regarded as having constructive notice of the terms of the trust, whence the trustee derives his power to act. . . . In Story, Eq. Jur. §400, it is laid down that "a purchaser is . . . supposed to have knowledge of the instrument under which the party with whom he contracts as executor, or trustee, or appointee derives his power"; and quite lately this court has affirmed that doctrine. Such an inquiry was called for in this case as was reasonably possible to the plaintiff. . . . The proof shows that the Broadway Bank, whose stock was offered to be pledged, had transferred the title thereto to Hotchkiss as trustee, upon the requirements of an order of the Connecticut court, which appointed him as trustee in succession to a prior trustee. This order referred to "the matter of the Imlay trust, dated January 17, 1857," . . . [which] would, presumably, have disclosed further facts about the trust. . . . Its examination would have shown that the only power which the trustee had to deal with the trust securities was to sell the same, and invest the proceeds thereof in other good bank stocks "in his own name as trustee." It would have shown that Georgiana's interest in them was only that of a life beneficiary. . . .

I see nothing unreasonable in holding the plaintiff to such a rule of diligence as would require the examination of the trust instrument before it undertook to loan moneys upon trust property in behalf or for the benefit of any person. The burden was upon it to prove what inquiry was made, and failing that proof, the presumption should obtain that it was made up to the instrument of trust itself, an inspection of which would show that the trustee could not pledge the trust securities. . . . Doubtless, the circumstances of each case must determine whether the person has acted prudently and cautiously. Whether he was constructively notified in the transaction with the trustee may depend upon how far those circumstances pointed out the path of inquiry.

On the face of this stock, the plaintiff's attention was called to the fact that it was dealing with a trustee, and inquiry of the Broadway Bank would have produced the order appointing Hotchkiss trustee "in the matter of the Imlay trust, dated January 17, 1857." It then became chargeable with the knowledge of such facts about the trustee's duty and power as would have been revealed by such an inquiry as a prudent regard for the rights of others, if not for its own interest, would, naturally, dictate. That a knowledge of the limitations of the trustee's power of disposition would have, or should have, deterred the plaintiff from advancing moneys to a business concern upon a pledge of the stock, is not to be doubted. That such knowledge was obtainable, if not through the trustee himself, then through other available means, is also clear. . . .

But I do not think we should affirm the judgment below in so far as it denies the plaintiff's claim upon the life interest of Georgiana Hotchkiss in the dividends accumulated and to be declared upon the stock. . . . I think she is estopped by her acts from setting up any claim to the income upon the stock received, and which may be hereafter, during her life, received, by way of dividends, by the trustee. If this were not so, then the court would be aiding her in the perpetration of a fraud upon the plaintiff. . . .

Compare Kurowski v. Burch, 8 Ill. App. 3d 716, 719-720, 290 N.E.2d 401, 404-405 (1972):

[A]lthough it be assumed that the purchasers knew they were dealing with trustees and receiving a conveyance of trust property, there is absent from the second amended complaint any allegation that the purchasers knew or should have known that they were dealing with trustees who were committing a breach of trust in making the conveyance of the property in question. In order to declare the purchasers trustees and impress a trust upon the property it must appear that they either knew or should have known that the trustees with whom they were dealing were committing a breach of trust in conveying the property to them. The purchasers would have notice that a breach of trust was taking place if they had actual knowledge of the breach or if they possessed knowledge of facts that would lead a reasonably intelligent and diligent person to make further inquiry as to whether the trustees were committing a breach of trust. . . . [A] trustee is presumed to act rightfully, and in the absence of facts putting purchasers on inquiry they are not bound to presume wrongful conduct on his part.

UNIFORM TRUST CODE
(Draft, Feb. 2000)

§1012. *Protection of Person Dealing with Trustee.*

(a) A person other than a beneficiary who in good faith assists a trustee or who in good faith and for value deals with a trustee without knowledge that the trustee is exceeding or improperly exercising the trustee's powers is protected from liability as if the trustee properly exercised the power.

(b) A person other than a beneficiary who in good faith deals with another person knowing that the other person is a trustee is not required to inquire into the extent of the trustee's powers or the propriety of their exercise.

(c) A person who in good faith delivers assets to a trustee need not ensure their proper application.

(d) A person other than a beneficiary who in good faith assists a former trustee or who for value and in good faith deals with a former trustee without knowledge that the trusteeship has terminated is protected from liability as if the former trustee were still a trustee.

(e) The protection provided by this section to persons assisting or dealing with a trustee is superseded by comparable protective provisions of other laws relating to commercial transactions or to the transfer of securities by fiduciaries.

UTC §103 (*Definitions*) provides: "(9) 'Know,' with respect to a fact, means to have knowledge of the fact or have reason to know that the fact exists based upon all of the facts and circumstances known to the person at the time." See also Adler v. Manor Healthcare Corp., 7 Cal. App. 4th 1110, 9 Cal. Rptr. 2d 732 (1992), giving effect to Cal. Prob. Code §18100 that similarly alleviates the problems created by the common law rule.

Uniform Trust Code §1013 further provides for a "certification of trust," which the comment explains as follows:

> This section, based on California Probate Code §18100.5, is designed to protect the privacy of a trust instrument by reducing requests by third parties for complete copies of the instrument . . . to verify a specific and narrow authority of the trustee to engage in a particular transaction. While a testamentary trust, because it is created under a will, is a matter of public record, an inter vivos trust instrument is private. Such privacy is compromised, however, if the trust instrument must be widely distributed among third parties. A certification of trust is a document signed by all currently acting trustees that may include excerpts from the trust instrument necessary to facilitate the particular transaction. . . . Persons acting in reliance on a certification may assume the truth of the certification even if they have a complete copy of the trust instrument in their possession.
>
> To encourage compliance with this section, persons demanding a trust instrument despite having already been offered a certification may be liable for damages if their refusal is determined not to have been made in good faith.

UNIFORM PROBATE CODE

§3-714. *Persons Dealing with Personal Representative; Protection.* A person who in good faith either assists a personal representative or deals with him for value is protected as if the personal representative properly exercised his power. The fact that a person knowingly deals with a personal representative does not alone require the person to inquire into the existence of a power or the propriety of its exercise. . . . A person is not bound to see to the proper application of estate assets paid or delivered to a personal representative. . . . The protection here expressed is not by substitution for that provided by comparable provisions of the laws relating to commercial transactions and the laws simplifying transfers of securities by fiduciaries.

18

Management Functions

In order that the administration of a decedent's estate or trust can be carried out, the fiduciary must have the power to act. The powers of a fiduciary may be expressed or implied. The practice today is to extend the powers of fiduciaries by broad grants of powers in the controlling document or by statutory presumptions in favor of certain powers. A power that is not granted by the instrument or by statute may be implied so that the purposes of the administration may be carried out.

In this chapter we consider first whether certain powers need be expressed or may be implied. Then we explore the significant function of investment and problems associated with the fiduciary's investment power. Throughout, the student should consider how particular matters might be dealt with in the planning and drafting of wills and trust instruments.

A. Powers of Fiduciaries

1. General Managerial Powers

RESTATEMENT (SECOND) OF TRUSTS

§186. *Extent of Trustee's Powers.* Except as stated in §§165-168 [dealing with impossibility, illegality, and change of circumstances], the trustee can properly exercise such powers and only such powers as

(a) are conferred upon him in specific words by the terms of the trust, or

(b) are necessary or appropriate to carry out the purposes of the trust and are not forbidden by the terms of the trust.

Case law in some states may still be more restrictive than suggested by the above excerpt. See W. Fratcher, Trustee's Powers Legislation, 37 N.Y.U. L. Rev. 627 (1962). Because of concern over the continuing tendency in many states to narrowly construe grants of fiduciary authority in documents and to take a narrow view of powers implied by law, some states offer for the convenience of drafters a statutory list of fiduciary powers that may be incorporated into documents by reference, either in whole or in part. See, e.g., N.C. Gen. Stat. §§32-26, 32-27. (With the Restatement view, above, compare the UTC and UPC rules infra.)

In the absence of express authority granted in a governing instrument or statute, certain common business transactions have been the subject of doubt and thus controversy. Typical issues include the power to sell or improve land, the power to borrow money or to mortgage fiduciary property, the power to make secured or unsecured loans, and powers to grant options or to lease beyond the period of estate or trust administration. In Russell v. Russell, 109 Conn. 187, 145 A. 648 (1929), for example, the court found no authority in the will to make improvements but concluded that, on remand, the probate court could grant this authority and power to borrow money to finance the improvements where, as a result of fire damage, rentals from the trust property would otherwise be insufficient to pay the necessary charges upon it. (Compare the doctrine of equitable deviation in Chapter 14, supra.) See also Purdy v. Bank of America, 2 Cal. 2d 298, 304, 40 P. 2d 481, 484 (1935), expressing the view that the power to borrow money is a "dangerous power" that may nevertheless be implied "where the facts establish the necessity and the trustee has acted in good faith."

In the case of personal property, particularly securities held as an investment, a *trustee* normally has an implied power of sale even though the property in question is proper as a trust investment. Courts have traditionally been less willing, however, to imply a power to sell land when not necessary to accomplish the purposes of the trust. Although the modern tendency is to do away with the assumption that land is to be retained, the inference that a power of sale does or does not exist may be strengthened or weakened by the circumstances, such as: the propriety of the property as a trust investment; whether it is or is not reasonably productive of income; whether the instrument suggests that the property is to be held for the use of the life beneficiary or is to be distributed in specie to the remainder beneficiaries; and the role the property may play in carrying out the purposes of the trust. See generally III W. Fratcher, Scott on Trusts §§190-190.3 (4th ed. 1988). See also Smith v. Mooney, 5 N.J. Misc. 1087, 139 A. 513 (1927), implying a power to sell land where the trustee was directed to divide the corpus among numerous beneficiaries and some of the shares would be as small as one seventy-second of the whole.

The power of a *personal representative* to sell property of a decedent's estate, as well as the manner of its exercise, is frequently determined by statute. Often, approval by a court is required. The powers and procedures may be different as between real and personal property, although the trend is to abolish this distinction in administration of estates. The contrasting functions of personal representatives and trustees may suggest significant differences in the powers to be implied for the two types of fiduciaries. Nevertheless, legislative and drafting tendencies are to set out a broad set of powers for executors and administrators or to confer on them powers typically granted to trustees.

Where sales must be confirmed by court, what if a trustee or personal representative contracts to sell privately or at auction but receives a higher offer before the court has confirmed the sale? In re Strass's Trust Estate, 11 Wis. 2d 410, 105 N.W.2d 533 (1960), held that the policy in favor of stability of contracts warranted sale at the lower price, but the dissent and some other cases would refuse confirmation of the lower price.

UNIFORM TRUST CODE
(Draft, Feb. 2000)

§815. *General Powers of Trustee.*

(a) A trustee, without authorization by the court, may exercise:
    (1) powers conferred by the terms of the trust;
    (2) except as limited by the terms of the trust:
        (A) all powers over the trust property which an unmarried competent owner has over individually owned property;
        (B) any other powers appropriate to achieve the proper management, investment, and distribution of the trust property; and
        (C) any other powers conferred by this [Act].
(b) Except as modified by the terms of a trust, the exercise of a power is subject to the fiduciary duties prescribed by this [article].

UNIFORM PROBATE CODE

§3-711. *Powers of Personal Representatives; In General.* Until termination of his appointment a personal representative has the same power over the title to property of the estate that an absolute owner would have, in trust however, for the benefit of the creditors and others interested in the estate. This power may be exercised without notice, hearing, or order of court.

In addition to the general grants of powers in the above Codes,[1] each also spells out a full set of powers the trustee or personal representative may exercise, unless denied by the terms of the trust or will. UTC §816; UPC §3-715.

PROBLEM

18-A.   *T* administers a trust estate consisting of about $400,000 worth of securities and one parcel of land. The trust terms expressly empower *T* either to sell the land or to retain it as an investment. Having carefully weighed the alternatives available to her, *T* believes she should accept an offer she has received from *P*, who wishes to purchase the land for $300,000. One-third of this price is to be paid in cash, and the remaining $200,000 is to be in the form of a note, bearing an appropriate rate of interest, payable in installments over a fifteen-year period and secured by a first mortgage on the land. *T* wishes to know whether she can properly accept this offer. How would you advise her?

DURKIN v. CONNELLY
84 N.J. Eq. 66, 92 A. 906 (Ch. 1915)

[The testator's will authorized the executor to sell real estate and to invest the proceeds "at her discretion." She contracted to sell estate land for $45,000, to be paid $5,000 in cash, $16,000 by proceeds of a bank loan secured by a first mortgage, and $24,000 by note secured by a second mortgage to her as executor. The executor later refused to perform, alleging lack of power to do so, and the purchaser filed a bill for specific performance.]

LEAMING, V.C.

---

1. Noting the recent tendency to reverse "the law's negative attitude toward delegation by trustees" (see Chapter 17, section C.5, supra) and that a "fundamental premise of the prudent investor rule" (see infra section B) is that "no investment or course of action is *per se* impermissible," E. Halbach, Uniform Acts, Restatements, and Other Trends in American Trust Law at Century's End, 25 ACTEC Notes 101, 121-122 (1999), predicts that counterparts of these trends "can be expected to apply pervasively to matters of trust administration" and that, absent restrictive trust provision or statute, "the trust law of the future will not ask whether or for what purpose a particular power exists but will simply focus on the circumstances and manner of its exercise." That is, the prudence of a trustee's conduct in a particular case will be judged in its full context — and without arbitrary prohibitions — in light of the [purposes and circumstances] of the trust, as well as the trustee's general duty to act with prudence (i.e., care, skill and caution) and to comply with the fundamental fiduciary duties of loyalty and impartiality." Also compare the recent, general approach to powers in English Trusts of Land and Appointment of Trustees Act of 1996 §6(1).

It is obvious that this court cannot by its decree require the specific performance of a contract of sale which has been made by a trustee if by the terms of the trust the trustee had no power to do what he contracted to do; in such circumstances a trustee will not be compelled to commit a breach of his trust. Repetto v. Baylor, 61 N.J. Eq. 501, 506 [which] also held that a mere power to sell does not include any power to arrange terms of postponed payment of price, or to accept a mortgage or anything else than money in satisfaction of it. . . .

With the power of sale here involved there is added the power "to invest the proceeds," but this added power cannot be made the basis of a decree herein, for, if the acceptance of a second mortgage on the property sold to secure the payment of a part of the purchase price is regarded as an investment of a part of the proceeds of sale, such investment is proposed to be secured in a manner not authorized by our Orphans Court Act (3 Comp. Stat. p. 3864 §137); the trustee cannot be properly required by decree of this court to make such an investment.

It is urged in behalf of complainant that Repetto v. Baylor, supra, is not in harmony with the earlier case of Woodruff v. Lounsberry, 40 N.J. Eq. 545. In that case a will authorized and directed executors to sell and convey real estate and to invest the proceeds thereof upon first bond and mortgage on property worth double the amount or in stocks or bonds of the United States or the State of New Jersey, and pay the income to testator's widow. The executors sold certain real estate at a good price and accepted in payment forty percent cash and purchase-money mortgages — first liens — to secure the sixty percent deferred payments. Losses having been sustained on these mortgages, the question before the court was whether the executors should be compelled to make good these losses. It will be observed that the mortgages accepted by the executors were in amount the percentage of value of the mortgaged premises authorized by the Orphans Court Act. In determining that the executors should not be charged the losses, the learned ordinary said:

> . . . Those mortgages were not taken as an investment of proceeds of sales, but to secure the payment of part of the price at which the property was sold. They were themselves proceeds of sales. In taking the mortgages for which the accountant asks allowance, the executors appear to have acted in good faith and for the best interest of the estate. They, therefore, ought not to be charged with them.

It is, therefore, insisted in behalf of complainant that Woodruff v. Lounsberry recognizes a power to sell as including a power to postpone payments of the purchase price . . . and . . . that the acceptance of a purchase-money mortgage for a part of the purchase price is not to be regarded as an exercise of the power of investment. I am unable to adopt that view. In Woodruff v. Lounsberry the primary inquiry was whether under the special circumstances of that case the executor should be compelled to bear the loss which had arisen from shrinkage of the value of the tracts of land on which he had taken purchase-money mortgages. The learned chancellor points out with clearness and emphasis that the sales had been made at good prices . . . in good faith and for the best interest of the estate. . . . It may well be . . . that in a suit in which the primary issue is whether an executor shall be made personally liable for losses . . . a purchase-money mortgage should not be regarded as so clearly an unauthorized investment as to justify an imposition of personal liability. . . . But in a suit for specific performance of a contract of sale made by an executor the primary inquiry is whether the contract is one which the executor had power to make and which a court of equity should compel him to specifically perform. . . .

. . . [T]his court is committed to the view that a mere power of sale does not include any power to arrange terms of postponed payments of price, or to accept a mortgage or anything else than money in satisfaction of it. If the added power to invest proceeds of sale justifies the arrangement . . . it is necessarily because the purchase-money mortgage is [a proper] investment.

. . . The testimony at the hearing disclosed that $16,000 was the largest amount that could be procured as a loan on first mortgage security. This court is therefore asked to compel this executrix, in effect, to invest $24,000 of trust money in a second mortgage. . . . It is clear that no court would advise such an investment of trust funds. . . .

I am obliged to advise a decree denying the relief sought by the bill.

ALLARD v. PACIFIC NATIONAL BANK
99 Wash. 2d 394, 663 P.2d 104 (1983)

[Plaintiffs Allard and Orkney are life beneficiaries of inter vivos trusts [the Stone trusts] established by their parents, and Pacific Bank is the trustee. The sole asset of the trusts was the "Third and Columbia property" in downtown Seattle. The property was subject to a 99-year lease the settlors had entered into in 1952 with Seafirst Bank at a fixed rental for the entire period, with the lessee holding a right of first refusal in the event the lessor wished to sell the property. In 1977 Seafirst Bank assigned its leasehold interest to Credit Union, which 8 months later offered to purchase the property for $139,900. The trustee's insistence on at least $200,000 led to Credit Union's offer of $200,000, which Pacific Bank accepted, deeding the property to Credit Union in August of 1978. About six weeks later the trustee informed the plaintiffs of the sale, and this action for breach of fiduciary duties was commenced on May 1, 1979. The trial court entered judgment after trial dismissing plaintiffs' action, determining that Pacific Bank "acted in good faith and in conformance with its duties under the Stone trust instruments," and awarded Pacific Bank attorney fees and costs payable from the trusts. Plaintiffs appeal.]

DOLLIVER, J. . . .

The beneficiaries of the Stone trusts essentially allege Pacific Bank improperly depleted the trust assets by selling the Third and Columbia property for less than its fair market value. . . . [Their] argument regarding Pacific Bank's alleged breach of its fiduciary duties is twofold. First, Pacific Bank had a duty to inform them [in advance of the contemplated] sale of the Third and Columbia property. Second, Pacific Bank breached its fiduciary duties by failing either to obtain an independent appraisal of the . . . property or to place [it] on the open market prior to selling it to . . . Credit Union. We agree with the plaintiffs' position in both instances and hold defendant breached its fiduciary duty in its management of the trusts. . . .

The Stone trusts gave Pacific Bank "full power to . . . manage, improve, sell, lease, mortgage, pledge, encumber, and exchange the whole or any part of the assets of [the] trust estate." Under such an agreement, the trustee is not required to secure the consent of trust beneficiaries before selling trust assets. The trustee owes to the beneficiaries, however, the highest degree of good faith, care, loyalty, and integrity.

Pacific Bank claims it was obligated to sell the property to Credit Union since Credit Union, as assignee of the lease agreement with Seafirst Bank, had a right of first refusal to purchase the property. Since it did not need to obtain the consent of the beneficiaries before selling trust assets, Pacific Bank argues it also was not required to inform the beneficiaries of the sale. We disagree. The beneficiaries could have offered to purchase the property at a higher price than the offer by Credit Union, thereby forcing Credit Union to pay a higher price to exercise its right of first refusal as assignee of the lease agreement. Furthermore, letters from the beneficiaries to Pacific Bank indicated their desire to retain the Third and Columbia property. While the beneficiaries could not have prevented Pacific Bank from selling the property, they presumably could have outbid Credit Union for the property. This opportunity should have been afforded to them.

On a previous occasion, we ruled the trustee's fiduciary duty includes the responsibility to inform the beneficiaries fully of all facts which would aid them in protecting their interests. . . .

The duty to provide information is often performed by corporate trustees by rendering periodic statements to the beneficiaries, usually in the form of copies of the ledger sheets concerning the trust. G. Bogert, Trusts §141 (5th ed. 1973). For example, such condensed explanations of recent transactions may be mailed to the beneficiaries annually, semiannually, or quarterly. G. Bogert, Trusts, supra. Ordinarily, periodic statements are sufficient to satisfy a trustee's duty to beneficiaries. . . .

The trustee must inform beneficiaries, however, of all material facts in connection with a nonroutine transaction which significantly affects the trust estate and the interests of the beneficiaries prior to the transaction taking place. The duty to inform is particularly required in this case where the only asset of the trusts was the property on the corner of Third and Columbia. Under the circumstances found in this case failure to inform was an egregious breach of fiduciary duty and defies the course of conduct any reasonable person would take. . . .

We also conclude Pacific Bank breached its fiduciary duties regarding management of the Stone trusts by failing to obtain the best possible price for the Third and Columbia property. Pacific Bank made no attempt to obtain a more favorable price for the property from Credit Union by, for example, negotiating to cancel the restrictive provisions in the lease originally negotiated with Seafirst Bank. . . . The bank neither offered the property for sale on the open market, nor did it obtain an independent, outside appraisal of the Third and Columbia property to determine its fair market value.

Washington courts have not yet considered the nature of a trustee's duty of care regarding the sale of trust assets. . . . Some courts specifically require trustees to obtain an independent appraisal of the property. . . . Other courts merely require that a trustee determine fair market value by placing the property on the open market. . . .

We agree with the Oregon Court . . . that a trustee may determine the best possible price for trust property either by obtaining an independent appraisal of the property or by "testing the market" to determine what a willing buyer would pay. The record discloses none of these actions were taken by the defendant. . . .

Finally, we consider whether the trial court improperly awarded attorney fees to Pacific Bank. A trial court may allow and properly charge attorney fees to a trust estate for litigation that is necessary to the administration of the trust. The award . . . is vested in the discretion of the trial court. A trial court's discretion to award attorney fees, however, is not absolute. . . .

The court's underlying consideration must be whether the litigation and the participation of the party seeking attorney fees caused a benefit to the trust. A trustee who unsuccessfully defends against charges of breach of fiduciary duties obviously has not caused a benefit to the trust. Therefore, a trial court abuses its discretion when it awards attorney fees to a trustee for litigation caused by the trustee's misconduct.

. . . A trustee may be awarded attorney fees and costs for litigation alleging breach of the trust agreement only if the trustee successfully defends against the action. . . .

We also hold that since defendant breached its fiduciary duty plaintiffs should be granted their request to recover all attorney fees expended at both the trial and on appeal on behalf of the plaintiffs and all minor . . . and unknown beneficiaries. . . .

The case is remanded for a determination of the damages caused to plaintiffs by defendant's breach of its fiduciary duties . . . and a determination of the amount of attorney fees to be awarded plaintiffs from the trustee individually.

[On remand plaintiffs were awarded approximately $2.5 million in damages and almost $1 million in attorney fees. The awards were sustained on appeal, even though the fee award was based on a consideration of both hourly compensation and a contingent fee agreement, the ultimate issue being whether the attorney fees, "as a whole, were reasonable." Allard v. First Interstate Bank, 112 Wash. 2d 145, 768 P. 2d 998 (1989).]

2. Power to Continue Decedent's Business

PROBLEM

18-B. The testator, who died recently, left a simple will that devised one-half of his property to his wife and one-half to his eight-year-old child. His wife is named executrix. The testator operated an explosives delivery and storage service as a sole proprietorship. The storage igloos are located in a small secluded valley on land that he had owned. Four expert and trusted employees drive the trucks and handle the dynamite and other explosives. This is a highly profitable business but with an obviously high risk of loss and liability. The surviving spouse, who has run the business office, comes to you for advice. She would like to keep the business operating through administration and indefinitely thereafter, but she is concerned about insurance costs, the risks involved, and her child's interests. What problems do you foresee, and what advice would you give regarding possible solutions and why?

Consider how her situation would be affected by Uniform Probate Code §3-715, which empowers a personal representative, "acting reasonably for the benefit of the interested persons," to:

> (16) borrow money with or without security to be repaid from the estate assets or otherwise; and advance money for the protection of the estate; . . .

(24) continue any unincorporated business or venture in which the decedent was engaged at the time of his death (i) in the same business form for a period of not more than 4 months from the date of appointment of a general personal representative if continuation is a reasonable means of preserving the value of the business including good will, (ii) in the same business form for any additional period of time that may be approved by order of the Court in a formal proceeding to which the persons interested in the estate are parties; or (iii) throughout the period of administration if the business is incorporated by the personal representative and if none of the probable distributees of the business who are competent adults object to its incorporation and retention in the estate.

(25) incorporate any business or venture in which the decedent was engaged at the time of his death.

T. ATKINSON, WILLS
(2d ed. 1953)

§121. A representative who continues the decedent's business without authority incurs personal obligation to those with whom he deals and is liable for all losses and must account to the estate for all profits.

Authority to operate the business of the deceased may exist temporarily to preserve the assets of the estate or to realize thereon, and also by reason of:

(1)   Express provision of testator's will, or
(2)   Consent of the interested parties, or
(3)   Order of the court (at least if the statute so provides).

The personal representative who is so authorized to conduct the business has the same liabilities as the unauthorized representative, except that he is not obliged to bear the losses incurred in good faith.

In re ESTATE OF KURKOWSKI
487 Pa. 295, 409 A.2d 357 (1979)

EAGEN, CHIEF JUSTICE. [Footnotes and case citations omitted] . . .
Carl J. Kurkowski died intestate on November 22, 1973, survived by his wife, the administratrix, and two minor sons from a prior marriage. . . . At the time of his death, decedent was president and sole shareholder of Monroe Cycle Center, Inc. . . . The business was valued in the estate inventory by administratrix at $43,797.88. Decedent also owned a home valued at $75,000.00, subject to a mortgage, in addition to furniture, fixtures, and tools. Further, the decedent's life was insured for

approximately $90,000.00 of which approximately $75,000.00 was paid to Monroe Cycle Center, Inc. as beneficiary. The administration of the estate was undertaken by Ellen Kurkowski Simon in January 1974 upon the posting of a $500.00 bond.

After her husband's death, Ellen Kurkowski Simon was elected president, secretary, and treasurer of Monroe Cycle Center, Inc. Prior to his death, she had served as a corporation's vice-president and had worked part-time in the business. Shortly after her election, the two other members of the Board of Directors, including the attorney for the estate, resigned. Thereafter, the administratrix ignored corporate procedures and formalities. The administratrix paid herself a salary in excess of $33,000.00 during the twenty-month period she continued to operate the business. One of decedent's sons worked part-time in the business as a mechanic and received compensation of $1,148.86. Administratrix utilized a car titled in the corporate name for her personal use and subsequently traded it in on a new car which she titled in her own name without any accounting to the corporation for the value of the car. She paid the decedent's funeral bill from the corporate assets and subsequently included the bill in her final account as an expense of the estate without having repaid the corporation the cost of the funeral.

The business operated at a continuing loss for the entire twenty-month period. During this period, administratrix made no attempt to sell the business or its assets. She testified she intended to operate it indefinitely. The record indicates some attempts to sell were made after administratrix closed the business. However, when these efforts were not successful, administratrix made no provision for disposition or liquidation of the corporate assets or for payment of the corporate debts. At the time administratrix closed the doors of the business, the corporate accounts reflected over $120,000.00 in assets.

In June 1976, nine months after it ceased operating, the corporation was placed into state receivership to avoid the landlord's execution on a judgment for past due rents. Several months later, all of its assets were sold by the receiver for $22,759.00. This fund was exhausted after the payment of administrative expenses and priority claims. . . . In the interim, the house was sold and administratrix posted an additional bond.

In October 1976, decedent's sons petitioned for an accounting of the estate which was filed by administratrix in January 1977. Objections to the accounting were sustained in part and the court entered a decree directing administratrix to perform certain administrative tasks and surcharging her $119,000.00 for having continued to operate the solely owned corporation . . . without court approval. . . . The amount of the surcharge was determined by the value of the capital stock of the corporation at the time of decedent's death — viz. $43,000.00 — and the $76,000.00 paid into the corporation from insurance proceeds. . . . [A]dministratrix appealed.

The court below concluded administratrix should not have continued to operate decedent's solely owned corporation without first securing the court's authorization as required by 20 Pa. C.S.A. §3314 (1975). In this appeal, administratrix argues the court's application of section 3314 to a corporation was error. We need not decide this question. Even assuming the statutory procedures contained in section 3314 were not applicable to decedent's business, administratrix nevertheless breached her common law fiduciary duty in failing to liquidate the estate for purposes of distribution to decedent's heirs and, therefore, is chargeable with the losses incurred.

. . . [A] personal representative breaches his trust if he continues to operate a trade or business on behalf of an estate in the absence of testamentary direction, court order, or the consent of all interested persons. If he does so, he will be liable for any loss thereby resulting to the estate.

This general rule is subject to the limitation that the personal representative may continue operating a business of the decedent for a limited time without liability for the purpose of selling the business as a going concern or winding up the business by converting the assets into cash or performing existing contracts of the decedent.

In this case, administratrix clearly breached her fiduciary duty as personal representative of the decedent by continuing to operate the business at a loss for a period of twenty months after decedent's death while realizing personal gain in the form of salary and fringe benefits and by eventually abandoning the business without making provision for disposition or liquidation of its assets or payment of the corporate debts.

Administratrix argues she should not be liable to the heirs for any loss sustained by continued operation of the business since they consented both expressly and implicitly to the continuance. A personal representative relying on consent for authority to continue a business must show the consent of all interested parties was procured or given after full information and a fair representation of the risks involved was communicated to them. See 31 Am. Jur. 2d §222. Neither the express nor implied consent of decedent's minor sons was established in this case. . . .

Decree affirmed. Costs on appellant.

See also *Spivak v. Bronstein,* 367 Pa. 70, 79 A.2d 205 (1951), where a partner in a restaurant business died intestate, survived by a widow and a minor son. The widow was appointed administrator but did not obtain formal appointment as guardian. Acting individually and as administrator, and also as guardian of her son, but without court approval, the widow entered into a new partnership with her late husband's partner. As administrator, she later sued the defendant partner for an accounting of profits owed to the estate. The court said that the defendant was bound to know that personal representatives may not carry on the business of a decedent unless authorized by a will or by the court. The widow was bound personally as an heir by her agreement, "but in her representative capacity of fiduciary representing possible creditors of the estate and as [natural] guardian, she was utterly without authority to risk the assets of the estate and certainly not the share of the minor in what was virtually a continuation of the business." The partner was therefore required to account for the son's interest in the business and share of the profits.

In re ESTATE OF MULLER
24 N.Y.2d 336, 248 N.E.2d 164, 300 N.Y.S.2d 341 (1969)

JASEN, J. . . .

One of the issues raised by the objectant bears on the right of an executor to use assets of the general estate to pay corporate obligations where the testator specifically conferred the executor with the power to continue decedent's businesses.

The intention of a testator to confer upon an executor power to use general assets of the estate to continue various businesses of the testator "must be found in the direct, explicit and unequivocal language of the will, or else it will not be deemed to have been conferred."

Although the will did authorize the executor to continue the various businesses of the testator "if in his discretion it [was] for the best interest of [the] estate," such authorization merely grants to the executor the power to conduct the various businesses with the funds already invested in them at the time of the testator's death, and to subject only these funds, and not the general assets of the estate, to the hazards of the businesses.

Moreover, a clause in the will giving the executor authority to sell, invest and reinvest the general assets of the estate will not be taken as authority to invest additional money in the decedent's businesses. . . .

Willis v. Sharp, 113 N.Y. 586, 21 N.E. 705 (1889), however, regarded a clause empowering the executors "to sell or make such other disposition of [the testator's] real and personal estate as the safe conduct of the business shall seem to require" as indicating an intention to subject the general assets of the estate to the debts of the business. But cf. Hillyard v. Leonard, 391 S.W.2d 211 (Mo. 1965).

If the donor's business has been incorporated before it passes to a personal representative or trustee, are the considerations any different for the fiduciary? What is the explanation for Uniform Probate Code §3-715(24)(iii), supra?

Reduced to its essentials, is not the question of retention of a closely held business interest, and possible use of other estate assets to continue the business, ultimately a question of the fiduciary's investment authority and the propriety of the investment? See Durand, Retention of Decedent's Business, 95 Tr. & Est. 907 (1962), Restatement (Third) of Trusts: The Prudent Investor Rule §229 (1992), and section B of this chapter, infra. Why might a closely held business not be a prudent investment? See section B, infra.

Clearly the disposition of a business interest by will or trust requires careful planning and drafting. Liquidity and marketability are often problems, as is the general duty and importance of diversification if the recipient is a trust. Competent successor management is difficult to find, and corporate fiduciaries may be reluctant to assume management responsibilities. On the other hand, the business may be quite valuable, even after an entrepreneur's death. Buy-sell agreements sometimes provide a solution. See generally Durand, supra.

Uniform Trust Code §816(6) is more permissive than the Uniform Probate Code (which in turn is more permissive than the common law). The UTC authorizes a trustee "with respect to an interest in a proprietorship, partnership, limited liability company, business trust, corporation or other form of business or enterprise, [to] continue the business or other enterprise and take any action that may be taken by shareholders, members, or property owners, including merging, dissolving or otherwise changing the form of the business organization or contributing additional capital." Why might the law be more permissive for trustees than for personal representatives?

3. Powers of Successor Fiduciaries

TATMAN v. COOK'S ADMINISTRATRIX
302 Ky. 529, 195 S.W.2d 72 (1946)

DAWSON, J. . . .

The only question presented on this appeal is whether the power of sale conferred by the will is personal to the executors named therein, or whether such power passed to the administratrix with the will annexed. . . .

In the Restatement of the Law of Trusts, Vol. 1, Section 196, in treating the question under consideration, subsections b., d., and f. state the rule as follows:

> b. Powers which are essential to the trust or powers which relate to the effective administration of the trust can ordinarily be exercised by successor trustees. Thus, a power of sale can ordinarily be exercised by successor trustees.
>
> d. Where the exercise of a power is not discretionary, the inference is that the settlor intended that it might be exercised by successor trustees. There is ordinarily the same inference where the trustee is given discretion and there is a standard by which the reasonableness of the exercise of the discretion can be judged. If the exercise of a power is within the discretion of the trustee and there is no such standard the inference is not as strong, but ordinarily the power may be exercised by successor trustees, unless it appears from the terms of the trust that the confidence placed in the original trustee should be personal to him.
>
> f. The relation between the settlor and the original trustee may be such as to show an intention to place confidence in him personally and only in him. It is less difficult to draw an inference that the settlor intended powers to be exercised by successor trustees where the original trustee was a person not related to or closely connected with the settlor, especially where the original trustee was a corporate trustee, than it is where the trustee was a near relative or close friend of the settlor. . . .

Taking the will as a whole, it is apparent that the testator had one purpose uppermost in his mind, and that was that his executors convert his estate, including his realty, into cash and have the proceeds invested for the benefit of his sister and niece. . . . Applying the rule set out in the Restatement of the Law we are impelled to hold that the testator's intention was to confer the power of sale upon the executors by virtue of that office. It follows that the power passes to the administratrix with the will annexed. . . .

Uniform Probate Code §3-716 is similar to the Restatement rule quoted in the above case.

B. The Investment Function

It has already been noticed that the functions of the personal representative and the trustee are likely to be quite different, particularly as affects the matter of power and duty to invest.

Most of our attention in this section is focused on situations, such as the typical trust situation, in which it is assumed that the fiduciary has an obligation to make the property productive. We might begin, however, with a brief look at the situation of a decedent's estate and the limitations traditionally placed on the personal representative. "Ordinarily it is not the function of an executor or administrator, as such, to invest the money even in land mortgages or government bonds, though this is authorized by statute in some jurisdictions and under certain circumstances would be proper even in absence of such legislation." T. Atkinson, Wills §124 (2d ed. 1953).

In Jones v. O'Brien, 58 S.D. 213, 235 N.W. 654 (1931), the question was whether the administrator, and thus the surety on his bond, was absolutely liable for losses sustained in connection with estate funds placed on deposit in a bank that subsequently failed. There was no allegation of negligence or bad faith but only that the placing of funds on a time deposit at interest constituted an improper investment. The court's opinion (at 218-227, 235 N.W. at 656-660) stated:

> The general rule is universally held to be that an executor or administrator may deposit money in a bank temporarily as a trust account. . . . [T]here is some question . . . where a deposit is not payable on demand. . . .
>
> . . . It has been held that any deposit in a bank which bears interest is an "investment," whether the deposit is for a fixed period or not. . . . [T]here was a very considerable tendency among the earlier cases to treat every time deposit as a loan upon time. . . .
>
> . . . We do not wish to establish any general rule to the effect that an executor or administrator is authorized to part with control of trust funds in his hands for any fixed period of time, either to a bank or to anyone else. . . . In the instant case, however, we think the defendant administrator was justified, by reason of [general custom and practice in the community] in believing that the money would be paid him at any time upon demand (without interest if demanded prior to six months).

UNIFORM PROBATE CODE

§3-715. *Transactions Authorized for Personal Representatives; Exceptions.* Except as restricted or otherwise provided by the will or by an order. . . , a personal representative, acting reasonably for the benefit of the interested persons, may properly:

(1) retain assets owned by the decedent pending distribution or liquidation including those in which the representative is personally interested or which are otherwise improper for trust investment; . . .

(5) if funds are not needed to meet debts and expenses currently payable and are not immediately distributable, deposit or invest liquid assets of the estate, including moneys received from the sale of other assets, in federally insured interest-bearing accounts,

readily marketable secured loan arrangements or other prudent investments which would be reasonable for use by trustees generally. . . .

DICKINSON, APPELLANT
152 Mass. 184, 25 N.E. 99 (1890)

FIELD, C.J.

The general principles which should govern a trustee in making investments, when the creator of the trust has given no specific directions concerning investments, have been repeatedly declared by this court. . . .

The rule in general terms is, that a trustee must in the investment of the trust fund act with good faith and sound discretion, and must, as laid down in Harvard College v. Amory, [26 Mass. (9 Pick.) 446,] at page 461, "observe how men of prudence, discretion, and intelligence manage their own affairs, not in regard to speculation, but in regard to the permanent disposition of their funds, considering the probable income, as well as the probable safety of the capital to be invested."

It is said in the opinion in Brown v. French, [125 Mass. 410]: "If a more strict and precise rule should be deemed expedient, it must be enacted by the Legislature. It cannot be introduced by judicial decision without working great hardship and injustice." It is also said, "The question of the lawfulness and the fitness of the investment is to be judged as of the time when it was made, and not by subsequent facts which could not then have been anticipated." . . . [Life income beneficiaries] desire a large income from the trust property, but they are only entitled to such an income as it can earn when invested in such securities as a prudent man investing his own money, and having regard to the permanent disposition of the fund, would consider safe. A prudent man possessed of considerable wealth, in investing a small part of his property, may wisely enough take risks which a trustee would not be justified in taking. A trustee, whose duty is to keep the trust fund safely invested in productive property, ought not to hazard the safety of the property under any temptation to make extraordinary profits. Our cases, however, show that trustees in this Commonwealth are permitted to invest portions of trust funds in dividend paying stocks and interest bearing bonds of private business corporations, when the corporations have acquired, by reason of the amount of their property, and the prudent management of their affairs, such a reputation that cautious and intelligent persons commonly invest their own money in such stocks and bonds as permanent investments.

   The experience of recent years has, perhaps, taught the whole community that there is a greater uncertainty in the permanent value of
rail-road properties in the unsettled or newly settled parts of this country than was anticipated nine years ago. Without, however, taking into
consideration facts which are now commonly known, and confining
ourselves strictly to the evidence in the case, and the considerations
which ought to have been present to the mind of the appellant, when
in May and August, 1881, he made the investment in the stock of the
Union Pacific Railroad Company, we think it appears that he acted in
entire good faith, and after careful inquiry of many persons as to the
value of the stock and the propriety of the investments. We cannot say
that it is shown to our satisfaction that the trustee so far failed to exercise a sound discretion that the investments should be held to be wholly
unauthorized. Still, it must have been manifest to any well informed
person in the year 1881, that the Union Pacific Railroad ran through
a new and comparatively unsettled country; that it had been constructed at great expense, as represented by its stock and bonds, and
was heavily indebted; that its continued prosperity depended upon
many circumstances which could not be predicted; and that it would
be taking a considerable risk to invest any part of a trust fund in the
stock of such a road.
   . . . On May 9, 1881, the trustee bought thirty shares of the stock of
the Union Pacific Railroad Company at $119 per share. . . . This is an
investment of between one fourth and one fifth of the whole trust fund
in this stock, and is certainly a large investment relatively to the whole
amount of the trust fund to be made in the stock of any one corporation. After this, on August 16, 1881, he purchased twenty shares more
at $123 per share. . . . The last investment, we think, cannot be sus-
tained as made in the exercise of a sound discretion. While we recognize the hardship of compelling a trustee to make good out of his own
property a loss occasioned by an investment of trust property which he
has made in good faith, and upon the advice of persons whom he
thinks to be qualified to give advice, we cannot on the evidence hold
that the trustee was justified in investing in such stock as this so large
a proportional part of the property.
   . . . It does not appear that, when the first account was allowed, there
was any adjudication of the questions now before us, and they are not
therefore res judicata, and no assent to these investments is shown on
the part of the persons now entitled to the trust property. The result
is, that this last investment is disallowed, and that the trustee must be
charged with the amount of it, to wit: $2,475, and with simple interest
thereon from August 16, 1881, and must be credited with any dividends
therefrom which he has received and paid over, with simple interest
on each, from the time each dividend was received. . . .
   Decree accordingly.

ST. LOUIS UNION TRUST CO. v. TOBERMAN
235 Mo. App. 559, 140 S.W.2d 68 (1940)

[This is a suit by a trust company seeking instructions with respect to the character of investments it may be permitted to make as trustee under a will. The court below decreed, inter alia, that the plaintiff was authorized to invest "in corporate preferred and common stocks" selected with "reasonable care."]

BENNICK, C. . . .

. . . A trustee . . . may take only such risks as an ordinarily prudent man would take in the investment of the funds of others, bearing in mind that it is the preservation of the estate, and not an accumulation to it, which is the chief object and purpose of his trusteeship. . . .

In many jurisdictions the question of . . . the investments that a trustee may make . . . [have] come to be explicitly regulated by statute, but such is not the case in our own jurisdiction. . . .

Neither is there any decision in our own state which purports to arbitrarily classify, define, or limit the character of investments that a trustee may or may not make for his estate. . . .

Apart from the requirement of statutes . . . and in the absence of any specific authority conferred by the instrument creating the trust, there would seem to exist two rules having to do with the general investment powers of trustees, the one, the New York, or more strict, rule, which holds that a trustee may not invest trust funds in common or preferred stocks, and permits investment only in government securities and first mortgages on real estate; and the other, the Massachusetts, or more liberal, rule, which permits the reasonable investment of trust funds in corporate stocks, where the corporations have acquired, by reason of the amount of their property and the prudent management of their affairs, such a reputation for safety and stability that cautious and prudent persons commonly invest their own money in such stocks as permanent investments. . . .

As we view the situation, not only do reason and experience establish the soundness of the [Massachusetts rule], but indeed a proper conception of judicial power and authority would hardly warrant a court in holding otherwise. By this we mean that a court . . . has no function to perform with respect to arbitrarily classifying and defining the character of investments[a trustee] may make. . . . On the contrary, if there is to be an arbitrary classification of the character of investments that a trustee may be permitted to make for his estate, the making of such classification would seem to be purely a legislative, and not a judicial, function. . . .

With [this] in mind, we know of no reason why a court . . . should attempt to say, as a matter of law, that corporate stocks, as such, can never be a proper form of investment for money held in trust. We appreciate that many years ago there may have been sound reason for a holding to the contrary. The corporations were in their infancy, and at that time a contemplated investment in such new and unproved enterprises necessarily involved a contemplated investment of a more or less speculative nature. Now, however, there are many corporations in the land with years of good management and demonstrated stability and earning capacity behind them, in the stocks of which the most prudent and cautious persons are accustomed to invest their savings with a primary view to the safety and permanency of their investments. . . .

Contrast the "New York rule" as expressed in Taylor's Estate, 277 Pa. 518, 121 Atl. 310 (1923): "Pennsylvania has long stood with the majority of jurisdictions favoring the view that, in the absence of express authority, a fiduciary has no power to invest . . . in the stock or bonds of private corporations." Early in the development of American trust law and continuing well into the twentieth century, this highly restrictive approach to the investment authority of fiduciaries was reaffirmed or adopted by legislation in many of the states. These "legal list" statutes, prescribing with varying degrees of specificity the types and characteristics of permissible investments, still apply in a few jurisdictions to some or all trustees or to other fiduciaries.

Is it proper for trustees, in their investment policies, to take into account the effects of inflation on purchasing power and the prospect that market values and dividend levels of equity securities are likely to increase during extended periods of inflation, even though risk tends to be higher and income yield lower for these securities than for high-grade debt securities? See Bulk, Prudence Will Be Prosecuted, 39 Tr. Bull. 4 (1960). Consider the language of the traditional "prudent man [or "prudent person] rule" as stated by the Massachusetts court (supra) or as often codified in statutes instructing trustees to consider "the probable income as well as the probable safety of their capital."[2]

As you read the case that follows (and subsequent material in this chapter will be relevant as well), consider whether the trustees' invest-

---

2. In recent years questions have begun to arise (such as in meetings of boards of trustees), and occasionally even to surface in court, over the possibility of taking account of noneconomic (especially social or political) criteria in making investment decisions with respect to charitable, employee benefit, and even family trusts. How does the duty of undivided loyalty affect these questions? See, e.g., Withers v. Teachers Retirement Sys., 447 F. Supp. 1248 (S.D.N.Y. 1978) (upholding purchase of $2.5 billion of speculative city bonds to help stave off city's possible bankruptcy); Restatement (Third) of Trusts: The Prudent Investor Rule §227 (1992), comment *c* and Reporter's Notes thereto. Cf. the harsher statement in the Comment to Uniform Prudent Investor Act §5.

ment policy adequately took account of the interests of the remainder beneficiaries and whether the trustees appropriately balanced their duties to all of the various beneficiaries (see Chapter 17, section C.2, page 847). Is the court's concept of the duty to diversify and of the risks to be guarded against through diversification an adequate one in an age of long-run inflationary trends? Also consider whether, even if a trustee is not *required* to invest with one eye on the cost-of-living index, a fiduciary duty is or may be violated if the trustee adjusts — and admits to adjusting — investment policy to expectations regarding inflation.

COMMERCIAL TRUST CO. v. BARNARD
27 N.J. 332, 142 A.2d 865 (1958)

[In 1920 Isaac Guggenheim created a trust of 6 percent corporate bonds having a face value of $1,267,000. The net income was to be divided equally among the settlor's three daughters, the remainder of the share of each to her issue. A bank and an individual were cotrustees. From the time the original bonds were redeemed for $1,393,700 (1927) until the present intermediate accounting (1955), the corpus was invested in tax-exempt government bonds pursuant to the policy developed under the advice of the settlor's brothers while possessed of a veto power. Exceptions were filed by the three daughters, by the adult remainder beneficiaries, and by the guardians ad litem of unborn and infant remainder beneficiaries. The trial court disallowed the exceptions, refused to surcharge the trustees for their low-return investments, and approved the account as stated. Exceptants have appealed.

The evidence showed descending yields on the trust estate: an annual average of 4.27 percent in 1927, 2.34 percent in 1944, 2.17 percent in 1945, and 1.51 percent in 1955. Exceptants argued that a change of investment policy should have been considered, but was not, in 1945 when the yield went below $2\frac{1}{4}$ percent; they also introduced evidence to support their allegation that other trusts appropriate for comparison were averaging yields of $4\frac{1}{4}$ percent or better and sought surcharge for the difference. The trustees introduced evidence that during the period from 1945 through 1954 the tax brackets reached by one daughter averaged over 83 percent and the second daughter averaged over 68 percent. In comparing net disposable incomes after taxes for these two daughters, the trustees' policy produced decidedly better results than would have been produced by fully taxable yields at any reasonably likely trust rates.]

BURLING, J. . . .

Helen G. Ward [the third daughter] had an average tax rate of 64.8 percent of the years 1950 through 1954. . . . For the years 1945 through

1949 she had the status of a non-resident alien and was therefore only subject to a 15 percent federal income tax rate. This fact has no appreciable bearing on the duty of the trustees since they were required to deal with the corpus as a whole for the benefit of all three life income beneficiaries as well as the remaindermen. They could not be expected or required to change their investment policy because of the temporary tax status of one of the income beneficiaries. . . .

Exceptants' primary contention is that the trustees have failed to exercise any judgment with regard to the propriety of investing in higher-yield securities. They allege an adamant refusal over the years to even consider investments other than tax-exempts.

It is the duty of a trustee, imbued by the settlor with discretionary powers, to exercise active judgment and not to remain inert. The standard is set forth in 2 Scott on Trusts, §187.3, 995-996 (1939) as follows:

> Where by the terms of the trust a discretionary power is conferred upon the trustee and the exercise of the power is left to his judgment, the court will interpose if the trustee fails to use his judgment. This is true even though what is done by the trustee or what he fails to do would have been proper if he had used his judgment. . . .

The facts in the present case would not sustain a finding that the trustees have failed to exercise judgment with respect to investments. . . .

Exceptants contend that by investing solely in governmental securities the trustees have breached their duty to diversify investments. Exceptants have misconceived the import of the doctrine that the trustees have a duty to diversify investments.

The Restatement [Second] of Trusts, §228, comment (a) provides: "The trustee is under a duty to the beneficiary to exercise prudence in diversifying the investments so as to *minimize the risk of large losses,* and therefore he should not invest a disproportionately large part of the trust estate in a particular security or type of security."

The italicized phrase is the reason for the rule, i.e., avoidance of large losses resulting from the deflation in value of a particular security. It is difficult to perceive how the trustees could have better protected the trust assets from the hazards of the market than by investing in governmental securities.

In Scott on Trusts, supra, §227.3 p. 1203, it is stated:

> The primary purpose of a trustee should be to preserve the trust estate, while receiving a reasonable amount of income, rather than to take risks for the purpose of increasing the principal or income. In other words, a trustee must be not merely careful and skillful but also cautious.

The law requires that a trustee exercise that degree of care, prudence, circumspection and foresight that an ordinary prudent person would employ in like matters of his own.

We conclude that the trustees have fully acquitted the duties imposed upon them by pursuing the investment policy that they have, bearing in mind the high income status of the beneficiaries. . . .

Note the assertion at the outset of the above opinion that the trustees could not be expected to change their investment policy because of the markedly different income-tax status of the three daughters, beginning in 1945. Why not? How could the trustees have changed their investment policy to accommodate the different status? If the issue had been foreseen, how could the drafter have solved the problem? Instead of changing their investment policy, how might the trustees have deviated from the trust design in order to accommodate the different status? See Chapter 14, sections D.1 and 2, supra.

The investments of trustees are judged primarily on two bases under traditional doctrine: (1) whether the investment is of a type in which the trustee can properly invest; and (2) whether the particular investment chosen from the permissible types is proper. The latter depends on the care, skill, and caution exercised by the trustee, whose actions may be defended by showing compliance with these standards as long as the type of investment is permissible under the first test, which has to do with the outer limits of the trustee's discretion. The first test is often controlled by statutory provision or by the terms of the particular trust, which may serve to enlarge or restrict the range of investments permissible under applicable common law rule or statute. Compliance with the general fiduciary duty to exercise care, skill, and caution is not a defense when the investment is of a type not permitted to the trustee.

Even in the absence of a statutory rule or restriction in the governing instrument, courts have often developed from the general standard of prudence, particularly the duty of caution, subsidiary rules regarding the characteristics and categories of investments that are and are not permissible. This has been true even in jurisdictions that have adopted the more flexible "prudent man" doctrine rooted in the early Massachusetts cases and now recognized in judicial opinions or adopted by legislation in many jurisdictions, and in nearly all states until the early 1990s. In such situations it was recognized several decades ago that "what was decided in one case as a question of fact tends to be treated as a precedent establishing a rule of law." 3 A. Scott, Trusts §227 (2d ed. 1956). Rules of thumb have thus tended to forbid investment in bonds and stocks of "new and untried" enterprises, a prohibition that has applied as well to the securities of small, closely held businesses under ordinary circumstances. Such rules, of course, preclude all "speculative" investments or courses of action. At the more conservative end of the spectrum, however, traditional doctrine allows trustees to invest in the bonds of federal, state, and municipal governments, and normally also in high-grade corporate bonds and in first mortgages or deeds of trust secured by land of sufficient value to offer a comfortable margin of safety, always assuming that care, skill, and caution are exercised. In between are significant areas of authorized investment that now generally include the preferred and common shares of stable, well established, and financially sound corporations.

Trust Investment Law under the Third Restatement. A reformulated "general standard of prudent investment" was approved by the American Law Institute in 1990, and §227 of the Restatement (Third) of Trusts: The Prudent Investor Rule (1992) instructs a trustee to "invest and manage the funds of the trust as a prudent investor would, in light of the purposes, terms, distribution requirements and other circumstances of the trust." The blackletter of the section goes on to explain that this standard "requires the exercise of reasonable care, skill and caution, and is to be applied to investments not in isolation but in the context of the trust portfolio and as a part of an overall investment strategy." That strategy must ordinarily provide for reasonable diversification of trust investments and incorporate "risk and return objectives reasonably suitable to the trust." The rule further directs the trustee, in making and implementing investment decisions, to "conform to fundamental fiduciary duties of loyalty and impartiality," to "incur only costs that are reasonable in amount and appropriate to the investment responsibilities of the trusteeship," and to "act with prudence in deciding whether and how to delegate authority and in the selection and supervision of agents."

The manner in which these investment duties, and the trustee's authority and responsibilities, may be affected by the terms of a trust or applicable statute is discussed in §228. The duty with respect to "inception assets" is then dealt with in §229. That section calls for the trustee, "within a reasonable time after the creation of the trust, to review the contents of the trust estate and to make and implement decisions concerning the retention and disposition of original investments in order to conform to the requirements of §§227 and 228."[3]

---

3. Both §228 and §229 struggle to offer guidance to fiduciaries and courts in the difficult matters of interpretation presented by increasingly common but unfortunately casual authorizations or grants of discretion with respect to the acquisition or retention of particular trust investments. The struggle particularly involves a conflict between (a) the objective of giving respect and meaning to the terms of a trust or statute and (b) concerns over the possible nonexercise of judgment or disregard of basic prudence by trustees who are sometimes willing to rely on permissive provisions as a source of

Codification of §§227-229 and their commentary has been facilitated by the 1994 promulgation of the Uniform Prudent Investor Act. By the turn of the century, the prudent investor rule has become law in over two-thirds of the states, by enactment of the Uniform Act or otherwise (e.g., Ill. Ann. Stat. ch. 17, ¶1675, §5 (1992)). M. Begleiter, Does the Prudent Investor Need the Uniform Prudent Investor Act? — An Empirical Study of Trust Investment Practices, 51 Maine L. Rev. 27 (1999), concluding with an affirmative answer to the question in the title.

UNIFORM PRUDENT INVESTOR ACT

Prefatory Note . . .

Objectives of the Act. UPIA makes five fundamental alterations in the former criteria for prudent investing. All are to be found in the Restatement of Trusts 3d: Prudent Investor Rule.

(1) The standard of prudence is applied to any investment as part of the total portfolio, rather than to individual investments [sic]. In the trust setting the term "portfolio" embraces all the trust's assets. UPIA §2(b) [but contrast its wording with prior sentence, above, marked [sic].]

(2) The tradeoff in all investing between risk and return is identified as the fiduciary's central consideration. UPIA §2(b).

(3) All categoric restrictions on types of investments have been abrogated; the trustee can invest in anything that plays an appropriate role in achieving the risk/return objectives of the trust and that meets the other requirements of prudent investing. UPIA §2(e).

(4) The long familiar requirement that fiduciaries diversify their investments has been integrated into the definition of prudent investing. UPIA §3.

(5) The much criticized former rule of trust law forbidding the trustee to delegate investment and management functions has been reversed. Delegation is now permitted, subject to safeguards. UPIA §9.

§1.   *Prudent Investor Rule.*

(a) Except as otherwise provided in subsection (b), a trustee who invests and manages trust assets owes a duty to the beneficiaries of the trust to comply with the prudent investor rule set forth in this [Act].

(b) The prudent investor rule, a default rule, may be expanded, restricted, eliminated, or otherwise altered by the provisions of a trust.

---

exculpation or as justification for simply giving no attention to "authorized" portions of their portfolios.

A trustee is not liable to a beneficiary to the extent that the trustee acted in reasonable reliance on the provisions of the trust.

§2.   *Standard of Care; Portfolio Strategy; Risk and Return Objectives.*

(a) A trustee shall invest and manage trust assets as a prudent investor would, by considering the purposes, terms, distribution requirements, and other circumstances of the trust. In satisfying this standard, the trustee shall exercise reasonable care, skill, and caution.

(b) A trustee's investment and management decisions respecting individual assets must be evaluated not in isolation but in the context of the trust portfolio as a whole and as a part of an overall investment strategy having risk and return objectives reasonably suited to the trust.

(c) Among circumstances that a trustee shall consider in investing and managing trust assets are such of the following as are relevant to the trust or its beneficiaries:

(1) general economic conditions;

(2) the possible effect of inflation or deflation;

(3) the expected tax consequences of investment decisions or strategies;

(4) the role that each investment or course of action plays within the overall trust portfolio, which may include financial assets, interests in closely held enterprises, tangible and intangible personal property, and real property;

(5) the expected total return from income and the appreciation of capital;

(6) other resources of the beneficiaries;

(7) needs for liquidity, regularity of income, and preservation or appreciation of capital; and

(8) an asset's special relationship or special value, if any, to the purposes of the trust or to one or more of the beneficiaries.

(d) A trustee shall make a reasonable effort to verify facts relevant to the investment and management of trust assets.

(e) A trustee may invest in any kind of property or type of investment consistent with the standards of this [Act].

(f) A trustee who has special skills or expertise, or is named trustee in reliance upon the trustee's representation that the trustee has special skills or expertise, has a duty to use those special skills or expertise.

§3. *Diversification.*   A trustee shall diversify the investments of the trust unless the trustee reasonably determines that, because of special circumstances, the purposes of the trust are better served without diversifying.

§4. *Duties at Inception of Trusteeship.*   Within a reasonable time after accepting a trusteeship or receiving trust assets, a trustee shall review the trust assets and make and implement decisions concerning the retention and disposition of assets, in order to bring the trust portfolio into compliance with the purposes, terms, distribution requirements, and other circumstances of the trust, and with the requirements of this [Act].

§5. *Loyalty.*   A trustee shall invest and manage the trust assets solely in the interest of the beneficiaries.

§6. *Impartiality.*   If a trust has two or more beneficiaries, the trustee shall act impartially in investing and managing the trust assets, taking into account any differing interests of the beneficiaries.

§7. *Investment Costs.*   In investing and managing trust assets, a trustee may only incur costs that are appropriate and reasonable in relation to the assets, the purposes of the trust, and the skills of the trustee.

§8. *Reviewing Compliance.*   Compliance with the prudent investor rule is determined in light of the facts and circumstances existing at the time of a trustee's decision or action and not by hindsight.

§9.   *Delegation of Investment and Management Functions.*
         [See Chapter 17, section C.5, supra] . . .

[Sections 10 and 11 of the Act provide, respectively, that document language referring to "legal" or "authorized" investments or to the "prudent man" or "prudent person" rule, or the like, does not render the Act inapplicable, and that the Act applies to preexisting trusts but only as to decisions or actions occurring after its effective date.]

The evolution of the traditional "prudent man rule" over the years resulted in considerable rigidity and arbitrariness, despite the generality and flexibility of the language in which that rule was originally expressed in the classic dictum of Harvard College v. Amory, quoted in *Dickinson, Appellant,* supra. As we have seen, decisions dealing with essentially factual issues tended later to become crystallized into rather specific subsidiary rules prescribing the permissible types or required characteristics of trust investments. These rules in turn were usually based on some perceived but unarticulated degree of risk that was abstractly viewed as excessive not only for a particular trustee but for trustees in general. Typically, little or no concern was shown for the portfolio context or role of a challenged investment, or for the particular trust's purposes or risk tolerance. In short, the tendency to judge and classify investments in isolation generally resulted in broad categories of assets (such as venture capital) or courses of action (e.g., borrowing, in many contexts) being labeled "speculative" or imprudent per se, and thus impermissible, normally without regard to the degree of care and skill exercised by the trustee.

Knowledge, experience, and practice in the modern investment world have demonstrated that arbitrary restrictions on trust investments are generally unwarranted and likely to be counterproductive, not to mention their potential for inhibiting the judgment of skilled trustees and even for causing unjustified fiduciary liability. The need for change in trust investment law has been well documented in scholarly research and in legal and financial literature in recent years. The need is also evidenced by recent legislative trends at both federal and state levels, even if rather selectively, and by the judgments and behavior of expert fund managers. Particularly concerned are fiduciaries whose circumstances would otherwise invite, or at least permit, management strategies that would include some relatively high risk-and-return investment programs (involving, for example, venture capital or real estate), or some abstractly high-risk courses of action of types that are now widely employed by fund managers for the purpose of reducing the risk level of a portfolio as a whole (e.g., certain uses of options and futures).

The American Law Institute's prudent investor project was undertaken with a clear recognition that trust investment law should reflect and accommodate current concepts and knowledge within the financial community. It had become evident that trust investment law must be general and flexible enough both (a) to adapt to changes that have occurred and will continue to occur in the financial world and in our economic knowledge and (b) to take account of the differing needs and circumstances of the broad variety of trusts, trustees, and settlor purposes to which that body of law will inevitably apply. These objectives required that revised Restatement doctrine draw only on consistent themes of legitimate financial theories and express only those principles upon which general agreement exists. Thus, the objectives called for a prudent investor rule the mandates of which would not exceed what was needed in order to articulate standards by which the conduct of trustees may be guided and judged, while also protecting settlor objectives and the interests of trust beneficiaries.

Principles of Prudence. With these various goals in mind, the modernized prudent investor rule begins with the fundamental proposition that no investments or courses of action are imprudent per se. In addition, given the broad variety in the goals and composition of different trust estates, the rule also recognizes that it would be inappropriate for the law to attempt to prescribe some universal standard of acceptable risk, or even of risk characteristics for permissible investments and techniques. Each investment or course of action is thus to be judged by its role in the trust portfolio and in relation to the objectives and circumstances of the particular trust in question. The rule of §227 and its commentary then go on to prescribe a few more specific yet relatively flexible principles of prudence — or, one might say, fiduciary duties — for the guidance of trustees, their counsel, and the courts.

First, sound diversification is fundamental to risk management[4] and is therefore ordinarily required of trustees as a means of moderating the dangers inherent in investing and, most notably, as a means of minimizing "uncompensated" risk.[5] Thus, a trustee has the duty to

4. Risk is generally defined as variability in predicted outcomes, or is sometimes viewed in financial writings as "volatility." Often the expression "standard deviation" is used, being a measure of the dispersion of returns of an asset (variation from the arithmetic mean); the greater the degree of dispersion, the greater the risk. There is no agreed way of measuring or expressing risk, although the most commonly used (despite increasing doubt about its utility in recent years) is "beta," a measure of a stock's volatility compared to the stock market in general. A *beta* of one means that the stock is likely to go up or down as much as the market in general. A *beta* of two means that a stock is expected to go up or down twice as much as the market generally, while a *beta* of .5 means the stock is half as volatile as the market generally. (In speaking of market changes, the press — "the market was up 43 points today" — usually refers to the Dow-Jones Industrial Average, an unweighted average of 30 large industrial stocks. Most investment professionals are likely to use the S&P 500, a market-weighted index of the shares of the 500 largest, publicly traded corporations.)

The commentary and Reporter's Notes to §227 contain, in addition to suggested readings for a lawyer audience, rather lengthy explanations of the nature and types of risk, as well as discussion of efficient market theories, modern portfolio theory, and other financial background and concepts that are important to a proper understanding of modern trust investment principles. See also J. Macey, An Introduction to Modern Financial Theory (ACTEC, 2d ed. 1998).

5. Uncompensated risk, as the term suggests, is risk that is not rewarded by the market. It is generally described by financial economists as unique to a particular company or industry group, and can be virtually eliminated by diversification. By buying assets that move in opposite directions from each other as a result of a given economic event or stimulus, i.e., that "negatively covary," the investor can reduce uncompensated ("nondiversifiable" or "specific") risk. Empirical studies show that a carefully diversified portfolio of 10 different stocks can eliminate 88.5 percent of uncompensated risk, and a diversified portfolio of 20 different stocks can eliminate 94.2 percent of uncompensated risk. See Macey, supra note 4, at 24-25. Since diversification (which results in a portfolio risk far lower than the average risk of the individual holdings) occurs without reducing the portfolio return expectation (which is simply the weighted average of the return expectations of the holdings), this is a bargain that should not lightly be resisted — thus the expression "diversification pays," as it normally is a true "free lunch." It is often said that, because uncompensated risk can be so readily eliminated, there is no need for the market to reward it. A simpler but more obviously valid explanation is that the market has no way of knowing whether one is buying stock, for example,

diversify investments unless, under the circumstances, the objectives of both prudent risk management and impartiality (primarily as between income and remainder beneficiaries) can be satisfied without doing so, or unless special considerations make it prudent not to diversify in a particular trust situation.

Second, "compensated" risk and expected return are so directly related that a trustee has a duty to consider, and to make conscious decisions concerning, the level of risk appropriate to the purposes, distribution requirements, and other circumstances of the particular trust being administered. Although carrying "uncompensated" (i.e., diversifiable) risk is viewed negatively, the same cannot be said of risks that are rewarded by expectation of increased return.[6] This so-called "compensated" (or "market" or "systematic") risk is unavoidable in investing, and fiduciary decisions are therefore concerned with the appropriate degree of that risk. As an integral part of investment strategy, these decisions call for the trustee to make reasonable judgments about a suitable level of risk and reward for the trust. These decisions are thus to be made and reviewed with due regard for portfolio context and objectives and in light of such factors as the particular trust's return requirements and risk tolerance.[7]

---

to add to a diversified or undiversified portfolio and thus has no way of rewarding this kind of risk.

6. Investors are risk-averse. Therefore, the greater the nondiversifiable risk assumed in buying an asset, the greater the return the investor will require as compensation for bearing that risk. (Simple examples include a bank's willingness to lend at the "prime" rate to its most credit-worthy customers while demanding much higher rates from poor credit risks; the fact that *equity* investments ordinarily have higher returns than *debt* investments, with long-term bonds bearing higher interest rates than short-term and with newer or small cap (capitalization under $1 billion) company stocks involving more risk than the shares of well established or large cap (over $5 billion), or mega cap, companies.) This *compensated* (or "market" or "systematic") risk is, in effect, rewarded through ordinary market mechanisms. Most simply, among individual stocks with like long-term return expectations, the highly volatile ones sell for lower prices than those that are less volatile, whose similar predicted returns are subject to a lesser degree of expected variability. Because of the direct correlation between this type of risk and legitimate return expectations, the question of how much the trust portfolio as a whole should bear is properly a matter for an educated, trust-by-trust judgment call.

7. Risk management begins with what are called "asset allocation" decisions, often referred to as the key to successful investing. Asset allocation involves deciding what portion of a trust's (or other investor's) portfolio should be allocated to equity investments, to debt investments, and to cash equivalents. (Recall the numerous articles in newspapers and periodicals reporting the embarrassingly simplistic interviews with financial planners and investment advisers who state their rules-of-thumb or recommended percentage breakdown between stocks and bonds solely based on customer age categories.) Although there are no established categories of investments for this purpose, asset allocation does not end with the foregoing groups of asset types. For example, *equities* include real estate (including pools or REITs) as well as stocks (with subcategories including, for example, *growth* and *value* shares, *venture capital* and *large cap* stocks and other groupings based on risk characteristics, and a variety of mutual

Third, trustees and the rules that govern their investment activities must be sensitive to the competition between the needs of the present and the future, and also to the different meanings impartiality might have depending on the nature, purposes, and circumstances of different trusts. This sensitivity is especially important in light of modern experience with inflation and taxation and with the differing impact these factors may have on different beneficiary interests. Conflicting objectives in these matters are especially but not exclusively evident between income and principal beneficiaries. In particular, the prudent investor rule recognizes that traditional concern for protection of principal should include reasonable consideration of an objective of preserving purchasing power and real, after-tax values. It also recognizes that life beneficiaries' concerns over trust-accounting income are not the same (or even necessarily present) in all trusts, and in any event that productivity requirements focus on the portfolio as a whole, rather than on each investment. The rule further recognizes that family financial and tax circumstances and settlor objectives will sometimes justify a deliberate effort to achieve real growth in the value of the trust estate. Accordingly, the new Restatement seeks to increase, or at least clarify, both the flexibility of the duty of impartiality and the breadth of the concerns it addresses.[8]

---

funds that may be actively managed or passive [e.g., various types of index] funds), and bonds may be categorized by due date (long-, mid-, or short-term) or by risk of default (AAA to "junk") or by type of bond mutual fund. Both stock and bond holdings may include international or foreign securities, generally by region or by developing countries or emerging markets, with each category available through mutual funds. Asset allocation decisions should implement the trustee's strategy for risk management — i.e., reflect both the diversification plan and the targeted level of risk and reward.

8. An associated or companion feature of the duty of impartiality is the duty to make the trust estate reasonably "productive" for the benefit of income beneficiaries — i.e., productive of trust accounting income. These duties obligate the trustee to balance the competing objectives and concerns of the diverse beneficial interests in typical private trusts, and the frequent counterpart concerns in charitable trusts, with the interests of the "present" to be balanced against those of the "future." These issues arise whenever distributions or expenditures are tied in whole or in part to trust "income." In other words, income productivity issues do not arise with respect to wholly discretionary trusts or pure annuity or unitrust arrangements, and the problems are eased by trusts with flexible powers to invade principal or by the Uniform Management of Institutional Funds Act (UMIFA). Both the common law stated in the Third Restatement and the statutory view of the Uniform Act make clear that a trustee's *productivity* concerns and the duty to take account of the risks that *inflation* may pose to purchasing power and real values relate to the portfolio as a whole, and in a manner and to an extent consistent with the nature and objectives of the particular trust. (This, of course, does not mean that a trustee who has acted with prudence is liable for failing to achieve a particular goal.) Modernized investment law under both the Third Restatement and the Uniform Act emphasizes strategies and objectives consistent with the purposes of each individual trust and also portfolio theory and the benefits of investing for total return (i.e., income yield *plus* increase in corpus value), stimulating the interest of trust practitioners in

Fourth, prudence may require or at least benefit from expert assistance in investment matters. Accordingly, the prudent investor rule views delegation by trustees much more positively than has traditional doctrine accompanying the "prudent man" standard. In very different ways, delegation is likely to advance the management activities of trustees ranging from skilled professional fiduciaries (who may seek, for example, to pursue challenging investment strategies) to family members or friends selected as trustees for quite valid reasons other than financial expertise.

Finally, trustees should avoid incurring unwarranted expenses in fulfilling their investment responsibilities. Cost-conscious administration should take account of market efficiency concepts and the importance of comparing the additional research and transaction costs of active management strategies with realistically appraised prospects for increased return from such strategies.[9] It should also take account of in-

---

achieving an understanding of finance, or at least of financial theory. (see J. Macey, supra note 4; B. Malkiel, An Update on Modern Financial Theory, 24 ACTEC Notes 127 (1998 Trachtman Lecture) (emphasizing *index* investing and efficient market theory, on which see note 9, infra). Particularly useful for the foreseeable future will be the recent professional writings about and legislative proposals reflecting the importance of, and techniques for avoiding, unfortunate investment inhibitions and conflicts between the productivity requirement and the optimality of total-return investment objectives, specifically: (1) through revision of statutes governing principal and income accounting (or the drafting of private instruments) to include some form of special *adjustment power* to be used when proper and beneficial investment programs lead to inordinately low "income" yields (see the power in §104 of the recently promulgated Uniform Principal and Income Act, and see Chapter 19); and (2) through creative trust design, often emphasizing *unitrust* life interests. See opening pieces in a growing dialog, R. Wolf, Defeating the Duty to Disappoint Equally — The Total Return Trust, 23 ACTEC Notes 46 (1997), W. Hoisington, Modern Trust Design: New Paradigms for the 21st Century, 31 U. of Miami Heckerling Inst. on Est. Plan. ch. 6 (1997), and J. Dobris, Why Trustee Investors Often Prefer Dividends to Capital Gain and Debt Investments to Equity — A Daunting Principal and Income Problem, 32 Real Prop. Prob. & Trust J. 225 (1997); and then J. Horn, Prudent Investor Rule, Modern Portfolio Theory, and Private Trusts: Drafting and Administration Including the "Give-Me-Five" Unitrust, 33 id. 1 (1998), and the somewhat contrarian but valuable J. Garland, The Problems with Unitrusts, 1. J. of Private Portfolio Mgmt. no. 4 (1999).

9. Compelling economic evidence shows that the major capital markets of this country and some others are highly efficient, in the sense that available information is rapidly digested and reflected in the market prices of securities. Thus, investors are confronted with potent evidence that the application of expertise, investigation, and diligence in efforts to "beat the market" (by finding underpriced securities) in these markets ordinarily promises little or no payoff, and usually negative results after taking account of research and transaction costs. Empirical research supporting the theory of efficient markets reveals that in such markets skilled professionals have rarely succeeded (although some successes are inevitable) in attempts to outguess the market with respect to price and future return with any regularity. In fact, evidence shows that there is little correlation between fund managers' earlier successes and their ability to produce above-market returns in subsequent periods. (Better-than-average return from higher-than-average risk is not *beating* the market but merely consistent with its theories.) It

creased legal acceptance of delegation and pooled investing by trustees, as well as the availability and continuing emergence not only of investment products with significantly varied characteristics but also of virtually identical products being offered at significantly different costs.[10]

Related portions of the initial volume of the Restatement (Third) of Trusts give particular attention to several issues of trustee liability.

Damages Issues. Frequent criticism of the anti-netting rule (Chapter 17, section D.1) stems from a mistaken belief that the long-standing, general rule that forbids offsetting gains against losses from multiple breaches of trust prevents a trustee from relying on modern portfolio theory in investing. This belief fails to recognize that a breach of trust depends on fiduciary *conduct* rather than on investment *performance,* so that the anti-netting rule is not involved in determining *whether* there

---

is fair to say that efficiency is normally a relative matter and that all markets are not efficient. On degrees and significance of market efficiency, see Gordon & Kornhauser, Efficient Markets, Costly Information and Securities Research, 69 N.Y.U. L. Rev. 761 (1985); Brealey & Myers, Principles of Corporate Finance (3d ed. 1988). Current assessments of the degree of efficiency certainly support the adoption of various forms of passive strategies by trustees, such as reliance on index funds. On efficient market hypotheses that undergird the index fund concept, see B. Malkiel, A Random Walk Down Wall Street (rev. ed. 1999). On the other hand, these assessments would not justify the law in barring prudent use of active management strategies by trustees, with normal adherence to informed diversification within these activities. (Note also that the inclusion of high-risk assets from inefficient markets has the effect of reducing *overall* portfolio risk by improved diversification, while increasing return expectations — a benefit that the more confining "prudent man rule" denied to trusts, much as it denied the use of derivatives as a means by which even cautious trustees might prudently reduce risks or escape significant costs.) The additional expenses associated with active management strategies, however, are not to be ignored. Typical actively managed mutual funds charge annual fees (separate from any *loads* infra note 10) averaging 1.5 percent of the value of the assets under management, while a well-run S&P 500 index fund may charge annual fees of 0.2 percent or less. As noted in Restatement Third's Prudent Investor Rule, §227, cmt. *h,* realistic and cautiously evaluated return expectations from active management must justify its extra costs; the greater the trustee's departure from passive strategies, the greater the appropriate burden of justification, and also of monitoring, whether an active program is undertaken in-house or through mutual funds. There is no evidence that load funds outperform no-load funds to make up for the reduced amount available for initial investment. (Why, therefore, do you suppose people buy load funds? And why do you suppose people use retail brokers instead of discount brokers?)

10. For example, comparable mutual funds may be sold with no *load* charge or with modest or heavy *loads* (perhaps ranging from 3 to 8 percent of the amount invested (front-end loads) or perhaps a back-end or exit load if redemption occurs within some period after purchase); and their annual management fees may differ significantly. Certainly, the trustee's duties include some reasonable obligation to inquire into and compare these costs — and also to take account of the costs of delegation or investment advice in determing its own compensation requests (not ordinarily on a one-for-one basis, but considering the trustee's originally contemplated and continuing investment responsibilities and the prospect of value added).

has been a breach of trust but only in determining the measure of damages when breaches do occur. Nevertheless, the commentary to §213 of the Third Restatement (Prudent Investor volume) attempts to be more careful than its predecessors in identifying when breaches should be treated as "separate and distinct" so as to preclude offset.

In addition, as a part of the prudent investor rule's effort to be more careful about the distinction between "total return" and income "yield," the new Restatement generally measures a trustee's liability for improper investment conduct by reference to total return. It thus allows, in most situations, for example, recovery for the trustee's failure to produce gains or portfolio appreciation that would reasonably have been expected from an appropriate investment program. As noted in Chapter 17, section D.1, this seeks to assure that trustees who have ignored important aspects of their fiduciary obligations by employing inadequate investment strategies will not be insulated from liability merely because their portfolios escaped loss of dollar value during periods of significantly rising markets. Restatement (Third) §§205 and 208-211 recognize that earlier concern over the "speculative" character of such damages is alleviated today by the availability of relevant data and the suitability of current investment principles to serve as guides in identifying reasonably appropriate "benchmark portfolios" for this purpose.

PROBLEM

18-C. *S* devised $1 million in cash to *T* as trustee to pay the income for life to *S*'s widow, *W*, with *T* having power to invade principal for her in the event of serious need, and upon her death to distribute the trust property outright to the then-living issue of *S*'s prior marriage (two adult children, each with minor children). *T* was a close friend of *S*, with a good understanding of the family and its dynamics but no investment experience. The terms of the trust provide no investment guidance, and *T* consults you for advice on his general investment powers and duties. Aside from keeping a reasonable reserve of cash or such equivalents as certificates of deposit or money market funds, he asks you about the propriety of investing the balance in the following specific ways:

(a) As recommended, or determined, by *T*'s financial planner.
(b) Entirely in U.S. Treasury bonds or municipal bonds rated AAA (the highest rating).
(c) Entirely in a diversified portfolio of selected common stocks.
(d) The bulk in bonds and common stocks but small portions in international stocks, real estate, and venture capital.

(e) In a mixture of 40 percent Treasury and AAA-rated municipal bonds and 60 percent in a diversified portfolio of common stocks.

(f) As above except that, instead of holding diverse common stocks, to invest the stock portion in an actively managed stock mutual fund.

(g) As above except that the stock portion would be invested entirely in an index fund.

Respond first under traditional trust investment law and then under the prudent investor rule. Consider also the appropriate role of the lawyer in advising a trustee on these matters and what additional information you might need to know to advise *T*. Consider further how you would advise *T* if, because of his social beliefs, he wishes to avoid investing in the securities of companies that produce nuclear power or tobacco products. Or, if instead, because of the social and political views of *S*'s children, *T* is considering emphasizing investments in companies that manufacture handguns or publish textbooks that teach creationism.

DENNIS v. RHODE ISLAND HOSPITAL TRUST NATIONAL BANK
744 F.2d 893 (1st Cir. 1984)

[The plaintiffs, beneficiaries of a testamentary trust (and sole surviving issue of the settlor), claim that the bank trustee had breached various fiduciary obligations in its handling of interests in three commercial buildings in downtown Providence, all constructed before 1900. Property values declined markedly in the area over the last 30 years, during which the trust held (although expressly authorized to sell) the interests in the buildings, which were leased to a number of different tenants. The district court rejected many of plaintiffs' arguments but found the trustee had failed to act impartially, having favored the income beneficiaries over the remainder beneficiaries. The court imposed a surcharge of $365,000, concluding that, to avoid improper favoritism, the trustee should have sold the real estate interests and reinvested the proceeds at least by 1950, when it must or should have known that the character of downtown commercial Providence was changing and that the buildings' values would seriously decline.]

BREYER, CIRCUIT JUDGE. . . .

The trustee first argues that the district court's conclusions rest on "hindsight" . . . [and] that a trustee can indulge a preference for keeping the trust's "inception assets". . . .

The trustee's claim might be persuasive had the district court found that it had acted *imprudently* in 1950, in retaining the buildings. If that were the case, one might note that every 1950 sale involved both a pessimistic seller and an optimistic buyer; and one might ask how the court could expect the trustee to have known then (in 1950) whose prediction would turn out to be correct. The trustee's argument is less plausible, however, where, as here, the district court basically found that in 1950 the trustee had acted not imprudently, but *unfairly*, between income beneficiaries and remaindermen.

Suppose, for example, that a trustee of farmland over a number of years overplants the land, thereby increasing short run income, but ruining the soil and making the farm worthless in the long run. The trustee's duty to take corrective action would arise from the fact that he knows (or plainly ought to know) that his present course of action will injure the remaindermen; settled law requires him to act impartially, "with due regard" for the "respective interests" of both the life tenant and the remainderman. . . . The district court here found that a sale in 1950 would have represented one way (perhaps the only practical way) to correct this type of favoritism. . . .

To be more specific, in the court's view the problem arose out of the trustee's failure to keep up the buildings, to renovate them, to modernize them, or to take other reasonably obvious steps that might have given the remaindermen property roughly capable of continuing to produce a reasonable income. This failure allowed the trustee to make larger income payments during the life of the trust; but the size of those payments reflected the trustee's acquiescence in the gradual deterioration of the property. In a sense, the payments ate away the trust's capital.

The trustee correctly points out that it did take certain steps to keep up the buildings; and events beyond its control made it difficult to do more. . . . [T]he depression made it difficult during the 1930's to find tenants who would pay a high rent and keep up the buildings. After World War II the neighborhood enjoyed a brief renaissance; but, then, with the 1950's flight to the suburbs, it simply deteriorated.

Even if we accept these trustee claims, however, the record provides adequate support for the district court's conclusions. There is considerable evidence indicating that, at least by 1950, the trustee should have been aware of the way in which the buildings' high rents, the upkeep problem, the changing neighborhood, the buildings' age, the failure to modernize, all together were consuming the buildings' value. . . . There is no indication in the record that the trust's officers focused upon the problem or consulted real estate experts about it or made any further rehabilitation efforts. Rather, there is evidence that the trustee did little more than routinely agree to the requests of the trust's income beneficiaries that it manage the trust corpus to produce the largest possible income. . . .

The district court also found that the trustee had at least one practical solution available. It might have sold the property in 1950 and reinvested the proceeds in other assets of roughly equivalent total value that did not create a "partiality" problem. . . . "[A] trustee is under a duty to the beneficiary who is ultimately entitled to the principal not to . . . retain property which is certain or likely to depreciate in value, although the property yields a large income, unless he makes adequate provision for amortizing the depreciation." Restatement (Second) of Trusts §232, comment *b*. . . .

Contrary to the trustee's contention, the case law it cites does not give it an absolute right under Rhode Island law to keep the trust's "inception assets" in disregard of the likely effect of retention on classes of trust beneficiaries. . . .

The judgment of the district court [on a matter of damages that is omitted here] is modified and as modified affirmed.

TAYLOR'S ESTATE
277 Pa. 518, 121 Atl. 310 (1923)

[William Taylor died in 1899, leaving part of his residuary estate to the Fidelity Trust Company in trust to pay the income to his daughter for her life, remainder to her children who survive her.]

MOSCHZISKER, C.J. . . .

The present account was filed, at the instance of the daughter and her son, to determine whether the will authorized either the retaining or acquiring of certain classes of securities in which the funds of the estate were invested.

The auditing judge decided that the will did not authorize the purchase or undue retention of nonlegal securities, and surcharged sums aggregating $9,087.60 for losses . . . [on] bonds . . . , which originally had come to accountant as trustee from itself as executor, [plus] $43,018.75 representing the price of sundry nonlegal securities originally purchased and still held by the trustee. . . .

Perry on Trusts, 6th ed., sec. 465, correctly states:

There is said to be a distinction between an original investment improperly made by trustees, and an investment made by the testator himself and simply continued by a trustee, but it is a distinction that cannot be safely acted upon (as controlling). . . . It is true, a testator during his life may deal with his property according to his pleasure, and investments made by him are some evidence he had confidence in that class of invest-

ments; but, in the absence of directions in the will, it is more reasonable
to suppose that a testator intended that his trustees should act according
to law. Consequently, in states where the investments which trustees may
make are pointed out by law, the fact that the testator has invested his
property in certain stocks, or loaned it on personal security, will not authorize trustees to continue such investments beyond a reasonable time
for conversion and investment in regular securities.

In Pennsylvania we have a number of cases where this court refused
to surcharge executors with losses sustained through holding, for several years after a testator's death, dividend-paying corporate stocks purchased by their decedent . . . ; and the rule in respect to holding
nonlegal securities owned by a decedent, which governs . . . personal
representatives with their presumably short-duration trusts, should for
obvious reasons, be more liberal than that governing trustees fixed with
the duty of managing an estate during a long period of years.

. . . The general rule, — in jurisdictions which, like Pennsylvania,
limit the investment of trust funds, — is that ordinarily a fiduciary has
no right to retain, beyond a reasonable period, investments made by
the decedent in unauthorized securities, unless specially empowered
so to do; that when a trustee continues to possess such nonlegal investments after a time when he could properly dispose of them, and a loss
occurs, he may be held liable for a failure of due care, unless he shows
that his retention of the securities in question represents, not a mere
lack of attention, but the honest exercise of judgment based on actual
consideration of existing conditions; in other words, he is expected to
be ordinarily watchful and to exercise normally good judgment. . . .

Are the last seven lines of the above opinion really consistent with
its "correctly state[d]" quotation from Perry?

With the question of inception assets, compare the situation in which
the governing instrument expressly grants the trustee broader investment authority than otherwise implied by law, or grants the trustee
"discretion" in making investments or authorizes retention of certain
assets. For example, in Miller v. Pender, 93 N.H. 1, 34 A.2d 663 (1943),
the trustee was authorized to invest "in such securities as said trustee
shall deem proper (even though the same shall not be classified as
trust investments under the laws of New Hampshire)" and the court
concluded: "Clearly the defendant had authority to invest in securities
that were not legal under our statutes, but in view of the fact that the
trial Court adopted the standard of care and skill of a man of ordinary
prudence in dealing with his own property rather than that of a prudent man whose duty is to conserve the property, this exception [to

the trustee's accounts] is sustained and there should be a new trial."
The court also observed that "provisions enlarging [investment] powers . . . are strictly construed" and quoted from an early edition of a
leading treatise that where "by statute or judicial decision the scope
of [permissible] trust investments is narrow, . . . authorization to the
trustee to make investments 'in his discretion' is ordinarily interpreted
to enlarge his powers so that he can properly make such investments
as a prudent man would make," but where the prudent man rule is in
effect, an authorization "to make investments 'in his discretion' ordinarily does not extend his powers."

FIRST ALABAMA BANK v. SPRAGINS
515 So. 2d 962 (Ala. 1987)

[The Spragins family, as beneficiaries, brought suit against First Alabama (sometimes "the Bank") as trustee of a trust created for them
under the will of Marion Beirne Spragins, Sr., for breach of fiduciary
duty and mismanagement. The Bank was permitted to withdraw as
trustee following a jury verdict against it, which, on earlier appeal, was
reversed and remanded with instructions to the trial court that the case
should not have been tried to a jury and that no reasonable inferences
existed to support a finding of bad faith or willful mismanagement that
could justify an award of punitive damages. On remand the trial judge
found for the plaintiffs and ordered the Bank to pay $685,560 in com-
pensatory damages and $79,224 in interest, which the Supreme Court
affirms.]

ADAMS, J. . . .

The facts reveal that Marion Beirne Spragins, Sr., was formerly the
president and later chairman of the board of trustees of the defendant
(appellant) Bank. . . . After settlement of his estate, the net value of
the trust was $556,881.73, at least 70% of which consisted of stock in
First Alabama's own holding company. . . . The Bank argues that the
trial court's award of damages was based on First Alabama's failure to
diversify the trust holdings, when in fact, the power not to diversify was
[expressly] granted to the Bank by the trust agreement. [Also, the]
alleged "loss" suffered by the trust, the Bank argues, is illusory because
the trust principal increased and "substantial income" was earned
throughout the Bank's tenure as trustee. First Alabama contends that
the court erroneously based its finding that the trust suffered a com-
pensable loss on the Spraginses' calculations of what the trust might
have earned had the trust portfolio been more diversified. The Bank

argues that no loss was suffered, and, therefore, that the law will not recognize any loss to the trust.

We noted in our earlier consideration of this case, 475 So. 2d at 516, that although a trustee's duties and obligations are governed largely by the trust agreement, that agreement cannot be employed to vitiate "the duty imposed by the 'prudent person' standard." . . .

The Spraginses argue that . . . [t]he Bank's concentration of the trust property in its own stock, First Alabama Bancshares, was a violation of its duty of loyalty to the trust beneficiaries and constituted self-dealing . . . [and] that the Bank's failure to diversify the trust portfolio was "at least, insensitivity" by the trustee to the duty of loyalty it owed the trust beneficiaries. We agree . . . with the circuit court that the donor did not intend to vest in the trustee Bank a power to diversify so little as to prejudice the interests of the beneficiaries.

. . . Testimony by the Bank's senior trust officer revealed that eight years after the Bank had assumed administration of the trust, i.e., by 1982, the needs of the testator's grandchildren had still not been determined by the trustee, a basic step which should have preceded formulation of a prudent plan for management of the trust property. The Bank argued, nevertheless, that it had adopted an investment strategy of "moderate income and moderate growth," in its management of the trust. Again, from the facts presented, the circuit court had more than ample evidence from which to conclude that the plan of investment which the Bank claims to have adopted to manage the Spragins trust was "designed to provide a justification for the failure of the trustee Bank to more fully diversify the trust holdings by selling all or substantially all of the First Alabama Bancshares stock." At a time when the trustee Bank's own investment advisory service was recommending that investment in bank stock be limited to five percent of a trust's portfolio, approximately seventy-five percent of the Spragins trust assets were invested in First Alabama Bancshares. We hold that the circuit court was not in error in concluding that the trustee Bank's management of the Spragins trust was, at least, imprudent, and demonstrated the insensitivity of the trustee Bank in the performance of its duty of loyalty to the trust's beneficiaries.

The appellant argues, however, that liability is irrelevant; that even if the Bank is guilty of a breach of trust, no damages should have been awarded because the Trust suffered no loss. Again, we disagree.

The net value of the Trust was $556,881.73 when the testator's estate was settled. The court found that the trust property, 70 to 75% of which was composed of First Alabama Bancshares during the Bank's tenure as trustee, fluctuated in value from a low of approximately $200,000.00 in 1975 to $776,168.00 by 1983. By contrast, the Spraginses offered the testimony of James C. King, a recognized expert in the field of trust management, to show what active, prudent management might have achieved. The Bank disputes King's conclusion, attributing his estimation of loss suffered by the trust to hindsight and speculation. We conclude that the circuit court was not in error in finding that the trust suffered a compensable loss and, further, that the method employed by Mr. King was not mere speculation and hindsight. . . .

Mr. King's approach, the court said, was one of fiscally sound, conservative, active management of the trust estate. His alternative to the Bank's investment in First Alabama Bancshares was to concentrate the assets in the Standard and Poor's 500 index and in fixed income treasury bills. Although the Bank argues strenuously that Mr. King's approach was speculative and mere hindsight, the trial court had substantial evidence upon which to base its conclusion that King's approach was a responsible investment alternative to the Bank's management method. Indeed, the Bank's investment approach appears to have been based upon the assumption that, at all times during its tenure as trustee, First Alabama Bancshares represented the best possible investment of the trust property. More than sufficient evidence supports the circuit court's finding that the Bank's continued investment of 70 to 75% of the trust assets in bank stock was not in the best interest of the beneficiaries. . . .

Affirmed. . . .

TORBERT, CHIEF JUDGE (dissenting).

. . . [T]he trust instrument authorized the very conduct at issue . . . [and] the supposed breach resulted in no actual loss. . . .

. . . The specific issue is whether the bank was imprudent in failing to diversify the portfolio, which consisted primarily of bank stock [which the instrument authorized the bank to retain "regardless of any lack of diversification"]. . . .

We have been very restrictive with regard to allowing recovery for lost profits, primarily because such awards would often be based on very questionable evidence. The Restatement appears to take a similar view, by limiting recovery for lost profits for breach of trusts in the absence of a breach of loyalty to situations where the trustee had a duty to purchase a specific piece of property. Restatement (Second) of Trusts §205(c) and comment (c) and §211. . . . Lost profits are easily ascertained with respect to failure to purchase a specific item, such as shares of XYZ Corporation. . . .

. . . [Furthermore,] Mr. King starts with the premise that all bank stock would be sold and reinvested. However, Mr. King agreed that the bank stock was a good investment in general, and his objection was solely that the trust res was too heavily concentrated in that stock. "[T]he trustee is liable only for such loss as results from the investment of the excess beyond the amount which it would have been proper so

to invest." Restatement (Second) of Trusts §228 comment 1. Therefore, Mr. King began from the wrong starting point.

UNION COMMERCE BANK v. KUSSE
251 N.E.2d 884 (Ohio Prob. Ct. 1969)

[The executor's petition for instructions asks whether a will provision *precluding* the executor and trustee from selling securities received
from the probate estate relieves them from possible liability for holding
the securities.]

ANDREWS, CHIEF REFEREE (opinion approved by MERRICK, P.J.). . . .

The answer to that question is definitely "no." Even though a fiduciary is without power of sale, he is still not relieved from his duty to
manage the estate with due care and prudence. If the circumstances
are such that it becomes imprudent to retain a certain security or other
item of property, the fiduciary must apply to the court for permission
to sell it. And in an emergency or what the fiduciary reasonably believes
to be an emergency, if he has no opportunity to apply to the court,
he may sell the security without first obtaining the court's permission,
although his action is subject to the court's later approval. 1 Restatement, Trusts 2d, sec. 167(2) and Comment *e* [dealing with equitable deviation from trust terms based on changed circumstances (see
Chapter 14, section D.1)]. . . .

Questions relating to the retention of investments coming to a fiduciary at the beginning of his service start with the common law rule
that where the fiduciary receives securities which are not proper trust
investments (often called "nonlegals"), it is his duty to dispose of them
within a reasonable time.

Statutes or provisions in wills or trust instruments authorizing the
fiduciary to retain any property coming to him relieve the fiduciary of
this common law duty. But they do not relieve him of his duty to exercise due care and prudence with reference to the retention or disposal
of such property. . . .

Mr. Kusse's will also grants to his executor and trustee the power to
invest in any property without regard to statutory or judicial restrictions. Consequently, no investments made by either fiduciary can be
classed as nonlegals, and the same is true of the property originally
coming to the fiduciary. 3 Scott, Trusts (3d ed.) sec. 230.1, p. 1870.

But even the unlimited investment authority given in Mr. Kusse's
will does not relieve the fiduciary from the obligation of due care and
prudence. . . .

When the fiduciary is a corporate executor and trustee, with greater
skill and facilities for handling trust estates than those possessed by the

"ordinary prudent man," such fiduciary is held to a higher degree of care, consonant with its greater skill and facilities. . . .

BOSTON SAFE DEPOSIT & TRUST CO. v. BOONE
489 N.E.2d 209 (Mass. App. 1986)

[The will of W. T. Pearson, who died in 1968, established a marital deduction trust giving his widow income for life and a general power to appoint the remainder by her will, with a gift in default of appointment to Brown University. Pearson's attorney, who had died by the time this action was brought, and Boston Safe were cotrustees. When Mrs. Pearson died in 1972, a codicil to her will provided for various appointments of the trust remainder with any balance to go to her estate. Brown University contested the appointments, delaying for a period during which a severe decline and a partial recovery in the stock market reduced the estate assets by about $100,000, so that no balance was available for Mrs. Pearson's executors.]

KAPLAN, J. . . .

Boston Safe recognized, as a general proposition, that [on termination] a trustee should consider itself . . . a "stake holder" with some obligation to "back off to a conservative position." . . . Usually the "stake holder" will discharge its duty by liquidating and distributing with reasonable promptness. There is, however, no iron or absolute duty to do so, and prudence may indeed suggest (or even demand) that liquidation be deferred. . . . Where distribution will necessarily be long deferred, common sense tells us that a trustee can properly consider keeping the corpus of the trust reasonably productive meanwhile. . . . One can well imagine a claim of surcharge if a trustee in these circumstances liquidates precipitately, say upon an obviously depressed market. . . .

Neither the record or common experience suggests that the trustee could fairly be held for failing to predict the movement of stock prices after April, 1974, and in this period it faced the problem of what to do in a declining market. . . . In consideration of the vagaries of the market, our courts have not been harsh about charging trustees for investment judgments which, on reflection after the event, appear to have been mistaken, although an extreme case could warrant surcharge. . . .

Mr. Pearson's will provided: "No one of them [executors and trustees] shall be liable for any act or omission except for his or its own willful default or bad faith." In light of the discussion above, we are not required to deal with the effect of this "exculpatory" clause. However, we note our agreement with the judge that the trustee's behavior cannot in any view be properly characterized as having involved "willful default" or "bad faith." The judge's evident view that the clause was effective according to its terms and not against public policy, is supported by past decisions.

The executors [of Mrs. Pearson's estate] attempt on this appeal for the first time to argue the point that one who drafts a will in which he is named as a fiduciary should not include an exculpatory clause that might apply to himself, without first advising the testator specifically of the effect of this provision. . . . [A]ny claimed delict of the cotrustee should have been brought forward by the executors at an early stage. . . .

The judgments dismissing the executors' objections to the accounting and allowing the accounts are affirmed.

SPRINGFIELD SAFE DEPOSIT & TRUST CO. v. FIRST UNITARIAN SOCIETY
293 Mass. 480, 200 N.E. 541 (1936)

RUGG, C.J. [Petition for allowance of trustee's accounts] . . .

The facts relating to the original investment [objected to] were these in substance: In 1925 the trust department of the petitioner, from uninvested funds held by it in various trusts, lent $65,000 to William M. Young, a man of substantial means and owner of a considerable amount of real estate, on his note payable on demand after three years with interest at five and a half percent per annum, payable quarterly, and secured by a first mortgage in usual form on real estate in the business section of Springfield. . . . The officers of the petitioner appraised the land at $100,000 and the buildings at $20,000. The executive committee of the petitioner, consisting of its president and five directors, all men of extensive experience in real estate matters, approved the loan as a conservative mortgage and a proper investment for the trust estates contributing thereto. The note and mortgage ran to the petitioner without designation as trustee. This method was for the convenience of the various trust estates interested therein and to enable the petitioner as trustee to hold, administer and deal with the note and mortgage for the best interests of the trusts. This method was in accordance with uniform practice of other similar institutions and was the only practicable way to manage such an investment. The money advanced on this note and mortgage was derived exclusively from various trust funds in the control of the trust department of the petitioner; no portion of it belonged to the commercial department of the petitioner. When the loan was made and the necessary funds contributed by the various trust estates from uninvested capital in the several trust estates, proper entries were promptly and duly made upon the books of the trust department of the petitioner showing the sums respectively advanced from each contributing trust estate, the proportion of each contribution to the amount of the note and mortgage, and the face amount of the participating beneficial interest therein received by each contributing trust estate, which participating beneficial interests were evidenced and represented by "Certificates of Interest in Real Estate Mortgage," so called, identical in form, which were on the same date duly executed by the petitioner and placed in the portfolio of each contributing trust estate. These certificates showed that the particular trust estate had a participating interest in the mortgage with a face value equal to the amount contributed by it. . . . In 1932, during the depression, it became necessary to foreclose this mortgage. The property was sold at a loss. A new note and first mortgage were taken by the petitioner covering the same property and a new participating interest certificate issued to represent the share of the Spaulding trust on the same plan as before. This was known as the Okum mortgage. The loss thus suffered by the Spaulding trust was in no respect due to the method of holding the Young mortgage or caused by the fact that it was a participating mortgage. The same loss would have occurred if the mortgage had been held entirely by one trust estate. It is stated in the agreed facts:

> Investment of trust funds held by corporate fiduciaries in participating interests in mortgages, similar to those held in this trust, have been made since 1892 and continuously thereafter. . . .

Conditions which have led to this form of investment are narrated at some length in the record but need not be here recited. This device was adopted and has grown in favor because of the difficulty which corporate fiduciaries have experienced in obtaining first mortgages upon real estate in the Commonwealth in amounts small enough to be held in smaller trusts and to provide the diversification desired in larger trusts. The plain inference from the facts stated is that this form of investment for trust funds has been regarded as safe and conservative by the men charged with the responsibility of managing large and small trusts by trust companies. . . .

The precise question is whether as a matter of law such investments are permissible. That question has not arisen hitherto in this Commonwealth. Investment of trust funds in securities of this nature has been upheld in other jurisdictions. . . . It was said in Matter of Union Trust Co. 219 N.Y. 514, 519:

> The advantages that are frequently to be secured by combining trust funds to make a large and more satisfactory investment than can be made

of the funds of one trust without combination are of sufficient importance and value to the several trust funds to overcome any disadvantage that may arise from the fact that the several owners of the investment may thereafter differ in the matter of handling the same. Trust funds have been from time to time combined for investment with satisfactory results and the practice is generally recognized as proper for a trustee. . . .

Individual trustees ought to be scrupulously careful not to make investments of trust funds in their own names but always to indicate that they are made in a trust capacity. They are held to strict liability for violation of this duty. But the books of account of the petitioner, the stringent provisions of statute as to the separation of trust investments, and the constant public supervision of its affairs show that no harm has come to the beneficiaries. . . .

It is the duty also of trustees holding two or more distinct trust funds to keep them separate and ordinarily not to invest them together. . . . That principle has not been violated in the case at bar in its essential features. The mortgage was a single investment, but it was divided forthwith by the issuance of the certificates of interest to the several trusts, which became at once a matter of record in its trust department and subject to periodical inspection and examination by the bank commissioner. Objection based on the possibility of transfer of certificates from one trust to another by the trustee, if in good faith, and otherwise not open to just criticism, is without merit. . . .

In the case at bar there is no contention that the petitioner did not exercise good faith and act for a proper purpose. The loss that has resulted to the beneficiaries is not due to conduct of the petitioner or the kind of investment made, but to adverse general financial conditions. In such circumstances there is no liability for breach of trust. . . .

The contention is made by the beneficiaries that the Young mortgage was not a proper investment in point of security when originally made in 1925. The circumstances attendant upon making that investment have already been stated. The amount of the loan seems large in view of what happened since it was made. The propriety of an investment must be determined with reference to facts and conditions existing at the time it was made and not in the light of subsequent and unforeseen events. The depreciation in the value of the real estate resulting from the depression and the consequent loss on the mortgage occurring after it was taken have no direct bearing on the soundness of the original investment. . . .

Decree may be entered allowing each account. Ordered accordingly.

About a dozen years later similar doubts were recognized with regard to the propriety of trustees investing in mutual funds but, again, with an outcome supportive of the practice. In re Rees' Estate, 53 Ohio L. Abs. 385, 85 N.E.2d 563 (1949), reads as follows:

> Because of the lack of judicial authority on the subject in this state, the Court has had to look elsewhere and has been benefited by a recent article written by Mayo Shattuck . . . in 25 Boston University Law Review (1945) at pages 12 and 13, where he states:
>
>> When we are speaking of acquiring shares of an investment trust are we describing an *abandonment* of the duties of a trust in any real sense or are we describing a *discharge* of those duties by participation in a reputable management enterprise, the evidence of which participation consists of a readily marketable certificate? Is the trust management in any real or practical sense abandoned? To me it seems that exactly the opposite has taken place. Nor am I alone in this view. Men of prudence, intelligence and discretion are every day acquiring the shares of well seasoned management type investment companies and investment trusts as desirable securities. . . .
>>
>> Now, if it is the intention of modern trust law to place the trustee as nearly as possible in the position of the man of prudence, intelligence and discretion who is making permanent disposition of his own capital, why should not the trustee be extended the same privilege which is everyday being exercised by the prudent man who is his model? My answer is that the trustee ought to have that privilege; that there is no sound reason for denying it to him and that the law must therefore be expected to advance in this direction.
>
> This court believes that the arguments of Mr. Shattuck are well founded. Therefore the exceptions to the account are overruled.

Typical of state banking and financial codes at the time of the *Rees* decision was the following provision:

> Any trust company may establish and administer common trust funds composed of property permitted by law for the investment of trust funds, for the purpose of furnishing investments to itself as fiduciary, and may invest funds held by it as fiduciary in interests in such common trust funds, if not prohibited by the instrument, decree, or order creating such fiduciary relationship.

Such statutes came to insist, as did case law, that a bank make no separate charge for operating and investing trust funds in its common trust fund(s). (Many banks today are terminating their common funds in favor of participation in and compensated services to outside "proprietary" mutual funds, with statutory blessing. What do you suppose the effect of this should be on regular trustee fees paid by participating trusts? See Chapter 17, sections B and C.2, supra).

Index funds (and other forms of indexing) may still raise special problems. See Committee Report, Current Investment Questions and the Prudent Person Rule, 13 Real Prop., Prob. & Tr. J. 650, 654-657 (1978):

To the extent that estimates are available as to the relative value of portfolios declared to be "indexed," a figure in the neighborhood of 1 percent [a seriously outdated figure today — EDS.] of institutional portfolios appears to be realistic. . . .

For those trust portfolios which must be judged by the "Prudent Person Rule," whether in one of its common law or statutory permutations, how does indexing meet the standard of prudence?

One challenge to indexing is improper delegation of duty. A trustee who invests in an index fund has, it may be presumed, taken two steps. First, he has examined the index fund concept and concluded that the concept has validity and that a prudent person would invest in such funds. Second, he has selected a particular fund. . . . It is unrealistic to assume that a trustee investing in an index fund will investigate the individual securities held by the fund. . . . The mix of stocks in each index is changed from time to time . . . imposing a further independent decision on the trustee's investment. . . . The counter argument would take a unitary approach to the index fund investment. That is, the fund as a whole is the investment. A change in its parts is no more the creature of an improper delegation than is corporate management's decision to sell off a division of a corporation whose stock is held by a trust.

A second challenge to index fund investing is the general prohibition against offsetting gains and losses. . . . Here again, the counter argument is bottomed on the unitary concept, with the speculative stock included in the index no more significant than the new division in the diversified corporation.

A third question is the general wisdom of index funds. There is evidence that index funds have in recent years outperformed individually managed portfolios. If such is the case presumably a prudent trustee should give serious consideration to the concept in the performance of his duties within the prudent person rule. Knowledgeable fiduciaries and investors have established and invested in index funds, and [fiduciaries are] "to observe how men of prudence, discretion and intelligence manage their own affairs. . . ." Also, an index fund certainly enables a trustee to diversify to a degree beyond that which could be achieved by most trustees without an unwarranted increase in administrative costs. . . .

The Report, id. at 662-663, then considers "modern portfolio theory":

[Securities] which might be quite risky when taken alone may, according to the theory, decrease total portfolio risk and, accordingly, be a more "prudent" purchase than a security which appears less risky by itself. . . .

In any event, modern portfolio theory and its methodology have not yet been endorsed by the courts, although the Department of Labor offers a ringing endorsement for ERISA purposes. Ian Lanoff's announcement April 21, 1978 of proposed regulation section 2550.401a-1 states that the Act goes beyond what he alleges to be the common law doctrine of judging prudence of an investment alone, without regard to its role in the total investment portfolio. [Reality check! — only in tax regs and rulings: the self-defeating, silly suggestion in the preamble to the *final* ERISA regulations (1979) to the effect that, to use an index fund, weeding would be required to screen out high-risk companies.]

Perhaps the *Spitzer* case [below] comes closest to addressing the portfolio issue, and its consideration is balanced. The Court of Appeals decision held that . . . individual investment decisions are properly affected by considerations of the portfolio as a whole, as, e.g., diversification and sound tax planning. But the focus, nevertheless, is on the individual security as such, with factors relating to the entire portfolio to be weighed only along with others in reviewing particular investment decisions. . . .[11]

MATTER OF BANK OF NEW YORK ("THE *SPITZER* CASE")
35 N.Y.2d 512, 323 N.E.2d 700 (1974)

[The bank as trustee of its own common trust fund submitted an accounting for a four-year period (as prescribed by N.Y. Banking Law §100-c) ending September 30, 1968. The guardian ad litem (as "attorney for principal") challenged four investments; after examination of witnesses, summary judgment on the four objections was granted, two

---

11. Because of ERISA's general similarity to the prudent investor rule, the treatment of a different issue in a recent ERISA case may be instructive. In Laborers National Pension Fund v. Northern Trust Quantitative Advisors, 173 F.3d 313 (5th Cir. 1999), an investment manager for an ERISA pension plan purchased interest-only mortgage-backed securities (IOs) that resulted in a $4.2 million loss in a year in which the portfolio as a whole experienced a gain of $18 million. IOs are derivatives (financial instruments whose performance is derived from the performance of underlying assets) that "can result in significantly greater price and yield volatility than traditional debt securities . . . [but] can serve as a hedge to prevent significant losses due to interest rate [increases] because IOs generally increase as interest rates rise." The federal district court had determined that purchase of the IOs was imprudent, but this finding was reversed on appeal. The circuit court of appeals said that under ERISA the appropriate inquiry is whether the manager acted "as a prudent investment manager under . . . modern portfolio theory"; that neither ERISA nor the plan documents prohibited investment in IOs; and that the test for prudence "is how the fiduciary acted in his selection of the investment, and not whether his investments succeeded or failed." The court found prudent conduct in the manager's review of literature on IOs, discussion of the merits of IOs with brokers, and utilization of electronic stress simulation models to project, under various market conditions, the performance of IOs and of the fund's portfolio as a whole.

by the Surrogate and the other two by modification in the Appellate Division.]

JONES, J. . . .

We now affirm the [dismissal] of all objections raised by the guardian [ad litem]. . . .

The guardian had completed the examination desired by him both of the trustee's records and its personnel. . . . There is no factual dispute between the parties as to what the trustee and its representatives did or omitted to do. The difference between them relates only to the legal conclusion to be drawn from conceded facts — the one contends that the trustee did not meet the duty imposed on it by law; the other, that such duty was discharged. . . .

[W]e do not agree with what appears to have been in part the basis on which the majority at the Appellate Division reached its conclusion. The fact that this portfolio showed substantial overall increase in total value during the accounting period does not insulate the trustee from responsibility for imprudence with respect to individual investments for which it would otherwise be surcharged (cf. King v. Talbot, 40 N.Y. 76, 90-91; 3 Scott, Trusts [3d ed.], §213.1, pp. 1712-1713). To hold to the contrary would in effect be to assure fiduciary immunity in an advancing market such as marked the history of the accounting period here involved. The record of any individual investment is not to be viewed exclusively, of course, as though it were in its own water-tight compartment, since to some extent individual investment decisions may properly be affected by considerations of the performance of the fund as an entity, as in the instance, for example, of individual security decisions based in part on considerations of diversification of the fund or of capital transactions to achieve sound tax planning for the fund as a whole. The focus of inquiry, however, is nonetheless on the individual security as such and factors relating to the entire portfolio are to be weighed only along with others in reviewing the prudence of the particular investment decisions. . . .

The record discloses that with respect to each investment the trustee acted in good faith and cannot be said to have failed to exercise " 'such diligence and such prudence in the care and management [of the fund], as in general, prudent men of discretion and intelligence in such matters, employ in their own like affairs.' " . . . It was not shown in any instance that the losses to the trust fund resulted from imprudence or negligence. There was evidence of attention and consideration with reference to each decision made. Obviously it is not sufficient that hindsight might suggest that another course would have been more beneficial: nor does a mere error of investment judgment mandate a surcharge. Our courts do not demand investment infallibility, nor hold a trustee to prescience in investment decisions. . . .

Whether a trustee is to be surcharged in these instances, as in other cases, must necessarily depend on a balanced and perceptive analysis of its consideration and action in the light of the history of each individual investment, viewed at the time of its action or its omission to act. In our opinion no sufficiently useful purpose would be served by a detailed description of the analysis by which we reach the conclusion that there is no basis for surcharge with respect to any of the four investments here called into question. . . .

Decree affirmed. . . .

In the recent case of Matter of Estate of Janes, 90 N.Y.2d 41, 681 N.E.2d 332 (1997), the New York Court of Appeals rejected the trustee's argument that there was no duty to diversify in the absence of additional elements of hazard. Seventy-one per cent of the trust property received from the testator consisted of stock in a single blue-chip company, Eastman Kodak. The trustee retained the stock as it declined from a date-of-death value of $135 per share to about $47 per share. Relying in part on language in the *Spitzer Case,* the court surcharged the trustee for the excessive concentration. The court used as the measure of damages the value of the lost capital rather than a lost profits or market index measure.

ESTATE OF KNIPP
489 Pa. 509, 414 A.2d 1007 (1980)

FLAHERTY, J. . . .

[T]he Orphans' Court . . . denied a claim for surcharge . . . against the appellee corporate executor, Central Penn National Bank, for alleged mismanagement of estate investments. . . .

On November 9, 1972, letters testamentary were issued to appellee as executor of decedent's estate. His will created a testamentary trust, the beneficiaries of which included the appellants, and designated appellee to serve as trustee. The estate property included 4314 shares of Sears Roebuck & Co. common stock valued at the commencement of the estate's administration at approximately $470,000, a figure which represented 71% of the estate's total asset value and 97% of the value of all stocks in the estate. Only 400 of the Sears shares were sold by the executor during the first year of administration, the sales being made primarily to cover costs of administration rather than for reinvestment purposes. The will gave appellee, as executor and trustee, an absolute discretionary power either to retain or sell such property. . . .

After a thorough review of the record, we find, at least minimally, sufficient evidence to support the conclusion of the court below that the appellee exercised the degree of care, skill, and judgment required of a fiduciary. . . . The evidence establishes that Sears stock was, during the period in question, reasonably believed to be a sound, national, broadbased stock worthy of investment by a fiduciary.

As it turned out, however, performance of the Sears stock was poor. . . . Hindsight, however, is not the test of liability for surcharge. . . .

On the other hand, we are not prepared to say that authorization to retain assets gives an executor or trustee an absolute and unbridled discretion to sit idly by while those assets depreciate in value. Rather, when challenged, every such administration should be carefully scrutinized to determine whether an expert corporate fiduciary has performed according to the higher standards required of it.

In addition to the heretofore discussed assertion of a lack of attention to the estate account, appellants contend that the trustee's failure to substantially diversify the stock holdings within three months of commencement of administration constituted unskillful and imprudent trust asset management. Where, as in the present case, a testator vests a fiduciary with discretion to retain assets, the fiduciary is not thereby excused from the duty of making the retention decision prudently. . . . It is not, however, per se imprudent for an executor, vested with absolute discretion to hold property, to refrain from immediately diversifying a large block of stock received at the commencement of administration. In Saeger's Estates, 340 Pa. 73, 76-77, 16 A.2d 19, 21-22 (1940), where a surcharge was sought solely on the ground that the trustee had not diversified holdings, we said:

> Nor does it appear that in any case thus far brought before this Court has a trustee been surcharged solely for the reason now urged. In the absence of controlling precedent and particularly in the absence of such requirement in the statutory law relating to the investment of trust funds, we conclude that . . . there is no authority in the law of this State for the doctrine, contended for by appellants, that trust investments, otherwise legal and entirely proper under all the recognized standards, are necessarily improvident per se for any claimed lack of proper diversification.

Although many financial authorities advocate diversity of investment as a desirable course for trust management, a judicial decision declaring non-diversification to be presumptively imprudent would arbitrarily foreclose executors and trustees from opportunities to retain beneficial holdings. The preferable approach, therefore, is to determine on a case by case basis whether the particular investment approach meets the standard in Killey Trust, supra. Here we cannot say that the record does not adequately support the determination of the court below that retention of the Sears stock, without diversification, was not imprudent.

Decree affirmed. Each party to pay own costs.

CHURCH AND SNITZER, DIVERSIFICATION, RISK AND MODERN PORTFOLIO THEORY
124 Tr. & Est. 32 (Oct. 1985)

The investment industry has undergone dramatic changes in recent years reflecting in part its efforts to convert ever-increasing amounts of information into knowledge. And while investors have always been concerned with diversification and risk, only recently have they had the tools to adequately quantify them.

Traditionally, professional investors, including bank trust departments, have relied on analysts to research companies and industries and provide reports for review by their organizations' investment committees. Portfolio managers, in turn, translated these recommendations into action for their assigned accounts. Though the methodology varied, the process remained essentially subjective.

Conventional wisdom held that diversification served to reduce risk, but that notion could not be proved quantitatively. . . .

In 1952, Prof. Harry Markowitz, in a pioneering effort to quantify these factors, conceived Modern Portfolio Theory. This theory held that all investors are risk-averse and will seek the highest rate of return at a particular level of risk. Prof. Markowitz also concluded that since most investors used basically the same precepts and quickly factored all published information into their investment decisions, markets tended to be efficient.

Prof. Markowitz recognized, however, that by creating a sufficiently large portfolio, non-market risk could be largely eliminated. . . . As computers became available and professional managers [were recognized as] underperforming popular market averages, Modern Portfolio Theory gained in popularity. By the mid '70s passive or index funds became fashionable. These funds, however, raised an important question — should the holdings of an indexed portfolio be confirmed by independent research?

By the late '70s the notion of efficient markets had become less credible. A consensus developed that large, well-researched and efficiently priced companies were appropriate for passive core holdings, but that opportunities for superior investment results lie in the inefficient market, i.e., small companies that are not fully researched.

Concurrently, the concept of covariance emerged. This is a measurement of how a security moves in relation to other securities and to the market. Covariance has become an accepted portfolio management tool. Simply, different types of stocks tend to move in opposite directions; this phenomenon can be quantified by itself, as well as in terms of its effect on a particular portfolio.

Covariance, then, represents a further evolution and refinement of Modern Portfolio Theory. . . .

Today's version of Modern Portfolio Theory is characterized by analysis of greater amounts of data — some unconventional such as earnings and price momentum, volatility and others — while reducing decision time. Moreover, it reflects the need to increase productivity through use of computer databases and screens to identify specific issues for constructing portfolios with optimal characteristics.

In March of this year, the Chase Lincoln First of Rochester, New York obtained approval from the New York State banking authorities to use stock index options and market futures in common trust funds.

The investment world is changing rapidly and professional trustees may not be able to cling to past procedures and strategies to protect themselves from surcharge.

The basics of this approach are probably here to stay, particularly quantification of risk and portfolio characteristics vis-à-vis client investment objectives. The new methods are less subjective and more precise, thereby substantially enhancing the odds for successful investment performance.

By way of example, in the Estate of Knipp [supra] the Supreme Court of Pennsylvania held that a bank would not be surcharged for losses sustained by failure to diversify stock holdings of an estate within the first 90 days of account administration. . . .

Modern Portfolio Theory teaches that the financial principle underpinning the duty to diversify, is the need to modulate the effect of unanticipated events on the performance of a portfolio and to reduce risk.

One generally accepted measurement of portfolio risk is the standard deviation of return, a statistical method measuring the extent to which the actual return of a portfolio differs from its average return. For example, if a portfolio over time returned 10 percent on average, but could have returned from −20 percent to +40 percent, in any one time segment, its standard deviation is said to be 30 percent. Such a portfolio would seem volatile, and therefore more risky, than one with an average return of 10 percent and a standard deviation of 10 percent.

Now let us examine the *Knipp* portfolio vs. Standard & Poor's over a 12 year period (Jan. 1961 to Dec. 1972). . . .

. . . [O]n a total return basis with dividends and capital gains reinvested, a dollar in January 1961 of Sears stock became $4.52 by 1972.

On the same basis, a dollar of the S&P 500 became $2.75. Sears was 60 percent riskier than the S&P 500. The risk, in retrospect, was worth it (.45 is better than .36). (However, it certainly was not worth the risk from Jan. 1, 1973 to Jan. 1, 1983 when the S&P 500 outperformed Sears by a margin of three to one even though Sears was 85 percent riskier than the market in *that* period.) The odds of securing such risk-adjusted results are between 5 and 50 percent.

The court did not address the issue now quantified by professional money managers: How much risk was the bank taking and was it appropriate for its beneficiaries? . . .

It is not often that a fiduciary for widows and children takes 60 percent greater risk than market, a risk comparable to the most aggressive portfolio managers. A trustee who does not know the past and current risk of a portfolio is ignorant of what modern financial ideas can teach of an important element of fiduciary duty.

As for the legal implications, because it is now possible to define with reasonable mathematical precision the past risk of individual securities and portfolios, a criteria of investment competence should be that a trustee *know* such risk.

The excerpt below is in one sense most directly related to principal/ income accounting questions, and thus may usefully serve here as an introduction to the next chapter. It may be more significantly related, however, to an understanding of investment principles and decisions in an inflationary economy, including issues about possible applications of portfolio theory and at least about portfolio balance.

YOUNG, RUSSELL, ET AL., CURRENT INVESTMENT QUESTIONS AND THE PRUDENT PERSON RULE
13 Real Prop., Prob & Tr. J. 650, 664-668 (1978)

Based on our current inflation trends and projections for the future, is the purchase of long-term bonds with high interest rates prudent, considering what is apt to be left for the remaindermen after the passage of time? It has been suggested that some of this "interest" is an inflation factor which should be added to principal.

Such an adjustment to the income of a life income beneficiary is at present unsupported by the law. Does the law need changing, or should trust documents direct the trustee to undertake such an allocation? . . .

Interest rates (yields) on long-term bonds are a function of a "real" interest rate and the degree of "risk" incurred by the lender or investor. . . . The "risk" component represents the premium demanded and obtained to compensate for the risk assumed, [and inflation is] incorporated into the rate, or yield, structure . . . as a risk [causing] devaluation in the purchasing power of money. . . .

Conceptually, this interest rate now consists of two components, "a real rate of interest . . . and an inflation premium." Indeed, "inflation has almost always coincided with rising interest rates, and interest rates have rarely risen without inflation."

A possible way to avoid this might be to allocate some portion of the nominal interest rate return to principal. . . .

The problem, of course, is that it is not precisely known how much of the nominal interest rate is attributable to inflation factors . . . because many factors may be involved in the setting of an interest rate. . . .

. . . [T]he practical problem of measurement probably vitiates any substantial interest in making such an allocation and an amendment to our principal and income laws to accomplish this purpose seems remote.

The real problem here is one of "overproductivity" with regard to the portfolio as a whole. As you proceed into Chapter 19, consider whether an effort has been made, in a different way than suggested above, to deal with this problem.

19

Matters of Accounting and Successive Enjoyment

Some of the more technical and troublesome problems in fiduciary administration are considered in this chapter. Here we take up the day-to-day detail of allocating receipts and expenditures to the appropriate accounts, particularly as between principal and income. Most trusts and estates have purposes for which income is to be used or beneficiaries to whom income must be paid. At the same time usually there will be purposes and beneficial interests to which principal is allocable. At the time of each receipt or disbursement the fiduciary is forced to decide whether it is to be charged or credited to income or to principal, or whether it is to be apportioned between these accounts. Charged with the duty of impartiality, the fiduciary must make corrections or recover erroneous distributions, or will be subject to surcharge for improper allocation on any of these many transactions.

In the course of administering a trust or decedent's estate, a fiduciary will also find it necessary to make certain choices that will affect the various beneficial interests differently. Thus, the problem arises: How does the fiduciary's duty of impartiality to successive or multiple beneficiaries affect administrative decisions, and, if a decision benefits one beneficiary to the detriment of another, is any adjustment required or permitted?

Each item of a fiduciary's account is reviewable by the beneficiaries and, if objected to, must be supported as to its accuracy and propriety. This means not only that the allocation to the proper account or beneficiary must be correct but also that the validity and amount of the entry must be sustained. Thus, the fiduciary must show that each expenditure has been made for a proper purpose and in a reasonable amount and has been charged to the appropriate account. Only after this burden has been sustained will the fiduciary's accounts be approved.

In the case that follows, note the two types of problems it introduces. First, there is the question of a fiduciary's possible duty to insure, arising out of the obligation to protect and benefit potentially diverse interests. This type of problem quite often reflects itself in the investment function, where it affects the selection of properties to be held by the fiduciary. Second, there is the question of how the costs of fulfilling a fiduciary duty are to be borne by the various interests. This is one side of the general principal and income problem, which is a fundamental burden of fiduciary life.

WILLIS v. HENDRY
127 Conn. 653, 20 A.2d 375 (1940)

MALTBIE, C.J. . . .

We are asked whether it is the duty of the trustees to insure the premises given to them in the fourth article against loss by fire, and if so, whether the premium should be apportioned between the widow and the remaindermen. It is the duty of the trustees to exercise that care and prudence which an ordinarily prudent person would who was entrusted with the management of like property for another. . . . It is today a general custom among prudent business men to insure buildings in their charge against loss by fire; and ordinarily it is the duty of trustees holding property for remaindermen to see that such provision is made. . . . We are not informed of any facts in this case which would make inapplicable this rule. The premises are not to become a part of the residuary trust in the will until the widow dies, and, so long as she occupies them, the trustees are without any income from the property with which to pay such charges. The apparent intent of the testator was that the widow should bear all ordinary charges incident to the maintenance of the property so long as she lives on it, and the word "upkeep" is to be so construed. . . . In the absence of any facts taking the case out of the general rule, we advise that it is primarily the duty of the widow to insure the buildings; but if she fails to do so, the trustees should insure them and charge the premiums against her. Should the term of any policy run beyond the life of the widow, the portion of the premium representing the period thereafter would be a charge upon the trustees and the widow's estate would be entitled to reimbursement to the extent. . . .

A. Principal and Income

In the area of principal and income matters there have been many legislative attempts to spell out the rights of the various parties. These statutes on the whole have been helpful, but, as is seen below, many problems remain and new ones have arisen either in spite of or because of the statutory provisions. The administration of a decedent's estate has its principal and income problems and also the related problems of interest and increase. Thus, the interests of residuary beneficiaries are regularly at odds with those of the recipients of specific or general devises. Particular attention is required, however, to trust problems, and legislative efforts emphasized *trust* accounting until the 1997 Uniform Act, which also encompasses decedents' estates.

1. Introductory Matters

a. Typical Principal and Income Issues

The following excerpt provides an overview of common principal and income issues, as well as some basic (especially common law) accounting concepts, but note its date — pre-1997 Uniform Act.

P. HASKELL, PREFACE TO WILLS, TRUSTS & ADMINISTRATION
298-304 (2d ed. 1994)

Assets delivered in trust by the settlor of a living trust are principal. Assets owned by the testator at the date of death allocable to a testamentary trust are [usually] principal. Any gain realized on the sale of principal is principal. If land is held in trust, the net rents are income. If corporate stock is held in trust, the ordinary cash dividends are income. If bonds, debentures, notes, certificates of deposit, or savings accounts are held in trust, the interest received is income.

There is a problem, however, if that which is ordinarily income relates to a period immediately prior to the creation of the living trust, or, in the case of the testamentary trust, the testator's death. Suppose settlor creates a living trust on May 15 consisting of land, bonds and common stock. The rents from the land are payable on the last day of each month for that month. On May 31 the trustee receives the $1,000 rent for May. Approximately half the rent was attributable to the period in May prior to the creation of the trust. That portion appears to have been, in effect, delivered in trust as principal. But that is not the way the common law treated it. At common law, rent did not accrue. That means that it is allocable wholly to principal or wholly to income in accordance with the date on which it was payable. The $1,000 is income because it was payable after the trust was created. By statute in many jurisdictions, however, rent accrues, as described in the next paragraph.

Bond interest accrues. Let us assume that a $1,000 bond delivered in trust on May 15 pays 6% annual interest, one-half on February 15 and one-half on August 15. On August 15 the trustee receives the semi-annual interest payment. Is the entire payment allocable to income? It is not. One half is allocable to income and one-half is allocable to principal. The portion attributable to the period from February 15 to May 15 is deemed to have been delivered in trust as principal. The portion attributable to the period following the creation of the trust is allocable to income. Interest on notes, debentures, certificates of deposit and savings accounts accrue in the same manner.

[Ordinary cash dividends] on corporate stock do not accrue. Suppose 1,000 shares of ABC Corporation common stock was delivered in trust on May 15. On May 1 the board of directors of the corporation declared a dividend of one dollar per share, payable on June 15 to stockholders of record on May 25. The dividend belongs entirely to the trust, and it is wholly allocable to income. Dividends are allocated in accordance with the "stockholder of record" date, regardless of when they are declared or payable. If the dividend was declared on May 1 to stockholders of record on May 14, payable on June 15, the dividend would be paid directly to the settlor because he was the stockholder of record on May 14. If there is no "stockholder of record" date, then the determinative date for these purposes is the date on which the dividend was declared.

The same issue is presented when an income payment is received which relates in part to the period after the death of a life income beneficiary and in part to the period prior thereto. Suppose the life income beneficiary in our previous example dies exactly five years later on May 15, and the remainderman then becomes entitled to the principal. The same assets were held in trust at the life income beneficiary's death, and the same rent, interest and dividend payments were made on the same dates except five years later. Rent payable on May 31 would belong wholly to the remainderman at common law because there is no accrual; under statutes providing for accrual, however, the rent would belong one-half to the life income beneficiary's estate and one-half to the remainderman. The bond interest payment on August 15 would belong one-half to the estate of the income beneficiary and one-half to the remainderman, because bond interest accrues. The dividend payable to stockholders of record on May 25 would belong wholly to the remainderman; a dividend payable to the stockholder of record on May 14, however, would belong wholly to the estate of the income beneficiary. The allocations parallel those which are made at the creation of the trust.

Another problem area has to do with the allocation of income which is received by the executor during the administration of the estate and prior to the distribution to the testamentary trust or trusts. As we have discussed previously, there are three types of testamentary trusts, the specific bequest or devise in trust, the general bequest in trust, and the residuary bequest and devise in trust. If the testator specifically bequeaths 5,000 shares of ABC Corporation common stock in trust, the executor retains the shares during administration and is likely to receive dividends on the shares during the period of administration. Although the trust does not come into existence until the distribution to the trustee, for principal and income purposes the trust is treated as if it came into existence at the date of the testator's death. The dividends received on the shares during administration are distributable to the trustee together with the stock and are payable as income to the income beneficiary. This parallels the treatment of income received during administration on specifically bequeathed property that is not in trust; the specific legatee is entitled to the income earned on the asset during administration.

If the testator makes a general bequest in trust of $200,000, the trust does not come into existence until distribution to the trustee, but for principal and income purposes the trust is treated as if it came into existence at the date of the testator's death. When the executor of the estate distributes the principal to the trustee, he also distributes income which is deemed to have been earned by the $200,000 during the administration of the estate. The principal of the trust is not designated in the will as specific property and is not precisely identifiable during estate administration, and so there is no income that is precisely attributable to the $200,000 that is ultimately transferred to the trustee by the executor. There is allocated, therefore, to the income beneficiary that proportion of the income received on the entire estate, except for specific bequests and devises, that $200,000 bears to such portion of the estate. This is different from the treatment of the $200,000 bequest that is not in trust. The legatee of $200,000 is usually not entitled to interest on the bequest from the date of the testator's death, but in some jurisdictions he is entitled to interest on the bequest at the so-called legal rate after some period of time following the testator's death, [usually] one year.

If the testator creates a residuary trust, for income purposes the trust is treated as if it came into existence at the testator's death. The executor distributes the residue of the estate to the trustee, including the income earned on the estate other than that which is allocated to specific and general bequests. The income is payable by the trustee to the residuary trust income beneficiary. This parallels the treatment of the residuary bequest which is not in trust, where the legatee receives all that is not otherwise distributed including income received during administration.

We have stated previously that ordinary cash dividends are income. Cash dividends, however, which are in partial or total liquidation of the assets of the corporation are usually allocated to principal. There is authority, however, that liquidating cash dividends are to be apportioned between principal and income on the basis of the source of the distribution; that is to say, to the extent that the distribution appears to have been paid out of earnings accrued since the creation of the trust, the distribution is allocated to income, and the rest is allocated to principal. In most states, stock dividends are always principal, but there is limited authority that they are apportioned between principal and income in accordance with the source of the earnings capitalized in connection with the issuance of the stock dividend. Capital gains dividends of investment companies are principal.

Wasting assets also present a principal and income issue. Copyrights and patents are wasting assets because of their limited life. When the period of the copyright or patent expires, there no longer is any value. Copyrights and patents constitute monopolies for a period of time, and during such period revenue is derived because of the monopoly. The copyright or the patent when it is received in trust is principal, and in order to prevent the wasting of that principal, a portion of the revenue received on account of the monopoly during its life should be allocated to principal to maintain its value. The copyright or the patent has a market value at the time it is received in trust, and it is this value which the law attempts to maintain out of the revenues; the income beneficiary is entitled to a reasonable return on that amount which also comes out of the revenues. In other words, the revenues should be allocated in a manner which would produce substantially the same result as if the copyright or patent were immediately sold by the trustee upon receiving it and the proceeds invested in a nonwasting asset such as a bond. Accordingly, from the revenues of the monopoly as received from time to time, an allocation is made between principal and income which provides for a reasonable rate of return, such as 5% per annum, on the market value of the copyright or patent at the time of the creation of the trust.

Mining land is, of course, a wasting asset also. The common law concerning the allocation of revenues between principal and income for trust purposes is rather surprising. If prior to the creation of the trust, a mine or mines were opened, the revenues from such mine or mines during the period of the trust are entirely allocable to income. Revenues derived from mines opened during the period of the trust by the trustee are entirely allocable to principal; the income earned on the revenues derived from the newly opened mines, however, is allocable to the income account. This follows the law of waste as between legal life tenants and remaindermen of mining property, which provides that the life tenant is entitled to exploit previously opened mines for his own benefit, but is forbidden to open any new mines. The Revised Uniform Principal and Income Act [the 1962 Act] §9 provides for an apportionment between income and principal of the revenues of mining property in certain circumstances.

There is also the issue as to whether there should be an allocation to principal from the rents derived from buildings held in trust on account of depreciation. A building is a wasting asset although it usually "wastes" much more gradually than the mining property or the patent. There is authority that with respect to buildings which form a part of the original trust estate, the trustee is not required to allocate a fraction of the rents to a depreciation account for the benefit of the principal beneficiaries. If, however, the trustee purchases a building for the trust, there should be a provision for depreciation out of the rents. The Revised [1962] Act §13 appears to provide for an allocation to principal out of rental income on account of depreciation, regardless of whether the building was part of the original trust estate or was purchased by the trustee.

A bond purchased by the trustee at a premium, that is, at a price in excess of its face value, such as $1100 for a $1000 bond, is a form of wasting asset because the debtor will pay only $1000 to the holder at maturity. The price is $1100 because the interest paid on the bond is higher than the current interest rate in the market for the same quality of security. The value returns to $1000, however, on maturity. The income return calculated on the premium price will be slightly higher than the money market calls for to compensate for the inevitable decline of the value of the bond to $1000 at maturity. In effect, the income beneficiary benefits at the expense of the principal beneficiary. With respect to bonds purchased by the trustee at a premium, there is authority that the trustee should allocate [an appropriate] fraction of the interest received to the principal account to compensate for the wasting nature of the bond, but there are statutes to the contrary. If a bond was part of the original trust estate and had a value above its face value at the establishment of the trust, there is authority that the trustee is not to make any allocation to the principal account out of the interest received.

It should be emphasized that the rules concerning principal and income we have been discussing are all subject to the terms of the trust instrument which may define principal and income differently in one or more respects. For instance, the trust instrument may provide that stock dividends are to be considered income for purposes of the trust, or that bond interest payments payable after the death of the life income beneficiary shall belong to the remainderman regardless of any accrual prior to the death.

Now a few words about the allocation of trust expenses to the principal and income accounts. Interest on mortgage debt, income taxes on ordinary income, and where real estate is held in trust, repairs, insurance and land taxes, are usually charged to income. Payments on the principal of mortgage debt, taxes on capital gains, capital improvements on real estate, and expenses incurred in the acquisition and sale of investments are usually charged to principal. Trustees' fees, expenses of accountings, and expenses of litigation are often split between principal and income. The trust instrument is, of course, controlling if it provides for the charging of a particular expense to income or principal contrary to the rules of law which are otherwise applicable.

What Is Income? Professor Haskell gives some useful examples, but matters are not always as simple as they seem. Principal and income accounting involves three differing concepts of income: (1) fiduciary or trust accounting income; (2) federal income tax accounting income; and (3) generally accepted accounting principles (GAAP) income.

Our focus will be on fiduciary or trust accounting income (TAI) or net accounting income (NAI). These accounting concepts are determined by reference to state law, e.g., a Principal and Income Act. They determine the net amount that a trustee has available for distribution to the "income" beneficiaries (NAI), generally calculated by subtracting total trust expenditures *that are charged to income* from the total trust receipts *that are credited to income.*

For federal income tax purposes, the key concept is that of "distributable net income" (DNI). This is a fundamental tax concept of Subchapter J of the Internal Revenue Code and is used in determining whether an amount of income is ultimately taxable to distributees or to the trust. (Recall the discussion in Chapter 8, section F.2.b, supra.)

Another key concept is "generally accepted accounting principles" (GAAP). For some purposes, what is income or not for business accounting purposes may or may not be treated as having the same character for trust accounting purposes — and properly so. After all, should business purposes necessarily be the same as *trust accounting* purposes? Business accounting purposes do not even control for *tax* purposes — thus, the legitimate and essential maintaining of a "double set of books." *Fiduciary* accounting principles, however, are for the most part honored in determining DNI. On these various definitions of income, see generally B. Abbin, D. Carlson & M. Vorsatz, Income Taxation of Fiduciaries and Beneficiaries §202 (1998 ed.).

b.   Introduction to Principal and Income Legislation

There are three Uniform Principal and Income Acts. The original Act, the "1931 Act," is still in effect in about ten states, often with significant modifications.[1] The Revised Uniform Principal and Income Act, the "1962 Act," is in effect in about thirty jurisdictions, frequently with modifications.[2] In response to the need to modernize the 1962 Act and an increasing understanding of and growing desire for the optimal total-return in trusts encouraged by the prudent investor rule, the Uniform Principal and Income Act (1997) (the "1997 Act") was promulgated by NCCUSL.[3] The 1997 Act has been adopted in about seven states, Oklahoma being the first and California (with significant modifications) being the most prominent. It is scheduled for introduction in other states. A few enactments have deleted or modified §104 (Trustee's Power to Adjust), which is considered in detail, infra. The 1997 Act promises to be the dominant (and probably controversial) influence on principal and income legislation for the foreseeable future. Hence, it affords a frame of reference for our study, although comparisons to the still important 1962 Act and case law will be made from time to time.

The 1959 Restatement (Second) of Trusts also covers principal and income issues and sometimes differs from the 1962 Act. The principal and income provisions of the Restatement (Third) of Trusts remain to be drafted, although some of the completed portions of the Third Restatement, for example the Prudent Investor Rule and its associated revisions, bear on principal and income issues.

c. Related Problems of Decedents' Estates

For purposes of the present subject and certain other matters it is often important to classify bequests and devises (or simply devises). Classification was considered in Chapter 11, section A. Briefly, a *specific* devise is a gift of a particular thing or parcel of land, such as a devise of Blackacre or of "my twenty-five shares of Acme Corp. stock." A *general* devise is one payable out of the general assets of the estate, typified by a legacy (a stated or formula sum of money). A devise of "twenty-five shares of Acme Corp. stock" would be general if the testator intended the executor to purchase the shares out of the general funds

---

1. See generally C. Clark, Interpretation of Proposed Uniform Principal and Income Act, 54 Tr. Co. 723 (1932).

2. A discussion of the pros and cons of the 1962 Act can be found in J. Gamble, The Revised Principal and Income Act (Mich. Inst. Contin. Legal Ed. 1966). Mr. Gamble was Co-Reporter (with Professor Joel Dobris of the University of California–Davis) for the *1997* Act.

3. For an explication of the 1997 Act, see J. Gamble, If It's the 1990s, It Must Be Time for Another Principal and Income Act, 32 U. of Miami Inst. on Est. Plan. ch. 8 (1998). See also Keister & McCarthy, 1997 Principal and Income Act Reflects Modern Trust Investing, 26 Est. Plan. 99 (March/April 1999).

of the estate. The term *residuary* devise is more or less self-explanatory. A *demonstrative* devise is a hybrid, usually a legacy, payable from a particular source, and if that source is insufficient then out of the general assets of the estate.

A specific devise normally carries with it any increments that are not separable from the property itself. The devisee is also entitled to the income from specifically devised property *after* the death of the testator. Because the devisee is not entitled to income received by the testator during life, it becomes necessary to know what receipts by the testator constitute *income* from, rather than the *principal* of, the property involved.

There are also problems of when income is deemed to arise, because the specific devisee gets only the income after the death of the testator. Certain general rules have been developed for application in the absence of provision to the contrary in a will or statute. For example, *interest,* as distinguished from other forms of income, is "earned from day to day" for purposes of apportioning receipts between income and principal at the beginning of a trust or at the termination of a right to trust income. At common law, a devisee is entitled to rent becoming due after the testator's death, even though it might cover a period preceding death, but is not entitled to rent payable in advance during the testator's lifetime. Statutes now generally apportion rents received after the testator's death, but compare Article 2 of the Uniform Principal and Income Act (1997). Dividends declared to *stockholders of record* during the testator's lifetime, though paid to the executor or administrator, are held not to pass to the devisee of the specifically devised stock.

Unless the contrary is provided by will, legacies (general devises) are usually held to bear interest at the legal rate beginning a year after the death of the testator, or, under some statutory rules, as of some other date. At common law and by statute, exceptions are typically recognized for devises in payment of debts, in lieu of dower, or for support of a minor child, and frequently for the creation of testamentary trusts under which the income is payable to a designated beneficiary. In the exceptional cases interest commences at death.

Because income received by the personal representative and not allocable to specific devises enlarges the residue, and because interest charges are borne by the residuary estate, residuary gifts do not bear interest.

Where Devisee Is a Trustee.   The income beneficiary of a trust is ordinarily entitled to the earnings of the trust property commencing with the testator's death. Generally speaking, specific and general gifts in trust cause no difficulty because the earnings accruing to the trustee (as devisee) under the above rules are simply allocated to the income beneficiary in most states. On the other hand, if the trust is residuary, as is typically the case in modern wills, the determination of income and principal for the period of estate administration is likely to become more complex. There is disagreement among the cases regarding the rights of income and the remainder beneficiaries on a variety of matters.

PROBLEMS

19-A.   The decedent died leaving a gross estate of $550,000 and a will bequeathing:

1. My 1,000 shares of stock in W.G. Corporation to *G.*
2. $20,000 to *A.*
3. $100,000 to *X* Trust Co. to pay the income to *B* for life, remainder to *C.*
4. $100,000 to *Y* Trust Co. to pay the income to *D* for life, remainder to *D*'s surviving children or their issue by representation.
5. Residue to *T* Trust Co. to pay the income to *E* for life, remainder to *F.*

(1) At the end of one year, the executor delivered 1,000 shares of W.G. Corporation stock (worth $25,000) to *G* and paid $100,000 to *X* Trust Co. in trust for *B* and *C.* (2) At the end of eighteen months, the executor paid $20,000 to *A* and $100,000 to *Y* Trust Co. to fund the *D* family trust. (3) Then at the end of twenty-four months, the executor paid $150,000 in debts, costs of administration and taxes, and is now ready to distribute the residue to *T* Trust Co.

The estate earned income of:

(a) $6,000 in the first year after the decedent's death, including a $500 cash dividend on the W.G. stock;
(b) $13,000 during the period from twelve to eighteen months after the decedent's death; and
(c) $10,000 during the period eighteen to twenty-four months after decedent's death.

How are these items of income to be accounted for in a state that has adopted the 1997 Act? In your state? Are interest payments due to any of the beneficiaries?

19-B.   In Problem 19-A above, suppose instead that the decedent had no will but made the same gifts under a revocable living trust reserving the income to the decedent for life, remainder as provided in the problem. The 1931 and 1962 Acts did not cover this situation. What result under the 1997 Act? In your state? Are interest payments due to any of the beneficiaries?

TILGHMAN v. FRAZER
199 Md. 620, 87 A.2d 812 (1950)

MARKELL, J. . . .

The basic question now before us is whether, as between life tenant and remainderman, in the absence of indication of a contrary intent by the testator, income received, during the period of administration, from that part of the testator's assets which eventually was sold and used to pay debts, administration expenses and legacies, goes to the life tenant as income, or, together with the assets so sold and used, is part of the corpus. This question was decided by this court, by holding that such income goes to corpus, fifty-eight years ago. Wethered v. Safe Deposit and Trust Co., (1894) 79 Md. 153, 28 A. 812. . . .

The *Wethered* case was followed in [York v. Maryland Trust Co., 150 Md. 354, 133 A. 128 (1926)], in which the court said,

> We do not find in the testator's will any expression of intention that the debts should be paid from income, but we do think there is an indication that the wife was only to receive the income from the residue of the estate, after the payment of the debts, and under these circumstances it is clear that the rules laid down in the *Wethered* case and the other authorities heretofore cited should apply, and these rules are: (1) that the debts and expenses are payable from the corpus and not from the income; and, (2) that where a life tenant is entitled to the income, such income, in the absence of a contrary intention expressed in the will, is confined to that received from the residue, and does not ordinarily include the income derived from that part of the principal used to pay debts, expenses and specific legacies. It accordingly follows that in this case the . . . items should have been charged against the corpus of the estate, but it also follows that, since there was no contrary intention expressed in the will, the life tenant was not entitled to receive the dividends derived from the securities sold to pay the testator's debts. . . .

Long since the *Wethered* case . . . a conflict in the authorities has developed. In the greater number of jurisdictions the law is in accord with the Maryland law, but a few jurisdictions have adopted a so-called "Massachusetts rule," which is at variance with the "general," or Maryland, or former New York, or "English" rule. In [Proctor v. American Security and Trust Co., 98 F.2d 599, 601–606] the court, by Judge Vinson, said,

It is fair to say that there are two irreconcilable rules which have grown up in this country in respect to the point involved. There is the general rule, supported by the decided weight of authority in this country, and, likewise, the English cases, that the earnings upon testator's property, derived during the course of administration, used to pay costs of administration, debts and legacies, if not disposed of by the express terms of the will, are added to the residuary trust as part of its corpus. Then there is the so-called Massachusetts rule, which crystallized in 1929 (Old Colony Trust Co. v. Smith, 266 Mass. 500, 165 N.E. 657), which holds that the earnings upon testator's property used to pay costs of administration, debts and legacies derived during the course of administration, if not disposed of by the express terms of the will, are distributable to the life beneficiaries as income. The general rule finds support in the courts of New York, Maryland, Connecticut, Kentucky, New Hampshire, Delaware, New Jersey and the English cases. The Massachusetts rule is followed in the courts of Rhode Island and North Carolina.

In New York the former rule was changed by statute. Laws of 1931, c. 706, Personal Property Law, sec. 17-b, McK. Consol. Laws, c. 41. In Maryland the Act of 1949, ch. 672, Code, Art. 93, sec. 372, apparently modeled after the New York statute, is applicable only to testators who die after the passage of the act. Appellant says the Act of 1949 substitutes the Massachusetts rule for the *Wethered* case. As to the construction or operation of the Act of 1949 we express no opinion.

The merit of the Massachusetts rule is simplicity, i.e., it can be applied, without the use of arithmetical — or algebraical — formulas in more or less complicated computations. The defects of the rule are that it (1) is unsound in principle in distributing, as income of the residue, income from property that never was part of the residue, and (2) consequently is unsound in practice in giving the life tenant more income from the initial year or years than for subsequent years. When administration of an estate is promptly completed the defects of the rule are often mitigated by the circumstance that the difference between the results of the two rules is small. In the instant case the results of the defects of the rule are magnified by the inordinate delay in administering the estate.

This court has not had occasion to express in a formula the principle established and applied in the *Wethered* and *York* cases. In the instant case the auditor followed the formula stated in Section 234, comment *g*, of the Restatement of Trusts:

> *g. Income on property used in paying legacies, debts and expenses.* To the extent to which the income received by the executor during the period of administration is derived from property which is subsequently used in paying legacies and discharging debts and expenses of administration,

and has not been applied to the payment of interest on such legacies, debts and expenses, the trustee is entitled to receive the same, but it should be added to principal and not paid to the beneficiary entitled to income. A proper method of determining the extent to which legacies, debts and expenses of administration should be paid out of principal is by ascertaining the amount which with interest thereon at the rate of return received by the executor upon the whole estate from the death of the testator to the dates of payment would equal the amounts paid. This amount is charged to principal and the balance of the amount paid is charged to income.

Illustrations: 3. *A* bequeathes $30,000 to *B* and all the residue of his property to *C* in trust to pay the income to *D* for life and on *D*'s death to pay the principal to *E*. The value of *A*'s estate at his death is $100,000. During the year after his death the income received by his executor is $5,000. At the expiration of the year the executor pays the legacy of $30,000 to *B* and pays $10,000 in discharging *A*'s debts and the expenses of administration. Of the $40,000 so paid, $38,095.23 (the sum which with interest at five percent for one year would equal $40,000) is charged to principal, and $1,904.77 is charged to income. *D* is entitled to receive as income for the first year after *A*'s death $3,095.23; the remainder of the estate amounting to $61,904.77 is principal of the trust estate. . . .

The auditor followed the correct method. . . .

Order affirmed and cause remanded, costs to be paid by appellant individually.

In drawing wills, lawyers often find it desirable to include special provisions covering questions of the types raised above. For example, it is not uncommon for drafters to make special provision to prevent the "doubling up" of payments to a surviving spouse that results from the recurring situation in which the spouse is entitled to (1) an allowance from the decedent's estate for support during the period of estate administration and (2) the income of the residuary trust created by the decedent's will. Compare In re King's Estate, 367 Mich. 503, 116 N.W.2d 897 (1962), where the widow was to receive a stated amount monthly from the trust under her husband's will and was also awarded a monthly allowance for the statutory period of one year during probate. Although recognizing that the testator could provide for a different result, the court held that the widow was entitled to both payments for the period of her allowance. Even though an annuity or a right to trust income generally runs from the date of the testator's death, actual payment to the beneficiary is usually not made until the estate is distributed by the executor to the trustee. Typically, however, courts of probate can authorize preliminary distributions before completion of administration under appropriate circumstances.

UNIFORM PRINCIPAL AND INCOME ACT
(1997)

§201. *Determination and Distribution of Net Income.*

After a decedent dies, in the case of an estate, or after an income interest in a trust ends, the following rules apply:

(1) A fiduciary of an estate or of a terminating income interest shall determine the amount of net income and net principal receipts received from property specifically given to a beneficiary under the rules in [Articles] 3 through 5 which apply to trustees and the rules in paragraph (5). The fiduciary shall distribute the net income and net principal receipts to the beneficiary who is to receive the specific property.

(2) A fiduciary shall determine the remaining net income of a decedent's estate or a terminating income interest under the rules in [Articles] 3 through 5 which apply to trustees and by:

(A) including in net income all income from property used to discharge liabilities;

(B) paying from income or principal, in the fiduciary's discretion, fees of attorneys, accountants, and fiduciaries; court costs and other expenses of administration; and interest on death taxes, but the fiduciary may pay those expenses from income of property passing to a trust for which the fiduciary claims an estate tax marital or charitable deduction only to the extent that the payment of those expenses from income will not cause the reduction or loss of the deduction; and

(C) paying from principal all other disbursements made or incurred in connection with the settlement of a decedent's estate or the winding up of a terminating income interest, including debts, funeral expenses, disposition of remains, family allowances, and death taxes and related penalties that are apportioned to the estate or terminating income interest by the will, the terms of the trust, or applicable law.

(3) A fiduciary shall distribute to a beneficiary who receives a pecuniary amount outright the interest or any other amount provided by the will, the terms of the trust, or applicable law from net income determined under paragraph (2) or from principal to the extent that net income is insufficient. If a beneficiary is to receive a pecuniary amount outright from a trust after an income interest ends and no interest or other amount is provided for by the terms of the trust or applicable law, the fiduciary shall distribute the interest or other amount to which the beneficiary would be entitled under applicable law if the pecuniary amount were required to be paid under a will.

(4) A fiduciary shall distribute the net income remaining after distributions required by paragraph (3) in the manner described in Section 202 to all other beneficiaries, including a beneficiary who receives a pecuniary amount in trust, even if the beneficiary holds an unqualified power to withdraw assets from the trust or other presently exercisable general power of appointment over the trust.

(5) A fiduciary may not reduce principal or income receipts from property described in paragraph (1) because of a payment described in Section 501 or 502 to the extent that the will, the terms of the trust, or applicable law requires the fiduciary to make the payment from assets other than the property or to the extent that the fiduciary recovers or expects to recover the payment from a third party. The net income and principal receipts from the property are determined by including all of the amounts the fiduciary receives or pays with respect to the property, whether those amounts accrued or became due before, on, or after the date of a decedent's death or an income interest's terminating event, and by making a reasonable provision for amounts that the fiduciary believes the estate or terminating income interest may become obligated to pay after the property is distributed.

§202.   *Distribution to Residuary and Remainder
        Beneficiaries.*

(a) Each beneficiary described in Section 201(4) is entitled to receive a portion of the net income equal to the beneficiary's fractional interest in undistributed principal assets, using values as of the distribution date. If a fiduciary makes more than one distribution of assets to beneficiaries to whom this section applies, each beneficiary, including one who does not receive part of the distribution, is entitled, as of each distribution date, to the net income the fiduciary has received after the date of death or terminating event or earlier distribution date but has not distributed as of the current distribution date.

(b) In determining a beneficiary's share of net income, the following rules apply:

(1) The beneficiary is entitled to receive a portion of the net income equal to the beneficiary's fractional interest in the undistributed principal assets immediately before the distribution date, including assets that later may be sold to meet principal obligations.

(2) The beneficiary's fractional interest in the undistributed principal assets must be calculated without regard to property specifically given to a beneficiary and property required to pay pecuniary amounts not in trust.

(3) The beneficiary's fractional interest in the undistributed principal assets must be calculated on the basis of the aggregate value of those assets as of the distribution date without reducing the value by any unpaid principal obligation.

(4) The distribution date for purposes of this section may be the date as of which the fiduciary calculates the value of the assets if that date is reasonably near the date on which assets are actually distributed.

(c) If a fiduciary does not distribute all of the collected but undistributed net income to each person as of a distribution date, the fiduciary shall maintain appropriate records showing the interest of each beneficiary in that net income.

(d) A fiduciary may apply the rules in this section, to the extent that the fiduciary considers it appropriate, to net gain or loss realized after the date of death or terminating event or earlier distribution date from the disposition of a principal asset if this section applies to the income from the asset.

Notice the wording in the first sentence of §202(a), "using values as of the distribution date." This is a change from §5(b)(2) of the 1962 Act, which used inventory values. Why do you suppose the drafters changed the valuation date?

PROBLEM

19-C.   A testator created a trust to pay the income to her husband, *H,* for life, then to pay the income to her children for life, remainder to her grandchildren. The trust property included: (1) an interest-bearing bank account that paid interest on the 15th day of each month; (2) a promissory note that paid interest on the 20th day of each month; and (3) rental property for which rent was due on the 25th of each month. Assume that *H* died on July 31. At that time: (1) the July 15 bank account interest had been received by the trustee but not yet distributed to *H;* (2) a check for the July 20 promissory note interest had been mailed on time but not yet received; and (3) the July 25 rent had not been paid. The check for the July 20 interest was received on August 2. The July 25 rent was paid on August 4. The August payments due in August for all three obligations were made on time. *H* died owing substantial debts and leaving a will that devised his entire estate to the State University Athletic Foundation. How should these items be accounted for in a state that has adopted the 1997 Act? See 1997 Act §303, Comment. How should these items be accounted for in your state?

As a drafter, what language might you provide in the will to cover these kinds of situations? Compare Appeal of New Britain Bank & Trust Co., 39 Conn. Supp. 157, 472 A.2d 1305 (1983) (deceased wife/life tenant's estate entitled to income accrued but not actually received by trustees at the time of the life tenant's death, despite direction in trust "to pay over the net income to or for the maintenance or support of my wife . . . during the term of her natural life); Davidson's Estate, 287 Pa. 354, 135 A. 130 (1926) (similar result, despite direction in trust that the "interest arising from [the trust property] . . . shall every three months be divided into nine equal shares," four of which were to be paid to the wife/life tenant "while she lives and remains my widow"); W. McGovern, S. Kurtz & J. Rein, Wills, Trusts and Estates Including Taxation and Future Interests 686–687 (1988).

UNIFORM PRINCIPAL AND INCOME ACT
(1997)

§301. *When Right to Income Begins and Ends.*

(a) An income beneficiary is entitled to net income from the date on which the income interest begins. An income interest begins on the date specified in the terms of the trust or, if no date is specified, on the date an asset becomes subject to a trust or successive income interest.

(b) An asset becomes subject to a trust:

(1) on the date it is transferred to the trust in the case of an asset that is transferred to a trust during the transferor's life;

(2) on the date of a testator's death in the case of an asset that becomes subject to a trust by reason of a will, even if there is an intervening period of administration of the testator's estate; or

(3) on the date of an individual's death in the case of an asset that is transferred to a fiduciary by a third party because of the individual's death.

(c) An asset becomes subject to a successive income interest on the day after the preceding income interest ends, as determined under subsection (d), even if there is an intervening period of administration to wind up the preceding income interest.

(d) An income interest ends on the day before an income beneficiary dies or another terminating event occurs, or on the last day of a period during which there is no beneficiary to whom a trustee may distribute income.

§302. *Apportionment of Receipts and Disbursements When Decedent Dies or Income Interest Begins.*

(a) A trustee shall allocate an income receipt or disbursement other than one to which Section 201(1) applies to principal if its due date occurs before a decedent dies in the case of an estate or before an income interest begins in the case of a trust or successive income interest.

(b) A trustee shall allocate an income receipt or disbursement to income if its due date occurs on or after the date on which a decedent dies or an income interest begins and it is a periodic due date. An income receipt or disbursement must be treated as accruing from day to day if its due date is not periodic or it has no due date. The portion of the receipt or disbursement accruing before the date on which a decedent dies or an income interest begins must be allocated to principal and the balance must be allocated to income.

(c) An item of income or an obligation is due on the date the payer is required to make a payment. If a payment date is not stated, there is no due date for the purposes of this [Act]. Distributions to shareholders or other owners from an entity to which Section 401 applies are deemed to be due on the date fixed by the entity for determining who is entitled to receive the distribution or, if no date is fixed, on the declaration date for the distribution. A due date is periodic for receipts or disbursements that must be paid at regular intervals under a lease or an obligation to pay interest or if an entity customarily makes distributions at regular intervals.

§303. *Apportionment When Income Interest Ends.*

(a) In this section, "undistributed income" means net income received before the date on which an income interest ends. The term does not include an item of income or expense that is due or accrued or net income that has been added or is required to be added to principal under the terms of the trust.

(b) When a mandatory income interest ends, the trustee shall pay to a mandatory income beneficiary who survives that date, or the estate of a deceased mandatory income beneficiary whose death causes the interest to end, the beneficiary's share of the undistributed income that is not disposed of under the terms of the trust unless the beneficiary has an unqualified power to revoke more than five percent of the trust immediately before the income interest ends. In the latter case, the undistributed income from the portion of the trust that may be revoked must be added to principal.

(c) When a trustee's obligation to pay a fixed annuity or a fixed fraction of the value of the trust's assets ends, the trustee shall prorate the final payment if and to the extent required by applicable law to accomplish a purpose of the trust or its settlor relating to income, gift, estate, or other tax requirements.

2.   General Principles: Trust Estates

UNIFORM PRINCIPAL AND INCOME ACT
(1997)

§102.   *Definitions. In this [Act]:* . . .

(12) "Terms of a trust" means the manifestation of the intent of a settlor or decedent with respect to the trust, expressed in a manner that admits of its proof in a judicial proceeding, whether by written or spoken words or by conduct.[4]

§103.   *Fiduciary Duties; General Principles.*

(a) In allocating receipts and disbursements to or between principal and income, and with respect to any matter within the scope of [Articles] 2 and 3, a fiduciary:

(1) shall administer a trust or estate in accordance with the terms of the trust or the will, even if there is a different provision in this [Act];

(2) may administer a trust or estate by the exercise of a discretionary power of administration given to the fiduciary by the terms of the trust or the will, even if the exercise of the power produces a result different from a result required or permitted by this [Act];

(3) shall administer a trust or estate in accordance with this [Act] if the terms of the trust or the will do not contain a different provision or do not give the fiduciary a discretionary power of administration; and

(4) shall add a receipt or charge a disbursement to principal to the extent that the terms of the trust and this [Act] do not provide a rule for allocating the receipt or disbursement to or between principal and income.

(b) In exercising the power to adjust under Section 104(a) or a discretionary power of administration regarding a matter within the scope of this [Act], whether granted by the terms of a trust, a will, or this

---

4.   Restatement (Third) of Trusts §4 (Tent. Draft, approved 1996); Uniform Trust Code §103(20) (Draft, Feb. 2000), and Restatement (Second) of Trusts §4 are similar. See also Restatement (Third) of Property: Wills & Other Donative Transfers §11.3 (Tent. Draft, approved 1995).

[Act], a fiduciary shall administer a trust or estate impartially, based on what is fair and reasonable to all of the beneficiaries, except to the extent that the terms of the trust or the will clearly manifest an intention that the fiduciary shall or may favor one or more of the beneficiaries. A determination in accordance with this [Act] is presumed to be fair and reasonable to all of the beneficiaries.

The Prefatory Note to the 1997 Act begins: "This revision of [the 1931 and 1962 Acts] has two purposes." One is to revise the content of those Acts to reflect "the now widespread use of the revocable living trust as a will substitute, to change the rules in those Acts that experience has shown need to be changed, and to establish new rules to cover situations not provided for in the old Acts, including rules that apply to financial instruments invented since 1962." The other purpose is to support "investment regime[s] based on principles embodied in the Uniform Prudent Investor Act, especially [the principles that make it permissible for trustees to invest] for total return rather than [for a suitable] level of 'income' as traditionally perceived in terms of interest, dividends, and rents." On the first of the above purposes, the *Prefatory Note* explains:

> The prior Acts and this revision of those Acts deal with four questions affecting the rights of beneficiaries:
>
> (1) How is income earned during the probate of an estate to be distributed to trusts and to persons who receive outright [devises] of specific property, pecuniary gifts, and the residue?
>
> (2) When an income interest in a trust begins (i.e., when a person who creates the trust dies or when she transfers property to a trust during life), what property is principal that will eventually go to the remainder beneficiaries and what is income?
>
> (3) When an income interest ends, who gets the income that has been received but not distributed, or that is due but not yet collected, or that has accrued but is not yet due?
>
> (4) After an income interest begins and before it ends, how should its receipts and disbursements be allocated to or between principal and income?
>
> ... **New Rules** ... deal with situations not covered by the prior Acts. ...
>
> (1) The application of the probate administration rules to revocable living trusts after the settlor's death and to other terminating trusts. Articles 2 and 3.
>
> (2) The payment of interest or some other amount on the delayed payment of an outright pecuniary gift that is made pursuant to a trust

agreement instead of a will when the agreement or state law does not provide for such a payment. Section 201(3).

(3) The allocation of net income from partnership interests acquired by the trustee other than from a decedent (the old Acts deal only with partnership interests acquired from a decedent). Section 401.

(4) An "unincorporated entity" concept has been introduced to deal with businesses operated by a trustee, including farming and livestock operations, and investment activities in rental real estate, natural resources, timber, and derivatives. Section 403.

(5) The allocation of receipts from discount obligations such as zero-coupon bonds. Section 406(b).

(6) The allocation of net income from harvesting and selling timber between principal and income. Section 412.

(7) The allocation between principal and income of receipts from derivatives, options, and asset-backed securities. Sections 414 and 415.

(8) Disbursements made because of environmental laws. Section 502(a)(7).

(9) Income tax obligations resulting from the ownership of S corporation stock and interests in partnerships. Section 505.

(10) The power to make adjustments between principal and income to correct inequities caused by tax elections or peculiarities in the way the fiduciary income tax rules apply. Section 506.

Clarifications and changes in existing rules. A number of matters provided for in the prior Acts have been changed or clarified in this revision, including the following:

(1) An income beneficiary's estate will be entitled to receive only net income actually received by a trust before the beneficiary's death and not items of accrued income. Section 303.

(2) Income from a partnership is based on actual distributions from the partnership, in the same manner as corporate distributions. Section 401.

(3) Distributions from corporations and partnerships that exceed 20% of the entity's gross assets will be principal whether or not intended by the entity to be a partial liquidation. Section 401(d)(2).

(4) Deferred compensation is dealt with in greater detail in a separate section. Section 409.

(5) The 1962 Act rule for "property subject to depletion," (patents, copyrights, royalties, and the like), which provides that a trustee may allocate up to 5% of the asset's inventory value to income and the balance to principal, has been replaced by a rule that allocates 90% of the *amounts received* to principal and the balance to income. Section 410. [Emphasis added]

(6) The percentage used to allocate amounts received from oil and gas has been changed — 90% of those receipts are allocated to principal and the balance to income. Section 411.

(7) The unproductive property rule has been eliminated for trusts other than marital deduction trusts. Section 413.

(8) Charging depreciation against income is no longer mandatory, and is left to the discretion of the trustee. Section 503.

Coordination with the Uniform Prudent Investor Act

[Trust investment law recently] has been modernized [in most of the states]. See Uniform Prudent Investor Act (1994); Restatement (Third) of Trusts: Prudent Investor Rule (1992). Now it is time to update the principal and income allocation rules so the two bodies of doctrine can work well together. This revision deals conservatively with the tension between modern investment theory and traditional income allocation. The starting point is to use the traditional system. If prudent investing of all the assets in a trust viewed as a portfolio and traditional allocation effectuate the intent of the settlor, then nothing need be done. The Act, however, helps the trustee who has made a prudent, modern portfolio-based investment decision that has the initial effect of skewing return from all the assets under management, viewed as a portfolio, as between income and principal beneficiaries. The Act gives that trustee a power to reallocate the portfolio return suitably. To leave a trustee constrained by the traditional system would inhibit the trustee's ability to fully implement modern portfolio theory.

See further on modernized trust investment law and underlying investment principles: the Preface and commentary to the Uniform Prudent Investor Act, supra; the commentary to the Restatement 3d: Prudent Investor Rule, supra, and the discussion in the §227 Reporter's Notes by E. Halbach, Jr.; and J. Langbein, The Uniform Prudent Investor Act and the Future of Trust Investing, 81 Iowa L. Rev. 641 (1996). On earlier law or underlying investment principles, see Bevis Longstreth's critique of prior law, Modern Investment Management and the Prudent Man Rule (1986), the reviews of underlying principles in R.A. Brealy, An Introduction to Risk and Return from Common Stocks (2d ed. 1983), and Jonathan Macey, An Introduction to Modern Financial Theory (2d ed. 1998). On the related need for principal and income reform, see R. Wolf, Defeating the Duty to Disappoint Equally — the Total Return Trust, 23 ACTEC Notes 46 (1997); W. Hoisington, Modern Trust Design: New Paradigms for the 21st Century, 31 U. of Miami Heckerling Inst. on Est. Plan. ch. 6 (1997); J. Horn, Prudent Investor Rule, Modern Portfolio Theory, and Private Trusts: Drafting and Administration Including the "Give-Me-Five" Unitrust, 33 Real Prop., Prob. & Tr. J. 1 (1998); and the valuable, somewhat contrarian, J. Garland, The Problems With Unitrusts, 1 J. Private Portfolio Mgmt. no. 4 (1999).

At the early stages of preparing both the 1962 and 1997 Acts, the drafting committee considered but rejected a one-sentence principal and income act that would have provided something like: "The trustee shall reasonably allocate receipts and disbursements to principal and income." Why do you suppose this approach has twice been rejected? Also, the drafting committee for the 1997 Act considered but rejected providing, instead of the adjustment power in id. §104, a default rule that would treat a right to trust income as a right to a unitrust interest of some statutory percentage. Why do you suppose this approach was rejected?

a.   Trustee's Discretionary Allocation Power Granted by Instrument

If a trustee is given by the terms of the trust "the power exercisable in the trustee's discretion to allocate receipts and disbursements to income or principal," and the trustee charges to income a disbursement for a capital improvement on income-producing trust land that under the 1997 Act would ordinarily be allocated to principal, is there an inference of abuse of the power? Compare the 1962 Act §2(b) language that "no inference of imprudence or impartiality arises from the fact that the trustee has made an allocation contrary to the provisions of the Act." See also Dumaine v. Dumaine (below), and Sherman v. Sherman and State Street Trust Co. v. United States (both noted below). But see Englund v. First National Bank, 381 So. 2d 8 (Ala. 1980) (discretionary power did not extend to allocating capital gains to income beneficiary, where proper allocation was not a matter of doubt). Compare Robinson v. Commissioner, 75 T.C. 346 (1980) (trustee-beneficiary's allocation power not a taxable general power because of trustee's duty to treat remainder beneficiaries fairly); State Street Trust Co. v. United States, 263 F.2d 635 (1st Cir. 1959) (broad investment and principal/income allocation powers together constituted taxable general power), *overruled,* Old Colony Trust Co. v. United States, 423 F.2d 601 (1st Cir. 1970) (*semble*); Restatement (Second) of Trusts §187; Id. §233, cmt. *p.*

PROBLEM

19-D.   In Dumaine v. Dumaine, below, suppose the trustee offers two reasons for his allocation of capital gains to income: (1) The stock investments had been underproductive of income but had grown in market value because of a combination of inflated markets and corporate policies to retain earnings; (2) The remainder beneficiaries were significantly wealthier than the two income beneficiaries, who were closer to the settlor, had more need for the money and would make better use of it. Would either of these reasons be an appropriate justification for the trustee's allocation? After 1997?

DUMAINE v. DUMAINE
301 Mass. 214, 16 N.E.2d 625 (1938)

. . . The sole question for determination is the power of the trustee under the following clause of the trust indenture:

> The trustee under this instrument shall have full power and discretion to determine whether any money or other property received by him is principal or income without being answerable to any person for the manner in which he shall exercise that discretion.

Frederic C. Dumaine, Jr., the plaintiff trustee, and Frederic C. Dumaine, Sr., a defendant, are the life tenants under the trust indenture, and the [other] trustees of "Dumaines," defendants, are the remaindermen. By the terms of the trust instrument certain property was conveyed to the plaintiff in trust "[t]o hold, manage, invest and reinvest the same with all the powers hereinafter set forth, and, after paying the expenses of administering the trust in this instrument set forth," to pay the net income as therein directed. The trustee is not required to give any bond, and

> [n]o trustee under this instrument shall ever be held responsible for any act or omission of any other person nor for any loss or depreciation of any of the trust property unless such loss or depreciation shall have been directly caused by his own dishonesty or gross negligence. . . . He shall not be responsible for any loss which may occur if he shall have in his absolute and uncontrolled discretion mortgaged, pledged or otherwise encumbered any of the property of this trust fund for the benefit of "Dumaines."

Absolute and uncontrolled discretion is given the trustee as to the purchase and retention of securities. . . .

Our inquiry will be limited to the question raised by the amendment to the bill, that is, whether the trustee may, in his discretion, distribute to himself, as life tenant, as income, the profit derived by the sale of certain shares of stock in 1938, over and above their cost. The general rule is that, in case of a trust, gains resulting from the purchase and sale of securities are accretions belonging to the principal of the trust fund, rather than income. . . .

The defendant trustees do not appear to argue that a settlor has no power to confer a discretion upon his trustees to determine what is income and what is principal, but do contend that, under the trust instrument in question, the trustee has no power to determine, contrary to established rules of law in this Commonwealth, what money or other property received by him as trustee is principal or income. This court has uniformly held that trustees in whom a discretion is vested are under an obligation to exercise a "sound judgment and a reasonable and prudent discretion," Davis, appellant, 183 Mass. 499, 502; that kind of "power and discretion which inheres in a fiduciary relation and not that illimitable potentiality which an unrestrained individual possesses respecting his own property," Corkery v. Dorsey, 223 Mass. 97, 101; a "soundness of judgment which follows from a due appreciation of trust responsibility," Boyden v. Stevens, 285 Mass. 176, 179, unless the settlor has expressed an intention that the power of discretion conferred is such that "the court will not interfere except upon clear proof that the trustees are abusing their authority and acting in perversion of the trust." . . .

On the other hand "full power and discretion" to determine whether any money or other property received by the trustee is principal or income, in the light of attendant circumstances and the language of the trust instrument as a whole, would have little significance if construed to mean a discretion so to determine only in cases where there is no settled law to guide. By the terms of the trust instrument he is to have that power and discretion "without being answerable to any person for the manner in which he shall exercise that discretion."

The court may properly have in mind that, when a settlor reposes a discretion in a trustee, he does so because he desires the honest judgment of the trustee, perhaps even to the exclusion of that of the court. In reposing a discretion he must be held to have known that human judgment is not infallible. It is not for the court to read into a trust instrument provisions which do not expressly appear or which do not arise by implication from the plain meaning of the words used, and the court will not substitute its discretion for that of the trustee except when necessary to prevent an abuse of discretion. It has been said that doubtless a trust might be created which by its terms would make his judgment, however unwise it might be, the final test.

The power, if uncontrollable, to determine whether any money or other property received by the trustee is principal or income, coupled with the power to pay over to the present life tenant so much of the net income as in his absolute and uncontrolled discretion he shall determine, would give the trustee power to destroy the trust. The settlor has no such intention. In deciding the question which is before us, we think that the scope of our inquiry properly embraces the needs of the life tenants, the continuance of the trust until its manifest purposes are accomplished, and the protection and well-being of the "Dumaines," of which latter trust the plaintiff is not only a trustee but also a beneficiary. We do not think the clause in issue confers an absolute and uncontrolled discretion. Nor do we think that it limits the trustee to the determination of the matter involved in cases where there is a question of doubt or no rule of law to guide him. We have nothing before us to show the amount of the trust fund. The trust known as "Dumaines" was created on July 31, 1920, twelve years prior to the trust involved. It made immediate provisions for the children of Frederic C. Dumaine, with ultimate provisions for a substantial educational charity. The power is reserved, in the trust before us, in Frederic C. Dumaine, to make additions to the trust property, and to appoint other trustees instead of or in addition to the one named in the instrument. The trust known as "Dumaines" stands out as an important consideration in the mind of the settlor of the trust before us. Clearly he contemplated no destruction of his trust by any discretionary act of the trustee. But he did intend to give the trustee a power to determine what was principal and income, although he refrained from conferring that power as an absolute and uncontrolled discretion, and we regard this as significant, in the light shed upon the inquiry by a consideration of all factors. The discretion conferred is not an empty one. It confers an important responsibility to make a determination which, if honestly exercised, calls for no revision by the court. Am. Law Inst. Restatement: Trusts, §§187, 233. . . .

Upon consideration of the entire matter, we are of the opinion that the trustee under the clause in question has full power and discretion, after serious and responsible consideration, short of arbitrary or dishonest conduct or bad faith or fraud, when he has to determine whether any money or other property received by him is principal or income; and that upon this record there is nothing disclosed to prevent him from distributing to himself, in his personal capacity, the profit derived during the year 1938 as the result of selling certain shares of stock, a part of the trust property, at a price "over and above cost." . . .

Ordered accordingly.

In Sherman v. Sherman, 5 Ohio St. 2d 27, 213 N.E.2d 360 (1966), the question before the court was whether, for purposes of a clause giving trustees "discretion" to allocate "all receipts" between principal and income, certain stock dividends (clearly otherwise allocable to principal under Ohio law) were "receipts" to which the trustees' power would apply. A four-judge majority held the power did apply, but three judges dissented on the ground that "stock splits and stock dividends are not *receipts* which may be allocated to income by a trustee unless the trust instrument specifically confers [that authority] by unequivocal and express language."

In the much-discussed case of State Street Trust Co. v. United States, 263 F.2d 635 (1st Cir. 1959),[5] the question was whether the powers

5. This case was overruled ostensibly on the basis of changed Massachusetts trust doctrine in Old Colony Trust Co. v. United States, 423 F.2d 601 (1st Cir. 1970).

retained by the settlor as cotrustee were such as to render the property of an irrevocable trust includible in his gross estate for federal estate tax purposes. This question in turn depended on whether the powers amounted to a retained right "to designate the person who shall possess or enjoy the property or the income therefrom." (See Internal Revenue Code §§2036, 2038.) The court held that the settlor, as cotrustee, possessed such a right because of the express power (at 638)

> to exchange property for other property; . . . to retain and invest and reinvest in securities or properties of a kind . . . ordinarily . . . not considered suitable for a trust investment, including, but without restriction, investments that yield a high rate of income or no income at all and wasting investments, intending hereby to authorize . . . investments [which] might not otherwise be proper; . . . to determine what shall be charged or credited to income and what to principal notwithstanding any determination by the courts and specifically, but without limitation, to make such determination in regard to stock and cash dividends . . . and to decide whether or not to make deductions from income for depreciation, amortization or waste and in what amount; . . . all such acts and decisions made by the Trustees in good faith shall be conclusive.

The majority opinion further stated (at 638–639):

> It is true that it is not at all unusual to clothe trustees with power to invest trust assets in securities other than so-called "legals." And it is also true that it is far from uncommon to provide that trustees shall have the power in their discretion to allocate accretions to the property they hold in trust to principal or to income, at least when there is no settled rule of law to apply and proper allocation is open to honest doubt. Certainly in the exercise of one or both of these powers trustees can to some extent affect the interests of the various beneficiaries. Indeed, even in a trust wherein investment is limited to "legals," a trustee can effect some shifting of benefits between life beneficiaries and remaindermen by his choice of investment with respect to rate of income return or growth potential. [And here] the trustees' discretionary power to allocate trust assets to corpus or income is not limited to situations where the law is unsettled and there is honest doubt whether a given accretion or receipt should be classified as capital or income. . . . Furthermore, the trustees may make deductions from income for depreciation, amortization or waste in whatever amounts they see fit. . . .
>
> We may . . . assume that a Massachusetts court of equity at the behest of a beneficiary would intervene not only in the event of a wilful act or default by the trustees, but would also intervene in the event the trustees should act in utter disregard of the rights of a beneficiary. . . . But short of utter disregard of the rights of a life tenant or a remainderman . . .

a Massachusetts court would have no external standard with which to measure the trustees' conduct. The area of the trustees' discretion, although not untrammelled, is about as broad as language can make it and the law permits, and within that area the trustees can act in the administration and management of their trusts to confer or withhold very substantial benefits as between the life tenants and remaindermen.

Chief Judge Magruder, dissenting, argued (at 641–642):

The investment powers, although obviously designed to permit a more imaginative program of investment than trustees usually may pursue, were not uncontrolled. . . .

The accounting power given to the trustees is obviously corollary to this investment power and necessary to the successful maintenance of this balance; I believe it must be limited to this purpose and restricted to the best interests of the trust as a whole.

PROBLEMS

19-E.   A testamentary trust calls for the trustee, *T*, to pay the income to *L* for life, remainder to *R* or his issue. The terms of the trust are silent concerning investments. The jurisdiction has enacted the Uniform Prudent Investor act and the 1997 Uniform Principal and Income Act. *T* invests prudently, but after later examining the return from each investment, concludes that some of the investments have had "underproductive" income yields, with some of these investments having provided appreciation, but others not. In order to be fair and reasonable to *L*, *T* decides to use the 1997 Act §104 adjustment power to transfer part of the capital appreciation on the low-income investments to income. May *T* do so? What would be *T*'s alternatives in absence of these statutes?

19-F.   *T*, trustee of an irrevocable trust, is to pay *L* annually the greater of $24,000 or the net trust accounting income, and on her death to distribute the trust estate to *R* or his issue. The terms of the trust are silent with regard to *T*'s investment authority. The jurisdiction has enacted both the Uniform Prudent Investor Act and the 1997 Uniform Principal and Income Act. *T* invests prudently, but later determines that the investments have unduly favored *R* over the years and produced income during this past year of only $20,000 on a trust corpus of $2 million. In order to be fair and reasonable to *L*, *T* plans to use the power to adjust under 1997 Act §104 by distributing to *L* an additional $40,000 from principal, thereby giving her total payments from the trust of $60,000 (3 percent of corpus) for the year. May *T* do so?

UNIFORM PRINCIPAL AND INCOME ACT
(1997)

§104.   *Trustee's Power to Adjust.*

(a) A trustee may adjust between principal and income to the extent the trustee considers necessary if the trustee invests and manages trust assets as a prudent investor, the terms of the trust describe the amount that may or must be distributed to a beneficiary by referring to the trust's income, and the trustee determines, after applying the rules in Section 103(a), that the trustee is unable to comply with Section 103(b).

(b) In deciding whether and to what extent to exercise the power conferred by subsection (a), a trustee shall consider all factors relevant to the trust and its beneficiaries, including the following factors to the extent they are relevant:

(1) the nature, purpose, and expected duration of the trust;

(2) the intent of the settlor;

(3) the identity and circumstances of the beneficiaries;

(4) the needs for liquidity, regularity of income, and preservation and appreciation of capital;

(5) the assets held in the trust; the extent to which they consist of financial assets, interests in closely held enterprises, tangible and intangible personal property, or real property; the extent to which an asset is used by a beneficiary; and whether an asset was purchased by the trustee or received from the settlor;

(6) the net amount allocated to income under the other sections of this [Act] and the increase or decrease in the value of the principal assets, which the trustee may estimate as to assets for which market values are not readily available;

(7) whether and to what extent the terms of the trust give the trustee the power to invade principal or accumulate income or prohibit the trustee from invading principal or accumulating income, and the extent to which the trustee has exercised a power from time to time to invade principal or accumulate income;

(8) the actual and anticipated effect of economic conditions on principal and income and effects of inflation and deflation; and

(9) the anticipated tax consequences of an adjustment.

(c) A trustee may not make an adjustment:

(1) that diminishes the income interest in a trust that requires all of the income to be paid at least annually to a spouse and for which an estate tax or gift tax marital deduction would be allowed, in whole or in part, if the trustee did not have the power to make the adjustment;

(2) that reduces the actuarial value of the income interest in a

trust to which a person transfers property with the intent to qualify for a gift tax exclusion;

(3) that changes the amount payable to a beneficiary as a fixed annuity or a fixed fraction of the value of the trust assets;

(4) from any amount that is permanently set aside for charitable purposes under a will or the terms of a trust unless both income and principal are so set aside;

(5) if possessing or exercising the power to make an adjustment causes an individual to be treated as the owner of all or part of the trust for income tax purposes, and the individual would not be treated as the owner if the trustee did not possess the power to make an adjustment;

(6) if possessing or exercising the power to make an adjustment causes all or part of the trust assets to be included for estate tax purposes in the estate of an individual who has the power to remove a trustee or appoint a trustee, or both, and the assets would not be included in the estate of the individual if the trustee did not possess the power to make an adjustment;

(7) if the trustee is a beneficiary of the trust; or

(8) if the trustee is not a beneficiary, but the adjustment would benefit the trustee directly or indirectly.

(d) If subsection (c)(5), (6), (7), or (8) applies to a trustee and there is more than one trustee, a cotrustee to whom the provision does not apply may make the adjustment unless the exercise of the power by the remaining trustee or trustees is not permitted by the terms of the trust.

(e) A trustee may release the entire power conferred by subsection (a) or may release only the power to adjust from income to principal or the power to adjust from principal to income if the trustee is uncertain about whether possessing or exercising the power will cause a result described in subsection (c)(1) through (6) or (c)(8) or if the trustee determines that possessing or exercising the power will or may deprive the trust of a tax benefit or impose a tax burden not described in subsection (c). The release may be permanent or for a specified period, including a period measured by the life of an individual.

(f) Terms of a trust that limit the power of a trustee to make an adjustment between principal and income do not affect the application of this section unless it is clear from the terms of the trust that the terms are intended to deny the trustee the power of adjustment conferred by subsection (a).

Comment

Purpose and Scope of Provision. The purpose of Section 104 is to enable a trustee to select investments using the standards of a prudent investor without having to realize a particular portion of the portfolio's total return in the form of traditional trust accounting income such as interest, dividends, and rents. Section 104(a) authorizes a trustee to make adjustments between principal and income if three conditions are met: (1) the trustee must be managing the trust assets under the prudent investor rule; (2) the terms of the trust must express the income beneficiary's distribution rights in terms of the right to receive "income" in the sense of traditional trust accounting income; and (3) the trustee must determine, after applying the rules in Section 103(a), that he is unable to comply with Section 103(b). In deciding whether and to what extent to exercise the power to adjust, the trustee is required to consider the factors described in Section 104(b), but the trustee may not make an adjustment in circumstances described in Section 104(c).

Section 104 does not empower a trustee to increase or decrease the degree of beneficial enjoyment to which a beneficiary is entitled under the terms of the trust; rather, it authorizes the trustee to make adjustments between principal and income that may be necessary if the income component of a portfolio's total return is too small or too large [to provide beneficiaries with the income or growth to which their interests entitle them] because of investment decisions made by the trustee under the prudent investor rule. The paramount consideration in applying Section 104(a) is the requirement in Section 103(b) that "a fiduciary must administer a trust or estate impartially, based on what is fair and reasonable to all of the beneficiaries, except to the extent that the terms of the trust or the will clearly manifest an intention that the fiduciary shall or may favor one or more of the beneficiaries." The power to adjust is subject to control by the court to prevent an abuse of discretion. Restatement (Second) of Trusts §187 (1959). See also id. §§183, 232, 233, Comment *p* (1959).

Section 104 will be important for trusts that are irrevocable when a State adopts the prudent investor rule by statute or judicial approval of the rule in Restatement of Trusts 3d: Prudent Investor Rule. Wills and trust instruments executed after the rule is adopted can be drafted to describe a beneficiary's distribution rights in terms that do not depend upon the amount of trust accounting income, but to the extent that drafters of trust documents continue to describe an income beneficiary's distribution rights by referring to trust accounting income, Section 104 will be an important tool in trust administration. . . .

Factors to consider in exercising the power to adjust. Section 104(b) requires a trustee to consider factors relevant to the trust and its beneficiaries in deciding whether and to what extent the power to adjust should be exercised. Section 2(c) of the Uniform Prudent Investor Act sets forth circumstances that a trustee is to consider in investing and managing trust assets. The circumstances in Section 2(c) of the Uniform Prudent Investor Act are the source of the factors in paragraphs (3) through (6) and (8) of Section 104(b) (modified where necessary to adapt them to the purposes of this Act) so that, to the extent possible, comparable factors will apply to investment decisions and decisions involving the power to adjust. If a trustee who is operating under the prudent investor rule decides that the portfolio should be composed of financial assets whose total return will result primarily from capital appreciation rather than dividends, interest, and rents, the trustee can decide at the same time the extent to which an adjustment from principal to income may be necessary under Section 104. On the other hand, if a trustee decides that the risk and return objectives for the trust are best achieved by a portfolio whose total return includes interest and dividend income that is sufficient to provide the income beneficiary with the beneficial interest to which the beneficiary is entitled under the terms of the trust, the trustee can decide that it is unnecessary to exercise the power to adjust.

Assets received from the settlor. Section 3 of the Uniform Prudent Investor Act provides that ''[a] trustee shall diversify the investments of the trust unless the trustee reasonably determines that, because of special circumstances, the purposes of the trust are better served without diversifying.'' The special circumstances may include the wish to retain a family business, the benefit derived from deferring liquidation of the asset in order to defer payment of income taxes, or the anticipated capital appreciation from retaining an asset such as undeveloped real estate for a long period. To the extent the trustee retains assets received from the settlor because of special circumstances that overcome the duty to diversify, the trustee may take these circumstances into account in determining whether and to what extent the power to adjust should be exercised to change the results produced by other provisions of this Act that apply to the retained assets. See Section 104(b)(5); Uniform Prudent Investor Act §3, Comment, 7B U.L.A. 18, at 25–26 (Supp. 1997); Restatement of Trusts 3d: Prudent Investor Rule §229 and Comments *a–e*.

Limitations on the power to adjust. The purpose of subsections (c)(1) through (4) is to preserve tax benefits that may have been an important purpose for creating the trust. Subsections (c)(5), (6), and (8) deny the power to adjust in the circumstances described in those subsections in order to prevent adverse tax consequences, and subsection (c)(7) denies the power to adjust to any beneficiary, whether or not possession of the power may have adverse tax consequences. . . .

Release of the power to adjust. Section 104(e) permits a trustee to release all or part of the power to adjust in circumstances in which the possession or exercise of the power might deprive the trust of a tax benefit or impose a tax burden. For example, if possessing the power would diminish the actuarial value of the income interest in a trust for which the income beneficiary's estate may be eligible to claim a credit for property previously taxed if the beneficiary dies within ten years after the death of the person creating the trust, the trustee is permitted under subsection (e) to release just the power to adjust from income to principal.

Trust terms that limit a power to adjust. Section 104(f) applies to trust provisions that limit a trustee's power to adjust. Since the power is intended to enable trustees to employ the prudent investor rule without being constrained by traditional principal and income rules, an instrument executed before the adoption of this Act whose terms describe the amount that may or must be distributed to a beneficiary by referring to the trust's income or that prohibit the invasion of principal or that prohibit equitable adjustments in general should not be construed as forbidding the use of the power to adjust under Section 104(a) if the need for adjustment arises because the trustee is operating under the prudent investor rule. Instruments containing such provisions that are executed after the adoption of this Act should specifically refer to the power to adjust if the settlor intends to forbid its use. See generally, Joel C. Dobris, Limits on the Doctrine of Equitable Adjustment in Sophisticated Postmortem Tax Planning, 66 Iowa L. Rev. 273 (1981).

Most corporate trustees enthusiastically supported the promulgation of the Uniform Prudent Investor Act and its subsequent enactment by individual states. An American Bankers Association representative participated as an observer in the drafting meetings for the 1997 Uniform Principal and Income Act and expressed serious reservations about §104, as have many individual bank trust officers and representatives of state bankers associations. Why do you suppose corporate trustees might have reservations about the adjustment power?

Given the duty of impartiality (scarcely itself a bright-line rule), the trustee's investment powers may be seriously constrained by the need to provide an income flow that is, under the purposes and circumstances of the trust, suitable for the income beneficiary and for preservation of the purchasing power of trust principal. Regardless of the investment climate at the time, a trustee with an obligation to balance impartially these claims for trust accounting income might allocate a significant portion (possibly 40 percent or so) of trust investments to bonds or other investments that primarily yield income, while a remaining portion (perhaps 60 percent or less) is allocated to investments, such as common stocks, that emphasize capital appreciation. To let this duty of impartiality determine investment policy seems to put the cart before the horse, given that modern investment principles and trust concepts would ordinarily call for an investment program designed to produce maximum (or at least optimal) *total* return, regardless of the traditional handcuffs of the duty of *impartiality* and the rules of trust principal-income accounting.

How did trust law and drafting get to the present state of affairs? Probably because of accidents of history. First, during the formative years of trust law and practice, and for a considerable period of inadequate sensitivity thereafter, inflation was not an economic problem in this country. Second, the forerunner of the modern trust, as you may recall from Chapter 9, was the *use*, with the feoffee to uses holding legal title to land to the use of the cestui or cestuis que use, who had what we now call equitable title. Most wealth was represented by land, and one estimate indicates that by the fifteenth century a majority of land in England was held to the use of others, with someone entitled to rents, issues, and profits (after paying costs of cultivation and harvest and saving enough seed for the next year's crop) and another to the land at the death of this cestui for life. We became accustomed early to thinking about the trust as a device for *preserving* the corpus while consuming the "net income" from it — even as most wealth and entrusted wealth evolved away from land and into financial instruments, such as stocks and bonds.

Recent empirical research, Modern Portfolio Theory, and the variety of current trust purposes all suggest that the traditional income-principal and impartiality lens is a distorted one through which to view the trust world of today. Investing for optimal total return, with whatever elements and definitions of income and principal, simply makes sense as a matter of the best interests of the trust beneficiaries as a whole. As one writer put it (W. Hoisington, Modern Trust Design: New Paradigms for the 21st Century, 31 U. of Miami Inst. on Est. Plan. ¶6-10 (1997):

> Property is property. Money is fungible. Accretions to wealth derived by an owner from cash payments made by issuers of securities (interest and dividends) have no essential characteristic that distinguishes them from those derived from cash payments made by the purchasers of securities sold by the owner (realized capital appreciation). And absent the antiquated model and associated slogans, no one in his/her right mind would ever have thought otherwise.

All trust investments are not marketable securities. Trust property may consist of a family business or a ranch, and psychology tells us that our property holdings may represent more than wealth: it may represent who we are, what we do, how we express ourselves, and how we relate to, or even control, others. Thus, how we give it away may have powerful symbolic meaning, see T. Shaffer & C. Mooney, The Planning and Drafting of Wills and Trusts 19-22 (3d ed. 1991).

Evidence clearly shows that stocks and other equities significantly outperform bonds and other fixed-income investments over the long term, and that over the last three quarters of the twentieth century the real value of equity portfolios greatly outperforms debt portfolios — i.e., the dollar value of these portfolios, respectively, outstrip inflation (less than 3.1 percent over the same period) by large or modest amounts. For example, bonds ordinarily yield more income but produce no, or little or even negative, capital appreciation, while stocks ordinarily produce considerably greater total return, a much smaller part of which is income and much greater part of which is capital appreciation. When taxes and real-world costs of fiduciary and counsel fees and other expenses are factored into the equation, the trustee is almost doomed to failure: if investments are skewed toward bonds, remainder beneficiaries will be disappointed (and the gradual decline of the purchasing power of distributions to income beneficiaries who have long life spans can produce quite a surprise); if investments are skewed toward stocks, the income beneficiary will be disappointed. In fact, the return from a traditionally "balanced" portfolio can be expected to produce a disappointing overall performance and disappoint all beneficiaries in the long run.

In most states, distributions or expenditures by nonprofit institutions such as universities, hospitals, and nonprofit corporations and many charitable trusts are not governed by traditional principal and income rules. They are subject to the Uniform Management of Institutional Funds Act (UMIFA), which allows them to expend endowment appreciation for operating purposes despite trust terms or provisions in other donative instruments limiting disbursements to "income" or "net income." Experience of nonprofits under UMIFA has suggested that an annual payout in the range of 4 percent or even as high as 6 percent might be sustainable without impairing the real value of the fund. Of course, the fund and its expenditures are normally tax-exempt, and various "smoothing rules" have evolved to deal with year-to-year fluctuations in the value of the fund on which the percentage is calculated (e.g., a three-year trailing average of the fund's value). In fact, this basic concept in UMIFA and the frequent combination of generosity in expenditure formulas and lack of concern over maintenance or even enhancement of the real economic value of the corpus of the fund are made acceptable when the fund receives continuing contributions from the general public. Contrast the sustainable distribution rate for a private trust that is hoped to maintain the purchasing power of principal, for which a distribution rate in the range of 3 (or maybe 3.5) percent is often suggested. Would you have suspected the payout rate to be so low? Would the settlor of a private trust have expected, or the income beneficiary be satisfied with, a 3 percent distribution rate?

There are a variety of drafting designs to escape these "distorted lens" problems, the most prominent of which seem to be the use of discretionary or unitrust (but at what rate?) interests, depending on trust objectives and circumstances or more flexibly by using combinations of these interests in a given plan. There are variations of these ideas to meet various concerns, such as volatile fund values (which might be eased by, e.g., the three-year trailing average approach, supra) and marital deduction qualification (for which the greater of a unitrust amount or trust accounting income might be used). Arguments are also made for distributing dividends plus some additional percentage of that figure, or the dividend rate on the S&P 500 plus some percentage of that amount. There is a growing literature on these issues and ideas. See, e.g., J. Garland, A Market-Spending Rule for Endowments and Trusts, Financial Analysts J. 50-60 (July/Aug. 1989); J. Dobris, Real Return, Modern Portfolio Theory, and College, University, and Foundation Decisions on Annual Spending from Endowments: A Visit to the World of Spending Rules, 28 Real Prop., Prob. & Tr. J. 49 (1993); Holding & Reid, The Private Unitrust vs. The Discretionary Trust as a Paradigm for the New Century — A Different Viewpoint, 18 The Will and the Way no. 2, pp. 1-5 (N.C. Bar Ass'n, Feb. 1999); J. Garland, "A Market-Yield Spending Rule" Revisited: An Update Through 1998, *www.jeffreyco.com* (Aug. 16, 1999).

The 1997 Act §104 (*Trustee's Power to Adjust*) is a commendable concept for solving the current tensions between investment objectives and traditional principal/income accounting rules, although it is neither a simple statute nor free of understandable criticism. For a modified rule to substitute for §104 (and *comparable* to the unitrust concept recommended early in the 1997 Act deliberations), see Proposed Changes to the Definition of Trust Accounting Income . . . , Fifth Report of the EPTL — S.E.P.A. Leg. Advisory Comm. (May 11, 1999). A key lesson from all of this is that planners and drafters of trusts need to reexamine some of their basic assumptions and approaches. The provisions of the 1997 Act are, after all, default rules that yield to the terms of the trust.

In drafting private trusts, popular substitutes for the "income" rule or payout trust, are discretionary trusts, unitrusts, annuity trusts, or some variation or combination of these, or some different approach. What are the pros and cons of each? Consider, inter alia, freedom to use optimal investment plans, likely settlor intentions, beneficiary expectations, avoidance of conflict among beneficiaries, predictability, ease of administration, general notions of fairness, flexibility of distribution decisions, trustee skills and concerns, and adaptability to changes in economic circumstances or beneficiary needs or wishes.

b. The Principle of Impartiality

The fiduciary's duty of loyalty to the beneficiaries imposes more than an obligation to avoid conflicts of interest and personal profit arising from its fiduciary activities. Those are simply problems an alert and scrupulous fiduciary will normally avoid. More pervasive, and usually unavoidable, are the problems of conflicts among the various beneficial interests that the fiduciary must represent and to which are owed duties of care and loyalty. Consequently, purely fiduciary obligations are in conflict, giving rise to what is usually called a *duty of impartiality*. We have previously encountered various manifestations of this duty, most notably in connection with the investment function (Chapter 18, section B). In a sense, this duty is the fundamental principle underlying principal and income accounting, including the exercise of discretionary authority granted with respect to accounting matters (see especially subsection A.2.a, above).

RESTATEMENT (THIRD) OF TRUSTS: PRUDENT INVESTOR RULE

§183.   *Duty to Deal Impartially With Beneficiaries.*

When there are two or more beneficiaries of a trust, the trustee is under a duty to deal impartially with them.

Comment

a. Applicability of Section. The rule stated in this Section is applicable whether the beneficiaries' interests in the trust property are concurrent or successive.

By the terms of the trust the trustee may have discretion to favor one or more beneficiaries over others. The court will not control the exercise of such discretion, except to prevent the trustee from abusing it. . . .

In re DWIGHT'S TRUST
204 Misc. 204, 128 N.Y.S.2d 23 (Sup. Ct. 1952)

DICKSTEIN, J.

Upon this application to settle the accounts of a trustee, the guardian ad litem has interposed an objection which presents one of the facets of a recurring problem in trust administration today. Due to increased income tax rates, trustees are being met with demands by life beneficiaries, who are in high income tax brackets, to invest in tax exempt securities. In most cases such securities sell at a premium, with the result that upon maturity there is a loss in principal, even though the securities are redeemed at par. Such loss is visited upon the remaindermen of the trusts. It is unnecessary in the instant case to decide the broad questions of the liability of trustees under such circumstances, for here it is undisputed that the trustee, when informed of the high tax bracket in which the life beneficiary found herself, deliberately sold United States Savings Bonds, which it held as principal in the trust, at a loss to the estate, so that it could invest the proceeds in tax free securities. The redemption of the United States Bonds resulted in a loss of $3,290.70. I hold that the objection of the guardian to such loss is well taken and that the action of the trustee constituted an unwarranted subordination of the interests of the remaindermen to that of the life beneficiary. There was no power in the trustee to redeem the bonds at a loss for the sole purpose of effecting a higher net income for the life beneficiary. The trustee will, therefore, be surcharged the amount of the loss so sustained. The motion to settle the accounts is otherwise granted.

The problem of impartiality is particularly acute today in the context of tax burdens and the related allocation decisions of personal representatives and trustees. Examples are the alternate valuation date election under the federal estate tax and the types of situations in the cases below. As these opinions are studied, consider the effect of the fiduciary's duty of impartiality on (1) the actual decisions to be made in tax matters arising in the course of administering a decedent's estate or trust and then on (2) the allocation or apportionment of the benefits or detriments flowing from these decisions. This array of tax-related issues is both significant and interesting in its own right, as well as being revealing for purposes of other fiduciary situations. These problems, recognized or not, confront the fiduciary as everyday matters although yet remaining doctrinally on the frontiers of the law. See generally J. Dobris, Equitable Adjustments in Post-Mortem Tax Planning: An Unremitting Diet of *Warms*,[6] 65 Iowa L. Rev. 103 (1979); M. Moore, Conflicting Interests in Postmortem Planning, 1975 U. of Miami Est. Plan. Inst. ch.19. The cases that follow are fairly representative of the still modest number of decisions on these matters.

---

6. The reference is to Estate of Warms, 140 N.Y.S.2d 169 (Surr. Ct. 1955).

ESTATE OF BIXBY
140 Cal. App. 2d 326, 295 P.2d 68 (1956)

Fox, J. . . .

The executor or administrator . . . represents all the beneficiaries of the estate and must not favor one over another.

Estates are treated for tax purposes as separate entities, the tax on whose income is payable by the executor or administrator. The tax applies to the entire taxable income of the estate.

Bearing these principles in mind, we turn now to a consideration of who must bear the thrust of income taxes paid by the executor upon income accruing to the estate while in the course of administration. In the instant case, we are concerned with the dividends amounting to $76,000 which the executor received upon the 19,000 shares of stock of which Mrs. Bixby was the outright legatee. As legatee of this stock, title thereto vested in her eo instante as of the date of the testator's death, at which time there also originated her right to receive the income (dividends) produced by this stock subsequent to the testator's death. Had the legatee received this income when her right thereto accrued, it is undisputed that the payment of an income tax on these funds would have been the legatee's obligation. However, distribution not having as yet been made and the estate being a taxable entity, the executor was required to pay an income tax on this and other income received by him during the course of administration. Since such taxes are the subject of and measured by the income, it seems only fair that they should be paid therefrom and not from the principal of the residue of the estate. . . .

We pass now to the problem presented by the trustees' appeal, viz.: What is the effect on the rights of the beneficiaries of the executor's utilization of expenses of administration as federal income rather than federal estate tax deductions? In order to strip the problem of its esoteric trappings and place it in its proper perspective, a few prefatory observations are in order by way of clarification of the treatment of deductions in connection with the fiduciary returns which an executor is required to file under the provisions of the Internal Revenue Code, 26 U.S.C.A.

The taxable income of an estate, with certain exceptions not here germane, is computed in the same manner as that of an individual. The tax imposed upon the taxable income of an estate must be paid by the executor. The period of administration or settlement of the estate is, of course, the period actually required by the executor to perform his normal administration functions. During this period administration expenses accrue, and these expenses, in the case at bar, have been paid from the principal of the residue of the estate. The propriety of using that fund as the source of payments is not challenged. Taxwise, administration expenses of estates may be treated as a deduction under the income tax return or under the estate tax return. However, to obviate double deductibility, administration expenses are allowable as a deduction only once, and the executor is afforded an election as to whether he will apply the deduction against the estate tax or against the income tax. (§162(e), Internal Revenue Code, 26 U.S.C.A., reenacted as §642(g) of the Internal Revenue Code of 1954.) This gives the executor an opportunity of determining under which return it would prove more advantageous taxwise to claim the administrative expense deduction, and places him in a position to minimize the aggregate of taxes paid by the estate. Confronted with this elective treatment of deductions, the discreet executor will, of course, study the applicable estate tax and estate income rates and if he finds that there is a wide disparity between them, it would be judicious to avail himself of the deduction in the place where the optimum advantage will accrue to the estate, that is, by diminishing the aggregate amount of taxes payable to the federal government.

In the case at bar, the executor discharged his responsibility wisely under the circumstances by electing to utilize the administration expenses as an income tax deduction, although such expenses were borne by the principal of the residuary estate. In so doing, having reported an income of some $160,000, he paid a tax of $18,728.16. Had he not utilized this deduction on the estate income tax return, the tax would have been $120,378.11. He thus effected a tax saving of $101,649.95, resulting in a very substantial benefit to the legatees and beneficiaries entitled to the income. While this is a most obviously desirable result, its correlative effect on those entitled to corpus is unfortunate. For had the administrative expenses been used as a deduction in the federal estate tax return, the succession taxes payable from decedent's estate would have been reduced by $58,932.44. To that extent the remainder beneficiaries of the residuary trusts have been penalized to effect the income tax saving previously described.

It is at once manifest that the election to effect a tax saving afforded the executor under the Revenue Code does not justify the severe disruption and disarrangement of what would otherwise constitute the beneficial interests of the legatees and remaindermen under the will. Recognizing this inequity, the court below charged Mrs. Bixby's income account with the sum of $8,713.40, this sum being the part of the $18,728.16 in federal and state income taxes paid by the executor which is allocable to the dividends on the stock bequeathed to her. This, however, does not go far enough in adjusting the rights of the parties and in repairing the detriment occasioned to the corpus of the estate by giving only the income beneficiaries the benefit of the deduction for administration expenses. The total income tax saving, as we have seen was $101,649.95. The consequent impairment of corpus was $58,932.44, the amount by which the estate tax was increased by being deprived of the deduction of administration expenses. The impact of this loss to corpus is borne by the remaindermen. In such a situation, the equitable solution is to reallocate enough of the tax saving to the principal account to make whole the detriment suffered by corpus. (Estate of Warms, 140 N.Y.S.2d 169.) The virtue of this approach is that while a significant benefit in the form of tax saving still accrues to Mrs. Bixby, and the income beneficiaries, it is not exacted in the form of an unjust enrichment at the expense of the residuary beneficiaries. . . .

Such a rule commends itself to the conscience of the court as one under which no one is injured by an unjust encroachment on his inheritance. Apart from its simplicity of application, we adopt this rule because it places the burden of the income tax on the income legatee, where it properly belongs, and obviates any dislocation of the testator's bounty by shifting the burden of an income tax to a residuary legatee. While the executor's election as to the use of deductions under the present circumstances still enables the income beneficiaries to receive an actual cash benefit in the form of tax savings, by the process of reallocating an appropriate portion of such savings to principal, no part of any beneficiary's inheritance is diminished so that another may reap a profit at his expense. It is within the province of the probate court to bring to its aid the full equitable powers with which as a superior court it is invested to insure that income beneficiaries do not profit at the expense of the remaindermen. . . .

On the *equitable adjustment* doctrine generally, also see Will of Pross, 90 Misc. 2d 895, 396 N.Y.S.2d 309 (Surr. Ct. 1977); Cooper v. Parkinson, 186 So. 2d 844 (Fla. App. 1996); and Hill v. Estate of Richards, 142 N.J. 639, 66 A.2d 695 (1995). The Comment to §506 of the 1997 Act (permitting the trustee to make adjustments between principal and income because of taxes) explains:

Discretionary adjustments. §506(a) permits the fiduciary to make adjustments between income and principal because of tax law provisions. It would permit discretionary adjustments in situations like these: (1) A fiduciary elects to deduct administration expenses that are paid from principal on an income tax return instead of on the estate tax return; (2) a distribution of a principal asset to a trust or other beneficiary causes

the taxable income of an estate or trust to be carried out to the distributee and relieves the persons who receive the income of any obligation
to pay income tax on the income; or (3) a trustee realizes a capital gain
on the sale of a principal asset and pays a large state income tax on the
gain, but under applicable federal income tax rules the trustee may not
deduct the state income tax payment from the capital gain in calculating
the trust's federal capital gain tax, and the income beneficiary receives
the benefit of the deduction for state income tax paid on the capital
gain. See generally Joel C. Dobris, Limits on the Doctrine of Equitable
Adjustment in Sophisticated Postmortem Tax Planning, 66 Iowa L. Rev.
273 (1981).

3. Allocation or Apportionment of Receipts

Most of the issues remaining to be examined in the rest of this section A involve trust accounting. The first set of problems, however, in
subsection a, below, has both decedents' estates and trust accounting
contexts, the former deferred to this point because of the useful insights likely to result from examining both prototypical forms of the
problem together.

a. Receipts from Entities

Stock Dividends and Splits. No satisfactory answers have yet been found
for recurring questions involving, essentially, whether a corporation's
distributions of its own shares, either by stock dividend or stock split,
should be treated as a form of "income" or as a part of the principal
of the issuing corporation's shares (1) owned by the testator and devised to a particular devisee or (2) held by a trustee as a trust investment. Let us initially examine a form of the issue as it arises in
decedents' estates.

Does a devise of corporate stock carry with it additional shares attributable to that devised stock but received by the testator, via stock dividend or split, after the execution of the will but before the testator's
death? Or are the additional shares instead a form of "income" to the
testator and thus general assets of the estate at death, thereby belonging to the residuary beneficiaries?

The common law and early statutes struggled with the issue. Cases
were unpredictable, turning on such factors as whether the devise was
general or *specific*, whether the additional shares were the result of a
stock *split* or a stock *dividend*, whether the testator's probable intention
was the key determinant, or whether the nature of the underlying cor-

porate accounting was significant. When precedents pointed to a result that seemed to a court inappropriate, it might seek such escape hatches as a "time-of-death" construction, "mere change in form," or a finding that the particular devise was general rather than specific. Overall, it would probably be fair to summarize common law decisions as tending to award additional shares received by testators via stock split as belonging to specific but not general devisees, and shares received via stock dividend as passing to neither general nor specific legatees, falling instead (as *cash* dividends do) into the residue. Uniform Probate Code §2-605 ordinarily includes the additional shares in the devise, treating stock dividends and splits alike without regard to the specific or general character of the devise.

PROBLEM

19-G.   *T* executed a will reading, in relevant part, as follows: "I bequeath 800 shares of *X* Co. stock to my Sister, *S*. The residue of my estate I give to the children of my deceased Brother, *B*." Ten years later, *T* executed a valid codicil, simply stating, "I hereby bequeath $1,000 to my nurse, *N*."

At the time the original will was executed *T*'s portfolio of listed securities included 1,000 shares of *X* Company common stock. Seven years thereafter, *X* Company distributed to its common stockholders one additional share of common stock for each two shares previously held, thereby increasing *T*'s holdings to 1,500 shares, which are now in the estate. Your investigation reveals that *X* Company designated this distribution a dividend and transferred to capital stock and capital surplus an amount of its retained earnings equal to the fair market value of the newly issued shares. *X* Company's retained earnings had grown considerably over the preceding ten-year period because of high earnings and relatively low cash dividends.

T died a year ago, and it is now time for *T*'s estate to be distributed. Instructions are sought regarding the rights of *S* and the two children of *B*. To what is *S* entitled? How would you argue her case? How would you argue the case for *B*'s children?

Consider what additional facts, if any, you would want determined. Consider, along with the preceding materials in this section, the notes and the cases that follow. Cf. Knight v. Bardwell, 32 Ill. 2d 172, 205 N.E.2d 249 (1965); Loeb's Will, 206 So. 2d 615 (Miss. 1968).

The second of these prototypical problems involving stock dividends and splits arises in the context of trust accounting, and is illustrated by the problem below.

PROBLEM

19-H.   *T* holds a diversified portfolio of securities, including stock of *X* Co., in trust to pay the income to *L* for life, remainder to the settlor's issue. *T* is about to receive one new share of *X* Co. (labeled a "stock dividend") for each two *X* Co. shares presently held. *T* asks for your advice on how to account for these additional shares — are they income or principal? What additional information do you need to know to advise *T*? Consider the 1997 Act. If the state has the 1962 Act, consider the key section 6(a), which states: "Corporate distributions of shares of the distributing corporation, including distributions in the form of a stock split or stock dividend, are principal."

The first four cases discussed below were all decided at about the same time by different courts. Each involved a *stock split* and the question of whether the increased number of shares passed to the legatee of a stated number of shares in a named corporation.

In Igoe v. Darby, 343 Mass. 145, 177 N.E.2d 676 (1961), the testatrix owned seventy-six shares of certain common stock ($100 par value) and gave twenty-five shares to *A*, twenty-five to *B*, and twenty-six to *C*. A three-for-one split (reducing par to $33.33) occurred prior to the death of the testatrix. The Supreme Judicial Court of Massachusetts (343 Mass. at 147-148, 177 N.E.2d at 677-678) stated:

> Usually a gift of stock (such as "*X* shares of *Y* stock") is general; but . . . the testator's intent must prevail if it can be ascertained. . . . Doubtless the tendency of courts to favor general, rather than specific legacies, is chiefly to avoid the harshness of ademption [under which a specific bequest is extinguished if the thing bequeathed is not a part of the estate at the testator's death;]. . . .
>
> But ademption is not involved here and the reason for preferring to treat a bequest of stock in a named corporation as a general legacy does not exist. At all events, the rule of preference in such a case is merely one of construction and must yield in a case where the intent of the testator to make a specific legacy can be, as we think it can be here, ascertained from the entire will. . . . It will be noted that the number of shares bequeathed corresponds exactly with the number of shares (76) owned by the testatrix at the time of the execution of the will. This may not be very significant in the case of round numbers, but it is of considerable significance in the case, as here, of an odd amount. . . . Following the stock split the interest of the testatrix in [the company] remained precisely the same; the change was one of form rather than substance. In receiving all of the shares the legatees are getting no more than they would have received had there been no split. It would be manifestly un-

just to hold that they were not entitled to the additional shares resulting from the split.

In Shriners Hospital v. Emrie, 347 S.W.2d 198 (Mo. 1961), a bequest of 200 shares of stock, without possessory words, was held specific even though the testatrix owned many more shares in the named corporation at the date the will was executed. In holding that the legatee was to receive 1,000 shares when the stock was split five for one before the testatrix died, the court said that in the case of a specific bequest "a will speaks as of the time of execution and . . . is not ambulatory as to the meaning of . . . such a bequest."

On the other hand, in Matter of Brown's Will, 26 Misc. 2d 1011, 1017-1018, 209 N.Y.S.2d 465, 472 (Surr. Ct. 1961), additional shares acquired through a stock split were held not to pass to the legatees because a bequest of stock "available for purchase on the open market is a general legacy where the testator does not specify any particular share of stock . . . despite the fact that the testator may own on the date of the execution of his Will an equal or larger amount of shares than the legacy."

In re Helfman's Estate, 193 Cal. App. 2d 652, 14 Cal. Rptr. 482 (1961), in giving the legatee the enlarged number of shares resulting from a stock split, the court did not consider it important whether a bequest of X shares of Y stock was general or specific because in either case the issue was a matter of the testator's intent when the will was executed.

More recently, the case of Egavian v. Egavian, 102 R.I. 740, 232 A.2d 789 (1967), a case of first impression, reviewed the decisions of other states and adopted a rather forceful position on this problem. The court began by observing that many courts have struggled to permit the new shares resulting from a split to pass to the legatee as a part of the shares originally bequeathed, and that the unmanageable distinction between general and specific bequests invited manipulation to that end. The opinion then referred to sophisticated recent cases that recognize that a stock split "in no way alters the testator's total interest or rights in the corporation" but merely divides the "outstanding shares of a corporation into a greater number of units without disturbing the stockholder's original proportional participating interest." It quotes from one case to the effect that in today's world it seems "logical to assume that, in absence of language to the contrary, a testator, in making a gift of a given number of shares of stock in a corporation, intends that the legatee be entitled to the future profits of the corporation in the same fractional share as the testator received at the time of the will," and from another that a court should not so construe a will "as to deprive a beneficiary of a value which the testatrix intended to be given." The court concluded:

To rely [on] a formalistic and almost arbitrary analysis as to how this gift should be classified is clearly lacking in common sense and reason. It would give undue credence to pure fiction to hold that a testator's true intent as to whether a legatee should receive the increased number of shares due to a stock split could be determined from the degree of specificity with which the bequest was drafted when the contingency which has subsequently occurred was one the testator had little reason to anticipate at the time he drew his will and was one over which he had little control.

It is our firm belief that the rule first expressed by the Pennsylvania supreme court . . . and subsequently adopted in four other jurisdictions, which removed the distinction between specific, general or demonstrative legacies as a necessary incident when considering the effects of a stock split, is far sounder, and more just than the others which require an initial classification. In Allen v. National Bank, 19 Ill. App. 2d 149, 160, 153 N.E.2d 260, 265, an Illinois court said " . . . that in the absence of an intention to the contrary, a legatee of shares of stock is entitled to additional shares issued as a result of a stock split occurring after execution of the will." Whereas it has in the past been generally held that a legatee receives the surplus shares of stock split only if the testator is deemed to have specifically bequeathed the stock in question, today we embrace the rule as announced in *Allen*, supra, and hold that it is presumed that the prime intent of the testator is that the legatee is to benefit from any increased shares coming by way of a stock split provided no contrary intent is evident in the will.

See also In re Estate of Marks, 435 Pa. 155, 159, 255 A.2d 512, 515 (1969): "Other jurisdictions . . . have not been unanimous in their views; however, the more recent case law would award the fruits of a stock split to the legatees to whom stock gifts were provided in the will."

After reviewing the *Helfman, Egavian,* and *Marks* cases, among others, and its own earlier dicta in *Igoe* about splits producing a change of form and not substance, the Massachusetts Court has abandoned its prior distinction between general and specific bequests in order to reflect both corporate realities and probable testamentary intent, holding that presumptively the additional shares resulting from a stock split go to the legatee regardless of the elusive, litigation-breeding distinction previously employed in that state. Bostwick v. Hurstel, 364 Mass. 282, 304 N.E.2d 186 (1973). Compare Estate of Holmes, 821 P.2d 300 (Colo. App. 1991), where bequests of "my" 180 X Company shares and of "my" 124 Y Company shares passed, respectively 360 and 248 shares, the additional shares in each case having been acquired by splits during testator's lifetime, the court concluding that the "conflict" between "my" and the numbers of shares should be resolved by holding that the testator had intended to bequeath all of her shares in the X and Y companies.

AMERICAN INSTITUTE OF CERTIFIED PUBLIC ACCOUNTANTS COMMITTEE ON ACCOUNTING PROCEDURE, ACCOUNTING RESEARCH BULLETIN
No. 43, ch. 7(B) (1953)

Stock Dividends

10. As has been previously stated, a stock dividend does not, in fact give rise to any change whatsoever in either the corporation's assets or its respective shareholders' proportionate interests therein. However, it cannot fail to be recognized that, merely as a consequence of the expressed purpose of the transaction and its characterization as a *dividend* in related notices to shareholders and the public at large, many recipients of stock dividends look upon them as distribution of corporate earnings and usually in an amount equivalent to the fair value of the additional shares received. Furthermore, it is to be presumed that such views of recipients are materially strengthened in those instances, which are by far the most numerous, where the issuances are so small in comparison with the shares previously outstanding that they do not have any apparent effect upon the share market price and, consequently, the market value of the shares previously held remains substantially unchanged. The committee therefore believes that where these circumstances exist the corporation should . . . account for the transaction by transferring from earned surplus to the category of permanent capital . . . an amount equal to the fair value of the additional shares issued. . . .

11. Where the number of additional shares issued . . . is so great that it has, or may reasonably be expected to have, the effect of materially reducing the share market value, the committee believes that the implications and possible constructions discussed in the previous paragraph are not likely to exist and that the transaction clearly partakes of the nature of a stock split-up. . . .

13. Obviously, the point at which the relative size of the additional shares issued becomes large enough to materially influence the unit market price of the stock will vary with individual companies and under differing market conditions and, hence, no single percentage can be laid down as a standard for determining when capitalization of earned surplus in excess of legal requirements is called for and when it is not. However, . . . it would appear that there would be a few instances involving the issuance of additional shares of less than, say, 20% or 25% of the number previously outstanding where the effect would not be such as to call for the procedure referred to in paragraph 10.

New York E.P.T.L. §11-2.1(e)(2) provides:

> A distribution by a corporation or association made to a trustee in the
> shares of the distributing corporation or association held in such trust,
> whether in the form of a stock split or a stock divided, at the rate of six
> percent or less of the shares of such corporation or association upon
> which the distribution is made, is income. Any such distribution at a
> greater rate is principal.

See also 20 Pa. Purdon's Stat. §8105 (1984). Compare Matter of Fos-
dick's Trust, 4 N.Y.2d 646, 152 N.E.2d 228 (1958), where a trust of
General Electric stock directed that "all stock dividends" be distributed to the settlor or his executor. Subsequently GE cancelled all old
stock, issued 36 million new shares of $5 par value stock (aggregate
capital of $180 million) for the old capital of $180 million, and issued
50 million new shares of $5 par value stock, backed by a capitalization
of earned surplus in the amount of $250 million; the latter shares repre-
sented 7/12 of the total new shares (figures are approximate). The
court held that 7/12 of the new stock constituted a stock dividend
within the meaning of the trust instrument.

UNITED STATES TRUST CO. v. COWIN
121 Neb. 427, 237 N.W. 284 (1931)

GOOD, J.

Plaintiff, as trustee, brings this action, seeking direction and guidance as to the proper disposition of a stock dividend, declared upon
corporate stock constituting a part of the trust estate. . . .

The question is new in this jurisdiction. It has been a fruitful source
of litigation in other courts. Their holdings are not harmonious. The
courts of last resort in this country which have passed upon the question have taken three distinctly divergent views. They are generally referred to as the Massachusetts rule, the Kentucky rule, and the
Pennsylvania rule.

Briefly speaking, the Massachusetts rule is that [stock dividends are]
not income but a part of the corpus of the trust. The Kentucky rule is
that a stock dividend, declared during the existence of the trust, is income and belongs to the life tenant or settlor, regardless of whether
the stock dividend was declared from earnings accumulated before or
after the creation of the trust, or partly before and partly thereafter.
The Pennsylvania rule, under such circumstances, apportions the stock
dividend, holding that so much of the stock dividend as represents
earnings of the corporation prior to the creation of the trust is a part
of the corpus of the trust, and that such part of the stock dividend as

represents earnings, made subsequent to the creation of the trust, is income and belongs to the settlor or life tenant.

Plausible arguments have been adduced in support of each of these rules. Practically all of the courts, regardless of which rule obtains, hold that the intention of the settlor, if sufficiently specific and violative of no statute or rule of public policy, shall guide the courts in the determination of the question. . . . In the instant case the settlor has not evinced by the language used any specific direction with regard to a stock dividend. . . .

It may be observed that the Kentucky rule has not been generally accepted and followed by other jurisdictions.

The Pennsylvania rule appears to have been first specifically announced in Earp's Appeal, 28 Pa. St. 368, decided in 1857. That rule has been followed in a number of jurisdictions, but has been severely criticized, and we think the more recent trend of authority is in favor of the Massachusetts rule. The Ohio supreme court, in the case of Lamb v. Lehmann, 110 Ohio St. 59, after reviewing the reasons supporting the various rules, announced its adherence to the Massachusetts rule. Commenting upon this decision in 34 Yale Law Journal, 195, it is said (p. 196):

> The apportionment rule (meaning the Pennsylvania rule) is unfortunately blessed with an implication of fairness. . . . The first cases figured the value of the corpus from the market value of the shares on the day of testator's death. It was soon seen that this measure of value was inadequate, and the test in later Pennsylvania cases seems to be "actual value." In New York we find the courts making findings of "intrinsic value" from the books, records, and reports of the corporation. In a very recent case the court made its findings on the basis of a report of capital and earnings furnished by the executor. Through all of the decisions one is conscious of faulty methods of valuation. To ascertain the value of the corpus the courts must order an independent and complete inventory of assets as of the time of the testator's death. In cases where the courts must find value of the assets of one of our modern industrial giants, the cost is so great as to render the rule of apportionment impracticable.

In the comment it is further said:

> The decisions, therefore, have been based upon an approximation of "value." They represent, not apportionment, but a more or less arbitrary allotment of stock dividends a part of the life tenant, and at times a part to the remainderman. . . .
>
> Out of sympathy for the life tenant the apportionment rule might be condoned were it not for certain other legal consequences which seem to have been entirely overlooked. Valuable legal relations attach to the

ownership of stock, and those legal relations have a value which is a part of the value of the corpus. . . .

The fairness of the apportionment rule is only theoretical and illusory. Its application is dangerously variable, and it is really unfair to the remainderman. The supreme court of Ohio has chosen wisely in its adoption of the Massachusetts rule. The advantage of simplicity is obvious.

It seems to us that the inherent fallacy of the Pennsylvania rule is that it regards the corpus of the trust as of its value at the time the trust was created, while the fact is, where the trust property consists of corporate stock, the stock, itself, is the corpus, and it may rise or fall in value. Still, the corporate stock is the corpus or principal. If corporate stock, held in trust, greatly increases in value for a time, and a stock dividend is declared and goes to the life tenant, and thereafter the stock falls in value until it is worth much less than when the trust was created, by what process can the value of the corpus be maintained? We know of no means by which it can be maintained. If real estate is conveyed in trust the corpus is the realty. It may rise or fall in value as the market goes up or down; so corporate stock, placed in trust, remains the corpus or principal of the trust; its value may rise or fall with the market; but because its value rises with the market it should not be reduced by declaring a stock dividend and thereby dividing the corpus.

One of the best expositions of the Massachusetts rule may be found in Gibbons v. Mahon, 136 U.S. 549, wherein it is said (p. 557):

> [T]he intention of the testator, so far as manifested by him, must of course control; but when he has given no special direction upon the question as to what shall be considered principal and what income, he must be presumed to have had in view the lawful power of the corporation over the use and apportionment of its earnings, and to have intended that the determination of that question should depend upon the regular action of the corporation with regard to all its shares.
>
> Therefore, when a distribution of earnings is made by a corporation among its stockholders, the question whether such distribution is an apportionment of additional stock representing capital, or a division of profits and income, depends upon the substance and intent of the action of the corporation, as manifested by its vote or resolution; and ordinarily a dividend declared in stock is to be deemed capital, and a dividend in money is to be deemed income, of each share.
>
> A stock dividend really takes nothing from the property of the corporation, and adds nothing to the interests of the shareholders. Its property is not diminished, and their interests are not increased. After such a dividend, as before, the corporation has the title in all the corporate property; the aggregate interests therein of all the shareholders are represented by the whole number of shares; and the proportional interest

of each shareholder remains the same. The only change is in the evidence which represents that interest, the new shares and the original shares together representing the same proportional interest that the original shares represented before the issue of new ones. . . .

In the case of Hayes v. St. Louis Union Trust Co., 317 Mo. 1028, decided in 1927, there is a full and thorough review of all the cases. In that case it is held:

> If . . . the corporate stock so held in trust increases in value through the accumulation of corporate earnings after the beginning of the trust, and if no dividends are declared, the whole increase belongs to the corpus, even upon a sale of the stock. . . .
>
> The earnings and profits of a corporation remain the property of the corporation until severed from corporate assets and distributed as dividends. . . .
>
> A stock dividend is in no true sense a dividend. A dividend implies a division, a severance from the corporate assets to the amount of the dividend, and a distribution thereof among the stockholders. A stock dividend is the increasing of the fixed capital of the corporation; it takes nothing from the corporation; it gives nothing to the shareholder; the title to all corporate property remains in the corporation as before, and the proportional interest of the stockholder continues the same. . . .

In our view, the Massachusetts rule is the more logical and based on the better reason. We therefore adopt that rule, and hold that where corporate stock is placed in trust, reserving the income therefrom to the settlor, a stock dividend, declared during the existence of the trust, is not income, but is a part of the corpus of the trust and goes to the beneficiary of the trust.

It follows that the judgment of the district court is right, and it is therefore affirmed.

Accord, Bowles v. Stilley's Executor, 267 S.W.2d 707 (Ky. App. 1954). Is there any statutory solution that might be considered, other than one representing one of the three views already discussed? Is the 1962 Act's allocation of both stock splits and dividends to principal fair to the income beneficiary? Assuming a desirable statutory solution is enacted, is it to be applied prospectively only or retroactively? Consider the problems that may arise in either approach. See In re Dunham's Estate, 433 Pa. 273, 249 A.2d 531 (1969); South Carolina National Bank v. Arrington, 165 S.E.2d 77 (S.C. 1968). If a trustee held a substantial block of stock of a company that pursued a regular policy of retaining its earnings and declaring periodic stock dividends in lieu of cash dividends, could the trustee retain the stock without fear of surcharge? Is this danger a good thing for trusts generally, especially where the beneficiaries are or may be in high income tax brackets? How might the settlor's drafter provide an adequate solution without becoming (or forcing the trustee to become) involved in excessive detail?

TAIT v. PECK
346 Mass. 521, 194 N.E.2d 707 (1963)

CUTTER, J.

Letitia M. Tait (the widow) seeks a declaratory decree with respect to an inter vivos trust (the trust) executed in 1935 by her late husband (the settlor). She asks the court to determine whether a certain distribution of capital gains to the trust, made by Broad Street Investing Corporation (Broad Street) in December, 1961 is to be treated as principal or income of the trust. The widow, life beneficiary of the trust, asserts that the capital gains distribution is income. The individual remaindermen and the trustees assert that it is a return of capital and hence should be added to principal. . . .

In 1961, . . . Broad Street paid to the trustees of the trust two cash dividends from income and in addition, in December, 1961, Broad Street delivered to the trustees 1,463 additional shares of Broad Street as "distributions of gain," as distinguished from "dividend from income," on the shares then held by the trustees. The trustees paid to the widow the 1961 dividends from income paid to them by Broad Street in 1961 (less expenses and taxes) "but refused and still refuse to transfer" to the widow the 1,463 shares of Broad Street (less any expense or taxes thereto allocable). The trustees, in support of their position, state that under Int. Rev. Code of 1954 §852, the trustees must pay a Federal capital gains tax on these shares of Broad Street so received as "distributions of gain." . . .

In its statements to the public, Broad Street says that its investments have two goals — (1) favorable current income, and (2) long term growth in both income and capital value. Dividends payable out of net income are paid quarterly, whereas distributions of gain realized on the sale of investments are paid at the end of each year. . . . The 1,463 shares were paid to the trustees in December, 1961, at their request. At their option, they could have received the equivalent of these shares in cash.

1. No party contends that the inter vivos trust shows what the settlor's intent was with respect to capital gains dividends. . . .

2. The usual Massachusetts rule for the allocation of dividends was stated in Minot v. Paine, 99 Mass. 101, 108:

> A trustee needs some plain principle to guide him; and the cestuis que trust ought not to be subjected to the expense of going behind the action of the directors, and investigating the concerns of the corporation, especially if it is out of our jurisdiction. A simple rule is, to regard cash dividends, however large, as income, and stock dividends, however made, as capital.

. . . This simple rule, in practice, has come to be based . . . upon the substance . . . of the transaction as carried out by the entity declaring the dividend. Dividends in cash in substance paid out of capital or in liquidation have been treated as belonging to principal. The substance of a transaction has been examined to determine whether it was equivalent to a stock dividend. Where the trustee, as shareholder, is given the option to receive a dividend in stock or in cash, the later cases, in effect, treat the dividend as a cash dividend and as income. We look at the substance of the capital gain distribution made by Broad Street in December, 1961, against the background of these authorities. No prior Massachusetts case has presented the question whether such a distribution, received by a trustee, is to be treated as capital or income. . . .

Some commentators have felt that dividends from net capital gains from the sales of securities held in a mutual fund's portfolio are income from the ordinary conduct of the fund's business, that the portfolio holdings are bought and sold like inventory or other corporate property of a business corporation, and that distribution from such gains, at least where there is opportunity to receive the distribution in cash, should be treated as income. Weight is given by these commentators to the circumstances that investors in investment companies rely on both income and capital gains as a part of the expected yield. It is suggested by at least one author (Professor Bogert) that to invest in mutual funds would be a breach of trust, about which the life beneficiary could complain, unless the investment produced a normal trust investment yield. The contrary view is that the sale of a security in an investment company portfolio involves the sale of a capital item, so that, if the gain is distributed the capital is necessarily reduced. In some years such a company may experience net losses. It is argued that if capital gain distributions of other years have been paid to the income beneficiary, the trust principal will inevitably suffer in years of losses, which must be expected even in an era generally inflationary, so that, in effect, the investment company shares may become a wasting investment. It is also urged that a trustee's investment in an investment company is in substance nothing more than a fractional ownership in a diversified portfolio of securities, as to which the trustee should account as if he held the portfolio securities directly. The special character of regulated investment companies and their specialized tax treatment under the Internal Revenue Code also have some tendency to give capital gains distributions the aspect of principal.

If the dividends and distributions of a regulated investment company should be regarded as inherently the same as those of an ordinary industrial company, then the rule of Smith v. Cotting, 231 Mass. 42, 48-49, 120 N.E. 177, should be applied to Broad Street's 1961 capital gain distribution, which the trustees, at their option, could have received either in cash or in shares. It seems to us, however, that, when a fiduciary invests in investment company shares, he is entering into an arrangement more closely like participation in a common trust fund (see G.L. c. 203A) than like an investment in the shares of an industrial company. His purpose generally will be to obtain for his trust beneficiaries (usually of a small trust) the same type of a spread of investment risk which the trustee of a common trust fund can obtain for its participating trusts, or which the trustee of a large trust fund can obtain by a well conceived program of diversified direct investment. . . .

The method of determining the purchase and sales prices of investment company shares, in relation to the net asset value of shares, is consistent with the concept that the trustee is obtaining diversification by an indirect participation in the investment company's portfolio. It is apparent that if a fiduciary were to redeem his shares at a profit just before a capital gain distribution, he would necessarily allocate any gain to principal. No practical reason requires treating the capital gain distribution, when made, in any different way, or prevents retaining it as a part of the principal of the trust.

One major virtue of our Massachusetts rule for allocation between principal and income has been its simplicity as a rule of convenience. To treat capital gains distributions of registered investment companies as principal will not impair the simplicity of our rule, for no inquiry need be made as to the source of the distribution. The source must be announced [§19 of the Investment Company Act of 1940, 15 U.S.C. §80a-19 (1958)], as it was in respect of Broad Street's capital gain distribution in December, 1961.

Since no binding precedent controls our decision, we are guided by the substance of the situation. We adopt the rule that distributions by a regulated investment company, from capital gains (whether made in the form of cash or shares or an option to take or purchase new shares), are to be allocated to principal. This is essentially the view adopted by the Commissioners on Uniform State Laws in 1962 after full deliberation. The Commissioners' action can be taken as reflecting a considered current view of what is in the public interest. In effect, we think that the regulated company, from the standpoint of a trustee investing in its shares, is merely a conduit of its realized gains to the trust fund and that, in the hands of the trustee, the gains should retain their character as principal. . . .

UNIFORM PRINCIPAL AND INCOME ACT
(RECEIPTS FROM ENTITIES)
(1997)

§401. *Character of Receipts.*

(a) In this section, "entity" means a corporation, partnership, limited liability company, regulated investment company, real estate investment trust, common trust fund, or any other organization in which a trustee has an interest other than a trust or estate to which Section 402 applies, a business or activity to which Section 403 applies, or an asset-backed security to which Section 415 applies.

(b) Except as otherwise provided in this section, a trustee shall allocate to income money received from an entity.

(c) A trustee shall allocate the following receipts from an entity to principal:

(1) property other than money;

(2) money received in one distribution or a series of related distributions in exchange for part or all of a trust's interest in the entity;

(3) money received in total or partial liquidation of the entity; and

(4) money received from an entity that is a regulated investment company or a real estate investment trust if the money distributed is a capital gain dividend for federal income tax purposes.

(d) Money is received in partial liquidation:

(1) to the extent that the entity, at or near the time of a distribution, indicates that it is a distribution in partial liquidation; or

(2) if the total amount of money and property received in a distribution or series of related distributions is greater than 20 percent of the entity's gross assets, as shown by the entity's year-end financial statements immediately preceding the initial receipt.

(e) Money is not received in partial liquidation, nor may it be taken into account under subsection (d)(2), to the extent that it does not exceed the amount of income tax that a trustee or beneficiary must pay on taxable income of the entity that distributes the money.

(f) A trustee may rely upon a statement made by an entity about the source or character of a distribution if the statement is made at or near the time of distribution by the entity's board of directors or other person or group of persons authorized to exercise powers to pay money or transfer property comparable to those of a corporation's board of directors.

§402. *Distribution from Trust or Estate.*

A trustee shall allocate to income an amount received as a distribution of income from a trust or an estate in which the trust has an interest other than a purchased interest, and shall allocate to principal an amount received as a distribution of principal from such a trust or estate. If a trustee purchases an interest in a trust that is an investment entity, or a decedent or donor transfers an interest in such a trust to a trustee, Section 401 or 415 applies to a receipt from the trust.

---

4. Underproductive or Overproductive (or Wasting) Property

a. Underproductive Assets

PROBLEM

19-I. The trust estate in question, as originally constituted, included a note in the principal amount of $100,000, bearing annual interest at 6 percent. No interest payments have been received for a five-year period, at the end of which the debtor, following insolvency proceedings, paid $60,000 in discharge of this obligation. The trustee was unable to dispose of this note or to realize on it earlier, despite diligent efforts since the time of default. He now asks you to advise whether the $60,000 he has received belongs to principal or whether some of this amount is allocable to income. What answer would you give under the 1962 Act? Under §413 of the 1997 Act? What result in absence of statute?

In re PAGE'S ESTATE
199 Cal. App. 2d 550, 18 Cal. Rptr. 886 (1962)

Fox, P.J.

This litigation arose by way of a petition for distribution to the remaindermen of the assets of a testamentary trust upon the death of the income beneficiary. The pleadings constitute an accounting, report and petition filed by the trustees (who are also the remaindermen) and objections thereto filed by the widow and executrix of the estate of the income beneficiary.

Lottie Page died testate in 1938, leaving four children as her sole heirs. In August of 1940 the estate was distributed pursuant to a Decree of Distribution which was based on Lottie's holographic will. Pursuant to the Decree each of the three children, Lottie Ray, Mary Simonsen and Albert Johnson, were given an undivided one-fourth interest in the entire estate. The remaining undivided one-fourth interest was distributed to the same three children as trustees, with the income attributable to that interest to be paid to John Johnson for his life. On John's death the trust estate was to be distributed to the trustees as remaindermen.

The estate, insofar as is here pertinent, consisted in part of completely unproductive desert land, together with some income properties. The income properties and some of the desert properties were never sold. A number of the desert properties were sold in 1957 and 1958 [during the life estate]. None of the desert properties ever became productive of income. All of the properties appreciated substantially in value. By her objections to the accounting, John Johnson's executrix, whom we shall call "contestant," seeks two things: A portion of the appreciated value of the properties in the estate as "delayed income"; and a surcharge upon the trustees for an alleged breach of trust in not making productive the portion of the estate which produced no income and in not making more productive the remaining portion.

By its judgment the trial court awarded contestant a portion of the appreciated value of the desert properties (both those which were sold and those retained), held that she was not entitled to any of the appreciated value of the income properties, and refused to surcharge the trustees. Both sides, being unsatisfied with the judgment, have appealed.

At this point it would seem appropriate to set forth . . . Civil Code §730.13 of the Principal and Income Law, originally enacted in 1941, on which the judgment is based. [See similar provision in Revised Uniform Principal and Income Act §12 (1962)]

> (1) Where any part of a principal in the possession of a trustee consists of realty or personalty which for more than a year and until disposed of as hereinafter stated has not produced an average net income of at least 1 per centum per annum of its inventory value as fixed by the appraiser or appraisers regularly appointed by the court, or in default thereof its market value at the time the principal was established or of its cost where purchased or otherwise acquired later, and the trustee is under a duty to change the form of the investment as soon as a reasonable price, not representing an undue sacrifice of value, may be obtained and such change is delayed, but is made before the principal is finally distributed, then the tenant shall be entitled to share in the net proceeds received from the property as delayed income to the extent hereinafter stated.

(2) Such income shall be the difference between the net proceeds received from the property and the amount which, had it been placed at simple interest at the rate of 5 per centum per annum for the period during which the change was delayed, would have produced the net proceeds at the time of change, but in no event shall such income be more than the amount by which the net proceeds exceed the inventory value of the property, or in default thereof its market value at the time the principal was established or its cost where purchased later. The net proceeds shall consist of the gross proceeds received from the property less any expenses incurred in disposing of it and less all carrying charges which have been paid out of principal during the period while it has been unproductive.

(3) The change shall be taken to have been delayed from the time when the duty to make it first arose, which shall be presumed in the absence of evidence to the contrary, to be one year after the trustee first received the property if then unproductive, otherwise one year after it became unproductive.

(4) If the tenant has received any income from the property or has had any beneficial use thereof during the period while the change has been delayed, his share of the delayed income shall be reduced by the amount of such income received or the value of the use had.

(5) As between successive tenants, or a tenant and a remainderman, delayed income shall be apportioned in the same manner as provided for income by Section 730.06.

It will be noticed that 1 percent is the stated test of productivity for the purpose of apportionment. The trial court found that the desert properties which were sold were unproductive and that the trustees were under a duty to sell them within a year, and "imprudently neglected [to sell them] within a reasonable time." The same was found as to the unsold desert properties, and delayed income was computed, the record reveals, according to the formula in Section 730.13(2). Concerning the income properties in question, it was found "That the net income from the trust's interest in inventory items #1 and #3 did not at any time fall below one percent per annum of the appraised value of said interest." This finding is not challenged and it of course takes the income properties out of the operation of Section 730.13. In its conclusions of law the trial court sets forth certain amounts as "delayed income apportionable to John Johnson" from the desert properties. Concerning the income properties, the trial court concluded "That inasmuch as the net income from inventory items #1 and #3 did not at any time fall below one percent per annum, the trustees are deemed to have acted as prudent men in the management of the trust's interest in said inventory items."

Contestant challenges the judgment in two ways. She claims that certain allegations of fraud on the part of the trustees were improperly stricken, and that if she were allowed to prove these allegations she would be entitled to a surcharge equal to all the appreciated value of the estate. She further contends that although the one percent figure is the dividing line between productive and unproductive property for purposes of Section 730.13, the fact that one percent was earned on the income properties does not mean that as a matter of law the trustees met their trust responsibility to the income beneficiary with respect to those properties. The trustees' appeal is based on claims that the evidence is insufficient to establish a duty or the amount of the judgment; that the trial court erred in failing to find on the question of estoppel and various other matters; and that there were certain evidentiary errors.

The contention of the trustees that is dispositive of this appeal is that Section 730.13 does not apply to this trust. The Decree of Distribution establishing the trust became effective in August of 1940. Section 730.02 of the Principal and Income Law reads in part:

> This chapter [of which §730.13 is a part] shall apply to all transactions by which principal shall be established which become legally effective on or after September 13, 1941. It shall also apply to all revocable trusts existing on and prior to that date and to all other trusts to the extent to which they may be at that time or any later time amendable by the settlor in respect to matters covered by this chapter. . . .

This section was apparently included to protect the constitutionality of the law. (See Annot. 69 A.L.R.2d 1137.) It clearly does not embrace the instant trust within its terms.

This is not to say that the principle of apportionment does not exist in this State independent of statute. Estate of Bothwell, 65 Cal. App. 2d 598, 151 P.2d 298, 868, was the first appellate decision in California to consider the question. It adopted the Restatement rule. Section 241 of the Restatement of Trusts reads:

> (1) Unless it is otherwise provided by the terms of the trust, if property held in trust to pay the income to a beneficiary for a designated period and thereafter to pay the principal to another beneficiary is property which the trustee is under a duty to sell, and which produces no income or an income substantially less than the current rate of return on trust investments, or which is wasting property or produces an income substantially more than the current rate of return on trust investments, and the trustee does not immediately sell the property, the trustee should make an apportionment of the proceeds of the sale when made, as stated in Subsection (2).
>
> (2) The net proceeds received from the sale of the property are apportioned by ascertaining the sum which with simple interest thereon at the current rate of return on trust investments from the day when the duty

to sell arose to the day of the sale would equal the net proceeds; and the sum so ascertained is to be treated as principal, and the residue of the net proceeds as income.

(3) The net proceeds are determined by adding to the net sale price the net income received or deducting therefrom the net loss incurred in carrying the property prior to the sale.

It will be noted that there are several important differences between Section 730.13 and the Restatement rule. The "one percent" rule of Section 730.13 becomes "no income or income substantially less than the current rate of return on trust investments" in the Restatement. Section 730.13 uses 5 percent in calculating the amount to be apportioned to income, whereas the Restatement uses "the current rate of return on trust investments." There are many other differences which should receive judicial comment only when interpretation is necessary in the resolution of a case. It is sufficient here to say that the differences are such as to alter substantially the complexion of the litigation. It is impossible to ascertain what the trial court would have done had it applied Estate of Bothwell, supra, and Section 241 of the Restatement instead of Section 730.13. . . .

Since the other matters giving rise to alleged error are less than likely to occur on a new trial, it would not be appropriate to discuss them here.

Because of the unusual circumstances of this case, each side will bear its own costs on appeal.

The judgment is reversed.

For other cases involving problems of "unproductive" property, see Bowen v. Safe Deposit & Trust Co., 188 Md. 482, 53 A.2d 413 (1947) (involving proceeds from the sale of rights to new securities received pursuant to the reorganization of a corporation whose bonds were in default and on which no interest was paid during the period of the trust); Matter of Rowland, 273 N.Y. 100, 6 N.E.2d 393 (1937) (involving proceeds of sale of real estate on which the rental activities had produced a large net loss); In re Nirdlinger's Estate, 327 Pa. 171, 193 A. 30 (1937) (involving proceeds of foreclosing a mortgage that had been in default and on which less than the principal amount of the mortgage was realized).

The terms "unproductive" and "underproductive" are pre-1997 Act concepts. "Un [or under] productive" means underproductive of trust accounting income. See 1997 Act §413, cmt. How do you explain the 1997 Act treatment of the issue?

UNIFORM PRINCIPAL AND INCOME ACT
(1997)

§413.   *Property Not Productive of Income.*

(a) . . . If a marital deduction is allowed for all or part of a trust whose assets consist substantially of property that does not provide the spouse with sufficient income from or use of the trust assets, and if the amounts that the trustee transfers from principal to income under Section 104 and distributes to the spouse from principal pursuant to the terms of the trust are insufficient to provide the spouse with the beneficial enjoyment required to obtain the marital deduction, the spouse may require the trustee to make property productive of income, convert property within a reasonable time, or exercise the power conferred by Section 104(a). The trustee may decide which action or combination of actions to take.

(b) In cases not governed by subsection (a) [which applies to most marital deduction trusts], proceeds from the sale or other disposition of an asset are principal without regard to the amount of income the asset produces during any accounting period.

b.   Depreciable and Wasting Assets

PROBLEM

19-J.   When *H* died three years ago, he left a life insurance policy payable to his widow, *W.* On the advice of an insurance agent, *W* elected an option under which she would receive annual payments of $8,000 for the rest of her life but providing that even in the event of death within ten years the payments were to continue until ten such annual payments were made. Because of her failing health at the time of election, *W* believed this "term certain" option was preferable to the straight life annuity under which the annual payments to her would have been larger.

Recently, *W* died. Her will, executed before *H*'s death, left her entire estate to *T* Trust Company to pay the income to *M,* the widowed mother of *H,* and then to distribute the corpus on *M*'s death to *B* and *S,* who were *W*'s brother and sister. Among the assets of *W*'s estate was the right to receive the seven remaining annual payments under the insurance settlement option previously mentioned. The other assets paid over to the trust estate consisted of about $160,000 worth of securities.

T consults you and informs you that *B* and *S* insist that *M* is not entitled to receive the $8,000 payment to be received by *T* from the insurance company each year, while *M* insists that she is. How would you advise *T*? What possibilities are open? Should a court give instructions to *T*, and if so what should the instructions be? Cf. Matter of Pennock, 285 N.Y. 475, 35 N.E.2d 177 (1941) (deceased life insurance agent's right to percentage of renewal premiums). Assume that the cases below were decided in your state. What would be the result under the 1997 Uniform Principal and Income Act?

In Union County Trust Co. v. Gray, 110 N.J. Eq. 270, 159 A. 625 (1932), the testamentary trust contained almost 50,000 shares of the Gray Processes Corporation, the assets of which consisted primarily of a patented process invented by the testator. The corporation also received about $110,000 of insurance proceeds on the testator's death in April 1931, increasing the company's "surplus" to $275,000. Thereafter in June 1931 the corporation declared a "regular" dividend of $50,000 and an "extra" dividend of $50,000, each being payable in January 1932, first out of earnings since July 1, 1931, and if insufficient then out of prior earnings. The question of whether these dividends were income or principal or were to be apportioned was presented to the court, which stated:

> A neat answer, that [one] . . . dividend is extraordinary and the other is not, would be of no assistance, for solution of the meritorious question is not to be found in nomenclature. The tags "regular" and "extra" are presently of no significance. . . .
>
> The regular and extra dividends of June 11th, 1931, are apportionable. . . . So much of the dividends as represents life insurance, obviously was capital; the earnings for the six months preceding the dividend, $3,769.30 are apportionable to corpus and income. . . .
>
> The income from license fees and royalties will end with the life of the patent, and, meanwhile, paying it out in dividends to the life tenants may result in disappointing the remaindermen. . . . [F]or the protection of the remaindermen, the value of the certificates is to be ascertained as of the testator's death and the life tenants paid interest on the sum, as in Helme v. Strater, 52 N.J. Eq. 591, where the principle was laid down and applied by Chancellor McGill:
>
>> Where a testator bequeaths the residue of his property without specific description, or, in other words, indicating an intention that it shall be enjoyed in specie, first to a tenant for life and then to a remainderman, and thus manifests that the same fund shall be successively enjoyed by both, the necessary inference and established rule in equity is that it must be invested as a permanent fund so that the successive takers shall enjoy it in an equally productive capacity. But where it consists in whole or in part of property which is in its nature perishable, which for some reason cannot be converted into money or cannot be so converted without great sacrifice of both principal and interest, the tenant for life will not be entitled to the annual product which the property thus perishing

is actually making, but to interest from the testator's death on the value thereof estimated as of that time.

. . . The rule of the court (says Lewin) under which perishable property is converted does not proceed upon the assumption that the testator in fact intended his property to be sold, but is founded upon the circumstance that the testator intended the perishable property to be enjoyed by different persons in succession, which is accomplished by means of a sale. . . . Lewin, Trusts 300. Here . . . the power given to the trustees to "invest and reinvest" the estate implies that it should be converted. There is no indication of intention to vary the relative rights of the legatees, or, that the rule of conversion should not obtain. Constructive conversion will be ordered. . . .

There will be a reference to a master to determine the value of the certificates, and lawful interest will be allowed if the annual income equals the rate.

It is the fact that only about ten per cent of the oil industry is presently using the patented process, and that the rest of the field is open to exploitation which may greatly swell the annual profits. The possibility requires that the valuation be periodically adjusted to increased annual profits.

110 N.J. Eq. at 274-279, 159 A. at 628-630.

CHAPIN v. COLLARD
29 Wash. 2d 788, 189 P.2d 642 (1948)

[Action by trustees for declaratory judgment. Included among the assets originally received by the trustees from the settlor's estate were two apartment houses, two commercial buildings, and several other buildings. The trustees requested authority to deduct reasonable depreciation on these buildings from gross income before arriving at distributable net income. The trial court decreed that depreciation was not authorized by the will or by law and directed that amounts previously withheld be paid over to the income beneficiary and that no such deductions be made in the future.]

ROBINSON, J. . . .

In Laflin v. Commissioner of Internal Revenue, 69 F.2d 460, the law is tersely stated:

It is a rule of general application that the beneficiary of a trust entitled thereunder to receive the income from such property may not be required to suffer a deduction from such income for the creation of a sinking fund to provide for depreciation and obsolescence, unless, indeed, the trust instrument or the law of the state makes provision therefor.

Appellants concede this to be the general rule, but urge that the language of the whole will . . . manifests an intention on the part of the testator that a reserve for depreciation be established.

This is no more than wishful thinking. The trustees were directed, "after payment of the necessary expenses of this trust," to pay to the named beneficiaries "the entire net income from said trust." There is nothing in the will to evidence any intention that a reserve for depreciation be deducted from that income, and no ambiguity that warrants the admission of extrinsic evidence of such an intention. . . .

Appellants then invite us to say that the rule referred to is outmoded, and to declare that modern business conditions and practice justify the establishment of a rule of law in this state that trustees of a trust including rental property may deduct a depreciation reserve from rental income which would otherwise be distributed to a life tenant. . . .

In re Roth's Estate, 52 A.2d (N.J.) 811, [in denying a request for depreciation charges the court] said:

> Such a course is in harmony with modern accounting practice, but generally, as between life tenant and remainderman, the latter must bear any loss due to depreciation and obsolescence. . . . A tenant for life is bound to repair only to the extent of preventing permissive or actual waste. . . . But he is under no obligation in respect to the loss of economic value of a building which normally occurs.

We find no substantial authority, either "old" or "modern," supporting the position of the appellants, and both the number and the reasoning of the cases which adhere to the rule as stated in the *Laflin* case, supra, impel us to decline the invitation to establish a different rule in this state.

The courts diligently protect the right of the life tenant to enjoy the full benefits intended for him or her, because, as Mr. Justice Swayze said, in McCracken v. Gulick, 92 N.J. Eq. 214, 112 A. 317:

> Clearly when he [the testator] has created a trust fund and directed that the income be paid a beneficiary for life, he intends to secure that income to the life tenant; that is the very object of the fund . . . the testator can hardly mean to starve the life tenant for the benefit of remaindermen, whom he often has never seen.

That statement is particularly appropriate in this case, where the trust terminates on the death of the life tenant. . . .

Note that, in following the traditional view rather than modern accounting practice, the above court was considering depreciation on assets initially received by the trustee. Should the result be different as to properties acquired, buildings erected, or improvements made by the trustee? See section A.5, infra. An important California decision established the rule providing for depreciation on the *trustee's* investments and then reasoned back to modify the traditional rule on property received from the settlor over which the trustee had power of sale. (After this decision, the California legislature made it a matter of the trustee's "absolute discretion" whether to provide "a reasonable allowance for depreciation under generally accepted accounting principles.") This case, Estate of Kelly, 63 Cal. 2d 679, 685-690, 408 P.2d 353, 357-359 (1965), states:

> Ordinary repairs are those incidental repairs that do not materially add to the value of the property or appreciably prolong its life, but keep it in efficient operating condition. They are customarily treated as charges against income by accountants and accepted as such for both federal and state tax purposes. . . . The renovation of the store building constituted a capital improvement. The work was undertaken, not to maintain a state of repair existing when the property was received by the trustees, but to offset obsolescence brought about by changes in merchandising techniques. It materially increased the value of the property. . . . The installation of new fixtures was also a capital improvement. Although replacement of fixtures, component parts of a structure, or of mechanical apparatus may be ordinary repairs when done to maintain operating efficiency, that was not the purpose of the expenditures here. The purpose was to provide the lessee with essentially a new store, adapted for modern merchandising techniques. The trial court therefore erred in treating the expenditures for fixtures as ordinary repairs. . . .
>
> The improvement generates additional income for the life beneficiary, but if it depreciates in value with the passage of time, it will not benefit the remaindermen unless the trust terminates before the end of the useful life of the improvement. To require the remaindermen to pay the entire cost of a trust activity undertaken for the benefit of all the beneficiaries would contravene both the intent of the testator and the express provisions of the Principal and Income Law that ordinary expenses of trust management be met by income. . . .
>
> Allocation of the amounts withheld from income to a depreciation reserve account will provide a fund to meet the expense of making the improvements and of needed upkeep [by replacement of fixtures].

>> It avoids the necessity of speculating upon the probable duration of the trust and deducting immediately a gross sum from the income for the whole period. It results in an equalization of the income from year to year instead of the deduction of a large amount all in one year. If the life beneficiary lives as long as the probable duration of the improvements, he will ultimately have paid for the improvements, which is just, because in that case the remainderman ordinarily will have no advantage from the improvements. If the life beneficiary dies within a short time after the improvements are made, he pays for no more than the actual enjoyment he has had, and the remainderman who profits in that case pays the balance of the cost.

(3 Scott, Trusts (2d ed.) §233, p. 1760.) . . .

Depreciation of commercial or rental realty that formed part of the original trust corpus is also a proper trust expense unless the testator has expressed a contrary intent. Rules to the effect that the remainderman must bear the burden of shrinkage of trust capital due to depreciation were the outgrowth of concepts developed during the last century to govern the relation between legal life tenants and remaindermen. Such rules are not adequate to assure either profitable or equitable administration of a contemporary trust. . . . [A trustee can invest in realty] only if the interests of both the income beneficiary . . . and the remainderman . . . are protected. When a trustee who has the power to sell realty held in the trust and to invest the proceeds therefrom elects instead to retain the property, the duty to preserve corpus remains. . . . [H]e must adopt a method of accounting that will prevent the impairment of the principal unless the testator has clearly indicated a contrary intent. . . . An awareness that sound trust management requires that business properties be managed by trustees in such a way that they are not permitted to deteriorate at the expense of the remainderman is reflected in the decision of the Commissioners on Uniform State Laws to provide for a depreciation reserve account in the Uniform Revised Principal and Income Act (1962). . . .

When realty other than that to be occupied by the beneficiary is retained in a trust, the trustee must administer it as a business, allocating expenses in accordance with accepted accounting procedures if he is to fulfill his obligation to income beneficiary and remainderman and fulfill the normal intentions of the testator. . . . Property used in a trade or business continued by trustees is depreciable. As commercial or rental realty retained by trustees cannot be meaningfully distinguished from property used in a trade or business, it should be treated in a similar manner. . . .

. . . [T]he trustees should establish a depreciation schedule under which the improvements to the store building, including fixtures, will be depreciated on a straight line basis over their anticipated useful life. . . . Additionally, the value of the store building itself, before the modernization, is subject to depreciation. . . .

UNIFORM PRINCIPAL AND INCOME ACT
(1997)

§501. *Disbursements from Income.*

A trustee shall make the following disbursements from income to the extent that they are not disbursements to which Section 201(2)(B) or (C) applies:

(1) one-half of the regular compensation of the trustee and of any person providing investment advisory or custodial services to the trustee;

(2) one-half of all expenses for accountings, judicial proceedings, or other matters that involve both the income and remainder interests;

(3) all of the other ordinary expenses incurred in connection with the administration, management, or preservation of trust property and the distribution of income, including interest, ordinary repairs, regularly recurring taxes assessed against principal, and expenses of a proceeding or other matter that concerns primarily the income interest; and

(4) recurring premiums on insurance covering the loss of a principal asset or the loss of income from or use of the asset.

Comment

Trustee fees. The regular compensation of a trustee or the trustee's agent includes compensation based on a percentage of either principal or income or both. . . .

§502. *Disbursements from Principal.*

(a) A trustee shall make the following disbursements from principal:

(1) the remaining one-half of the disbursements described in Section 501(1) and (2);

(2) all of the trustee's compensation calculated on principal as a fee for acceptance, distribution, or termination, and disbursements made to prepare property for sale;

(3) payments on the principal of a trust debt;

(4) expenses of a proceeding that concerns primarily principal, including a proceeding to construe the trust or to protect the trust or its property;

(5) premiums paid on a policy of insurance not described in Section 501(4) of which the trust is the owner and beneficiary;

(6) estate, inheritance, and other transfer taxes, including penalties, apportioned to the trust; and

(7) disbursements related to environmental matters, including reclamation, assessing environmental conditions, remedying and removing environmental contamination, monitoring remedial activities and the release of substances, preventing future releases of substances, collecting amounts from persons liable or potentially liable for the costs of those activities, penalties imposed under environmental laws or regulations and other payments made to comply with those laws or regulations, statutory or common law claims by third parties, and defending claims based on environmental matters.

(b) If a principal asset is encumbered with an obligation that requires income from that asset to be paid directly to the creditor, the trustee shall transfer from principal to income an amount equal to the income paid to the creditor in reduction of the principal balance of the obligation.

Comment

Environmental expenses. All environmental expenses are payable from principal, subject to the power of the trustee to transfer funds to principal from income under Section 504. However, the Drafting Committee decided that it was not necessary to broaden this provision to cover other expenditures made under compulsion of governmental authority. See generally the annotation at 43 A.L.R. 4th 1012 (Duty as Between Life Tenant and Remainderman with Respect to Cost of Improvements or Repairs Made Under Compulsion of Government Authority).

Environmental expenses paid by a trust are to be paid from principal under Section 502(a)(7) on the assumption that they will usually be extraordinary in nature. . . .

Insurance premiums. Insurance premiums referred to in Section 502(a)(5) include title insurance premiums. They also include premiums on life insurance policies owned by the trust, which represent the trust's periodic investment in the insurance policy. There is no provision in the 1962 Act for life insurance premiums.

b. Depreciation

§503. *Transfers from Income to Principal for Depreciation.*

(a) In this section, "depreciation" means a reduction in value due to wear, tear, decay, corrosion, or gradual obsolescence of a fixed asset having a useful life of more than one year.

(b) A trustee may transfer to principal a reasonable amount of the net cash receipts from a principal asset that is subject to depreciation, but may not transfer any amount for depreciation:

(1) of that portion of real property used or available for use by a beneficiary as a residence or of tangible personal property held or made available for the personal use or enjoyment of a beneficiary;

(2) during the administration of a decedent's estate; or

(3) under this section if the trustee is accounting under Section 403 for the business or activity in which the asset is used.

(c) An amount transferred to principal need not be held as a separate fund.

Comment

Prior Acts. The 1931 Act has no provision for depreciation. Section 13(a)(2) of the 1962 Act provides that a charge shall be made against income for " . . . a reasonable allowance for depreciation on property subject to depreciation under generally accepted accounting principles. . . ." That provision has been resisted by many trustees, who do not provide for any depreciation for a variety of reasons. One reason relied upon is that a charge for depreciation is not needed to protect the remainder beneficiaries if the value of the land is increasing; another is that generally accepted accounting principles may not require depreciation to be taken if the property is not part of a business. The Drafting Committee concluded that the decision to provide for depreciation should be discretionary with the trustee. The power to transfer funds from income to principal that is granted by this section is a discretionary power of administration referred to in Section 103(b), and in exercising the power a trustee must comply with Section 103(b). . . .

c. Expenses and Other Disbursements

PROBLEM

19-K.   *X* is executor and trustee under the will in question. The entire estate was left to *X* as trustee, and probate administration is now ready to be closed. One of the main assets of the estate is an apartment building the trustee is authorized to retain. It is appraised at $500,000. Two matters have been brought to your attention as attorney for *X*. The first is that the taxes on the apartment building had not been paid for several years preceding the testator's death and were paid from the rental receipts during estate administration. The second is that the municipality in which the building is located recently built a new sewage disposal plant. An ordinance was adopted increasing real estate taxes for a period of five years by raising the tax base from 60 percent to 75 percent of appraised values. It is anticipated that the increased revenue will enable the city to pay for the sewage plant in five years after which the tax base is to return to 60 percent. How should *X* account for the taxes he has paid and expects to pay in the future, as between income and principal?

MATTER OF CRONISE
167 Misc. 310, 6 N.Y.S.2d 392 (Surr. Ct. 1937)

FEELY, S.

In this final judicial settlement of the account of the executor, several matters are to be determined, mainly, the apportionment of the estate or death taxes laid both by the Federal government and by the State of New York; and next the allocation of certain disbursements of the executor as between the life beneficiary and the residuary legatees.

Testatrix was domiciled in Rochester, N.Y., where she made her last will on April 2, 1933, and died on the eighteenth of the next August. After the will had been probated in this court, it was re-probated in Stockton, Cal., where testatrix also had both real and personal property. Her last will was that her debts and funeral expenses be paid; and also $5,000 be given to Mills College for a scholarship. By the third paragraph she gave to her sister, Mrs. Eliza F.H. Middlecoff, now by marriage, Mrs. Emery, of Stockton, Cal., "all real estate owned by me situate in the State of California"; and by the next paragraph to the same sister there was given "as her absolute property all my personal effects such as jewelry, clothing, household furniture and all other articles of domestic and personal use." These personal effects lay in Rochester, N.Y. The general residue of her estate was given to Security Trust Company, in trust, "(a) to collect and receive the rent, issues, income and profits thereof, and after paying therefrom all lawful dues and expenses in respect thereof, to pay the net income thereof to my said sister, Eliza F.H. Middlecoff, in monthly payments as long as she shall live; and (b) on the death of my said sister, the corpus, with any unpaid net income to" two named nephews, who are the children of the life beneficiary, and are residents of the State of California.

1. There is nothing else in the will that bears on the matter of allocation or apportionment.

The general rule, as shown by Surrogate Wingate in Matter of Shepard, 136 Misc. 218, is to charge principal only with such expenses as tend to enhance the value of the principal of the trust while income must bear all ordinary expenses connected with the continuance of the property in substantially its existing state; and this is especially so where the will gives only the "net" income. See, also, Matter of Lichtenstein, Rochester Daily Record of July 11, 1932.

In other words, Mr. H. W. Jessup summarizes the rule by saying that expenditures to protect the integrity of the corpus, to avert wastage, etc., are charged to principal; but those made to assure productivity, or for ordinary administration costs are charged to income.

In Matter of Brewster (148 Misc. 390, 392), from which the foregoing summary of the rules is copied, the same distinction is also expressed by referring to one class as items made to assure productivity, but to the other class as items of a structural or defensive character.

The facts bearing on the allocation of outlays, other than for death or estate taxes, are undisputed. The homestead is a large, spacious house, on a large city lot, in a somewhat central section of this city and in a neighborhood that has changed from a fine residential section to one of a boarding house and professional office class; and at death of testatrix was not the kind of a house that could be let to an ordinary family. This real property is valued at $15,000. Despite the executor's efforts, the house was neither sold nor leased, except that the life tenant was in occupancy of it from November 1, 1933, till December twentieth following; and thereafter it stood idle until October, 1935, when it was let at a rental that hardly meets the carrying charges. The expenses of fitting up the property for this tenant is one of the items in question.

In the meantime, the executor paid a caretaker to watch the property and keep the yard and walks in condition; and in the house there were living for a time, for the purpose of caring for the house and its contents, a maid and a sister-in-law of the testatrix, for whom food, etc., was supplied by the executor until the arrival here of the life beneficiary. These outlays kept the property in good condition, and protected it from the dangers to which vacant houses are nowadays exposed, especially when filled, as this house was, with furniture, etc., of the appraised value of $5,612 (New York tax deposition), which had been specifically bequeathed to the life beneficiary as the latter's absolute property. This movable property the executor could as well have put into a public storage warehouse at the charge of the specific legatee. On the basis of the value of the lot and house alone at about $15,000, and this specific legacy at $5,612, one-fourth of these caretaking charges, with insurance premiums on personalty, should be borne by the specific legatee, and the remaining three-fourths should be apportioned between the life beneficiary and the residuary legatees in such ratio as the value of the life estate bears to that of the residuary, because to that extent a common benefit was derived therefrom by both parties in interest. A like apportionment should be made of the expense of caretaking (other than fire insurance) from the time the life beneficiary moved out, taking the personal property with her, until the present tenant was found in October, 1935. The city and county taxes that became liens before the death of testatrix for ordinary purposes other than for local improvements, must be borne wholly by the residuary legatees, but those that became liens after the death of testatrix fall entirely to the charge of the life beneficiary under the provision of the will giving her only "net" income.

On September 14, 1933, a plumbing bill of six dollars was incurred, which was paid December 13, 1933. This appears to have been an ordinary repair. The fact that it was the culmination of wear that probably was given it mainly in the lifetime of the testatrix does not lessen the obligation of the life beneficiary, now that the latter has accepted benefits under the will, from bearing the whole of this charge, as she is deemed to have accepted the condition of the property as it was on the date of the death of the testatrix. No authority for apportionment of any such repair charge has come to the attention of this court.

Most of the other outlay in question arose out of the fitting up of the large outmoded family residence so that it could be used as a boarding house. In this adaptation, the making of a new bathroom was required in addition to the existing two; and $22 was laid out on a partition, $10 on resetting a door, and $100.63 for decoration after these changes. The plumber's bill for the fixtures installed in this new bathroom, with ventilation, amounts to $233. As the only call in this neighborhood is for a lay-out suitable either for boarding house purposes or for the offices of medical or dental doctors, this adaptation was necessary rather than optional, and was designed to "assure productivity," and at the same time it consisted of a permanent addition to the structure of the house; and the cost should be apportioned.

The same is true of the bill of thirty-five dollars spent to run a new pipe line from the heater to the old front bathroom on the second floor, which never before had been heated, except by the seepage from adjoining rooms. Likewise, the seven dollars and five cents spent for new door bells; and the forty-eight dollars and sixty-six cents spent for new wire screens for windows that never had been so equipped before; and the thirty dollars spent for firebelt and rope to comply with the ordinance in respect of the apartment on the third floor. All of these should be apportioned between the life beneficiary and the residuary legatees in such ratio as the value of the life estate bears to that of the residuary interests. (Matter of Laytin, 2 Con. Surr. 106. See, also, Peerless Candy Co. v. Kessler, 123 Misc. 735; Matter of Whitney, 75 id. 610; Peck v. Sherwood, 56 N.Y. 615.)

Then there is a group of replacement of outworn items, like the ninety-one dollars spent to replace a worn-out water heater with a new one. The residuaries were not required either to repair or to replace it (Stevens v. Melcher, 80 Hun. 514, 524); but the life beneficiary would find her income impaired without one, in the peculiar circumstances of this case. Similarly, the removal of the old coal range, and the replacing of it with a used one, at a cost of fourteen dollars and sixty-three cents; and also the replacement of an old ice box with a used electric refrigerator at a cost of $139.50; and likewise in the heating system, an old oil burner, that had been fitted to the furnace had worn to uselessness, and was replaced with a used burner, and the furnace reset, at a cost of $150; these replacements were substantial, and were all put in to stay as long as they should last; although the manner in which some were connected or fastened was not in itself enough to indicate the permanency of the intention with which they were installed. All these replacements, in the circumstances, should be apportioned between the life beneficiary and the residuaries, as aforesaid.

Then there is a group of ordinary repairs, such as the leak in the water pipe, repaired at a cost of fifteen dollars; the repairs to the trap under the tile floor in the old bathroom, at a cost of fifty-nine dollars and seven cents; also the two dollars and forty-seven cents paid to relieve stoppage in the laundry trays; the synchronizing of the thermostat, and repair of leaks, at a cost of six dollars and twenty-four cents; the twenty-five dollars paid for painting the living room; and the twenty-three dollars and thirty cents paid for repairs to the oil burner; and the replacement of the fallen ceiling with plasterboard at a cost of seventeen dollars and twenty-five cents, probably necessitated by the leaks mentioned above — all these fall entirely to the charge of the life beneficiary. To this class should be added the ten dollars paid to clear the garage of the two useless and worthless old safes.

2. The executor's expense in probating this will in California inured to the benefit of the legatee to whom testatrix had devised specifically "all real estate owned by me situate in the State of California"; and it also benefited the residuary trust inasmuch as there was considerable personal property, also situate in that State, which will go into this trust. May the expense be allocated or apportioned for that reason? An executor, by accepting the nomination as such, becomes obliged to execute the last will; and to that end a decree of probate is practically indispensable. The will is thus formally established in several respects — as one integral act, and also conclusively as to all parties in interest, and as to all the property of the testatrix wheresoever situate — at least, such is the policy of New York as to regularly foreign-made wills that are in writing and subscribed by testator. Re-probate is usually not required in New York, although it is practiced in some other jurisdictions. The integral character of the act of probate — whatever be its procedural incidents in other jurisdictions — whether by record there of an exemplified copy, or by a decree re-probating the original instrument — appears to have caused it to be ever regarded here as a fundamental administrative expense, properly chargeable to corpus on account of its general structural nature. While the executor was not obliged, in an amply solvent estate like this, to take possession of the sometime property of the testatrix situate in other jurisdictions that had been specifically devised or bequeathed by her, nor to make actual physical delivery thereof to its specific legatee (Matter of Columbia Trust Co., 186 App. Div. 377), still the executor was obliged to execute the last will whereby the property had been given, and also to establish title thereto in the ordinary manner as an inseparable part of the integral will he undertook to execute. To ask the legatee of specified property, other than the residue, to pay the expense of formally establishing the wish that the legatee should have it before others were served — as is usually the intention of testators — is not in line with that intention, nor justified by any authority known to this court. This applies not only to the specified land but also to the rest of the California property, to wit, the personalty there, which will go into the residuary trust for the respective benefit of the life beneficiary and of the residuaries solely by virtue of the indivisible act of probating and establishing the wish that it should ultimately benefit them, among others also remembered in the last will. It is not the practice, and to a large extent impracticable to apportion or allocate any such fundamental expense among all the

various interests created or benefited by the will, including tax gatherers, lawyers and funeral directors. None of the expense of the California probate, nor that of obtaining possession of the movable property situate there should be apportioned, but should all be borne by the corpus of the estate as a general administrative expense.

3. Some of the ordinary taxes of the California real estate had become liens on January 1, 1933, three months before the date of her will and eight months before the death of the testatrix. While she may not have been liable therefor personally, still they had become liens on her landed interests in her lifetime, and for that reason fall wholly to the charge of the estate at large, to wit, the residue; and without any right of apportionment, because they antedate the inception of the estate and the erection of the trust therein. (See Matter of Babcock, 115 N.Y. 450.) These liens fall in the statutory class of "taxes assessed on property of the deceased previous to his death," which are to be paid as debts in the order or priority defined in subdivision 2 of section 212 of the Surrogate's Court Act.

Mrs. Emery, having paid $7,659.96 of taxes on the California land which had been assessed in the lifetime of the testatrix, is now entitled to credit therefor.

4. As to apportionment of death or estate taxes, . . . New York in 1930 enacted [legislation] for the apportionment of Federal and State estate taxes, and authorized therein the executor either to deduct the apportioned share from the distribution, or to recover it from the person benefited. . . .

The objectant, Mrs. Emery, being subject to the New York law of apportionment, is thereby made liable to an action to recover the portion of the Federal estate tax allotted to her in respect either of her specific legacy, or of her right to income from the residuary trust. To facilitate a prompt settlement of this estate, and to avoid the delay and expense of pursuing that administrative cause of action in some other jurisdiction, this court under its broadened equity powers will decree that enough of her income may be impounded to fully satisfy this obligation now and be applied thereto, unless sooner met otherwise.

5. The outlays made to preserve the lien of certain mortgages subject now to the Alberta Moratorium Act, as set out in Schedule H, should be temporarily charged to principal, until that matter can be finally adjusted.

On notice to counsel, or on voluntary appearance, submit for signature and enter a decree in accord with this decision.

The problem of the estate tax burden and apportionment in the above case is considered further in a subsequent section. One particular aspect of the apportionment problem in the *Cronise* case should be noted, however. As a practical matter the New York apportionment rule was enforced against the devisee of the California land through her interest in the residuary trust, which was under the control of the New York court. If this devisee had received no interest under the will other than the land in California, how might the matter of the tax burden have been handled? Could the testator have required apportionment?

The allocation and apportionment of expenses of a trust estate are treated in §13 of the Revised Principal and Income Act (1962). Compare id. §5; and §§501 and 502 of the 1997 Act, supra.

ESTATE OF LOPEZ
79 Cal. App. 2d 399, 179 P.2d 621 (1947)

GOODELL, J. . . .

The respondent trustee filed in the superior court its first account and report in each of two trusts created by the will of Robert F. Lopez. . . .

In the orders settling the accounts the court allowed compensation to the trustee and its attorneys for their services during said first year of administration and charged one-half thereof against the corpus and one-half against the income, of the respective trusts. From those orders this appeal was taken. . . .

The appellant [contends "that] the trustee may not impair the principal of the trust estate by paying therefrom compensation for itself and its attorneys but must pay such out of the income." . . . The testamentary provision creating each trust provides:

> 2. The said trustee shall collect and receive any . . . income, issues and profits . . . and shall dispose of all such cash revenue from said trust fund:
>
> (a) By first paying . . . taxes and the reasonable expenses of this trust which shall include the reasonable compensation of said Trustee for its service as Trustee hereunder, and the reasonable compensation of any attorney employed by said Trustee in the administration of said trust fund; and
>
> (b) By paying . . . the surplus to [the life beneficiary] for her support and maintenance during her life.

Appellant contends that the provisions of paragraph (a) that the net income shall be arrived at after the deduction, inter alia, of the trustees and attorney's compensation from the gross income so circumscribes the court's action that it cannot make any charge whatever against corpus. She also invokes section 2 of the Principal and Income Act . . . which provides that:

> This act shall govern the ascertainment of income and principal, . . . except that . . . the person establishing the principal may himself direct the manner of ascertainment of income and principal and the apportionment of receipts and expenses or grant discretion to the trustee or other person to do so, and such provision and direction, where not otherwise contrary to law, shall control notwithstanding this act.

The year covered by these two accounts, it must be remembered, was the first year of the administration of both trusts. The duties of the trustee and its attorneys during that first year embraced the acceptance of the trust property which, in turn, involved putting both trusts into operation, the determination of questions of corpus and income in organizing the trust funds, the settling of tax problems consequent upon the new administration, setting up the necessary accountancy machinery, and in the case of the Leonardini trust, the purchase of a home in Stockton for the use and occupancy of Mrs. Leonardini, the life beneficiary. None of these can be classified as ordinary, routine, recurring, or year-round duties any more than the tasks connected with the distribution or winding up of a trust can be.

Section 12 of the act provides that the trustee's compensation upon or for acceptance or distribution of principal shall be paid out of principal, [but as] we view this case it is not necessary for us to decide whether or not the court's action was taken under the Principal and Income Act.

In Estate of Kruce, 10 Cal. App. 2d 426, 51 P.2d 1174, the testamentary provision was not substantially different from that in paragraph 2(a) of the Lopez will quoted above. . . . The court said, page 430:

> We do . . . not think the provisions of the will depart from this rule. *The direction of the will would seem to apply to the current compensation and expenses of the trustees and not to anything of an extraordinary nature.* The services for which the allowances were made consisted of closing the trust and distributing the property remaining therein after the death of the life tenant. They were performed necessarily for the benefit of the remaindermen and were unrelated to the management of the trust for the benefit of the life estate. *They were not such ordinary and current expenses as would have to be deducted from the income periodically in order that the net income might be computed and paid to the life tenant each month as directed by the will.*

(Emphasis added.)

The language just quoted is particularly applicable to this case and we think is controlling. . . .

The orders settling the two accounts and approving the trustees' reports are affirmed.

Cf. Creed v. McAleer, 275 Mass. 353, 358-359, 175 N.E. 761, 763 (1931).

d. New Financial Instruments

UNIFORM PRINCIPAL AND INCOME ACT
(1997)

§414. *Derivatives and Options.*

(a) In this section, "derivative" means a contract or financial instrument or a combination of contracts and financial instruments which gives a trust the right or obligation to participate in some or all changes in the price of a tangible or intangible asset or group of assets, or changes in a rate, an index of prices or rates, or other market indicator for an asset or a group of assets.

(b) To the extent that a trustee does not account under Section 403 for transactions in derivatives, the trustee shall allocate to principal receipts from and disbursements made in connection with those transactions.

(c) If a trustee grants an option to buy property from the trust, whether or not the trust owns the property when the option is granted, grants an option that permits another person to sell property to the trust, or acquires an option to buy property for the trust or an option to sell an asset owned by the trust, and the trustee or other owner of the asset is required to deliver the asset if the option is exercised, an amount received for granting the option must be allocated to principal. An amount paid to acquire the option must be paid from principal. A gain or loss realized upon the exercise of an option, including an option granted to a settlor of the trust for services rendered, must be allocated to principal.

Comment

... **Definition of "derivative."** "Derivative" is a difficult term to define because new derivatives are invented daily as dealers tailor their terms to achieve specific financial objectives for particular clients. Since derivatives are typically contract-based, a derivative can probably be devised for almost any set of objectives if another party can be found who is willing to assume the obligations required to meet those objectives. ...

A derivative is frequently described as including futures, forwards, swaps and options, terms that also require definition, and the definition in this Act avoids these terms. . . .

Section 415 of the 1997 Act deals with asset-backed securities, defined as "an asset whose value is based upon the right it gives the owner to receive distributions from the proceeds of financial assets that provided collateral for the security." The Comment lists among asset-backed securities "arrangements in which debt obligations such as real estate mortgages, credit card receivables and auto loans are acquired by an investment trust and interests in the trust are sold to investors." Under §415 if a trust receives a payment, the portion which the payer identifies as being from interest or current return is allocated to income, and the balance is allocated to principal. Payments received in exchange for the trust's entire interest in an asset-backed security in one accounting period are allocated entirely to principal, and similar payments received over more than one accounting period are allocated 10 percent to income and the balance to principal.

B.   *Special Problems Posed by Business Interests Administered in Trust*

A sophisticated but not unusual problem for an estate planner, or a trustee's counsel, is how to deal with a closely held business, and particularly what trust provisions are helpful if such a business, incorporated or not, is to be continued in trust. Sensitive issues include those having to do with trust principal-and-income accounting. Often the bulk of the wealth of an estate owner is tied up in a family business, in one of several increasingly diverse forms. The considerations are likely to be much more complicated even than the challenging dividends and split problems examined above — not to mention that other branches of law, family dynamics, and business finance become important in planning, drafting details, and administration.

HOLMES v. HROBON
93 Ohio App. 1, 103 N.E.2d 845 (1950)

[Action for declaratory judgment instituted in 1946 by H. B. Holmes, as trustee under the will of C. M. Thomas, seeking construction of the will and instructions concerning the administration of the trust.

Thomas died testate in 1938 leaving the residue of his estate to Holmes, his attorney for many years, in trust to pay his widow, Mae Thomas,

> all the income after the payment of operating expenses and taxes and other charges from my business at The Atlas Linen Laundry [an unincorporated business], or any other income that I may have after the payment of the other monthly legacies which I herebefore have set out.

A codicil authorized continuation of any business of the testator and added the "wish that the said trustee shall continue my linen and laundry business as long as the same may be profitable." The trust was to terminate on the widow's death, and the property was then to be distributed to the testator's "legal heirs." The trust property consisted of the assets of the Atlas business (net worth about $75,000) and certain unrelated real estate.

During the period until August 1946 the widow, who has remarried and is now Mae Thomas Hrobon, received from the trustee an average of nearly $33,000 annually, or a total in excess of $260,000. In September 1946 she demanded additional sums primarily as income of the Atlas business from prior periods. Her demands included amounts of income expended for the purchase of five competing businesses ($104,000) and for the purchase of machinery and equipment, designated in the subsequent report of a referee as "replacements" ($140,000) and "additions" ($62,000). Other facts appear in the opinion of the Court of Appeals printed below; certain issues have been omitted.]

WISEMAN, J. . . .

The referee held that income payable to the life tenant should be arrived at by computing the gross income from the operation of the Atlas Plant and other income producing properties of the decedent; and deducting therefrom all operating costs recognized . . . for [federal] income tax purposes; [and] that in the operating costs of the Atlas Plant there should be included maintenance, *expansion necessary to keep pace with the increase or progress and continued operation of the business of the plant,* the cost of the management of the trust, including the trustee's compensation, court costs, fees of counsel necessarily incurred in the administration of the trust, *and the interpretation of the will, also expenses occasioned by litigation and other charges incurred under the supervision and control of the court.* . . . We disagree with the referee with respect to that part of the finding which is [italicized]. . . .

The words in the will, the meaning of which is in dispute, are "other charges." The life tenant contends that the rule of ejusdem generis applies, restricting the meaning of the term to items of expense similar to operating expenses and taxes. We do not believe that the testator intended to give these words such a restricted meaning.

The trustee and remaindermen contend that the words "other charges" should be given a broad meaning because of the broad powers conferred on the trustee [to continue the business]. The trustee and the remaindermen contend, and the referee finds, that the powers thus conferred authorized the trustee to conduct the laundry business in the same manner as if it were his own enterprise [including discretion whether] any of the income from the business should be used for expansion purposes, such as purchasing competing businesses, purchasing additional land and additional machinery for such expanded business, in order that the laundry business "may be profitable." In other words, the trustee interpreted the will, and the referee agreed, that it was the intention of the testator that the trustee could do anything necessary to operate successfully. Record, p. 917. We do not agree. The testator had in mind that the trustee may not be able to operate the business profitably and so provided for the sale of the business.

We recognize that in operating a business, such as a laundry business, it would be advisable to confer wide discretionary power on the trustee in determining whether a certain given expense, such as money expended for the purchase of competing businesses and for additional land and machinery for the operation of the expanded business, would be for the best interest of the trust. However, unless the provisions of the will expressly provide that the trustee shall have such wide discretionary power to take income, which would otherwise be distributed to the life tenant, and to use it for such purpose, the trustee has no authority to make such expenditures. Authority to operate does not confer power on trustee to allocate the costs of replacements and additions to the detriment of the life tenant and benefit of the remaindermen. . . . We find no provision in the will which would permit a construction that it was the intention of the testator that the trustee in the operation of the laundry business could deprive the life tenant of a portion of her income to expand the business, thereby increasing the corpus at her expense. . . .

We now apply the principle herein announced to several controversial matters in which the trustee expended from the income substantial sums of money in the conduct of the laundry business.

A. Cost of Linens — Float

The referee found that "float" is a term used to denote linens and garments in use; that is, in the hands of customers, in trucks, and at the Atlas Plant being laundered. The life of these linens and garments, according to the evidence, is considerably less than one year. The referee properly found from the evidence that "float" is expensed as soon as it is put into use, and appears as an "operating expense" on the statement of income. The referee also found that the testator in the operation of the laundry business and in his income tax returns followed the policy of expensing float as of the date it went into use, and that the trustee, upon assuming charge of the trust, followed the same policy. . . .

The increase in the value of material in stock, and also the material in use, known as float, was largely due to the persistent effort on the part of the trustee to expand the business and particularly in the purchase of like competing businesses. . . . [T]he purchase of competing businesses, which will be treated later under an additional heading, resulted in the expansion of the business and necessitated the purchase of additional machinery, additional trucks, additional supplies, and resulted in a tremendous increase [$14,000 to almost $100,000] in the amount and value of float. . . . All of the cost of float was paid from income.

It is the contention of the trustee and the legatees that the life tenant was the direct beneficiary of this expansion of the business and this manner of operation for the reason that her income increased correspondingly each succeeding year. The life tenant contends that since the material in stock and float has been tremendously increased in value a credit should be given the life tenant at this time for the increased inventory value of the material on hand and for float over and above the inventory value for such material and float at the beginning of the trust. If these were done the effect would be to permit the life tenant to receive the income from the use of float in the business and, also, a credit for the estimated value of float at the end of the accounting period. We cannot accept this view of the matter, since it is the fact that linens, etc., are totally consumed and depreciated within a few months after being taken out of stock and put into use, and that it is the accepted practice to expense linens, etc., as soon as such material is taken from stock and put into use.

The life tenant has received and now claims the income derived from the use of float in the business. In order to keep the business operating on a high level of income, the trustee must annually expend large sums for material which goes into stock. The purchase of such material is properly charged to income. The increased cost of material going into stock in turn produces an increase in net income distributable to the life tenant.

We are in accord with the contention of the life tenant to the extent that the trustee should not be permitted to gradually build up the inventory of such material during the conduct of the trust and charge it to income and at the termination of the trust regard such material in inventory and float as corpus. In respect to float we fail to find any injustice resulting to the life tenant during the continuation of the trust. It is upon the termination of the trust that an adjustment must be made, otherwise the remaindermen would be unjustly enriched at the expense of the life tenant. Then, too, in the event of the sale of the business material in inventory and in float would be a substantial item in determining the value of the business. It would be at that juncture in the relationship of the parties that an adjustment would be required. . . .

B. *Expansion — Businesses Purchased*

The referee found from the record that from January 18, 1940 to and including the 19th day of May, 1945, the trustee purchased five similar competing businesses. The total costs of purchase of the several businesses were paid out of the gross income of the trust. The trustee contends that since the will placed no limitation upon the trustee respecting the purchase of new businesses that, therefore, the trustee may do so. This Court holds to the proposition that the trustee has not the power to purchase new businesses unless the will expressly confers the power on him to do so. "Full power and authority to conduct and carry on the laundry business," and "to do all things necessary or proper in the usual course of said business," which was the power conferred on the trustee in the will, does not authorize him to purchase new businesses. To do "all things necessary" means to do all things necessary as trustee and not as sole proprietor. . . . A private individual may use income to expand at will; a trustee may not unless authority is clearly given.

But it is claimed that the life tenant consented to the purchase of other businesses by the trustee. The record does not show that the trustee discussed with the life tenant the purchase of the first three businesses. . . . However, it does appear that an application was filed in the Probate Court by the trustee to purchase The 5¢ Towel and Supply business and The Bowden Towel and Supply Company. The Court in an ex parte order granted the application. The life tenant had no notice and such order would not be binding on her. . . .

This situation presents two questions: First, the power and authority of the trustee under the will to make the purchases. On this issue we conclude that the trustee exceeded his powers in the purchase of these businesses. Second, the trustee, having made the purchases, against whom should the cost be charged? . . . The physical assets received through these purchases fall into the category of additional equipment and machinery purchased by the trustee. The physical assets received by the trustee, such as trucks, machinery, etc., should be charged to corpus in the same manner as any other additional equipment and machinery, and depreciated over a period of years in the same manner; the life tenant to be charged annually for depreciation during the life of such assets. The difference between the value of the physical assets and the purchase price is the amount paid for good will and becomes a part of and should be charged to corpus. This method of accounting is discussed more fully under the next sub-heading.

C.   Replacements — Additions to Laundry Building

It is conceded that repairs to machinery, equipment and buildings are properly charged to income.

The referee found from the record that between May 1, 1938 and August 31, 1946, new property assets, such as machinery and equipment, were purchased during this period at a total cost of $201,883.33, of which amount $140,091.20 was for replacements and $61,792.13 was for additions. The purchase price of these various property assets was deducted from the net income as "other charges" in the year purchased, so that the distributable income to the life tenant was reduced over this period by reason of the cost of these property assets. The referee further found that in each year the amount of depreciation on the items so purchased was credited to net income in determining the distributable income to the life tenant [thereby relieving distributable income of depreciation charges on the replacements and additions]; that during this period these credits amounted to $39,823.18 for replacements and $18,163.25 for additions, or a total of $57,986.43. The difference between the latter figure and $201,883.33, the total cost of such assets so purchased up to the year of 1946, will be credited back to net income of life tenant in succeeding years so that by 1955 the total depreciation credits will equal the amount of the cost of the assets.

The trustee and the legatees contend . . . that in the event of the death of the life tenant at a time prior to the receiving by the life tenant of all of such depreciation credits there will be due her estate the balance of such depreciation credits. . . . This method of operation of the trust, and this system of accounting of charges and credits forces the life tenant to finance the operation of the business out of her income from year to year, and because of the increase of the business and the expansion of the business by the trustee from year to year, the life tenant is required to forego each succeeding year a larger share of her income; so that at no time during the operation of the trust would she receive the total amount of income due her for any current year. As a result there would be from year to year an increasing total amount of depreciation credits due her. It is contended by the remaindermen that at her death her estate could make claim against the trust for the total amount of such depreciation credits due her.

The life tenant is not interested in depreciation credits. The life tenant is entitled to receive each calendar year the net income from the Atlas business after deducting operating expenses, taxes and other charges as defined by this Court. If some of the assets which are considered to be corpus are replaced the cost [should be] charged to the corpus and a depreciation charge should be made against the income of the life tenant for each year during the life of such replacement. The same is true with respect to additions which depreciate through use and produce income. In Restatement of the Law, Trusts, Vol. I, Section 233, Note 1, page 688, the author states:

> . . . [T]he result is that if the trust does not terminate before the end of the probable life of the improvements, the whole cost of the improvements will be paid out of income. This is fair because the beneficiary entitled to the income gets the full benefit of the improvements and the remainderman gets no benefit. On the other hand, if the trust terminates prior to the end of the probable life of the improvements, the payments from income will cease on the termination of the trust. This is fair because the beneficiary entitled to the income has not received the full benefit from the improvements but the remainderman receives a part of the benefit. . . .

However, the trustee now contends that he will experience financial difficulty if he is required to operate the trust as directed by this Court. The trustee contends that since he has no working capital, and the net income is distributed to the life tenant, he is required of necessity to charge the cost of replacements and additions to income and give the life tenant a depreciation credit each year during the useful life of the article. As we have heretofore stated, we have rejected this method on the ground that it forces the life tenant to finance the operation of the trust out of income, and therefore deprives the life tenant of a substantial portion of her income each accounting period. In our judgment this method is neither fair nor just to the life tenant, and is contrary to fundamental principles of trust law.

We do not believe the trustee will experience serious difficulty in operating the trust as directed by this Court. We have found that the trustee has no power to purchase additions except machinery and equipment required to take care of the normal increase of trade. Had the trustee, in the conduct of the trust thus far, confined his purchases of replacements and additions to take care of the normal increase of trade, it is our opinion he would have been able to conduct the trust by making bank loans and mortgaging trust property. As a matter of fact the record shows that the trustee did make repeated bank loans and applied to the Probate Court for authority to mortgage the trust res. This is the accepted procedure to be followed by the trustee where there is no working capital. However, it is the duty of the trustee to find working capital. There are assets in the trust, exclusive of the laundry business, which may be liquidated and the proceeds placed in a working capital account or a reserve account. . . . See Scott on Trusts, Section 233.3 in the 1951 supplement, page 116, which reads as follows:

> Where a trust is created for successive beneficiaries, the trustee cannot properly set up a reserve out of income for future improvements. . . .

The finding of the referee is sustained in part and overruled in part. . . .

[Dissenting opinion omitted.]

HOLMES v. HROBON
158 Ohio St. 508, 110 N.E.2d 574 (1953)

[The opinion that follows involves the next reported step of the litigation in the above case. Parts of the opinion of the Supreme Court of Ohio are omitted; these deal with issues omitted in the printed portions of the preceding opinion.]

MIDDLETON, J. . . .

Giving full consideration to the desire of the testator that the Atlas business be continued, the history of its past operation, the fact that it had always been operated and expanded out of earnings, the complete lack of capital with which the trustee could operate, the amount of the profits realized from the business during the latter years of operation by the testator and the impossibility of operation by the trustee without using a portion of the income as capital, we conclude that it was the intention of the testator to and he did authorize the use by the trustee of income in the operation and expansion of Atlas, even though such use reduced the amount of profits currently available for payment to the widow. The right of the trustee to so use income would exist only so long as the business was operated profitably and the widow received a reasonable amount of the income. That the widow has not suffered hardship is evidenced by payment to her of $263,299.72 up to August 31, 1946. Although the record does not contain evidence of the amounts paid to the widow since 1946, photostatic copies of checks in her favor included in the briefs indicate payment of $100,000 to her during the first ten months of 1952.

The right of the trustee to use income in operation extends to all phases of operation which sound business judgment would approve, but such right of the trustee to use a portion of the income does not authorize accounting such as will result in currently increasing the corpus of the trust estate or confiscation of income payable to the life tenant.

This court does not undertake to direct the detailed manner in which the trustee's accounts should be kept. It is hoped, however, that such general principles may be herein stated as will enable accountants to rewrite or amend the trustee's books of accounts so that they will satisfy all legal requirements. . . .

The first item of capital is the value of the corpus of the trust. The "corpus" of the trust as here used is that portion of the total assets of the estate remaining after deduction of all debts of the testator as they existed at the time of his death, all taxes, the widow's year's allowance, the amount exempt from administration and the entire cost of the administration. Upon determination of that amount it should be shown in the books of account and it will represent the amount as to which the remaindermen were entitled to the protection of law at the inception of the trust. The corpus of the trust is an amount of money representing the net assets of the estate as above stated. It does not consist of specific property. When so set up on the books of account, the amount of money representing the corpus of the trust will not be reduced as a result of the operation of the business. On the other hand, the use of income by the trustee in the operation, maintenance or expansion of the business must not be permitted to result in currently increasing the value of the corpus of the trust.

Expenditures by the trust out of income may, and in all probability will, result in increasing the total net assets used in operation of the business. This may be considered as increasing the capital. Since, as we have stated, such increase does not currently change the value of the corpus of the trust, that increase in the capital belongs to the widow and she is entitled to receive it upon sale of the business or termination of the trust. The books of account must be so kept that annual statements will reflect the total net assets of the trust and reflect both the unchanging value of the corpus and the additional capital resulting from expenditure of income. It would seem obvious that at a given time the latter element of capital, to wit, the amount thereof resulting from investment of income, will be the difference between the total net assets and the original and unchanged value of the corpus.

The court is mindful of the fact that upon sale of the business or termination of the trust there may be an item of intangible value, goodwill or going value, not represented by physical assets or cash in the hands of the trustee, the disposition of which may call for the court's determination at that time. No such issue is now before this court and this decision is not to be considered as dispositive of any such questions or issues except to the limited extent herein stated. . . .

The words "other charges," which appear in item V of the will have been given much consideration by the lower courts and have been discussed in briefs at great length. Is their meaning to be limited to items similar to operating expenses and taxes under the rule of ejusdem generis or should they be given a broader interpretation in harmony with the broad powers given to the trustee? We adopt the latter interpretation.

Referring to specific transactions affected by that interpretation, we hold that the trustee had the right and authority to use income as needed with which to purchase five competing businesses. We do not, however, approve the accounting now in the records of the trustee with respect to those purchases. . . . The trustee included the items of equipment in appropriate accounts but charged the entire balance covering "float" (linen in service) and intangibles to operating expense in the years of the respective purchases. Such accounting does not protect the interests of the life tenant. . . . [T]he amount of the purchase price remaining after deduction of cost of equipment and value of linen in service — in other words, the amount representing intangible ["goodwill"] value — should be included in the capital assets but should be amortized and written out of the capital account over a period of years. . . . Income of the widow would thus be used to purchase those items of goodwill but, the investment having been made in the exercise of sound business judgment, it is to be assumed that the income of the widow during the succeeding years would be increased by reason of such expenditure of income. . . .

Upon sale of the business or termination of the trust, the unamortized portions of the cost of goodwill of the five businesses purchased [may] still be present in the statement of capital assets and the widow would be entitled to receive such unamortized amounts, provided, however, that such payment to her may not effect any reduction in the stated value of the "corpus."

Since the life of linen in service is shown to be less than one year, the trustee's practice of charging the linen to expense when put into service is approved. For like reasons we approve of charging the value of "float," purchased with the five businesses, to expense in the year of purchase. . . .

The judgment of the Court of Appeals is affirmed in part and reversed in part, and the cause is remanded for accounting consistent herewith.

For a thorough and informative examination of the above litigation and related problems, see Krasnowiecki, Existing Rules of Trust Administration: A Stranglehold on the Trustee-Controlled Business Enterprise, 110 U. Pa. L. Rev. 506 (Part I, The Unincorporated Business), 816 (Part II, The Incorporated Business) (1962).

How might the drafter attempt to deal with such problems of operating an unincorporated business in trust, such as setting up reserves for depreciation, depletion, replacement, or expansion? Does statutory or testamentary authorization "to continue the decedent's business" mean the trustee can do anything an owner could do? Does the customary business practice reflected in the income tax law, federal or state, impliedly authorize a trustee to establish depreciation reserves in order to obtain a tax benefit for the trust or some beneficiaries? Compare Uniform Trustees Powers Act §3(b), (c)(3), (21); Revised Uniform Principal and Income Act §§8, 13. Would these problems be any different if the business interest bequeathed to the trustee had been in the form of the capital stock of an incorporated business? How would these matters be affected if the corporate shares involved represented a controlling interest in the business but not all of the outstanding stock? Can the trustee who receives an unincorporated business interest hope to solve these problems by incorporation? Compare Uniform Trustees Powers Act §3(c)(3). If the law of the state does not authorize the trustee to incorporate a business, could the matter be resolved by the executor of the decedent's estate before distribution to the trustee? Compare Uniform Probate Code §3-715(24), (25); cf. supra Chapter 18, section A.2. Be prepared to discuss these questions, particularly in the context of an inflationary economy.

It would appear that the attorney has three opportunities to suggest solutions to these problems of handling business interests in the decedent's estate or trust: (1) lifetime and testamentary estate planning during the owner's life; (2) postmortem estate planning during the administration of the decedent's estate; and (3) postmortem planning during the administration of the trust. The opportunities and available alternatives decrease sharply with the passage of time in each instance. Does this failure of the attorney to see the problems and take corrective steps at the earliest opportunity constitute malpractice or only excusable incompetence?

C. Burden of Death Taxes

Recall the doctrines of abatement and exoneration from Chapter 11, supra. A related and more common problem that arises in all substantial estates is that of allocating or apportioning the burden of estate and inheritance taxes. The nature of an inheritance tax, often levied by states, is an excise tax on the privilege of *receiving* property at death: the burden is borne by each distributee on whose interest an inheritance tax is levied, assuming no express provision for its payment from another source. The federal estate tax, to the extent it is based on probate assets and nonprobate assets for which no contrary provision is made in the Internal Revenue Code, is payable by the personal representative and generally from the residuary estate unless state legislation or will provision prescribes a different result. Most states, however, either by statute or by judicial decision, now provide for some form of equitable apportionment of the estate tax among the various recipients of the taxable estate on a basis of the tax attributable to their respective shares. See Scoles & Stephens, The Proposed Uniform Estate Tax Apportionment Act, 43 Minn. L. Rev. 907 (1959); Scoles, Estate Tax Apportionment in the Multi-State Estate, 5 Miami Inst. Est. Plan. 7-1 (1971). Nonprobate assets often contribute to the total tax imposed upon an estate. The Internal Revenue Code (§§2206, 2207, 2207A, and 2207B) directs that certain of these assets (life insurance proceeds, property subject to a general power of appointment, qualified terminable interest property (QTIP), and property in which the decedent retained a life estate) are to bear the tax attributable to them, while other taxable nonprobate assets remain a source of uncertainty and diverse results in the absence of well-tailored estate plans. A 1995 study listed thirty-seven states plus the District of Columbia as providing for apportionment; eight states providing for limited apportionment, i.e., apportionment between probate and nonprobate property, but no apportionment among the probate property; and five states as not apportioning. John E. MacKenty (Compiling Editor), ACTEC Study No. 12, Apportionment of Death Taxes (March 1995). The clear majority in favor of apportionment instead of placing the entire burden on the residue is consistent with modern estate plans, in which the residue often carries the most important gifts to the primary objects of the donor's bounty.

The most common statute is the Uniform Estate Tax Apportionment Act, which is copied into the UPC:

UNIFORM PROBATE CODE

§3-916.   *Apportionment of Estate Taxes. . . .*

(b) Except as provided in subsection (i) and, unless the will otherwise provides, the tax shall be apportioned among all persons interested in the estate. The apportionment is to be made in the proportion that the value of the interest of each person interested in the estate bears to the total value of the interests of all persons interested in the estate. The values used in determining the tax are to be used for that purpose. If the decedent's will directs a method of apportionment of tax different from the method described in this Code, the method described in the will controls.

(c)(1) The Court in which venue lies for the administration of the estate of a decedent, on petition for the purpose may determine the apportionment of the tax.

(2) If the Court finds that it is inequitable to apportion interest and penalties in the manner provided in subsection (b), because of special circumstances, it may direct apportionment thereof in the manner it finds equitable. . . .

(d)(1) The personal representative or other person in possession of the property of the decedent required to pay the tax may withhold from any property distributable to any person interested in the estate, upon its distribution to him, the amount of tax attributable to his interest. If the property in possession of the personal representative or other person required to pay the tax and distributable to any person interested in the estate is insufficient to satisfy the proportionate amount of the tax determined to be due from the person, the personal representative or other person required to pay the tax may recover the deficiency from the person interested in the estate. If the property is not in the possession of the personal representative or the other person required to pay the tax, the personal representative or the other person required to pay the tax may recover from any person interested in the estate the amount of the tax apportioned to the person in accordance with this Act. . . .

(e)(1) In making an apportionment, allowances shall be made for any exemptions granted, any classification made of persons interested in the estate and for any deductions and credits allowed by the law imposing the tax.

(2) Any exemption or deduction allowed by reason of the relationship of any person to the decedent or by reason of the purposes of the gift inures to the benefit of the person bearing such relationship or receiving the gift; but if an interest is subject to a prior present interest which is not allowable as a deduction, the tax apportionable against the present interest shall be paid from principal.

(3) Any deduction for property previously taxed and any credit for gift taxes or death taxes of a foreign country paid by the decedent or his estate inures to the proportionate benefit of all persons liable to apportionment.

(4) Any credit for inheritance, succession or estate taxes or taxes in the nature thereof applicable to property or interests includable in the estate, inures to the benefit of the persons or interests chargeable with the payment thereof to the extent proportionately that the credit reduces the tax.

(5) To the extent that property passing to or in trust for a surviving spouse or any charitable, public or similar purpose is not an allowable deduction for purposes of the tax solely by reason of an

inheritance tax or other death tax imposed upon and deductible from the property, the property is not included in the computation provided for in subsection (b) hereof, and to that extent no apportionment is made against the property. The sentence immediately preceding does not apply to any case if the result would be to deprive the estate of a deduction otherwise allowable under Section 2053(d) of the Internal Revenue Code of 1954, as amended, of the United States, relating to deduction for state death taxes on transfers for public, charitable, or religious uses.

(f) No interest in income and no estate for years or for life or other temporary interest in any property or fund is subject to apportionment as between the temporary interest and the remainder. The tax on the temporary interest and the tax, if any, on the remainder is chargeable against the corpus of the property or funds subject to the temporary interest and remainder. . . .

(i) If the liabilities of persons interested in the estate as prescribed by this act differ from those which result under the Federal Estate tax law, the liabilities imposed by the federal law will control and the balance of this Section shall apply as if the resulting liabilities had been prescribed herein.

If the marital or charitable share were subject to taxes, a circuitous computation would be introduced: the amount passing to the spouse or charity would be reduced, thus increasing the taxes, which would further reduce the charitable or marital gift, and so on. The Uniform Estate Tax Apportionment Act avoids this problem, by freeing the marital and charitable gifts from the burden of estate tax. What language in the Act (UPC §3-916) accomplishes this result? Courts have reached a similar solution in the absence of statute, the reasoning being that the transferor sought the largest possible deduction or that equitable principles would place the tax burden on the property which generated the tax.

As noted above, there are two basic problems in transfer tax apportionment. First, within the probate estate, which gifts bear the burden of taxes? Second, if there are nonprobate assets, should they bear any burden of taxes? If nonprobate assets generate large amounts of tax, and the tax is payable entirely out of the probate estate, the transferor's plan may be greatly distorted. These matters call for careful planning and drafting. You will note that UPC §3-916 is a default rule that yields to contrary provisions in the testator's will.

Johnson v. Hall, 283 Md. 644, 392 A.2d 1103 (1978), illustrates the first drafting issue. There the court apportioned the federal estate tax among the beneficiaries, rather than placing the burden entirely on the residuary legatee. In the court's view, the state statute directing apportionment could only be overcome by a clear intent in the will. A boilerplate clause "direct[ing] that all lawful debts I owe at the time of my death, including . . . all estate and inheritance taxes, be paid as soon after my death as can lawfully and conveniently be done" was not sufficient to overcome the statute and shift the burden to the residue. The clause in Johnson v. Hall indicated no source from which the debts and taxes were to be paid, but some courts reaching an opposite result have reasoned that the linking of taxes with debts implies that taxes are to be paid from the same source as debts, typically the residue. Of course, some of these clauses directing the executor to pay "just debts" and taxes are meaningless, since the executor is bound to pay them anyway. Further, they may require payment of obligations that are otherwise barred by the statute of limitations.

McLaughlin v. Green, 136 Conn. 138, 69 A.2d 289 (1949), illustrates a second issue that continues to trouble courts and to arise from imprecise drafting. Under an apportionment statute, does a will clause directing payment "from my residuary estate of all estate, inheritance and other death taxes imposed on my estate" (or "all succession, transfer and inheritance taxes," as in *McLaughlin*) include taxes payable with respect to joint tenancy property, life insurance proceeds, and other nonprobate assets (inter vivos trust properties in *McLaughlin*)? Or is this direction insufficiently "clear" to overcome the statute's allocation of a portion of the tax burden to the recipients of all nonprobate assets that contribute to (that is, are not deductible or excludable in determining) the estate's overall tax liability? Like many such cases, *McLaughlin* concluded that the language of the clause in question applied only to the testamentary estate and failed to show the requisite intention to overcome the statutory apportionment. Compare Yoakley v. Raese, 448 So. 2d 632 (Fla. App. 1984), where both statute and will provision were clear enough in placing the primary burden for all death taxes on the residuary estate, with respect to probate and nonprobate assets alike, but the residue proved inadequate to pay the taxes — in what should not have been a surprise to the lawyer who handled the planning for that estate.

Conflict of Laws. For a case involving the burden of estate taxes where the nonprobate asset that was subject to tax was located in a state (Massachusetts) other than that of the testator's domicile (Maine), see Isaacson v. Boston Safe Deposit & Trust Co., 325 Mass. 469, 91 N.E.2d 334 (1950). The Massachusetts court refused to give the Maine apportionment statute an extraterritorial effect. Professor Scott commented, "the question of the allocation of the tax was one of interpretation or construction, a question of the intention or probable intention of the decedent. That question was ignored by the court." VA W. Fratcher, Scott on Trusts §576, at 211-212 (4th ed. 1989).

If a revocable inter vivos trust established by the decedent directs the payment of all death taxes on both probate and nonprobate assets from the trust estate and if the decedent's will also directs payment of all taxes from the residue of the probate estate, how are these contradictory directions to be resolved? Should the will prevail if executed later than the trust? Estate of Cord, 462 N.Y.S.2d 622, 449 N.E.2d 402 (App. Div. 1983) held that the later document prevailed. The *Cord* rule was modified by a statute requiring the later instrument to make specific reference to the tax direction in the earlier instrument. See Matter of Hoffman, 165 Misc. 2d 146, 627 N.Y.S.2d 524 (Surr. 1995), holding that the statute did not apply where the two instruments were executed concurrently and finding that a direction in the trust to pay the trust's share of taxes "out of the trust property" was sufficient to overcome the general rule of apportionment. In First National Bank v. Shawmut Bank, 389 N.E.2d 1002 (Mass. 1979), the later will did "not qualify as an amendment to the trust" (amendment of which required the trustee's signature), and the Supreme Judicial Court reversed the trial court's exclusion (based on the will's "clarity") of extrinsic evidence intended primarily to show the size of the nontrust estate at the time the will was executed. The opinion states:

> If these conflicting provisions appeared in a single document, such as a will, we would admit extrinsic evidence to assist in resolving the ambiguity. . . . [W]hen a slip-up has obviously occurred in the estate planning process, evidence of the circumstances known to a testator-settlor may be particularly instructive in achieving the ultimate goal of recognizing and carrying out the testator-settlor's intention. Here, if the allegations of the Florida executor concerning the tax obligations of [the] estate are proved, the view espoused by the trustees would result in total failure of all testamentary gifts, including the gift of income to [testatrix'] friend, who is not an income beneficiary of the trust. There may be no logic in a result which would fully achieve an expressed testamentary purpose of paying all taxes from the residue while in the process destroying the only gifts expressed in the will.

389 N.E.2d at 1006. The court also observed:

> We need not decide at this time whether the suggestion of the *Isaacson* and *Warfield* [Warfield v. Merchants National Bank, 337 Mass. 14, 147 N.E.2d 809 (1958)] opinions on choice of law would be accepted today. Refusal to apply the law of the decedent's domicil has been criticized. See Scoles, Apportionment of Federal Estate Taxes and Conflict of Laws, 55 Colum. L. Rev. 261 (1955). In several jurisdictions the law of the decedent's domicile has been applied. . . . The application of the law of the decedent's domicil, if followed universally, would tend to ensure unifor-

mity of treatment among nonprobate assets included in the decedent's gross estate.

389 N.E.2d at 1007.

Finally, note Doetsch v. Doetsch, 312 F.2d 323 (7th Cir. 1963), applying the apportionment law of the settlor's domicile, where the settlor's inter vivos trust was established and administered in one state (Illinois) and the settlor died domiciled in another state (Arizona). The court said, "The domicile provides an easy and convenient point of reference for the solution of these problems." Finding no Arizona authority, the court opined that Arizona would follow the rule of apportionment. When the question was squarely put to an Arizona court some thirty-four years later, it held that Arizona followed the common law residuary rule. Estate of Mason, 190 Ariz. 312, 947 P.2d 886 (1997).[7]

7.   For a thorough treatment of the conflict of laws problems involved in cases such as the case at bar see Scoles. Apportionment of Federal Estate Taxes and Conflict of Laws, 55 Colum. L. Rev. 261 (1955).

20

Rules Regulating Perpetuities

Rules regulating perpetuities are the natural conclusion to our study of decedents' estates and trusts. These rules illustrate again the tension between transferor autonomy and other social policies. They strike a balance between the dead hand and the desires of the living to control the ownership and use of property. The immediately preceding chapters deal with issues raised by time-divided ownership; perpetuities rules control the fundamental question of how long the ownership may be time-divided, whether in trust (the usual case) or not. We shall see that the long-accepted approach to these questions has been a rule against remote vesting, but that the historical approach is under renewed scrutiny.

An excellent, comprehensive, yet reasonably brief introduction to the Common Law Rule Against Perpetuities can be obtained through careful study of Professor W. Barton Leach's Perpetuities in a Nutshell. Much of this classic summary is reproduced below. For another relatively short and complete treatment of the rule, see Chapter 24 of Simes, Future Interests (2d ed. 1966). A reading of different presentations of the same material may be the answer to your difficulties in attempting to master this subject matter, some selected aspects of which will be treated in greater depth through cases and other materials later in this chapter.

Before proceeding further, it may be helpful to re-read the brief introduction at the end of Chapter 10 of this book. That material attempted to provide some background on the rule and its policy underpinnings, as well as introduce the rule in a container smaller than a nutshell.

A. Summary of the Common Law Rule

LEACH, PERPETUITIES IN A NUTSHELL[1]
51 Harv. L. Rev. 638 (1938)

. . . Gray's statement of the Rule, adopted by practically every court which has dealt with the subject, is as follows:

---

1. Many footnotes have been omitted and others have been renumbered.

No interest is good unless it must vest, if at all, not later than twenty-one years after some life in being at the creation of the interest.

The whole law of perpetuities cannot be put in a single sentence. Gray's formulation would be more realistic if it were preceded by the words *Generally speaking* and if the word *vest* were put in quotation marks. But this formulation has proved workable, solves the great bulk of cases that arise and serves as a convenient starting point for the solution of those which it does not solve.

II.   Nature of the Rule

The Rule Against Perpetuities is a rule invalidating interests which *vest* too remotely. Indeed, it is often called the rule against remoteness of vesting.

It is *not* a rule invalidating interests which *last* too long. Thus a gift to A for life, remainder to B in fee is entirely valid, although the remainder may last forever. Similarly a gift to A for life, remainder to A's children for their lives, remainder to B in fee is valid, although the life estates in A's children may last longer than the period of perpetuities; B's remainder is vested at once, though it may not become possessory until beyond the period of perpetuities.

The Rule Against Perpetuities is *not* a rule against suspension of the power of alienation of property through the creation of interests in unborn or unascertained persons; and it is not satisfied by the fact that there are persons in being who can together give a complete title to a purchaser. Thus, where land is given to A in fee, but if liquor shall ever be sold on the premises then to B in fee, the executory interest in B is bad even though A and B together can give a complete title to the land.

The Rule Against Perpetuities must be distinguished from the rules against restraints on alienation, though, like these rules, it stems from the general policy against withdrawal of property from commerce. A restraint on alienation is some provision which, even after an interest has become vested, prevents the owner thereof from disposing of it at all or from disposing of it in particular ways or to particular persons — the most common example being the spendthrift trust. An interest which is void under the Rule Against Perpetuities fails because it vests too remotely; it may be, and usually is, freely alienable at all times.

III.   Elements of the Rule

A.   The Period of Perpetuities

The period within which interests must vest or fail is: twenty-one years after any reasonable number of lives in being at the creation of the interest, plus actual periods of gestation. Rules to be noted with reference to this period are the following:

A. The 21-year period may be in gross as well as connected with the minority of any person. Thus the following are valid:

1. Bequest "to all descendants of mine who shall be born within 21 years after my death."

2. Bequest to a trustee "to pay the income to A for life and then to pay the principal to such children of A as reach the age of 21."

B. The 21-year period cannot precede the measuring lives; or, to put it more exactly, the measuring lives must be in being at the creation of the interest (i.e., the death of the testator in a will, the delivery of a deed); it is not sufficient that they come into being within 21 years.

3. Bequest "to accumulate the income for 21 years and then to pay the income to such of my grandchildren as shall then be living for life and upon the death of the survivor to pay the principal to my great-grandchildren then living." The life estates to the grandchildren are valid, since they vest within 21 years; but the remainders to great-grandchildren are invalid.[2]

C. The measuring lives need not be mentioned in the instrument, need not be holders of previous estates, and need not be connected in any way with the property or the persons designated to take it.

4. Bequest "to my grandchildren who shall reach the age of 21." This is valid, since all grandchildren must be born in the lives of the testator's (*T*'s) children and these must perforce be lives in being at *T*'s death.

5. Inter vivos trust for "my grandchildren who shall reach the age of 21." This is bad, since (unlike the case of a bequest) other children may be born to the settlor and the children cannot, therefore, be taken as the lives in being.

6. Bequest "to *A*'s grandchildren who shall reach the age of 21." This is bad since, *A* still being alive and presumptively capable of having more children, his children cannot be taken as the lives in being.

7. Bequest "to such of my children and more remote issue as shall be living 21 years after the death of the survivor of *R, S, T, U, V, W, X, Y* and *Z*" (these being nine healthy babies selected at random). This is valid.

D. Any number of lives may be selected, provided they are not so numerous as to make it impossible to ascertain their termination.

8. Bequest in 1926 to "my descendants who shall be living 21 years after the death of all lineal descendants of Queen Victoria now living."

---

2. It is, of course, assumed that the testator (*T*) had children living at his death and that, consequently there was a possibility that other grandchildren would be born. If this is not so, the grandchildren are themselves the lives in being and the gift to great-grandchildren is valid.

There were 120 such descendants. The gift was held valid, but it certainly represents the outside limit of the permissible number of lives.

E. Actual periods of gestation are included in the period of perpetuities.

9. Bequest "to my children for their lives, remainder to my grandchildren who shall reach 21." The testator (*T*) at his death has one living child, *C1,* and one child *en ventre sa mere, C2,* who is born 8 months later. *C2* at his death leaves a child *en ventre sa mere, G,* who is born 8 months later. *G* reaches 21. The gift to grandchildren of *T* is valid and *G* takes a share in it. But,

10. A bequest to "such of my descendants as shall be living 21 years and 9 months after the death of *A*" is invalid. Periods of gestation are included in the period of perpetuities only so far as they actually occur.

B.   The Required Certainty of Vesting

A future interest is invalid unless it is absolutely certain that it must vest within the period of perpetuities. Probability of vesting, however great, is not sufficient. Moreover, the certainty of vesting must have existed at the time when the instrument took effect (i.e., the testator's death in the case of a will; the date of delivery in the case of a deed or trust). It is immaterial that the contingencies actually do occur within the permissible period or actually have occurred when the validity of the instrument is first litigated.

It is at this point that the rule becomes a trap to the draftsman. Many perfectly reasonable dispositions are stricken down because on some outside chance not foreseen by the testator or his lawyer it is mathematically possible that the vesting might occur too remotely. Mistakes of this sort are readily classifiable into frequently recurring types. Such possibilities of salvation as exist are discussed under each type.

First comes the "fertile octogenarian" type.

11. T has a widowed sister, *A,* aged 80. He leaves property in trust to pay the income to *A* for life, then to pay the income to the children of *A* for their lives, then to pay the principal to the children of such children.

By the traditional English view the gift of the principal is bad; for the *children* of *A* include after-born children and *A* is conclusively presumed to be capable of having children until death.[3] Plainly this is silly on two grounds: (1) When *T* used the word *children* he never intended to include after-born children of *A* because he never considered that after-born children were within the realm of possibility. Hence, although *children* usually means *children whenever born,* it should mean

---

3. Jee v. Audley, I Cox Eq. Cas. 324 (1787); Johnston v. Hill, 39 Ch. D. 155 (1888); Ward v. Van Der Loeff [1924] A. C. 653.

children now living when used by *T* in these circumstances. One American court has adopted this view.[4] (2) It is physically impossible for *A* to have children and a conclusive presumption to the contrary flies in the face of medical knowledge; thus the certainty required by the Rule Against Perpetuities exists except so far as the court chooses to blind its eyes. But no court, English or American, has failed to follow the presumption in a perpetuities case. The draftsman plainly should restrict class designations (children, nephews, nieces, etc.) to living persons where this coincides with the testator's desires.

Second comes the "unborn widow" type of case.

12. T has a son, *A*, 45 years old. The son has a wife and grown children. *T* leaves property in trust "to pay the income to *A* for his life, then to pay the income to *A*'s widow, if any, for her life and then to pay the principal to the children of *A* then living."

Incontestably the gift of principal is invalid. *A* may marry again and his second wife may be a person who was unborn at *T*'s death. Hence the gift to children of *A* (including after-born children) contingent on their surviving the widow is too remote. Of course, everyone knows that *A* will not marry a woman 45 years his junior; but it is a mathematical possibility. A provision in the will that the life estate to the widow is dependent upon her being born in the life of *T* saves the remainder.

Third comes the "administration contingency" type. In this class of case the testator foresees the possibility that some of the objects of his bounty will die during the relatively short time that is required for the administration of his estate or for the carrying out of very short trusts which he sets up for specific purposes; and, desiring to avoid the additional shrinkage which is bound to attend the passage of his property through another decedent estate, he provides that the property shall pass only to persons who are living at the time when administration is completed and distribution is made. What he fails to observe is that, although everyone expects the administration of his estate or of the trust to be completed within a very short time, it is mathematically possible that it will take more than a period of perpetuities (which, in the absence of an available measuring life, is 21 years). For example:

13. T was in the sand and gravel business. He owned gravel pits which, at the time of his death, would have been exhausted in 4 years if worked at the rate which was habitual with *T*. *T* died, leaving a will which devised to trustees the gravel pits in trust to work until the same were exhausted, then to sell the pits and divide the proceeds among *T*'s issue then living. The pits were actually exhausted in 6 years. But the gift to issue was held bad on the ground that they might not have been exhausted within 21 years.[5]

4. Wright's Estate, 284 Pa. 334, 131 A.188 (1925).

5. In re Wood, [1894] 3 Ch. 381. Valid gift ". . . to work the pits for 20 years or until they are exhausted, whichever happens first, and then to sell the property and

14. T owned Blackacre subject to a mortgage upon which a balance of £1000 was still due, payable £200 per year. The rents from the property were sufficient to meet this payment, plus interest, taxes and insurance with a substantial margin. *T* devised Blackacre to trustees to pay off the mortgage out of the rents and then to transfer the property to his issue then living. The gift was held bad, since it was possible that the income from the property would decrease so that the mortgage would not be paid off within 21 years.

15. T devised Blackacre to *A* "from and after the date of probate of this will." The devise was held bad on the ground that "it cannot be said that it [probate] is a condition that must inevitably happen within 21 years from the death of the testatrix."

16. T left his property to such of his issue as should be living when his debts were paid and his estate settled. The gift was held bad.

It is less relevant to discuss whether these cases are the proof of Mr. Bumble's proposition that "the law is a ass, a idiot" than to recognize that this is the law with which a draftsman must deal and against which he must protect the instruments which he draws. There is, however, some solace in the approach of the Connecticut court to this type of problem. In Belfield v. Booth,[6] a gift which was to vest 14 years after the settlement of the testator's estate was held valid. The court reasoned that the holder of the will was in duty bound to produce it promptly and that the executor had a fiduciary obligation to settle the estate promptly; that the testator expected both of these things to be done; and therefore that, as a matter of construction, the 14-year period "will commence at the time when the accounts of the executor or administrator of his estate are, or should be, settled in the due course of administration; and that this time cannot be delayed so long as seven years from his decease." Such an approach would have saved all the gifts in Cases *13* to *16.*

The certainty required by the Rule Against Perpetuities may be produced by the fact that, at the testator's death, relevant persons have died or reached particular ages. Thus,

17. T makes a bequest "to such children of *A* as shall reach the age of 30." Prima facie this gift is bad. But (1) if *A* is dead at the death of *T,* the gift is good, since the children of *A* may themselves be treated as the lives in being; and (2) even though *A* is alive, if one of the children has reached 30 at the death of *T,* this closes the class to future

---

divide the proceeds among such of my issue as shall be living 20 years after my death or at the exhaustion of the pits, whichever happens first." Observe also that if the gift had been to *T*'s *children* living at the time of sale, it would have been valid; for the children are lives in being at *T*'s death, and the gift to them will vest if at *all* in their lives.

6. 63 Conn. 299, 27 A.383 (1893).

born children, and again the children of *A* can be treated as the lives in being.[7]

18. T makes a bequest in trust "for *B* for life and then for such children of *A* as shall reach the age of 30." Prima facie the remainder is bad. But (1) if *A* is dead at the death of *T,* the gift is good, on the same grounds as in Case *17*(1). Or (2) if *B* is dead and a child of *A* has reached 30 at the death of *T* the gift is good on the same grounds as in Case *17*(2). However (3) if *B* is living, the fact that a child of *A* has reached 30 at *T*'s death is immaterial, for the intervening life estate of *B* keeps the class open to unborn children of *A* until *B*'s death; the children of *A* cannot therefore be treated as the lives in being; and the gift is still bad.

C.   "Vesting" in Interest

The metaphysical common law notion that a future estate can vest in interest before it vests in possession is incorporated into the Rule Against Perpetuities. A remainder complies with the requirements of the rule as soon as it becomes vested, regardless of when it becomes possessory. Thus in a devise to *A* for life, remainder to *A*'s children for their lives, remainder to *B*, *B*'s interest is good; it is presently vested, though clearly it may not come into possession until the death of a child of *A* yet unborn — a point well beyond the period of perpetuities. Again,

19. T bequeaths a fund in trust to pay the income to *A* for life, then to pay the income to *A*'s children for their lives, then to pay the principal to his residuary legatees (*B, C, D* and *E*) if they should then be living but, if not, to the heirs of the residuary legatees. The remainder is good. It is not presently vested; but it must become vested within the lives or upon the deaths of the residuary legatees, who are lives in being. If, at the death of the children of *A*, a residuary legatee is living, his share then becomes vested in possession; if he dies before that time his heirs are ascertained at his death and as to them the gift is thenceforth vested in interest.

Possibilities of reverter are not subject to the Rule Against Perpetuities. It is sometimes said that this is because they are reversionary interests and hence, in common law theory, vested. Thus,

20. T devises Blackacre "to the *A* Church so long as the premises are used for church purposes." Upon the cessation of the prescribed use the property reverts to *T* and his heirs, even if this occurs centuries

---

7. Picken v. Matthews, 10 Ch. D. 264 (1878). The "rule of convenience" as to class gifts, universally recognized, is that the class closes to later born members at any time when a class member is entitled to require a distribution of principal. 2 Simes, Future Interests §§373 et seq. (1936).

later. This exemption of possibilities of reverter from the rule theoretically makes possible fantastic dispositions. For instance,

21. T leaves the residue of his estate "to the *A* Trust Company so long as it pays to my oldest living descendant for the time being 80% of the income received from the fund." The balance of 20% of the income would presumably constitute a sufficient inducement to assure the payment of 80% of the income as stipulated.

However, execution interests do not have the capacity of vesting in interest before they vest in possession. Thus the Rule Against Perpetuities requires that executory interests become possessory within lives and 21 years.

22. T devises Blackacre to *A,* but if liquor shall ever be sold on the premises then to *B. B*'s interest is a shifting executory devise; it need not become possessory within the period of perpetuities; and it therefore fails.

23. T grants Blackacre "to *B* at such time as lime shall cease to be burned on the premises." *B*'s interest is a springing executory devise; it need not become possessory within the period of perpetuities; and it therefore fails.[8]

IV. *Application of the Rule to Gifts to Classes*

In England the rule became settled that a gift of property to be divided among a class of persons was totally invalid if it was possible that the interest of any member of the class would vest beyond the period of perpetuities. Or, to put it differently, a class gift is not "vested" within the meaning of that word as used in the Rule Against Perpetuities until the interest of each member of the class is vested. Thus,

24. T bequeaths a fund in trust for *A* for life and then in trust for *A*'s children who shall reach the age of 25. Four children of *A* are living at the death of *T.* Standing alone, the gift to these children is valid, since they must reach or fail to reach 25 within their own lives. Yet the fact that a later child of *A* might be born and might reach 25 more than 21 years after the death of all persons in being at *T*'s death invalidates the whole gift.[9]

8. Walker v. Marcellus & Otisco Lake Ry., 226 N.Y. 347, 123 N.E. 736 (1919). But suppose the gift is upon a certain event as well as to a designated person, e.g., "to *A* 25 years after my death." Analytically this is also bad; but such a result is incongruous, since a gift "to *X* for 25 years, remainder to *A*" would be vested and valid. The authority is slight, Mann v. Registrar. [1918] 1 Ch. 202; Gray, Perpetuities §§114, 317 (3d ed. 1915).

9. Leake v. Robinson, 2 Mer. 363 (Ch. 1817). The same result would follow even though all four of the living children had already reached 25 at *T*'s death! See Case 18, supra.

No satisfactory rationalization of this application of the rule has ever been advanced. Yet, as is too often the case with regard to problems of future interests, the English cases have been followed in the United States where the issue has arisen without independent examination of the question involved.[10]

Two important limitations on the class-gift rule must be mentioned.

First is the rule that where there is a gift of a specific sum to each person described by a class designation (as distinguished from a gift of a fund or piece of land to be divided between the class) some members may take their gifts though the gifts to others are void. Thus,

25. *T* bequeaths $100 to each child of *A* who reaches the age of 25. Four children of *A* are living at the death of *T*. Each of these children is entitled to receive $100 if he reaches 25, although the gifts of $100 each to children of *A* born after the death of *T* are too remote.

Second is the rule that where there is a gift to a class of sub-classes the gift to a particular sub-class can be valid even though the gift to another sub-class is too remote. Thus,

26. *T* bequeaths a fund in trust to pay the income to *A* for life, then to pay the income to the children of *A* for their lives, and upon the death of any child of *A* to pay the principal upon which such child was receiving the income to the children of such child. *A* has two children: *C1*, who was born before the death of *T*, and *C2*, who was born after the death of *T*. Plainly the life estates to both *C1* and *C2* are valid. Equally plainly the remainder to the children of *C2* is invalid. The question concerns the remainder to the children of *C1*. The share which is to be divided between them will be known at the death of *A*, since thereafter no children of *A* can be born; the fraction which each of the children of *C1* is to take in the share will be known at the death of *C1*; therefore all interests will vest within the life of the survivor of *A* and *C1*, both of whom were in being at *T*'s death, and the gift is, of itself, valid. The fact that the contemporaneous gift to the children of *C2* fails is immaterial. However, this limitation applies only if the testator separates the ultimate remainder into sub-classes.

---

10. See Gray, Perpetuities §374 (3d ed. 1915); 2 Simes, Future Interests §528 (1936). The jurisdictions in which this issue has arisen are, however, relatively few. There is no reason why a court before which the problem arises de novo should not reach an opposite conclusion. Properly the problem is one of separability, not of perpetuities; a question of construction, not of application of a rule of law. Where there is a gift to the children of *A* who reach 25 and one reaches 25, such child has a vested interest subject to partial divestment in favor of other children who later attain the prescribed age. If the other children are unborn it is the divesting contingency which is remote, not the gift to the child who was living at *T*'s death and has reached 25. As in other cases of partial invalidity the valid portion should be allowed to stand unless *T*'s dispositive intent will be better carried out by declaring the whole gift bad. See heading VII, infra. I hope to elaborate these views in a subsequent article. [Done, See 51 Harv. L. Rev. 1329.]

27. *T* bequeaths a fund in trust to pay the income to *A* for life, then to pay the income to the children of *A* for their lives and then to pay the principal to the grandchildren of *A*. The remainder to grandchildren is void.

V.   Powers of Appointment

In any discussion of powers of appointment the distinction between general and special powers is so vital that it is well to define the terms at the outset. A general power is one which permits appointment to anyone including the donee of the power or his estate — e.g., a devise "to *A* for life and then to such person or persons as *A* shall appoint." A general power can be testamentary (that is, exercisable by will only — e.g., a devise "to *A* for life and then to such person or persons as *A* shall *by will* appoint"); in that case the donee plainly cannot appoint to himself, but he still can appoint to his estate. A special (sometimes called limited) power is one which permits appointment only to a designated class — e.g., a devise "to *A* for life, and then to such of *A*'s children as *A* shall appoint." A special power also can be testamentary; but this has no particular significance with reference to perpetuities problems.

With reference to the Rule Against Perpetuities two problems arise: (1) Is the power valid? (2) Assuming the power to be valid, is the interest which has been appointed in the exercise of the power valid? The first of these problems is fairly simple, the latter quite complex.

A.   The Validity of the Power

A special power is void if it is capable of being exercised beyond the period of perpetuities. Thus any special power given to an unborn person is invalid unless the time of exercise is specially restricted.

28. *T* bequeaths a fund in trust to pay the income to *A* for life, then to pay the income to *A*'s children for their lives and then to pay the principal to such of *A*'s grandchildren as the oldest child of *A* shall appoint. *A*'s oldest child, born after *T*'s death, makes an appointment in *A*'s lifetime to grandchildren of *A* then living. The appointment has no effect because the power is void ab initio.

This type of case is rather fantastic; but there are two types which involve the same principle and which are at once much more likely to occur and much more deceptive. The first type consists of cases in which a power is created in the exercise of a special power or a general testamentary power.

29. *T* bequeaths a fund in trust for *A* for life and then in trust for *A*'s issue as *A* shall appoint, with power to create new powers. *A* by will appoints to his son, *B*, for life, remainder to such of *B*'s children as

B shall appoint. *B* was born after *T*'s death. As will later appear, *A*'s appointment has to be "read back" into *T*'s will; and, thus read back, it gives a special power to *B*, a person unborn at *T*'s death. This power is void.

The second type consists of cases in which a "discretionary trust" is created to last during unborn lives. Such a trust is in essence a power of appointment and the discretionary power is void if it can be exercised too remotely.

30. *T* bequeaths a fund in trust for *A* for life and then for the children of *A* for their lives, with power in the trustees to determine how much of the income shall be applied to each of the children of *A*. This power is void.

A general testamentary power stands on the same footing as a special power. It is void if it can be exercised during the whole life of the donee, a person unborn at the creation of the power.

A general power exercisable by deed or will, however, is different. It is the equivalent of ownership since it enables the donee of the power to become the owner at any time by appointing to himself. Therefore a general power exercisable by deed or will is valid if the donee must *acquire* the power within the period of perpetuities.

31. *T* bequeaths a fund in trust to pay the income to *A* for life, then to pay the income to the children of *A* for their lives, then to pay the principal to such person or persons as the eldest child of *A* (unborn at *T*'s death) shall appoint. The power is valid.

B.   The Validity of Appointed Interests

Where an appointment is made under a special power, the appointment is read back into the instrument creating the power (as if the donee were filling in blanks in the donor's instrument) and the period of perpetuities is computed from the date the power was created [except in Delaware]. Thus,

32. *T* (the donor) bequeaths a fund in trust for *A* for life and then in trust for such issue of *A* as *A* shall appoint. *A* appoints to his child, *B* (unborn at *T*'s death), for life, remainder to *B*'s children. The gift to *B*'s children, when read back into *T*'s will, is a gift to the children of an unborn person and hence too remote.

However, facts and circumstances existing at the date the appointment is made must be considered in determining the validity of the appointment. Thus if, in Case 32, *B* is in fact a child of *A* who was born within the life of *T*, then the appointment to his children is valid.

Where an appointment is made under a general testamentary power the same rules apply: the validity of the appointment is determined by reckoning the period of perpetuities from the date of creation of the power.

Where an appointment is made under a general power exercisable by deed or will the validity of the appointment is determined by reckoning the period of perpetuities from the date of the appointment. The fact that the donee of the power can appoint to himself makes him in substance the owner and makes it reasonable to treat his appointments as dispositions of owned property.

VI. Severability of Invalid Conditions and Modifying Clauses

Where a testator makes a gift to A upon either of two expressed contingencies, one being remote and one not, the gift takes effect if the valid contingency occurs. Thus,

33. T bequeaths a fund in trust to pay the income to A for life, then to pay the income to any surviving wife of A for life; then, upon the death of A, or upon the death of A's wife if he leaves one surviving, to pay the principal to A's children then living. At A's death no wife survives. Although the gift to the children would have been too remote if A had left a surviving wife,[11] it was not too remote if he left none. Therefore the children take. However, if the testator has *expressed* only one contingency and this may occur too remotely, the gift is invalid, even though two or more contingencies are implicit in the expressed contingency and the one of them that occurs is not too remote. Thus,

34. T bequeaths $1000 to the first son of A who shall become a clergyman; but if no son of A becomes a clergyman, then to B. (The gift over to B "if no son of A becomes a clergyman" plainly includes at least two contingencies: (a) A having no son — which must occur, if at all, at A's death; (b) A having one or more sons, none of whom becomes a clergyman — which cannot be known until the death of A's sons, a time well beyond the period of perpetuities.) A dies without ever having had a son. Nevertheless the gift to B fails.[12] This distinction is all a matter of the form of words and of chance expressions used by the testator. It has been widely criticized but almost invariably followed.

Another matter of form is the doctrine of "modifying clauses." This permits a gift to be valid in spite of the imposition of an invalid qualification thereof, if the gift and qualification are verbally separable. The fact that such separation rarely occurs does not diminish the usefulness of this doctrine in those few cases to which it can apply. Thus,

35. T bequeaths a fund in trust to pay the income to A for life "and upon the death of A to pay the principal to A's children. As to the

11. The wife might be a person unborn at T's death. See Case 12, supra.

12. Proctor v. Bishop of Bath, 2 H. Bl. 358 (C. P. 1794). The gift would have been good if T had said "but if A have no son, or none of the sons born to A becomes a clergyman, then to B." See previous case.

share thus given to any daughter I direct that it shall be held in trust for her until her age of 25 and then paid to her if and when she reaches that age; but if she dies under that age, then to my other children then surviving." Upon the death of A the principal is paid outright to all children including daughters. The modifying clause which imposes the invalid condition is ignored.

VII.   Effect of Invalidity of an Interest Under the Rule

Where an interest is void under the Rule Against Perpetuities, it is stricken out; and (apart from the principles of infectious invalidity, considered in the three succeeding paragraphs) the other interests created in the will or trust instrument take effect as if the void interest had never been written. Thus,

36. T bequeaths the residue of his estate in trust to pay the income to A for life *and then to pay the principal to such children of A as shall reach the age of 25.* The remainder is void. Thus the italicized words are ignored; the trustee pays the income to A for life and then holds the principal upon a resulting trust for the next-of-kin of T.

37. T devises land to A and his heirs, *but if the premises shall be used for the sale of liquors, then to B and his heirs.* The executory devise is void. Thus the italicized words are ignored; A has a fee simple absolute.

38. T devises land to A and his heirs so long as no liquor is sold on the premises, *but if liquor shall be sold on the premises then to B and his heirs.* The executory devise is void. Thus the italicized words are ignored; A has a fee simple determinable and the heirs of T have a possibility of reverter.

If an ultimate interest is void under the Rule Against Perpetuities, does this cause the failure of prior interests which, standing alone, are not too remote? This is properly a problem of severability whose solution depends upon the answer to the question: Will the general dispositive ideas of the testator or settlor be better carried out by holding the prior limitations valid or by striking them down? Or, to put the question in another way: Is the invalid limitation so essential to the dispositive scheme of the testator or settlor that it can be inferred that he would not wish the prior limitations to stand alone? Generally, courts are very reluctant to strike down a portion of the disposition which is, of itself, valid; but in Pennsylvania and Illinois the decisions have given evidence of a punitive spirit which invalidates many entire wills and trusts which would be given partial effect in other states.

If one of two alternative interests is too remote, does that necessarily cause the other alternative interest to be void? The answer is No. If the contingency occurs upon which the second limitation is to take effect, and if the second limitation is of itself valid, it will be given effect.

39. T bequeaths a fund in trust for *A* for life and then, if children of *A* survive him, to such of the children as reach the age of 25, but if no children of *A* survive him, then to *B*. If, but only if, *A* dies without surviving children, *B* takes.

If a limitation is too remote, do subsequent limitations necessarily fail? This question has not arisen in the United States and the customary American types of dispositions are unlikely to raise it. The English law seems to be that all limitations subsequent to a void limitation are necessarily void; but this result has been severely criticized.

VIII.   *Construction and Perpetuities*

The question is: As between two possible constructions of a gift, how far is it proper to select one of the constructions on the ground that it is valid under the Rule Against Perpetuities while the other is invalid?

Gray said, "Every provision in a will or settlement is to be construed as if the rule did not exist, and then to the provision so construed the rule is to be remorselessly applied." But he added, "When the expression which a testator uses is really ambiguous, and is fairly capable of two constructions, one of which would produce a legal result, and the other a result that would be bad for remoteness, it is a fair presumption that the testator meant to create a legal rather than an illegal interest." This distinction is rather nebulous, but it plainly leans in the direction of severity. It is the accepted formula in England, violated at convenience.

But in the United States we have a precedent which is lacking in England. It has become well settled that, in the construction of a statute, that interpretation will be selected which renders the statute constitutional rather than unconstitutional, even to the extent of a warping of words which cannot be described otherwise than as violent. The rationale of this rule is directly applicable to the construction of wills and trusts under the Rule Against Perpetuities. One starts with the inference that the testator (like Congress) intended to do a legal act rather than an illegal one, and one permits this basic intention to overcome inferences as to minor intentions, which would ordinarily be drawn from particular words, unless those words are clear. Such an attitude seems increasingly to represent the trend of American authority.

Almost invariably problems of construction in which the Rule Against Perpetuities can play a part involve the question whether references to *children* or *grandchildren* in a will include persons who are born after the testator's death. The ordinary rule of construction is that class designations such as *children* or *grandchildren* include all who are born prior to the period of first principal distribution. But this ordinary meaning (itself a product of a "rule of construction" of the courts) should yield to a more restricted meaning where there is nothing in the words used by the testator or in the circumstances of the execution of his will which would indicate that the restricted meaning was not intended. Thus,

40. *T* devised his homestead to trustees to allow his "children and grandchildren" to live in the house until there was only one survivor, and then to convey the house to such survivor. At his death *T* had two sons and four grandchildren. It was held that "grandchildren" meant grandchildren living at *T*'s death. Thus construed, the devise was valid.

41. *T* bequeathed the residue of his estate "to the grandchildren of my brother Charles, to be by them received when they and each of them shall attain the age of 25." At *T*'s death 7 grandchildren were living. It was held that the gift included only these 7 grandchildren. Thus construed, the bequest was valid.

IX.   Application of the Rule to Various Types of Interests

Thus far we have been considering the application of the Rule Against Perpetuities to remainders and executory interests created in the course of gift transactions, with or without the use of powers of appointment. This was the field in which the rule grew up and in which it has its usual application. We now turn to a consideration of the rule with reference to types of interests which are more or less off this beaten track.

A.   Contracts, Particularly Options

The Rule Against Perpetuities is a rule of property law, not a rule of the law of contracts. It is no objection to the enforceability of a contract that the liability thereunder does not accrue until a time beyond the period of perpetuities. Thus insurance and suretyship contracts (both contingent obligations) are valid without reference to the time when the contingency may occur or payment may be required.

However, if a contract for the transfer of property is specifically enforceable, there is created in the promisee an equitable interest in the property; and the question arises whether this equitable interest, based upon the specific enforceability of a contract, is subject to the Rule Against Perpetuities. At the outset it should be stated that this question *ought* to be answered in the negative. Assuming that it is desirable to have some restriction upon the equitable interests created by specifically enforceable contracts, the Rule Against Perpetuities does not offer an appropriate limitation. The period of lives in being and 21 years, which works admirably with regard to gift transactions for family purposes, has no significance in the world of commercial affairs.

Options to purchase in gross. It has been held both in England and the United States that an option in gross to purchase land is void if it can be exercised beyond the period of perpetuities. The objection to this rule is not in the options that it strikes down but in those that it permits. An option in gross is an effective preventative of the improvement of the land over which it exists, unless (as is rarely, if ever, the case) the purchase price under the option fluctuates in accordance with the improved value of the land. As long as the option lasts the owner in possession cannot afford to make improvements which can be snatched away from him without compensation by the exercise of the option. To allow such a restraint to last for the period of perpetuities is monstrous. However, the common sense of land owners suffices to prevent this problem from being particularly important.

Options to purchase in leases. In England it was held that an option to purchase by a lessee stood on the same footing as an option to purchase in gross: it was void if it could be exercised beyond the period of perpetuities. Thus an option to purchase at any time during a lease for 30 years failed. It was not observed that the situation was the exact opposite of that which exists where there is an option in gross. The improvement of the land is stimulated, not retarded, by the existence of an option in the lessee. If the lessee has an option to purchase he can safely improve; for, by the exercise of the option, he can preserve to himself the benefit of the improvement. If he has no option he cannot economically make an improvement which will still have a substantial value at the termination of the lease. Thus, a rule which invalidates options in lessees for the full term of their leases defeats the policy favoring free alienation and full use of property which the Rule Against Perpetuities was designed to further. Several American jurisdictions have recognized this fact and have held valid such options: but the English cases still have some following in the United States. The English rule is particularly surprising in view of the fact that it is well settled that perpetual options to *renew* leases have always been held valid.

Stock option warrants and conversion privileges in bonds. As contracts, options to purchase stock have nothing to do with the Rule Against Perpetuities. However, if (1) such an option should refer to particular shares and (2) the stock should be so unique that specific performance of the option would ordinarily be granted, an equitable interest in the stock would ordinarily arise, and this would be void if the option could be exercised beyond the period of perpetuities.

B. Revocable Trusts; Insurance Trusts

The question with regard to revocable trusts and insurance trusts is whether the period of perpetuities is computed from the creation of the trust or from the death of the settlor.

Suppose *A* creates a trust to pay the income to himself for life, then to pay the income to his children, then to pay the principal to his grandchildren, reserving to himself the power to revoke the trust at any time during his life. If the period of perpetuities is computed from the creation of the trust, the possibility that A will have further children causes the gift to the grandchildren to be too remote; but if the period is computed from the death of A, the impossibility of further children of A being born allows them to be taken as the lives in being and causes the gift to grandchildren to be valid. The existence of the power of revocation should cause the period of perpetuities to be computed only from the expiration of the power — i.e., from the death of A — and it has been so held. So long as one person has the power at any time to make himself the sole owner, there is no tying-up of the property and no violation of the policy of the Rule Against Perpetuities. If the power is not exercised the future interests which could have been destroyed by the exercise of the power are in substance gifts made by the holder of the power at the time of the power's expiration, and they should be so treated under the Rule Against Perpetuities. The situation is analogous to future interests after an estate tail, where the period of perpetuities is computed from the date of expiration of the estate tail; the power to disentail makes the tenant in tail the substantial owner and causes interests after the estate tail to be in substance gifts by the last tenant in tail at the time of expiration of his estate. The situation is also analogous to gifts in default of the exercise of a general power by deed or will, the period of perpetuities being computed from the expiration of the power — i.e., the death of the donee.

With regard to insurance trusts, the problem of deciding whether the period of perpetuities is computed from the creation of the trust or from the death of the assured-settlor is complex. There is substantially no authority. If the trust is revocable, the decision should be the same as in the case of any other revocable trust; and it has been so held. But if the trust is irrevocable, variations in the terms of the policies (notably, whether they are "assigned" or "unassigned") and in the trust instrument (notably, whether the trust is "funded" or "unfunded") may produce one or the other result. Any settlor should be advised to create a trust which is valid under a computation of the period of perpetuities from the creation of the trust.

C.   Rights of Entry for Condition Broken; Possibilities of Reverter

It is the settled American law that both of these types of interests are exempt from the operation of the Rule Against Perpetuities. Thus, a gift "to the A church so long as the premises are used for church purposes" creates a possibility of reverter in the grantor which will become possessory whenever the contingency occurs. Similarly, a gift "to the

A church in fee simple, but if the premises are ever used other than for church purposes the grantor and his heirs may re-enter and repossess the premises as of their former estate" creates a right of entry for condition broken in the grantor, and this right of entry can be exercised whenever the named contingency occurs.

D.   Powers of Sale in Trustees and Mortgagees

We have seen that a power of appointment (unless it is a general power exercisable by deed or will) is void if it can be exercised beyond the period of perpetuities. There is no such restriction upon powers of sale in trustees during the continuance of a trust. Such powers facilitate rather than hinder the free circulation of property, and to strike them down frustrates the policy of the Rule Against Perpetuities. Likewise, there is no such restriction upon powers of sale in mortgagees. Such powers are ancillary to the security title of the mortgagee, are administrative rather than dispositive in character, and do not give rise to the abuses which the Rule Against Perpetuities was designed to remedy.

X.   Associated Rules

In addition to the Rule Against Perpetuities (i.e., the rule invalidating interests which vest too remotely) there are a few other bodies of legal doctrine relating to the imposition of time limitations for the purpose of preventing property from being tied up. The rules forbidding restraints on alienation might be considered as "associated rules", since they, like the Rule Against Perpetuities, are designed to foster the free circulation of property; but they are not here treated, because most of such rules invalidate a restraint in toto without reference to the time during which it is imposed. So far as the validity of a restraint is dependent upon a time duration analogous to the period of perpetuities, it is hereinafter treated.

A.   Restrictions on Accumulations

In the famous case of Thellusson v. Woodford,[13] it was held that a trust to accumulate the income of property for the period of perpetuities was valid. But it has several times been stated that a court will invalidate accumulations even within the period of perpetuities if the accumulation is found to last so long that public policy will be violated.

13. 11 Ves. Jr. 112 (Ch. 1805).

Statutes commonly prescribe more stringent limits for periods of accumulation — the commonest provision being that the accumulation "must be made for the benefit of one or more minors" and must terminate before their majority. This is not the place for an extended discussion of these statutes; but it is desirable that two warnings should be given.

(1) The requirement that the accumulation be "for the benefit" of the minor and terminate at majority means that when the minor reaches 21 the accumulations must be paid over to him outright; and if the instrument does not so provide, the accumulation provision is void. Thus,

42. Under such a statute *T* bequeaths his estate in trust to pay to his minor child, *A,* so much of the income as should be needed for his support and education during minority; to accumulate the balance of the income during *A*'s minority and add the same to principal; upon *A*'s majority to pay to him the whole income of the combined fund of principal and accumulations during his life; and upon *A*'s death to pay the combined fund of principal and accumulations to *A*'s children. The provision for accumulation is void, and *A* is entitled to the full income of the fund during his minority.

(2) Many usual and harmless provisions in wills and trusts create "accumulations" without superficially appearing to do so. For example, a provision that trustees shall use income to discharge a mortgage on real estate in the trust, a provision that, if the market value of the principal and accumulations during his life; and upon *A*'s death to pay creation, income shall be used to make up the deficiency, a provision that stock dividends shall all be treated as principal in a jurisdiction where some of them would otherwise be treated as income, have all been held to create invalid accumulations.

B. Time Restrictions upon Restraints Otherwise Valid

The rules as to restraints upon alienation strike down certain attempts to prevent the free circulation of property, regardless of the time element. Thus a provision in a conveyance in fee simple from *A* to *B* declaring that the property shall not be conveyed by *B* is wholly ineffective, and it generally makes no difference that the restraint is limited in time — say, to ten years. But some important types of restraints do not fall within the general prohibitions of these rules. For example:

a. Restraints upon alienation of equitable life interests in trusts — the familiar "spendthrift trusts" — are held valid almost everywhere.

    b. Restraints upon anticipation of equitable fee interests in trusts —
        e.g., "To A trustee in trust to pay the income to B until he
        reaches the age of 40 and then to pay the principal to him" —
        are recognized in most states.
    c. Restraints upon alienation of legal life estates seem to be finding
        greater favor in the courts.

It is probable, though there is no clear American authority on the
point, that any one of these restraints which escapes the general rules
as to restraints upon alienation is nevertheless invalid if it may last
longer than the period of perpetuities. Thus,

43. *T* bequeaths the residue of his estate in trust for *A* for life, remainder for such issue of *A* and in such manner and for such estates as *A*
shall by will appoint. *A* by will appoints one-half of the fund to his son
B (living at *T*'s death) for life and one-half of the fund to his son *C*
(unborn at *T*'s death) for life, with survivorship between the sons for
life, remainder to such of *B*'s and *C*'s children as shall be born within
21 years of the death of all descendants of *T* who were living at *T*'s
death. *A*'s will contains a clause as follows: "No interest of any beneficiary of this trust, whether in principal or in income, shall be assignable
or subject to the claims of creditors of such beneficiary." All interests
created by the trust are valid; the interests of *B* and *C* vest at the death
of *A*, who was a life in being at *T*'s death; the interests of the remaindermen vest within 21 years after the termination of a reasonable number of lives in being at *T*'s death. The restraint on alienation of *B*'s
interest is valid because he was in being at *T*'s death. But it is *probable*
that the restraints on *C*'s life estate and upon the remainders is invalid,
since they may last longer than the period of perpetuities.

C. Time Limitations on the Duration of Trusts

There is no objection, upon principle or by the great weight of authority, to a trust which lasts longer than the period of perpetuities. Thus
a trust for *A* for life, and then for *A*'s children for their lives and then
for Harvard College is perfectly good. However, at least one court has
held trusts bad because they exceed the period of perpetuities in duration; and a few others have rendered decisions or uttered dicta which
tend in the same direction.

    Assuming, however, that in the particular jurisdiction there is no objection per se to a trust which lasts beyond the period, there are still
disadvantages to such an arrangement. If the trust instrument contains
restraints on alienation (e.g., spendthrift provisions), these may be invalidated by lasting too long. If the instrument contains provisions for
accumulations, these also may fall with resulting litigation as to the

disposition of the income thus set free. If the English cases on the application of the Rule Against Perpetuities to powers of sale and lease in the trustees should be followed, such powers would be invalid.

For these reasons the preferable draftsmanship practice is to limit the duration of trusts to the period of perpetuities — i.e., to lives in being and 21 years from the death of the testator or creation of the trust, or, if a special power or a general testamentary power is being exercised, from the creation of the power. This is no great hardship because, as has been heretofore indicated, a little care in the selection of the lives in being will cause any trust to last approximately a century.

XI.   Charities

There is some relaxation of the Rule Against Perpetuities in favor of charities, but not much. Where there is a gift to the *A* charity, with a gift over to the *B* charity upon a remote contingency, the disposition is wholly valid. But if either the first or second of these gifts is to a noncharity the second gift fails. Thus,

44. T bequeaths a fund to the municipality of Reading for certain charitable purposes in that town with a direction that, if the said municipality shall for one year omit to perform the directions, the property shall pass to the municipality of London for the benefit of Christ's Hospital. The entire gift is valid.

45: T devises land to the *A* Church for use as a residence for its minister, but if the land shall ever cease to be used for such purpose, then to *T*'s nephew, *B*. The executory devise to *B* is invalid.

46. T devises land to his nephew, *A*, until Gloversville shall be incorporated as a village, and then to Gloversville for the purpose of establishing a library. The gift to Gloversville is invalid.

An *accumulation* for charity is not limited to the period of perpetuities; but the courts have frequently stated that they have power to strike down an accumulation for charity which exceeds the bounds of reason.

XII.   Some Suggestions as to Draftsmanship

Practically anything a testator is likely to want can be done within the limits of the Rule Against Perpetuities. Wills fail because of inept work of lawyers, not because of excessive demands of testators. . . . In drafting instruments . . . the following suggestions are worth noting:

1. Examine *every* will for possible violations of the rule. The cases dealt with under heading III*B*, supra, are sufficient proof that the most innocent limitations may fail to comply with the requirement of absolute certainty of vesting within lives and 21 years.

2. Investigate fully the question whether the will disposes of property which is subject to a power of appointment; for, as indicated under heading V*B,* supra, the period of perpetuities is computed from the creation of the power where the power is either special or testamentary.

3. Describe beneficiaries by name rather than by a class designation wherever that is possible; for this will eliminate many of the casualties of the "fertile octogenarian" type. Where *T* wishes to benefit an aged sister and her children and grandchildren, say "To my sister, Mary, for life, remainder to John, Henry and William, children of my said sister, for their lives; and upon the death of any one of these three the share of the property in which he had a life estate is to pass in fee simple to his children him surviving, or if no children survive him, then to such children of his two brothers as shall then be living per capita." Do not say "To my sister, Mary, for life, remainder to her children for their lives, remainder to her grandchildren in fee."

4. Regard with particular suspicion any gift which is contingent upon the taker attaining an age in excess of 21. Such gifts constitute the largest single group of invalid limitations.

5. Discourage gifts which are contingent upon the taker being living at the time when the estate is settled, or the will probated, or the debts paid. Such gifts can be drafted so that they are valid; but they do little good and often run substantial risks. It is not sufficient that a gift be valid; it is necessary that it be so clearly valid that litigation cannot develop.

6. Limit the duration of trusts to the period of perpetuities. Longer trusts may be valid; but they involve substantial difficulties with certain doctrines related to the Rule Against Perpetuities.

The competent drafting of wills is a difficult business which offers only austere rewards. . . . But the counsellor who leaves behind him a will book which succeeds in placing property where his clients wished it without those uncertainties as to validity and ambiguities as to meaning which breed litigation, can sleep the eternal sleep in the comforting knowledge that he has upheld the finest traditions of his craft.

B.   *Review and Application: A Perpetuities Quiz*

The basic perpetuities questions that follow can be used to provide a fairly comprehensive review of the common law Rule Against Perpetuities and of Leach's explanation of it. If not taken too seriously — for some questions, being essentially "openers" for discussion, will seem tricky or less specific than one would expect in a real test — the quiz offers a basis for a light but instructive examination of important features of the rule. Some instructors may find it more provocative and effective, either for class discussion or for independent discussion by students outside of class, if students are provided a set of "answers" but without the explanations or qualifications that discussion is intended to develop.

Answer QUESTIONS 1-35 either TRUE or FALSE

_____ 1.   Except in the case of future interests in class gift form, the rule is satisfied as to the interest in question if that interest must *either* vest or fail within the period of the rule.

_____ 2.   The rule is *not* satisfied by the mere fact that it is *certain* that, by the time the period expires, there will be a combination of persons in being who will then be able to convey a perfect title to the property.

_____ 3.   The rule does *not* require complete title to vest in one person within the period.

_____ 4.   In some cases the rule may invalidate even vested remainders.

_____ 5.   The "twenty-one year period" is really 21 years and (approximately) 9 months.

_____ 6.   The 21-year period can *not* precede the measuring lives.

_____ 7.   The following bequest is valid in its entirety: "... in trust to pay the income to my children for 21 years, and then to pay the income for life to my youngest grandchild living at the end of that 21 year period, and upon such grandchild's death, remainder to *A*." (Be careful!)

_____ 8.   The grantor may select the measuring lives (but probably not to exceed a reasonable number) and is not confined in so doing to the lives of beneficiaries.

_____ 9.   A bequest to be divided among all of one's own grandchildren who shall attain the age of 25 will be invalid regardless of the circumstances. (Careful!)

_____ 10.   "To my wife if she is living at the date administration of my estate is completed and distribution is made, otherwise to my children then surviving, and if none, to the heirs of *X*." This devise is valid in its entirety. (Careful!)

_____ 11.   A bequest to "such of *X*'s children as reach age 30" is valid under the rule if either *X* is dead or one of *X*'s living children has reached 30 at the time of the gift.

_____ 12.   *X*, an unmarried man, creates an irrevocable trust for himself for life and then "equally to my children, but if any child shall die before age 50 then to Z and his heirs." The remainder to the children is invalid.

_____ 13. Under a deed to "A Church for so long as used for church purposes and then to B and his heirs," the gift to B is valid. (Incidentally, what is A's interest? B's?)

_____ 14. Under a deed "to A, but if liquor shall ever be sold on the premises then to B," the gift to B is valid. (Again, what does A have?)

_____ 15. A deed "to X in fee simple, but if X shall ever become bankrupt then to such of my descendants as shall then be living" is valid in its entirety.

_____ 16. A bequest of "$100,000 for life to my son A [who is alive at the testator's death], then to be divided equally among such of my grandchildren as shall reach age 25" is invalid even as to grandchildren alive at the testator's death. (Incidentally, would it matter if a grandchild or two were already 25 when the testator died?)

_____ 17. A bequest of "$1,000 to each of my grandchildren who reaches age 25" is valid as to any grandchildren alive at the testator's death.

_____ 18. Any general power of appointment is valid if it is *certain* that the donee will *acquire* the power, if at all, within the period.

_____ 19. A special power of appointment is valid if it is certain that such a power will be capable of being exercised within the period.

_____ 20. The period for determining the validity of interests appointed under a special power is measured from the date of the creation of the power.

_____ 21. Whenever a power of appointment is classified as a general power, the perpetuities period for appointed interests is measured from the date of exercise.

_____ 22. Even when the period is measured from the origin of the power, the validity of an appointment is judged in the light of facts which *actually* (rather than those which might) have occurred between the dates of the power's creation and exercise.

_____ 23. *T*'s will devises Blackacre "to A for life, then equally for life to A's children who are living from time to time, and on the survivor's death, or upon A's death without children surviving, remainder to such issue of B as may then be living, such issue to take per stirpes." There is a valid contingent remainder created by the provision for the described issue of B. (Careful!)

_____ 24. The validity of the above provision would *not* be improved by the fact that *B* had predeceased *T* leaving issue who survived *T*.

_____ 25. But the provision set out in question 23 could not in any way violate the rule if *A* had predeceased the testator.

_____ 26. *T*'s will devises "to my surviving children for life, then equally to my then surviving grandchildren for life, remainder to the then surviving children of *B*." The ultimate remainder in *B*'s children is valid.

       _____ a. cf. (answer if the final provision had been) "remainder to the children of *B*."

       _____ b. cf. "remainder to the children of *B*, but if any child should die before receiving possession then to his or her issue."

       _____ c. cf. "remainder to the children of *B* who are alive at the trust's termination or to the issue of any who are then dead."

_____ 27. The gift to *B*'s children in the original form of question 26 conceivably might be valid even if the testator had followed the grandchildren's life estates with life estates to each of his then surviving great-grandchildren (and then remainder to the children of *B* who are then surviving), even though we further assume that children of the testator do in fact survive him.

_____ 28. According to Gray, who is thought to have known something about some of these things, instruments should be construed as if the rule did not exist, and then the rule is to be applied remorselessly to the interests so interpreted.

_____ 29. Leach, of whom like thoughts are thought, says by way of elaboration that even where the terms of an instrument are ambiguous, they are construed by courts as if the rule did not exist, since the rule is applied despite the grantor's intent.

_____ 30. The rule has no application to options.

_____ 31. The common law rule does not apply to rights of entry or to possibilities of reverter in America, but it does apply to executory interests as well as remainders.

_____ 32. The duration of a trust is not limited to the perpetuities period where all interests therein are vested.

_____ 33. A direction to accumulate income for longer than the perpetuities period is valid in a trust which lasts beyond the period.

_____ 34. But a provision in such a trust would be invalid if it authorized accumulations beyond the period at the trust-

ee's discretion (i.e., a discretionary power to pay out or
accumulate income.)

_____ 35. Future interests to charity are exempt from the rule.

In QUESTIONS 36-38, check ALL ANSWERS which accurately
complete the statement

_____ 36. A testamentary disposition to "my son _A_ for life, then to
_A_'s surviving spouse for life, remainder to such of _A_'s
children as are then surviving" is _valid_ in its entirety if:
_____ _A_ in fact predeceased the testator.
_____ _A_ had children living at the date of the testator's
death.
_____ _A_ was unmarried when the testator died.

_____ 37. A transfer by _A_ "to such of _B_'s grandchildren as shall
attain the age of 21" may be _invalid:_
_____ if made by will.
_____ if irrevocably made inter vivos.
_____ if the transfer is revocable.

_____ 38. The last person to own Blackacre outright was _X_. A gift
of Blackacre "to all of _X_'s great grandchildren living
when the youngest reaches the age of 21" may be _invalid_
if made by:
_____ inter vivos trust established by _X_, reserving the
absolute power to revoke.
_____ _X_'s will, though _X_ outlived his children.
_____ a special power of appointment created by _X_'s
will and exercised by the will of _X_'s wife when
_X_'s only living descendants were grandchildren
actually born in _X_'s lifetime.

Trust Duration. The Rule Against Perpetuities is a rule against remote
vesting, not a rule against interests that last too long. Nevertheless, the
common law rule does indirectly limit the duration of private trusts,
since at some point the settlor will run out of lives in being in which
to vest the beneficial interests.

Recall the _Claflin_ doctrine from Chapter 14, section C supra, that
the beneficiaries of a trust may not terminate the trust if its continuance
is necessary to fulfill a material purpose of the settlor. The Restatement
(Second) of Property, Donative Transfers (1983) indicates that even
a material purpose trust becomes terminable by agreement of all the
beneficiaries at any time after the perpetuities period expires. Id. §2.1.
Reflecting appreciable judicial and statutory authority, the Restatement (Second) states that a provision for accumulation of trust
income expires at the end of the perpetuities period, and any accumu-

lation thereafter is invalid. Id. §2.2; see also Restatement (Third) of Trusts §29 & Id. cmts. *b* & *c* (Tent. Draft approved 1999).

C.   Selected Aspects of the Rule Against Perpetuities

1.   General Nature, Requirements, and Scope of the Rule

PROBLEMS

20-A.   *D* bequeathed his residuary estate to *T* Trust Co. in trust to pay the net income to *A* for life, then providing: "On *A*'s death the trust shall continue and the trustee shall pay the net income in equal shares to *A*'s children for their lives, and on the death of the last of *A*'s children the trust shall terminate and the principal shall be distributed to *A*'s heirs." At *D*'s death *A* is alive, well, married and the father of one small child. *T* Trust Co. consults you concerning this trust and wishes to know what problems it is stepping into. What issues, if any, do you see with regard to the meaning and validity of the quoted provisions of *D*'s will? So far as perpetuities and related issues are concerned, be prepared to explain fully the arguable solutions, the results you think most likely and the reasoning underlying those expected results.

20-B.   *T*'s will provided: "It has always been my hope that one of my grandsons would enter the clergy. I therefore bequeath $50,000 to the first grandson of mine to do so. If my children have no such son, then I give the $50,000 to St. Anne's Chapel, Kennebunkport." *T* was survived by his widow, two sons and one daughter, plus six grandchildren. At the time of *T*'s death he was paying the expenses of a grandchild, *G*, who was age 20 and a seminarian, and *T* had intimated to *G* that *G* could expect a "rather spectacular graduation present." The widow (*T*'s wife by a second marriage late in life), as residuary legatee of *T*'s will, the trustees of St. Anne's Chapel, and *G*, who graduated and was ordained into the clergy several months after *T*'s death, all claim the $50,000. What arguments would each make, and what result should be reached? Why? How could the drafter have avoided the difficulties here?

20-C.   *X* died twenty-five years ago, survived by a son, *S*, and a daughter, *D*, as his only heirs. *X* bequeathed $100,000 in trust "to pay the income to *S* for life, then the income to *S*'s widow for life; on the death of *S*'s widow, or on *S*'s death should he leave no widow, to pay the principal equally to *S*'s then living children and by right of representation to the then living issue of any deceased children of *S*." The will, which left $100,000 outright to *D*, contained no residuary clause. At

X's death *S* was married to *W* and they had three children. Five years ago *W* died, and now *S* has just died leaving legacies of $10,000 each to his two daughters and the residue of his estate to his oldest child (and only son), *E. D, E,* and the daughters of *S* all seek to claim as much of the trust fund as possible. What would each claim and on what basis? How should the trust estate be distributed? Explain, and respond to each contention that is rejected.

JEE v. AUDLEY
1 Cox 324, 29 Eng. Rep. 1186 (Ch. 1787)

Edward Audley, by his will, bequeathed as follows, "Also my will is that £1000 shall be placed out at interest during the life of my wife, which interest I give her during her life, and at her death I give the said £1000 unto my niece Mary Hall and the issue of her body lawfully begotten, and to be begotten, and in default of such issue I give the said £1000 to be equally divided between the daughters *then* living of my kinsman John Jee and his wife Elizabeth Jee."

It appeared that John Jee and Elizabeth Jee were living at the time of the death of the testator, had four daughters and no son, and were of a very advanced age. Mary Hall was unmarried and of the age of about 40; the wife was dead. The present bill was filed by the four daughters of John and Elizabeth Jee to have the £1000 secured for their benefit upon the event of the said Mary Hall dying without leaving children. And the question was, whether the limitation to the daughters of John and Elizabeth Jee was not void as being too remote; and to prove so, it was said that this was to take effect on a general failure of issue of Mary Hall; and though it was to the daughters of John and Elizabeth Jee, yet it was not confined to the daughters living at the death of the testator, and consequently it might extend to after-born daughters, in which case it would not be within the limit of a life or lives in being and 21 years afterwards, beyond which time an executory devise is void.

On the other side it was said, that though the late cases had decided that on a gift to children generally, such children as should be living at the time of the distribution of the fund should be let in, yet it would be very hard to adhere to such a rule of construction so rigidly, as to defeat the evident intention of the testator in this case, especially as there was no real possibility of John and Elizabeth Jee having children after the testator's death, they being then 70 years old; that if there were two ways of construing words, that should be adopted which would give effect to the disposition made by the testator; that the cases, which had decided that after-born children should take, proceeded on the implied intention of the testator, and never meant to give an effect to words which would totally defeat such intention. . . .

MASTER OF THE ROLLS [Sir Lloyd Kenyon]. Several cases . . . have settled that children born after the death of the testator shall take a share in these cases; the difference is, where there is an immediate devise, and where there is an interest in remainder; in the former case the children living at the testator's death only shall take; in the latter those who are living at the time the interest vests in possession; and this being now a settled principle, I shall not strain to serve an intention at the expense of removing the land marks of the law; it is of infinite importance to abide by decided cases, and perhaps more so on this subject than any other. The general principles which apply to this case are not disputed: the limitations of personal estate are void, unless they necessarily vest, if at all, within a life or lives in being and 21 years or 9 or 10 months afterwards. This has been sanctioned by the opinion of the judges of all times, from the time of the Duke of Norfolk's case to the present: it is grown reverend by age, and is not now to be broken in upon; I am desired to do in this case something which I do not feel myself at liberty to do, namely to suppose it impossible for persons in so advanced an age as John and Elizabeth Jee to have children; but if this can be done in one case it may in another, and it is a very dangerous experiment, and introductive of the greatest inconvenience to give a latitude to such sort of conjecture. Another thing pressed upon me, is to decide on the events which have happened; but I cannot do this without overturning very many cases. The single question before me is, not whether the limitation is good in the events which have happened, but whether it was good in its creation; and if it were not, I cannot make it so. Then must this limitation, if at all, *necessarily* take place within the limits prescribed by law? The words are "in default of such issue I give the said £1000 to be equally divided between the daughters *then* living of John Jee and Elizabeth his wife." If it had been to "daughters now living," or "who should be living at the time of my death," it would have been very good; but as it stands, this limitation may take in after-born daughters; this point is clearly settled . . . and the effect of law on such limitation cannot make any difference in construing such intention. If then, this will extended to after-born daughters, is it within the rules of law? Most certainly not, because John and Elizabeth Jee might have children born ten years after the testator's death, and then Mary Hall might die without issue 50 years afterwards; in which case it would evidently transgress the rules prescribed. I am of opinion therefore, though the testator might possibly mean to restrain the limitation to the children who should be living at the time of the death, I cannot, consistently with decided cases, construe it in such restrained sense, but must intend it to take in after-born children. This therefore not being within the rules of law, and as I cannot judge upon subsequent events, I think the limitation void. Therefore dismiss the bill, but without costs.

——————————

For a keen analysis of Jee v. Audley, see Leach, The Rule Against Perpetuities and Gifts to Classes, 51 Harv. L. Rev. 1329, 1338-1341 (1938). *Jee* is infamous as the source of four principles that were not inherent in the common law Rule but came to be part of its lore. What are they? Note, too, Sir Lloyd Kenyon's gratuitous dictum that "If [the gift over] had been to 'daughters now living,' or 'who should be living at the time of my death,' it would have been very good. . . ." How good would it have been?

2. Class Gifts and the Rule

PROBLEM

20-D. *W* established a revocable inter vivos trust, funding it with securities and providing that the income be paid to her for life "and thereafter income to my husband, *H*, and my daughter, *D*, in equal shares or to the survivor." On the death of the last of *H, D*, and *W* "the Trustee shall divide the trust estate into equal shares and shall set aside and designate one such share as a separate trust fund for the benefit of each grandchild of mine who is then living." The trust terms then provide that each grandchild is to receive the net income (and, in the trustee's discretion, principal as needed for support) from his or her trust for its duration and is "to receive one third of the principal at age 25, half of the remaining principal at age 30 and the rest at age 35, at which time the trust is to terminate; if said grandchild does not live to receive his or her full share of my trust, the corpus of that share is to go to his or her issue per stirpes, if any, and otherwise to the other trusts for my other grandchildren."

W died eleven years ago, survived by *H, D*, and *D*'s two children. *H* was the sole beneficiary of her will. Soon thereafter *H* designated *W*'s trust as payee of a $100,000 life insurance policy of which *W* had previously been the primary beneficiary. A month ago *H* died, intestate, survived by his second spouse, *S*, and by *D* and her four children.

The trustee asks your advice concerning the rights that might be asserted in the trust estate, which now consists of the proceeds of *H*'s life insurance policy and securities presently valued at about $200,000. Can the trust be carried out as drawn? What claims do you anticipate being asserted contrary to the terms of the trust, and how do you evaluate those claims? Do you need to know other facts than those set out above?

LEAKE v. ROBINSON
2 Mer. 363, 35 Eng. Rep. 979 (Ch. 1817)

[The testator left certain property in trust, with income to be applied as needed for the support and education of his grandson, William Rowe Robinson, until age twenty-five, and thereafter to pay him the income for life; after Robinson's death, the trustees were to apply income for the benefit of Robinson's children "until (being sons) they should respectively attain twenty-five, or (being daughters) they should attain such age or marry" and then to transfer "an equal proportion of [principal] to such child or children," and if only one child qualified "then the whole to such . . . child." If no child qualified or Robinson died without issue, the principal was to go equally to Robinson's brothers "upon attaining twenty-five" and sisters "at such age or marriage." At the testator's death Robinson had one brother and four sisters; thereafter two more brothers were born before and another sister after the death of Robinson, who died without issue. The question was whether the limitation to Robinson's brothers and sisters was good or "was void, as being too remote."]

THE MASTER of the ROLLS [Sir Wm. Grant]. The first point to be determined in this case is: Who are included in the description of brothers and sisters of William Rowe Robinson . . . those only who were in being at the time of the testator's death, or all who might come in esse during the lives of the respective tenants for life? . . .

. . . According to the established rule of construction, and what I conceive to have been the actual intention of the testator, all who were living at the time of William Rowe Robinson's death must be held to be comprehended in the description.

Having ascertained the persons intended to take, the next question is what time the interests given to them were to vest.

. . . [T]here being no direct gift to the grandchildren [i.e., Robinson's brothers and sisters] . . . none were to take vested interests before the specified period. The attainment of twenty-five is necessary to entitle any child to claim a transfer. . . . The direction to pay is the gift, and that gift is only to attach to children that shall attain twenty-five. . . .

Then, assuming that after-born grandchildren were to be let in, and that the vesting was not to take place till twenty-five, the consequence is, that it might not take place till more than twenty-one years after a life or lives in being at the death of the testator. It was not at all disputed that the bequests must for that reason be wholly void, unless the Court can distinguish between the children born before, and those born after, the testator's death. Upon what ground can that distinction rest? Not upon the intention of the testator; for we have already ascertained that all are included in the description he has given of the objects of his bounty. And all who are included in it were equally capable of taking. It is the period of vesting, and not the description of the legatees, that produces the incapacity. Now, how am I to ascertain in which part of the will it is that the testator has made the blunder which vitiates his bequests? He supposed that he could do legally all that he has done; — that is, include after-born grandchildren, and also postpone the vesting till twenty-five. But, if he had been informed that he could not do both, can I say that the alteration he would have made would have been to leave out the after-born grandchildren, rather than abridge the period of vesting? I should think quite the contrary. It is very unlikely that he should have excluded one half of the family of his daughters, in order only that the other half might be kept four years longer out of the enjoyment of what he left them. It is much more probable that he would have said. ''I do mean to include all my grandchildren, but as you tell me that I cannot do so, and at the same time postpone the vesting till twenty-five, I will postpone it only till twenty-one.'' If I could at all alter the will, I should be inclined to alter it in the way in which it seems to me probable that the testator himself would have altered it. That alteration would at least have an important object to justify it; for it would give validity to all the bequests in the will. The other alteration would only give them a partial effect; and that too by making a distinction, which the testator himself never intended to make, between those who were the equal objects of his bounty. In the latter case, I should be new-modelling a bequest which, standing by itself, is perfectly valid; while I left unaltered that clause which alone impedes the execution of the testator's intention in favour of all his grandchildren. Perhaps it might have been as well if the Courts had originally held an executory devise transgressing the allowed limits to be void only for the excess, where that excess could, as in this case it can be clearly ascertained. But the law is otherwise settled. . . .

To induce the Court to hold the bequests in this will to be partially good, the case has been argued as if they had been made to some individuals who are, and to some who are not, capable of taking. But the bequests in question are not made to individuals, but to classes; and what I have to determine is, whether the class can take. I must make a new will for the testator, if I split into portions his general bequest to the class, and say, that because the rule of law forbids his intention from operating in favour of the whole class, I will make his bequests, what he never intended them to be, viz. a series of particular legacies to particular individuals, or what he had as little in his contemplation, distinct bequests, in each instance, to two different classes, namely to grand-children living at his death, and to grandchildren born after his death.

If the present case were an entirely new question, I should doubt very much whether this could be done. But it is a question which appears to me to be perfectly settled by antecedent decisions, and in cases in which there were grounds for supporting the bequests that do not here exist. In Jee v. Audley (1 Cox 324), there were no after-born children — no distinction therefore to be made between persons capable and persons incapable — (all were capable) — no difficulty, consequently, in adjusting the proportions that the capable children were to take, or in determining the manner, or the period, of ascertaining those proportions. I am asked why the existence of incapable children should prevent capable children from taking. But, in Jee v. Audley, the mere possibility that there might have been incapable children was sufficient to exclude those who were capable. It is said, the devise there was future. Certainly; but only in the same sense in which these bequests are future; that is, so conceived as to let in after-born children, which was the sole reason for its being held to be void. Unless my decision on the first point be erroneous, the bequests in this case do equally include after-born children of the testator's daughters, and are therefore equally void. . . .

A question has been made, whether the particular bequests thus declared void do or do not fall into the residue. I have always understood that, with regard to personal estate, everything which is ill-given by the will does fall into the residue; and it must be a very peculiar case indeed, in which there can at once be a residuary clause and a partial intestacy, unless some part of the residue itself be ill-given. It is immaterial how it happens that any part of the property is undisposed of, whether by the death of a legatee, or by the remoteness, and consequent illegality of the bequest. Either way it is residue, — i.e. something upon which no other disposition of the will effectually operates. It may in words have been before given; but if not effectually given, it is, legally speaking, undisposed of, and consequently included in the denomination of residue. . . .

STORRS v. BENBOW
3 DeG.M.2G 390, 43 Eng. Rep. 153 (Ch. 1853)

The LORD CHANCELLOR. . . . The question arises upon a clause in a codicil which is in these words, — "Item. I direct my executors to pay by and out of my personal estate exclusively the sum of £500 apiece to each child that may be born to either of the children of either of my brothers lawfully begotten to be paid to each of them on his or her attaining the age of twenty-one years without benefit of survivorship." This is a money legacy to each child of any nephew the testator had or might have. The testator had brothers living, [so] there might be legacies too remote, because the gift included legacies to children of a child not yet born.

The bill was filed twenty or thirty years ago; and the cause was heard before Sir John Leach. The argument then was, that the gift was too remote, but Sir John Leach thought that, according to the true construction of the clause children born in the lifetime of the testator were meant, and therefore he said the gift could not be too remote. . . . The Master found that the Plaintiff was in esse in this sense, namely that the testator died in October and the Plaintiff was born six months afterwards; and I think he was so. . . .

. . . I must add however that I do not say that the gift [to the Plaintiff] was at all remote if [the clause included children] to be born at any time, because this is not the case of a class, it is a gift of a pecuniary legacy of a particular amount to every child of every nephew which the testator then had, or of every nephew that might be born after his death, and is therefore good as to the children of the nephews he then had, and bad as to the children of nephews to be born after his death.

It would be a mistake to compare this with Leake v. Robinson (2 Mer. 363) and other cases where the parties take as a class, for the difficulty which there arises as to giving it to some and not giving it to others does not apply here. The question of whether or not the children of after-born nephews shall or shall not take, has no bearing at all upon the question of whether the child of an existing nephew takes; the legacy given to him cannot be bad because there is a legacy given under a similar description to a person who would not be able to take because the gift would be too remote. I give therefore no positive opinion upon the point of remoteness generally in this case, because I think that quacunque via, on the construction of the will, there is nothing to justify the exclusion from taking of a child who was conceived at the death of the testator and born six or seven months afterwards. If the words in question meant children who though not then in existence should be in existence at the death, the Plaintiff was in existence at the death; and if they meant children born at any time, he was born and must have been born if at all within such a time as made his legacy not remote. I am therefore of opinion that in any way he is entitled.

SECOND BANK-STATE STREET TRUST CO. v. SECOND BANK-STATE STREET TRUST CO.
335 Mass. 407, 140 N.E.2d 201 (1957)

CUTTER, J. . . .

On May 8, 1930, the settlor transferred certain securities to himself[1] and a bank in trust to pay the income to the settlor for life and thereaf-

---

1. The Lonach trust provides that after the settlor's death the bank is to be sole trustee.

ter to the settlor's wife, Josephine, for life. Paragraph Third of the instrument provides in part: "After the decease of both the" settlor and "Josephine, the said trust estate shall be held in trust for the benefit of the children of the said Allan, and the issue of any child who may have deceased, each child to receive an equal share of the net income therefrom during his or her life. The share of any child who shall die leaving no issue surviving him or her shall be held in trust for the equal benefit of the surviving children of the said Allan, and the issue of any deceased child, taking by the stocks; and the net income therefrom shall be paid over equally to such surviving children during their lives, and to the issue of any deceased child, such issue taking their parents' share. If any child of the said Allan shall die leaving issue, his or her share shall be held in trust for the benefit of such issue, and the net income therefrom paid over to such issue, per stirpes, or to their legal guardian or guardians, until the termination of this trust. At the expiration of twenty-one years after the death of the last survivor of the children of the said Allan, this trust shall terminate, and the trust estate shall then be distributed among such issue, per stirpes, and not per capita; and until the termination of this trust, the trust estate shall be held together, and administered as one trust."

No power of revocation or amendment is contained in the Lonach trust, which includes a spendthrift clause and trust powers.[2]

The settlor has died. His widow, Josephine Forbes, and four children of the settlor are now living. One son, Robert, died before the settlor leaving two children, Elizabeth and Phyllis Forbes, both born after May 8, 1930, and now minors. After May 8, 1930, the settlor had no further children. The youngest child of the settlor was born in 1925. . . .

The question for determination is whether the remainder interests (other than the admittedly valid life estates of the settlor's widow, Josephine, and his children) are void as in violation of the rule against perpetuities so that a resulting trust in favor of the settlor's estate may exist. This question arises, of course, because the Lonach trust is an irrevocable, inter vivos instrument as to which the period of the rule against perpetuities starts running from the effective date of the instrument, . . . and not a will or a revocable trust, as to either of which the period of the rule against perpetuities would start running at the death of the testator or settlor. . . .

Possible invalidity of the remainder interests under this irrevocable inter vivos trust would not be prevented by the provision in paragraph

2. We expressly leave undecided all questions (which do not affect the validity of any interest, see Restatement, Property, s. 444) relating to whether the restraints on alienation contained in the spendthrift clause will be binding and whether all the trust powers may be exercised during the whole period of this trust, which viewed as of 1930 might not have terminated until twenty-one years after the death of a child of the settlor not then born.

Third for ultimate termination of the trust and distribution of the corpus at "the expiration of twenty-one years after the death of the last survivor of the children of the said Allan." We assume that an appropriate provision . . . for (a) termination of all the trusts under paragraph Third at the end of a period of twenty-one years after the death of specified or ascertainable persons living at the effective date of the trust in 1930 and (b) for distribution of the corpus at the date of such termination to persons then ascertainable, would have assured the validity of all the gifts in paragraph Third, even if those gifts might otherwise have been in violation of the rule against perpetuities. However, if the term "the children of the said Allan" refers to all the children of the settlor, whether born before or after the effective date of the trust instrument then the provision for ultimate termination of the trusts and distribution of the corpus, actually found in paragraph Third (because of the possibility existing in 1930 that further children of the settlor might be born thereafter) does not necessarily limit termination to the expiration of twenty-one years after lives in being in 1930. Viewed as of 1930, this termination could conceivably take place more than twenty-one years after the death of the last survivor of the settlor's children living in 1930. For example, a son of the settlor might have been born in 1932. If that child turned out to be the last survivor of the widow and all the children of the settlor, the vesting of an interest under paragraph Third twenty-one years after his death would be at too remote a time.

The executors in effect rest their contentions upon the possibility, just mentioned, that the termination date (viewed as of the effective date of the trust in 1930) might occur at too remote a date. They seem to construe the fourth sentence of paragraph Third as giving the corpus of the trust at the termination date to a general class consisting of the settlor's issue, then living, per stirpes. This gift, they say, is void "because it was possible that the class . . . could both increase and decrease in number for a period beyond that allowed by the" rule against perpetuities. We think, however, that paragraph Third is not to be viewed as making a general class gift, but that it contains limitations governed by the doctrine of severable or severed shares. . . .

We view paragraph Third as setting up a separate share of the trust corpus for each child of the settlor and such child's issue, with the devolution of that share to be dealt with separately from the devolution of the other shares. On our construction of paragraph Third, no remainder interest in any share of the trust corpus will vest later than the death of a child of the settlor. As all the children of the settlor were living at the effective date of the trust in 1930, all remainder interests will vest within the period of the rule against perpetuities. They thus will be unaffected by the possibility (which existed in 1930 but which never eventuated) that the settlor might have children born later in whose separate and severable shares the remainder interests might vest more than twenty-one years after the end of lives in being in 1930.

We are guided to this construction of paragraph Third by the principle that if there are two or more reasonable interpretations of a dispositive scheme, one of which does not result in holding the remainder interests void under the rule against perpetuities when others do so, the interpretation leading to a holding of validity should be adopted, if consistent with the settlor's general intention and with the public policy behind the rule itself. . . . However, apart from this general principle, paragraph Third shows that the settlor and his draftsman intended to set up a separate share of the trust property for each child of the settlor and that child's issue. This is apparent (a) from the frequent use of the word "share" in the early sentences of the paragraph . . . ; (b) from the provision that until "the termination . . . the trust estate shall be held together, and administered as one trust," which would have been unnecessary[3] if the settlor had intended the remainder interests to be a single general class gift (instead of gifts of severable shares); and (c) from the direction that, at termination, the trust estate shall "be distributed among such issue, per stirpes," which continues the concept of a separate share for the line or stock of each child of the settlor. . . . In addition to the foregoing, it should be pointed out that a provision of paragraph Third, not quoted earlier in this opinion, authorizes the trustees to pay over to any child "a sufficient amount, not exceeding, however, the share of such child or children in the trust fund," to enable such child to purchase certain real estate. This is additional proof that the settlor treated the shares as severable, for obviously the settlor, who has treated his children throughout paragraph Third with equality, intended each such advance to be charged against some share. . . .

A decree [is to be entered] declaring the rights of the defendants in accordance with this opinion. . . .

So ordered.

3.   Powers of Appointment and the Rule

PROBLEMS

20-E.   *T* bequeathed a fund in trust to *A* for life and the remainder "outright or in trust for such persons as *A* should by will appoint" and

---

3. A single trust for a class would normally have been administered as a unit. Of course, separate and independent shares of a single trust, held together for investment and economical administration purposes, frequently must be regarded as severable for purposes of devolution and accounting. . . .

in default of appointment the remainder was "to go to such of A's children as attain the age of 25." In addition, A was given the power "to invade or consume principal in such amounts as she should by instrument in writing request of the trustee." A died twelve years after T without appointing or consuming any principal; she left children aged 2, 6, and 10. The trustee petitions for instructions for distribution of the principal. What result? Would it matter if A had died fifteen years after T, leaving children aged 5, 9, and 13?

20-F.   Shortly before his marriage, S established a trust with the T Trust Co. as trustee; the trust income was payable to S for life, then to his wife, W, for her life, then to S's children for their lives. The income was then payable to the grandchildren of S that "are living at the death of the settlor for their lives. At the death of the last survivor of such grandchildren living at the settlor's death, the trustee shall pay the principal to the then living issue of the settlor, per stirpes." S reserved power to appoint the principal by will or deed to such persons as he saw fit. On his thirtieth wedding anniversary, when the youngest of S's three children was 25, S executed an instrument releasing the power of appointment and delivered this instrument to his adult children and the trustee. S died three years later, survived by his wife, his three children, and seven grandchildren. He left a will devising the residue of his estate to D, his youngest grandchild, who was 5 at S's death. On a petition for construction of the will and trust, D's guardian ad litem asserts D's claim to all the trust assets, to become possessory at the death of W. To what extent, if any, do you expect D to prevail? Why? What are the interests of other parties, born and unborn? Explain the arguments underlying each interest that might be asserted.

20-G. A, recently married, transferred $200,000 to a corporate trustee, creating a revocable inter vivos trust by which the income is to be paid to A for life, then to his wife, W for life, then in equal shares to A's children for life, and on the death of each child the share of principal from which he or she had been receiving income to go as the child shall appoint by deed or will and in default of appointment income equally to that child's children for life, with appropriate portions of the principal to pass as each grandchild shall appoint by deed or will, and in default of appointment income equally to the grandchild's children for life, with an appropriate share of the remainder to go as each great-grandchild shall appoint by deed or will and in default the share to go that great-grandchild's then living issue by right of representation.

(a) The trustee asks you to explain what interests are created and to what extent they are valid. A has as yet no children. How would you answer? Why? Does the answer trouble you as a matter of social policy?

(b) Two years after the creation of the trust above, A and W had a child, C. Thereafter, A released his power of revocation. The trustee returns to ask you if this changes the advice you gave earlier. How would you respond?

NORTHERN TRUST CO. v. PORTER
368 Ill. 256, 13 N.E.2d 487 (1938)

[Caroline McWilliams died in 1913, leaving a will by which she established a trust, known as the McWilliams fund, for the benefit of her daughter, Frances Lee Porter, for life. Mrs. Porter was also given a general power to appoint the fund by her will. In 1933 Mrs. Porter, as a compromise settlement of certain litigation with her son, Washington Porter II, contracted to appoint half of the fund in further trust for the primary benefit of the son. Mrs. Porter died in 1935, appointing the McWilliams fund by her will, executed in 1934, substantially as follows: two-thirds in trust for her daughter, Pauline Porter White, for life, and after her death for the benefit of her descendants, providing that upon the death of Pauline's last surviving child "or twenty-one years after the death of the last surviving child of Pauline Porter White who is living at the time of my death, whichever event shall happen first, I direct that the principal [shall be paid per stirpes to] the then surviving lawful descendants of my deceased child." The same provision was made for Washington Porter II with regard to the remaining third of the fund. None of Pauline's children was in being at the death of Mrs. McWilliams; Washington is unmarried and has no children.]

JONES, J. . . . It is obvious that, if the period of the rule against perpetuities is computed from the time of the creation of the power by the donor, the gift of the McWilliams fund violates the rule against perpetuities. It is equally clear that if the period is computed from the date of the exercise of the power by the donee, that the gift does not violate the rule against perpetuities. The question presented for decision is whether the period of perpetuities begins to run from the date of the creation of the power or from the date of its exercise. It must be borne in mind that we are concerned only with general power of appointment by will, and not with special power of appointment or a power to appoint by deed or will. This question has not been presented to this court before. It may therefore not be amiss to review the authorities.

Professor Gray asserted that the period of perpetuities begins to run from the date of the creation of a general testamentary power. On the other hand, Professor Kales argued that the date of the exercise of the power was the time from which the period should be computed. 26 Harv. L. Rev. 64, id. 720-727. Both Gray and Kales agreed that the test as to when the period of perpetuities should start to run depended upon whether the donee was "practically the owner" of the appointive fund. Gray contended, with forcefulness, that the donee of a testamentary power of appointment "is not practically the owner; he cannot appoint to himself; he is, indeed, the only person to whom he cannot possibly appoint, for he must die before the transfer of the property can take place." Gray on Perpetuities, §526 (b) (3d ed.). Kales replied that the time for determining whether or not the donee was "practically the owner" was at the moment of exercising the power. It was his view that the donee of a general power to appoint by will is, at the moment when he may exercise the power, practically the owner. Kales, Estates and Future Interests, §695/2d ed. To this, Gray countered: "But a man cannot, in the eye of the law, be at the same time alive and dead. So long as he is alive, the condition necessary for the exercise of the power is not fulfilled, and after he is dead, he cannot be an appointee." Gray on Perpetuities, §952.

On the side of Kales are [a series of] English cases. [Citations omitted.] The Supreme Court of Wisconsin has agreed with Kales in holding that the donee of a general testamentary power of appointment was "practically the owner" at the time of the exercise of the power and, therefore, that the period of perpetuities was to be computed from the date of the exercise of the power. Miller v. Douglass, 192 Wis. 486, 213 N.W. 320.

The weight of the American decisions, however, supports the view of Gray. [Citations omitted.]

The most recent text writer upon this subject is Professor Simes of Michigan. He sums up the law as follows: "There has been some controversy over the question whether, in determining the validity of an appointment under a general power to appoint by will, the period should be calculated from the creation of the power or from the time of its exercise. The weight of authority in the United States, and, it is believed, the better reason is in favor of the view that a general power to appoint by will should be treated as a special power in this respect, and that the period should be computed from the time of the creation of the power. It has been argued that, since the donee of a general power to appoint by will may appoint to his own estate or to any person for a consideration, he is in substance the owner to almost the same extent as if he had a general power to appoint by deed as well as by will, and that, being substantially the owner, the rule should only apply from the time the power is exercised. It is believed, however, that from a practical standpoint the position of the donee of a general power to appoint by will is very different from that of the donee of a power to appoint by deed. Wills are not, as a rule, commercial transactions. The fact that a man has an unrestricted power to appoint property by will does not mean that he is likely to put the property on the market and sell it. The very fact that he is limited to a disposition by will means that he will probably dispose of it to members of his family or to charities by way of gift. The property, during the existence of this power, is, from a practical standpoint, removed from commerce. And it is proper, in determining remoteness, to count the period from the creation and not from the exercise of the power."

After a careful consideration, we prefer to adopt the views expressed by Professors Gray and Simes, and we hold that the attempted exercise of the power violated the rule against perpetuities. The purpose of the rule against perpetuities is to prevent property from being kept out of the channels of commerce for too long a period of time. Since the donee of a general testamentary power of appointment cannot appoint the property during his lifetime, and restraint on alienation begins at the time of the creation of the power by the donor, the validity of an appointment, under a general testamentary power, must be determined by considering the donee's appointment as part of the instrument created by the donor. Thus, we must look to see whether or not the remainders will vest in interest (although not necessarily in possession) within the period measured from the time of the creation of the power by the donor. Of course, events as they actually exist at the time of the appointment by the donee may be considered in this determination, and a ground of invalidity apparently existing under such a gift as of the date of the creating instrument, which can no longer occur, need not be considered. This was apparently the view of Hopkinson v. Swaim, 284 Ill. 11, 119 N.E. 985, which considers a special power of appointment, to which the same rule should apply.

This holding necessarily raises the question whether the valid portions of the appointment can be separated from the invalid portions. We are of the opinion that they cannot. The trust presents one entire, connected scheme for the disposition of the McWilliams fund, and the provisions are interdependent. There is no gift of the fee to the children of the donee followed by an invalid successive interest. It is our opinion that the donee would have preferred to die intestate as to the power of appointment rather than to have the appointment take effect with the void clause left out. [Citations omitted.]

The entire appointment failing, what should become of the McWilliams fund? Should it pass by intestacy to the heirs of Mrs. Porter or should it pass in default of appointment as provided by the donor? This question is one of intention of the donee. . . .

The blending of an appointment with the rest of the property of the donee indicates an intention that, if the appointment is ineffective, the appointed property should go into the estate of the donee rather than to the beneficiaries in default. In the instant case, the exercise of the power of appointment is made a separate and distinct clause of the will of the donee and is not mingled with her own property. . . .

. . . It is our belief that Frances Lee Porter would have preferred that the McWilliams fund pass by default of appointment rather than by intestacy. . . .

Since the McWilliams fund passes under the will of the donor by default of appointment, the question of damages, due to Mrs. Porter's failure to appoint the fund in accordance with the settlement agreement, remains. The settlement agreement provided for execution of the power of appointment, and an execution, ineffective because of the Rule Against Perpetuities, is as much a breach of the agreement as would be an execution contrary to the terms of the agreement or nonexecution of the power.

The only claim of the defendants is for damages from the estate of Mrs. Porter, including the McWilliams fund, which damages consist of the value of the McWilliams fund at the time of Mrs. Porter's death, with interest thereon from the date of her death. It is conceded that the contract is not specifically enforceable. . . .

Our view is in accord with that of the reporters of the American Law Institute, who state, in the Restatement of Property, tentative draft No. 7, §463, comment *a*: "By giving a testamentary power or a power otherwise not presently exercisable, the donor expresses an intent that the discretion as to the exercise of the power shall be retained until the donee's death or such other time as is stipulated. To specifically enforce a promise to appoint under such a power would be to permit the donor's intent as to disposition of his property to be directly defeated. Moreover, to allow the donee to render himself liable in damages for breach of such promise would be to permit the donor's intent to be defeated by indirection; for the compulsion of a prospective suit for damages would be sufficient to eliminate any practical freedom of choice after the making of the contract. These considerations are especially strong where the power is special and consequently the duty to postpone the exercise of discretion is one of the fiduciary duties owed to the objects of the power, but even where the power is general the fulfillment of the donor's lawful wishes is a sufficient reason for denying validity to promises to appoint." The reporters evidently preferred not to follow the case of In re Parkin, 3 L.R. (Ch. Div. 1892) 510, 1892 Probate 591, and with them we agree. . . .

In re BIRD'S ESTATE
225 Cal. App. 2d 196, 37 Cal. Rptr. 288 (1964)

STONE, J. This appeal from a decree determining interests in an estate, presents a question of the manner in which the rule against perpetuities (Civ. Code §715.2) is to be applied to general testamentary powers of appointment. The case was tried before the 1963 amendments to the Civil Code pertaining to the rule against perpetuities became effective.

Jeannette Miller Bird and Geoffrey Andrew Bird, her husband, executed their wills simultaneously February 17, 1961. Jeannette died June 16, 1961, and her will, which was admitted to probate, provided, insofar as here pertinent:

"2. This trust shall exist and continue for and during the life of my said husband, GEOFFREY ANDREW BIRD, and shall cease and terminate upon his death. I give and grant to my husband the exclusive power to dispose of the corpus, and undistributed income, under the terms of his Last Will and Testament, and should he have failed to exercise this power as aforesaid, or should his said Last Will and Testament be deemed invalid for any reason whatsoever, then the corpus and any undistributed income shall become a part of the estate of my said husband, and shall be distributed to his heirs at law according to the laws of succession of the State of California then in effect."

Geoffrey Bird died just three months later, September 16, 1961. He exercised the power of appointment created by Jeannette's will, by the following provisions in his will:

"FIFTH: I will, devise and bequeath to CITIZENS NATIONAL BANK, in trust, all of the rest, residue and remainder of my property of every nature, kind and description, including the property and assets which are included in the Marital Deduction Trust as set forth in my wife's Will, and I do now specifically exercise my power of testamentary disposition by including such assets in this trust.

(a) Said property is to be held by the Trustee for the following purposes:

"1. The net income shall be distributed in monthly or other convenient installments to or for the benefit of my said children in equal shares for life. . . .

"3. This trust shall terminate on the death of the last survivor of my children and my grandchildren living at the time of my death, and the entire corpus and undistributed net income shall go and be distributed to the children of my grandchildren per capita."

Counsel for both appellant and respondent agree that the matter is one of first impression in California, and they pose two questions: First, whether the period prescribed by the rule against perpetuities (Civ. Code §715.2) is determined as of the time the power was created, that is, at Jeannette's death, or at Geoffrey's death when the power was exercised. Second, if the time the power is created governs, is the determination made according to the facts existing at the time of creation of the power, or are the circumstances existing at the time the power is exercised, controlling? We hold that the period is counted from the time the power of appointment is created, but that the facts and circumstances are considered as of the time of its exercise. This holding disposes of both questions raised.

The applicable statute is Civil Code section 715.2, which provides:

"No interest in real or personal property shall be good unless it must vest, if at all, not later than 21 years after some life in being at the creation of the interest and any period of gestation involved in the situation to which the limitation applies. The lives selected to govern the time of vesting must not be so numerous or so situated that evidence of their deaths is likely to be unreasonably difficult to obtain. It is intended by the enactment of this section to make effective in this State the American common law rule against perpetuities."

Simes and Smith, in their work, The Law of Future Interest, section 1276, page 214, tell us that the common law rule is:

". . . in determining the validity of an appointment under a special power or a general testamentary power, though the period is counted from the creation of the power, facts and circumstances are considered as of the time of its exercise."

Respondent points out that the New York Courts have held to the contrary, that is to say, that circumstances are considered as of the time of creation of the power of appointment in determining whether the statute against perpetuities has been violated. In support thereof In re Baiter's Estate, 152 Misc. 177, 273 N.Y.S. 962, is cited. The Baiter opinion is based upon a New York statute, Real Property Law, McK. Consol. Laws, c. 50, §179, and the court quotes that part of the statute it deems applicable. No language is quoted that is similar to the final sentence of California Civil Code section 715.2, to wit: "It is intended by the enactment of this section to make effective in this State the American common law rule against perpetuities." This language appears to us to be decisive insofar as California is concerned. In fact, a 1957 New York case, In re Estate of Huntington, 10 Misc. 2d 932, 170 N.Y.S.2d 452, recognized that California follows "[t]he common law rule of powers."

The Restatement of Property adopted the common law rule applicable to general testamentary powers of appointment, which Civil Code section 715.2 directs us to follow in California. The rule is expressed in section 392 as follows:

". . . an appointment under either a general testamentary power or a special power is invalid, because of the rule against perpetuities, only to the extent that its limitations, (a) construed in the light of the circumstances existent when the power is exercised, but (b) measured, for the purpose of applying the rule against perpetuities, from the time when the power was created, violate that rule."

In commenting upon the rationale of the rule, the Restatement points out that:

"The element of the stated rule embodied in Clause (a), mitigates the destructive effect of the doctrine of 'relation back.' In applying the rule against perpetuities to the limitations of an attempted appointment made under either a general testamentary power or a special power, no useful end would be served by finding an invalidity because of some possible uncertainty, present when the power was created, but actually and definitively excluded by the course of events which has already occurred and which is known at the time of the exercise of the power. By the part of the rule embodied in Clause (a) the fiction of 'relation back' is prevented from having destructive effects greater than those required for the reasonable effectuation of the underlying social policy of the rule against perpetuities." (I'p. 2308-2309.)

This is in accord with the liberal approach toward the rule against perpetuities taken by the California Supreme Court in the recent case of Wong v. Di Grazia, 60 A.C. 505, 35 Cal. Rptr. 241, 386 P.2d 817. A like liberal intendment was manifested by the State Legislature in enacting Civil Code sections 715.5 through 715.8, subsequent to the trial of this action. Without quoting these sections, we note that they mollify the harshness of the rule against perpetuities.

The facts of this case demonstrate the reasonableness of the common law rule embodied in section 392 of the Restatement of Property, supra. By reason of the proximate deaths of Jeannette and Geoffrey, only three months elapsed between creation of the power and its exercise. There was no factual change during that short interval. The lives in being at the time the power was exercised were in being when the power was created, so that the power of appointment did not, in fact, violate the rule against perpetuities. To defeat the purposes and the wishes of Jeannette and Geoffrey because a violation of the rule against perpetuities was theoretically possible, but in fact did not occur, seems to us to be unnecessarily restrictive. It is the sort of rigid mechanistic application of the rule which the Supreme Court decried in Wong v. Di Grazia, supra.

In any event, we find Civil Code section 715.2 and the common law rule to which it refers, controlling. Applying this test, there was no violation of the rule against perpetuities at the time the power of appointment was created, when considered in the light of the facts and circumstances as of the time the power of appointment was exercised.

The judgment is reversed.

GRIFFIN, P. J., and COUGHLIN, J., concur.

SEARS v. COOLIDGE
329 Mass. 340, 108 N.E.2d 563 (1952)

WILKINS, J. . . . The fundamental issue is whether the remainder interests [under an inter vivos trust] violate the rule against perpetuities. Paragraph 5 of the trust instrument provides that the capital of the trust is to be distributed "in equal shares to and among my issue living" at the time of distribution. Distribution is to take place upon "whichever shall first happen" of two events: (1) "the death of the last survivor of those of my children, grandchildren and great-grandchildren who shall be living at my death"; or (2) "the attainment of fifty years by the youngest surviving grandchild of mine who shall be living at my death." The second event first happened. . . .

[F]or present purposes we accept the [appellees'] position that the phrase "the youngest surviving grandchild of mine who shall be living at my death" is not to be interpreted as excluding grandchildren who might be born after the trust instrument was created.

The appellants make the contention that the settlor in the trust deed reserved a power which was at least equivalent to a special power of appointment, and that the validity of the remainders must in any event be determined in the light of the facts existing at his death when it was known that his only grandchildren had been lives in being at the time the trust was created. This has been referred to in the arguments as "a second look." . . .

The point, which, so far as appears, has not been pressed upon an appellate court before, is based upon the analogy of Minot v. Paine, 230 Mass. 514, 120 N.E. 167, 1 A.L.R. 365. The theory is that at the settlor's death the expiration of the power to divert the property from the takers in default was the same in effect as an appointment of the remainders by the settlor's will.

The reserved power is, at the very least, akin to a power of appointment. [Citations omitted.] And, for present purposes, we treat it as having attributes of a special power to appoint by deed. . . .

Since it is permissible to make use of the circumstances known when a power, which is special or testamentary, is exercised to determine validity under the rule, it seems reasonable to afford the same opportunity in cases where such a power is not exercised. . . . Upon his death it could be learned for the first time what definitely were to be the terms of the trust. It then could be seen for the first time that there was to be no failure to vest within the period limited by the rule. No further grandchildren had been born. In these precise circumstances there is no compelling decision which prevents taking advantage of facts known at the moment when the power ceased to be exercisable. American Law of Property, §24.36. We are unwilling to apply the rule so as to invalidate the trust instrument.

The appellees strongly urge that the doctrine of a "second look" has no place in reading the original limitations in default of appointment, which were capable of examination when created, and which should retain the same meaning throughout. They argue that its adoption would be a nullification of the rule "that executory limitations are void unless they take effect ex necessitate and in all possible contingencies" within the prescribed period. Hall v. Hall, 123 Mass. 120, 124. But this rule, while recognized, was assuaged as to the exercise of a power of appointment in Minot v. Paine, 230 Mass. 514, 522, 120 N.E. 167, 1 A.L.R. 365. It was there deemed wise not to apply unmodified a remorseless technical principle to a case which it did not fit. That principle seems equally inappropriate here. . . .

So ordered.

The Delaware Tax Trap.   Delaware has a curious statute providing that the perpetuities period begins to run from the time of exercise for all powers, not just general ones. See Del. Code Ann. tit. 25, §501. What this means is that a settlor may create a trust that can last forever and seemingly avoid all federal estate tax in the estates of the beneficiaries. For example, the settlor could create a trust to pay the income to her child, *A*, for life, remainder to such of *A*'s descendants as *A* might appoint by will, with power to appoint in trust and to create further life estates and powers of appointment, etc. To eliminate this technique, Congress in 1942 added §2041(a)(3) to the Internal Revenue Code. It includes in the donee's estate any property with respect to which the decedent:

> exercises a power of appointment created after October 21, 1942, by creating another power of appointment which under the applicable local law can be validly exercised so as to postpone the vesting of any estate or interest in such property, or suspend the absolute ownership or power of alienation of such property, for a period ascertainable without regard to the date of the creation of the first power.

Thus the usual lesson to draw from the Delaware Tax Trap for persons in all states is not to exercise a special power by creating a new presently exercisable general power (e.g., a power of withdrawal).

Nevertheless, since the advent of the generation-skipping transfer (GST) tax, it is sometimes advisable for donees of special powers to deliberately fall into the Delaware Tax Trap. Recall from the discussion in Chapter 8, page 303 supra that the GST is imposed at a flat rate of 55 percent. The GST is not imposed if the generation-skipping trust assets are subject to federal estate tax in the donee's estate. By exercising the special power to create a new presently exercisable general power that triggers the Delaware Tax Trap, the donee of the special power is taxed at estate tax rates. See Blattmacher & Pennell, Adventures in Generation-Skipping, or How We Learned to Love the "Delaware Tax Trap," 24 Real Prop., Prob. & Trust J. 75 (1989).

D. Trends and Reforms in Perpetuities Rules

1. Reform of the Rule Against Perpetuities (Other Than the Uniform Statutory Rule Against Perpetuities)

At one time a number of states adopted more or less complete statutory schemes relating to perpetuities, either replacing or operating alongside the common law rules. These statutory rules were quite distinct from the common law and were generally patterned after early New York legislation dealing with suspension of the power of alienation rather than with remoteness of vesting. These early statutory systems should be distinguished from legislative modifications of the common law Rule Against Perpetuities and from attempted legislative declarations of the common law. There is an understandable trend away from these distinct statutory systems, back to the common law rules. This modern trend has been accompanied — also understandably — by legislative and occasionally by judicial efforts to reform the common law Rule Against Perpetuities.

PROBLEM

20-H.   As an interested future expert in future interests you are invited to testify before a state legislative committee on the merits of a proposed statute, which reads:

"Any interest in real or personal property which would violate the Rule Against Perpetuities shall be reformed, within the limits of that rule, to approximate most closely the intention of the creator of the interest. In determining whether an interest would violate said rule and in reforming an interest the period of perpetuities shall be measured by actual rather than possible events."

Briefly, what points would you make, what questions would you anticipate and what response would you make to those questions?

Largely as a result of the lifetime crusade of Professor Leach, reform of the Rule Against Perpetuities came to the attention of legislatures and judges in the United States and the Commonwealth countries. At least three major approaches to limiting the rule can be identified. One is to sustain dispositions as far as possible by invalidating only so much of dispositive provisions as are remote, construing and modifying the disposition to approximate the intended disposition. This is the so-called *cy pres* technique utilized not only in legislation but also by a few courts on their own. The second technique is the "wait-and-see" approach of not striking down interests as excessively remote if the facts, as they actually occur, do not result in vesting beyond the period of the rule. Arguably, this is an extension of the tack taken by the courts in the *Bird* and *Sears* cases, supra.

The third approach has been legislation to correct specific facets of the rule believed to be unduly harsh or lenient and to prune the rule in a series of detailed sections or statutes, dealing with the presumption of lifelong fertility, the exemption from the rule of possibilities of reverter and rights of entry for condition broken, the administrative contingency and unborn widow rules, and the like.

a.   Cy Pres (or Reformation)

T. BERGIN & P. HASKELL, PREFACE TO ESTATES IN LAND AND FUTURE INTERESTS
218-219 (2d ed. 1984)

Now let us examine the reformation principle. A group of states have enacted broad cy pres, or reformation, statutes, of which the Vermont statute is an example:

> Any interest in real or personal property which would violate the rule against perpetuities shall be reformed, within the limits of the rule, to approximate most closely the intention of the creator of the interest. In determining whether an interest would violate said rule and in reforming an interest the period of perpetuities shall be measured by actual rather than possible events.

It should be noted that this statute provides for wait-and-see as well as reformation, and that reformation may be employed only after invalidity is determined under wait-and-see. In those states which have adopted cy pres but not wait-and-see, reformation may be done at the time of the creation of the invalid future interest or at some time thereafter, depending upon the time suit is brought. A court may be inclined to defer reformation until close to the time the invalid future interest would become possessory in order to have the benefit of all relevant facts with respect to the situation.

Several states have enacted limited reformation statutes that provide for the reduction of an age contingency to 21 in situations in which there is an age contingency in excess of 21 which renders an interest invalid. The Illinois statute is an example:

. . . where any interest . . . would be invalid because it is made to depend upon any person attaining or failing to attain an age in excess of 21 years, the age specified shall be reduced to 21 years as to every person to whom the age contingency applies. . . .

Restatement (Second) of Property, Donative Transfers §1.5 provides for reformation as follows:

If under a donative transfer an interest in property fails because it does not vest or cannot vest within the period of the rule against perpetuities, the transferred property shall be disposed of in the manner which most closely effectuates the transferor's manifested plan of distribution, and which is within the limits of the rule against perpetuities.

Several cases have employed the reformation principle in the absence of statute to reduce age or time contingencies to 21 years to make valid a future interest which was invalid in its original form.

Some of the statutes cited by Professors Bergin and Haskell have since been repealed in light of subsequent enactment of the Uniform Statutory Rule Against Perpetuities. Nevertheless, legislative or judicial adoption of cy pres survives in a handful of jurisdictions, notably Illinois, New York, and Texas.

PROBLEM

20-I. Under the Restatement (Second) of Property (Donative Transfers) §1.5 quoted by Professors Bergin and Haskell, how would the following cases be resolved? Assume that the common law Rule Against Perpetuities is in effect (no wait-and-see), except as modified by §1.5.

(a) *O* devises property to *T* in trust to pay the income to *A* for life, then to accumulate the income until *A*'s youngest child attains the age of 40, and then to distribute the trust property to *A*'s children who attain the age of 40. At *O*'s death, *A* is alive and has two children, *B* (age 25) and *C* (age 15). One year after *O*'s death, *A* has another child, *D*. *B* dies at age 30; *C* and *D* attain age 40. See Restatement (Second) of Property (Donative Transfers) §1.5 illus. 5; In re Estate of Chun Quan Yee Hop, 52 Haw. 40, 469 P.2d 183 (1970); Edgerly v. Barker, 66 N.H. 434, 31 A. 900 (1891); J.C. Gray, The Rule Against Perpetuities §§869 to 871 (R. Gray 4th ed. 1942) (comment on Edgerly v. Barker); Carter v. Berry, 243 Miss. 321, 140 So. 2d 843 (1962); T. Bergin & P. Haskell, Preface to Estates in Land and Future Interests 220 (2d ed. 1984).

(b) *O* devises property to *T* in trust to pay the income to *A* for life, then to pay the income to the children of *A* for their respective lives, and upon the death of each child of *A,* to pay over the percentage of the principal equal to the percentage of the income the child was receiving, to the issue then living of such child per stirpes. At *O*'s death, *A* is alive and has one child, *B,* and no grandchildren. Five years later another child, *C,* is born to *A. A* then dies, and twenty-five years later *C* dies leaving issue surviving her. *B* is alive at *C*'s death. See Restatement (Second) of Property (Donative Transfers) §1.5 illus. 8; T. Bergin & P. Haskell, Preface to Estates in Land and Future Interests 220-221 (2d ed. 1984).

b. Wait-and-See

MERCHANTS NATIONAL BANK v. CURTIS
98 N.H. 225, 97 A.2d 207 (1953)

[The testatrix devised certain land to her children for life, remainder (clause Fourth) "to my granddaughter Margaret May Curtis and her heirs forever." The will, however, further provided (clause Fifth) that if either of her children leave "other heirs of their body surviving them such heir or heirs shall share equally with Margaret" and (clause Sixth) that if Margaret or "other grandchildren survive both of my children and shall have and leave no heirs of her or their body, then . . . unto my brothers and sisters then living and to the representatives of those not living, and to my late husband's niece, Almeda, . . . in equal shares." The rights in the property depend in part on whether clause Sixth violates the Rule Against Perpetuities.]

KENISON, C.J. . . . The rule . . . prevails in this state, but it has never been "remorselessly applied" as advocated by Gray [citation omitted]. . . .

The rationale of [Edgerly v. Barker] was that, whenever possible, a will should be construed to carry out the primary intent to accomplish a legal testamentary disposition even though the will may have inadvertently exposed a secondary intent to accomplish the testamentary disposition in an ineffective manner. That rationale has been applied in many recent will cases that have not involved the rule itself. . . .

The rule is a technical one, difficult of application and is often enforced to frustrate testamentary intent although the policy of the rule may not require such enforcement in a particular case. It is not surprising, therefore, that there has been an increasing tendency to avoid the application of the rule by various judicial techniques. There is a constructional preference for considering interests vested rather than contingent. Upton v. White, 92 N.H. 221, 29 A.2d 126. "The public interest in keeping *the destructive force of the rule against perpetuities within reasonable limits* is a considerable present factor supporting the public interest in that construction which accomplishes the earlier vesting." 3 Restatement, Property, §243 comment *i.* (Emphasis supplied). If a gift is made upon alternative contingencies, one of which might be remote, while the other is not, the gift is valid where the second contingency actually happens. This doctrine is used to prevent the application of the rule in many cases. Annotation 64 A.L.R. 1077. "Essentially this represents a revulsion against the rule requiring absolute certainty of vesting as viewed from the creation of the interest . . . courts have a strong tendency to 'wait and see' wherever possible." 6 American Law of Property §24.54 (1952). These techniques have the salutary effect of avoiding the punitive and technical aspects of the rule but at the same time confirming the policy and purpose of the rule within reasonable limits. Wentworth & Co. v. Wentworth, 77 N.H. 400, 92 A. 733.

Clause Sixth of the will is capable of at least two possible constructions. The first construction is that clause Sixth created two contingencies upon which it would take effect: one to occur, if at all, on the death of Margaret May Curtis; the other to occur, if at all, on the death of unborn grandchildren. Since the first contingency actually occurred and is within the period of perpetuities, the gift may be considered valid. . . . Under this construction the event occurs at the death of Margaret May Curtis, a life in being, and clause Sixth would not be considered violative of the rule.

The second possible construction of this Sixth clause is the one urged by the Beanquirin interests. They argue that the will gives the brothers and sisters an executory interest upon a single contingency which may occur at the death of as yet unborn grandchildren. While this is not the only construction that the clause is susceptible of, it is not a labored one. There is no doubt that, if there had been another grandchild who died after Margaret May Curtis without leaving heirs of his body, this event would have occurred beyond the period allowed by the rule against perpetuities.

Assuming this second construction to be permissible, we come to the crucial question whether we are justified in deciding the perpetuities issue on the facts which actually occurred rather than on facts that might have happened viewed as of the death of the testator. There is little case authority for deciding upon facts occurring after the testator's death in a case such as the one before us. However, recognized modern commentators present convincing arguments for doing so. Leach, Perpetuities in Perspective: Ending the Rule's Reign of Terror, 65 Harv. L. Rev. 721 (1952); 6 American Law of Property §24.10 (1952); and a full study by a Pennsylvania law revision commission resulted in a statute that permits such events to be considered. Pa. Estates Act of

1947, §4, Pa. Stat. Ann. (Purdon, 1947) tit. 20, §301.4. There is no precedent in this state that compels us to close our eyes to facts occurring after the death of the testator.

In the present case we are called on to determine the validity of a clause of a will that did not in fact tie up property beyond the permissible limit of lives in being plus twenty-one years. There is no logical justification for deciding the problem as of the date of the death of the testator on facts that might have happened rather than the facts which actually happened. It is difficult to see how the public welfare is threatened by a vesting that might have been postponed beyond the period of perpetuities but actually was not. The recent decision in Sears v. Coolidge, 329 Mass. 340, 108 N.E.2d 563, allows the court to take a "second look" under powers of appointment. While this is not direct authority for doing the same thing with a devise or bequest, it is bottomed on the same proposition that the glacial force of the rule will be avoided where the interests actually vest within the period of perpetuities. 6 American Law of Property, §24.35 (1952). When a decision is made at a time when the events have happened, the court should not be compelled to consider only what might have been and completely ignore what was. Analogy may be found in cases where the validity of a remainder interest is not considered until the facts existing on the death of the life tenant can be established. See Orr v. Moses, 94 N.H. 309, 52 A.2d 128; B. M. C. Durfee Trust Co. v. Taylor, 325 Mass. 201, 89 N.E.2d 777.

At the death of the survivor of the life tenants, Edward Harrington and Delana B. Curtis, both of whom were lives in being at testatrix' death, it became certain that no grandchildren of the testatrix would be born after her death. This in turn made it certain that the gift in clause Sixth of the will would in fact vest at the death of Margaret May Curtis Reynolds Vreeland, also a life in being at testatrix' death. Consistent with the principles above stated, the facts existing at the death of the two life tenants are taken into consideration in applying the rule.

We therefore conclude that clause Sixth does not violate the rule against perpetuities. The individuals who are entitled to participate in the distribution of the trust moneys and the extent of their interests are to be determined under this clause.

c. Specific Corrections

A good example of a statute preserving the common law rule but correcting specific aspects that seem unduly harsh or capricious is the Illinois Statute Concerning Perpetuities, Ill. Comp. Stat. Ann. ch. 765, §§305/4 & 305/5 (1998). See also the article by Professor Schuyler of Northwestern, entitled The Statute Concerning Perpetuities, 65 Nw.

U. L. Rev. 3 (1970). Among the statute's features are subsections that presume that an interest was intended to be valid, that an administrative contingency must occur, if at all, within the perpetuities period, that a reference to a widow or widower is to a person living at the time the perpetuities period commences to run, and that no person under the age of 13 or over the age of 64 shall be deemed capable of having a child. Another article advocating specific corrections is Bloom, Perpetuities Refinement: There Is an Alternative, 62 Wash. L. Rev. 23 (1987).

2. The Uniform Statutory Rule Against Perpetuities

By 1986 none of the various approaches to reform illustrated in the preceding materials had achieved widespread acceptance, but the Restatement (Second) of Property (Donative Transfers) took the position that wait-and-see and cy pres were the law of the land. Although no court or legislature has adopted the Second Restatement's method of determining the measuring lives, the approval of wait-and-see and cy pres in the Second Restatement probably paved the way for the next stage of perpetuities reform.

In 1986, the Uniform Law Commissioners approved the Uniform Statutory Rule Against Perpetuities (USRAP). This was a project of the Joint Editorial Board for the Uniform Probate Code, with Professor Lawrence Waggoner of Michigan serving as Reporter. USRAP quickly gained the endorsement of key bar groups and has been adopted in 26 states and incorporated into the UPC. A recent movement to abolish the Rule Against Perpetuities in various ways, described infra, is eroding the USRAP's majority status.

UNIFORM STATUTORY RULE
AGAINST PERPETUITIES
Prefatory Note

. . . *Rationale of the 90-year Permissible Vesting Period.* The myriad problems associated with the actual-measuring-lives approach are swept aside by shifting away from actual measuring lives and adopting instead a 90-year permissible vesting period as representing a reasonable approximation of — a proxy for — the period of time that would, on average, be produced by identifying and tracing an actual set of measuring lives and then tacking on a 21-year period following the death of the survivor. The selection of 90 years as the period of time reasonably approximating the period that would be produced, on average, by using the set of actual measuring lives identified in the Restatement (Second) or the earlier draft of the Uniform Act is based on a statistical study published in Waggoner, Perpetuities: A Progress Report on the Draft Uniform Statutory Rule Against Perpetuities, 20 U. Miami Inst. on Est. Plan. Ch. 7 (1986). This study suggests that the youngest measuring life, on average, is about 6 years old. The remaining life expectancy of a 6-year-old is reported as 69.6 years in the U.S. Bureau of the Census, Statistical Abstract of the United States: 1986, Table 108, at p. 69. (In the Statistical Abstract for 1985, 69.3 years was reported.) In the interest of arriving at an end number that is a multiple of five, the Uniform Act utilizes 69 years as an appropriate measure of the remaining life expectancy of a 6-year-old, which — with the 21-year tack-on period added — yields a permissible vesting period of 90 years.

The adoption of a flat period of 90 years rather than the use of actual measuring lives is an evolutionary step in the development and refinement of the wait-and-see doctrine. Far from revolutionary, it is well within the tradition of that doctrine. The 90-year period makes wait-and-see simple, fair, and workable. *Aggregate dead-hand control will not be increased beyond that which is already possible by competent drafting under the Common-law Rule.*

Seen as a valid approximation of the period that would be produced under the conventional survivor-of-the-measuring-lives-plus-21-years approach, and in the interest of making the law of perpetuities uniform, *jurisdictions adopting this Act are strongly urged not to adopt a period of time different from the 90-year period.* . . .

§1. *Statutory Rule Against Perpetuities*

(a) [Validity of Nonvested Property Interest.] A nonvested property interest is invalid unless:

(1) when the interest is created, it is certain to vest or terminate no later than 21 years after the death of an individual then alive; or

(2) the interest either vests or terminates within 90 years after its creation.

(b) [Validity of General Power of Appointment Subject to a Condition Precedent.] A general power of appointment not presently exercisable because of a condition precedent is invalid unless:

(1) when the power is created, the condition precedent is certain to be satisfied or become impossible to satisfy no later than 21 years after the death of an individual then alive; or

(2) the condition precedent either is satisfied or becomes impossible to satisfy within 90 years after its creation.

(c) [Validity of Nongeneral or Testamentary Power of Appointment.]   A nongeneral power of appointment or a general testamentary power of appointment is invalid unless:

(1) when the power is created, it is certain to be irrevocably exercised or otherwise to terminate no later than 21 years after the death of an individual then alive; or

(2) the power is irrevocably exercised or otherwise terminates within 90 years after its creation.

(d) [Possibility of Post-death Child Disregarded.]   In determining whether a nonvested property interest or a power of appointment is valid under subsection (a)(1), (b)(1), or (c)(1), the possibility that a child will be born to an individual after the individual's death is disregarded.

(e) [Effect of Certain "Later-of" Type Language.]   If, in measuring a period from the creation of a trust or other property arrangement, language in a governing instrument (i) seeks to disallow the vesting or termination of any interest or trust beyond, (ii) seeks to postpone the vesting or termination of any interest or trust until, or (iii) seeks to operate in effect in any similar fashion upon, the later of (A) the expiration of a period of time not exceeding 21 years after the death of the survivor of specified lives in being at the creation of the trust or other property arrangement or (B) the expiration of a period of time that exceeds or might exceed 21 years after the death of the survivor of lives in being at the creation of the trust or other property arrangement, that language is inoperative to the extent it produces a period of time that exceeds 21 years after the death of the survivor of the specified lives.

§2.   *When Nonvested Property Interest or Power of*
      Appointment Created

(a) Except as provided in subsections (b) and (c) and in Section 5(a), the time of creation of a nonvested property interest or a power of appointment is determined under general principles of property law.

(b) For purposes of this [Act], if there is a person who alone can exercise a power created by a governing instrument to become the unqualified beneficial owner of (i) a nonvested property interest or (ii) a property interest subject to a power of appointment described in Section 1(b) or 1(c), the nonvested property interest or power of appointment is created when the power to become the unqualified beneficial owner terminates. [For purposes of this [Act], a joint power with respect to community property or to marital property under the Uniform Marital Property Act held by individuals married to each other is a power exercisable by one person alone.]

(c) For purposes of this [Act], a nonvested property interest or a power of appointment arising from a transfer of property to a previously funded trust or other existing property arrangement is created when the nonvested property interest or power of appointment in the original contribution was created.

§3.   *Reformation*

Upon the petition of an interested person, a court shall reform a disposition in the manner that most closely approximates the transferor's manifested plan of distribution and is within the 90 years allowed by Section 1(a)(2), 1(b)(2), or 1(c)(2) if:

(1) a nonvested property interest or a power of appointment becomes invalid under Section 1 (statutory rule against perpetuities);

(2) a class gift is not but might become invalid under Section 1 (statutory rule against perpetuities) and the time has arrived when the share of any class member is to take effect in possession or enjoyment; or

(3) a nonvested property interest that is not validated by Section 1(a)(1) can vest but not within 90 years after its creation.

§4.   *Exclusions From Statutory Rule Against Perpetuities*

Section 1 (statutory rule against perpetuities) does not apply to:

(1) a nonvested property interest or a power of appointment arising out of a nondonative transfer, except a nonvested property interest or a power of appointment arising out of (i) a premarital or postmarital agreement, (ii) a separation or divorce settlement, (iii) a spouse's election, (iv) a similar arrangement arising out of a prospective, existing, or previous marital relationship between the parties, (v) a contract to make or not to revoke a will or trust, (vi) a contract to exercise or not to exercise a power of appointment, (vii) a transfer in satisfaction of a duty of support, or (viii) a reciprocal transfer;

(2) a fiduciary's power relating to the administration or management of assets, including the power of a fiduciary to sell, lease, or mortgage property, and the power of a fiduciary to determine principal and income;

(3) a power to appoint a fiduciary;

(4) a discretionary power of a trustee to distribute principal before termination of a trust to a beneficiary having an indefeasibly vested interest in the income and principal;

(5) a nonvested property interest held by a charity, government, or governmental agency or subdivision, if the nonvested property interest is preceded by an interest held by another charity, government, or governmental agency or subdivision;

(6) a nonvested property interest in or a power of appointment with respect to a trust or other property arrangement forming part of a pension, profit-sharing, stock bonus, health, disability, death benefit, income deferral, or other current or deferred benefit plan for one or more employees, independent contractors, or their beneficiaries or spouses, to which contributions are made for the purpose of distributing to or for the benefit of the participants or their beneficiaries or spouses the property, income, or principal in the trust or other property arrangement, except a nonvested property interest or a power of appointment that is created by an election of a participant or a beneficiary or spouse; or

(7) a property interest, power of appointment, or arrangement that was not subject to the common-law rule against perpetuities or is excluded by another statute of this State.

§5. *Prospective Application*

(a) Except as extended by subsection (b), this [Act] applies to a nonvested property interest or a power of appointment that is created on or after the effective date of this [Act]. For purposes of this section, a nonvested property interest or a power of appointment created by the exercise of a power of appointment is created when the power is irrevocably exercised or when a revocable exercise becomes irrevocable.

(b) If a nonvested property interest or a power of appointment was created before the effective date of this [Act] and is determined in a judicial proceeding, commenced on or after the effective date of this [Act], to violate this State's rule against perpetuities as that rule existed before the effective date of this [Act], a court upon the petition of an interested person may reform the disposition in the manner that most closely approximates the transferor's manifested plan of distribution and is within the limits of the rule against perpetuities applicable when the nonvested property interest or power of appointment was created. . . .

§9. *[Supersession] [Repeal].* This [Act] [supersedes the rule of the common law known as the rule against perpetuities] [repeals (list statutes to be repealed)].

Saving Clauses. When Professor Leach wrote the original Nutshell article in 1938 (supra, page 1072) perpetuities saving clauses were not widely used. His later (1965) article encouraged the use of saving clauses, and informed, careful drafters now include them.

LEACH, PERPETUITIES: THE NUTSHELL REVISITED
78 Harv. L. Rev. 973, 985-986 (1965)

XII.   Some Suggestions as to Draftsmanship

The Rule Against Perpetuities is not always perfectly understood by the bar or wisely applied by the bench. Anyone can make a mistake in drafting an instrument and the reports are full of decisions that are demonstrably wrong. Generalized precepts of draftsmanship, even if they have come to the attention of a particular attorney, may themselves be misunderstood. Faced with this problem, Dean James K. Logan of Kansas and I, . . . concocted a Standard Perpetuity Saving Clause . . . :

> In any disposition in this instrument, or in any instrument exercising a power of appointment created herein, I do not intend that there shall be any violation of the Rule Against Perpetuities or any related rule. If any such violation should inadvertently occur, it is my wish that the appropriate court shall reform the gift or appointment in such a way as to approximate most closely my intent, or the intent of the appointor, within the limits permissible under such Rule or related rule.

J. PRICE, CONTEMPORARY ESTATE PLANNING
§10.48 (1992)

Form 10-9.   Perpetuities Savings Clause

If this trust has not terminated within 21 years after the death of the survivor of my issue living on my death, it shall terminate at the end of such 21-year period, and the trust property shall be distributed outright to my issue then living, such issue to take per stirpes.

What would be the effect of a direction to pay the income from a trust to the settlor's spouse and descendants from time to time living "for as long a period as is legally possible" and finally to distribute the principal to the settlor's then living descendants per stirpes? See Estate of Holt, 75 Haw. 224, 857 P.2d 1355 (1993). Does a drafter have any business drafting wills and trusts if he does not know whether the instrument violates the Rule Against Perpetuities? Would it be malpractice not to include a saving clause? Cf. Lucas v. Hamm, 56 Cal. 2d 583, 364 P.2d 685 (1961); Wright v. Williams, 47 Cal. App. 3d 802, 809 n.2, 121 Cal. Rptr. 194, 199 n.2 (1975).

Effect of Certain "Later-of" Language. In a USRAP jurisdiction, what would be the effect of a saving clause that provided that the maximum time of vesting or termination of any interest or trust must occur no later than the later of (A) twenty-one years after the death of the last to die of specified lives in being at the creation of the trust or (B) ninety years after the creation of the interest or trust? See USRAP §1(e), supra. For alternative explanations of how this subsection came to be, see USRAP §1 Comment G [Reporter's account] and Dukeminier, The Uniform Statutory Rule Against Perpetuities and the GST Tax: New Perils for Practitioners and New Opportunities, 30 Real Prop., Prob. & Tr. J. 186, 189-191 (1995) [critic's account].

In re TRUST FOR WOLD
310 N.J. Super. 382, 708 A.2d 787 (1998)

HAMLIN, P.J., Ch. Div.

This written decision amplifies an earlier oral bench opinion rendered on plaintiff's petition for interpretation and direction regarding the application of the New Jersey Uniform Statutory Rule Against Perpetuities N.J.S.A. 46:2F-1-8 to a proposed exercise by the beneficiary of her power of appointment under the terms of this 1944 Trust. It is an issue of first impression requiring the court to determine if the ninety-year period of N.J.S.A. 46:2F-1-8 enacted on July 3, 1991, may be invoked by the beneficiary in regard to the exercise of that power of appointment vested in her by the 1944 Trust. The issue arises following inquiry by Elaine Johnson Wold, the life beneficiary of the Trust, to the Trustees. More specifically she advised the trustees that she wishes to create a testamentary Trust appointing the proceeds of the 1944 Trust in further trust for the benefit of her spouse and surviving issue. The proposed testamentary trust would create non-vested property interests in one or more issue. By way of illustration the proposed exercise of the power in a new testamentary trust created by Mrs. Wold would permit property held for one of her children, upon the death of that child, to continue in trust for the benefit of that child's own issue. Thus, the trust interest of that child would be considered non-vested since it would pass to the next generation upon the occurrence of a specific event, i.e. the death of the child.

The proposed exercise of Mrs. Wold's power of appointment under the 1944 Trust through the creation of her own testamentary trust would permit such generational structure to continue for the full period permitted under the Rule Against Perpetuities. In delineating the maximum term of the trust she would create for her spouse and issue, Mrs. Wold has expressed to the trustees her intention to rely on the ninety-year "wait and see" perpetuities period as codified in the 1991 legislation.

In order to ensure the validity of her long term estate planning and to make certain that the trustees will be permitted to make distributions of the trust estate in accordance with her expressed intentions Mrs. Wold, through the trustees, asks this court to determine the applicability and construction of the New Jersey Rule Against Perpetuities Act as it applies to the exercise of her special power of appointment. In the absence of clear and binding precedent or other authority, neither Mrs. Wold nor the trustees can be assured that the intended disposition will not be later found to violate the applicable rule against perpetuities. Without a present determination, there exists the possibility that the testamentary trust created by Mrs. Wold might, after her death, be voided or reformed in a manner that is inconsistent with her expressed intention.

In addition, the trustees seek direction from the court regarding the proposed testamentary exercise of Mrs. Wold's power of appointment under the terms of the 1944 instrument. They assert that they are in doubt as to whether the power granted Mrs. Wold to dispose of the trust res includes the power to appoint the trust assets by a successive testamentary trust. The trustees seek to invoke the traditional equitable power of the Chancery court to resolve their concerns about the exercise of their fiduciary duty as governed by the provision of the original trust which states:

> Upon the death of Elaine Johnson Wold, the Trustees are directed to divide, transfer and pay over absolutely, outright and forever, the trust property as follows: to the surviving spouse and issue of Elaine Johnson (Wold) or any of them in such shares as she may direct by her Last Will and Testament duly admitted to probate. . . .

All persons having an interest in the issue presented have been served and have chosen not to take a position on the application.

Creation of the 1944 Trust

J. Seward Johnson (hereinafter Seward) created this trust on October 20, 1944 to benefit his daughter Elaine Johnson Wold. It was one of several trusts he created contemporaneously for each of his children. Each was identical in language with the exception of the named beneficiaries. Subsequently the settlor created at least two additional charitable lead trusts to further benefit his issue. The trust plan was neither haphazard nor one dimensional. The trusts were initially funded by substantial shares of the health care corporate giant, Johnson and Johnson (J & J). Seward and his brother, Robert Wood Johnson, were the principal heirs of the controlling stock of J & J, which was already a major national corporation at that time. Robert Wood Johnson succeeded to the leadership of the company. Through his efforts and subsequent astute business management, J & J has become a major international diversified business presence. Thus, the original 15,000 shares of J & J stock which initially funded the trust have multiplied in value so that they now constitute one of the most significant family fortunes in America. Since J & J has been headquartered in New Brunswick, New Jersey for over a century and the trusts were created here, the Middlesex County Courts and more specifically the Chancery Division of this venue, have had long interaction with the construction and administration of the various trusts created by Seward. Many accountings have been presented over the years. Specific previous applications by trustees have been the subject of decisions and unpublished opinions. Likewise there has been significant litigation involving the trusts, their creation and purpose, which resulted in published opinions that are helpful to our overall understanding of the trust scheme established by Seward with the assistance of sophisticated estate planning counsel. See Hill v. Estate of Mary Lea Johnson Richards, 142 N.J. 639, 667 A.2d 695 (1995); Wiedenmayer v. Johnson, 106 N.J. Super. 161, 254 A.2d 534 (App. Div. 1969), aff'd 55 N.J. 81, 259 A.2d 465 (1970); Barbara P. Johnson v. J. Seward Johnson, Jr., 212 N.J. Super. 368, 515 A.2d 255 (Ch. Div. 1986); and Burke v. Director, Division of Taxation, 11 N.J. Tax 29 (1990).

The trust instrument itself is comprehensive and clearly designed to accomplish several salutary ends. Foremost is the provision for support and income to the beneficiary and such of her heirs as she may select. Such income was maximized to the fullest by utilizing tax saving devices permitted by law. While not directly related to this application the trusts facilitated the corporate advancement of J & J by reposing the voting control of trust stock in J & J executives who would have an interest in increasing the value of the res.

Under the terms of the Trust, the trustees were directed during the lifetime of Elaine Johnson Wold to collect and receive the income and profits from the trust property and, after deducting those expenses of "the trust" which are payable out of the income, to accumulate the net income and add it at the end of each calendar year to the trust property. Once Elaine Johnson Wold attained the age of twenty-one (21) years, the trust agreement authorized the trustees to pay to her so much of the net income in any year as the trustees in their absolute and uncontrolled discretion deemed to be for her best interest. The trust instrument further permits the trustees to transfer and pay over to the life beneficiary ". . . any or all of the Trust property." Upon the death of Elaine Johnson Wold, the trust agreement directs the trustees to divide, transfer and pay over absolutely, outright and forever, the trust property as follows:

> a. To the surviving spouse and issue of Elaine Johnson (Wold) or any of them in such shares as she may direct by her last Will and Testament duly admitted to probate, or failing such testamentary direction, then, (emphasis added)
>
> b. To her issue in equal shares per stirpes, or failing such issue, then
>
> c. To divide the trust property into as many equal shares as there shall be children of the Grantor now in being and then surviving and the issue collectively of any child of the Grantor now in being who may predecease Elaine Johnson (Wold) leaving issue surviving, one such equal part for the benefit of each such surviving child of the Grantor, and one such equal part for the issue collectively of each such deceased child of the Grantor; and to pay over such share so set apart for the benefit of a surviving child of the Grantor to the Trustees of a child by agreement bearing even date herewith, and to distribute and pay over such share so set apart for the issue collectively of a deceased child of the Grantor to such issue in equal shares per stirpes; or failing all such issue of the Grantor, then,
>
> d. To those persons, other than the Grantor, who under the laws of New Jersey then in force would be entitled to inherit from Elaine Johnson (Wold) (had she died intestate domiciled in New Jersey) personal property located in New Jersey of which she died possessed and in the same proportions as they would be so entitled; or failing such persons, then
>
> e. To and among such education, religious or charitable corporations as the Trustees in their discretion may select and designate and in such amounts respectively as they may determine.

The Trustees' Right to Seek Instructions

The Trustees have been notified by the life beneficiary, that it is her intention to protect the future financial well being of "her surviving spouse . . . and issue or any of them" through the utilization of a testamentary trust for the benefit of her spouse, children and grandchildren. To accomplish that purpose she intends to leave a portion of the trust assets for the direct benefit of those persons named in the Trust including her two granddaughters through the utilization of trust concepts.

The Trustees have also been informed that Mrs. Wold, in establishing the aforementioned testamentary trust, would create non-vested property interests. Therefore, in establishing the trust, Mrs. Wold intends to avail herself of the ninety-year perpetuities period contained in the New Jersey Uniform Statutory Rule Against Perpetuities, N.J.S.A. 46:2F-1 to 8. There is no question as to the Trustees' right and duty to seek judicial instruction where a valid question exists as to an appropriate construction of a trust instrument. . . . The question raised by the expressed intention of the beneficiary presents substantial and timely issues for the Trustees to answer with the guidance of the court. The beneficiary has substantial and immediate choices to make regarding her estate planning which hinge upon the application of the law. Neither she nor the trustees can afford error which, by the time it was so determined, would be irreparable. The issue before this court presents a real and present justiciable issue. The Court's decision is necessary to govern the trustees' present action and the beneficiary's execution of her power of appointment under the terms of the 1944 trust.

Does the Trust Prohibit the Proposed Exercise?

At the threshold this court notes that the trust instrument, by its very language, vested in the trustees the broadest possible discretion that may be found in any trust instrument. They are to be guided solely by their evaluation of the beneficiary's best interest. Clearly the settlor intended to repose in the Trustees maximum flexibility in addressing the needs of the beneficiaries. By way of illustration it is clear that had the Trustees distributed the entire income and corpus to Mrs. Wold during her lifetime, leaving nothing to be appointed to subsequent heirs, it would have been permissible absent claim of corruption, intentional misconduct or gross negligence. In regard to the instant matter this court is mindful that the sole inference from the unambiguous language of the trust instrument was the desire of the settlor to create a flexible instrument to meet the developing needs of his children both at the time of the creation of the trust and for unforeseen events that would occur. It is an expansive rather than a restrictive instrument.

The law of trusts lends support to Mrs. Wold's position that she should be able to exercise the special power of appointment created by her father, Seward, in a testamentary trust by her for the benefit of her granddaughters [by creating further trusts]. . . . Restatement (Second) of Trusts §17. . . . Further, it is clear that one can infer that the donor of a special power intended the donee to have the same discretion in making an appointment that he had in the disposition of his own property, so far as the extent and nature of the interests which he might give to the members of the class are concerned. Id.; see also Restatement (Second) of Property, §19.3 (1984). . . .

While the trust instrument speaks in terms of appointment including distribution of the corpus in fee simple, if the beneficiary saw fit, it should not be construed as a form of limitation. The hallmark of this trust, as the others, is the flexibility of the trustees, and implicitly the donee of the power, to be permitted maximum discretion.

The court is not unmindful of the clear purpose of the settlor to protect the trust from tax burdens to the fullest extent permitted by law. There can be no question that the proposed testamentary trust exercise of the power will effect significant tax savings. As this court observed in a matter involving another long term trust created by Seward, one of the significant purposes of the Trust scheme was ". . . that the Grantor was able to shelter the fund and its appreciation in value from his estate for estate tax purposes and to incorporate then permissible generation skipping features." Such a purpose, as evidenced by the sophisticated estate planning devices used by Seward, are to be given effect in the exercise of the power of appointment rather than restricted. The proposed creation of the testamentary trust as described by Mrs. Wold is well within the contemplation and intent of the trust instrument. The trustees may honor the proposed exercise of the power of appointment at the appropriate time and make a consistent distribution of the trust assets.

The Application of N.J.S.A. 46:2A-1-5

New Jersey adopted the Uniform Statutory Rule Against Perpetuities on July 3, 1991. In so doing it adopted the "wait-and-see" approach long advocated by reformers of the common law rule against perpetuities so painfully committed to memory by generations of law students. The statute may well sound the death knell for Leach's "Perpetuities In A Nutshell." . . .

The Statute, in a specific and distinguishable fact pattern, was applied prospectively. In Juliano & Sons Enterprises, Inc. v. Chevron U.S.A. Inc., 250 N.J. Super. 148, 593 A.2d 814 (App. Div. 1991), which is the only reported New Jersey decision that has addressed the new statute, the court held that the statutory rule was not retroactive and intended to apply only to property interests created on or after the effective date of the statute. See also U.L.A. Perpetuities §5 (1990). Thus, an interest created under a trust established in 1944 would arguably not fall under the new legislation.

However, while the statute may not apply retroactively as a general matter, for purposes of determining the applicability of the new statutory period the law specifically provides that an interest created pursuant to a power of appointment is deemed to be created upon the exercise of power. N.J.S.A. 46:2F-5(a). Therefore, even if created under a pre-existing power of appointment, the New Jersey Uniform Statutory Rule Against Perpetuities would apply to an interest created under that power, whether general or specific, if exercised after July 3, 1991.

This interpretation is supported by the clear language of the statute as well as by the comments to the Uniform Laws Annotated. "All provisions of the [Uniform] Act except section 5(b) apply to a non-vested property interest (or power of appointment) created by a donee's exercise of a power of appointment where the donee's exercise, whether revocable or irrevocable, occurs on or after the effective date of [the] Act." (Section 5(b) allows reformation of non-vested interests created before the new law). The ULA comment also makes clear that the special rule bringing a non-vested interest created under a preexisting power of appointment within the scope of the new law "applies to the exercise of all type of powers of appointment — presently exercisable general powers, general testamentary powers, and non-general powers."

The court in Will of Charles Pratt, 94 Misc. 2d 1020, 405 N.Y.S.2d 995 (Sur. Ct. 1978), adopted a similar approach, although that case did not involve application of the Uniform "wait-and-see" perpetuities period. Nevertheless, the petitioners in that case requested a determination of whether the testator's son violated the rule against perpetuities in exercising a power of appointment granted to him under his father's will. In finding that there was no violation of the rule against perpetuities, the court held that "the permissible period of the rule against perpetuities is determined by the law in effect when the power is exercised and not by the law in effect when the power was created." Id. (Emphasis added). The general principle expressed by the court in this matter is consistent with the statutory interpretation that is contained in the U.L.A., as adopted by New Jersey.

Consistent with the language of the statute as well as the persuasive analysis of secondary authority this court concludes that the statutory period applies to the non-vested interest that would be created pursuant to the exercise of the power and measured from the creation of the 1944 Trust.

Did the *Wold* court correctly apply the USRAP?

Nondonative Transfers. Although our focus is donative transfers, some of the modern perpetuities litigation has concerned nondonative transfers. Usually a nondonative transfer is a commercial one, for example an option in gross, a preemptive right, a lease to commence in the future, or a nonvested easement in gross. A possibility of reverter, right of entry, or executory interest where the future interest depends on an event affecting the use of land could also be nondonative. Rights in pension plans, stock options, and conversion privileges in bonds might also be in jeopardy.

The common law Rule Against Perpetuities should never have been applied to commercial interests. The measuring period of the Rule (lives in being plus twenty-one years) makes sense in a will or trust. It allows the donor to provide for persons he knows (lives in being), plus twenty-one years to allow their children to reach majority. It has no necessary relationship to a commercial transaction, and may be too short or too long. See Continental Cablevision v. United Broadcasting, 873 F.2d 717 (4th Cir. 1989), holding, sensibly, that performance under a contract is presumed to be within a reasonable time, which is not more than twenty-one years.

The drafters of the USRAP were well aware of the nondonative transfer cases and therefore exempted them from the operation of the USRAP. See USRAP §4 Comment A. With the §4 exclusions from the USRAP, what rule now governs nondonative transfers?

A few states, notably Illinois and Massachusetts, have enacted flat thirty-year time limits on certain commercial transactions. One state, North Carolina, has enacted a comprehensive set of time limits for certain interests in land. The statute provides a thirty-year time limit for the exercise of options and rights of first refusal, or the commencement of leases to commence in the future and nonvested easements. It also provides a sixty-year time limit for possibilities of reverter, rights of entry and executory interests that depend on events affecting the use of land. See N.C. Gen. Stat. §§41-28 to 41-33; Link & Licata, Perpetuities Reform in North Carolina: The Uniform Statutory Rule Against Perpetuities, Nondonative Transfers, and Honorary Trusts, 74 N.C.L. Rev. 1783 (1996).

PROBLEM

20-J.   Would the attorney who drafted the following instruments be liable for malpractice? Assume there was no saving clause in the instruments. Also, assume no statute of limitations or damages issues.

Devise to *A* for life, remainder to such of *A*'s grandchildren, living at the testator's death or born within five years thereafter, as should reach 21. *A* was a widow of 67 with two children and one grandchild. See Re Gaite's Will Trusts, [1949] 1 All. Eng. Rep. 459 (Ch. Div.); J.H.C. Morris, Comment on Re Gaite's Will Trusts, 13 the Conveyancer (N.S.) 289 (1949); W.B. Leach, Comment on Dr. Morris's Comment, 68 L.Q. Rev. 46.

For some guidance, compare Lucas v. Hamm, 56 Cal. 2d 583, 364 P.2d 685 (1961); Megarry, Note, 81 L.Q. Rev. 465, 478-481 (1965); Wright v. Williams, 47 Cal. App. 3d 802, 809 n.2, 121 Cal. Rptr. 194, 199 n.2 (1975); Millwright v. Romer, 322 N.W.2d 30 (Iowa 1982).

Dynasty Trusts. The expression "dynasty trust" seems to be used in at least three senses. In its original sense, it is a trust created to last as long as possible under the applicable Rule Against Perpetuities. The next meaning of "dynasty trust" seems to be a trust designed to take advantage of the $1 million exemption from the generation-skipping transfer tax for as long as possible. The third sense of "dynasty trust" is a trust designed to last forever. Is such a perpetual trust possible? What if the Rule Against Perpetuities is abolished?

3. Abolition of the Rule Against Perpetuities

What was once unthinkable became a serious possibility in the 1990s. About a dozen states have, in one form or another, abolished their Rule Against Perpetuities. How did a rule that began with the 1682 Duke of Norfolk's Case, 3 Ch. Cas. 1, 22 Eng. Rep. 931, and endured for three centuries into the reaffirming 1983 Restatement (Second) of Property and the 1986 USRAP, suddenly be questioned? Despite the nonsense applications of the common law Rule, did it not draw a fair balance between social recognition of the desires of the dead hand to control the disposition of property and the desires of the future generation to control it?

Several states abolished the Rule Against Perpetuities as part of an effort to attract trust business by enhancing certain tax motivated benefits. Without much attention, the 1950 Wisconsin case of In re Walker's Will, 258 Wis. 65, 45 N.W.2d 94 (1950), quietly began this revolution. It involved a New York-style suspension of the power of alienation rule, and held "that because of such power of sale the absolute power of alienation has not been suspended." In 1969 this was codified, Wis. Stat. Ann. §700.16. Then South Dakota followed Wisconsin, S.D. Codified Laws Ann. §43-5-8. See Foye, Using South Dakota Law for Perpetual Trusts, Prob. & Prop., Jan./Feb. 1998, at 17. Idaho followed. Idaho Code §55-111.

The movement gained momentum in 1995, as Alaska and Delaware vied to attract trust business by creating the most settlor-friendly laws. In 1995 Delaware abolished the Rule for trusts of personal property. Del. Code Ann. tit. 25, §503. In 1997 Alaska effectively abolished the Rule. Alaska Stat. §34.27.050(a)(3). Delaware now allows trusts of personal property to last forever and trusts of real property to last for 110 years. Del. Code Ann. tit. 25, §503. Florida, Illinois, Maine, Maryland, New Jersey, Ohio, and Rhode Island joined in the race by repealing the Rule to one degree or another, typically by permitting perpetual trusts of personal (and sometimes even real) property if the trustee has a power of sale. See, e.g., 2000 Fla. Laws ch. 245 (changing USRAP 90-year period to 360 years); Ill. Con. Stat. ch. 765, §305/3; Me. Rev. Stat.

Ann. tit. 33, §101-A; Md. Est. & Trusts Code Ann. §11-102(e); N.J. Stat. Ann. §§46:2F-9 & 46-2F-11; Ohio Rev. Code Ann. §2131.09(B); and R.I. Stat. §34-11-38.

Where will all this lead? Has the Rule outlived its purposes? What are its purposes? Has it in effect been abolished by the USRAP? Will we see a revival of the traditional reforms, whether cy pres, wait-and-see, or specific corrections? Will the IRS stand idly by as dynasty trusts avoid federal estate tax and the generation-skipping transfer tax? Is not the existing federal transfer tax system premised on a Rule Against Perpetuities that exposes property to tax approximately every generation?

PROBLEM

20-K. You are counsel to a legislative study commission. The jurisdiction still follows the common law Rule Against Perpetuities. Bills have been introduced and referred to the commission that would: (1) abolish the Rule and not replace it; (2) abolish the Rule and replace it with the Uniform Statutory Rule Against Perpetuities; or (3) preserve the Rule but make specific corrections along the lines of the Illinois Statute Concerning Perpetuities. Which alternative would you recommend? Would you recommend some other alternative and, if so, what? Consider the following:

RESTATEMENT OF PROPERTY (1944)
Intr. Note to Div. IV, 2129-2133

[At this point, you should reread the Restatement material at pages 409-412.]

See also Restatement (Second) of Property Part I, Rationale, at 8-18 (1983) (almost identical to 1944 Restatement); Simes, The Policy Against Perpetuities, 103 U. Pa. L. Rev. 707 (1955), which is also published in Simes, Public Policy and the Dead Hand (1955); L. Simes & A. Smith, The Law of Future Interests §1117 (2d ed. 1956). An excellent collection of references to both proposed and enacted statutes, together with discussions of policies and concerns, pro and con, is published by the Committee on Rules Against Perpetuities, Section of Real Property, Probate and Trust Law of the American Bar Association, in the Perpetuity Legislation Handbook (3d ed. 1967), 2 Real Prop., Prob. & Trust J. 176, 220 (1967).

Table of Cases

Index